R.1986   Mike Kerwin

THE GREAT
CONTEMPORARY
ISSUES

LABOR
AND
MANAGEMENT

p434 LBJ on minimum wage law

THE GREAT
CONTEMPORARY
ISSUES

LABOR
AND
MANAGEMENT

𝕿𝖍𝖊 𝕹𝖊𝖜 𝖄𝖔𝖗𝖐 𝕿𝖎𝖒𝖊𝖘

ARNO PRESS

NEW YORK/1973

RICHARD B. MORRIS

Advisory Editor

Copyright © 1973 by The New York Times Company.
Library of Congress Catalog Card Number: 72-5019
ISBN 0-405-04163-2
Manufactured in the United States of America by Arno Press, Inc.

The editors express special thanks to The Associated Press, United Press
International, and Reuters for permission to include in this series of
books a number of dispatches originally distributed by those news services.

A HUDSON GROUP BOOK
Produced by Morningside Associates. Edited by Gene Brown.

Contents

Publisher's Note About the Series

It would take even an accomplished speed-reader, moving at full throttle, some three and a half solid hours a day to work his way through all the news THE NEW YORK TIMES prints. The sad irony, of course, is that even such indefatigable devotion to life's carnival would scarcely assure a decent understanding of what it was really all about. For even the most dutiful reader might easily overlook an occasional long-range trend of importance, or perhaps some of the fragile, elusive relationships between events that sometimes turn out to be more significant than the events themselves.

This is why "The Great Contemporary Issues" was created—to help make sense out of some of the major forces and counterforces at large in today's world. The philosophical conviction behind the series is a simple one: that the past not only can illuminate the present but must. ("Continuity with the past," declared Oliver Wendell Holmes, "is a necessity, not a duty.") Each book in the series, therefore, has as its subject some central issue of our time that needs to be viewed in the context of its antecedents if it is to be fully understood. By showing, through a substantial selection of contemporary accounts from THE NEW YORK TIMES, the evolution of a subject and its significance, each book in the series offers a perspective that is available in no other way. For while most books on contemporary affairs specialize, for excellent reasons, in predigested facts and neatly drawn conclusions, the books in this series allow the reader to draw his own conclusions on the basis of the facts as they appeared at virtually the moment of their occurrence. This is not to argue that there is no place for events recollected in tranquility; it is simply to say that when fresh, raw truths are allowed to speak for themselves, some quite distinct values often emerge.

For this reason, most of the articles in "The Great Contemporary Issues" are reprinted in their entirety, even in those cases where portions are not central to a given book's theme. Editing has been done only rarely, and in all such cases it is clearly indicated. (Such an excision occasionally occurs, for example, in the case of a Presidential State of the Union Message, where only brief portions are germane to a particular volume, and in the case of some names, where for legal reasons or reasons of taste it is preferable not to republish specific identifications.) Similarly, typographical errors, where they occur, have been allowed to stand as originally printed.

"The Great Contemporary Issues" inevitably encompasses a substantial amount of history. In order to explore their subjects fully, some of the books go back a century or more. Yet their fundamental theme is not the past but the present. In this series the past is of significance insofar as it suggests how we got where we are today. These books, therefore, do not always treat a subject in a purely chronological way. Rather, their material is arranged to point up trends and interrelationships that the editors believe are more illuminating than a chronological listing would be.

"The Great Contemporary Issues" series will ultimately constitute an encyclopedic library of today's major issues. Long before editorial work on the first volume had even begun, some fifty specific titles had already been either scheduled for definite publication or listed as candidates. Since then, events have prompted the inclusion of a number of additional titles, and the editors are, moreover, alert not only for new issues as they emerge but also for issues whose development may call for the publication of sequel volumes. We will, of course, also welcome readers' suggestions for future topics.

Introduction

At a time when American labor is entering a new phase, one which challenges many of its past goals and questions many established interpretations, this account of its struggles, leadership and achievements, as revealed in the pages of *The New York Times*, will surely for the years ahead serve as a valuable documentary record and reference source. Ranging from eye-witness reporting of classic confrontations between labor and capital to in-depth analyses of the labor movement, the *Times'* back files constitute a comprehensive history of labor in the United States since the Civil War.

Appropriately, the starting point for this volume is also the take-off point for American labor. The burning stacks of steel mills lighting the skies over Pittsburgh in the post-Civil War years signalized the coming of the Industrial Age to America. That age of industrial capitalism and business concentration posed a challenge to labor to organize successfully on a national level. The early reporting from *The New York Times* covers such pioneer efforts as those of William H. Sylvis to create a National Labor Union, an organization perhaps more concerned with political reform than with bread-and-butter issues, and with Terence V. Powderly's valiant efforts to forge a national union of all wage-earners, an industrial rather than a craft organization, the Knights of Labor, which was tried and found wanting in the strife-torn 1880's.

Initially sympathetic with the goals of organized labor, the *Times* was repelled by the violent confrontations of labor and capital in the years between the great Railway Strike of 1877, to which President Hayes dispatched Federal troops, and the Haymarket Riot of 1886, with its spectacular trial, convictions, and executions. To the even more violent decade that followed the *Times* gave full coverage, with detailed accounts of the Homestead Strike at the plant of the Carnegie Steel Company, the dispatch of Federal troops to Coeur d'Alene, Idaho, as a result of the escalation of violence between silver miners and strikebreakers, and the Pullman Strike. The last confrontation saw President Cleveland, over the protest of Illinois' governor John Peter Altgeld, dispatch Federal troops ostensibly to safeguard the mail and protect inter-state commerce. The jailing for contempt of Eugene V. Debs, the labor leader, dramatized the increasing use of the labor injunction, whose effectiveness against strikes was not to be blunted until the passage of the Norris-LaGuardia Act of 1932.

Samuel Gompers through his American Federation of Labor held the center of the labor stage for almost a half century after 1886. Concentrating on the crafts and confining his objectives to business unionism, Gompers was an avowed opponent of theorists and radicals in the labor movement, opposing an independent labor party and eschewing political commitments by labor to any of the existing parties. The notable exception, the Presidential campaign of 1924, which saw the A. F. of L. give half-hearted endorsement to the unsuccessful candidacy of Senator Robert M. La Follette, coincided with Gompers' last months in office. On balance, in the years down to World War I the A. F. of L.'s conservative and traditionalist program yielded such dividends as substantial gains in trade union membership and considerable influence in its lobbying for pro-labor legislation.

In its coverage of labor-management relations for the years 1900—14 the *Times* documents a zigzag pattern of labor victories and stunning defeats. Labor's gains in militancy and membership drew a response from management through the National Association of Manufacturers, which since 1895 had been conducting a vigorous anti-union campaign. Meantime, as the *Times* reported, government, labor and business each initiated approaches toward allaying friction between capital and labor and reducing the economic cost of work stoppages. By the early 20th century the Federal government had begun to play a significant role. The *Times* reports President Theodore Roosevelt's intervention in the anthracite coal strike of 1902, the enactment by Congress of legislation, beginning with the Erdman Act of 1898 and continuing down to 1934 with the passage of the Railway Labor Act, to provide for the mediation of railway labor disputes, always stopping short of compulsory arbitration.

At the same time labor undertook some initiatives of its own. The cloak and suit industry pioneered arbitration machinery in 1910, a protocol initiated by Louis D.

Brandeis, out of which the noteworthy impartial chairmanship evolved. Business also reacted, as the *Times'* pages record. In the early years of the 20th century the National Civic Federation, with organized labor's support, proved an effective instrument in mediating labor disputes, and on the eve of World War I nationwide, even worldwide, attention was drawn to the paternalistic program of Henry Ford, with its eight-hour day and five-dollar daily wage.

In this period, however, of the three branches of the Federal government, the Supreme Court proved to be the most inimical to the labor movement. In 1905 the high court invalidated a New York law setting maximum hours for bakers (*Lochner* v. *New York*), only to uphold an Oregon law three years later setting maximum hours for women. The latter case, *Muller* v. *Oregon*, was noteworthy for the socioeconomic brief submitted by Louis D. Brandeis, counsel for the state. The notorious *Danbury Hatters' Case* (1908), in which the Supreme Court held that a secondary boycott by a labor union was a conspiracy in restraint of trade within the meaning of the Sherman Act, sent shock waves throughout the labor movement, as previously that act had not been applied to labor organizations. To reverse the effect of this decision Congress in 1914 enacted the Clayton Act, presumably exempting labor unions and activities from the antitrust laws. Hailed by Gompers as the "Magna Carta" of labor, the guarantees of the Clayton Act proved to be largely illusory.

The New York Times did not neglect labor during World War I. It reported the enactment of the La Follette Seaman's Act of 1915, regulating conditions of employment for maritime workers; the Adamson Act of 1916 fixing an eight-hour day for railway workers; and the literacy test passed by Congress over President Wilson's veto—a first step toward the policy of immigration restriction which labor had so long demanded. The National War Labor Board, which served as a final court of appeals to settle industrial disputes, forecast a new governmental relationship toward labor to be institutionalized by the New Deal. The Board recognized the right of labor to organize and bargain collectively, the eight-hour day so far as practicable and the principle of equal pay for equal work, a concession to the expanding share of the labor force now held by women.

Labor's gains and new-found power were abruptly reversed with the coming of peace. The fomenting of strikes by left-wing elements contributed to the "Red Scare" of these postwar years, with a hardening of the public attitude toward labor. The *Times'* labor coverage of postwar years reported a succession of labor setbacks: the decision of the Supreme Court in *Hammer* v. *Dagenhart*, invalidating the Child Labor Act of 1916; failure of the strike against United States Steel (1919-20); a chain of Federal and state court decisions supporting company unions, "Yellow Dog" contracts and other anti-union devices. The result: a drastic weakening of labor's power and a sharp decline in union membership between 1921 and 1933.

The New Deal ushered in a new era for labor, and the *Times* assigned labor coverage to their top-notch labor reporter Louis Stark, whose remarkable *Times'* story of the execution of Nicola Sacco and Bartolomeo Vanzetti in August 1927, had already established him in the front rank of newspapermen. Throughout the thirties and forties Stark's depth reporting of labor events carried nationwide authority, and revealed at the same time a perceptible shift in *Times'* coverage and editorial policy toward the objectives of labor. The passage in 1933 of the National Industrial Recovery Act, which guaranteed to labor the right to bargain through representatives of its choosing, a right reiterated by the National Labor Relations Act (Wagner Act) of 1935, bestirred labor to a frenzy of organizing. The *Times* covered the effort to form industrial unions promoted by the Committee for Industrial Organization (CIO), which seceded from the A. F. of L., with close attention to the struggle to organize the automotive and steel industries. The year 1937 began with a spectacular 44-day sitdown strike at the General Motors' plants in Flint, Michigan, and culminated in the tragic "massacre" on Memorial Day, when striking workers were shot at Republic Steel. To the pages of *The New York Times* one may confidently turn for reports of such pathmaking legislation as the Social Security Act of 1935 and the Fair Labor Standards Act (Wages and Hours Law) of 1938.

Governmental controls over production, prices and labor were introduced on an unprecedented scale at the beginning of World War II. The *Times* exceeded all other American newspapers in the lineage devoted to the activities of the War Manpower Commission and the War Production Board and to price control and rationing. Crucial to the relations of government with management and labor in wartime were the activities of the National War Labor Board under the chairmanship of William H. Davis. The Board not only granted unions maintenance of membership if backed by a majority of union employees, but tied wage increases to the rise in living costs ("Little Steel" Formula, 1942).

The *Times'* reporters also covered the take-over of the anthracite coal mines ordered by President Roosevelt in 1942 to deal with a work stoppage called by mine union-leader John L. Lewis and the temporary seizure and operation of the railroads that year to prevent a strike of railway workers. Congress reacted to work stoppages threatening war production by the passage over President Roosevelt's veto of the Smith-Connally Anti-Strike Act (1942), which broadened Presidential power to seize plants where interference with war production was threatened by a labor disturbance, made illegal the instigation of strikes in plants seized by the government and held unions liable for damage suits for failure to give 30 days' notice of intention to strike in war industries.

In this period, too, the *Times* began to focus attention on the problem of discrimination in employment against minorities, giving considerable space to the activities of the Fair Employment Practice Committee (FEPC) set up in 1941 to curb discrimination in war production and government employment. The Committee's objectives were bolstered by an Executive order in 1943 calling for the mandatory incorporation of nondiscrimination clauses in war contracts and subcontracts.

It is to the postwar story of labor-management relations that the fullest coverage is reserved in this volume. Marking a new era for labor, it introduced to *Times'* readers the full and sympathetic labor reportage by A. H. Raskin. The experience of management with the operation of the Wagner Act brought increasing pressures for its modification. The Taft-Hartley Act, passed by Congress over President Truman's veto in 1947, condemned unfair union practices and forbade union coercion of employees who refused to bargain collectively, excessive membership fees, secondary boycotts and jurisdictional strikes. The act expressly banned the closed shop, circumscribed the union shop and required unions to give 60 days' notice for the termination or modification of any agreement. In the case of strikes found to imperil national health and safety the President was authorized to apply through the Attorney General for an injunction restraining all strike activity for 60 days. Despite gloomy prophecies the Taft-Hartley bill failed to choke off labor power, to curtail union membership or to end strikes and work stoppages—which increased in response to the postwar inflationary cycle. The most dramatic confrontation of management and labor in these postwar years was the seizure in 1952 by President Truman of the steel mills when the companies refused to abide by a wage mediation award of higher wages to workers without a corresponding rise in steel prices. The Supreme Court ruled the seizure unconstitutional.

Unable to secure the repeal of the Taft-Hartley Law and confronted with a rash of state "right-to-work" laws outlawing the union shop, the A. F. of L. and the CIO put aside their philosophic and jurisdictional differences and merged in 1955 under the presidency of George Meany. Biographical sketches of Meany and the United Auto Workers' Walter Reuther appear in the *Times* under the byline of A. H. Raskin. The *Times* documented the changing emphasis from issues of wages to "fringe" benefits like pension and early retirement rights, health care and the guaranteed annual wage, important aspects of the new welfare unionism. The *Times* has given increasing attention to the new social attitude of the worker

toward his job and his disenchantment with automation, which he finds offers tasks both boring and unfulfilling, perhaps best epitomized by coverage of the trouble in 1972 at the automated Chevrolet plant at Lordstown, Ohio.

In the years between the Korean and Vietnam wars public attention came to be spotlighted on such disturbing developments within the labor union movement as crime, corruption, mismanagement of health and welfare funds and, most persistently, discrimination. Each in turn was covered by *Times'* reporters, as was the increasing political conservatism within labor. Thus, the *Times'* pages covered crime on the New York waterfront and the activities of Senator McClellan's committee investigating racketeering in labor-management relations, especially in the Teamsters' Union, with focus on the actions of its president, Dave Beck, and its then vice-president and subsequent president, James R. Hoffa. The *Times* followed the legislative career of the Landrum-Griffith Act (1958), which in its final form embodied a cluster of proposals to suppress gangsterism, racketeering and blackmail in labor organizations. It also reported the murder of United Mine Workers' official Joseph Yablonski in 1970 and the trial and conviction of certain principals and accessories.

The *Times* documented the attempts of the Kennedy and Johnson administrations to combat unemployment by increasing over-all economic activity without inflation. With inflation a major domestic concern of the Nixon administration, the *Times'* reporters have devoted considerable attention to the guidelines set in Washington to keep wage raises in line with productivity gains and to the determined resistance of A. F. of L. officials to the wage policies laid down by the Pay Board.

The massive balance of payment deficits reported for the United States in recent years attest to the inroads that the Japanese and our other trading partners have made in the American market. The response of American management has been the multinational corporation able to exploit low-wage foreign labor abroad to the benefit of American investors, to be sure, but to the detriment of high-cost American labor. The latter sees to its chagrin certain entire industries eliminated by foreign competition and other industries in headlong flight to cheap labor areas. One way management has found to meet competition is by improving efficiency by introducing advanced technology to promote gains in labor productivity. A probable response of labor in the United States will be to build worldwide coalitions of labor and in effect form multinational unions to equalize labor competition and raise labor standards on a worldwide basis. Initiatives in that direction are by no means new, but are likely to be spurred in the coming new era of economic and political relationships among nations.

Whether or not a new pattern of labor power and

organization may emerge, one thing is clear. Old line craft and industrial unions no longer command the headlines. Rather the focus is on the organization of public employees, including teachers, policemen, firemen and hospital workers; on continuing discrimination on the part of both labor unions and management against blacks and other ethnic groups; on the extraordinary gains secured by farm labor under the dynamic leadership of Cesar Chavez and finally on the increasing conservatism of blue collar workers.

In the opening decade of the 20th century Hutchins Hapgood, a labor writer, commented: "The world of labor is so big—it has so markedly not only the character of a great human thing, but also connects itself so definitely with history and politics—it has so many aspects, so many threads, that no man can possibly stand at the center of it." If this observation was true in 1907, it is even more apt today. As these pages from the back issues of *The New York Times* abundantly demonstrate, labor unions in America have raised the expectations of all labor, both organized and unorganized, men and women, black and white, assembly line and white collar, and these expectations have received the sanction of laws and administrative agencies, and are periodically embodied in the platforms of the major political parties. They are an essential part of the American Dream, and no business executive or responsible labor leader can jauntily ignore them. Labor today constitutes a complex sociocultural element in American life. Its interests transcend economic goals, and it is proving to be less manipulable than ever by labor leaders, by management or by political parties.

Richard B. Morris

Columbia University

x

LABOR
AND
MANAGEMENT

WORKMEN CANNONADING THE BARGES.

SOLDIERS IN CAMP.

WORKMEN ATTACKING THE BARGES.

GREAT BATTLE
OF HOMESTEAD.
Defeat and Capture of the
PINKERTON INVADERS
July 6th 1892.

SURRENDER OF THE PINKERTON MEN.

PINKERTON'S CAPTIVES ON THEIR WAY TO PRISON.

CHAPTER **1**

The Lines Are Drawn

Industrial warefare in Pennsylvania.

The New York Times.

The Interests of the Laboring Man.

In connection with the recent difficulties between the bricklayers and the master masons, some considerations are suggested to us, which, though not directly involved in this conflict, are of the greatest importance to all laboring men.

Labor in this country has a dignity which attaches to it in no other. No limitations are imposed upon it other than those which belong legitimately to political economy, and which regulate all industrial competition. Any attempt to interfere with these laws cannot result in permanent benefit to the workingman. And generally it is true that coöperative societies, organized for the purpose of such interference, only tend to place the lazy and the incompetent upon a level with their superiors in skill and industry.

The best course for the laborer to take is to absolve himself from this factitious aid, and depend upon himself. Whether or no, he will have to come to that in the end, since nothing else can avail him anything in the long run.

Skill and perseverance—these are the great requisites of success to the workingman: the former regulates brute force by intelligence; the latter secures the full result of intelligent experience. They are the secrets of power, and those who avail themselves of them are invincible, except by fate. But these are not the only requisites to complete success. Only through temperate habits of life and economy in the expenditure of money can the laborer realize either happiness or certain profit. The unskilled laborer who earns $2 a day and spends it all, is no worse off than he who, by greater skill, earns $5 and has nothing to show for it.

The great vice of the laboring classes is wasteful expenditure of their daily earnings. Comparatively little, as a rule, goes for food, necessary clothing and shelter; the rest is too frequently squandered either by the husband in dissipation, or by the wife and daughters at the milliner's. The wife, by her extravagance, leads the husband to more dissolute habits; and he, by his absence from home, drives her to other resorts than his society for pleasure, and thus increases her extravagance.

Let the laborer select a wife who will indeed prove a helpmeet to him, whose temper and moral disposition will elevate instead of depressing him, and whose society will be more desirable than that to be found in the gin-shop. Such a marriage is salvation. It is the beginning of a home; it is the fountain of household pleasures, of spiritual and physical health, and of worldly prosperity. The home thus becomes both the incentive to industry and its reward. It furnishes motives for labor, and it also affords relaxation and rest.

But, says the honest and sober laborer, "I have been blessed with such a wife; I have trusted solely to my own skill and experience for promotion: I earn good wages as the result of persevering industry—but, for all that, the demands of a large family consume all my hard earnings. I can simply clothe and feed my family and pay my rent; there is nothing left over. I can only obtain for $6 what six years ago I could get for $2. If I should die suddenly, I leave nothing to my wife and children; I cannot afford the yearly cost of an insurance policy. What am I to do?"

In reply, we say, go out of the City and secure a residence where land is cheap and rents are low. All around New-York are places where those doing business in the City can live at nearly one-half the expense which must be incurred within the limits of the metropolis. Every year the facilities of rapid locomotion between the City and the country are growing greater. Soon by economy you can purchase a lot which will include a garden sufficient to supply your family with vegetables all the year round. As soon as you have done this you can build a house. The interest upon the mortgage which you allow will not be nearly so great as your present expense for rent; and very soon, with good management, you will be free from even that burden. Your children will be healthier, for they will have fresh air, pure milk, and abundant room and motive for exercise.

This plan is practicable; it has been tried by many with the most satisfactory results. How much wiser it is for the workman to adopt such a plan than to spend his earnings for that which is not bread, but poison. How much better for his wife to coöperate with him for this end, than to ruin both her own, her children's and her husband's prospects for the sake of indulging for a few years in extravagance and vain show.

The best interests of the workingman, then, are not to be secured through arbitrary coöperative associations, but through skill, industry, temperate habits, economy, and wisdom in the conduct of his domestic affairs.

OUR WORKING CLASSES.

Their Condition and Prospects—Concentration of Capital in the Hands of the Few—Employers Becoming Fewer and Laborers More Numerous—The Rich Richer, the Poor Poorer.

"The rich become richer, the poor poorer," is a pregnant phrase; but it is less the force and vigor than the startling truth of the expression which has given it of late such extended and powerful currency. It was the early recognition of this truth, to which Commissioner WELLS in his report on the revenue gave such eloquent voice, that instigated years ago the organization of Trades' Unions and Protective Associations, and in later years suggested Coöperative Societies among the laboring classes. It was the realization of this bitter truth which actuated the numerous "strikes" among the workingmen of various trades during the past year; and the present strikes among the printers, sailors, painters, slate-roofers, tailors and coopers, are simply rebellions against the same hard fate.

The idea that there must of necessity be an antagonism between Capital and Labor is a most obnoxious one; almost as much argument has been wasted, as many earnest appeals have been thrown away in attempts to convince capitalists and laborers that their interests were mutual and identical, as in attempts to reconcile the various religious sects. There has never been a condition of society since the beginning of the world, when this antagonism did not exist. Nor can there ever be a millennium of this sort—capital and labor must of necessity always be antagonistic. He is blind to facts and figures who does not see this antagonism between the employing capitalists and the workingmen of this country increasing daily in bitterness. Capital is annually concentrating in the hands of the few; great manufacturing establishments are swallowing up the small ones; competition is less extensive, and hence the prices of manufactured commodities are not lessened, nor the wages of labor advanced, as they should be by such wholesome rivalry, while tariff protections are greater, and hence the cost of all manufactured articles is increased to the consumer and laborer, whose wages are also thereby reduced. While laborers are rapidly increasing, the employing manufacturers are becoming fewer in number; one capitalist employs five men now where he employed one twenty years ago; and thus there is gradually developing at the North a system of slavery as absolute if not as degrading as that which lately prevailed at the South. The only difference is that there agriculture was the field, landed proprietors were the masters and negroes were the slaves; while in the North manufactures is the field, manufacturing capitalists threaten to become the masters, and it is the white laborers who are to be slaves.

Doubtless the capitalists of the country repudiate any such purpose; and we do not doubt that they can honestly do so, for it is not a well arranged and thoroughly organized conspiracy. We do not charge them with the deliberate intention to establish any such relations between themselves and their employes. Doubtless the laborers themselves will at first be inclined to laugh at the assertion, as at the cry of "Wolf" when there is no wolf near, and sneer at the power which is supposed to be capable of thus enslaving them. But a deliberate study of the facts and figures of this subject of the relations of capitalists and laborers will reveal that the inevitable tendency of the industrial interests of the North is to reduce the laboring classes to the same condition of absolute dependency, in which 22,000,000 of the English manufacturing and agricultural laborers now struggle. In proof and explanation of the truth of this we propose in this paper to show:

1. That capital is being concentrated in the hands of the few;

2. That small manufacturing establishments are being absorbed by the large ones;

3. That competition, which is the protection of the consumer, has been in a great measure abolished; and, in short,

4. That the rich are becoming richer.

And all this at the expense, directly in the reduction of wages, and indirectly in the increase in the cost of food and of all manufactured commodities, of the mass who form the laboring classes of the country.

The manufacturing interests of the country from 1810 to 1860 increased ten-fold, at a ratio twice as great as that of the population; and this was shown not only in the increased capital and labor employed and profits realized in all kinds of domestic industry, but in the increase also of the number of establishments. But since 1850, while the capital, labor, and product of nearly all kinds of industry have continued to increase at an equal if not greater ratio, the actual number of industrial establishments and employing capitalists have largely decreased. There is probably not a mechanic of mature age in the New-England and Middle States who cannot recall more than one instance of the absorption of small manufacturing establishments by the larger ones. Every one has noticed this tendency in all the trades. Small manufacturers are far less common than they were before the war. A casual observer, walking the streets of a city familiar to him ten years ago, cannot fail to notice this fact. It has also been observed that the smaller manufacturers thus swallowed up have become workmen on wages in the greater establishments, whose longer purses, labor-saving machines, &c., refused to allow the small manufacturer a separate existence. The immense contracts made during the war were given to the larger establishments at high rates, because of the greater financial responsibility and political influences of the proprietors, and their ability to furnish the needed articles with dispatch and in vast quantities. To fill these contracts the smaller establishments, machinery, workmen and all, were largely employed, but either by sub-letting the contracts at low prices, or else by the absorption of the small factories and factors—mainly the latter.

But this decrease in the number of the manufacturing establishments was not owing entirely to the war. It was greater for the ten years before the war than during its continuance and since it ended; and this consolidation of manufacturing interests, and concentration of the capital employed in manufacturing enterprises of all kinds, has been going on so systematically as to appear as if by design for the last twenty years. There has been, to speak more definitely, no increase in the number of manufacturing establishments or proprietors in this country since 1860, except in new branches of manufacture just beginning to develop, as sewing machines, newspapers, &c., &c.

It is the common belief that the inventior and substitution of labor-saving machines for hand labor is detrimental to the interests of the laborer. But, while we have found this not to be so practically, it is undoubtedly true that these inventions are favorable to the interests of employers. Almost every new machine put in practical use, instead of decreasing the force of laborers, increases it by developing new branches of industry. A firm in this City, engaged in manufacturing paper-collar boxes, employed a newly-invented machine for cutting the pasteboard in proper shape. Instead of discharging the several hands whose work this machine accomplished, the employer soon found that these hands were needed in a new direction,—the making of another kind of box for tobacco, which the machine itself had originated by its facility in cutting pasteboard into all conceivable shapes. This is but an illustration of how almost all machines for saving labor increase the laboring force in other directions. The manufacture of sewing machines alone has given employment to many more persons than were temporarily discharged by its use. But at the same time the increase of machinery is favorable to employers, and tends to the concentration of capital, as we have argued, by making it more difficult, because more costly, for a laborer to become an employer.

The following table illustrates in detail the assertions we have made, and will be found, on examination, to fully bear us out in the theory advanced:

Table of Manufactories in 1850 and 1860.

Manufactures.		No. of Establishments.	Capital.
Woolen Goods	1850	1,817	$26,071,542
	1860	1,260	30,862,654
Cotton Goods	1850	1,074	76,032,578
	1860	1,091	98,585,269
Clothing	1850	4,278	12,509,161
	1860	3,793	24,939,193
Hats and Caps	1850	1,048	4,427,798
	1860	622	4,128,572
Iron Castings	1850	1,319	14,722,749
	1860	955	13,580,512

Manufactures.		Value of Products.	No. of Hands.	Annual Wages.
Woolen Goods.	1850	$43,552,285	34,895	$7,167,900
	1860	61,896,217	41,360	9,803,254
Cotton Goods..	1850	69,135,418	94,956	....
	1860	115,681,774	122,028	....
Clothing.......	1850	48,311,709	96,551	15,032,340
	1860	73,219,765	98,903	18,942,838
Hats and Caps	1850	14,318,864	15,200	3,179,700
	1860	16,665,475	10,341	3,638,596
Iron Castings.	1850	20,111,517	18,969	....
	1860	20,000,267	15,225	....

Take, in illustration of this statement, any of the large and long-established branches of industry. In the manufacture of woolen goods, for instance, there existed, in 1850, 1,817 establishments, with a capital of $26,071,542; but though the capital in the next ten years increased to $30,862,654, the number of establishments decreased to 1,260. The number of these establishments increased during the war, as also did the capital, but this was owing to the transformation of a large number of cotton mills into woolen factories, controlled, however, by the same class of large capitalists. Although twenty years ago cotton manufactures had really only begun to develop in this country, there was during the decade 1850–60 an increase of only 17, or less than two per cent. in the number of mills, while the capital increased over 30 per cent.; the product was nearly doubled in value, and the laborers increased 33 per cent. in number. The decrease in the number of cotton mills during the war was, or has been stated, very great, and it does not appear that they have increased since the war ended. The machine shops of the country increased their laboring force from 1850 to 1860 at the rate of 35 per cent., and the value of their products 66 per cent., but the establishments themselves (in spite of the fact that this is one of the most rapidly increasing industries of the country, owing to the great railroad extensions, unparalleled in any other country) increased only at the rate of about eight per cent.

Take other branches of the great iron interest. There were 404 iron furnaces in full blast in 1850, but only 286 in 1860. There were 1,319 establishments in the country engaged in 1850 in the manufacture of various kinds of iron castings, from cannon and hydraulic rams to kitchen stoves and patent gridirons. In 1860 there were only 955 of these left, but these few were more extensive in their operations, owned more capital, employed more hands and produced greater amounts and values at greater profits than did the larger number for the ten years previous. The clothing manufacturers, as will be seen from the table above, also largely decreased in number from 1850 to 1860; and our information is to the effect that this decrease during the war was still greater, owing to the extension of the large establishments in filling large army contracts, the small ones being absorbed and their proprietors employed as laborers. It is calculated by men engaged in the manufacture of clothing that there are 1,000 less establishments to-day than there was in 1850, though the capital and products have been trebled.

Take minor interests, such as the manufacture of hats and caps—1,048 in 1850, only 622 in number in 1860, but the smaller number doing the larger business,—and the figures, as given in the census and other Government reports, bear out the theory we have advanced, that the capitalists or masters are becoming fewer and stronger and richer, while the laborers or slaves are becoming more numerous and weaker and poorer.

One of the natural, and to the laborer and consumer deplorable, consequences of this concentration of capital is the decrease in the competition or rivalry between manufacturers. This affects the working classes in their dual character of laborers and consumers. First, it reduces their wages. Instead of a sharp competition among manufacturers to secure the best skilled labor by offering the best wages, the rivalry is wholly among the laboring men to secure situations by underbidding each other. In the second place, in the absence of brisk competition, the prices of the manufactured commodities are kept up and the working classes are thus compelled to pay the highest prices for the product of their labor at the lowest rates. The decrease in competition, for instance, between the 4,278 small clothing manufacturers who existed in 1850, was much less than that between the 3,793 who were in operation in 1860. The fact is, that practically there was no competition; in all the great branches of industry there is, on the contrary, a half-recognized union, an implied though unexpressed coöperation among manufacturers to sustain prices and keep down wages. The absence of this competition must of necessity affect the rate of wages, since it is regulated entirely by the laws of demand and supply—save where positive Protective Unions are organized among laborers to counteract the effect of this half-organized coöperation among employers.

This coöperation among employers, though negative and unacknowledged as regards the keeping down of wages, is positive and open and cordial in the other direction for the sustaining of prices of manufactured commodities. This they accomplish, not only as we have shown, by abolishing competition to a great extent, but by coöperation in efforts to secure protective tariffs. There are numerous instances of the active coöperation of great capitalists, who in the days when "competition is the life of trade" was an orthodox commercial doctrine, would have been considered rivals in trade, for the purpose of influencing legislation, testing legal decisions, &c., &c. Almost every branch of business has its "ring," and each seeks its own protection at the expense of all others, and particularly at the expense of the laboring classes, who are also the consumers, and whose cost of living is much enhanced by the indiscriminate protection which unwise legislation grants, to the destruction of all wholesome competition.

Thus, while the laborers have been increasing for the last twenty years in this country, the capitalists have been decreasing; while the average wages of labor have practically decreased, its products have increased in value. The rich have become richer and the poor poorer.

We are rapidly approaching in this country the condition, industrially, of England, where 22,000,000 of agricultural and mechanical laborers are virtually the slaves of a few thousand large landed proprietors and great manufacturers. Of course, the social aspect of the question in the two countries can never be the same, so long as the workingman here enjoys the political privileges and educational advantages denied him in England; but already the financial aspect of the case is painfully alike in both countries. The concentration of capital is going on even more rapidly with us than with the English, as we have shown. We reserve for another paper the evidence that the laboring man in this country is at this time even worse paid than the "White Slaves of England," and is rapidly becoming even poorer than at present.

Meeting of Trade Employers.

A large meeting of employers in the different pursuits connected with house-building, took place yesterday afternoon at No. 51 Liberty-street. Mr. DENNIS HENNESSY, a master carpenter, took the chair, and Mr. WM. H. JACKSON, a master plasterer, was chosen Secretary. The following resolutions were read and commented upon:

Whereas, The repeated and continued agitation of the various relations existing between the employers and the employed are constantly a source of disturbance to the welfare and quietude of the business community; and,

Whereas, It is highly essential to the interests of the people that an expression should be given of the views entertained by the several branches of trade here represented on the foregoing matters of issue; and,

Whereas, We, as citizens of the Empire City and the country at large, in common with all good citizens, have an important interest at stake, namely, in keeping the credit of the country unimpaired, and that a nation, like a corporation or private individual, can never pay its debts by growing less industrious or energetic, and that a reduction of the working hours from the present rates, once initiated in this city, will become general throughout the different States, and thereby reduce the productive labor of the nation one-fifth, or in other words, take away twenty per cent. of the means of the nation to pay its debts; therefore, be it

Resolved, That at present we deem it inexpedient to reduce the number of working hours constituting a day's work. The consequences of such reduction we consider would be fatal to business generally, enhance the value of all commodities of life, and fall heaviest upon the mechanic and workman seeking such reduction; that the system of trades unions is uncalled for on this continent, and the principles by which they are governed, anti-Republican, demoralizing, and damaging to the skillful, the industrious, and energetic, depriving them of the opportunity of earning all they are worth, and encouraging the unskillful and idle, whose only merit often consists in being a member of a Union in good standing. We deny the assertions of the Unions that they have a tendency to improve and combine those who are skilled in their trades. On the contrary, the Unions prevent the apprentices and their members from becoming experts as mechanics, by dividing one and the same trade into three or four distinct branches.

Resolved, That we will pay the industrious a full remuneration for their services, whether they be members of a Union or not, and will not submit to any arbitrary rules or dictations as to the manner in which we, as employers, shall conduct our business, or whom we shall employ. That we will employ as many apprentices as our business may warrant, and make it our duty to have them well provided for, serve a regular apprenticeship with one master, and seek employment for them with others to finish a regular time of apprenticeship where the master is unable to retain them by reason of retirement from business, death, or otherwise; and be it further

Resolved, That we will sign no contract, limiting the time for completion of work, without adding the following clause, as passed upon by the Master Masons' Association, viz.: "The time lost by strikes, caused by any unreasonable demands of the trades-unions, shall be added to the time given to finish the work."

Resolved, That the body as now convened select a standing committee, consisting of two representatives of each branch of the trade represented, which shall organize itself and appoint a regular time of meeting, and that they be empowered to add to their number, call meetings of any one or all branches of the building trade, and take the necessary steps to act upon any questions arising and conflicting with the resolutions passed, and also collect the necessary funds to defray their expenses; and be it further

Resolved, That in adopting these resolutions we harbor no ill-feeling against the mechanics and working-men in our employ, personally; on the contrary, we think that we are advocating their cause more than our own by issuing our views to them and the public at large, and by trying, if possible, to prevent strikes, so detrimental to business generally and fatal to the employés and their families.

Mr. ROSS, a master bricklayer, said that trades-unions were not only anti-Republican, but were an outrage on the community. He denied the right of men to dictate to their employers how many hours they should require them to work, how much they should pay them, or how many apprentices they should employ. Mechanics were worse at present than before trades' unions were established. They could then do several things well, but now could rarely do any one thing thoroughly. There were more household-ing mechanics, twenty years ago, who owned the houses in which they lived, than now, though the journeymen are now from five to ten times as numerous as then.

Mr. M. EIDLITZ objected specially to that part of the system of trades-unions that denied the right of union bricklayers to act as plasterers, unless they belonged also to the Plasterers' Union, and paid $25 or $50 to the Society to become members.

Mr. TOSTEVIN coincided with the previous speakers, and urged polite and conciliatory manners to journeymen on the part of employers. He cited a case where he had recently heard an employer, in reply to a question from a journeyman, say insultingly that "He (the journeyman) had no business to address him, but should go to the foreman." Mr. TOSTEVIN thought the unfair dealing was not altogether on the journeymen's side.

In this Mr. ROSS coincided, and said there were natural hogs in all business pursuits.

Mr. McLANE complained of an article which had appeared in the TIMES, wherein it was stated that journeymen had a right to combine.

Mr. JAMES WEBB, a mason, wished the advocacy of ten hours as a day's work in the resolutions distinctly understood. Mr. M. EIDLITZ, also a mason, said that the question of hours was not now at issue. When it should arise it would be time to take measures in favor of it.

Mr. TOSTEVIN was glad that neither eight nor ten hours had been named in the resolutions.

Mr. WILSON, of the brown-stone workers, also objected to the naming of ten hours.

The Chairman coincided with the above, and desired to have no disagreement with labor.

Eight-Hour Strikes.

There is no question that almost everybody nowadays works too hard. If the whole European and American world would consent to reduce their productions and their wants one-fifth, we believe they would be at least that proportion better off, mentally and morally. The grandest products of the human mind have come from those regions where climate and custom permit the needs of the body to be less, and the leisure for calm and elevated mental efforts to be proportionately greater. The religions of the world and its language of devotion have all come from the East. The Parthenon could never have been built, or the Apollo molded, in the midst of the intense competition and struggling haste of English and American civilization.

There is no nook or corner of Great Britain or the United States calm and undisturbed enough, with so little of the "struggle for existence," as to even permit the existence of a modern Socrates or Plato. The fact that in Greece, and Palestine, and India, nature permitted man to live with so little labor and exposure, alone almost accounts for the great contributions these countries have made to the highest thoughts of the race. If all people in Great Britain and this country would unanimously give up one-fifth of their labor and one-fifth of their luxuries, we should certainly have a simpler and healthier life, and would perhaps add more to the world's real treasures. But as this is impossible, the question arises, "Can one class cut off one-fifth of its labor and its wants?" The laboring classes of this City are not, however, exactly attempting this. They are trying to burn the candle at one end, and to keep as much of the other as they can. They will reduce their labor, and retain their wants. They will cut off one-fifth of their toil, and keep the full equivalent of labor; in other words, they claim twenty per cent. higher wages.

This claim, if supported by rational and legal means, is perfectly proper and legitimate. There is no exact division of the profits of capital; there is no fixed "wage-fund;" labor may at one time get more of this profit and at another less. The laborers are now in fact striking for higher wages; they may not get all they ask, but they will get something. There are, however, several dangers before them in this effort which they would do well to consider. For the past few years, capital has not had a very successful career. Our taxation has fallen upon it with great heaviness. We suspect that the laborer's wages have taken a large proportion of its profits. It is clear that in certain branches, such as the manufacture of machinery, the taxation and the strikes have fairly driven capital from the field. Our machine-shops and engine-yards are closed, and the laborers are left in destitution.

It is among the possibilities that the masons, and brick-layers, and plumbers, and carpenters may produce a similar effect in their trades; that is, capital may find it more profitable to build railroads or work farms at the West than to build houses here and our population may be still further driven from the City by high rents. There is a limit to the exactions of labor, and capital may be approaching it. Then, again, strikes of course add to the prices of the commodities the laborers produce. A rise of twenty per cent. in wages means a certain rise in commodities. These strikes will make every house, and store, and shop dearer in New-York next year. Rents will be higher, and then the prices of almost every article sold in shops. Labor itself may be driven away from the City by them. If the strikes spread through the county, all commodities will rise, and the laboring classes will be but little better off.

But how will the laborers of this City use their eight hours? The upper mechanics will, we believe, be benefited by a shorter day's labor. Many will remove to the country, and be enabled to have their families in little houses of their own, at cheaper rent and lower expenses, because the new rule gives them time to go in and out to their work. Others will improve themselves at the Cooper Union and the public libraries, or will be more with their families. The lower class of workmen, we think, will be nowise benefited by this new privilege. They will only the more frequent liquor-shops and work for politicians. Their new leisure will be a new temptation. Probably, however, both classes of workmen will be tempted by higher wages to longer days' labor, and both laborers and the community will be compelled to pay the additional expense of protection. If the movement is guided with judgment and reason, it will command respect; if it be not so guided, it will only react on the laboring class.

THE LABOR QUESTION.

DARK PROSPECTS FOR THE OPERATIVES.

MEN THROWN OUT OF WORK IN ALL BRANCHES—REMEDIES SUGGESTED.

The condition of the working classes this Winter, and the privations which they must encounter by reason of money stringency in all branches of business, must excite attention and kindle solicitude in their behalf. Thousands have already been thrown out of work, and many more must soon have the same misfortune and endure it, in some degree, throughout the entire Winter. Already the act, in all its aspects, has been presented to attentive observation, and extraordinary measures of a local character have been adopted for the extension of relief in various places. It is gratifying to note these preparations, though many are convinced that whatever provision may be made it will fall far short of absolute requirements.

Groups of anxious men yesterday discussed the probabilities, and the best means to meet the coming rants. Hundreds on Saturday were discharged from the sugar-refineries and oil works at the foot of Cherry street. In the former place they only received $9 per week, and those who were retained have been reduced to $6 a week. In the oil works all operations have ceased. The majority of the discharged men have large families to support. It is claimed that there is much work to be done in the City in the way of improvements, which would keep many men engaged this Winter. Within the past month several working men's organizations have petitioned the Mayor and Common Council in regard to the matter, but the petitions have not been taken into consideration up to this. Important action was had in this regard yesterday, in the Federal Council of the International Working Men's Association, which met in Turn Hall, Spring street. The delegates represented German, French, Swiss, and English speaking portions of the laboring classes. A delegation from the French revolutionary group was also present. It was resolved to unite with the other associations and call a congress. A committee was appointed to draw up a petition to the Mayor and Common Council, asking for the establishment of markets where the working classes could provide themselves with the necessaries of life at cost price, in view of approaching distress. The petition recommends the appointment of a commission similar to the Chicago Relief Committee in that city. Attention is called to the City's wants and the chances for work if any effort to supply them be made. There are, it says, elevators to be constructed, houses to be built, sewers to be improved, parks to be laid out, a rapid-transit road to be constructed, and streets to be opened; and concludes with the assertion "Relief we must have; peaceably if we can, forcibly if we must." A motion for its adoption was carried unanimously, and the committee was ordered to present it to-day to the Mayor.

MASS-MEETING OF THE UNEMPLOYED IN CHICAGO.

AN EXCITED GATHERING — COMMUNISTIC TALK—THE DEMANDS MADE—A RIOT ANTICIPATED.

Special Dispatch to the New-York Times.

CHICAGO, Dec. 21.—An immense meeting of laboring men and mechanics who are out of work was held on West Twelfth street this afternoon. Upward of 5,000 participated. The meeting was highly exciting, and speeches were made in the English, German, French, and Polish languages. A large number of policemen were present, and had they not been a terrible riot might have occurred. The speeches were all of an incendiary character, and created great excitement. The speakers announced that the working men had met, not for political purposes, but to devise some means "to bring the laboring classes out of their present terrible calamity." Distinctions in society, it was stated, are to be broken up. The working men must band together to sustain themselves in their rights. Thousands of men are out of employment, and something must be done to sustain them. The crisis was denounced as the result of overproduction and of monopoly. The laboring men, rated as so many machines, are actually in a starving condition, and help must be demanded. They must combine against capital. If there was no other remedy, then they must resort to force. The city must be compelled to give them work, or money and provisions. It was said that slavery is abolished in the South, but a worse serfdom than that ever was now exists in the North. The rich were denounced as caring more for luxury than for human lives. An organization similar to that of the grangers was urged upon the meeting. Hopes were expressed (and the sentiment was loudly cheered) that the day was near at hand when an equitable division of wealth would be made. In specific terms it was demanded that the city furnish work for the suffering many. Then a preamble and resolutions were adopted, addressed to the Mayor and Common Council, embracing the following propositions: First, demanding employment for all who are willing and able to work, at the rate of eight hours per day, with sufficient wages; second, that advances, either in money or provisions, be made to those for whom there is no work; third, that these advances shall be distributed by a committee to be appointed by the working classes; and fourth, that in case the funds of the city are insufficient, the city credit shall be resorted to for the purpose of obtaining a loan. In order that the resolutions may be promptly brought before the Mayor, a special committee was appointed for that purpose. They will go before the Common Council to-morrow evening. The men out of employment will assemble at 7 o'clock, and will march in solid phalanx to the Court-house square, where they will await the return of their committee. It is hardly possible that the delegation to visit the Mayor will be cordially received, and it is certain that their resolutions will be referred to a standing committee. This, it is believed, will anger the men congregated in the public square, and grave consequences are anticipated.

THE DESPERATE STRIKERS.

A RIOT AT BALTIMORE.

MILITIA REGIMENT ORDERED TO THE FRONT BY GOV. CARROLL—THE SOLDIERS, WHILE ON THE MARCH, FIRED ON BY A MOB—THE FIRE RETURNED—NINE PERSONS KILLED AND THIRTEEN KNOWN TO BE WOUNDED—BUSINESS OF THE BALTIMORE AND OHIO ROAD VIRTUALLY DEAD.

Special Dispatch to the New-York Times.

BALTIMORE, Md., July 20.—This has been a terrible and bloody day for Baltimore, and at midnight the city is in a ferment of excitement. The streets are thronged with people, and the vicinity of the Baltimore and Ohio Railroad Depot is besieged with anxious crowds discussing the situation, while the southern horizon is lit up with the flames of burning buildings along the line of the track which the rioters have set fire to. The history of the sad events of the day begins with the issuance about noon of Gov. Carroll's proclamation, warning the mob in Maryland to disperse, and his orders calling out the Fifth Regiment Maryland National Guards to proceed to Cumberland under command of Gen. James R. Herbert, commanding the First Brigade of the State Militia. This action was taken in consequence of the attacks of the strikers at Cumberland upon the west-bound freight train which left Martinsburg on Thursday. Gov. Carroll had advised with the railway authorities on the subject, and as it seems clear that the strikers were extending their operations into Maryland, they called upon him for aid, and he immediately placed himself in communication with Gen. Herbert with the result stated. Although the afternoon papers announced that the Fifth Regiment had been ordered out, there was not the slightest apprehension of trouble in the city. No one dreamed that there would be any opposition to their departure for the seat of war. The first indications of coming trouble were manifested in the jeering of the soldiers hurrying singly or in squads to the armory by men and boys along the streets. Occasionally a soldier would be stoned, and as the evening approached a great throng of men assembled around the armory of the Fifth Regiment. At this point some one ordered the sounding on the City Hall bell of the signal of 151, which means that a riot is in progress, and the mustering of the Militia is demanded. The Fifth Regiment assembled in force, and about 7 o'clock marched out of the armory on the way to Camden Station with about 250 muskets in line. They marched down to the depot, the crowd following them, hooting and yelling, but not making any actual attack on them. At the corner of Pratt and Eutaw streets, three blocks from the depot, a rush was made upon the regiment. Stones and bricks were thrown, but not a shot was fired, and the troops, with fixed bayonets, steadily kept their march to the station. They entered it. The fusilade of stones grew heavy, and the rioters, charging around the lower end of the platform, met them again. A charge was ordered, and the mob fell back without waiting for a taste of the cold steel. The troops then entered a train that had been drawn up to take them west, but the strikers gathered around the locomotive and drove the engineer and fireman away from it.

PROCLAMATION BY THE PRESIDENT.

WASHINGTON, July 18.—The following was issued to-night by the President of the United States:

Whereas, It is provided in the Constitution of the United States that the United States shall protect every State in this Union on application of the Legislature or the Executive, when the Legislature cannot be convened, against domestic violence; and

Whereas, The Governor of the State of West Virginia has represented that domestic violence exists in said State at Martinsburg and at various other points along the line of the Baltimore and Ohio Railroad in said State, which the authorities of said State are unable to suppress; and

Whereas, The laws of the United States require that in all cases of insurrection in any State, or of obstruction to the laws thereof, whenever it may be necessary in the judgment of the President, he shall forthwith by proclamation command such insurgents to disperse and retire peaceably to their respective abodes within a limited time.

Now, therefore, I, Rutherford B. Hayes, President of the United States, do hereby admonish all good citizens of the United States, and all persons within the territory and jurisdiction of the United States, against aiding, countenancing, abetting, or taking part in such unlawful proceedings; and I do hereby warn all persons engaged in or connected with said domestic violence and obstruction of laws to disperse and retire peacefully to their respective abodes on or before 12 o'clock noon of the 19th day of July inst.

In witness whereof I have hereunto set my hand and caused the seal of the United States to be affixed.

Done at the City of Washington, this eighteenth

Rutherford Birchard Hayes

day of July, in the year of Our Lord eighteen hundred and seventy-seven, and of the Independence of the United States, the one hundred and second.

R. B. HAYES.

By the President.
F. W. SEWARD, Assistant Secretary of State.

July 19, 1877

In the meantime, while these events were occurring in the western section of the city and around Camden Station, the bloody work was going on down town. The armory of the Sixth Regiment is at the corner of Front and Fayette streets, in East Baltimore. The men had been instructed to hold themselves in readiness since Tuesday, and when the alarm was rung on the City Hall bell they gathered at head-quarters. It was about half past 6 o'clock when the alarm was struck, and half an hour later there were over 400 men at the Armory. Gen Herbert sent an order to Col. Peters, commanding the regiment, to detail three companies, under command of Adjt. George W. Bishop, to report to him at Camden Station immediately. Lieut. Bishop started out with Companies B, I, and C, and they had not reached the street before they were set upon by a mob of not less than 2,000 that had gathered around the armory. Stones were thrown at the soldiers and several shots fired. As the column turned from Front-street into Baltimore-street the mob made a rush, and one of the companies commanded by Capt. Duffy was cut off from the other two. The first two marched on up the street, leaving the rioters between them and Capt. Duffy's command. It is hard to say who first commenced the firing, but from the Centre Market up to the corner of Baltimore and St. Paul streets there was a running fight. The mob was swelled in numbers by sympathizers pouring in from side streets until the sidewalks swarmed with them. Having isolated Capt. Duffy's company, they devoted most of their attention to it. Seeing that a fight was inevitable, and the men were ordered to defend themselves, and after passing

Centre Market they fired right and left. The sharp, quick crack of musketry rang out along the street incessantly during the half hour occupied in traversing the distance marched, and the soldiers successfully fought their way through. At the commencement they fired in the air, but as the mob pushed them closer they leveled their rifles with terrible effect. The first man killed was shot at the corner of Frederick and Baltimore streets, and the battle was continued from thence five blocks westward. It is not likely that the first two companies under Adjutant Bishop did serious damage, as the efforts of the mob were mainly directed upon Capt. Duffy's little squad of less than 30 men. The mob was not intimidated by the fire, or even by the killing of one or two men, but continued to crowd the troops and pour missiles into their ranks.

It was just after dusk of a lovely Summer evening, and Baltimore-street, the principle thoroughfare of the city, was densely thronged. Men, women, and children ran panic-stricken into the stores to escape the pattering rain of bullets, but the rioters continued their assault on the soldiers, and as the latter returned the fire, man after man fell dead along the sidewalk. At this writing (midnight) there are known to have been ten citizens killed and seven wounded seriously.

THE KILLED.

The following are the names of the dead as far as ascertained:

Thomas B. Byrne, Register of the Fifth Ward, shot in the head and killed instantly; age, 40 years; resided on Gay-street.

William Horan, a newsboy, aged 14 years;

shot in the head and killed instantly at the corner of Baltimore and Holliday streets.

Lewis Jahowitz, a young shoemaker, who lived at No. 4 Albemarle-street.

Cornelius Murphy, shot through the spinal column ; aged 23 ; an Arab.

Patrick Gill, a stranger, who had been here only a few days, and was living at No. 9 South Front-street. He was shot in the groin.

John H. Frank, aged 23, clerk in his father's grocery store at No. 88 South Central-avenue. He was shot through the heart.

Otto Manecke, aged about 40 years, who lived at No. 53 Granby-street. He was shot in the left cheek. He was a fresco painter.

The bodies of the remaining three have not yet been identified.

THE WOUNDED

The wounded are James Roke, aged 25, a laborer in a bottling establishment ; shot through the buttock, the ball coming out in the groin ; dangerously.

George Kemp, huckster, aged 23 ; shot through the thigh, at the corner of Baltimore and Frederick streets, while on his way home ; seriously.

Cary Williams, No. 117 East Pratt-street ; dangerously in abdomen.

Michael E. Heiman, a boy ; in the back ; not dangerously.

Jacob Wagner, No. 25 Calverton-road ; thigh ; not dangerously.

John Norton, boy, No. 18 Front-street ; not dangerously.

Mark Dowd, Adam's Express Company ; sabre cut on the back of the head ; will not live through the night.

William E. Callendar, Front, near Forest-street ; shot in thigh ; compound fracture.

John Groh, Marshmarket space ; shot in the back ; dangerously.

Jacob Klump, No. 31 Forrest-street, thigh ; not dangerously.

John Neville, Fort Road, shot in toe of left foot.

Miller, No. 48 Bourke-street, shot in left foot.

W. H. Young, Company E, Sixth Regiment, No. 42 South High-street, back of head ; not dangerously.

The determined temper of the soldiers is evinced by the circumstance that all the men killed were shot through the head or heart. The Central Station and Washington University Hospital presented a sad

scene to-night with the dead laid out on stretchers, and the wounded groaning and writhing in pain. Of the soldiers none were seriously hurt. Private William H. Young, of Company E, of the Sixth Regiment, was shot in the head by a rioter and had his face crushed with a brick, but the physicians are hopeful for him. Some 30 40 men of the the Fifth and Sixth Regiments were struck with stones but not badly hurt.

The blame for the ringing of the alarm, which precipitated the riot, is said to be placed between Gov. Carroll and Gen. Herbert. The troops could have been quietly called together and dispatched out of the city without attracting any attention, but the sounding of the alarm was a signal to the whole city of what was to be done, and it brought together the worst and most disorderly elements who were glad of a chance for a riot. Really, the strikers had nothing to do with the attack upon the three companies of the Sixth Regiment. The mob that provoked it, was mostly composed of working men from the neighboring factories, and gangs of roughs who sympathized with the strikers. They began by hooting, and in the inflamed feeling of both sides it did not require much provocation to bring on the most serious consequences. As usual in affairs of this sort innocent men were the sufferers. So far as is known not one of the men killed were engaged in hostilities. They appear to have been either spectators or among the throng that filled, at that hour of the evening, the main street of the city. After the detachment of the Sixth Regiment had fought its way up to Camden Station there was a cessation of belligerant operations. The remaining seven companies of the Sixth Regiment were ordered to remain at the armory and are still there under arms. The Fifth Regiment and the three companies of the Sixth are still at Camden Station. Outside of the depot everything is in the hands of the rioters. They have burned the freight sheds at the lower end of Camden Station, and are supposed to have done further damage on the outskirts of the city of the same kind. They seized a locomotive at Camden Station this evening, and started to run it up the road, but some of their own men had left a switch open a few hundred yards outside of the depot, and the engine was jumped from the track. No passenger trains have arrived or departed since 7 o'clock this evening.

A report has just come in that there has been a fight between the rioters and the Police at Bailey's, a station two miles outside of Camden Station, and that several have been killed on each side. The business of the Baltimore and Ohio Railroad is virtually dead for the time being, and it can transact neither freight nor passenger business. The events of to-morrow are looked forward to with intense anxiety. The strikers along the road have ceased operations in view of the occurrences at Baltimore, and things are quiet to-night at Martinsburg and points westward.

WASHINGTON

THE GOVERNMENT AND THE STRIKES.

THE INTERRUPTION TO THE RUNNING OF TRAINS BELIEVED AT AN END—MAJ.-GEN. HANCOCK'S AND LIEUT.-GEN. SHERIDAN'S DISPATCHES—THE FIRST THROUGH MAIL BY WAY OF PITTSBURG SENT LAST NIGHT.

Special Dispatch to the New-York Times.

WASHINGTON, July 30.—The strike, so far as it interferes with the running of trains, is regarded as ended. In his dispatch to-day to the War Department Gen. Hancock thus tersely describes the situation : " Have heard from Cumberland and Pittsburg this morning ; everything on the railroad within reach of my communications seems to be quiet and progressing well. A very little time and reflection, I think, will accomplish the rest." Both the Baltimore and Ohio, and Pennsylvania Roads are passing freight trains over their lines, and the mails will be dispatched by them to-morrow with the usual regularity. The first through mail to the West by way of Pittsburg, since the strike commenced, will be sent out to-night. The Treasury Department is sending out and receiving money by express as usual. To-day there was received for redemption from national banks nearly $1,500,000, being the first money received for redemption for eight days.

The following telegram was received from Lieut.-Gen. Sheridan to-day at the War Department :

CHICAGO, July 30, 1877.

To Gen. E. D. Townsend :

I have the honor to inform the Secretary of War that this city is tranquil to-day. Gen. Pope came here yesterday morning and will return to St. Louis this evening. I don't regard the troubles here as fully settled, but affairs have an improved look to-day.

P. H. SHERIDAN, Lieutenant-General.

Gen. Sheridan arrived in Chicago yesterday, having left Gen. Sherman and party on the Big Horn River, all well. Gen. Schofield left Washington for New-York to-night, it being considered at the War Department that his presence here is no longer necessary. He left his duties at West Point on short notice, and left here to resume them. He will return here should his services be needed.

The statement that there is on the part of the United States Government any sympathy with, or disposition to recommend, any compromise whatever with the strikers and rioters, is without any foundation in fact. It is known that neither the President nor any member of his Cabinet entertains such views as have been in some instances imputed to them ; but their purpose is to restore and enforce law and order throughout the entire land. In view of the disposition of communistic organizations, trades-unions, and other means of combining men in opposition to law and order, much satisfaction is expressed by the President and members of the Cabinet with the success which has attended the placing promptly of United States troops at points most exposed to the attacks of the railroad strikers and their immediate sympathizers. Commendation is bestowed on Adjutant-Gen. Townsend, Assistant-Adjutant-Gen. Vincent, and other gentlemen of that bureau, and on the general officers, all having acted in perfect accord in carrying out the purposes of the Administration, which will continue the same course should any similar disturbances again occur.

The War Department to-night was closed at 9 o'clock for the first time since the troubles growing out of the railroad strike began. The few dispatches received to-day and this evening show an improved feeling all over the country and no fear of further violence is entertained.

A COOL PROPOSITION.

BILL FOR TRANSPORTING TROOPS TO PROTECT ITS LINE PRESENTED TO THE GOVERNMENT BY THE BALTIMORE AND OHIO RAILROAD COMPANY.

Special Dispatch to the New-York Times.

WASHINGTON, Aug. 10.—Much to the surprise of the War Department officials, the Baltimore and Ohio Railroad Company has presented a claim for payment for transporting United States troops from Washington to different points along its line to protect the road from the strikers. This seems a little like impertinence. Without the aid of the troops the railroad company would have been completely at the mercy of the strikers, for the Militia were of no service whatever, and in some cases expressed their sympathy for the rioters in an unmistakable manner. If the military had been sent over the road to protect private or public property, the case would have been different; but no property required protection except that belonging to the railroad company. During the war of the rebellion many precedents were established under which this claim could be paid, but it is stated at the War Department that there was an understanding when the troops were sent that the railroad companies should furnish transportation. If this is the case the matter will probably go to the courts for settlement. No railroad but the Baltimore and Ohio has yet presented its bill, and at the Cabinet meeting to-day, when this matter was brought up, it was decided that no action should be taken until all the other railroads should be heard from, when it will be submitted to the Attorney-General for an opinion.

August 11, 1877

A DEFENSE OF TRADES-UNIONS.

To the Editor of the New-York Times:

We of the trades-unions are so used to being belabored in the press that the process no longer causes us any great amount of pain; yet, hardened and toughened as we are by this sort of thing, some of us are sometimes moved to make an outcry. Without knowing whether I am welcome or not, I take the liberty of offering a few observations upon several recent articles in THE TIMES relating to strikes and the alleged attitudes of the unions toward apprenticing.

In the article of Thursday the writer asserts that experience has proved these trade combinations to be a failure so far as protection to the working man is concerned; that "striking" is wrong in principle and unprofitable in practice, and that the employé could make better terms (conceding that a rearrangement is sometimes desirable) with his employer individually than by acting in concert. What grounds exist for these assertions I am at a loss to conceive; and, having worked in the shops for a matter of 15 years, I beg to say that I know what I am talking about. If the paying of wages were a matter of conscience or of equity, and all employers were honest and fair-dealing men, the laborer could well afford to trust them. But the deuce of it is that the average employer don't see it in that noble light at all; with him it is an affair of interest and business, pure and simple—to get his labor at the least possible cost. On the part of the workman—would you believe it?—the wretch actually wants, not what he can get, but the most he can get, for his labor! As to strikes, I don't think we can consent to give them up. They may, and do, cause loss and annoyance to a certain extent, but in the long run they are useful to us—even unsuccessful strikes. They strengthen the bond of fellowship between our members, show what we are capable of, and lessen the temptation of the employer to take an unfair advantage. And to show that this temptation exists everywhere and has to be closely watched, I may incidentally mention that upon the comparatively recent introduction of coolie labor—the cheapest of all kinds of labor—into the British West Indies, it became at once necessary to enact the most stringent ordinances to prevent their being outrageously wronged. Mr. Editor, the unions are the workman's only safe reliance; and they are such because they are able, if need be, to exert a positive amount of pressure. To give them up is to yield everything, and our being pauperized would be only a question of time. Individualism in this case means simply "every one for himself, and the devil for us all."

As to the charge made against the unions of opposing the employment of apprentices and of hostility to the old indenture system, it is wholly unjust. That the unions should wish to make some regulations to prevent the shops being overrun with boys seems to me both natural and proper, but the truth is that, with the exception of one body, there is practically no hindrance whatever. The indenture law yet stands on the statute-books of this State, if I am not mistaken, or if repealed, it was certainly not done at the instance of the trades-unions. The employers never liked it, and disregarded it almost entirely, although there were, I believe, some pretty severe penalties attached to the law. It is now rather antiquated. The conditions have greatly changed. Under the modern system of "division of labor" a trade cannot be completely learned—only parts of it —and the time required for proficiency in a branch is correspondingly shortened, so that indenturing is hardly worth while.   TRADES-UNIONIST.

May 5, 1880

NOTES FROM WASHINGTON.

WASHINGTON, Feb. 8, 1883.

The Senate Committee on Education and Labor resumed its inquiries this morning and examined Frank K. Foster, of Cambridge, Mass., Secretary of the Massachusetts Federation of Trade and Labor Unions. The witness made a general statement as to the condition of the laboring classes of New-England in general and of Massachusetts in particular. Speaking of the moral, intellectual, and physical condition of the printers as a class he said the lines of "caste" were growing more and more clearly defined each year, and that in New-England, at least, the assumed worship of God has ceased to level all distinctions among men. The mill operatives of New-England as a class are perhaps the worst off, and their present condition is sure to produce an enfeebled race of men and women in the next generation, as the same conditions have already done in England. The working people of Massachusetts are better off than those of the other New-England States on account of the enforcement of the ten-hour law. The hours of work in Massachusetts are 60 per week, while in the weaving districts of England they are only 56; the wages are about the same. Since 1878 the average wages have increased 6.9 per cent., while the average cost of the necessities of life, including meats, breadstuffs, vegetables, dry goods, boots, board, &c., has increased 21.2 per cent.

February 9, 1883

Organized labor was finding its strength. During the railway strike of 1894 cavalry escorted a meat train out of Chicago.

April 20, 1941

CONDITION OF THE WORKING CLASS.

THE ABUSES PRACTICED BY MILL OWNERS—HARDSHIPS OF WORKING GIRLS.

WASHINGTON, Feb. 9.—The examination of Frank K. Foster, of Cambridge, Mass., was continued this morning before the Senate Committee on Education and Labor. Mr. Foster said that most of the tenement-houses in the manufacturing cities of Massachusetts were owned by the mill-owners, and that the lessees were compelled to furnish so many operatives. The houses are generally small, ill ventilated, and uncomfortable. and the operatives are compelled to live in the companies' houses or be dismissed. The sewerage and sanitary facilities are terribly bad, and on Summer nights the stench from the sess-pool is nearly overpowering. The French Canadians are to New-England what Chinese are to California and the Pacific coast. Their morals are lower, their necessities fewer, and their only aim seems to be to see how much money they can get to take, out of the country. They do not wish their children to attend schools, and when compelled to send them, often move to another place. They seldom accept the right of franchise. Out of a population of 88,653 in 32 cities in New-England only 5,996 are naturalized and 2,859 property owners. Mr. Foster spoke strongly against the employment of children of tender years. In Massachusetts there is a law against the employment in mills of children under 10 years of age, and providing that those from 10 to 14 must attend schools 13 weeks in the year. This law does not include the little cash boys and girls employed in large numbers in the city stores; these little ones are not old enough in many cases to be away from their mothers, and are employed during the busy season from 8 A. M. to 9 and 10 P. M. The weary look of these little ones toward the close of their day's work is pitiful. The girls employed as shop women are paid on an average about $2 50 per week, and out of this they are expected to beard themselves and provide for all the necessaries of life, and to dress themselves well. Society demands that they should be virtuous, yet with the meagre stipend received and the snares often thrown around them by those over them. it is not a wonder that many of them fail. The condition of the mill girls is to be deplored. Away from home influences and restraints, thrown among those depraved of both sexes in low tenement-houses, what wonder is it that their morals are too often low? "I speak advisedly," said Mr. Foster, "that the city of Lowell, Mass., alone presents a wide field for philanthropic work. There is more need there and a better object than the building of places for decayed gentlewomen or giving large sums to Harvard College. Large strides have been made in Boston toward giving the working people the benefit of art galleries and libraries by opening them on Sunday." Mr. Foster's examination will be continued to-morrow.

February 10, 1883

THE LABOR INVESTIGATION.

WASHINGTON, Feb. 12.—Frank K. Foster, Secretary of the Federation of Trade and Labor Unions of Massachusetts, continued his testimony before the Senate Committee on Education and Labor this morning. He spoke of the black-listing system in the New-England mills, and said that employes who had been prominent in labor organizations during the strikes were put on the black-lists, and that, no matter how good workmen they might be, they could not find employment afterward. He cited the case of the strike in the Pacific Mills at Lawrence last year, in illustration of this system. To cure existing evils, Mr. Foster recommended the following remedies as the most practicable and desirable at present: First, the establishment of a national bureau of labor statistics; second, the establishment of boards of arbitration wherever practicable; third, the enforcement of the national eight-hour law; fourth, the abolition of child labor so far as possible by legislation; fifth, the repeal of all "conspiracy" laws which interfere with the right of working men to combine for their own protection and the incorporation of their unions like other corporations; sixth, the abolition of the convict labor contract system.

Senator Blair read a letter from the witnesses now in attendance, saying it was evident that the great pressure of business in the Senate at this late stage of the session will not leave sufficient time for them to present their views fully, and therefore suggesting that their examination be postponed to some more convenient season. The committtee thereupon agreed that it was impossible at this time to give the witnesses the necessary attention, and dismissed them with the understanding that they shall be given precedence in the future hearing of testimony.

February 13, 1883

SOME INOPERATIVE LAWS

PASSED BY THE "FRIENDS OF WORKING MEN."

DEMAGOGUES OF THE PAST WHOSE ACTS ARE RECALLED BY THOSE PRACTICED TO-DAY.

ALBANY, Feb. 3.—How true it is that history repeats itself in legislative as in other matters, is illustrated in the attempts of the professional friends of the working men to secure labor legislation this Winter. It is doubtful if any of the representatives of this particular class of professionals are aware of the fact that there is already on the statute-book an eight-hour law. Nobody knows where it is enforced. It certainly is not right here on the Capitol, but that is overlooked by the professionals. In all the debate in the Assembly over the bill of Mr. Earl, of Brooklyn, to reduce to 12 hours a day the labor of car drivers and conductors, nobody referred to the existence of such a law. It had passed out of mind completely, of so little practical value is it. Yet it has been a part of the law of the State for 14 years. It was unearthed by that studious book-worm Van Duzer, of Chemung, who will bring it before the Assembly when the professionals next bring up their Drivers' bill for its third reading. The forgotten act was passed April 26, 1870. It reads as follows:

AN ACT to regulate the hours of labor of mechanics, working men, and laborers in the employ of the State, or otherwise engaged on public works.

The People of the State of New-York, represented in Senate and Assembly, do enact as follows:

SECTION 1. On and after the passage of this act eight hours shall constitute a legal day's work for all classes of mechanics, working men, and laborers, excepting those engaged in farm and domestic labor, but overwork for an extra compensation by agreement between employer and employe is hereby permitted.

SEC. 2. This act shall apply to all mechanics, working men, and laborers now or hereafter employed by the State, or any municipal corporation therein, through its agents or officers, or in the employ of persons contracting with the State or such corporation for performance of public work.

SEC. 3. Any officer or officers or agents of this State, or of such corporation who shall openly violate or otherwise evade the provisions of this act, shall be deemed guilty of malfeasense in office, and be liable to suspension or removal accordingly, by the Governor or head of the department to which such officer is attached.

SEC. 4. Any party or parties contracting with the State, or any such corporation, who shall fail to comply with, or secrectly evade, the provisions hereof, by exacting and requiring more hours of labor for the compensation agreed to be paid per day than is herein fixed shall, on conviction thereof, be deemed guilty of a misdemeanor, and be punished by a fine of not less than $100 nor exceeding $500, and in addition thereto shall forfeit such contract at the option of the State.

SEC. 5. Chapter 856, of the laws of 1867, entitled "An Act to Limit the Hours of Labor Constituting a Day's Work to Eight Hours," passed May 9, 1867, is hereby repealed.

SEC. 6. This act shall take effect immediately.

The legislative history of this act is interesting, because it discovers of how little importance to working men is this species of legislation. It brings into prominence the fact that an eight-hour law, similar to one which Speaker Sheard has introduced, but which makes 10 hours a legal day's work in manufactories. once stood on the statute books, and was found so utterly worthless that it had to be repealed. That act was passed in 1867. It was the one which the fifth section of the act of 1870 repeals. It was introduced into the Assembly early in January of that year by the Hon. Patrick Keady, of Brooklyn, now a well-known lawyer of that city. Mr. Keady was identified with the working men's interests, being himself a sign painter at the time, and in their behalf he offered his bill making eight hours of labor a legal day's work. Petitions in favor of its passage poured in upon the Assembly from Buffalo, Lockport, Rochester, Oswego, Troy, Albany, New-York, and Brooklyn. It progressed to the Committee of the Whole and was there denounced by some of the members as a "piece of demagoguery," "clap-trap," "humbug," &c. By John C. Jacobs, then as now the parliamentarian of the Democrats in any body of which he is a member, it was brought out of the committee and sent to its third reading. The motion to effect this was adopted by 60 to 12. Among those who were recorded in the affirmative were Assemblymen Jacobs, Keady, Littlejohn, Murphy, (now Senator,) and Speaker Edmund L. Pitts. Two days afterward it passed the Assembly by a vote of 73 to 39. Mr. Littlejohn voted neither for nor against it. He was absent. Within 16 days after being sent to the Senate it was passed. Senator Folger (now Secretary of the United States Treasury) was one of those who was interested in its passage, and it was on his motion that it was given a third-reading number. On its final passage 23 votes were favorable to it and 5 against it. The affirmative comprised names that have played an important part in the history of the State. Ezra Cornell, the founder of the university; Andrew D. White, to-day the President of that institution; John O'Donnel, now a member of the Board of Railroad Commissioners; Henry R. Low, who again represents his district in the Senate this year: Henry C. Murphy, afterward President of the Brooklyn Bridge Trustees; Thomas Murphy, subsequently Collector of the Port of New-York, and Richard Crowley, he of Lockport, whose name is so frequently mentioned for every office within the gift of the President—all these gentlemen were members of that memorable Senate of 1867 and voted for the eight hour law of Mr. Keady. Gov. Fenton signed the bill, and for three years it was bound in calf along with other statutes. It is interesting reading at this particular time, and it ran as follows:

AN ACT to limit the hours of labor constituting a day's work in the State to eight hours.

The people of the State of New-York represented in Senate and Assembly do enact as follows:

SECTION 1. On and after the first day of May, 1867, eight hours of labor, between the rising and setting of the sun, shall be deemed and held to be a legal day's work, in all cases of labor and service by the day, where there is no contract or agreement to the contrary.

SEC. 2. This act shall not apply to or in any way affect farm or agricultural labor or service by the year, month, or week, nor shall any person be prevented by anything herein contained from working as many hours over-time, or extra work, as he or she may see fit, the compensation to be agreed upon between the employer and employe.

SEC. 3. All other acts, or parts of acts, relating to the hours of labor which shall constitute a day's work in this State are hereby repealed.

At the expiration of three years, this law having been found, as its opponents declared it would be, impractical and inoperative, more tinkering was thought to be the proper thing, and it was repealed. Working men employed by the State and by the cities of the State were now deemed to be objects of legislative pity. An eight-hour law for their benefit was introduced by John R. Hennessy, of the Fourteenth District of New-York. It barred out entirely those unfortunates who had not the political good luck to secure State or municipal employment. A hard mob from the City of New-York was in the Legislature that year, but all of its members were, as New-York members are to-day, "friends of the working-man." The bill passed by a vote of 68 to 2. "Billy" Hitchman was Speaker. Among those who voted in favor of its passage were Messrs. Alvord, Jacobs, Husted, Littlejohn, and Tim Campbell. The Senate, which also passed it 18 days later by a unanimous vote, had among its members Tweed, Harry Genet, "Tom" Creamer, Jarvis Lord, Henry C. Murphy, and Woodin. Gov. Hoffman by his signature gave it the form of law, and for 14 years this law of 1870 has stood on the statute-books, its existence barely known, its value *nil*.

The dusty archives in the Assembly library point out one other attempted piece of legislation, almost identical with Mr. Earl's bill for the alleged benefit of car drivers and conductors. Singularly enough, it also came from Brooklyn. Fourteen years ago Assemblyman Samuel T. Maddox, of the Seventh District of Kings, grew excited over the horrors of horse car life, and in the same philanthropic spirit which has since been exhibited by Mr. Earl he sought to give the managers of the front and rear platforms relief. He introduced a bill entitled "an act to authorize the Common Council of the City of Brooklyn to regulate the employment of conductors and drivers on the horse railroads in that city." His bill went to the Judiciary Committee, of which Tom Fields, of New-York, was Chairman. It was promptly reported and passed by a vote of 72 to 9. Two well-known gentlemen, ex-Speakers Alvord and Littlejohn, recorded themselves against the measure. Gen. Husted happened to be in the affirmative. The bill went to the Senate and was referred to the Committee on Municipal Affairs, of which Tweed himself was Chairman. It was never heard of more. Even that "stanch friend" of the working men, "the Boss" himself, could not see enough merit in it to warrant him in ever reporting favorably upon it.

February 4, 1884

WORKMEN AND DYNAMITE.

The introduction of dynamite into trade disputes is regarded by some of the so-called workingmen's leaders as an event of great promise for the workingmen's cause. It is really one of the gravest and most threatening misfortunes that have ever happened or could happen to the real workingmen. Doubtless it would help some of the "leaders," not the men of sense and conscience who know what work is and have the lasting good of their fellows at heart, but the idle, tricky, greedy men who seek to give themselves notoriety and to make money by exciting the passions of the workers for wages. These men can play on the imagination by their threats and can awaken envy and distrust and hatred for employers more readily with a weapon in their hands so powerful for evil. But for the genuine workingmen who have to labor for wages—and these are considerably the greater number of the people of all countries—this particular form of violence will work mischief just in proportion as it is resorted to or even seriously talked about.

And for a very simple reason. The amount of wages paid in any one year depends entirely on the amount of the product for that year. It has been shown over and again, and becomes more clear the more it is studied, that the whole world taken together produces each year very little more than it consumes. When production is checked the amount to be consumed is checked in like degree. When production increases—as it steadily tends to increase—the amount to be consumed and the share for each consumer increases also. Comparing any one period with an earlier one it is seen that while the gain of capital increases in amount, its share of the annual product tends to become smaller, while the amount paid to labor is not only larger but forms a larger share of the whole. This is due to the fact that, thanks to machinery and invention and improved skill in management, the competition of capital grows faster than the competition of labor.

But this wholesome and beneficent process can go on only while capital is practically free to compete, and it goes on most securely and rapidly where capital is most free. For instance, it is much more certain and steady in England than in Germany or France, where the large standing armies and the dangers of disturbance from war interfere with it. It is still more regular and rapid in the United States than in England, because here the natural resources of the country are richer and more varied and, owing to the freedom with which land can be bought, sold, and worked, are far

more available. But it is plain that this process would be very seriously interfered with were there to grow up the feeling that violence and destruction of property were likely to be resorted to in trade disputes. No man of sense and prudence would as readily put his money in a business requiring the employment of workmen if he thought that when his workmen differed with him as to wages or hours of work they were liable to blow up his buildings or smash his machinery with dynamite. Capital would not only be withheld under such fears from new enterprises; it would be withdrawn from those already started, and it would seek employment somewhere else, if any place could be found where security from such dangers could be had.

The immediate loss from this sort of operation would fall upon the workingmen, and would be most sorely felt by them. The owners of capital would lose the gains they might otherwise make, but they would have most of the capital itself left to them. The workingmen would lose the chance of making wages, and would have little or nothing to fall back upon. The longer the fear of violence was allowed to be cherished, or the more widely it spread, the worse it would be for the workingmen. In the end their suffering would be intolerable, and they would of their own accord put down sternly and completely all those who gave occasion for this blighting and ruinous fear. But it would be far better for them if they would see from the outset that the man who uses, or counsels or suggests the use of, destructive agents to bring employers to terms is their worst enemy and should be promptly and completely silenced. In this country not only is the resort to any such agency wildly foolish but it is wholly unneeded. Workmen can almost without obstruction combine to carry out any fair purpose of their own—to refuse to work themselves, to dissuade others from working, to start co-operative factories in rivalry with their employers, and so on. The laws, so far from restraining them in the free exercise of their rights, protect them. But if they encourage men who try to put them outside the law, to inveigle them into acts of violence and wrong to their employers, they will do themselves more and more lasting mischief than their most vindictive foes could possibly devise. They simply help to bring about a condition of things worse than slavery itself, for under slavery there was forced production, from which the slaves got at least their poor food and clothing and shelter. In proportion as dynamiters have their way production will become impossible, and all the conditions of life for workingmen will be made constantly harder.

JAY GOULD ON THE STAND

HIS TALK TO THE COMMITTEE ON RAILROAD MATTERS.

HE DEFENDS MR. HOXIE, CHARGES MR. POWDERLY WITH MISREPRESENTATION, AND TALKS ON ARBITRATION.

WASHINGTON, April 22.—The doors of the room of the House Committee on Elections were kept closed this morning until the special committee investigating the causes and extent of the labor troubles in the Southwest were prepared to proceed with the examination of Mr. Jay Gould. As that gentleman arose to take the oath all eyes were fixed upon him, and his response, " I do," was given in a low tone.

The Chairman—It is the desire of the committee, Mr. Gould, that you give us testimony in respect to the investigation in which we are engaged, and for the time I leave the examination to Mr. Burnes.

The witness wished to know the scope of the resolution under which the committee was acting.

Mr. Burnes stated that the select committee had been authorized by the House of Representatives to investigate the causes and extent of the disturbed condition now existing between railroad corporations engaged in carrying inter-State commerce and their employes in the States of Illinois, Missouri, Kansas, Arkansas, and Texas.

Mr. Gould—It is true that the Missouri Pacific runs through some of those States, but at this time we have no difference with our men, and are not, strictly speaking, within the rule of that resolution. But I will be very glad to spend my time talking to the committee, though I hardly think they want to spend their valuable time in talking to me.

Being requested, however, to proceed. Mr. Gould read a statement showing in detail the number of men employed by the Missouri Pacific system. He recited the story of his interview with Mr. Powderly and the committee prior to his West Indian cruise, during which he said the Knights declared that the Missouri Pacific had lived up to its agreement, and agreed not to strike again, but to come to him, "man fashion," and settle any future grievances they might have. Then the strike came after his departure, yet, said Mr. Gould, "your men told Mr. Hoxie that they had no grievances and were told so when. What followed the strike?" asked Mr. Gould, showing signs of deep feeling. " They seized St. Louis, Kansas City, Sedalia, Texarkana, and terminal facilities; they took possession and said : 'No man shall run a train over that road.' Our loyal employes could not run a train, and were deprived of the power to earn their wages. That was what followed the strike—forcible possession. I can't call it anything else; something the Czar of Russia would hesitate to do with his millions of soldiers behind him." Mr. Gould said that when he returned to New York he had agreed to meet Messrs. Powderly and McDowell as individuals. "My motive was to brace them up," said the witness. " because the sentiments which he [Powderly] expressed in his circular were so different from the acts of the association that I thought he needed bracing up." Mr. Powderly, he said, had told him that the men were in rebellion against the order, that they had struck without cause, and he had it in contemplation to vindicate himself by taking away their charter. As he wished to be equally frank, witness had showed Mr. Powderly the dispatch he intended to send to Mr. Hoxie next morning, in which he stated that he saw no objection to arbitration. He declared that Messrs. Powderly and McDowell had no right to make public that dispatch. Yet they had changed their plans upon seeing the telegram, and in the morning it had been published broadcast that Jay Gould had consented to their (Powderly and McDowell) plan of arbitration. That was untrue—utterly untrue—said the witness.

In answer to Mr. Burnes Mr. Gould said that his telegram to Mr. Hoxie referring to arbitration was not even advisory in its nature; he meant to leave the entire matter in Mr. Hoxie's hands and hold him responsible for the result. I want to say, said Mr. Gould very distinctly, that there have been no instructions issued other than those embodied in my letter to Mr. Hoxie. They have been lived up to by the company from that time to this. Mr. Gould here read the various telegrams and correspondence which have been already made public, including the proclamation of March 29 issued by the Executive Board of the district assemblies at St. Louis.

Mr. Burnes—Have you any other documents that you wish to submit?

Mr. Gould—I have just received a telegram from Mr. Hoxie stating that the St. Louis papers to-day publish this dispatch sent from here yesterday :

Push the strike. We have plenty of money to carry it through. (Signed.) JOHN HAYES.

Mr. Hayes is, I believe, one of the Executive Committee of the Knights of Labor. He is the same man who addressed the dispatch to me holding me responsible for the murders in East St. Louis.

Mr. Burnes—You spoke of a resolution of the Board of Directors of the Missouri Pacific Railroad with reference to the duties and powers of Mr. Hoxie. Did you understand that resolution as limiting or controlling your powers as President of the corporation?

Mr. Gould—That happened while I was away. When I left on the 5th of January an acting President was appointed, and I surrendered (for the time being) my position as President of the board. I did not consider the resolution as having anything to do with the question of the duties and powers of the President.

Mr. Burnes—When you prepared your dispatch to Mr. Hoxie, did you intend at that time to leave him entirely free to act according to his own judgment? Did you intend it as a peremptory order or merely as advisory?

Mr. Gould—Not even as advisory. I intended it as a matter of precaution. I meant to put the whole matter in his hands, to give him entire control, and to hold him responsible for the results.

Mr. Burnes—Did you send to Mr. Hoxie, or did you cause to be sent to him, either on the Monday or on the Sunday or Saturday preceding, any other telegram or any other advice?

Mr. Gould—No, sir. My telegram to Mr. Hoxie means just what it says, and we have not changed from that day to this by the crossing of a t or the dotting of an i.

Mr. Burnes—In your testimony as to this dispatch to Mr. Hoxie you seem to favor the principle of arbitration for the settlement of contentions between employers and employes. Give us the results and experience of your observations as to how that principle can be carried out practically.

Mr. Gould—Arbitration is getting to be a very easy and popular way of settling difficulties between individuals and corporations and between corporations and their individual employes. I have always been in favor of arbitration. I regard the employes of a railroad company as upon a different footing from the employes of a manufacturing or other private corporation. A railway corporation acts in two senses, first, as a private organization, and second as a public corporation, having a contract with the State by which it has certain duties to perform. These duties are to be performed, not by the rails and engines alone, but by the entire organization, and they clothe themselves with public duties, from the President to the lowest employe. They clothe themselves with the public duties which appertain to the operation of that railroad as an entirety.

Mr. Burnes—Have you considered the question as to whether there is any mode by which the whole working force of a railroad can be put under the control of the people?

Mr. Gould—Yes, Sir. The laws do that now. The difficulty is only in enforcing them. You see that on roads operated by Receivers strikes are rapidly overcome, because there is respect for the United States courts. The public has a right to have railroads operated. Any law which defines that right and complies with its provisions for arbitration would be a practical solution of the question. But the arbitration should not be after men had struck and seized the property of the railroad company. It should be the duty of the men to keep on at their work. A railroad is not merely the rails, ties, gradings, locomotives, and cars; but it is the whole thing. It is the duty of somebody to manage it.

Mr. Burnes—Might not the General Government license, and thereby govern and control, the officials of a railroad, from the Superintendent down.

Mr. Gould—I think the officials assume that to be their duty now. It might be made more distinct by some enactment, and then, if any injustice be done, there should be a mode of arbitration. I have been always in favor of that. I think that Mr. Powderly is undertaking to do too much. All that I can do is to manage the Missouri Pacific, and I have no end of trouble with that. But Mr. Powderly is running the shoemakers, the men who make pegs and leather, all other tradesmen, and not only the employes of the Missouri Pacific Railroad, but all the employes on 130,000 miles of railroad. I do not wonder that he has broken down under the load. I think the Government should have such right to govern and control railroads as to have troubles arbitrated, even without consulting the companies or its employes.

Mr. Burnes—You mean compulsory arbitration?

Mr. Gould—Public opinion on these questions is all powerful. Perhaps voluntary arbitration would have greater effect than compulsory arbitration.

Mr. Burnes—And yet, for some reason, you and Mr. Powderly and Mr. McDowell were in consultation and endeavoring to bring about a settlement of alleged grievances, and it was not brought about.

Mr. Gould—Oh, no; I was not endeavoring to do that.

Mr. Burnes—You were not endeavoring to arbitrate?

Mr. Gould—No, Sir. We met as individuals to have a talk over the situation. The matter was in Mr. Hoxie's hands, and I never changed it in any shape or form. I said at the start that I would not, I so stated in my letter, and have always stated so.

Mr. Burnes—Why were not your views, that are friendly to arbitration, carried out at St. Louis?

Mr. Gould—Mr. Hoxie has been always ready to carry them out. That has been always our policy. We are ready to arbitrate any grievances between the company and its employes. But the interpretation which Mr. Powderly put upon it was that the Knights of Labor were to step in and oversee this arbitration. There are 10,000 men employed by the Missouri Pacific Company who are not members of that order, but are members of other organizations which deal with us directly. After the strike in 1885 we terminated our relations with the order of the Knights of Labor. They had taken possession of our road. Then there was a new deal. We put them on a different footing. We took back the men, but we took them back as individuals. We did not ask them whether they were Knights of Labor, or Methodists, or Baptists, or anything else. We did not propose to deal with Knights of Labor as an organization. Mr. Powderly understood that distinctly, because I stated it distinctly in that interview.

Mr. Burnes called attention to the order referred to in the testimony yesterday directing that no Knights of Labor should be employed as foremen.

Mr. Gould denied any knowledge of that order, but justified it on the principle of not putting on guard any except those who could be trusted. He added: "The last words that I said to Mr. Powderly were: 'Mr. Powderly, if you have any grievances you may come to my house or my office at any time. But do not bring McDowell. Come yourself.' I was overrun with people who said to me: 'Look out for McDowell. You will have him presenting you with a bill to-morrow of $20,000 for settling this strike, and he will put it in the hands of a lawyer and sue you.'"

Mr. Gould was asked by Mr. Crain as to the ways of construction companies in issuing stock to themselves out of proportion to the work done, but Mr. Gould denied any knowledge of such dark and questionable transactions. He was asked his opinion as to the cause of the strike and the only reason that occurred to him was the desire of some of the leaders to obtain notoriety and consequence. He had never heard of the cheating of employes in the matter of hospital taxation, homesteads, and stores belonging to Superintendents and foremen. Such statements were ridiculous. He knew nothing of stock speculations growing out of the strike, and so far as he was himself concerned, he had not made a transaction in stock, either long or short, since Jan. 1, and had no speculative interest in the market. He was sure none of the Directors of the Missouri Pacific had any dealings in the stock of the road on the days following his interview with Powderly.

Mr. Outhwaite—Wherein would the public interests or the interests of the company have suffered by the representatives of the company accepting the proposition of the Knights of Labor?

Mr. Gould—To arbitrate what? That was the question.

Mr. Outhwaite—You certainly knew what you differed about.

Mr. Gould—I do not know that we differed at all. I read my proposition over to Mr. Powderly, and he said he agreed to every word of it.

Mr. Outhwaite—But what injury could have come to the company if it had accepted and acted upon Mr. Powderly's view of the case?

Mr. Gould—I do not know what subject their arbitration would cover. If it covered the question whether we should discharge men whom we had employed after the strike, we would not admit that to be a subject of arbitration.

Mr. Outhwaite—Then you did not intend or want to have any arbitration or effort to settle any difficulties with Knights of Labor who had struck, or were out of your employment at the time. Was that the understanding?

Mr. Gould—Yes; that is it distinctly.

Mr. Burnes inquired as to the general effect of the pooling system and Mr. Gould replied that its general effect was beneficial to the public, because, without it, most, if not all, the railroads of the country would be in the hands of Receivers.

Mr. Burnes—Why would that be the result?

Mr. Gould—Because of low rates from excessive competition.

Mr. Burnes—Then competition is not the life of trade.

Mr. Gould—No, Sir. And the result would be that wages would have to be cut down 50 per cent.

Mr. Burnes—If pooling is beneficial to the railroad companies, is it also beneficial to the people?

Mr. Gould—I think it is. The public is interested in having strong, able roads, well equipped. I have always found that real estate sells higher and the people would rather live on the lines of railroads that are financially strong.

This closed Mr. Gould's examination, which extended over four hours. He gave his testimony very briefly and in a low tone of voice, and did not volunteer any statement, confining himself merely to answering the questions asked him.

Mr. Hopkins, the Vice-President of the Missouri Pacific, was then examined. He corroborated generally Mr. Gould's account of the interviews with Mr. Powderly, at which he was present. He had always believed in arbitration as a means of settlement, but such arbitration would have to be between the employes themselves (actually at work) and the company. That was the point in this whole matter. Railroad employes had no better friends than the managers of the road. There were no antagonistic interests between them. The managers wanted to accomplish the best results, and in order to do so they should have good men, and should be in accord with their men and on friendly relations with them. He thought it should be made a criminal offense to have a strike on a railroad. There was no objection to men quitting work; and if, in the present case, the strikers had confined themselves to that the company would never have stopped running trains. He was asked as to whether he had any knowledge of Wall-street speculations in connection with the strike, but all that he knew on that point was that he had been informed that persons connected with Knights of Labor had been noticed in brokers' offices. He promised to give the names of such persons as had been mentioned to him in that connection. He closed by paying a high compliment to Mr. Hoxie for the manner in which he had administered the affairs of the company. The committee adjourned till 11 o'clock to-morrow.

April 23, 1886

EDITORIAL

Politically the men engaged in the protected industries of mining coal and iron in Pennsylvania feel a remarkable solicitude for the wages of their workmen. They think the whole country should cheerfully endure a tax for their maintenance. Practically they are quite willing for their own profit to deprive those wages of a considerable part of their nominal value by paying them in store orders, which have to be taken out in cheap merchandise at high prices. This practice of paying in store orders has flourished many years in the mining regions of Pennsylvania and been subject to many abuses. A law was passed in 1881 requiring the payment of all wages in lawful money or in orders redeemable in money within thirty days, with interest, and the courts are beginning to decide that where payment has not been made in this way the wages may be recovered, notwithstanding the store orders that have been previously received. These decisions ought to have a wholesome effect in doing away with the mean practice of compelling workmen to submit to an indirect shave for the profit of the "pluck-me" storekeepers.

April 14, 1885

ANARCHY'S RED HAND

RIOTING AND BLOODSHED IN THE STREETS OF CHICAGO.

POLICE MOWED DOWN WITH DYNAMITE.

STRIKERS KILLED WITH VOLLEYS FROM REVOLVERS.

THE SLAUGHTER FOLLOWING AN ANARCHIST MEETING—TWELVE POLICEMEN DEAD OR DYING—THE NUMBER OF KILLED OR INJURED CIVILIANS UNKNOWN BUT VERY LARGE — THE BRAVERY OF THE POLICE FORCE.

CHICAGO, May 4.—The villainous teachings of the Anarchists bore bloody fruit in Chicago to-night, and before daylight at least a dozen stalwart men will have laid down their lives as a tribute to the doctrine of Herr Johann Most. There had been skirmishes all day between the police and various sections of the mob, which had no head and no organization. In every instance the police won. In the afternoon a handbill, printed in German and English, called upon "workingmen" to meet at Des Plaines and Randolph streets this evening. "Good speakers," it was promised, "will be present to denounce the latest atrocious act of the police—the shooting of our fellow-workmen yesterday afternoon."

In response to this invitation 1,400 men, including those most active in the Anarchist riots of the past 48 hours, gathered at the point designated. At Des Plaines-street, Randolph-street, which runs east and west, widens out, and is known as the Old Haymarket. The plaza thus formed is about 2,900 feet long and 150 feet wide. It was just off the northeastern corner of this plaza and around the corner into Des Plaines-street, 100 feet north of Randolph, that the crowd gathered. A light rainstorm came up and about 800 people went away. The 600 who remained listened to speeches from the lips of August Spies, the editor of the *Arbiter Zeitung*, and A. R. Parsons, an Anarchist with a negro wife. The speeches were rather mild in tone, but when Sam Fielden, another Anarchist leader, mounted the wagon from which the orators spoke, the crowd pressed nearer, knowing that something different was coming.

They were not disappointed. Fielden spoke for 20 minutes, growing wilder and more violent as he proceeded. Police Inspector Bonfield had heard the early part of the speech, and, walking down the street to the Des Plaines-street police station, not 300 feet south of where Fielden stood, called out a reserve of 60 policemen and started them up the street toward the crowd. The men were formed in two lines stretching from curb to curb. The Inspector hurried on ahead, and, forcing his way through the crowd, reached a point close to the wagon. Fielden had just uttered an incendiary sentence, when Bonfield cried:

"I command you in the name of the law to desist, and you," turning to the crowd, "to disperse."

Just as he began to speak the stars on the broad breasts of the blue coats, as they came marching down the street so quietly that they had not been heard, reflected the rays of light from the neighboring street lamp. From a little group of men standing at the entrance to an alley opening on Des Plaines-street, opposite where Fielden was speaking, something rose up into the air, carrying with it a slender tail of fire, squarely in front of the advancing line of policemen. It struck and sputtered mildly for a moment. Then, as they were so close to it that the nearest man could have stepped upon the thing, it exploded with terrific effect.

The men in the centre of the line went down with shrieks and groans, dying together. Then from the Anarchists on every side, a deadly fire was poured in on the stricken lines of police, and more men fell to the ground. At the discharge of the bomb the bystanders on the sidewalk fled for their lives, and numbers were trampled upon in the mad haste of the crowd to get away. The groans of those hit could be heard above the rattle of the revolvers, as the police answered the fire of the rioters with deadly effect. In two minutes the ground was strewn with wounded men. Then the shots straggled, and soon after all was quiet and the police were masters of the situation.

The situation was appalling in the extreme. The ground was covered with the bodies of men writhing in agony and apparently dying. The men who were uninjured were ministering to their comrades as best they could, and as soon as possible the wounded were removed to the station house. The first death was that of Officer Joseph Deegan, who rose from the ground where he was thrown by the explosion, walked a hundred feet toward the station house, and, dropping down, expired. All around within a radius of a block of the field of battle men were seen limping into drug stores and saloons or crawling on their hands, their legs being disabled. Others tottered along the street like drunken men, holding their hands to their heads and calling for help to take them home. The open doorways and saloons in the immediate vicinity were crowded with men. Some jumped over tables and chairs, barricading themselves behind them; others crouched behind the walls, counters, doorways, and empty barrels. For a few minutes after the shooting nobody ventured out on the street.

A hospital was hastily improvised in the squad room at the station house, and thither the wounded were carried by tender hands. The room presented a harrowing sight. Half a dozen men, from whom the blood literally flowed in streams, were stretched upon the floor. Others were laid out on tables and benches, and others not so badly wounded were placed in chairs to await, with what patience they could, the assistance of the surgeon. Mattresses and other bedding were dragged down stairs, and dozens of willing hands did their utmost to assuage the pain of the sufferers. Very soon the doctors were busy with needle, lancet and probe. Priests passed from one wounded man to another administering brief words of consolation and hope and the sacrament of extreme unction to others. Officers and volunteer assistants went around with stimulants, or helped to bind up wounds, or held the patient down while the Surgeon was at work, or carried some of the wounded to the other apartments, or in some other way did what could be done to help in easing pain or saving

The popular image of the anarchist of old is shown in the print; by contrast, today's anarchist is typically youthful—he may even be too young to grow a beard.

July 14, 1968

life. Pools of blood formed on the floor and was tramped about until almost every foot of space was red and slippery.

The groans of the dying men arose above the heavy shuffling of feet, and, to add to the agony, the cries of women, relatives of officers reported to have been wounded, could be heard from an outer room, beyond which the women were not permitted to enter. Men who had only got a foot or an arm wounded, even though the blood poured from it in streams, sat still, claiming no help in the face of the greater agony. "O Christ! Let me die!" "O merciful God!" and similar expressions were continually wrung forth as the surgeon's knife or saw was at work or when attempts were made to move those more badly wounded. The sacrament of extreme unction was administered to eight of the wounded before they were moved from the spot where they had been first laid.

As the bodies were picked up from the ground it was found that one man, an unknown Bohemian, was dead, making, with Officer Deegan, two victims already of the crime. The following is a partial list of the 33 injured policemen. It is impossible to say at this hour (1:15 A. M.) how many will die, but it is believed that the number will be nearly, if not quite, a dozen.

JOSEPH DEEGAN, West Lake-street station; fell dead in front of the Desplaines-street station in the arms of Detective John McDonald.

He had sufficient vitality to walk from the scene of the shooting to the spot where he expired.

Lieut. JAMES STANTON, West Lake-street station; shot in both legs; not badly hurt.

JACOB HANSEN, West Lake-street station; shot in both legs.

THOMAS SHANNON, Desplaines-street station; shot in foot, leg and arms; married and has three children.

JOHN K. MCMAHON, West Chicago-avenue; shot in thigh and calf of right leg; married and has three children.

JOHN E. DOYLE, Desplaines-strreet, bomb wounds in leg, knee, and back; married and has one child.

TIMOTHY FLAVIN, Ranson-street station; shot in leg; resides at station; married.

JOHN H. KING, Desplaines-street station; bomb wound in neck, feet, and arms.

JAMES PLUNKETT, Desplaines-street station; shot in the hand.

EDWARD BARRETT, West Chicago-avenue; shot in knee and ankle; has wife and six children.

J. SIMONS, West Chicago-avenue; shot in side; has wife and two children.

A. C. KELLER, Desplaines-street station; shot in side.

L. J. MURPHY, Desplaines-street; shot in neck and hand; foot hurt by bomb; married.

T. BUTTERLY, West Lake-street; shot in hand; has wife and one child.

H. T. SMITH, Desplaines-street; shot in the right ankle; single.

ARTHUR CONLEY, Desplaines-street; bullet wound in leg and right shoulder and bomb wound in right leg; married.

C. WHITNEY, West Lake-street; wounded in the breast by a bomb; married.

Lieut. Bowler, who was in charge of the Second Company of 24 men, said: "Every man in my company is wounded, with only three exceptions. I led the company up to the wagon from which the speeches were being made. Inspector Bonfield and Capt. Ward were immediately in front of me. The Inspector told Fielden they would have to stop, as he had orders to disperse the meeting. As he finished speaking a bomb was thrown from the wagon and fell directly in the centre of my company, where it exploded."

"Are you positive the bomb was thrown from that wagon?"

"Yes, I am. I could make no mistake about it, for I saw it thrown. Officers Reid and Doyle were knocked down by it. Bonfield, Ward, and myself were the only three to escape. Every one behind me was wounded—just mowed down."

Several of the men listening to Felden had their revolvers in their hands under their coats, and were prepared for an attack. These drifted around to the northern end of the crowd, where the street was much darker. The windows of the brick building in the northeastern corner of Randolph and Desplaines streets were filled with the heads and faces of men and women. One of the wounded officers says he saw the bomb coming from one of these windows. Officer Marx said he saw the bomb coming from the wagon in which the speakers stood. It is probable that both of the officers were mistaken and that the bomb came from the sidewalk.

When the first shots were fired most of the crowd scampered east and west in Randolph-street. The bullets followed the fleeing ones and many of them dropped on the way before they got out of danger. A number of women were also seen in the crowd and several scampered screaming down Randolph-street. More were seen falling 500 and 600 feet up Randolph-street, west of Desplaines. Hats were lost, and several, stopping to pick something they had dropped, were trampled on by the mad mob. In the neighboring stores everything was confusion. Men in their haste to get away from the bullets broke open the doors of the stores and entered, hiding in the first convenient place they could find. The proprietors struck at the intruders with clubs and threatened them with pistols, but they pushed past these and entered.

The feeling among the police when they fully realized the extent of the calamity which had befallen their comrades rose to a frenzy, and nothing but the discipline among them and the presence of Inspector Bonfield, who was one of the very few cool men in the station, prevented their rushing out and taking summary vengeance on the crowds of loiterers on the sidewalks, who jeered the flying patrol wagons as they passed filled with officers on the way to the scene of the disaster. The cruel heartlessness of the men who exulted over the fact that more than a score of policemen had fallen victims to the deadly Nihilist bomb surpasses belief, and yet it is a fact that, crowded along the sidewalks on both sides of Desplaines-street, from Madison-street to the station, were hundreds of Communistic sympathizers who exulted in the fiendish work which had been perpetrated but a few moments before. The big bell in the police station tower had tolled out a riot alarm, while the telegrapher sent dispatches to other stations calling for

aid. Ten minutes later patrol wagons were dashing toward the scene of the riot from all directions, bringing stalwart policemen. The mob shouted wildly as the wagons dashed by, and several missiles were thrown, all of which missed the bluecoats on the wagons. The Anarchists slunk back as a large company of policemen on foot marched down Desplaines-street.

Several times the mob advanced with wild shouts from the north, but they were kept back as far as Randolph-street. The Anarchists, led by two wiry, whiskered foreigners, grew bolder and made several attempts to renew the attack, but the police stood their ground. At 11:30 o'clock the police made a grand drive at the mob, which was growing larger instead of diminishing. Blank cartridges were fired from hundreds of revolvers in two volleys, which set the crowd flying in all directions. The police gave chase as far as the Lyceum Theatre, firing again, and the crowd, covering Madison-street from curb to curb, did not stop running until Halstead-street was passed. This fusillade from the officers practially dispersed the mob, and at 11:45 there were few people in the streets near the station.

The celerity with which the leaders of the dynamite movement got out of the way as soon as the explosion occurred was little short of marvelous, and this fact led many to believe that they had knowledge of what was to be done and therefore took occasion to escape the consequences they knew would follow.

As soon as the superior officers could collect their wits orders were at once issued for the arrest of the dynamite orators, and they, therefore, will be behind the bars as soon as the detectives can get hold of them. Some said that when persons in the mob fell to the ground their friends picked them up and carried them away. It is therefore impossible to give any estimate of the number of citizens shot. That the number is large there can be no doubt, and that some were fatally wounded, if not killed outright, is more than probable. Fifteen persons were picked up by the police, and one or two of these will, in all probability, die. The people injured are in the main men who were on their way home from a cheap theatre, where the performance had come to an end early. Among them are the following:

ROBERT SHULTS, a waiter, on his way home from the theatre; shot in the leg.

JOHN SACHMAN, who was walking in Randolph-street; shot in the leg.

FRANK WROVSCH; shot in the shoulder and sides, and will die.

CHARLES SHOEMAKER, tailor; shot in back.

EMIL GOLTZ, shoemaker; shot in shoulder.

JOSEPH KUCHER; shot in back.

JOHN EDLUND; shot in head.

PETER LEY; shot in the back.

B. LE PLANT, of Earl Park, Ind.; on his way home from the theatre; shot in the leg and shoulder.

It should be borne in mind that the men who were present at the Anarchist meeting were, with few exceptions, fellows with no visible means of support and professional agitators. They were not there to right any specific wrong, but to listen to wild harangues, such as they hear upon the lake front and in the Anarchist halls on Sunday. The meeting was of precisely the same nature as those held Sundays, differing only from the usual gatherings in that it was held in the night instead of the day time. The street where the meeting was held was narrow, but

the crowd was gathered very compactly. Everything points to a preconcerted plan on the part of Spies, Parsons, and Fielden to try the effect of one of their bombs. The speeches were planned to rouse the mob gradually to a point where police interference could reasonably be hoped for, and then a man, screened by others, at the end of a convenient dark alley, down which he could run, was detailed to throw a bomb when the proper time came.

This evening 200 Bohemian sausagemakers at Armour's left the establishment and marched down to Ashland - avenue, carrying red flags, beating drums, and shouting "Down with the police." They paraded around all night, and about 11 o'clock reached the corner of Forty-eighth and Laflin streets. Officers Doran, McManus, and J. W. Murphy, of the town of Lake, were met, and the mob commenced to beat them, when Officer McManus drew his revolver and fired. Matthew Blank, one of the strikers, ran a few yards and then dropped dead.

May 5, 1886

EDITORIAL

No doubt the workmen on strike in Chicago mean what they say in denouncing the ruffians who have used the name of "labor" as a pretext for murder. They would prove their sincerity still more completely if they were to abandon, for the present, their demand for a change in their hours of work. This demand was made the occasion, though without any fault of theirs, for the outrages that have disgraced Chicago, and public feeling is so excited that a persistence in their demand may precipitate outrages that will disgrace it still more deeply. It would be absurd to say that a reduction which they have done without all their lives they cannot do without a few weeks longer, when the excitement has abated and the demand has a better chance for consideration. Nothing will be lost by this course, since the question must be decided in each trade by itself. A general stoppage of business, even when not accompanied by riot, diminishes the wage-paying capacity of every employer. If the strikers should resume work, reserving their demand for a change in its conditions till a more convenient season, they would not only prove the sincerity of their denunciation of the murderers by dynamite, but they would deserve and receive the gratitude and sympathy of the community at large, and these are of very great value in any labor dispute.

May 8, 1886

WHAT IS A BOYCOTT?

The indignation of the American people against the boycotters is virtually universal, and it is as intense as it is general. It is an old saying that the American people are the most conservative people on the face of the earth. The saying is true, and it is true for the obvious reason that a larger number of the American people than of any other have something to conserve which they feel to be of value, and which they know the institutions of the country help them to protect. This feeling is shared by a very large proportion of the class of workers for wages. It would not be unfair to say that it is shared by all the workers for wages except the lazy and extravagant; for the industrious and frugal, in any branch of skilled labor at least, find no difficulty in saving something. They can save enough at any rate to make them members of the "capitalistic" class in the estimation of those who have saved nothing, and have no purpose of saving anything.

This enormous number of laborers who are also capitalists it is that makes the community with us more nearly unanimous against anything that threatens the right of a man to his own than any other people. In most countries of Europe the class of workers for wages would sympathize very generally with an attempt to boycott a man who treated persons in his employ in a manner of which those persons did not approve. Here there is a disposition among workers for wages to inquire both into the merits of the case and the methods used by the parties to a dispute. The result is that boycotting is defended only by a few professional friends of labor, while it is regarded in the same light by a skilled mechanic and a bank President.

This very unanimity of opposition to boycotting makes it desirable that we should define very clearly to ourselves in what boycotting consists. It does not consist in expressing an unfavorable opinion of the moral character or commercial methods of another, and of announcing one's purpose to have no further dealings with him. This is the right of every man, and every man exercises it whenever he changes his tailor or his grocer, or stops his newspaper. If he has a right to make such a change, he has an equal right to give his reasons for making it, and by so doing to dissuade other people from dealing with him. The right of criticism everybody exercises every day, and it is by the exercise of it that the reputation of men is fixed among their neighbors. It is a very valuable right, and it would be an injustice if it should be abridged by any proceedings against boycotters.

But the exercise of this right is not and cannot become a "boycott" within the meaning of the sections of the Penal Code in relation to coercion or to conspiracy. The extortion of blackmail under the pretense of collecting the expenses of the boycott, and the interruption of a man's business by the gathering of boycotters at the place where it is done, are offenses that do not properly belong to boycotting. They may be incidents of a boycott or not, but they are so plainly unlawful that no labor union is likely to get itself into trouble by authorizing them again. The essence of boycotting is that the boycotters do not rely upon the strength of their case, or upon their powers of suasion or dissuasion. They undertake to coerce others, whether the others agree or not upon the sufficiency of their reasons, into imitating their action. In the Landgraf case it has been shown that people were frightened out of dealing with Mrs. LANDGRAF because she was under the ban of the boycotters, and because they feared that the same ban would fall upon them. This is the result at which all boycotts are aimed, and it is a result the accomplishment of which is inconsistent with the rudiments of civilization. Where this coercion, or an attempt at this coercion, is shown, the crime which is called boycotting has been committed, and it is a crime to which no mercy ought to be shown.

July 10, 1886

KILLED BY PINKERTON'S MEN.

AN INNOCENT MAN THE VICTIM OF NEEDLESS SHOOTING.

CHICAGO, Oct. 19.—A crowd composed mainly of half-grown boys stoned a train loaded with workmen and Pinkerton men on their way into the city from Packingtown this morning, and a dozen of the officers fired out of the windows of the train. Terence Bigley, a hard-working, reputable cart driver, who happened to be passing, was struck by one of the shots, and received a wound from which he died this evening. The shooting of Bigley occasioned intense excitement in the southwestern part of the city, and had the Pinkerton men not been beyond reach they would undoubtedly have been hanged by a mob. The train was composed of eight passenger coaches. Six of these were filled at the packing houses by 100 of the new men who had been given work by Armour in place of his striking employes, and 123 Pinkerton men who were coming back to the city, the termination of the strike having rendered their further presence at the packing houses useless. The Pinkerton men, most of whom were around with rifles, were also serving as guards to the workmen who had come to the conclusion that they had better resign their positions in Armour's employ than remain and work side by side with the defeated strikers.

When the train crossed Halsted-street a few men and boys who were hanging around the crossing discovered that it was carrying some of the hated Pinkerton men. The train backed on to a switch and up to the stock yards gates, where two more coaches were attached. As it reached the Halsted-street crossing on its way back it was seen that the crowd had largely increased. There were several Pinkerton men standing on the platforms of the coaches and they were greeted with cheers, taunts, and epithets.

Although different stories are told, there seems no doubt that some of the persons in the crowd threw sticks and stones at the train. A Pinkerton man standing on the platform of one of the coaches drew a revolver and fired a shot. Many of the other Pinkerton men had the muzzles of their rifles pointing out of the windows and they fired ten or a dozen shots. One of these struck Begley in the right side of the abdomen and bored its way through his body, passing out on the other side. The train had not stopped, and it continued on its way to the city. The shooting occurred in the town of Lake, and Capt. Markey, of the town police, was at once notified. He telephoned the Chicago Central Station to hold the Pinkerton men until his arrival, and started for the city. Orders were sent out from the Central Station, and details of officers boarded the train at Twenty-second and at the Lake Shore station at Van Buren street.

The Pinkerton men and the 100 workmen were placed under arrest and taken to the Harrison-street station. Capt. Markey soon arrived with a brother of Begley and three boys, who said they could identify the Pinkerton man who fired the first shot. The Pinkerton men were brought before the boys and they picked out Walter Andrews and Joseph Hill, being unable to agree on one man. The police officer disarmed the men and examined their arms to ascertain which had been emptied. Emmons Shaw was found to have emptied his gun, and three others admitted having fired at the Halsted-street crossing. At this juncture William Pinkerton put in an appearance, and upon being told what the examination had thus far disclosed, stepped out into the middle of the room and asked the men who had fired the shots to come to his side. Four men responded, and then, with Hill and Andrews, were locked up to await the result of the Coroner's inquest. All the other men, including the workingmen, were discharged.

There are two distinctly different stories of the trouble. Persons who stood with or near the crowd outside say the men and boys composing it were generally contenting themselves with abusing the Pinkerton men, using epithets likely to enrage any man to whom they were employed. They admit that there were a few stones thrown, but say that no harm was done the train or anybody on it. It is certain that Bigley was not with the crowd, and that he simply chanced to be driving past at the moment. The Pinkerton men are extremely reticent, but it would seem that the shot fired by one of their number led them to hastily infer that they were being attacked and without waiting for orders several of them pulled the triggers. It is probable that no aim was taken and that the shot which struck Begley was not intended for him or anybody in particular. The Pinkerton men have had a hard time of it in Packingtown for the last week, two or three of them having been brutally beaten by friends of the strikers or strikers themselves. The feeling in the neighborhood of the stock yards is very bitter against any man wearing a Pinkerton badge, and the unfortunate occurrence of to-day has served to intensify it to an extraordinary degree.

October 20, 1886

A MENACE TO TRADES UNIONS.

The men employed in TIFFANY'S factory who were recently on strike went back to work again after having succeeded in abolishing for themselves the piece-work system. The circumstance is worth more than a mere passing comment, particularly so because of the antagonism which the trades unions and the Knights of Labor have shown toward that system. To men who think it would seem that in this antagonism are contained elements which may eventually lead to a disruption of labor organizations as now carried on.

The piece-work system is a plan of work in which employés are paid, not by the time consumed by them in their labors, nor at a fixed stipend per day or week, but ratably according to the amount of finished product which each man turns out. It is not satisfactory to labor organizations which insist upon fixed rates—so much per hour or day or week. The fundamental error underlying this latter system is that it places all men belonging to a union on the same level. It takes no heed of such things as skill and industry. A poor workman or a lazy one, provided he belong to the union, must receive just as much wages as his more skilled and more diligent comrades. The fixed rate system also fails to take into account individual ambition or necessities. If the majority of the union men in any trade happen to be bachelors or married men with small families or persons who are content to struggle along in a hand-to-mouth existence they curtail hours of labor and forbid others with greater needs or an ambition to accumulate property from supplying their wants or advancing in the world. The tendency and influence of the unions as now carried on is to keep men on the same level.

This arrangement, it is manifest, is for the advantage of the less skilled and less industrious. It has already had the effect of discouraging individual efforts to excel and of taking away a needed spur to industry. It tends to "slop" work and "slop" workmen. Why should a man strive to perfect himself or why should he labor very hard if neither of these things will give him any advantage over his fellows who do not? Suppose one man has a large family or a sick wife or child, and is therefore under a greater expense than another person who is not in such a position. Why should the first be compelled to work for no more than the other is willing to accept?

The aspect of the question which unfortunately does not seem to be regarded at all is the inalienable right of every person to work as long as he pleases and to earn as big wages as he can get. This right is confined within certain legal limitations, principally as to the age and surroundings of the worker. The limitations are only such as are necessary for the health and wellbeing of the community. Within them the right is absolute. This right or liberty of the individual will assert itself some day. Sooner or later the man with greater needs will demand an opportunity of honestly laboring to supply them, and the man with an ambition to be more than a mechanic all his days will assert his right to work overtime so that he may increase his savings. The skilled workman will insist on being paid at a higher rate than the dullard, and the hard-working man will claim a greater compensation than the drone. Demands like these must succeed in the end because they are just. Then, when once a premium is put, as it should be, upon skill and industry, will come a clash. The unions will be obliged to recede from the position they are now insisting upon, and, if they resist they will break up. The most skillful and industrious workers will have no difficulty in getting work at higher wages. But it will be bad for the unskilled and the lazy. These considerations should be taken into account by labor organizations if they would truly be of service to workingmen. Such organizations will have more to fear from internal dissensions in the future than from any coalition without, and they should be prepared to meet the emergency which will surely come.

November 8, 1886

THE BLOODSHED AT HOMESTEAD.

It is not necessary to discuss the dispute between the Carnegie Steel Company and its employés in order to fix the responsibility for the outbreak of violence at Homestead. The company may have been wrong in the course it took in regard to the scale of wages, but it had the right to employ men in its works at whatever rate of pay they were willing to accept. After its former employés had abandoned its service they had no right to interfere with the employment of others or with the operation of the works. Their relations with the company were severed, and while it was their right to use persuasion to induce others not to enter its service, they had no right to use force or resort to violence. If the company was able to operate its works without the help of the strikers, it might prove fatal to the latter in their contest over the question of wages, but that was the misfortune of their position, and gave them no right to interfere with property which was not theirs or with workmen who were willing to work on the terms offered.

When the officers of the company called upon the Sheriff of Allegheny County to protect its property, and to protect them in their efforts to operate the works with men whom they were employing, the strikers declared that the property was in no danger, and offered to guard it themselves. They even went so far as to prevent the Sheriff's deputies from entering the grounds, and forced them to return to Pittsburg, escorting them one by one to the boat to protect them from the crowd. It was for the officers of the company, and not for the citizens of Homestead who had formerly been in its service, to judge of the necessity for protection. The latter had no business to interfere with the property or assume its protection. It was for the company to protect its own property, and to call upon the authorities of the county if it was prevented from doing so or if it was threatened by a mob. In calling upon Sheriff MCCLEARY, the company was clearly within its right, and it had ample cause for doing so, as subsequent events have proved.

The company had also an undoubted right to employ whatever number of watchmen it deemed necessary for the protection of its works, and to obtain them wherever it saw fit. Nevertheless, the employment of "Pinkerton men" was, in the circumstances, a move sure to lead to violence and bloodshed, and for that reason was certainly unwise. The strikers put themselves in the wrong in attempting to interfere with the company's property and workmen, in resisting the Sheriff and driving off his deputies, and in trying to prevent the landing at Homestead of the guards brought there for the protection of the steel works. But it was quite plain that they would do all this, and it was bad policy to give them the opportunity to do just what many of them really wanted to do. The statements are conflicting as to the side from which the first shot was fired in yesterday's riot and bloodshed, but there is no doubt that an unlawful mob was gathered to prevent the landing of the Pinkerton men, trampling upon private rights, and defying public authority. The mob practically took possession of the place, and by violence and disorder overpowered the men employed by the company and defied the authorities of the county.

There is no question as to the duty of the authorities of Allegheny County and of the State of Pennsylvania. It is to enforce law and order at Homestead, to quell the mob, to put the property of the Carnegie Steel Company in possession of its owners and to protect them in their lawful rights. It is not a question of sympathy in a labor controversy, but of the maintenance of law and the enforcement of public authority, and all considerations relating to the labor trouble should be postponed until that is accomplished. No State can afford to let its citizens take the law into their own hands and wage bloody warfare among themselves in defense of what they claim to be their rights. The first duty of the public authorities in Pennsylvania is plainly to establish order at Homestead and compel its people to submit to the rule of law.

July 7, 1892

ANDREW CARNEGIE

THE CARNEGIE ULTIMATUM

STRIKERS INVITED TO RETURN TO THEIR WORK.

IF THEY FAIL TO RESPOND BY THURS-
DAY THEIR PLACES WILL BE FILLED
WITH NON-UNION MEN—ADMIRABLE
DISCIPLINE MAINTAINED BY THE
NATIONAL GUARD AT HOMESTEAD.

HOMESTEAD, Penn., July 16.—Seven of the
ten Carnegie mills have had steam started up
since yesterday morning, and by Monday the
future of the strike, its success or failure, will
be pretty well established.

This morning every one of the 3,800 workingmen who were employed in the mills received
an invitation from the company to resume
work. The notification reads as follows:

THE CARNEGIE STEEL CO., LIMITED, HOMESTEAD.
STEEL WORKS, July 15, 1892.
DEAR SIR: Repairs will be resumed on Monday
morning, July 18, 1892. We invite you to return to
your old position, work to commence at the usual
time. Respectfully, J. A. POTTER.
GENERAL OFFICE.

The men received the invitations with more
or less sullenness. Some of them promptly destroyed the circulars, others threw them in the
gutter. Every workman who was questioned
declared that not a man would return. The
leaders said that after the demonstration yesterday in the rink there was no mistaking the
firmness and determination of the men.

More workingmen were seen about the mills
to-day than yesterday. The current report
about Homestead is that at least 100 non-union
men are in possession, working under the lead
of some of the old foremen. Certain it is, that
numbers of strange men entered the place during the morning and afternoon.

The policy of the company is slowly developing. They propose to give the old men a chance
to resume their old places except those who
shot at the Pinkertons. If they refuse, non-
union men will be brought in in bulk. This afternoon a huge placard was posted at various
points along the high board fence and at all the
entrances. It is the company's ultimatum, and
was drawn by a clear-headed lawyer. It reads
as follows:

THE CARNEGIE STEEL COMPANY, (LIMITED).

Notice—Individual applications for employment at
the Homestead Steel Works will be received by the
General Superintendent either in person or by letter
until 6 P. M. Thursday, July 21, 1892. It is our desire to retain in our service all of our old employes
whose past record is satisfactory and who did not
take part in the attempts which have been made to
interfere with our right to manage our business.

Such of our old employes as do not apply by the
time above named will be considered as having no
desire to re-enter our employment, and the positions
which they held will be given to other men, and
those first applying will have the choice of unfilled
positions for which they are suitable.

The Carnegie Steel Company, (Limited,)
H. C. FRICK, Chairman.

The military authorities expressed no opinion
on the notification or the placard. They fell
back on the old statement that the military will
preserve peace. One thing was manifest, however, that the troops will remain here a week
longer, unless the strikers yield. Thus far the
only troops admitted to the works with arms
are those who work the pumps for water for the
Second and Third Brigades. In order to permit the soldiers to obtain some acquaintance
with the works, entire companies, except those

detached for guard duty and special service, march through them in command of their Captain or a Lieutenant.

Major Wetherill of the division staff to-day used the heliograph to signal over to Col. Hawkins's quarters, with brilliant results. Several messages were sent without a break. The Signal Corps is not authorized by the State, but consists of detachments from the various regiments.

The town this morning is completely invested from a military standpoint. There is not an inch of exposed ground within the fences that is not covered by the lines of artillery or infantry fire.

Last night, Col. Elliott of Gen. Snowden's staff, accompanied by Major Campbell, started out to place a company of infantry at Munhall Station and to establish a post of observation on the high hill in the rear. When half way down Carnegie Hill the clouds opened, and for three-quarters of an hour the troops were exposed to the heaviest thunderstorm of the year without the slightest shelter. Not a murmur was made, however, and when the storm ceased the troops marched to their station drenched to the skin. Col. Elliott posted them in their positions, the guard that climbed the hill having anything but an easy time of it.

Every guard in camp now carries his piece loaded. At division headquarters the guard is doubled at taps. All passes for the day expire at 10 P. M.

Commissioned officers fare no better than privates when they encounter the guard. Last night two officers of the division staff on a return from a scouting expedition were halted by the guard. The Corporal and the Sergeant of the guard were called for and failed to recognize their superiors. It was not till the Lieutenant of the guard was summoned that the belated officers were permitted to go to their quarters.

The discipline in the camp in all respects is as vigorous after taps as if the troops were in an enemy's country. The sentries have orders to fire if their challenge is unheeded. Every night scouting parties of officers from division and brigade headquarters are sent out on the hills and in the ravines to the south and east of the camp.

A delegation left here to-night for Duquesne to be present at a meeting of the workmen in the Duquesne mill of the Carnegie Steel Company, Limited. The meeting has been gotten up by the Homestead leaders, and the best talkers among them are going to hold forth to-morrow in the hope of inducing the Duquesne men to go on a sympathetic strike. The men at Duquesne, all of whom are "scabs," have already declared against a strike, but O'Donnell and his coadjutors hope to win them over.

The Homesteaders are losing heart the more they think of the gyves of iron which the militia have bound around their brawny wrists. Non-union men have been coming into the Carnegie mills this afternoon and to-night on every train in small parties of from two to six persons. Each party is escorted into the mill yard under a strong guard of State soldiers. Some of these men have come from Pittsburg and some from the South. They have arrived on the Pennsylvania Railroad and on the Baltimore and Ohio on the opposite side of the river. The Little Bill has been landing men and provisions at the mill all day long.

To-night a squad of sharpshooters was posted at a point commanding the houses of the Hungarians near the mill yard. The houses have been under suspicion for several days, because it is believed that there is a chance that trouble may break out there.

Homestead to-night is filled with a holiday crowd, and presents an appearance far different from that it bore last Saturday night. The streets are thronged with women and young girls, many of them in from the country to see the sights, and especially the soldiers and their camp on the hill. Last Saturday night the streets were crowded, but only with men, and the lights were all extinguished at 9 o'clock. To-night there were hundreds of both sexes abroad at midnight.

There will be religious services in camp to-morrow.

July 17, 1892

LABOR AND ANARCHY.

The would-be assassin of Mr. FRICK of the Carnegie Steel Company appears to have been a fanatical Anarchist seeking to strike down a man who to his disordered mind seemed to be a conspicuous enemy of the poor and the oppressed. His dastardly deed was probably the result of the labor trouble at Homestead only in the sense that this trouble made Mr. FRICK stand out conspicuously for the time being as a representative of what Anarchists and Socialists are wont to denounce as the "capitalistic class," and that the excitement produced by the contest directed the attention of such wild fanatics especially to him as an enemy to be destroyed. These pestilent creatures have been fostering the notion that violence and destruction are justifiable in a warfare against what they prate about as the wrongs of labor, and have been breeding possible assassins in a class that hardly knows what honest labor means. There are no worse enemies of the workingmen of this country than these same ignorant and reckless Socialists and Anarchists of foreign origin, who make so much noise about the rights and wrongs of society of which they have no intelligent comprehension.

But while the strikers at Homestead cannot in any sense be held accountable for the act of this crack-brained Anarchist, they have given an indirect encouragement to lawless notions of which such an act is always a possible outcome. They have set agoing impulses the consequences of which are beyond their control. When they met the Pinkerton men on the banks of the Monongahela River with weapons in their hands, and began to shoot them down as they attempted to land, they taught a lesson of violence and disregard of the restraints of law which carried with it all the possibilities of anarchy. The difference between the shooting of Pinkerton men as the hired foes of organized labor and the shooting of Mr. FRICK as the arch-enemy of all workingmen in the fevered imagination of the rabid Anarchist is a difference only of degree. The latter was an extreme manifestation of the spirit displayed in the former. And yet none of these workingmen who claim to be peaceable American citizens and who make professions of regard for law and order have yet acknowledged the wrongfulness of that lawless attack of July 6.

Their disregard of law has not been confined to that violent and bloody resistance of the landing of Pinkerton men at Homestead. They assumed to prevent the Carnegie Company from entering upon its own property and taking control of its works; they defied the authority of Allegheny County, and yielded to that of the State of Pennsylvania only when it was represented by a military force that it was useless to resist. It is a humiliation which these men do not yet seem to appreciate that a display of military force should be necessary to induce American workingmen to submit to the law and to constituted authority and show respect for the rights of others. The spectacle at Homestead for nearly three weeks past has been that of a practical suspension of civil authority, due solely to the fact that the people had refused to submit to it. What is the essence of Anarchy but a refusal to submit to law and authority and a subversion of the constituted order of civil society? In these proceedings the people of Homestead have been giving encouragement to the worst enemies of the cause of honest labor.

Why is a military force still maintained at Homestead at great expense to the State of Pennsylvania and at a serious sacrifice of members of the militia? Is it not because the stand taken and the disposition shown by the former workmen of the mills make it practically certain that if the force should be withdrawn there would be an immediate resumption of lawlessness to the extent of preventing the Carnegie Company from running its works without first yielding to the demands of the strikers? The question is not whether their demands were just, or whether the course taken by the company was right, but whether the property would be safe in the hands of the owners, whether the company would be allowed to proceed with its business without interference, and whether other workingmen than the strikers would be left at liberty to go and come at will. In other words, it is whether the sway of the law would be resumed and peaceably submitted to, and private rights under the protection of law would be respected. Not until an assurance of that normal state of things exists can the workmen vindicate their claim of being law-abiding citizens and free themselves wholly from the charge of giving encouragement to the spirit of anarchy. Not until then can they regain the full sympathy of those who regard the maintenance of law and order as the first condition of the settlement of disputes between labor and capital.

July 25, 1892

EDITORIAL

The moment it became a question of endurance between the Homestead workmen and the great corporation that owns the Carnegie Steel Works the struggle of the strikers became a hopeless one. In such a test capital has an enormous advantage. Workingmen cannot long remit their labor without suffering, and they invariably find that the funds of the unions cannot be depended upon for support. At Homestead the wages of comparatively few of the men were affected by the new scale, and those were among the best paid. With the mass of them want would speedily become the alternative of work. But capital could wait without suffering, and it could even recoup its losses from a suspension of activity out of increased prices through a shortening of its output. Moreover, labor was sure to suffer from the pressure of the competition of other labor seeking employment, while capital had no fear that other capital would come in and take its place. Not until labor is more thoroughly organized than at present and has a greater solidarity of interests can it hope to win in a trial of endurance with corporate capital unless it has a cause that commands universal sympathy and support.

July 28, 1892

DECLARES THE STRIKE LOST.

THE "LOCAL NEWS" ADVISES HOMESTEAD MEN TO ADMIT DEFEAT.

PITTSBURG, Oct. 15.—The *Local News*, a Homestead paper, created a sensation to-day by coming out with a long editorial declaring that the strike is lost. This same paper was, during the inception of the wage struggle, an organ for the locked-out men, and the Advisory Committee published statements in its columns.

To-day's editorial was, therefore, unexpected, and causes much comment. Many strikers are angry and are stopping their subscriptions, but that Editor Scholley's article was submitted to several prominent locked-out men, and was admitted to be correct before publication, is a f ct. The paper says:

"The only results the strikers can show are that they are keeping themselves well in line and are causing the steel firm loss and trouble. Thus the situation stands at present, to say nothing of charges in the courts on both sides. The candid observer, taking a view of the situation, can come to the following conclusions only:

"*First*—The Carnegie Steel Company is gradually succeedin g.

"*Second*—The great Homestead strike is gradually dying out."

October 16, 1892

Editorial

The miners of the Cœur d'Alêne district in Idaho have carried to their logical consequences the teachings of the steel workers at Homestead, Penn. They are probably a more lawless set of men, and they live in a region where regard for law and respect for authority are less habitual, but not until they heard of the bloodshed at Homestead did they resort to open violence. Once incited to that course they proceed without restraint to take possession of the mining property, to kill workmen, and to blow up the mills with dynamite. In principle their course differed very little from that of the Pennsylvania strikers. They have forced the discharge of non-union men and compelled a suspension of all work. There was no local authority sufficient to control them, and it turns out that the State of Idaho has practically no militia force with which to support its authority. It has been compelled to call upon the National Government for troops, which have been promptly ordered to the scene of trouble. These are not welcomed by the rioters and nothing but a display of superior force will bring them into subjection. The trouble is of long standing, growing out of a reduction of wages some months ago, which seems to have been necessary, as the mining works were closed for some time because they could not be run at a profit, except with non-union men at the reduced wages.

July 14, 1892

EMBRACING MORE RAILROADS

PULLMAN BOYCOTT EXTENDING, THE MEN BEING DETERMINED.

Big Lines West of Chicago Crippled by the Action of the Strikers, Who Will Endeavor to Bring in All Labor Organizations—Estimated that 40,000 of the Workers Are Out—May Change Headquarters to St. Louis —The Managers Stand Firm.

CHICAGO, June 28.—With the simple beginning of a few hundred discontented strikers at Pullman, Ill., who were attempting to force a local issue, the Pullman strike and consequent boycott has assumed the proportions of the greatest battle between labor and capital that has ever been inaugurated in the United States.

In three days' time the Pullman trouble has spread to nearly all of the important railroads in the United States west of Chicago, with the result that entire systems are tied up and powerless in the hands of employes.

Within three days, over 20,000 men have either quit work or have announced their intention of so doing in Chicago, and added to this are the many thousands on the systems all through the West who have gone out on strike in obedience to requests from the officers of the American Railway Union.

It was estimated to-day at the headquarters of the American Railway Union that fully 40,000 men were now out on a strike on account of the refusal of the Pullman Company to settle the differences with its employes in the shops.

By to-morrow night nearly double that number will have been ordered out, and the strikers will include not only members of the union, but Knights of Labor, brotherhood men, and other organizations which can in any way affect the interests of the roads which have decided to stand by Mr. Pullman.

It was given out at headquarters to-day that to-morrow morning the different railroads out of Chicago handling Pullman cars would be sufficiently crippled to warrant the removal of the base of operations of the officers of the American Railway Union from Chicago to St. Louis.

Martin Elliott, a representative of the union, was sent to St. Louis to-night to call out the men in all but two roads entering the St. Louis Union Station with Pullman Palace cars in their trains. To-morrow night, if necessary, President Debs and Vice President Howard will go to St. Louis to take charge of the strike there.

It is confidently asserted that within two days all railroads out of St. Louis handling Pullman cars, excepting the Missouri Pacific, will be asked to cancel Pullman contracts or incur a strike.

Vice President Hoard said to-day that the union would not exempt a single road in the West or Southwest, and if necessary all of the more important of the Eastern roads would be tied up in order to force a settlement of the Pullman strike. From the showing made within the last three days by the union, railroad men are inclined to believe that the statement is no idle boast.

A new deal was sprung this evening, when orders were issued to tie up the Chicago and Alton, the Burlington, and the Rock Island. The instructions to strike were given late this afternoon, and while the committees appointed to act with the employes began work at once it was not expected that the men would go out before 12 o'clock to-night.

Trains on all of the roads were gotten out in fair shape to-day, although the most of them were made up by the officials and their assistants.

The feature of the union's work to-day was the speedy settlement effected with the Chicago, Milwaukee and St. Paul. This morning a special committee was sent to the General Manager of the Milwaukee with a request that the road refuse to haul Pullman sleepers. Through a misunderstanding a number of the Milwaukee men struck before an answer was given, and this led to the report that the road was tied up.

The company officials lost no time in informing the committee that no Pullmans would be hauled over the road, and within an hour the nine objectionable cars which are run on that line were side tracked. President Debs immediately ordered the men back to work, and the road suffered but little inconvenience.

The United States Government has taken a hand in the strike so far as it concerns the Santa Fé system. Late this afternoon United States District Attorney Milchrist received a dispatch from Attorney General Olney intimating that advices had been received from the Postmaster General indicating that transportation of the United States mail on the road in question was either obstructed or in danger thereof.

The Attorney General instructed the United States District Attorney to proceed against all individuals concerned in such obstruction, and to place warrants in the hands of the United States Marshal, who in turn was instructed to appoint all the Deputy Marshals necessary for the proper enforcement of the law, and to arrest all persons interfering with or interposing obstacles to the government of trains carrying the mails of the United States.

This action of Attorney General Olney was predicated upon a dispatch forwarded early in the afternoon by the receivers of the Santa Fé to Postmaster General Bissell, setting forth the condition caused by the strike, and asking relief.

Rumor was set abroad to-day that the meeting of General Managers had determined that the strike must end and that Pullman must consent to arbitration with his striking employes.

Asked by a United Press reporter if it were true, General Manager C. H. Chappel of the Chicago and Alton Railroad said: "There is not a word of truth in the statement. On the contrary, we have organized to resist this strike to the bitter end.

"We have opened at No. 732 Rookery Building an employment office, and John M. Egan, formerly President and General Manager of the Chicago and Great Western Road, has taken charge of the work of securing men to take the places of those men who decline to switch or draw Pullman cars. More than that, we have already opened a branch office in every important city in the country, and by Saturday night we shall have hundreds of men here to fill the places as fast as vacant."

The strikers had much the best of the situation to-day on the Illinois Central. That road is almost entirely tied up in this city and the Illinois Division, and thousands of dollars are being lost along the line by the inability of the company to handle freight, the practical abandonment of its vast suburban service, and the timidity of the traveling public. The greatest loss to the road is probably in the demoralization of suburban traffic.

The express firemen who went out early in the day returned to work late in the afternoon. Besides the order issued this morning declaring that the Illinois Central would receive no more perishable freight or stock freight, a later one was sent out which orders that all kinds of freight be refused at all points of the road, whether subject to delay or not.

Seventy-five cars of perishable and merchandise freight to-night lie side-tracked at Fordham, the men there refusing to move them. One hundred carloads of bananas are between New-Orleans and Chicago, and it is not thought they can be delivered.

The Baltimore and Ohio has also suspended the reception of perishable freight.

The section men at Grand Crossing, Burnside, and Fordham, and several construction gangs, have struck. The water supply has been cut off at Weldon, and matters are hourly growing more serious.

All day the strikers in the Van Buren Street yards tried to induce the train and engine men to strike, with success in a few cases. It is reported that the firemen were ordered out by their Brotherhood, but the rumor cannot be confirmed.

All the engineers in the suburban express service but two quit work.

At Archer Avenue and Halstead Street a mob prevented the handling of milk trains. It was difficult for the company to keep the gatemen at Grand Crossing at work on account of intimidation by strikers.

The 125 men in the yards of the Northwestern who are out comprise the "make-up" and "break-up" crews in the yards and the freight switchmen.

Only perishable freight was moved to-day, and the company officials, such as the Assistant Superintendent, yardmaster, &c., made up these trains. The company is hiring all the men that apply for work, and an official of the road expressed his opinion that by to-morrow fully half of the strikers' places would be filled.

Six interlocking switch tower operators and as many ground switchmen employed on the joint tracks of the Pittsburg, Fort Wayne and Chicago; the Chicago, Burlington and Quincy, and the Chicago and Alton Railroad, at the Union Depot and south to Twenty-first Street, left their switches and levers at 3 o'clock this afternoon, when they received orders from headquarters to strike in support of the Pullman boycott.

Although few in number, the striking of these men brought confusion and delay to the officials and thousands of patrons who use the suburban and local trains on the Burlington, Panhandle, and Alton Roads entering the Union Station.

In two hours the blockade was raised. The trains on an average were half an hour late. Among them was the Pennsylvania Limited, for New-York, which should have left at 5:30. It pulled out at 5:50, and the Pullman cars contained but thirty passengers. The 6 o'clock train on the Alton was half an hour late.

The Baltimore and Ohio Pittsburg express, which is scheduled to leave at 7 P. M. from the Grand Central Station, was completely stalled inside the city limits for more than four hours by the strikers at Western Avenue. Riot was narrowly averted between the train crew and the strikers, and a squad of police was ordered to the scene from the West Thirteenth Street Station.

An attempt was made by the officers to start the train at 11 o'clock, but it was found that the cars had been uncoupled. It was made known to the crowd that the train was carrying United States mail for Washington, and that any interference with it would subject the culprits to prosecution, but this had no effect.

No fight occurred, but all attempts to start the train were baffled by the crowd. The inbound Baltimore and Ohio mail train due here at 9 P. M. was also held by the crowd until after midnight.

At the request of the railway employes in the East, twenty-five men were sent out by the American Railway Union to-day to aid organization in that part of the country. They are bound for New-York, and will begin work among the employes of the New-York Central Railroad Company.

The strike of the Northwestern and the Pan Handle, followed by that of the employes of the Fort Wayne to-day, greatly increased the strength of the union.

Not a train was sent out of the city after 8 o'clock to-night by any of the roads using the Polk Street Station. Most of the regular passenger trains were made up by officials and left the station all right, but at midnight they are all stalled at Thirty-first Street.

A number of in-bound trains on the roads affected are also stuck outside the city, and their passengers had to make their way to town by street cars or hacks.

Among the trains between Thirty-first Street and Fortieth Street are the Chicago and Eastern Illinois through passenger train from Terre Haute; the Chicago and Eastern Illinois locals, the Wabash local from St. Louis, the Wabash Short Line train from New-York, the Monon through train for Cincinnati, carrying four Pullman cars, and a number of freight trains.

Most of the trouble was caused by the Chicago and Eastern Illinois yardmen joining the Chicago and Western Indiana Terminal employes. In addition to this, two of the firemen on the stalled Eastern Illinois trains left their cabs, and the engineers refused to proceed with green men.

All efforts to get the firemen back to work failed, and as a last resort an attempt was made to get these two engines back into the Thirty-first Street roundhouse, so as to clear the track and let the other trains go ahead.

It was found that the switch leading to the roundhouse had been spiked and set. At midnight there was little probability of the blockade's being raised to-night.

At 10 o'clock to-night only a few of the switchmen were out in the Fort Wayne and the Alton in Chicago. The Burlington men were ordered out, but concluded to review the situation in mass meeting before acting. The Rock Island had not been touched by the strikers at 9 P. M.

The tying up of the Rock Island would result in the tying up of the Lake Shore at this point.

At 4 o'clock this afternoon orders were issued to the employed of the Union Pacific and the Denver and Rio Grande to strike at once. The Chicago and Eastern Illinois men were ordered out at 6 o'clock to-night and responded promptly.

At 10 o'clock between 3,000 and 4,000 people had gathered at the Fortieth Street crossing, and four or five trains were held there unable to break through the gates and the crowd. All efforts on the part of the officials to get the trains through met with failure.

Considerable excitement was created to-day by the announcement that the trainmen and all other employes at the stock yards and packing houses had gone out. A meeting was held to-night and it is likely that the stock-yards men will go out to-morrow.

There is considerable talk about the shutting down of the large manufactories in Chicago on account of the strike and owing to the inability to ship goods or get in material. The first to notify its employes of a shut-down was the Chicago Sugar Refining Company. This throws 2,500 employes out of work.

The tie-up of the Northern Pacific is complete from St. Paul to Missouri. Reports up to 8 P. M. were to the effect that the Pacific Division of the road was still open. The tie-up in Minneapolis is complete.

Every switchman on the Northern Pacific and Omaha Lines at Duluth, and all of the Northern Pacific switchmen in Superior are out.

Not a wheel turned on the Northern Pacific in Montana to-day. Express trains are held at Missoula, Helena, and Livingston. About 500 through passengers are laid up.

The Northern Pacific and its branches in Washington and Idaho are completely tied up. At Cairo all trains are stopped, except on the Big Four. That road hauls no Pullmans.

George M. Pullman,
President Pullman Palace Car Company.

MR. PULLMAN'S STATEMENT.

Men Struck After the Company Had Made Sacrifices for Them.

George M. Pullman, President of the Pullman Palace Car Company, who is now in Chicago, has issued a comprehensive statement to the public with regard to the efforts of the company to keep its works open and give employment to its men. Among other things, he says:

"At the commencement of the serious depression last year we were employing at Pullman 5,816 men and paying out in wages there $305,000 a month. Negotiations with intending purchasers of railway equipment that were then pending for new work were stopped by them, orders already given by others were canceled, and we were obliged to lay off a large number of men in every department, so that by Nov. 1, 1893, there were only about 2,000 men in all departments, or about one-third of the normal number. I realized the necessity for the most strenuous exertions to procure work immediately, without which there would be great embarrassment, not only to the employes and their families at Pullman, but also to those living in the immediate vicinity, including between 700 and 800 employes who had purchased homes and to whom employment was actually necessary to enable them to complete their payments.

"I canvassed the matter thoroughly with the manager of the works, and the result of this discussion was a revision in piece-work prices, which, in the absence of any information to the contrary, I supposed to be acceptable to the men under the circumstances. Under these conditions, and with lower prices upon all materials, I personally undertook the work of the letting of cars, and by making lower bids than other manufacturers I secured work enough to gradually increase our force from 2,200 up to about 4,200, the number employed, according to the April pay rolls, in all capacities at Pullman.

"This result has not been accomplished merely by reduction in wages, but the company has borne its full share by eliminating from its estimates the use of capital and machinery, and, in many cases, even going below that and taking work at considerable loss.

"During the night of May 10 a strike was decided upon, and accordingly next day about 2,500 of the employes quit, leaving about 600 at work, of whom very few were skilled workmen. As it was found impracticable to keep the shops in operation with a force thus diminished and disorganized, the next day those remaining were necessarily laid off, and no work has since been done in the shops. The pay rolls at the time amounted to about $7,000 a day, and were reduced $5,500 by the strike, so that during the period of little more than six weeks which has elapsed the employes who quit their work have deprived themselves and their comrades of earnings of more than $200,000."

CARS MUST NOT BE STOPPED

SWEEPING INJUNCTION AGAINST RAILROAD STRIKERS.

EX-EMPLOYES PRACTICALLY HELPLESS

To Prevent Operations of Trains Is to Violate the Interstate Law.

END OF STRIKE NEAR AT HAND.

The Restraining Order Enjoins All Strikers, Their Friends, Sympathizers, and Those Whom They May Incite from Interfering in Any Way in Illinois, Portions of Indiana, and Wisconsin with Any Inter-State Commerce Traffic — Railroads Will Passively Allow Strikers to Act, for the Purpose of Having the Injunction Enforced — Strikers Think the Order a Boomerang—Meantime, the Railroad ex-Employes Have Strengthened Their Vantage—Troops Will Be Necessary to Restore Operation of Trains.

CHICAGO, July 2.—The crucial point in the railroad strike will be reached within twenty-four hours from midnight. This is the opinion confidently expressed at the headquarters of the railroad managers at a late hour to-night.

It is likewise the first expression emanating from the managers' end since the commencement of hostilities with which the representatives of the strikers are in complete accord. Both elements are sanguine that the beginning of the end will be in sight before sundown Tuesday.

As to the means by which this desirable consummation is to be attained, however, there is a radical difference of opinion.

The General Managers profess to believe that the extraordinary injunction issued to-day by Judges Woods and Grosscup will prove to be worthy of the terse yet epigrammatical designation given to it by the members of the Federal judiciary first named, "A Gatling gun on paper."

It is a veritable dragnet in the matter of legal verbiage, one of those peculiar instruments that punishes an individual for doing a certain thing, and is equally merciless if he does not do it, so it is difficult to understand how the strikers can maintain their present policy and at the same time evade its operation or escape its influence.

Even personal service is not an absolute necessity to its legal enforcement.

According to the law as expounded by United States District Attorney Milchrist to-night, the publication of the decree in a widely-circulated paper, its posting in a public place where it is certain to be read, and its contents disseminated, or the formal reading to a demonstrative crowd by a Deputy Marshal, may be ruled upon as constituting sufficient service to place those guilty of a breach of its provisions under the ban of the law.

Under this interpretation thousands of strikers might be arrested day after day and be arraigned and summarily dealt with for contempt of court, and this is precisely the policy, according to the reports at the Government Building to-night, that it is intended to pursue.

If it is carried out, there will be no need, so it is believed, for the employment either of State militia or Federal troops.

A goodly force of Deputy Marshals armed with power to make arbitrary arrests and with the knowledge on the part of the strikers that, once within the clutches of the law, peremptory sentence to prison for contempt instead of a preliminary hearing, bail, and a final trial months hence, when the echoes of the strike may have died away, will be their portion, should, so reason the railroad managers, create such a combination of circumstances as to induce the strikers to pause and reason before proceeding further in their present course.

But the strikers themselves reason differently. At their headquarters this evening the interference of the Federal court was denounced in vigorous language by one and all of the hundreds, if not thousands, of railroad men that passed in and out, and the most intelligent of the number voiced the general sentiment in the declaration that the far-reaching and dragnet character of the injunction would tend toward defeating the very ends to which it was directed.

Instead of inducing men to return to work, so it was contended, it would result in driving out thousands of members of railroad organizations not affiliated with the union or apparently in sympathy with its present operations, simply because these men would not tolerate the cracking over the shoulders of their fellows of a Government whip that some day or other, under similar circumstances, might be used as a lash for their own shoulders.

The opinion was confidently expressed in the strikers' camp to-night that the engineers and firemen of every road that attempted to resume operations by virtue of the injunction would immediately leave their posts, and that consequently the last state of such roads would be worse than the first.

Not only this, but it was asserted that it needed simply the formal request of the officers of the union to bring out every man, woman, and child in Chicago identified with organized labor in accordance with the formal resolutions adopted at yesterday's meeting of the federated trades.

Such a step, it was argued, would be meeting Greek with Greek, and the tug of war could not result otherwise than in a speedy and absolute victory for the labor element. Such a situation and such an ending the leaders of the strike prognosticate for the next twenty-four hours.

The day was more prolific of rumors and scares than of actual developments. A feeling of unrest and semi-excitement pervaded every section of the community.

Stories that the entire militia force had been called out, that the regulars from Fort Sheridan were on the move, that Deputy Marshals and Sheriffs who had been sent to suburban points were being massacred by the score, were passed from mouth to mouth, and received implicit credence until authoritatively contradicted.

The railroads were content to allow things to run along as they had on Saturday and Sunday, reserving for to-morrow the supreme effort to break the backbone of the strike.

The Federal and county officials continued to swear in deputies, and an army of over 2,000 of the toughest-looking citizens that Cook County can produce, armed and wearing the insignia of State or national authority, is subject to orders to-night, and will doubtless be brought into service to-morrow.

Lights were burning in the windows of the Government and county buildings at midnight, and the authorities were prepared for any emergency.

The strike is tying up lake traffic effectually. The grain trade is completely paralyzed, as the railroads are unable to get any corn or oats to the elevators, and the stocks for shipment are well-nigh exhausted.

Several cars containing flour and other freights bound for the seaboard and foreign ports are lying on the side track, the companies being powerless to get them to the steamboat docks.

In the meantime the steamers have been bringing in large amounts of freight here, which they have been unable to deliver to the railroads, and all the river warehouses are filled to overflowing. Nearly a score of boats are on the market to-day for cargoes, but are unable to obtain any. Hard coal is still the only fuel to be had here.

Lodge No. 238 of the Brotherhood of Locomotive Firemen at Brighton Park gave up its charter in the old organization to-day and joined the American Railway Union. The lodge includes firemen on the Chicago and Alton and the Santa Fé.

Six Grand Trunk passenger trains are in the yards at Battle Creek, and at least 500 passengers are waiting to get out. The yards are blocked with freight and passenger cars. The Grand Trunk shopmen went out this morning, and the large thrashing machine works closed down to-night. The authorities have closed all the saloons.

The Grand Trunk has canceled all its trains on the Chicago Division out of Port Huron, Mich., on account of the suspension of traffic west of Battle Creek.

All freight trains have been abandoned on the Hannibal and Decatur Branch of the Wabash, and all passenger trains are very late.

The Missouri Pacific shops at Fort Scott, Kan., have been closed down on account of the strike.

When Mr. Debs's attention was called to the rumors that have been in circulation for the past two days, to the effect that negotiations looking to a settlement of the strike were being conducted between himself and Mr. Studebaker for the Pullman Company, he declined to answer direct questions, but consented to outline the terms upon which the officers of the union would settle the strike.

"First," he said, "we will settle with the Pullman Company upon any terms that the employes of the company may desire. We will settle with the railroads on the condition that they restore their striking employes to their former places. We want the settlement to take place with all the corporations at once, however."

Fifty engineers and firemen on the Wabash met and organized at Thirty-ninth and State Streets to-day. They received an American Railway Union charter this afternoon. These men quit work at 10 o'clock. It is claimed that this ties up the Wabash very effectually as far as running trains in and out of Chicago is concerned. A committee of the Wabash employes came to Uhlich's Hall to-day and requested instructions for striking.

It is now planned to tie up the line from Chicago to St. Louis and from Chicago to Detroit.

At Joliet, Illinois, the blockade on the Rock Island continues, although the roads employes at that place are not on strike. The switches are filled with passenger trains, and the trains with passengers. Not a train has left for Chicago since midnight Monday, and no train has arrived from Chicago since Saturday noon.

The mails remain here, no attempt being made to transfer them to other roads which are running into Chicago. The passengers are suffering for water and food, and some sickness prevails among them.

Grand Trunk officers announced to-day that they would be compelled to abandon the funeral train service to Mount Olivet. This decision was conveyed to the strikers, and a meeting was called to consider the subject. Resolutions were passed by the employes by which they agreed to operate funeral trains and to prevent interference with them.

The committee reported that the company refused to operate funeral trains until it was allowed to run Pullman sleepers on its other trains.

Following is the telegram General Master Workman Sovereign of the Knights of Labor sent to President Debs of the American Railway Union to-day:

"Have I left anything undone? Am willing to call a general strike."

The general situation, as summed up by the General Managers, who are in close telegraphic communication with all lines, is, briefly, as follows:

The Illinois Central and the Rock Island are in the worst straits. Rioting has been general along both lines, with the principal battle ground at Blue Island, on the latter road. Some four hundred Deputy

Marshals and Deputy Sheriffs were simply powerless in the hands of the 2,000 strikers and sympathizers.

Late to-night Marshal Arnold telegraphed to the United States Attorney General for the Fifteenth Infantry, stationed at Fort Sheridan.

All the night suburban trains of the Wisconsin Central and Chicago and Northern Pacific were abandoned.

The Michigan Central is having serious trouble over the employment of new men, as the engineers and firemen refuse to work with them. No freight has been moved in or out of Chicago over the Chicago, Milwaukee and St. Paul to-day. Passenger trains have been moved on time, but suburban service is delayed. The office force of the road has been discharged. All the passenger trains on the Baltimore and Ohio, with full equipment, went out on time, but three engines and cabooses were stalled at Twenty-first Street.

The Santa Fé is working its freight handlers in the yards under protection of United States Marshals. No perishable freight is received. The main trouble is in the West. The shops at Topeka have been shut up in anticipation of a strike.

The Chicago and Calumet terminals are tied up tight, and no attempt to operate is being made.

Passenger trains on the Burlington have not been interfered with, but freight, especially stock, cannot be handled. The general situation is much more serious.

Strikers have been stoning the Wabash trains out of the city, and the road is not attempting to handle any freight. Trains are tied up at Decatur.

The Chicago and Alton is filling the places of the strikers. No freight is moving as yet. The delayed trains at Slater have been released.

GOV. ALTGELD MAKES COMPLAINT.

He Tells the President He Should Not Send Troops into Illinois.

WASHINGTON, July 5.—The President, Secretary Lamont, Attorney General Olney, Postmaster General Bissell, and Gen. Schofield remained at the White House to-night until nearly 12 o'clock. Many telegrams were received and sent during the course of the evening.

When the conference ended Secretary Lamont, acting as spokesman for the President, announced that there was nothing to make public, except the telegram from Gov. Altgeld of Illinois and the President's response thereto.

Gov. Altgeld protests against the presence of United States troops in Chicago. To this the President responds:

John P. Altgeld, Governor of Illinois, Springfield, Ill.:

Federal troops were sent to Chicago in strict accordance with the Constitution and laws of the United States, upon the demand of the Post Office Department that obstruction of the mails should be removed, and upon the representations of the judicial officers of the United States that process of the Federal courts could not be executed through the ordinary means, and upon abundant proof that conspiracies existed against commerce between the States.

To meet these conditions, which are clearly within the province of Federal authority, the presence of Federal troops in the City of Chicago was deemed not only proper, but necessary, and there has been no intention of thereby interfering with the plain duty of the local authorities to preserve the peace of the city.

GROVER CLEVELAND.

Gov. Altgeld's telegram to the President is as follows:

I am advised that you have ordered Federal troops to go into service in the State of Illinois. Surely the facts have not been correctly presented to you in this case, or you would not have taken this step, for it is entirely unnecessary and, as it seems to me, injustifiable.

Waiving all questions of courtesy, I will say that the State of Illinois is not only able to take care of itself, but it stands ready to-day to furnish the Federal Government any assistance it may need elsewhere. Our military force is ample, and consists of as good soldiers as can be found in the country. They have been ordered out promptly whenever and wherever they were needed.

We have stationed in Chicago alone three regiments of infantry, one battery, and one troop of cavalry, and no better soldiers can be found. They have been ready every moment to go on duty, and have been and are eager to go into service. But they have not been ordered out because nobody in Cook County, whether official or private citizen, asked to have their assistance or even intimated in any way that their assistance was desired or necessary.

So far as I have been advised, the local officials have been able to handle the situation. But, if any assistance were needed, the State stood ready to furnish 100 men for every man required and stood ready to do so at a moment's notice. Notwithstanding these facts, the Federal Government has been applied to by men who had political and selfish motives for wanting to ignore the State Government.

We have just gone through a long coal strike, more extensive here than in any other State, because our soft coal field is larger than that of any other State; we have now had ten days of the railroad strike, and we have promptly furnished military aid wherever the local officials needed it.

In two instances the United States Marshal for the Southern District of Illinois applied for assistance to enable him to enforce the processes of the United States court, and troops were promptly furnished him, and he was assisted in every way he desired. The law has been thoroughly executed, and every man guilty of violating it during the strike has been brought to justice.

If the Marshal for the Northern District of Illinois or the authorities of Cook County needed military assistance they had but to ask for it in order to get it from the State.

At present some of our railroads are paralyzed, not by reason of obstructions, but because they cannot get men to operate their trains. For some reason they are anxious to keep this fact from the public, and for this purpose are making an outcry about obstructions in order to divert

attention. I will cite to you two examples which illustrate the situation:

Some days ago I was advised that the business of one of our railroads was obstructed at two railroad centres, that there was a condition bordering on anarchy there, and I was asked to furnish protection, so as to enable the employes of the road to operate the trains. Troops were promptly ordered to both points.

Then it transpired that the company had not sufficient on its line to operate one train. All the old hands were orderly, but refused to go. The company had large shops, in which worked a number of men who did not belong to the Railway Union, and who could run an engine. They were appealed to to run the train, but flatly refused. We were obliged to hunt up soldiers who could run an engine and operate a train.

Again, two days ago, appeals which were almost frantic came from officials of another road, stating that at an important point on their lines trains were forcibly obstructed, and that there was a reign of anarchy at that place, and they asked for protection, so that they could move their trains.

Troops were put on the ground in a few hours' time, when the officer in command telegraphed me that there was no trouble, and had been none at that point, but that the road seemed to have no men to run trains, and the Sheriff telegraphed that he did not need troops, but would himself move every train if the company would only furnish an engineer.

The result was that the troops were there over twelve hours before a single train was moved, although there was no attempt at interference by anybody.

It is true that in several instances a road made efforts to work a few green men, and a crowd standing around insulted them and tried to drive them, and in a few other cases they cut off Pullman sleepers from trains. But all these troubles were local in character, and could easily be handled by the State authorities.

Illinois has more railroad men than any other State in the Union, but as a rule they are orderly and well-behaved. This is shown by the fact that so very little actual violence has been committed. Only a very small per cent. of these men have been guilty of any infractions of the law. The newspaper accounts have in some cases been pure fabrications, and in others wild exaggerations.

I have gone thus into details to show that it is not soldiers that the railroads need so much as it is men to operate trains and that the conditions do not exist here which bring the case within the Federal statute, a statute that was passed in 1861 and is in reality a war measure. This statute authorizes the use of Federal troops in a State whenever it shall be impracticable to enforce the laws of the United States within such State by the ordinary judicial proceedings. Such a condition does not exist in Illinois.

There have been a few local disturbances, but nothing that seriously interfered with the administration of justice, or that could not easily be controlled by the local or State authorities, for the Federal troops can do nothing that the State troops cannot do.

I repeat that you have been imposed upon in this matter, but even if by a forced construction it were held that the conditions here came within the letter of the statute, then I submit that local self-government is a fundamental principle of our Constitution.

Each community shall govern itself so long as it can and is ready and able to enforce the law, and it is in harmony with this fundamental principle that the statute authorizing the President to send troops into States must be construed. Especially is this so in matters relating to the exercise of the police power and the preservation of law and order.

To absolutely ignore a local government in matters of this kind, when the local government is ready to furnish any assistance needed, and is amply able to enforce the law, not only insults the people of the State by imputing to them an inability to govern themselves, or unwillingness to enforce the law, but is in violation of a basic principle of our institutions.

The question of Federal supremacy is in no way involved. No one disputes it for a moment, but under our Constitution Federal supremacy and local self-government must go hand in hand, and to ignore the latter is to do violence to the Constitution.

As Governor of the State of Illinois, I protest against this, and ask the immediate withdrawal of the Federal troops from active duty in this State. Should the situation at any time get so serious that we cannot control it with the State forces, we will promptly and freely ask for Federal assistance, but until such time I protest, with all due deference, against this uncalled-for reflection upon our people, and again ask the immediate withdrawal of these troops.

I have the honor to be, yours respectfully,
JOHN P. ALTGELD.

DEBS IN THE LAW'S GRASP

INDICTED AND ARRESTED WITH HIS ASSOCIATES.

HIS RELEASE SECURED ON $10,000 BAIL.

All Charged with Interfering with the Mails and Hindering Execution of Laws.

ARRESTED MEN ARE INDIFFERENT.

The United States Grand Jury, After a Strong and Able Charge by Judge Grosscup, in Which He Clearly Defined the Rights of Labor Men, Brought in the Indictments After a Careful Consideration—After the Men Had Been Arrested They Were Taken to the District Attorney's Office to Arrange for Bail—Debs and Howard Laughed and Joked and Appeared Unconcerned—Their Supporters Greeted Them with Cheers When They Returned to Headquarters—Officers Made a Search of Debs's Office and Seized Records, Letters, and All Documents.

CHICAGO, July 10.—Eugene V. Debs, President of the American Railway Union; George W. Howard, Vice President; Sylvester Keliher, Secretary; L. W. Rogers, Director and editor of The Railway Times, and James Murwin, an engineer, who is said to have thrown a switch on the Rock Island Road some time ago, endangering the lives of many persons, were arrested this afternoon on warrants sworn out pursuant to indictments issued by the Federal Grand Jury, which convened to-day at 12 o'clock. The full list of indictments was as follows:

Eugene V. Debs, George W. Howard, Sylvester Keliher, L. W. Rogers, James Murwin, Lloyd Hotchkins, A. Paizybak, H. Elfin, James Hammond, William Smith, John Westerbrook, Edward O'Neil, Charles Nailer, John Duffy, William McMullen, E. Shelby, Fred Ketcham, and John W. Doyle.

They are accused of interfering with the business of the United States, obstructing the mails, and also of preventing and hindering the execution of the laws of the United States.

Bail was fixed at $10,000 in each case, which was furnished. The penalty is a fine of from $1,000 to $10,000.

Eugene V. Debs,
President American Railway Union.

Although to some extent it had been anticipated, the arrest of President Debs and his associates was the sensation of the day.

The President of the American Railway Union and his colleagues were brought in quietly and without any of the outbursts of popular indignation that sensationalists had predicted.

The Federal Grand Jury, composed almost entirely of out-of-town residents, occupied less time than had been expected in reaching the decision that the evidence presented for its consideration was sufficient to justify the return of true bills against the leaders of the union.

No other result had been expected by those who listened to the charge of Judge Grosscup, and which, although denounced with fury at the headquarters of the various labor organizations to-night, is generally commented upon in commercial and professional circles as a masterly exposition of the line between the legal and justifiable methods of trades organizations, and defiance of the laws, or rebellion against the authority of the United States.

The jurists took the ground emphatically that, while the right of labor to organize could not be successfully attacked, and that while it was the imperishable right of a free man to work or quit work, as he saw fit, and that while, moreover, he was entitled to all the fruits and strategy of work or of cessation from work, yet, at the same time, trades organizations are subject to the same laws as other associations; that their leaders are also subject to the same laws governing all other men, and that no organization, nor the leaders of such organizations, could with impunity violate the laws enacted for the government of inter-State commerce or the protection of the mails.

Judge Grosscup said that the present emergency was to vindicate the law, and that only, and that if that law had been violated there should be quick, prompt, and adequate indictment.

When the jury turned toward its consulting chamber there was not a man, prob-

ably, within reach of the Judge's voice, who had not already made up his mind that a return of indictments against the leaders of the union would be as quick and prompt as those responsible for the putting into operation of the machinery of the Federal courts could possibly desire.

Organized labor was prompt to strike back at the latest manifestation of Federal power and authority. Hardly had the word been flashed across the half a mile of intervening ground between the Government Building and labor headquarters that indictments had been returned and warrants for Debs and his associates placed in the hands of the officers of the law than the committee appointed by the trades and labor associations of the city to urge upon the Pullman Company the desirability of submitting the dispute with its employes to arbitration, and which had been endowed with autocratic authority in the event of a refusal being returned, attached its signatures to the order calling out every union man in the city from midnight.

Almost before the ink was dry on this document General Master Workman Sovereign of the Knights of Labor placed the official seal of the order upon a manifesto addressed to members of the organization throughout the country, declaring that "a crisis had been reached in the affairs of the Nation that endangered the peace of the Republic, that the flames of discord were being purposely fanned by the railroad corporations at the risk of the life of the Government," and appealing to the order, and, through it to the whole people, to lay down the implements of toil for a short season and under the banner of peace and with patriotic impulse to create, through peaceable assemblage, a healthy public sentiment in favor of the amicable settlement of the issues involved.

The manifesto was couched in somewhat qualified terms, for, while in one portion it appealed to the order as though its executive officer was at the moment of writing a little doubtful of his ground or the scope of his authority, it later on specifically requested the membership not to return to its usual vocations until a settlement of the pending trouble had been made known through authentic sources.

This order, or request, or whatever it might properly be designated, was wired at once to the officers of every district assembly throughout the country, with instructions looking to its immediate transmission to the executive heads of each local assembly.

The organization of the Knights and its means of communicating with the individual members are so perfect that it was the opinion at headquarters that every Knight of Labor in the land would be made acquainted with the ultimatum by the midnight hour.

District Assembly No. 24, representing every local assembly in Chicago and surrounding towns, was the first to respond to the executive appeal, and this evening, by formal resolution, it declared it to be the duty of all members within its jurisdiction to carry out the suggestions contained in the appeal and at the same time declared that during the crisis it was the duty of all members of the order to refrain from congregating in crowds upon the street and to use every endeavor to maintain peace and order in the community.

Around town the news of the arrests, while it intensified the strained feelings already referred to, produced many manifestations of approval. People that had been assuring one another that the arrest of Mr. Debs would be the signal for a movement by the masses upon the building in which he might be temporarily confined proved themselves false prophets.

The arrested men took the situation in a nonchalent mood. They were not handcuffed. They joked, laughed, and enjoyed the hospitality of the District Attorney's office while waiting for bail, put their signatures to the bonds as a matter of personal recognizance, and then returned to their headquarters to resume the work that had been temporarily interrupted.

Their reappearance was the signal for enthusiastic cheers and greetings from the crowd in waiting, and which, in the meantime, had been venting its fury over the arrests by denouncing the action of the Government and hurling maledictions upon the heads of those of the Federal officers responsible for the proceedings.

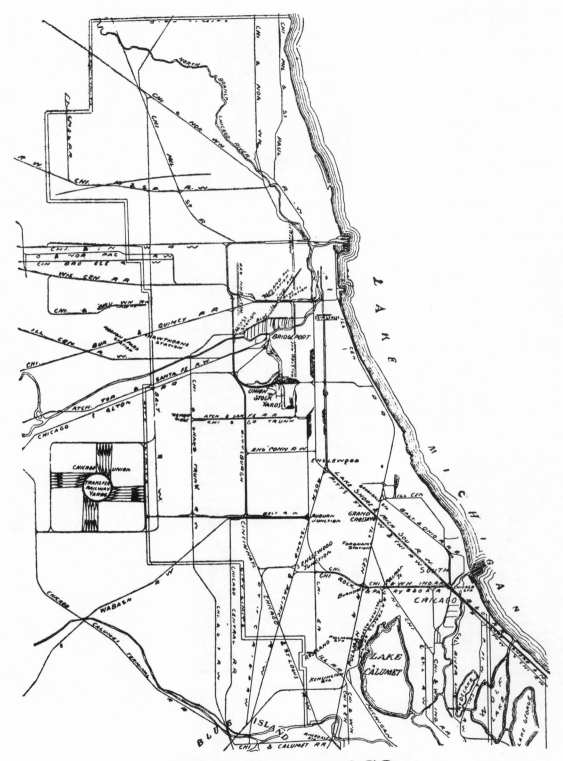

MAP OF CHICAGO.

Showing the Points and Localities Where Disorders and Rioting Have Taken Place and the Railroad Systems Involved in the Strike.

July 13, 1894

MR. PULLMAN ON THE STAND

VOLUNTARY WITNESS BEFORE THE LABOR COMMISSION.

Says the Capital Stock of $36,000,000 Represents Cash Actually Paid in, and that Since the Company Was Organized $73,000,000 Has Been Paid Out for Materials, $32,847,924 for Wages and $25,000,000 Has Gone to the Profit Account.

CHICAGO, Aug. 27.—George M. Pullman appeared before the National Labor Commission this afternoon as a voluntary witness. Mr. Pullman said that the reasons for reducing the wages were purely a matter of business, as the manufacturing department was losing money. He saw no reason why the company, although it had this year declared a dividend of $2,800,000, should raise the wages of men in a department which was losing money. As to matters of detail, the witness referred the commission to Vice President Wickes, who followed him on the stand. The morning session was of little interest.

Edward F. Bryant, cashier and manager of the Pullman Loan and Savings Bank, said that all wages at Pullman were paid in the form of checks on the Pullman Bank. Each man got two checks, one for the amount of rent due, and one for the remainder of his salary. Savings bank depositors were paid 4 per cent. per annum interest. The money was largely invested in real estate mortgages on land in Pullman and vicinity. The maximum of savings deposits was $677,000, and the minimum, $366,000. On pay days employes were requested to pay a part of their rent. Many had only paid $1 every two weeks during the hard times. Many had paid nothing. It was optional with the men whether they paid rent or not.

The accumulation of three or four years were drawn out during the strike. May 1, 1893, the bank had bills to the amount of $3,891 to collect from employes. One year later this amount reached $28,247, showing forcibly the difference made by the cut in wages. Aug. 1, this amount reached $58,773. These bills represented only those placed in the hands of the bank for collection.

The Rev. Charles H. Eaton of New-York testified that he found the destitution at Pullman not nearly so great as reported.

When George M. Pullman took the stand he stated that the Pullman Palace Car Company was organized July 31, 1867, with a capital of $1,000,000. The town of Pullman was established in 1880.

"The plan was," said Mr. Pullman, reading from a typewritten manuscript, "to establish a community for workingmen which would enable them to live in harmonious relations with the company. The relations of the Pullman Company are, however, simply those of a landlord in regard to its employes, which it treats as tenants. The basis of profit was 6 per cent. per annum, which at that time was a fair profit on the investment. The cost of establishing the streets and improvements was of course considered in making this calculation. This does not include the cost of the manufacturing plant."

The Pullman Company, Mr. Pullman said, did not sell property within the limits of the town of Pullman, because the company did not wish objectionable characters to establish themselves in the town. There were in consequence no saloons nor disorderly houses, as there might otherwise have been.

Mr. Pullman explained that the clause in the lease, which provides that either party may terminate it by giving ten days' notice was for the protection of the Pullman Company, so that it might exclude all objectionable characters.

"What is the capital of the Pullman Company?" asked Chairman Wright.

"Thirty-six million dollars."

"It has been stated in the public press that the Pullman Company has a surplus of $16,000,000."

"It is more than that," said Mr. Pullman. "This represents individual profits, and is for the most part invested in assets."

"Are the dividends you pay based on a capital of $36,000,000?"

"They are. The dividends are 2 per cent. quarterly. The company has paid dividends since the beginning. For three years it paid 3 per cent. quarterly, and for a while 9½ per cent. annually. Latterly it has paid 8 per cent. annually."

"Has it been the practice of the company to reduce wages from time to time, and, if so, will you tell us of such reductions?" asked Mr. Wright.

"I am not familiar with the daily workings of the town of Pullman. I will have to refer the commission to the Second Vice President for those details. I will say, however, that for months we did not have an order for a car. I realized that, unless something was done, there would be suffering at Pullman, and, after a consultation with Vice President Wickes, I determined to make bids under the actual cost of construction. We did this, and I remember the first order was for fifty-five cars. I put in a bid for these cars at from $300 to $400 below the cost of a car, making up my mind to make this contribution rather than see my men idle. I believe many other car builders in the country felt the same way. As evidence of this, the next lowest bid to mine was only $24 higher than mine. On another occasion I bid for a lot of 250 cars at a loss of $15 on each car, preferring to do this rather than see the freight shops closed. I underbid the next competitor only $1 a car. It cost us about $50,000 to keep the men in work as long as I did. I explained all this to Mr. Heathcote, the leader of the strikers, who said to me: 'We want the wages of 1893.' I informed him that that was impossible. I told him it would be a most unfortunate thing if the wages of 1893 were restored; that there were only six or eight weeks' work here as it was, and there was none in sight at the rate on which the wages of 1893 were based."

Mr. Pullman told Mr. Heathcote that as long as he remained in the employ of the company he could have access to the highest officials, and could even see the books if he pleased.

"Were the books, as a matter of fact, shown to the Strike Committee?" inquired the Chairman.

"They were not, because the men made no effort to see them."

"Are you at the town of Pullman much?"

"Not a great deal. I don't have time."

"What attempts, if any, did you make for a satisfactory adjustment of the troubles at Pullman?"

"An answer to that will come better from Vice President Wickes."

"It has been stated publicly, very freely, that you were approached by the strikers, who looked for a settlement of the troubles, and that you said you had nothing to arbitrate."

"I did not use exactly those words. I may have told them something of the sort."

Judge Worthington asked if the Pullman Land Association was a separate corporation from the Pullman Car Company.

Mr. Pullman replied that it was. The latter company owned the 500 acres on which the town was built and the improvements. There was no community of interest. The witness said he had used his influence to keep the land immediately surrounding Pullman from being sold, because he was afraid "baneful influences might be established on the border after being shut out of the town itself."

"Do the same parties control the Pullman Land Association and the Pullman Car Company?"

"There is no control. They own all the stock of the land coporation, so that they are practically one. The average increase of the capital stock of the car company has been $1,000,000 a year. One year it increased $6,000,000. There are about 4,200 actual stockholders. When the company was established, the capital stock was $1,000,000, and the other $35,000,000 represents cash actually paid in. The individual profits have been $25,000,000. There has never been any stock watered, any extra dividend paid."

"Can you tell approximately the total amount of dividends declared?"

"I cannot now, but I will do so."

"Can you tell the amount of wages paid the men since the formation of the company?"

"Thirty-two million eight hundred and forty-seven thousand nine hundred and twenty-four dollars. For materials we have paid out in that time $73,000,000."

"The success of the company has been phenomenal, has it not?"

"I aimed to make it so. I tried to make it good for the public, good for the employes, and, incidentally, good for the company."

Mr. Pullman then related his experience as an inventor and projector of the modern sleeping car. Under questioning by Judge Worthington, he made the following statement:

"The profits fell off nearly $500,000 in the month of August alone last year, as compared with the same month in 1892. As to the reduction of wages, I shall have to refer you to the people who had that matter in charge. I do not remember of any efforts at arbitration made by the Pullman Company. I expressed myself as decidedly opposed to arbitration."

"Has the company made or lost money during the last year?"

"It has made money. It paid its usual dividend of 8 per cent., about $2,800,000 in all."

"Do you not think it would have been right, Mr. Pullman, for a company making as much money as the Pullman Company has, which last year declared a dividend of $2,800,000, to have in some measure shared its profits with the employes at Pullman?"

"The manufacturing department of Pullman is entirely separate from any other department of the company. The manufacturing department was losing money, and I see no reason why we should, simply because the company was prosperous, raise the wages in a particular department which was losing money."

"Has the company ever in years of unusual prosperity increased the wages of its employes?"

"It has not."

"What did you see that was so objectionable in submitting to a third party the question whether you should raise the wages of your employes or not?"

"I refer you to my written statement, which declares in effect, that I am able to manage my own business. I still think that after twenty-seven years of experience I am better able to tell the position of the Pullman Company than any third party."

"Do you not think it would have been just to have divided with these employes a little while, so as to give them at least fair living wages?"

"I do not. It would have amounted to a gift of money to these men. It was simply a matter of business. The company and the men had to make a mutual sacrifice. The men were required to work harder, while the company lost money on the contracts."

Mr. Pullman denied any collusion with the railroads in regard to resisting the strikers. Judge Worthington read a copy of the Pullman lease, which requires the tenant to do all the repairing. "Now, this is not true, is it?"

Mr. Pullman seemed embarrassed. He said the Pullman Company repaired the roofs. He knew that much, but he could not say as to other repairs. The lease also provided that in case the tenant did not make these repairs, an amount of money sufficient to do the work should be deducted from his wages; also, that his rent could be deducted from his wages. When Mr. Pullman heard all these statements read he declared he could not swear to that lease as a Pullman lease. Mr. Doty, the acting Pullman landlord, gave it to him, he said. "I think the American Railway Union was the cause of the trouble at Pullman," continued the witness. "We will retain no man in our employ who is a member of the American Railway Union."

"Were rents reduced when wages went down?" asked Judge Worthington.

"They were not. So little income was coming from rents that we could not afford to reduce them further."

"Were your wages and those of the other officers of the company reduced?"

"They were not."

"Why was this not done?"

"Well, if the wages of the superior officers were reduced they might have quit us."

Second Vice President Thomas H. Wickes then took the stand and supplied the details which Mr. Pullman had been unable to give, using a bulky typewritten document. He said many statements made by the strikers were not true. He declared that the statements in regard to wages were in nearly all cases false. He submitted a table taken from the books, which shows a rate of wages much higher than those submitted by Mr. Heathcote, Mr. Rhodie, and others in these particular cases. Instead of making money like water, Mr. Wickes said, the company lost $500,000 monthly.

The examination of Mr. Wickes will be continued to-morrow.

August 28, 1894

DEBS TO SERVE HIS TERM

The Supreme Court Refuses a Writ of Habeas Corpus.

OPINION OF THE JUDGES UNANIMOUS

The Nation Has Power to Protect Inter-State Commerce from Obstruction by Mob Violence.

WASHINGTON, May 27.—The habeas corpus case of Eugene V. Debs and others, growing out of the great railroad strike at Chicago last Summer, was decided in the Supreme Court of the United States to-day, the unanimous opinion being read by Justice Brewer.

The opinion recited the facts connected with the origin of the case—a suit by the United States in the Circuit Court for the Northern District of Illinois for an injunction to restrain Debs and his associates of the American Railway Union from interfering with the movement of inter-State traffic; the issuing of the injunction prayed for; the violation of the injunction by Debs and others; their arrest and punishment by Judge Woods for contempt of court, and the application of the petitioners for a writ of habeas corpus. The case was argued some weeks ago by Attorney General Olney for the Government and C. S. Darrow for the petitioners, the contention of the latter being that the Circuit Court had no jurisdiction of the original bill, and therefore there could be no contempt of court in failing to observe the terms of the injunction issued thereunder.

After presenting the facts, the opinion proceeds:

Two questions of importance are presented: First—Are the relations of the General Government to inter-State commerce and the transportation of the mails such as authorize a direct interference to prevent a forcible obstruction thereof? Second—If authority exists, as authority in governmental affairs implies both power and duty, has a court of equity jurisdiction to issue an injunction in aid of the performance of such duty?

First—What are the relations of the General Government to inter-State commerce and the transportation of the mails? They are those of direct supervision, control, and management. While under the dual system which prevails with us the powers of Government are distributed between the State and the Nation, and while the latter is properly styled a Government of enumerated powers, yet within the limits of such enumeration it has all the attributes of sovereignty, and, in the exercise of those enumerated powers, acts directly upon the citizen and not through the intermediate agency of the State.

If the inhabitants of a single State or a great body of them should combine to obstruct inter-State commerce or the transportation of the mails, prosecutions for such offenses had in such a community would be doomed in advance to failure. And if the certainty of such failure was known, and the National Government had no other way to enforce the freedom of inter-State commerce and the transportation of mails than by prosecution and punishment for interference therewith, the whole interests of the Nation in these respects would be at the absolute mercy of a portion of the inhabitants of a single State.

Power of the Government.

But there is no such impotency in the National Government. The entire strength of the Nation may be used to enforce in any part of the land the full and free exercise of all national powers and the security of all rights intrusted by the Constitution to its care. The strong arm of the National Government may be put forth to brush away all obstructions to the freedom of inter-State commerce or the transportation of the mails. If the emergency arises, the army of the Nation and all its militia are at the service of the Nation to compel obedience to its laws.

But, passing to the second question, is there no other alternative than the use of force on the part of the executive authorities whenever obstructions arise to the freedom of inter-State commerce or the transportation of the mails? Is the army the only instrument by which the rights of the public can be enforced and the peace of the Nation preserved? Grant that any public nuisance may be forcibly abated, either at the instance of the authorities or by any individual suffering private damage therefrom, the existence of this right of forcible abatement is not inconsistent with nor does it destroy the right of appeal in an orderly way to the courts for a judicial determination and an exercise of their powers by a writ of injunction and otherwise to accomplish the same result.

It is more to the praise than to the blame of the Government that, instead of determining for itself questions of right and wrong on the part of these petitioners and their associates and enforcing that determination by the club of the policeman and the bayonet of the soldier, it submitted all those questions to the peaceful determination of judicial tribunals, and invoked their consideration and judgment as to the measure of its rights and powers and the correlative obligations of those against whom it made complaint. And it is equally to the credit of the latter that the judgment of those tribunals was by the great body of them respected, and the troubles which threatened so much disaster terminated.

Neither can it be doubted that the Government has such an interest in the subject matter as enables it to appear as party plaintiff in this suit. It is said that equity only interferes for the protection of property, and that the Government has no property interest. A sufficient reply is that the United States have a property in the mails, the protection of which was one of the purposes of this bill. Every Government, intrusted by the very terms of its being with powers and duties to be exercised and discharged for the general welfare, has a right to apply to its own courts for any proper assistance in the exercise of the one and the discharge of the other, and it is no sufficient answer to its appeal to one of those courts that it has no pecuniary interest in the matter. The obligations which it is under to promote the interest of all and to prevent the wrongdoing of one, resulting in injury to the general welfare, is often of itself sufficient to give it a standing in court. This proposition in some of its relations has heretofore received the sanction of this court.

Can Protect the General Public.

It is obvious from these decisions that, while it is not the province of the Government to interfere in any mere matter of private controversy between individuals, or to use its great powers to enforce the rights of one against another, yet, whenever the wrongs complained of are such as affect the public at large, and are in respect of matters which by the Constitution are intrusted to the care of the Nation, and concerning which the Nation owes the duty to all the citizens of securing to them their common rights, the mere fact that the Government has no pecuniary interest in the controversy is not sufficient to exclude it from the courts or prevent it from taking measures therein to fully discharge those constitutional duties.

The National Government, given by the Constitution power to regulate inter-State commerce, has by express statute assumed jurisdiction over such commerce when carried upon railroads. It is charged, therefore, with the duty of keeping those highways of inter-State commerce free from obstruction, for it has always been recognized as one of the powers and duties of a Government to remove obstructions from the highways under its control.

It is said that the jurisdiction heretofore exercised by the National Government over highways has been in respect to waterways—the natural highways of the country—and not over artificial highways, such as railroads; but the occasion for the exercise by Congress of its jurisdiction over the latter is of recent date.

Up to a recnt date commerce, both inter-State and international, was mainly by water, and it is not strange that both the legislation of Congress and the cases in the courts have been principally concerned therewith. The fact that in recent years inter-State commerce has come mainly to be carried on by railroads and over artificial highways has in no manner narrowed the scope of the constitutional provision, or abridged the power of Congress over such commerce. On the contrary, the same fullness of control exists in the one case as in the other, and the same power to remove obstructions from the one as from the other.

Constitutional provisions do not change, but their operation extends to new matters as the modes of business and the habits of life of the people vary with each succeeding generation. The law of the common carrier is the same to-day as when transportation on land was by coach and wagon, and on water by canal boat and sailing vessel, yet in its actual operation it touches and regulates transportation by modes then unknown—the railroad train and the steamship. Just so is it with the grant to the National Government of power over inter-State commerce. The Constitution has not changed. The power is the same. But it operates to-day upon modes of inter-State commerce unknown to the fathers, and it will operate with equal force upon any new modes of such commerce which the future may develop.

It is said that seldom have the courts assumed jurisdiction to restrain by injunction in suits brought by the Government, either State or national, obstructions to highways either artificial or natural. This is undoubtedly true, but the reason is that the necessity for such interference has only been occasional. Ordinarily the local authorities have taken full control over the matter, and by indictment for misdemeanor or in some kindred way have secured the removal of the obstruction and the cessation of the nuisance.

The Court Was Justified.

That the bill filed in this case disclosed special facts calling for the exercise of the powers of the court is not open to question. The picture drawn in it of the vast interests involved, not merely of the City of Chicago and the State of Illinois, but of all the States and the general confusion into which the inter-State commerce of the country was thrown; the forcible interference with that commerce; the attempted exercise by individuals of powers belonging only to Government, and the threatened continuance of such invasions of public right, presents a condition of things which called for the fullest exercise of all the powers of the courts. If ever there was a special exigency presented, one which demanded that the court should do all that courts can do, it is apparent on the face of this bill, and we need not turn to the public history of the day, which only reaffirms with clearest emphasis all its allegations.

Again, it is objected that it is outside of the jurisdiction of a court of equity to enjoin the commission of crimes. This, as a general proposition, is unquestioned. A Chancellor has no criminal jurisdiction. Something more than the threatened commission of an offense against the laws of the land is necessary to call into exercise the injunctive powers of the court. There must be some interferences, actual or threatened, with property or rights of a pecuniary nature, but when such interferences appear the jurisdiction of a court of equity arises, and is not destroyed by the fact that they are accompanied by or are themselves violations of the criminal law.

The law is full of instances in which the same act may give rise to a civil action and a criminal prosecution. An assault with intent to kill may be punished criminally, under an indictment therefor, or will support a civil action for damage, and the same is true of all other offenses which cause injury to person or property. In such cases the jurisdiction of the civil court is invoked, not to enforce the criminal law and punish the wrongdoer, but to compensate the injured party for the damages which he or his property has suffered, and it is no defense to the civil action that the same act by the defendant exposes him also the indictment and punishment in a court of criminal jurisdiction. So here the acts of the defendants may or may not have been violations of the criminal law. If they were, that matter is for inquiry in other proceedings. The complaint made against them in this is of disobedience to an order of a civil court, made for the protection of property and the security of rights. If any criminal prosecution be brought against them for the criminal offenses alleged in the bill of complaint, of derailing and wrecking engines and trains, assaulting and disabling employes of the railroad companies, it will be no defense to such prosecution that they disobeyed the orders of injunction served upon them and have been punished for such disobedience.

It must be borne in mind that this bill was not simply to enjoin a mob and mob violence. It was not a bill to command a keeping of the peace; much less was its purport to restrain the defendants from abandoning whatever employment they were engaged in. The right of any laborer, or any number of laborers, to quit work was not challenged. The scope and purpose of the bill was only to restrain forcible obstructions of the highways along which inter-State commerce travels and the mails are carried. And the facts set forth at length are only those facts which tended to show that defendants were engaged in such obstructions.

No Heroism in Mob Violence.

A most earnest and eloquent appeal was made to us in eulogy of the heroic spirit of those who threw up their employment and gave up their means of earning a livelihood, not in defense of their own rights, but in sympathy for and to assist others whom they believed to be wronged. We yield to none in our admiration of any act of heroism or self-sacrifice, but we may be permitted to add that it is a lesson which cannot be learned too soon or too thoroughly that under this government of and by the people the means of redress of all wrong are through the courts and at the ballot box, and that no wrong, real or fancied, carries with it legal warrant to invite as a means of redress the co-operation of a mob, with its accompanying acts of violence.

We have given to this case the most careful and anxious attention, for we realize that it touches closely questions of supreme importance to the people of this country. Summing up our conclusions, we hold that the Government of the United States is one having jurisdiction over every foot of soil within its territory and acting directly upon each citizen; that, while it is a Government of enumerated powers, it has within the limits of those powers all the attributes of sovereignty; that to it is committed a power over inter-State commerce and the transmission of the mail; that the powers thus conferred upon the National Government are not dormant, but have been assumed and put into practical exercise by the legislation of Congress; that in the exercise of those powers it is competent for the Nation to remove all obstructions upon highways, natural or artificial, to the passage of inter-State commerce or the carrying of the mail; that, while it may be competent for the Government (through the executive branch and in the use of the entire executive power of the Nation) to forcibly remove all such obstructions, it is equally within its competency to appeal to the civil courts for an inquiry and determination as to the existence and character of any alleged obstructions, and if such are found to exist, or threaten to occur, to invoke the powers of those courts to remove or restrain such obstructions; that the jurisdiction of courts to interfere in such matters by injunction is one recognized from ancient times and by indubitable authority; that such jurisdiction is not ousted by the fact that the obstructions are accompanied by or consist of acts in themselves violations of the criminal law; that the proceeding by injunction is of a civil character and may be enforced by proceedings in contempt; that the penalty for a violation of such injunction is no substitute for and defense to a prosecution for any criminal offenses committed in the course of such violations; that the complaint filed in this case clearly showed an existing obstruction of artificial highways for the passage of inter-State commerce and the transmission of the mail, an obstruction not only temporarily existing, but threatening to continue; that under such complaint the Circuit Court had power to issue its process of injunction; that, it having been issued and served on these defendants, the Circuit Court had authority to inquire whether its orders had been disobeyed, and when it found that they had been, then to proceed under Section 725, Revised Statutes, which grants power to "punish, by fine or imprisonment, * * * disobedience, * * * by any party * * * or other person, to any lawful writ, process, order, rule, decree, or command," and enter the order of punishment complained of, and, finally, that, the Circuit Court, having full jurisdiction in the premises, its finding of the fact of disobedience is not open to review of habeas corpus in this or any other court.

We enter into no examination of the act of July 2, 1890, (26 Stat. 209,) upon which the Circuit Court relied mainly to sustain its jurisdiction. It must not be understood from this that we dissent from the conclusions of that court in reference to the scope of the act, but simply that we prefer to rest our judgment on the broader ground which has been discussed in this opinion, believing it of importance that the principles underlying it should be fully stated and affirmed.

The petition for a writ of habeas corpus was denied.

May 28, 1895

FEMALE AND CHILD LABOR.

The Assembly Committee Wants More Time for Investigation.

ALBANY, N. Y., May 1.—The special committee of the Assembly of which Philip W. Reinhard, Jr., is Chairman, which has been investigating the condition of female labor in New-York City, to-day submitted its report to the Assembly, and it was ordered printed. The report, in part, is as follows:

In the investigation into the condition of female labor in the dry goods establishments, the committee has examined a number of employers and a number of experts interested in the welfare of the employes. The committee has ascertained to some extent the ages of children employed, the wages paid to female employes, the hours of labor, the vacations, the systems of fines and discipline, and the sanitary conditions prevailing in the large mercantile establishments.

From the examination thus far had, it appears that in these establishments the working day is from 8 A. M. to 6 P. M., witn from 30 to 45 minutes for lunch, except on Saturday, when in many stores the employes work until 9 P. M. and 10 P. M., and except also for a period of from ten to fourteen days during the Christmas holidays, when the employes remain until 9 P. M. and 11 P. M., without extra compensation. In one of the smaller stores, where thirty-one persons were employed, of whom nineteen were women, the hours of labor were from 8 A. M. to 9 P. M., and on Saturday till 11 and 12 P. M., and some of the employes also worked on Sunday from 8 A. M. to 12 A. M. for an extra compensation of 75 cents. Large numbers of girls from 14 to 16 years of age are employed at wages ranging from $1.50 a week upward, but it is impossible to ascertain the average rate of wages until further testimony is taken.

The inspection of mercantile houses by the Board of Education in the City of New-York through its attendance officers is not as thorough as the law and the necessities demand. These officers appear to rely largely upon the statements, unverified, of the employers of the various mercantile establishments, and not upon a personal inspection. It is claimed by the Superintendent of Public Schools of the City of New-York that his force of attendance (truancy) officers is insufficient. Whatever may be the cause of such inadequate inspection it is imperative that some means should be employed to stringently enforce the truancy laws.

The committee has further ascertained from the testimony of employers that, from their standpoint, there is no need for the employment of children under fourteen years of age, and suggests that it should be a matter of careful consideration on the part of the Legislature to inquire into the advisability of enacting a law which should absolutely prevent the employment of children under said age.

Up to the present time it has been impossible for the committee to examine any of the employes in the large mercantile establishments by reason of the fact that it has been stated to the committee that the employes are afraid of testifying truthfully as to the exact existing conditions. Whether this fear is well founded or not, it is apparent to the committee that the only satisfactory way to examine these witnesses is at executive sessions, where no employers are present, and the committee believes that it cannot ascertain the whole truth unless it has the opportunity to hold such executive sessions, and supplement them by personal investigations of a fair number of representative mercantile establishments. The committee finds thus far that the sanitary conditions and arrangements of the mercantile houses are on the average fair, though violations of existing laws and regulations of the local Board of Health have been found in some of the large establishments.

The committee further finds that the law requiring employers to provide seats for female employes. (Chapter 298, Laws of 1888,) has not been generally observed, and, to be of any value, must be amended so as to make it more definite and thereby capable of enforcement.

In regard to the "sweat shops," the committee has been able thus far to examine to any extent only into the condition of labor employed by manufacturers of clothing. The committee has ascertained that there is a general and constant violation of the factory laws, and of the rules and regulations of the Board of Health by persons who employ labor in the shops and tenement houses in the section of the city known as the down-town east side. From the testimony already had, the committee is of the opinion that large numbers of persons are employed in tenement houses, in flagrant violation of the factory law, and that great danger constantly threatens the community by reason of the infection of clothing.

The case of Morris Braun of 11 Rutgers Place of the City of New-York, is an apt illustration of this great danger. Braun had four rooms at that place, three of which he used as living, eating, and sleeping rooms, and one as a workroom, where he employed never less than ten men and four women in making up into coats clothing which he received from Messrs. Sinsheimer, Levison & Co., of 546 Broadway. Braun's child became sick with scarlet fever. The case was reported by the attending physician to the Board of Health on March 31, 1895, and a Medical Inspector of the Board of Health visited Braun, and testified that he ordered him to close the door betwen the living rooms and the workroom. Thereafter the Factory Inspector visited Braun, and testified that he ordered him to stop work, but nevertheless the coats from this infected shop were sent to Messrs. Sinsheimer, Levison & Co., the wholesalers, and it was not until April 9, 1895, that the Board of Health procured the goods for fumigation, and took them to its fumigating station.

The committee found that under the practice of the Board of Health it was discretionary with the Medical Inspector to stop work, and also found that the Factory Inspector failed to tag the goods of the workshop, as required by Section 13 of the factory law. From the testimony of the Assistant Sanitary Superintendent, the Chief of the Bureau of Contagious Diseases, and the Medical Inspector of the Board of Health in charge of this case, it appears unquestionably to the committee that the present law and the rules and regulations of the Board of Health are inadequate to protect public health against the grave danger of infection which exists in cases of this kind.

Whether the tax law (Section 13 of Factory act) would have been effective cannot be determined because of the negligence on the part of the Factory Inspector in failing to tag the goods. In this connection it is clear to the committee that legislation is needed in order to protect public health and welfare against similar cases, and that some further and more stringent legislation is demanded with which to deal with the problem of goods manufactured in tenement houses. Many cases of a similar character undoubtedly have occurred which the committee can discover if it has more time to pursue its investigations.

Another existing evil is the employment of child labor contrary to law. It has been made very plain to your committee that the so-called "parents' certificates," by which Factory Inspectors and truancy officers are obliged to be governed, are in a great many cases worthless, for the reason that parents who are willing to let their children work under age are often equally willing to swear that these children are of legal age. Then, too, among people of certain nationalities, many of whom do not understand English, the touching of a pen to paper in making their mark is not regarded as having the force and solemnity of an oath. Whether the substitution of birth certificates would be practicable or advisable your committee cannot determine without the authority of more certain knowledge. The employment of these young children has enabled sweat-shop keepers to pay from $1.75 to $2 a week for at least sixty hours' work, which would be done by older children at any small wages.

The committee likewise finds that the wages of the younger employes are entirely disproportionate to the work done and the number of hours employed. The committee believes that there are other reasons than the natural one of supply and demand why wages of the young employes are so small as they are. Some of these reasons are the minimizing of expense by keeping the premises in a condition contrary to law, and by working in tenement houses contrary to law. The committee has not been able to ascertain the wages of adult labor to its satisfaction thus far, as it has only had an opportunity to call employers, and the testimony of the employers has been unreliable on its face, as the committee, in a number of instances, has discovered to its own satisfaction.

Illustrations of this unreliability can be found in the testimony of Nathan Vagler and Nathan Levy. In the former case, Vagler had given up his work as an employe to become an employer, unquestionably to better himself, and yet from his own testimony it appeared that he paid weekly in wages and rent $9.40 more than he received for the goods which he manufactured. From this testimony and the appearance of the witness, the committee, of course, concluded that he was not telling the truth, the difficulty which has been found among nearly all of these sweat-shop employers who have been examined. In the Levy case, it appeared that Levy was prosperous and had a bank account, and yet, according to his own testimony, after he had paid his employes and his rent, he was only able to make 25 cents a week. It is clear to the committee that the real wages paid can only be ascertained by an examination of adult employes in executive session, so that the employes may be assured that they will not lose their places by giving truthful testimony; and this examination should be supplemented by a personal investigation of the work places.

The "sweat-shop" system, as a whole, is undoubtedly the cause of physical wretchedness and moral degradation to thousands of women in the City of New-York, and it involves for a large number of children a hopeless childhood, initiating them into a still more hopeless adult existence.

The committee believes that in justice to the present Assembly and its honorable record it should have further opportunity to carry on its investigations and make them as searching and earnest as the subject demands, and your committee prays that this request be granted, and that an extension of time and a further appropriation adequate to the demands of the investigation be given.

May 2, 1895

THE SWEATING SYSTEM

OPINION OF THE SECRETARY OF THE WORKERS OF AMERICA.

What Is Sweating?—Contractors and Sub-Contractors—How the Toilers Suffer—Number of Small Shops—How Can Fourteen Inspectors, Half of Them Women, Inspect New-York?—Mrs. Humphry Ward on Sweating in London.

Mr. Henry White, General Secretary of the United Garment Workers of America, in the last bulletin of the Department of Labor, publishes an extended article on the sweating system. During the last six months this subject has remained in a quiescent state, not that sweating does not exist, the same sad conditions ever presenting themselves, but for the reason that in some small way remedial efforts were used by the sweated, and some very slight aid was given the workers in garments by State legislation.

As usually understood, the "sweating system" has a vague meaning. What it really is is a condition of labor "in which a maximum amount of work in a given time is performed for a minimum wage, and in which the ordinary rules of health and comfort are disregarded." It is rightly understood as being contract work, and the main trouble arises from sub-contracting.

If there were to be a large contract given there would seem no harm in that. It is apparently within the rules of legitimate business. The trouble comes in when the contractor puts out the work to sub-contractors. Then starts up a competition which means work to be done at starvation prices, and necessarily under the very worst physical conditions.

Where there is an excess of population, which hives in a dense quarter, there is eagerness to take in work. It seems paradoxical that thrift and industry should work ruin. Where there is a large foreign population, always being renewed, it must earn some little money or starve. These people are then willing to submit to the most cruel of taskmasters. It is this form of labor, Mr. Henry White says, which has "outcompeted and displaced" all other forms, and becomes the standard of the particular industry in which it is introduced.

Fingers in the making of garments have been replaced somewhat by machinery. The sewing machine runs on forever, but it has made only subdivisions of labor. It has helped to create fifty times more clothes, but it has not enhanced the value of the time of the man or woman who works the treadle. It is because, then, the machine can be run by almost any one who wants a job, no matter what, that there is an overabundance of workers.

The necessary attainments of the operator are, however, kept within a narrow sphere. He has no knowledge of anything more than his own piece work. That particular work he may after a while do well and quickly, but there are thousands of others who are just as rapid or skillful. "The class of workers, therefore, becomes wholly dependent upon the knowledge that they have acquired of one small part of the trade, and are incapable of advancement through individual effort."

There is one factor, which is never to be overlooked in crowded New-York, and it is the high rents. If rents were cheaper, as Mr. White explains it, there might be an advantage in a family working together. In such localities in New-York where rents are moderate, the evils of the sweating system are not apparent, or if noticed, are less acute. With excessively high rents there comes the huddling together of many toilers. The loft, the garret, is packed, and to save money, the health of the workers is imperiled. Crowded, insalubrious workshops have for positive resultants sickness and death. The mother of a healthy child works alongside of another mother whose child has smallpox. The contagion at once spreads. The garment, fashioned in such surroundings, may be bought by any one, and then there is propagation of disease. In 1894 a smallpox epidemic prevailed in Chicago, and was, in a measure, confined to the clothing districts in the city, and no less than 273 tenement houses were declared by the health officers to be infected. And then by no means had all of the houses been inspected. It may be remembered that during this same time there were several outbreaks of smallpox in various parts of the State of Illinois, and in the States west of it, not to be accounted for in any other way than by the distribution of infected garments.

Suppose we look, as does Mr. White, at the sweating shop in an impartial manner. In its primitive guise it was the small shop, where father, mother, and children worked together. In Japan not only for the making of clothes, but for the weaving, not so long ago, exactly similar conditions existed, and with good results. In Eastern Europe, Mr. White tells us, nearly all the clothing and cloak making is carried on in this way. But in the primitive shop And the sweating shop, as to the getting rid of the output, or the selling of it, the difference is great. In the former the employer was also the dealer, and the contract system had no existence. "As the shopkeeper or master depended for patronage on his immediate neighbors, the keen competition of modern business was not a factor, and the present leveling struggle for employment was unknown. The workers labored more leisurely, their wages were naturally lower, and their wants were few."

"The beginning of the sweating system dates from just after our civil war. First, the markets had been stripped bare then, and, second, there came a great and steady stream of immigrants. It can hardly be believed that thirty-five years ago the wholesale manufacture of clothing scarcely existed. Even the large wholesale boot and shoe manufacturers, save for the use of negro brogans in the South, were restricted before 1865. Mr. White tells us that in England, Ireland, France, and Germany the conditions of the clothing trade were forty years ago of minor importance. Then foreign countries took to the sweating system, and more particularly England, for after the Franco-Prussian war and the religious persecutions in Russia, there set in in England precisely the same influx of emigrants.

In Europe, our authority states that to-day "ready-made custom work" is by no means in as large an excess as in the United States, and that on that account "very little outside help is employed."

To do work at home, no matter of what kind, cannot be in itself objectionable. It is the combination "of living apartment and factory, and the employment of outsiders therein, which constitute the detrimental features which in time become of menace to the community."

We have before stated that the term "sweating" seems to be solely applied by the public to the tailoring, cloak, and shirt or underwear business, but it exists in a terrible degree in cigar making, but with this latter occupation at present we have nothing to do. Mr. White, who should know, says that the business of garment making is confined mainly to the following cities, in the order of their rank, viz.: New-York and vicinity, (including Brooklyn and Newark,) Chicago, Philadelphia, Rochester, Baltimore, Boston, Cincinnati, Syracuse, Cleveland, St. Louis, Utica, and Milwaukee. We believe, however, within the limit of a certain cost in freight, (to be deducted from the wages of the worker,) that within a distance of fifty miles of New-York City an immense amount of clothing is made up. The estimate is presented that there are, counting all the branches, no less than 60,000 persons employed in garment making in New-York and its vicinity, and of these 70 per cent. work in the small shops and on contract work. In some branches the work is fitful, and comes in with a rush, as in cloak making. Now cloak making requires a certain amount of skill and rapidity, and so these workers, who are invariably foreigners, are to be classed among the élite. They have been the more fortunate from their ability. Employed directly by large firms, they have been more independent. Their wages have been good—the standard being between $15 and $24 per week, a good and reliable cloak maker earning by hard and constant work $20 a week. It has been direct employment, not indirect, and without middlemen or subcontractors. Where there is a middleman he must live, and his percentage comes from the toiler, and the more there are of contractors or sub-contractors, the greater their parings.

In the sweating shops, says Mr. White, conditions of labor as degrading may exist as in other industries, "but no class of laborers is so desperately situated, owing to the difficulty of introducing reforms in the numerous small shops abounding in the dark corners of the great cities, the helplessness of the victims, and the ignorant tenacity with which they cling to their tasks."

Grant that there are evils attending the **intervention of a middleman. Just as** long, however, as trade exists and time has its value, it is the broker who saves both the seller and buyer their time. In the lower grades of tailoring the contractor—the sub-contractor—in order to live must associate his business with those who exist only from hand to mouth, and through dire necessity work under the most unwholesome of physical conditions.

"The petty contractor," writes our authority, "has made possible the sweating evil, and he is inseparable from it." It takes a very little money and a small acquaintance with the business to keep the sub-contractor going. There are so many of them that, eager for gain, they enter into the keenest competition with one another, and it is the toiler who suffers the most.

The natural question which at once suggests itself is this: Why do not wholesale manufacturers conduct their own large shops, just as the cutting of clothes is done? The answer of the manufacturer is that the made-up goods would cost him more, and, besides, even though the contractor made a profit, under the present system the trouble and expense of supervision are avoided. "This really means," adds Mr. White, "that the wholesale merchant, under the contract system, shirks all responsibility for the conditions under which the employes work. Moreover, large shops would become more amenable to the State factory laws, and it would be impossible to impose conditions so near the life line."

Who, then, is at fault? If the contractor agrees to deliver garments at a fixed price, the lowest possible, 3 cents on a coat being even in his favor, he will be indifferent as to whether a day's work be twelve or twenty hours—he will tax the toiling man or woman past all power of endurance.

It has been supposed that it was only the

common and cheap clothing which was made in the sweating shops, but such, Mr. White says, is far from the absolute facts, for if we understand him correctly, it is a necessity that a well-fashioned coat, as far as the sewing of it goes, should be made at home, and there have the care only to be found in the small shop. Let us take a survey of the laws of New-York in regard to the hours of labor. For persons under eighteen years of age and women under twenty-one it is sixty hours per week, and no woman under twenty-one or person under eighteen years of age can be employed before 6 A. M. or after 9 P. M. The factory laws of this State include registers for the use of Inspectors, and there is something which will be novel to most readers, and it is that if any article for wear is made in a tenement there shall be conspicuously affixed to such article "a label containing the words, 'tenement-made' printed in small pica capital letters on a tag not less than two inches long." Then, too, there are sanitary rules as to size and conditions of workroom.

"The evil is so extensive and so difficult to reach that the ordinary Factory Inspectors, whose duties are not alone to investigate the sweating evil, are plainly unable to cope with the abuses." There is laxity in the enforcement of the laws. It is manifestly impossible that short handed as are the Inspectors for New-York City, they can do much. There are 25,400 factories in this city, and how can fourteen Inspectors, of whom one-half are women, grapple with such an enormous business? Take the prosecutions for violations of the law regulating the manufacture of clothing in tenement workshops of New-York last year. In all there were 88 complaints, and the fines were $1,870. For the whole State in 1894 there were 10,425 notifications.

Mr. White tells about the investigations made by a select committee of the House of Lords, 1890, which studied the sweating system in London and other English cities, and the committee believed that it arose (1) from an unduly low rate of wages, (2) excessive hours of labor, (3) the unsanitary state of the houses in which work was carried on. The fines and penalties in England for violation of the factory laws very much exceed ours, but the main point is that the regulations, as they are printed, are unflinchingly carried out. That the cure has been found in London and the canker of the sweating system extirpated is not probable.

In Mrs. Humphry Ward's "Sir George Tressady" can be read the details of the sweating system. The scenes are absolutely realistic, and never could have been penned by Mrs. Ward if she had not been in absolute contact with the poor sewing women in the East End of London. It is a clergyman who at times gives his experiences. "The difference between now and twenty years ago is that the women work much more, the men less. * * * Their lives seem to be mere refuse, the rags and shreds that are thrown every day into the mill, and ground to nothing, without a thought, without a word of pity, an hour of happiness. * * * Then when the parish has buried her the man has only to hold up his finger to find some one else to use up in the same way." Mrs. Humphry Ward writes feelingly of "those ragged, hollow-eyed creatures newly arrived from Russia, Poland, Austria, or Roumania—men whose strange faces and eyes under their matted shocks of black or reddish hair suggested every here and there the typical history and tragic destiny of the race." All, irrespective of creed or nationality, were "the victims of a huge world struggle that does but toss them on its surge."

There is no political tremor in Europe which is not first felt in London, next in New-York. God only knows, but can we forbid the instinct of self-preservation which actuates these people? But we do recognize what are the effects of overstocking the labor market. Sooner or later the sediment subsides, falls as if by force of gravity into the sweating shop, and the contractor and the sub-contractors faster on their victims.

INVESTIGATING SWEAT SHOPS.

Dr. Feeney Says Many on the East Side Are in Bad Condition.

Dr. Michael B. Feeney, Chief Sanitary Inspector of the Health Department, expressed surprise yesterday at the condition of numerous east side sweatshops. He explained that he had ascertained that numbers of uniforms for the soldiers during the late war had been made in these places.

"During my many years' experience," said he, "I have frequently seen the children of those who live in the sweatshops asleep on piles of unfinished clothing. The families are so poor in these quarters that they are unable to buy bedding, and make use of the unfinished clothes.

"The other day I found in one of these places a woman suffering with grip in the same room where others were employed in making nursery clothing. The odor in the room was nauseating. We have also found cases of diphtheria, scarlet fever, and other diseases in these sweatshops."

Dr. Feeney added that he had entered complaint after complaint against the landlords of such places. They say they can do nothing, because of the cold weather. This, the doctor explained, was—in a measure true, because the water supply in the tenements had, in many cases, been cut off during the cold weather, and tended in a way to bring about congested conditions. A number of Health Board Inspectors are investigating the matter.

HOLDS BLACKLIST IS LEGAL.

Chicago Judge Says Employers Have a Right to Agree to Bar Strikers.

Special to The New York Times.

CHICAGO, June 10.—Suit brought to test the blacklist law by eight girls who had been refused work by packers because they quit their jobs with Libby, McNeil & Libby, was decided for the defendants by Judge Waterman to-day. He at the same time declared that strikes, lock-outs, and boycotts are not illegal. He said:

"The defendants agreed not to re-employ those who went out on a strike; this they have a right to do. According to the allegations of the girls' declaration, the purpose for making this agreement was bad, because by such agreement the plaintiffs cannot get employment at their trade, and are thus injured. This gives them no right of action—for a bad motive does not make a lawful deed actionable.

"Each girl exercised her undoubted right, by agreement and combination with her fellow-employes, to strike and leave the service of one of the defendants. She and her co-workers may have done this for the purpose of breaking up the business of and ruining such defendant, and such might have been the result; yet the defendant could not have recovered damages therefor from the plaintiffs. The consequence of a refusal to employ any man may be deleterious and pitiful; so the consequence of refusing to work for another may be disastrous and ruinous; but the fact that one refuses to employ another because he wishes to see him come to want does not give a cause of action."

June 14, 1896   February 26, 1899   June 11, 1901

MOB SPIRIT IN UNIONS

D. M. Parry at Chautauqua Arraigns Organized Labor.

Declares That the Unions Constitute a Standing Mob and Override the Constitution.

CHAUTAUQUA, N. Y., Aug. 13.—At today's discussion of the mob violence question the subject was "The Labor Unions and the Mob Spirit," and an address was delivered by D. M. Parry, President of the National Association of Manufacturers. He said, in part:

"Mob spirit is a relic of the barbarous stage of human development. It harks back to the time when the race relied upon the purely physical for maintenance. In essence it is a hatred or contempt for all regulations of government, and an attempt by the vicious and ignorant to impress their will upon others by the exercise of physical force.

"Mobs may be spontaneous in growth or their formation may extend over a long period. They may be poorly organized or they may be under good discipline. In this country in the last year there have been many mobs of different kinds, but to my mind the most dangerous of them all is the mob of organized labor. No man, I take it, can object to any kind of an association, labor or otherwise, which is organized for lawful and beneficent purposes, but organized labor, as it is conducted today, stands convicted by its own leaders as a lawless organization.

"In that it seeks by physical force to override individual rights and its continually railing against the laws and denouncing courts and public officials for enforcing these laws it fulfills all the requirements of the definition of mobocracy. Unlike the lynching bees and the vigilance committees it is what might be termed a standing mob, under fair discipline by its officers, and ready upon occasion to commit the overt acts of outrage and destruction which are the outward manifestation of the mob spirit. It declares in effect that its will is superior to customs, traditions, government regulations, and even the Constitution of the country. It asserts that the individual has no inherent rights that cannot be taken from him, and that, therefore, it has the right to say that no man shall work and that no industry shall run without its consent.

"In its attempt to compel a recognition of its pretensions to sovereignty it relies not on reason, but upon coercion, intimidation, and the bludgeon. In its continual preachments against law and its constant appeal to the baser passions of men it is doing more than any other agency to inculcate the mob spirit and to encourage the unfurling of the red flag of anarchy.

"The President of the Chicago Federation of Labor recently declared in an interview: 'The President deals a death blow to organized labor when he declares that he cannot discriminate in its favor. It sounds fair on the face of it but without discrimination we are just where we started. What we have been fighting for is union labor to the exclusion of all others.'

"These are the words of a conservative among union leaders, and they voice the sentiment of the agitators the country over. To their mind if you deny the right of their organization to commit illegal acts you are attempting to crush it. If organized labor has only lawless purposes it but without ought to be crushed.

"During the last year the attempts to force men to give allegiance to strike bosses in their plans to set up an oligarchy that will control industry independent of the laws of the country have resulted in mob conditions in many of the leading centres. Not only has the supremacy of law and order sustained many severe shocks, but the Nation has also lost millions of dollars by the organized idleness of thousands of men. This loss must fall heavier upon the man who depends upon his daily wage than upon those who have something to fall back upon. It is time that the workmen of this country were learning that for the millions of dollars they pay in salaries to the agitators they are receiving in return nothing but ceaseless trouble, enforced idleness, and less of the comforts of life. They are also bidding for the destruction of their most precious possession—that of industrial liberty. Their investments in mobocracy are mighty poor investments."

In the discussion which followed Mr. Parry's paper, Thomas Kidd said that thousands of workingmen have been embittered by the conditions of their childhood and that experiences in later life with the company store and the other evidences of greed and power arrayed against them have made them more desperate.

Mr. Kidd insisted, however, that the percentage of riot in labor troubles was very small, saying that records of 25,000 strikes in seven years show less than 1 per cent. attended by riots. He did not believe Mr. Parry correctly represents the employers of the country.

The employment of detectives and agents who excite the men to violence, said Mr. Kidd, places much responsibility upon certain employers.

LAWLESSNESS AND "LABOR."

Those were bitter words, but not more bitter than true, that Mr. PARRY, President of the National Association of Manufacturers, uttered yesterday at Chautauqua upon "The Mob Spirit in Organized Labor." It was in continuation of the discussion on lynching that he spoke, and when he said that the most dangerous mob in this country is the mob of organized labor, he spoke words not only of truth but of soberness.

For an occasional eruption of the mob spirit in the murder by a crowd of a man who has committed a crime particularly adapted to excite popular indignation, though very deplorable and very properly punishable, is a far less serious symptom than the existence of what may fairly be called a permanent mob. That is a fair description of organized labor as now, in very many cases and very many communities, it is managed. It does set itself above the law. It relies not in the least upon reason and justice, but upon lawless force and lawless intimidation for the accomplishment of its object. It deliberately and avowedly sets itself to weaken the forces that make for the maintenance of law and order, and chief among them of that "well-regulated militia" which the Constitution of the United States declares to be "essential to the security of a free State."

And all this for what? Practically to support without manual labor a band of demagogues who call themselves labor leaders. They have been encouraged by political demagogues of a higher class until they have waxed exceeding bold and come out into the open with their demands. That is all that is necessary to call the public attention to the dangerous and criminal character of so many of the labor organizations, and to the dangerous and criminal spirit which, we are sorry to have to say, is coming to characterize labor organizations. When the public once fairly understands the danger with which it is threatened by the leaders of standing mobs, it will find means of maintaining order in spite of them, and of crushing them if they resist.

BATTLE AGAINST BOYCOTT

Work of Organization Which Has Suits Against Labor Leaders.

Contention That the Boycott Is a Conspiracy In Restraint of Trade Is to be Tested.

Suits now pending in State and United States Courts in Connecticut in connection with the Danbury boycott troubles, and actions commenced or about to be commenced along similar lines in other sections of the country, where labor unions have called in the boycott as a weapon with which to enforce their demands, have brought just now to attention the development attained by the American Anti-Boycott Association, which, organized only in June of this year, has already become an important factor in the industrial world.

The American Anti-Boycott Association secret as to the personnel of its membership, but entirely open in respect to its organization and methods, which was formed as the result of a belief that the boycott as a device of labor warfare was unjustifiable and illegal, and could be made the basis of action in State and National courts. The Anti-Boycott Association had no quarrel with labor unions, nor did it undertake to choose sides on the issues involved in individual contests when the boycott was not called into play. It was specifically determined by the business men who drew the constitution that the association should not be the ally of the employer rather than the employed, and suits now in process seeking to recover damages for individuals who have been kept from earning a livelihood by union boycotts have given practical demonstration of the purposes in this latter connection.

Some eighteen months ago the movement started very quietly and with the express understanding that no definite steps should be taken until a membership of 100 was obtained. This number was reached last Summer, and with the formal organization these officers were chosen: General Executive Agent—Daniel Davenport of Bridgeport, Conn.; Chairman of the General Executive Board—Charles H. Merritt of Danbury, Conn; Secretary—Charles Biggs of 13 Astor Place, New York. Ex-Assistant United States attorney General James M. Beck of this city is general counsel for the association and A. C. Allen of Allen & Weseman of Chicago counsel in that city. It was provided that funds should be raised by a payment of one-tenth of 1 per cent. of the monthly pay rolls of members.

There are two fundamental propositions upon which the association rests its intention to go into court on boycott cases. The first of these is that members of a union, as members of a voluntary association, are individually liable for the consequences of the acts of their officers or agents when the constitution delegates to these latter certain powers. The second is that the boycott is a violation of the Sherman law defining conspiracy in restraint of trade.

The Connecticut cases mentioned are typical of the activities of the association. In them considerable attention is centred, because it is believed that the points involved are fundamental in the fight against the boycott. Both cases were brought on account of the boycott against the hat manufacturing firm of D. E. Loewe & Co., in Danbury, a concern running on "open shop."

One of these cases was brought in the State courts, with 241 members and officers of the American Federation of Labor and of the United Hatters, including among the former Samuel Gompers and John Mitchell, as defendants, and the other, in the State courts, with the same defendants. Damages were asked in the sum of $100,000 in the first instance, and attachments levied on real estate and bank accounts of the various defendants amounting in value to between $150,000 and $160,000.

For the result of these suits great hope is expressed by officers of the Anti-Boycott Association. They are encouraged also by results attained in Chicago in the late Summer, when their organization was instrumental in dissuading the teamsters from entering upon a sympathetic strike, and from the prospects in several other pending cases, and the constantly growing membership, it is believed that the association in its particular field will be a powerful influence toward the re-establishment of fair relations between employer and employe.

November 11, 1903

UNIONS SUSPECT SPY SYSTEM.

Delegate Wilson Tells How Employers' Emissaries Are Treated.

In reference to reports that a Cleveland company supplies an organized spy system to employers in order that they may keep tab on the doings of the unions, James Wilson, delegate of the International Association of Machinists, said yesterday:

"It has been an open secret for many years that employers have their spies in nearly all the unions. We have found it so ourselves, and have a system of spying on the spies themselves. When a man suspected of being a spy gets into a union he is watched, his description taken, and when he goes to another city the local union is warned, and when he is found to be a spy he is expelled from the union and all the other unions are notified."

According to reports the Cleveland company pays the spies $65 a month, gives them periodical instructions, and posts them as to the best methods of learning the secrets of the union.

March 21, 1904

THE "CLOSED SHOP" IN LAW.

Gradually the body of the law relating to the rights of organized labor is building up, through decisions involving important principles in the relations of employers and workingmen. The latest decision of this character is that of the Appellate Court of Illinois sustaining the Superior Court of Cook County in an order to punish the officers of the Chicago Brass Workers' Union and other unions for contempt of court in violating an injunction restraining them from interfering improperly with the business of a manufacturing company of that city. The chief interest of the decision of the Appellate Court is that it declares unlawful the demand of the unions that the manufacturer referred to shall execute an agreement to make his factory a "closed shop." It holds that such an agreement would be contrary to public policy in restricting the right of contract and discriminating in favor of one class of citizens and against another, both results being in violation of the Constitution of Illinois and that of the United States. It also holds that the action of the union representatives in endeavoring to compel the execution of a contract to this effect constituted duress and criminal conspiracy, and that each conspirator was responsible for the acts and declarations of every other conspirator made in furtherance of the common purpose. Of the employment of pickets the court says:

The appellants deny that they personally used force, threats, or intimidation of any sort and say that they were very peaceable and mildly persuasive. But the very presence of a large number of pickets with the avowed purpose of preventing complainant's employés from remaining in its employ and those seeking employment with it to desist therefrom was itself intimidation.

This is wholesome doctrine. If it assists the leaders of organized labor to understand that they cannot safely further their ends by acts deliberately destructive of the rights of others it will have accomplished a very good purpose.

May 28, 1904

CITIZENS INDUSTRIAL ASSOCIATION. | CITIZENS INDUSTRIAL ASSOCIATION. | CITIZENS INDUSTRIAL ASSOCIATION.

The SQUARE DEAL

Printed in an Open Shop.

VOL. 1. No. 9.   NEW YORK, APRIL, 1906.   Price, 10 Cents.

Labor's Anti-Injunction Bill

A direct bid for Anarchy

The Labor Trust is pressing before Congress an anti-injunction measure to take from federal courts any power to issue restraining orders or injunctions to prevent injury threatened to property or personal rights.

The present power of the Courts established by the people is used for the protection of property and person.

The Labor Trust want all obstacles to their lawlessness removed for a purpose, plain enough to any peace-loving American.

LABOR TRUST ANARCHY.
Citizens Must Rise for Protection.

As the law of the land now stands, courts can issue restraining orders frequently called "injunctions" to prevent acts by strikers or others that may result in destruction of property or interference with the rights of free American citizens.

The labor unions object to any power that will prevent their members from wreaking vengeance on men or property when their "orders" are not implicitly obeyed, therefore they have the astonishing audacity and impudence to "demand" of Congress an "Anti-Injunction" law to take from the courts any power to thus protect the people. When they succeed in this there will be No use for the wife to plead for her husband's protection.

No use for the children to ask that the father be allowed to work for them in safety.

No use for either mother or children to hope for any power to prevent insult, assault, or the home being blown up by labor union strikers.

No use for a property owner to ask for any order to prevent union strikers from destroying it.

No use for any community to apply to the courts to preserve order and prevent the rioting and destruction by strikers and other union men.

The operations of the labor trust (unions) during the past five years in America include the most appalling list of crimes imaginable. Over five thousand free workmen were assaulted and injured in Chicago in one year. Hundreds of murders have been committed and millions of dollars of property destroyed.

Is this true or not? Simply turn to the files of the daily newspapers and observe that scarcely a day passes but some act of bloody violence is done by "union" men. The leaders of the labor trust are quick to deny, in the papers, any complicity in these crimes, but the actual facts when brought out show that the crimes are committed by the labor union members and frequently in conspiracy with the leaders.

The labor papers, including the yellow journals, during the civil war inaugurated in Colorado during the operations of the Western Federation of Miners, bitterly denounced the state military authorities for attempting to preserve the peace, and the lives of the state officials were threatened, and frequent attempts made upon them.

Finally ex-Governor Steunenberg was blown to pieces by dynamite and the president and other officers of this labor trust are charged with being among the conspirators who arranged for his murder, and are now held for trial in Idaho.

The denials are useless and the labor unions are compelled to bear the denunciation of the public until the union men cease such criminal acts and the leaders cease supporting and aiding them. The public is not deceived by announcements that the leaders counsel against lawlessness when the American Federation of Labor or labor union money is freely spent to support lawless strikers and defend them in the courts when apprehended. The people must see "union" money spent freely to convict criminal strikers before they will have any sort of faith in the honesty of union talk in favor of law. Every act so far points all too clearly in an opposite direction, and the common newspaper announcement of a strike includes a statement of the steps taken to protect the people from violence and destruction of property, showing that strikers are considered aliens and probable criminals when they dare be.

Any man has a right to quit work, but no man has a right to do criminal acts to try and force some one to hire him.

It is the duty of every employer to get the record of each man who applies for work and absolutely cut out the agitator and violent, discontented man with criminal instincts.

Altogether too many labor unions contain criminals ready whenever their demands are refused to commit crime, and the peace and safety of the common citizens demand protection through the courts with their free right to issue restraining orders.

The operations of these criminals are certainly not in the interest of the common man, and so long as labor unions conduct their affairs in a manner that puts power in the hands of criminals, so long will such labor unions be a menace to the community.

The labor trust must be forced to conduct its affairs on the lines of common commercial law. A labor union has labor to sell. It has a right that labor for sale the same as any commodity is offered for sale in a legitimate commercial way, and the buyer of labor has a right to refuse to purchase. Then the owners of labor have a right to offer it peaceably to other purchasers, and sell where they can obtain the best price, but all of this must be done without resort to crime, and the people must insist upon the labor unions conducting their affairs in a peaceful and legitimate manner.

Upright liberty-loving desirable citi-

zens who are unfortunate enough to be connected with criminally conducted labor unions have a right and owe it as a duty to other citizens to withdraw from such conspiracies.

There is a way to obtain good prices and good conditions for labor without resort to crime, and the common citizen must demand a cessation of all these criminal procedures.

Suppose an employer should hire an "entertainment committee" to go out and dynamite the house of a man because he struck and refused to come back to work and incidentally this "committee" beat the man to death, then the employer planning to attack the property of other strikers would apply for an "anti-injunction bill" to take away from the courts any power to issue an injunction to prevent such outrage and allow the employer free rein to carry on such lawlessness without restraint. What a howl would go up from the labor unions and in fact from every lawabiding citizen protesting against such a bid for anarchy and unrestrained lawlessness. And yet the employer has exactly the same right to do this as the labor unions which are now using every power in their ranks to bring about the emasculation of the courts established for the protection of the people.

The desire of the labor unions to tie the hands of the courts and prevent them from protecting the people is plain evidence of a desire to do criminal acts without interference of the courts, and it is the duty of every citizen to write his Congressman and Senator to vote to support the courts in their power to issue restraining orders. In other words to defeat this anti-injunction bill presented by these anarchists seeking to make crime safe and easy. Citizens must act to protect themselves and their property. Let every man—merchant, workman, doctor, lawyer, and farmer—write his protest to his Senator and Congressman at once in order to protect the people and save this country from such a blot from the hands of the anarchists.

The SQUARE DEAL magazine is published monthly to keep the people advised of the facts. It is sold by the year for $1.00 and by Elevated and Subway as well as other newsstands at 10 cents per copy. If your newsdealer hides it or refuses to keep it, know he is under the thumb of the labor trust, and transfer your business to a dealer that furnishes a free people with such magazines as they call for.

Citizens Industrial Ass'n, St. James Bld'g, New York.

C. W. POST.

NEW YORK 10-HOUR LAW IS UNCONSTITUTIONAL

U. S. Supreme Court Holds It Violates Freedom of Contract.

BIG STRIKE IS THREATENED

Justice Harlan, Who Dissents, Calls Court's Decision One of Most Important in a Century.

WASHINGTON, April 17.—In an opinion by Justice Peckham the Supreme Court of the United States to-day held to be unconstitutional the New York State law making ten hours a day's work and sixty hours a week's work in bakeries in that State. Justices Harlan, White, Day, and Holmes dissented, and Justice Harlan declared that no more important decision had been rendered in the last century.

The decision was based on the ground that the law interferes with the free exercise of the rights of contract between individuals.

The case that gave rise to it was that of Lockner vs. The State of New York. Lockner is a baker in the city of Utica and was found guilty of permitting an employe to work in his bakery mo than sixty hours in a week and fined $50.

The Court of Appeals of the State upheld the law and affirmed the judgment of the trial court finding Lockner guilty. Judge Parker wrote the opinion, holding that the measure was within the police power of the State for the protection of the public health from improper conditions surrounding the preparation of food.

To-day's opinion dealt entirely with the constitutional question involved. Justice Peckham said that the law was not an act merely fixing the number of hours which should constitute a legal day's work, but an absolute prohibition on the employer permitting under any circumstances more than ten hours' work to be done in his establishment. He continued:

"The employe may desire to earn the extra money which would arise from his working more than the prescribed time, but this statute forbids the employer from permitting the employe to earn it. It necessarily interferes with the right of contract between the employer and employes concerning the number of hours in which the latter may labor in the bakery of the employer."

"The general rights to make a contract in relation to his business is part of the liberty of the individual protected by the Fourteenth Amendment to the Federal Constitution. Under that provision no State can deprive any person of life, liberty, or property without due process of law. The right to purchase or to sell labor is part of the liberty protected by this amendment unless there are circumstances which exclude the right."

"The question whether this act is valid as a labor law pure and simple may," he said, "be dismissed in a few words. There is no reasonable ground for interfering with the liberty of persons or the right of free contract by determining the hours of labor in the occupation of a baker. Bakers are in no sense wards of the State. Viewed in the light of a purely labor law, with no reference whatever to the question of health, we think that a law like the one before us involves neither the safety, the morals, nor the welfare of the public and that the interest of the public is not in the slightest degree affected by such an act.

"It is a question of which of two powers or rights snall prevail—the power of the State to legislate or the right of the individual to liberty of person and freedom of contract. The mere assertion that the subject relates to the public health does not necessarily render the enactment valid.

"It seems to us that the real object and purpose was simply to regulate the hours of labor between the master and his employes, all being men sui juris, in a private business, not dangerous in any degree to morals or in any real and substantial degree to the health of the employes. Under such circumstances the freedom of master and employe to contract with each other in relation to their employment and in defining the same, cannot be prohibited or interfered with without violating the Federal Constitution."

Justices Holmes and Harlan delivered dissenting opinions and Justices White and Day concurred in the views of Justice Harlan, who said in part:

"I do not stop to consider whether any particular view of this economic question presents the sounder theory. The question is one about which there is room for debate and for an honest difference of opinion. No one can doubt that there are many reasons, based upon the experience of mankind, in support of the theory that, all things considered, more than ten hours steady work each day, from week to week, in a bakery or confectionery establishment, may endanger the health, impair the usefulness, and shorten the lives of the workmen.

"Our duty then is to sustain the statute as not being in conflict with the Federal Constitution, for the reason—and such is an all-sufficient reason—it is not shown to be plainly and palpably inconsistent with that instrument.

"Let the State alone in the management of its purely domestic affairs, so long as it does not appear beyond all question that it has violated the Federal Constitution. This view necessarily results from the principle that the health and safety of the people of a State are primarily for the State to guard and protect, and is not a matter ordinarily of concern to the National Government."

CAN DISCHARGE MAN FOR JOINING UNION

Supreme Court Upsets the Law Forbidding Discrimination Against Labor Organizations.

WILL HAVE POLITICAL EFFECT

Presidential Candidates and Congressmen Cannot Ignore It — Act Was a Strike Remedy.

Special to The New York Times.

WASHINGTON, Jan. 27.—A blow was administered to organized labor to-day by the United States Supreme Court in a decision declaring that any railroad or other common carrier engaged in handling inter-State commerce may discharge an employe and assign no reason beyond the fact that he belongs to a labor organization.

The decision was in the case of William Adair, plaintiff in error, against the United States. Adair was master mechanic of the Louisville and Nashville Railroad, and his discharge of William Coppage, a locomotive engineer, because he belonged to a labor union, was made the basis of the action, brought under the Erdman act, approved July 1, 1898.

Labor leaders will regard to-day's court decision as the most disastrous of the series of setbacks they have received from the courts within the last few weeks. It is conceded to be more far-reaching than the action of the District of Columbia Supreme Court in granting an order to restrain the American Federation of Labor from printing the name of the Buck Stove and Range Company in the "unfair" list; by many it will be regarded a greater blow than that administered by the United States Supreme Court in declaring the Employers' Liability act unconstitutional.

Aside from the effect the decision will have on labor sentiment there is bound to be an important political side to the decision that will have to be met by Presidential candidates. Coming just at this time the decision cannot be ignored from its political side. It will make the statesmen more anxious than ever to get on the right side of labor legislation at the present session of Congress.

The opinion handed down to-day was by Justice Harlan. Justices Holmes and McKenna dissented, and Justice Moody did not participate.

Invades Personal Liberty.

The tenth section of the Erdman act prohibits all common carriers from discriminating against members of labor organizations, and forbids their dismissal because of such membership. Adair was sued in a District Court in Kentucky and was fined $100. An appeal was taken to the Supreme Court. The decision by Justice Harlan expressly says that the tenth section of the Erdman act is unconstitutional, but expressly limits the decision to that section. The opinion of the court, in part, follows:

"The first inquiry is whether that part of the Tenth Section of the Act of 1898, upon which the first count of the indictment was based, is repugnant to the Fifth Amendment of the Constitution declaring that no person shall be deprived of liberty or property without due process of law. In our opinion that section, in the particular mentioned, is an invasion of the personal liberty as well as the right of property guaranteed by that amendment.

"As agent of the railroad company and as such having control of the business of one of its departments, it was the defendant Adair's right—and that right inhered in his personal liberty, and was also a right to property—to serve his employer as best he could, so long as he did nothing that was reasonably forbidden by law as injurious to the public interests. It was the right of the defendant to prescribe the terms upon which the services of Coppage would be accepted, and it was the right of Coppage to become or not, as he chose, an employe of the railroad company upon the terms offered to him.

Equal Rights Guaranteed.

"While, as already suggested, the rights of liberty and property guaranteed by the Constitution to every person within the jurisdiction of the United States against deprivation without due process of law, are subject to such reasonable restraints as the common good or the general welfare may require, it is not within the functions of Government—at least in the absence of contract between the parties—to compel any person in the course of his business and against his will to accept or retain the personal services of another, or to compel any person against his will to perform personal services for another.

"The right of a person to sell his labor upon such terms as he deems proper is, in its essence, the same as the right of the purchaser of labor to prescribe the conditions upon which he will accept such labor from the person offering to sell it. So the right of the employe to quit the service of the employer, for whatever reason, is the same as the right of the employer, for whatever reason, to dispense with the services of such employe. It was the legal right of the defendant, Adair, however unwise such a course might have been, to discharge Coppage because of his being a member of a labor organization, as it was the legal right of Coppage, if he saw fit to do so, however unwise such a course on his part might have been, to quit the service in which he was engaged, because the defendant employed those who were not members of some labor organization. In all such particulars the employer and the employe have equality of right, and any legislation that disturbs that equality is an arbitrary interference with the liberty of contract which no Government can legally justify in a free land."

This law was passed by Congress as a result of the great Chicago strike, and was designed to prevent such conditions as caused it.

BOYCOTT BY UNIONS UNDER COURT BAN

Individual Members Liable in Threefold Damages to Firm Attacked.

IS IN RESTRAINT OF TRADE

Supreme Court Unanimous in Decision Against the Hatters' Union —Gompers Silent

Special to The New York Times.

WASHINGTON, Feb. 3.—The Supreme Court rendered another anti-labor decision to-day, of more far-reaching effect than either of the two which preceded it. The court held unanimously that a boycott which is of such character as to restrain trade is actionable under Section 7 of the Serman anti-trust law, which provides for the recovery of threefold damages. There was no explicit pronouncement on this point, but the inference was that such an action would lie against the individual members of any labor union causing such a boycott.

It is the most damaging blow that organized labor has received, and, carried to its full import, means that hereafter any union which undertakes a boycott renders every one of its members personally liable for threefold damages to the firm or individual boycotted.

The case was that of Dietrich Loewe & Co., hat manufacturers of Danbury, Conn., against Martin Lawlor and 200 other members of the United Hatters of America. The American Federation of Labor was not named as a defendant, but is involved directly in the suit, having assisted in the boycott which the United Hatters waged against Loewe & Co.

The United Hatters, with the assistance of the American Federation of Labor, were undertaking to unionize all the hat factories in the country. In 70 of the 82 shops they succeeded. Loewe & Co. were one of the twelve concerns that held out, and they determined to fight to the finish. Thereupon the boycott was declared, under lead of Martin Lawlor, head of the hatters. The Federation took up the fight and printed the name of the Loewe concern in the "We don't patronize" list in The Federationist, the official organ of the Federation.

Loewe Alleged $80,000 Damages.

Loewe alleged that he had sustained actual damages to the amount of $80,000 and sued Lawlor and 200 other members of the hatters for $280,000, under Section 7 of the Sherman act, which says:

"Any person who shall be injured in his business or property by any other person or corporation by reason of anything forbidden or declared to be unlawful by this act, may sue therefor in any Circuit Court of the United States in the district in which the defendant resides or is found, without respect to the amount in controversy, and shall recover threefold the damages by him sustained, and the costs of suit with a reasonable attorney's fee."

The hatters demurred to Loewe's complaint on the ground that neither the manufacture nor distribution of hats is inter-State in character, and asked that the case be dismissed. The manufacturers did an extensive business, reaching to a number of States, and the boycott therefore covered the business done in these States. The Circuit Court decided that the Sherman act was not sufficiently broad to cover a case of this character, and held that the distribution of hats did not involve the inter-State transportation. Accordingly the complaint was dismissed on the demurrer.

The question of whether Section 7 of the Sherman act should apply was of such importance that the Court of Appeals, without delay or investigation, affirmed the decision of the Circuit Court and certified the case directly to the Supreme Court of the United States. The decision to-day overrules the decision of the Appellate Court. The case was remanded to the Circuit Court for trial for the action for threefold damages.

Supreme Court's Opinion.

Chief Justice Fuller said:

"In our opinion the combination described in the declaration is a combination 'in restraint of trade or commerce among the several States' in the sense in which those words are used in the act, and the action can be maintained accordingly, and that conclusion rests on many judgments of this court, to the effect that the act prohibits any combination whatever to secure action which essentially obstructs the free flow of commerce between the States, or restricts, in that regard, the liberty of a trader to engage in business.

"The combination charged falls within the class of restraints of trade aimed at compelling third parties and strangers involuntarily not to engage in the course of trade except on conditions that the combination imposes; and there is no doubt that, to quote from the well-known work of Chief Justice Erle on trades unions, 'at common law every person has individually, and the public has also collectively, a right to require that the course of trade should be kept free from unreasonable obstruction.'

"But the objection here is to the jurisdiction, because, even conceding that the declaration states the case good at common law, it is contended that it does not state one within the statute. Thus, it is said that the restraint alleged would operate to entirely destroy the defendant's business and thereby include inter-State trade as well; that physical obstruction is not alleged as contemplated, and that defendants are not themselves engaged in intra-State trade.

"We think none of the objections are tenable and that they are disposed of by previous decisions of this court."

Samuel Gompers, President of the American Federation of Labor, declined to comment upon the decision. He was equally reticent when the court previously declared unconstitutional the Employers' Liability act, and later delivered a like blow to the Erdman act by declaring that a corporation may discharge an employe without naming any ground other than that the employe was a member of a labor organization.

The decisions must have an effect on the political situation. It is one which would seem to call for another message from the President.

THE POSITION OF WOMAN.

That woman is a ward of the State, that she is set apart in a class by herself, and placed under the fostering care and special protection of the law, not because of consideration for her individual comfort and interests, but in the interest of the human race and of posterity, is a principle that has just been affirmed by the Supreme Court of the United States. It is held, even, that she may be constitutionally deprived of certain rights in the exercise of which she might incur risk, rights with which, in the case of the male sex, the State would not upon any similar ground interfere.

The case was that of CURT MULLER versus The State of Oregon. By a statute of Oregon, approved in 1903, the employment of women in any mechanical establishment or factory or laundry " more than ten hours in any one day " is forbidden. MULLER, in his suit, attacked the law as unconstitutional on the ground that it limits the right of contract. The statute was sustained by the Oregon Supreme Court as a proper exercise of the police power. That decision was affirmed on Tuesday by the Supreme Court, Justice BREWER writing the opinion, from which we here quote the essential passage:

Differentiated by these matters from the other sex, she is probably placed in a class by herself, and legislation designed for her protection may be sustained, even when like legislation is not necessary for men, and could not be sustained. It is impossible to close one's eyes to the fact that she still looks to her brother and depends upon him. Even though all restrictions on political, personal, and contractual rights were taken away, and she stood, so far as statutes are concerned, upon an absolutely equal plane with him, it would still be true that she is so constituted that she will rest upon and look to him for protection; that her physical structure and a proper discharge of her maternal functions—having in view not merely her own health but the well-being of the race—justify legislation to protect her from the greed as well as the passion of man. The limitations which this statute places upon her contractual powers, upon her right to agree with her employer as to the time she shall labor, are not imposed solely for her benefit, but also largely for the benefit of all. Many words cannot make this plainer. The two sexes differ in structure of body, in the functions to be performed by each, in the amount of physical strength, in the capacity for long-continued labor, particularly when done standing, the influence of vigorous health upon the future wellbeing of the race, the self-reliance which enables one to assert full rights, and in the capacity to maintain the struggle for subsistence. This difference justifies a difference in legislation and upholds that which is designed to compensate for some of the burdens which rest upon her.

It would appear that the doctrine here set up is on its way to become the public policy and practice of the land. In twenty States of the Union laws have been enacted forbidding the employment of women for more than ten hours a day in factories. The other nineteen are Massachusetts, Rhode Island, Louisiana, Connecticut, Maine, New Hampshire, Maryland, Virginia, Pennsylvania, New York, Nebraska, Washington, Wisconsin, North Dakota, South Dakota, Oklahoma, New Jersey, Colorado, and South Carolina. Massachusetts led the way in this legislation in 1874. The New York law was enacted in 1899, and embodied, with amendments, in the statutes of 1907. Curiously enough, this act was declared unconstitutional by the New York Court of Appeals in June last. Judge GRAY, in writing the opinion, seems to have taken a view of the position of woman diametrically opposite to that which guided the Supreme Court in affirming the constitutionality of the Oregon law. We find in Judge GRAY's opinion these views, expressed:

Under our laws men and women now stand alike in their constitutional rights, and there is no warrant for making any discrimination between them with respect to the liberties of persons or of contract.

He expressed the opinion, therefore, that the legislation had overstepped the limits set by the Constitution of the State to the exercise of the power to interfere with the rights of citizens. " An adult female," he said, " is not to be regarded as the ward of the State, or in any other light than the man is regarded when the question relates to the business, pursuit, or calling." It is to be noted, however, that Judge GRAY failed to find in the language of the law anything suggesting the purpose of promoting health. He leaves it to be inferred that, had such a purpose been expressly stated, the court might have delivered a different opinion. Judicial constructions of the scope of the police power have always been extremely liberal. It has been repeatedly held by the Supreme Court, in effect, that the police power comprehends all general laws of internal regulation " necessary to secure peace, good order, health, and the comfort of society, private interest being subservient to the general interests of the community "; and, further, " the possession and enjoyment of all rights is subject to such reasonable conditions as may be deemed by the governing authority essential to the safety, health, peace, good order, and morals of the community." This is plainly the ground upon which Judge BREWER bases his reasoning. To deny a woman the right to work more than ten hours a day in a factory may work a hardship to her individually, since her freedom of contract is interfered with and her power to earn a subsistence may be diminished. But, says the court, the policy embodied in the statute has in view " not merely her own health, but the well-being of the race." This repeats with great exactness the principle of Nature, as expressed by TENNYSON:

So careful of the type she seems,
So careless of the single life.

It accords, also, with the policy of exemptions in favor of woman that prevails in all civilized countries, and largely, even, among primitive savages; exemptions, that is, from jury duty and military and constabulary service. It is in harmony, likewise, with the laws that compel support of the wife by the husband, and provide for alimony when divorces are granted. It will be observed that these laws, and the opinion of the court sustaining their constitutionality, do not spring from sentiment. They rest rather upon a maxim of highest social policy. To the end that the race may be preserved, that the health, vigor, and soundness of posterity may be assured, that class of society charged with the chief functions of race preservation must be surrounded with peculiar safeguards, and securely sheltered against risks and perils that the law permits men freely to incur in their daily affairs.

We leave to the advocates of woman suffrage to say whether this decision makes for, or against, the success of their cause.

DOORS WERE LOCKED, SAY RESCUED GIRLS

Workers Huddled Against Them as Fire Spread, According to Strike Leader.

MASS MEETING OF PROTEST

Arranged by Women's Trade Union League—Triangle Employes Underpaid, Miss Dreier Charges.

Speaking to delegates from twenty philanthropic organizations and settlement workers, who met yesterday in the headquarters of the Women's Trade Union League to plan a mass meeting to discuss problems suggested by the Triangle Waist Company's fire, Leonora O'Reilly, a leader in the strike in the company's plant last year, declared that to her certain knowledge the doors on the eighth and ninth floors of the building were locked fast Saturday afternoon.

"I have just come from a luncheon we prepared for the unfortunate girls who escaped," Miss O'Reilly declared. "They all told me one thing—that the doors were locked. Eighteen of our workers have been going the rounds of the families of those having employment. In every family they tell the same story.

"And while at first this thing may seem strange to you, I assure you it is not strange at all. The girls are locked in while they work in nearly every factory. We exploited this fact when we declared the strike in the Triangle plant, and later saw it grow into the revolt of the entire trade.

"And since that strike the rule about keeping the doors locked has been enforced more strictly than ever. It had an economic basis and it was to the advantage of the employer in more ways than one.

"In the first place, employers do not trust their help. In many factories they search them at night to see that they do not carry off the shirtwaists they have made.

Planned to Prevent Tardiness.

"To enforce rules regarding tardiness the idea of locking the doors was first inaugurated. It was found that if girls understood they could not get into the factories after the minute of commencing work in the morning, they would be more sure to come on time.

"But, in trying to lock the late-comers out, they overlooked the fact that they were also locking those in who were at work. After the strike the locked doors gave another protection, for it was when agents entered the rooms of all shirtwaist factories simultaneously that the girls all walked out to join the revolt. The locked doors were a permanent guarantee that there would be no more sudden notices to cease work passed simultaneously to all factories.

"The girls with whom I lunched to-day were very excited, and could tell but little with definiteness. But they did say that they had seen large numbers of girls huddled against the locked doors, and the reports of the fire agree that girls were found in just this position on the eighth, and especially on the ninth floor."

The meeting Miss O'Reilly addressed passed resolutions denouncing the administrative policies which did not provide better means of egress. It also appointed committees to confer with labor organizations and employers and see if a co-operative plan cannot be worked out to bring about an improvement of exit facilities in loft structures.

Miss Mary E. Dreier, President of the Women's Trade Union League, who was arrested in the strike while doing picket duty in front of the Triangle Waist Company's place of business, said she recognized among the dead many who had passed with her through the strike experiences.

"The worst of all the firms we had to deal with was that of Harris & Blanck," Miss Dreier declared. "When both sides had been wearied by the long struggle and it seemed they could get together, Mr. Blanck came to our representatives and pleaded with us that he had a business reputation to sustain—that he didn't want it to seem that we had beaten him into making changes. He said if we would only help him save his face and let the girls go back he would see that the improvements were speedily made and every sanitary regulation suggested was complied with.

"His words were reassuring. We thought he had seen the justice of our demands for decent working conditions. He was the largest man in the business, controlling factories in Newark and Philadelphia, as well as in New York. We trusted him, and let our girls go back.

"They found that each experienced girl was required to teach six Italian girls all she knew about the business—these six being seated near her machine to see her sew. Then we found the experienced girls, as soon as they had done the instructing necessary, were dismissed.

"All who had joined in the strike as leaders were dismissed, one by one, whenever excuses, however slight, could be found. The union girls were put exclusively on the eighth floor, after others had been instructed to do their work, and thus it is that there are so many employes other than Jews who met their death. The employes, up to the time of the strike adjustment, were nearly all Jewish."

Says Girls Were Underpaid.

Miss Dreier recounted the manner in which she was arrested in front of the place, and then received apologies from the police when her identity became known and reproaches from the policeman who had taken her into custody for not telling him who she was, so that he could have avoided the "mistake." She said that in every union shop the girls were paid 60 cents a dozen for doing work for which the girls in the Triangle shop got 85 cents a dozen, and that it was because of this low rate that the girls were still at work at an hour when employes had left off work in nearly all the factories of the city.

"The poor Italian girl," she said, "has no conception, when she first arrives, of how short a distance $6 a week will go in this country. She thinks the wage is fair; her more experienced sisters know that $10 a week is less than needed to keep decently alive. And there you have the game Harris & Blanck played—they exploited the newly arrived and unsophisticated and turned out those to whom they pledged that they would change conditions in their shop."

Ida Rowe, a field worker for the league, told of her experiences trying to get the Mayor and the Building Department to take action against known firetraps, following the Newark disaster.

"We found the authority scattered all through the City Government," she said; "the Building Department referred us to the Fire Department, and the Fire Department to the Factory Inspectors, and so it went.

"Chief Croker told me how anxious he was to gain complete control. I think we are anxious to see him have it, or see it centred in his department, since it knows more than the others about the toll in death lists that the improper facilities have. I think a monster mass meeting, which we are here to provide for, should put itself on record as in favor of such consolidation and revision of the laws."

To Seek Data from the Workers.

The question of gathering information about conditions in factories was brought up by Morris Hillquit. Miss O'Reilly said that it was more than any girl's head was worth to speak openly about the conditions of her employment. "I propose that we name a committee," she said, "which will advertise that it will guard as secret any information brought to it." She proposed that the girls of all factory buildings be asked these questions:

  Do you work in a fire trap?
  Are the doors locked while you work?
  Are there bars on the windows?
  Are there fire escapes on all floors?
  Are the escapes readily accessible?
  Are scraps or waste allowed to accumulate near the motors or steam plant?

If so, you work in a fire trap. You may secretly describe your condition by calling at the homes or writing to Mrs. Stephen Wise, 23 West Ninetieth Street; Leonora O'Reilly, 680 Seventh Avenue; Mrs. Root, 501 West 120th Street; Mrs. Ollesheimer, 6 East Fifty-eighth Street, or Helen Marot, 43 East Twenty-second Street.

Circulars as suggested were ordered sent out, the data gathered to be turned over to a steering committee of twenty-five citizens to be named by the mass meeting's Chairman, to plan for a general assembly on Thursday or Friday night in the largest hall available.

Rabbi Stephen Wise declared that he was willing to take no man's word—especially no official's word—about what the facts of the shirtwaist fire were. "We have seen," he said, "the terrible evidences of what officials can do in the way of avoiding the search for facts in the case of the recent legislative investigating committee, which passed so skillfully all opportunities really to find out the scandals of race track gambling.

"I want the citizens of New York to find out for themselves, through the medium of a committee named at a general mass assembly. If this thing was avoidable I want to see those responsible punished. If it was due to some corrupt failure to enforce the law I want to see that determined. And I do not trust public officials to determine it for us; it is our own task as citizens to do that for ourselves."

The Resolutions.

Benjamin C. Marsh of the Mayor's Committee on Congestion of Population, William J. Schieffelin, President of the People's Union, and others spoke in favor of the resolutions which were adopted, and which read:

  Whereas, So soon following the frightful holocaust in our neighboring city of Newark, and in spite of the solemn warning to our officials in a leading New York magazine, that conditions were as bad, or worse, here, this dreadful disaster has come to the most helpless of our people, the working women of our city and those dependent upon them; and

  Whereas, It is most evident that there has been neglect on the part of many, both officials and private citizens, and especially lack of co-operation to prevent such accidents, and that such neglect is immediately the cause of this most deplorable affliction; and

  Whereas, Yet deeper lie causes, such as the continuation of industrial warfare, the failure to exact and enforce proper factory inspection, the inexcusable delay about adopting measures, which in other countries have minimized such dangers and provided for the compensation of the victims of industrial accidents in a manner, which results in a maximum of prevention; and

  Whereas, These, our sisters and our brothers will have died in the occasion pass without a full and firm expression of the indignation, shame, and grief, with which the horror has been received by all, now therefore be it

  Resolved, That we, who are here assembled, deplore and condemn the blindness of public officials, who fatuously permit such conditions to continue, the insufficiency of the number of factory inspectors, the greed of employers, who do not welcome, but instead punish with dismissal, employes, who demand safe conditions under which to work, and the inertia of the great, busy public, which does not render such unprofitable, both in the public servant and the employer; and

  Be it resolved, That we call upon the people of our city, State, and Nation to bring to account all who are responsible for such conditions, and to take steps to render it impossible that we should ever again be compelled to bow our heads in helpless grief, and rage, and shame at that which human forethought could so easily prevent; and

  Be it resolved, That we call upon the working people of New York, and all in sympathy with them, to join in the funeral procession of the victims, and thus give expression alike to their sorrow and to their resolve to prevent such horrors in future.

The committee of twenty-five called for to arrange a mass meeting, it was announced, would be appointed this morning from among the city's most representative men and women.

BAYONET CHARGE ON LAWRENCE STRIKERS

Riotous Assaults Numerous Till Militia Attack and Battery Unlimbers Its Guns.

30,000 OPERATIVES ARE OUT

New York Strike Leader Makes New Wage Demands—Mills to Reopen To-day Under Guard—Many Arrests.

Special to The New York Times.

LAWRENCE, Mass., Jan. 15.—Every mill in Lawrence will throw open its gates to-morrow morning and start the million of wheels whirring in defiance of the 15,000 strikers, who sit to-night in stuffy halls and crowded tenement houses, peering out of narrow windows with angry eyes at the soldiers pacing the streets through the snow and slush guarding the mills.

Half a thousand militiamen, 300 policemen, and a company of artillery were sufficient to overawe the strikers to-day. One of their number lies dying of a bayonet thrust, scores are nursing broken heads from policemen's clubs, and the long ash sticks of Battery C, twenty-eight of the leaders arrested to-day have been sentenced to jail, several for two years, the others for one year, yet to-night the most enthusiastic mass meeting the strikers have had jammed City Hall full, overflowing into the square and the common.

Fiery speeches that the struggle be prolonged were shouted in many languages to surging throngs which had entered the hall through a double line of bayonets. No one believes to-night that the fight has yet been won by the mill men. The mass of soldiery has served to infuriate rather than to subdue the strikers.

The only way that further rioting and bloodshed possibly can be avoided, according to men in a position to know, is by the mill owners shutting down every mill and leaving the strikers to starve. This the mill owners will not listen to. They are rushed with orders. The strike has come at the busiest season of the year, and they are determined not to concede a point to the strikers.

Mayor Scanlon is plainly in sympathy with the millowners. He had a conference with Lawrence Maroney, one the strike leaders, this afternoon.

"Why don't you go out there and tell those strikers to go home," said the Mayor to Maroney. "I want you to understand that a crowd of bandits is not going to run this city. I will keep order here if I have to call on the whole Federal army, and believe me when I tell you that if to-day's riots are repeated to-morrow there will be an awful slaughter."

Wage Increase Demanded.

Although the strike was originally instituted in protest of a reduction in pay because of the operation of new fifty-four-hour law, which makes the working week two hours shorter, the strikers now declare that they will not return to work without a 15 per cent. increase in wages and other concessions, including double pay for overtime work and the abolition of the premium or bonus system. The decision of the strikers to enforce these new demands was made known at a conference between strike leaders and members of the City Government this afternoon.

Joseph J. Ettor of New York, National Organizer of the Industrial Workers of the World, is the leader of the strike. As a result of the conference the strikers were granted the use of the City Hall for a mass meeting, which was held this evening. It was also agreed at this conference that the strikers be allowed to place tickets about the approaches to the mills to-morrow with the understanding that any signs of violence on the part of the picketers will be cause for arrest.

Mayor Scanlon suggested that it might relieve the situation if Ettor should return to New York, but the latter declared his intention of remaining in the city as long as the strike continues. Throughout the day there were outbreaks in rapid succession, the police finding the strikers and their sympathizers particularly hard to deal with because of the many nationalities represented.

No less than forty-five tongues are spoken by employes of Lawrence mills, and the workers are said to represent no less than fifty-two different nationalities.

Defended With Fire Hose.

The opening of the mills at 7 o'clock this morning was the signal for the first outbreak, when strikers stormed the gates of the Wood, Washington, Prospect, and other mills. The attacking parties were repulsed by police and mill employes with streams of water, but their tactics resulted in the closing down of nearly two-thirds of the plants.

Later there were clashes between the strikers and the soldiers and mill officials about the lower Pacific, Atlantic, and Arlington, and other mills, in which shots were exchanged and several persons slightly injured. The police fired into the air in the hope that it would frighten the rioters, but the firehose proved more effective.

The three local militia organizations, Companies F of the Ninth and L of the Eighth Regiment, both infantry companies, and Battery C, light artillery, were called out early when it was seen the police could not cope with the situation.

Until awed by the show of arms at the Pacific Mills the strikers pressed forward, when Capt. Radlett of Company L ordered his men to fix bayonets and charge. In the charge several persons were injured, a Sicilian boy, Dominic Raprasa, being so badly hurt that he will probably die.

Battery Unlimbers Guns.

The militia have orders to shoot if necessary, and at one time Battery C unlimbered its guns to clear the streets. Police from other cities arrived to-night to aid the forces already in the city.

The greatest crowd gathered at the Wood Mill this morning before the hour of opening. Pickets were on duty as early as 5 A. M. to prevent operatives from entering the plant. Force was often used, and women and children were roughly handled by the strikers when they insisted on going to work. About 1,000 hands

reached their places in the mill only to be met there by other strikers who, having evaded the police and watchmen, brandished clubs in an effort to force the operatives out. These agitators had their way until the mills were shut down shortly after 7 o'clock.

Meanwhile the crowd of strikers clamoring at the mill gates made two attempts to storm the doors which had been closed against them. Several of the men were able to enter the mill and were immediately arrested. One of these gave his name as Santo Fagaro. When the Wood mill was closed the strike sympathizers marched to the Prospect mills and dashed at the gates which had been closed against them. They assumed a more belligerent attitude and resisted strenuously the attempts of the police to force them back.

Striker Armed to the Teeth.

Vincenzo Lamarest, 23 years old, was one of the most violent in the crowd, and he was arrested for assault. State Officer Flynn found a .38 calibre revolver with an ammunition belt containing twenty-two cartridges, a long dirk knife in one pocket, and a stiletto in another. When Marshal O'Sullivan arrived at the Prospect Mills during this outbreak, strike sympathizers cut the tires of his automobile and left him stranded.

Another crowd of over a thousand gathered at the big Washington mills. They swarmed over the bridge leading to the mills across the canal and had several minor scrimmages with the police. When snow began to fall the mob dispersed. On the way to the halls the woolen mill strikers ran into a disturbance at the Pacific Cotton Mills. Here a body of more violently inclined strike sympathizers had worked themselves into a fighting mood and had just emerged from an assault on the mill gates when the Washington mill crowd arrived. Soon all was in an uproar. The mob raided coal cars on a siding, and bombarded the windows of the Pacific weave shed. On the canal and Matheum Street sides of the mills the windows were shattered. Six operatives inside were hurt, but none seriously. The police then charged the mob and fired a number of shots in the air. The shots did not scare the strikers, and orders were then given to turn on the water in the mill hose.

The situation at the lower Pacific mills ... so strained at 9:30 o'clock that it ... had the assistance of the militia ... Accordingly Company L ... ...ment and Company F ... ...rdered out for serv... ... Company ... ...f the en... ...lls, while ...

MINER'S STORY OF PEONAGE.

Says He Was Brought to Work by Deception and Held by Force.

DENVER, Feb. 10.—Further testimony designed to establish charges of peonage in the Colorado coal fields was introduced to-day before the sub-committee of the House Committee on Mines and Mining, which is investigating the coal miners' strike.

Salvatori Valentin, a Sicilian, told the committee that he had been brought from Pittsburgh through deception and forced to work in the Delagua Mine. One of his fellow-strikebreakers, he said, was shot and killed in the mine by an unknown person.

Valentin said he signed a contract on Dec. 13, in which he was told, according to his statement, there was no strike in Colorado.

James Adams, the young Missourian who last night testified that he was held prisoner in the Delagua mine, was recalled to identify the contract under which he said he was brought to Colorado. He was unable to identify positively his own signature. The alleged contract produced by counsel for the mine operators bound the signer to work in the mines as a strike breaker.

February 11, 1914

PATERSON STRIKERS NOW BECOME ACTORS

Madison Square Garden the Scene of Melodramatic Reproduction of Silk Strike.

1,029 ON GIGANTIC STAGE

Biggest Cast Ever Seen in a New York Production Stages Its Own Show.

It is doubtful if Madison Square Garden, even at the close of the bitterest of political campaigns, ever held a larger audience than that which packed that great auditorium last night to witness the first production of "Big Bill" Haywood's "Paterson Strike Pageant,' a spectacular production in which 1,029 Paterson strikers of many nationalities and ages played the leading as well as all of the minor parts.

The spectacle was in six scenes, and was intended to give a picture of the strike from the dawn of that morning, almost sixteen weeks ago, when the silk mill workers of the New Jersey city deserted their looms until the present moment, when practically every mill in the greatest silk manufacturing city in America is still idle and when every other industry there is feeling the pinch of hard times due to the self-enforced idleness of more than 25,000 silk weavers and dyers.

It was said by the Industrial Workers of the World leaders, who managed last night's spectacle, that more than 12,000 persons had paid their way into the fair, and these, with the New Jersey strikers, who were admitted free, brought the total number of the audience to a figure that it was said closely approximated the 15,000 mark.

It was an audience every man, woman, and child in which seemed to be enthusiastic for the Haywood organization and all that it stands for.

American Flag Eliminated.

There was not an American flag in the whole scheme of decoration, a scheme that covered every inch of the Garden except the floors and the roof.

There were red I. W. W. emblems everywhere. As a matter of fact, everything was red except a single sign that held a commanding position near the stage on the Twenty-seventh Street side of the third gallery. It was a huge sign, the letters of which were painted green on a background of white, and this is how the sign read:

"No God, no master."

The sign had not figured in the original scheme of the decoration and was placed in position by two New York men, both of whom it was said were of the Industrial Workers of the World, but who were not concerned in any way in the management or the agitation of the great Paterson strike.

The sign was in place, and the great audience was wondering why it was there before Patrick Quinlan, the Industrial Workers of the World leader, Haywood, Elizabeth Gurley Flynn, and Carlo Tresca knew anything about it. Quinlan, when his attention was called to the sign, rushed up to the gallery with Theodore Haefeli, one of the Paterson strikers. Quinlan tore the sign from its place, and turning to those responsible for hanging it denounced them in true Quinlanesque fashion.

"You are a fine gang of bums," he cried, "to try and discredit us by doing such a thing as this. Now you get out of here, and if I catch you doing any more of this sort of thing I will see to it that every one of you is arrested and locked up."

Quinlan was cheered to the echo when he apepared on the main floor with the big sign crumpled to pieces in his hands.

"That was an infernal outrage," he said to the newspaper men, "and I hope you will do us the justice to let it be known that every man and woman connected with the Paterson strike repudiates it."

Police Stop Overcrowding.

At 9 o'clock the New York police ordered the entrances to the Garden closed and gave instructions that no more tickets were to be sold or any more persons permitted to enter the Garden. At that hour every seat on the main floor, in the balcony, and in the galleries was occupied, while perhaps a thousand persons were standing in the rear of the Garden.

Every box was occupied, many of them by fashionably dressed men and women, while down in front sat Sheriff Harburger, who said he was present to see to it that no man or woman said or did anything that could in the remotest way be termed a desecration of the American flag.

"Just let anybody," said the Sheriff, "say one word of disrespect to the flag and I will stop the sho so uickly it will take their breath away."

"Why don't you stop the Marseillaise?" somebody asked the Sheriff.

"I can't," he answered, "for the courts have decided that the Marseillaise is legal."

At 9:01 o'clock the lights in the roof of the Garden went out, and those on the giant stage were turned on. The stage was said by I. W. W. leaders to be the biggest ever erected in New York for show purposes. It was on the Fourth Avenue side of the Garden, and extended from the Twenty-sixth to the Twenty-seventh Street side. Every man, woman, and child who appeared on it was, according to the strike management, a bona-fide Paterson silk mill striker or the child of a striker.

The company—for that is what they call it now—had been brought to New York on a special train over the Lackawanna, and arriving here, had been joined by 3,000 strikers from Hudson County, N. J., and 800 from New York City, but only the Paterson contingent appeared in the Garden spectacle. The others were there for cheering purposes.

Spent $1,200 for Scenery.

The scenery used last night was painted for the spectacle and cost the Industrial Workers of the World $1,200. It showed a dozen Paterson silk mills, one big one taking up all the canvas on the Fourth Avenue side of the Garden. The other mills, all smaller ones, formed the wings.

When the first scene was announced by the turning on of the lights, the stage was deserted. The Paterson strikers' brass band struck up the strike march. The whistles of the mills sounded, calling the weavers to work. They came in from the wings and down the aisles a thousand strong. They walked as if they were ill fed. Some were reading newspapers and the pantomime showed that all were talking strike.

It was just before the opening time in the morning. The sun had not risen and the windows of the mill showed the glare of electric lights within. The whistles blew and the workers entered the mill to begin work. The whirr of the looms was heard.

Everything indicated industrial peace and contentment. Then something happened. Men and women gathered in small groups in front of the mill. The action was in pantomime, but it did not take more than one good eye to see that the subject being so heatedly discussed had to do with going on a strike. Suddenly the workers rushed from the mill, all of them shouting at the top of their voices: "Strike! Strike!"

The stage was crowded by a mob of excited men and women, all shouting the news that the big silk-mill strike had started. As a climax the band struck up the Marseillaise, and the strikers both on and off the stage joined in the singing that follows. As the curtain went down the strikers, still singing the Marseillaise, were seen marching away from the mills.

In the second scene the pickets were shown at work. The scenery was still the same, but the lights in the mills were missing. The I. W. W. programme said the mills were idle. The strikers were marching up and down in front of the mills by twos and threes, their eyes searching the crowds that passed for a possible worker who was not of the I. W. W. and who might want to stay at work. Such a person finally appeared. He was under police escort and was on his way hoping to earn a day's pay. He was "booed" all the way across the stage, but the police managed to get him into the mill.

Then the strike actors turned on the police and unmercifully "booed" the Captain in charge and the men under his command. The police—those in the show—got angry, and charged the crowd, beating men and women with their clubs, and when it was all over forty strikers were under arrest. The prisoners were marched to the Paterson Police Headquarters, the strikers following, a thousand strong, cheering the prisoners and booing the police at every step. And that was the end of the second scene.

Next a Funeral March.

There was no cheering either on the stage or among the audience during Scene 3. The band played the "Dead March in Saul," and the scene pictured the funeral of Valentino Modestino, the Paterson laborer who was killed by a stray bullet in one of the clashes between the police and the strikers. Modestino was not a striker, but the I. W. W. proclaimed him a martyr just the same. Four strikers came on the stage, carrying on their shoulders a plain black coffin, covered with a flag. The flag was not American, but the red emblem of the Industrial Workers of the World. The coffin was opened, and the strikers filed by, one by one, and as each passed dropped into the coffin a red carnation.

Then, Carlo Tresca, who is under indictment in Paterson, and is soon to go on trial, made a speech. It was the funeral oration. Then Tresca stopped and Haywood spoke. He pledged the I. W. W. to care forever for Modestino's widow and child.

Next the funeral procession formed and, as the coffin disappeared from the stage, the curtain went down and scene three was at an end.

The green in the centre of the Borough of Haledon, on the outskirts of Paterson, was the scene of the next act. Two thousand strikers appeared in this scene. The regular Haledon programme followed every Sunday since the strike began, was acted. There was singing by Italian quartettes and German quartettes and by an octette that sang in English. Then the speaking began, the little fellows leading off, the big fellows and Miss Flynn being saved for the climax. Haywood, Miss Flynn, Tresca, Quinlan and Lessig all spoke in the fourth scene last night, and Haywood called on the strikers to vote their disapproval of the conviction of Quinlan and Scott. The strikers voted as requested and likewise voted to stay out on strike. With a chorus of strike songs, the red curtain was drawn on the fourth scene.

Scene five was intended to show the departure from Paterson of the strike children, who were sent to New York and other cities to be cared for by I. W. W. families. Elizabeth Gurley Flynn had a prominent part in that scene. She gave the children to the "strike mothers,' as those who received them are known. Hundreds of boys and girls were featured in this scene, and each one wore a red sash, a red tie, or both. Miss Flynn also made another speech. The scene ended with the children on the way to their temporary homes in New York and elsewhere.

The last scene showed Helvetia Hall, now closed to the strikers as a result of police action in Paterson. Haywood and Tresca and Miss Flynn and Quinlan spoke again, the strikers swore to stay on strike until the strike was won, the band played the "Marseillaise," and the "Paterson Strike Pageant" was ended.

From Paterson and from Hoboken and other New Jersey towns, where the men and women and boys and girls weave silk ribbons and cloths, the strikers who are affiliated with the Industrial Workers of the World advanced upon New York.

Every age from 6 years up and many nationalities were represented in the army of red-ribboned people that walked singing and cheering through the streets of New York. The Paterson delegation led the way, with the New York contingent bringing up the rear. At the front of the procession marched "Big Bill" Haywood, the I. W. W. leader.

Plenty of Red Flags.

There were many flags, most of them the fiery red ones of the I. W. W., not to mention many banners on which short, pithy paragraphs in bright golden letters told the story of the alleged sufferings of the strikers at the hands of the authorities of Paterson and the silk mill owners.

The strikers' band played just one tune from the ferry to the Garden and that was the Marseillaise. The route of the parade had not been advertised and for that reason no great crowds lined Fifth Avenue to watch the strikers as they proceeded on their way to Madison Square Garden.

It was announced at the Garden last night that, after paying the rent of the Garden, paying for the special train, the painting of the scenery, and feeding the Paterson "players," the "I. W. W." cleared $6,500 as a result of tht first production of "The Paterson Strike Pageant."

June 8, 1913

ROCKEFELLER, JR., DEFIES UNION RULE

Will Sacrifice All in Colorado Rather Than Subject Miners to Union Dictation.

FIRM FOR "OPEN SHOP"

Americans, He Tells Congressmen, Must Have Right to Work Where They Please.

SAYS HE DOES HIS DUTY

Is a Director, but Must Trust Details to Trained Officers—Testifies for Four Hours.

Special to The New York Times.

WASHINGTON, April 6.—John D. Rockefeller, Jr., testifying to-day as a Director of the Colorado Fuel and Iron Company in the inquiry which the House Committee on Mines is conducting into the Colorado coal strike, declared unequivocally on the principle of the "open shop," and assented that he and his associates would prefer that they should "lose all of their millions invested in the coal fields than that American workingmen should be deprived of the right under the Constitution to work for whom they pleased."

Mr. Rockefeller said that he thought his chief duty as a Director was to place honest and capable officers in control of the business. He said he would rather relinquish his interests in Colorado and close down the mines than to recognize the unions under the circumstances. He was not opposed to unions as such, he said, but he did object to unions which tried to force men to join them and which deprived men of the liberty of working for whom they pleased. He said that a recognition of the Mine Workers' Union would mean the repudiation of the employes who had been faithful enough to remain with the company during the strike.

Might Consider Arbitration.

Mr. Rockefeller said he favored arbitration in industrial disputes generally, but in the present instance had supported the officers of the company in their refusal to submit the question of unionizing the mines to arbitration. Later in his testimony he said that he would consider arbitration of the dispute in the Colorado field if he could be assured that a fair and unbiased Board of Arbitration could be obtained. He suggested Federal Judges as the best qualified to serve on such a board.

It was brought out that John D. Rockefeller, Sr., owned about 40 per cent. of the securities of the Colorado Fuel and Iron Company. The witness testified that his father's interest on the Board of Directors was represented by Starr J. Murphy and John D. Green, as well as by the witness himself, and that J. H. McKenna and L. M. Bowers were "indirect representatives."

It was the younger Rockefeller's début before a Congressional investigating committee. Although steadily interrogated for four hours, scored with intimations of non-interest in employes, indirectly rebuked for having assumed no personal supervision during the strike, and in a way baited with the accusation that he was a sociological uplifter who had not taken a direct interest in the striking miners in Colorado, Mr. Rockefeller stood his ground solidly and refrained from getting excited over the unexpected trend of the hearing.

Mr. Rockefeller was called as a witness not only because he is a Director of the Colorado Fuel and Iron Company, which has a big steel plant at Pueblo, the "Pittsburgh of the West," but also on account of the virtual control of that great property by his father. The witness said that he himself held just enough stock in the company to qualify him as a Director.

When pressed hard by Chairman Foster for an explanation of his alleged lack of personal interest in the welfare of the men and questioned as to his duty in the matter, Mr. Rockefeller said that he had conducted his business just as his father and he had conducted their philanthropies, by employing the best men to look after the details and upholding those men so long as they attended to business, and were considered capable and worthy. He said that he had absolute confidence in the officers of the Colorado Fuel and Iron Company, and was willing to rely upon those men.

Never ruffled over the way in which Chairman Foster and other members of the committee questioned him, Mr. Rockefeller, polite and thoroughly suave, insisted that he was doing all he could to keep in touch with the situation. He said his office had a man of exceptional ability on the ground in L. M. Bowers, Vice President of the company, and that the members of the Rockefeller family were disposed to stand by him in the Colorado affair or in any other matter in which he might be a representative of the Rockefeller investments.

Rely Upon Trained Agents.

When pressed closely by Chairman Foster for an opinion as to whether, while Mr. Rockefeller was paying close attention to sociological, welfare, and religious work, the company in which he represented his father's interests was allowing a severe industrial warfare to develop in Colorado, Mr. Rockefeller pointed to the large batch of correspondence he had had with Vice President Bowers, and reminded the committee that specially trained agents had been employed in many of the more important social investigations of the Rockefeller interests.

"I believe," said Chairman Foster, "that you are connected with sociological and uplift movements and that you were recently the foreman of a Grand Jury which reported upon the white slave traffic. Do you not think you might have paid some attention to these bloody strike conditions out in Colorado, where you have 1,000 employes in whose welfare you seem not to have taken any deep personal interest?"

"I have done what I regard as the very best thing in the interest of these employes and the large investment I represent," said Mr. Rockefeller. "We have gotten the best men obtainable and are relying on their judgment. We follow the very same policy in philanthropic and social work that we are following in business; that is, we put the best men we can in charge."

"While you were engaged in social uplift work," said Chairman Foster, "did it ever occur to you to investigate conditions among your own employes?"

"When I was foreman of the Grand Jury," replied Mr. Rockefeller, "I did not personally acquaint myself with vice and white slavery, because there were other men so much better qualified to make an investigation and report. They were experienced in the business. I was not. I sent Dr. Flexner to Europe for the same reason."

Not a "Dummy Director."

Replying to questions, Mr. Rockefeller said he had not attended a Directors' meeting of the Colorado Company in ten years, nor had he seen the Colorado properties in that period.

"Are you a dummy Director?" asked

Representative Byrnes of South Carolina.

"I do not so regard myself," replied Mr. Rockefeller.

"I believe," said Chairman Foster, "you are affiliated with certain philanthropic and sociological organizations, including the Rockefeller Foundation?"

"Yes," said Mr. Rockefeller, "we contribute to them."

"You were also interested, I believe, in the Chicago Vice Commission's work and were the foreman of a New York Grand Jury which investigated the white-slave traffic," said Mr. Foster. "Still, with 10,000 striking miners in Colorado, what have you done to look after them?"

"I have done," said Mr. Rockefeller, "what I regard as the best thing I could have done in the interest of the employes and the large amount we have invested. I do not know what else I might have done."

"What have you done personally to end this strike?"

"I have done nothing personally," said Mr. Rockefeller. "My only knowledge comes from the correspondence I have had with the men in charge there. So long as we have officials there we must let them handle the situation, and the position taken by the officers will be upheld by us as long as we deem them worthy of confidence. I have every confidence in the ability of Mr. Welborn and Mr. Bowers."

"Do you think the fact that the Government is taking some interest in this strike ought to be a hint to you to take at least a passing interest in the affairs at your mines?"

"I have not taken just a passing interest," Mr. Rockefeller replied very quickly, but without the least excitement. "The strike has caused us great concern, but all we can do is to keep in touch with the men we trust. Should we reach the conclusion that they are not doing the right thing, then we would take the matter up with them."

Father's Interest in Company.

When asked as to the Rockefeller holdings in the Colorado Fuel and Iron Company, the witness said his father held the following securities of that concern: Common stock, 139,807 out of 342,355 shares; preferred stock, 7,943 out of 20,000. Bonds, Colorado Industrial Company 5 per cents, $14,450,000 out of $33,437,000. General 5 per cents of the Colorado Fuel and Iron Company, $266,000 out of $5,658,000.

According to the witness, the only dividends paid by the company were in 1912. He said a cumulative dividend of 8 per cent. due on the preferred stock had at that time accumulated to 75 per cent. He said that 35 per cent. was paid on the accumulated dividend and 4 per cent. on the 8 per cent. dividend due that year.

Mr. Rockefeller told the committee that Vice President Bowers had been looking after the Rockefeller interests for many years. He did so formerly in the East. Mrs. Bowers's health failed and she had to be taken West in 1907. Mr. Bowers asked whether he could be of service in the West, and was asked to investigate some investments that the Rockefellers had in the West at that time. Then he became Treasurer of the Colorado Company, and afterward was made Chairman of the board by the board itself, without "any knowledge on our part." Mr. Rockefeller said he mentioned these things to show that Mr. Bowers's "long continued relationship with the company has been controlled by the board because of his great value to the enterprise."

Q. (by Chairman Foster)—You have never taken the time personally, nor have any of the Directors, to find out for yourselves from personal knowledge whether these miners had a grievance or not? A.—Just the minute I have the slightest lack of confidence in the man in charge—

Q.—I know, but you have not done that? A.—I have not found it necessary in the discharge of my duty.

Q.—As a Director of the company you thought that all necessary for you to do was put your name on the roster of officers as a Director, not even attending the stockholders' meeting, turn the matter over to somebody else, and say "Go ahead"? A.—W— spent ten years testing out the man that is one of the men in charge.

Q.—Do you think your duty goes further than that? A.—I do not know of any way in which I could more adequately and completely discharge my duty than in that way.

Q.—Don't you believe that you, looking after the welfare of other civilians of the United States—that somewhat closer relations between officers and that class of men, these 6,000 coal diggers who work underground, many of them foreigners, ignorant and unacquainted with the ways of the country, would be an uplift to them and make them better citizens? A.—It is because I have such a profound interest in these men and all workers that I expect to stand by the policy which has been outlined by the officers, and which seems to me to be first, last, and always, in the greatest interest of the employes of the country.

Q.—But you do not regard it as a matter personal to you to look into these matters yourself? A.—Oh, I am giving it constant and close attention.

Q.—You have spent a lot of money, thousands of dollars, looking to the civic uplift in different parts of the country, have you not? A.—We have spent some money in those ways.

"And yet, with 10,000 employes, you have simply trusted it to two or three men out there?" asked Chairman Foster.

Strike Costing $1,000,000

According to the estimate of the President of the company, Mr. Rockefeller said, it was costing the Rockefellers "about $1,000,000 to stand for the principle which we believe is to the ultimate interest of those men."

"And," interjected Chairman Foster, "that is to fight the union?"

"That is to allow them to have the privilege of determining the conditions under which they shall work," replied the witness.

Q.—And not that men shall get together and talk over their own interests? A.—They have every right to do that.

Q.—Collective bargaining and sale of their labor—you want to fight that? A.—I do not say that. Not that outside men, who have no interest in them or in their employers, shall come in and impose upon them that organization.

Q.—You are an outsider with respect to Colorado, are you not? A.—I do not live there. I am an outsider, except in a representative capacity.

Q.—You have not been there for ten years? A.—I have never lived there. I am an outsider to the extent of being one who is spending a million dollars in helping to look out for the interests of those people.

Q.—And is the man who works to be excluded from going in and looking out for the interests of that class of men? A.—I think that when we help a class of persons you have to give them a right to say whether they will be helped or not.

Q.—But are the outsiders who invest their money there the only ones? A.—Certainly not, but the men have not expressed any dissatisfaction with their condition. The records show that the conditions have been admirable. If the men should express themselves as dissatisfied—

Q.—You have had a strike there within a year? A.—A strike has been imposed upon the company from outside.

Q.—How can you have a strike without dissatisfaction? They could not make men go out of the mines for nothing. A.—They could not make the men go out? Then I do not think you have as much knowledge of the conditions as I have.

Strike Brought On by Threats.

Mr. Rockefeller said that "Black-Hand" letters had been received, along with threats of violence to the wives and daughters of workmen, and that these were the ways in which outsiders "make men go out."

Chairman Foster wanted to know whether that was the way they had brought on the strike, and Mr. Rockefeller said it was.

"I assume," said Mr. Rockefeller, "the technical way in which the fight was brought on was the calling of this convention, in which there was no bona-fide representative or delegate from any of our men. I claim it is hardly a republican method of dealing to have a strike brought on in convention without any representatives of the men who are to strike being present."

Mr. Rockefeller said the miners had no grievances that he knew of, whereupon Mr Foster said he would send Mr. Rockefeller a copy of the testimony taken at the hearings.

"Very well," said Mr. Rockefeller, "All the things contended for during the strike had been conceded by the company previous to the strike."

Q.—Do you think that a Director like you are, of a company, like the Colorado Fuel and Iron Company, should take the responsibility for the conduct of that company? A.—In these days, when interests are so diversified and numerous, of course it would be impossible for any man to be personally responsible for all the management of the various concerns in which he might be a larger or smaller stockholder. It would be simply impossible to do that, and all that any man can do is to find the ablest men that he can find and put the responsibility squarely on them.

Q.—You think that relieves the stockholder or Director of any responsibility for the management of that company? A.—I do not know of any way in which a company can be run except by putting the responsibility upon the officers, and then holding them to it, and seeing that they perform in a proper way the tasks imposed upon them.

Q.—Do you think there is a difference between a man who represents his own interests or somebody else's interests, which he is willing to turn over to a third party in the management of a company? A.—Do you mean, does it make any difference in his responsibility?

Q.—In his responsibility. A.—Not the slightest. I hold myself just as responsible as though I owned this stock myself.

Q.—You do not consider yourself a dummy Director in the Colorado Fuel and Iron Company? A.—I do not.

Q.—But you do represent some one else, and not yourself? A.—I do, because since his retirement from business some fifteen years ago, my father has given no personal attention to the conduct of any of the private businesses in which he is an investor.

Q.—And you have attended no meetings of the Board of Directors since this strike started in Colorado? A.—I have not, but I have kept in close touch with the affairs of the company.

As to Guns and Ammunition.

When Chairman Foster asked Mr. Rockefeller what he knew about "the purchase of guns and ammunition in Colorado," Mr. Rockefeller said he knew nothing about it. He said he had not the slightest idea whether his company had bought any guns or ammunition.

"How much has this strike cost your company directly?" asked Chairman Foster.

"I do not know definitely," replied the witness. "Mr. Bowers told me it was estimated that before the end of the fiscal year the loss resulting from the strike would be in the vicinity of $1,000,000."

Q.—You do not know directly how much it has cost you? A.—I can only know what he said. If he says that is his opinion, I presume it is as good a guess as any one could make.

Q.—I will give you the information that he has testified that directly it has cost your company $250,000. Do you know whether a considerable sum of money has been spent for guns and ammunition? A.—I have not the slightest idea whether any part of that money was spent for that.

Q.—Do you know there have been imported into Colorado from West Virginia the machine guns that were used in the West Virginia strike? A.—I do not.

Q.—What do you think about that? A.—If the local authorities in Colorado have not been able to provide adequate protection for the employes of the Colorado Fuel and Iron Company, I should regard it as the first duty of the officials of the company to provide such protection.

Q.—Buy machine guns? A.—I would not undertake to suggest to them how to do it.

Q.—To buy plenty of guns and plenty of ammunition? A.—I would not undertake to suggest to them how to do it, but I would say, Be sure you protect our men who are faithful to us.

Q.—As a Director, did you authorize the expenditure of this money for guns and ammunition? A.—No, it would not come to us to authorize any expenditure for the conduct of the strike. That is left in the hands of the officers.

Q.—Did you authorize the employment of the Baldwin-Felts detectives? A.—I have never heard of anything of the kind. All these matters have been cared for by the officers.

Q.—You do not know what this money has been spent for? A.—Except that I know it has been spent in proper ways, to conserve the interests of the employes.

Asked whether the officers of the company had ever taken any interest in Colorado politics, Mr. Rockefeller replied:

"I should hope that the officers of any company in which I was interested would, as citizens, take a very active interest in the politics of the country in which they live."

Chairman Foster wanted to know how many liquor saloons there were on the Rockefeller Colorado property.

"I have not the slightest idea," said Mr. Rockefeller. "I should hope there are not any."

"Does your company own the saloon buildings?"

Dealing With the Liquor Evil.

"I do not know that, but I know that when I was in Colorado one of the things that interested me most was to see the earnest efforts which had been made by the then officials of the company to deal with the liquor question. They realized that the employes, being largely foreigners, were in the habit of drinking, and their study was to see how the liquor evil should be reduced to a minimum; and they tried different methods of handling that.

"One method was to have a saloon in which the bartender was paid a salary and received no commission on the drinks. Another that interested me deeply was the establishing in several places of clubs for the employes, of which the local officials of the company and the employes themselves were officers. In these clubs drinks were served; treating was not allowed, and drinks were not allowed to be sold to a man that was under the influence of liquor in any degree. In those various towns the officers have studied with the utmost care to see how they might reduce to a minimum the evils of intemperance among the men."

Mr. Rockefeller told the committee he did not know whether the company or an outside individual held the licenses for the saloons, and, when asked why he had never looked into that, said he had absolute confidence in the men in charge, knew their views and felt satisfied they were doing "the very best that can be done in the common interest."

Mr. Foster asked Mr. Rockefeller whether he had built any churches "out there." The witness answered that there was reference in the correspondence to the church which was recently built, and another which was built by the company, and another which was undergoing repairs when the strike began, but that other than that he had no information.

Mr. Foster wanted to know whether Mr. Rockefeller was aware of the charge that the schools were crowded and that the children received insufficient privileges. Mr. Rockefeller answered that it would be somewhat surprising to him if that were true, because the officers of the company had not only provided school facilities, but the very best teachers obtainable, according to his information from the officers. Asked whether there were any high schools in the Rockefeller mining camps, the witness said he did not know.

"Well," eclaimed Mr. Foster, "you have not. I can tell you that."

Q.—The miners who work for the company are compelled to rent your property? A.—They are not compelled to work for the company.

Q.—I say, if they work they are compelled? A.—If they work they must live somewhere, and you say all the land is owned by the company. Where could they live?

Knew Nothing of Company Checks.

Q.—Do you think that's the way to conduct an industrial concern? A.—Certainly; we must house the men somewhere.

Q.—Do you know that in these incorporated towns usually the store manager is the Postmaster? A.—I think that is usually true in most small towns, is it not, whether they are mining camps or otherwise?

Q.—That is the condition out there. Do you know your company up to a short time ago—it is claimed it is stopped now—was issuing company checks in competition with the Government in issuing postal money orders, so that your company has been getting a profit out of that? A.—I do not.

Q.—That is true, Mr. Rockefeller. It is claimed it was stopped last Fall, but it was done up to the time this investigation began. A lot of these conditions have gone on there which you know nothing about? A.—It would be inevitably so.

Q.—Do you not think, Mr. Rockefeller, it was your duty to know just what the conditions were? A.—We have often thought that the companies in which we were interested were somewhat favored investments, and we have usually found that employes of such companies were about as happy, about as contented, and about as well treated as any employes.

Chairman Foster told Mr. Rockefeller that "they had a strike out in Colorado about once every ten years," whereupon Mr. Rockefeller retorted that 90 per cent. of the employes were not in favor of the present strike, adding without raising his voice:

"Sometimes one has a burglary, but is it one's fault? I know that there was a strike ten or about a dozen years ago brought about the same way. There are no mining camps in this country where there have been less trouble and fewer strikes than in the camps owned by the Colorado Fuel and Iron Company. I think that must inevitably reflect very creditably upon the Directors and management."

When the Chairman asked Mr. Rockefeller if he knew anything about an automobile being protected with armor plate by his company, he responded: "It sounds very interesting, but I have not heard of it."

"It was built," said Chairman Foster, "in the shops of the Colorado Fuel and Iron Company."

"I did not know they produced automobiles as well," said Mr. Rockefeller.

"They put machine guns on it, going around through the country," said Mr. Foster.

The Duty of Employers.

Mr. Foster said that when the militia was ordered out many of the mine guards were sworn into the service of the State and kept on the payrolls of the Colorado Fuel & Iron Company. Asked whether he thought that made the militia a non-partisan preserver of the peace, Mr. Rockefeller said:

"If the local authorities in any community were unable or did not render adequate protection to the workers, it was the duty of the employers of the laborers to supplement that protection in any way they could."

When asked whether he thought it was better to swear in the mine guards as part of the militia than to get them outside, Mr. Rockefeller said he would not undertake "to form an opinion as against the opinion of the Governor of the State."

"All this disturbance and loss of life—killing upon both sides—out there has not been of enough importance to you to cause you to say, 'Let us have a meeting of the Directors,' and find out more about it?" asked Mr. Foster.

"I have been so greatly interested in the matter and have such a warm sympathy for this very large number of men that work for us that I should be the last one to surrender the liberty under which they have been working and the conditions which to them have been entirely satisfactory to give up that liberty and accept dictation from those outside who have no interest in them or in the company."

Q.—But the killing of people and shooting of children has not that been of enough importance to you for you to communicate with the other Directors and see if something might be done to end that sort of thing? A.—We believe the issue is not a local one in Colorado. It is a national issue whether workers shall be allowed to work under such conditions as they may choose. As part owners of the property our interest in the laboring men in this country is so immense, so deep, so profound that we stand ready to lose every cent we put in that company rather than see the men we have employed thrown out of work and have imposed upon them conditions which dare not of their seeking and which neither they nor we can see are in our interest.

Q.—You are willing to let these willings take place rather than to go there and do something to settle conditions. A.—There is just one thing that can be done to settle this strike, and that is to unionize the camps, and our interest in labor is so profound and we believe so sincerely that that interest demands that the camps shall be open camps, that we expect to stand by the officers at any cost. It is not an accident that this is our position—

Q.—And you will do that if that costs all your property and kills all your employees? A.—It is a great principle.

Q.—And you would do that rather than recognize the right of men in collective bargaining? A.—No, Sir—rather than allow outside people to come in and interfere with employes who are thoroughly satisfied with their labor conditions. It was upon a similar principle that the War of the Revolution was carried on. It is a great national issue of the most vital kind.

45 DEAD, 20 HURT, SCORE MISSING, IN STRIKE WAR

Women and Children Roasted in Pits of Tent Colony as Flames Destroy It.

HID FROM HAIL OF BULLETS

Miners' Store of Ammunition and Dynamite Exploded, Scattering Death and Ruin.

TO RESUME BATTLE TO-DAY

Men from Other Union Camps Join Fighters in Hills to Avenge Their Slain.

MILITIA TROOP HEMMED IN

Decisive Engagement Planned by the Soldiers, Who Are Preparing a Machine Gun Sortie.

Special to The New York Times.

TRINIDAD, Col., April 21.—Forty-five dead, more than two-thirds of them women and children, a score missing, and more than a score wounded, is the result known to-night of the fourteen-hour battle which raged with uninterrupted fury yesterday between State troops and striking coal miners in the Ludlow district, on the property of the Colorado Fuel and Iron Company, the Rockefeller holdings.

The Ludlow camp is a mass of charred débris, and buried beneath it is a story of horror unparalleled in the history of industrial warfare. In the holes which had been dug for their protection against the rifles' fire the women and children died like trapped rats when the flames swept over them. One pit, uncovered this afternoon, disclosed the bodies of ten children and two women. Further exploration was forbidden by the position of the camp, which lies directly between the militia and the strikers' positions.

To Resume Battle at Dawn.

With arms ready, both sides after a day of ominous quiet, now await the coming of dawn, when, it is predicted, the battle will be resumed with greater bloodshed than that which has occurred. The militia, which yesterday drove the strikers from their tent colony, and, it is charged, fired it, involving thereby the greatest loss of lives, are preparing for a machine gun sortie at daybreak from their position along the Colorado & Southern Railroad tracks at each side of the Ludlow Station.

On the surrounding hills, sheltered by rocks and boulders, 400 strikers await their coming, while their ranks are being swelled by grim faced men who tramped overland in the dark, carrying guns and ammunition from the neighboring union camps.

Italian, Greek and Austrian miners have appealed to their consular representatives for protection, and John McLennan, President of the local union district, wired the Red Cross in Denver to-day to be prepared to render aid.

On the outcome of the engagement to-morrow may depend the fate of the strike. Both sides face it as a battle to the death with no thought of quarter asked or received. At a late hour it was said here that the battle could only be averted by the arrival of overwhelming reinforcements for the troops of Denver.

Both strikers and militia have a plentiful supply of ammunition on hand. Five thousand rounds were run into the troops at Ludlow on a Colorado & Southern train from Denver early this morning, and this supply was later supplemented by a shipment from Trinidad. The strikers, by the seizure of an engine in the Denver & Rio Grande yards at El Moro, were also able to replenish their stock at Barnes.

The militia number 200. Detachments from Walsenburg and Lamar got through the lines early yesterday. They occupy a line approximately three miles in length.

No train service through the war zone is permitted. A command of the troops is hemmed in on all sides by the strikers' lines, which extend back three miles. Through this cordon only the dead wagon is allowed to pass.

In Trinidad the situation is no less acute. Men throng the streets about the union headquarters and demand guns with which to work vengeance upon the militia, whom they hold responsible for the destruction of their homes and the death of their women and children.

Throughout the day yesterday and intermittently during the night the fighting raged over an area of approximately three square miles, bounded on the west by Berwind and Hastings, on the east by Barnes Station, on the north by the Ludlow tent colony, and on the south by Rameyville. The battlefield was completely isolated by the cutting of telegraph and telephone wires.

Within the doomed camp last night explosions of cartridges which had been stored there by the miners added to the horror of the flames which swept over it amid a hail of lead with which the soldiers raked the tents.

An unidentified man driving a horse attached to a light buggy dashed from the tents waving a white flag, just after the fire started. When ordered to halt he opened fire with a revolver and was killed by a return volley from the militia.

Terrified by the bullets which whistled through the blazing canvas above their heads, the women and children apparently more afraid of the lead than the flames, remained huddled in their pits until the smoke and heat carried death to them.

Some, braver than the rest, ran into the open and dashed aimlessly among the two hundred tents, which by that time, had become so many torches which swirled their fire and sparks and lighted the scene with ghastly brilliancy.

Two women dashed toward the militia position.

"Dynamite," they screamed.

An instant later the ammunition remaining in the camp exploded sending a shower of lead in all directions.

A seven-year-old girl dashed from under a blazing tent and heard the scream of bullets about her ears. Insane from fright, she ran into a tent again and fell into the hole with the remainder of her family to die with them. The child is said to have been a daughter of Charles Costa, a union leader at Aguilar, who perished with his wife and another child.

Instances of individual heroism were numerous. James Fyler, financial secretary of the Trinidad local union and a witness in the recent Congressional investigation, died with a bullet in his forehead as he was attempting to rescue his wife from the flames.

A bystander, Premo Larsie, 18, son of Louis Larsie, a Trinidad brewery worker, was among the first to fall. On his way from Ludlow to Hastings to visit a friend he paused to witness the encounter, which had just started. A bullet struck him in the head.

Lewis Tikas, leader of the Greek colony and one of the most prominent organizers in the district, was shot as he attempted to lead a group of women away from the camp in the direction of an arroya which offered shelter. According to witnesses of his death, Tikas threw up his arms to show that he carried no weapons. The troopers yelled at him to run, and shot him as he fled.

In an effort to rescue his sister from danger, Frank Snyder, 10 years old, son of William Snyder, a striker, met death in the colony later in the afternoon. The girl ventured from the pit where the family had taken refuge. The boy jumped out to draw her back and a bullet struck him in the back of the head, killing him instantly.

When it appeared that no more men remained in the colony the militia ceased firing and went to the work of rescue. Women ran from the burning tents, some with their clothing afire, carrying their babies in their arms. Many, in order to save the babies at their breasts, were forced to abandon their older children to their fate. Among these was Mrs. Marcelina Pedragon. With her light skirt ablaze in several places she carried her youngest child to the open, but left two others behind. Hope for them has been abandoned.

Trembling, hysterical, some apparently dazed, the women were escorted by the troops to the Ludlow, where they were held until this morning, when a Colorado & Southern train brought them into Trinidad. In the haste of departure families became separated. Efforts to unite them by the United Mine Workers in many instances proved in vain.

The camp was abandoned to its fate following the departure of the women, and for hours the light of the fire lit the sky a bright red. By its light the strikers retreated to the arroyas back of the colony and to the surrounding hills. The camp fell at 8:30, just fourteen hours after the fight commenced.

Denies Soldiers Fired the Camp.

Major Hamrock denied to-night that his men had started the conflagration.

"It started spontaneously, apparently, from the west end of the camp and spread through the flimsy structures like wildfire. When that occurred my men were at quite a distance and could have had nothing whatsoever to do with it."

He placed the responsibility for the opening of the engagement upon the strikers, who, he said, fired first upon the militia encampment from the hills. This was denied at union headquarters, where it was said the militia opened hostilities with the machine guns.

He also reiterated the statement that the fighting was precipitated by a band of Greek strikers under Louis Tikas, who opened fire upon military tents at Ludlow. Tikas, he added, had promised a few minutes previously to go out among a party of strikers that had entrenched in an arroyo west of the colony and induce them to disarm.

The soldiers were driven out of their camp by bullets, according to the officer. Later, he said, the strikers moved around back of the colony and took a position along the Colorado & Southeastern tracks and attacked Lieut. Linderfelt's detachment.

The first wagon load of five bodies was brought in late this afternoon and a second wagon load is expected to-night. Among the bodies is that of Private A. Martin of Company A. Officers of the militia charge that though merely wounded in the neck, Martin, who lay where the strikers subsequently passed by him, was shot in the side of the head and through the mouth as he lay wounded on the round. The charge is denied by officials of the union.

Trinidad is horror stricken by reports of the number of women, children, and non-combatants who lost their lives in the fight and in the fire that followed.

"It is horrible," said John McLennan, President of District No. 15 of the United Mine Workers of America, who is in charge at local headquarters. "They were trapped without a chance of escape. The bodies of two women and ten children were seen in one trench, it was announced at the Ludlow military camp to-night. God only knows how many yet will be found."

More than 200 women and children refugees from the burned colony are being cared for here. The hall of the Trinidad Trades Assembly has been turned into a temporary dormitory and hospital. Many are suffering from burns and injuries. Food and bedding are being provided by the union.

TRUCE DECLARED IN MINERS' WAR

Governor Appeals for Federal Aid and Is Told Troops Can't Be Spared.

STRIKERS FLEE TO HILLS

Lynn and Aguilar Occupied by Gen. Chase After One Bloodless Skirmish.

MINE DEFENDERS RELIEVED

Result of Five Days' Strife Probable Total of 60 Killed and Property Damage of $1,000,000.

Foster Would Arbitrate.

By Telegraph to the Editor of The New York Times.

WASHINGTON, April 24.—Statements are conflicting. I am unable to tell who is to blame. It seems there should be some means to arbitrate the differences, whatever they may be, between the operators and employes and save the loss of life and property. It is deplorable that such conditions should exist. I hope that a peaceful settlement may come soon. M. D. FOSTER.

The above dispatch from the Chairman of the House Committee on Mines, which has been investigating conditions in the coal and copper regions of Colorado and Michigan, was sent in reply to a request for an expression of his opinion on the strike war in Colorado.

Special to The New York Times.

DENVER, Col., April 24.—A truce was declared here this evening in the industrial war which for five days has virtually paralyzed the State, caused a loss of life that probably will be found to total sixty, and destruction of property estimated at upward of $1,000,000 in value.

Gov. Ammons arrived in Denver to-night from Washington. While en route he called on the Federal Government for troops to aid in settling the strike situation in Colorado, and to-night received answer that the War Department could spare no soldiers for this purpose. This answer was conveyed in a telegram signed by Congressman Edward Taylor.

Acting Governor Fitzgerald and Horace N. Hawkins, attorney for the United Mine Workers of America, made the agreement for the truce after a conference in which State Auditor Kenehan and Justice George W. Musher of the Supreme Court participated.

The terms of the truce were contained in a telegram read to Gen. Chase over the telephone in the presence of Mr. Hawkins, attorney for the United Mine Workers of America. It follows:

Release John McLennan at once. There will be no shooting by either side. Indefinite truce is on. We must observe it. Go no farther south than Lynn.

John McLennan is President of the State Federal Union of Labor and district of the United Mine Workers of America. He had been arrested to-day near Ludlow by the militia under Major P. J. Hamrock.

Seat of Mining War in Colorado.

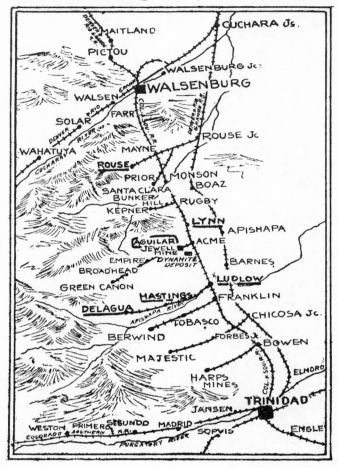

"His release was requested," explained Mr. Hawkins, "as we need his aid in any steps taken to avert further bloodshed. It was also understood that I should call union headquarters throughout the State and notify them of the agreement and urge that any hostile steps contemplated be abandoned. This I did."

Interest to-day centred in the progress of the troop train sent from Denver to the Ludlow district. One thousand armed strikers met last night to halt the progress of the train. A dispute over the exact point upon which to make the attack, coupled with precautions taken by Gen. John Chase, in command, prevented a battle.

Part of the miners went to Lynn. These belonged to the Aguilar camp. The Ludlow men wanted to intercept the train at a point nearer Trinidad. As a result, the forces were divided. Gen. Chase, fearful of dynamite explosions, held the troop train at Walsenburg, twenty-six miles this side of Ludlow, until daybreak, and when the soldiers appeared on foot, having detrained six miles away, the strikers at Lynn retreated. They are believed to be intrenched with the rest of the miners' army in the Black Hills, near Ludlow.

TRINIDAD, Colo., April 24.—State troops under command of Adj. Gen. John Chase advanced to-night toward Ludlow after occupying Lynn and Aguilar without resistance. At Aguilar the militiamen released the company men, who had been imprisoned in the Empire Mine and Southwestern mines since Wednesday. All the prisoners, including J. W. Siple, President of the Southwestern Fuel Company, were said to be alive and unharmed.

The whereabouts of the strikers, who this morning suddenly abandoned their plan of resisting the troops at Lynn, was not definitely known. It was generally believed, however, that they executed the manoeuvre began early in the day and massed their forces in the Black Hills, about 2 miles north of Ludlow.

The bloodless capture of the strikers' capital at Aguilar was effected several hours after a brief skirmish near Bunker Hill, on the way from Walsenburg. This fight was between an advance force of about seventy mounted militiamen and a party of strikers. After a brisk exchange of shots, with no casualties reported, the strikers retreated. The main body of State troops son afterward reached Lynn. No strikers were found there or at Aguilar.

The territory into which the troops penetrated, and which for two days has been practically controlled by the strikers, extends northwest and southeast for about fifteen miles. At its widest point it is perhaps four miles in extent. The zone is bounded on the south by Ludlow, where the station and immediate surrounding territory have been held by militia since the battle of Monday. On the north is Rouse, where a strongly fortified mine of the Colorado Fuel and Iron Company offered an effective barrier. To the southwest is the Hastings Canyon, where on Wednesday the strikers were beaten back in a sharp brush with guards and militiamen.

Throughout this district until the arrival of the State troops the martial rule of the strikers was supreme, except at the mines where besieged defenders held out desperately after the aboveground works had been burned. Strike leaders in command of a force of men estimated as high as 1,000, held absolute sway over that portion of the population which had not fled to the hills.

A train which reached Trinidad last night was crowded with refugees from the centre of the disturbed district. Many families have also fled to neighboring ranches and other towns out of the strike zone.

The town's water supply is cut off by the destruction of the pumping plant, which also supplied the camps at Hastings, Delagua, and Berwind. Similar conditions exist in probably a dozen mining camps in Huerafano and Las Animas Counties.

Fifteen hundred men, women and children crowded in front of the Holy Trinity Church to-day while open air funeral services were held for fourteen victims of the Ludlow fire. Two heavy trucks draped in black conveyed the flower laden caskets from the morgue to the church and Catholic cemetery.

The aged father of Charles Costa, who with his wife and two children were killed last Monday, created a demonstration at the morgue by a violent verbal attack on the Colorado militia.

Separate services will be held for Louis Tikas, leader of the Greek strikers who was killed.

STRIKERS VETERANS OF BALKAN WAR

Can't Speak English and Have Been Made Anarchists by Labor Leaders, Says J. S. Osgood.

THINK THEY OWN MINES

Colorado Fuel and Iron Co. Founder Gives History of the Troubles in the Mine Districts.

J. C. Osgood, founder and for many years President of the Colorado Fuel and Iron Company and now Chairman of the Board of Directors of the Victor American Fuel Company, whose principal mines are in the section of Colorado in which the strikers and the militia are battling, gave yesterday the history of the troubles and their causes.

In reviewing the situation in southern Colorado, with which he has been keeping in touch by telegraph, Mr. Osgood, who is at the Vanderbilt, charged that all the violence and lawlessness that have taken place have been instigated by the leaders of the United Mine Workers. The majority of the people in the tent colonies are Italians, Greeks, Bulgarians, and Montenegrins, many of the last three nationalities veterans of the Balkan wars. They have been turned into anarchists, Mr. Osgood says, by labor agitators who have taught them that the mines really belong to them and that they cannot be punished for anything they do. Many of the men with the strikers, according to Mr. Osgood, have been imported from West Virginia and other States for the prime purpose of fighting.

"The coal mines of Colorado have been operated for the last thirty years, since mining has been conducted on any considerable scale, on the open shop basis, employing union and non-union men indiscriminately, but not having any contract with labor organizations," said Mr. Osgood. "During this period there have been but two general strikes—the so-called 'Debbs' strike in 1894, which was nation-wide, and a strike in the Fall of 1903 called by the United Mine Workers of America under the Presidency of John Mitchell. This strike was a failure in the largest portion of the State and was called off in the following May. At this time, however, the mines of northern Colorado, producing about 15 per cent. of the coal tonnage of the State, signed contracts with the United Mine Workers of America, and for the following six years attempted to work under such contracts, but with frequent strikes and interruptions.

Declined to Renew Contract.

"At the end of that time, the operators declined to renew the contract with the Union, and procured non-union labor sufficient to operate their mines to their full capacity. The resulting strike on the part of the members of the United Mine Workers of America has been kept in force since

that time, and the existing strike in Colorado was called by the United Mine Workers of America as a State-wide strike on Sept. 23, when the northern Colorado strike had become hopeless. The labor organizers established tent colonies in close proximity to the mines for the occupation of the striking miners and their families. Violence was commenced the day following the calling of the strike and has been continued by the strikers ever since.

"In the testimony given before the Congressional Investigation Committee, evidence was introduced showing that the officers of the United Mine Workers had purchased ammunition and arms, and shipped them into the district a week prior to the beginning of the strike. Violence continued and increased to such an extent that on October 23 Gov. Ammons was obliged to call out the entire State militia.

"With the protection of the militia, many of the men who had gone on strike returned to work and with these and men procured elsewhere the operators were enabled to produce all the coal required by the demands of the market. The troops under command of Adjt. Gen. Chase acted with energy and great discretion in maintaining order, as evidenced by the fact that although they were frequently attacked, and sorely tried at times, not a single striker was killed or seriously injured.

"The State of Colorado had no fund from which to pay the troops or their expenses, but public-spirited merchants and bankers of the State cashed the warrants to a large extent for that purpose. It became difficult, however, for Gov. Ammons to obtain funds to maintain the troops in the field, and in the early part of March he began to withdraw them gradually.

Acts of Violence Resumed.

As the troops were withdrawn, acts of violence were resumed by the strikers. The largest camp established by the strikers was at Ludlow, from one to two miles from the mouths of canyons in which were situated some of the largest mines in the State. The high ridges surrounding these canyons, covered with heavy underbrush, gave an excellent opportunity for the strikers in small bands to take positions overlooking the mines, from which they would shoot into the camps for the purpose of killing and intimidating the men who were working and their families. A small detachment of troops was left at Ludlow to prevent as far as possible these attacks on the part of strikers.

The number of men remaining on strike was approximately 2,000, or 15 per cent. of the total number of men working in the State at the time the strike was called. The remaining men who went on strike have either returned to work or left the State. The majority of the men remaining in the Ludlow and other tent colonies, are foreigners, most of whom do not speak the English language, and include Italians, Greeks, Bulgarians, and Montenegrins. Many of these men are veterans of the Balkan War and accustomed to the use of firearms, and the Greeks particularly have been among the leaders in the violence which has occurred during the strike.

"These ignorant foreigners have practically been made anarchists by the labor organizers and agitators sent among them by the officers of the United Mine Workers of America. They have been led to believe that the mines really belong to them and that the organization behind them is so powerful that they cannot be punished for any acts of violence they commit. Many of the men now in these camps have never worked in the mines of Colorado, but have been brought there as fighting men by the labor leaders from West Virginia and other sections.

Start of the Present Conflict.

"On Monday, April 20, a small body of militia, seventeen in number, attempted to intercept some of the strikers who were trying to get on to the ridges overlooking the coal camps. They were fired on by the strikers who outnumbered them at least five to one, and found that they were surrounded on all sides. Under command of Capt. Linderfeldt, who had formerly been in the United States Army, they succeeded in repulsing the strikers, who retreated to their tent colony, from which they continued to fire on the militia which, by this time, had been reinforced. In some manner which has not yet been investigated or explained, a fire started in the tent colony at a point furthest remote from where the militia was stationed. This fire spread rapidly and practically destroyed the colony. Some of the women and children who had taken refuge in caves prepared for the purpose, were smothered to death by smoke from this fire.

"It is of course possible that the rifle fire of the militia may have set fire to the tents through the explosion of ammunition which they contained in large quantities, particularly the private tent occupied by John Lawson, strike leader. The strikers have attempted to gain sympathy for their cause by claiming that the militia fired on defenseless women and children, and were responsible for the deaths of those who were smothered. Of course, with fair-minded people the responsibility of the strikers themselves is apparent. In attacking the militia from their tent colony, they must have expected that their fire would be returned, putting their woman and children at jeopardy. The militia knew that every tent contained a rifle pit, and that there were caves and other places where the women could be placed for safety in the event of a fight, and had no reason to suppose that any women or children were exposed to their fire.

"The final result of this fight was the dispersal of the strikers, with considerable loss of life on both sides. The strikers scattered into the hills, where they received reinforcements from all the camps in the district, and on the following day, commencing at daybreak, attacked the mining camp at Delagua, firing into the houses where there were defenceless women and children. This attack resulted in the death of five of the employes of the company and an unknown number of the strikers. On Wednesday and Thursday, with constantly increasing numbers, they attacked the mining camps in the immediate vicinity, killing and destroying property to an extent not yet fully known.

"At the Empire mine, near Aguilar, the officials and employes when fired upon retreated into the mine for protection. The strikers dynamited the entrance to the mine, thus imprisoning them and burned down the surrounding buildings, including the ventilating shaft and fan, with the expectation of suffocating the occupants of the mine. Latest reports, however, seem to indicate that they did not succeed in this purpose. In the absence of the Governor, the Lieut. Governor called out the militia the second time, and they arrived in the strike zone this morning.

Labor Leaders Blamed.

"All of the violence and lawlessness have been instigated by the leaders of the United Mine Workers, who are morally responsible for the present condition of anarchy. The purpose for which the strike was called, out of which this violence has grown, was to force the operators to sign contracts with the union and employ only union labor, discharging any of their own employes who did not care to join the union.

"Wages in Colorado are higher than in any of the unionized States. Mining and living conditions are as good, or better, than elsewhere. It has been necessary for the operators to pay such wages and furnish such conditions as would enable them to procure a sufficient amount of labor from mining States east of them, which are nearer to the ports where immigrants arrive, and which is the only source from which labor can be procured for the constant growth of the coal mining business of the State. In employing non-English speaking immigrants the operators are not acting from choice, but necessity."

"What outcome do you expect?" Mr. Osgood was asked.

"The Adjutant General of the State, Gen. Chase, is a very efficient officer," he replied. "I believe he will be able to regain control of the situation."

Gen. Sherman Bell, former Adjutant General of Colorado, who settled the famous Cripple Creek strike about nine years ago, also is at the Vanderbilt, but when seen yesterday declined to speak of present conditions in Colorado. It is said by friends of Gen. Bell that as a result of his work in pacifying that part of Colorado he had to fight suits aggregating $2,100,000, which were carried all the way to the Supreme Court of the United States, where he finally won out, and that the cost of defending himself swallowed up a modest fortune.

FROM THE WORKERS' SIDE.

An Analysis of the Strike Conditions from Prof. Seligman.

Prof. R. A. Seligman, of Columbia University, has written for the current number of The Annalist, out to-day, an analysis of the industrial and social conditions which brought about the present crisis in Colorado. After reviewing the seven demands of the strikers he says that five of them are guaranteed under severe penalty by the laws of Colorado, but the miners contend that these laws were never enforced.

"Whether that is so or not," says Prof. Seligman, "is it not a very remarkable commentary on the state of American civilization that individuals should be compelled to resort to a strike in order to enforce laws which it is the obligation of the employers to obey and the State to enforce?"

Prof. Seligman characterizes the attempt of the operators to defend some of these extra legal practices as far from ingenuous. "Thus," he says, "we are told that in one of the mining camps only 22 per cent. of the wages of the men were expended in the company's stores; but we are not told what happened in all the other camps; nor that according to our Federal statistics the average expenditure for food of a workman receiving $1,200 a year is 36 per cent. of his wages—so that even in this single camp the company's stores swallowed about two-thirds of a miner's average expenditure for goods ordinarily bought at such stores; nor are we told that such company stores have universally earned the name of 'pluck-me' stores and have everywhere else fallen under the ban of enlightened public opinion.

"It is claimed by the operators that this is a fight against the closed shop, whereas in reality it is a fight against the recognition of the union. The two things are by no means the same. The closed shop means that none but union men may be employed; the recognition of the union means that the employers should consent to discuss matters of common interest with the representatives of the union. Under conditions of complete freedom these would normally in a short time represent most of the workers. If any of the workers, however, desire to remain out of the union, the favorable conditions obtained by the union representatives would nevertheless apply to them. The existing protocol in the clothing industry in New York shows that the recognition of the union does not necessarily imply a closed shop.

"The question is asked by the operators, Why should mines be unionized when only 10 per cent. of the men belong to the union? The reply is obvious. Do the union men number 10 per cent. because only 10 per cent. sympathize with the union or because 90 per cent. are either ignorant of what the union means or afraid to lose their jobs if they show any active interest in the union? And what would happen to the 90 per cent. if all the employes were actually given complete liberty to participate in union activities, and if collective bargaining became the rule?"

With reference to the acts of violence, Prof. Seligman admits, there is unfortunately not much to choose between the workmen and the operators. Human nature is about the same in all classes, and, given sufficient provocation on one side or the other, violence is bound to ensue. It is well worth while, however, he says, to compare the bitter and incendiary language used in the recent letter of the coal operators, refusing to arbitrate, with the expressions employed by the officials of the union.

His conclusion is that too much stress is placed upon the sacredness of a "principle" which has been abandoned almost everywhere else in the coal fields of England and of the United States, and the disappearance of which is leading toward industrial peace and social progress.

FILES ROCKEFELLER LETTERS ON STRIKE

Commission Puts Correspondence on Record, Perhaps for Foundation Inquiry.

WAS PLEASED AT ELECTION

Said Colorado Result Indicated Victory for "Law and Order"—Foundation Incorporators Were Active.

Special to The New York Times.

DENVER, Dec. 12.—It is believed here by persons who have followed closely the hearings of the Federal Commission on Industrial Relations that the huge volume of communications between President Jesse F. Welborn of the Colorado Fuel and Iron Company and John D. Rockefeller, Jr., and his associates will figure in the proposed investigation of the Rockefeller Foundation planned by the commission. There are 8,000 words in all in the telegrams and letters, and all were read into the record of the commission now investigating the causes of the great coal strike.

The line of questions propounded to Mr. Welborn by Chairman Frank P. Walsh and other members of the commission indicated a belief that these men hold the Rockefeller Foundation and allied corporate interests responsible for the uncompromising resistance to recognition of the miners' union.

The chief figures in the correspondence are J. D. Rockefeller, Jr., J. H. McClement, Starr J. Murphy, and Jerome D. Greene, all Directors of the Colorado Fuel & Iron Company. Messrs. Rockefeller, Murphy, and Greene are incorporators of the Rockefeller Foundation.

Beginning with May 23, 1914, the letters and telegrams cover a period of six months, the last being dated Nov. 24, 1914. The first letter read into the record was one from Mr. Welborn to J. H. McClement, dated at Denver. Following is an extract:

The general press reports have been very incorrect, and in many cases absolutely false. I assume, however, that you saw a copy of the operators' telegram to Dr. Foster, (referring to Chairman of Congressional Committee,) in reply to one he sent Mr. Rockefeller April 29, which was handled by the Associated Press. I am, however, inclosing a copy of this, together with copy of second telegram sent Dr. Foster, supplementing the first; also copy of a telegram to President Wilson and signed by all of the principal operators except the C. F. & I. Co.

On May 26 Mr. McClement replied to this letter, saying that he had read the clippings with great interest, and that several of them had not been published in Eastern newspapers. He also expressed a desire to know what the mines were doing. Under date of May 27 Mr. Welborn wrote an extended review to Mr. McClement of the battles at Ludlow and vicinity between the coal mine strikers and the militia. After describing the opening of the Ludlow engagement, he wrote:

Reinforcements were obtained from two troops just previously organized at Trinidad and Walsenburg and made up of mine employes. The wisdom of having enlisted men available cannot be questioned.

After describing other incidents Mr. Welborn says regarding Lieut. Gov. Fitzgarrald:

Under heavy pressure we induced the Lieutenant Governor, in the absence of Gov. Ammons on a trip to Washington, to order the militia back into the field. Before they reached the real trouble zone, however, the Lieutenant Governor had established a truce with the attorney representing the United Mine Workers, under one of the conditions of which the militia were not to move south of Ludlow, and that the strikers would cease their attacks on the militia and mine property. This truce was, in my judgement, nothing short of a conspiracy, and I so informed the Lieutenant Governor when he told me about it.

In the same letter further on, he says:

Early in the morning of Wednesday, the 29th, assistance was given us from the military force that had been established at Ludlow, which is about twenty-five miles south of Walsenburg, and maintained there under the peace pact. These men were under what I consider a very incompetent Colonel, and his work was of a very negative character. * * * After the establishment of the truce, Dr. Lester, engaged in treating a wounded soldier and wearing the Red Cross badge, was killed. Because of what I consider the cowardice of the Colonel, his body was not recovered until 9 o'clock that night.

The policy of the Federal troops is not satisfactory to us. They will not permit us to bring in any men from outside the State. * * * I am sure they are obtaining valuable information, and that in a general way they know where the guns which the strikers failed to deliver are hidden. They are, however, unquestionably acting under directions from Washington and without authority to search for arms until specifically ordered by Washington to do so.

Under date of May 30, from 26 Broadway, New York, John D. Rockefeller, Jr., wrote to Mr. Welborn:

I am sending you, under separate cover, a copy of my testimony before the Committee of the House on Mines and Mining in Washington.

On June 3, Mr. Rockefeller wrote to Mr. Welborn from New York calling his attention to an inclosed letter and in reply, on June 8, Mr. Welborn wrote:

My Dear Mr. Rockefeller: I have yours of the 3d inst., inclosing a letter from Des Moines purporting to contain information of value concerning certain incidents in connection with the attacks on mines and employes last month. I think it advisable to learn more about this, and will take immediate steps to do so.

Reports on Ludlow.

On the following day Mr. Welborn wrote to Starr J. Murphy inclosing newspapers containing statement by two militia officers about the battle of Ludlow, as well as a blue print map of Ludlow and vicinity. Mr. Murphy replied to this on June 12, saying the statements in all essential particulars bore out those made by Major Boughton, but were more valuable as they were from eye-witnesses. In another letter to Mr. Murphy, June 16, Mr. Welborn introduced the Rev. R. E. Chandler of Trinidad, saying that Mr. Chandler had been a good friend to the Colorado Fuel and Iron Company.

John D. Rockefeller, Jr., on June 27 sent to Mr. Welborn a letter containing a report from a Burns detective he had employed to watch "Gen." John Brown, an I. W. W. leader who was driven away from Tarrytown, and Mr. Welborn, in reply, told of Brown's activities in Colorado as a fighter. On July 22 Mr. Welborn wrote to Mr. Rockefeller as follows:

Acting on the suggestion contained in yours of the 10th instant I have ordered from Mr. John H. Moore, (Commander in the United States Navy,) Chairman of the Committee of Information of Aliens, 3,300 copies of his pamphlet printed in various languages. We will use most of these at our own properties and I will find distribution for the remainder through some of the other companies.

Inquiries by Mr. Rockefeller.

From 26 Broadway, on Aug. 7, Mr. Rockefeller wrote to Mr. Welborn about a Colorado Springs labor newspaper which offered to publish the company's bulletins for a consideration and asked Mr. Welborn to investigate. He reported that the newspaper was of small circulation and influence and refused to advertise. Mr. Rockefeller, on Aug. 3, wrote to Mr. Welborn, inclosing a letter containing charges made by Lieut. Lawrence of the Colorado National Guard. Part of Mr. Welborn's reply said:

I have seen Mr. Lawrence only once, and that was on the occasion of his coming to my office to secure cash on his State warrant. I had a few moments' conversation with him at that time, when I took occasion to congratulate him on the good work he had done, and, unless I am mistaken, he expressed satisfaction at the treatment he had received at the hands of our employes in the district where he was stationed.

Mr. Welborn, on Oct. 2, sent to Mr. Rockefeller a copy of the original brief of the striking miners presented before the Congressional committee headed by Dr. Foster. Three days later, Starr J. Murphy, in reply to a letter of Oct. 1, wrote to Mr. Welborn thanking him for inclosing an editorial published by the Pueblo Star-Journal. In this article, Mr. Rockefeller was praised as a philanthropist, and the company's publicity methods were commended. Mr. Murphy wrote:

I have yours of Oct. 1 inclosing clipping from The Pueblo Star-Journal. This is fine, and shows how effective intelligent publicity can be. I hope it will be kept up.

On Oct. 8, some time after a series of conferences at Tarrytown and 26 Broadway, at which the Colorado situation and the world-wide plan of the Rockefeller Foundation for an investigation into industrial conditions had been discussed, Mackenzie King wrote to Mr. Welborn. In reply Mr. Welborn said:

Nothing of moment has developed in connection with our affairs since I left you in New York. I have a strong feeling, however, that Washington is not going to press the truce proposal any further without some material modification. Personally, of course, I hope they will not ask us to consider that particular plan in any modified form.

Mr. Welborn later testified that at the conferences in New York, which preceded his interview with President Wilson at the White House, there were present John D. Rockefeller, Sr., his son, Ivy Lee, King, Charles P. Neill, former United States Labor Commissioner and now with the Guggenheim smelting interests; McClement, Murphy, and Dr. Fred Gates.

On Oct. 31, replying to a letter from Starr J. Murphy relative to charges he had received from the wife of a minister at Sunrise, Wyo., Mr. Welborn promised to investigate, and said that he had thought of removing the minister, but had refrained from taking a course that would indicate a prejudice against him because of indiscreet statements he had made relative to the Ludlow affair.

On Nov. 6, three days after the State election, Mr. Welborn wrote to Mr. Rockefeller on the success of the Republican candidate for Governor, George A. Carlson, and the Democratic candidate for Attorney General, Fred Farrar. Of Mr. Farrar he said, among other things, "He has been about the only reliable force for law and order in the State House." In reply to this, on Nov. 24, Mr. Rockefeller wrote to Mr. Welborn as follows:

26 Broadway, New York,
Nov. 24, 1914.

Dear Mr. Welborn: I have just returned to the city after an absence of several weeks in the South with my wife and find your letter of Nov. 6 regarding the gratifying plurality of Carlson for Governor and Farrar for Attorney General. It would seem that the election of this Republican Governor and the re-election of this Democratic Attorney General, both of whom have established clear records as to their strong stand for law and order, would indicate that the sentiment of the people of Colorado is for law and order, quite irrespective of party lines.

Thank you for sending me this gratifying news. Very cordially,

JOHN D. ROCKEFELLER, Jr.

Among the letters are several referring to the payment of money to the members of the Colorado National Guard. On Nov. 10 Mr. Rockefeller sent to Mr. Welborn a letter from William Park Athey, a guardsman living at Holly, Col. Mr. Welborn, after turning the case over to E. H. Weitzel, general manager of the Colorado Fuel and Iron Company, wrote to Mr. Rockefeller in part as follows:

We have found it necessary to cash a good many of the certificates of indebtedness issued to members of the State Militia, or have considered it advisable to do so, and if this young man's circumstances are as he has stated them, I believe we should accommodate him.

I suggest, therefore, that you refer him to me, and by the time he receives your reply I will have learned enough about him to know whether or not we are justified in taking up his certificates.

These certificates are exchangeable for State warrants bearing 4 per cent. interest.

Mr. Rockefeller wrote to the young man along the lines suggested, while the Colorado Fuel and Iron Company investigated the case, which involved $41.

On the witness stand Mr. Welborn, in reply to questions by Chairman Walsh, said that the Colorado Fuel and Iron Company had taken up between $75,000 and $80,000 in certificates of indebtedness held by the militiamen. Part of this, he said, was paid in cash and part in merchandise provided for the militiamen by the company's stores.

Mr. Welborn caused to be read into the record a telegram to President Wilson, signed by fifteen or more coal operators, in which they assured the President that their refusal to deal with the United Mine Workers of America should not be attributed to John D. Rockefeller, Jr., or any of his aids. It concluded:

The position we have taken is entirely our own, and we deplore the unjust attacks to which Mr. Rockefeller has been subjected.

At this morning's meeting of the Federal Commission, Edward L. Doyle, Secretary-Treasurer of District 15, United Mine Workers of America, told about his two trials for contempt of court on charges of violating the injunction against the Northern Colorado coal miners. The trials, he said, were farcical. There was no jury, he said, and during the proceedings the prisoners were identified by witnesses according to the chairs in which they sat in court.

Most of the men convicted, he added, had not been in a street fight with strike-breakers as was charged. In the first case the union men were sentenced to a year in jail and a fine. Before an appeal could be heard in the Supreme Court, Doyle testified, the convicting Judge released them.

Doyle said that freedom was offered to him after his second conviction if he would make an apology for articles he had written for the official organ of the United Mine Workers of America.

December 13, 1914

ROCKEFELLER AID IS MOTHER JONES

"Easy to Misjudge You," Says Agitator, Who Will Call on Him About Colorado.

FORD'S PLAN NOT FEASIBLE

Capitalist Tells Industrial Commission It Would Be Unfair to Fuel Co. Investors.

DESCRIBES FATHER'S POLICY

Education and Eradication of Misery of Disease His Aims—Strike Violence Akin to Burglary.

John D. Rockefeller, Jr., faced two separate attacks at the hands of the Federal Commission on Industrial Relations yesterday. At the morning session in the Council Chamber of the City Hall he was questioned more searchingly than even on Monday about the strike in Colorado and the action the officials of the Colorado Fuel and Iron Company had taken in connection with it.

Most of the time in the afternoon was given to the immense benefactions which his father has set up, and Chairman Walsh tried to make him admit that in the existence of funds measured by the tens of millions in the hands of self-perpetuating trustees lay the germ of much harm to the community.

As Mr. Rockefeller discussed the strike question with the calmness and self-possession that never had left him on the stand, there was interjected one assertion of the point of view of the capitalist. When strikers resorted to violence and to the destruction of property, he suggested, it was impossible to be nice about methods, as it would be to choose one's measures in tackling a burglar.

Father's Gifts of $250,000,000.

Chairman Walsh was at a greater disadvantage in the examination about the benefactions than he was in the discussion of Colorado conditions. He brought up all kinds of possibilities that might arise from the establishment of the great funds, but Mr. Rockefeller was able to reply by an appeal to the character of the men who had been selected as trustees, and he even contended that the very size of the philanthropies, necessarily attracting the public attention, was a safeguard against their misuse. He gave a summary of his father's reasons for setting up the General Education Board, the Rockefeller Institute for Medical Research, and the Rockefeller Fund at a cost of approximately $250,000,000 as the best answer to all the criticisms which had been aimed against them.

The crowd which went to hear Mr. Rockefeller was quite as large yesterday as on Monday, and among them was Mother Jones, the Colorado coal agitator. As soon as Mr. Rockefeller entered, he caught sight of her, and going up to her said:

"I wish you would come to my office and tell me what you know of the Colorado situation."

"Nice of You," Says Mother Jones.

"Well, that's nice of you," replied the aged woman. "I've always said you could never know what those hirelings out there were doing. I liked the way you testified yesterday, and I can see how easy it is to misjudge you."

There was some talk of Mother Jones going to the Standard Oil Building at noon, but it was decided there was not time, and it was better to leave the conference to some other day this week. Vice President Hayes of the United Mine Workers, will be present at the conference.

Mr. Rockefeller also let it be known through Ivy L. Lee, when he returned after luncheon, that he had objected to the guard of detectives, which the police had provided for him, and, once he had got away from the City Hall and the crowds at the hearing at any rate, he did not want to be so officiously looked after.

Commissioner Walsh began his questioning by referring to the Colorado strike of 1903, and asked if men had not been deported from the mining camps and if their constitutional rights had not been taken away. Mr. Rockefeller did not recall anything in detail about that, and the Chairman shifted his attack to the control which it is alleged the Fuel Company exercises over ministers and school teachers in its district.

"Would you discharge an executive official who presumed to dictate what a minister should say?" Mr. Walsh

Control Over a Minister.

"I do not want to evade your questions," answered Mr. Rockefeller, "but in fairness to the official I should want to know the full circumstances before answering such a question. I say unhesitatingly that freedom of speech should be accorded in any instance."

Chairman Walsh quoted a letter written by J. F. Welborn, President of the Colorado Company, to Starr J. Murphy on Oct. 31, 1914, in which it was stated that the minister at Sunrise, Wyo., had been outspoken against the company; that he was Socialistic in his tendencies; that his wife was a Greek, and that the writer was about to investigate the case. Mr. Welborn was represented as saying that the company had thought of changing the minister, but this had not been done in order not to be unfair to the minister or to do anything which might seem prejudiced on account of the stand he took in the Ludlow outbreak.

Mr. Rockefeller admitted having seen the letter, and that at the Ludlow affair several miners had been killed.

"I should not care," he said, "to express an opinion on the question of the minister until all the facts were before me. As you read the letter I got the impression that several charges were made."

"Yes; that the minister was of Socialistic tendencies and had married a Greek," retorted the Chairman.

Mr. Walsh took up the question of Jeff Farr, Sheriff of Huerfano County, in which the fuel company owned mines. He prefaced this attack by the general question:

"Are you opposed to the use of violence in labor disputes or in any other circumstances?"

"I certainly am."

"Do you believe that the duty of the citizen to uphold the law applies also to the Directors of corporations?"

"I certainly do."

"Then do you know," asked Mr. Walsh sternly, "that Jeff Farr on Sept. 1, 1913, before there was a strike, swore in 326 deputies; that he did not know these men personally, and that as far as he could tell they might have been red-handed murderers or criminals? Do you know that these men were not paid by the county, but that Farr was told by Supt. Madison that arms would be supplied to them by the Colorado Fuel and Iron Company, and that payment would be made by the company? If these facts be true, would you consider this a menace to the peace of the community and the republican form of government?"

Mr. Rockefeller objected to such a long question, but added:

"I don't know how I could express an opinion on the measures taken to protect life and property when I was not present, and do not know all the circumstances. Anything that interferes with democratic government I should deplore but I cannot say whether a situation did not arise that made it necessary to take extraordinary measures to protect life and property. A man may enter my house as a burglar, and I may have to take action to defend my wife and family. Such would be deplorable, but the ordinary methods of preserving peace might be insufficient."

That did not satisfy Mr. Walsh, and he had the question reread. Mr. Rockefeller in response referred to the remote part of the country where the incident occurred, and the impossibility of trusting to ordinary measures to keep the peace.

Mr. Walsh reminded the witness that the deputies were sworn in before the strike started, and that they might have been criminals. To this Mr. Rockefeller retorted:

"Yes, but they might not have been anything of the kind. Moreover, the officers may have thought that danger to life and property was impending, and their first duty was to protect it. So they felt justified in taking emergency steps."

Capital and Politics.

Political activity on the part of the Colorado Fuel and Iron Company was the next point selected, and Mr. Walsh suggested that one of its officials had used money to influence elections, Constitutional Conventions, and the selection of candidates.

"I am entirely against such practices," replied Mr. Rockefeller. "As for an official who used such practices I should, as a Director, want to disassociate him entirely from the corporation. A man who was dishonest in one thing I think might be dishonest in others. I cannot make it too strong how opposed I am to anything destructive of the principles of democratic government."

The witness excused himself from discussing the amount of influence a mine Superintendent might exercise in selecting school trustees, on the ground that he never had had the time to go into the matter. Chairman Walsh retorted with asperity:

"Please describe how you are occupied?"

Mr. Rockefeller spoke of the time the business of the Rockefeller benefactions took up.

"Have you ever thought of delegating such work to others," said Mr. Walsh, "so that you could think of your Colorado employes? I believe you could get reports on Colorado conditions and look over them in a week."

Mr. Walsh referred to the recent testimony of Henry Ford before the commission, which Mr. Rockefeller said he had "skimmed over." After banging several quick questions at the witness, apparently to show that Mr. Rockefeller's information about Colorado was not very exact, the Chairman asked:

"Could not a sociological department such as Mr. Ford established, if it was set up in New York, keep you thoroughly informed concerning your employes?"

"It would be entirely possible," answered Mr. Rockefeller without any show of irritation. "But Mr. Ford showed that he was making many millions of dollars, and so he could develop such a department with entire justice to his stockholders. But I think you will agree in the case of the Colorado Company, where the common stockholders have had no returns for many years, it would not be fair to undertake sociological work."

Might Close Up Entirely.

"Don't you think that if you cannot look after the workers properly it might be better to close entirely?"

"It might come to that," said Mr. Rockefeller placidly.

Mr. Walsh seemed to think he had pressed the argument too far.

"My question was," he said, "if the industry goes on should you not undertake this sociological work?"

"Why, certainly. We are trying to do it," said Mr. Rockefeller, quietly but firmly. "The alternative might be to abandon these sociological attempts altogether, but I prefer to try to do them imperfectly rather than not at all."

Mr. Walsh elicited that Mr. Rockefeller had only looked through the evidence taken by the Congressional investigation of the Colorado situation, as it was so voluminous, and that he merely had glanced at the headlines of the New York newspapers on the strike.

"What newspapers do you read?" asked Mr. Walsh.

Mr. Rockefeller looked over at the crowd of the reporters in the well beneath the witness table and said with a smile:

"It would be embarassing to answer in the presence of this fraternity."

"These gentlemen do not matter," replied Mr. Walsh.

"THE TIMES in the morning," said Mr. Rockefeller, "and The Sun and Post in the evening."

"Do you believe a company should maintain a black list?" asked the Chairman.

"Please define a black list."

"It is a list of men considered by the company as undesirables and it is kept open for the inspection of other companies."

"I have no knowledge of such a list. I think every company should take steps to prevent undesirables being employed, but I do not think it should be shown to other companies."

"Can the employers be trusted to guard the rights and interests of the employed?"

The witness replied indirectly that it would be highly desirable if the workers had a participation in directing such matters. Mr. Walsh asked the question four times, and at last had to be satisfied with the reply that Mr. Rockefeller had not given enough thought to the question to be more definite. After luncheon Mr. Rockefeller said his attention had been called to this question, and he wished to say he had failed to grasp it, and was now willing to say that, of course, it was impossible to trust employes implicitly in such matters.

Upholds Non-Union Rights.

After several other matters had been briefly dealt with Mr. Walsh said:

"At Washington you testified that

you took a profound interest in labor matters and would fight for the open camp as a great principle. Why did you take so determined a stand?"

"That testimony has been construed as a declaration on my part of warfare on the unions. It is not fair to take it as such. The principle we were resisting was that our company should discharge all the non-union men, while we believe that every man under the Constitution has the right to choose whether he should belong to a union or not. My testimony was in no way a declaration of antagonism to unionism."

Mr. Rockefeller a little later said he would be glad to get some suggestions from the commission.

"Do you depend on outside Governmental agencies for suggestions?" asked Mr. Walsh, sarcastically.

"No, but we shall be glad of your assistance," answered Mr. Rockefeller, quietly.

At the afternoon session there was read a long letter to Mr. Rockefeller from Mackenzie King last August, in which Mr. King expressed the opinion that times were likely to be so bad that the unions would no longer bother about recognition simply for the sake of recognition, but would be glad to work with companies big enough to keep up the standard of wages as they were at present. It was shown that in the last twelve years Mr. Rockefeller, Sr., had received, in addition to the $376,000 on his stock investment, $9,260,000 interest on his Colorado bonds. In that period the 15,000 employes had received $92,000,-000 in wages.

"Would you consider it just," asked Mr. Walsh, "that the 15,000 employes, some of whom had been crippled at the times, should receive ten times as much as the man who had never visited the property?"

"I can't see the connection," said the witness. "Capital must get its return, and two-thirds of 1 per cent. on the capital investment is utterly inadequate to attract it when it might go into a savings bank."

Mr. Walsh turned to the Rockefeller benefactions, the Rockefeller Fund, the General Education Board, and the Rockefeller Medical Institute. Asked to give the total amount of his father's public appropriations the witness said:

"Not accurately as a statement, but it would approximate $250,000,000; $100,-000,000 to the Rockefeller Foundation, $34,000,000 now in the hands of the General Education Board, besides larger gifts under the board of which my father has reserved the right to designate the destination, as to the University of Chicago and the Rockefeller Institute.

Describes His Father's Views.

"Then there are the gifts outside of the Foundation, such as $1,000,000 to the Institute of Medical Research, which does not include $2,250,000 not yet paid to it. The University of Chicago has received between $33,000,000 and $34,-000,000."

"Do you not think that your father would have done more for the public interest if he had given the money to workers in industries?"

The question drew from Mr. Rockefeller a defense of his father's policy:

"I think my father held that one of the best forms of giving was the building up of productive industries. But other things could best be done by giving to such things as education. To a small extent these great foundations have been intended to carry on my father's private philanthropies. As his ability to contribute toward education increased we thought it desirable to crystallize in one organization the several activities he had carried on himself.

"First came the General Education Board. Up to that time my father had given to education, guided by the studies and inquiries of his associates. He thought it better not to confine himself to one group necessarily small, and so he set up the board, and as the personnel shows tried to bring in as broad, intelligent and representative a group as he could get together.

"Then my father had the growing impression that the great cause of human misery was disease, and if he could find any way to contribute toward information that might prevent or eradicate disease he would be making a real permanent contribution to the world at large. So the idea of medical research came to his mind, because frequently it is so unproductive and costly that it does not recommend itself to philanthopists. He began quietly and modestly with a gift of $300,000, and got the most competent men to investigate, to study disease in various laboratories. There was at first no separate plant, no endowment. He made no suggestion how the work should be done, but always got the best men for it.

"This gift was enough to develop men of special ability, and the question as to where the institute should be was not decided by my father, but was left to a board of special experts created for the purpose. Now we have a laboratory and a hospital, and contemplate additional laboratories. The study has been along special lines, and we have been successful in reducing the average

JOHN D. ROCKEFELLER, JR., ON THE STAND BEFORE THE INDUSTRIAL RELATIONS COMMISSION

death toll in cerebro-meningitis from 75 per cent. to 25 per cent. That is to say, in 600 cases, 300 owe their lives to the institute. The remedy has been used in different parts of the world and has been turned over to the public for public use.

For Succeeding Generations.

"The Rockefeller Foundation was the most recently organized in order that various kinds of altruistic endeavors might continue to receive attention from the persons in charge of the fund. Its organization was purposely made broad, because my father thinks that each generation can best tell what are its specific needs, and the man who tries to prophesy in advance is not likely to do as much good as he who leaves it to each generation to act to the best advantage."

Mr. Rockefeller described how an attempt was made to get the best possible men for the Trustees of the foundations, and how they succeeded in finding men of experience and vision who would come thousands of miles without remuneration to take part in a work for the public good.

"Do you consider such endowments a menace to the cause of industrial progress or education?" Mr. Walsh asked.

"I rather thought," answered Mr. Rockefeller, "that they would be of service to humanity. I never considered it necessary to think they could be a menace. Besides the Legislature could always repeal their charters."

"Should such foundations be compelled to consume their incomes?"

"I should not consider it necessary," the witness replied.

Neither did Mr. Rockefeller see any necessity to have a limitation of the life of such funds as the Chairman suggested for fifty years, although he showed that the Trustees of the Rockefeller Foundation and the General Education Board were at liberty to distribute the money they held.

He denied that the funds of a $100,-000,000 corporation could be used to affect the stock market; he saw no value in limiting the salaries of the officials, he explained the exemption of the real estate the foundations occupied simply on the ground of custom; he denied that the General Education Board would ever give money to a college except absolutely, as it would not desire to limit the discretion of the college in its activities.

Finally Mr. Rockefeller denied absolutely that the view of the man who gave the money for these funds would ever reach to men who received them so as to limit free action.

Mr. Rockefeller is to take the stand again this morning at 10 o'clock.

ROCKEFELLER OFFER TO MINERS IN WANT

Says Foundation Will Aid if Colorado State Officials Request It to Do So.

IF NEED IS STATEWIDE

Trinidad Business Men Told That Fuel and Iron Company Is Looking After Its Own Men.

John D. Rockefeller, Jr., has notified the Chamber of Commerce of Trinidad, Col., that the people of Colorado may call upon the Rockefeller Foundation for assistance in the relief of unemployed miners if they desire. The offer applies particularly to other parts of Colorado than that in which lie properties of the Colorado Fuel and Iron Company because, according to Mr. Rockefeller's telegram to the Chamber of Commerce, the company is doing all it can to prevent suffering among its own men.

The statement in the telegrams that the Colorado Fuel and Iron Company, of which John D. Rockefeller, Jr., is the dominant stockholder, is helping its men in all ways possible stands somewhat in contrast with the report on the Colorado situation submitted to the House on Tuesday by the Committee on Mines and Mining. The report contained this reference to Mr. Rockefeller's attitude toward the miners:

Mr. Rockefeller, a large stockholder of the most powerful company in the State, has done a great deal for the uplift of people in other parts of the country and in foreign lands, spending millions of dollars in this work, yet he has not endeavored to improve the condition of the more than 6,000 employes in the company with which he is connected, and has not visited the State for more than ten years.

The correspondence between Mr. Rockefeller and business men of Trinidad was made public yesterday at 26 Broadway. It shows that a labor leader who was a striker during the prolonged troubles between the Colorado Fuel and Iron Company and its employes telegraphed to Mr. Rockefeller late in February that suffering was widespread and immediate aid was needed.

Needy Miners Appeal.

After the receipt of the message Mr. Rockefeller sent this telegram of inquiry to the head of the Chamber of Commerce:

Feb. 25, 1915.
Chairman Trinidad Chamber of Commerce, Trinidad, Col.:
I have received from Joe Rizzi of your city a telegram stating that at a mass meeting on Saturday a committee was appointed to appeal to me for immediate relief in aid of needy miners. At my request Mr. Welborn has had an investigation made, and advises that Mr. Weitzel has reported to him that, in conference with several representative citizens of Trinidad, including some of your Directors, none of them could give the names of any former employes of the Colorado Fuel and Iron Company in need of help. As you doubtless know, the company is seeking to do all that it properly can for its former employes and their families. The co-operation of the Chamber of Commerce toward that end will be greatly appreciated.
JOHN D. ROCKEFELLER, JR.

In response came this telegram:

Trinidad, Col., Feb. 26, 1915.
John D. Rockefeller, Jr., 26 Broadway, New York City.
We find that the local officials of the Colorado Fuel and Iron Company are doing all that is possible to relieve the distress of its former employes. There is great distress among the working class caused by the recent trouble. We suggest that you could do a great good for mankind by helping relieve the distress in this community among other than your former employes by enlarging the scope of the work being done by the local officials of your company, and we stand ready to co-operate with you in any way you suggest.
TRINIDAD CHAMBER OF COMMERCE.
F. J. RADFORD, President.
C. F. DONAHUE, Secretary.

Mr. Rockefeller thereupon telegraphed Mr. Radford that the Rockefeller Foundation would consider applications for assistance if presented through satisfactory channels. The message read:

March 2, 1915.
F. J. Radford, President, Chamber of Commerce, Trinidad, Col.:
Your telegram suggesting that I could do "a great work for mankind" by helping to relieve the distress of your community would indicate that the need existing among miners and their families in Colorado has assumed such proportions and has become so acute that the community itself is unable to adequately meet it. So far as former employes of the Colorado Fuel and Iron Company and their families are concerned, as stated in my previous telegram, the officers of that company have expressed the hope that the company itself will be able to provide such relief as is necessary.
If the civic and State authorities are of the opinion that what other mining companies, existing agencies, and local aid may be able to accomplish will prove insufficient to meet other cases of distress, and that widespread suffering and want will ensue among miners and their families unless assistance from without the State is provided, a situation would be presented which the Rockefeller Foundation might properly consider, on representations from leading bodies and the Governor of the State as to the extent of their inability to cope with the need.

Wants Official Representations.

I have already intimated to the officers of the Colorado Fuel and Iron Company that I should be willing to make a personal contribution to the company to aid it in relieving distress among its former employes, should that become necessary, but without official representations in regard to the general distress I should fear that the citizens of Colorado might not welcome and that the Foundation would not be justified in acting upon the suggestions made to me in your telegram to make the aid general.
JOHN D. ROCKEFELLER Jr.

No intimation was made at the Rockefeller offices that plans were under way as to ways and means for carrying on the work in Colorado in case the authorities ask help of the Foundation It was understood that nothing would be done, probably, until further word was received from the Western State.

$1,000,000 LIMIT ON BIG FORTUNES

Industrial Board Reports, as Times Forecast, on Plans to Confiscate Wealth.

MULTIPLICITY OF FINDINGS

Three Reports from Commissioners Unable to Agree on Social Remedies.

DRASTIC INHERITANCE TAX

To Prune Big Estates—Savings to Go to Education, Social Service and Public Works.

CHICAGO, Aug. 22.—Summaries of three reports of the United States Commission on Industrial Relations were made public here tonight. The commission, which ceases to exist tomorrow, was composed of three representatives each of the employers, the employed, and the general public. The Commissioners were unable to agree on a single report, but it is said that none of the reports given out tonight can properly be called a "majority" report.

The commission was composed of Frank P. Walsh, Missouri, (Chairman;) John R. Commons, Wisconsin, and Mrs. J. Borden Harriman, representing the public; R. H. Aishton, Illinois; Harris Weinstock, California, and S. Thurston Ballard, Kentucky, representing the employers; and John B. Lennon, Illinois; James O'Connell, District of Columbia, and A. B. Garretson, Iowa, representing the employed.

The report of the representatives of the employes, drawn up by Basil M. Manly, Director of Research and Investigation for the commission, was signed by Commissioners Walsh, Lennon, O'Connell, and Garretson. This report finds that the causes of industrial unrest group themselves almost without exception under four main sources:

1. Unjust distribution of wealth and income.
2. Unemployment and denial of opportunity to earn a living.
3. Denial of justice in the creation, in the adjudication and in the administration of law.
4. Denial of the right and opportunity to form effective organizations.

Dissipation of Great Fortunes.

Under the head of the unjust distribution of wealth, the Manly report, as already announced in THE NEW YORK TIMES, proposes the return to the people of all fortunes in excess of $1,000,000. The report summarizes evidence showing that forty-four families possess aggregate incomes totaling at the least $50,000,000 per year, while between one-fourth and one-third of male workers in factories and mines, 18 years of age and over, earn less than $10 per week, and only about one-tenth earn more than $20 per week.

"In effect," says the report, "the American law of inheritance is as efficient for the establishment and maintenance of families as the English law, which has bulwarked the British aristocracy through the centuries. Every year, indeed, sees this tendency increase, as the creation of 'estates in trust' secures the ends which might be more simply reached if there were no prohibition of 'entail.'

"According to the income tax returns for ten months of 1914, there are in the

United States 1,598 fortunes yielding an income of $100,000 per year or over. Practically all of these fortunes are so invested and hedged about with restrictions upon expenditure that they are, to all intents and purposes, perpetuities.

"An analysis of fifty of the largest American fortunes shows that nearly half have already passed to the control of heirs or to trustees, (their vice regents,) and that the remainder will pass to the control of heirs within twenty years upon the deaths of the 'founders.'

"We have, according to the income tax returns, forty-four families, with incomes of $1,000,000 or more, whose members perform little or no useful service, but whose aggregate incomes, totaling at the least fifty millions per year, are equivalent to the earnings of 100,000 wage earners, at the average rate of $500."

How the Money Would Be Spent.

As a remedy the report urges "the enactment of an inheritance tax so graded that while making generous provision for the support of dependents and the education of minor children, it shall leave no large accumulation of wealth to pass into hands which had no share in its production." The report suggests that a limit of $1,000,000 be fixed on the amount that shall pass to the heirs. It recommends that the revenue from this tax be reserved by the Federal Government for three principal purposes:

1. The extension of education.
2. The development of other important social services which should properly be performed by the nation.
3. Development, in co-operation with States and municipalities, of great constructive works, such as road building, irrigation, and reforestation, which would materially increase the efficiency and welfare of the entire nation.

Other recommendations made in the Manly report are:

Land and Other Reforms.

Vigorous and unrelenting prosecution to regain all land, water power, and mineral rights secured from the Government by fraud.

A general revision of our land laws, so as to apply to all future land grants the doctrine of "superior use," as in the case of water rights in California, and provision for forfeiture in case of actual non-use.

The forcing of all unused land into use by making the tax on non-productive the same as on productive land of the same kind, and exempting all improvements.

That Congress should forthwith initiate an amendment to the Constitution providing in specific terms for the protection of the personal rights of every person in the United States from encroachment by the Federal and State Governments and by private individuals, associations, and corporations.

That Congress immediately enact by statute or, if deemed necessary, initiate a constitutional amendment specifically prohibiting the courts from declaring legislative acts unconstitutional.

That Congress enact that in all Federal cases where the trial is by jury, all qualified voters in the district shall be included in the list from which jurors are selected and that they shall be drawn by the use of a wheel or other device designed to promote absolute impartiality.

That Congress should drastically regulate or prohibit private detective agencies and private employment agencies doing business in more than one State, employed by a company doing an interstate business, or using the mails in connection with their business. Such regulation, if it is feasible, should include particularly the limitation of their activities to the bona fide functions of detecting crime, and adequate provision should be made for the rigid supervision of their organization and personnel.

That, the militia of the several Seates being subject to regulation by Congress, carefully drawn rules for their personnel, organization, and conduct in the field should be drawn up to insure their impartiality during industrial disputes.

Trades Unionists' Rights.

Incorporation among the rights guaranteed by the Constitution of the unlimited right of individuals to form associations, not for the sake of profit, but for the advancement of their individual and collective interests.

Enactment of statutes specifically protecting this right and prohibiting the discharge of any person because of his membership in a labor organization.

Enactment of a statute providing that action on the part of an association of individuals not organized for profit shall not be held to be unlawful, where such action would not be unlawful in the case of an individual.

That the Federal Trade Commission be specifically empowered and directed by Congress in determining unfair methods of competition to take into account and specially investigate the unfair treatment of labor in all respects, with particular reference to the following points: a. Refusal to permit employes to become members of labor organizations. b. Refusal to meet or confer with the authorized representatives of employes.

That the Department of Labor, through the Secretary of Labor or any other authorized official, be empowered and directed to present to the Federal Trade Commission, and to prosecute before that body, all cases of unfair competition arising out of the treatment of labor which may come to his attention.

That such cases, affecting as they do the lives of citizens in the humblest circumstances, as well as the profits of competitors and the peace of the community, be directed by Congress to have precedence over all other cases before the Federal Trade Commission.

Commons-Harriman Report.

The greatest cause of industrial unrest is the breakdown in the administration of labor laws and the distrust of our municipal, State and National Governments on the part of a large portion of our people, according to the report signed by Professor John R. Commons and Mrs. J. Borden Harriman, and concurred in with some exceptions by Harris Weinstock, S. Thruston Ballard, and R. H. Aishton, the employers' representatives.

Recommendations for additional legislation would be futile, says the report, until methods are provided for making enforceable the laws now on the statute books, through the creation of administrative machinery that will be entirely removed from political influences. To remedy the conditions criticised the report recommends the creation of a Federal fund for social welfare, maintained by an inheritance tax on large fortunes, and administered by a commission on industrial relations aided by an advisory council composed of representatives of employers and employes.

The advisory council would be composed of ten persons representing the different associations of employers and farmers in the country; ten representing organized labor, and the Secretary of Commerce and the Secretary of Labor to be members ex-officio. The Industrial Commission, in addition to the twenty persons thus selected, may appoint ten additional members interested in social legislation and industrial education. The members of the advisory council are to be appointed by the President from names submitted to him by the associations interested, and they shall serve without compensation other than actual expenses.

The Industrial Commission, it is recommended, shall be composed of three persons, appointed by the President and confirmed by the Senate. The commission shall have full power to administer all labor laws, but shall not interfere with the duties of the Department of Labor in making investigations and recommending legislation. For the purpose of adjusting labor disputes the Industrial Commission is to appoint a chief mediator and such assistant mediators as may be necessary.

Inheritance Tax Again.

To provide funds for the maintenance of the Industrial Commission and further social welfare, without increasing taxation of the people, the report recommends an inheritance tax on large fortunes. The rate of the inheritance tax is graduated from 1 per cent. on the excess of $25,000 fortunes left to direct heirs, to 15 per cent. on fortunes over $1,000,000. The tax on estates going to distant heirs is greater.

The inheritance tax proposed would be collected by the federal government through existing machinery that collects the income tax, and a portion would be turned over to each State. The various States now collect a sum equal to about $25,000,000 in inheritance taxes, but the rate is low in some States. By increasing the rate as proposed it is estimated that a fund of $200,000,000 a year would be collected, of which $50,000,000 would be returned to the various States.

The principal of this fund it is proposed to invest in homes for workingmen, hospitals, rural credits for farmers, and such other purposes of a social nature as would insure an income. The income from the fund, which would be administered by the Industrial Commission, would be used to meet the expenses of the commission; to promote the social well-being in the shape of establishing sickness and unemployment insurance, old-age pensions, the establishment of employment offices, the promotion of industrial education through subsidies paid to the various States and enabling tenant farmers to acquire possession of their farms.

Another recommendation in the report is the establishment of a system of national and State employment offices, under the control of the Federal and State Industrial Commissions, co-operating with employers and labor unions. The various State employment offices would be brought under the Federal Industrial Commission, through subsidies granted them for complying with certain standards which the commission would establish.

Foundations Indorsed.

The report says that no legislation should be enacted that would abolish privately endowed institutions unless a substitute is provided. It points out that the proposed Federal Fund for Social Welfare would provide the means for doing many of the things being done, or attempted by endowed foundations, and would be much more social and democratic.

The report recommends a combination of the Irish and Australasian land laws. Under the plan proposed the Government would extend credit to enable tenant farmers to become land owners.

On the Colorado situation the report says that a condition of feudalism exists in the mining regions, but it decries any attempt to hold responsible any single individual. It emphasizes the fact that the whole situation in Colorado, West Virginia, and other places where industrial warfare has existed, is due to a system which cannot be remedied by the public abuse of an individual. It recommends that corporations and labor unions alike be removed from the control of politics, and says that the Industrial Commission, with its Advisory Council and civil service rules; the initiative, referendum and limited recall, proportional representation, direct primaries, and anti-lobbying legislation, would accomplish this purpose, which is essential before any permanent remedy can be effected.

Capital and Labor.

In a separate report, Commissioners Weinstock, Aishton and Ballard dissent from the recommendation that the secondary boycott be legalized. They "find that the alleged findings of fact and, in a general way, the comments thereon made in the report of the staff of this commission, under the direction of Mr. Basil M. Manly, which has been made a part of the records of this commission without the indorsement, however, of the commission, so manifestly partisan and unfair that we cannot give them our indorsement."

"There is an abundance of available testimony in our record," these Commissioners say, "to show that many employers are frightened off from recognizing or dealing with organized labor for fear that to do so means to put their heads in the noose and to invite the probability of seriously injuring, if not ruining, their business. The prime objections that such employers have to recognizing and dealing with organized labor is the fear of sympathetic strikes, jurisdictional disputes, labor union politics, contract breaking, restriction of output, prohibition of the use of non-union made tools and materials, closed shop, contest for supremacy between rival unions, acts of violence against non-union workers and the properties of employers, apprenticeship rules.

"Organized labor will never come into its own, and will indefinitely postpone the day when its many commendable objects will be achieved in the broadest sense, until it will cut out of its program sympathetic strikes, until it can prevent cessation of work in jurisdictional disputes, until it can more successfully prevent labor union politics, until it can teach many in its rank and file to regard more sacredly their trade agreements, until it can penalize its members for resorting to violence in labor disputes, and can make it a labor union offense to limit output. If these evils are eliminated by organized labor from its program, much will have been done to stimulate collective bargaining and to minimize the existing causes of industrial unrest.

For Strong Organizations.

"The ideal day in the industrial world will be reached when all labor disputes will be settled as a result of reason, and not as a result of force. This, of course, means the strongest kind of organization on both sides. It means that employers must drive out of the ranks of their associations the law breaker, the labor contract breaker, and the exploiters of labor. It also means that, in the interest of fairness, every Board of Directors of an industrial enterprise should have within its organization a committee for the special purpose of keeping the Board of Directors advised as to the condition of their workers."

Owing to its length, it was impossible for the printers to provide the full summary of the Manly report. This latter report consists of three sections, only the first of which was given out today. The second section will be made public on Aug. 24 and the third section on Aug. 26.

"Supplemental Opinions and Suggestions" of Commissioners Garretson and Ballard were made public today, while those of Walsh, O'Connell, and Lennon are expected to be given out at a later date.

The commission will make public on Aug. 27 a report on the Colorado strike, and a few days later a report on the structural iron workers.

FIND IN LOW WAGES CAUSE OF UNREST

Industrial Board Chairman and Two Associates See Menace to Nation's Peace.

THEY PLEAD FOR AGITATION

Urge Efforts to "Eliminate the Injustices" of Present Education —Charge Oppression of Labor.

KANSAS CITY, Mo., Aug. 28.—Low wages is ascribed as the basic cause of industrial unrest in the report which Frank P. Walsh, Chairman of the Federal Commission on Industrial Relations, and the labor members of that body will present to Congress as a result of the commission's two-year investigation into the subject.

The report, embodying the personal findings of Mr. Walsh and concurred in by Commissioners John B. Lennon, James O'Connell, and Austin B. Garretson, was made public here today. In part it says:

"We find the basic cause of industrial dissatisfaction to be low wages, or, stated in another way, the fact that the workers of the nation, through compulsory and oppressive methods, legal and illegal, are denied the full product of their toil.

"We further find that unrest among the workers in industry has grown to proportions that already menace the social good will and the peace of the nation. Citizens numbering millions smart under a sense of injustice and oppression.

"The extent and depth of industrial unrest can hardly be exaggerated. State and national conventions of labor organizations, numbering many thousands of members, have cheered the names of leaders imprisoned for participation in a campaign of violence, conducted as one phase of a conflict with organized employers.

"Employers have created and maintained small private armies and used these forces to intimidate and suppress their striking employes by deporting, imprisoning, assaulting and killing their leaders. Elaborate spy systems are maintained to discover and forestall the movements of the enemy. The use of State troops in policing strikes has bred a bitter hostility to the militia system.

Accuses the Courts.

"Courts, Legislatures and Governors have been rightfully accused of serving employers to the defeat of justice; and, while countercharges come from employers and their agents, with almost negligible exceptions, it is the wage-earners who believe, assert and prove that the very institutions of their country have been perverted by the power of the employer.

"To the support of the militant and aggressive propaganda of organized labor has come, within recent years, a small but rapidly increasing host of ministers, college professors, writers, journalists and others of the professional classes, distinguished in many instances by exceptional talent, which they devote to agitation with no hope of material reward.

"We find the unrest here described to be but the latest manifestation of the age-long struggle of the race for freedom of opportunity for every individual to live his life to its highest ends.

"The unrest of the wage-earners has been augmented by recent changes and developments in industry. Chief of these are the rapid and universal introduction and extension of machinery, by which unskilled workers may be substituted for the skilled, and an equally rapid development of means of rapid transportation and communication, by which private capital has been enabled to organize in great corporations.

"Now, more than ever, the profits of great industries under centralized control pour into the coffers of stockholders and Directors who never have so much as visited the plants, and who perform no service in return. And while vast inherited fortunes, representing zero in social service to the credit of their possessors, automatically treble and multiply in volume, two-thirds of those who toil from eight to twelve hours a day receive less than enough to support themselves and family in decency and comfort.

Find Liberty Imperiled.

"We find that many entire communities exist under the arbitrary economic control of corporation officials charged with the management of an industry or group of industries and we find that in such communities political liberty does not exist, and its forms are hollow mockeries.

"In larger communities where espionage becomes impossible, the wage-earner who is unsupported by a collective organization may enjoy freedom of expression outside the workshop, but there his freedom ends. And it is a freedom more apparent than real. For the house he lives in, the food he eats, the clothing he wears, the environment of his wife and children, and his own health and safety are in the hands of the employer through the arbitrary power he exercises in fixing his wages and working conditions.

"The responsibility for the conditions which have been described above, we declare, rests primarily upon workers, who, blind to their collective strength and oftentimes deaf to the cries of their followers, have suffered exploitation and the invasion of their most sacred rights without resistance. A large measure of responsibility must, however, attach to the great mass of citizens. But, until the workers themselves realize their responsibility and utilize to the full their collective power, no action, whether governmental or altruistic, can work any genuine and lasting improvement.

"We call upon our citizenship, regardless of politics or economic conditions, to use every means of agitation, all avenues of education and every department and function of Government to eliminate the injustices exposed by this commission, to the end that each laborer may secure the whole product of his labor."

GOVERNMENT FIRST TO GRANT 8-HOUR DAY

Congress by Law, in 1868, Reduced Working Hours of Federal Workmen.

FIRST BIG STRIKE IN 1877

Railways Were Then Tied Up In 14 States—U. S. Troops Called Out In Many Strikes.

With the possibility of a great railroad strike being averted by Congress by law, granting in part the demands of the workers, interest attaches to the fact that a survey of the strikes which have occurred in the industrial history of this country reveals that the first strike of national importance was conducted by railway employes and is known in the histories as the railroad strike of 1877. It tied up roads in fourteen States, caused much violence and disorder, and, even at that date, brought up the question of Federal interference.

Many of the questions of the present crisis have played their part in past industrial disputes. The eight-hour day demand was first made in 1868, when Congress established the eight-hour day for all laborers, workmen, and mechanics employed by the Government, and President Grant by proclamation later ordered there be no reduction of pay because of the shortened time of labor. President Van Buren had in 1840 by Executive order established the ten-hour system for Federal employes, though it was not lived up to at first.

A list of the most important strikes in the history of the United States follows:

1877.
July—Railway employes of fourteen States; cause, railroads reduced wages; State and Federal troops in service; much violence and disorder; ended in two weeks; each side claimed victory.
July—Anthracite coal miners of Pennsylvania demanded higher wages; rioting suppressed by State authorities; ended gradually during August; companies agreed to 10 per cent. wage increase.

1880.
May 26—Leadville, Col.; 5,000 miners participating; cause, ostensibly wage increase, but real grievance understood as strict

rules maintained by companies; 5,000 miners participated; martial law proclaimed; total loss of $4,000,000 estimated; result, concessions by both sides.

1882.
March—Cumberland, Md.; coal miners asked wage increase; lasted six months; employers won.
May 9—Cleveland, Ohio; steel and iron workers demanded wage advance; 75,000 men with fund of $500,000; lasted many months; strikers lost; old wage scale resumed.

1886.
February—On Gould system of railroads in Texas, Missouri, Kansas, and Illinois; cause, rights of Knights of Labor; considerable disorder and several deaths; lasted seven weeks; result, complete failure for unions.
May—Chicago; freight handlers and then other industries employing 60,000; cause, eight-hour day; Haymarket riot, in which anarchists took part, with seventy killed and wounded, occurred during this strike, which was more a general demonstration than an individual effort.
November—Chicago stock yards strike; largest since railroad troubles of 1877; militia called out.

1892.
July—Homestead, Pa.; steel and iron workers opposed reduction in wages and non-recognition of union; conditions approximating warfare, with even the use of cannon; entire State militia called out, strike ended Nov. 20, by which time company had displaced about 4,000 old workmen by nonunion men, less than 1,000 old employes being able to secure employment in the mills.
July—Coeur d'Alene mining regions of Idaho; much disorder; strikers dynamited railroad bridges to prevent entrance of troops, but military order was established on the 17th and leaders placed under arrest.
August—Buffalo; Erie and Lehigh Valley switchmen; loaded freight trains burned on Aug. 14; entire militia called out; strike failed because of nonsupport from other unions.

1894.
May 11—Pullman, Ill., a suburb of Chicago; Pullman Company employes resisted cut in wages, which developed into a boycott of handling cars of the Pullman Company and sympathetic strikes in twenty-seven States; action centred in Chicago, where terrorism prevailed and mobs tried to prevent running of cars; Federal troops finally granted by President Cleveland over protests of Governor Altgeld; Eugene V. Debs, President of the union, arrested for violating the " blanket injunction " of the United States District Court; strike lasted until July 17, when it dwindled away, lacking the leadership of Debs, who refused to give bail and went to prison; strike caused great discussion of question of " government by injunction."

1895.
January—Brooklyn employes of electric system on strike; much rioting during month that strike lasted; strike subsided when militia was sent to scene.

1902.
May 12—Anthracite coal miners of Pennsylvania struck over wage conditions and recognition of union; John Mitchell led strikers and George F. Baer headed officials of coal-carrying railroads; in October President Roosevelt held conference with leaders of both sides in Washington; en-

listed aid of J. Pierpont Morgan in winning operators to Arbitration Committee, which Mitchell had accepted; miners at once went back to work and relieved coal famine; five months later commission made findings which were called a victory for miners, though involving compromise on certain points.

1903.
August—International Association of Bridge and Structural Ironworkers declared general strike against American Bridge Company for sub-letting contract in New Haven to firm with which union was unfriendly; the interest in the strike itself was lost sight of in the development which grew out of the situation, the dynamiting cases, among them that of the plant of The Los Angeles Times, where twenty-one men were killed; William J. Burns fixed the blame on union officials.

1907.
August—Los Angeles; telegraphers started strike against Western Union, which in a few days spread over practically the whole country and took in the Postal Telegraph Company. Union recognition and matters of regulation were important factors in causing the strike, which lasted until November. It ended in a return to conditions existing before the strike.

1911.
November—New York strike of street cleaners, which left the streets littered with unremoved garbage for weeks; strike broken by Street Cleaning Commissioner Edwards, who brought in outside men.

1912.
January—Lawrence, Mass.; textile workers strike; much disorder and rioting; strike led by I. W. W.; State militia called on Jan. 15; several deaths; strikers' children sent out of town; ended March 24, strikers obtaining substantial advantages.

1913.
January—Garment workers strike, paralyzing industry; protocol signed between Ladies' International Garment Workers' Union and Dress and Waist Manufacturers' Association on Jan. 18; strikers won preferential union shop and concessions on hours and wages.
Sept. 23—Trinidad, Col., mine workers begin strike which extends over Colorado, involving the Colorado Fuel and Iron Company, the Rockefeller property; great director; " Mother Jones " indignities and alleged massacre of miners' families involved; Federal troops sent into district for months; situation attracted widest attention all over country and many prominent men took sides; President Wilson appointed commission; lasted until December, 1914.

1916.
Aug. 5—New York; employes of all surface lines in Borough of Manhattan and others; demand increases in pay and recognition of union; settled Aug. 7 by Mayor Mitchel and Commissioner Straus, with victory for men.

Another fact revealed by a study of labor history is that, next to the Typographical Union, the organization of the Locomotive engineers, established in 1863, is the oldest union founded on a national basis which has existed up to the present day. The railway conductors and the railway firemen also appear in the list of the earliest six national organizations now existing.

September 1, 1916

SIGNS CHILD LABOR BILL.

President Says It Will Mean Health and Vigor to the Country.

WASHINGTON, Sept. 1.—President Wilson today signed the child labor bill. The ceremony was witnessed by Secretary Wilson, Senator Robinson, Representative Keating, Miss Julia Lathrop, chief of the Children's Bureau of the Labor Department, and a large group of men and women interested in the legislation.

"I want to say that with real emotion I sign this bill," the President said, " because I know how long the struggle has been to secure legislation of this sort and what it is going to mean to the health and to the vigor of the country, and also to the happiness of those whom it affects. It is with genuine pride that I play my part in completing this legislation. I congratulate the country and felicitate myself."

September 2, 1916

CHILD LABOR LAW UPSET BY COURT

Action of Congress Declared Unconstitutional by 5 to 4 on Final Test.

HELD TO EXCEED POWERS

Holmes Reads Dissenting Opinion—Move for New Law or Constitutional Amendment.

Special to The New York Times.

WASHINGTON, June 3. — On the ground that Congress, in passing the child labor law, unwarrantably invaded the rights of the States to control their own commerce, the Supreme Court today declared the law unconstitutional.

The decision was concurred in by five of the nine members of the court, Chief Justice White, and Justices Day, Van Devanter, Pitney, and McReynolds. Justice Holmes read a dissenting opinion, concurred in by Justices Brandeis, Clarke, and McKenna.

The court's action caused the utmost surprise. It was received with much regret by those who worked for nearly fifteen years in Congress for the passage of the law, which prohibited the shipment in interstate commerce of the products of child labor.

"The controlling question for decision is," said Justice Day, who handed down the prevailing opinion, "Is it within the authority of Congress in regulating commerce among the States to prohibit the transportation in interstate commerce of manufactured goods, the product of a factory in which, within thirty days prior to their removal therefrom, children under the age of 14 have been employed or permitted to work, or children between the ages of 14 and 16 have been employed or permitted to work more than eight hours in any day, or more than six days in any week, or after the hour of 7 o'clock P. M. or before the hour of 6 o'clock A. M.?"

Called Purely Local Question.

This question the majority opinion answered as follows:

"To sustain this statute would not be in our judgment a recognition of the lawful exertion of Congressional authority over interstate commerce, but would sanction an invasion by the Federal power for the control of a matter purely local in its character, and over which no authority has been delegated to Congress in conferring the power to regulate commerce among the States."

Justice Day said:

"All will admit that there should be limitations upon the right to employ children in mines and factories. That such employment is generally deemed to require regulation is shown by the fact that every State in the Union has a law limiting the right thus to employ children.

"We have neither authority nor disposition to question the motives of Congress in enacting this legislation. The purposes intended must be attained consistently with constitutional limitations, and not by an invasion of the powers of the States. This court has no more important function than that which devolves upon it the obligation to preserve inviolate the constitutional limitations upon the exercise of authority, Federal and State, to the end that each may continue to discharge, harmoniously with the other, the duties intrusted to it by the Constitution.

Boundaries of Trade Freedom.

"In our view, the necessary effect of this act is, by means of a prohibition against the movement in interstate commerce of ordinary commercial commodities, to regulate the hours of labor of children in factories and mines within the States, a purely State authority. Thus the act in a twofold sense is repugnant to the Constitution. It not only transcends the authority delegated to Congress over commerce, but also exerts a power as to a purely local matter to which the Federal authority does not extend.

"The far-reaching result of upholding the act cannot be more plainly indicated than by pointing out that if Congress can thus regulate matters intrusted to local authority by prohibition of the movement of commodities in interstate commerce all freedom of commerce will be at an end, and the power of the States over local matters may be eliminated, and thus our system of Government be practically destroyed."

Justice Day pointed out that the making of goods or the mining of coal were not in themselves commerce, even though the goods or the coal were afterward to be shipped in interstate commerce. He cited this in support of his argument that the law in effect aims "to standardize the ages at which children may be employed in mining and manufacturing."

"If the mere manufacture or mining were part of interstate commerce," Justice Day said, "all manufacture intended for interstate shipment would be brought under Federal control to the practical exclusion of the authority of the States, a result certainly not contemplated by the framers of the Constitution when they vested in Congress the authority to regulate commerce among the States."

Dissenting Opinion by Holmes.

In the dissenting opinion, Justice Holmes stated that Congress in his judgment was clearly within its rights, as defined by the Constitution, in enacting the law, even if it constituted interference with the individual rights of States to regulate commerce.

"The national welfare," said Justice Holmes, "is higher than the rights of any State or States, and Congress was clearly justified in using all its efforts along that line."

Justice Holmes expressed surprise that this question of the right of Congress to invade State rights of commercial control should have entered into the decision. He pointed out that in the oleomargarine case, various cases under the Sherman anti-trust law, and under the Pure Food and Drug act, as well as under the Mann act, the Supreme Court had decided that in the broad general interest of the nation, Congress had a right to trample upon the individual rights of States.

The suit decided today was brought by Roland H. Dagenhart in behalf of his children, Roland, Jr., Reuben, and John, who were employed in the mill of the Fidelity Manufacturing Company at Charlotte, N. C. Mr. Dagenhart sought an injunction to prevent the concern from discharging his children.

The Federal Court for the Western District of North Carolina decided that Mr. Dagenhart's contention that the law was unconstitutional was well founded. The Government was at once appealed, and today's decision is the result.

Representative Keating of Colorado and Senator Kenyon of Iowa, ardent supporters of the child labor law, stated today they would immediately begin a campaign for a new law, or for an amendment to the Constitution, which would permit Congress to enact such a law. Mr. Keating suggested that the situation might be met by taxing the products of factories employing children.

A meeting will be held in Washington soon to plan a new campaign for a child labor law that will meet the Supreme Court's objections.

MINIMUM WAGE LAW FOR WOMEN IS VOID

Supreme Court, by 5 to 3, Rules District of Columbia Act Is Unconstitutional.

CONGRESS CANNOT FIX PAY

Justice Sutherland, for Majority, Declares Employer and Employe Must Be Free to Contract.

TAFT GIVES MINORITY VIEW

Twelve States Have Measures to Protect Women and These May Be All Upset.

Special to The New York Times.

WASHINGTON, April 9.—The law passed by Congress fixing the minimum wage for women and minor girls in the District of Columbia was declared unconstitutional by the United States Supreme Court this afternoon. The decision is regarded as one of the most important the court has ever rendered, and indeed a nation-wide precedent, for minimum wage laws are in effect in more than a dozen States, six of which, New York, Kansas, California, Oregon, Wisconsin and Washington, got permission to intervene in the case as friends of the court. No less than 12,500 women and girls in the District of Columbia are directly affected by the ruling.

Associate Justice Sutherland, who delivered the opinion of the court, took the ground that the law interfered with the liberty of contract guaranteed under the Constitution and was also discriminatory in that it favored women, who, the opinion stated, were today fully as able to make contracts as men.

Chief Justice Taft submitted a dissenting opinion in which he held that it was not the function of the Supreme Court to hold a Congressional act invalid merely because these statutes carried out economic views which the court considered unsound. Associate Justice Sanford agreed with Mr. Taft in this dissent. Another dissenting opinion was delivered by Associate Justice Holmes. Associate Justice Brandeis took no part in the case. He once appeared in a minimum wage case involving an Oregon decision. His daughter, Miss Elizabeth Brandeis, is Secretary of the District of Columbia Minimum Wage Board.

The case came to the Supreme Court from the Court of Appeals of the District of Columbia, which once, after sustaining the law, ordered a rehearing and reversed itself, declaring the law unconstitutional in that it restricted the liberty of contract. The action arose when suits were brought by the Children's Hospital and by Willie A. Lyons, a woman elevator operator at a hotel, against the Congress Hall Hotel.

Gompers Deplores Ruling.

Wade H. Ellis, former assistant to the Attorney General of the United States, who appeared for the plaintiffs, said tonight he believed the decision had more profound consequences than any other rendered by the Supreme Court in a generation. Samuel Gompers, President of the American Federation of Labor, issued a statement deploring the action of the court.

The opinion by Justice Sutherland held that the Minimum Wage law of the District did not come within any of the exceptions to the general rule forbidding legislative interference with freedom of contract, in that it did not touch on contracts of public interest, emergency and other considerations of a similar public nature.

"It is simply and exclusively a price-fixing law," he said, "confined to adult women who are legally as capable of contracting for themselves as men. It forbids two parties having lawful capacity—under penalties to the employer—to contract freely with one another in respects of the price for which one shall render service to the other in a purely private employment where both are willing, perhaps anxious, to agree, even though the consequence may be to oblige one to surrender a desirable engagement and the other to dispense with the service of a desirable employe.

"The price fixed by the board need have no relation to the capacity or earning power of the employe, the number of hours which may happen to constitute the day's work, the character of the place where the work is done or the circumstances or surroundings of the employment; and while it has no other basis to support its validity than the assumed necessities of the employe, it takes no account of any independent resources she may have. It is based wholly on the opinion of the members of the board and their advisers—perhaps an average of their opinion if they did not precisely agree—as to what will be necessary to provide a living wage for a woman, keep her in health and preserve her morals.

"It applies to any and every occupation in the District of Columbia without regard to its nature or the character of the work."

Turning to an Oregon statute forbidding the employment of women in certain industries for more than ten hours, Justice Sutherland read that the act was upheld as a measure of protection to the health of women.

Finds No Inequality of Sexes.

"But the ancient inequality of the sexes," the majority opinion continued, "otherwise than physical, as suggested in the Muller vs. Oregon case has continued without 'diminishing intensity' in view of the great—not to say revolutionary—changes which have taken place since that utterance in the contractual, political and civil status of women culminating in the Nineteenth Amendment. It is not unreasonable to say that these differences have now come almost if not quite to the vanishing point. In this aspect of the matter, while the physical differences must be recognized in appropriate cases and legislation fixing hours or conditions of work may properly take them into account, we cannot accept the doctrine that women of mature age sui juris require or may be subjected to restrictions upon their liberty of contract which could not be lawfully imposed in the case of men under similar circumstances. To do so would be to ignore all the implications to be drawn from the present day trend of legislation as well as that of common thought and usage by which woman is accorded emancipation from the old doctrine that she must be given special protection or be subjected to special restraint in her contractual and civil relationships."

The wage standards furnished by the statute were held by Justice Sutherland to be so vague as to be impossible of application with any degree of accuracy. In addition, he held that earnings and morals could not be standardized in as far as morality rests on other considerations than wages. The opinion held the

law failed to consider whether the employe was capable of earning the minimum wage specified by the board and that no equivalent was demanded of the employe.

As examples of the uncertainty of the statutory standards the opinion recited that the minimum wage for a woman employed in a place where food is served or in a mercantile establishment is $16.50 a week, and in a printing establishment $15.50 a week, while in a laundry it was $15 a week, with a provision reducing it to $9 in the case of a beginner.

"The feature of this statute, which perhaps more than any other," the opinion continued, "puts upon it the stamp of invalidity is that it exacts from the employer an arbitrary payment for a purpose and upon a basis having no casual connection with his business or the contract or the work the employe engages to do. The declared basis is not the value of the service rendered, but the extraneous circumstances that the employe needs to get a prescribed sum of money to insure her subsistence, health and morals.

"The ethical rights of every worker, man or woman, to a living wage may be conceded. One of the declared and important purposes of trade organizations is to secure it, and with that principle and with every legitimate effort to realize it in fact, no one can quarrel, but the fallacy of the proposed method of obtaining it is that it assumes that every employer is bound to furnish it."

Justice Sutherland argued that the minimum wage law ignored the moral requirement implicit in every contract that the amount paid and the service rendered shall be equal. In principle, he contended there can be no difference between the case of selling labor and the case of selling goods.

Fears Power for Maximum Wage.

"Finally, it may be said," the Court continued, "that if in the interest of public welfare the police power may be invoked to justify the fixing of a minimum wage, it may, when the public welfare is thought to require it, be invoked to justify a maximum wage. The power to fix wages connotes by like course of reasoning the power to fix low wages.

"If in the face of the guarantee of the Fifth Amendment this form of legislation shall be legally justified, the field for the operation of the police power will have been widened to a great and dangerous degree. To sustain the individual freedom of action contemplated by the Constitution is not to strike down the common good but to exalt it; for surely the good of society as a whole cannot be better served than by the preservation against arbitrary restraint of the liberties of its constituent members."

In a long discussion of the validity of the law, Justice Sutherland considered the powers of the Supreme Court in declaring laws unconstitutional.

"This is not the exercise of a substantive power to review and nullify acts of Congress," he said, "for no such substantive power exists. It is simply a necessary concomitant of a power to hear and dispose of a controversy properly before the court to the determination of which must be brought the test and measure of the law * * * but if by clear and indubitable demonstration a statute be opposed to the Constitution we have no choice but to say so."

The majority opinion said a long line of decisions from John Marshall down protected the liberty of individuals to contract on their private affairs. Such restrictions which had been placed on this right, it was held, covered exceptional cases.

Taft Gives Minority View.

The dissenting opinion by Chief Justice Taft, in which Justice Sanford concurred, stated:

"Legislatures in limiting freedom of contract between employer and employe by a minimum wage proceed on the assumption that employes, in the class receiving less pay, are not upon a full

level of equality of choice with their employers and by necessitous circumstances are prone to accept pretty much anything that is offered. They are peculiarly subject to the overreaching of the harsh and greedy employer. The evils of the sweating system and long hours and low wages which are characteristic of it are well known. Now, I agree it is a disputable question in the field of political economy how far a statutory requirement of maximum hours or minimum wages may be a useful remedy for these evils and whether it may not make the case of the oppressed employe worse than it was before. But it is not the function of this Court to hold Congressional acts invalid simply because they are passed to carry out economic views which the Court believes to be unwise or unsound.

"The right of the Legislature under the Fifth and Fourteenth Amendments to limit the hours of employment on the score of health of the employe, it seems to me, has been firmly established."

Chief Justice Taft then referred to decisions in other cases relating to maximum hours of employment. He continued:

"However, the opinion herein does not override the Bunting case in express terms and therefore I assume the conclusion in this case rests on limiting of liberty to contract. I regret to be at variance with the Court as to the substance of this distinction. In absolute freedom of contract, the one term is as important as the other, for both enter equally into the consideration given and received. A restriction as to one is not any greater in essence than the other and is of the same kind."

Congress, said Mr. Taft, had taken the view that low wages and long hours were equally harmful upon the health of the employe. He continued:

"With deference to the very able opinion of the Court and my brethren who concur in it, it appears to me to exaggerate the importance of the wage term of the contract of employment as more inviolate than its other terms. Its conclusion seems influenced by the fear that the concession of power to impose a minimum wage must carry with it a concession of the power to fix a maximum wage. This, I submit, is a non-sequitur. Certainly the wide difference between prescribing a minimum wage and a maximum wage could as a matter of degree and experience be easily affirmed.

"I am not sure from reading the opinion whether the Court thinks the authority of Muller vs. Oregon is shaken by the adoption of the Nineteenth Amendment. The Nineteenth Amendment did not change the physical strength or limitations of woman upon which the decision in this case rests. The amendment did give women political power and makes more certain that the Legislative provisions for their protection will be in accordance with their interests as they see them, but I do not think we are warranted in varying constitutional construction based on physical differences between men and women because of the amendment."

Samuel Gompers in commenting on the decision said:

"It is regrettable that the Court should have taken away from the women wage earners of the district this sorely needed protection.

"Presumably the Court followed what in its mind is a certain philosophy of government and a certain construction of the Constitution. It is notable, however, that in practically every case of importance involving employment relations and the protection of humanity, the Court ranges itself on the side of property and against humanity.

"The woman wage earners of the District of Columbia are less favorably situated than women wage earners elsewhere. Not only are they less able to defend themselves on the economic fields, but they are absolutely without means of defense in the political field. This is a situation peculiar to this voteless oasis.

"The Supreme Court has declared the Child Labor law unconstitutional, and this new decision taking a proper and needed protection from women is a logical next step in perfecting the doctrine that those who cannot help themselves shall not be helped."

CHAPTER 2

The A.F. of L. and Business Unionism

Terence Powderly of the Knights of Labor
addresses a meeting.

Courtesy U.S. Department of Labor.

OUR WORKING CLASSES

Protective Unions and Co-operative Associations.

The Means by which Workingmen Protect Themselves.

Operations and Results of State and National Unions.

We attempted to show, in the first paper of this series, that the great manufacturing establishments and the employing manufacturers of the country were less in number, but more extended and prosperous in their operations, than they were twenty years ago; while, on the contrary, the working classes had largely increased in number and skill, yet were receiving comparatively less pay. In short, we argued and illustrated the undeniable fact that capital was being concentrated in the hands of the few, to the cost and independence of the many; that "the rich are becoming richer, and the poor poorer." We reserve for this paper an account of the means by which workingmen in most branches of manufacture are endeavoring to regain their independence, and restore their wages to an adequate basis and themselves to the position of employers once more.

PROTECTIVE UNIONS.

The most practical and effective of the means devised for this purpose have been found to be "protective or trades unions," and coöperative associations. During the continuance of the late strikes in this City,—some of them still continue,—protective unions of the following thirty-nine different trades and occupations were developed and took active part in encouraging and sustaining the strikers belonging to their various unions:

Bakers,	Paper-stainers,
Blacksmiths,	Pastry cooks,
Bricklayers,	Patternmakers,
Cabinetmakers,	Pencil-case makers,
Carpenters and Joiners,	Piano-forte makers,
Carvers,	Plasterers,
Cigarmakers,	Plumbers,
Clothing cutters,	Printers,
Coopers,	Quarrymen,
Copperworkers,	Sailors,
Iron-moulders,	Shoemakers,
Iron, sheet, workers,	Slate-roofers,
Laborers, common,	Stair-builders,
Longshoremen, (stevedores,)	Stone-cutters,
	Stone-mounters,
Machinists,	Tailors,
Marble-cutters,	Tin-workers,
Masons,	Varnishers,
Millers,	Waiters,
Painters,	Woolen-spinners.

During this same period of the January and February strikes, the fifth annual Convention of the "Workingmen's Assembly" of the State of New-York was held at Albany, and it was found that there were in existence in the State no less than 303 such organizations, twenty-five of which had been organized during the year 1868. Over 30,000 workingmen were represented in that Convention from this State alone, and it was represented that the number of unions and members were annually increasing, and that consequently the funds, power and influence of the associations were daily enlarging. It is only a few years since the Typographical Union was the only one of any importance or power in the coun-

try, and its development was strongly opposed as an improper interference between laborer and employer. The system is now extended to nearly all trades. The "union people," as the members of such organizations are called, claim that their policy is not aggressive, but that they simply seek mutual protection by united action and an organization which will prevent workmen at the same trade from underbidding each other or laboring for such wages as the employer may dictate. In the pursuance of this policy they claim they are justified by the past experience of laboring men in all countries; and by advancing these ideas and arguments they have succeeded in building up very strong and effective associations, which are protective not only in regulating the rates of wages, but as providing for members in ill-health and out of employment. The fund of the Workingmen's Assembly of this State for this purpose and for sustaining members engaged in strikes is very large; and the raising of an additional sum, to vary from $25,000 to $100,000, according to the necessities of the "strikers," was provided for in the late convention of the "State Workingmen's Assembly."

Very naturally many manufacturing employers deprecate the existence of these unions, and denounce them as unwarrantable and aggressive. There is no doubt that they are very powerful; but it cannot be said, we think, that they are more dictatorial than the manufacturers themselves. There is no clear proof that the manufacturers suffer by the occasional demands of the workingmen, through their unions, for advanced wages, or their refusal to submit to a decrease in their pay; while it is very evident that those workingmen without "trades unions" or those possessing ineffective unions suffer at the hands of the employers.

We lately published a table showing that certain classes of workmen at trades were making wages at which they could live comfortably and save something, but that a great many others were laboring at wholly unprofitable rates. That table showed that the more prosperous were the best skilled workmen. It will also be found that these more prosperous workmen belonged to the best organized, most general and effective, and richest "trades unions;" and that those who obtained the least wages were without organization, or their unions were in a demoralized state. The bricklayers throughout the country have a most perfect organization; each community has a lodge; each State a general organization; and a "National Bricklayers' Convention" meets annually. In the last Convention held in Washington, Jan. 11, 1869, thirty-six unions were represented, thirteen of them being from this State. Through the operation of these unions the wages of bricklayers in this City have advanced from $12 per week in 1860 to $30 in 1869. The same may be said of the plasterers. The bakers, on the contrary, are almost wholly without effective organization; their unions are demoralized, without much money, and their members do not represent one-third of the number of bakers in the City. The consequence is that the employing bakers dictate the terms, and the laborers at the trade, each acting for himself, underbid each other to obtain situations, and are now working for less money than they were in 1860. It was represented in the late State Workingmen's Assembly, by the Bakers' Society, "that bakers in many places in this City were working twenty hours a day and getting only $6 a week." At the last quarterly meeting of the Journeymen Bakers' Society, Mr. Ennis, formerly President of the Workingmen's Assembly, declared that

journeymen bakers in New-York were "compelled to work 120 hours a week, while the plasterers work only 48 hours at $4 50 per day." He held that "the bakers of New-York are more shamefully overworked than were ever the slaves of the South." Mr. BEATTY, the Chairman of the Society, said he "knew some shops where the men worked twenty-two hours out of the twenty-four." Mr. STERRITT declared that "the French bakers in this City had not one day out of the seven;" and subsequently stated that during the month of January, 1869, bakers not belonging to the Union had been cut down to $4 per week, and suggested that it was a bad illustration of the argument against unions. The condition of the journeymen shoemakers is very nearly the same; they may not be as much overworked as the bakers, but they are as badly paid, and there is little doubt that it is a consequence of the absence of an effective organization. The tailors are receiving but a fraction more wages to-day than they did in 1860; their condition is not much better than that of the bakers and shoemakers, but what little of superiority they possess is owing, without doubt, to the greater effectiveness of their trade organizations. They have only lately improved their organizations, and the principal advance in wages since 1860 was obtained only last year. They now have seven unions, and others are being formed, with a view to make a vigorous strike this Spring for higher wages.

Some years ago the Legislature of this State passed a law prohibiting strikes. It has been known as the "Conspiracy law," and it was believed at the time of its adoption that it would prevent the success of these embryo Trades Protective Unions. It only served to stimulate the workingmen. They have not only established their organizations, but have already secured the eight hour law; and a bill was introduced in the New-York Assembly on Jan. 28, repealing the "Conspiracy law" and authorizing "all classes of mechanics, journeymen, tradesmen and laborers to form associations for mutual aid and protection." These are clear proofs of the growing power of the "trade unions." As another proof, it is stated that "the employers in trades connected with house-building are taking measures to obviate any pecuniary inconvenience that may arise from strikes during the coming season. Their contracts with owners will contain a clause stipulating that in case of strikes they shall not be required to complete work in the time named." A mass meeting of workingmen of different trades is to be held on March 23 at Cooper Institute, the object being to consolidate all workingmen in a political union in which the interests of labor will be considered above all others.

COÖPERATIVE ASSOCIATIONS.

A later developed but not less promising means devised by workingmen to make themselves independent of the capitalists is the establishment, in imitation of the English and Germans, of coöperative associations. At present coöperative labor is an experiment with the workingmen of most of the trades; but a complete success with the printers and iron moulders. Some success has been attained also by "building" and by "building lot associations," but as these are not wholly confined to conducting mechanical trades, for the benefit of the members and shareholders, we simply mention them.

The iron moulders were the first workingmen in America to enter actively in the business of "coöperative foundries." In 1866 a number of workmen at Troy, N. Y., being out of employment, conceived the idea of setting up in business for themselves; and subscribing their labor and a little money, they established a small foundry for making stoves. It proved so successful that it now employs over one hundred men; and two smaller foundries have been started at the same place, and the third at Albany, which has become even more extensive in its operations than the pioneer foundry at Troy. Similar foundries now exist at Rochester, N. Y., Chicago and Quincy, Ill., Louisville, Ky., Pittsburg, Penn., and two at Cleveland, Ohio, making ten in successful operation in the United States. Two associations are now forming in New-York City. The sales of shares in one have reached nearly $60,000. The other has been started during the present year; its shares were fixed at 2,000 of $100 each, and of these a large number have been taken by 150 practical moulders.

Emulating the example of these printers, others of the craft now on strike are engaged in efforts to establish another on a larger scale. At a meeting of those interested, on March 13, it was reported by the Secretary-Treasurer that 1,600 shares had been applied for—150 by merchants desirous of encouraging the project, while donations to the amount of $900 had been promised. The first installment of 10 per cent. was promptly paid on demand on 879 shares, and the success of the undertaking appeared most promising.

In addition to these associations, there have been established coöperative carpentering shops at Buffalo and Poughkeepsie, each employing fifteen men, and a coöperative laundry at Troy, N. Y. All of these are in a thriving condition. We have an incomplete account of another association at Boston owning a new patent of a peculiar bed, but know nothing of its success.

The Coöperative Printer's Society, at No. 166 William-street, is doubtless the most successful association of the kind in this branch of industry. In 1865 twenty-five printers made an agreement to lay aside $2 each per week to form a capital on which to go into business for themselves. In two years they raised $5,000. For half of this sum they bought a second-hand establishment which originally cost $6,000, and with the rest bought stock to begin work with. Two of the members of the Association were detailed to attend the Coöperative Printing Office. The remainder continued at work at their old places until business should call them to their own establishment. From May 1, 1867, to May 1, 1868 the profits of the establishment, employing six members of the Association, was $8,000. All of this was wisely expended in stock, and at the commencement of the second year the Association, after supporting six men at good wages, found their $5,000 represented by an office, material, &c., worth not less than $12,000. On the first of next May the Association expects to move into larger quarters, and to retain in its employ all of the twenty-five stockholders.

Workingmen are also agitating and discussing the subject of establishing savings banks on the German and English principle combined—that is, to secure the largest interest on their deposits and to loan principally to those of their own trade, in order to establish them in business, and then in building homes and in purchasing building lots, and even farms. There is every evidence of the increasing power of the trades unions, and the disposition among the workingmen to unite in efforts to advance their interests, industrially and politically, was never so great as at the present time.

March 24, 1869

NATIONAL LABOR UNION.

Annual Convention of Workingmen—Numerous and Intelligent Attendance—The President's Report—The Relations of Labor and Capital Considered.

The second annual session of the National Labor Union, consisting of delegates from the different Trades' Unions throughout the United States, assembled yesterday morning at the Germania Assembly Rooms. Among the representatives were Miss SUSAN B. ANTHONY, of the Workingwoman's Association No. 1, of New-York; Mrs. M. R. PUTNAM, of the Workingwoman's Association No. 2, and Mrs. M. H. MACDONALD, of the Mount Vernon Woman's Suffrage and Labor Protective Association.

Mr. J. C. C. WHALEY, of Washington, President of the Union, called the meeting to order, and called for an election of a Secretary *pro tem.*, in the absence of the Secretary of the Union. Mr. HENRY D. MULHALL, of the Workingmen's State Association, was chosen. The call for the meeting was then read, stating that the Union intended instituting reforms, and carrying out those already instituted, in the interests of the working masses, and by establishing reciprocal relations between their different organizations, unite them in a common effort to protect themselves, and keep back the enactments of centralized wealth upon the rights of labor, and to secure legislation that will improve their condition and advance them in the scale of prosperity and intelligence. The following are the articles of the Constitution of the Union relative to representation:

"The National Labor Union shall be composed of such labor organizations as may now or hereafter exist, having for their object the amelioration of the condition of those who labor for a living.

Every international or national organization shall be entitled to three representatives and a Vice-President; State organizations to two. Trades' Unions and all other organizations to one representative in the National Labor Congress, provided that representatives shall derive their election direct from the organizations they claim to represent.

Ex-representatives, upon presentation of certificate of good standing in their organizations, shall be entitled to a voice, without a vote, in the National Labor Congress."

WM. J. JESSUP, President of the New-York Workingmen's Union; A. C. CAMERON, of the Chicago Union, and AARON W. STOCKTON, of the Ship Joiners' Union of Baltimore, were appointed a committee on credentials. After the presentation of credentials by the delegates, an adjournment took place until 2 o'clock.

On reassembling, the delegates were present from New-York, Maryland, Illinois, New-Jersey, Massachusetts and of several national organizations.

THE REPORT OF THE PRESIDENT.

The Secretary then read a report of Mr. J. C. C. WHALEY, President of the Union, which enlarged upon the importance of workingmen to the world; urged the enforcement of the Eight-hour law, and gave a history of its inception and birth in Congress and the Legislature of this State. Coöperation was forcibly touched upon and considered the key to the prosperity of the masses.

FEMALE LABOR.

On the subject of female labor, the report says, The question of female labor is one of paramount importance to the industrial classes, and merits the attention of trade organizations, local and national. The extent to which female labor is introduced into many trades makes it a serious question with workmen therein as to what course shall be pursued in reference thereto, and how they can protect themselves from its depressing influences; for the effect of introducing female labor is to undermine prices, that character of labor being usually employed, unjustly to the woman, at a lower rate than is paid for male labor on the same kind of work—an injustice that I sincerely hope to yet see removed, for there is no good reason why a woman should not receive as much pay as is given a man if she executes a quantity and quality of work equal to that executed by him. It would be well could government be induced to set the example of equal compensation for male and female labor. I believe that every effort should be made to encourage and assist in the formation of female societies and then they should be brought into coöperation with the men's societies. To bring up the lowest to the level of the highest is the true principle of reform, and by making that noble purpose the underlying principle of our action, the happiest of results must ultimately ensue.

It would be a great reform to relieve the poorly paid and overburdened workingwomen of the damaging physical effects and demoralizing tendencies of the prevailing system, and to contribute to that result would be an action worthy of your best endeavors."

POLITICAL ACTION.

"The subject of political action," says the report, "is one of interest to the National Labor Union at present, the Labor Congress at Chicago having enunciated broad, national principles on the financial and land questions, the discussion of which leads to the political arena. In my judgment, the true position to hold, though an exceedingly difficult one, is that of independence of both political parties, as thus may be wielded the balance of power. In no instance should the identity of the organization be lost, or, in other words, merged into any political party; but moving from the Trades' Assemblies in this or that direction, according as this or that party is sustaining your principles, by allying yourselves with them you can generally manage to secure the election in your favor. Thus you would become the followers of principles, and not the slaves of party; the advocates of measures for your own good, and not the noisy worshippers of men who care much more for their own preferment than for either you or your principles. One injury that arises to the masses of this country, but which would be somewhat obviated, were the workingmen to organize and keep organized into trades assemblies, comes from the fact that nominations are generally made by a few individuals who are brought together temporarily for that purpose; the election shortly after takes place, and all combination is lost, and with it goes the check-string of responsibility that holds the representative loyal to the discharge of his trust. If there be a permanent organization with political influence, there is an existing authority to hold him responsible and keep him from forgetting and performing his pledges, and from returning near the close of his term and making his own organization through which to hoodwink his constituency and secure a re-election.

The unfortunate condition of the laboring masses in this country demands, if they would relieve themselves of the thraldom of capital and taxation, that they should organize themselves and use their political power to counteract the evil influences of subsidized legislation. The burdens must be lessened or they will become intolerable.

It has been tersely written that if 'to do were as easy as to know what were good to do, chapels had been churches and poor men's cottages princes' palaces,' and if to carry out plans of reforms were as easy as to prescribe them, it would not be long ere the workingmen of this country would be so organized as to directly wield a powerful influence in the affairs of this nation, and the voices of many of their chosen representatives would be heard influentially speaking in its councils. They would then exercise such an influence as their numerical strength and intelligence would entitle them to, and which they will have to exercise if they successfully inaugurate reform and secure the legislation that their rights and interests may demand.

OTHER REPORTS.

A report of WM. J. JESSUP, Vice-President of the National Labor Union of the State of New-York, was then read. Among other matters it stated that there were 50,000 men in the different Trades' Unions of the State of New-York. He had received every aid from the officers of the various labor associations in procuring matter for circulars in regard to the present meeting. He had received the addresses of 1,000 labor organizations in the United States, and they had proved of great service to him in sending circular notices of the present meeting, and in appealing for aid for the New-York bricklayers on strike. He had sent 700 circulars to labor organizations. He had received 252 letters, eight of which were from Great Britain.

A report of JOHN HINCHCLIFFE, Treasurer of the Union, was then read, which stated that $475 96 had been received and $449 57 paid. Mr. HINCHCLIFFE concluded his report by resigning.

Mr. A. M. KENADAY, Vice-President of the National Labor Union, in California, in his report stated that California had an eight-hour law, and though no penalty was inforced for its infringement with regard to adults, yet the compelling of children to work more than eight hours, was punished as a misdemeanor by a fine of not less $10 or more than $100, or imprisonment for twenty days.

Committees were then appointed on finance, coöperation, ways and means, female labor, a constitution, a platform and prison labor.

Miss SUSAN B. ANTHONY announced that a meeting of the Working Women's Association would take place in the evening at the office of the *Revolution*, and they would be glad to see any gentlemen present and receive their suggestions.

A discussion then ensued about the propriety of forming a workingmen's political party, without action being taken. The meeting then adjourned until to-day at 9 o'clock. At a committee meeting to appoint an evening for consideration of a workingmen's political party, time was lost in irrelevant discussion, and no time was appointed.

September 22, 1868

AN ORDER OF WORKING MEN

THE AIMS AND PRINCIPLES OF THE KNIGHTS OF LABOR.

INTERVIEWS WITH TWO OF THE SOCIETY'S CHIEF OFFICERS—ITS MAIN OBJECT TO REVOLUTIONIZE THE LABOR SYSTEM—THE OVERTHROW OF THE GOVERNMENT IN A DAY SAID TO BE WITHIN ITS POWER.

SCRANTON, Penn., April 17.—The rapid growth of the Knights of Labor throughout the United States, and especially in Pennsylvania, has awakened considerable apprehension in the public mind concerning the true character of this secret organization, whose ramifications extend almost into every town and hamlet in 28 States of the Union. The agents of the order are now working with renewed activity to extend its influence, and so effective is its machinery, and so great its membership, that it is claimed it could, in 24 hours, overthrow our entire system of government, were it as desperate as it has on several occasions been represented to be. Ascertaining that the Grand Secretary of the Order for the United States, Representative Charles H. Litchman, of the Massachusetts Legislature, was visiting the Grand Master Workman, Mayor T. V. Powderly, of this city, the TIMES correspondent called on these gentlemen with a view to learning something official from those who are authorized to speak on a question that is now engaging so much attention. At first they refused to speak of the organization, which, they said, had been so frequently vilified and misrepresented by the press. The Mayor was especially anxious to be relieved from the interview, and finally referred the correspondent to the Grand Secretary.

Representative Litchman is young, of medium stature, pleasing face, penetrating eye, and well-developed perceptive faculties. He paced the floor of the Mayor's office leisurely during the interview, and his statements were made with as much deliberation and earnestness as if he were addressing a thousand men.

The TIMES correspondent began: "Having seen it stated that you are Grand Secretary for the Knights of Labor in the United States, and, therefore, in a position to know all about the order, I have come to ask you something of its origin, aims, and political character."

Mr. Litchman hesitated several seconds, and then said: "I have very great reluctance in making a favorable answer to your question, for fear of a misconception of the motives under which I may be supposed to act by those with whom I am connected in the grand movement for the unification of labor. Again, the press at large has so vilified and falsified our organization and the zealous men who are conscientiously striving for a higher plane of action in labor reform, that I feel little patience in responding to any inquiry such as you make. Perhaps, after all, your inquiry presents an opening by which we can get a fair hearing from the press and an opportunity to state such things as we would be allowed to state of the aims and objects of our organization. The order is divided into three branches —Local, District, and General Assembly. The local organization is intended to be an association for productive distribution and saving co-operation. The District Assembly, which must be composed of not less than five local bodies, is intended to be, in like manner, the productive, distributive, and saving agency of the section of country covered by the local bodies under its jurisdiction. The General Assembly is the supreme head of authority in the order, and composed of representatives of the various District Assemblies, meeting annually. It has already held three annual meetings. The office of the General Assembly is to have a general supervision of the workings of the order, and to form a grand, wholesale agency, by which, through the District Assemblies, the local co-operative agencies are to be supplied. The theory is that, in time, if necessary, the General Assembly shall own and operate mines, railroads, factories, and farms, and thus produce and supply at cost price everything that can feed, clothe, or shelter mankind. That is the end which we will reach some day. It is a secret organization, not, as has been charged, for unlawful purposes, but for the purpose of shielding from oppression those members who, in the infancy of the order, were compelled to assume positions of leadership, and to protect them until such time as the operations of the organization furnish the means for employment to those who are "black-listed" or victimized by their employers for participation in the order. In many parts of the country branches are working openly, under the name of the order, while in most localities, though strong and powerful in numbers, its existence is not even suspected.

Q.—How long has the order been in existence? A.—About 11 years.

Q.—What is its present strength in this country? A.—To that I must give an apparently indefinite answer, for the following reason: When the organization started, those who conceived it had in view the founding of an order or association of working men whose very existence should never be made known—the names of whose members were to be kept profoundly secret, and whose places of meeting were never to be divulged. The work of the order was conducted orally, and only those were given authority to organize branches or "Assemblies" who showed mental fitness for the position. Such members were given what was practically a roving commission, with authority to organize wherever and whenever the requisite number of working men suitable to the purpose could be had. Thus the seeds of the organization were sown broadcast through the land. While this resulted in extending the order from Philadelphia, its birthplace, even to Oregon, it resulted unfavorably in one respect, namely, that no complete or systematic record of work done was ever made or attempted until the General Assembly was organized in January, 1878. The work of my office as Grand Secretary since that time has in a large measure been to gather up the scattered threads and weave them together. I am constantly hearing of localities where assemblies have been formed whose existence was before unknown. This makes it difficult to state definitely its membership, for not until recently has an attempt been made to gather statistical facts which might render an answer to such a question possible. Various fabulous numbers have been given concerning the membership of the Knights of Labor, some ranging as 1,500,000 men, but I have no knowledge of more than 500,000 members. It would not be fair to claim that this number is in active affiliation with the General Assembly, principally because of the difficulty before mentioned.

Q.—In what sense is the order a trades-union? A.—To this I should answer, in the highest and noblest sense. The old trades-union was organized upon a corner-stone of selfishness—thinking, knowing, and caring for nothing but the members of the particular trade therein represented. Thus my own craft—that of shoe-making—had its trade organization, numbering nearly 100,000 men at one time, with a fast hold throughout the United States and Canada, wherever the craft had sufficient numbers to form a lodge. The cigar-makers, the machinists, the blacksmiths, and the miners had their separate trades-unions in like manner. The shoe-maker cared little for the miner or the blacksmith, provided he obtained good wages for his own labor. In this way, at least in a negative sense, the member of each trades-union was a sort of Ishmael of labor. The new order of things under the rule of this organization seeks a higher plane of action. It recognizes the fact that when one branch of labor is idle it is from causes which in like manner affect all branches of trade, and so when one prospers all prosper—everything being equal. It was for this end that the leaders sought to establish a union which should combine in one grand universal brotherhood all branches of honorable toil, knowing no sect, no nation, no creed, but seeking the elevation and benefit of all who obeyed the divine injunction "By the sweat of thy brow shalt thou eat bread."

Q.—Is the organization political in its aims? A.—It is not, in the sense of being a political party, because we have men in our ranks who are conscientious members of all political parties. Political party action cannot be taken in the Local Assembly, but political economy touching upon those points set forth in our preamble may, and should be, in a fraternal and candid spirit freely discussed therein. I might here quote a decision of a former Grand Master Workman, which clearly defines our position. He says: "The Knights of Labor is not a political party. It is more and higher, and must be kept so. It is the parent of principles. In it are born and crystallized sentiments and measures for the benefit of the whole people, and it allows legitimate results and consequences to fall where and when and upon whom they will."

Q.—Which of the parties now existing is the order most in favor of? A.—As an organization, the General Assembly would take no action, nor would its officers presume for a moment to dictate, or even indicate, which way the votes of the members should be cast. But from my correspondence with members individually I do not hesitate to say that in my judgment three-fourths of the members would work heartily for the candidate of the Greenback Party if nominated upon a platform which opposed monopoly in land, labor, and money. Being originally a Republican, I have acted with the Greenback Labor Party, so called, because, in my judgment, it comes the nearest to being the exponent of the principles whose triumph we seek of either of the existing political organizations. No man is required, or expected, to change his political affiliations by becoming a member of our organization, but we feel confident no intelligent man can listen long to the teachings of our ritual and the discussion of the principles of our constitution without realizing keenly that the old political parties furnish no hope of relief. Therefore, the necessity of action independent of those two parties —Republican and Democratic—seems imperative. The order exists in 28 States of the Union, in some of which it has such a controlling influence that, whatever direction its combined power may be thrown in political action, it cannot fail to prove an important factor in the coming campaign.

Q.—What is the position of the order in relation to strikes? A.—We do not approve of strikes; in fact, we resolutely set our faces against them. We regard the strike as a relic of the past, which it would be well to bury from sight forever. One grand aim of our order is to educate working men and teach them that there are better and cheaper methods of attaining the same ends which they formerly thought the strike could reach. We believe that the money spent in making a strike can be much more advantageously employed in developing and extending the principle of co-operation. Our plan is, if a difficulty occurs, instead of sustaining the strike, to take, if need be, the branch of labor represented, invest sufficient capital in the name of the General Assembly, and make the strikers producers, instead of consumers of the bread of idleness.

Q.—How far is the organization a beneficial one? A.—There is no system of mutual benefit as yet engrafted on the laws of the General Assembly. In many places, however, Local Assemblies have a system of weekly and funeral benefits.

Mayor T. V. Powderly, of Scranton, the Grand Master Workman, or chief officer of the Knights of Labor for the United States, stood by during the interview, occasionally suggesting an amplification of some of the Grand Secretary's answers of which he approved. On asking him what his views were, Grand Master Workman Powderly answered by saying: "I hold the same views in regard to granting an interview for publication as the Grand Secretary does. Yet I feel that it is due to the members of our organization and the public generally that truthful answers should be given by those having a right to speak for the Knights of Labor. I have frequently read garbled accounts in the press of interviews on our association with different persons who are supposed to be members. Some of the points touched upon in those interviews are correct, and others very far from the truth. Anything which I might say would not better the statement made by the Grand Secretary, for it is the truth. I have read in several papers of late that steps are being taken to secure the co-operation of the Knights of Labor (through its leaders) for the purpose of electing certain candidates of either one of the different political parties. That assertion is made and scattered broadcast for the purpose of creating distrust and suspicion in the minds of the members, in order that they may lose confidence in their leaders. While speaking on this point, I would say, by way of warning to those who desire to purchase votes, that they must beware of pretended leaders of the Knights of Labor who seek to sell, for, no matter what contract or agreement any one of the officers might make, he could not deliver the goods, and the first intimation he gave looking toward that end would be the signal for him to write out his resignation, and retire from his position in disgrace. He may entertain such views as he pleases, and, as a private citizen, may strive for the political advancement of any man he chooses, but the moment he approaches a brother-member "officially," either in person or by letter, then he leaves the path chosen for him to walk in, and is open to censure and disgrace. The organization has been grossly misrepresented as to the law-abiding character of its members. If it were as black as it has been painted, so effective and thorough in its machinery that at a signal, which could be easily given by its leaders, the whole system of the United States Government could be overturned in 24 hours. But no danger need be apprehended, as the Knights of Labor are men who would sacrifice their lives to save the Union.

April 19, 1880

THE FEDERATION OF LABOR

TRADES UNIONISTS FORM A NEW ORGANIZATION.

THE KNIGHTS OF LABOR IGNORED AND A CONSTITUTION FOR THE NEW BODY ADOPTED—OFFICERS ELECTED.

COLUMBUS, Ohio, Dec. 11.—It will doubt-less prove a trifle galling to Terence Vincent Powderly and his old Executive Board to learn that the trades unionists, who have been in session here for the best part of a week, have elected as President of their new organization, the American Federation of Labor, Samuel Gompers, the man he so vilified in the "secret" circular that was printed in to-day's TIMES. The fact that Mr. Gompers was elected without opposition may give Mr. Powderly an idea of the estimation in which he is held by trades unionists. The latter are now prepared to go their own way. They did not invite interference or opposition, in the first place, and if Mr. Powderly's lieutenants with his knowledge had not abused their powers so grossly there would be peace to-day between organizations that are now rivals. The new organization has no fear of the Knights, for its membership was in existence long before they were thought of. It begins life with 25 trades unions as a nucleus. There is reason to suppose that as many more will join the fold before another convention is held. Its primary object is to secure as members every trade and labor union in the country, and some of the steps it has taken to attain this object show the shrewdness of the builders.

Heretofore the Knights have been enabled to enroll all the workers in small communities. A glance at the Federation's constitution will show that such a field will no longer be left exclusively to the "noble order." The Knights have been enabled to secure many members by a promise of general assistance in case of a strike or lockout. Such assistance has proved by experience but a broken reed. The Federation's constitution provides that, under certain circumstances, assistance of a general character will be given in case of strikes or lockouts, and unionists know that their treasuries are seldom empty, and that among them a promise has usually amounted to fulfillment. Then members of the Federation will be allowed self-government. As among the Knights, a cigarmaker will not, among trades unions, be allowed to march into a silk mill and order a strike. The leaders of the new movement are tried men. The work is not new to them. They are acquainted with the weak spots in the "noble order" as well as in trades unions, and they have labored hard to construct such an organization that will not need constant interference. They think that they have succeeded, and they talk like men who have satisfactorily accomplished a difficult task, upon adjournment late this afternoon.

The salient points in the constitution of the new organization are as follows:

This association shall be known as the American Federation of Labor, and it shall consist of such trades unions as shall conform to the rules and regulations.

The objects of the Federation shall be the encouragement and formation of local trades and labor unions and the closer federation of such societies throughout the organization, of central trades and labor unions in every city, and the further combination of such bodies into State, Territorial, and provincial organizations, to secure State legislation in the interests of the workingmen.

The establishment of national and international trades unions based upon a strict recognition of the autonomy of each trade.

To secure national legislation in the interests of the working people and influence public opinion by peaceful and legal methods.

The basis of representation in the convention shall be from national and international unions of less than 4,000 members, one delegate; 4,000 or more, two delegates; 8,000 or more, three delegates; 16,000 or more, four delegates, and so on, and from each local trade district or union not connected with a national head, one delegate.

No organization which has seceded from any local, national, or international organization shall be allowed representation or recognition in the Federation.

The officers shall be an Executive Council, with power to watch legislative measures directly affecting the interests of working people and to initiate, whenever necessary, such legislative action as the convention may direct.

This council shall use all possible means to organize new national and international and local trades unions, and to connect them with the Federation.

While we recognize the right of each trade to manage its own affairs, it shall be the duty of the Executive Council to secure the unification of all labor organizations so far as to assist each other in any justifiable boycott, and with voluntary financial help in the event of a strike or boycott duly approved by the Executive Council. When a strike has been approved by the latter, the particulars of a difficulty, even if it be a lockout, shall be explained in a circular issued by the President of the Federation. It shall then be the duty of all affiliated societies to urge their local unions and members to make liberal financial donation in aid of the working people involved.

The revenue of the Federation shall be derived from a per capita tax of ½ cent. per month from each member in good standing.

The salary of the President shall be $1,000 per year, with mileage and expenses.

Whenever the revenues shall warrant it the Executive Council shall authorize the employment of speakers in the interest of the Federation.

The remuneration for loss of time by the Executive Council shall be $3 per day and traveling and incidental expenses.

Any seven wage-workers of good character and favorably to trades unions, and not members of any body affiliated with this Federation, shall subscribe to the constitution, shall have power to form a local body to be known as a Federal Labor Union, and they shall have power to form their own rules in conformity with the constitution, and shall be granted a charter by the President of the Federation, provided the request for a charter be indorsed by the nearest local or national trades union cars connected with this Federation.

This constitution shall go into effect March 1, 1887.

The committee that conferred with the Knights of Labor who had been sent here by Mr. Powderly made the following recommendation:

"That the Executive Council of the newly organized Federation shall issue an address to the public upon the subject of our differences with the Knights of Labor. We might have terminated the conference the first half hour of the meeting, for it was evident the Knights of Labor committee had no power to act. In the interests of harmony we deemed it wiser to spend three hours in a friendly discussion with the hope of coming to an understanding."

The Federation elected as its President Samuel Gompers, of New-York. He is Vice-President of the International Cigarmakers' Union, and is considered one of the cleverest leaders in the trades unions of the country. He was born in London of Dutch parents. He has been a resident of this country since his thirteenth year, and worked at his trade, cigarmaking, since he was 10 years old. He is now 37, and has been a member of his union since its organization in 1864.

George Harris, of Reynoldsville, Penn., was elected First Vice-President. He was born in England in 1853. In 1883 he was elected President of the Miners and Laborers' Amalgamated Association of Pennsylvania, and still holds the office. His association has, he said to-day, a membership of over 35,000. The Knights, he thought, should not organize with "unfair" material or in districts in which unions were able to take care of workingmen's interests.

J. W. Smith, the Second Vice-President, is a member of the National Tailors' Union, and a resident of Springfield, Ill.

Gabriel Edmonston was elected Treasurer. He is a member of the Brotherhood of Carpenters and Joiners, and resides at Washington, D. C.

The Secretary of the Federation is P. J. McGuire, who occupies a similar office in the Brotherhood of Carpenters and Joiners. He is a man of brains as well as labor in the labor movement, and to him more than to any other single man is due the successful organization of the Federation. Secretary McGuire is a most successful organizer, and is at the head of a union that has few equals. He believes the Federation has a bright future. He will not invite a contest with the Knights, but if it comes he will be their principal opponent.

Adolph Strasser, President of the International Cigarmakers' Union, expressed himself as follows, after adjournment:

"Our work will result in amalgamating all national and international trades unions. The Knights of Labor are defunct; it's no use talking about a corpse. They have lost 75 per cent. of the order in Massachusetts since Oct. 1 through the collapse of the Peabody strike."

J. R. Winders, San Francisco, said:

"I think the difficulties existing between the Knights and trades unions could be satisfactorily settled if No. 49, of New-York, was thrown into the ocean. Some of our radicals might be disposed of in the same way without causing a national loss."

Henry Emerich, of the National Furniture Makers, said:

"We have laid the foundation of a great labor movement."

George Block, National Bakers' Union, said:

"We will soon have all the trade and labor unions of the country in the Federation."

Christopher Evans, President of the Federation of Miners and Mine Laborers, said:

"The convention could not have accomplished more."

Among the unions which were represented at the convention and are now members of the Federation are the Brotherhood of Carpenters and Joiners, organized in 1881 with a membership of 2,342; its membership now is 26,742; it has obtained an advance in wages of from 25 to 75 per cent.; the International Cigarmakers' Union, organized in 1864. Its membership is 34,000. It has paid out in benefits $700,000. Its treasury contains $270,000. It has increased wages 50 to 80 per cent since 1873. The Iron Molders' Union was organized in 1859. Its membership is 20,000. The Bricklayers' International Union has a membership of 18,000. It was organized in 1885. The International Typographical Union was organized in 1850. It has a membership of 30,000. The National Federation of Miners and Mine Laborers was organized in 1885. Its membership is 30,000. The Granite Cutters' Union has a membership of 3,000. It was organized in 1877. The National Furniture Makers' Union, organized in 1873, membership 9,000. National Bakers' Union, organized 1886, membership 6,000. Miners' and Laborers' Amalgamated Association of Pennsylvania, organized 1883, membership 35,000. Waiters' Union, organized 1855, membership 1,200. German Typographical Union, organized 1873, membership 1,400. Operative Painters, of New-York, organized 1842, membership 1,800. International Bootmen's Union, organized 1886, membership 1,080. It has doubled wages.

The unions which favor the Federation have a membership of 350,000. Letters expressive of sympathy with the cause were received from unions having an almost equal membership. All the delegates took night trains for their homes. They seemed certain of having accomplished a good bit of work.

MR. POWDERLY'S FOE.

A TALK WITH THE HEAD OF THE LABOR FEDERATION.

The bitter feeling on the part of the Knights of Labor, of which Mr. Powderly is the head, against the American Federation of Labor, of which Mr. Samuel Gompers, of this city, is the President, will not be sweetened in the least by the announcement that since the Columbus Convention there have been three applications for charters under the new federation and a very large correspondence offering sympathy and aid. It would not do to mention the names of the applicants at present for obvious reason; the principal one being that it might incite the Knights to further attempts at coercion, notwithstanding their vain efforts in that direction heretofore. Neither will it be pleasant news for the Knights that the Amalgamated Association of Iron and Steel Workers, who were not represented at the Columbus Convention, greatly to the joy of antagonistic anti-unionists, have practically agreed to join hands with the federation. Furthermore, Mr. Powderly and his colleagues will be interested to know that the Executive Committee of the rival association intends to exercise its power of sending competent speakers through the States to preach its doctrines, and they will also shortly begin the publication of an official journal to be called the *Union Standard*. It will be under the editorial management of the President, who is no novice in journalism.

Thus is the new organization advancing slowly but surely, without any symptoms of mushroom growth. Already it has assumed formidable proportions, having attained a membership not far from 370,000. At the head of this great democratic—not politically—association is one who said last night that he would not exchange his position with any man in the land. The emoluments of the office are not to be envied, but "Sam" Gompers, as he is known to all those under him, is none the less gratified and proud of his constituents. He has an abiding faith in the principles of the association, and believes them to be the only ones by which the great army of skilled labor can remain steadfast. He bears the friendliest feeling toward the Knights of Labor, and hopes and expects them to adopt a conciliatory policy. This will probably happen, he thinks, when Mr. Powderly's anger is tempered by sober second thought. It may be that the head Knight will continue an antagonistic course because he knows his following is numerically larger than that of Mr. Gompers. In that case a settlement of the difficulty is unlikely until the Federation has drawn materially from his forces and swelled their own ranks.

"All we ask," said Mr. Gompers, "is that the Knights keep clear of our field by changing their course toward trades unionists. By this method only can anything like harmony be maintained and the interests of the laboring men advanced. If the fight is kept up I fear it will prove disastrous to the Knights and to the organized labor movement generally. The fact of the matter is that the Knights have interfered in disputes between employers and employes, contrary to common decency. They have taken into their order persons expelled or suspended from trades unions for violations of obligations. It is this policy that we object to and which we hope to change in time. Whether we will accomplish our aim or not remains to be seen. We hope that brother Powderly will see the folly of his course and make overtures.

"You can judge something of the strength of our organization when I tell you that it includes 34,000 cigarmakers, 22,000 bricklayers, 40,000 coal workers, 29,000 printers, 27,000 iron molders, and 30,000 carpenters and joiners. The iron and steel workers of the Amalgamated Association will undoubtedly join us. They have decided by an almost unanimous vote not to go with the Knights. The President wrote a letter to the Columbus Convention, in which he gave assurances of co-operation if we omitted a free trade plank in the platform. That was done, hence it is safe to say that the iron and steel workers are with us. The policy of our organization is distinctively union, and that means strength. We are confident and hopeful."

Action in the matter on the part of the General Executive Board of the Knights of Labor is likely to take place soon, because the figurehead committee sent to the Columbus Convention have submitted a report. The nature of that report has not been made public, but it cannot amount to very much, as the committee received no recognition after it was learned that it had no power to act.

December 19, 1886

KNIGHTS AND UNIONISTS

THEIR VARYING FORTUNES OF A COUPLE OF YEARS.

A POLICY THAT HAS WRECKED ONE ORGANIZATION—METHODS THAT HAVE STRENGTHENED THE OTHER.

In the Spring of 1886 half a dozen men met in one of the parlors of a hotel at Cleveland, Ohio. With one exception they displayed a tendency to anger and an inclination to talk at the same time. The exception was the biggest man in the room. His shoulders were square and broad. The head they carried was large and covered with closely-cropped dark red hair. Partly hidden by a black slouched hat was a forehead that betokened intelligence, if not something rarer. For five minutes or more this man listened to the exciting talk of his companions, and then stood up and stretched his arms as if his body wanted to yawn and, in his opinion, deserved the privilege. His companions ceased their talk to look at him, and while they looked he said his say. Unlike his companions, he had evidently determined what to say before he opened his mouth. His manner was composed but earnest, and in a very short time his opinion was the general opinion. The burden of his talk was: "Let us wait." At the outset the advice would not have been palatable to a single man in the room, but the reasons that accompanied it were sound, and once accepted it seemed to give a great deal of relief to those who had nothing so good to offer. The man who gave the advice was then a resident of Cleveland, but is now a resident of Philadelphia, and his name is P. J. McGuire. Like his companions, he was and is a trades unionist. He and they had met to discuss the situation. To them it seemed studded with so many difficulties that they were upon the point of losing their heads when the owner of the slouched hat brought them to their senses. McGuire may or may not have had, at the time, a policy more definite than one of waiting. The chances are that he had not, and like an able General made the one suggestion that could do no harm and might do his side much good. He had been a trades unionist all his life and was Secretary of the Brotherhood of Carpenters and Joiners. In spite of his quiet manner he was an enthusiast, and in order to push the labor movement had thrown down his tools to work with his head alone, though he lost money by the change. He had a heart as well as brains, and he felt for his fellows in their struggle for a livelihood. He was firmly convinced that there should be organization among wage workers. He firmly believed that each trade should have the administration of its own affairs. Trades unions were gray-haired before the Knights of Labor were born. The new broom had been doing a desperate lot of sweeping and its handlers seemed determined to sweep trades unions out of existence. A good many of McGuire's fellow-unionists had been dazzled by the cyclonic-like advance of the new order, but he maintained his composure, and when he felt it necessary to express his opinion maintained that trades unionism had not seen its last days. He was constrained to admit that its prospects had looked more encouraging.

.

The situation was briefly this: The Knights of Labor, in the order's infancy, had opened its arms to trades unionists. Its policy was pacific. While the Knights of Labor conferred more benefits upon its members than any other labor organization possibly could, there was room for all. A man could be a unionist and a Knight of Labor also. The policy was a wise one, and unionists flocked to the standard of the Knights. The latter soon equaled, then surpassed the trades unions in numbers. The increase in membership and in wealth developed a change of policy. War, not peace, was breathed. Unionists who had fallen from grace were made Knights. The labor market became divided into three instead of two classes. Prior to the birth of the Knights it had consisted of unionists and men who belonged to no organization, and the latter was divided into men who had been unionists and had broken the rules and those who had always preferred entire independence. Between these subdivisions the Knights in 1886 apparently saw no difference. If the Knights had any preference it was apparently for men who had been marked "unfair" by unions from which they had been expelled. The scheme was to convince unionists that they could defy their own organization and still be eligible to membership in a body that boasted of far more power. The unions were discomposed. They asked for a parley. They appointed a committee to wait upon the special General Assembly that met at Cleveland in May, 1886. This committee made a strong plea for fair dealing. It suggested that Knights and unionists work in common, and that all who transgressed the rules of either organization should be labeled "unfair" by both. The conservative element among the Knights recognized the justice of the plea. All the morning New-York newspapers were specially represented at Cleveland during the session of the special assembly. Prior to the meeting of this assembly hardly a paper in the country except THE TIMES had printed a criticism touching the Knights that was not of the most favorable character. When THE TIMES discovered the Knights in an attempt to coerce an opponent on the ground that might was right it very promptly demonstrated to the Knights that neither their numbers nor threats were of the slightest consequence. But until the meeting at Cleveland THE TIMES had been alone in its attitude toward the order. Subsequent to the Cleveland meeting THE TIMES had plenty of assistance. It was the first to print an exposé of the Home Club's purposes and to show how entirely Powderly had surrendered himself to the worst elements in the order. It was prompt to denounce the Knights for their treatment of their fellow-workmen, the trades unionists, who were contemptuously informed that their desires might be considered, but not at the Cleveland Assembly. Since the Cleveland Assembly the Knights have missed the almost solid support of the press, to which they had grown so accustomed as not to appreciate it.

.

There was nothing for the unionists to do but wait. McGuire, however, had no notion of idly waiting. He meant to be up and doing while the Summer was slipping away. The Knights were too powerful for the unions while each union stood on its own tub. A pitched battle was out of the question. A dishonest peace was bad enough to endure, but it was at least better than extermination. So McGuire said "wait," and rolled up his sleeves.

***

The trades unions waited to some purpose. In less than a year from the date of the rebuff administered by the Knights at Cleveland representatives of a large number of trades met at Columbus, Ohio, and accomplished a federation. It has not occupied so much space in the newspapers as has been given to the Knights of Labor, and fortunately for it. The Knights now get into print solely because of their inability to keep their quarrels and other mistakes from becoming public property. And it has come to pass that the Knights are now talking of doing even more than the unions thought of suggesting two years and a half ago. In 1886 the Knights, or their leaders rather, advised the expulsion of members who would not sever their connection with the unions. A few days ago at the General Assembly in session at Indianapolis Master Workman Lewis of District Assembly No. 135—composed of miners—offered a resolution providing for the appointment of a committee of five to meet with a similar committee of the American Federation of Labor to prepare a plan for the consolidation of the Knights and the federation. At the same time Lewis suggested that the plan should be based upon the constitution of the federation rather than upon the alleged constitution of the Knights. The latter are really without a constitution. They had one with which to begin business, but when it interfered with the schemes of the leaders it was overridden, and it has been overridden so often that it long since became valueless. Lewis could hardly have expected his resolution to bear much fruit of the kind relished by Powderly and his sort. Lewis is a man of some sense, and he has evidently been a Knight of Labor long enough to discover that to the rank and file the order has been simply a sponge. That a good many miners are of the same opinion Powderly knows, for recently he issued a "secret" circular—a weakness of his—to Lewis's assembly that contains some amusing matter. To the miners he wrote that "the prospects are that every bitterness of the past will vanish, and it is not fair to these miners whom we represent to ask them to step back again to the bottom of the ladder and begin anew to build an organization of that craft simply because the officers differ as to methods. The same trouble will face the miners in or out of the Knights of Labor." The chief beauty of Powderly's appeal lies in the last paragraph, which is as follows: "If a new organization is formed it will have to fight its way to where the Knights of Labor now stand."

***

If that be so, the new organization will simply have to fight by sliding down hill. Lewis knows this, and in a reply to Powderly he administered a few thrusts that must have hit the five-thousand-dollar General Master Workman in a tender spot. Lewis tells him: "Look at your own homes, where, in the territory covered by District Assembly No. 16, there are about 40,000 miners, the most oppressed and tyranny-ridden people in the United States. Out of that vast multitude of working people District Assembly No. 16 has about 4,000 or 5,000 members, of whom about 2,000 are miners, having their affairs looked after by men who dig coal in the court houses and shoe and clothing stores." He finishes his reply to Powderly with this parting salute: "For nearly two years has District Assembly No. 135 tried to organize those men and for nearly two years the officers of District Assembly No. 16, backed by yourself upon some flimsy pretext, have defeated the work of organization." Two years and a half ago Lewis would not have talked in such fashion, but, like thousands of other workingmen, he has watched the downward course of the Knights and the gradual rise of the unionists.

***

Neither the Knights nor the public would have been favored with a statement of something approaching their actual condition had the treasury not been empty. Hundreds of thousands had left the order because they could obtain no information of what became of the money that was poured into the general treasury. Even the small remnant of the faithful had grown so tired of putting its hands in its pockets that, as a last resort, some figures were vouchsafed to it. A couple of years ago the leaders claimed that the Knights numbered 750,000. The same leaders are still at the head of affairs and under their management, according to their own figures, the Knights now number 259,518. These figures are probably much too large, but if a decrease of a half million in membership in two years is not enough to demonstrate unfitness for office it is difficult to imagine what could convince the Knights that their leaders are incompetent or worse.

***

The figures given in the official reports presented to the Indianapolis Assembly are instructive in two ways. They show how demoralized the Knights have become. They prove that the men who made the reports have lied about the strength of the order. According to the membership report District Assembly No. 30 of Boston had fallen away from 31,644 in July, 1887, to 9,179 in July of the present year. At the Richmond Assembly it was stated that this assembly had a membership of over 60,000. It was stated at the same assembly that No. 1 of Philadelphia had a membership of over 30,000. The official report states that the membership has fallen away from 11,294 to 2,314. It looks as if the men at the head of the order, having determined to lie, decided to do so on a large scale. How they must have squirmed when they found it absolutely necessary to confess that the order had dwindled away, and to show that District Assembly No. 198 had decreased from 5,163 to 229; No. 24 of Chicago, from 10,483 to 3,507; No. 57 of the same city, from 4,656 to 761; No. 41 of Baltimore, from 7,549 to 2,248; No. 43 of Cincinnati, from 14,519 to 4,527; No. 55 of Gloversville, N. Y., from 3,402 to 149; No. 70 of Philadelphia, from 3,267 to 228; No. 77 of Lynn, Mass., from 2,450 to 358; No. 106 of Indianapolis, from 2,140 to 377; No. 108 of Milwaukee, from 3,178 to 595; No. 61 of Hamilton, Ontario, from 2,070 to 386; No. 184 of Pottsville, Penn., from 2,680 to 421.

***

The loss of membership could probably have been borne by the leaders with equanimity if it were not accompanied by a loss of income. To start a year with over $200,000 in the treasury and to end it with nothing but a lot of debts is not convincing evidence of a capacity for financial management, but in order to squeeze more money out of the remnant of the order it was necessary to give it a few facts or parts of facts. Disheartening as these forced disclosures must be to men who really expected great things of the order, they must be in the nature of a relief after the everlasting doses of bombast and untruth so lavishly dealt out by the leaders. They must be in the highest degree encouraging to McGuire and his fellow-unionists. While the Knights have indulged in bluster and untruth, the unionists have been at work quietly but steadily. Each month has added to their numbers and to their strength. Numbers were only a source of weakness to the Knights. Not so to the unionists. Each union is composed of a separate trade, and when a union gets into difficulties with the employers of its members the latter are not compelled to take orders from a person totally unacquainted with their work and their needs. The employer of a lot of carpenters is not dictated to by a cigarmaker or a baker, but the rights of his fellows are stated by a carpenter, who has some knowledge of both sides of the case and is not transformed into an insufferable brute by a little brief authority.

***

In short, the changes that have occurred in the labor world in two years and a half are far greater than McGuire and his companions at that Cleveland meeting could possibly have hoped for. The Knights have gone to pieces. The unionists have grown strong. The lost membership of the Knights can be found in the federation. A large percentage of the present membership of the Knights will soon be found in the unions. The latter are at peace and are prosperous. The former are at war with themselves and are bankrupt. Powderly talks; McGuire works. Powderly has at last gained his point and is an autocrat. McGuire is apparently in favor of the largest possible division of authority; at least he has made no effort at centralization. Powderly is hungry for notoriety and a large salary. McGuire has never attempted to rush into print, and asks no more for his services than he can earn at his trade. Powderly is fond of sounding titles and insists upon being head, body, and tail of the Knights. McGuire, though by far the ablest man among the unionists, is satisfied with the title of Secretary, and keeps in the background. Powderly, judged by the history of the Knights, is for self. McGuire, according to his record and that of the Federation of American Labor, is for the workingman. Powderly talks of what he will do. McGuire makes no boasts of what he has done. He does not even slap his fellow-workmen on the shoulders and say, "Didn't I tell you so?" Perhaps he is still waiting. Certainly he is watching the course of events, and has probably determined how to take advantage of them, not for the benefit of P. J. McGuire, but for the aid of trades unionism.

T. B. F.

December 7, 1888

THE TRADES FEDERATION.

Mr. MULRANEY, a delegate to the "Congress of Federated Trades," at Columbus, has given his views upon the labor question to a Chicago reporter. "When I have trouble as a bricklayer," remarked Mr. MULRANEY, "I do not want a butcher, a shoemaker, and a blacksmith to act upon any troubles that my union becomes involved in."

This remark touches the point of the whole business of the organization of labor. It is so obviously sensible that it seems strange that an enormous organization should have grown up for the purpose of violating the principle which it expresses. The motto of the Knights of Labor is that "an injury to one is the concern of all." In practice this has been taken to mean not only that a butcher, a shoemaker, and a blacksmith shall adjudicate the disputes of bricklayers, but also that the butchers and shoemakers and blacksmiths shall quit work whenever the bricklayers go on strike. Sometimes this general strike is meant as a means of coercing the employers of the bricklayers by causing a public inconvenience which the strikers imagine will be laid to the charge of the employers. More often it is made simply as a means of enabling the strikers to "show their power."

Men who follow a useful calling are in general more exercised about supporting their families than about showing their power, when this latter performance means also showing their lack of sense. One would suppose beforehand that skilled workmen would leave to unskilled laborers the showing of their power by quitting work and turning out in processions, and this is exactly what has happened. The idea of the Knights of Labor is that when any Knight anywhere has any trouble with his employer, all other Knights everywhere shall strike work and show at once their power and their sympathy with the discontented workingman. The skilled laborer who desires to keep at work and not be mixed up in anybody else's quarrels finds some difficulty in doing this when the people who are in favor of mixing themselves up with the quarrels of everybody else are numerous, well organized, and excited. The locomotive engineers employed on the Missouri Pacific and its tributaries were subjected to a very strong pressure last year to induce them to join the striking switchmen, yardmen, and unskilled laborers generally who had been employed upon that road. They were able to do so because of belonging to at once the strongest and the most intelligent trades union in the country, and of being bound not to strike work without consulting the authorities of their order. If the Brotherhood of Locomotive Engineers had not been so strong and so intelligently managed it is to be feared that the strikers would have dragged the engineers along with them.

It is this difficulty which the followers of one trade find in withstanding the pressure of an organized mob that accounts for the formation of the Trades Federation. It may seem strange that mechanics should find it necessary to organize a union of different trades in order to mind their own business, but it seems to be the fact that they do. At least if the Trades Federation does not mean to accomplish that it would be hard to say for what purpose it exists. A carpenter and a compositor and a plasterer have no more in common than a stevedore and a car driver and a street sweeper. They have this in common as against unskilled laborers of all kinds that they are skilled laborers, and that their labor commands a comparatively high price in the market, while the unskilled laborer will work for the minimum of subsistence, so greatly does the supply of him exceed the demand. He cannot, except under very unusual circumstances, command higher wages unless he has an organization competent to intimidate the unemployed workmen who would be glad to take his place at that rate, and whom he calls "scabs."

Such an organization is the Knights of Labor, or at least the controlling element in the organization is of this kind. Strikes, followed by mob violence, and boycotts are the chief of its weapons. It is a necessity of such an organization that men who desire to get a living without working should be anxious to control it, either in order to be supported by it directly or in order to use it in politics. The proceedings of the Montauk Assembly, in its meeting in Brooklyn on Sunday, shows to what dissensions such an ambition may give rise.

It is not to be expected that the Trades Federation will employ such methods or be subject to such temptations. With skilled laborers the question how much money they can earn is not a question of the limit of subsistence. It is a question of the condition of the market for their products. They have no occasion to employ intimidation, for if their trades union is complete there are no men outside their own ranks who can do their work at short notice. For a like reason boycotts are of no use to them. Accordingly nearly all the lawless representatives of labor, the Anarchists and rowdies and loafers, are to be found among the unskilled laborers represented in the Knights of Labor, and not among the skilled laborers represented in the Trades Federation. The organization into one body of all labor, skilled and unskilled, is a foolish dream. The Trades Federation may be needful in order to show that workingmen acting in concert are not necessarily fools. At any rate, the Trades Federation demonstrated that fact when it voted down a resolution offered by a Chicago labor union denouncing the verdict against the Anarchists as an outrage, and substituted another declaring that the trades of the country "are dependent on law and order for continued existence and support."

December 14, 1886

WHAT TWENTY YEARS HAS DONE FOR THE WORKINGMAN.

Notwithstanding the complaints about hard times, the general condition of the workingman and workingwoman in this city is much better to-day than it was some twenty years ago. The rates of wages have in most instances been increased, the hours of labor have been lessened, the sanitary arrangements in the shops and factories where they work have been greatly improved, measures have been taken to guard against injuries and loss of life from machinery, fire, and defective scaffolding, and child labor has been practically abolished. The State Legislature has done a great deal for the workingman, and influential and professional philanthropists now champion his cause, sometimes with so much professed zeal as to evoke a smile of doubt from the hard-handed son of toil.

It is, however, in a great measure due to the workingman's own efforts, through unions and combinations of unions, and to their agitation that these improvements have been brought about. The old-established unions of to-day are different from those organized twenty years ago. The men then came together to redress what they called certain wrongs or to get an advance of wages. Some of the hot-headed and more eloquent among them aroused them with extemporary harangues that had often been mainly inspired by beer and whisky, and goaded them on to strike and fight anyhow, and show the employers their strength. If the men won a strike they only became more elated and wanted more, and then often made absurd and impossible demands. If they lost they became disheartened, like an undisciplined mob, and scattered in all directions and remained quiet, sometimes for a long period. Defeats, however, often proved very salutary to them, as it taught them the value of caution and deliberation, and to respect the rights of others. It taught them to listen to the counsels of cooler and experienced heads, and gradually unions took the form of sober, deliberative bodies. Occasionally, when the success of a union attracted a large number of men who had stayed outside there was a setback to old conditions of disorder, caused by the very new, inexperienced men who imagined that they knew it all and could do better than the older members. But on the whole the tendency was forward. The men learned that a slow pace was safer, and that deliberation enabled them to avoid many mistakes. The agitations of the Socialists also considerably interfered with the progress of American trades unionism. These Socialist missionaries called all capitalists thieves and robbers who had no rights that workmen were bound to respect, and told the men that as their labor had produced the goods in their respective trades, all of right belonged to them and nothing to the employer who had simply paid them money that he unlawfully obtained from others. They urged an overthrow of the present

order of society and of the Government, and the substitution of the Socialist leveling system, where what they called the people should own everything—lands, mines, industries, systems of transportation and communication — and where all citizens should get equal remuneration for their labor. To this end they urged that all unions should become political bodies as well, and, of course, vote the Socialist ticket. Of course the leaders of the Socialists regarded themselves as "the people" who were to control the country and its enormous resources and industries, for were they not the wise men, and the masses of workingmen their obedient pupils?

Unfortunately for these leaders of Socialism, the masses of workingmen could not digest their theories. After the novelty had worn off they saw that those wild theories were utterly impracticable, inasmuch as a dead level could not be maintained under the laws of nature, and that the best and wisest thing for them to do was to go on with their work, trying to get better wages and more leisure time. Many of the unions tried politics again and again, but they obtained no benefit therefrom. Workingmen found it impossible to think alike in politics, and partisan loves and prejudices continued strong within the unions and caused dissensions, and thus weakened their usefulness for the purposes for which they had been organized. Some of the leaders, who under ordinary circumstances were honest enough, did not hesitate to manipulate the unions and sell them out to professional politicians.

The unions also found out that the politicians of both parties were willing to do them favors in the hope of catching votes for one side or the other. The Socialists have confined their efforts to propaganda among newly arrived immigrants from Continental Europe, among whom they have made some headway. But even the children of many Socialists who have been brought up in this country discard their fathers' doctrines in favor of American institutions. Among the benefits that New-York workingmen have obtained, both from the Legislature and their own efforts, are the creation of the Bureau of Factory Inspectors, the Bureau of Statistics of Labor, a Public Employment Bureau, advances in wages, reduction of the hours of labor, and the adoption of the eight hour system in the building and several other trades, the prevention of child labor in dangerous occupations, the prohibition of the employment of women and children at night work, the adoption of the Australian system of voting, the abolition of convict labor, the Labor Day holiday, and the union label system.

THE BUILDING TRADES INTERESTS.

Strikes and Long Struggles Between Contractors and Their Employes.

The men engaged in the building trades in

this city number many thousands and are among the most important of the working elements. These trades are numerous, bricklayers, stone masons, artificial-stone masons and cement laborers, hod carriers, plasterers and their helpers, carpenters and joiners, derrickmen, electrical workers, elevator constructors, architectural iron workers, lathers, house and fresco painters, varnishers, paper hangers, gilders, housesmiths, plumbers, gas and steam fitters, tin and sheet-iron and cornice workers, slate and metal roofers, mosaic and encaustic tile layers, marble workers, hod-hoisting engineers, and stair builders. Their total number is estimated as between 40,000 and 50,000. Of bricklayers there are about 4,000, and most of their struggles have been for a reduction of their hours of labor. They generally commanded good or fair wages, except when building was very slack, receiving $4 and $4.50 a day when the season was brisk and $3 when the season was good. Formerly a good many of the bricklayers and stone masons had their families in Ireland and Scotland, and Germany, and later also in Italy. In Summer, when the building season opened, they came over, leaving their families behind, and by careful living they saved enough to take them back and keep themselves and families during the Winter months in Europe, where living was much cheaper. This system, however, became unpopular, and finally most of the men settled here with their families.

The numerous strikes by the members of the building trades occasioned great loss to contractors, who were bound by their contracts to complete their work within a certain time under penalty of heavy forfeits. Finally the contractors combined, and had a strike clause inserted in their contracts which freed them from responsibility in cases of delays caused by strikes. The bricklayers and masons, with their laborers, then came to the sensible conclusion that an amicable understanding with their employers was preferable to strikes that hurt them as well as the contractors, and they made yearly agreements as to wages and hours of labor and apprentices, and pledged themselves not to strike for any alleged grievances of their own, nor to participate in any sympathetic strike. At the same time they broke loose from the other building trades and all other trades unions, and have kept their agreements. Bricklayers and stone masons formerly worked ten hours a day, but they complained that that was too long to work, at bending and unbending the body under a burning sun, and believed that if allowed more rest they could accomplish just as much work in eight hours as they had been doing in ten hours. A compromise on nine hours was made, and the time was then further reduced to eight hours, which is the rule now.

The former hod carriers now call themselves simply laborers, and their unions here come under the head of the General Council of the Laborers' Protective Society. Although their work of carrying hods of bricks and mortar up an almost perpendicular ladder two, three, and four stories high was intensely wearing, yet when the hod-hoisting engines were invented and began displacing them the men became greatly alarmed, and opposed the innovation as hard as they could. The hod-hoisting machine carried the day, the numbers of human carriers were reduced, and those who did remain in the business blessed the new invention, as all that they had to do was to fill the hods with bricks or mortar and carry them a distance of a few feet to the hoisting machine. They also work eight hours, and get $2.40 a day.

This new invention gave rise to a new set of workmen, with a certain amount of mechanical skill, for they had to know how to handle a stationary engine. In fact, they were engineers, and they adopted the name of portable hod-hoisting engineers. Of this class of workingmen there were about 1,000, who organized themselves into a union and joined the Board of Walking Delegates, to which organization they are still attached. As the bricklayers work only eight hours, the hod-hoisting engineers are not required to work any longer. They easily won all their demands, and most of the strikes on which they have gone have been sympathetic ones to help out the other unions in the building trade. They get $4 a day. Another new class of workmen in the building trades who have come into prominence are

the electrical workers, formerly known as electrical wiremen. They lay all the electrical wires and fixtures in the buildings. This work, in the incipiency of the electric lighting and bell industry, was formerly done by bricklayers and carpenters. Even after the electrical workers had become special craftsmen, quarrels arose between them and the bricklayers as to who should pass the wires through walls, and strikes were threatened. In 1890 the electrical workers of New-York organized themselves into Local Assembly No. 5,468, Knights of Labor, but in the Board of Walking Delegates they were known as Electrical Workers' Union No. 3, and are still so called. They received $2.75 a day, and worked eight hours, but now they wanted more, and went on strike. Their places were filled principally by men from other cities, the strike was lost, and the organization almost went to pieces. Many of those who went out left the Knights altogether, and organized another union, which they called No. 5, and affiliated themselves with the American Federation of Labor, the great and deadly rival of the Knights. This caused a feud between the two electrical unions, and last Winter and Spring No. 3, having the backing of the Board of Walking Delegates, got that body to order general strikes on buildings where No. 5 men were employed. This caused serious inconvenience to the contractors all around, and the electrical contractors got together and locked out all the men of No. 3, who were working for them on all buildings. The Board of Walking Delegates threatened strikes on all buildings in the city, but the workmen who had already experienced hard times, refused to obey a senseless, capricious order, and so No. 3 and the Board of Walking Delegates were brought to terms, abandoned the arbitrary position they had taken, and begged the electrical contractors to let up on them.

Of carpenters there are between 8,000 and 9,000 in the city, and those that are organized belong to three different National organizations—the United Brotherhood of Carpenters and Joiners, that has 60,000 members in the country; the Amalgamated Society of Carpenters and Joiners, an international organization that includes Canada, Great Britain, and Australia, and the Progressive Carpenters, who are Knights of Labor. There is no difference in the terms on which they work, as their rates are $3.50 for eight hours, but there exists a great deal of ill feeling between the Brotherhood carpenters that belong to the American Federation of Labor and the Progressives, each trying to break up the other's organization. Formerly both belonged to the Board of Walking Delegates, but the Brotherhood men got out, and the Progressives instigated the board to order strikes against them. This attempt failed, like that of the Knights of Labor electrical workers against their rivals. The carpenters in this city have had to fight hard for what they have obtained. Formerly they got $2.50 a day and worked ten hours, and sometimes more, as long as daylight lasted. Next to the bricklayers, they were the first among the building trades to make a fight for eight hours by going on strike. They won in two days. Later on the hours of labor were again increased, and wages were reduced, but when business revived they regained what they had lost, and this seesaw business still goes on in the trade.

The tile layers are a comparatively new set of workmen in the building trades, as fourteen years ago there were only twenty of them here, and now there are about 200. They worked nine hours a day, and got $3.50, but as tile laying became more fashionable, more men of that craft were attracted here, and they easily obtained $4 for eight hours' work. The granite cutters number about 500 men in New-York. In 1872 they worked ten hours a day for $2.50, but, after organizing themselves, they gradually improved their condition, and now they receive $4 for eight hours' work when times are good. The number of painters is very large, and this trade has various ramifications—house painters, decorative painters, fresco painters, sign painters, and so on—but the great mass are house painters, who have lately combined their different unions into one. Although a good many of the painters are workmen of mediocre ability, a considerable number are quite skillful, and have been encroaching upon the work of other men of kindred trades. First, they attacked the gilders, who are weak, and forbade them working in buildings. The gilders protested, but got no satisfaction. Then they attacked the varnishers, whom they also undertook to drive out of buildings and to do the varnishing themselves. The varnishers appealed to the Board of Walking Delegates, which suggested a compromise, by dividing the work between painters and varnishers. The painters defied the board

and were suspended, and now they threaten to get up a new and rival Board of Walking Delegates. Their union rates are $3.50 a day, but many work for $2.50 and for $2.

Plumbers and steam and gas fitters formerly did the same work, but improvement in building separated them into two distinct trades. The wages of plumbers have undergone few changes, and they have generally averaged $3.50 a day. Formerly they worked ten hours, and now eight. Most of their fights were to prevent boys from learning the trade, as they feared their numbers would increase too much, and wages go down. In one strike against apprentices, a number of years ago, the employers won, and they received a further check through the school of Col. Auchmuty, where young men were taught the plumbing, bricklaying, and some other of the building trades. The steam and gas fitters received between $2.50 and $3 a day.

The housesmiths, of which there are about a thousand, also comprise a comparatively new trade, which has come into prominence since the system of erecting iron skeleton buildings was introduced. About three-fourths of their number organized about 1890 and joined the Knights of Labor, and soon started an agitation for an increase of wages and a reduction of the hours of labor to eight. They ordered a strike and were supported by the Board of Walking Delegates, who called out all the men of the building trades under its jurisdiction. This led to the organization of the Iron League, a federation of all the principal iron manufacturers in this city, and the league was supported in the fight against the housesmiths by the Building Trades Club, composed of the contractors in the building business. The fight was a stubborn one, but the employers won, and the housesmiths' union went to pieces. Their wages then averaged $2 a day, and now they get about 21 cents an hour for nine hours' work. They reorganized and are preparing for another strike. The architectural iron workers have not cut much of a figure in the labor troubles, and their wages have remained almost stationary for nearly ten years at $2 a day. They did succeed in having their working hours reduced from ten hours to nine.

The tin and sheet-iron makers have also obtained a reduction of hours from ten to nine, and an increase of wages. Twelve years ago they got from $2 to $2.50 a day, and now the latter figure is the minimum rate, and the maximum $3.

The present outlook for fewer strikes in the building trades is very promising. Even the Board of Walking Delegates is tired of strikes that injure the men as much as they do the employers, and impede trade. Some time ago the board suggested the appointment of a joint arbitration board, to be composed of members of the unions and of employers, to whom all disputes should be submitted for settlement. The master masons' association approved of the suggestion, and now negotiations are going on between the board and the employers with a view of adopting the joint arbitration system.

TYPOGRAPHICAL UNION NO. 6.

Brief History of the "Big Six" Organization.

The printers have been called the swells of labor, and whenever they turned out in force on Labor Day parades they never failed to appear in black coats, with silk hats, and canes. Their union—Typographical Union No. 6—is known as "Big Six," and has for many years been regarded as one of the strong unions of this city. "Big Six" was formally organized in 1853, and it also combines out-of-work and death benefit features. It was in 1853 that "Big Six" got up its first scale of prices. Previous to organization compositors on morning papers were paid $14 a week, and when on piece work received 32 cents per 1,000 ems. They worked twelve hours a day. On afternoon newspapers they got $12 a week, or 25 cents to 28 cents per 1,000 ems, and worked nine hours a day. Compositors on book and job work were paid $9 and $10 a week, and worked ten hours a day.

The first scale of prices arranged by the printers, who were then known as the "New-York Printers' Union," was sent to the Employers' Association and was accompanied by a polite letter, in which the printers said that at that time of unparalleled increase of rents and high rates of living they felt it imperative to receive an advance on the existing rate of remuneration for their labor. They requested the employers to appoint a delegation to meet a delegation of the workmen for the purpose of adopting a fair and just increase on the scale. The employers did not respond to the call, so the union committee went ahead with the work of getting up a new scale to the best of their judgment, which scale was adopted by the union. The letter sent to the employers was signed by I. D. Boyce, Robert Peake, and J. C. Johnson, the committee, and concluded with a postscript asking for the acceptance of the scale by the employers within a few days.

The union grew stronger, and then went through various vicissitudes, the men trying, whenever they felt themselves strong enough, to advance the rates of composition, and at other times resisting reductions of wages. In the early seventies the printers began to take an active interest in politics, and wanted to have one of their number represent labor in one of the county or municipal offices. Nelson Young, Sr., was a prominent figure in the councils of the union at the time, and aspired to high political honors. The ruling political party in the city, to secure the votes of the printers and other workingmen, gave their candidate the nomination for Coroner, and "Nelse" Young, as he was affectionately called by his colleagues, was elected to that office and served his full term. The Coroners at that time were paid by fees, which were received from every inquest, and the office was considered quite a lucrative one, the average income of a Coroner being estimated at $15,000 a year. In those days every Coroner's case was always promptly attended to, and sometimes there was a race between two or more Coroners for a case in order to secure the fees, until they finally came to an understanding in the matter.

Dabbling in politics as members of trades unions, while it benefited certain ambitious individuals, did not help the printers any more than it did other union men. It caused jealousies and dissensions that weakened them. When Mr. Young's term of office expired he became a labor politician, and for a number of years after he held a clerkship in one of the municipal offices. In 1876 the membership of "Big Six" rose to 2,500, and then the hard times again weakened the organization. Many were thrown out of work, were unable to pay up their dues, and dropped out of the organization. They then looked for work at reduced wages. The union itself, while it nominally kept up its scale, either ignored the reductions in rates made in a good many offices, or allowed the employers who still recognized the union certain rebates which practically amounted to the same thing as the positive reductions made in other offices. By the end of 1877 the union scale was practically suspended, each printer taking what he could get.

A strike was tried at last on a morning newspaper just as the reports of the news of the day were being sent up to the composing rooms to be set up in type, but was unsuccessful. The reports were immediately condensed and several of the other employes who had learned to set type in their early days were impressed into the service; and there happened to be on hand a good many galleys of special stories and correspondence that had already been set up. The paper came out a little later than usual the next morning. There was a dearth of news and a good many typographical errors, but the paper came out, and by evening a sufficient number of non-union printers was secured. For a good many years thereafter that paper was known as a non-union office.

More and more men kept dropping out of the organization until in 1881, the membership had dwindled down to 1,000. In 1883, when business began to revive, the leaders began to bestir themselves, and about 300 men were induced to return to the union, and within a year the membership rose to 3,500, and the old scale of wages was restored in the larger offices that did not care to incur the risk of strikes. The agitation of the Knights of Labor was carried on among the printers, and a good many of them joined the order, at the same time retaining their membership in the open union. They belonged to District Assembly No. 49, and when numbers of pressmen and stereotypers also joined, a separate district assembly was formed, consisting of locals of printers and kindred trades, and was known as District Assembly No. 64. Florence F. Donovan, then an aspirant for political office, and who later was made one of the State Commissioners of Mediation and Arbitration, and is now a liquor dealer in Brooklyn, was elected District Master Workman. This organization did not last long. Political rancor and divisions upon the questions of supporting and opposing the Home Club drove out those who cared about neither, and the constituent local assemblies lapsed one after another.

The membership of "Big Six" is now estimated at 4,500, but there are a good many printers who are still out of the union, and who work at various offices at less than union rates. The union rates now are 50 cents per thousand ems on morning newspapers, and 40 cents on evening newspapers, the men working not more than fifty-nine hours in one week. The introduction of typesetting machines has materially interfered with the prosperity of printers on newspapers, on account of the rapidity with which machine work is done. It was agreed that only union men should be employed on the machines, and a scale of $27 a week on morning papers and $24 on evening papers was agreed upon. In job offices the wages are 40 cents to 43 cents per 1,000 ems for setting type from manuscript, and 37 to 43 cents for reprint, or a salary of $18 per week.

The typesetting machines and keen competition among printing offices have thrown many printers out of work. So the union, to keep up its membership and help out the unemployed, levied an assessment upon its working members for two weeks in 1893. This amounted to $6,000. In 1894 more assessments were levied, and $30,858.52 was paid out to the unemployed. This, with death, strike, and sick benefits and other expenses, amounted to $42,466.06. The amount of benefits paid during the past year is estimated between $50,000 and $60,000.

HARDSHIPS OF CLOTHING WORKERS

Strikes Against Wage Reductions and the Shops.

Of working people who are engaged in the manufacture of clothing for men and women, there are some 50,000 in this city, and the greater part of these have come to this country within the past fifteen years, principally from Russian, Austrian, and German Poland. The proportion from Russian Poland and from Russia itself is very large, and they left their native land at the time that the Russian Government resumed its policy of restricting the Hebrews to the "pale." Many thousands left the country altogether, and large numbers found their way to America and settled principally in New-York. Many of them had learned the trade of tailoring in Russia, for the Jews have a peculiar aptitude for the trade, and make excellent cutters. Many are now large manufacturers.

Before the influx of Hebrews, a large proportion of the journeymen tailors in this city were Germans, and the rest were Americans, Englishmen, and Irishmen. The clothing industry, while extensive, had not nearly attained the enormous proportions of the present day, and many of the journeymen knew the trade of tailoring thoroughly, and could cut and sew together an entire suit of clothes, including a cloak. An entire change has taken place since those days, and now there are basters, bushelmen, buttonhole makers, buttonhole carriers, cloakmakers, coatmakers, finishers, cutters, operators, overall makers, trousers and knee-pants makers, pressers, and tailors, besides cloakmakers.

First in the business came the cutters, the aristocracy of the trade, and a skilled cutter in the custom trade—merchant tailors who make clothes to order—could easily earn $40 a week. These cutters had such a high opinion of themselves that at one time they seriously discussed the question as to whether they should call their union the Sartorial Artists' Society. They at least managed to keep up their rates of wages for a good many years. The cutters in the ready-made clothing factories, which were gradually growing larger and more numerous, could earn $25 a week, and sometimes a little more, while the tailors could earn $16, and in some instances $18.

Merchants from near and distant parts of the country began buying large quantities of clothes in New-York, and many city men who formerly had their clothes made to order patronized the ready-made clothing stores, where they could get suits of as good cloth as they wore cheaper, although they did not fit as well. Large numbers of tailors were attracted here, where they could find work at almost any season of the year. This caused a surplus of labor in the tailor market, and employers began to cut down wages. The men and their unions struggled against the reductions, but the tendency was downward.

Soon after the influx of the Hebrew element began, the clothing industry of New-York grew still larger, and new methods were introduced. Large clothing factories employed hands by the hundreds and by the thousands, and many of the Jewish tailors aspired to become employers themselves. They saved all the money they could, and purchased machines, on which they and their families and a few hired hands worked. This was the beginning of the contractor and sweating system. The small contractor would take a lot of cut cloth from the manufacturer to make up at a certain price, and then had it made up at his home by hands that he would himself hire. At first the contractor made large profits, and his men a comfortable living. But new contractors kept constantly coming into the field, competing with each other and underbidding each other. Necessarily their margins of profit grew smaller and smaller, and they in turn cut the wages of their men and increased their hours of labor. This was the task system, and from early morning until 10 and 11 o'clock at night, and occasionally later, men, women, boys, and girls were seen huddled together in stifling hot rooms, working the sewing machines, stitching, and pressing, many of them in various stages of undress, to get some relief from the overpowering heat.

There was considerable difficulty in getting these people to organize for their own benefit. They looked with suspicion upon the Gentile fellow-workers, who gave them the advice. But when they did understand, there was a rush to join some union or other. Many joined the Knights of Labor, but after some experience in the order they again left it; and finally a number of unions were organized, which became affiliated with each other under the name of the United Hebrew Trades. As soon as they won a couple of strikes they seemed to become smitten with a strike fever. They wanted to strike for any petty grievance. The inroads that the Socialists and Anarchists made into their ranks rendered them still more irritable, and they were taught to regard liberty as a general hatred of all capitalists. For a time John Most, Emma Goldman, and other Anarchist ranters were their heroes, but eventually thousands upon thousands became disgusted, forsook the Socialists, and affiliated themselves with the conservative central organization known as the United Garment Workers of America, of whom many are Americans, and others foreigners who have lived many years in the country, and their children.

The creation of the office of State Factory Inspector has been the means of greatly improving the condition of these poor tailors, especially by the breaking up of the sweatshops, and the improvements in the sanitary conditions in the rooms where clothing is made.

The struggles of the tailors have been mainly to prevent reductions of wages, and they have not always succeeded. Rarely have they won fights for the restoration of old rates of wages. Union maximum rates of tailors' wages are $16 a week, and for assistants about $10, but $12, and even less for tailors, is the more general rule, and assistants get from $5 to $7. The clothing industry has been slack for the last two years, and contractors have been cutting wages, alleging that the employers have also cut their prices. The tailors had a strike last Spring, and compelled the contractors to sign an agreement to pay union wages, but the ink had scarcely dried on the paper when the cutting process began again. The members of the Brotherhood of Tailors are now preparing to order another general strike on July 1.

The tailors have succeeded in one thing, and that is a reduction of the hours of labor; but that is as much due to legislation regulating the hours of labor of women and children as to their own efforts. Where they formerly worked fifteen and sixteen hours out of the twenty-four, they now rarely work over twelve hours, and sometimes under ten hours.

THE BAKERS' UNION AFFAIRS.

Legislation Finally Comes to the Relief of the Trade.

The bakers' unions in this city have had as many ups and downs as any other labor organization. They were organized early and began blazing up, and as a sudden rainstorm struck them the fire hissed, and the flames were subdued and seemed to go out into outer darkness. Then again a faint spark appeared, and as it grew brighter and kindled more fuel many members were drawn into the vortex of politics, the maelstrom of trades unions, and disappeared. Again they reorganized, and again went down through inexperience and because they probably demanded more than under the circumstances of the times they could get. But they persisted, and when public opinion was aroused an agitation was gotten up in their favor, and the Legislature enacted laws that brought the bakeries, many of which were underground hells, under the inspection of the State Factory Inspectors. The first bakers' union in this city was organized in 1869. The city was not so large and competition among master bakers was not so keen as now, and, although journeymen did not get over $6 or $7 a week, they were not required to work as hard or produce as much bread in fourteen or fifteen hours work a day as they were later on. There was also a better feeling between masters and workmen, and the latter were to a certain extent treated as members of the family.

The year previous the Federal eight-hour law for work done on Government works was passed, and this so tickled the vanity of trades unions which had agitated in its favor that many of them resolved to go into politics, and among these were the bakers. It, however, proved a serious and almost fatal mistake. Dissensions and quarrels followed, and the bakers' union was one of those that were knocked out of existence. The condition of the bakers gradually became worse, and when the Knights of Labor began to agitate more openly and actively the English-speaking bakers organized a union in 1878, and other unions were organized in Boston and elsewhere. But when the union undertook to start bakers' intelligence bureaus, which they called "Houses of Call," it met with decided opposition and was extinguished. No other bakers' union was heard of until 1880, and in the meanwhile large numbers of bakers came here from Germany and Great Britain, and Jewish bakers from Southwestern Russia. Competition became keener, their hours of labor were increased, and heavier tasks were imposed upon the journeymen, and they found that they were being worked harder than they had ever worked before in their lives. Agitations were gotten up in this city and in other large cities in the country, but no satisfactory results were obtained.

In the following year, in May, the New-York bakers to the number of 6,000 went out on strike and went in a large procession to Irving Hall. Here they made several demands, the first of which was a reduction of the time of labor to twelve hours a day, and the second was to have the journeymen board outside of their employers' houses, and get in cash the $4 a week that was deducted from their wages for board. This demand was made because the employers made their men do menial housework besides their regular work, and not infrequently awakened them out of their sleep to do odd jobs. A third demand was the abolition of the vampire system, and the recognition of the union labor bureau.

Under the vampire system, certain beer saloons were recognized by the master bakers as employment bureaus, and journeymen looking for work were compelled to wait at these saloons and spend their money in drink to get a chance to work. The man who spent the most money would be the first to get a job, and if he wanted to keep it he had to visit the saloon at least on every pay day and spend part of his wages there. These vampire saloon keepers, most of whom had themselves been bakers, had their agents about Castle Garden and the immigrant boarding houses, and whenever they found an immigrant baker with about $50 in his possession they inveigled him to the vampire caves by promise of work and good wages. But these poor fellows were not given any employment until they had spent all their money at those places.

The strike lasted for four weeks, and then the men were compelled to go back to work, and the unions that they had hurriedly formed were discontinued as trades organizations, but were kept up under the name of benevolent societies. This was done to keep the men together as much as possible; but many became disheartened and dropped out. Later, Bakers' Union No. 1 was declared organized, and a journeymen bakers' organ called the Bäcker-Zeitung was published, and copies were sent to all the shops urging the men to reorganize, as their strength lay only in union. This acted as a stimulus, and a few months later the unions began cropping up again. In 1884 the benevolent societies resumed their names as unions, and repeated their demands for a reduction of the hours of labor, the abolition of the employers' boarding house and vampire systems, and the recognition of the union labor bureau.

Their efforts were attended with a little more success. They had succeeded in getting the ear of the public through the newspapers, and the employers were constrained to make them even larger concessions than they had asked for, at least nominally. The hours of labor that had been increased to sixteen, seventeen, and also eighteen, and which the men had asked to be reduced to twelve were fixed at eleven, and the wages were raised to $16 a week for foremen, or first hands; $12 for second hands, and $10 for third hands. The first hands do the baking, the second hands knead the dough and make up the loaves, and the third hands are the general helpers. The men were allowed to board wherever they pleased, and the employers agreed to employ men from the union labor bureau. Gradually, however, matters drifted back to old conditions, as the small employers, taking advantage of the fact that new bakers kept constantly arriving from all parts, again reduced wages and made their men board with them, giving them inferior food and making them work longer time.

In the early part of 1886 a Bakers' National Convention was held in Pittsburg, at which twenty-six unions were represented, and that led to the organization of the Bakers' International Union of the United States and Canada. The New-York bakers succeeded in abolishing Saturday night work for bread baking and Sunday work for cake baking. Having gained so much, the unions turned their attention to the improvement of the sanitary condition of the bakeries, and for this they sought aid from the Legislature, and they asked that State Factory Inspectors be authorized to inspect them. The condition of many of these places was found to be filthy, abominable, and disgusting in the extreme. Most of them were situated in cellars, and often the sewage leaked on the floor, sometimes close to the kneading troughs. Fetid gases rising from the ground, combined with the vile stenches from the sewage, and stenches from other causes were inhaled by the workmen in an overheated temperature, while rats, cockroaches, and other vermin roamed about at will over dough and barrels of flour, while the men themselves often slept on boards loosely laid on barrels.

It was not until 1892 that a law was passed empowering Factory Inspectors to inspect bakeries, and later an amendment was passed forbidding the employment of youths under eighteen years of age in bakeries between the hours of 9 P. M. and 6 A. M. It was claimed that this was necessary, on account of the very unhealthy occupation; but the unions favored this law as a check upon the large number of apprentices. The conditions under which journeymen bakers now work, said Henry Weissman, the editor of the Bäcker-Zeitung, are twelve hours a day. The State Bureau of Statistics of Labor gives their present maximum wages as $2.66 2-3 per day, as against $3 in 1893. There is no change in wages of second hands, but third hands get a trifle less now than in 1893. The average wages are larger than before the bakers were organized, and they work fewer hours a day. A few weeks ago the Hebrew bakers' unions, which are also affiliated with the Bakers' International Union, struck for a reduction of hours of labor and for an advance of wages. They were generally successful, and then some of the smaller employers attempted to make up for their losses in this direction by raising the price of bread 1 cent per loaf. Competition, however, compelled them to drop the price again. There are about 8,000 bakers in New-York.

THE CIGARMAKERS' UNION.

Struggles and Tribulations of the Workers in Tobacco.

The cigarmakers—that is, the workers on the cheap brands that are smoked by the millions—form a considerable proportion of the working population of this city. Their numbers are estimated at about 12,000, New-York being the largest cigar manufacturing centre in the country. Nearly all the cigarmakers here are of foreign birth or extraction, the majority of them being Bohemians who had come over with a knowledge of the trade that they had learned in the Austrian Empire, where the Government holds the monopoly of the tobacco trade and cigar manufacture. As a rule, the Bohemian cigarmaker is not an ambitious or provident individual, and although many of them came here when the great cigar industry was still in its infancy, very few of them have become manufacturers on their own account, while, on the other hand, the old manufacturers, who have built up colossal fortunes, in several instances amounting to millions, have nearly all been graduated from the workman's bench. The profit of the manufacturer was enormous, and although the large increase of cigar factories and the keen competition that has resulted, and the prevailing fashion among many of smoking cigarettes, have materially curtailed the profits, they are still considerable, and a failure in a cigar factory is rarely heard of. The Bohemian, having long been oppressed by the Austrian Government, has not yet been able to recover his elasticity, and is content to plod along for his daily bread, making a fight only when his wages have been reduced to the starvation point. When he gets an advance of wages he is happy, and talks of Bohemia and the hated German that has kept him down for ages.

It was about 1875 that the cigarmakers of New-York began to agitate against gradual but steady reductions of wages. A good many of the factories were then situated in old Chatham Street, Chatham Square, the Bowery, and also east of that thoroughfare, where most of these establishments were simple tenement houses, in which the people worked and lived. They could earn about $15 a week, and when a man, with his wife and children, all worked together as they still do, they managed to make a comfortable income. They received a certain amount for making a thousand cigars, and the family divided itself up into bunchers, rollers, &c. These wages were gradually reduced until a man could hardly make $8 a week, and the remainder of his family a little more, while the manufacturer, who generally owned the tenement factory and compelled him to live there, taxed him a higher price for rent than he could have got from workmen of any other trades. The sanitary condition of many of these tenement factories was abominable. In a couple of rooms an entire family worked all day and late into the night, and there they also cooked, washed, and slept. Tobacco dust caused by the handling of the weed filled the atmosphere, and with the odors arising from the cooking and washing, made the place unbearable to persons unaccustomed to such stenches, and some such visitors were known to hurry out again with a feeling of dizziness in the head and of sickness at the stomach.

About 1877 thousands of the workers declared that their condition was unbearable. They held mass meetings on the east side, organized a union, and started a great strike. Adolf Strasser and Samuel Gompers, both of whom were then working at that trade, were elected respectively President and Vice President. They were both able and energetic men, and encouraged the strikers to hold together. The strike was a long one, and a cigarmakers' mutual benefit organization was merged into the new union. Some aid was received from unions of other trades and from out-of-town cigarmakers, and the men succeeded in slightly improving their condition. Several of the largest manufacturers decided to discontinue tenement-house work altogether, and built large and well-ventilated factories up town, and here the hands worked only by day. Other manufacturers also moved up town and erected large tenement factories, where the sanitary conditions were much improved. The union became a National and then an international one, and strike and death benefit features were introduced. "In time of peace prepare for war!" became the motto of the leaders, and a part of the dues of the members was laid aside for those purposes, and a very large sum of money was thus raised. The strength of the unions, however, tempted many of the workers to launch into hurried and unnecessary strikes, and to put a stop to this the international union, that was now becoming conservative, made a rule that no local union should order a strike except after receiving permission to do so by a majority of all the unions in the United States and Canada, under penalty of forfeiting the strike benefit.

The fight against the tenement-house work system was kept up, as most of the cigar factories were still tenements. The newspapers of this city advocated the cause of the men, and the Legislature passed a law to abolish that system. The manufacturers, however, fought the law in the courts, and it was decided that the law was unconstitutional. Thereupon the men adopted another method, and got up a union blue label, to be affixed to the cigar box, which guaranteed that the cigars inside had been made in a regular factory. These were furnished to manufacturers who stood by the union men, and an appeal was made to all workingmen and the public in general to smoke only union label cigars, although union men continued working in tenement shops. One or two of these manufacturers undertook to imitate the label, and pasted them on their cigar boxes, but the union appealed to the courts, and after a long litigation succeeded in getting a permanent injunction against them. The men in the large factories received advanced wages, and were able to earn between $10 and $12 a week, working eight hours a day, but in the smaller tenements their wages were reduced whenever opportunity offered, and ten and twelve hours a day was the rule there.

Large numbers of cigarmakers joined the Knights of Labor, including Samuel Gompers, but the dissensions that broke out in that order disgusted many, and they left. Then the union ordered all its members who had joined the Knights to come out or leave the union. Most of them complied, but a good many, of Socialistic tendencies, remained behind, and called themselves the progressive cigarmakers. They adopted a red cigar label in opposition to the blue label of the open union. A fierce war broke out between the blue and the red label men, and each boycotted the other, and whenever the blue-label men went out on strike the red-label men took their places. The blue-label men finally won the day.

THE DEMANDS OF LABOR.

Laws Wanted to Regulate Hours of Work, Injunctions, Convict Labor, and Immigration.

WASHINGTON, Jan. 7.—The Legislative Committee of the American Federation of Labor, consisting of President Samuel Gompers, Secretary Frank Morrison and Andrew Furnseth, has issued an address to the members of the Fifty-fifth Congress. After calling attention to the introduction of modern machinery and new business methods and the competition of convict labor, by which it is alleged wage workers are forced into idleness and want, the committee asks the enactment of laws as follows:

First—An eight-hour work day on all public works, such law to provide that all contracts or sub-contracts for materials furnished or work done must contain a proviso that eight hours shall be the maximum labor of any one individual in any one calendar day; further, that it shall be the duty of officials vested with the power of signing such contract to withhold their signatures until such proviso is inserted therein.

Second—A law to stop the indiscriminate and dangerous use of the writ of injunction.

Third—A law to prohibit the transportation of prison made goods from one State into any other State or Territory.

Fourth—A reasonable law to restrict undesirable immigration, such law to be based upon an educational qualification.

VULTURES, SAYS GOMPERS.

He Denounces the Industrial Workers of the World, a New Body.

President Gompers of the American Federation of Labor, who has from time to time expressed his disapproval of the organization of the Industrial Workers of the World, formed by the Socialists at a convention in Chicago to fight the American Federation of Labor, issued his first formal denunciation of it yesterday. He says that the movement calls to mind the meeting of the "three tailors of Tooley Street," and says that it is a futile attempt to destroy the labor movement.

He denounces the leaders of the new movement. Among them he mentions Daniel De Leon, the founder of the Socialist Trade and Labor Alliance, and Eugene V. Debs, twice Socialist candidate for President of the United States.

"There were also in the movement," he says, "a few who pretended to represent the American Labor Union. This is the whole conglomeration! The Socialist Trade and Labor Alliance, with its vulturelike record, preying on the remains of those who have fallen in labor's battle, the American Labor Union, which is confessedly dying."

He says that the leaders of the new movement have shown "colossal nerve," and that the two and a half millions of organized workingmen in this country, besides those in other countries, are happily oblivious of the fact that they are included in the new movement.

June 28, 1896

January 8, 1898

August 6, 1905

UNIONS REJECT SOCIALISM

American Federation Refuses to Adopt Principles of That Party.

John Mitchell and President Gompers Speak Against Proposal, Which Is Defeated by Big Majority.

BOSTON, Nov. 18.—In historic Faneuill Hall to-day, at the end of a session remarkable because of the fervor of its oratory, the attempt of the Socialist delegates to have the organization pledge itself to Socialism was signally defeated at the convention of the American Federation of Labor. Nine resolutions presented by followers of Socialism calling for the adoption of the principles of that political party had been reported upon unfavorably by the Committee on Resolutions, and delegates representing a voting strength of 11,282 registered themselves in support of the committee's recommendation, while delegates with 2,185 numerical votes threw their power against the report of the committee and in favor of the resolutions.

The issue was discussed all to-day as well as part of yesterday. All the leaders of both sides engaged in debate. Just before the vote was taken this afternoon the convention became tumultuous over the question of the right of certain delegates to have their time extended, as well as Delegate Carey's heated condemnation of Vice President Duncan's attack upon the Socialists.

The discussion to-day was opened by Delegate D. W. Richmond, President of the Railway Clerks' International Association, who declared that his organization would withdraw if the federation adopted Socialistic ideas.

Charles Lavin, the venerable delegate from Wilkesbarre, made an impassioned speech against the Resolution Committee's action in bunching the Socialist resolutions in reporting to the convention. He urged the convention to adopt the resolutions, arguing that there was something wrong with the body politic, and that Socialism would cure the evils. The delegate declared that boys and girls are taken from school early and put to work in the factories and mills, and he pointed out that the more boys there are the worse it is for the men, and declared: "I see no political party that will stop these conditions except the Socialist."

Delegates Kreft of Philadelphia and Slayton of Newcastle, Penn., addressed the Chair in opposition to the committee's unfavorable report. Delegate Kreft stated that no political party except the Socialist had made reference in its platform to the coal strike.

After several other Socialist delegates had spoken, John Mitchell, President of the United Mine Workers, gave his views as follows:

"I do not desire to detract from the credit due our Socialist friends for the assistance rendered us during the coal strike. On the contrary, I wish to make grateful acknowledgment to them for the assistance they gave to us. But I wish to deny the statement made by Delegate Kreft that the Relief Committee in Philadelphia was organized by or was under the supervision of the Socialist body. The Socialists of Philadelphia, as in all other parts of the country, contributed as liberally as other trades unions did. They did as much —they did no more.

"I have no desire to discuss the relative merits of the trades unions and Socialism. I recognize the right of every man to believe as he pleases. I wish to say that I regard it as a very great mistake on the part of our Socialist friends to attempt to commit this movement to the principles in which they believe. It would be a sad day, indeed, if trades unions were made the tail-end of a political organization."

When the convention reassembled after luncheon, an hour remained for debate and a proposition was made that two speakers for each side be heard in conclusion. Objection was made, and Delegate Quick of St. Louis spoke for the resolutions. Vice President Duncan opposed them. Then Delegate Carey addressed the convention, making an extended argument in favor of Socialism. He concluded just before 3 o'clock, and although the convention had decided to vote at 3, consent was given that President Gompers should be heard on the question before the ballot was taken.

President Gompers spoke in defense of the position, and the words of Vice President Duncan, which had been attacked by Delegate Carey. After stating that with the constant increase in wages it would be found there was a steady increase in the purchasing power of wages, notwithstanding the increased cost of the things that go to make up the necessaries of life, Mr. Gompers declared that the philosophy of the Socialists was all askew, although their ideas of economic conditions were true. Mr. Gompers pointed out that a vote for the resolutions presented would be construed by the world as an indorsement of Socialism. The Socialists did not want trade unionists elected to office, he said. Wherever there have been Socialists they have always opposed the trade unionists who were running for office outside the Federation of Labor. Mr. Gompers asserted that the Socialists were constantly making indiscreet remarks, and cited one or two instances. The speaker later became very earnest and even bitter in his statements against Socialism, and was interrupted frequently from the floor. In closing, he said:

"I am at variance with your philosophy. Economically you are unsound, socially you are wrong, and industrially you are an impossibility. I have an abiding faith in the trades union movement because it is the protector of labor to-day, and if emancipation comes some time it must be the trades union movement that will achieve it."

The vote was then taken, the result being greeted with prolonged applause.

November 19, 1903

Labor's Issues as Samuel Gompers Sees Them

President of American Federation of Labor Discusses Workmen's Movements in the Past Year and Makes Forecast of Future

By Samuel Gompers
President of the American Federation of Labor.

LABOR DAY, 1916, brings to the workers of America the right to cheer and confidence in the trade union movement. There have been tests and crises that have proved its fundamental principles; there have been opportunities that have tested its practical efficiency. Through them all the trade union movement has made sure progress and gained in confident vision for the future.

Every national and international, every local union affiliated to the American Federation of Labor has made definite progress in securing for its members greater advantages in those things which are fundamental of betterment in all relations of life. In some organizations the success has been phenomenal.

Taking the labor movement as a whole, there has been greater progress in securing the eight-hour day or the shorter workday than in any other similar period of time. The meaning of these victories can be interpreted only in the light of full understanding of the meaning of the eight-hour day. The shorter workday is something more than an economic demand. It is a demand for opportunity for rest, recuperation, and development; things which make life more than mechanical drudgery.

The workers whose whole periods are short are essentially different from those who are so worn by toil that they have neither energy nor mind for other things in life. They become more energetic, more resourceful workers with keener mentality and greater producing power. It inevitably follows that the short-hour workers are the best paid workers. With every reduction in hours there is always a corresponding increase in wages. Wherever demands for the shorter workday and higher wages have been presented and urged by organized workers during the last year they have met with success. These economic gains have a potent relation to the social side of life.

Shortening the period of work lengthens the period for development, and for all of the other activities that belong to the normal individual. Increases in wages give the workers the means for taking advantage of the increased opportunities of the shorter workday. The workers of short hours and better wages become very different citizens from those who are so exhausted by the daily grind that they have neither the time nor the energy for thought or aspiration. These gains mean better homes, better food, better clothing; time and opportunity for the cultivation of the best and the highest that is possible in the life of man.

Economic achievements are the basis upon which the workers can secure social and political progress. The power which secures these achievements is the power that will secure justice for them in every other relation. Shorter hours and higher wages give the opportunity and the means to live better, more purposeful lives.

Power through economic organization means political power. There must be an economic basis in order to give political activity reason for existence and a program. By organizing its economic power to secure political protection and by adhering strictly to a non-partisan political program the American Federation of Labor has won glorious legislative victories.

The object of legislation which organized labor has sought to obtain is always to establish larger and better opportunities for life and freedom. Organized labor does not seek through legislation to do things for the workers that they can do for themselves. It only seeks to establish for them opportunities. This principle applies to workers in private industry. In the case of workers in Governmental employment, where the Government is the employer and conditions of employment can be fixed only by legislation, then the organized labor movement seeks to do something more than merely establish opportunity. It must secure legislation regulating conditions of employment.

The record of the legislative achievements of the labor movement since 1906, when the non-partisan political party was inaugurated, is one of splendid victories. The two most important are the Seamen's act and the labor sections of the Clayton Anti-Trust law. The greatest thing in both of these acts is the advancement of human freedom.

The problem of human freedom was not ended by the work of Lincoln. There still remained a class bound to involuntary servitude—the seamen. The Seamen's act brings freedom to these workers. It makes American soil sacred to freedom, a country upon which a bondman may not step without losing his legal fetters. Freed and given an opportunity to protect themselves, the seamen are pressing their demands for higher wages and better conditions. Section 6 of the Clayton Anti-Trust act contains the most advanced concept of freedom: "The labor of a human being is not a commodity or article of commerce."

According to old-time philosophy, political economy, and legal thought, labor power was a commodity and article of commerce, in no way different from coal, potatoes, and iron. Under this concept the most recent attempts have been made to hold workers in oppression and under the domination of employers, but the power to produce commodities is something different from the commodities themselves. It is personal, human, a part of life itself. Under the concept that labor was a commodity, and therefore property, employers have tried to repress efforts of workers for progress and for larger liberty by punishing these efforts under anti-trust legislation and by attempting to restrain them through the injunctive process. It was to protect the workers against these abuses and to establish recognition of the concept that the workers and all of their attributes were human, that the labor sections of the Clayton act were enacted. In addition to these big achievements, many other important humanitarian laws have been enacted by Congress, increasing in number with every session of Congress since the fifty-ninth session.

As Labor Day, 1916, comes in with one of the most critical political campaigns since the civil war period, it is well to call attention to the big issue of the campaign, which has a national as well as an international relation. The issue is the attitude of the political parties toward questions of humanity and human welfare. The party now in power has in its legislative achievements placed the highest valuation upon human life and human attributes that has ever been declared and enacted by any political party in power.

The question that concerns the workers is how to hold their present advantages and how to secure from political parties still greater opportunities for freedom. The thing which is fundamental is Section 6 of the Clayton Anti-Trust act—that the labor of a human being is not a commodity or an article of commerce. The representatives of the American Federation of Labor went to the political parties and asked them to declare themselves upon this principle. The answers that the political parties gave are in their platforms, where all may read.

The Democratic Party openly and favorably declared and emphasized its position. The Republican Party took no notice of labor's request that it declare itself upon that which the workers considered of greatest importance to them.

The international issue that now comes closest to the labor movement is the policy of our Government toward Mexico. The cause of humanity is in the balance in Mexico. The people there are trying to work out their own problems and to establish their own ideals of political, social, and economic justice. The labor movement in Mexico has developed, that is, the most power and the most constructive product of the revolution. Representatives of the labor movement of Mexico have joined with representatives of the labor movement of America to insure to the workers and the citizens of Mexico the rights of human beings, opportunities for freedom and for independence. Many of the problems of the Mexican workers are problems of the workers of the United States. Their welfare is our welfare. The boundary line between the two countries is only an artificial division that has little or no effect upon the course and the nature of industrial and commercial development.

The problem of industrial welfare in the States of the Southwest is largely a Mexican problem. With low standards

Samuel Gompers.

of life and work prevailing among the 15,000,000 Mexicans, there exists an obstacle to the establishment of higher standards within the United States. There are capitalists and exploiting interests of the United States who, because they have property in Mexico, (often corruptly and dishonestly obtained,) desire to maintain Governmental agencies by which they can hold the people in subjection and deny to them the opportunity for protecting themselves through the organized labor movement and other opportunities for growth and development.

These selfish exploiting interests are concentrating their political power in the present campaign to secure a different policy on the part of our Government toward Mexico. Even under the guise of intervention, no matter how unnecessary and unwarrantable, the advocates of that policy really aim at the conquest and annexation of Mexico. A few of the most reckless come out brazenly in the demand for intervention, invasion, conquest, and annexation of Mexico. Of course, every effort must be made to safeguard the lives and the property of our people living along the border line, but who can honestly say that the Mexican marauders were the only offenders? The allied forces of greed and profit would deny the Mexican people the opportunity for their development; they would gladly embroil the United States in an unnecessary and unwarrantable war with Mexico. To them property, property rights, and profits are held far more sacred than human life, international honor, and human liberty.

These are some of the issues that primarily concern the workers and all liberty-loving citizens of the United States; they are the issues upon which every wage-earner—every citizen—will make his own decision, not only in his every day activity, but also at the polls on election day.

THE SEARCH FOR LABOR PEACE

THE PRESIDENT ON STRIKES

HE URGES CONGRESS TO TAKE PROMPT ACTION.

A UNITED STATES COMMISSION ATTACHED TO THE LABOR BUREAU AND WITH POWER TO ARBITRATE SUGGESTED.

WASHINGTON, April 22.—The President to-day sent a message to Congress on the subject of the labor troubles. The message in full is as follows:

To the Senate and House of Representatives:

The Constitution imposes on the President the duty of recommending to the consideration of Congress from time to time such measures as he shall judge necessary and expedient. I am so deeply impressed with the importance of immediately and thoughtfully meeting the problem which recent events and a present condition have thrust upon us, involving the settlement of disputes arising between our laboring men and their employers, that I am constrained to recommend to Congress legislation upon this serious and pressing subject.

Under our form of government the value of labor as an element of national prosperity should be distinctly recognized and the welfare of the laboring man should be regarded as especially entitled to legislative care. In a country which offers to all its citizens the highest attainment of social and political distinction, its workingmen cannot justly or safely be considered as irrevocably consigned to the limits of a class and entitled to no attention and allowed to protest against neglect. The laboring man, bearing in his hand an indispensable contribution to our growth and progress, may well insist, with manly courage and as a right, upon the same recognition from those who make our laws as is accorded to any other citizens having a valuable interest in charge; and his reasonable demand should be met in such a spirit of appreciation and fairness as to induce a contented and patriotic co-operation in the achievement of a grand national destiny.

While the real interests of labor are not promoted by a resort to threats and violent manifestations, and while those who, under the pretext of an advocacy of the claims of labor, wantonly attack the rights of capital, and for selfish purposes or the love of disorder sow seeds of violence and discontent, should neither be encouraged nor conciliated, all legislation on the subject should be calmly and deliberately undertaken, with no purpose of satisfying unreasonable demands or gaining partisan advantage.

The present condition of the relations between labor and capital are far from satisfactory. The discontent of the employed is due in a large degree to the grasping and heedless exactions of employers and the alleged discrimination in favor of capital as an object of governmental attention. It must also be conceded that the laboring men are not always careful to avoid causeless and unjustifiable disturbance. Though the importance of a better accord between these interests is apparent, it must be borne in mind that any effort in that direction by the Federal Government must be greatly limited by constitutional restrictions. There are many grievances which legislation by Congress cannot redress, and many conditions which cannot by such means be reformed.

I am satisfied, however, that something may be done under Federal authority to prevent the disturbances which so often arise from disputes between employers and the employed, and which at times seriously threaten the business interests of the country, and in my opinion the proper theory upon which to proceed is that of voluntary arbitration as the means of settling these difficulties. But I suggest that instead of arbitrators chosen in the heat of conflicting claims, and after each dispute shall arise, there

be created a Commission of Labor, consisting of three members, who shall be regular officers of the Government, charged among other duties with the consideration and settlement, when possible, of all controversies between labor and capital. A commission thus organized would have the advantage of being an able body, and its members, as they gained experience, would constantly improve in their ability to deal intelligently and usefully with the questions which might be submitted to them. If arbitrators are chosen for temporary service as each case of dispute arises, experience and familiarity with much that is involved in the question will be lacking, extreme partisanship and bias will be the qualifications sought on either side, and frequent complaints of unfairness and partiality will be inevitable. The imposition upon a Federal court of a duty foreign to the judicial function as the selection of an arbitrator in such cases is at least of doubtful propriety. The establishment by Federal authority of such a bureau would be a just and sensible recognition of the value of labor and of its right to be represented in the departments of the Government. So far as its conciliatory offices shall have relation to disturbances which interfere with transit and commerce between the States its existence would be justified under the provisions of the Constitution, which gives to Congress the power "to regulate commerce with foreign nations and among the several States." And in the frequent disputes between the laboring men and their employers, of less extent and the consequences of which are confined within State limits and threaten domestic violence, the interposition of such a commission might be tendered, upon the application of the Legislature or Executive of a State, under the constitutional provision which requires the General Government to "protect" each of the States "against domestic violence." If such a commission were fairly organized the risk of a loss of popular support and sympathy resulting from a refusal to submit to so peaceful an instrumentality would constrain both parties to such disputes to invoke its interference and abide by its decisions. There would also be good reason to hope that the very existence of such an agency would invite application to it for advice and counsel, frequently resulting in the avoidance of contention and misunderstanding. If the usefulness of such a commission is doubted because it might lack power to enforce its decisions, much encouragement is derived from the conceded good that has been accomplished by the railroad commissions which have been organized in many of the States, which, having little more than advisory power, have exerted a most satisfactory influence in the settlement of disputes between conflicting interests.

In July, 1884, by a law of Congress, a bureau of labor was established and placed in charge of a Commissioner of Labor, who is required to "collect information upon the subject of labor, its relations to capital, the hours of labor and the earnings of laboring men and women, and the means of promoting their material, social, intellectual, and moral prosperity." The commission which I suggest could easily be ingrafted upon the bureau thus already organized, by the addition of two more Commissioners and by supplementing the duties now imposed upon it by such other powers and functions as would permit the Commissioners to act as arbitrators when necessary between labor and capital, under such limitations and upon such occasions as should be deemed proper and useful. Power should also be distinctly conferred upon this bureau to investigate the causes of all disputes as they occur, whether submitted for arbitration or not, so that information may always be at hand to aid legislation on the subject when necessary and desirable.

GROVER CLEVELAND.

EXECUTIVE MANSION, April 22, 1886.

April 23, 1886

LABOR DAY A NATIONAL HOLIDAY.

President Cleveland Signs the Bill—Samuel Gompers to Have the Pen.

WASHINGTON, June 28.—Representative Cummings (Dem., N. Y.,) this afternoon took to the White House the bill making Labor Day a national holiday, and President Cleveland immediately signed it.

The pen and holder will be sent by Mr. Cummings to Samuel Gompers, President of the American Federation of Labor.

June 29, 1894

FOR INDUSTRIAL ARBITRATION.

Committee of Employers and Employes Formed to Settle Trade Disputes.

Capital and labor, it was announced yesterday, are to work hand in hand all over the United States for the promotion of good feeling between employers and employes and the adoption of arbitration instead of strikes as a means of settling trade disputes.

The movement was started by the National Civic Federation some time ago, which organized a permanent Committee on Industrial Conciliation and Arbitration, composed of employers and employes. Secretary Easley of the National Civic Federation, who is now in this city, announced yesterday that Cardinal Gibbons and Bishop Potter have agreed to serve on the committee, along with Seth Low, Felix Adler, and others who have taken an interest in arbitration of labor troubles. Among those who are on the committee are the following:

Adolphus C. Bartlett of Spencer, Bartlett & Co., Chicago; Samuel Gompers, President of the American Federation of Labor; S. R. Callaway, President of the New York Central and Hudson River Railroad Company; Chauncey H. Castle, President of the Stove Founders' National Defense Association; William J. Chalmers, Secretary of the National Metal Workers' Association, Chicago; E. E. Clark, Grand Chief Conductor, Order of Railway Conductors; Martin Fox, President of the Iron Molders' Union of North America; John Mitchell, President of the United Mine Workers of America; E. D. Kenna, Atchison, Topeka and Santa Fé Railway; Henry White, General Secretary of the United Garment Workers; Frank Sargent, Grand Master of the Brotherhood of Locomotive Firemen, and about fifteen or twenty other representative employers and labor men.

March 3, 1901

SYNOPSIS OF COAL STRIKE.

Genesis of the Trouble, Chief Events During the Struggle, and an Estimate of the Cost.

The anthracite mine workers, after eighteen months of uncertainty as to action, voted to strike May 15, when in convention at Hazleton, Penn. It was then assumed that 145,000 men would be in conflict with the operators. The strike was voted for by 461¼ yeas to 349¾ nays. At the convention President John Mitchell plainly and forcefully advocated peace. The strike once declared, he zealously supported the action of the convention and planned to have a special National convention of United Mine Workers, so as to have the bituminous coal workers involved in the struggle and 450,000 men out, with the idea of forcing a compromise, as the railroads and business of the entire country would be tied up. Before the strike was declared, hard coal in New York was $5.35 a ton on an average daily consumption in the city of 13,000 tons. In a few days the price advanced $1 a ton. Soft coal advanced 50 cents a ton within a week, and its use began to be general, with the result of interference by the Health Department, especially with the Manhattan Railway.

When the strike was declared, the wages of miners netted from $60 to $100 a month for from four to six hours' work daily. He blasted out the coal, which was picked up by laborers paid by him, he paying for powder and other requirements. He averaged six cars a day at $1 each. The laborers worked eight ten hours daily, each receiving $2 a day from the miner. Engineers and breaker boys who were called out received, respectively, $60 to $80 a month and 75 cents a day.

The strike demands were 20 per cent. increase to miners and an eight-hour work day for men paid by the day, such as engineers, pumpmen, and breaker boys, and that 2,240 pounds and not 2,750 pounds shall constitute a ton. The plight of the laborers was ignored. For them there was no demand made for increase of wages or shorter hours.

The strike's importance was gradually evidenced in various ways, until the situation dominated all factors in business and financial interests. Phases of it were conferences at all points, including this city, between President Mitchell and others identified with the strikers and those identified with the operators. Views on the subject were expressed by laymen, clergy, and leading economists, including Abram S. Hewitt. In the mining district were scenes of riot, incendiarism, mine flooding, a state of siege where mines were operated or attempts made to this end, lives were lost in riot, murders were committed, and scores of persons were injured. After attempts to deter the strikers with paid police had failed, appeals for protection were made vainly to Gov. Stone of Pennsylvania.

The attempt of the strikers to draw the bituminous coal workers into the struggle was abandoned, and the hard-coal men were left to fight it out alone. The first appeal to the Chief Executive of the Nation was made June 4 by the New York Board of Trade and Transportation, which asked President Roosevelt to mediate, without result. Like appeals to J. Pierpont Morgan availed nothing. Gov. Stone refused July 10 to order out the National Guard of Pennsylvania, but July 30 the situation was so acute that part of the State Militia took the field under the command of Gen. J. P. S. Gobin.

President Baer of the Philadelphia and Reading Railroad went down to history early in August in replying to an appeal, asking him as a Christian to settle the strike, by replying:

The rights and interests of the laboring man will be protected and cared for not by the labor agitators, but by the Christian men to whom God in His infinite wisdom has given control of the property interests of the country.

President Mitchell Sept. 20 set forth the claims and cause of the miners at Madison Square Garden. The situation had grown more tense and serious when, Oct. 1, President Roosevelt in his desire to mediate asked President Mitchell and the leading anthracite coal operators to come to Washington and confer with him. Naught came of this, as on Oct. 4 the operators rejected the offer of the miners to arbitrate and to mine coal pending a decision. Affairs in Pennsylvania were at their worst Oct. 6, when Gov. Stone yielded and ordered on duty the entire National Guard of the State, putting 9,000 militiamen in the disturbed districts.

Anthracite coal, domestic grades, had then in New York City reached famine prices, dealers demanding from even old customers from $20 to $25 a ton, and were unwilling to dispose of more than half a ton to one person. The price of soft coal had risen to $10 a ton. More than 300,000 tons of anthracite had been ordered in Europe.

During the next few days the President exerted his influence to induce the miners to go back to work, and several conferences were held between Mitchell and Senators Quay and Penrose. Gov. Odell on Oct. 11 issued an appeal to the operators to make concessions, but they would not yield their ground. At this time the Erie Railroad asked the striking miners to resume work, and guaranteed them protection.* A proposition to abolish the tariff of 67 cents a ton on coal was also discussed. The final and eventually successful negotiations for a settlement began on Oct. 11, when Secretary of War Root paid a visit to J. P. Morgan, then on his yacht, lying in the North River. Two days later, at nearly midnight, Mr. Morgan laid before the President the statement of the coal operators, in which they agreed to leave the matter to be adjusted by arbitration, and, pending arbitration, to work the mines on the condition that the union men did not interfere with the workers.

The President, after a consultation with Mr. Mitchell, appointed as arbitrators Gen. John M. Wilson, E. W. Parker, Judge George Gray, Bishop John L. Spalding, E. E. Clark, and Thomas H. Watkins. On the following day, Oct. 17, the strike was practically ended by the acceptance of the commission by the miners' Executive Committee

The cost of the strike, figured at Wilkesbarre last night, was:

Loss to operators in price of coal.... $55,100,000
Loss to strikers in wages............. 29,700,000
Loss to employes other than strikers.. 6,900,000
Loss to railroads in earnings........ 13,400,000
Loss to business men in the region.. 16,800,000
Loss to business men outside the region.................... 10,300,000
Cost of maintaining coal and iron police.................... 2,300,000
Cost of maintaining non-union men.. 650,000
Cost of maintaining troops in the region.................... 850,000
Damage to mines and machinery..... 6,500,000

Total...................... $142,500,000

Items overlooked in the computation of losses and outlays would swell the total to about $147,000,000.

ARBITRATORS GRANT MORE PAY
TO THE ANTHRACITE MINERS

Strike Commission Awards a General Advance of About Ten Per Cent. in Wages and a Sliding Scale Providing for More—Suggests a Permanent Board of Conciliation -- Recognizes Labor Organizations, but Not Mr. Mitchell's Union.

WASHINGTON, March 21.—Increase of wages and shorter hours for the anthracite coal miners are awarded by the report of the coal strike commission, which was made public to-day. It provides that the award shall remain in effect from April 1 next to March 31, 1906, and that disputes between the miners and their employers shall be referred to a permanent board of arbitration, lockouts and strikes being absolutely forbidden. The awards in brief are:

Ten per cent. increase in wages of all employes from Nov. 1, 1902, when the commission began its labors, to April 1, 1903, when the general award takes effect.

Eight-hour day after April 1 for engineers who hoist water at the rate of wages now paid.

Five per cent. increase of pay and Sundays off for other engineers and pumpmen.

Eight-hour day for firemen at the present rate of wages.

Nine-hour day instead of ten hours, with the present wages, for other employes.

In addition an increase of 1 per cent. in wages to all employes for each 5 cents added to the price of coal free on board at New York Harbor, an accountant appointed by a Federal Circuit Judge to determine the price monthly.

Establishment of a permanent Board of Conciliation composed of six members, the operators in each of the three districts to appoint one and "an organization representing a majority of said miners" in each district to appoint one. In case of a deadlock an umpire to be appointed by a Federal Circuit Judge. All strikes and lockouts forbidden and the decision of the board made absolute.

Check weighmen and check docking bosses may be provided by the miners.

Cars shall be distributed equitably. No attempt must be made by the miners to limit the output of the mines except by mutual agreement. For larger cars than those now provided higher pay must be allowed.

No discrimination by miners' organizations or the operators against men because of non-membership or membership in such organizations.

Direct payment of wages by operators to laborers employed by contract miners.

No formal recognition of the United Mine Workers, but recognition in various transactions of "an organization representing a majority of said miners."

The report is signed by all the members of the commission, which was composed of Judge George Gray of Delaware, Labor Commissioner Carroll D. Wright, Brig. Gen. John M. Wilson, and Edward W. Parker if this city; Bishop John L. Spalding of Illinois, Thomas H. Watkins of Pennsylvania, and E. E. Clark of Cedar Rapids, Iowa.

SUMMARY OF THE AWARDS.

Following is the commission's own summary of the awards:

"I. That an increase of 10 per cent. over and above the rates paid in April, 1902, be paid to all contract miners for cutting coal, yardage, and other work for which standard rates or allowances existed at that time, from and after Nov. 1, 1902, and during the life of this award. The amount of increase under the award due for work done between Nov. 1, 1902, and April 1, 1903, to be paid on or before June 1, 1903.

"II. That engineers who are employed in hoisting water shall have an increase of 10 per cent. on their earnings between Nov. 1, 1902, and April 1, 1903, to be paid on or before June 1, 1903, and from and after April 1, 1903, and during the life of the award they shall have eight-hour shifts, with the same pay which was effective in April, 1902, and where they are now working eight-hour shifts, the eight-hour shifts shall be continued and these engineers shall have an increase of 10 per cent. on the wages which were effective in the several positions in April, 1902.

"Hoisting engineers and other engineers and pumpmen, other than those employed in hoisting water, who are employed in positions which are manned continuously, shall have an increase of 10 per cent. on their earnings between Nov. 1, 1902, and April 1, 1903, to be paid on or before June 1, 1903; and from and after April 1, 1903, and during the life of the award, they shall have an increase of 5 per cent. on the rates of wages which were effective in the several positions in April, 1902; and in addition they shall be relieved from duty on Sundays, without loss of pay, by a man provided by the employer to relieve them during the hours of the day shift.

"That firemen shall have an increase of 10 per cent. on their earnings between Nov. 1, 1902, and April 1, 1903, to be paid on or before June 1, 1903, and from and after April 1, 1903, and during the life of the award they shall have eight-hour shifts, with the same wages per day, week, or month as were paid in each position on April 1, 1902.

"All employes or company men other than those for whom the commission makes special awards shall be paid an increase of 10 per cent. on their earnings between Nov. 1, 1902, and April 1, 1903, to be paid on or before June 1, 1903, and from and after April 1, 1903, and during the life of this award, they shall be paid on the basis of a nine-hour day, receiving therefor the same wages as were paid in April, 1902, for a ten-hour day. Overtime in excess of nine hours in any day to be paid at a proportionate rate per hour.

"III. During the life of this award the present methods of payment for coal mined shall be adhered to unless changed by mutual agreement. In all of the above awards it is provided that allowances like those made shall be paid to the legal representatives of such employes as may have died since Nov. 1, 1902.

Permanent Board of Conciliation.

"IV.—Any difficulty or disagreement arising under this award, either as to its interpretation or application, or in any way growing out of the relations of the employers and employed which cannot be settled or adjusted by consultation between the Superintendent or manager of the mine or mines and the miner or miners directly interested, or is of a scope too large to be so settled or adjusted, shall be referred to a permanent joint committee to be called a Board of Conciliation, to consist of six persons, appointed as hereinafter provided.

"That is to say, if there shall be a division of the whole region into three districts, in each of which there shall exist an organization representing a majority of the mine workers of such district, one of said Board of Conciliation shall be appointed by each of said organizations and three other persons shall be appointed by the operators, the operators in each of said districts appointing one person.

"The Board of Conciliation thus constituted shall take up and consider any question referred to it as aforesaid, hearing both parties to the controversy and such evidence as may be laid before it by either party, and any award made by a majority of such Board of Conciliation shall be final and binding on all parties. If, however, the said board is unable to decide any question submitted or point related thereto, that question or point shall be referred to an umpire, to be appointed, at the request of said board, by one of the Circuit Judges of the Third Judicial Circuit of the United States, whose decision shall be final and binding in the premises.

"The membership of said board shall at all times be kept complete, either the operators' or miners' organizations having the right at any time when a controversy is not pending to change their representation thereon.

"At all hearings before said board the parties may be represented by such person or persons as they may respectively select.

"No suspension of work shall take place by lockout or strike pending the adjudication of any matter so taken up for adjustment.

"V.—Whenever requested by a majority of the contract miners of any colliery, check weighmen or check docking bosses, or both, shall be employed. The wages of said check weighman and check docking bosses shall be fixed, collected, and paid by the miners in such manner as the said miners shall by a majority vote elect, and when requested by a majority of said miners, the operators shall pay the wages fixed for check weighmen and check docking bosses out of deductions made proportionately from the earnings of the said miners, on such basis as the majority of said miners shall determine.

"VI.—Mine cars shall be distributed among miners, who are at work, as uniformly and as equitably as possible, and there shall be no concerted effort on the part of the miners or mine workers of any colliery or collieries to limit the output of the mines or to detract from the quality of the work performed, unless such limitation of output be in conformity to an agreement between an operator or operators and an organization representing a majority of said miners in his or their employ.

Sliding Scale of Wages.

"VII.—In all cases where miners are paid by the car, the increase awarded to the contract miners is based upon the cars in use, the topping required, and the rates paid per car which were in force on April 1, 1902. Any increase in the size of car, or in the topping required shall be accompanied by a proportionate increase in the rate paid per car.

"VIII.—The following sliding scale of wages shall become effective April 1, 1903, and shall affect all miners and mine workers included in the awards of the commission—the wages fixed in the awards being the basis of and the minimum under the sliding scale:

For each increase of 5 cents in the average price of white ash coal of sizes above pea coal, sold at or near New York, between Perth Amboy and Edgewater, and reported to the Bureau of Anthracite Coal Statistics, above $4.50 per ton free on board, the employes shall have an increase of 1 per cent. in this compensation, which shall continue until a change in the average of said coal works a reduction or an increase in said additional compensation hereunder; but the rate of compensation shall in no case be less than that fixed in the award.

That is, when the price of said coal reaches $4.55 per ton, the compensation will be increased 1 per cent., to continue until the price falls below $4.50 per ton when the 1 per cent. increase will cease or until the price reaches $4.60 per ton, when an additional 1 per cent. will be added, and so on.

These average prices shall be computed monthly, by an accountant or Commissioner, named by one of the Circuit Judges of the Third Judicial Circuit of the United States, and paid by the coal operators, at such compensation as the appointing Judge may fix, which compensation shall be distributed among the operators in proportion to the tonnage of each mine.

"In order that the basis may be laid for the successful working of the sliding scale provided herein, it is also adjudged and awarded: That all coal operating companies file at once with the United States Commissioner of Labor a certified statement of the rates of compensation paid in each occupation known in their companies, as they existed, April 1, 1902.

"IX. No person shall be refused employment, or in any way discriminated against, on account of membership or non-membership in any labor organization; and there shall be no discrimination against or interference with any employe who is not a member of any labor organization by members of such organization.

"X. All contract miners shall be required to furnish within a reasonable time before each pay day a statement of the amount of money due from them to their laborers, and such sums shall be deducted from the amount due the contract miner, and paid directly to each laborer by the company. All employes so paid shall be furnished with an itemized statement of account.

"XI. The awards herein made shall continue in force until March 31, 1906; and any employe, or group of employes, violating any of the provisions thereof shall be subject to reasonable discipline by the employer; and, further, that the violation of any provisions of these awards, either by employer or employes, shall not invalidate any of the provisions thereof."

Reforms Urged by the Board.

The commission also makes recommendations which may be summarized as follows:

This discontinuance of the system of employing "the coal and iron police," because this force is believed to have an irritating effect, and a resort to the regularly constituted peace authorities in case of necessity.

A stricter enforcement of the laws in relation to the employment of children.

That the State and Federal Governments shall provide machinery for compulsory investigation of difficulties similar to the investigation which this commission has made. The commission expresses the opinion that, with a few modifications, the Federal act of October, 1888, authorizing a commission to settle controversies between railroad corporations and other common carriers could be made the basis of a law for arbitration in the anthracite coal mining business.

The commission, however, take a decided position against compulsory arbitration. On this point they add quite a lengthy commentary, which closes in this language: "The chief benefit to be derived from the suggestion herein made lies in placing the real facts and the responsibility for such condition authoritatively before the people, that public opinion may crystallize and make its power felt. Could such a commission as that suggested have been brought into existence in June last, we believe that the coal famine might have been averted—certainly the suffering and deprivation might have been greatly mitigated."

General conditions affecting the anthracite industry are discussed in the report.

"There is probably no other commodity entering into human consumption which possesses so much the character of a natural monopoly as the anthracite coal of Pennsylvania," it says. "The only other known deposits of anthracite coal of economic value in the United States are in Colorado and New Mexico, but these are all comparatively insignificant, yielding less than 100,000 tons annually. Practically, therefore, the entire source of supply of this fuel is confined to an area of 496 square miles, in nine counties in Pennsylvania.

"The output of anthracite coal in 1901 amounted to 60,242,560 long tons, with a value at the mines of $112,504,020. As an indication of the comparative importance of this industry it may be stated that the value of this product exceeded that of any other non-metallic product of the United States in 1901, with the exception of bituminous coal, and exceeded the value of any metallic product, with the exception of pig iron. It amounted to considerably more than 10 per cent. of the entire value of the mineral output of the United States in 1901."

Prices Likely to be Higher.

Figures are given on the supply of anthracite, and an estimate given that it will be exhausted in 200 to 250 years.

"However we may make our estimates of future production, it is apparent that the maximum output has been almost if not quite reached," says the report. "The production henceforth will be from lower levels and thinner seams than those previously worked. This will necessitate greater expense in mining, and consequently higher prices for the fuel. With higher prices will necessarily follow more economy in consumption, greater restriction of the market, and the increased competition of other fuels. All conditions seem to combine for the conservation of the supply of anthracite coal.

"It is interesting to note to what an extent the production is now controlled by the large corporations engaged in the business. Mr. Griffith in a contribution to The Bond Record states that the railroads either own or control 96.20 per cent. of the anthracite deposits, nearly 91 per cent. being actually owner by the transportation companies.

"The endeavor to control this natural monopoly has led many to miscalculate the anticipated increase in value of anthracite coal, due to said increase being more gradual than they had thought, causing in the past undue competition, unwarranted development of the mines, and financial disaster to many of the interests participating in this competition, so that the business has been subject to violent fluctuations. The gradual concentration of anthracite mining properties in the hands of fewer corporations, and the gradual increase in consumption of the product, have contributed to secure more uniform conditions in mining and the management of the business.

"There has been a decided improvement in the past three years in the conditions controlling the anthracite business; among others, the general prosperity of the country has led to an increased consumption of anthracite more nearly approaching the capacity to produce, consequently removing to a great extent the strong competition on the part of the operators.

"Anthracite, though regarded largely as a necessity, is not free from competition, and unreasonably high prices limit the use of it. Owing to its gradual exhaustion and the consequent greater expense of mining the poorer veins, and the increased labor cost due to higher wages, the tendency of the price of anthracite coal is probably upward. The effect of higher prices will undoubtedly be to limit consumption.

"We were impressed with many important features regarding the anthracite industry that are not generally known, and particularly with the capital required in the development of the mines and the production of the coal, as well as with the great waste occurring and the cost of handling the output under present conditions in the preparation of the marketable sizes. The cost of opening a colliery, with its equipment, varies from $200,000 to $750,000, which must be returned by the time the coal is exhausted or the investment results in loss, as the plants are worthless when all of the coal has been mined.

"In the study of anthracite conditions one cannot but be struck by the thought that a commodity so valuable and indispensable, lying within a small area, limited in quantity, should not be wastefully mined, and that the needs of future generations should be considered and their interests conserved."

Hazards in the Mines.

Taking up the conditions of mining, the report says:

"Considering the compensation to be paid for any class of labor, the danger to life and limb to those engaged should be taken into account. Coal mining is more hazardous than any other class of underground work, for, in addition to the usual dangers from falling rock and premature blasts, the coal miner runs risk of fire, explosion, and suffocation. The occupation must therefore be classed among those of a hazardous nature, the fisheries, certain classes of railway employment, and powder manufacture being among the few in which the danger exceeds that of coal mining.

"It has been asserted that the mining of anthracite is more dangerous than the mining of bituminous coal. This contention is evidently based upon a comparison of anthracite mining with favorable bituminous conditions.

"In an accompanying table it is shown that the number of fatal accidents per 1,000 employes in the anthracite mines of Pennsylvania in a period of ten years has exceeded those in the bituminous mines of the same State and of Illinois, Indiana, Iowa, Kansas, Kentucky, Maryland, Missouri, and Ohio, while the bituminous mines of Colorado, Indian Territory, New Mexico, Utah, West Virginia, and Washington show death rates per 1,000 considerably in excess of those in the anthracite mines.

"It does not seem, therefore, that the average hazard in anthracite mining is greater than that in bituminous coal mining. The table in which the statistics are presented shows also the death rate per 1,000 in a number of other countries for the years for which statistics are obtainable. Generally speaking, the accident death rates in the United States do not make a favorable showing for this country."

"There are, unfortunately, no annual statistics of fatalities in other employments (except railway service) in the United States with which comparisons can be made. Statistics compiled by the labor department of the British Board of Trade show the fatalities per 1,000 employes engaged, respectively, in mining, quarrying, factories, railway service, and shipping. The last named only present a higher death rate than that of anthracite coal mining in Pennsylvania." The table affecting railways shows a greater death rate from accidents.

Figures are given of the losses from the strike, the report saying:

"It is impossible to state with accuracy the losses occasioned by the strike, but fair estimates may be given. The total shipments of anthracite coal in 1902, according to a statement by William W. Ruley, Chief of the Bureau of Anthracite Coal Statistics, were 31,200,890 long tons. As compared with 1901, when the shipments amounted to 53,568,601 long tons, this indicates a decrease of 22,367,711 long tons, or over 40 per cent. If the same decrease is assumed for the coal mined for local trade and consumption, the total decrease in production in 1902 amounted to 24,604,482 long tons, which at the price received in 1901 meant a decrease in the receipts of the coal-mining companies for their product at the mines of $46,100,000.

"Assuming the average wage cost to be about $1.25 per ton on marketable coal, and allowing for the wages paid to engineers, pumpmen, and others who remained at work during the strike, the mine employes lost in wages a total of about $25,000,000. According to reports made at the recent convention of mine workers in Indianapolis, there were expended about $1,800,000 in relief funds.

"Assuming that 60 per cent. of the total shipments represents the sizes above pea coal, the decrease in the shipments of these larger sizes in 1902, as compared with 1901, was 13,420,627 long tons. With an average price at New York Harbor of $4.00 per ton, and with 35 per cent. of the receipts charged to transportation expenses, the decrease in freights paid to the railroad companies on these larger sizes, if it had all been sent to New York Harbor, would have been about $19,000,000; and, assuming the freight rate of $1 per ton on the smaller sizes, the total decrease in freight receipts on the transportation companies would have been about $28,000,000."

Attitude of the Commission.

The commission then enters into an explanation of their methods and purposes. They say in part:

"In reviewing the whole case they have been impressed with the importance of the issues involved, as well as with the intricacy and difficulty of many of the problems presented to them for solution, and they have striven diligently to get a clear understanding of each point upon which they were required to make a finding, and to do exact justice as nearly as possible to all parties concerned.

"There has been practical unanimity among them, and, though differences of opinion have from time to time arisen, there has not been a moment during the nearly five months in which they have been in session when there was an unpleasant word, or any indication whatever of thought or desire of aught save truth and justice. It has been their constant aim to keep themselves from bias, that they might see things as they are and weigh them dispassionately.

"All through their investigations and deliberations the conviction has grown upon them that if they could evoke and confirm a more genuine spirit of good-will—a more conciliatory disposition in the operators and their employes in their relations toward one another—they would do a better and a more lasting work than any which mere rulings, however wise or just, may accomplish. Fairness, forbearance, and good-will are the prerequisites of peace and harmonious co-operation in all the social and economic relations of men.

"The interests of employers and employes are reciprocal. The success of industrial processes is the result of their co-operation and their attitude toward one another, therefore, should be that of friends, not that of foes; and since those who depend for a livelihood on the labor of their hands bear the heavier burdens and have less opportunity to upbuild their higher being, the men of position and education, for whom they labor, should lead them not more in virtue of their greater ability and capital than in virtue of their greater loving kindness.

"Where production is controlled despotically by capital there may be a seeming prosperity, but the qualities which give sacredness and worth to life are enfeebled or destroyed. In the absence of a trustful and conciliatory disposition the strife between capital and labor cannot be composed by laws and contrivances. The causes from which it springs are as deep as man's nature, and nothing that is powerless to illumine the mind and touch the heart can reach the fountain head of the evil.

"So long as employers and employes continue to look on one another as opponents and antagonists, so long shall their relations be unsatisfactory and strained, requiring but a slight thing to provoke the open warfare which is called a strike.

"Naturally, some questions have been presented to the commission that are incapable of final solution, owing to the difficulties which are inherent in human nature. Nevertheless, while conscious of fallibility, the members indulge the hope that substantial justice will have been achieved by their findings and award, and that better relations between the parties concerned will hereafter exist."

How the Coal Miners Live.

Taking up the demand of the contract miners for more pay, the report says:

"The commission finds that the conditions of the life of mine workers outside the mines do not justify, to their full extent, the adverse criticisms made by their representatives, in their contentions at the hearings and in their arguments before the commission in support of the proposition 'that the annual earnings of the mine workers are insufficient to maintain the American standard of living.' There was evidence that during the last twenty years a general though gradual improvement in miners' houses has taken place. In any locality where those occupying the houses presumably receive or have opportunity to receive substantially the same earnings, the best houses, if they are in a majority, and not the worst, should be the standard.

"This should be borne in mind especially when there is a question of the homes of recent immigrants, as to whose houses, where they do not approach a proper standard, it is impossible to say how much choice and volition have had to do with their inferiority. The homes and surroundings of the English-speaking miners and mine workers are generally superior to those of the class just mentioned, and show an intelligent appreciation of the decencies of life and ability to realize them.

"During the hearings much comment was made on so-called company houses—that is, houses erected and owned by the coal companies and rented to their employes. The statistics produced at the hearings show that the percentage of employes living in company houses is not large. As the villages and towns have grown up around the mining camps the companies have gradually abandoned their earlier syst n, the employes living wherever they choose. Some of the older company houses are in poor condition, but it will not be many years before they are of the past.

"The commission also finds that the social conditions obtaining in the communities made up largely of mineworkers are good. The number and character of the public schools accessible in all these communities are fully up to the American standard. The number of churches in proportion to the population is rather above the average, and the opportunities generally for mental and religious instruction appear to be adequate.

"Another contention of the miners, to wit, that the wages of contract miners are necessarily so low that their children are prematurely forced into breakers and mills, has not been fully sustained, and the commission does not think that the testimony warrants it in finding as a fact the allegations so made.

"As to the general contention that the rates of compensation for contract miners in the anthracite region are lower than those paid in the bituminous fields for work substantially similar, or lower than are paid in other occupations requiring equal skill and training, the commission finds that there has been a failure to produce testimony to sustain either of these propositions."

Discussion of the cost of living is entered into, but the commission finds that this phase of the controversy need not be taken strongly into consideration. It also dismisses the contention that the miners earn more annually than other classes of laborers.

Awards which are summarized above are then made.

Passing to the demand that payment for mining should be made by weight, the commission cites a law of Pennsylvania bearing on this subject.

"It is a fact that during the whole period of twenty-eight years since the passage of this act no question seems to have been raised as to its requirements, or complaint made that they have been violated, or the prescribed penalty invoiked for any alleged violation thereof. The inference is not unfairly drawn from this state of things that the situation with which the statute purported to deal has been, on the whole, not unsatisfactory to either miners or operators, and that the provisions of the statute referred to never attracted the notice of the parties affected, and were thus practically ignored.

"The situation being thus anomalous, the commission has not been able to see clearly its way to an attempt to change it by an obligatory award. Many of the operators, in order to accommodate themselves to the change, would have to reconstruct the breakers or place the scales at the foot of the shaft, and, when there is more than one level in the mine, at the foot of each level."

Discussion of the Union.

The demand for recognition of the United Mine Workers of America is discussed at some length. It is decided that under the conditions of its organization the commission cannot give such recognition. The report says:

"Whatever the jurisdiction of this commission under the submission may be, the suggestion of a working agreement between employers and employes embodying the doctrine of collective bargaining is one which the commission believes contains many hopeful elements for the adjustment of relations in the mining regions, but it does not see that, under the terms of the submission from which the powers of the commission are derived such an agreement can be made to take the place of or become part of its award.

"Trades unionism is rapidly becoming a matter of business, and that employer who fails to give the same careful attention to the question of his relation to his labor or his employes, which he gives to the other factors which enter into the conduct of his business, makes a mistake, which sooner or later he will be obliged to correct. In this, as in other things, it is much better to start right than to make mistakes in starting which necessitate returning to correct them.

"Experience shows that the more full the recognition given to a trades union, the more businesslike and responsible it becomes. Through dealing with business men in business matters its more intelligent, conservative, and responsible members come to the front and gain general control and direction of its affairs. If the energy of the employer is directed to discouragement and repression of the union, he need not be surprised if the more radically inclined members are the ones most frequently heard.

"The commission agrees that a plan under which all questions of difference between the employer and his employes shall first be considered in conference between the employer or his official representative and a committee chosen by his employes from their own ranks is most likely to produce satisfactory results and harmonious relations, and at such conference the employes should have the right to call to their assistance such representatives or agents as they may choose, and to have them recognized as such.

"In order to be entitled to such recognition, the labor organization or union must give the same recognition to the rights of the employer and of others which it demands for itself and for its members. The worker has the right to quit or to strike in conjunction with his fellows when by so doing he does not violate a contract made by or for him. He has neither right nor license to destroy or to damage the property of the employer; neither has he any right or license to intimidate or to use violence against the man who chooses to exercise his right to work, nor to interfere with those who do not feel that the union offers the best method for adjusting grievances.

"The union must not undertake to assume, or to interfere with, the management of the business of the employer. It should strive to make membership in it so valuable as to attract all who are eligible, but in its efforts to build itself up it must not lose sight of the fact that those who may think differently have certain rights guaranteed them by our free Government. However irritating it may be to see a man enjoy benefits to the securing of which he refuses to contribute, either morally or physically or financially, the fact that he has a right to dispose of his personal services as he chooses cannot be ignored.

"The non-union man assumes the whole responsibility which results from his being such, but his right and privilege of being a non-union man are sanctioned in law and morals. The rights and privileges of non-union men are as sacred to them as the rights and privileges of unionists. The contention that a majority of the employes in an industry, by voluntarily associating themselves in a union, acquire authority over those who do not so associate themselves is untenable.

"The present constitution of the United Mine Workers of America does not present the most inviting inducements to the operators to enter into contractual relations with it. Minors are represented in conventions called for the consideration of strikes; while boys do not go as delegates, only one case having been noted, they send delegates to such conventions, and as the boys in the union in the anthracite region constitute about 20 per cent of the membership, it is easily seen that their representatives, who may be obliged to act on instructions, may have the balance of power, and thus carry a vote for a strike when the more conservative and experienced members might be opposed to it.

"An independent and autonomous organization of the anthracite mine workers of Pennsylvania, however affiliated, in which the objectionable features above alluded to should be absent, would deserve the recommendation of this commission, and, were it within the scope of its jurisdiction, the said fourth demand of the statement of claim, for collective bargaining and a trade agreement might then be reasonably granted."

Disorder During the Strike.

Touching the question of discrimination, lawlessness, boycotting, and blacklisting, the commission states that during the continuance of the late strike disorder and lawlessness existed to some extent over the whole region and throughout the whole period. Continuing, the commission says:

"It is admitted that this disorder and lawlessness was incident to the strike. Its history is stained with a record of riot and bloodshed, culminating in three murders, unprovoked save by the fact that two of the victims were asserting their right to work and another, as an officer of the law, was performing his duty in attempting to preserve the peace.

"Men who chose to be employed or who remained at work were assailed and threatened and they and their families terrorized and intimidated. In several instances the houses of such workmen were dynamited or otherwise assaulted and the lives of unoffending women and children put in jeopardy.

"The armed guards employed to protect the colleris and the men who worked them appear not to have been an unnecessary precaution, and the Governor of the State was, as the evidence before the commission shows, justified in calling out the citizen soldiery of the Commonwealth to preserve its peace and vindicate its laws.

"The resentment expressed by many persons connected with the strike at the presence of the armed guards and militia of the State does not argue well for the peaceable character or purposes of such persons. No peaceable or law-abiding citizen has reason to fear or resent the presence of either.

"It is also true, and justice requires the statement, that the leaders of the organization which began and conducted the strike, and notably its President, condemned all violence, and exhorted their followers to sobriety and moderation. It would seem, however, that the subordinate local organizations and their leaders were not so amenable to such counsels as to prevent the regrettable occurrences to which reference has been made.

"In making this arraignment, we are not unmindful of what appears to be the fact, that the mine workers of the anthracite region are, in the main, well disposed and good citizens of the Commonwealth of Pennsylvania, and that it is in the power of a minority of the less responsible men and boys, together with the idle and vicious, unless properly restrained, to destroy the peace and good order of any community."

Punishment for the Boycott.

Regarding the boycott the commission says: "What is popularly known as the boycott (a word of evil omen and unhappy origin) is a form of coercion by which a combination of many persons seek to work their will upon a single person, or upon a few persons, by compelling others to abstain from social or beneficial business intercourse with such person or persons.

"Carried to the extent sometimes practiced in aid of a strike, and as was in some instances practiced in connection with the late anthracite strike, it is a cruel weapon of aggression, and its use immoral and anti-social, and the concerted attempt to accomplish it is a conspiracy at common law, and merits and should receive the punishment due to such a crime."

"Some weak attempt was made at the hearings to justify the boycotts we have been describing, by confusing them with what might be called, for convenience sake, the primary boycott, which consists merely in the voluntary abstention of one or many persons from social or business relations with one whom they dislike. This, indeed, might amount to a conspiracy at law, if the ingredient of malicious purpose and concerted action to accomplish it were present, but whether this be so or not, the practical distinction between such a boycott and the one we have been reprobating is clear.

"It was attempted to defend the boycott by calling the contest between employers and employes a war between capital and labor, and pursuing the analogies of the word to justify thereby the cruelty and illegality of conduct on the part of those conducting a strike. The analogy is not apt, and the argument founded upon it is fallacious. There is only one warmaking power recognized by our institutions, and that is the Government of the United States and of the States in subordination thereto when repelling invasion or suppressing domestic violence. War between citizens is not to be tolerated, and cannot in the proper sense exist. If attempted it is unlawful, and is to be put down by the sovereign power of the State and Nation.

"The practices, which we are condemning, would be outside the pale of civilized war. In civilized warfare, women and children and the defenseless are safe from attack, and a code of honor controls the parties to such warfare which cries out against the boycott we have in view. Cruel and cowardly are terms not too severe by which to characterize it.

"Closely allied to the boycott is the blacklist, by which employers of labor sometimes prevent the employment by others of men whom they have discharged. In other words, it is a combination among employers not to employ workmen discharged by any of the members of said combination. This system is as reprehensible and as cruel as the boycott, and should be frowned down by all humane men.

"Happily there was little evidence of its existence among the operators in the anthracite region, one case only having been distinctly proved, and in that the refusal to employ the tabooed men continued but for a short time. Whenever it is practiced to the extent of being founded upon an agreement or concerted action, it, too, comes within the definition of the crime of conspiracy, and as such should be punished. There is also a civil remedy open to one who suffers from having been blacklisted, in an action against those who are a party to it, to recover damages compensatory of the injury received."

TERMS OF THE ARBITRATION.

Under the agreement entered into on Oct. 21, 1902, by the mine operators and the miners for the appointment of the arbitration commission, both are bound for three years to the acceptance of the findings and terms that are made by the commission.

The plan of the commission was formed by the operators, in response to action taken by President Roosevelt to end the strike by arbitration. In their communication the operators for the first time receded from their original position, and consented to treat with the miners through the proposed commission. This was signed for the mine owners and operators by George F. Baer, President of the Philadelphia and Reading Coal and Iron Company, Lehigh and Wilkesbarre Coal Company, and Temple Iron Company; E. B. Thomas, Chairman Pennsylvania Coal Company and Hillside Coal and Iron Company; W. H. Truesdale, President Delaware and Lackawanna Railroad; T. P. Fowler, President of Scranton Coal Company and Elkhill Coal and Iron Company; R. M. Olyphant, President of Delaware and Hudson Company, and Alfred Walters, President Lehigh Valley Coal Company.

It outlined the plan for the appointment of the commission, under the following conditions:

It being the understanding that immediately upon the constitution of such commission, in order that idleness and non-production may cease instantly, the miners will return to work and cease all interference with and persecution of any non-union men who are working or shall hereafter work. The findings of this commission shall fix the date when the same shall be effective and shall govern the conditions of employment between the respective companies and their employes for a term of at least three years.

President Roosevelt immediately appointed a commission composed of the following members:

Brig. Gen. John M. Wilson, United States Army, retired, representing the Engineer Corps of the United States Army; E. W. Parker of Washington, as a representative mining engineer; Judge George Gray, Wilmington, Del., representing the Federal courts; E. E. Clark of Cedar Rapids, Iowa, as a sociologist; Thomas H. Watkins, Scranton, Penn., as a practical coal mine operator, and Bishop John L. Spalding of Peoria, Ill. Later Carroll D. Wright, United States Commissioner of Labor, was added to the commission, but as recorder only.

The commission and the plan and terms offered by the mine operators were accepted by the United Mine Workers of America, through its Executive Committee, and this action later was ratified by a general meeting of the union miners at Wilkesbarre. Under the agreement, all matters concerned in the strike were referred to the arbitration committee, and the strike officially was ended on Oct. 22.

March 22, 1903

CLOAK STRIKE ENDS; AGREEMENT SIGNED

Men Win All Their Demands Except That for the "Closed Shop."

"VICTORY," BOTH SIDES SAY

Employers to Maintain "Preferential" Shops, Grant More Pay, Shorter Hours, and Better Conditions.

The strike of 70,000 cloakmakers which began early in last July ended yesterday with the acceptance by both the strikers and the employers of a peace protocol, based principally upon the agreement suggested by Louis D. Brandeis of Boston in the last days of July, when he conducted a series of conferences between employers and strikers. In all but a few of its provisions the peace agreement also is a duplicate of that arranged by Louis Marshall and rejected by the strikers last week.

Yesterday's settlement was reached after a conference between Julius Henry Cohen, counsel for the Cloak, Suit, and Skirt Manufacturers' Protective Association, and Meyer London, attorney for the unions, in Mr. Marshall's office, 37 Wall Street. The agreement was signed by Mr. Cohen on behalf of the manufacturers and by Mr. London and the Executive Committee of the unions on behalf of the strikers.

The principal change in the present agreement and the rejected one of last week is that the strikers accept the "preferential shop" as suggested by Mr. Brandeis, instead of the "closed shop" which they had demanded while the employers accept the principle that those who desire the benefits of unionism should share in its burdens. In announcing the settlement, Mr. Marshall said:

"Although the principle of the union shop has been adopted, it has been accompanied with such limitations and conditions as will minimize those features of the system which ordinarily have proved objectionable to employers, while at the same time the existing obligations of employers, including those to present employes are to be respected. The terms "union standards" and "preferential employment of union men" have been defined carefully and definitely.

"I have been impressed with the conciliatory attitude and the apparent desire to act justly displayed by the employers."

Mr. Cohen issued a statement giving credit to Mr. Brandeis and Mr. Marshall for ending the eight weeks' strike, and calling attention to the few important changes in the agreement of a week ago on which the present settlement was reached.

"The most important change is that instead of leaving to future arbitration the questions of wages and hours each side has yielded a little, and has settled upon definite terms. No principle has been surrendered by the manufacturers, yet the unions may truly claim that they have won a great victory for their people."

The protocol provides for the installation of electric power for the operation of machines by next Dec. 31 without charge for power by the employers and also for the institution of a uniform deposit system of $1 in each case where employes receive tools or implements from the employers.

Time contracts with individual employes are done away with as is the old custom of giving work to employes to be done at home. The ten legal holidays recognized by the State are to be observed with full pay for operatives employed by the week and provision is made that piece workers shall fix upon their prices by a conference between a committee of employes and the employer in each shop.

Hours of labor are limited to fifty weekly, nine hours constituting a day's work for five days in the week, with five hours' work on the sixth rounding out the week. Overtime work is limited, and when performed must be paid for at double the usual pay. A minimum scale of wages, which is slightly higher in some instances than the scale proposed by the manufacturers and in others slightly lower than that suggested by the strikers, will be maintained hereafter.

Section 14 of the agreement defines the attitude of the employers toward the unions. It reads:

Each member of the manufacturers is to maintain a union shop; a "union shop" being understood to refer to a shop where union standards as to working conditions, hours of labor, and rates of wages as herein stipulated prevail, and where, when hiring help, union men are preferred, it being recognized that since there are differences in degrees of skill among those employed in the trade, employers shall have freedom of selection as between one union man and another, and shall not be confined to any list nor bound to follow any prescribed order whatever.

Three boards are established by the agreement—a sanitary board, to consist of two nominees of the manufacturers, two nominees of the unions, and three representatives of the public, to be selected by counsel for both sides. This board is to establish standards of sanitary conditions to which the manufacturers and the unions shall be committed and shall, obligate themselves to maintain to the best of their ability.

An arbitration board will consist of a member from the employers, one from the unions, and a representative of the public, and to it "shall be submitted any differences hereafter arising between the parties hereto, or between any members of the manufacturers and any members of the unions."

The third board will consider and pass upon all grievances of a minor nature which arise between employers and employes and will consist of two members each from the manufacturers and the unions.

An important provision of the agreement states that there shall be no strike or lockout in the future because of differences between employers and men until the questions involved shall have been submitted to the Arbitration Committee.

The settlement of their difficulties was hailed alike by strikers and employers with delight. The manufacturers celebrated in their headquarters in the Hoffman House and there was rejoicing in strike headquarters, at 161 West Thirty-fourth Street.

Mr. Cohen voiced the sentiments of employers and employes alike when he declared that the protocol furnished "a great opportunity to build up a strong working relation between the unions and the manufacturers. Nothing is accomplished by large groups of men except by strong organization. Trades unions are not only necessary, but must be guided and strengthened."

In Jefferson Market Court several cloakmaker strikers were arraigned before Magistrate House, most of them charged with loitering in front of cloak houses. The Magistrate discharged all but those who had committed a specific act of disorder. In discharging them he said:

"These strikers in the act of picketing have committed no crime, although they may be punished by the Supreme Court. This court can take notice only of acts that constitute a crime or a breach of the peace."

September 3, 1910

ARBITRATION FOR RAILWAYS.

The Bill Providing for a Conference with Employes in Dispute Passes the House.

WASHINGTON, May 5.—The House to-day passed the bill for the arbitration of disputes between railroads and their employes.

When the bill came up for consideration Mr. Maguire (Cal.) attacked the provisions requiring employes to not leave their e... ployers under three months after the filing of the award without giving thirty days' notice. He said the provision left the question of punishment of violations of the provision open.

Mr. Grosvenor, (Rep., Ohio.,) explaining the bill, in reply to questions said the measure was not compulsory, did not require employes or employers to arbitrate, but merely opened a clear way to arbitration should the parties desire to avail themselves of it, and offered a way to carry out, under Governmental direction, an award reached through mutual and voluntary agreement. Criticism of the bill, as being unsafe, indefinite in many of its clauses, and open to possible abuse in the matters of judgment and execution, was made by Mr. Lewis, (Washington.)

Mr. Cochran (Dem., Mo.,) spoke in support of the bill as being a step in the right direction, though not perfect in its provisions.

Mr. Cummings (N. Y.) declared his purpose to support the bill as a member of Congress and a member of Typographical Union No. 6 of New York, and criticised briefly the Government for failure to pay union wages to its employes. He took occasion to deny a London dispatch in a Philadelphia paper to-day naming him as a Congressman on the payroll of a New York paper.

Mr. Sulzer, (N. Y.,) Mr. Gardner, (Rep., N. J.,) and Mr. Walker, (Mass.,) spoke in support of the measure.

Mr. Lewis (Wash.) moved to recommit with instructions favoring numerous amendments. This motion was defeated and the bill then was passed.

It provides that in case a serious controversy concerning wages, hours of labor, or conditions of employment shall arise between a carrier subject to the act and the employes, the Chairman of the Inter-State Commission and the Commissioner of Labor, upon the request of either party, endeavor to amicably settle the dispute by mediation, and in case the endeavor shall fail, then the controversy may be submitted to arbitration of a board of three persons, each party to the controversy to name one arbitrator, and the two thus named shall name a third. The agreement to submit must contain stipulations that the arbitration shall be begun within five days, and the award shall be filed within twenty days from the appointment of the third arbitrator; that the award shall be filed in the Circuit Court of the United States for any district wherein the employer carries on business; that the parties shall consider the award final and conclusive, and faithfully execute the same; that the award shall continue in force as between the parties for one year, and that the employer shall not dismiss nor shall any employe, dissatisfied with the award, quit work under three months without giving thirty days' notice.

The award shall become final and operative ten days after filing unless an appeal shall be taken within the ten days on exceptions to matter of law. The act recognizes organized labor and provides penalties for employers discriminating against employes by reason of their connection with or purpose to join such organization.

At 4:35 P. M. the House adjourned to Monday.

WILSON AVERTS RAILROAD STRIKE

Heads of Roads and Unions Agree on Erdman Act Changes and Are Ready to Arbitrate.

BILL BECOMES LAW TO-DAY

Managers Hint That Roads' Grievances Be Arbitrated Causes Flurry—Truce Till Wednesday.

Special to The New York Times.

WASHINGTON, July 14.—President Wilson helped to-day to avert the threatened strike of nearly 100,000 trainmen and conductors on the Eastern railroads, when, after a conference at the White House, representatives of the railroad companies and the brotherhoods agreed with legislative leaders on the terms of the Newlands bill, amending the Erdman Arbitration act, and promised to submit their differences to adjudication under the amended law.

The Newlands bill will be passed by both houses of Congress to-morrow with a few minor amendments, and will be signed to-morrow night by President Wilson, who described to-day's meeting as "simple and satisfactory."

Pending the passage of this legislation, no strike will be declared, officials of the brotherhoods agreeing to an armistice until Wednesday night.

The conference which resulted in this momentous decision was the largest that has been held since President Wilson took office, and assembled at 3 o'clock in the afternoon in the President's room in the executive office. Those participating in the gathering were:

Senator Newlands, Chairman of the Interstate Commerce Committee.
Senator Kern, Democratic floor leader.
Representative Clayton, Chairman of the Judiciary Committee.
Representative Mann, Republican floor leader.
Secretary William B. Wilson of the Department of Labor.
President Samuel Rea of the Pennsylvania Railroad.
President Daniel Willard of the Baltimore & Ohio Railroad.
President George W. Stevens of the Chesapeake & Ohio Railroad.
President William C. Brown of the New York Central Railroad.
Frank Trumbull, Chairman of the Executive Committee of the Chesapeake & Ohio Railroad.
Seth Low, President of the National Civic Federation.
Marcus M. Marks, Chairman of the Committee on Mediation and Arbitration Legislation of the National Civic Federation.
Ralph M. Easly, Chairman of the Executive Committee of the National Civic Federation.
President A. B. Garretson of the Order of Railway Conductors.
President W. G. Lee of the Brotherhood of Railway Trainmen.
Grand Chief Warren S. Stone of the Brotherhood of Locomotive Engineers.
President W. S. Carter of the Brotherhood of Locomotive Firemen.

Vital Questions Involved.

Seth Low was the principal spokesman concerning the character of legislation that would satisfy both the railroad Presidents and the brotherhoods. It was explained that the railroads were unwilling to submit to arbitration under the existing Erdman Act, which provides for only three arbitrators. They held that while three arbitrators might be sufficient in a controversy between one road and its employes, a board of that size could not handle all complexities of a problem involved in a controversy between fifty-four railroads

and 100,000 trainmen and conductors, such as that concerned in the pending dispute.

Both the railroad Presidents and the brotherhood Presidents were willing to submit such disputes to an arbitration board of six, as provided in the Newlands bill, but were opposed to an arbitration board of nine, as contemplated by the Clayton bill.

It was made plain that both sides wished to have a board of conciliation, independent of all governmental departments. This was not so much because of dissatisfaction with mediation under the old Erdman Act, but because both sides felt the matter would be taken more seriously if provided for independently. Under the original Erdman law, the Commissioner of Labor and the President of the Interstate Commerce Commission were allowed to mediate, and that was regarded as an independent arrangement. The Interstate Commerce Commission was not connected with any department and the Commissioner of Labor was also independent.

By various changes of law, the Commissionership of Labor ceased to be independent becoming first a subordinate part of the Department of Commerce and Labor and then being transferred into a department of its own. Consequently one of the problems that confronted the conference to-day was how to accomplish the aim of the original Erdman law and provide a wholly independent board of conciliation.

President Wilson thought that the suggestions, made for the adoption of the Newlands bill, were wholly just and that there was no reason why Congress should not immediately pass the Newlands measure and thus avert a disastrous struggle.

The Bases of Settlement.

The great points at issue were settled as follows, to the complete satisfaction of the railroad Presidents and the labor leaders, as well as the Federal officials, attending the conference:

First—Whenever a controversy arises between the railroads and their employes that cannot be settled by mediation and conciliation, the dispute is to be submitted to an arbitration board of six members, the employers and the employes, parties to the agreement to arbitrate, each naming two arbitrators, and the four arbitrators thus chosen being allowed by a majority vote to choose the remaining two arbitrators. If, within fifteen days, the four arbitrators fail to name the other two the latter must be named by the Board of Mediation and Conciliation.

Second—The proposed board of mediation and conciliation, instead of being under the Department of Labor, is to be independent of every Government department. The board will consist of a Commissioner of Mediation and Conciliation to be appointed by the President for a term of seven years and two other officials of the Government to be designated by the President.

The bill introduced in the House by Representative Clayton, Chairman of the Judiciary Committee, was originally identical with that introduced in the Senate by Senator Newlands, but was amended at the instance of Secretary Wilson of the Department of Labor, who wished the arbitration board to consist of nine members, who were to be under the jurisdiction of his department.

At to-day's conference, however, Secretary Wilson, while still expressing preference for the Clayton bill, said he would not insist on it, and an agreement was reached to put through the Newlands bill, of which both parties to the controversy had previously expressed approval, with two minor provisions of the Clayton bill incorporated.

One of these changes will correct an inconsistency in the Newlands bill, which provided originally that original papers in connection with proposed arbitrations should be filed in two different places. The other change was the insertion of a proviso that no mandatory process of any court should oblige an individual workman to work against his will.

The Senate originally intended to adjourn to-day until Thursday, but Senator Kern, the Democratic floor leader, who participated in the White House conference, made arrangements for the Senate to hold a special session to-morrow to pass the amended Newlands bill.

Result Pleases Both Sides

Both union leaders and railroad executives expressed approval of the result of the conference.

The brotherhood Presidents could not, of course, say whether their men would be satisfied with what had been done, but they themselves assured the President of their complete satisfaction with the proposed legislation, and it was stated at the White House to-night that President Wilson has not the slightest doubt that the men in the brotherhoods would indorse the position taken by their representatives in the conference.

"We have until Wednesday night in which to effect an amicable settlement," said Mr. Garretson, after the meeting. "We are willing to avail ourselves of every means for a reasonable settlement. Should the Congress fail to act then the entire subject will be referred to the committee of 1,000 for action.

W. C. Brown, President of the New York Central, said:

"The result of the conference was entirely satisfactory to the railway managers. It is exactly what had been agreed upon by the railways and the unions. When the Newlands measure shall have become a law it will furnish the best means of settling future wage troubles. We are pleased in every way."

The other railway Presidents concurred in this view.

President Wilson expressed his gratification that an agreement had been reached. He said that while the Erdman act originally contemplated a controversy between a single railroad and its employes the scope had now been widened so as to deal with a series of railroads. He referred to the suggestions made as "just and reasonable," and said he would name the new commission as quickly as possible.

Features of Proposed Law.

The perfected Newlands bill will create a Board of Mediation and Conciliation to be composed of a Commissioner appointed by the President, with the consent of the Senate, with a salary of $7,500, and a tenure of seven years, and not more than two other officials of the Government already appointed by the President, with the consent of the Senate, who shall be designated by him as the two other members of the board. An Assistant Commissioner, with a salary of $5,000, is also provided for, and willl be authorized to act in the Commissioner's absence.

In case of a controversy arising, either party may apply to the Board of Mediation for an adjustment of the trouble. Where the controversy threatens to interrupt traffic, the board may offer its services.

If the board's efforts prove futile, it must seek to persuade both parties to submit their differences to arbitration by a board of three or six, as they prefer.

Agreements to arbitrate must be written and must specfically state that a majority of the Arbitration Board shall have power to make a binding award. Awards made by the board are to be executed by the Federal courts, with which appeals may be filed.

July 15, 1913

PRESIDENT SIGNS 8-HOUR BILL IN HIS PRIVATE CAR

Will Affix His Signature Again on Tuesday to Clinch Question of Legality.

ALL CEREMONY IS AVOIDED

Mrs. Wilson Sees Him Make Adamson Measure a Law and Engineer Toots a Whistle.

UNION HEADS QUIT CAPITAL

Four Pens Used to Sign the Bill Will Go to the Railway Brotherhoods Leaders.

Special to The New York Times.

WASHINGTON, Sept. 3.—Seated in his private car, the "Federal" at the Union Station, President Wilson signed the railroad eight-hour bill at 9:11 o'clock this morning, thereby consummating the successful effort of the Government to avert a national railroad strike, which had been set for 7 o'clock tomorrow morning.

The only persons who saw the signing of the measure were Mrs. Wilson, her brother, John R. Bolling, Rudolph Forster, the White House Executive clerk, and a group of trainmen in their overalls, who paused in their work and looked through the car window. An engineer, passing in a yard engine, celebrated the occasion with several prolonged blasts of his whistle.

The President used four pens to write across the bill "Approved, 3 September, 1916, Woodrow Wilson." The pens, one for each syllable of his name, will be presented to the four heads of the railway brotherhoods. To meet any question of the legality of the act being signed on Sunday, the President will sign it again when he returns to Washington on Tuesday.

The President's train reached Union Station at 7:10 o'clock this morning from Long Branch, N. J., where he delivered his speech of acceptance yesterday. It had been supposed at the White House that the President would go there to sign the measure, but he decided to have it brought to his car, and at 9 o'clock Mr. Forster reached the station with the bill passed in a memorable forty-eight hours by Congress. After signing it the President went for an automobile ride with Mrs. Wilson, returning to his car in time to leave at 11:30 o'clock for Hodgenville, Ky.

Railway Heads Leave Capital.

The signing of the eight-hour bill by President Wilson was the fulfillment of his promise to the brotherhoods through Secretary of Labor W. B. Wilson to prevail upon the labor leaders to issue the strike recall order last night, in order that there might be no doubt of its delivery by 7 o'clock tomorrow morning.

Wearing no boastful air, but proud of their achievement, the brotherhood heads today closed their offices in Washington, which they established three weeks ago, and most of them left the capital tonight.

Elisha Lee, Chairman of the National Conference Committee of the Railways, who led the opposition of the railroads to accepting the eight-hour day voluntarily, left Washington with his attachés at 11 o'clock this morning for Philadelphia. He was the last of the railroad executives to go. He took with him copies of the eight-hour law, which will be laid before the railway attorneys on Tuesday, to get their opinions as to its constitutionality.

The eight-hour law settlement, as made by Congress, puts on the railroads a heavier burden than they would have sustained through an acceptance of the terms offered by President Wilson, which they rejected. The President's plan would have applied only to engineers, firemen, conductors, and trainmen on freight trains. The bill as passed prescribes the eight-hour day for all employes on trains engaged in interstate commerce. This means, of course, that the Government has prescribed the eight-hour day for passenger as well as freight workers.

Other Railway Workers Benefit.

It means also, according to the labor chiefs, that the army of negro trainmen in the South, excluded from the negotiations for the eight-hour day as conducted by the brotherhoods, are also included. They also say that telegraphers and switchmen will be benefited. Furthermore, while the negotiations between the four brotherhoods and the Conference Committee of managers were conducted on behalf of 125 railway systems, the eight-hour law applies as well to the seventy-five systems engaged in interstate commerce which were not represented by the Conference Committee. These seventy-five roads constitute, it is estimated, one-fifth of the total railway mileage of the country. All in all, the labor leaders are very much pleased with what Congress gave them.

"I have always considered the Sabbath as one of the best days of the week," said A. B. Garretson, leader of the labor chiefs, when asked how he felt now that the bill was signed.

Mr. Garretson gave the assurance that there was no danger of a strike in the near future over the application of the Adamson law. He said that if the law was not obeyed the brotherhoods would bring action in the Federal courts against the railroads, instead of resorting to another strike threat. He pointed out that the strike vote under which the brotherhoods have been operating in their negotiations since Aug. 6 is now ineffective. Mr. Garretson said that he and the other labor leaders were ready at any time to do all they could to aid the railroad managers to work out new schedules in conformity with the eight-hour law. He does not share in the common belief that the law means merely a 25 per cent. increase in wages.

"When a man has a run that cannot be cut it will mean to him simply a 25 per cent. increase in pay," he explained. "But to many of the 400,000 men concerned it will mean the same pay with two more hours of their time at their own disposal. The railroad managers themselves did not mean what they said when they declared that the eight-hour day meant merely an increase in wages."

Put Cost At $20,000,000.

He said there were thousands of schedules which could be changed without cost to the railroads so that a man could do in eight hours all the work he now does in ten. This is how the brotherhood chiefs explain the difference between $60,000,000, the railroads' estimate of what it would cost to give the trainmen the eight-hour day, and $20,000,000, the estimate of the unions.

The labor leaders today made no effort to defend the unprecedented action of Congress in legislating wages for them. They argued that the President and not the brotherhoods took the matter to Congress, and that it was the legislators' own affair whether they paid the price the unions demanded to call off the strike. Whether or not the action of the lawmakers leads to demands from other workers for the eight-hour day, the unions consider as no concern of theirs.

"However, it must be remembered," said Mr. Garretson, "that Congress has power to legislate wages only for workers engaged in interstate commerce, as I look at it, and that of course narrows the field considerably."

Mr. Garretson admitted that it was most likely that the success of the brotherhoods in getting the eight-hour day would lead to concerted action by the 1,600,000 workers on railroads who are not engineers, firemen, conductors, or trainmen.

"It is only human," he said, "that these men should try to get the eight-hour day, and I hope to God they succeed."

Mr. Garretson said it was absurd to hold that all classes of workers would be running to Congress for the eight-hour day, because, he said, Congress could not, under the Constitution, do anything for them unless they were engaged in interstate work. He thought that outside of railroad workers, only sailors would be justified in appealing to Congress under the precedent the lawmakers set in legislating more wages for the railroad workers. He pointed out that in the Seamen's bill Congress had already legislated for sailors.

To Press Underwood Proposal.

While the railroad executives have declared that they will press the Underwood proposal for regulating of wages on railroads by the Interstate Commerce Commission, defeated in the Senate yesterday, before the next Congress, the labor leaders do not believe that such a law will be enacted. They believe that the force of organised labor, which insists on retaining the right of collective bargaining, will halt the adoption of such a measure.

But what the labor leaders do believe is that the action of Congress should lead to the enactment of a measure giving the Federal Government entire regulation of the railroads, taking that power away from the States. This is one thing the brotherhoods and the railroads agree upon—that the dual regulation of railways by the Federal Government and State Governments puts an unnecessary burden on the carriers.

"At present," said Mr. Garretson, "under the dual regulation it is unlawful for a railroad to do something on one side of an imaginary State line, and unlawful for the railroad not to do it a mile further along in another State. This is a nuisance, and just so far as the Federal Government keeps on legislating as affects the railroads it should grant the relief that would come by a sane and comprehensive system of Federal regulation. Right now I pledge myself to do all that I can to bring that about."

Sees Government Ownership.

Mr. Garretson said that as he believed the action of Congress in legislating the eight-hour day on the railroads leads logically to Federal regulation of all railways, so he believed that Federal regulation would lead to Government ownership of railroads.

"If the Government keeps on regulating," said the labor leader, "the inevitable question will arise in vital form, 'What of the road that does not make a profit under such regulation?' Will not the Government be responsible for guaranteeing an income on the investment? This means but one thing—that the Government must take over that road and operate it. But if the Government must operate the roads that do not make money under its regulation, why should it not take over the roads that flourish under the same regulation? Why should it not get the profit if it makes good the deficit?

"Therefore, I say that I would vote for Government ownership as the lesser of two evils. There are many arguments against it, not the least of which is that nowhere in the world is there such service as has been built up in America under the competitive operation of railroads. On the other hand, some Governments have made a sorry business of conducting railroads. But the Post Office is the great example that the American Government can operate a great business successfully. Perhaps the example of the Post Office answers the argument that because of politics the Government could not successfully operate the railroads."

Mr. Garretson did not believe that the outcome of the strike crisis meant that there would never be the danger again of a national railroad strike.

"I might say that there would never be the danger again unless the railroad managers blinded themselves to the seriousness of the situation," he said. "But that is just what happened in this case. You may say that Congress can act again, but I tell you that Congress would not act if the President didn't wish it to act. In this case if we hadn't had a President of the United States who was willing to stake his own fortunes in a supreme effort to head off the strike it would have taken place before this."

Mr. Garretson was asked to say, now that the crisis was over, whether he would insist that the labor leaders would have "gone through" with the strike.

Garretson Expected a Strike.

"We would," he snapped. "I believed all along the strike would come. I despaired of Congress taking the action it did. It was not until Friday, when I was notified that the Republican Senators would not filibuster, that I had any real hope that it would be averted."

While some persons believe seriously that President Wilson's rôle will hurt him in the Fall campaign, that belief is not shared by the labor leaders. They say that before Nov. 4 the people will have forgotten all about every phase of the situation except that President Wilson averted the strike.

Incidentally, it became known today that Senator Penrose of Pennsylvania perhaps deserves large credit for the passage of the eight-hour bill in the Senate. When the Republican Senators held a caucus before the Senate took up the bill for final passage the political aspect of the situation was taken into consideration.

There were Republican Senators who wished to filibuster against the measure. It was finally decided, however, that it would not be the best policy to do so, and it was arranged that Republican Senators should make speeches for The Congressional Record against the measure and vote against it, but they would not, by filibustering, prevent the Democratic members from averting the strike. In this way the Republicans not only dodged all responsibility for the so-called indignity of the legislation, but they avoided responsibility for bringing the strike upon the nation.

Penrose Plan Carried Out.

It is known that Senator Penrose had much to do with arriving at this solution of the dilemma in which the Republican Senators found themselves. That this plan was well carried out is shown by the fact that there was only one Republican Senator who voted for the measure, La Follette of Wisconsin, and he did not attend the conference of Republican Senators.

While the Congressmen, with the strike crisis off their hands, are preparing to get away Wednesday or Thursday, they continue to say that they will do something at the next Congress to work out a solution of the situation. But there are many who believe that the rest of President Wilson's program will not be carried out, and that the result of the whole thing will be that if the report of the commission created in the eight-hour measure shows that the railroads deserve an increase in freight rates the Administration will look favorably upon an action by the Interstate Commerce Commission granting such an increase.

Before leaving Washington the labor leaders are tonight preparing a circular to be sent to all the 400,000 members of the brotherhoods telling them just what they have won.

Mr. Garretson was asked if he would tell just what the measure meant to a worker.

"That is a very complicated question," he said. "But take the example of the man who now earns $2,000 a year. If his run can be shortened or adjusted so that he works eight hours, the bill gives him two more hours a day to himself at the same pay. If his run cannot be shortened, it gives him $2,500 a year instead of $2,000.

"It should be pointed out that everything the members of the brotherhoods get applies also to the workers in the same classes of labor who are not members of the brotherhoods."

When he leaves Washington tomorrow morning, Mr. Garretson will go to Grand Rapids, Iowa, his home, where on Sept. 14 he will celebrate his sixtieth birthday. As soon as he can so arrange his affairs, he expects to leave New York on a sailing ship for a trip around Cape Horn.

W. G. Lee, President of the Order of Railway Trainmen, and W. S. Carter, President of the Brotherhood of Railroad Firemen and Enginemen, left Washington tonight. W. S. Stone, Grand Chief of the Brotherhood of Engineers, will leave tomorrow.

While the railroads are preparing to attack the constitutionality of the law as soon as possible, and while some of the executives had hoped that it might be declared void before Jan. 1, the day it goes into operation, the opinion was advanced today by those familiar with the course of such procedure that the attorneys for the railroads would probably not begin a legal attack upon the law until after it was put in operation.

CONFEREES AGREE ON RAILROAD BILL

Labor Provision Changed to Provide for a Single Federal Board.

ITS DECISION MADE FINAL

Unionist Officials Reiterate Opposition to Clauses in Pending Measure.

WASHINGTON, Feb. 16.—Final agreement on railroad reorganization legislation was reached late today by the House and Senate conferees, who planned to have the report ready for their signatures tomorrow, so that it could be presented to the House the following day.

Aside from textual changes, the general features of the compromise bill follow the lines agreed upon recently by the conferees, with the exception of the labor provision, which was modified so as to provide for a Federal appeal Board appointed by the President and consisting of nine members equally divided between the employes, the employers and the public. As previously agreed upon this board was to have been composed of five members.

Director General Hines of the Railroad Administration submitted tonight the new provision to the railroad bill dealing with the settlement of disputes by boards of arbitration, which was accepted by the conferees.

Original Plan Changed.

As originally proposed, five boards composed equally of employes and employers, would have been established to deal with labor disagreements, and their conclusions would have been subject to the approval of a Federal board of five members appointed by the President with the Senate's consent. This plan was changed by the conferees to provide that, while adjustments of labor differences might be made by representatives of the men and the carriers in cases where a strike was threatened which would tie up interstate commerce, submission of the dispute to the Federal Board was made compulsory before a cessation of work occurred, and the findings of this board would be final.

To prevent discrimination against the public, the conferees inserted a provision requiring the board's decision to be made by a majority, one of which must be a representative of the public.

"Was the labor provision agreed on so that this board can take jurisdiction of the pending wage controversy?" Senator Cummins was asked.

"That was in mind," he replied.

Hopes President Will Wait.

Attention was called to the fact that the President's reply to the railroad men indicated that he might appoint a separate board to deal with their grievances.

"I hope that he will not do that, but that he will regard this board as well qualified to take hold of the situation," Senator Cummins said. "If he doesn't, it will cause some confusion, for it will be this board's duty to consider the dispute."

Senator Cummins said he and Chairman Esch, of the House managers, would meet tomorrow to go over the final draft of the bill.

Representative Esch announced tonight that he would submit the conference report to the House on Wednesday, when it also will be presented in the Senate. He plans to ask for unanimous agreement to restrict debate on the bill in the House to four hours, and believes the House will complete action on the measure on Saturday.

Frank Morrison and other officers of the American Federation of Labor conferred tonight with twenty members of the House who are favorable to organized labor, and reasserted their opposition to certain provisions of the railroad bill. These Representatives, including Messrs. Nolan of California and Garland and Casey of Pennsylvania, promised to exert their influence in aid of organized labor.

Resolutions were adopted by the conference reiterating that control of railroads should be exercised by the Government for not less than two years in order that a proper test might be made as to Government control; opposing legislation making strikes of workers unlawful, and that penalty clauses against workers ceasing their employment should be eliminated.

Enactment of the beneficial features which tend to establish better relations between employes and the carriers was favored, and the resolutions proposed that they be extended to sleeping car and Pullman Company employes.

The labor leaders urged elimination from the Esch bill of the clause providing "that it shall be the duty of all carriers subject to this act, and their agents, officers and employes, to exert every reasonable effort and adopt every available and reasonable means to avoid interruption to the operation of a carrier subject to this act. growing out of controversy or dispute over any question of wages, working conditions, or discipline of employes," and the accompanying penalty clause.

After declaring that the federation officers have never indorsed or approved of either the Esch or Cummins bill, except that part of the Esch bill known as the Anderson amendment, the resolutions continue:

"All classes of employes can be properly represented on three boards of adjustment, and by three commissions on labor disputes, and there is no necessity for additional boards. The present bona fide and regular labor employes' organizations have protected, and will properly protect, all railway employes. The creation of additional boards will cause confusion and create friction, thereby interfering with the present orderly process of disposing of labor disputes.

"Suppose the conferees recommend to Congress for adoption a bill that contains provisions for the settlement of disputes between railroads and employes different than herein stated, we must urge that the proposed law be defeated in its entirety."

RAIL LABOR BILL PASSED BY SENATE

By 69 to 13 the Upper Branch Accepts the House Measure Without Amendment.

HARD FIGHT FOR CHANGES

Curtis Fails to Get Commerce Board Power Over Wages— Coolidge's Approval Expected.

Special to The New York Times.

WASHINGTON, May 11.—The bill to abolish the Railroad Labor Board and permit railways and their employes to settle disputes over wages and working conditions by mutual agreement was passed by the Senate by a vote of 69 to 13 late this afternoon. As the Senate approved the bill in identically the same form it passed the House no conference will be necessary and the bill will become law when the President affixes his signature.

Before the Senate passed the bill it was stated at the White House that it was not an Administration measure. The President, it was said, was interested in it to the extent that he believed it would work well because a majority of the railroad managers and employes favored it. But it was also understood that he did not entirely approve the bill as passed, he having suggested that it be amended so as to protect the public interest.

The detailed vote follows:

FOR THE BILL—69.
Republican—39.

Borah, Howell, Robinson
Butler, Johnson, (Ind.),
Cameron, Jones (Wash.) Sackett,
Couzens, LaFollette, Schall,
Cummins, Lenroot, Shortridge,
Dale, McMaster, Smoot,
Deneen, McNary, Stanfield,
Edge, Means, Wadsworth,
Ernst, Metcalf, Warren,
Fess, Norris, Watson,
Frazier, Nye, Weller,
Gillett, Oddie, Willis.
Gooding, Pine,
Harreld, Reed (Pa.)

Democrats—29.

Ashurst, Glass, Sheppard,
Blease, Harris, Simmons,
Bratton, Heflin, Steck,
Broussard, Jones (N. M.), Stephens,
Bruce, Kendrick, Swanson,
Copeland, McKellar, Trammell,
Dill, Mayfield, Tyson,
Edwards, Neely, Walsh,
George, Overman, Wheeler.
Gerry, Pittman,

Farmer-Laborite—1.

Shipstead.

AGAINST THE BILL—13.
Republicans—9.

Bingham, Keyes, Norbeck,
Curtis, McLean, Phipps,
Hale. Moses. Williams.

Democrats—4.

Bayard, Robinson Underwood.
Ransdell, (Ark.),

Provisions of the Measure.

The bill, which was agreed upon last year by most of the railway executives and heads of the four brotherhoods, and which the President endorsed in principle in his message to Congress, provides:

1. That the railroads and employes shall establish adjustment boards to arrange disputes.

2. That the President shall appoint, with the consent of the Senate, a board of mediation of five persons, none of whom has a pecuniary interest on either side, to intervene when the adjustment boards fail.

3. That boards of arbitration shall be created when both parties consent to arbitration.

4. That when the above methods fail the Board of Mediation shall notify the President, who may appoint an emergency board to investigate and report to him within thirty days. For thirty days after the report has been made there shall be no change in the conditions of the dispute except by agreement of the two parties concerned.

There has been a long and determined fight against the bill on the ground that the public is not mandatorily represented on any of the boards and on the ground that there is nothing in the bill to make any settlement final, but nevertheless the Senate voted the measure through by more than five to one majority, resisting all efforts to change it in any particular.

Curtis Amendment Rejected.

Sentiment against altering the bill was demonstrated when the Senate earlier in the day defeated an important amendment which was designed to afford the public definite protection.

This amendment, submitted by Mr. Curtis, the Republican leader, provided that the Interstate Commerce Commission could suspend any agreement between the railroads and their employes if the commission considered the compact might involve a wage increase against the public interest.

The amendment, which has approval of the National Association of Manufacturers and the American Farm Bureau Federation, was lost by a vote of 64 to 12. The dozen men voting for it were: Bayard, Delaware, and Underwood, Democrats; Bingham, Curtis, Hale, Keyes, McLean, McMaster, Moses, Norbeck, Weller and Williams, Republicans.

It came as a surprise that many Democrats and also radical Republicans, who are ordinarily "against the railroads," declined to vote for the Curtis amendment, but in the lobbies the charge was made that the railroads exerted force on some of these and the railway unions used their influence with others.

Likewise, it was regarded as surprising that some of the Republican stalwarts voted for the Curtis amendment, but here it was rumored that the pressure from industrial interests was felt by some of the Senators and that messages from agricultural organizations influenced others.

"Guarantee Clause" Is Retained.

Just before the final vote on the bill, Senator Norbeck, the near-radical from North Dakota, startled the Senate by proposing an amendment which would have eliminated from the Esch-Cummins law the provision assuring the railroads a return of approximately 6 per cent. on their earnings.

Opponents of the bill have contended that its passage will mean a compact between the railroads and employes to raise wages and then to demand higher rates.

The attempt to strike out Section 15 A was defeated by a vote of 54 to 2. Those voting to kill the "guarantee clause" were Borah, Curtis, Frazier, Howell, Keyes, La Follette, Lenroot, McMaster, Norbeck, Norris and Nye, Republicans; and Edwards, Harris, Heflin, McKeller, Mayfield, Neely, Sheppard, Simmons, Trammell, Walsh and Wheeler, Democrats.

Senator Phipps tried to put an anti-strike clause in the bill by offering an amendment that no strike should be ordered pending a decision by the Board of Mediation, but was voted down viva voce.

Opposition to the bill was sounded by Senator Robinson, the Democratic leader, who said the railroads and employes could already do what the bill empowered them to do.

"The bill really gives them the moral support of the public for anything they do, and anything they fail to do," he asserted.

"Doesn't its passage pave the way for a wage increase without the trouble of a strike?" Senator Norbeck queried.

"I think it does," replied Senator Robinson. "I think the railways could well say the Government makes it obligatory on them to enter into agreements with their employes for increased wages. If the increases are large this would probably prompt demands for higher rates."

"Is the Senator in favor of compulsory arbitration?" asked Senator Watson.

"Yes, I would like to bind the two parties to continuation of transportation," replied Senator Robinson.

"While I don't want to make anybody work, I realize, and they realize, that the people of this nation can't live if there is a general strike."

One of the most determined opponents of the bill, Senator Bruce of Maryland, fought hard for changes in it. He was so insistent in his efforts that he aroused Senator Neely of West Virginia.

"There's no way to prevent the Senator from making two or three hundred more speeches, but regardless of petulant objections I am going to take every parliamentary advantage to shut off those who have spoken more than fifty times," Senator Neely assured Senator Bruce.

"Your song is sung," he added to Senator Bruce. Every one expected the Marylander to reply with sarcasm, but he merely called for the final vote.

After the last roll-call Senator Norbeck moved to name the measure "A Bill to Increase the Farmers' Working Day From Fourteen to Sixteen Hours, and to Reduce the Railroad Man's Day From Eight to Seven Hours."

The element of compulsion is totally absent from the new bill. There is nothing in it making the findings of any of the boards arbitrary. Even the Presidential Emergency Board has no authority to enforce its findings, and there is no language in the bill to show what would happen should this last court of resort fail to bring about a settlement.

Neither is there any direction in the bill that the public shall be represented on any board, not even upon the Emergency Board, for while the President is empowered to create the Emergency Board, nothing is said about its composition.

The Railroad Labor Board, which goes out of existence with the signing of the new law, has three representatives, one each from labor, the railroads and the public. The board was supposed to be clothed by law with mandatory powers, but the Supreme Court decided that it had no authority to enforce its decisions.

LABOR PORTFOLIO CREATED.

Senate Now Passes Bill Adding Another Member to the Cabinet.

Special to The New York Times.

WASHINGTON, Feb. 26. — After last night's bitter filibuster the Senate passed the bill this morning creating a new Department of Labor without a roll call and practically without debate. The efforts of its opponents under the active leadership of Senator Simon Guggenheim of Colorado to amend the bill out of all resemblance to its original purpose were abandoned this morning. The measure adopted is so similar to that already passed by the House that it is practically certain there will be ten members in President Wilson's Cabinet.

Senator William E. Borah handled the bill in the Senate, and it is understood that he used plain language to the opponents of the measure. At any rate, when he asked for consideration of the measure, which seemed last night to have been indefinitely postponed by a short filibuster, he got it without difficulty. The only practical amendments adopted were one including the Children's Bureau in the new department, and another dividing the Bureau of Immigration and Naturalization into two bureaus.

A formal amendment adopted out of courtesy to the office of President eliminated the express provision that the Secretary of Labor should sit in the Cabinet. It was explained that the Cabinet is extra-constitutional, and that the President may call to its councils whomsoever he pleases. It is understood, of course, that the new Secretary will be a Cabinet officer, but technically his seat will depend upon the President's invitation.

CLAYTON BILL PROGRESSES.

House Conferees Agree to Accept Senate's Labor Union Amendments.

Special to The New York Times.

WASHINGTON, Sept. 12.—At the conference of the managers of the two houses on the Clayton Trust bill, the House conferees today virtually agreed to accept the Senate amendment relating to the exemption of labor unions from the operations of the Sherman law, and restricting the use of injunctions in labor disputes. In the form in which the bill passed the Senate the provisions regarding labor unions, while fully protecting the rights of organized labor, are less broad than the provisions of the House measure.

In general, Section 19 of the bill as thus agreed to provides that no restraining order shall prohibit any individual or individuals from terminating any relation of employment or from recommending or persuading others by peaceful means so to do. It also provides that such orders of a court shall not be issued to prohibit such persons from attending at any place where any such person or persons may lawfully be, for the purpose of peacefully obtaining or communicating information or from peaceably persuading any person to work or abstain from working.

The remainder of the section provides that no restraining order or injunction " shall prohibit persons from paying or giving to, or withholding from, any person engaged in such dispute, any strike benefits or other moneys or things of value, or from peaceably assembling in a lawful manner and for lawful purposes, or from doing any act or thing which might lawfully be done in the absence of such dispute by any party thereto; nor shall any of the acts specified in this paragraph be considered or held to be violations of any law of the United States."

The conference will continue next week, amendments to paragraphs covering price discrimination, " tying contracts," and prohibitions against interlocking Directors still being in dispute.

September 13, 1914

SEAMEN'S BILL SIGNED.

President Does Not Think It Will Interfere with Our Treaty Obligations.

WASHINGTON, March 4.—President Wilson today signed the Seaman's bill, improving working conditions of American seamen and increasing life-saving equipment requirements.

It was said the President had carefully examined the objections of some Senators that the bill would interfere with the treaty obligations of the United States, but concluded that it was so drawn that he could handle those questions with full recognition of the rights of other nations.

The provisions of the bill do not go into effect for fifteen months.

SAN FRANCISCO, March 4.—R. P. Schwerin, President of the Pacific Mail Steamship Company, which operates seven trans-Pacific steamships, declared today that enforcement of the Seamen's bill signed this morning by President Wilson would drive the Pacific Mail steamers off the seas. " With the enactment of such a law the Pacific Mail can do nothing but go out of business." he said. " It will be impossible for us to compete with the Japanese steamships employing Oriental labor and subsidized by their Government. Under this bill our operating expenses would be increased 200 per cent. The total increase would be $800,000, and the company has never earned more than $200,000 in any one year."

March 5, 1917

"Human Cussedness" Causes Labor Disputes

By Richard Barry.

IT was *not* Mark Twain I talked with the morning of the Mayor's conference with the appointees of the Secretary of Labor, though he had Mark Twain's shock of white hair, Mark Twain's profile, Mark Twain's shyly voluble manner, and wore the same sort of white clothes that Mark used to wear.

Instead, it was the Chief Statistician of the Bureau of Labor Statistics, from the United States Department of Labor, Washington, D. C., Ethelbert Stewart, who had been sent to New York by William B. Wilson, Secretary of Labor, as one of three Commissioners to make a final effort at mediation between the striking garment workers and the manufacturers.

This commission has become known, familiarly, in the underworld of strike manipulation, as " the forlorn hope brigade." In this instance it had been called in when all else had failed, when the State Commissioners, who really have some power in the matter, had given up the idea of a settlement of the strike as hopeless.

Mr. Stewart explained that because of the peculiar delicacy of his present position in the labor controversy now engulfing New York he did not wish to be quoted regarding the merits of that affair, but he was willing to elucidate for THE TIMES SUNDAY MAGAZINE the nature of the work on which he was engaged, what the Department of Labor has been able to accomplish in similar cases, and, what seemed to me most interesting of all, his personal view of strikes in general.

"This is the fourth time I have been employed on such an errand," said Commissioner Stewart. "I was first asked to go to the Colorado Coal and Iron strike in 1913. That strike lasted, as you will remember, for fourteen months, and resulted in a complete victory for the mining companies. I was in Ludlow the day the soldiers fired on the strikers and saw most of the bloodshed. I utilized every known power of mediation then and failed to bring about even a promise of arbitration from the company. It stood like adamant and finally wore out the men.

" My second effort was at the Indianapolis car strike in December, 1913. This was a signal success for our commission. We managed to secure the consent of both sides to a settlement by arbitration. Moreover, we were able to avoid the abuses of arbitration which have been so frequently observed in similar English cases by arbitrarily limiting the time in which settlement was to be made and in influencing the men to return to work under an agreement to be reimbursed for back pay immediately upon the finding of the arbitration commission. This was composed of the members of the State Public Utilities Commission, which had been appointed previous to the origin of the strike and which was, therefore, free from any suspicion of bias in the matter. It was provided that all the hearings should be completed within ten days, and that the findings should be announced not more than thirty days thereafter. It was finally agreed by both sides to abide by the findings of the commission for at least three years. These agreements and provisions were lived up to strictly to the letter, and Indianapolis today is abiding by the terms of that arbitration.

"My third effort also, I believe, would have been successful if the strikers had held out. This was in Philadelphia in 1914, at the strike of the cloak, skirt, and coat workers. There, within twenty-four hours of my arrival, I found the manufacturers willing to come to some such agreement as was made in Indianapolis, but that very day the opposition of the workers vanished because the support they had been receiving from New York was withdrawn; they were left without funds, and the individual workers returned to their tasks without demanding any terms.

"So I have had one success, one failure and one draw. I sincerely hope that, with my confreres, I may be of real service to the City of New York in the present emergency."

Mr. Stewart then explained that his personal experience involved a very small part of the record of the Bureau of Labor in the settlement of disputes.

"There is a provision in the organic law of the Department of Labor," he said, "for the establishment of a Bureau of Mediation and Conciliation. It is a mistake to suppose that the Government gives us any real authority in these matters. What it does do is to clothe us with the plenipotentiary powers of the Government, arm us with special knowledge, and direct our attention to the individual cases of trouble with a well-established reputation for disinterestedness.

"The bureau was established in 1913, but for the first year very little was done. However, our record for the last three years speaks for itself. From May 4, 1913, to June 6, 1916, we have mediated in a total number of 234 controversies between employers and employes. These involved nearly 250,000 employes directly and about 300,000 indirectly. They do not include fifteen cases in which the number of employes concerned was not reported, and a very large number of cases in which the number indirectly affected was unknown.

"Of these 234 cases we succeeded in amicably adjusting 149. We were unable to adjust 33; and there are still pending for settlement 52 cases.

"So you will see that the Government has been successful at least 63 per cent. of the time. This percentage will be considerably increased when we are able to reckon in the 52 cases now pending, for of those nearly all will be settled amicably.

"Among the more celebrated strikes which we have been able to mediate were:

"The West Virginia coal miners' strike, 15,000 men; the Westinghouse Electric Company, 13,000 men; the Illinois Railway shopmen, 8,000 men; the Eastern Ohio coal strike, 18,000 men; the Buffalo building trades strike, 4,000 men; the Bayonne, New Jersey, oilmen's strike, 8,500 men; the American Graphophone strike, 2,100 men; the Norristown, (Penn.) textile workers, 1,000 men; the Arizona copper miners' strike, 4,500 men; the Washington, D. C., railway strike, 1,500 men; the Cramp shipbuilding strike, 1,100 men; the Westinghouse East Pittsburgh strike, 36,000 men; the Pittsburgh street railway strike, 3,000 men, and the Pittsburgh & Lake Erie Railway strike, 4,000 men.

"The labor controversies involving over a thousand men which we have been unable to adjust during the last four years are:

"The Père Marquette Railway shopmen, 1,500 men; The Colorado Coal and Iron strike, 10,000 men; the Providence street railway strike, 5,000 men; the Meriden (Conn.) silver workers' strike, 2,600 men, and the Providence (R. I.) Brown & Sharpe Company, 5,000 men.

"The other cases in which we have been concerned, except a few now pending settlement, have involved less than a thousand men, and, while serious locally, have seldom been known to the country at large."

Earlier Mr. Stewart had told me that he had been engaged in the Department of Labor, and concerned with the statistics division, for twenty-seven years, and before that he had been a newspaper man. So I asked him:

"From your long and disinterested observation of labor disputes in America what, in your opinion, is their trend? Are they growing more or less frequent; are they becoming more or less bitter?"

"The day of the little strike is over," he said, "what I call 'the old-fashioned strike' is a thing of the past. I mean the trouble which was once frequent and may even yet be observed here and there: A demand for shorter hours, more pay, different working conditions, made by a small group of men. These strikes, which, in the last analysis, are perhaps the essence of labor troubles, will soon be extinct, I believe.

"I refer to the kind of strikes settled in a few days and sometimes in five minutes. People don't have time for them any more. Perhaps they haven't the grievances; I don't know. The strike in vogue today is a deeper matter, a more serious matter. It comes out of the big cities; it spreads over whole States and sections; it involves vast numbers of allied workers; it draws in thousands who have no grievances at all except perhaps imaginary ones. And it takes weeks and months to settle; often more than a year. It grows until it becomes practically civil war.

"That sort of strike, instead of decreasing, is constantly becoming a greater and greater menace to permanent industrial peace. It is very difficult to say what is the foundation cause of these huge strikes. Certainly the cause is not merely a desire for more wages, or shorter hours, or even for the so-called 'recognition of the union.'

"That phrase 'recognition of the union,' I have often observed, befuddles both sides to a controversy. Often I have known the employers to be willing to grant everything meant by the phrase except the use of the phrase itself. Again I have known employes to refuse to accept everything but the phrase, and then get the use of the phrase without what it means.

"But even that moot point of contest, 'recognition of the union,' hardly explains a deeper and indefinable cause of conflict that surely exists and which men like myself constantly observe. I don't mean class antagonism, or mass hatred or any of those ideas so beloved by writers on sociology and political economy. I would rather call it downright human cussedness. In almost every strike you will find a group of men, and they never are confined to one side, who would sooner fight than settle, no matter what the terms of settlement may be.

"There can be no industrial peace until both sides to a labor argument want industrial peace, and when both sides really want peace, and not a fight, a settlement is bound to come. There must be concession on both sides and a willingness on both sides to abide by a settlement. But, unfortunately, in America it seems that there is a large class of men, by no means confined either to the laboring or to the capitalistic class, who prefer fighting, for its own sake, to industrial peace and all that such peace means."

"What solution do you offer for this condition?" I asked.

Mr. Stewart answered indirectly, but effectively.

"Back in 1886," he said, "the Stove Foundrymen and the Iron Molders' Union locked horns with the manufacturers in the stove industry. It began with the Bridge Beach strike in St. Louis, and soon involved the entire country. They fought until both sides were utterly exhausted and each had barely a single breath left. Finally both sides used that last breath to say, 'Let us forget it.' They saw that if they did not stop then and stop forever the stove industry would go to pieces, and for the salvation of the industry to which they all owed life they came together, settled their differences, appointed committees of arbitration from both sides, and established machinery for the settlement of all disputes that might possibly arise in the future. Each year since that time these committees have met and adjusted amicably all the differences in the stove industry.

"However, that is the only industry in the United States which has been at peace for thirty years; the only industry which apparently has learned that warfare is destructive, not so much to the individuals who participate in it, as it is destructive to the very industry itself. When that fact is once firmly grasped by all strikers and by all lockers-out the labor disturbances will depreciate astoundingly."

MILLIONS MORE FOR LABOR IN 1916

Many Firms Besides Transportation Companies to Give Advances Jan. 1.

PROOF OF OUR PROSPERITY

Building Trades and Other Union Demands Cause Concern in Some Quarters.

75,000 MILL HANDS GET MORE

Northern New England Cotton Operators Grant Voluntary Raises, Averaging 5 Per Cent.

Increases in the pay of workers in New York were announced from many quarters yesterday, and it was estimated that fully 200,000 employes would be benefited, and that payrolls, beginning Jan. 1, would be heavier by millions of dollars.

Among the increases announced yesterday was that of the Second Avenue Railroad Company, which operates cars along Second Avenue from Worth to One Hundred and Twenty-ninth Street, and along First Avenue from Fifty-ninth to One Hundred and Twenty-fifth Street. One cent an hour was added to the pay of motormen, conductors, switchmen, and others, and more than 400 employes are affected.

Similar action has been taken within a few days by the other transit lines. On last Friday the Brooklyn Rapid Transit Company announced an increase of 1 cent an hour for carmen on its surface lines, as well as advances for men on the elevated roads, aggregating $250,-000 a year. Between 6,000 and 7,000 workers on the surface and about 2,000 on the elevated lines are affected.

On Tuesday the Interborough Rapid Transit Company, the New York Railways Company, and the Third Avenue Railroad Company raised the pay of their motormen, conductors, and others. The Interborough advance reaches about 11,000 employes and the Third Avenue about 300.

Ross Tompkins, Secretary of the United Board of Business Agents for the Building Trades of New York, announced yesterday that the following had received increases:

Trades.	Increase per Day.	Workers Affected.
Metallic lathers	$5.30 to $5.50	1,400
Machinists	5.00 to 5.50	5,000
Tile layers	5.50 to 6.00	900
Wood lathers	5.00 to 6.40	1,000

Others affiliated with the building trades whose agreements with their employers expire tomorrow with one exception and who are demanding increases, with the expectation of receiving them, are:

Trades.	Increase Asked.	No. of Workers.
Asbestos workers	$4.75 to $5.00	900
Boilermakers	5.00 to 5.50	...
Carpenters	5.00 to 5.50	18,000
Decorators	4.50 to 5.00	2,800
Mosaic workers	4.50 to 5.00	750
Painters	4.00 to 4.50	7,000
Subway excavators	2.50 to 2.80	3,500
House movers	3.75 to 4.25	2,500

In Manhattan, where building operations are largely suspended in January and February, the demands of the unions are not causing as much concern as in Queens and the Bronx, where many large structures are under way, Mr. Tompkins explained.

Increases in pay have been granted to 12,000 girls in the millinery trade, to 8,000 waiters, to Pullman porters, conductors, and others employed on sleepers, and to 1,200 mechanics in the Brooklyn Navy Yard.

"I do not remember a time when more organizations were asking larger pay than now," said a large employer yesterday, "nor do I remember a time when so many were getting it.

"If a way could be found, without a canvass of employers, for totaling the additional money the workers in New York will receive in the coming year, the sum would be startling. It would give proof of prosperity such as has not been presented before. In some lines these demands are causing uneasiness, for the improvement in conditions is not as great in some trades as in others. Nevertheless, almost all employes, regardless of conditions, are asking more money."

Labor Costs Are Increasing.

The manufacturing of war munitions is having its effect on labor costs in lines that are not at all allied to that business. Textile producers in the New England towns in which "war plants" are located are having their own troubles with their employes. The wage increases granted to one class of labor make the others in the same district envious, and the only way to avert strikes is to pay all of the workers more. This condition of affairs, together with the increasing cost of the raw materials required in manufacturing, is naturally having its effect on the prices of textiles.

August 14, 1915

REPORT ON WAGE CHANGES.

Merchants' Bureau Takes Up Extra Compensation and Living Cost.

The Industrial Bureau of the Merchants' Association recently conducted an inquiry into the matter of extra compensation paid employes to enable them to meet the increased cost of living, and the results are printed in the issue of Greater New York, the association's bulletin, published today. The investigation was made through about fifty important employers.

The bureau found, according to the report, that in the case of factory and unskilled labor wage increases had nearly, if not completely, offset the cost of living for many. Office help of all kinds, employes of special skill and aptitude for the particular positions held by them, and employes who, for many reasons, were reluctant to change their positions, were found to be the ones still working for wages received two and three years ago, and most of the extra compensation payments made were for the benefit of these.

Many employers advised against an increase in wages for such employes, on the ground that the present high cost of living was temporary, while increased wages could not be decreased later without serious difficulties to affected persons. Extra cash payments were recommended in lieu of increased salaries by some employers, but others said that they had found a bonus system unsatisfactory.

December 30, 1915

September 24, 1917

STRIKES BARRED DURING THE WAR

Labor and Capital Announce Plan Adopted for Mediation of All Disputes.

UMPIRE'S DECISION FINAL

National War Labor Board to be Created to Keep Production at Maximum.

MUTUAL CONCESSIONS MADE

Union and Open Shops Both Protected—Text of Conferees' Recommendations.

Special to The New York Times.

WASHINGTON, March 30.—A comprehensive program for the settlement of disputes between labor and capital by the general adoption of which strikes and lockouts would be averted and production kept at a maximum during the period of the war, was submitted today to William B. Wilson, Secretary of Labor, by the War Labor Conference, which has been in session here several weeks. It is believed that Mr. Wilson will approve the recommendations and that the machinery necessary to carry out the plan will be created within a short time.

One of the most important recommendations contained in the report places in the hands of an umpire power to make final decisions, from which there can be no appeal, when all other channels of conciliation have been exhausted. The umpire is to be selected either by the unanimous vote of a National War Labor Board, the creation of which is recommended in the report, or drawn by lot from a list of ten persons to be nominated by the President of the United States.

The agreement to accept such a provision received the full approval of the five representatives of capital and five representatives of organized labor participating in the conference, the latter selected by the American Federation of Labor. Should the recommendations receive the approval of Secretary Wilson and the President and be put into effect it is the general understanding that those who refuse to abide by the plan will be looked upon as outlaws and obstructionists.

Ex-President William H. Taft and Frank P. Walsh, selected respectively as counsellors by capital and labor, have both given full approval to the recommendations. In statements today they expressed the belief that the adoption of the program would prove the longest step yet taken in putting an end to the danger of industrial unrest during the war.

Concessions were made by both capital and labor in reaching the agreement. It was agreed for one thing that women on work ordinarily performed by men must be allowed equal pay for equal work.

Organized labor agrees to abandon any demand for the closed shop. Their right to extend their organizations, however, is carefully protected upon the agreement that coercive methods shall not be employed. The complete program proposed is given in this letter submitted today to Secretary of Labor Wilson:

Text of the Recommendations.

The Hon. William B. Wilson, Secretary of Labor.

Sir: The commission of representatives of employers and workers, selected in accord with the suggestion of your letter of Jan. 28, 1918, to aid in the formulation, in the present emergency, of a national labor program, present to you, as a result of their conferences, the following:

(a) That there be created, for the period of the war, a National War Labor Board of the same number and to be selected in the same manner and by the same agencies as the commission making this recommendation.

(b) That the functions and powers of the National Board shall be as follows:

1. To bring about a settlement by mediation and conciliation of every controversy arising between employers and workers in the field of production necessary for the effective conduct of the war.

2. To do the same thing in similar controversies in other fields of national activity, delays and obstructions in which may, in the opinion of the National Board affect detrimentally such production.

3. To provide machinery by direct appointment or otherwise for selection of committees, or boards, to sit in various parts of the country where controversies arise, to secure settlement by local mediation and conciliation.

4. To summon the parties to the controversy for hearing and action by the National Board in case of failure to secure settlement by local mediation and conciliation.

(c) If the sincere and determined effort of the National Board shall fail to bring about a voluntary settlement, and the members of the board shall be unable unanimously to agree upon a decision, then, and in that case, and only as a last resort, an umpire appointed in the manner provided in the next paragraph shall hear and finally decide the controversy under simple rules of procedure prescribed by the National Board.

(d) The members of the National Board shall choose the umpire by unanimous vote. Failing such choice, the name of the umpire shall be drawn by lot from a list of ten suitable and disinterested persons to be nominated for the purpose by the President of the United States.

(e) The National Board shall hold its regular meetings in the City of Washington, with power to meet at any other place convenient for the board and the occasion.

(f) The National Board may alter its methods and practice in settlement of controversies hereunder, from time to time, as experience may suggest.

(g) The National Board shall refuse to take cognizance of a controversy between employer and workers in any field of industrial or other activity where there is by agreement or Federal law a means of settlement which has not been invoked.

(h) The place of each member of the National Board unavoidably detained from attending one or more of its sessions may be filled by a substitute to be named by such member as his regular substitute. The substitute shall have the same representative character as his principal.

(i) The National Board shall have power to appoint a Secretary and to create such other clerical organization under it as may be in its judgment necessary for the discharge of its duties.

(j) The National Board may apply to the Secretary of Labor for authority to use the machinery of the department in its work of conciliation and mediation.

(k) The action of the National Board may be invoked in respect to controversies within its jurisdiction by the Secretary of Labor or by either side in a controversy, or its duly authorized representative. The board, after summary consideration, may refuse further hearing if the case is not of such character or importance to justify it.

(l) In the appointment of committees of its own members to act for the board in general or local matters and in the creation of local committees the employers and the workers shall be equally represented.

(m) The representatives of the public in the board shall preside alternately at successive sessions of the board, or as agreed upon.

(n) The board, in its mediating and conciliatory action, and the umpire, in his consideration of a controversy, shall be governed by the following principles:

THERE SHOULD BE NO STRIKES OR LOCKOUTS DURING THE WAR.

RIGHT TO ORGANIZE:

1. The right of workers to organize in trade unions and to bargain collectively, through chosen representatives, is recognized and affirmed. This right shall not be denied, abridged, or interfered with by the employers in any manner whatsoever.

2. The right of employers to organize in associations of groups and to bargain collectively, through chosen representatives, is recognized and affirmed. This right shall not be denied, abridged, or interfered with by the workers in any manner whatsoever.

3. Employers should not discharge workers for membership in trade unions nor for legitimate trade union activities.

4. The workers, in the exercise of their right to organize, shall not use coercive measures of any kind to induce persons to join their organizations, nor to induce employers to bargain or deal therewith.

EXISTING CONDITIONS:

1. In establishments where the union shop exists the same shall continue, and the union standards as to wages, hours of labor and other conditions of employment shall be maintained.

2. In establishments where union and nonunion men and women now work together, and the employer meets only with employes or representatives engaged in said establishments, the continuance of such conditions shall not be deemed a grievance. This declaration, however, is not intended in any manner to deny the right or discourage the practice of the formation of labor unions, or the joining of the same by the workers in said establishments, or guarantees in the last paragraph, nor to prevent the War Labor Board, or any umpire from urging, or granting, under the machinery herein provided, improvement of their situation in the matter of wages, hours of labor, or other conditions as shall be found desirable from time to time.

3. Established safeguards and regulations for the protection of the health and safety of workers shall not be relaxed.

WOMEN IN INDUSTRY:

If it shall become necessary to employ women on work ordinarily performed by men, they must be allowed equal pay for equal work, and must not be allotted tasks disproportionate to their strength.

HOURS OF LABOR:

The basic eight-hour day is recognized as applying in all cases in which existing law requires it. In all other cases the question of hours of labor shall be settled with due regard to Governmental necessities, and the welfare, health, and proper comfort of the workers.

MAXIMUM PRODUCTION:

The maximum production of all war industries should be maintained, and methods of work and operation on the part of employers or workers which operate to delay or limit production, or which have a tendency to artificially increase the cost thereof, should be discontinued.

MOBILIZATION OF LABOR:

For the purpose of mobilizing the labor supply, with a view of its rapid and effective distribution, a permanent list of the number of skilled and other workers available in different parts of the nation shall be kept on file by the Department of Labor, the information to be constantly furnished:

1. By the trades unions.

2. By State employment bureaus and Federal agencies of like character.

3. By the managers and operators

of industrial establishments throughout the country.

These agencies should be given opportunity to aid in the distribution of labor, as necessity demands.

CUSTOM OF LOCALITIES:

In fixing wages, hours, and conditions of labor, regard should always be paid to the labor standards, wage scales, and other conditions prevailing in the localities affected.

THE LIVING WAGE:

1. The right of all workers, including common laborers, to a living wage is hereby declared.

2. In fixing wages, minimum rates of pay shall be established which will insure the subsistence of the worker and his family in health and reasonable comfort.

Loyall A. Osborne,   Frank J. Hayes,
L. F. Loree,   W. L. Hutcheson,
W. H. Van Dervoort,   Thomas J. Savage,
C. E. Michael,   Victor A. Olander,
B. L. Worden,   T. A. Rickert,
William H. Taft,   Frank P. Walsh.

Statements By Taft and Walsh.

Ex-President Taft, as spokesman of the group representing capital, made this statement:

"I am profoundly gratified that the conference appointed under the direction of Secretary Wilson has reached an agreement upon the plan for a national labor board to maintain maximum production by settling obstructive controversies between employers and workers. It certainly is not too much to say that it was due to the self-restraint, tact, and earnest patriotic desire of the representatives of the employers and the workers to reach a conclusion. I can say this with due modesty, because I was not one of such representatives.

"Mr. Walsh and I were selected as representatives of the public. Personally, it was one of the pleasant experiences of my life. It brought me into contact with leaders of industry and leaders of labor, and my experience gives me a very high respect for both. I am personally indebted to all of the board, but especially to Mr. Walsh, with whom, as the only other lawyer on the board, it was necessary for me to confer frequently in the framing of the points which, step by step, the conference agreed to.

"Of course the next question is: 'Will our plan work?' I hope and think it will, if administered in the spirit in which it was formulated and agreed upon."

For the group representing organized labor, Frank P. Walsh made this announcement:

"The plan submitted represents the best thought of capital and labor as to what the policy of our Government with respect to industrial relations during the war ought to be. Representing capital were five of the largest employers in the nation, but one of whom had ever dealt with trade unions, advised and counseled by ex-President Taft, one of the world's proved great administrators, and of the very highest American type of manhood. The representatives of the unions upon the board were the national officers of unions engaged in war production and numbering in their ranks considerably over 1,000,000 men and women.

"The principles declared might be called an industrial chart for the Government, securing to the employer maximum production and to the worker the strongest guaranty of his right to organization and the healthy growth of the principles of democracy, as applied to industry, as well as the highest protection of his economic welfare while the war for human liberty everywhere is being waged.

"If the plan is adopted by the Government, I am satisfied that there will be a ready and hearty acquiescence therein by the employers and workers of the country, so that the volume of production may flow with the maximum of fruitfulness and speed. This is absolutely essential to an early victory. The industrial army, both planners and workers, which are but other names for employers and employes, is second only in importance and necessity to our forces in the theatre of war. Their loyal co-operation and enthusiastic effort will win the war."

March 31, 1918

INSISTS AFTER-WAR WAGES MUST DROP

W. H. Barr, National Founders' Head, Says Eight-Hour Day and High Pay Can't Go On.

ASSAILS LABOR UNIONISTS

Declares They Have Been Utilizing Every Power to Intrench Their Position.

William H. Barr of Buffalo, President of the National Founders' Association, speaking yesterday at the opening session of the annual convention of the organization in the Hotel Astor, warned the 250 foundrymen present that the first and greatest post-war problem to engage the attention of the association and industry in general was the liquidation of labor. He asserted that the war level wage schedule could not be maintained by private industry in peace times if the nation's needs were to be met.

"There is no one who will seriously contend," Mr. Barr said, "that with the return of peace we can continue to operate our mines and factories and compete in the world of trade if we are to operate on a national eight-hour day and pay the wages which have been imposed during the stress of political opportunity. When the Government ceases to be the great common employer, and Government money no longer pays the present extravagant wages, can private industry so order its affairs as to continue to furnish employment to the millions of our workmen? This question, broad and comprehensive, is the labor problem which will come with the end of the war.

"With the return of peace the needs of the war will no longer furnish work or determine labor relationships. The vogue of those who have strange solutions for our social and industrial problems, and who are willing to experiment with a sorely tried nation in the midst of its great crisis, will cease. The present determination on the part of certain forces among the workers to attempt to cling to all that union labor has gained on an unsound basis during an abnormal and artificial period will doubtless occasion some trouble and friction.

Mr. Barr charged that the trade unionists had been utilizing every method, power and force, political or otherwise, to put themselves in a position of strength irrespective of the ultimate cost to the country or industry. He said it was clearly their hope that when the soldiers of the American Armies returned from Europe they would be unable to obtain positions in many industries without the consent of the unions. Mr. Barr said he thought, however, that the returning soldiers would "have a word to say almost immediately concerning conditions here." He added that the soldiers would become a dominant factor in politics and said they would entertain no maudlin sympathy for experimental industrial socialism.

In conclusion, Mr. Barr said the manufacturers of the country may now properly "demand the dissolution of the throttling agreement between politics and unionism at the expense of industry, and urge the cessation of usurpation of power by Government officials or appointees." He insisted that in the new peace era the manufacturers should not be asked to surrender the open shop.

"Now, what is this force which is dictating to the President of the United States, to the departments of the Government, to Congress, to politicians, and, presumably a little later on, to the Church?" he asked. He said it was trade unionism, which represented only about 2 per cent. of the workers of the population of continental United States and 8 per cent. of the workers of the country. He then enumerated the small percentage of organized labor employed in shipyards and other war industries.

Mr. Barr scored the United States Employment Service and alleged that a large percentage of the managers of offices opened up all over the country were officers of labor unions, who discriminated against the open shop and used their powers to promote union organization. But he said credit should be given to the National War Labor Board for its splendid efforts to win the war by bringing about maximum production.

At the victory dinner of the association in the Hotel Astor last night, Dr. George E. Vincent, President of the Rockefeller Foundation, predicted that the United War Work Campaign would be a great success. The Rev. Dr. Robert Johnston, pastor of the American Church of Montreal, who was Lieutenant Colonel of the 166th Canadian Regiment, also spoke.

November 14, 1918

LABOR WILL FIGHT WAGE REDUCTION

Gompers Gives Warning That Advantages Gained by the War Must Be Maintained.

TO AID IN RECONSTRUCTION

But Asserts That "Bourbons" Cannot Bring Back Pre-War Conditions.

REPLY INSPIRED BY BARR

Head of Labor Federation Resents Founders' Chief's Recent Assertions Here.

Special to The New York Times.

LAREDO, Texas, Nov. 16.—The advantage in wages and hours won through the war must be maintained, and organized labor will fight to the last gasp to secure them, according to a declaration concerning reconstruction, made before the Pan American Labor Conference this afternoon by Samuel Gompers, its presiding officer and recognized chieftain of organized labor in America. Mr. Gompers asserted that he was making this statement with a full sense of the responsibility it involved.

Mr. Gompers's statement was inspired by a recent utterance of William H. Barr of Buffalo, President of the National Founders' Association, that the eight-hour day would have to be abolished and wages materially lowered from their present scale.

"This is not the first time," said Mr. Gompers, "that the association of which this gentleman is President, or the employers of America, have undertaken to reduce wages and lengthen hours. It was the policy of employers in every crisis, industrial, economic, and financial, to try to force down wages and lengthen the hours of labor as their remedy for the misery of the people.

"With the understanding of the responsibility which goes with my words, notice is given here and now that the American working people will not be forced back by either Barr, his association, or all the Bourbons in the United States.

"The time has come in the world when the working people are coming into their own. They have new rights and new advantages. They have made the sacrifices, and they are going to enjoy the better times for which the whole world has been in a convulsion.

"The American labor movement, wholeheartedly, supported this world struggle. We went the fullest length in support of that struggle, and we knew what was involved. And the Barrs, whether it be this individual or others of his type, must understand that their day of absolutism in industry is gone, the same as absolutism in government has been destroyed.

"The American labor movement will co-operate with all other agencies to help in this reconstruction time. Our movement is not to destroy, but to construct, and all may just as well understand now as at any other time that the advantages which the workers of America and the allied countries have gained, and which we hope even to extend to the peoples of the conquered countries, are not going to be taken away from us, and we will resist the attempt to the uttermost."

The Mexican delegates to the conference today offered several proposals based upon the existence of the European war. These had been limited by their committee resolutions. Mr. Gompers's peace plan for labor was then taken up. The Mexicans debated the parts of it which in substance reiterated the declaration of the interallied labor program adopted at the London conference of last September and relating to the rights of nations and universal freedom and national self-determination. They expressed doubt as to their ability to satisfy their home organizations of the advisability of discussing international political affairs at this conference.

A recess was taken to enable the Mexicans to debate the matter among themselves, following which there was a unanimous agreement upon Mr. Gompers' proposals, with the Mexicans reserving the right to submit them to a referendum vote of the Mexican labor organizations. The representatives of other Central American Republics unanimously favored the Gompers' suggestions.

Mr. Gompers then arose and, prefacing his remarks by reference to the adoption of his peace treaty program by the conference, referred to a newspaper dispatch from New York, dated Nov. 14, which contained the remarks by Mr. Barr.

A permanent organization of the conference was effected following the presentation of the report of the Committee on Permanent Organization by Chairman John R. Alpine, under the name of the Pan-American Labor Congress.

It was determined to hold annual sessions in July, and the next meeting was scheduled for July, 1919, at Panama. Samuel Gompers was elected First President of the congress, to serve until the next meeting, and John Murray was selected as English-speaking and Canulo Vargas of Mexico as Spanish-speaking Secretary.

The conference adjourned after President Gompers had again warned against the evils of disorganization and Bolshevism and had urged unity of purpose for the workers throughout the Americas.

TROOPS ON GUARD IN SEATTLE STRIKE

Soldiers from Camp Lewis Hurried There Upon Call from Governor Lister.

ENTIRE CITY IS TIED UP

Street Cars Stopped, Schools Closed, and Newspapers Suspended.

SEATTLE, Feb. 6.—Federal troops from Camp Lewis are quartered tonight in Seattle and Tacoma to "stand ready for any emergency," as army officers said today, in connection with the general strike this morning of 45,000 union men, in sympathy with 25,000 shipyard workers who walked out on Jan. 21 to enforce demands for higher wages.

Major John L. Hayren commands the contingent of 800 soldiers in Seattle, and General Frank B. Watson has under him in Tacoma, thirty-six miles from here, two battalions and a machine-gun company. Equipment of the soldiers included 200 hand grenades. Authority for the use of troops was granted by Secretary of War Baker upon advices from Governor Ernest Lister.

Thirty-five thousand union men in the vicinity of Seattle quit work today, labor leaders said, but in Tacoma the response was not so general, and the principal unions involved there were the carmen, timber workers, barbers, and retail clerks.

Street cars stopped running in Seattle, schools closed, restaurants and theatres closed their doors. Newspapers suspended and other industries ceased operating. Twelve "soup kitchens" were established by culinary unions to feed strikers and others who depend upon restaurants for meals. Patrons of the kitchens were lined up and served in military mess fashion. Barber shops closed and elevators stopped running.

Only emergency telegraph business from Seattle was handled by the telegraph companies. The telephone system continued in service.

The city government is prepared for any emergency, Mayor Ole Hanson said, and ten thousand extra police will be sworn in if necessary.

"Any man who attempts to take over control of municipal government functions here will be shot on sight," Mayor Hanson declared when told of a statement by Senator Thomas in the Senate today.

"Strikers have not taken over government functions in Seattle," the Mayor said. "They will not be allowed to take over any government functions despite their published statements that they intend to operate the light plant and help police the city. The seat of city government is still at the City Hall."

Police Have Machine Gun.

Seattle police said they were ready for any emergency. A big truck carrying a machine gun, with sand bags built up around its edges, stands at the police station. Three former army Lieutenants have been assigned to the truck.

Motor cycle police were instructed to watch sharply for offenders who might possibly spread tacks on the streets to puncture automobile tires. For several days stories of enormous sales of tacks for this purpose have been circulated here.

A statement issued by the Strike Committee of the Central Labor Council, which is directing the strike, said the walkout was a success. All lines of industry in which union workmen were employed were crippled, the statement said.

Steamship operators and others were worried over the handling of fresh fish shipments, due from Alaska, and fruits and vegetables coming from California, because of the strike of the longshoremen who, defying their international officers, have virtually tied up coastwise and off-shore traffic.

Vessels coming here to discharge, it was said, would be diverted to other ports nearby. Two Japanese steamers, the Hozan Maru and Mandasan, were ordered to San Francisco to load cargo for the Orient.

February 7, 1919

54 FOREIGN REDS ON THE WAY EAST TO BE DEPORTED

Train Passes Through Chicago with Two Carloads of Alien Prisoners.

ROUNDED UP IN FAR WEST

Some Are from Seattle, Where Bolsheviki and I. W. W. Started Big Strike.

ARRESTS MADE QUIETLY

Immigration Officials Determined to Rid the Country of European Anarchists.

Special to The New York Times.

CHICAGO, Monday, Feb. 10.—The Chicago Tribune this morning prints the following:

Deportation is the answer of the United States Government to the challenge of I. W. W. and Bolshevist agitators who come to this country with the avowed purpose of stirring up trouble in industry and social life.

The first Federal blow against the wave of Anarchism already launched on the Pacific Coast came to light yesterday when fifty-four labor agitators passed through Chicago in two heavily-guarded tourist sleepers bound for immediate deportation from an Atlantic port.

A motley company of I. W. W. troublemakers, bearded labor fanatics, and red flag supporters were huddled in crowded berths and propaganda-strewed compartments of the prison train, which slipped in and out of the city so quietly that few Federal officials were aware of its existence. As far as is known, no movement of the kind has ever before been attempted by the Government and the train blazed a trail which, immigration authorities agree, will entirely solve the greatest danger of an industrial unrest during the reconstruction period.

Three leaders of the Seattle uprising, one prominent Spokane agitator, a dangerous I. W. W. leader from Denver and five alien convicts arrested in Chicago, were among the prisoners gathered into the Federal net and now well on their way toward the land of their birth, after trial and conviction as undesirable citizens.

The remainder were alien labor agitators picked up by officers of the United States Immigration Service during a year of quiet campaigning in industrial centres of the Pacific coast.

They were guarded by fourteen heavily armed immigration officers, who paced up and down the length of the train from the time it reached the Chicago yards until it pulled from the city with clearance orders over all traffic. A. D. H. Jackson, chief of the Seattle office of the Immigration Service, was in command.

Dragnet Set Two Years Ago.

"The proceeding against enemies of this type is simple," declared an official with the train. "Just two hours before the Seattle strike was called we had gathered forty agitators into these cars with everything cleared away between them and the middle of the Atlantic Ocean. For more than a year the Immigration Service has been working quietly in all industrial centres, checking up on the strange aliens who appeared during war months and gathering evidence against I. W. W. leaders and trouble makers who call themselves Bolsheviki.

"When the evidence was compiled against this particular crew each case was brought to a Federal hearing, and all court findings sent to Washington, where they were reviewed by Secretary of Labor Wilson. The Secretary has the power to order this type of prisoner deported or released, and so far there has been little trouble in getting quick action.

"While labor circles were seething with trouble along the coast, our prison train slipped out for the Atlantic long before strike leaders were aware that some cherished members of thir organisation had left their midst. We picked up additions to the party in Spokane and one joined us from Denver.

Habeas Corpus Failed.

"The surprise seemed to take the wind from the sails of the agitators. Only one man rebelled when told of Uncle Sam's decision to rid the country of his presence. He got out a writ of habeas corpus against deportation, which was promptly quashed by a Federal Judge in Spokane. The courts have opened every facility and given every co-operation in this work."

When the prison train reached Chicago, red flags that waved from the cars on the first day's run, I. W. W. banners, and strike placards were piled on the littered tourist berths which held all of the earthly goods of the prisoners. One I. W. W. songbook, with its flaring red cover, was propped in a car window, but it was hastily removed when a big guard passed by and tapped on the glass. The prisoners seemed thoroughly cowed and convinced at last that Uncle Sam means business in dealing with their class.

"We let 'em howl and wave the red flag as much as they wanted to after we left Seattle," said a train guard, "and when they found that they could do it without causing anybody trouble, they quit and have been quiet ever since.

"Before we reached the State of Montana Mr. Jackson went through and told the prisoners that for their own good they had better remain quiet and not allow red stuff to show from the windows.

"'The cowboys of this State don't like I. W. W.'s,' he told them. 'If they see you coming through with a lot of racket and find out who you are, they might let loose with some fireworks. These cowboys are mighty quick on the trigger hereabouts.'

"That was enough. The Bolshevist Army pulled in its banners and faded from sight as we passed through Montana towns."

Avoided Mob at Butte.

The one and only attempt at a mob delivery of the prisoners was frustrated by the foresight of the Federal officers. Before the prison train reached Butte, Mont., officers were warned that I. W. W. leaders in that city and Helena had learned of the deportations and were massing to deliver their comrades. The two cars, then attached to a regular train, were cut off at a junction and put into another train which made a wide detour, missing both Butte and Helena and striking the main line well to the east of the danger point, while the I. W. W. mob spread over Montana in a futile attempt at rescue.

One thousand men in a typical I. W. W. mob stormed the Butte station when the original train reached that point, according to reports received here by the guards. Three hundred members of the mob swept gatemen and police officers aside and insisted on searching the train. They were allowed to do so and left without causing further trouble when they found what had happened up the line.

Throughout the trip railroad men and Federal officers are co-operating to keep the route and running schedule secret. Chief Jackson has no fear of running into any additional trouble on the remainder of his journey. While in Chicago, his fourteen guards were placed in complete command of the train and although Federal officers and railroad men were notified of the movement, the immigration guards did not require assistance of any kind.

Only one woman, the wife of a Finnish agitator arrested in Spokane, was among the prisoners.

Handcuffs for All.

She hugged a car window and gloomily watched the guards as they paced their beats. In a forward compartment a blanket concealed fifty-four pairs of business-like handcuffs to be used in emergencies or when the prisoners leave their cars.

"The handcuffs helped convince these birds that they are not appreciated in America," remarked a stocky little guard who wore a civilian overcoat over his infantry uniform. He received his discharge just in time to serve in the first active campaign of Uncle Sam's war against the reds.

"We don't need the cuffs now," said the guard. "What we need is a number of good gags. This is a musical gang. They sing foreign songs for hours. Some of 'em wake up in the night to do it."

The majority of the prisoners will be sent back to Russian provinces. Some are Norwegians, some Scandinavians, and some Finns, according to their guards.

The five prisoners who were added to the party here have been sentenced to deportation under the 1917 act for some time past. They are not connected with the I. W. W. or Bolshevist movement, as far as could be learned. One of the Chicago prisoners served a sentence in the House of Correction for failure to register.

Practically all of the prisoners have been in the United States more than a year, according to the Finn leader and spokesman of the party, who has been a Bolshevist representative in every city west of the Mississippi. He led a half-hearted cheer from his barred window yesterday and exhibited the tattered end of a red flag when he was sure no "quick trigger" cowboy lurked in the vicinity.

The immigration service bases its new policy of deportation on the immigration act passed by Congress in October, 1917.

Incomplete Washington Survey Accounts for 121 Walk-Outs, with 53 Others Threatened

STRIKES are on the increase throughout the country, according to reports received at Washington. In the number of strikes and lockouts now going on, and the number threatened, labor unrest is at its highest point since the armistice, and in the variety of them is without precedent, so far as bases of comparison are available.

The strike data that follow were obtained from the Department of Labor and from other sources at Washington. These show that there are 121 strikes now under way in the country, indicated on reports received in the seven days preceding Sept. 18. The data are admitted to be incomplete. The Statistical Bureau of the Department of Labor collects strikes and lockouts by quarters of the year. The last available is for the quarter ending in March. There is no segregation by weeks, but in the four weeks of February, the highest of the quarter, the total was 193 strikes. Of the 121 strikes now under way, comparatively only a few are a month old, indicating that, at the present rate, when September is finally footed up, the February total will be surpassed.

Fifty-three strikes are threatened. At the head stands the menace of the strike of the country's steel workers, due for a walkout tomorrow. Beyond the largest cloud is that of the miners, which looms for Nov. 1 unless peace is made.

On Sept. 17 the Conciliation Bureau of the Department of Labor had fifty-eight strikes before it for settlement. In addition there were ninety-seven controversies which had not reached the strike stage. The grand total is 155 and 36 were new cases brought to the attention of the department during the week. This, compared with 19 and 35, respectively, for the two preceding weeks, points to an upward trend.

On the brighter side is the fact that many of the strikes are apparently of short duration. Nineteen are reported to have been settled in the seven days preceding Sept. 17. In most cases the strikers gained an advantage. In the demands made by strikers and those who threaten to strike are numerous instances in which $1 an hour is asked. Master and steam fitters of St. Louis, Mo., demand $12 a day.

Below is given the list of strikes under way, those threatened, and those case where obtainable. The number of new strikes is not segregated, but it is estimated to be not largely in excess of those reported to be adjusted:

Strikes Pending.

300 cigarmakers, Cleveland; ask for 50 per cent. increase in wages.

Building trade crafts at San Antonio, Texas; in sympathy with union electricians.

Employes of the Monumental Tailoring Company of Baltimore, Md.

Employes of the Moran Paving Company of Ogden, Utah; ask for $5 a day.

Blacksmiths in the Ralph Shipyards, Eureka, Cal.

155 gas workers employed by the Seattle Lighting Company of Seattle, Wash.

500 hodcarriers, plasterers, and laborers at Portland, Ore.; ask an increase of $5 a month.

Candymakers at Portland, Ore.

1,000 journeymen tailors at San Francisco, Cal.; ask for $1 an hour and a forty-four-hour week.

100 tailors at San Diego, Cal.; want $36 a week and an eight-hour day.

Milk drivers at Minneapolis, Minn.

Leather workers of the Ohio Leather Company, Girard, Ohio.

30,000 coal miners at Troy, Belleville, Peoria, and Collinsville and Marisa, Ill.

Employes of the B. F. Avery & Sons Company, Louisville, Ky.

Window cleaners of New York City; demand a minimum wage of $39 a week and a forty-hour week.

Policemen, Tulsa, Okla.

Members of the building trades, Seattle, Wash.; want higher wages.

Butchers and meat cutters at New Orleans, La.

Employes of the Eck Dynamo Company of Belleville, N. J.; want a 10 per cent. increase in wages.

Stationary engineers, Omaha, Neb.

Carpenters, Providence, R. I.

Cooks and waiters, Omaha, Neb.

Employes of the Louisville Street Railway Company, Louisville, Ky.

38,000 cigarmakers in the United States and Canada.

Employes of fourteen Walton restaurants at Boston, Mass.; ask for an increase of $ a week.

Publishers' pressmen of New York City.

Brewery workers of Youngstown, Ohio; demand $36 a week.

Employes of the Rogers Peet Company, New York City.

Dock workers at Duluth, Minn.

Bricklayers on all Government projects at Philadelphia, Penn.; want $1.25 an hour.

4,500 silk workers at Paterson, N. J.; want a forty-four-hour week.

Employes of the National Equipment Company, Springfield, Mass.

1,400 policemen at Boston, Mass.; want recognition and increase in wages.

Employes of the Worcester Gaslight Company, Worcester, Mass.

Journeymen tailors of St. Louis, Mo.; ask for an eight-hour day and abolition of piecework.

Mill workers of the Mount Nebo Marble Company of Salt Lake City, Utah; demanding an increase of 50 cents a day.

300 shopmen on the New York Central at Buffalo, N. Y.

Employes of the F. Blumenthal Company, leather manufacturers, Wilmington, Del.

1,000 employes of the Bibb Manufacturing

3,000 miners and laborers of the Standard Steel Car Company, Hammond, Ind.

Paper box makers at New York City.

Sheet metal workers at Washington, D. C.

Employes of the Cudahy Packing Company, Milwaukee, Wis.

Employes of the Malleable Casting Company, Richmond, Ind.

Employes of the Shore Line Electric Railway Company, Hartford, Conn.

Plumbers at Pawtucket, R. I.; ask $1 an hour.

120,000 building trade workers at Chicago; demand $1 an hour.

Painters in Cincinnati, Ohio.

6,000 stevedores at San Francisco, Cal.

6,000 waiters at New York City.

3,000 clothing and textile workers in mills at Utica, N. Y.

200 plumbers at Youngstown, Ohio.

500 blacksmiths, helpers, woodworkers, and machine hands employed in fifty wagon shops at St. Louis, Mo.

200 employes in the Worcester Machine Company, Worcester, Mass.

Employes in Armour's plant, Omaha, Neb.

Garbage collectors in Providence, R. I.

600 metal workers, Salt Lake City, Utah.

Clerks in cigar stores, New York City.

3,000 machinists in twenty-four factories at Akron, Ohio.

Miners in the coal district, Logan County, W. Va.

Meat cutters and butchers in two slaughter houses at St. Louis, Mo.

Employes of the East St. Louis and Suburban Company, St. Louis, Mo.

Employes of the Berkshire Street Railway Company, Pittsfield, Mass.

Miners of the Coeur d'Alene district, Idaho.

Employes of the T. G. Plant Shoe Company, Boston, Mass.

Employes of the Southern Public Utilities Company, Charlotte, N. C.

Garbage men of Newark, N. Y., asking for a flat rate of $10 a day.

900 employes of the Lucey Manufacturing Company of Chattanooga, Tenn.

Journeymen tailors of Boston, Mass.; demanding minimum wage increase of $33 a month.

500 employes of the Gates Rubber Company, Denver, Col.

Employes of the Columbus Power and Light Company, Columbus, Ohio; ask an increase of 35 per cent and other concessions.

Carmen of the Ashtabula Rapid Transit Company, Ashtabula, Ohio.

1,000 yardmen of the Southern Pacific Company, San Francisco, Cal.

Central Manufacturing Company and the Dodge Brothers Auto Company of Macon, Ga.; want higher wages and decrease in hours.

Employes of the Willingham Sash and Door Company, the Willingham-Chambers Lumber Company.

19,000 miners in the Wyoming and Lackawanna Valleys, Pennsylvania.

Operators of the Southwestern Bell Telephone Company, Shawnee, Okla.

50 employes of the Empire City Rice Mill and 135 employes of the Otis Manufacturing Company, New Orleans, La.; want higher wages and union recognition.

Department store tailors, St. Louis, Mo.; demand minimum wage of 75 cents an hour and an eight-hour day.

Employes of the moving and storage companies, St. Louis, Mo.

150 fishermen on the menhaden fleet, Atlantic City; protesting against cut in wages.

3,000 tobacco workers at Key West, Fla.

Employes of the J. J. Regan Manufacturing Company and the Hockanum Mills Company, Rockville, Mass.

18,000 silk mill workers at Scranton, Penn.; demand an eight-hour day and minimum pay of $15 a week.

Painters at Denver, Col.

200 employes of the Globe Milling and Elevator Company and the Sperry Flour Company of Ogden, Utah; ask for $5 a day.

Operators in the Home Telephone Exchange, Hillsboro, Ohio; want better wages and increased hours.

Bricklayers at Wilmington, Del. ask wage of $1 an hour.

Drug clerks at Louisville, Ky.; want increase of wages.

100 cobblers at Elizabeth, N. J.; demand $25 a week and a forty-eight-hour week.

Slashers in the Lancaster Mills, Clinton, Mass.

400 machine men in Miami Paper Company mills, West Carrollton, Ohio; want increase in wages.

Moving picture operators, Indianapolis, Ind.; demand $1 an hour.

Stokers in the power plant of the Metropolitan Building, New York.

Journeymen tailors, Louisville, Ky.; demand a minimum wage of $36 a week, a forty-four-hour week, and the abolition of piecework.

Journeymen tailors of Springfield, Mass.; ask for a minimum wage of $30 a week.

Employes of the Utah Power and Light Company, Ogden, Utah.

Linemen of the Columbus Railway, Light and Power Company, Columbus, Ohio.

Journeymen tailors at St. Louis, Mo.; demand a minimum wage of $36 a week and a forty-eight-hour week.

Printers at Tacoma, Wash.; demand from $3.50 to $3.75 a day for a six-and-a-half-hour day.

6,000 ladies' tailors at Boston, Mass.; demand forty-four-hour week and increased pay.

Union musicians at Philadelphia, Penn.; in protest against the employment of nonunion men in the Knights Templars parade.

500 gasmakers in the Brooklyn plants, New York City; demand 25 per cent. increase.

6,000 members of the building crafts at Seattle, Wash.; want higher wages.

Pressmen at Seattle, Wash.; ask for $7 a day.

Barbers at Philadelphia; ask for higher wages.

Plumbers and steam fitters at Idaho Falls, Idaho; demand $9 for an eight-hour day.

48,000 coal miners, employed by the Delaware and Hudson Coal Company, Scranton, Penn.

Employes of Chicago, Illinois & Midland Railway, Taylorville, Ill.

Employes Peters Cartridge Company, King Mills, Ohio.

1,100 employes of Wisconsin Motor Company, Milwaukee, Wis.; demanded 5 per cent. increase by July 1 and another 5 per cent. increase by Aug. 1.

Molders, Minneapolis, Minn.

200 employes of Surpass & Forderer Leather Company.

Blacksmiths, Schuylkill Forge Company, Philadelphia, Penn.

Machinists, Rutenbor Motor Works, Marion, Ind.; demand increase of wages and eight-hour day.

Machinists' Union of Tilton Optical Company of Tilton, N. H.; discrimination alleged by union.

Chemical workers of Lanman & Kemp of New York City.

Chemical workers of McKesson & Robbins, New York City.

Wire drawers employed by Waterbury Wire Rope Company, Brooklyn, N. Y.

Strikes Threatened.

1,000 employes of the Central Railroad, Elizabeth, N. J.; want increase of 17 per cent. in wages.

Firemen, Holyoke, Mass.; ask for increase in wages.

150,000 shipworkers on Pacific Coast; want wage increase.

Butchers at San Francisco, Cal.; want $40 a week.

Stock yard workers at Chicago, Ill.; want wages raised 20 per cent.

10,000 shipworkers in the Brooklyn, Queens, Staten Island, and New Jersey yards; ask for $1.25 an hour.

Employes of the Pennsylvania car shops at Trenton, N. J.; ask for 83 cents an hour.

Moving picture employes, Portland, Ore.

Park employes of Boston, Mass.; demanding a 20 per cent. increase in wages.

Steel workers at Portland, Ore., demanding an 8-cent-an-hour increase.

Journeymen tailors at Youngstown, Ohio; demanding a minimum wage of $30 a week and a forty-eight-hour week.

Employes in the Bay State Street Railway Company, Boston, Mass.; want wage increase.

Employes of the Eastern Massachusetts Railway; want wage increase.

600,000 maintenance of way and shop-workers in the United States and Canada; demand an increase of $1 a day in wages.

4,500 street cleaners in New York City; ask for from $33 to $44 a week.

Garbage men in New York City; ask for 100 per cent. increase.

Technical men, New York City.

300,000 steel workers set for Sept. 22; American Federation of Labor demands recognition of unions and collective bargaining through national unions.

Employes of Childs restaurants of Philadelphia; protest against being sent to Atlantic City for week-end rush.

Machinists of Hamilton, Ohio; ask for nine-hour day and half holiday Saturday.

3,000 drug clerks in New York City; ask eight-hour day, six-day week, and 40 per cent. increase in pay.

11,000 miners in Guyam Valley coal fields.

Railroad telegraphers in United States and Canada; ask for 50 cents an hour.

General strike at Peoria, Ill., in support of the street railway strike.

General strike of organized labor supporting policemen's strike at Boston, Mass.

Negro plumbers at Washington, D. C.; demanding $6 a day.

Journeymen tailors at Providence, R. I.; ask for $36 a week for journeymen and $17 for helpers.

Job printers at Denver, Col.; ask for $39 a week for day and $42 for night work.

Bituminous coal miners throughout the country; threaten to strike Nov. 1 unless granted demands for shorter work day and higher wages.

Employes of the Washington Railway and Electric Company; demand higher wages.

5,000 railroad shopmen at Cleveland, Ohio.

Journeymen tailors in Philadelphia.

Pawnbrokers' clerks in New York City; want to do away with working Saturday nights.

California Central Fruit Workers' Union; want 17 per cent. increase.

Textile Workers of Windsor Print Works, North Adams, Mass.

Bricklayers, Wilmington, Del.

Employes of the North Alabama Traction Company, Albany, Ala.

Employes of the Manhattan and Queens Traction Company.

Employes of the water plants at St. Louis, Mo.

Federated railway shopmen of Chicago district.

Carpenters at Newark, N. J.; demand $7 a day.

Machinists in Denver, Col., shops; refuse to accept 4 cents an hour increase.

Master plumbers and steamfitters of St. Louis; demand $12 a day.

Street car men at Portland, Ore.; demanding 25 per cent. increase.

Policemen, Portland, Ore.

General strike at Los Angeles, Cal.

150 journeymen tailors at Portland, Ore.; demand increase in wages running from $34.50 to $40 a week for a forty-four-hour week.

Painters at Wilmington, Del.; want 87½ cents and hour.

50,000 employees of the City of New York: want an increase of from 10 to 20 per cent.

Journeymen tailors of Philadelphia, Penn.: demanding wage of $36 a week, an eight-hour day, and recognition of the union.

250 boilermakers employed in the St. Louis-San Francisco shops; decline to accept 4 cents an hour increase offered by President Wilson.

Metal trade workers at Salt Lake City; in protest of high cost of living.

2,000 carpenters at Newark, N. J.: demand $1 an hour.

Strikes Ended.

Cigarmakers of Newark, N. J.: received an increase in wages of from $2 to $3.50 per 1,000 cigars.

Women tailors of New York City: won a minimum wage of $50 a week and a forty-four-hour week.

Employes of the Baltimore & Ohio Railroad, Cumberland, Md.

Employes of the Columbus Railway and Light Company, Columbus, Ohio: ended in compromise.

Employes of Commercial Cable Company of New York City: resulted in compromise.

300 Americans, in defiance of 1,200 alien workers at the Standard Steel plant, Hammond, Ind.: returned to work.

400 movers in St. Louis, Mo.: chauffeurs, movers, and packers receive $27 a week and helpers $24.

Job pressmen, Salt Lake City, Utah; ended in a compromise.

Carpenters at Chicago, Ill.: granted 90 cents an hour until May, 1920; after that will be placed on the same basis as other trades.

Employes of the C. E. Miller and B. E. Cole Company of Haverhill, Mass.: return to work pending settlement of grievances.

Miners at the Comstock Mine at Virginia City, Nev.: returned to work at regular wage scale.

Employes of Eureka Lumber Company, Eureka, Mon.: ten hours' pay for eight hours' work and recognition of union granted.

260 employes of abattoirs of New Orleans, La.: all demands, including eight-hour day, granted; wage increase referred to arbitration.

Employes of the Hudson Valley Electric Company, Lake George, N. Y.: hourly rate increased from 34½ to 40 cents, and eight-hour day established.

Street and electric railways of Charlotte, Winston-Salem, N. C., and Greenville, N. C.: granted 263 employes increase of 9½ cents an hour.

450 employes of Underwood Computing Machine Company, Hartford, Conn.; eight-hour demands granted; wage increase of from 12 to 20 per cent.

Foreman & Clark Clothing Company, Chicago, Ill.

Brick and clay workers of Coffeville, Kan.; promise to readjust wage scale and working hours.

Employes of Schuette & Koerting Company of Philadelphia, Penn.; granted 55 hours' pay for 48-hour week.

Employes of the Wilmington and Philadelphia Company; received 10 cents an hour increase.

Employes of the Columbia Graphophone Company.

Mine workers of the Nevada Consolidated Copper Company, Ely, Nev.; granted a company commissary and better working conditions.

Clothing workers of the Sherman & Sons plant, Louisville, Ky., recognition of union, $4 increase a week and forty-four-hour week.

Steel car repairmen of the Silver Grove Yards of the Chesapeake & Ohio Railroad, Cincinnati, Ohio.

2,000 B. & O. shopmen at Cumberland, Md.

Actors' Equity, New York.

Text of the President's Labor Day Message Urging Economy and Telling His Wage Plan

Special to The New York Times.

WASHINGTON, Aug. 31.—*Here is President Wilson's Labor Day message:*

I am encouraged and gratified by the progress which is being made in controlling the cost of living. The support of the movement is widespread and I confidently look for substantial results; although I must counsel patience as well as vigilance, because such results will not come instantly or without team work.

Let me again emphasize my appeal to every citizen of the country to continue to give his personal support in this matter, and to make it as active as possible. Let him not only refrain from doing anything which at the moment will tend to increase the cost of living, but let him do all in his power to increase the production; and, further than that, let him at the same time himself carefully economize in the matter of consumption. By common action in this direction we shall overcome a danger greater than the danger of war. We will hold steady a situation which is fraught with possibilities of hardship and suffering to a large part of our population; we will enable the processes of production to overtake the processes of consumption; and we will speed the restoration of an adequate purchasing power for wages.

I am particularly gratified at the support which the Government's policy has received from the representatives of organized labor, and I earnestly hope that the workers generally will emphatically indorse the position of their leaders and thereby move with the Government instead of against it in the solution of this greatest domestic problem.

I am calling for as early a date as practicable a conference in which authoritative representatives of labor and of those who direct labor will discuss fundamental means of bettering the whole relationship of capital and labor and putting the whole question of wages upon another footing.

WOODROW WILSON.

September 21, 1919

September 1, 1919

LABOR GROUP QUITS THE CONFERENCE; GOMPERS WILL PRESS STEEL STRIKE; RAILWAY WORKERS MAKE NEW THREAT

GOMPERS LEADS MEN OUT

Labor Group Withdraws When Employers Defeat Bargaining Plan.

WILSON'S APPEAL FUTILE

Leaders Say That Federation Will Back Steel Strike with Full Power.

CONFERENCE WILL GO ON

President's Message Appealed to Delegates to Unite on Definite Program.

Special to The New York Times.

WASHINGTON, Oct. 22.—The labor group late this afternoon withdrew from the Industrial Conference following the refusal of the employers' group to accept a final resolution, submitted by Samuel Gompers, on collective bargaining, in which the public group concurred, and despite the reading of President Wilson's sick-bed letter pleading with the conference to adjust its differences and get together on a constructive program.

The withdrawal of the labor delegates, however, does not mean the breaking up of the conference, which will continue in session with the employers' and public groups and meet again tomorrow.

The resolution on which the conference split was offered by Mr. Gompers as follows:

"The right of wage earners to organize without discrimination, to bargain collectively, to be represented by representatives of their own choosing in negotiations and adjustments with employers in respect to wages, hours of labor, and relations and conditions of employment is recognized."

When the employers' group by a majority of one vote had defeated this resolution Mr. Gompers said:

"The word you have spoken here means nothing. You have defeated the labor group in its declaration, but we will meet you again in conference, and when we do meet you there you will be glad to talk collective bargaining."

Then he announced that the Executive Council of the American Federation of Labor in a meeting last night had voted to devote all its moral and financial support to aid the steel strikers in en-

forcing their demand for collective bargaining.

The action taken by the labor group was presaged at the morning session of the conference when, after the delegates had given the President a rising vote of thanks, following the reading of his letter, Mr. Gompers and his followers declined to vote for a resolution, offered by John Spargo, pledging the conference to leave no stone unturned to agree on a program before adjourning.

After expressing his own and his associates' concurrence in those parts of the Spargo motion which "expressed deep sympathy for the President" as well as the hope of the President's speedy recovery, Mr. Gompers said he could not without consulting his associates undertake to vote for the assurance and pledge which were included in the motion.

Chairman Lane then suggested that the labor group withdraw for consultation. This was agreed to, and Mr. Gompers announced that he would have a motion on behalf of labor to put before the conference when the afternoon session convened.

Gompers Offers Resolution.

When the afternoon session opened Mr. Gompers at once took the floor.

"When we heard read this morning," he said, "the letter addressed to this conference by the President of the United States, a letter which the whole world will read with the deepest interest, it disclosed to us one thing at least, that must give hope to every American and every liberty-loving man and woman in our country and the whole world; a letter emanating from the President of the United States from his bed of illness, where he is stricken as the result of his great contributions to the freedom and the justice and democracy of the world. It disclosed the one fact, also, that the mind of the President is as clear as it ever was during his entire life and gives true Americans the hope and encouragement that with time and rest he may be restored to health and to strength and to the activity that his wonderful nature will give to the whole world, and particularly to our own country.

"No man could hear that letter read but to be moved by it to the very innermost recesses of his soul. Under its influence and its spell th labor group asked for an adjournment or a recess. During recess we have met and discussed the present situation in this conference in almost every particular."

He then read the resolution approved by the labor group, adding that he might have something to say after members of other groups had discussed it, and moved that it be taken up for immediate decision without reference to the Committee of Fifteen. This was agreed to. Frederick P. Fish of Boston, of the employers' group, then advanced views which proved to be a forecast of the adverse action later taken by that group.

"It seems to me," he said, "as argument in this conference, has developed, it has been clear that the sum and substance of the resolutions with reference to collective bargaining that have been presented heretofore, excepting the substitute from the employers' group, the Chadbourne resolution and the substitute offered for it by the employers' group, have in substance meant this and nothing else—that this conference is asked to take action

which will force, if possible, the hundreds of thousands of employers in industries throughout this country to recognize the labor unions whether they will or will not, and to force their organizations to deal with the labor unions against their will. Now, that that is the issue of this whole situation has been most definitely determined, I believe, in the mind of every man in this conference, and I believe that our friends in the labor group would concede that that has been and now is their thought.

"Now they produce this resolution, which as a matter of words does not go as far as that, but words do not count—it is the thought behind the words; and if this resolution should be adopted by the employers' group, for example, it would go out to the world as a concession on the part of the employers' group that they recognize the necessity of the unionization of all the industrial establishments in the country, and the kind of collective bargaining that the labor unions insist upon as distinguished from other kinds. The labor men, the working men throughout the country, would not be allowed or called upon to discriminate. The public would not be allowed to discriminate, and could not discriminate. Therefore I shall personally feel obliged to oppose this resolution unless there is a plain definition as to what is meant by bargaining collectively, and the reservation upon which the employers' group insisted in its substitute resolution that the employers in the industrial establishments in this country shall not be required and forced against their will to deal with men chosen as representatives by their own employes, who are not of the number of their own employes, for that particular substantial issue cannot be evaded by any form of words.

Defeated by One Employer.

Louis Titus of San Francisco, of the public group, argued that a resolution which practically meant the same thing had been introduced by the employers' group. Collective bargaining had been in every resolution introduced by any of the groups and the collective bargaining principle had been recognized by all the elements represented in the conference.

A. A. Landon of Buffalo, another of the public group, stated his sympathy with the resolution, as did also H. B. Endicott, the shoe manufacturer, of the public group. Without labor as a partner, peace, said Mr. Endicott, was impossible. He told of a meeting of the Committee of Fifteen at which the controversy had been threshed out, but the effort came to naught because of the attitude of the representatives of the employers' group. Charles Edward Russell and Dr. Charles W. Eliot, also of the public group, indorsed the resolution, while Herbert F. Perkins of the International Harvester Company, of the employers' group, opposed it.

"I would not have the country convinced that we are not willing to take into partnership with us today the men we hailed as partners during the war and without whose aid the war could not possibly have been won," said Mr. Endicott.

He insisted that the employers' delegates had not yielded an inch during the conference, but that the labor group had been "dignified" and had "attempted to meet the real difficulties in the way of an agreement."

"Since all the civilized world has acknowledged the right of wage earners to bargain collectively, why deny that right in this industrial conference?" asked Mr. Russell. It was the "foundation" of all of labor's demands, he contended. He believed a revolution of a certain type was not impossible in the United States.

"Where justice rules there is no dissension," said he.

The only personal clash of the conference came after Perkins had called unwarranted an intimation by Mr. Endicott that a certain member of the employers' group had withdrawn from it after introducing a resolution not acceptable to his conferees.

John Spargo asked Mr. Gompers whether, if the resolution was adopted, the labor group would understand it to mean that the principle of collective bargaining would then be rationally and carefully worked out by the conference. Mr. Gompers said such was his understanding.

L. F. Loree, President of the Delaware & Hudson Railroad, of the employers' group, said "We are not going to be led into the adoption of any resolution of this kind that does not set out plainly on its face all of the circumstances under which collective bargaining can be conducted."

J. W. O'Leary, also of the employers' group, expressed the hope that the votes of those who opposed the resolution would not be taken as a denial of the right of wage earners to bargain collectively "under such forms as experience and good practice have shown to be productive of the best relationship between capital and labor."

A vote was then called for. The public group, after a few minutes' deliberation, indorsed the resolution, and Bernard M. Baruch cast its vote. The labor group voted aye, of course, and the employers no, a majority of one deciding the vote.

Gompers Makes Final Plea.

Mr. Gompers, when the vote was announced, was immediately on his feet.

"I feel it incumbent upon me at this juncture," he said, "to ask that I may be heard in connection with the present situation. As I stated or tried to state upon our convening early this afternoon the group of which I am a part felt impressed very deeply with the urgent request of the President, and under its influence prepared for submission to this conference a resolution which by the vote of the employers' group has been rejected. The situation thus created can bring satisfaction to no man. It is regrettable beyond what words can express. It is regrettable from every viewpoint.

He referred to the fact that in a previous speech in the conference he had called attention to the activities of the I. W. W. The employers' group, he added, "are placing themselves in exactly the same position as the I. W. W. by the attitude assumed by the group during the course of the conference."

"I admit that our movement is not perfect. I concede that errors may be made, and it is quite true and quite natural, but I submit that there is not a single voluntary organization in this or any country which has contributed so much to a constructive policy within

rational lines as has the American trades union movement.

"My associates and I in this labor group in this conference are not here by sufferance; we are here, as are the employers, at the direction of the President, for our representation and the group representing the public were appointed by the President directly. Is it imaginable that we as the representatives of the organized workers of America—at least, the organized workers—you may dispute whatever claims we may make—but representing, with the representatives of the railroad brotherhoods, four and a half million wage workers in the United States, can enter into this conference and remain members of it, with a refusal on the part of the employers' group to admit the right of the wage workers to organize for collective bargaining? Is it possible that such a construction can be placed upon the President's call? I doubt it.

"Is there anything that any man can say against the declaration that we have submitted, and which the employers' group by their vote defeated? Is there in that anything that any man can say is unfair or improper? We hear this talk of the individual workers. Do we not say in that declaration 'the right to organize without discrimination'?"

Leader and Delegates Walk Out

He referred to the steel strike and said that a meeting of the Executive Council of the Federation of Labor last night the council had voted "to more fully, if possible, bring the moral and the financial support of the workers of America to aid the steel and iron workers in their just contention for a conference with a view to collective bargaining.

The longer, he added, the rights of labor are denied, the more difficult will be the job of the employers. In conclusion, he said:

"Gentlemen. I have sung my swan song in this conference. You have, by your action, the action of the employers' group, legislated us out of this conference. We have nothing further to submit and we feel great regret that we are not enabled with a clear conscience to remain here longer. We have responsibilities to the millions of workers and those dependent upon them. We must fulfill these obligations. Our regret is that the rejection of anything like a fair proposition on our part has occurred. It has been done and the die is cast; and we were endeavoring

by all means within our power to comply with the request made by that great man, now stricken on a bed of illness, the President of the United States, for whom we have an admiration and a love inexpressible.

"Mr. Chairman, and gentlemen, for the courtesy which you have extended to us we are profoundly grateful, but we cannot longer remain with you."

As he ended Mr. Gompers walked from the room, followed by Frank Morrison, Michael F. Tighe, and the other representatives of the American Federation of Labor. The representatives of the railway brotherhoods did not immediately quit the room. They did so a little later, after L. E. Sheppard of the conductors and W. G. Lee of the railway trainmen had expressed their sympathy with the stand taken by Mr. Gompers and his Federation colleagues.

Sheppard accused some of the delegates with being actuated by political motives, with a Presidential election only a year away. He asserted those who had defeated the collective bargaining resolution "want to achieve their political ends." The representatives of the railroad administration were the only members of the capital group who "know anything about labor by direct contact," he added, saying that the "railroad men are the key to the situation in the country, and that while they would live up to their contracts, it might be necessary for them to fight for their rights."

He charged that a representative of the employers' group had asserted that "if we could only defeat the American Federation of Labor, we could take care of the Bolsheviki and the I. W. W."

Members of the employers' group asked that it be made plain that they had not brought about the defection of the labor group. They said they were willing to remain in Washington indefinitely in an effort to bring about the success of the conference on the lines laid down by President Wilson.

After John Spargo had offered a resolution for the continuance of the conference with a proviso that an effort be made to get the labor group back, Chairman Lane announced adjournment until 9:30 o'clock tomorrow morning.

"This conference is not at an end," said Mr. Lane, "and we shall have a session tomorrow."

He was asked if an effort would be made to get the labor group back. He did not answer. He did say that if necessary the President might appoint a new group to represent labor. But it was evident that he did not think such action on the part of the President would be necessary.

October 23, 1919

Chairman Gary's Letter to Subsidiary Companies Telling Why He Won't Deal With Labor Unions

PITTSBURGH, Sept. 17.—A letter from Chairman E. H. Gary, addressed to the Presidents of the subsidiary companies of the United States Steel Corporation, giving the reasons for declining to deal with labor unions, was made public by the Carnegie Steel Company today. The letter, which is dated New York, Sept. 16, reads:

Not long since I respectfully declined to meet for the purpose of discussing matters pertaining to labor at our various plants a number of gentlemen representing certain labor unions. They claim this furnishes cause for complaint and have stated that they intend, if possible, to prevent a continuation of operations at our mills and factories.

I deem it proper to repeat in a letter what heretofore has been said to you verbally. I entertain no feeling of animosity toward the gentlemen personally and would not hesitate to meet them as individuals, but I did not and do not consider it proper to confer with them under the circumstances.

The declination was made for two reasons: First, because I did not believe the gentlemen were authorized to speak for large numbers of our employes, whose interests and wishes are of prime importance; secondly, because a conference with these men would have been treated by them as a recognition of the "closed shop" method of employment. We do not combat labor unions as such. We do not negotiate with labor unions because it would indicate the closing of our shops against non-union labor; and large numbers of our workmen are not members of unions and do not care to be.

The principle of the "open shop" is vital to the greatest industrial progress and prosperity. It is of equal benefit to employer and employe. It means that every man may engage in any line of employment that he selects and under such terms as he and the employer may agree upon; that he may arrange for the kind and character of work which he believes will bring to him the largest compensation and the most satisfactory conditions, depending upon his own merit and disposition.

The "closed shop" means that no man can obtain employment in that shop except through and on the terms and conditions imposed by the labor unions. He is compelled to join the union and to submit to the dictation of its leader before he can enter the place of business. If he joins the union he is then restricted by its leader as to place of work, hours of work, (and therefore amount of compensation,) and advancement in position, regardless of merit; and sometimes, by the dictum of the union leader, called out and prevented from working for days or weeks, although he has no real grievance, and he and his family are suffering for want of the necessities of life. In short, he is subjected to the arbitrary direction of the leader, and his personal independence is gone. Personal ambition to succeed and prosper is stifled.

This country will not stand for the "closed shop." It cannot afford it. In the light of experience, we know it would signify decreased production, increased cost of living, and initiative, development, and enterprise dwarfed. It would be the beginning of industrial decay, and an injustice to the workmen themselves, who prosper only when industry succeeds. The "open shop" will generally be approved by them, for this permits them to engage in any employment, whether they are or are not members of a labor union.

It is appropriate to further emphasize what has been said many times in regard to our employes. Every one, without exception, must be treated by all others justly and according to merit. In accordance with our established custom, one of our workmen, or a number of our workmen from any department, will continue to be received by the management to consider adjustment of any question presented.

It is the settled determination of the United States Steel Corporation and its subsidiaries that the wages and working conditions of their employes shall compare favorably with the highest standards of propriety and justice. Misrepresentations have already and will hereafter be made; unfavorable criticisms may be indulged in by outsiders, especially by those who have little knowledge of the facts; our employes may be threatened and abused in the effort to influence them to join the unions against their own desire; but, whatever the circumstances may be, we should proceed with the conduct of our business in the usual way and should give evidence to our employes that we mean to be fair with them.

NEGROES OPEN FIRE ON DONORA STRIKERS

Reply to Attack with Bricks on Men Returning to Work in Steel Mills.

TWO FOREIGNERS WOUNDED

Senate Committee Is Expected Today to Visit the Plants and to Hear Both Sides.

Special to The New York Times.

PITTSBURGH, Oct. 9.—Two men were shot and several were hit with bricks in a riot at Donora this morning when a number of negroes, returning to work at the plant of the American Steel and Wire Company, opened fire with revolvers in return for an attack with missiles by strikers.

Both of the wounded men are foreigners, who can not speak English. One was shot in the right ankle and the other in the knee. Several more negro laborers were hurt. State police arrived immediately after the shooting and scattered the crowd.

Bricks, clubs, and revolvers were brought into play again in the evening when the shift was changed. One woman and several men were hurt by bricks. Several shots were fired without injuring any one. The workmen leaving the plant defended themselves with fists and missiles for a time and then broke and ran, pursued by the strikers. The battle had raged only a few minutes when it was broken up by mounted police.

The mill at Donora was closed by the strike, but reopened this week with several hundred new men, replacing strikers, among them many negroes. Strike organizers have been bitter for several days because of the employment of negroes in large numbers to take the places of strikers. The negroes have been drifting in from all parts of the East to the large plants about Pittsburgh and are being employed as common laborers as fast as they arrive. Another grievance of the strikers against the negroes is that those employed before the strike have remained at their work almost to a man, in spite of every effort to induce them to join the strikers.

Look to Industrial Conference.

Strike leaders refused today to discuss their financial plight, and their efforts to obtain aid for the further conduct of the strike from American Federation of Labor organizations. The organization of the strike, which covered a period of thirteen months, and the conduct of the strike during its eighteen days is said to have cost, in round numbers, $1,000,000, which would make it probably the most expensive strike in history.

It was reported today that several of the international Presidents are opposed to making further appropriations for the strike, and that no money is available for the payment of strike benefits. While the subject of finances was taboo at strike headquarters, it was said that the committee directing the strike had been surprised at the smallness of the number of requests for assistance which they had received.

It was announced at strike headquarters that the plant of the Alleghany Steel Company at Brackenridge, which was closed by the strike and reopened, has been closed again. At the offices of the company in Pittsburgh it was said that this was not only untrue, but that the company was running with a full force of men, and that 700 foreigners who had struck would never be able to get back into the plant. The strikers also claimed gains in the plant of the West Penn Steel Company at Brackenridge, and further gains at Vandergrift and East Leechburg.

The Committee on Education and La-bor of the Senate, which has been investigating the strike, is due to arrive here tomorrow, and is expected to make a tour of the mills during the day. Tomorrow and Sunday it is expected to hold hearings here, while on Monday it will go to Youngstown, Ohio.

A bulletin was issued today by the strikers entitled, "The scabs can't win the strike." The bulletin is the first evidence of uneasiness manifested by the strikers, because of the numbers of men arriving daily from other sections to take jobs as common laborers in the mills.

At the offices of the Carnegie Steel Company it was said that the number of strikers to return to work today equaled yesterday's figure of 500. One furnace was put into operation at Carrie today, and another will be started tomorrow, which will make six blast furnaces in operation in the plant out of a total of seven. The seventh furnace, it was said, is being relined. Another blast furnace put into operation today was that on Neville Island. It was announced that the eighth furnace would be put in operation tomorrow at the Edgar Thompson plant at Braddock, leaving three furnaces idle. Two finishing mills of the Carnegie Steel Company in Pittsburgh, which have been running with the day shift only, started night shifts tonight.

October 10, 1919

SENATORS VISIT STRIKE DISTRICT

Kenyon's Committee Gets First-Hand Evidence in Pittsburgh Mills and Homes.

QUESTION MANY WORKERS

Hear Numerous Complaints on Hours and Pay and Find Few Foreigners Naturalized.

Special to The New York Times.

PITTSBURGH, Penn., Oct. 10.—The Senate Committee on Education and Labor, which is investigating the steel strike, put in a long day visiting the largest steel plants in the Monongahela Valley, where they met mill officials, employes, strikers strike organizers, and members of the Pennsylvania State Constabulary, and heard every side of the strike.

They found little visible evidence that the strike was still on at Homestead, Duquesne, Clairton, and McKeesport, where they inspected the plants and visited the homes of strikers in the neighborhood. These big mills, which are the backbone of the steel industry in the Pittsburgh district, after being threatened with shutdown on the opening of the strike, were running today with from 75 to 95 per cent. of those employed before the strike.

By a singular coincidence a shooting affray connected with the strike occurred on a street car in front of the Homestead plant, within 100 yards of the party of Senators, without their knowing it. Paul Stodlitz, a workman, who was being heckled by two strikers on a street car, drew his revolver and fired two shots at a distance of about five feet from the men, but missed them. Stodlitz was arrested, but later discharged when he said that he had fired wildly to scare the men.

It was apparent from conversations with the Senators that they were impressed with the fact that the strike, if not broken, was waning in the Pittsburgh district. They were also impressed by the earnestness and unanimity with which the strikers argued that 42 cents an hour would not support their families decently in these times. Another point which was remarked by the Senators was that only a very small proportion of the strikers were naturalized, though most of them could speak some English and many could express themselves without difficulty.

The investigation is being made by Senators Kenyon, Phipps, McKellar, and Sterling.

They talked freely about what they had observed, but were unwilling to be quoted lest their offhand statements might be unfair to the steel companies or the strikers.

Interviewed Many Strikers.

Each talked individually with about fifty or sixty strikers to get an idea of their reasons for striking. The chief reason given in practically every instance was that they could hardly live on 42 cents an hour and that they believed the strike was a means of getting more money. The second was that they had to work long hours, either ten or twelve hours a day.

Although Judge Gary testified that the men were paid time and a half for overtime, every man interviewed by the Senators said that he had never heard of extra pay for overtime in the steel mills. Before they were through with their rounds the Senators were convinced that the strikers were sincere in believing that they had a grievance on the wages and hours, whether they were misled in other respects by agitators or not.

One striker at Homestead included among the reasons for the strike that of having "the Government run the steel mills," which, he said, had been promised by organizers. But generally the strikers talked only of wages and hours, mainly of wages. They usually mentioned that they wanted a union, but mentioned it as an afterthought. When asked what they thought they ought to get for their work the strikers suggested figures ranging from 75 to 90 cents an hour, which they said were the rates mentioned by organizers at their meetings.

When asked how many men were on strike at Homestead the strikers gave the standard reply of 9,000, but the company officials at Homestead gave their employment records to the Senators, which indicate that the number of jobs vacant is less than 3,000.

The employment chart submitted to the Senate Committee gives an interesting history of the strike at the Homestead plant. This chart shows that 35 per cent. of the employes walked out on September 22, the first day of the strike. The mill lost more men in the next two days of the strike until only 62 per cent. of their employes appeared at work. On the fourth day this went up to 63 per cent. It has gained steadily ever since until the record showed that today slightly more than 75 per cent. of the normal force was at work.

After going through the mill, which appeared to be operating near normal, Senators drove to the Second Ward of Homestead, one of the poorest sections, where they interviewed strikers whom they picked haphazard standing on the sidewalk or sitting in front of their own homes.

Question Young Worker.

Senator Kenyon questioned a young man in his shirt sleeves who said he was supporting his mother, his wife, two children and himself on his pay of 42 cents an hour or $5.04 for a twelve-hour day, and that with prices what they are today he could put nothing by for an emergency.

As Senator Kenyon continued his questions throngs began to gather. Soon there were hundreds on the sidewalk, including many mothers with babies in their arms and scores of children, generally neat and well-looking. The men and women questioned each other in various languages to find out what it meant, and a little boy ran up shouting, "What the hell is it?"

Senators McKellar, Phipps, and Stanley also questioned strikers and their families.

The crowd grew until it brought several policemen to the spot. They had nothing to say, however, when they learned what was going on.

A photographer, shouting and waving his arms, drew the children after him, and lined up about 200 for a group picture, while their mothers clucked and gesticulated, showing a great deal of anxiety to get prominent places for their children.

Senator McKellar did not rest until, after shaking hands heartily with the men and doffing his campaign hat chivalrously to the women of one large, complex family, he got himself invited into their crowded two-story dwelling and made some first-hand notes of the manner in which they lived.

The party then went to the big plant of the Carnegie Steel Company at Duquesne, where they had luncheon and interviewed officials of the company. After that they went through the mill, which is now running normally.

This mill was practically unaffected by the strike, but its escape is laid by Secretary Foster to the suppression of meetings and the activity of the State Police. There were no strikers to interview here and the Senators moved on to Clairton where they went through the large mill of the Carnegie Steel Company, which was hit hard at the beginning of the strike, but has recovered considerable ground in the last two weeks.

P. H. Grogan, the strike organizer in the district, attached himself to the party and went through the mill with the men, somewhat to the displeasure of the mill officials. The news spread in a few minutes through Clairton that the Senators were visiting the mill, and a large crowd gathered when the Senators finished their inspection, and who stopped and questioned some of the strikers.

Senator Sterling became the centre of a group of five, and he found that his companions were an Italian, a Turk, a Croat, and a Lithuanian.

Senators Kenyon and McKellar questioned an intelligent young Serb, who called himself George Miller, and explained the hardships of trying to keep a family on 42 cents an hour.

Their next witness was a Slovene, calling himself Frank Smith. He was a neatly dressed young man, who seemed to be less than thirty years old, but he said that he had a wife and five children, and others in the crowd bore him out in this. He said he worked ten hours a day and got $4.67 for it, but that it was far from being enough for him and his family.

"You manage to dress very neatly," said Senator McKellar. "Yes, but that is because I saved money before I was married," he said. "I have to spend the money I had saved."

Some of the men complained of conditions, saying that they were mistreated and discharged for trifles, but Smith said that he could not honestly make any complaint about conditions, as his bosses had always treated him well. He said that he had lived in this country for seven years and that he was not naturalized, his reason being that mills closed down so often and he had to move so often that he couldn't settle long enough in one place for naturalization.

One man after another gave some excuse for not being naturalized, and Senator McKellar called for a show of hands to indicate how many had been naturalized. Few hands went up in a crowd of more than 100.

The Senators were very much struck by this.

A young Greek, who was questioned, said that he could live very well on his 42 cents an hour and save money, but that he was striking to help married men who could not "feed their children" on the money they were receiving.

One Austrian who said that 42 cents an hour was not enough to live on was asked how much he earned a day in the old country.

"Three kronen," he replied, "but that was ten years ago."

One of the Senators asked the crowd at Clairton how many of them had bought Liberty bonds. Most of them answered the question in English, and three or four interpreters relayed the question to the others. Every man put up his hand, and began eagerly to tell how much they had given for the Red Cross, the Y. M. C. A., and other war funds. They said they had given a day's pay in each of the three Red Cross drives. The crowd was made up mainly of men from countries of the Allies or oppressed Austrian States, who were eager to support the war.

The curious contrast between the response to this question and the poor showing on naturalization was commented on by members of the committee.

At McKeesport, the Senators talked with members of the State Constabulary. The conduct of the mounted police was vigorously defended by Sergeant Peter Murphy, who has been in charge of McKeesport, which has been kept free from disorder. The mill officials told the Senators that they lost 2,261 men out of a total of 7,500 on the first day of the strike, but that all except about 500 had returned.

The Senate Committee will hear witnesses representing the strikers, the steel companies, the State Constabulary, and the public at its hearing in the Federal Building today.

John Andrews, 35 years old, was arrested in New Kensington today and lodged in the county jail here, on the charge of having offered his services to strike leaders as a setter of bombs.

Andrew Chekok was shot in the right leg and three others were hurt at Clairton early in the morning in a row which started when several foreigners announced that they were going back to work.

The Central Labor Union of Pittsburgh, which met last night at the call of W. B. Rubin, counsel for the strikers, adopted a resolution calling for a meeting of the Pennsylvania State Federation of Labor on or before Oct. 26, for the purpose of taking drastic action as a protest against the alleged suppression of the right of free speech and arrest of strikers and pickets in connection with the steel strike. Speakers urged that a general strike of organized labor in the State of Pennsylvania should be called for the purpose of compelling fair treatment of labor.

STEEL STRIKE ENDS, FOSTER RESIGNS

National Committee Blames Courts, Press, Troops and Officials for Collapse.

AND THE SECRETARY QUITS

Will Redouble Organization Efforts, He Says, Professing No Discouragement.

PITTSBURGH, Pa., Jan. 8.—The strike in the steel mills and furnaces, called Sept. 22, and which at its inception involved 367,000 men, officially was called off here tonight by the National Committee of the Steel Workers' Union after an all-day meeting.

Announcement that the National Committee had decided to proceed no further was contained in a telegram sent to the headquarters of the American Federation of Labor in Washington, heads of all international unions interested and organizers and field men in all strike districts. The committee at the same time accepted the resignation of William Z. Foster as Secretary-Treasurer, effective Feb. 1.

Foster was the storm centre of the strike, the alleged vehicle, it was asserted, by which radicals of labor, "boring from within," were aiming to wrest control of the American Federation of Labor from President Gompers and the conservative leaders. He will be succeeded as Secretary-Treasurer by James G. Brown, former President of the Timber Workers' International

Union and Foster's chief aid in the conduct of the strike.

"The Steel Corporation, the telegram said, "with the active assistance of the press, the courts, the Federal troops, State police and many public officials, have denied the steel workers their rights of free speech, free assemblage and the right to organize, and, by this arbitrary and ruthless misuse of power, have brought about a condition which has compelled the national committee for organizing iron and steel workers to vote today that the active strike phase of the steel campaign is now at an end.

"A vigorous campaign of education and re-organization will be immediately begun, and will not cease until industrial justice in the steel industry has been achieved. All steel workers now are at liberty to return to work, pending preparation for the next big organization movement."

The telegram was signed by John Fitzpatrick, Chairman; D. J. Davis, Vice President of the Amalgamated Association of Iron, Steel and Tin Workers; Edward J. Evans, International Union of Electrical Workers; William Hannon, International Union of Machinists, and William Z. Foster, Secretary of the committee.

Mr. Fitzpatrick declined to discuss the action of the committee, but Secretary Foster said:
"The strike has encouraged the steel trade unions to redouble their efforts. It has been proved that the men in the steel industry can be organized and they have secured the confidence of men in other unions."

Reviewing the strike, Mr. Foster said that it had its inception at St. Paul in 1918 and he was called in as secretary of the committee then formed to organize the steel trades. All preliminary work was completed and the strike called Sept. 22 last. Nine States were affected and 367,000 quit work.

Steel Corporation executives said they were not surprised that the strike had been called off, as the strikers have been drifting back to work for several months. Many mills, it was added, had long ago been able to operate full time with full forces, the principal trouble being the lack of common labor, which formed the backbone of the strike.

LABOR FEDERATION OUSTING RADICALS

Foster and Fitzpatrick, Steel Strike Leaders, Are Dropped from Unionizing Committee.

WANT TO CUT IMMIGRATION

Influx of Foreign Born Is Adding to Unemployment, Now Regarded as a Growing Menace.

WASHINGTON, Nov. 17 (Associated Press).—Direct steps to eliminate radicalism from any control in organized labor and to meet the menace of increasing unemployment are being taken by the American Federation of Labor through its Executive Council, which is in session here.

A decisive victory over radical elements within the organization has already been achieved at one point, and the conferences of the council for the last week, dealing with the economic problems, appeared tonight to foreshadow action looking to closer co-operation between labor and capital to meet the problem of unemployment.

Conservative leaders in the Federation have pounded away on the radical question for months, insisting on a more determined stand by the controlling body, but the reports of increasing unemployment have now brought that subject into a position of equal importance.

Although leaders were reticent today, it developed that there was a feeling among members of the council that it should deal emphatically with the attempts of radicals to "bore from within." They were said to feel that conservatism must characterize labor's leadership.

This sentiment was based on two premises: First, that organized labor cannot hope to exert great power in coming years if its foundations are weakened by the permeation of radical doctrines; and, second, that the next Administration will be conservative. As to the latter, it was said in some quarters that labor could gain little from the new Congress unless it established policies of a conservative nature.

In the reorganization of the committee to unionize the steel workers the conservative element showed its strength. It eliminated from the committee John J. Fitzpatrick, Chairman, and William Z. Foster, Secretary, both of whom participated in the direction of the steel strike last Winter, around which clustered outspoken radicalism. Fitzpatrick was displaced by M. F. Tighe, a recognized conservative in labor politics, and Foster gave place to J. G. Brown, also conservative.

President Gompers has declared against the unrestricted admission of radicals from Europe, and the Federation itself is having no intercourse with foreign labor groups of the radical sort. Federation leaders expect to go before Congressional committees at every opportunity to urge a check on the rush of immigrants from radical areas of Europe and Asia. Increased restrictions will be pressed.

Immigration also has a bearing on the question of unemployment, which is recognized by the labor men to be increasing at a rapid rate. The situation was characterized by several labor officials today as somewhat alarming and they felt that the council should take steps to deal with it.

Continued admission of immigrants, thousands of whom are without skill or trade, was regarded as adding fuel to the fire in the face of an already menacing condition.

The Department of Labor made public today statistics showing that during October there were decreases in the number of employes in ten industrial plants as compared with October, 1919, while only four plants had enlarged payrolls. Although the number of reporting concerns was small, officials accepted the figures as indicating the general trend.

29 TO 40 KILLED BY MINE STRIKERS, TWENTY OTHERS MISSING, MAY BE DEAD; GOVERNOR ORDERS TROOPS MOBILIZED

MASSACRED WHILE BOUND

Eyewitnesses of Both Factions Describe Slaughter by Crazed Strikers.

15 BODIES THROWN IN POND

Some Hanged to Roadside Trees—Survivors Say All Had Surrendered.

WORKERS BLAME EMPLOYERS

Assert They Did Not Know They Were to Be Strike-Breakers— Say Guards Started Firing.

1,000 State Troops Ordered Mobilized by Governor Small

WAUKEGAN, Ill., June 22.—Governor Small tonight ordered 1,000 State troops mobilized at once and held under arms to be sent to Herrin if needed.

At midnight the Governor telegraphed Brig. Gen. Black, Adjutant General, to assemble the 132d Infantry and the machine gun companies of the 130th and 131st Infantries, with such other companies as necessary to make a force of at least 1,000 men, and hold them at the 132d Infantry Armory, Chicago, to be moved under further orders from him. The Governor directed that the troops should be given full field equipment. He told General Black that he was reliably advised that life and property are in jeopardy in the vicinity of Herrin, Williamson County.

Special to The New York Times.

MARION, Ill., June 22.—At least twenty-nine coal miners, perhaps forty, met death at the hands of a striking union mob in the Southern Illinois coal mining district yesterday and today.

The strip mine of the Southern Illinois Coal Company, eight miles northwest of Marion, is in ruins. Tracks, buildings and hundreds of thousands of dollars' worth of equipment were dynamited as today's battle closed shortly before noon, amid the uproar of 2,000 blood-drunk miners and the admiring plaudits of their women folk.

But reports tonight from Herrin, from which the deadly assault was directed, indicated that soberness was setting in. Worn by twenty-four hours of fighting, the victors had stacked their arms, but within easy reach.

Of the dead many were massacred in cold blood while being marched as prisoners toward Herrin. Some were shot, some clubbed to death, and some hanged to trees near the roadside.

Colonel Samuel N. Hunter, returning to Marion from Herrin as the representative of Adjutant General Carlos Black, said State troops had not been ordered out and would not be unless requested by local authorities. He was to submit a report to his chief tonight.

Seventeen Dead in Herrin.

Colonel Hunter said his investigation indicated that there were seventeen dead in a Herrin undertaking establishment and seven still were lying out on the field, where six of them were shot down in cold blood as, presumably, they were being marched under armed guard to Herrin from the coal mine upon which they had hoisted the white flag of surrender. The seventh was a union man, probably the victim of wild firing.

Three wounded were in the hospital at Herrin, he said, and a like number in a hospital at Carbondale. One of the latter, an ex-soldier and a Chicago man, will die.

Other casualty reports were at wide variance with that received by Colonel Hunter, the death toll, in most instances, mounting considerably higher.

Before noon today a reporter for THE NEW YORK TIMES had counted thirteen bullet-riddled bodies in the timber field two miles southeast of Herrin, where the vanquished workers, already battered and bleeding, had been herded into a clearing like cattle in a round-up, and shot in their tracks.

Squatted near this group of thirteen was a fourteenth, still living. Sitting bolt upright, he surveyed approaching newspaper men with unseeing eyes. He was sobbing, his clothing was torn to shreds, matted in blood. So he sat for some minutes, then toppled back, dead.

Many union men who witnessed the massacre, and were sickened by the spectacle, talked freely tonight. Some of these were authority for the charge that the captured strike-breakers were deliberately run into a field by their armed captors and then made targets for pot shots.

The battle that started yesterday afternoon after John L. Lewis, President of the United Mine Workers of America, said in a telegram that "representatives of our organization are justified in treating this crowd as an outlaw organization," resulted in fourteen dead and missing before sunset.

Firing, which had been intermittent throughout the night, was resumed at daybreak this morning. During the night the attackers had crept upon the mine and set off a fuse under the car in which two guards were doing sentinal duty. Guards and car were blown to atoms.

Defender Tells of Fight.

This and other incidents of the night and day battle were recounted by one of the three mine defenders known to have escaped after being disarmed. This man is Fred Bernard, 38 years old, Jefferson Hotel, Chicago. The password of a fraternal order, of which three of his assailants are members, saved him.

Text of Telegram from Miners' President Which Preceded Bloodshed at Illinois Mine

HERRIN, Ill., June 22 (Associated Press).—The twenty-four hours of bloodshed in the mining district here yesterday and today followed publication of a telegram from John L. Lewis, President of the United Mine Workers of America, saying that the employes of the Southern Illinois Coal Company, members of the Steam Shovelmen's Union, were "common strikebreakers."

Lewis's telegram was in reply to one from State Senator Sneed, a sub-district official of the miners' union, asking the status of the Shovelmen's Union. Sneed's telegram to Lewis follows:

"Is there an agreement by the American Federation of Labor that the Steam Shovelmen's Union has the right to man shovels, strip and load coal? Some men here claim they have jurisdiction granted by the Mining Department of the American Federation of Labor. J. W. Tracy of Chicago, district representative of the Steam Shovelmen's Union, is furnishing men to load coal in this district. We do not believe such an agreement exists. Wire answer after investigation if agreement exists and have the proper authorities stop the steam shovel men scabbing of union coal miners."

Lewis replied: "In reply to your wire of the 18th the Steam Shovelmen's Union was suspended from affiliation with the American Federation of Labor some years ago. It was also ordered suspended from the Mining Department of the American Federation of Labor at the Atlantic City convention.

"We now find that this outlaw organization is permitting its membership to act as strikebreakers in strip mines in Ohio.

"This organization is furnishing steam shovel engineers to work under armed guard with strikebreakers.

"It is not true that any agreement exists by and between this organization and the Mining Department or any other branch of the American Federation of Labor permitting it to work under such circumstances.

"Two of our representatives have taken this question up with officers of the Steam Shovelmen's Union and have failed to secure any satisfaction.

"Representatives of our organization are justified in treating this crowd as an outlaw organization and in viewing its members in the same light as they would view any other common strikebreakers."

"I was engaged," said Bernard, an overseas veteran, "by the George T. Bertrand Employment Agency, 561 West Madison Street, as a cook on what I was told was a steam shovelers' union job. I reported at the strip mine on Tuesday, just twenty-four hours before the trouble started. When I got on the job, I found that many other men had come under the same representations which induced me to ship out.

"I have not a very clear idea of what happened after we were attacked yesterday afternoon. I know that inside of our barricade of heaped-up slack there were three tracks, on each of which there was a line of gondolas. When the shooting started the mine guards—there were about thirty of these, I believe—wanted me and my kitchen crew of six men to take arms.

"But we declined and crouched down in one of the gondolas of the second line. Bullets struck all around us throughout the afternoon, and even during the night, but we never budged. This morning the first attack was made about 4 o'clock. But the strikers did not get over the huge pile of stacks on the side they had selected. They withdrew. But in less than two hours they were back with reinforcements.

"About a dozen colored men led the renewed assault. I don't know what came over the guards, because they had lots of ammunition, rifles and machine guns, but some one raised a white flag.

"Then the enemy, yelling like Indians, swarmed over the top and down on to us. We were helpless.

"First we were 'frisked' for firearms, and then lined up outside the mine. Perhaps some of our men did not suspect what was in store for them, but I felt it was all over just as soon as I got a look at the blood-shot eyes of some of our captors.

"Many of them were reeling drunk. First they struck us with their fists, and then, as they tasted blood, they started in to hammer us with butts of revolvers. I was not beaten.

"McDowell, superintendent of the mine, who, crippled, walked with a distinct limp, headed our line. It seemed to me everybody took a crack at him."

Bernard then described the spectacle of fifty-two men whipped into line by clouts and curses, forced more dead than alive, into a march between flanks of armed men.

Two newspaper men, driving over from Carbondale, fifteen miles southwest of Herrin, met this formidable army.

Their automobile, pulled to the edge of a narrow road, barely left room for captors and captives to pass.

The advanced guard, rattling by in scores of flivvers, had screeched the news, " We got 'em. They're coming."

And they came, the limping mine superintendent, blinking, and trying to ward off further blows. Others were about as much battered. All now apparently realized their plight, although it is doubtful whether they sensed death. In fact, it is equally doubtful whether such was the plan of the striking miners at the outset of the march. But blows brought blood, and the sight worked the men into a frenzy that swept away all self-control.

The line of marchers, followed by still other flivvers, prevented the newspaper men from turning in the narrow road. They waited until the line had passed, turned and then took a short cut into Herrin, planning to intercept the miners. But they swept through the town, and back out again, without sighting the army.

On every street corner were men and women and scores of small children eagerly awaiting the triumphant entry of the conquerors. But they did not enter. Instead, men in cars that had originally brought up the rear of the line, dashed into the town. To favored acquaintances who lined the roadway on the outskirts they shouted the tidings: " They're not coming in—they broke away."

Bernard, and, as already related, some of the miners, maintain they did not break away. Instead, they were called up in groups and ordered to " run into that field " on the roadside, and as they ran rifles cracked and the driven men pitched forward, one by one.

Superintendent McDowell, according to some accounts, was the first man shot, just a few hundred yards beyond the point at which the line passed the newspaper men.

One Saved by Fraternity Sign.

Bernard said that, when told to run, he did so, but as he saw or instinctively felt the rifles leveled at his back, he pitched forward, face down. Joseph Williams, 4,142 Lake Park Avenue, Chicago, a waiter at the mine, followed suit. That Williams was playing " possum " was discovered first. And Bernard was yanked to his feet a moment later. Then it was he asked if there was a " brother in the crowd." One man responded and Bernard gave the countersign, the others stepped to his side.

One of these fellow lodge members escorted him to safety while the attention of the mad band was engaged in winging the other two, who, hounded like hares, were seeking shelter in the underbrush.

There were cries of " there he goes " and " here he is," followed by yells and shots.

After losing track of the line that was headed for Herrin, the newspaper men did not encounter action again until they saw wild groups of the strikers beating the brush for human quarry. Then they saw two men, clothes torn and blood soaked, driven out from the timber. The prisoners, pleading but with hope obviously abandoned, had their hands raised high. Whether these were two of six men who were later walked out to the South Side School and on to the cemetery at Herrin, has not been established. It is known that at the cemetery these six had their shoes and stockings torn from their feet, and they were pounded forward.

An old woman stepped out in the roadway with arms extended, pleading. " Oh, what are you going to do," she asked. A strong arm felled her, and the marchers marched on.

But the elderly woman was an exception. Young matrons and even maidens egged on their men folk.

" Let's make soap of them," one of them suggested, as the six, banded together with a three-quarter inch rope, were shot down with one volley. An examination showed that one of the six still breathed. An executioner, with ready knife, completed what the bullets had left unfinished.

One of four men found under a tree in Harrison woods, where the body of a fifth was suspended from a branch, had offered a gold watch and $25 to his tormentors when he saw all was about over. " You're a good scout," taunted one of his tormentors. " Make a run for it." The man was shot down by the man who jeered at him.

" Be one of us, keep moving, and ask no questions," seemed to be the order of the day in the theatre of operations, which centred about Herrin. A few women sought to take kodak snapshots. Their kodaks were trampled under foot and the women were roughly handled.

Six small mines known as slope mines shut down today upon the request of county authorities, who feared outbreaks in the vicinity of Carbondale.

The union men had not objected to the operation of these mines in putting out supply for local consumption.

One of the three men known to have escaped from the mob today staggered into Cartersville, a few miles from Herrin, where he dropped in front of the First National Bank.

Police officers took him to Carbondale, where he was given refuge in the City Jail for thirty minutes. Chief of Police J. M. Anderson, fearing mob violence, shipped him out on the first freight.

MINERS VOTE TODAY ON HARD COAL PEACE

All Indications Point to Ratification by a Big Majority at Wilkes-Barre.

SAYS HARDING URGED CUTS

Lewis Withstood President, Even Before the Strike Began, Phil. Murray Asserts.

Special to The New York Times.

WILKES-BARRE, Pa., Sept. 8.—By noon tomorrow, it is expected, 690 delegates representing 155,000 anthracite strikers will have voted on the Pepper-Reed plan for settling the anthracite strike. Ratification is expected by a majority of 260 votes at the least and possibly as high as 500.

International President John L. Lewis, Vice President Phil Murray and District Presidents W. J. Brennan, Thomas Kennedy and Chris Golden are convinced tonight that the opposition has been beaten and that all danger of the insurgents controlling the vote has been eliminated. "Ratification will come tomorrow by an overwhelming majority," said Lewis tonight. Murray declared: "I look for ratification tomorrow by an almost unanimous vote."

Insurgents admitted tonight that the Lewis forces will win, but say they will go down fighting.

So bitter are some of the radical leaders that a meeting of their forces in the Pittston district was called and they are threatening to keep the men out of the mines there when the compact is finally ratified. They claim they will form a district of their own and break away from District No. 1, of which they are now a part. So dangerous has this situation become that Mayor Brown of Pittston announced today that no further meetings of the insurgent group will be allowed in the city.

The afternoon session of the convention was turned over to the delegates. George Evans of Olyphant was first to talk. He declared that each miner's family has gone $700 in debt in the five months' strike, besides the loss of wages, and that a one-year contract does not allow sufficient time to get on their feet to strike again if such an emergency is necessary when the proposed contract ends.

William Mates of Wilkes-Barre answered. He said the miners had gained one of their greatest victories. He urged immediate acceptance of the agreement.

After District President Kennedy had concluded his report on the work done by the Scale Committee at the morning session, a delegate moved its adoption. President Lewis pointed out that this meant ratification of the peace offer. A motion to lay the agreement on the table was ruled out.

Phil Murray summarized the provisions of the agreement, saying it was the greatest victory the laboring classes had ever won. "This is," he said, "an unusual period in the life of the nation. There has been a concerted drive to cut wages, yet the miners escaped this fate."

The bituminous men, he said, got only a seven months' contract. He told of President Harding summoning Lewis to Washington in 1921, telling him he understood he was marshaling his forces for an industrial fight and informing him that the miners, as well as everybody else, would have to accept wage cuts. Lewis stood before the President of the United States and told him that the miners would not accept a wage cut with his consent.

Murray told how the President had stated to Lewis that he would make himself an outstanding figure in the nation if he would have the miners take a cut in wages, but Lewis refused to make any such recommendation, and, on the contrary, said he would lead his men in their fight for justice for themselves.

GOMPERS REJECTS THIRD PARTY IDEA

Declares That Organized Labor Should Not Identify Itself With the Movement.

SAYS IT MEANS DIVISION

Federation Head Holds Third Party Draws From Progressives and Weakens Their Cause.

Special to The New York Times.

WASHINGTON, July 3.—On the eve of the Cleveland convention which plans to nominate Senator Robert M. La Follette of Wisconsin as an independent and third party candidate for the Presidency in opposition to President Coolidge and the nominee of the Democrats, Samuel Gompers, President of the American Federation of Labor, has come out in opposition to the support of any third party movement by organized labor in America.

The attitude of Mr. Gompers is stated in the leading editorial in the July issue of The American Federationist, the official magazine of the American Federation of Labor, just off the press, and in which he indicates what he thinks should be the attitude of labor in the 1924 campaign.

Declaring that the Federation is a "labor organization," emphasizing the word "labor" in black face type, Mr. Gompers asserts that it can achieve greater results in politics by devotion to principles rather than to parties and should not join or align itself with any third party movement.

"Now, as before, the average result of so-called third party adventures will be victory for reaction," declares Mr. Gompers.

"Practically, this is what happens: The 'third party' draws from the most progressive of the other candidates. The more conservative candidate loses no votes to a 'third party' candidate.

"Thus progressive votes are divided, the progressive cause weakened.

"When progressives divide among themselves reaction wins. History records altogether too many sad cases of this 'one foot forward and two feet backward' kind of frog-in-the well advancement."

Shows Labor Is Not United.

The declaration by Mr. Gompers is regarded as important, as coming from the recognized leader of organized labor in America. It shows that organized labor as a whole is not behind the movement launched at Cleveland for the nomination of Senator La Follette, despite the fact that certain labor leaders affiliated with the A. F. of L. are active in the Cleveland convention.

One of these is William H. Johnston, head of the International Machinists, who is national Chairman of the Conference for Progressive Political Action, which called the Cleveland convention, and is to act as permanent as well as temporary Chairman of the convention and, as such, will deliver the "keynote" speech at Cleveland tomorrow.

While third party movements, in the opinion of Mr. Gompers, "may gratify certain ambitions," he thinks labor should not align itself with any third party, but that if "the time ever comes when neither of the now dominant parties responds to the will of the people then the people will either rebuild one or both of them or abandon both of them in a great revolt and rebuilding." But that, he contends, will not be the sort of thing known today as a third party movement.

"That," he asserts, "will not be the carbonated performance of little coteries, nor the calculated political sabotage of revolutionists."

Says Eyes Are on Labor.

"With a national political campaign already under way, many eyes are turned in the direction of labor's efforts in that struggle," says Mr. Gompers. "Various so-called third party movements are under way, none of them of any particular promise, but all more or less confusing in their locality.

"Those who turn to these so-called third party movements proclaim their profound disgust with what they term the reactionary policy of the American Federation of Labor. They are impatient, and they fail to see that their impatience is leading them to the kind of haste which makes only for delay.

"The political policy of the American Federation of Labor will bear examination at all times, and examination at this time may be helpful to some who do not fully comprehend its meaning, or who have been beguiled by the phrases of the experimenters and dreamers.

"It is the belief of the American Federation of Labor that the greatest results are to be achieved in politics by a devotion to principles rather than to parties, and that the surest way to advance principles is to support those candidates who accept the principles and to oppose those who reject them.

"There is nothing involved about this belief; nothing complicated about the practice. And it is the only way by which labor can avoid the dissensions and schisms that inevitably must come from party partisanship. Parties must take position on matters that are not in any sense purely labor questions. For example, they must deal with the tariff, a matter on which labor has taken no position for a great many years for obvious reasons.

First Concern for Wage-Earners.

"The American Federation of Labor is a labor organization. Its principal object is to protect and promote the interests of the toiling masses. It must, in the field of politics, press for these men and measures that advance the interests of the toiling masses. Labor has its broad interests of citizenship and general progress, but its first concern is solely with the welfare of the great masses of wage earners.

"Principles for which labor contends cannot be the private property of any political party. These principles have to do with humanitarian and libertarian issues. They are neither Republican nor Democratic, neither socialistic nor Populistic, not any more than that they are Presbyterian or Baptist.

"These principles must be considered by men and be accepted or rejected by men. If a whole political party organization wishes to support any or all of labor's principles, that is entirely agreeable to labor.

"But such an act could not put the party label on the principles to the exclusion of any other support.

Calls Labor's Principles Non-Partisan.

"Principles which labor supports may, on the other hand, be rejected entirely by an entire party organization, but that cannot signify that there has been any change in the principles. Politically, they remain as non-partisan as ever.

"Representatives of all parties have espoused measures for which labor has contended. Witness such measures as the seamen's act, the eight-hour act, the Clayton act, the suffrage amendment, the recent immigration act, and the still more notable child labor amendment to the United States Constitution.

"In each case a larger percentage of one party voted for these measures than was mustered by the other party, but that did not make them party measures. Labor was interested in the success of the measures, not in the fortunes of a party.

"Seldom has a labor measure been fought through Congress as a strict party measure, either Republican or Democratic, and labor has not had any wish that any party should seek to exclude the other party from sponsorship of and support of labor's demands.

"There is nothing inherent in any labor demand to stamp it as impossible of acceptance by men of any political allegiance. There is nothing in any labor demand to stamp it as Republican or Democratic. Nor is there any labor demand that inherently requires a new political party for its success.

"Labor's Demands Not Political."

"It is all condensed in the simple statement that essentially labor's demands are not political.

"To enter into a partisan relationship with any political party—even a party which might call itself a labor party—would necessitate the espousal of propositions that were not an outgrowth of the labor movement and its requirements.

"The labor movement would have to participate in the fight for or against propositions of a purely political nature having nothing to do with labor.

"And, regardless of what the intellectuals may say—they must be saying something at all times—there is no partisan political labor movement anywhere, in America, Europe or elsewhere, that has yet demonstrated its real value to labor or to the masses of the people generally. That is said not as a criticism, but as a judgment on the results achieved.

"The American trade union movement is a labor movement. It has to its credit achievements unrivaled anywhere else in the world. It has demonstrated the soundness of its own contention, which is that a labor movement cannot also be something else and maintain its labor character and secure its labor results.

"The so-called third party movements may gratify certain ambitions. They may suit certain purposes. If the time comes when neither of the now dominant parties responds to the will of the people, then the people will either rebuild one or both of them or abandon both of them in a great revolt and rebuilding, but that will not be the sort of thing we know today as a third party movement. That will not be the carbonated performances of little coteries, nor the calculated political sabotage of revolutionists.

Policy Developed by Experience.

"American labor has developed its non-partisan political policy out of long experience. If experience had shown a better method, that better method would have been adopted. No movement in the world responds more readily to the teachings of experience than the American trade union movement. None is less afraid to blaze the way along new lines, if there is proof that those lines are sound.

"In that connection the temptation is to speak frankly and to say that many of those who shout for partisan political action do so because they are afraid not to. They are afraid that they will lose caste in their surroundings, afraid they will no longer be considered good proletarians, good revolutionists, good uncompromisers. This is all very silly for human beings; but, after all, many human beings are silly and many are sadly lacking in conviction, purpose and courage.

"That is the political status of American labor as the great 1924 campaign gets under way. American labor will be partisan to principles.

"It will fight to the finish against every candidate who is opposed to those principles; it will fight to the last for every candidate who is for them; and it is all the same whether these are candidates for the Presidency, for Congress or for the least and most humble office in the last small village on the further border line. And labor is going to win tremendous victories this year."

'OPEN SHOP' WINS IN SUPREME COURT

Injunctions Are Upheld Restraining Miners' Union in West Virginia Cases.

GOMPERS ATTACKS DECISION

Says John Mitchell and Secretary Wilson Are "Stigmatized as Conspirators."

WASHINGTON, Dec. 10.—Decisions defining in general terms the rights of both organized labor and the employer were rendered today by the Supreme Court. While the right of workmen to organize for lawful purposes was reaffirmed, the court held that employers may legally operate their plants as " open shops " and prevent conspiracies to bring their non-union employes into labor organizations.

The opinions were rendered in the cases of the Hitchman Coal and Coke Company and the Eagle Glass Manufacturing Company of West Virginia, the court deciding that both were entitled to operate their plants as " open shops," and upholding injunctions issued by Judge A. G. Dayton restraining union officials from attempting to organize their employes. Lower court decrees holding that the United Mine Workers of America and the American Flint Glass Workers' Union were illegal organizations and that under the Sherman law they were secret conspiracies in restraint of trade were ignored by the Supreme Court opinion.

In the Hitchman case, the majority of the court held that the officials of the Miners' Union " deliberately and advisedly selected that method of enlarging the union membership which would inflict injury " upon the company and its loyal employes, and declared that the " conduct in so doing was unlawful and malicious."

The court also held that " it is erroneous to assume that all measures which may be resorted to in the effort to unionize a mine are lawful if they are peaceable—that is, if they stop short of physical violence or coercion through fear of it." It added that " the purpose of the defendants to bring about a strike at the mine in order to compel plaintiff through fear of financial loss to the unionization of the mine as the lesser evil was an unlawful purpose."

Justices Brandeis, Holmes, and Clarke dissented.

Companies' Rights Set Forth.

"The Supreme Court holds," the majority opinion set forth, " that the plaintiff was acting within its lawful rights in employing its men upon the terms that they should not be members of the United Mine Workers; that, having established this working agreement between it and its employes with the free assent of the latter, the plaintiff is entitled to be protected in the enjoyment of the resulting status as in any other legal right; that the fact that the employment was terminable by either party at any time made no difference, since the right of the employes to strike or to leave the work gave no right to defendants to instigate a strike; that plaintiff was and is entitled to the goodwill of its employes, precisely as a merchant is entitled to the good-will of his customers, although they are under no obligation to deal with him; that the value of the relation lies in the reasonable probability that, by properly treating its employes and paying them fair wages and avoiding reasonable grounds

of complaint, plaintiff will be able to retain them in its employ and to fill vacancies occurring from time to time by the employment of other men on the same terms, and that defendants could not be permitted to interfere with these rights without some just cause or excuse.

" By way of justification or excuse, defendants set up the right of workingmen to form unions and enlarge their membership by inviting other workingmen to join. The opinion of the court freely conceded this right, provided the objects of the union be proper and legitimate, which is assumed to be true in a general sense, with respect to the United Mine Workers of America.

Must Not Injure Others.

" But the court holds that it is erroneous to assume that this right is so absolute that it may be exercised under any circumstances and without any qualification; that in truth, like other rights that exist in civilized society, it must always be exercised with reasonable regard for the conflicting rights of others, according to the fundamental maxim ' So use your own property as not to injure the rights of another.'

" Hence, assuming that the defendants were exercising the right to invite men to join their union, nevertheless, since they had notice that plaintiff's mine was run nonunion, that none of the men had a right to remain at work there after joining the union, and that the observance of this agreement was of much importance and value both to plaintiff and to its men who had voluntarily made the agreement and desired to continue working union, it the defendants were under a duty to exercise care to refrain from unnecessarily injuring plaintiff, yet they deliberately and advisedly selected that method of enlarging the union membership which would inflict injury upon plaintiff and its loyal employes, by persuading man after man to join the union, and, having done so, to remain at work, keeping the employer in ignorance of their number and identity, until so many should have joined that by stopping work in a body they could coerce the employer and the remaining miners to organize the mines, and that the conduct of defendants in so doing was unlawful and malicious."

Contempt proceedings instituted last month by the Hitchman Coal and Coke Company against President Frank J. Hayes of the Miners' Union and fifteen other officials and members for alleged violation of the injunctions are still pending and according to the company's counsel will be pressed. The court today granted the defendants sixty days in which to present their case.

" Unwarrantable," Says Gompers.

Samuel Gompers, President of the American Federation of Labor, in a statement tonight characterized the decision as " far-reaching and unwarrantable." He said:

" To hold that the United Mine Workers of America is an unlawful organization or that it is a conspiracy is to hark back to the days when employers were monarchs of all they surveyed and their employes were servants or slaves. The miners' union undertook by perfectly lawful methods and means to reach the unorganized and underpaid miners of West Virginia so that they might be treated as men and as citizens, with the responsibility of maintaining families upon an American standard.

" At the time when the injunction was issued John Mitchell was President and William B. Wilson Secretary-Treasurer of the United Mine Workers of America. The former is now the Food Administrator of the State of New York. The latter is a member of the President's Cabinet, and these men with others of equal standing and character are stigmatized by the court as conspirators.

" President Wilson has justly declared that society has given its sanction that the eight-hour workday is justified. It is to bring light and hope and patriotism into the lives of the workers for which we are organized and are organizing and federating the toilers of America. And we shall go on to reach our goal for a better concept of not only political but industrial democracy."

EMPLOYERS' GROUP PRESENTS DEMAND FOR THE OPEN SHOP

Reports Platform to Industrial Conference, Also Opposing Collective Bargaining.

NOT HOSTILE TO UNIONS

But Declare Against Arbitrary Use of Power in Industrial Disputes.

HOLD POSITION LIKE GARY'S

Conference Adjourns Until Tuesday to Await Report from Committee of 15.

Special to The New York Times.

WASHINGTON, Oct. 10.—Insisting on the open shop and the right of the employer to deal only with his own employes without reference to outsiders, the representatives of the employers group presented their recommendations to the industrial conference today, which at the end of the day's proceedings adjourned until Tuesday. In the meantime the general committee of fifteen will consider the proposals of the three groups—labor, capital, and public.

The statement of the employers on the subject of the open shop says:

" There should be no denial of the right of an employer and his workers voluntarily to agree that their relation shall be that of the closed union shop or of the closed nonunion shop. But the right of the employer and his men to continue their relations on the principle of the open shop should not be denied or questioned. No employer should be required to deal with men or groups of men who are not his employes or chosen by and from among them."

The employers thus seem to have in effect lined themselves up behind E. H. Gary of the United States Steel Corporation.

Two propositions were submitted by the employers group. One being a statement of twelve principles "which should govern the employment relation in industry." The other was a resolution by Loren F. Loree, providing that the next census should contain facts and figures which would aid in investigating the industrial situation.

The Central Committee, or Committee of Fifteen, was asked by Chairman Lane to ascertain whether it could not make a report. After an hour's consultation the committee, through its Chairman, Thomas L. Chadbourne of New York, stated that the task before it was so difficult that it desired to adjourn until Monday at 10:30 o'clock. Thereupon the conference decided to recess until Tuesday.

A severe struggle in the committee is predicted when it comes to the ballot on the employers' plan and the steel strike resolution. Members of all three groups are included in the Central Committee.

Clash Over Communications.

While the declaration of the twelve principles of the employers was sanctioned by the entire group, it has been made plain that the assent of a group in ordinary circumstances does not mean that every member of the group, or even the majority, is in entire sympathy with a resolution. The group must give its "assent" or "refusal" to the presentation of a plan, but this does not commit the entire group to the fundamentals of that plan, as Secretary Lane, chairmen of the conference, put it.

"The group does not approve or disapprove of the substance of the proposition by presenting it to the conference but its decision or its assent is to be construed as meaning that, in the opinion of the group, the matter presented by the member of the conference is germane to the subject matter as to which the conference is called."

There was a clash today between Gavin McNab, of San Francisco and Samuel Gompers when Mr. Gompers thought Mr. McNab accused the labor leader of trying to shut off suggestions from outside the conference. Mr. McNab suggested that the communications coming to the conference from outside be referred to a committee of the chairmen of the three groups. Both Mr. Baruch and Mr. Gompers objected, the latter agreeing with Matthew Woll, one of the labor delegates, that communications must receive the assent of the groups.

Both John Spargo of the group representing the public and Frederick P. Fish of the employers' section said they would like to have the benefit of advice from outside sources. Secretary of Labor Wilson suggested copying the ideas in triplicate and letting the Chairman of each group have them.

To this Samuel Gompers agreed, but he added:

"I decline to rest under the insinuation that I am desirous of excluding expression by the general public. One of the very things for which my associates and I have contended is for open sessions, so that the world, by inquiry, might understand what we are trying to do and how we are going about it. I do not know whether the entire press of the country strongly reflects the sentiments of one or the other group in this conference. You look at this morning's Washington Post and you will find the most unfair attack on the attitude of the labor group in this conference and it is made to appear that it is a contest between Americanism and radicalism.

Mr. McNab replied that he had not intended to suggest that Mr. Gompers wished to obstruct suggestions from outside.

Six members of the Committee on the High Cost of Living were named, including Charles Edward Russell, Henry S. Dennison of Framingham, Mass., and O. E. Bradfute of Xenia, Ohio, for the public, and R. H. Aishton, Ernest T. Trigg, and C. S. Barrett for the employers. Samuel Gompers announced that one of three selected to represent labor could not serve, and so the labor members would be announced later.

In presenting the twelve principles from the employers, Harry A. Wheeler, Chairman of that group, said:

"The document was originally prepared by that section of the employers' group named by the National Industrial Conference Board, and referred by the group to a committee composed of the various elements of the group, and we advised in some particulars. Therefore it comes to the conference in that form, the authorship, consequently, being the original authorship of the representatives of the Industrial Conference Board, with such changes as they accepted readily from the committee of the group."

Employers' Principles in Full.

The declaration of the employers' principles, as read by Mr. Wheeler, follows:

"Responding to the call of the President of the United States that the industrial conference convene for the purpose of reaching, if possible, some common ground of agreement and action with regard to the future conduct of industry, and for the purpose of enabling us to work out, if possible in a genuine spirit of co-operation, a practicable method of association based upon a real community of interest which will redound to the welfare of all our people, the group representing the employers assents to the presentation of the following fundamental considerations by which these purposes may be accomplished, viz.:

"Sound industrial development must have as its foundation productive efficiency, and high productive efficiency requires not only energy, loyalty, and intelligence on the part of management and men, but sincere co-operation in the employment relation based upon mutual confidence and sympathy.

"This is true of all producing industries, large and small, of the farming industry as well as the manufacturing. While there are differences between the different branches of industry which call for special application as to underlying principles, these principles are the same in all.

"Without efficiency in production, that is to say without a large production economically produced, there will be no fund for the payment of adequate compensation for labor, management and capital, and high cost of living will inevitably continue. Moreover, without such efficiency it woll be impossible for American industry successfully to compete in foreign markets or with foreign competition in this country. The larger and more effective the production the greater will be the return to all engaged in the industry and the lower the cost of living.

"The requisite efficiency in production cannot be secured unless there is effective co-operation between employer and employe, such as is only possible where, with a full understanding of each other's point of view, management and men meet upon a common ground of principle and in a spirit of co-operation based upon good understanding and a recognition of what is fair and right between the two. Then only can there be that harmony which will insure the prosperity of those engaged in industry and of all the people.

"With full recognition of the vital importance of these conditions and with due realization of the great responsibility resting upon management to secure their practical application in industrial afafirs we submit the following principles which we regard as fundamentally sound in the interest of industry, of those employed or concerned in industry, and of the people as a whole.

"1—Production.—The industrial organization as a productive agency is an association of management, capital, and labor, voluntarily established for economic production through co-operative effort. It is the function of management to co-ordinate and direct capital and labor for the joint benefit of all parties concerned, and in the interest of the consumer and of the community. No employment relation can be satisfactory or fulfill its functions for the common good which does not encourage and require management and men to recognize a joint as well as an individual obligation to improve and increase the quantity and quality of production to as great an extent as possible consistent with the health and well-being of the workers.

"There should be no intentional restriction of productive effort or output by either the employer or the employe to create an artificial scarcity of the product or of labor, in order to increase prices or wages; nor should there be any waste in the productive capacity of industry through the employment of unnecessary labor or inefficient management.

"It is the duty of management on the farms and in industry and commerce as far as possible to procure the capital necessary for the increased production that is required, and of both management and labor to co-operate to promote the use of capital in the most efficient fashion.

"2—The establishment as a productive unit. Recognizing the co-operative relationship between management and men essential to productive efficiency as a prerequisite for national and individual well being, the establishment rather than the industry as a whole or any branch of it should, as far as practicable, be considered as the unit of production and of mutual interest on the part of employer and employe. Here, by experimentation and adaption, should be worked out and set up satisfactory means for co-operative relations in the operation of the establishment with due regard to local factors.

"Each establishment should develop contact and full opportunity for interchange of view between management and men, through individual or collective dealing or a combination of both, or by some other effective method, always predicated on both sides on honesty of purpose, fairness of attitude, and due recognition of the joint interest and obligation in the common enterprise in which they are engaged.

Conditions of Work.

"Mere machinery is not enough for this purpose. There must also be sympathy and good will, with earnest intent that whatever the means employed, they must be effective.

"3—Conditions of work. It is the duty of management to make certain that the conditions under which work is carried on are as safe and as satisfactory to the workers as the nature of the business reasonably permits. Every effort should be made to maintain steady employment of the workers both on their account and to increase efficiency. Each establishment should study carefully the causes of unemployment and individually and in co-operation with other establishments in the same and other industries should endeavor to determine and to maintain conditions and business methods which will result in the greatest possible stability in the employment relation.

"4—Wages. While the law of supply and demand must inevitably play a large part in determining the wages in any industry or any establishment at any particular time, other conditions must be taken into account such as the efficiency of the workers and the wage standard of the industry in the locality. The wage should be so adjusted as to promote the maximum incentive consistent with health and well-being and the full exercise of individual skill and effort. Moreover, the business in each establisment and generally in industry should be so conducted that the worker should receive a wage sufficient to maintain him and his family at a standard of living that should be satisfactory to a right-minded man in view of the prevailing cost of living, which should fairly recognize the quantity and quality of his productive effort and the value and length of his service, and reflect a participation on his part in the prosperity of the enterprise to which he is devoting his energy.

"Many plans are now under consideration for adding to the fixed wage of the worker, such, for example, as bonus payments, profit sharing, and stock ownership. All such plans should be carefully studied in each establishment. It may well be that in many instances the employer and the employe could work out an arrangement of such a character to their mutual advantage.

"In order that the worker may in his own and the general interest develop his full earning capacity and command his maximum wage, it should be a primary concern of management to assist him to secure employment suited to his ability, to furnish him incentive and opportunity for improvement, to provide proper safeguards for his health and safety, and to aid him to increase the value of his productive effort.

"Where women are doing work equal with that of men under the same conditions, they should receive the same rates of pay as men and should be accorded the same opportunities for training and advancement.

Work Schedules and Disputes.

"5. Hours of Work.—Hours of work schedules should be fixed at the point consistent with the health of the worker and his right to an adequate period of leisure for rest, recreation, home life, and self-development. To the extent that the work schedule is shortened beyond this point the worker as well as the community must inevitably pay in the form of a reduced standard of living.

"The standard of the work schedule should be the week, varying as the peculiar requirements of individual industries may demand. Overtime work should, as far as possible, be avoided, and one day of rest in seven should be provided.

"6. Settlement of Disputes.—Each establishment should provide adequate means for the discussion of all questions and the just and prompt settlement of all disputes that arise between management and men in the course of industrial operation, but there should be no improper limitation or impairment of the exercise by management of its essential function of judgment and direction.

7. **Right to Associate.**—All men have the right to associate voluntarily for the accomplishment of lawful purposes by lawful means. The association of men, whether of employers, employes, or others, for collective action or dealing, confers no authority and involves no right of compulsion over those who do not desire to act or deal with them as an association. The arbitrary use of such collective power to coerce or control others without their consent is an infringement of personal liberty and a menace to the institutions of a free people.

"8. **Responsibility of Associations.**—The public safety requires that there shall be no exercise of power without corresponding responsibility. Every association, whether of employers or employes, must be equally subject to public authority and legally answerable for its own conduct or that of its agents.

"9. **Freedom of Contract.**—With the right to associate recognized, the fundamental principles of individual freedom demand that every person must be free to engage in any lawful occupation or enter into any lawful contract as an employer or an employe, and be secure in the continuity and rewards, of his effort.

"The only qualification to which such liberty of contract is subject lies in the power of the State, within limits imposed by the Constitution, to regulate in the public interest, for example, for the promotion of health, safety, and morals.

The Closed and Open Shop.

"10. **The Open Shop.**—The principles of individual liberty and freedom of contract upon which our investigations are fundamentally based require that there should be no interference with the open shop—that is, the shop in which membership or non-membership in any association is not made a condition of employment. While fair argument and persuasion are permissible, coercive methods aimed at turning the open shop into a 'closed union' or closed non-union shop' should not be tolerated.

"There should be no denial of the right of an employer and his workers voluntarily to agree that their relation shall be that of the closed union shop or the closed non-union shop.

"But the right of the employer and his men to continue their relations on the principle of the 'open shop' should not be denied or questioned. No employer should be required to deal with men or groups of men who are not his employes or chosen by and from among them.

"Under the organization of the 'open shop' there is not the same opportunity for outside interference on the part of other interests to prevent close and harmonious relations between employer and employe. Their efforts to continue or secure such harmonious relationship are not complicated to the same extent by intervention of an outside interest which may have aspirations and plans of its own to promote which are not necessarily consistent with good relations in the shop.

"11. **The right to strike or lockout.** In the statement of the principle that should govern as to the right to strike or lockout, a sharp distinction should be drawn between the employment relations in the field of (a) of the private industry, (b) of the public utility service, and (c) of Government employment, Federal, State or municipal. In all three there are common rights and obligations but, in so far as the right to strike or lockout is concerned, the nature of the Government service and public utility operations requires that they should be considered from a somewhat different point of view than private industry.

"In private industry the strike or the lockout is to be deplored, but the right to strike or lockout should not be denied as an ultimate resort after all possible means of adjustment have been exhausted. Both employers and employes should recognize the seriousness of such action and should be held to a high responsibility for the same.

"The statement that the right to strike or lockout should not be denied does not cover the matter of the sympathetic strike or lockout, where, for mere purposes of coercion, there is a combination deliberately inflicting injury upon parties against whom the assailants have no grievance, for the purpose of accomplishing an ulterior result. The sympathetic strike is indefensible, anti-social and immoral. The same may be said of the blacklist, the boycott, and also the sympathetic lockout.

"In public utility service the public interest and welfare must be the paramount and controlling consideration. Modern social life demands the uninterrupted and unimpaired operation of such service, upon which individuals and communities are as dependent as is human life on the uninterrupted circulation of the blood. The State should therefore impose such regulations as will assure continuous operation, at the same time providing adequate means for the prompt hearing and adjustment of complaints and disputes.

"In Government employment the orderly and continuous administration of governmental activities is imperative. A strike of Government employes is an attempt to prevent the operation of Government until the demands of such employes are granted, and cannot be tolerated. No public servant can obey two masters. He cannot divide his allegiance between the Government which he serves and a private organization which, under any circumstances, might obligate him to suspend his duties, or agrees to assist him morally or financially if he does. Social self-defense demands that no combination to prevent the operation of Government be permitted. The right of Government employes to be heard and to secure just redress should be amply safeguarded.

"12. **Training.**—Practical plans should be inaugurated in industry and outside of it for the training and upgrading of industrial workers, their proper placement in industry, the adoption and adaptation of apprenticeship systems, the extension of vocational education and such other adjustments of our educational system to the needs of industry as will prepare the worker for more effective and profitable service to society and to himself.

"The foregoing is limited to a statement of principles. Only casual reference has been made to methods by which such principles may be carried into effect. The problems are so serious and difficult that such methods must be worked out by the individual establishments in conjunction with their employes and by industry as a whole."

Here is the resolution submitted by Mr. Loree:

"Resolved, That the Congress be requested to appoint a committee to consider the information collected and reports made by the various Government departments and agencies, with a view to their preparation and co-ordination, so that reasonably exact information may be had of the population, occupied and unoccupied, male and female, and their several activities, so far as they may be classified; the home income and the income received from foreign investments and the several sources of the same; the wages, salaries and profits of the principal industries and their aggregate; the surplus and the necessary deductions therefrom—depreciation; taxes, local, State, and Federal; contributions to charities, current and endowed; royalties, interest, rent, advertising, sales expenses, &c., the savings necessary for the progress of an increasing population and the spendable income of management and capital; and

"Resolved, That as the decennial census is to be taken in 1920, it is of the first importance that advantage be taken of this early opportunity to secure data that will aid in the prompt determination of facts illuminative of the industrial situation."

Alleging that there can be no industrial peace or any permanent reduction in the high cost of living until the principles of the program of the Farmers' National Council for Economic Reconstruction is adopted by the conference, the Farmers' Council today made this declaration of principles:

"1. Government ownership and development of the natural resources of the country now being privately developed with prodigious wastefulness.

"2. Government ownership and democratic operation of the entire transportation system of the country's railroad systems, pipe lines, and the merchant marine.

"3. The prompt enactment into legislation of the Federal Trade Commission's recommendations regarding the meat packing industry.

"4. A revision of our money and credit system to make credit as available and as cheap to farmers as to any other legitimate and responsible industry.

"5. The rapid retirement of the indebtedness incurred for the conduct of the war by heavy taxation of incomes, war profits, estates and natural resources in and on land held for speculation.

"6. The establishment of a sound and economic method of marketing farm products.'"

PLOT AGAINST UNIONS AS GOMPERS SEES IT

By SAMUEL GOMPERS
President, American Federation of Labor

ORGANIZATIONS NAMED BY MR. GOMPERS

MR. GOMPERS attempts to prove by documentary evidence that the following organizations are allied in a conspiracy to crush unionism through the "American Plan," or open shop:

The United States Chamber of Commerce, with more than 1,400 member organizations.

The National Association of Manufacturers, with about 6,000 individual and corporate members.

The National Founders' Association, with 540 organizations in 44 States and a total of 23 national industrial associations included in these agencies.

The National Erectors' Association.

The steel, coal, railroad and banking groups, controlled through interlocking directorates.

Space forbids including in the article the material on interlocking directorates, which Mr. Gompers presents from public records; and other detailed material is omitted for the same reason.

LABOR has repeatedly made the charge that there exists a conspiracy to destroy the trade-union movement—that there is under way a concerted movement on the part of the employers to restore and maintain autocratic control of American industry. This charge has been challenged by various persons, principally representatives of employers or employers' associations.

It has been suggested that the production of evidence might settle the question of whether there is or is not such a concerted effort; but those who are engaged in a conspiracy or in a concerted effort to bring about the destruction of an antagonist do not customarily send broadcast the full evidence of their intentions or of their plans.

In a recently published book entitled "Employers' Associations in the United States," written by Clarence E. Bonnett, Ph. D., this lack of direct evidence is clearly recognized. Dr. Bonnett's book is accepted by employers generally as an authentic study of the leading organizations of employers. The United States Chamber of Commerce freely suggests that inquirers consult its pages.

In this book Dr. Bonnett says:

There is much that is confidential or secret about associations. In the conflict, one must not let one's opponent know in advance one's plans or proposed methods, nor one's real fighting strength, unless that is so great as to intimidate one's opponent. For this reason, much of the work of the associations is conducted secretly. In some cases, list of members are not made public because some of the employers fear that the union may single them out and punish them. It also permits an employer apparently to be friendly to the union, because he dares not fight it openly, yet to fight it secretly. Then there are doubtful practices which the Association engaging in them does not wish to be made public. Illegal activities are of the latter sort.

Elsewhere in the same chapter Dr. Bonnett says:

Nor is the full extent of the belligerency of an association always expressed in a formal declaration of principles; the utterances of its leaders must also be considered. The National Association of Manufacturers furnishes an excellent illustration of such a situation.

The government of the associations, no matter under what guise, is in the hands of a few leaders. The government of associations is much like that of corporations, dominated by a few who choose what may be styled the Board of Directors, who in turn select the executive head under various titles. Some associations retain a greater degree of democracy than others by the use of the referendum on certain measures. It is characteristically the belief of association leaders that democracy does not conduce to efficiency.

More Bitter Since World War.

While the struggle to prevent the organization of workers has from the beginning engaged the attention of employers, there has been since the conclusion of the World War such a manifestation of united effort toward that end as to force upon any careful observer the conclusion that unusual forces have been at work and that unusual plans have been laid.

The fact is, as labor sees it, that while prior to the war there was what might be termed a normal opposition to the organizations of workers, there has been since the conclusion of the war an abnormal or stimulated opposition inspired and in all probability more or less actively directed from a central point. The evidence which labor possesses is naturally to a large degree circumstantial.

The basic industries of our country are steel, coal and railroads. Of these steel is the undisputed leader. And the three exercise a combined leadership which is felt down to the very bottom of our industrial structure.

Before the war was ended, and while, under the pressure of war necessity, the dominating industrial combinations were compelled to deal with some fairness in their relations with labor, the threat was commonly made, "Wait until the war is over!" It was common knowledge and it was commonly expected that when the war ended and there was no longer a national demand for production for war needs, the industrial monarchs would turn on labor in a great effort to smash their way back to autocratic domination.

How dramatic, then, was the leadership assumed by steel on the heels of the armistice. The steel workers, during the later days of the war, had taken some advantage of the state of public opinion to begin the organization of unions. They thought that at last they saw a way to escape from bondage, to put an end to the barbarous 12-hour day and the inhuman "long shift" of 24 hours at every week-end.

It suited the ends of the United States Steel Corporation to have these new organizations send their leaders with requests for conferences to discuss employment relations and conditions. The defiance then thundered forth by Steel, the monarch of industry and the leader of industrial reaction in America, was the battle call which had been forecast while the guns yet roared for freedom in France. "My terms or none," was the answer of Steel, voiced by Elbert H. Gary.

The railroads, their profit guaranteed by the Government, set to work a movement which finally resulted in the present deplorable conditions.

Coal, meanwhile, threw down the gauntlet and forced its workers into a strike, ending only after an injunction of sweeping and until then unheard of provisions.

Steel as the Leader.

But at the head of the pack stood Steel, itself master of more coal than any other corporation in the country, itself owning whole railroads and having tentacles creeping through others through interlocking directorates, itself the absolute master of a horde of lesser dependent industries and the arbiter of the fate of thousands upon thousands.

In West Virginia, Steel found a collateral opportunity to strike at Labor through its ownership of coal mines, the result of which has come to be known generally as "the West Virginia mine war."

I shall not attempt to burden the record with quotations, but it is important to point out that every subsequent national conference—those summoned by President Wilson, as well as those summoned by President Harding—has failed of constructive achievement for exactly the same reason that threw President Wilson's first industrial conference on the scrap heap—the determination of the representatives of high finance and big business to permit no action which might indicate an attitude of fairness or of constructive helpfulness in the field of industrial relations.

President Wilson's second industrial conference was a lamentable fiasco. President Harding's unemployment conference encountered the same brutality and arrogant anti-unionism. And President Harding's agricultural conference, though summoned to discuss agriculture, was dominated by the most sinister type of big business representatives and was sent to its doom by exactly the same sort of ultimatum that wrecked President Wilson's first effort two years previous.

Reverting again to Dr. Bonnett's volume, it is interesting to note that he calls attention in his introductory chapter to the increase of belligerency on the part of organized employers that has been manifest since the war. Dr. Bonnett states in his preface that his sources of information have been interviews with association leaders, letters from the associations, printed literature of the associations " some of which is not for general distribution," public documents, such as committee hearings, trade publications and other similar literature. His information, therefore, is from the employers and their organizations. Regarding this after-the-war onslaught Dr. Bonnett says:

The belligerent associations (during the war) did not make an unconditional surrender. The entire ground of the struggle is now being fought over again and with more bitterness than ever before. The records show that we have been passing through the greatest strike period in all history. Any one who has studied the attitude and activities of the belligerent associations during the past twenty years will be inclined to believe that the unions will lose much of the ground they gained during the war of 1914-1918. A survey of a combination of certain factors indicates that the unions must lose much of the advantageous ground formerly held.

In the same chapter he continues: During the period 1919-1921 many " open-shop " associations have been formed in various localities. Employers in many industries are attempting to free themselves from union domination fastened upon them during the war. One of the most discussed methods of fighting unionism is the "shop union"—that is, a union of only the employes in a shop. Such a union has no " entangling alliances " with any other union. This scheme is known under various names, such as shop representation plan," " work council," " shop-committee system." Elaborate methods of government for such unions have been worked out. Such a scheme is usually designed to displace the trade union of the A. F. of L. type, and the A. F. of L. vigorously denounces such organizations as "fake unions" or as "employers' unions."

Barr on the Open Shop.

William H. Barr, President of the National Founders' Association, is well qualified as a witness to show specifically what Dr. Bonnett has stated in general terms in the remarks just quoted. Dr. Bonnett declares that the belligerency of organized employers has increased since the signing of the armistice. This means that their militant hostility to the organizations of the workers has been intensified. Mr. Barr, who is proud of his hatred of organized labor, made a speech before his association on Nov. 17, 1920, in which he said:

A change has been brought about by the determination of men to free themselves from the unsound and unnatural control so imposed upon them. Today, that determination is manifest in the open-shop movement. Its progress is a matter of economy to those who began it; of consolation to those engaged in industry; and a stimulant to the patriotism of every one. A partial, but careful survey of irresistible activities in behalf of the open shop shows that 540 organizations in 247 cities of 44 States are engaged in promoting this American principle in the employment relations. A total of 23 national industrial associations are included in these agencies. In addition, 1,665 local Chambers

of Commerce, following the splendid example of the United States Chamber of Commerce, are also pledged to the principle of the open shop.

I wonder if it is possible to picture adequately the tremendous force which has been mobilized for the purpose of destroying the organizations of labor. There is no reason to question Mr. Barr's statistics. It is a part of his business to know about all organizations engaged in combating trade unions. He has for many years been recognized as the spokesman of organized hostility to trade unions.

The resolution of the United States Chamber of Commerce was adopted by a referendum which was issued on June 9, and which closed on July 24, 1919. This referendum was known as Referendum 31 and was entitled Employment Relations. The action of the United States Chamber of Commerce was intended to serve as a warning and a guide not only to Chambers of Commerce throughout the United States but to employers generally. In this resolution, which it may safely be said has become a text for the guidance of reactionary employers, it is provided:

The right of open-shop operation, that is, the right of employer and employe to enter into and determine the conditions of employment relations with each other, is an essential part of the individual right of contract possessed by each of the parties.

In the referendum on this section there were 1,676 votes in favor of adoption and 4 against, so it will be seen that Mr. Barr's figures, at least in so far as they relate to Chambers of Commerce, are underestimations falling short of the full truth.

Manufacturers on Record.

The National Association of Manufacturers, ranking in importance in its field with the United States Chamber of Commerce, is a militant union-hating organization. On Jan. 16, 1921, J. Philip Bird, described as general manager of the association, was quoted as saying that: " More than five hundred organizations in 250 cities have now endorsed the [open shop] plan and prominent manufacturers declare they could not stem the tide if they wished." It would seem sufficient to have the word of the leaders of three of the most powerful, if they are not in fact the three most powerful, anti-union organizations in the United States for what has transpired since the conclusion of the war. Mr. Barr of the National Erectors' Association, Mr. Bird of the National Association of Manufacturers and the official declarations and records of the United States Chamber of Commerce cannot well be disputed as to the extent of the campaign against labor. The effectiveness of that campaign is another matter.

The outstanding example of the manner in which the advice of national " open shop " organizations has been put into practice was furnished by Eugene C. Grace, President of the Bethlehem Steel Corporation, in his testimony before the Lockwood committee in New York City on Dec. 15, 1920. The following is from The Associated Press account of Mr. Grace's testimony:

The Bethlehem Steel Corporation will refuse to sell fabricated steel to builders and contractors in the New York and Philadelphia districts to be erected on a union shop basis.
The policy was disclosed by Eugene C. Grace, President of the corporation, who testified today before the joint legislative committee investigating the alleged " building trust," replying to charges that his concern was sponsoring the " open shop " movement by withholding steel from builders employing union men.
" I think it is a proper thing to protect the open shop principle," declared Mr. Grace, who explained that his stand would not be changed even if

building operations in New York were to be suspended because steel could not be obtained by union erectors.

Agreement on Wages.

With the policy adopted by the Bethlehem Steel Corporation the United States Steel Corporation is in full sympathy and agreement. This was made clear also in testimony before the Lockwood committee.

C. E. Cheney, Secretary of the National Erectors' Association, was called upon to testify regarding the National Fabricators' Association, one of a number of interlocking anti-union employers' organizations. He said that the National Fabricators' Association had " adjusted the policy of the members so that the steel fabricated by them is erected in open shops." He made clear, also, the attitude of the Iron League Erectors' Association, another of the interlocking organizations, saying that at a special meeting it had adopted a resolution to the following effect: " Complying with the order of the Board of Governors of the Building Trades Employers' Association, no advance in wages can be made, and the Secretary will so notify members."

Thus it appears that the Building Trades Employers' Association had reached a decision late in 1920 to the effect that there must be no advances in wages; and this arbitrary and dictatorial command was accepted by the Iron League Erectors' Association as a command to its members and was so transmitted.

That the Steel Corporation is in entire harmony and accord with the organized union-smashing steel fabricators and erectors is of record in various ways. It is shown by the whole policy and course of action of the steel trust from the time of the steel strike to the present. It is shown by Judge Gary's pronouncements in regard to the strike, by his conduct in President Wilson's first industrial conference, and by his later declaration to the stockholders. It is further shown in the appointment by the Erectors' Association at a meeting in Pittsburgh on Dec. 15 of a committee to " see the officers of the United States Steel Corporation as soon as possible to explain to them in regard to notifying the association before making any changes in the rate of wages, &c., on erection in the future.

Local Organizations Active.

In addition to the powerful national associations of employers there are throughout the country local and State organizations, some of which exercise tremendous power in their localities. In highly industrial sections these local organizations are frequently as powerful as many of the national associations. One of the most militant and belligerent of the local organizations is the Associated Employers of Indianapolis. The Manufacturers' News, published in Chicago, declared that Andrew J. Allen, Secretary of the Associated Employers " has perhaps done more to promote the ' open-shop ' cause than any other individual in the country; his friends call him the ' living exponent of the American plan of employment."

It is claimed for Allen that he originated the term " American plan." What is called the " American plan " is, of course, merely the non-union shop under another name.

Another local organization of more than local significance is the Builders' Exchange of San Francisco. This organization is at present under the scrutiny of the Federal Courts and of the United States Department of Justice for seeking to compel its members to refuse to sell building material to contractors employing union workers. This Builders' Exchange has made it a condition of membership that the member must sign an agreement not to sell building material to contractors who refuse to operate on the so-called American plan, or, in other words, those who employ union workers.

Practically every industrial centre has its organization of anti-union employers under one name or another. The title "Associated Industries" has become popular of late, and there are a number of organizations under this title. It may be interesting to present the names of a few in order to make clear the fact that they exist and in order to indicate the variety of names adopted:

The Detroit Employers' Association.
Associated Industries of Butte (and particularly the Master Builders' Division).
Associated Industries of Seattle.
Dallas Chamber of Commerce.
The Open-Shop Square Deal Association of Dallas.
The Southwestern Open-Shop Association, with headquarters in Dallas.
The Employers' Association of Atlanta.
The American Open-Shop Association of Quincy, Ill.
The Little Rock Board of Commerce and its Open-Shop Bureau.
The Chamber of Commerce of San Francisco.
The Industrial Association of San Francisco.
Associated Industries of Utah.
The Builders and Contractors' Association of Norfolk, Va.
The Builders' Association Exchange of Buffalo.
The Citizens' Alliance of Minneapolis.
The Associated General Contractors of Chattanooga.
The Chamber of Commerce of Cleveland.
The Builders' Exchange of San Francisco.
The Civic and Commercial Association of Denver.
Associated Industries of Tacoma.
San Antonio Open Shop Association.

It is scarcely more than a month since the President of the United States, in an effort to settle the railroad strike, put before the executives and the striking shopmen a proposal for settlement. This proposal was accepted by the shopmen and flouted by the executives. In an effort to induce the executives to change their minds, the President sent Mr. Hoover as his messenger to New York City to attend a meeting of the executives.

Mr. Hoover and the Bankers.

Prior to the meeting with the executives, however, Mr. Hoover met a group of bankers. Mr. Hoover has been throughout his entire career engaged in large industrial enterprises. He understands the world of industry and he understands the banking world. He is not a man to be associated with anything but an honest endeavor. He would not go to a meeting of bankers asking that they do a certain thing, unless he knew that they had the power to do that which he asked.

Mr. Hoover, Aug. 1, 1922, met a group of bankers, among whom the following were reported as in attendance: Benjamin Strong, Governor Federal Reserve Bank of New York; Charles E. Mitchell, President National City Bank; Edward R. Stettinius, a partner of J. P. Morgan & Co.; James E. Alexander, President National Bank of Commerce; Mortimer L. Schiff of Kuhn, Loeb & Co.; Frederick Straus, J. & W. Seligman & Co., Seward Prosser, President Bankers Trust Company, and Jacob Reynolds, President First National Bank.

Mr. Hoover was confronting the most powerful financial aggregation in the United States. The answer that he got from the throne of high finance in that meeting was the plain declaration that so far as the powers of finance were concerned, the railroads were free to use their utmost efforts to crush the organizations of labor.

Scarcely more than four weeks later Attorney General Harry M. Daugherty, going from the same Presidential presence, secured from Judge Wilkerson in Chicago an injunction which outraged the American people. What is more important, however, was the address of the Attorney General to the Court in asking for the injunction. These are his words:

* * * So long and to the extent that I can speak for the Government of the United States I will use the power of the Government to prevent the labor unions of the country from destroying the open shop.

These are some of the facts. Most prima facie evidence which would prove the charge that labor has made and that labor repeats must necessarily be found in the confidential records of such organizations as the National Association of Manufacturers, the National Erectors' Association, the National Industrial Conference Board, the United States Steel Corporation, the Bethlehem Steel Corporation, the National Open Shop Association, various Chambers of Commerce throughout the United States, the League for Industrial Rights, the National Metal Trades Association, the National Founders' Association, and a considerable number of other organizations of employers, bankers and commercial interests.

I may say two things in addition. First, it has not been possible to present all of the information which I possess; second, it has not been possible to recount the first-hand experiences of practically every organization of workers in the United States in the period that has elapsed since the armistice.

The fact is that these organizations have had to fight for their life. They do not need documents. They have had the *action*.

The final point is the effect which this tremendous effort has had on the workers. If we are to omit the period of severe unemployment which reached its peak in the Winter of 1921-22, I may state simply as a matter of fact and of record that the effect has been to stimulate the efforts of the workers toward organization, to make clear to them the paramount need for organization, to drive home to them the truth that their salvation depends upon their own economic strength and their own intelligence.

We have witnessed the mightiest onslaught of reaction through which our nation ever passed. We have witnessed the most brilliant and effective resistance ever offered by labor in defense of rights and standards and principles.

And how short-sighted it has all been, this boastful, trumpet-blaring, lying, deceptive war to destroy the organizations of the workers, the useful, toiling men and women of our country! How wasteful! History teaches that progress goes on, tyrants, fools, self-seekers to the contrary notwithstanding. Caesars, Napoleons, Hohenzollerns, all pass and their forces crumble. The race moves onward. So it must be, now and tomorrow and forever.

September 17, 1922

Rules Employer Can Insist On Pledge Not to Join Union

SAN FRANCISCO, Nov. 14.—A decision by the United States Circuit Court of Appeals yesterday declared void the California law forbidding employers to exact pledges from employes not to join labor unions.

The opinion affirmed the decision of the United States District Court of Los Angeles, which enjoined labor unions from organizing the non-union workers of the Pacific Electric Railway Company in Los Angeles. The injunction was made permanent against the Brotherhood of Railway Trainmen and the Brotherhood of Locomotive Engineers.

"Activities without lawful excuse," engaged in by the unions, the court found, were: Unionizing the employes of the railway company and drawing them into a controversy in which they had no substantial cause for complaint; calling strikes after organizing 1,200 of the 1,500 employes; striking when the country was at war in the face of the Presidential proclamation that there should be no strikes or lockouts during the war, and striking while the complaints of the employes were being submitted by the railway company to a representative of the United States Department of Labor.

The Court held these activities "interrupted the railway company's business in intrastate and interstate commerce to its irreparable damage."

November 15, 1923

COMPANY UNIONS AS STRIKE CURE

Success on Pennsylvania Road Starts Many Other Employers to Organize Men Along Similar Lines

By ROSE C. FELD.

SIMULTANEOUS with the settlement of the railroad strike has come the news that many of the railroads are turning to company unions. This is not a new departure in industrial arbitration, but it is new in the railroad field. Company unions of various sorts have been functioning in large and small corporations for a number of years. Most of them have been known as industrial representation plans. Those adopted by the Standard Oil Company, the Harvester companies, the General Electric Company and the great meat packing companies are but a few of the better known.

Early in 1921 the Pennsylvania Railroad inaugurated a system whereby the management was to meet in council with the representatives of its employes. So far as railroad history was concerned that was the first time a company union of this sort had been organized. As will be later explained, the plan had to weather many storms before it could properly and freely function. Today, however, it apparently is built on solid ground. So marked was its influence in the recent strike and so cordial the feelings between the management and the workers that other railroads whose losses were great and where antagonism was bitter have turned to the company organization as a panacea for future industrial ills. Among these are the Delaware & Hudson, the Nashville, Chattanooga & St. Louis, the Jacksonville Terminal Company, the Central Railroad of New Jersey, the Lehigh Valley and the New York, New Haven & Hartford. Others are being added.

Before taking up the railroad unions, it might be well to get an idea of the working of the plan in industries where trouble has been less marked. Ever since April 1, 1918, the Standard Oil Company of New Jersey has been successfully carrying on round table conferences with its employes. It started with an honest idea on the part of the management to come into closer contact with the mind of the rank and file. Previous industrial differences had been settled only when they came to the breaking point. Whenever the men came into the company offices it was, practically speaking, with a cudgel in their hands. If their demands were not met, they quit.

Equally arbitrary were the employers on the other side of the fence. If the books showed a need of cutting wages, wages were cut. If an increase of hours was decided necessary, the increase was made. There was a definite division of interest between the two factions of industry, with increasing misunderstandings and ill feeling. Capital, so called, did not know what was in the workers'

mind, except in the instances where labor was in a bulldog mood; labor did not know what was in capital's mind save when capital showed its teeth.

Standard Oil workers were not organized in labor unions to any great degree. The American Federation of Labor had concentrated its efforts on the organization of skilled workers. The men in the shops of the Standard Oil were mostly unskilled or semi-skilled laborers. Not more than 20 per cent. of the men belonged to unions. This is an important point to remember. The company was not working under an agreement with the unions, as in plants where the men were organized. The miners' strike, for instance, was called because the operators would not sign new national agreements. The same has been true in strikes of the garment trades. In this case about 1,000 skilled workers belonged to a national labor organization, but were not bound by any written agreement between them and the company. The other odd 4,000 laborers had no affiliation of any sort.

Relations on Good Basis.

There was no desire on the part of the management to break the union or to build up the machinery to oust it. Relations between union officials and members of the employing staff were of the best. There was little interference on the part of either with the workings of the other. The union leaders made no attempt to organize the unskilled laborers, the company was not interested in undermining the affiliation of their skilled workers. The important point to the company was to arrive at some plan whereby it could establish better cooperation with every worker, unorganized or not, as he might be.

An announcement was posted in the shops of the plant at Bayonne which read as follows:

"This company invites the co-operation of every employe in seeing to it that its long established policy for the fair treatment of all employes in matters pertaining to wages and working conditions is maintained and the company on its part desires to co-operate as far as may be helpful with each employe in his plans to provide satisfactory living and social conditions for himself and family.

"In order that each employe may be enabled to thus co-operate most effectively, the company invites employes to elect from their own number by secret ballot men in whom they have confidence, who shall represent them in dealing with officers and other representatives of the company in matters of mutual interest, this election to be on the general basis of one representative to every 150 employes, with at least two representatives in each division of the works."

To facilitate this election employes of the Bayonne works were grouped as follows: The boilermakers and blacksmiths got two representatives, the carpenters, painters, lead burners and machinists, two; the masons, pipefitters, tinsmiths, railroad and hoisting engineers, two; common labor, three; watchmen, 2; refining process men and pitch plant men, two, refiners, two; still cleaners, two; power department, two; paraffin process, three; barrel factory, three; cooperage department, three; case and can department, seven; chemical works, two, making a total of thirty-seven.

A similar letter was sent to each refinery and elections were held. Ninety to 100 per cent. of the employes voted in each division. With only slight modifications the plan was extended to the refineries at Baltimore, Md., and Parkersburg, W. Va.

One of the important clauses in the plan was a guarantee against discrimination, either by the company or by fellow-employes, because of membership or non-membership in any church, society, fraternity or union.

Periodic meetings around the table between representatives of the employes and those of the management have succeeded in building up the spirit of cooperation sought by the company. Matters which are frankly discussed and settled at these conferences concern wages, hours, methods of payment, promotions, discharges, working conditions, sanitation, housing, vacations, improvements on industrial representation and other miscellaneous questions. Some of the employe representatives are union members; others are not. The turnover in the plants is small, men stay at their jobs and do not seek their fortunes elsewhere. They know that they have the opportunity of airing any grievance, real or imaginary. Union officials have visited the plants a number of times, and left convinced that there was no need or chance of further organizing the workers.

Rail Problem Different

What the Standard Oil has accomplished also has been done by other organizations. But the Pennsylvania and other railroad employes are highly unionized. First of all, there are the five brotherhoods. These are labor organizations peculiar to the railroads and not affiliated with the American Federation of Labor. They are the switchmen's union, the conductors' union, the trainmen's union, the engineers' union and the locomotive engine men and firemen's union. The shopmen and the maintenance of way men are organized with the American Federation of Labor. It was the shopmen who waged the recent fight against the railroads.

When the railroads were handed back to their owners by the Government they were working under national agreements made with union representatives. That was a yoke from which the roads constantly tried to escape. The most serious damage brought on by the war, they maintained, was the demoralization of railroad personnel and the inroads made upon the domain of management.

At the beginning of 1921 the Pennsylvania Railroad proposed a company union or representation plan to its employes. That was an expression of a desire on the part of the company to deal with its own men, its own problems, in its own conference rooms. It did not deny the right of employes to organize in labor organizations outside the company. The point it stressed was that in dealing with problems peculiar to the Pennsylvania Railroad it wanted no outside spokesmen, but preferred to arrange the matter with men employed by the company.

A plan of co-operation was inaugurated in May. Representatives were chosen by ballot and working agreements were made for various departments at table conferences held with these representatives. A snag arose, however, which threatened to break the company union. Officers of the shop crafts' union affiliated with the American Federation of Labor instructed their membership on the Pennsylvania System not to vote in the election of employe representatives. Union officers employed by the company claimed the right to represent the railroad employes in any capacity necessary. They insisted that the men vote, if they voted at all, for System Federation No. 90, the shop crafts' union. The result was that many of the shop craft employes refused to vote. Representation on that body was therefore almost entirely limited to non-union men.

To get redress the union appealed to the Labor Board, which rendered a decision in favor of the unions and ordered the road to make changes in the methods of selecting employe representatives and to proceed to negotiate new agreements with representatives of the men thus chosen. This the railroad refused to

do and brought the question to a higher court. It was decided in favor of the Pennsylvania and full liberty given the roads to get together with its employes in its own way.

In several instances committees elected in different departments were union men. These were fully recognized by the railroads as empowered to speak for the employes and negotiations were concluded with them. In other instances, however, the representation was mixed. Here, too, negotiations were concluded for all. In still other instances representation was entirely non-union.

This is the second year the Pennsylvania plan has been in effect. Today it functions in almost every department. Engineers, firemen, conductors, trainmen, shop craft employes, signal men, maintenance of way men, clerical employes, telegraphers, marine employes and miscellaneous forces, all are organized. The reviewing committees in the case of each class of employe concerned are composed of an equal number of representatives of the employes and the management. All members of these committees have equal voting power. Two-thirds vote of the body is necessary to decide any question submitted. The chairmanship alternates between an employe member and a management member.

Better Co-operation Now.

Contracts and working rules are negotiated directly with employes. This has in a large measure built up the spirit of co-operation which the management found had disappeared when the roads were returned.

Ill feeling toward this company union has not died down on the part of the American Federation of Labor, it is asserted. The brotherhoods, however, do not believe that the company union is making any inroads upon their organization. They take the stand that company representation can go hand in hand with national union membership without incurring any damage to either.

Because of the spirit of loyalty shown by the Pennsylvania employes to the railroad during the recent strike, other railroads have taken up the idea of the

company union. The mechanical department of the Association of the New Haven Railroad System was one of the first to be organized. Already it has formulated rules and regulations, the preamble of which reads as follows:

" We believe that with unity, guided by intelligence, and with an intelligent association, we can acquire discipline necessary to enable us to act together, concentrate our strength and direct our efforts toward a common purpose."

All mechanics, helpers and apprentices who are actively engaged in the maintenance of equipment and machinery in the motive power department, and not acting in a supervisory capacity, are entitled to membership in the association.

A general board has been created whose jurisdiction includes the New York, New Haven, Hartford, Providence and Boston Divisions, the Midland, Old Colony, Waterbury, Danbury and Central New England Divisions, the Van Nest shops and members from the locomotive, passenger and freight departments. This board is to look after the interests of the association on the divisions reporting to the association. There is an Adjustment Board which is to place before the officers of the company all matters submitted to it by a local Adjustment Board or the general board and report to the general board the results. Any disputes which cannot be settled in conference between the system Adjustment Board and officers of the company will be handled in accordance with the provisions of the Transportation act.

Whether these company unions will function as effectively as the older representation plans, time will show. The principal objection against them seems to lie in the fact that they are not intended to bring all parts of the organization more closely together, but to serve as a meeting ground between the management and representatives of departments. They will have to do more than merely take over the work of the unions if they are to prove a really progressive step in industry. The tendency today is toward greater representation in every way, not only in matters of hours and labor.

THE SHIFT FROM THE UNIONS

SAMUEL GOMPERS used to declare that the American Federation of Labor "never would surrender the advantages gained through the war." Yet in the six years 1920-25 it fell off in mere numbers from its peak of over 4,050,000 to 2,877,297. According to a writer in Current History, there has been an even greater decline in prestige. As Research Director of the Pennsylvania Old Age Commission, ABRAHAM EPSTEIN lately inspected "1,500 of the larger concerns of the United States." Almost everywhere he found a shift away from the union. "If the labor movement is doomed," he asks, "what then?"

MR. EPSTEIN pays high tribute to the achievements of the Federation. Not only to its own members but to American labor in general it has brought shorter hours, higher wages, improved working conditions. But he quotes its very leaders as attesting that its "vitality and missionary zeal" are in decadence. In the Pensylvania Federation twenty-two out of twenty-six officials "unequivocally declared" to this effect. Some of them conscientiously took the blame upon themselves. Others found refuge in current patter—"the automo- "bile, the radio, the movies, the good "times, the bad times, President COOL- "IDGE, the ignorance of the workers, "the Communists, the gross material- "ism of the labor movement, the capi- "talist press, the lack of a labor press. "Our younger members, especially, have "gone jazzy." Mr. EPSTEIN finds, rather, that "the hopes and aspirations of the rank and file" are in process of being transferred from outside union leaders to the managerial forces within the workers' several shops.

A new and more liberal generation is slowly rising to control. The "old-line captain of industry," having "risen from the ranks," was deficient in "social mindedness toward the workers." These new leaders, often products of the departments of sociology or the business schools of our universities, hold it as cardinal principles that "a contented em- "ploye is the best asset to a prosperous "business"; that "capital can prosper "only as long as it secures the good-will "of its workers by providing better ad- "vantages for them"; that "production "is far more a matter of efficient men "than of improved machinery." Mr. EPSTEIN details the advances that have been made during the past decade or two in employers' participation in mutual benefit or relief associations, in group life insurance and sickness insurance, in industrial old-age pensions, in stock ownership by employes—advances as notable for their social and business intelligence as for the billions of dollars involved. He shows that strikes have occurred mainly in industries like that of anthracite coal, into which the new ideas have not penetrated. And, finally, he gives conclusive proof of the bitter, implacable enmity of the unions to the spread of such methods.

Mr. EPSTEIN concludes that "a new "industrial order is evolving and grow- "ing at an accelerated rate." Its present advances are largely the result of our prosperity; the real test will not come until the next slump sets in. But he harbors no doubt that the movement will continue. At the answer to the question with which he set out he barely hints. On the one hand is communistic control of industry through outright employe ownership. On the other is a new industrial unionism, the "industrial republic," in which the forces of labor, capital and management cooperate sanely and liberally for the common good.

NEW LABOR CHIEF GREEN IS ELECTED

Secretary of Miners Declares He Will Carry Out Policies of Gompers.

DUNCAN, PASSED BY, QUITS

Head of Federation Is 51 Years Old and Belongs to the Conservative Union School.

PLAN GOMPERS MEMORIAL

One Proposal Is to Change the Name of Rutgers Square in His Honor.

William Green, Secretary-Treasurer of the United Mine Workers of America, was elected President of the American Federation of Labor yesterday to fill in the term of the late Samuel Gompers, which would have expired on Jan. 1, 1926. He was chosen at the Elks Club by eight of the ten members of the Executive Council, and immediately announced he would adhere to Mr. Gompers's policies.

As a candidate Mr. Green refrained from voting. So did James Duncan, First Vice President of the federation for thirty years. Mr. Duncan, who had delivered labor's farewell at the bier of Mr. Gompers twenty-four hours earlier, quit the labor movement by tendering his resignation when the council passed over his claim to the Presidency.

The resignation was tabled until the next meeting of the council in Miami on Feb. 3. Mr. Duncan said he had no plans for the future but that his decision to retire was irrevocable.

Mr. Green was the only man nominated. The name of Matthew Woll, President of the Photo-Engravers' Union, was not presented to the council.

The Executive Council conferred for three hours. Those present were James Duncan, former President of the International Granite Cutters' Union; Frank Duffy, Secretary-Treasurer of the United Brotherhood of Carpenters and Joiners; Mr. Green; Jacob Fischer of the International Barbers' Union; Thomas Rickert, President of the United Garment Workers; Matthew Woll, President of the International Association of Photo-Engravers; Frank Morrison, Secretary of the Federation; Daniel Tobin, Treasurer of the Federation; Martin F. Ryan of the Brotherhood of Railway Carmen and James Wilson of the International Brotherhood of Pattern Workers.

Duncan's Plea Ignored.

Shortly after the meeting opened at 10:45 Mr. Duncan suggested that, inasmuch as he had served the Federation so long and had been actively identified with Mr. Gompers and his policies for thirty years, it was proper that he be permitted to round out his career as head of the organization.

Mr. Rickert nominated Mr. Green and suggested that it was necessary to choose a man whom the convention would be sure to re-elect at next October's convention in Atlantic City. Mr. Tobin arose and said he could not pledge himself to any man for an indefinite period. Re-election would have to depend on the man's record. The nomination of Mr. Green was seconded by Mr. Woll.

Mr. Ryan, while not placing Mr. Duncan's name in nomination, stressed his long labor record and asked that it be considered. An oral vote revealed the eight Vice Presidents who voted favoring Mr. Green. J. P. Noonan of the Electrical Workers was elected to fill the vacancy caused by Mr. Green's promotion.

The New Leader's Statement.

The newly elected President explained his policy in the following statement:

I have been chosen by the Executive Council of the American Federation of Labor to be the successor to our late lamented leader, Mr. Gompers. This high honor came to me unsolicited and unsought. I regard it as a call to service, and for that reason I feel it my solemn duty to accept and to serve. In making this momentous decision I am deeply conscious of the grave responsibilities which are being assumed. The high standard of excellence in service, efficiency in leadership and administrative ability attained by Mr. Gompers during his long official and useful career is a challenge to the best and highest of everything which any human being can give in the service of his fellow-men.

While organized labor feels most keenly the loss of our great leader, Mr. Gompers, every member may take courage and consolation from the fact that he left us a legacy of incomprehensible value. We have his trade-union creed, his trade-union philosophy, his writings, letters and recorded spoken words. All of this will serve as a guide in charting and shaping our course and in the formulation of our policies.

It shall ever be my steadfast purpose to adhere to those fundamental principles of trade-unionism so ably championed by Mr. Gompers and upon which the superstructure of organized labor rests. In cooperation with my colleagues upon the Executive Council of the American Federation of Labor and the chosen officers of all affiliated organizations we will carry forward the work of organization and education among the workers of our land. We will endeavor to promote collective bargaining, the observance of wage agreements and the acceptance of the organized labor movement by all classes of people as a logical, necessary moral force in the economic, industrial and social life of our nation. While striving for the attainment of these praiseworthy purposes we shall ever be mindful of our duties and obligations as American citizens. Our devotion to America and American institutions must never be successfully challenged. Our demand upon society for higher standards of life, better wages, independence and humane conditions of employment must ever be based upon our inalienable right to the enjoyment of life, liberty and the pursuit of happiness. Our problems must be met and solved upon the basis of American fair play and in accordance with American traditions and American ideals.

Mr. Green is of the conservative school and does not believe that unions should experiment in commercial enterprises. He was one of the four members of the Executive Council who opposed ratification of La Follette by the A. F. of L. He does not believe labor organizations should form a separate labor party. His was the only voice in the recent convention of the A. F. of L. which was raised against committing the Federation to ratification of the proposal to form a labor insurance company. He has consistently opposed recognition of Soviet Russia and has always frowned on radical innovations.

Memorial Is Discussed.

The council discussed the proposal of a memorial to be erected to the memory of Mr. Gompers. President Green was empowered to appoint a committee to make a report to the Executive Council on that subject.

The newly elected President is a ruddy man of medium size, with a powerful chest and broad shoulders. He does not drink or smoke. He is 51 years old and makes his home in Coshocton, Ohio, the town where he was born and where his 90-year-old father and his mother live. They came to this country from England in 1868. His father is English and his mother Welsh.

Mr. Green was educated in the district school of Coshocton and went to work in the mines at 16. Becoming President of Sub-District 6 in 1900, Mr. Green rose rapidly until in 1906 he was elected President of the State organization. His only venture out of the miners' organization was a period of four years, be-

ginning in 1911, when he became State Senator and Speaker of the Ohio Senate. In 1913 he became Secretary-Treasurer of the miners' organization. He married Miss Jane Mobley April 14, 1892. The Greens have six children—five daughters and one son. Three daughters are married.

Memorial services for Samuel Gompers will be held at the next meeting of the Central Trades and Labor Council of Greater New York and vicinity, Jan. 15. A joint memorial service for August Belmont and Samuel Gompers is being arranged for next month by the National Civic Federation, of which Mr. Belmont was President in 1904 and 1905 and Mr. Gompers Vice President since its inception. The United Hebrew Trades is sponsoring a movement to change the name of Rutgers Square to Gompers Square, because it was there that the late Federation President made his first stump speech. Memorial plans will be discussed on Dec. 22 at a meeting of the New York State Federation of Labor in Albany.

40-HOUR WEEK IS NOW LABOR'S GOAL

EVER since the labor movement began in the United States the struggle for shorter hours has occupied a prominent place in organized labor's program of immediate demands. At first the ten-hour day was the goal. But after fifty years of struggle this came to be fairly well established about the middle of the last century. Labor pressed on to a new goal—the eight-hour day. With the passage of the Adamson Eight-Hour law for the railroad brotherhoods, in 1916, eight hours came to be generally accepted as a normal working day. But, as before, having attained a new low-hour mark, labor was not content. It demanded the forty-four-hour week, and got it in all the needle trades soon after the end of the war. Now the campaign for the forty-hour week is well under way.

One union, the Furriers, has already written it into its agreement with the manufacturers. The Dressmakers' Department of the International Ladies' Garment Workers Union in New York has had it since 1923, and the cloakmakers are expected to strike for it when their agreement expires the first of July. The cloth, hat and cap makers are also preparing to strike for the forty-hour week, among other demands, at the same time. The Amalgamated Clothing Workers went on record for the new short week at their recent convention in Montreal.

Already the forty-hour week slogan, so effectively dramatized by the Furriers in the strike which has just been terminated, has fired the imagination of other labor groups throughout the country. On May 22 a monster demonstration was staged in its behalf in the New Madison Square Garden. Besides the needle trades representatives, John Sullivan, President of the New York State Federation of Labor, and John Coughlin, Secretary of the New York Central Trades and Labor Council, were there to give the forty-hour movement their official blessing. Telegrams of support were read from the Pennsylvania, California and Minnesota State federations of labor, from central trade bodies in Minneapolis, St. Paul, Milwaukee, St. Louis, Pittsburgh and Philadelphia and from William H. Johnston, who has since resigned from the Presidency of the Machinists' Union because of ill-health.

Ten-Hour Fight in 1829.

This big forty-hour-week demonstration recalls another similar mass meeting held in New York City ninety-seven years ago. The Morning Courier of April 30, 1829, records that it was "one of the largest public meetings ever held in New York." From five to six thousand persons jammed the hall, and "the avenue and street were thronged with people unable to obtain admittance." The mechanics who gathered there resolved in future not to labor "more than the just and reasonable time of ten hours a day." They won. Professor Commons and his associates, in their "History of Labour in the United States," record the fact that "the effort to lengthen the day's work was abandoned and was never again seriously attempted in New York."

The struggle went on in other cities, with the building trades unions always in the forefront, until by 1840 the principle of the ten-hour day was established by an Executive order, in which President Van Buren established the ten-hour day on all Government works. The first ten-hour law was passed in 1847 in the State of New Hampshire, to be followed in 1853 by California and later by other States.

The first instance of the adoption of the eight-hour day was the ship carpenters and caulkers in the navy yard at Charlestown, Mass., in 1842. Thereafter Massachusetts became the stronghold of the eight-hour movement. An eight-hour plank was inserted in the Republican State platform in 1865 and in the following year The Boston Voice started a campaign to send Wendell Phillips to Congress. "What John Bright is to Parliament," ran the motto, "the workingmen of the Third Massachusetts District can make Wendell Phillips to Congress." Phillips did not get there, however.

Illinois, California, Connecticut, Missouri, New York and Wisconsin passed eight-hour laws in 1867, but none of them had any teeth. A contract requiring ten or more hours would be perfectly legal. The National Labor Union declared that "for all practical intents and purposes they might as well have never been placed on the statute books, and can only be described as frauds on the laboring class." In 1868, however, Congress enacted an eight-hour law for Government employes, and in 1872 a strike of workers in New York City secured the eight-hour day for the bricklayers, carpenters, plasterers, plumbers, painters, brown and bluestone cutters, stone masons, masons' laborers, paper hangers and plate printers.

Battles of the '80s.

Agitation for the shorter workday died down for a while because of the depression of 1877, and, in fact, the labor movement as a whole disintegrated and many of the gains made in the eight-hour movement of 1872 were swept away. So the fight had to be waged over again when the labor movement got on its feet. The "eight-hour-day" slogan was, in fact, used to put new life into the trade union movement. The Federation of Organized Trades and Labor Unions, forerunner of the A. F. of L., took the lead and at its 1884 convention resolved "that eight hours shall constitute a legal day's labor from and after May 1, 1886."

The A. F. of L. had to launch another campaign in 1888. This time the plan of procedure was to have one union after another strike for the eight-hour day, beginning with the carpenters. This union won the eight-hour day in 137 cities and a nine-hour day in most others in 1890. One after another the unions achieved their goal, which is by no means won for all workers even today.

The next phase of the movement for shorter hours came at the end of the war, when the Needle Trades Unions launched a drive for the forty-four-hour week—the eight-hour day for five days, with a half holiday on Saturday. The Amalgamated Clothing Workers took the lead. Early in 1918 they foresaw what would happen when the war would be over and hundreds of former clothing workers would return in search of employment.

"The question for us," wrote Joseph Schlossberg and Jacob Potofsky in the 1919-20 American Labor Year Book was: "Shall we permit the employers to make room for them by displacing us, thus rendering them obedient tools of the employers against their own fellow-workers, or shall we make it possible for our brothers, when they come back, to work along side of us in the factories, in the union, and on the picket line if necessary? In order to make room for them the working week had to be reduced. Accordingly, we enacted a forty-four-hour week for the industry."

Clothing Union Wins.

On the day the armistice was signed the employers in New York locked the union out of its factories on the forty-four-hour issue. While the union was struggling to maintain itself here, the leaders in Chicago, on Jan. 17, 1919, signed an agreement with Hart, Schaffner and Marx establishing the forty-four-hour week in the latter's factory. This came as a boon to the workers in New York who finally won the short week about the middle of February. The Ladies Garment Workers immediately took up the slogan and secured the forty-four-hour week in New York City in April. By the end of 1919 they had won their campaigns in many other cities and established the forty-four-hour week throughout the industry. Since then, the other needle trades unions, many building trades unions and a few others have secured the short work week for themselves.

The chief arguments for shorter hours which have been advanced from time to time may be classified under four headings: (1) that long hours are injurious to health; (2) the "citizenship" argument—to allow the workers leisure for self-improvement so that they may obtain the knowledge requisite to the intelligent use of the ballot; (3) the philosophy of Ira Steward, the Boston machinist, who maintained that "a reduction of hours is an increase of wages," since the workers' standard of living rises with increased leisure and he is compelled to demand higher wages; and (4) the "make work" argument—in the words of Samuel Gompers, "that so long as there is one man who seeks employment and cannot obtain it, the hours of labor are too long."

The health argument was the principal one advanced by the furriers in the recent strike. "The air in fur shops is laden with harmful dust from animal skins that have been dyed with powerful chemicals," says the report which the Workers' Health Bureau prepared for the union. "The forty-hour week is an indispensable safeguard necessary to enable the workers to gain some strength to offset the effects of harmful working conditions."

The same argument was used by the painters when they won the forty-hour week in 1920 in New York. At that time they were working forty-four hours per week for $6 a day. They went into the strike with the slogan, "40-40"—forty dollars for forty hours' work, and came out victorious. Today statistics gathered by the Painters' Brotherhood show that from 30,000 to 32,000 painters are working the forty-hour week. They have it in the entire State of Oregon and in Boston, Seattle, Scranton, Newark and other cities.

Reasons for Shorter Day.

The plasterers' union also has the forty-hour week in some cities, having achieved it in 1915 in Philadelphia and in New York City by their last agreement signed May 1, 1926. In New York the printers have it on the night shift in book and job printing establishments and have incorporated a demand for a thirty-nine-hour week for all newspaper printers to be presented to their employers when their agreement expires this month.

The "make-work" argument is still very popular. Many members of the United Mine Workers believe that the six-hour day is essential in order to give employment to the unemployed members of the union. Workers in the needle trades also hope that the forty-hour week will tend to spread out the seasons and give more regular employment to their members. Whether or not this is possible is doubtful, to say the least. Since the introduction of the forty-four-hour week the contrary has been true in many cases; the seasons have shrunk instead of lengthening.

As far as production is concerned, it has been pretty clearly shown by studies of fatigue and efficiency in industry made in England and the United States that a decrease in hours from ten to eight has, if anything, increased output. It is probable, however, that further reductions would not materially increase production and may, therefore, hold out some hope to the unemployed.

For the present the forty-hour week campaign is on in the needle trades and the Typographical Union in New York is out to get a thirty-nine hour week. President Green of the A. F. of L. gave his endorsement to the principle in the furriers' campaign, and it is possible that the A. F. of L. will, within a few years, have something to say on the subject in its official program.

AGAIN GASTONIA DRAWS EYES OF THE NATION

Murder Trial of Strikers and Communists Is Closely Interwoven With a Difficult Labor Situation in New Industrial South

FOR the third time since the inception of the case, sixteen Communists, former strikers and union guards, members of the National Textile Workers' Union, accused of the murder of Chief of Police O. F. Aderholdt of Gastonia, will go on trial before Judge M. V. Barnhill in Charlotte, N. C., tomorrow. With the murder charge is coupled the charge of conspiracy resulting in the murder. The National Textile Workers' Union is a Communist organization affiliated with the Red Trade Union International in Moscow.

Thirteen of the defendants, headed by Fred Erwin Beal of Lawrence, Mass., strike leader, are indicted for first degree murder. The State has waived the death penalty against the three women defendants, Amy Schechter, Vera Buch and Sophie Melvin, all New York Communists. There are three other Northerners among the defendants. The rest are Southern men who took part, one way or another, in the strike at the Lorray Mill of the Manville-Jenckes Company in Gastonia. The Manville-Jenckes Company is a Northern corporation.

It was the strike at the Lorray Mill which, on June 7, led to the killing of Aderholdt and the wounding of three of his men when they visited the union headquarters in response to a call from a neighbor, later a witness for the State, who reported to the police that there was a disturbance on the union grounds. The State charges a deliberate conspiracy to murder Aderholdt. The accused plead self-defense.

New Conditions in the South.

The trial at Charlotte is closely interwoven with a labor situation that has arisen in the new industrial South.

The strikes in North and South Carolina and in Tennessee were the result of what are generally acknowledged as unsatisfactory conditions of work and wages, long hours and the so-called "stretch-out system," which has been characterized by a committee of the South Carolina House of Representatives as "putting more work on the employes than they can do." By this system a worker is called upon to attend a greater number of machines than has previously been his allotment. There is no corresponding increase in pay. On the contrary, it has been shown that workers under the "stretch-out" system have earned less than they did before.

The violence resulting from the various strikes has been due largely to the usual course taken by strikes in which efforts are made by the employers to resume operation with strikebreakers. The strikers try to resist by mass picketing and, in some cases, by resort to means other than peaceful persuasion.

In its report the South Carolina committee pointed out that the strikes were in no way caused by labor unions directly and were "in no sense a rebellion against improved textile machinery, for the stretch-out system is not brought into play by the introduction of any improved textile machinery."

"In the stretch-out system it is the employe who does the stretching," the report said also. "To illustrate, in a card room, in one mill, five sections were employed at $23 per man per week. This force was cut to four men and the pay also cut to $17.25 per week. Still later this force was reduced to three and the pay was raised a little—to $20.23 per man per week."

It is conditions such as these and the introduction of this type of "efficiency system" which have been responsible for the strikes, including the one at the Lorray Mill.

In Elizabethton, Tenn., where 3,500 workers were on strike last June, it had been shown that girls were employed ten hours a day, receiving from 16 to 18 cents an hour. Their weekly pay envelopes averaged from $8 to $10. The wages of spinners and washers, men with families, averaged $12 a week. The twelve-hour workday is common in Southern textile mills.

The workers live in mill villages, in houses supplied by the companies at a nominal rental, but living conditions in these villages, for the most part, leave much to be desired. Poverty, ignorance and lack of opportunity for education and cultural betterment are the widespread manifestations of the system. The workers, as a rule, are a hopeless lot and feel that they have little chance in any open struggle with the employers. Every now and then some of them go out on strike, but almost invariably defeat is their lot. There are a few model communities, but these are the exceptions.

Majority of Native Stock.

The majority of the textile workers in the South are of native stock. A large proportion of them come from the mountain areas. To them the whole complex industrial civilization into which they have been

cast is bewildering. Coming from poor, ignorant and illiterate agricultural communities, they remain for a while satisfied with the wages they receive and the opportunity to move about from mill village to mill village. After a while they begin to realize, however, that the wages, although above their previous income, are inadequate to meet their new necessities, however modest.

Most of the unionization activity among them has been carried on by the United Textile Workers, but in Gastonia the Communists have been active. Here the United Textile Workers have not attempted to interfere. It is possible that this organization may at a later date, when the present troubles are over, seek to gain a foothold in Gaston County, the largest textile community in the South, but for the present the policy of this A. F. of L. organization so far as Gastonia and Gaston County are concerned is one of hands off.

From Gastonia the Communists have sought to extend their activities to other areas but have met with no success. The Lorray mill is the only establishment in which they managed to gain a foothold. But this they have now lost. It is quite evident from the general nature of their program that they consider the Southern textile industry a particularly fruitful source of action and propaganda.

Communist Weakness.

Up to a certain point this has proved to be true, but where the Communists fail is in their ability to hold any ground they may have gained. This has also been the rule in the North, as exemplified in the needle trades of New York. Their leaders insist, however, that they intend to remain in the South and give the United Textile Workers a battle for the control of that region. The latter organization is pursuing its own course without regard to Communist activities. It cannot be said, however, that the success achieved by the United Textile Workers has been marked, although the organization is preparing to extend its activities. Its future, however, depends to a large extent not only upon its own enterprise but upon whether or not the Southern textile industry will come to realize that organization and collective bargaining is to be preferred to constant outbreaks of trouble.

But to return to the murder trial. The case was first called for trial in Gastonia on July 29, but on July 30 Judge Barnhill, in response to a

plea by the defense for a change of venue, moved the trial to Charlotte, twenty miles distant, where it was resumed on Aug. 26. only to be interrupted by a mistrial on Sept. 9, brought about by the fact that a member of the jury went violently insane under the stress of the proceedings.

The mistrial was a great disappointment to the defense when it was revealed that the jury had been strongly inclined to a verdict of acquittal on the basis of the evidence presented by the State. While the attitude taken by the jury came as no surprise to observers at the trial, Solicitor John G. Carpenter, in charge of the prosecution, discounted the jury's opinion, believing that a conviction was likely when the full facts were laid bare.

The strike which led to the slaying of Aderholdt was but an episode in the drama of social ferment and industrial unrest which has been agitating the South in recent months as a result of prevailing economic conditions and the efforts to unionize the 300,000 textile workers of the region. Into this drama the Communists, directed from their headquarters in New York, have introduced an added element of friction which, while quite familiar in the North, has served to inflame public and official sentiment in the South by its strange and aggravating mixture of passion and propaganda among the inexperienced, poorly educated and, as many authorities, among them prominent Southerners, have pointed out, much exploited workers of the textile mills.

To a visitor from the North the spectacle of Communist leaders and propagandists preaching to a crowd of illiterate Southern mill workers from mountaineer stock was but a repetition of the familiar agitation in which New York revolutionists like to engage. To the Southerners it was all very alarming. The Communists roused certain elements in Gaston County to a sense of fear and danger. This, coupled with an opposition to the idea of trade union organization, laid the basis for the counter-attacks and mob action which marked the situation both during the strike and since the abortive trial of Sept. 9.

Among the manifestations of mob action during the strike, which began on April 1, was the destruction of the union headquarters in Gastonia, the wrecking of the strikers' relief store and the formation of a so-called committee of 100 which,

Photo by Acme.   Photograph at Top by Times Wide World.

The Illustration at the Top Shows an Outdoor Demonstration at Gastonia, N. C., a Scene of Great Bitterness. A Picket Line Outside a
Mill Fence Is Shown in the Bottom Picture.

the strikers charged, made it its deliberate aim to terrorize the workers. The leaders and members of the masked mob which destroyed the union headquarters and relief store were never identified and punished.

It was this attack, the Communists contend, which compelled them to arm themselves to prevent a repetition. New headquarters were established in the vicinity of the Lorray mill and armed guards posted to protect the building and grounds. Connected with the grounds was a tent colony, where lived a number of former strikers and their families. From this embattled position the Communists sought in vain to bring the strike to life again.

On June 7 there was a meeting on the union grounds. About 150 persons, strikers and non-strikers, were present. Beal and others made speeches in which they urged the strikers to join in a mass picketing demonstration against the Lorray mill. Attending the meeting were two minor officials of the mill. Rocks and other missiles were thrown at Beal. A shot was fired which struck one of the union guards. Commotion and disturbance followed. The police were sent for.

Charges of the Prosecution.

In the first bill of particulars filed by the prosecution the charge was made that the call for the police came from union headquarters and that it was by this call that Aderholdt was lured to his death. In the second bill of particulars, filed at the opening of the trial in Charlotte, the prosecution abandoned this charge, however, revealing that the call came from a neighbor who took it upon herself to summon the police, and who at the trial told about it on the witness stand.

What happened on the union grounds on the night of June 7 was established with reasonable clarity at the proceedings in Charlotte. What remains to be fixed is the responsibility. Aderholdt and his men arrived, and after an altercation be-

tween one of his men and a strike guard, there is said to have followed a shot, then another and then a volley of shots. As Louis McLaughlin, one of the defendants, put it on the witness stand, "the whole bunch fired."

It is the contention of the defense that the police fired the first shot, that the strikers, in view of what had happened at the meeting preceding the picketing demonstration and of the attacks to which they had been subjected previously, honestly believed themselves in danger, and that they were, therefore, justified in unleashing the fusillade. This argument, according to the defense, is strengthened by the fact that the picketing demonstration which preceded the arrival of the police had been broken up and turned back to union headquarters, and that on that occasion, as on others, strikers were beaten and maltreated by the police.

That the jury was impressed with the self-defense argument of the accused was said to have been evident from the opinions expressed by nearly all of its members after the collapse of the Charlotte trial. How well the prosecution has utilized the interim in bolstering up its case remains to be seen.

The events that followed the mistrial of Sept. 9—the kidnapping and beating of Communist organizers and the shooting of Mrs. Ella May Wiggins, a former striker and the mother of five children—have complicated the general situation. While most of the people of Mecklenburg and Gaston Counties were content to leave the case in the hands of the court and were reluctant to see anything done that might interfere with the normal processes of justice, a mob of some 100 men in Gastonia, most of them described as irresponsible youths, led by a few regarded as professional union baiters, descended upon union headquarters and the office of the International Labor Defense.

They staged a hostile demonstration, destroyed some Communist literature and, proceeding to a board-

ing house sheltering some of the Communist leaders and organizers, kidnapped three of them, took one of them for a "ride" and beat him, invaded Charlotte in a caravan of automobiles, where they sought to seize other Communist leaders and attorneys for the defense, and staged a spectacle of mob rule which outraged all decent elements of the community.

Murder of Mrs. Wiggins.

This was followed by the kidnapping and beating of another Communist organizer, and by the murder of Mrs. Wiggins on the night of Sept. 14, when a truckful of workers bound for a meeting called by the Communists near Gastonia was fired upon by a mob. Seven men were held in this murder in only $1,000 bail each. The bail was furnished by J. A. Baugh Jr., resident manager of the Loray Mill.

The murder of Mrs. Wiggins produced a profound impression in Gaston and Mecklenburg Counties. In this connection there has been sharp criticism of the Communists in failing to call off the meeting when it was well known that the Gastonia mob had determined to break it up. None of the Communist leaders, with the exception of their official press agent, showed up at the meeting.

Attention is now directed, among other elements in the situation, on how the State will deal with those responsible for the murder of Mrs. Wiggins.

Certain liberals both in the South and North have demanded that the Communists withdraw from Gastonia on the ground that they can serve no good purpose and that by their methods and tactics they have managed to provoke a civil war without in the least advancing the solution of the tangled and extremely difficult problem confronting the textile industry of the South. This problem is only a part of the larger task confronting that section of the country—the task of adjusting itself to the industrial revolution.

LABOR COUNCIL ASKS UNION DRIVE IN SOUTH

Report to A. F. of L. Urges Vigorous Campaign to Meet Growing Industrialization.

DEMANDS IMMIGRATION CUT

Reduction by One-Half and Drastic Curb on Influx of Mexicans Are Called Imperative.

MACHINE-AGE EVILS CITED

Displacement of Workers and "45-Year Deadline" Discussed—Convention Opens Today.

From a Staff Correspondent of The New York Times.

TORONTO, Ont., Oct. 6.—The rapid industrialization of the South is a challenge that should be accepted by the international unions affiliated with the American Federation of Labor and aggressive unionization plans should be pushed during the next year, in the opinion of the Executive Council of the federation, whose annual report will be placed before the delegates when the annual convention of the federation opens tomorrow morning.

Referring to the Southern textile strikes the Executive Council regards the recent "awakening of the South" to the need for trades unions as the "outstanding labor development of the last year."

Although the A. F. of L. and the United Textile Workers' Union have been attempting to organize the Southern mills for thirty years, only a small number of scattered organizations were formed, it was said. With the coming of the "stretchout" system, the textile workers were lashed into a realization of their need for unionism and "revolts" occurred in Tennessee, North and South Carolina and Georgia.

The report recites that the federation sent aid and organizers into the South to assist the strikers, but the chief responsibility for continuing the work now rests upon the international unions.

An appeal to the affiliated unions for further assistance will be made tomorrow by President Thomas D. McMahon of the United Textile Workers, who will offer a resolution to that effect.

"It is a most opportune time for all organizations to strengthen their unions in the South," the report continues. "The development of unions simultaneously with further industrialization of the South will assure sounder, better balanced progress. Permanent progress cannot be built

on low wages, long hours and special concessions.

Asks All Unions to Aid.

"The South has raw materials, American workers, power resources and a need for more industries. But unless these industries are prepared to give a square deal to workers they are not only pillaging the resources of the South but are sowing the seeds of class conflict in most dangerous soil. The Southern worker will not meekly bear injustice when experience teaches him standards of justice.

"We urge all organizations to include in their organizing plans for the coming year definite provision for work in the South. Organizing work in the South cannot stop until all industries are thoroughly organized."

The report dwells in great detail on the immigration problem and calls upon the convention to "take a strong stand" on the question. While the executive council last February declared in favor of suspending all immigration for ten years, it is now realized that such a drastic policy is impossible.

Therefore it is proposed that immigration from Europe be reduced one-half, admission to this country being extended to but 76,843 persons. Recommendation is also made that Mexico, Central and South America and the adjacent islands be placed upon a quota of 2 per cent, based on the census of 1890. This would admit 1,557 from Mexico instead of the thousands that cross the Rio Grande annually.

The council recognizes that the Secretaries of State, Agriculture and of the Interior are opposed to the quota application to Latin America, but points out that Secretary of Labor Davis favors placing Mexico under the quota law.

Calls Curb Imperative.

"The increased use of machinery with the attendant decrease in employment makes further restriction of immigration imperative, but whatever law is passed it must be accompanied by a provision for the employment of a sufficient number of border patrol to carry out the legislation," the report states.

It is pointed out that organizations of beet-sugar growers, cattle raisers, cotton growers, citrus raisers and others, in Arizona, California, Colorado, Wyoming, Texas and New Mexico have appeared before the Senate Committee on Immigration in opposition to the proposal to place Mexico under the quota law.

In this connection the report asserts that there are more than 2,500,000 Mexicans in the United States at the present time "and that half of them are here illegally," while 10,000 Mexicans enter the United States every year to work in the harvest fields alone, "and few of them return."

The amount of space which the report gives to the discussion of technological unemployment, discrimination against middle-aged workers and old age pensions is an indication of the emphasis that will be accorded these subjects during the next ten day.

Beginning with the statement that mass production can continue only so long as there is mass consumption, the report refers to the unemployment wrought by changes in technical skill and asserts that the problem challenges attention. The council says that irregular employment or unemployment is not confined to backward industries such as coal and

textiles but has also struck the automobile industry, which is in the forefront of technical progress.

While the automobile manufacturing companies have used every technical aid in sales and manufacture they are accused of "following most primitive models in their labor policies."

Pleads for Older Workers.

After pointing out that there were 500,000 fewer wage earners in the first six months of 1929, as compared with the same period ten years ago, the council discusses the difficulty of men displaced by machinery finding new places and of the discrimination alleged to exist against the employment of middle-aged and old workers.

The council has received reports which indicate that 45 years is the average deadline for employment and it is regarded as "ironical" that while medical science is seeking to prolong human life, industry "is establishing practices to restrict the productive years while society makes no provision for old age income."

The widespread discrimination against older workers is alleged by the council to exist in practically all industries and trades as well as in Federal, State and county governments.

The causes for such discrimination are said to be the introduction of private industrial old age pensions, workmen's compensation risks, group insurance and the pace set by the machine. It is asserted that the railroad, oil, rubber, automobile and steel industry refuse to employ workers who have reached the age of forty-five.

"Labor realizes it is idle to oppose technical progress, but we lament the fact that technical progress has been permitted to usher in human want and suffering, so that in the past some wage earners have in despair even tried to destroy machines," the report continues.

"Labor believes introducing machines without considering what the effect will be on employed persons and without planning to prevent hardships, is most regrettable and an unnecessary social and economic waste which retards progress.

"We believe that job analysis would disclose that younger persons are now exclusively employed for some jobs that older workers might perform equally well if not better."

Urges Federal Employment Body.

The remedy proposed to remedy the conditions set forth are the establishment of a Federal employment service which would gather data on employment and coordinate the placement work done by local bureaus and the establishment of municipal employment bureaus.

Quoting a study of old age pensions made for the federation, the council declares that private industrial pension plans are inadequate to provide for old age as the average man has but one to five chances in a hundred of remaining long enough with one firm to obtain the pension.

"Society cannot evade the problem and must provide either charity or an acceptable plan that respects independence and integrity," the report asserts. "Charity and pauper relief are most expensive methods socially."

Discussing State old age pension laws the council says that some State statutes leave the enactment of pension system optional with the counties. The council urges compulsory laws "requiring a pension commission for every county, paying a pension of at least $300 annually" with 65 years as the age of applicants.

Continuing, the report adds: "We believe that in the coming year, a model compulsory old age pension law should be drafted by the federation and recommend to State federations of labor as a matter of first order of importance. We should then inaugurate an active campaign for the enactment of such laws in every State."

Unions are cautioned not to install old age pensions without exercising the greatest caution and study.

In a section dealing with wages it is claimed that at least 5,000,000 wage earners are receiving less than $19 a week, and Secretary of Labor Davis is quoted as saying that, together with their families and dependants, there are "among us from ten to twenty million people who do not share as they should in the prosperity enjoyed by the rest of us."

Membership Is 3,433,545.

Secretary Frank Morrison's report shows a paid-up and reported membership of 2,933,545, an increase of 37,482 members in the last year. Adding the 500,000 members for whom per capita dues were not paid because of strikes or lockouts, the secretary's total figure for membership is 3,433,545.

A routine meeting of the executive council with President William Green presiding was held this afternoon. Mr. Green announced that the convention hall would be turned over on Oct. 16 to those organizations which will entertain Prime Minister Ramsay MacDonald. The latter has informed the Federation his engagements will not permit him to address the delegates.

At the executive council the subjects discussed were the amalgamation of the tobacco workers and the International Cigar Makers' Union and also the jurisdiction dispute between the Teamsters' Union and the Railway Express Union.

Seeks Funds for Work in South.

The American Federation of Labor is called upon to appropriate $1,000,000 for the purpose of organizing Southern textile workers in a statement issued yesterday by A. J. Muste, progressive labor authority.

Mr. Muste's statement declares that the situation in the South is at once a critical problem and a golden opportunity for organized labor, and predicts that the attitude taken by the Federation with regard to the Southern situation will have much to do with the future of that organization.

With the working week ranging upward from sixty hours, the average wage $12 per week, and "abominable living and working conditions," Mr. Muste says that the workers there are ready to fight and make sacrifices to improve conditions if they are provided with adequate leadership.

A. F. OF L. RESOLVES TO UNIONIZE SOUTH

Responding to Eloquent Pleas, Convention Approves Plan to Organize All Crafts.

CALLED ON TO END SLAVERY

The Leaders Denounce Textile Killings and Exhort Labor to Fight for Workers' Rights.

$1,000,000 FUND IS URGED

Green Names Finance Board of Three—Federal Council of Churches Pledges Cooperation.

From a Staff Correspondent of The New York Times.

TORONTO, Oct. 15.—Amid an outpouring of enthusiasm seldom equaled at similar conventions the delegates to the annual convention of the American Federation of Labor today responded to the call of the Southern textile workers and voted to help finance the movement in the South and to form plans for organizing the Southern workers regardless of craft or calling.

A committee on organization will be appointed by President William Green to meet within thirty days and to take steps to draw up comprehensive plans.

Following an appeal by President William Canavan of the Stage Hands' Union that $1,000,000 be raised, a committee of three was appointed to gather funds for use in the present emergency while the executive council was empowered to call upon the international unions for contributions to the "war chest" that will finance a long organizing campaign.

Eloquence Stirs Deep Fervor.

The delegates were moved by eloquent appeals calling for "a resurgence of labor's militant spirit." An almost religious fervor pervaded the assembly as speakers outlined the problem of the South as one that called for "sacrifices such as were made by the early Christians."

Speakers recounted the story of Elizabethton, Tenn., and of the recent events at Marion, N. C., where five textile workers were killed early this month. They also told the "stretch-out" system, characterized as "a crude and ignorant efficiency system" to whose introduction was attributed the wave of restlessness among the Southern textile workers.

Margaret Bowen, a thin slip of a girl, in a simple narration of the occurences at Elizabethton, Tenn., after she was "hired on" in the rayon mills last Spring, moved the delegates to outbursts of applause and the entire gathering of nearly a thousand men and women rose to their feet in tribute to the girl who was presented to them as a type of textile worker anxious for union organization.

Church Council Pledges Aid.

The discussion of the Southern textile situation was introduced by President Thomas F. McMahon of the United Textile Workers of America, who was followed by President Andrew Furuseth of the International Seamen's Union, W. C. Birthright, secretary of the Tennessee Federation of Labor; Matilda Lindsay of the Women's Trade Union League, Vice President Francis Gorman of the Textile Union, President Green of the A. F. of L. and James William Fitzpatrick of the Associated Actors and Artists of America.

A letter was read from the Rev. Dr. Worth M. Tippy of the Federal Council of the Churches of Christ in America pledging the cooperation of the churches to the federation in its plan of organization.

In his address Mr. MacMahon reviewed the history of union organization in the South in the last quarter century. He contrasted the average wage of $9.56 for a fifty-five-hour week in South Carolina with an average wage of $16.47 in Massachusetts for forty-eight hours and asked how men could bring up families on such incomes.

Furuseth Sounds Battle Call.

Mr. Furuseth declared that Mr. MacMahon's speech was "a fighting address" and urged complete cooperation with the textile union. He warned the delegates that in extending union organization to the South they would be faced by "the real thing" in injunctions and opposition, but he was confident that they would realize that the fight was one of all organized labor, not for the textile workers alone.

"You cannot have decent wages in the North until you have decent wages in the South, because these two sections of the country will compete with each other," he declared.

"This is part of the fight that from now on is going to wage bitterly through the United States and in the rest of the world. Big buiness, or the Third Estate, is in the saddle. It is going to try to liquidate every gain made by labor.

"We must be prepared to walk the same road as the early Christian martyrs and agitators. We must go through the same struggle to get freedom on the industrial field as we did to get political freedom. There is no question of mercy or consideration that will be accorded us now. Now is the time to go in and take the consequences of going in, and may God give us all the strength to do it!"

Plight of Southern Workers Told.

After referring to the kidnapping of union organizers by a committee "of bankers and business men," Mr. Birthright spoke of the recent shootings in Marion, N. C., and asserted that "murder is the order of the day, and people are being shot in the back by those who call themselves guardians of the law."

He predicted the defeat of Governor Horton of Tennessee by organized labor at the next election.

Miss Lindsay quoted the Southern textile workers as saying to her after the "stretch-out" system was introduced that they were "only asking for mercy."

"They have put a task on us which we cannot do," the strikers stated, according to Miss Lindsay, who added that the rate of pay at present is below that of five years ago.

She told of the mill villages where the workers were isolated from outside contact in unpainted houses built on stilts, where they were compelled to trade at the company stores and found themselves most of the time in debt to the mill owners.

"These people look to you for help and they know you will give it," Miss Lindsay said.

New Worker of South Hailed.

Vice President Gorman of the Textile Union asserted that the funeral of the victims of the "Marion massacre" marked the "passing of industrial slavery in the South."

"The union men were murdered not in defiance of law but while obeying the law," he continued. "Most of them were shot in the back while running away from tear gas.

"The Southern worker was docile because he has been the victim of a conspiracy for years. The industry has been built on the blood of women and children by forces they were powerless to combat.

"These forces do not want to see any one spread the gospel of light and hope. But a new day has dawned in the South. The new generation of young men and women are taking a keen interest in the organized labor movement.

"The entire South is watching Marion and Elizabethton. The people of the South are ready for organization and enrolment in the American Federation of Labor."

Miss Bowen said that when she was engaged to work for the rayon plant in Elizabethton she was promised $16 a week and was paid $10.08. Out of this she had to pay $5 a week for a room and board, sharing a bed with another girl; $1 a week for taxi fare and $1 for laundry. After many protests her wage was increased 1 cent an hour, to $10.64 a week, she said.

After describing the three strikes in Elizabethton, which, she asserted, were caused by the failure of the management to live up to its promises, Miss Bowen declared: "We people in the South may not be educated because we come from the hills, but our hearts and souls are with the labor movement."

Green States Labor's Aims in South.

President Green followed with a tribute to Miss Bowen's "sincere, eloquent and convincing address." He then read a telegram from Governor Max Gardner of North Carolina regretting that illness prevented him from addressing the convention.

Discussing conditions in the South, Mr. Green asserted that the charge that organized labor went to the South at the behest of Northern business to destroy Southern industry was untrue.

"We are in the South because it is awakening and because the workers appeal to us for help," he said. "In their extremity, victims of greed and injustice, to whom can they turn except to the labor movement? They cannot expect help from chambers of commerce, from political organizations or from civic and fraternal organizations."

In conclusion, he expressed the hope that the international unions would send their best organizers to the South and that this would be an answer "to those who say that for thirty years we have ignored the South."

Fund Committee Named.

Mr. Fitzpatrick, the next speaker, said he was glad to "witness again the resurgence of that crusading spirit which was responsible for the formation of the federation."

John P. Burke of the Pulp and Sulphite Paper Makers Union announced an initial contribution of $1,000 to the cause of organizing the textile workers, and Mr. Canavan of the Stage Hands Union proposed that affiliated unions contribute 35 cents per member, or about $1,000,-000.

President Green named Mr. Burke, Mr. Fitzpatrick and Mr. Canavan on a committee to raise emergency funds.

In his letter to the convention Dr. Tippy told of the work of the Federal Council of Churches in the South to help improve industrial conditions and of the "torrent of abuse" heaped on the council "from certain journals."

"Now the storm we saw coming has broken upon this area," he said. "While there are notable exceptions, the employers in this industry have shown that they cannot be left to correct these abuses alone. They have also demonstrated that the labor of the South must organize to protect itself and to lift its own standards of life."

CHAPTER 3

A New Deal for Labor

Walter Reuther and Richard Frankensteen
of the United Auto Workers after
a 1937 encounter with Ford's private police.

Courtesy Wide World Photos.

Major Proposals for Help in the Depression As Outlined by Labor Unions and Employer Bodies

U. S. Chamber of Commerce

1. Limited amendment of the anti-trust laws.

2. Establishment of privately sustained systems of unemployment benefits, based upon definite reserves.

3. The setting up of a national economic council.

4. Local as opposed to national efforts to find jobs for the unemployed.

5. A curb by commodity and security exchanges in manipulative speculation.

6. Every step possible that will lead to international disarmament.

7. Planning and execution of public works.

American Federation of Labor

1. Calling of a national conference of employers and labor on spreading out of jobs.

2. Immediate inauguration of the five-day week and shorter day.

3. Establishment of a national economic council.

4. Maintenance of wage structure and wage standards.

5. Guarantee to the employed that they will keep jobs.

6. Prohibition of child labor.

7. Long-range scientific plan to stabilize industry.

October 5, 1931

Main Points of Industry Bill

Special to THE NEW YORK TIMES.

WASHINGTON, May 17.—*Outstanding provisions of the national industrial recovery bill sent to Congress today by President Roosevelt follow:*

INDUSTRY CONTROL.

The President would have far-reaching authority to encourage, promote and require organization within private industry for better control of production, elimination of unfair competitive practices, relief of unemployment, improvement of standards of labor, "and otherwise to rehabilitate industry and to conserve natural resources."

To make effective this policy, the President would be empowered for two years to use any agencies and persons, public and private; to prescribe such procedure as he deemed necessary; to pass upon and virtually superintend "fair competition codes"; to compel, by use of fines, and if necessary a system of government licenses, enforcement of these codes and to provide himself a fair competition formula for industries which declined to initiate their own by agreements.

The President would be permitted to delegate the broad powers granted him "to such officers, agents and employes as he may designate or appoint."

May 18, 1933

SEC. 7.—(a) Every code of fair competition, agreement and license approved, prescribed or issued under this title shall contain the following conditions: (1) That employes shall have the right to organize and bargain collectively through representatives of their own choosing; (2) that no employe and no one seeking employment shall be required as a condition of employment to join any organization or to refrain from joining a labor organization of his own choosing, and (3) that employers shall comply with the maximum hours of labor, minimum rates of pay and other working conditions approved or prescribed by the President.

May 18, 1933

'YELLOW DOG' BILL SIGNED BY HOOVER

Special to THE NEW YORK TIMES.

WASHINGTON, March 23.—The Norris bill forbidding the issuance of injunctions by Federal courts against strikers without evidence of danger or injury to the interests against which a strike is directed and providing for jury trials where persons are cited for violation of injunctions was signed by President Hoover this afternoon.

Attorney General Mitchell, to whom the bill was referred by the President for an opinion as to its legality, held that, while the measure was in many respects not as clear as it might be, it merited executive approval.

The Attorney General's opinion, addressed to the President, said:

"Objections have been made to this measure because of the alleged unconstitutionality of some of its provisions, among which are those relating to contracts between employers and employes by which the latter agree not to be members of labor organizations and which are commonly called 'yellow dog' contracts.

"One of the major purposes of the bill is to prevent the issuance of injunctions to restrain third parties from persuading employes to violate such contracts, the theory of the bill being that such contracts are exacted from employes not with the idea that they will be treated by the employes as binding obligations but as a basis for invoking the old common law rule against malicious interference with contracts by third persons, and in this way to enable employers to secure injunctions against peaceful persuasion directed at their employes.

"There are various other aspects of the bill, the unconstitutionality of which has been debated. It seems to me futile to enter into a discussion of these questions. They are of such a controversial nature that they are not susceptible of final decision by the executive branch of the government, and no executive or administrative ruling for or against the validity of any provisions of this measure could be accepted as final. These questions are of such a nature that they can only be set at rest by judicial decision.

"Many objections have been made to the supposed effect of various provisions of this bill. In a number of respects it is not as clear as it might be, and its interpretation may involve differences of opinion, but many of these objections are based on extreme interpretations which are not warranted by the text of the bill as it was readjusted in conference.

"It is inconceivable that Congress could have intended to protect racketeering and extortion under the guise of labor organization activity, and the anti-trust division of this department, having carefully considered the measure, has concluded that it does not prevent injunctions in such cases and that it does not prevent the maintenance by the United States of suits to enjoin unlawful conspiracies or combinations under the anti-trust laws to outlaw legitimate articles of interstate commerce. It does not purport to permit interference by violence with workmen who wish to maintain their employment, and, fairly construed, it does not protect such interference by threats of violence or that sort of intimidation which creates fear of violence.

*March 24, 1932

MEDIATION BOARD WILL COVER NATION

Counted On to Avert Strikes and Lockouts During War on Depression.

HAILED AS GREATEST STEP

Functions Will Parallel Those of Labor Body Organized by Wilson in War.

Special to THE NEW YORK TIMES.

WASHINGTON, Aug. 5.—The National Board of Arbitration, approved today by President Roosevelt in a statement issued at his Summer home, was created today by the National Recovery Administration, after several days of conferences of the Industrial and Labor Advisory Boards.

Underlying the formation of the body was the fear that, unless some such organization was established during the war on the depression, strikes and lockouts would throw the nation back to the jungle method of adjusting industrial disputes. The board, consisting of seven outstanding leaders of labor, industry and the public, will conciliate, mediate and arbitrate disputes arising out of differing interpretations of the President's re-employment agreement.

Its functions will parallel those of another emergency labor body, the War Labor Board, which was set up by President Wilson April 8, 1918.

With a joint announcement of the two advisory boards, describing the establishment of the National Board of Arbitration and an appeal to labor and industry for a moratorium on disputes which would impede progress of the President's recovery program.

The advisory boards appealed to employers and employes "to unite in the preservation of industrial peace," since the objective of overcoming unemployment through nation-wide reduction in hours and increases in wage rates could only be reached "through cooperation on the part of all those associated with industry."

In announcing the formation of the board and its approval by President Roosevelt, General Johnson asserted that the new body's appeal was even more important than "the wartime appeal for harmony between capital and labor issued by Samuel Gompers, president of the American Federation of Labor."

"Strikes and lockouts at this time are idiotic and foolish," declared General Johnson. "This is an appeal for industrial peace which I am confident will be heeded by all sides. The purpose is to have labor, in asking for its rights, not to

New York Times Studio Photo.
Senator Robert F. Wagner, Who Heads the Board.

proceed by aggression, and industry, in carrying out its industrial policies, not to act arbitrarily.

"Machinery is here set up for the adjustment of industrial disputes in peaceful fashion. This is real progress."

He pointed out that the new arrangement provided for the establishment of central and local organizations whose function it would be to seek an adjustment of disputes and settle them. The national board would hear appeals.

Earlier this week the cotton textile industry established a board of three members, one each for labor and the industry and one appointed by the Recovery Administration, for the adjustment of disputes.

Similar machinery, it is understood, is provided for in the cloak and suit code, which received the approval of the President today and which will be made public in a day or two.

Other industries, from the smallest plants, mills and shops to the largest, are expected to follow the lead of the textile and cloak industries in an endeavor to adjust all industrial disputes.

The nucleus of such an organization for the soft coal industry was embodied in the agreement announced yesterday for ending the strike of 50,000 Pennsylvania soft coal miners. Machinery was set up for a national arbitration board of three members to hear disputes and grievances arising out of the terms of settlement. The members of the coal board are Gerard Swope, Mr. Kirstein and George L. Berry, president of the Printing Pressmen and Assistants Union of North America.

An attempt was made to have the first meeting of the national board of arbitration today, but several of the members were out of town. Some of the members met informally to discuss the setting up of an office and detailed procedure and machinery. Further discussions will continue early next week.

RIOTS BRING ORDER FROM LABOR BOARD FOR END OF STRIKE

Terms Fixed by NRA Agency After Minneapolis Deputy, a Manufacturer, Is Killed.

OTHER BUSINESS MEN HURT

5,000, in Second Day of Truckmen's Rioting, Batter 31 Special Officers.

Special to THE NEW YORK TIMES.

MINNEAPOLIS, May 22.—The Regional Labor Board tonight ordered a cessation of the truck drivers' strike following another day of rioting in which a prominent business man, acting as a volunteer special officer, was fatally injured by pickets and more than a score of others, engaged in similar service, were cruelly beaten.

The Regional Labor Board, after an all-day session, presented its ruling to the strike leaders and the representatives of the trucking firms. The decision, unless overruled by the national board, is mandatory on both parties.

The board ruled as follows:

Each firm is to bargain collectively with its employes, or with representatives chosen by its employes; members of the union may be selected as representatives without discrimination; there will be no discrimination against employment of union members; hours of work are to be governed by code provisions in each industry, and the present wage scale is to remain in effect for at least a year, the minimum wage for drivers being 50 cents an hour.

Regular Police Driven Back.

Uniformed police, armed with rifles, shotguns and pistols, made no use of their weapons as they were driven back by a mob of 5,000 in the rioting in the produce market district. After the strikers had wreaked their vengeance on the special policemen, most of them volunteers from business firms, a truce was called.

While the mob was holding unchecked sway and beating special policemen who had surrendered, the Regional Labor Board, meeting with leaders of the strikers and the employers, was expressing confidence that an agreement for ending the strike would soon be reached.

The man mortally beaten by the strikers was C. A. Lyman, vice president of the American Ball Company. Felled by pickets' clubs, he was taken to the General Hos-

pital, where he died of a fractured skull. Other special officers injured were Chester Lyford, sales manager of the Minneapolis-Honeywell Heat Regulator Company; Henry Carlson, assistant chief inspector of Minneapolis-Honeywell, and Peter Erath, a contractor. All are suffering from skull injuries which may prove fractures.

Today's outbreak came suddenly at noon when a group of strike pickets and sympathizers estimated to number 5,000 set out to drive the special police out of the produce market area, where they had been trying to protect the passage of trucks containing produce, of which many districts of the city have been in need for several days.

Reenforcements Called.

Efforts made by the regular uniformed police assigned to the district to stem the assault were futile. A radio call was broadcast ordering all squad and detective cars to the scene.

Meantime, outnumbered, the special police turned and tried to escape. Many were cornered in the stalls of the municipal market place and in corners of projecting buildings and beaten by ruffians armed with clubs and metal pipe. Some were battered, even after they had met demands to surrender their badges.

Twenty-five special deputies sent to the scene in a transfer truck by County Commissioner Arthur Ferrin were hauled from the vehicle and belabored with clubs and metal pipe. The strikers held complete command of the area for a half hour. Windows were smashed, and fruit crates were thrown into the streets.

Ambulances had such difficulty in making their way through the streets that police squad cars were sent out to succor the wounded. A detachment of 100 firemen was sent to help the police. Squad cars were driven into the mob with sirens screaming, and several combatants were injured.

Finally every available regular policeman was in the market area. But they were not needed then. The mob, having vented its brutality on the objects of its wrath, the special police, and driven them from the field, was content with its victory. Only a few regular policemen had sustained injuries. So, with their chief opponents in hospitals or physicians' offices, the leaders of the strike mob counseled their followers to remain peaceable pending the action of the Regional Labor Board, which had been meeting while the rioting was going on.

Truce Is Declared.

Leaving a picket line behind, the crowd left the scene of battle. A special conference was held in the office of Sheriff John Wall, with the aim of preventing further bloodshed, and a truce was agreed on. Present were Governor Floyd Olson, Adjt. Gen. Ellard A. Walsh, Michael Johannes, Chief of Police, and representatives of strikers and employers.

The truce provided that "all picketing shall cease on the one hand and that all transportation in so far as it concerns those represented by the employers' committee shall cease; that order for suspension of truck service shall not apply to delivery of newspapers, nor to the delivery of garden produce by farmers for sale to grocery stores or to the general public, nor shall it apply to the delivery of any commodities which heretofore have been permitted by pickets, including deliveries to hospitals."

The Chief of Police and Sheriff are asked to exercise their powers so as to bring about suspension of all traffic by truck in the city until twenty-four hours after an order is filed by the Regional Labor Board with reference to the pending strike. If the strikers and employers accept the conditions of the order prior to the expiration of such twenty-four hours, the suspension of traffic shall cease on acceptance of the order.

Lyman Well Known in East.

Ceylon Arthur Lyman was a native of Minneapolis but was well know in the East. Born in Minneapolis forty-three years ago, he received his education at the Hotchkiss School at Lakeville, Conn., and Williams College, Williamstown, Mass. He was graduated from college in 1913.

In 1916, when the National Guard was ordered to the Mexican border, Mr. Lyman enlisted in the Minnesota cavalry and served on the border throughout the period of the emergency. After the United States entered the World War, he obtained a commission in the Field Artillery and served overseas as a captain.

In 1921, he married here Miss Rosamond Coates. They had five children, four of them boys. He was active in the civic affairs of Minneapolis.

Associated Press Photo.

AN OUTBREAK OF VIOLENCE IN THE MINNEAPOLIS STRIKE.

Striking truck drivers armed with clubs, metal bars and pieces of pipe battling police. This photograph was made Monday. Yesterday the rioting resulted in a death and injuries to thirty-one policemen.

May 23, 1934

TWO SLAIN, SCORE INJURED, AS NATIONAL GUARD FIRES ON TOLEDO STRIKE RIOTERS

SHOTS HURL BACK THE MOB

Enraged Young Soldiers Level Rifles After Three Taunting Attacks.

TOLEDO, May 24.—Two men were killed and more than twenty-five persons were injured here this afternoon and tonight in two fierce battles between Ohio National Guardsmen and strikers at the Electric Auto-Lite plant.

Enraged by taunts and injuries, the troops fired two volleys in the first encounter this afternoon, causing the two deaths. About twenty were wounded, some by the gunfire and others by missiles.

The troops had laid down a two-hour barrage of tear gas bombs prior to using their guns, but hundreds of strikers and strike sympathizers had continued to rain brickbats upon them.

The shooting quieted the situation temporarily, but two more civilians were shot and two others were felled by bricks when guardsmen opened up with their rifles again after nightfall to repulse a crowd of rioters which began to surge toward the plant

Still another man was injured later, struck by a flying brick.

In the face of gas attacks and the possibility of more rifle fire, the crowd still hung menacingly in the area.

Soldiers arrested twenty-two alleged Communists, charged with inciting the mob to riot.

More Troops Ordered Out.

As a result of the disorder, Adjt. Gen. Frank D. Henderson ordered four additional companies of militia to Toledo, and said he was coming here to keep the Auto-Lite plant closed while negotiations for peace were going on.

Soon afterward officials of the company agreed to keep the plant closed pending settlement of the strike, and it was believed this would prevent further serious clashes.

Meanwhile, the adjutant general called a meeting of union officials, labor representatives and Federal arbitrators for tomorrow, at which it is hoped some agreement can be reached.

Charles P. Taft of Cincinnati, son of the former President, was deputized by the Department of Labor as a special mediator in the seven weeks' dispute, and arrived this afternoon to begin negotiations.

Shots Terrify Mob.

The rifle fire this afternoon, which struck terror into the mob and brought several of their number to the ground, climaxed a thrilling battle on Chestnut Street, a block east of the Auto-Lite plant, which was closed yesterday when strikers laid siege to 1,500 workers within.

Hundreds of gas bombs, both of the tear and the stench-producing variety, were fired into the jeering, cursing crowd. The troops stood their ground while a hail of bricks fell into their midst, until members of the mob began picking up and returning the gas bombs.

As the tear gas enveloped and blinded the troops the strikers advanced upon them, recovered their lost ammunition of broken bricks and forced a retreat to the walls of the factory, where reinforcements were waiting.

Twice the guardsmen were driven back and twice they regained their ground by bayonet charges with the aid of reinforcements.

When the mob made its third assault the troops were ordered to hold their position and fire. The first volley was directed above the attackers' heads, but, finding this ineffective, the infuriated young soldiers leveled their rifles at the mob and let go.

Those killed, said to have been onlookers, were Frank Hubay, 27 years old, of Toledo and unemployed, and Stephen Cyigon, 20, of

124

Rossford, Ohio, former Civilian Conservation Corps worker.

Half a dozen others were wounded by the shots, and the militiamen and spectators previously injured by bricks brought the casualties to about a score.

Gas Bombs Bring Lull.

A truck load of tear gas bombs was dispatched by a roundabout route to the intersection of Chestnut and Champlain Streets after the shooting, and enough of these were exploded to send up a blanket of the fumes reaching a block in each direction. This brought a temporary lull.

During the fighting the strikers and sympathizers mounted house tops with their bricks, took pot shots under signboards and came through alleys to make flank attacks upon the guardsmen.

Women and children crowded the front lawns and porches to watch the fighting, oblivious of the danger.

One woman was struck in the chest by a brick which knocked her insensible.

A youth on the side of the mob was hit in the mouth by a tear gas bomb and went to a hospital with an unrecognizable face.

At least ten guardsmen were injured by the bricks badly enough to be taken away in ambulances, and many others kept fighting with bloody hands or faces, lame ankles or knees.

Lieutenant Harry Comiskey, who stood in the centre of the front line, was continually warned by militia comrades to watch out for the bricks, but he disdained and told his men not to be afraid. At last he was sprawled by a blow in the temple and carried away in an automobile.

A few minutes later his brother John, a private, received a blow fracturing his kneecap.

The men in the mob shouted vile epithets at the troopers and the women jeered them with suggestions that they "go home to mama and their paper dolls."

There were at least 5,000 persons in and around the scene of the afternoon.

The 900 guardsmen arrived shortly after dawn this morning to lift the siege on the imprisoned workers. A night of violence had preceded their coming.

A chill rain was falling at this early hour, and the soldiers encountered no trouble in evacuating the 1,500 weary workers, who had been held in the plant for fifteen hours.

There were increasing rumors today that a general strike would be called in Toledo if the Auto-Lite Company attempted to reopen without negotiating with the United Automobile Workers Federal Labor Union, which is affiliated with the American Federation of Labor.

The Auto-Lite officials, whose company produces automotive starting and lighting equipment, insist they will submit the dispute to arbitration by the National Labor Board of the NRA, but will not negotiate with the United union.

The Auto-Lite plant has continued in full operation during the strike, since only two or three hundred employes were members of the union. It is an open shop, and J. Arthur Minch, vice president, says it will continue to be.

Union organizers at first demanded a general wage increase of 20 per cent, recognition of their union and seniority rights for their members. The officials declined to deal on such a basis, pointing out that they had increased wages from 25 to 32 per cent since the adoption of the Automotive Parts Code and were now paying within 10 per cent of the 1929 peak.

Mr. Minch and C. O. Miniger, president of the company, surrendered at the Safety Building today on a warrant charging them with maintaining a public nuisance.

The warrant was sworn by a resident of the area, who charged them with releasing tear-gas bombs which compelled him and his family to flee their home. The men were released on their own recognizance.

Louis Francis Budenz of New York City, national secretary of the American Workers' party, was one of those arrested yesterday for leading a picket line before the Auto-Lite Company. He will go to trial for contempt of court tomorrow morning.

May 25, 1934

Strike Developments

Major developments in the San Francisco and other strike situations yesterday included:

The general strike which began in San Francisco at 8 A. M. crippled the city's business and transit facilities, inconvenienced its population and increased fears of a food shortage, but only minor instances of vandalism and violence were reported.

Although the tie-up was expected to include the East Bay cities of Oakland and Alameda today, the general strike committee ordered employes of the San Francisco municipal transit lines to return to work, directed highway pickets not to interfere with food trucks, relieved the restrictions on restaurants and "eased up" generally in an effort to win public sympathy and avert bloodshed.

National Guardsmen, 4,500 strong, with tanks, light artillery and machine guns mounted at strategic points, guarded the troubled area from the docks to the produce section. Mayor Rossi charged Communist agitators were fomenting the crisis.

Under the auspices of the Mayor, a committee of 500 was formed to cooperate with the authorities in keeping the district open for the transportation of food.

With General Hugh S. Johnson momentarily expected in the city, the new National Labor Relations Board sent P. A. Donaghue, its chief examiner, there by airplane from Washington to assist in restoring peace.

United States Senator Robert S. Wagner left Newark by airplane for Portland, Ore., to try to avert a general strike there.

Minneapolis truck drivers went on strike at midnight.

Employes of two mills walked out to start state-wide Alabama textile strike scheduled to go into effect at 8 A. M. today.

July 17, 1934

The Dill-Crosser Railway Labor Act.

Before the President for Signature.

Amended the Railway Labor Act of May 20, 1926, by rewriting it and making several far-reaching and important changes in the Mediation Board and in the operation of the adjustment boards to settle grievances.

Created a national railway adjustment board, which will have four divisions, the members to be selected by the rail carriers and labor organizations.

Provided for the establishment of regional or system boards of adjustment, if the railroads and the employes desire to set up such boards voluntarily.

Abolished the present Board of Mediation, consisting of five members, and established a new and smaller board called the National Mediation Board, with power to select and appoint employes to act as mediators under the instruction of the board with the same freedom to delegate its work as the Interstate Commerce Commission now possesses.

Prohibited any carrier from providing financial assistance to any union of employes from funds of the carrier; prohibited the railroads from interfering in any manner whatsoever with employes joining or refusing to join any organization or union, and specifically provided that the choice of representatives of any craft shall be determined by a majority of the employes voting on the question.

June 19, 1934

ROOSEVELT SETS UP A NEW LABOR BOARD

Appoints Garrison, Millis and Smith, and Abolishes the Old Organization

NRA ROLE IS ELIMINATED

All Agencies Made Subservient to 'Impartial' Body in Handling Disputes and Elections.

Special to THE NEW YORK TIMES.

WASHINGTON, June 30.—President Roosevelt moved today to use the authority granted him by Congress to settle labor controversies throughout the United States, naming an "impartial" board of three to investigate and mediate disputes during the remainder of the statutory life of the NRA.

By an executive order issued at the White House Mr. Roosevelt took this essential function out of the hands of the NRA and General Johnson, transferred it entirely to the new board, working in conjunction with the Labor Department, and decreed the end of the present national labor board on July 9.

The President designated the new agency the National Labor Relations Board and to its membership he named Lloyd Garrison, dean of the Wisconsin Law School, chairman; Harry Alvin Millis, head of the Department of Economics at the University of Chicago, and Edwin S. Smith, present NRA labor compliance officer for Massachusetts. The board members are to receive salaries of $10,000 a year each and must devote all their time to its work.

In a statement accompanying the executive order, President Roosevelt said that his new move "establishes upon a firm statutory basis the additional machinery by which the United States Government will deal with labor relations, and particularly with difficulties arising in connection with collective bargaining, labor elections and labor representations."

As expressed by the President, his order creates "in connection with the Department of Labor, but not subject to the judicial supervision of the Secretary of Labor," a board with power to investigate, hold labor elections, hear complaints of discharged employes and act as a voluntary arbiter.

THE PRESIDENT'S STATEMENT

The President's satement follows:

The Executive order that I have just issued carries out the mandate of Congress, as expressed in Public Resolution No. 44, Seventy-third Congress, approved June 19, 1934. It establishes upon a firm statutory basis the additional machinery by which the United States Government will deal with labor relations, and particularly with difficulties arising in connection with collective bargain-

ing, labor elections and labor representation.

For many weeks but particularly during the last ten days, officials of the Department of Labor, the National Recovery Administration and the National Labor Board have been in conference with me and with each other on this subject. It has been our common objective to find an agency or agencies suitable for the disposition of these difficult problems, and after making such selection to make clear to the public how this machinery works and how it can be utilized in the interest of maintaining orderly industrial relations and justice as between employers, employes and the general public, and enforcing the statutes and other provisions of law that relate to collective bargaining and similar labor relations.

The Executive order creates in connection with the Department of Labor, but not subject to the judicial supervision of the Secretary of Labor, a National Labor Relations Board composed of three impartial persons, each of whom will receive a salary of $10,000 a year. This board is given the power to make investigations, to hold labor elections, to hear cases of discharge of employes and to act as voluntary arbitrator.

May Recommend New Boards.

In addition, the board is authorized to recommend to the President that in such cases as they deem it desirable, existing labor boards such as the industrial boards already created in the cotton textile industry or the petroleum industry, and such as the various regional labor boards, should be re-established under the authority of the joint resolution just passed by Congress and approved by me on June 19, 1934; and also to recommend that additional boards of a similar character should be newly created.

Whenever any regional, industrial or special board is established or created under the authority of the joint resolution it will report for administrative purposes to the National Labor Relations Board, but the decisions of the regional, industrial or special board will be subject to review by the National Board only where it is clear that such review will serve the public interest. Furthermore, the board can utilize and refer cases to suitable State or local tribunal.

The existing National Labor Board is by this Executive order abolished effective July 9, 1934, but the new National Labor Relations Board will have the benefit of the expert personnel of the old board and of such of the subordinate regional labor boards as it may deem necessary. The new board will have the advantages of the experience of the old board.

And I cannot let this opportunity pass without expressing publicly to the chairman and members of the old board my personal appreciation as well as the appreciation of the country of their unselfish and effective services during the difficult days of this last year.

One of the most important features of the new arrangement is that the National Labor Relations Board and all subordinate boards will make regular reports through the Secretary of Labor to the President. The Secretary will not

have any power to affect the proceedings, findings, orders, regulations or recommendations of these boards, but will serve as the conduit through which information reaches the President. In this way it will be possible to have a close acquaintance with the work of the board.

Economic Operation Sought.

Moreover, reports furnished regularly in this manner will be invaluable in the event that any permanent legislation is later contemplated and in developing a systematic knowledge of the general character of the labor relations problems in the United States of America, which must be justly and expeditiously handled. Duplication of work between the Department of Labor and these boards will be avoided and economy of force will be effected.

The very presence of this board and any boards it may authorize will have undoubtedly a salutary effect in making it possible for individual conciliators to arrive at settlements of local grievances promptly. Indeed it is my hope that so far as possible adjustment in labor relations and the correction of labor abuses can be effectively made at the source of the dispute without bringing the parties before national authorities located in Washington.

To accomplish this purpose and to eliminate other forms of confusion, it is provided that persons and agencies in the executive branch of the government shall not disturb the exclusive jurisdiction of the National Labor Relations Board and such other industrial, regional or special boards as I may, in accordance with the recommendations of the national board, designate or establish; and that all persons or agencies in the executive branch of the government shall respect the findings and orders of such boards. This rule is of universal application and includes within its scope all permanent and emergency governmental agencies.

This executive order, I believe, marks a great step forward in administrative efficiency and, more important, in governmental policy in labor matters. It meets the universal demand not only of employers and employes, but of the public, that the machinery for adjusting labor relations should be clarified so that every person may know where to turn for the adjustment of grievances.

Miss Perkins Hails New Board.

In the President's decree that when the National Labor Relations Board asserted its jurisdiction over a given dispute all other agencies of the government, "permanent and emergency," must keep hands off, observers saw the elimination of General Johnson and the NRA from the field of labor settlements.

Secretary Perkins expressed confidence that the new board, with its broad powers, would do much toward solving the difficult labor problems.

"When the new board takes jurisdiction of a case," she said, "not only are its findings final and not subject to review in the executive branch of the government, but also its jurisdiction cannot be disturbed by any person or other agency in the executive branch of the government. This will save confusion and make clear to what instrumentality labor disputes should be referred."

Miss Perkins said that Mr. Garrison will be able to serve only temporarily as he has received a three months' leave of absence from the University of Wisconsin. She said that the board might be supplemented from time to time by officials of existing special boards and by advisory panels drawn from the ranks of employes and employers.

The Secretary likewise praised the record of the National Labor Board, adding that in consultation with NRA officials, it was agreed that labor problems could be most effectively handled in connection with the Department of Labor.

Careers of Board Members.

Following are sketches of the members of the new board as given out by the Labor Department:

"Lloyd Garrison was born in New York and is a graduate of the Harvard Law School. He served in the navy during the war and later was associated with the firm of Root, Clark, Buckner & Ballantine in New York for four years. He organized the law firm of Parker & Garrison in 1926, was counsel of the New York City Bar Association for five years and was active in investigations on ambulance chasing and on bankruptcy. He served as special assistant to the United States Attorney General under the Solicitor General, participated in the study of bankruptcy upon which the New York bankruptcy laws are based and has been acting dean for the Wisconsin Law School for two years.

"Harry A. Millis is chairman of the Department of Economics at the University of Chicago, having been a professor there since 1916, and is widely known as a labor economist. He previously taught at the University of Arkansas, Stanford University and University of Kansas. He is a graduate of Indiana University. He was director of investigations in the Rocky Mountain and Pacifc States for the United States Immigration Commission in 1908-10; director of investigations, Illinois State Health Insurance Commission, 1918-19; chairman, trade boards, and chairman, board of arbitration of men's clothing industry in Chicago, 1919-23. He is president of the American Economist Association, is on the Chicago Regional Board and is a member of the Social Science Research Council.

Smith Served at Geneva.

"Edwin S. Smith was born in Brookline, Mass., and is a graduate of Harvard. He was a reporter on the Springfield and Hartford newspapers for several years after which he engaged on a business career, becoming a specialist in labor relations. He was for three years with the Russell-Sage Foundation in the Division of Industrial Relations, then became employment manager at Filene's in Boston. He was appointed by Governor Ely as Commissioner of Labor and Industries of Massachusetts in 1931 and was appointed by President Roosevelt as an observer at the International Labor Organization conference in Geneva last year. He has been Chief Labor Compliance Officer for Massachusetts under the NRA. He was one of the sponsors of the Massachusetts Minimum Wage Law and helped initiate the recent interstate compact. He served on the Massachusetts Special Commission Stabilization of Employment in 1931 and was chairman of the Industrial Disease Commission in 1933."

INDUSTRIAL TRUCE AT VANISHING POINT; LABOR SEES STRIFE

Union Chiefs Swing Away From President's Appeal, Holding Sec. 7A Is Not Enforced.

STRIKES PUT TO THE FORE

Labor Board Aid Is Admitted, Criticism Being Directed at Justice Department.

By LOUIS STARK.

Special to THE NEW YORK TIMES.

WASHINGTON, Oct. 31.—President Roosevelt's proposal for an industrial truce, made a month ago, has all but vanished because of a crisis which has arisen between organized labor and the government.

From a series of events, the last of which was the Justice Department's failure to present the Houde case to the courts, leaders of the labor organizations have reluctantly as well as regretfully come to a conclusion that the Roosevelt Administration has decided not to press for enforcement of Section 7A of the Recovery Act.

Organized labor is now well on the road toward deciding that it will pay less attention to the various labor boards and more to legislation and economic action; that is, strikes. There is no intention of abandoning cooperation with the labor boards, but from now on labor will feel less confident in the ability of these boards to obtain enforcement of Section 7A if labor agrees to forego strikes.

Hearing Unlikely on Auto Code.

Whether its conclusions are correct or not, leaders of organized labor are of the opinion that the government's handling of the automobile, steel and other cases indicates that there is grave doubt in administration circles as to whether the courts will sustain decisions such as that of the National Labor Relations Board concerning majority rule in industry.

The automobile code expires Nov. 3 and labor's demand for a public hearing before the code is renewed or modified or changed in any way will be refused, it was reported.

The industry is standing pat on its readiness to renew the code with its present provisions. General Johnson promised labor that as a price for its last acquiescence in renewing the code without change he would see to it that there would be a public hearing before the code expired.

In support of the view that the labor boards have perhaps reached the maximum of their powers in defining collective bargaining and building up precedents for handling Section 7A cases, the organized labor groups point to a series of decisions, chief of which is that in the Houde case. In these rulings the National Labor Board awarded recognition to the spokesmen for the majority; it excluded the closed shop agreement when made by a company union to evade the board's definition of collective bargaining; it ordered a company union disestablished and it ruled out individual contracts.

In two months the new labor board, under the guidance of Lloyd K. Garrison, now resigned, built up precedents intended to guide all regional boards in handling section 7A cases. At the same time it turned over the cases at issue to the Justice Department for prosecution. With the exception of the Weirton case, none of the alleged violators has been brought into the courts.

The notable lack of vigorous prosecution by the Justice Department of alleged violators of the collective bargaining provision of the Recovery Act is regarded by the union spokesmen as valid proof that after sixteen months of waiting for action from the government a definite decision has been made to refrain from proceeding against such employers.

Labor is therefore preparing to go to Congress for legislation outlawing the company union and for strengthening the agency designed to handle labor cases. This probably will mean the introduction of a bill similar to the defeated Wagner Trades Dispute Act.

The labor board set up under that act would have been empowered to initiate legal proceedings similar to such powers granted to the Federal Trade Commission and other Federal bodies. At present, labor is unable to proceed promptly against alleged offenders, for such cases must pass through the Justice Department, which the labor groups feel is unsympathetic to enforcement of Section 7A.

Before leaving for his home in Wisconsin several weeks ago the Labor Board chairman, Mr. Garrison, visited the Attorney General's office and is reported to have made vigorous representations as to the need for pressing the Houde and other cases. At first Mr. Cummings announced that there was not sufficient legal backing for such action. Later he said that the department still had the matter under advisement.

In cases involving disputes concerning collective bargaining in the steel industry, the National Steel Labor Board has sought to act as mediator and is said to have had considerable success. But the question of an election in the Carnegie Steel Company at Duquesne, Pa., is still hanging fire.

This case goes back to last February, when employees presented a petition to the Wagner National Labor Board requesting an election. The United States Steel Corporation refused to consent to an independent election supervised by the board, announcing that the company union rules had been liberalized to permit non-employes to be elected as officers. On May 1, the board ordered an election without fixing the date. Union spokesmen have insisted that an independent election be held, and some weeks ago this matter was placed before the new Steel Labor Board.

Labor's contention during the troubles last Spring, which threatened a strike, was that the NRA was "the National Run Around." The delay in the new governmental board's Carnegie case decision is causing increasing dissatisfaction among "rank and file" union groups, although this board is regarded as being strongly sympathetic to prompt governmental adjudication of Section 7a.

R. E. Desvernine, counsel to the Steel Code Authority, questioned the steel board's jurisdiction in matters such as those presented to it by the steel union.

Judge Stacy's Reply to Counsel.

At a recent hearing in Pittsburgh, Judge Walter P. Stacy, chairman of the board, replying to the steel counsel's statement, said that "if within the confines of the Constitution this board is a mere ghost flying around in thin air, the sooner we find it out the better."

On the same occasion, after the Steel Corporation counsel had summed up his argument against an election in the Carnegie mill, Judge Stacy remarked to him that "power is seldom surrendered; it is always taken."

"It was so at the first battle of Duquesne," he continued," and maybe it will also be so at the second battle of Duquesne."

When the National Labor Board was formed by Presidential edict in August, 1933, labor and industry were called upon to submit their disputes to the board. Prompt adjudication was promised. Labor asserts that it cooperated with the Wagner board but that that organization broke down because of its bipartisan character and its inability to obtain prompt enforcement of decisions.

The new labor board, according to the labor view, has speeded up decisions, but the result has been the same in the end, lack of enforcement of Section 7a cases by the Department of Justice.

Labor has had no success in its desire to have the President abolish the National Automobile Labor Board and substitute for it a statutory board of neutrals.

For these reasons, the coming months will be marked by intensive activity by labor on strikes and labor legislation.

2,500,000 WORKERS IN COMPANY UNIONS

Twentieth Century Fund Report Holds Them Inadequate for Collective Bargaining.

RAPID SPREAD UNDER 7A

From 1919 to 1932 They Added 896,000, While A. F. of L. Lost 800,000—Jumped Since 1933.

By LOUIS STARK.

Special to THE NEW YORK TIMES.

WASHINGTON, April 28.—The so-called company union is not an adequate agency for genuine collective bargaining, according to a report on this form of organization, part of a study of the government in labor relations, made public today by the Twentieth Century Fund.

The company unions or employe representation plans have increased rapidly since the war, and particularly since June, 1933, when Section 7a of the Recovery Act was promulgated, the report states.

The fund's staff estimated that about 2,500,000 employees are organized under company union plans, compared with a total trade union membership of 4,200,000, making a total of 6,700,000 organized wage earners, or 21 per cent of the 32,000,000 wage earners.

Between 1919 and 1932 the number of employes in company unions increased from 404,000 to 1,300,000 while the membership of the American Federation of Labor fell from 3,300,000 to 2,500,000 in the same period.

The report points out that where the trade union was unwelcome the employe representation plan or company union was presented as "the obvious substitute," indicating in most cases "an attempt to comply with a collective bargaining law and yet not bargain with a trade union." Nevertheless, it is added, company unions "often supply effective machinery for adjusting grievances and correcting abuses when none would otherwise exist," and "in this respect they afford the employe a means of protection which he can seldom achieve under conditions of individual bargaining."

Job Threat Is Cited.

The report cites the following as specific reasons for the failure of company unions to function as genuine collective bargaining agencies:

1. While many plans have guaranties against discrimination, company union representatives, being on the employers' payroll, are handicapped by fear that they may be discharged, disciplined or otherwise penalized by the employer if they are too aggressive. The vital necessity for an employe to hold his job makes it impossible for him to represent his fellow-employes as energetically, as wholeheartedly, with respect to those matters that

November 1, 1934

count most—hours, working conditions and, above all, wages—as if he were not dependent on the employer for his livelihood or were protected by an outside organization.

2. The fact that "all expenses of operating company unions are usually met by management, and that management furnishes without charge all the necessary facilities constitutes a link which tends to fetter the employe organization to management."

3. Company unions can rarely back up their demands by a strike threat. "There have been a few strikes in plants where company unions exist, but strikes must be financed, and where there is no treasury they can seldom be successfully conducted. Bargaining equality cannot be obtained where one party has disproportionate economic power. Frequent recourse to striking may be condemned, but the power, and not merely the abstract right, to strike when necessary is a prerequisite to an equitable bargaining relationship."

Isolation Is Stressed.

4. Bargaining representatives of company unions are usually chosen from their own ranks, though by the nature of their lives and occupations they cannot be equipped to contend successfully with the specialists hired by the employers. The trade union customarily can use agents outside the payroll of the company concerned who are bargainers by profession and can, in addition, hire its own outside experts.

5. Company unions have no direct contact with employes of other employers in the industry, which, "not only deprives company unions of the support of other workers and their organizations, but also increases their difficulties in bargaining because they cannot conveniently obtain first-hand knowledge of conditions throughout the industry in which they work."

6. Company union plans do not ordinarily lead to signed agreements for fixed periods of time, as do those under the usual trade union practice.

The trustees of the fund who authorized the study and appropriated the funds to carry it on, but who do not assume responsibility for the findings include: Newton D. Baker, Bruce Bliven, Henry S. Dennison, John H. Fahey, Edward A. Filene, James G. McDonald and Roscoe Pound.

April 29, 1935

ALL NRA ENFORCEMENT IS ENDED BY PRESIDENT AS SUPREME COURT RULES ACT AND CODES VOID

COURT IS UNANIMOUS

President Cannot Have 'Roving Commission' to Make Laws by Code.

NO INTRASTATE WAGE PACT

Indirect Effect of an Activity on Interstate Commerce Is Held to Be Insufficient.

PARLEY AT WHITE HOUSE

AAA Officials Also Plunge Into Study of Effect of Opinion on Farm Legislation.

By ARTHUR KROCK.
Special to THE NEW YORK TIMES.

WASHINGTON, May 27.—By a unanimous decision in the Schechter poultry case the Supreme Court today held unconstitutional the National Industrial Recovery Act, due to expire by limitation on June 16, and, by voiding the 750 codes which are the heart of the National Recovery Administration and denying the right of Congress or its agents to fix wages and hours in intrastate trade activities, demolished the chief administrative recovery weapon of the New Deal.

Immediate cessation of NRA code enforcement was announced by Chairman Richberg of the National Industrial Recovery Board following a conference at the White House in which President Roosevelt, Attorney General Cummings, Solicitor General Reed and Mr. Richberg participated. Mr. Richberg coupled with his announcement a plea to employers not to scrap the achievements in the field of fair practice and labor relations which had flowed from the Recovery Act.

The court, speaking through the Chief Justice, who read the passages vehemently, once more declared that Congress cannot give to the President or to private persons what Justice Cardozo, in a separate assenting opinion, called "a roving commission" to make laws in the form of codes or otherwise. Congress must specify standards and list objectives and provide a definite range of action.

But even when Congress has done that, said the court, its delegation of authority cannot apply to those engaged in intrastate industry, which was defined as any not "directly" affecting the current or flow of interstate commerce. The court specifically included mining, agriculture and manufacture.

Hour and Wage Rules Collapse.

Justice Cardozo pointed out that the attempted regulation of wages and hours was "the bone and sinew of the codes," and that therefore by the decision of the court they "collapse utterly." Since industry directly affecting interstate commerce is too small a group on which to base the NRA recovery plan, the theory and practice of NRA were killed by the decision, even though Congress should rewrite the law.

Realizing this, Congressional leaders at once took steps to substitute for the fallen code system such interstate trade regulations as those contained in the Black Thirty-Hour Bill and the Guffey coal legislation, and such labor wage-bargaining as is provided in the Wagner bill.

Government attorneys had been optimistic about the Schechter case and to them the decision was a bombshell. Donald R. Richberg and Solicitor General Reed, who had defended NIRA, left the court room with downcast faces. The Attorney General in his office stopped chewing a ham sandwich. The argument between the House and Senate over the time extension of NIRA and the terms thereof was temporarily laid aside. At the headquarters of Triple-A, which is administering some of the codes, the opinions were studied to determine whether they foreshadow the doom of that recovery experiment also.

Conferences were held at the Department of Justice, and then the Attorney General, the Solicitor General and Mr. Richberg were summoned to a late afternoon conference at the White House—the first of many—to ascertain what could be salvaged in the brief time remaining between today and June 16.

Regret was heard on all sides that the administration had taken the advice of those, among whom Professor Felix Frankfurter is prominently mentioned, who counseled delay in testing the constitutionality of NIRA until it was too late to reform ranks before the June doomsday. The once despised "chicken-killing" case had taken rank with McCulloch v. Maryland. General satisfaction was expressed that at last, in a grave matter, the court had been united in its opinion.

Foes in Congress Rejoice.

The many foes of NRA in Congress rejoiced. Senator Borah welcomed the new proclamation of the Constitution and Senator King "thanked God for the Supreme Court." Republicans pointed happily to what they called the vindication of Herbert Hoover's recent attacks on the recovery methods of the New Deal. At NRA headquarters officials and employes sat in gloom, wondering what is to become of them, and Washington landlords and restaurateurs, who have prospered from the influx of government workers, sadly examined their scales of prices.

Politicians noted with deep interest that on this same day the Supreme Court overthrew the Huey Long radicals who forced the Frazier-Lemke farm debt cancellation through Congress by declaring it unconstitutional, and reasserted the judicial independence of government commissions by holding that the President acted improperly in removing a Federal Trade Commissioner for causes not listed by Congress as bases of dismissal in the act creating the commission.

Labor was shocked, but rallied instantly behind the Black, Guffey and Wagner bills, determined to rescue some of its protections from the recent adverse decisions of the Supreme Court.

FACA Sends Up Cry for Help.

At FACA and the office of the special adviser to the President on foreign trade, as well as in other agencies set up by NIRA, the cry went to Congress, "Save us quickly or we sink." Simultaneously a band was forming in the Senate to let the hair go with the hide and, by obstruction and delay until June 16, to make of NIRA and all its works only a memory.

Conservatives in the administration recalled how they had opposed NIRA on two grounds when Senator Wagner, Raymond Moley and certain industrial groups proposed it: that economically from the viewpoint of recovery, it defeated its own ends by putting the cart before the horse in fixing higher wages and shorter hours before business had the increases to absorb their costs; and that the delegation of law-making to code authorities was unconstitutional. In this opposing group at the time were notably Secretary of State Hull and Lewis W. Douglas, former Director of the Budget.

The NIRB held a meeting. There was desultory discussion of what to do. Remedial legislation was proposed to meet the flaws discovered by the Supreme Court. Some one thought it might be well to press for a constitutional amendment. Then everybody agreed there was no use in talking until the White House conferences were concluded. The meeting broke up without any clear program. It reflected the devastation wrought by the accurate aim and propulsive force behind the judicial cannonade today.

Two Sections to the Opinion.

The unanimous opinion of the court—for the addendum by Justice Cardozo, with the concurrence of Justice Stone, was only an expansion of the theme on the point of intrastate wages and hours—was divided into two sections.

In the first the National Industrial Recovery Act was held invalid through the unconstitutionality of Section 3 on the ground that this section turned over actual lawmaking to individuals outside Congress without specifying conditions or setting metes and bounds. In the second section the court reiterated that the indirect effect of an industrial activity on interstate commerce does not bring it within the purview of the Federal Government; that the effect must be direct to validate Federal regulation.

At the outset of the opinion it was to be seen that the dictum of the Circuit Court of Appeals, in reversing the conviction of Schechters on wages and hours violations, had the attention of the Supreme Court. After reviewing the nature of the Schechter business, the opinion curtly remarked: "Defendants do not sell poultry in interstate commerce." The Supreme Court then devoted a thousand words or so to the history of the Live Poultry Code of Fair Competition and held in passing that "the requirement of 'straight-killing' (prescribing that a customer must take the run of the coop) was really one of 'straight selling.'"

The government, continued the court, had stressed the point that consideration of the code statutes "must be viewed in the light of the grave national crisis with which Congress was confronted." This is a tenable request, said the court, but the argument "cannot justify action which lies without the sphere of constitutional authority." As on previous occasions, the court pointed out that "extraordinary conditions do not create or enlarge constitutional power."

Holds Codes "Are Codes of Law."

The NIRA was not a device for voluntary effort, said the court. It did not merely offer privileges or immunities to trade groups, voluntary or otherwise. It was coercive law-making, for "the codes of fair competition which the statute attempts to authorize are codes of law." They are imposed both on those who approve and those who object to them and they carry penalties.

In the "hot oil" case, the court reminded the government it had recognized the need to adapt legislation to cover details of industrial activity with which Congress could not specifically deal. That Congress could lay down policies and leave to individuals the making of rules within these limits, and the determining of facts, the court agreed. But this recognition "cannot be allowed to obscure the limitations of the authority to delegate, if our constitutional system is to be maintained."

The NIRA case is distinct from the oil case, said the court, because in the former statute the subject of the prohibition—oil—was defined, and the only question was whether Congress had bounded the range of action delegated to the President. But in this case the question was whether Congress had adequately defined the subject itself from which the codes depended. The NIRA, from which flowed the codes of "fair competition," did not define what fair competition means. But the widest definition of that phrase in the law does not reach the objective of the codes. The very concept of NIRA took the codes far afield from that.

Trade Board Powers Defined.

In the law setting up the Federal Trade Commission, the expression "unfair methods of competition" was carefully written into the statute as within the commission's purview, and an accepted judicial process of determination was set up.

The NRA dispenses with this procedure and the subject matter of review and action as well. The government, said the court, had repeatedly referred it to Title I of the NIRA for definitions. But justification for the codes was not to be found there. "Rather the purpose [of Section 3] is clearly disclosed to authorize new and controlling prohibitions through codes of laws which would embrace what the formulators would propose, and what the President would approve, or prescribe, as wise and beneficent measures for the government of trades and industries in order to bring about their rehabilitation, correction and development," according to the policy of Section 1.

There is no dispute that the goal of NIRA was national recovery, and that was the purpose of each code, including the one before the court. But, asked the Justices, can any one contend that Congress can delegate its authority to trade groups so that they may enact any laws they consider essential to the recovery of their trade? Do they become legislative bodies because they know intimately the details of their own business?

"Such a delegation of powers," wrote the court, "is unknown to our law and is utterly inconsistent with the constitutional prerogatives and duties of Congress * * * Congress cannot delegate legislative power to the President to exercise an unfettered discretion to make whatever laws he thinks may be needed or advisable for the rehabilitation and expansion of trade or industry."

Groups Could "Roam at Will."

What fetters were there in NIRA? asked the *court*. Trade groups must be truly representative. They must not promote or permit monopolies. But they may "roam at will," under Section 1 and make into law "what is really only a statement of opinion as to the general effect upon the promotion of trade or industry of a scheme of laws." And the President may impose his own conditions in addition.

The court cited with approval the statutes creating the Interstate Commerce Commission, the Communications Commission and the flexible tariff powers of the President as properly-devised delegations of power, and approved the methods by which the statutes are carried out. "But Section 3 * * * is without precedent. It supplied no standards for any trade, industry, or activity." It permits code-making to prescribe them. The discretion of the President is unfettered. It is "an unconstitutional delegation of legislative power."

This ended the first division of the opinion, and the remainder was devoted to a discussion of what activities affecting interstate commerce fall within the right of Congress to regulate. In the Schechter case, interstate transactions ended when the poultry was trucked to the Brooklyn slaughter-houses for local disposition. Facts not disputed repel the argument that the poultry was in a "current" or "flow" of interstate commerce and therefore within the regulatory power of Congress. The poultry came to "a permanent rest within the State."

There must, said the court, be a distinction between the direct and indirect effect of transactions on interstate commerce. Each case must be settled on the basis of the facts, but the principle is clear. For instance, the negligence of an intrastate railroad employe with a safety device used in interstate commerce has direct effect. But when effects are indirect "such transactions remain within the domain of State power." Otherwise the Federal Government through the commerce clause would control all the activities of the people and the States would have no authority, save by Federal sufferance.

The hours and wages of the Schechter employes, said the court, were imposed on persons with no direct relation to interstate commerce. The government argued that these conditions affect prices generally. "But the government proves too much." If it can regulate intrastate wages and hours because of their indirect effect on interstate commerce, "it would seem that a similar control might be exerted over other elements of cost, also affecting prices, such as the number of employes, rents, advertising, methods of doing business, &c."

Once more the court emphasized the dictum of the Minnesota moratorium decision. "It is not our province to consider the economic advantages or disadvantages of such a centralized system. It is sufficient to say that the Federal Constitution does not provide for it * * *. Without in any way disparaging this motive [to effect recovery] it is enough to say that the recuperative efforts of the Federal Government must be made in a manner consistent with the authority granted by the Constitution."

On both points, therefore, the court reversed the convictions of the Schechters.

Cardozo Amplifies Opinion.

Justice Cardozo in the amplifying opinion said that NIRA gave the President "a roving commission to inquire into evils and on discovery correct them." This, he and Justice Stone agreed with the rest of the court, was unconstitutional. But Justice Cardozo recalled that he had dissented from the "hot oil" decision because there, in his belief, "no roving commission" had been granted.

The two justices concurred that codes of fair competition would be lawful which sought to eliminate unfair methods of competition, "ascertained upon inquiry to prevail in one industry or another," if the President is told to inquire into and denounce such practices. But under the NIRA code conception, when a code includes "whatever ordinances may be desirable or helpful for the well-being or prosperity of the industry affected," its function is not merely negative but positive, and this is "delegation running riot." Such power cannot be transferred. "The licit and illicit sections [of NIRA] are so combined and welded as to be incapable of severance without destructive mutilation."

But even if the Poultry Code had been adopted by Congress and not the President, said Justices Cardozo and Stone, it would be void because the defendants' employes were engaged in intrastate activity, and there is no Congressional authority over those. Since wages and hours are the very "bone and sinew" of the NIRA plan, to take these from a code is to destroy it.

"There is no opportunity in such circumstances for the severance of the infected parts in the hope of saving the remainder," wrote Justice Cardozo. "A code collapses utterly with bone and sinew gone."

May 28, 1935

ROOSEVELT SIGNS THE WAGNER BILL AS 'JUST TO LABOR'

It Is Important Step Toward Industrial Peace but Will Not Stop All Disputes, He Says.

MEDIATION NOT AFFECTED

President Explains New Board Will Act Only on Violations of the Right to Organize.

Special to THE NEW YORK TIMES.

WASHINGTON, July 5. — The Wagner Labor Disputes Bill, enacting into permanent law a Federal authorization for labor to organize for the purpose of collective bargaining, a definition of unfair practices, the creation of an organization to review disputes between employers and labor, was signed by President Roosevelt today.

The signing had been postponed several days in an effort to arrange a ceremony, but after it had been found impossible to get together all the leaders who sponsored the legislation, Mr. Roosevelt approved the bill at the White House this morning before going to the executive offices.

Later he hailed the measure as "an important step toward the achievement of just and peaceful labor relations in industry," but at the same time warned the public that "it will not stop all labor disputes."

He used two pens in signing the bill, directing afterward that one be presented to Senator Wagner, co-author of the bill with Representative Connery, and that the other go to William Green, president of the American Federation of Labor, who has called the bill the "magna charta of labor."

The bill provides Federal machinery for the adjudication of disputes over the right of labor to organize when "violation of the legal right of independent self-organization would burden or obstruct interstate commerce," the President announced.

Adjudication would be placed in the hands of a permanent National Labor Relations Board, to supersede the board carrying the same title which was organized under the National Recovery Act.

None of the personnel of the new board had been designated or even considered finally by Mr. Roosevelt, he said today.

The temporary board, the tenure of which was recently extended to Aug. 1, is expected to lapse immediately. Francis Biddle, chairman of the NLRB, who had announced he would leave office upon signing of the Wagner bill, called at the White House today to bid good-bye to the President.

THE PRESIDENT'S STATEMENT

Mr. Roosevelt's statement of the bill's purposes read as follows:

"This act defines, as a part of our substantive law, the right of self-organization of employes in industry for the purpose of collective bargaining, and provides methods by which the government can safeguard that legal right.

"It establishes a National Labor Relations Board to hear and determine cases in which it is charged that this legal right is abridged or denied, and to hold fair elections to ascertain who are the chosen representatives of employes.

"A better relationship between labor and management is the high purpose of this act. By assuring the employes the right of collective bargaining it fosters the development of the employment contract on a sound and equitable basis. By providing an orderly procedure for determining who is entitled to represent the employes, it aims to remove one of the chief causes of wasteful economic strife.

"By preventing practices which tend to destroy the independence of labor, it seeks, for every worker within its scope, that freedom of choice and action which is justly his.

"The National Labor Relations Board will be an independent quasi-judicial body. It should be clearly understood that it will not act as mediator or conciliator in labor disputes. The function or mediation remains, under this act, the duty of the Secretary of Labor, and of the Conciliation Service of the Department of Labor.

Seeks to Avoid Confusion.

"It is important that the judicial function and the mediation function should not be confused. Compromise, the essence of mediation, has no place in the interpretation and enforcement of the law.

"This act, defining rights, the enforcement of which is recognized by the Congress to be necessary as both an act of common justice and economic advance, must not be misinterpreted. It may eventually eliminate one major cause of labor disputes, but it will not stop all labor disputes. It does not cover all industry and labor, but is applicable only when violation of the legal right of independent self-organization would burden or obstruct interstate commerce.

"Accepted by labor, management and the public, with a sense of sober responsibility and of willing cooperation, however, it should serve as an important step toward the achievement of just and peaceful labor relations in industry."

It was pointed out here today that plans of many industries to test the constitutionality of the Wagner bill in the courts probably would be centred on the clause in the measure taht it "is applicable only when violation of the legal right of independent self-organization would burden or obstruct interstate commerce."

The automobile and steel industries are among the large employer groups expected to begin action soon against the new law.

July 6, 1935

HOW SECURITY BILL AIDS AGED AND IDLE

Pensions Will Be Paid to the Indigent, Crippled and Dependent Mothers.

STATES MUST JOIN PLAN

Employers Will Pay Payroll Taxes and Higher Paid Workers May Contribute.

Special to THE NEW YORK TIMES.

WASHINGTON, Aug. 14.—When the Social Security Board is named by President Roosevelt in a few days it will face the enormous task of administering an act designed to protect the American wage-earner "against the major hazards and vicissitudes of life."

Created as an independent organization, not subsidiary to or connected with the Labor Department, it will evolve administrative procedure and take on personnel which will, in a comparatively short time, probably rank as one of the largest in point of numbers among government departments.

The act provides for old-age pensions of two types, each of which will embrace large numbers of persons, although they will not apply to every one who reaches the age of 65, the point at which the bill states a person may be considered "old."

Free Pensions for Indigent.

The free pension provisions of the law, under which persons of 65 and over may apply for grants to be paid in equal shares by the Federal Government and the State will be reserved exclusively for indigent persons without other income or means of support.

In some cases partial pensions may be given to old people who have an income not large enough to sustain them, but at all events payments from the public funds will be only of a character necessary to sustain the aged needy.

The second type of pension will consist simply of an annuity plan sponsored by the government, under which workers may be pensioned at the age of 65, payments being made to them from a fund built up by joint contributions of employers and employes. Contributing workers will receive such earned annuities regardless of other income.

There will be no pensions for the large mass of persons who are ineligible to receive benefits from the workers' pension fund and who reach 65 with some other means of support.

Workers who may be unemployed will receive benefits paid to them only in those States which have adopted unemployment insurance schemes. They will not benefit from the National Security Law if they live in States that have no State job insurance laws.

All Must Pay Tax.

However, employers in the latter States will be compelled to pay 3 per cent of their payrolls into the Treasury and this will be lost to them if they fail to enact unemployment insurance laws. Such forfeiture is expected to stimulate passage of the necessary laws in every State.

If they pay into State job insurance funds, the employers would get credit for such payments not exceeding 90 per cent of the Federal tax.

The law also provides assistance to the States in taking care of their dependent unemployables, such as the blind, physically disabled, mothers and destitute or neglected children.

Inasmuch as Congress refused to place the administration of the Security Law in the Department of Labor, the problem of administration will take on a more difficult aspect than confronts those nations with similar laws.

In England and elsewhere payment of unemployment insurance is made through the Labor Ministry, which has direction of a nation-wide system of employment exchanges. Under the Wagner-Peyser act passed two years ago there has been created in the United States a national system of employment exchanges which honeycomb the country.

The law creating this employment exchange system was passed in expectation of the ultimate passage of an act along the lines of that signed today by the President.

It was expected that the unemployed would register at Federal-State employment offices which would certify to the period of idleness, after which the applicants would go to another window in the same room or in an adjoining room or building where his unemployment check would be made out.

Cooperation Is Planned

Since the Social Security Board is an independent body, the problem of arranging for an efficient method of certifying the idle employe's books will be wholly in the province of that board, and a method different from that prevailing in other countries for handling payments may have to be evolved.

The old-age section of the law is divided into two parts: old-age assistance and compulsory contributory pensions.

States that follow standards set up in the law will receive half of the old-age pension payments provided that after 1940 all over 65 who require this form of relief shall receive it. Up to that time the age limit will be 70.

The government will not pay its 50 per cent share on pensions above $30 a month. On these it will pay $15 a month.

Some thirty-one States have old-age pension laws on their books but not all of them are paying pensions, due to delay in making appropriations.

The law requires that a State pension act, to be recognized for the purpose of the Federal appropriation, may not have a State residence requirement for the applicant exceeding five years in the last nine years.

The old-age assistance law which grants free pensions to the aged indigent is designed for the working man who has passed his period of employment and who is destitute, living possibly in an almshouse.

Supporters of the measure hope that in time all wage-earners in the nation will be protected under the second old-age section of the law, that covering contributory old-age pensions. This section provides for an annuity when a worker reaches the age of 65 after he and his employer or employers have made joint payments into the "old-age fund."

Payments into this fund begin on Jan. 1, 1937. The payment will be 1 per cent of the payrolls jointly for three years, and it will be increased gradually each three years until the total joint payments reach 3 per cent of the payrolls.

All industrial wage-earners will be expected to make contributions to the fund, no matter what their income. But the payroll deductions will cover only that part of their income up to $3,000. So that a $10,000-a-year man will be entitled to an annuity covering his contributions made up to $3,000 of his salary.

Pensions will vary in amount with the period of employment and the monthly salary. They may be from $17.50 to $81.25 a month. Thus a man with an average salary of $50 a month, with ten years of contributions, will receive $17.50 and this will increase to $32.50 after forty years of payments.

A man with an average monthly salary of $250 and ten years of payments would receive a monthly pension of $37.50, and $81.25 if he had paid contributions for forty years.

Lump sum payments will be made to estates of beneficiaries based on a return of payments together with the interest.

Under the unemployment insurance section of the law States may enact insurance laws to conform to certain standards. Funds to be paid to the unemployed will come from a payroll-excise tax paid to the Federal Treasury solely by the employers. Unlike the contributory pension scheme, the unemployment insurance arrangement is not a joint participating plan.

After Jan. 1, 1936, employers of eight or more persons will pay an amount equaling 1 per cent of their payrolls into the fund. They will pay 2 per cent in 1937 and 3 per cent in 1938 and subsequent years.

Wide latitude is allowed to the States in formulating unemployment insurance plans. States that enact such laws will be reimbursed up to 90 per cent of the payments made by employers in those States.

An unemployed man will not be denied his compensation on the ground that he refused to take a job when a strike is being conducted, or when the job offered to him provides for terms less favorable than those prevailing in the locality, or on condition that he must join a company union or refrain from joining any other organization.

There is no indication as to how much benefit an unemployed man may obtain under the State unemployment insurance laws, because these will vary with the State. New York State provides that after a three-weeks' waiting period an unemployed worker will receive insurance benefits up to $15 a week for a maximum period of sixteen weeks. Wisconsin provides a maximum of $10 for ten weeks.

The law creates a system of Federal aid for the care of the blind, for the medical care of crippled children, aid to homeless and neglected children and aid to dependent children.

An immediate outlay of $95,000,000 is authorized for benefits and administration purposes. The long-range provisions, such as old-age pensions and unemployment insurance, are expected to be self-financing.

August 15, 1935

MINIMUM WAGE LAW CONSTITUTIONAL

A 5-TO-4 DECISION

Washington Law Akin to Voided New York Act Is Sustained

ADKINS RULING REVERSED

Hughes Reads Opinion—Sutherland, Van Devanter, Butler and McReynolds Dissent

By TURNER CATLEDGE
Special to THE NEW YORK TIMES.

WASHINGTON, March 29.—By a 5-to-4 decision, the numerical division by which it struck down the New York Minimum Wage Law for Women and Children last June, the Supreme Court today held constitutional a similar statute of another State, the Minimum Wages for Women Act of the State of Washington.

But while the numerical division was the same, the line-up was changed. Justice Owen J. Roberts switched from the "conservative" to the "liberal" side and turned what for fourteen years had been a minority view, into the controlling opinion of the court.

Justice Roberts found sufficient reason today to join with Chief Justice Hughes and Justices Brandeis, Stone and Cardozo in validating the Washington act, leaving Justices Sutherland, Van Devanter, McReynolds and Butler, with whom he had acted in overthrowing the New York law, powerless to do anything but issue a vehement dissent.

Reports of the court's decision, rushed to the Senate floor by a messenger, found that body engaged in a heated debate over President Roosevelt's judiciary reorganization program. Breaking into the discussion to tell the Senate what had happened, Senator Robinson shouted that the Supreme Court had "reversed" itself.

Other States' Wage Laws Spared

Not only did the decision settle the constitutionality of the 24-year-old Washington statute, but it expressly reversed the basis upon which the New York law had been invalidated and the minimum wage laws of fifteen other States jeopardized.

That basis was the decision in the Adkins case, long considered a barrier against the fixing by Congress of minimum wages for women in Federal jurisdiction, and cited as the controlling factor in the adverse opinion in the New York case, even though the latter involved a State law. Senator Robinson told the Senate that the reversal on the Adkins case probably validated the New York case law, which was ruled unconstitutional ten months ago.

In the Adkins case the Supreme Court invalidated a minimum wage law for women enacted by Congress for the District of Columbia, a strictly Federal territory. In view of this new ruling of the court, Elwood Seal, Corporation Counsel for the District of Columbia, held tonight that the old law, which was in effect from 1919 to 1923, "is fully effective" and began preparations to re-establish the Minimum Wage Board which administered it.

The court's opinion today, read to a packed court room by Chief Justice Hughes, said specifically:

"Our conclusion is that the case of Adkins vs. Children's Hospital should be and is overruled."

The opinion pointed out that in the New York case the court had not been asked to overthrow the Adkins decision, and therefore could not, while in the Washington case it had been made a vital point by the refusal of the State Supreme Court, in its decision upholding the validity of the statute, to consider the Adkins case as controlling.

Doubt Effect on Congress Fight

With the disclosure of this new attitude of the court on State powers in dealing with industrial reform legislation, speculation sprang high as to its probable influence on President Roosevelt's plan to remake the tribunal with more "liberal" members.

The prevailing opinion was that there was little net effect; that while some of the President's chief reasons for wanting a remodeled court were discounted by the inherent liberality of the decision, the circumstances by which it was brought about, specifically the switch of one justice, added strength to the argument against 5-to-4 decisions.

Removing the Adkins decision from its pathway, the majority of the court said in its opinion that the essential question remaining was whether the need for protecting women by minimum wage standards was sufficiently in the public interest to outweigh the arguments of deprivation of property without due process of law, if set up in the exercise of a State's police powers.

The opinion pointed out that present-day social conditions, which must be considered in reaching a decision, required the "protection of law against the evils which menace the health, safety, morals and welfare of the people."

Close to the 'Public Interest'

"What can be closer to the public interest," the majority then asked, "than the health of women and their protection from unscrupulous and overreaching employers? And if the protection of women is a legitimate end of the exercise of State power, how can it be said that the requirement of the payment of a minimum wage fairly fixed in order to meet the very necessities of existence is not an admissible means to that end?"

The dissenting justices demurred to this line of reasoning. In their opinion, read by Justice Sutherland with an emphasis in striking contrast to his usual placidity, they insisted that the pressure of economic conditions did not change the meaning of the Constitution, the due process provisions of which they construed the minimum wage law to contravene.

Furthermore, the dissenting opinion saw no impelling reason why the Legislature should discriminate between men and women in enacting laws restricting the right to bargain for wages.

Discussion of the case at issue was prefaced by the dissenting justices with an extended discourse on the powers and duties of the Supreme Court in passing upon acts of Congress and the States. They contended the Constitution made it

clear that the court was intrusted with the power to determine cases arising within its jurisdiction, "and so long as the power remains there, its exercise cannot be avoided without betrayal of a trust."

"Reasonable Doubt" Issue Raised

The minority opinion discussed, too, the question of the court's rule of resolving all "reasonable doubt" in favor of the legislative branch, which has been raised in recent discussions on the court's activities. The dissenters concluded that a justice's responsibility in deciding a case was upon him and no one else, that his oath was an "individual" oath and not a "composite" one, and that the question of "reasonable doubt" was personal to the justice himself.

This was construed by observers as being in answer both to the arguments of Justice Stone in recent minority opinions of the court, and to certain contentions made by witnesses sponsoring the President's court reorganization before the Senate Judiciary Committee.

As to the Washington minimum wage case, the dissenting justices contended that it violated that section of the Fourteenth Amendment prohibiting States from passing acts depriving citizens of property without due process of law, in that it deprived women workers of freedom of contract—of their right to bargain freely for their labor, without restraint as to the amount they should receive.

Washington Woman Fought Case

The case which brought about this new alignment of the court and the speculation that revolved around it tonight originated with Elsie Parrish, a chambermaid in a hotel at Wenatchee, Wash.

Mrs. Parrish worked in the hotel intermittently from August, 1933, until May, 1935. When her job was ended $17 was offered to her in final settlement for her services, but she and her husband knew that a State board, acting under the State Minimum Wages for Women Law passed in 1913, had fixed $14.30 a week as the minimum for her work. She and her husband sued in the State court for the difference of $216, which she contended was due her under that scale.

After losing in the county court, they appealed to the Washington State Supreme Court, which upheld the law and ordered payment. The West Coast Hotels Company appealed to the United States Supreme Court, and the State of Washington through its attorneys intervened in defense of its law. The decision today affirmed the judgment of the Washington State Supreme Court.

Early in the prevailing opinion Chief Justice Hughes said that the Washington case had necessitated a re-examination of the Adkins decision. He pointed out quickly, moreover, that the New York minimum wage case had come to the Supreme Court on the contention of attorneys for the State that it was distinguishable from the Adkins case, not that this latter suit had been decided erroneously when it was determined on a 5-to-3 decision in 1923.

Way to Reconsideration Is Seen

"We think that the question which was not deemed to be open in the Morehead (New York mini-

mum wage) case is open and is necessarily presented here," read the Chief Justice.

Amplifying his reasons, the Chief Justice said that the importance of the pending question, in which many States are concerned by virtue of similar laws, the close division by which the Adkins decision was reached in the first instance, and "the economic conditions which have supervened, and in the light of the reasonableness of the exercise of the protective power of the State must be considered, make it not only appropriate, but we think imperative, that in deciding the present case the subject should receive fresh consideration."

Mr. Hughes said there was no doubt on the question of principle involved. The due process clause of the Fourteenth Amendment governed the States just as the due process clause of the Fifth Amendment governed Congress. In both the Adkins case and the pending case, the violation alleged by those attacking minimum wage regulation for women was that it deprived them of the freedom of contract.

As to the Freedom of Contract

"What is this freedom?" asked the Chief Justice, reading the opinion for himself and colleagues. "The Constitution does not speak of freedom of contract. It speaks of liberty and prohibits the deprivation of liberty without due process of law. In prohibiting that deprivation, the Constitution does not recognize an absolute and uncontrollable liberty. Liberty in each of its phases has its history and connotation. But the liberty safeguarded is liberty in a social organization which requires the protection of law against the evils which menace the health, safety, morals and welfare of the people."

The Chief Justice cited former language of the court to support the contention that the State had a direct interest in its citizens, their welfare and protection. "The whole is no greater than the sum of all the parts and when the individual health, safety and welfare are sacrificed or neglected, the State must suffer," he quoted from Holden v. Hardy, decided, as he said, nearly forty years ago.

"We emphasize the need for protecting woman against oppression despite her possession of contractural rights," the Chief Justice said.

He quoted from the late Justice Holmes, who dissented in the Adkins case, to the effect that the statute in question did not compel anybody to do anything; and from the late Chief Justice Taft, who also dissented, upholding the justice and the validity of such laws.

Women's Position a Factor

The court held that the Legislature of the State was clearly within its proper sphere when considering the situation of women in employment, "the fact that they are in the class receiving the least pay, that their bargaining power is relatively weak, and that they are the ready victims of those who would take advantage of their necessitous circumstances."

It held that the Legislature was entitled to adopt measures to reduce the evils of the "sweating system," the exploiting of workers at wages so low as to be insufficient to meet the bare cost of living, "thus making their very helpless-

ness the occasion of a most injurious competition."

The Legislature had the right, the majority decision said, to consider that its minimum wage requirements would be an important aid in carrying out its policy of protection. The adoption of similar requirements by many of the other States was cited as evidence of a "deep-seated conviction both as to the presence of the evil and as to the means adopted to check it."

"Legislative response to that conviction cannot be regarded as arbitrary or capricious and that is all we have to decide," read the Chief Justice. "Even if the wisdom of the policy be regarded as debatable and its effects uncertain, still the Legislature is entitled to its judgment."

Burden on Community Cited

The court said there was an additional "and compelling" consideration which recent economic experience had brought strongly into light—the exploitation of a class of workers who are in an unequal position with reference to bargaining power "and are thus relatively defenseless against the denial of a living wage."

The decision held that this was not only detrimental to the health and well-being of the workers themselves but cast a direct burden for their support upon the community.

"What these workers lose in wages, the taxpayers are called upon to pay," said the court.

The relief load, carried even now in the midst of evidences of recovery, was pointed out.

"The community is not bound to provide what is in effect a subsidy for unconscionable employers," the opinion said.

The majority recalled that the court had frequently held that the legislative authority, acting within its proper field, was not bound to extend its regulation to all cases which it might possibly reach. It is free to recognize degrees of harm and restrict its remedies to classes and groups as it sees fit.

Quoting a former decision of the court, the opinion said:

"If 'the law presumably hits the evil where it is most felt, it is not to be overthrown because there are other instances to which it might have been applied.'"

Sutherland Reads Dissent

Almost half of the dissenting opinion, as read by Justice Sutherland, was taken up with a discussion of the general constitutional problem. To this extent it might have been taken as an answer to many of the attacks on the present judicial system as made over the radio, in Congress and before its committees by proponents of the President's plan for judiciary reorganization.

The dissenters upheld the right of the Supreme Court to pass upon the constitutionality of acts of Congress coming within its jurisdiction, and emphasized the duty of a justice to vote according to his own convictions. A justice cannot subordinate his convictions and refuse to pass upon a constitutional question and keep faith with his oath "or retain his judicial and moral independence."

Specifically, answer was given to the suggestion, made by certain

Supreme Court justices themselves and repeated in the debate now raging over the court problem, that the only check upon the exercise of judicial power is a judge's own faculty of self-restraint. This suggestion, said the minority opinion, "is both ill considered and mischievous."

Meaning of Basic Law Stands

Taking up the point emphasized by the court majority, that the question involved should now receive fresh consideration because of economic conditions that have intervened, the minority said that "the meaning of the Constitution does not change with the ebb and flow of economic events."

They urged that if the Constitution stands in the way of desirable legislation, "the blame must rest upon that instrument and not upon the court for enforcing it according to its terms."

"The remedy in that situation—and the only true remedy—is to amend the Constitution," said the minority opinion.

Coming finally to the Washington case, the dissenting justices held that if the Adkins case was properly decided, as they insisted it was, it necessarily followed that the Washington statute was invalid. They termed the law exclusively one fixing wages for adult women, "who are legally as capable of contracting for themselves as men," and held that it would not be sustained unless upon principles apart from those involved in cases already decided by the court.

They contended that the sole basis upon which the question of validity of the act rested was the assumption that the employe is entitled to receive a sum of money sufficient to provide a living for her, keep her in health and preserve her morals, a question, which they insisted, could not be determined by any general formula prescribed by a statutory board.

Differ on Freedom of Contract

Furthermore, the minority contended that the clause of the Fourteenth Amendment forbidding a State to deprive any person of life, liberty or property without due process of law includes freedom of contract—a principle "so well settled as to be no longer open to question."

"Nor reasonably can it be disputed that contracts of employment of labor are included in the law," said the opinion.

The dissenters added that the law failed to recognize the rights of the employer and failed to distinguish between the "great and powerful" employer and him of weak bargaining power.

They construed as "significant and important" the fact that all State statutes to which the court's attention had been called referred to women employes, and left adult men and their employers free to bargain as they please.

"The common-law rules restricting the power of women to make contracts have, under our system, long since practically disappeared," said the minority opinion. "Women today stand upon a legal and political equality with men. There is no longer reason why they should be put in different classes in respect of their legal right to make contracts; nor should they be denied, in effect, the right to compete with men for work paying lower wages which men may be willing to accept."

The minority quoted copiously from the prevailing opinion in the New York minimum wage case, contending that the language was exactly applicable in the present case. They contended finally that fixing of wages by public authority, if followed to its final conclusion, would abrogate completely the right of contract so far as wages are concerned.

News Conveyed to the Senate

When word of the court's decision, and the fact that the former majority opinion holding States unable to enact minimum wage laws had been overturned, reached the Senate, Senator Wheeler of Montana was on his feet answering an attack upon the court by Senator McKellar.

Senator Robinson interrupted to refer to what the court had done. Swinging both fists above his head to emphasize his point, Senator Robinson said:

"I would like to refer to the fact that the Supreme Court has reversed itself in the Adkins case and probably in the New York wage case."

"I am sure the Senator from Arkansas is delighted because they did it," put in Senator Wheeler.

"Certainly, I am delighted," Senator Robinson replied.

Continuing for a moment, Senator Robinson read the concluding remarks of the court in its prevailing opinion today, expressly reversing itself in the Adkins case.

"Fine," interjected Senator Wheeler.

"Yes, fine," shouted Senator Robinson, "but what happens to the thousands of women and children in the great State of New York who are compelled to work unlimited hours in sweat shops and in factories on the basis of the decision resting on the Adkins case? The basis of the decision in the Tipaldo case ought to be reconsidered and reversed."

Glad Court Has "Faced About"

"Let me say to the Senator from Arkansas," Mr. Wheeler put in, "that I am sure he is very happy that the Supreme Court has seen the light with reference to this case."

"I was made miserable when the Supreme Court decided that Congress could not fix maximum hours of labor and minimum wages for women and children workers in the District of Columbia," Mr. Robinson replied.

"I was made more unhappy when, following that precedent, the Supreme Court said that the New York State law-making power could not do it in the State of New York. I am glad that the Supreme Court has completely faced about and recognized the necessity of overruling its former decision.

"Mr. President, talk about accepting in all cases Supreme Court decisions as binding and being above question! Here is a case where the minority opinion at last after many years becomes the majority opinion."

March 3, 1937

SUPREME COURT UPHOLDS WAGNER LABOR LAW; UNIONS SEE SWEEPING PROGRESS WITHIN A YEAR

FIVE CASES DECIDED

Three Apply Commerce Clause to Manufactures First Time

By ARTHUR KROCK

WASHINGTON, April 12.—For the first time in American history, industries organized on a national scale, though their products are locally manufactured, were held by the Supreme Court today to come specifically within the regulatory powers of the Congress. The court modernized the commerce clause of the Constitution to this degree when it upheld the National Labor Relations (Wagner) Act in four cases by a vote of 5 to 4, upholding a fifth unanimously.

The effect of the momentous decisions was electric, particularly since far narrower rulings had been expected in the manufacturing cases. Organized labor, affirmed in the right of union organization, affiliation and collective bargaining with large industry, moved to consolidate its victory.

The political community fell to instant argument over the question whether now the President's judiciary bill should be withdrawn. Another group, noting a passage written by the Chief Justice in one of the decisions, began to plan a Wagner act companion in behalf of the employers.

There was a general feeling that since the decisions today removed the factor of uncertainty about the Wagner act as a justification of the sit-down strike, the country might reasonably expect organized labor to abandon that device.

Look to Security Act Ruling

Government officials, concluding that the industrial powers of Congress are now widely established, expressed the hope that its taxing powers would be equally broadened by the new Supreme Court majority in the forthcoming decision on the Security Act. The President indirectly revealed his jubilation in a telephone message to Speaker Bankhead, congratulating him on his birthday, and adding: "It's been a pretty good day for all of us."

The five cases came to the Supreme Court on appeals from rulings of the National Labor Relations Board, set up by the Wagner act. All grew out of the discharge of employes who had been active in labor organization.

The Supreme Court, following the reasoning in the railway labor case decided two weeks ago, was unanimous in holding that the Washington, Virginia & Maryland Coach Company, having conceded that it is engaged in interstate business, must obey the Wagner act.

Four members of the court—Justices Sutherland, Van Devanter, McReynolds and Butler—reserving decision as to whether The Associated Press conducts an interstate business, dissented from the application to its staff of the Wagner act by the Chief Justice and Justices Brandeis, Stone, Cardozo and Roberts on the ground that this application invades the unrestricted freedom of the press as guaranteed in the First Amendment and threatens the objectivity of the news report.

Three Manufacturing Cases

But the more important cases, and those in which the commerce clause was broadened as never before, affected three manufacturers: the Jones & Laughlin Steel Corporation, the Fruehauf Trailer Company and the Friedman-Harry Marks Clothing Company, Inc. These had all relied on many previous decisions of the court excluding matters in local manufacture from Federal regulation, and the four dissenters agreed with them. All were overruled by the majority, Justice Roberts again joining the four justices who had dissented in the New York minimum wage case to make the new "liberal" majority of the Supreme Court.

The court room was crowded, expectant of the decisions as it had been on several previous Mondays. This time the throng was not disappointed, nor was it disappointed by the matter of the decisions, transcendently important as guides to future Federal legislation dealing with industrial conditions of national economic and social concern. Government lawyers, hailing the outcome, said that the court had put a twentieth century dress on Marshall's dictum in the famous case of Gibbons v. Ogden, reversing the line it has taken in recent years.

Decisions and Dissents in Brief

Taking the decisions and dissents in the order of their importance with reference to the broadening of the commerce clause, they were in substance as follows:

Majority decision in the Jones & Laughlin case, delivered by the chief justice—

After a hearing the National Labor Relations Board decided that this company had engaged in unfair labor practices affecting commerce. It was found to have been guilty of discrimination against union men, of coercion among its employes, and to have discharged active union men as a form of intimidation. On appeal from a cease-and-desist order from the board, the corporation lost and was granted certiorari by the Supreme Court.

(Here the chief justice summarized the provisions of the Wagner act, certified that procedure was properly pursued and cited the arguments of the corporation and attorneys for the labor board.) The Jones & Laughlin company has its principal office in Pittsburgh, with many subsidiaries in other States. It owns mines, railroads and steamships. Its manufacturing works at Pittsburgh and Aliquippa can be likened to "the heart of a self-contained, highly integrated body." Approximately 75 per cent of its product is shipped out of Pennsylvania.

The discharged employes were mostly leaders in the labor union. In the hearings before the board, although the company charged that the attitude of the board was hostile, it made no attempt to refute the accusations of intimidation and coercion. Therefore there is no basis for setting aside the labor board's order on the record of the facts, and the evidence supports the findings.

Commerce Definition Satisfactory

Turning to questions of law, it is indisputably important for the Supreme Court to maintain the distinction between what is national and what is local in commerce. But the court is not at liberty to deny effect to specific provisions within the right of Congress to make by drawing inferences from other provisions in the same act, as the company lawyers have asked the court to do. "The cardinal principle of statutory construction is to save and not to destroy."

"Between two possible constructions the court's plain duty is to save an act of Congress. By its text the Wagner act may be construed as constitutional, with especial note of Section 2(7), in which Congress defines the term "affecting commerce." This definition is exclusive as well as inclusive, and therefore satisfactory.

The act does not give the board authority over the relationships between all industrial employers and employes. It deals only with what may burden or obstruct commerce —a constitutional exclusion. The legal application is left by the statute to individual cases, and this case should be examined in that light.

Discrimination and coercion to prevent the free exercise of self-organization is properly within legislative authority to outlaw. Long ago this court stated and approved the reasons for unions, and reiterated them in the decision two weeks ago in the railway labor case.

NRA Decision not Binding

The company's attorneys held that the decisions in the NRA and Guffey Act cases are binding in this instance. The government makes a distinction. When industrial activities have a close and substantial relation to interstate commerce, their control is essential, and Congress cannot be denied that control. This control should not, however, be extended to effects of interstate commerce so remote as to obliterate the drawn line between what is national and what is local and "create a completely centralized government."

But the power of the Interstate Commerce Commission, through Congress, over intrastate railroad rates as affecting interstate ones reveals how a proper relationship can exist. The Supreme Court has validated this power. The fact that the Jones & Laughlin employes were engaged in production is not determining. In the Schecter (NRA) case the activities of the employes were found too remote, and in the Guffey Act there was found to have been improper delegation of legislative power. These decisions do not control in this instance.

In view of the "far-flung" activities of Jones & Laughlin, a stoppage of those activities by industrial strife "would be immediate and might be catastrophic." The court is asked to shut its eyes "to the plainest facts of our national life * * * to deal * * in an intellectual vacuum." Interstate commerce is, as this court has often said, a practical conception. Interferences with that commerce "must be appraised by a judgment that does not ignore actual experience." Refusal by employers to confer and negotiate has been "one of the most prolific causes of strife." The steel industry is basic, its strikes have far-reaching consequences. It falls properly within the purview of Congress.

Akin to Railway Labor Case

In the railway labor case this court held that the obligation of the employer to deal with the true representative of a majority was exclusive so far as collective bargaining was concerned. But the court did not preclude the making of such individual contracts as a company might choose to make. This same construction applies to the collective bargaining section of the Wagner Act. It does not compel agreements between employers and employes. Also it provides that any individual employe or group may at any time present grievances.

The theory of the act is that free opportunity for negotiation between accredited representatives of the body of employes makes for industrial peace which the act does not attempt to compel. It does not interfere with the right of the employer to hire and to discharge. Nor does it authorize the board to interfere with the right of discharge for reasons other than those stated in the act.

The Wagner act has been criticized as one-sided. But the court is dealing with the power of Congress, not with its policy, and a cautious advance, step by step, is not undesirable, perhaps better than trying to obliterate all evils in one sweep.

Reinstatement and reimbursement of the discharged employes is ordered, and the court finds that the Labor Board acted "within its competency and the act is valid as here applied." The lower court is reversed.

Dissenting opinion in the Jones & Laughlin case, delivered by Justice McReynolds, and serving also as a dissent in the Fruehauf Trailer Company and Friedman-Harry Marks Clothing Company cases, with concurrence of Justices Sutherland, Butler and Van Devanter.

The decisions of the three lower courts in these cases were sound, were based on Supreme Court decisions recently delivered and should be affirmed. On the authority of this court in the NRA and Guffey act cases, the lower courts have held that the power of Congress under the commerce clause does not extend to employer-employe relations in manufacture. "Every consideration brought forward to uphold the act before us was applicable to support the acts held unconstitutional in causes decided within two years."

Of the three petitioners, one is large, two relatively small. The act is applied to all of them. It invests the board with authority over purely local authority as never before permitted. (Here the opinions of the three lower courts are cited).

The activities of the Jones & Laughlin Company do not differ materially from those of many small producers and distributors. At its plants the movements of raw material ends, and the material often comes to rest for months before manufacture begins. The discharged employes took no part in any activity which preceded or followed manufacture. (Here is appended a description of the activities of the petitioners, an account of proceedings before the Labor Board and the rulings of that board).

States' Rights Held Invaded

The government argument was that validity depends upon whether industrial strife resulting from the practices complained of by the unions would be the sort the Federal power could control. That view of the power of Congress would extend it boundlessly. But consideration of the facts in these cases shows that any effect on interstate commerce of the discharge of the employes "would be indirect and remote in the highest degree." "A more remote and indirect interference with interstate commerce or a more definite invasion of the powers reserved to the States is difficult, if not impossible, to imagine." "The Constitution still recognizes the existence of States with indestructible powers; the Tenth Amendment was supposed to put them beyond controversy."

If a man raises cattle and delivers them for interstate shipment, may Congress regulate his labor conditions? Will it become the duty of the Federal Government to suppress any strike which, by any eventual possibility, may blockade the stream of commerce?" Whatever effect any cause of discontent may ultimately have upon commerce is far too indirect to justify Congressional regulation. Almost anything—marriage, birth, death— may in some fashion affect commerce."

The Wagner Act carefully exempts from its regulation the right to strike, though its basic theory of Federal regulation is that strikes cause the discontent which requires the erection of a barrier against discharge for union activities. And it abridges the right of contract, including that of a private owner to "manage his own property by freely selecting those to whom his manufacturing operations are to be intrusted. We cannot think this can lawfully be done." Congress has exceeded its powers.

While the court's action affected five cases, there were technically seven victories in all for the government, because the Fruehauf Trailer and Friedman—Harry Marks issues were each split into two law suits.

In delivering the majority decision in the automobile trailer and clothing company cases, the Chief Justice merely stated the case, reviewed the findings of the Labor Board, found them factual and held that the law applied for the reasons given in the Jones & Laughlin decision.

The unanimous decision in the bus company case was brief. It recited the petitioner's admission that the company is engaged in interstate commerce and applied the exclusive collective bargaining validation of the recent railway labor decision as binding.

Majority Ruling in A. P. Case

Majority decision in The Associated Press case, delivered by Justice Roberts:

In October, 1935, the petitioner discharged Morris Watson, an employe in its New York office. The American Newspaper Guild filed a charge with the Labor Board of violation of the Wagner Act. The Associated Press denied that the dismissal was for Guild activities and questioned the authority of the board on constitutional grounds.

When its motion to dismiss was rejected by a board trial examiner, who reserved only the interstate commerce question for discussion The Associated Press withdrew. On the examiner's findings that an order should be issued against the peti-

tioner, the board summoned The Associated Press, which declined to appear. Cease-and-desist orders were then issued by the board, and the press association was told to reinstate Watson and give him back pay. The Associated Press refused compliance, and on petition from the Labor Board the lower court ordered enforcement of the board's finding.

In its answer before the lower court The Associated Press did not challenge the board's findings of fact. Therefore, this court accepts it as established that Watson was discharged for his Guild activities. This makes the validity of Section 8 of the Wagner Act the issue before the court.

A. P. Held to Commerce Clause

Does the statute, as applied to the A. P., exceed the power of Congress to regulate interstate commerce? The board concluded that the A. P. was engaged in interstate commerce, that Watson's activities dealt with a portion of that commerce (rewriting news for wire transmission) and that therefore his case was covered by the Wagner Act. These findings are supported by this court.

Does the statute, as applied to the petitioner, abridge the freedom of speech or of the press safeguarded by the First Amendment? The court thinks it does not. The Associated Press has contended that it must keep its report free from bias, according to the will of all its members, and that, unless its management is free to determine whether an employe may bias the report, it cannot maintain that objectivity.

But the actual reason for Watson's discharge was his Guild activity, as undisputed before the Labor Board. The Associated Press does not assert that Watson had shown bias in the past. The Wagner Act does not attempt to preclude discharge on that ground; it forbids

discharge for what the board found was the "real motive." It does not compel The Associated Press to employ any one or retain on its staff an incompetent employe or one whom it believes to have revealed bias.

Watson's restoration by this decision "in no sense guarantees his continuance in the petitioner's employ. . . . The petitioner is at liberty. . . . to sever his relationship for any cause that seems proper," save those mentioned in the statute.

The publisher of a newspaper or the management of a press association have no special immunity from the application of general statutes. They are answerable to libel, contempt of court, violation of the anti-trust laws. This regulation has nothing to do with the impartial writing of news. The rights of The Associated Press to publish and edit, to adopt and enforce policies, and to discharge Watson or any other who fails to comply with those policies, remain intact. The lower court judgment is affirmed.

Minority Ruling in A. P. Case

Minority opinion in The Associated Press case, by Justice Sutherland for himself and Justices Van Devanter, McReynolds and Butler:

The lower court judgment should be reversed because it abridges the freedom of the press. Reserving our assent to what has been said by the majority about the interstate commerce feature of The Associated Press report and other points, we confine ourselves to freedom of the press.

There are no reservations to the First Amendment. "When applied to the press the term freedom is not to be narrowly confined; and it obviously means more than publication and circulation." It includes the right to adopt any policy without government restriction. Its judgment must be uncensored with

respect to the employment or discharge of agents to carry out policies. "Congress shall make no law abridging the freedom of the press."

Accepting the labor board's finding that Watson was discharged for his Guild activities, we should bear in mind the existing contention between labor and capital. An unbiased version of this is of utmost public concern. Watson had the authority to determine the news value of items received in rewriting the copy given to him. He was active in establishing the Guild. Inducements were held out to him by his employer to abandon them. He declined.

Employer's Aims Paramount

Congress has no right to interfere with the petitioner's conclusion that Watson's sympathies might involve the purity of its report. The application of this statute, if carried to a logical extreme, might give the Guild "a high degree of control over the character of the news service." "To hold that the press association must await a concrete instance of misinterpretation of the news before it can act is to compel it to experiment with a doubt when it regards certainty as essential."

"Does the people of this land * * * desire to preserve those [liberties] so carefully protected by the First Amendment: liberty of religious worship, freedom of speech and of the press, and the right as free men peaceably to assemble and petition their government for a redress of grievances? If so, let them withstand all beginnings of encroachment. For the saddest epitaph which can be carved in memory of a vanished liberty is that it was lost because it possessors failed to stretch forth a saving hand while yet there was time."

The court then recessed for two weeks.

April 13, 1937

Text of the Wage and Hour Bill as Drafted by the House and Senate Conferees

WASHINGTON, June 12.—Following is the text of the Wages and Hours Bill as drafted by Senate and House conferees:

THAT THIS ACT MAY BE CITED AS THE "FAIR LABOR STANDARDS ACT OF 1938."

Finding and Declaration of Policy

Section 2. (a) The Congress hereby finds that the existence, in industries engaged in commerce or in the production of goods for commerce, of labor conditions detrimental to the maintenance of the minimum standard of living necessary for

health, efficiency and general well-being of workers (1) causes commerce and the channels and instrumentalities of commerce to be used to spread and perpetuate such labor conditions among the workers of the several States; (2) burdens commerce and the free flow of goods in commerce; (3) constitutes an unfair method of competition in commerce; (4) leads to labor disputes burdening and obstructing commerce and the free flow of goods in commerce; and (5) interferes with the orderly and fair marketing of goods in commerce.

(b) It is hereby declared to be the policy of this act, through the exercise by Congress of its power to regulate commerce among the several States, to correct and as rapidly as practicable to eliminate the conditions above referred to in such industries without substantially curtailing employment of earning power.

Definitions

Section 3. As used in this act—

(a) "Persons" means an individual, partnership, association, corporation, business trust, legal rep-

resentative or any organized group of persons.

(b) "Commerce" means trade, commerce, transportation, transmission, or communication among the several States or from any State to any place outside thereof.

(c) "State" means any State of the United States or the District of Columbia or any territory or possession of the United States.

(d) "Employer" includes any person acting directly or indirectly in the interest of an employer in relation to an employe but shall not include the United States or any State or political subdivision of a State, or any labor organization (other than when acting as an employer), or any one acting in the capacity of officer or agent of such labor organization.

(e) "Employe" includes any individual employed by an employer.

Coverage as to Agriculture

(f) "Agriculture" includes farming in all its branches and among other things includes the cultivation and tillage of the soil, dairy-

135

ing, the production, cultivation, growing, and harvesting of any agricultural or horticultural commodities (including commodities defined as agricultural commodities in Section 15 (g) of the Agricultural Marketing Act, as amended), the raising of livestock, bees, fur-bearing animals, or poultry, and any practices (including any forestry or lumbering operations) performed by a farmer or on a farm as an incident to or in conjunction with such farming operations, including preparation for market, delivery to storage or to market or to carriers for transportation to market.

(g) "Employ" includes to suffer or permit to work.

(h) "Industry" means a trade, business, industry, or branch thereof, or group of industries, in which individuals are gainfully employed.

The Definition of "Goods"

(i) "Goods" means goods (including ships and marine equipment), wares, products, commodities, merchandise or articles or subjects of commerce of any character, or any part or ingredient thereof, but does not include goods after their delivery into the actual physical possession of the ultimate consumer thereof other than a producer, manufacturer or processor thereof.

(j) "Produced" means produced, manufactured, mined, handled or in any other manner worked on in any State; and for the purposes of this act an employe shall be deemed to have been engaged in the production, manufacturing, mining, handling, transporting, or in any other manner working on such goods, or in any process or occupation necessary to the production thereof, in any State.

(k) "Sale" or "sell" includes any sale, exchange contract to sell, consignment for sale, shipment for sale or other disposition.

Specifications as to Child Labor

(l) "Oppressive child labor" means a condition of employment which (1) any employe under the age of 16 years is employed by an employer (other than a parent or a person standing in place of a parent employing his own child or a child in his custody under the age of 16 years in an occupation other than manufacturing or mining) in any occupation, or (2) any employe between the ages of 16 and 18 years is employed by an employer in any occupation which the Chief of the Children's Bureau in the Department of Labor shall find and by order declare to be particularly hazardous for the employment of children between such ages or detrimental to their health or well-being; but oppressive child labor shall not be deemed to exist by virtue of the employment in any occupation of any person with respect to whom the employer shall have on file an unexpired certificate issued and held pursuant to regulations of the Chief of the Children's Bureau certifying that such person is above the oppressive child-labor age. The Chief of the Children's Bureau shall provide by regulation or by order that the employment of persons between the ages of 14 and 16 years in occupations other than manufacturing and mining shall not be deemed to constitute oppressive child labor if and to the extent that

the Chief of the Children's Bureau determines that such employment is confined to persons which will not interfere with their schooling and to conditions which will not interfere with their health and well-being.

(m) "Wage" paid to any employe includes the reasonable cost, as determined by the administrator, to the employer of furnishing such employe with board, lodging or other facilities, if such board, lodging or other facilities are customarily furnished by such employer to his employes.

Administrator

Section 4. (a) There is hereby created in the Department of Labor a Wage and Hour Division which shall be under the direction of an administrator, to be known as the administrator of the Wage and Hour Division (in this act referred to as the "administrator"). The administrator shall be appointed by the President by and with the advice and consent of the Senate and shall receive compensation at the rate of $10,000 a year.

(b) The administrator may, subject to the civil service laws, appoint such employes as he deems necessary to carry out his functions and duties under this act and shall fix their compensation in accordance with the Classification Act of 1923, as amended. The administrator may establish and utilize such regional, local or other agencies, and utilize such voluntary and uncompensated services, as may from time to time be needed. Attorneys appointed under this section may appear for and represent the administrator in any litigation, but all such litigation shall be subject to the direction and control of the Attorney General. In the appointment, selection, classification and promotion of officers and employes of the administrator, no political test or qualification shall be permitted or given consideration, but all such appointments and promotions shall be given and made on the basis of merit and efficiency.

(c) The principal office of the administrator shall be in the District of Columbia, but he or his duly authorized representative may exercise any or all of his powers in any place.

(d) The administrator shall submit annually in January a year report to the Congress covering his activities for the preceding year and including such information, data and recommendations for further legislation in connection with the matters covered by this act as he may find advisable.

Industry Committees

Section 5. (a) The administrator shall as soon as practicable appoint one or more industry committees for each industry engaged in commerce or in the production of goods for commerce.

(b) An industry committee shall be appointed by the administrator without regard to any other provisions of law regarding the appointment and compensation of employes of the United States. It shall include a number of disinterested persons representing the public, one of whom the administrator shall designate as chairman, a like number of persons representing employes in the industry, and a like number representing employers in the industry. In the appointment

of the persons representing each group, the administrator shall give due regard to the geographical regions in which the industry is carried on.

(c) Two-thirds of the members of an industry committee shall constitute a quorum and the decision of the committee shall require a vote of not less than a majority of all its members. Members of an industry committee shall receive as compensation for their services a reasonable per diem, which the administrator shall by rules and regulations prescribe, for each day actually spent in the work of the committee and shall in addition be reimbursed for their necessary traveling and other expenses. The administrator shall furnish the committee with adequate legal, stenographic, clerical and other assistance, and shall by rules and regulations prescribe the procedure to be followed by the committee.

(d) The administrator shall submit to an industry committee from time to time such data as he may have available on the matters referred to it and shall cause to be brought before it in connection with such matters any witnesses whom he deems material. An industry committee may summon other witnesses or call upon the administrator to furnish additional information to aid it in its deliberations.

Minimum Wages

Section 6. (a) Every employer shall pay to each of his employes who is engaged in commerce or in the production of goods for commerce wages at the following rates:

(1) During the first year from the effective date of this section, not less than 25 cents an hour.

(2) During the next six years from such date not less than 30 cents an hour.

(3) After the expiration of seven years from such date not less than 40 cents an hour, or the rate (not less than 30 cents an hour) prescribed in the applicable order of the administrator issued under Section 8, whichever is lower, and

(4) At any time after the effective date of the section, not less than the rate (not in excess of 40 cents an hour) prescribed in the applicable order of the administrator issued under Section 8.

(b) This section shall take effect upon the expiration of one hundred and twenty days from the date of enactment of this act.

Maximum Hours

Section 7. (a) No employer shall, except as otherwise provided in this section, employ any of his employes who is engaged in commerce or in the production of goods for commerce

(1) for a work week longer than forty-four hours during the first year from the effective date of this section,

(2) for a work week longer than forty-two hours during the second year from such date, or

(3) for a work week longer than forty hours after the expiration of the second year from such date, unless such employe receives compensation for his employment in excess of the hours above specified at a rate not less than one and one-half times the regular rate at which he is employed.

(b) No employer shall be deemed to have violated subsection (a) by

employing any employe for a work week in excess of that specified in such subsection without paying the compensation for overtime employment prescribed therein if such employe is so employed

(1) in pursuance of an agreement, made as a result of collective bargaining by representatives of employes certified as bona fide by the National Labor Relations Board, which provides that no employe shall be employed more than 1,000 hours during any period of twenty-six consecutive weeks,

(2) on an annual basis in pursuance of an agreement with his employer, made as a result of collective bargaining by representatives of employes certified as bona fide by the National Labor Relations Board, which provides that the employe shall not be employed more than 2,000 hours during any period of fifty-two consecutive weeks, or

(3) for a period or periods of not more than twelve work weeks in the aggregate in any calendar year in an industry found by the administrator to be of a seasonal nature, and if such employe receives compensation for employment in excess of twelve hours in any work day, or for employment in excess of fifty-six hours in any work week, as the case may be, at a rate not less than one and one-half times the regular rate at which he is employed.

(c) In the case of an employer engaged in the first processing of milk, whey, skimmed milk or cream into dairy products, or in the ginning and compressing of cotton, or in the processing of cottonseed, or in the processing of sugar beets, sugar-beet molasses, sugar cane or maple sap into sugar or syrup the provisions of subsection (a) shall not apply to his employes in any place of employment where he is so engaged; and in the case of an employer engaged in the first processing of, or in canning, perishable fresh fruits or perishable or seasonal fresh vegetables, or in the first processing, within the area of production, of any agricultural or horticultural commodity during seasonal operations, or in handling, slaughtering or dressing poultry or livestock, the provisions of subsection (a) during a period or periods of not more than fourteen work weeks in the aggregate in any calendar year, shall not apply to his employes in any place of employment where he is so engaged.

(d) This section shall take effect upon the expiration of 120 days from the date of enactment of this act.

Wage Orders

Section 8. (a) With a view to carrying out the policy of this act by reaching, as rapidly as is economically feasible without substantially curtailing employment, the objective of a universal minimum wage of 40 cents an hour in each industry engaged in commerce or in the production of goods for commerce, the administrator shall from time to time convene the industry committees for each such industry, and the industry committees shall from time to time recommend the minimum rate or rates of wages to be paid under Section 6 by employers engaged in commerce or in the production of goods for commerce in such industry or classifications therein.

(b) Upon the convening of an industry committee, the administrator shall refer to it the question of the minimum wage rate or rates to be fixed for such industry. The industry committee shall investigate conditions in the industry and the committee, or any authorized subcommittee thereof, may hear such witnesses and receive such evidence as may be necessary or appropriate to enable the committee to perform its duties and functions under this act. The committee shall recommend to the administrator the highest minimum wage rates for the industry which it determines, having due regard to economic and competitive conditions, will not substantially curtail employment in the industry.

(c) The industry committee for any industry shall recommend such reasonable classifications within any industry as it determines to be necessary for the purpose of fixing for each classification within such industry the highest minimum wage rate (not in excess of 40 cents an hour) which (1) will not substantially curtail employment in such classification and (2) will not give a competitive advantage to any group in the industry, and shall recommend for each classification in the industry the highest minimum wage rate which the committee determines will not substantially curtail employment in such classification. In determining whether such classifications should be made in any industry, in making such classifications, and in determining the minimum wage rates for such classifications, no classification shall be made, and no minimum wage rate shall be fixed, solely on a regional basis, but the industry committee and the administrator shall consider among other relevant factors the following:

(1) Competitive conditions as affected by transportation, living and production costs.

(2) The wages established for work of like or comparable character by collective labor agreements negotiated between employers and employes by representatives of their own choosing; and

(3) The wages paid for work of like or comparable character by employers who voluntarily maintain minimum-wage standards in the industry.

To Report to Administrator

(d) The industry committee shall file with the administrator a report containing its recommendations with respect to the matters referred to it. Upon the filing of such report, the administrator, after due notice to interested persons, and giving them an opportunity to be herd, shall by order approve and carry into effect the recommendations contained in such report, if he finds that the recommendations are made in accordance with law, are supported by the evidence adduced at the hearing, and, taking into consideration the same factors as are required to be considered by the industry committee, will carry out the purposes of this section; otherwise he shall disapprove such recommendations. If the administrator disapproves such recommendations, he shall again refer the matter to such committee, or to another industry committee for such industry, for further consideration and recommendations.

(e) No order issued under this section with respect to any industry prior to the expiration of seven years from the effective date of this act shall remain in effect after such expiration, and no order shall be issued under this section with respect to any industry on or after such expiration, unless the industry committee by a preponderance of the evidence before it recommends, and the administrator by a preponderance of the evidence adduced at the hearing finds, that the continued effectiveness or the issuance of the order, as the case may be, is necessary in order to prevent substantial curtailment of employment in the industry.

(f) Orders issued under this section shall define the industries and classifications therein to which they are to apply, and shall contain such terms and conditions as the administrator finds necessary to carry out the purposes of such orders, to prevent the circumvention or evasion thereof, and to safeguard the minimum wage rates established therein. No such order shall take effect until after due notice is given to the issuance thereof by publication in the Federal Register and by such other means as the administrator deems reasonably calculated to give to interested persons general notice of such issuance.

(g) Due notice of any hearing provided for in this section shall be given by publication in The Federal Register and by such other means as the administrator deems reasonably calculated to give general notice to interested persons.

Section 9. For the purpose of any hearing or investigation provided for in this act, the provisions of Sections 9 and 10 (relating to the attendance of witnesses and the production of books, papers and documents) of the Federal Trade Commission Act of Sept. 16, 1914, as amended (U. S. C., 1934 edition, Title 15, Sections 49 and 50), are hereby made applicable to the jurisdiction, powers, and duties of the administrator, the chief of the Children's Bureau, and the industry committees.

Court Review

Section 10. (a) Any person aggrieved by an order of the administrator issued under Section 8 may obtain a review of such order in the Circuit Court of Appeals of the United States for any circuit wherein such person resides or has his principal place of business, or in the United States Court of Appeals for the District of Columbia, by filing in such court, within sixty days after the entry of such order, a written petition praying that the order of the administrator be modified or set aside in whole or in part. A copy of such petition shall forthwith be served upon the administrator, and thereupon the administrator shall certify and file in the court a transcript of the record upon which the order complained of was entered.

Upon the filing of such transcript such court shall have exclusive jurisdiction to affirm, modify or set aside such order in whole or in part, so far as it is applicable to the petitioner. The review by the court shall be limited to questions of law, and findings of fact by the administrator when supported by substantial evidence shall be conclusive.

No objection to the order of the administrator shall be considered by the court unless such objection shall have been urged before the administrator or unless there were reasonable grounds for failure so to do. If application is made to the court for leave to adduce additional evidence, and it is shown to the satisfaction of the court that such additional evidence may materially affect the result of the proceeding and that there were reasonable grounds for failure to adduce such evidence in the proceeding before the administrator, the court may order such additional evidence to be taken before the administrator and to be adduced upon the hearing in such manner and upon such terms and conditions as the court may deem proper.

May Modify Findings

The administrator may modify his findings by reason of the additional evidence so taken, and shall file with the court such modified or new findings, which, if supported by substantial evidence, shall be conclusive, and shall also file his recommendations, if any, for the modification or setting aside of the original order. The judgment and decree of the court shall be final, subject to review by the Supreme Court of the United States upon certiorari or certification as provided in sections 239 and 240 of the judicial code, as amended (U. S. C., title 28, secs. 346 and 347).

(b) The commencement of proceedings under subsection (a) shall not, unless specifically ordered by the court, operate as a stay of the administrator's order. The court shall not grant any stay of the order unless the person complaining of such order shall file in court an undertaking with a surety or sureties satisfactory to the court for the payment to the employes affected by the order, in the event such order is affirmed, of the amount by which the compensation such employes are entitled to receive under the order exceeds the compensation they actually receive while such stay is in effect.

Investigations, Inspections and Records

Section 11. (a) The administrator or his designated representatives may investigate and gather data regarding the wages, hours and other conditions and practices of employment in any industry subject to this act, and may enter and inspect such places and such records (and make transcriptions thereof), question such employes, and investigate such facts, conditions, practices or matters as he may deem necessary or appropriate to determine whether any person has violated any provision of this act, or which may aid in the enforcement of the provisions of this act.

Except as provided in Section 12 and in subsection (b) of this section, the administrator shall utilize the bureaus and divisions of the Department of Labor for all the investigations and inspections necessary under this section. Except as provided in Section 12, the administrator shall bring all actions under Section 17 to restrain violations of this act.

(b) With the consent and cooperation of State agencies charged with the administration of State labor laws, the administrator and the chief of the Children's Bureau may, for the purpose of carrying out their respective functions and duties under this act, utilize the services of State and local agencies, and their employes and, notwithstanding any other provision of law, may reimburse such State and local agencies and their employes for services rendered for such purposes.

(c) Every employer subject to any provision of this act or of any order issued under this act shall make, keep and preserve such records of the persons employed by him, and of the wages, hours and other conditions and practices of employment maintained by him, and shall preserve such records for such periods of time and shall make such reports therefrom to the administrator, as he shall prescribe by regulation or order as necessary or appropriate for the enforcement of the provisions of this act or the regulations or orders thereunder.

Child Labor Provisions

Section 12. (a) After the expiration of one hundred and twenty days from the date of enactment of this act, no producer, manufacturer or dealer shall ship or deliver for shipment in commerce any goods produced in an establishment situated in the United States in or about which within thirty days prior to the removal of such goods therefrom any oppressive child labor has been employed; provided, that a prosecution and conviction of a defendant for the shipment or delivery for shipment of any goods under the conditions herein prohibited shall be a bar to any further prosecution against the same defendant for shipments or deliveries for shipment of any such goods before the beginning of said prosecution.

(b) The Chief of the Children's Bureau in the Department of Labor, or any of his authorized representatives, shall make all investigations and inspections under Section 11 (a) with respect to the employment of minors, and, subject to the direction and control of the Attorney General, shall bring all actions under Section 17 to enjoin any act or practice which is unlawful by reason of the existence of oppressive child labor, and shall administer all other provisions of this act relating to oppressive child labor.

Exemptions

Section 13. (a) The provisions of Sections 6 and 7 shall not apply with respect to (1) any employe employed in a bona fide executive, administrative, professional, or local retailing capacity, or in the capacity of outside salesman (as such terms are defined and delimited by regulations of the administrator); or (2) any employe engaged in any retail or service establishment the greater part of whose selling is in intrastate commerce; or (3) any employe employed as a seaman; or (4) any employe of a carrier by air subject to the provisions of Title II of the Railway Labor Act; or (5) any employe employed in the catching, taking, harvesting, cultivating, or farming of any kind of fish, shellfish, crustacea, sponges, seaweeds, or other aquatic forms of animal and vegetable life, including the going to and returning from work and including employment in the loading, unloading, or packing of such products for shipment or in propagating, processing, marketing, freezing, canning, curing, storing, or distributing the above products or byproducts thereof; or (6) any employe employed in agriculture; or (7) any employe to the extent that such employe is exempted by regulations or orders of the administrator issued under Section 14; or (8) any employe employed in connection with the publication of any weekly or semiweekly newspaper with a circulation of less than 3,000 the major part of which circulation is within the country where printed and published; or (9) any employe of a street, suburban, or interurban electric railway, or local trolley or motor bus carrier, not included in other exemptions contained in this section; or (10) to any individual employed within the area of production (as defined by the administrator), engaged in handling, packing, storing, ginning, compressing, pasteurizing, drying, preparing in their raw or natural state, or canning of agricultural or horticultural commodities for market, or in making cheese or butter.

(b) The provisions of Section 7 shall not apply with respect to (1) any employe with respect to whom the Interstate Commerce Commission has power to establish qualifications and maximum hours of service pursuant to the provisions of Section 204 of the Motor Carrier Act, 1935; or (2) any employe of an employer subject to the provisions of Part 1 of the Interstate Commerce Act.

(c) The provisions of Section 12 relating to child labor shall not apply with respect to any employe temporarily employed in agriculture while not legally required to attend school, or to any child employed as an actor in motion pictures or theatrical productions.

Learners, Apprentices and Handicapped Workers

Section 14. The administrator, to the extent necessary in order to prevent curtailment of opportunities for employment, shall by regulations or by orders provide for (1) the employment of learners, of apprentices and of messengers em-

ployed exclusively in delivering letters and messages, under special certificates issued pursuant to regulations of the administrator, at such wages lower than the minimum wage applicable under Section 6 and subject to such limitations as to time, number, proportion and length of service as the administrator shall prescribe, and (2) the employment of individuals whose earning capacity is impaired by age or physical or mental deficiency or injury, under special certificates issued by the administrator, at such wages lower than the minimum wage applicable under Section 6 and for such period as shall be fixed in such certificates.

Prohibited Acts

Section 15. (a) After the expiration of 120 days from the date of enactment of this act, it shall be unlawful for any person—

(1) To transport, offer for transportation, ship, deliver, or sell in commerce, or to ship, deliver, or sell with knowledge that shipment or delivery or sale thereof in commerce is intended, any goods in the production of which any employe was employed in violation of Section 6 or Section 7, or in violation of any regulation or order of the administrator issued under Section 14; except that no provision of this act shall impose any liability upon any common carrier for the transportation in commerce in the regular course of its business of any goods not produced by such common carrier, and no provision of this act shall excuse any common carrier from its obligation to accept any goods for transportation;

(2) to violate any of the provisions of Section 6 or Section 7, or any of the provisions of any regulation or order of the administrator issued under Section 14;

(3) to willfully discharge or in any other manner discriminate against any employe because such employe has filed any complaint or instituted or caused to be instituted any proceeding under or related to this Act, or has testified or is about to testify in any such proceeding, or has served or is

about to serve on an industry committee:

(4) to violate any of the provisions of Section 12;

(5) to violate any of the provisions of Section 11 (c), or to make any statement, report, or record filed or kept pursuant to the provisions of such section or of any regulation or order, thereunder, knowing such statement, report, or record to be false in a material respect.

(b) For the purposes of Subsection (a) (1) proof that any employe was employed in any place of employment where goods shipped or sold in commerce were produced, within ninety days prior to the removal of the goods from such place of employment, shall be prima facie evidence that such employe was engaged in the production of such goods.

Penalties

Section 16. (a) Any person who willfully violates any of the provisions of Section 15 shall upon conviction thereof be subject to a fine of not more than $10,000, or to imprisonment for not more than six months, or both. No person shall be imprisoned under this subsection except for an offense committed after the conviction of such person for a prior offense under this subsection.

(b) Any employer who violates the provisions of Section 6 of this act shall be liable to the employe or employes affected in the amount, as determined by the Administrator, of their unpaid minimum wages or their unpaid compensation as the case may be and in an additional equal amount as liquidated damages. Action to recover such liability may be maintained in any court of competent jurisdiction by any one or more employes for and in behalf of himself or themselves and other employes similarly situated or such employe or employes may designate an agent or representative to maintain such action for and in behalf of all employes similarly situated. The court in such action shall, in addition to any judgment awarded to the plain-

tiff or plaintiffs, allow a reasonable attorney's fee to be paid by the defendant and costs of the action.

Injunction Proceedings

Section 17. The district courts of the United States and the United States courts of the Territories and possessions shall have jurisdiction, for cause shown, and subject to the provisions of Section 20 (relating to notice of opposite party) of the act entitled "An Act to Supplement Existing Laws Against Unlawful Restraints and Monopolies, and for Other Purposes," approved Oct. 15, 1914, as amended (U. S. C., 1934 edition, Title, Section 381), to restrain violations of Section 15.

Relation to Other Laws

Section 18. No provision of this act or of any order thereunder shall excuse noncompliance with any Federal or State law or municipal ordinance establishing a minimum wage higher than the minimum wage established under this act or a maximum work week lower than the maximum work week established under this act, and no provision of this act relating to the employment of child labor shall justify noncompliance with any Federal or State law or municipal ordinance establishing a higher standard than the standard established under this act. No provision of this act shall justify any employer in reducing a wage paid by him which is in excess of the applicable minimum wage under this act, or justify any employer in increasing hours of employment maintained by him which are shorter than the maximum hours applicable under this act.

Separability of Provisions

Section 19. If any provision of this act or the application of such provision to any person or circumstance is held invalid, the remainder of the act and the application of such provision to other persons or circumstances shall not be affected thereby.

And the House agree to the same.

June 13, 1938

WAGE LAW UPHELD BY SUPREME COURT; OLD DECISION UPSET

Justice Stone Writes Opinion Overruling a 22-Year-Old Child Labor Case

By LEWIS WOOD
Special to THE NEW YORK TIMES.

WASHINGTON, Feb. 3—The constitutionality of the Federal Wage

and Hour Law, last of the major New Deal statutes to face a legal challenge, was unanimously sustained by the Supreme Court today in an opinion affecting minimum wages for millions of workers.

Justice Stone ruled that Congress was empowered to prevent shipment in interstate commerce of materials produced by employes receiving less or working longer than the standards set in the act. Remarking that Congress intended the Wage and Hour Law to bar interstate traffic in goods produced under substandard labor conditions, the court specifically overruled the twenty-two-year-old decision hold-

ing the Federal child labor law invalid.

Dealing with another phase of the Wage and Hour Law, the court, again through Justice Stone, upheld the validity of the determination of a special industry committee setting a 32½-cent minimum hourly wage for cotton textile workers. Southern cotton mills attacked the determination, which was made as part of an order fixing this minimum wage for all the 650,000 workers of the textile industry.

The Wage and Hour decision, together with another holding Federal anti-trust laws inapplicable to jurisdictional disputes of labor unions, stood out in a list of nearly

twenty decisions handed down from a bench reduced to eight justices by the retirement of Justice McReynolds, who was 79 years old today.

Lumber Company Is Involved

Justice Stone handed down his principal opinion in the case of the F. W. Darby Lumber Company of Statesboro, Ga., indicted for failure to pay the required 25-cent minimum hourly wage and time and one-half for hours longer than a forty-four week, failing to keep proper records and shipping into interstate commerce lumber produced by workers paid less than the provisions of the act.

The indictment was based on actions of the concern shortly after the law became effective in 1938. Since then the wage level has been raised to 30 cents hourly and the work week set at forty hours.

The challenge to the special industry committee finding came from the Opp Cotton Mills of Opp, Ala., and ten other Southern cotton mills.

In this case Justice Stone upheld the Fifth Circuit Court of Appeals. In the Darby case he upset the Southern Georgia Federal District Court. In the latter Judge William H. Barrett quashed the indictment on the ground that the Wage and Hour Law, which he interpreted as a regulation of manufacture within the States, was unconstitutional.

Almost at the outset of his ruling Justice Stone commented that while manufacture was not of itself interstate commerce, the shipment of manufactured goods in interstate commerce "is such commerce." He added that the prohibition of such commerce by Congress was "indubitably" a regulation of commerce.

Commerce Power Is Defined

"The power to regulate commerce," he continued, citing authorities, "is the power 'to prescribe the rule by which commerce is governed.' It extends not only to those regulations which aid, foster and protect the commerce, but embraces those which prohibit it.

"It is conceded that the power of Congress to prohibit transportation in interstate commerce includes noxious articles, stolen articles, kidnapped persons and articles such as intoxicating liquors or convict-made goods, traffic in which is forbidden or restricted by the laws of the State of destination.

"The power of Congress over interstate commerce 'is complete in itself, may be exercised to its utmost extent, and acknowledges no limitations other than are prescribed by the Constitution.'

"That power can neither be enlarged nor diminished by the exercise of State power. Congress, following its own conception of public policy concerning the restrictions which may appropriately be imposed on interstate commerce, is free to exclude from the commerce articles whose use in the States for which they are destined it may conceive to be injurious to the public

health, morals or welfare, even though the Senate has not sought to regulate their use.

"Such regulation is not a forbidden invasion of State power merely because either its motive or its consequence is to restrict the use of articles of commerce within the States of destination and is not prohibited unless by other constitutional provisions.

"It is no objection to the assertion of the power to regulate interstate commerce that its exercise is attended by the same incidents which attend the exercise of the police power of the States."

The motive and purpose of the Wage and Hour Law, Justice Stone said, is plainly to make effective "the Congressional conception of public policy that interstate commerce should not be made the instrument of competition in the distribution of goods produced under substandard labor conditions, which competition is injurious to the commerce and to the States from and to which the commerce flows."

"The motive and purpose of a regulation of interstate commerce are matters for the legislative judgment upon the exercise of which the Constitution places no restriction and over which the courts are given no control," he added.

Child Labor Decision Is Cited

At this point Justice Stone took up the 1918 decision in Hammer v. Dagenhart, in which the Supreme Court in a five-to-four decision ruled that Congress was powerless to exclude the products of child labor from interstate commerce. In this case the late Justice Oliver Wendell Holmes delivered what Justice Stone called "a powerful and now classic dissent." Justice Brandeis joined Justice Holmes in saying that Congress had the right to bar any interstate commerce it saw fit.

"The reasoning and conclusion of the court's opinion there," Mr. Stone said of the child labor case, "cannot be reconciled with the conclusion which we have reached, that the power of Congress under the commerce clause is plenary to exclude any article from interstate commerce, subject only to the specific prohibitions of the Constitution.

"Hammer v. Dagenhart has not been followed. The distinction on which the decision was rested, that Congressional power to prohibit interstate commerce is limited to articles which in themselves have some harmful or deleterious property, a distinction which was novel when made and unsupported by any provision of the Constitution, has long since been abandoned.

"The conclusion is inescapable that Hammer v. Dagenhart was a departure from the principles which have prevailed in the interpretation of the commerce clause both before and since the decision and that such vitality, as a precedent, as it then had has long since been exhausted. It should be and now is overruled."

Later Justice Stone discussed the interpretation of "production for commerce" and said that Congress evidently intended that these words meant woods which, at the time of production, the employer intended to move in interstate commerce.

"There remains," he remarked, "the question whether such restriction on the production of goods for commerce is a permissible exercise of the commerce power. The power of Congress over interstate commerce is not confined to the regulation of commerce among the States.

"It extends to those activities intrastate which so affect interstate commerce or the exercise of the power of Congress over it as to make regulation of them appropriate means to the attainment of a legitimate end, the exercise of the granted power of Congress to regulate interstate commerce."

Congress may, said Justice Stone, regulate "intrastate activities where they have a substantial effect on interstate commerce."

Wagner Act Is Recalled

"A recent example," he stated, "is the National Labor Relations Act for the regulation of employer and employe relations in industries in which strikes, induced by unfair labor practices named in the act, tend to disturb or obstruct interstate commerce.

"But long before the adoption of the National Labor Relations Act this court had many times held that the power of Congress to regulate interstate commerce extends to the regulation through legislative action of activities intrastate which have a substantial effect on the commerce or the exercise of the Congressional power over it.

"The Sherman act and the National Labor Relations Act are familiar examples of the exertion of the commerce power to prohibit or control activities wholly intrastate because of their effect on interstate commerce."

In the ruling sustaining the textile industry wage, Justice Stone denied that here was an invalid delegation of legislative power to the Wage and Hour Administrator.

"The mandate of the Constitution that all legislative powers granted

'shall be vested' in Congress has never been thought to preclude Congress from resorting to the aid of administrative officers or boards as fact-finding agencies whose findings, made in conformity to previously adopted legislative standards or definitions of Congressional policy have been made prerequisitive to the operation of its statutory command," the Justice stated.

"The adoption of the declared policy by Congress and its definition of the circumstances in which its command is to be effective constitute the performance, in the constitutional sense, of the legislative function."

In the same opinion the court sustained the validity of the procedure set up for establishing wage minima above those prescribed in the act and ruled that the cotton textile industry committee and the administrator had complied with that procedure.

The cotton mills challenged the wage-hour administrator's findings, which were based on the committee's study, on the ground that a wage differential should have been granted to the South because of the difference between conditions existing there and in other textile centers.

"We conclude that the administrator's findings are supported by substantial evidence," Justice Stone stated. "Any different conclusion would require us to substitute our judgment of the weight of the evidence and the inference to be drawn from it for that of the administrator, which the statute forbids."

Notwithstanding the pronouncement of Justice Stone on the Child Labor Law as it affects interstate commerce, Gerard D. Reilly, Labor Department solicitor, said that neither the opinion nor any Congressional enlargement of the Wage and Hour Law would remove the necessity of State ratification of the Child Labor Amendment if the labor of minors in intrastate commerce was to be protected.

According to experts, an interesting sidelight on the wage and hour decision and the setting aside of the child labor law was that by its action the court automatically resurrected the child labor law fostered by former Representative Edward Keating which had been declared illegal in 1918.

In the same way, the court, it was said, held valid a minimum-wage law which also had been adopted for the District of Columbia, a Federal territory, at Mr. Keating's motion, which was also declared unconstitutional in 1918.

ORGANIZE TO PUSH INDUSTRIAL UNIONS

WASHINGTON, Nov. 9 (Æ).—Industrial unionism, which was opposed by craft unions at the recent American Federation of Labor convention, will be pushed by an organization formed here today by representatives of seven international labor unions.

John Brophy of Pittsburgh, Pa., was named director, with John L. Lewis, head of the United Mine Workers of America, president, and Charles P. Howard, president of the International Typographical Union, secretary. The organization will be called the "Committee for Industrial Organization."

Proponents of industrial unionism favor having all workers in an industry included in one organization. Those favoring craft unionism would have each trade organized separately. Industrial union advocates contend that their type of organization would do away with inter-union jurisdictional disputes.

Today's meeting was attended by representatives of the United Mine Workers, Typographical Union, Amalgamated Clothing Workers of America, International Ladies Garment Workers Union, United Textile Workers of America, Oil Field, Gas Well and Refinery Workers of America, United Hatters, Cap and Millinery Workers International Union, and International Union of Mine, Mill and Smelter Workers.

Besides Mr. Lewis and Mr. Howard, members of the committee selected were Sidney Hillman, president of the Clothing Workers; David Dubinsky, president of the Ladies Garment Workers; Thomas E. McMahon, president of the Textile Workers; Harvey C. Freming, president of the Oil Field Workers; M. Zaritsky, president of the Cap and Millinery Department of the Hatters, and Thomas H. Brown, president of the Mine, Mill and Smelter Workers.

A statement given out tonight said that the committee would work in accordance with the "principles and policies enunciated by these organizations at the Atlantic City convention of the American Federation of Labor."

"It is the purpose of the committee to encourage and promote organization of the workers in the mass production and unorganized industries of the nation and affiliation with the American Federation of Labor," it added.

"Its functions will be educational and advisory and the committee and its representatives will cooperate for the recognition and acceptance of modern collective bargaining in such industries.

"Other organizations interested in advancing organization work along the lines of industrial unionism will be invited to participate in the activities of the committee and name representatives to join in its work."

November 10, 1935

A. F. OF L. ORDERED TO SHUN POLITICS

Green and Morrison Call for Adherence to Nonpartisan Policy in the Campaign.

COUNTER 'LABOR LEAGUE'

In Contrast to Berry-Lewis Move for Roosevelt, Federation Is Advised to Avoid Splits.

Special to THE NEW YORK TIMES.

WASHINGTON, April 26.—The American Federation of Labor will follow its traditions and "adhere to a nonpartisan policy" in the 1936 campaign, William Green and Frank Morrison, president and secretary, respectively, asserted in a letter sent today to 109 national and international unions and all affiliated organizations.

This nonpartisan stand, which was maintained except in one Presidential campaign, may be modified, it was indicated unofficially, after the nominations are made and the platforms of the two major parties are adopted. Most of the members of the federation are regarded as favorable to the Roosevelt administration.

John L. Lewis, president of the United Mine Workers and head of the Committee for Industrial Organization which is at odds with the Green régime, has formally endorsed the administration and is expected to be active in the campaigns in West Virginia, Pennsylvania and Illinois, particularly if the Supreme Court should invalidate the Guffey Coal Control Act.

The Green-Morrison declaration nonpartisan policy for the federation is in contrast to the appeal made several weeks ago to the Printing Pressmen's Union by George L. Berry, its president, to join "Labor's Nonpartisan League," whose avowed aim was to "put A. F. of L. unions on record for President Roosevelt" individually. Mr. Lewis is an associate of Mr. Berry in this league.

The letter to the federation cited a "preponderance of membership opinion" expressed in conventions that "the political and economic interests of the working people of the country can best be served, for the present at least, through the pursuit of a nonpartisan political policy."

It pointed to unity within the federation, regardless of political opinions, in behalf of candidates who have supported legislation approved by labor and against candidates opposed to labor. Warning members to "avoid division" by refraining from identifying themselves with "any political movement designed to serve as a substitute" for the federation's nonpartisan policy, the letter concluded:

"When the occasion seems appropriate, when candidates have been nominated, when it becomes publicly known who the candidates are, upon what platform they stand and what social, economic and political principles they espouse, the executive council through its nonpartisan political committee will officially communicate with all organizations affiliated with the American Federation of Labor advising them regarding the standing, qualifications and public records of candidates for political positions."

April 27, 1936

GREEN-LEWIS FEUD NEARS OPEN SPLIT

Miners' Chief Calls on Head of A. F. of L. to Quit and Return to Aid Ex-Comrades.

SAYS OUSTER IS PLANNED

Sharp Reply Accuses Foe of Making It Impossible to Organize Steel Labor.

By LOUIS STARK
Special to THE NEW YORK TIMES.

WASHINGTON, June 6.—John L. Lewis, president of the United Mine Workers of America, and William Green, president of the American Federation of Labor, exchanged communications today that widened the rift between opposing forces on the craft-industrial union issue and, in the opinion of labor observers, apparently insured a disastrous split in the labor movement.

The correspondence began with a warning to Mr. Green by the miners' chief that members of the Executive Council were preparing to name a successor to Mr. Green as president of the A. F. of L. Mr. Lewis urged Mr. Green to return to the miners' union, adding that he could not believe that the former secretary-treasurer of the coal-diggers would approve of the suspension from the federation of the ten unions working to organize industrial unions in the mass production industries.

Mr. Green replied by saying that the issue was whether or not the A. F. of L. would be maintained and preserved. He asserted that Mr. Lewis had opened the controversy by espousing the industrial union cause, and reiterated his charge that the action of the Committee for Industrial Organization, in aligning the steel workers' union with it, had made a joint campaign by the entire labor movement to organize steel impossible.

As president of the federation, Mr. Green said, he had undertaken to be governed by its decisions, but he declared that Mr. Lewis had refused to be bound by the federation's rulings.

Plan for Ouster Is Denied

Mr. Lewis's admonition to Mr. Green was the first public statement giving credence to reports that members of the Executive Council were dissatisfied with Mr. Green and that they were planning to name his successor, possibly at the next convention. Although members of the Executive Council were unavailable today, it was denied in labor circles that an agreement had been reached as to Mr. Green's successor.

Mr. Green, in his reply, called his former chief "Dear sir and brother," and taunted him with the statement that "truth is mightier than the sword." He flatly accused Mr. Lewis of having made it impossible to solidify the labor forces of the nation in an effort to help the steel workers, and said that this, and not any action that the federation may have taken, would console "the steel barons," as intimated in Mr. Lewis's communication.

Recalling that the United Mine Workers was "created" by the A. F. of L., Mr. Green said the federation had guarded the miners' union and saved it in 1927 by giving it $500,000.

Mr. Green said Mr. Lewis had taken part in the conventions of the A. F. of L., where policies were formulated and decisions made. There the industrial union issue had been dealt with, he said.

Lewis's Letter to Green

The correspondence follows:
Mr. William Green, president American Federation of Labor,
A. F. of L. Building,
Washington, D. C.
Dear Bill:
I overlook the inane ineptitude of your statement published today. Perchance you were agitated and distraught. The momentary satisfaction accruing to the employers of the steel industry as they perused your statement is also of little consequence.

It is inconceivable that you intend doing what your statement implies, i. e., to sit with the women, under an awning on the hilltop, while the steel workers in the valley struggle in the dust and agony of industrial warfare.

You are the custodian of your own honor. Nevertheless, your own union has declared itself for a definite policy. It calls upon its loyal sons for support of that policy. The imperishable words of Stephen Decatur in Norfolk in 1816 constitute an analogy.

Press accounts detail, without reserve, the intent of the executives of the American Federation of Labor to suspend on July 8 the ten national and international unions who plan to extend aid to the workers in America's unorganized industries. You have uttered no disclaimer. **Even so,** I cannot yet believe that you would be a party to such a Brutus blow. In addition, you would destroy yourself.

It is known to you that your shipmates on the Executive Council are even now planning to slit your political throat and scuttle your official ship. They are caviling among themselves over the naming of your successor when the perfidious act of separation is accomplished. Why not forego such company and return home to the union that suckled you, rather than court obloquy by dwelling among its adversaries and lending them your strength?

An honored seat at the council table awaits you, if you elect to return.

Very truly yours,
JOHN L. LEWIS.

Green's Reply to Lewis

June 6, 1936.

Mr. John L. Lewis, President International Union, United Mine Workers of America, Washington, D. C.

Dear Sir and Brother:

Truth is mightier than the sword. It cuts deeply. Evidently my press statement, filled with truth, affected you that way. That is the only reason I can assign for your most recent letter, which you sent me by special messenger today. No indulgence in any form of poetic language can change the facts. You have made it impossible for the American Federation of Labor to unite and solidify its forces in support of an organizing campaign in the steel industry. The steel barons may get some consolation out of that fact, not out of any action which the American Federation of Labor has taken.

The issue involved, which has grown out of the controversy you raised, is, Shall the federation be maintained and preserved? Shall it be divided or shall it be solidified? I am seeking to maintain it intact and united. This is the basis for every action I have taken and every move I have made. I have appealed, entreated and begged you to join with me in this supreme effort. If you persist in your determination to divide the forces of labor I will still continue to protect and preserve our common heritage, the American Federation of Labor. You, alone, can determine whether you will remain with or leave the American Federation of Labor. That decision rests with you.

Cites Gompers Tradition

The pioneers of the labor movement founded the American Federation of Labor. Samuel Gompers and his associates nurtured and protected it. It has been handed to us with a solemn admonition that we protect it and preserve it. This great parent body created the United Mine Workers of America. It guarded it and made it strong when it was weak. It saved it in 1927, which seems but yesterday, when those who still remain loyal and devoted to its principles and policies contributed more than half a million dollars in order to save it.

I am the president of the American Federation of Labor. I took a solemn obligation to uphold its laws, to be governed by its decisions and to be loyal to its principles and policies.

In the conventions of this great organization decisions and policies were made. You participated in them, submitting an issue which you considered as vital for decision. Every rule of honor and fair play would require that the decision of the tribunal to which you submitted an issue would be respected, obeyed and observed.

Nothing can be offered as a justification for the sacrifice of honor and a solemn obligation. The mandate of the American Federation of Labor convention becomes law to me. There will be no resort to subterfuge or expediency in order to evade the discharge of this solemn obligation. The members of the international union, United Mine Workers of America, would hold me in utter contempt, and rightly so, if I pursued any other course.

Fraternally yours,
WILLIAM GREEN.

Drive in Steel Mills Pushed

Special to THE NEW YORK TIMES.

PITTSBURGH, June 6.—The big guns of labor's militant drive will be turned full upon the United States Steel Corporation in its first major offensive to organize the nation's 500,000 steel workers into one big union, it was learned authoritatively today.

The big drive, to be launched in the name of the Amalgamated Association of Iron, Steel and Tin Workers, will have the support—moral and financial—of nine major industrial unions, composing one-third of the total membership of the powerful American Federation of Labor.

From A. F. of L. headquarters in Washington today came word of an impending action of the Executive Council to carry out the threat of President William Green to suspend the "rebellious" unions that have lined up solidly behind the defiant John L. Lewis, head of the United Mine Workers of America.

For obvious disciplinary purposes, it was said, it has become "more necessary than ever" to suspend the nine unions composing the "outlawed" Committee for Industrial Organization. Mr. Lewis and his militant associates, however, went determinedly ahead with plans to launch the 500,000 membership drive of the Amalgamated Association.

June 7, 1936

CARNEGIE STEEL SIGNS C. I. O. CONTRACT FOR PAY RISE, 40-HR. WEEK, RECOGNITION

STRIKE IS AVERTED

Company Grants Same Benefits to Employe Representatives

UNION IS NOT SOLE AGENT

$5 MINIMUM DAILY WAGE

By LOUIS STARK

Special to THE NEW YORK TIMES.

PITTSBURGH, March 2.—Possibility of a general steel strike this Spring was scrapped today when the Carnegie-Illinois Steel Corporation, the United States Steel Corporation's major subsidiary, signed an agreement with the Steel Workers' organizing committee on behalf of its members who are employes of the corporation.

The agreement covered union recognition, a wage increase, the eight-hour day and forty-hour week, time and a half for overtime, no discrimination against employes for joining the union, and agreement by the union not to solicit members in the plants on corporation time.

While the union group led by Philip Murray was conferring with Carnegie-Illinois officials led by President Benjamin F. Fairless, the corporation announced to its employe representatives in twenty-seven plants that it was granting them the same wage advances as those accorded to the union.

First Labor Agreement

Mr. Murray said that the agreement was the first "legitimate agreement" made on behalf of a unit of the United States Steel Corporation with an independent trade union, recalling that when the corporation was organized in 1901 it announced its opposition to making such union agreements.

The agreement calls for a minimum wage of $5 instead of the present $4.20 a day, and will be in effect for one year ending Feb. 28, 1938. A joint committee representing the corporation and the S. W. O. C. will meet not later than March 10 for the purpose of drawing up a written agreement covering work conditions, application of rates and other details.

Mr. Murray maintained that the agreement sounded the death knell of the employe representation plan, but admitted that the scrapping of the company union had not come before the conferees.

On this point, it was emphatically denied on behalf of the corporation that the employe representation plan had been put aside. It was said that the company was still adhering to its policy of dealing with any group of employes, and this had been reiterated today when employe representatives had been advised of the change in conditions which, it was said, had been requested by the district council of employe representatives three weeks ago.

All Wage Rates to Be Adjusted

No statement was made on behalf of the Carnegie-Illinois Corporation when the conference ended. The only announcement made today was the following, imparted to employe representatives:

"As a result of numerous requests from various plants for wage increases, we wish to announce the following schedule, effective March 16, 1937.

"The common labor rate of 52½ cents an hour will be increased to 62½ cents per hour.

"All other rates will be adjusted equitably.

"The basic forty-hour week will be established and time and a half paid for more than forty hours per week or eight hours per day. The adoption of the forty-hour basic week is made necessary in order to qualify for government contracts under the Walsh-Healey bill."

The Carnegie-Illinois agreement covers the union's membership among the 120,000 employes of the corporation. Mr. Murray did not divulge the number of union members in this corporation's plants.

The business of making public the results of the unheralded conferences of the last two days was turned over to Mr. Murray. He said that invitations would now go out from the union to the other subsidiaries of the United States Steel Corporation and that he expected that these organizations would, through their presidents, sign similar agreements covering in all the plants the union's members among the parent corporation's 550,000 workers.

At the same time Mr. Murray said that before the end of the week invitations would go to independent steel producers to confer with the S. W. O. C. in order to make an agreement similar to the one reached today. Mr. Murray said that the Carnegie-Illinois Corporation stated it would not object to the union men wearing their buttons in the plants, a privilege similar to that accorded automobile union members by the General Motors Corporation as a result of the recent strike.

C. I. O.-A. F. of L. Rift May Widen

The announcement today is likely to lead to the widening of the chasm that separates the craft and industrial union adherents in the A. F. of L. The gap has become greater in recent months, particularly since the glass workers' strike and that of the automobile workers. These unions are among the fifteen affiliates of the Committee on Industrial Organization.

There appear to be indications that the craft unions in the federation are likely to follow the example of the C. I. O. and take over the employe representation groups in some plants in order to use them as the nucleus for unionization drives.

On its side the C. I. O. probably will broaden the scope of its organization work to include not only other steel corporations but also other industries, notably oil and textiles.

Rivalry between the A. F. of L. and the C. I. O. is evidenced in the respective legislative programs which they are seeking to promote in Congress and in the State Legislatures.

Other Companies Raise Wages

Additional steel corporations today announced wage rises similar to those announced yesterday by independents and that made public today by the Carnegie-Illinois Corporation.

Jones & Laughlin announced that "as a result of collective bargaining with employe representatives a common labor rate of $5 a day has been granted, effective March 16."

"Adjustment will be made of other rates," it was said. "The question of limiting the work week to forty hours, with time and a half for overtime, is under consideration with employe representatives and a decision is expected shortly."

Three other subsidiaries of the United States Steel Corporation were among those which announced wage increases and establishment of the forty-hour basic week today. They were the American Steel and Wire Company, the Columbia Steel Company and the National Tube Corporation. The latter is the giant pipe-making subsidiary of the United States Steel Corporation.

In his formal announcement of the signing of the agreement Mr. Murray said:

"We are pleased to announce the execution of an agreement today between Carnegie-Illinois Steel Corporation and the Steel Workers Organizing Committee, on behalf of its members who are employes of the corporation. This agreement provides for an increase in wages,

March 3, 1937

4 KILLED 84 HURT AS STRIKERS FIGHT POLICE IN CHICAGO

Day's Strike Developments

Four were killed and eighty-four injured when about 1,000 C. I. O. strikers, marching on the Republic Steel plant in South Chicago, were repulsed by police. The strikers hurled rocks and bolts and fired some shots. The police used their clubs, tear gas and guns.

A battle line was drawn at Youngstown between steel strikers and civic authorities over the supplying of food to maintenance men within the plants.

Union planes failed to prevent company aircraft from dropping supplies for the besieged. P.

Rival steel worker rallies were held near the Weirton company's mills in West Virginia, with some members of the Security League booing a C. I. O. parade and snatching flags off cars.

The City Industrial Relations Board promised the C. I. O. taxi drivers' union to consider its request for a referendum of the employes of the Parmelee System.

May 31, 1937

REPUBLIC STEEL TO SIGN WITH C. I. O.

Four-Year Fight Ends With Stipulation for Contract if Union Proves Majority

GIRDLER EXPLAINS STAND

He Says Corporation Wishes to Avoid Any Letdown on Defense Orders

By W. H. LAWRENCE
Special to The New York Times.

WASHINGTON, July 15 — The Republic Steel Corporation ended today its four and a half year battle against the C. I. O.'s Steel Workers Organizing Committee and the National Labor Relations Board, and the corporation, the C. I. O. and the NLRB signed a stipulation settling all charges of Wagner Act violation against the company. Several hundred workers will be reinstated in their jobs and back pay totaling tens of thousands of dollars will be paid.

The company agreed to dispense with an NLRB election and to abide by the results of an NLRB check of union membership cards against payrolls at fifteen steel producing plants.

If the NLRB certifies that the C. I. O. has a majority, and if agreement is reached in collective bargaining, the corporation stipulated that "such agreement shall be reduced to writing and signed."

Recalls Little Steel Strike

The "signed contract" was the principal issue of the 1937 "Little Steel" strike, in which eighteen persons were killed.

Tom M. Girdler, Republic's board chairman, told Secretary Perkins's special Steel Mediation Board at that time that "Republic cannot and will not enter into a contract, oral or written, with an irresponsible party, and the C. I. O. as presently constituted, is utterly irresponsible."

Mr. Girdler also declared that "he would go back to the farm and dig potatoes before he would sign with the C. I. O."

Consequently, the Republic agreement was regarded in labor circles as second in significance only to the contract with the Ford Motor Company, in which Henry Ford recently granted not only all the union's wage demands but also gave the C. I. O. a closed shop and the check-off.

No accurate estimate of the back pay involved in the Republic case was available. In Ohio, the company and the union agreed to arbitrate if they were unable to agree on the amount of back pay claimed by 6,500 men involved in the 1937 strike.

Fewer numbers will be affected in plants in other cities.

As the agreement was signed here by attorneys for the board, the C. I. O. and the company, Mr. Girdler issued a statement in which he said:

"This procedure will eliminate the necessity of plant elections. It was adopted in the furtherance of collective bargaining in the plants and in the interests of national defense as it will avoid any interference with production which might result from plant electioneering campaigns.

"The agreement marks the union's first offer to submit proof of its membership in the company's plants. Membership in any plant will be established by union records checked against the company payrolls and verified by the National Labor Relations Board.

"Republic is operating at top speed and a good share of its output is for defense needs. We want to avoid any let-down in production from any cause."

The C. I. O. said 41,630 workers would be brought under the agreement at the company's plants.

July 16, 1941

LABOR BARGAIN IDEA DRAFTED BY SLOAN

General Motors Notifies Employes This Does Not Mean Employe Management.

BARS COERCION BY UNIONS

Pamphlet Sent to 130,000 Workers Provides Guide in All Grievances.

Special to The New York Times.

DETROIT, Oct. 15.—A statement by the General Motors Corporation, signed by Alfred P. Sloan Jr., its president, on basic policies governing employer-employe relations in all its divisions, enunciating in the main the broad "philosophy and principles" which "every element of the management" from foreman to president has been instructed to follow, was sent by mail today to the corporation's 130,000 employes.

In a letter accompanying the pamphlet, Mr. Sloan tells the corporation's views on collective bargaining, in this language.

"As you know, the subject deals with the problem of 'collective bargaining.' First, I want to make it clear that we, in General Motors, recognize 'collective bargaining' as a constructive step forward, both for the employes and the management.

"Regardless of any obligation that may exist, we propose not only to continue the idea but to develop it. How much can be accomplished will depend upon the cooperation of all concerned.

"To develop the maximum, we must both understand what we are trying to do, and how we are trying to do it, and then, again, must be patient with each other, because we are proceeding, in a way, along a new road. Mistakes are bound to develop and mistakes are sure to be made on both sides—that is inevitable—in establishing a new relationship of this character. However, experience and cooperation will, through evolution, correct all this if we approach the problem in the right spirit.

"From the standpoint of management, I am extremely anxious that every individual concerned in management, wholeheartedly and with an open mind, cooperate with the employes in making this potential step forward, a real step forward."

Appeal Tribunal Chosen.

Appeal procedure for employes or employe representatives is provided in a section which names the Department of Industrial Relations in Detroit as the high tribunal for such cases.

"The management is convinced that, given sincere and patient effort on both sides, there is no reason why problems arising out of relationships with employes cannot be satisfactorily adjusted within the organization," an introduction to the plan declares.

That embattled term "collective bargaining," out of which widespread strife has developed in various industries in the past year, receives the following simple and understandable definition:

"Collective bargaining is to be understood as a method of intercommunication and negotiation between employes and management, whose objective is the maintenance of harmonious and cooperative relations through mutual understanding and agreement with respect to terms and conditions of employment."

Recognition is given to social factors in another paragraph, which states: "Management should recognize the importance of social considerations as influencing broad policies governing industrial relations. For example, if medical research discovers that certain conditions of employment are inimical to the health of employes, management should take such action as is practicable to remedy the harmful conditions."

Inherent responsibilities of management are referred to and a declaration is made that this arrangement does not mean collective employer-employe management.

Outside Agencies Are Curbed.

Mention is made that the plan does not mean that impartial or judicial agencies have no place in collective bargaining. "On the contrary," it states, "controversial questions of fact, such as discrimination cases and questions of lay-off, may frequently be more amicably and speedily settled through an impartial, competent, fact-finding agency having the confidence of both sides."

Provision is attached, however, that "no case is to be submitted to the determination of any outside agency without the specific authorization of the executive committee."

A degree of flexibility in the matter of representation is allowed in the section which deals with procedure, stating:

"While there is the technical requirement that in collective bargaining negotiations the right to represent employes must be duly established, nevertheless the management should be reasonable in its willingness to listen to anyone desiring to discuss matters purporting to affect General Motors employes.

"In the event that an issue is raised by a particular group or their duly accredited representatives, the settlement of which involves the interests of non-represented groups, the management should satisfy itself that any decision arrived at provides fair treatment with respect to such non-represented groups."

Bargaining Procedure Explained.

The section which deals with "procedure with bargaining groups" provides:

"The procedure outlined in this subsection does not contemplate formal conferences between management and employes or their representatives, but rather the ordinary managerial consideration and attention to views and contentions indicated in behalf of employes.

"Questions raised by employes, or by accredited representatives, should be dealt with as expeditiously as practicable at all times. Routine matters falling within the scope of authority of the foreman, or the supervisory executive in immediate contact, should be settled on the spot whenever it is possible to arrive at a satisfactory understanding.

"When the matter is outside of the scope of the authority of the foreman or the supervisory executive in immediate contact, or if a satisfactory settlement cannot be made by him, the foreman or the executive should in all cases submit the matter to his superior.

"Similarly, if the matter is outside of the scope of the authority of the executive to whom it has been submitted, or if he cannot settle it satisfactorily, he, in turn, should submit it to his superior and successively the matter should be referred up through the organization until it reaches the executive whose scope of authority enables him to make final decision.

"Every effort should be made to effect an amicable settlement, even if this necessitates referring the matter all the way up to the general manager of the division. When a matter has been decided, not only the exact nature of the decision, but also the management's viewpoint thereon, should be made clear

to those down the line to the point of initial contact with the matter."

Procedure for Appeal.

Appeal procedure is provided as follows:

"In any case where it has not been possible to arrive at an amicable understanding through conference and discussion—even after the case has been referred to the general manager of the division—employes or their representatives may refer the case to the Department of Industrial Relations in Detroit. In such cases a complete statement of the facts, together with supporting evidence, should be submitted by both sides to the controversy.

"The Department of Industrial Relations will review the material submitted and make such independent investigations as may be necessary to determine if there has been either a violation of company policies or if the case involves matter beyond the scope of divisional authority. If it is found that the case falls within either of the above two categories, the complete facts will be referred to the executive vice president through the group executive for such action as may be required.

"The executive vice president will, for the information of the executive committee, make a report to it on all such appeal cases referred to him."

Freedom of discussion is provided in a clause which states: "It must be distinctly understood that it is contrary to the letter and the spirit of collective bargaining for the management to attempt by any means to prevent questions as regards same from being raised by the employes and fully discussed with them or their representatives.

Coercion Is Forbidden.

Recalling that coercion by unions as well as employers has been banned, the corporation's plan states that "all cases of attempted coercion by outside unions to force employes to join them should be thoroughly investigated" and referred to the Industrial Relations Department.

"Although the fact that employes are members of an employe association or of an outside union does not make such association or union the agent of these employes for collective bargaining," the rules hold. It is provided that "the Automobile Labor Board has laid down a general ruling that there should be no solicitation of membership during working hours." Impartial enforcement is demanded.

"It is important that all employment departments make every effort to hire local employes," the plan sets forth. Furthermore, it

provides a method of appealing to the NRA to get necessary exceptions to permit its existing working force to work longer hours, so as to avoid the economic and social consequences which result from the importation of employes for brief periods.

"The management has the full right to discharge an employe for cause, such as, for example, insubordination, inefficiency or infraction of shop rules," the plan continues. "The decision to discharge an employe, however, must rest upon clear and explicit cause and must be reasonable. Furthermore, the full reasons for discharge should be recorded and should be stated explicitly to the employe.

"The law is explicit in its prohibition of discharging employes for affiliation or non-affiliation with any labor or employe organization."

Change of status is covered as follows:

"When a man is separated from any division he should be given a release slip, clearly indicating the reasons. If he is discharged, he should know why; if laid off on account of reduction of force, it must be understood he is eligible for reemployment. When a man quits, his release slip should indicate this. The slip and the employment record should give the employe's status in plain English, not in code."

October 16, 1934

'SIT DOWNS' CLOSE FOUR BIG PLANTS OF GENERAL MOTORS

LEWIS BACKS UNION MOVE

Insists That Automobile Concern Must Deal With Workers on Nation-Wide Basis.

Latest Moves in Strike

"Sit-down" strikes in Fisher Body plants Nos. 1 and 2 at Flint, Mich., forced a general curtailment of parts orders for General Motors production plants. 25,200 out of work.

Labor moves have forced a shutdown of the Chevrolet assembly plant at Flint. That motor plant and also the Buick units are likely to suspend today.

Plants in many parts of the country supplying automotive parts prepared to curtail production.

John L. Lewis was quoted as say-

ing the C. I. O. was fully behind the fight, which might include the steel, coal and glass industries.

Flint Is Center of Trouble

Special to THE NEW YORK TIMES.

FLINT, Mich., Dec. 30.—Backed by the John L. Lewis Committee for Industrial Organization, the United Automobile Workers of America today started its campaign to include the nation's automobile industry within its ranks. It struck at the center of General Motors operations and halted activities in three of its unit plants here.

Affecting operations at all but one of the five General Motors units in Flint, Fisher Body Plant No. 1 was closed late tonight by a sit-down strike ordered by the United Automobile Workers of America.

This action brought to 25,200 the number of men thrown out of work, including employes of two Fisher Body plants, the Chevrolet assembly plant and the Buick Motor Company plant.

The strike at Fisher No. 1 tonight affected 1,600 men and women on the night shift and 5,500 others on the day shift. This plant supplies all bodies used by Buick and will prevent Buick from operating today.

Buick Workers Forced Out

A strike this morning at Fisher Body Plant No. 2, which supplies all bodies for the Chevrolet assembly plant here, caused operations to cease both at the Fisher plant and the Chevrolet assembly plant.

The situation now finds 8,200 men thrown out of work at the two Fisher plants, 1,000 at the Chevrolet assembly plant and 16,000 at Buick. Spark Plug plants have not been affected so far.

The sit-down at Fisher No. 1 late tonight came with the same suddenness which marked similar action at Fisher No. 1 earlier in the day. Returning from their usual lunch hour at 10 P. M., an undetermined number of men refused to return to work and all operations ceased. Nearly 300 women employed on the night shift immediately left the plant.

A spokesman for the strikers charged the company with discrimination, but individual strikers refused to discuss the situation with the management.

It was announced by an official spokesman for the company that the United Automobile Workers' representatives had presented a contract to the management and had informed the company that they expected it to be signed by Monday afternoon. The spokesman declared the union representatives

assured the company that no action of any kind would be taken by the workers until after Monday's conference.

Announced as an "extraordinary conference," United Automobile Workers Union national officials have scheduled a meeting in Flint Sunday afternoon with representatives of unions in ten other cities taking part.

They have announced they will prepare a basic policy for presentation to General Motors plants throughout the nation at this conference.

Because of the threatened strikes and the shortage of glass due to the present strikes in glass plants, General Motors officials announced that temporary stop orders had been sent to various companies supplying parts. Hundreds of supplying companies are affected.

Operations at Fisher Body Plant No. 2, supplying bodies for the Chevrolet assembly plant here, were halted this morning. The plant was forced to close when a group of less than fifty members of the United Automobile Workers Union sat down in the plant and refused to work.

Being in key positions, the plant operations were immediately halted. Within a few hours the lack of bodies forced the Chevrolet plant assembly line and car delivery department into idleness.

A few hours later, 137 employes of the Standard Cotton Products

144

Company, which makes seat materials for Fisher Body plants, sat down at their work, demanding a 20-cents-an-hour wage increase for every employe, an eight-hour day, and time and one-half for overtime, in addition to a minimum wage of 50 cents an hour for every employe.

Curtailment of operations in the General Motors units here was caused by a dispute over company policies. Because some employes belong to the United Automobile Workers Union and others do not, it is a rule of the company that inspectors on the assembly lines cannot hold membership in the union because of the opportunity for discrimination against non-union workers.

Men who were working as inspectors received an opportunity to accept transfer to other jobs or give up their union membership. This they refused to do and the sit-down followed.

Martin Asks for $100,000

Announcing that the United Automobile Workers Union was backing the strike, Homer Martin, international president, declared the Flint strike was called "as a warning to General Motors Corporation that we mean business." He also declared that "these strikes cannot be settled locally; settlement must be on a national basis."

The position of General Motors, as enunciated by an official spokesman, was that strikes in individual plants were the problem of individual plant managements, and should be settled locally.

That the union intends to adhere to its announced policy was evidenced in the fact that Robert Travis, an organizer here, went to Detroit today and asked labor officials for $100,000 to finance the strike in Flint. "We will need that much," he declared.

There was no disorder in the Fisher plants. Of the 1,200 at work in Plant No. 2 when the sit-down began, fewer than 500 remained in the plant tonight. Food was taken to them by other members of the union, with full permission of the company.

It was intimated late tonight that a sit-down would be ordered in the motor manufacturing plant of Chevrolet, which would affect every Chevrolet assembly plant, 66,000 workers being employed there.

Some Parts Completely Halted

In explaining the temporary stop orders sent to various companies supplying auto parts, officials of General Motors said the purpose was to keep shipments from suppliers in line with the demands of General Motors units.

Hundreds of supplying companies will be affected. Some of them were instructed to suspend shipments pending further orders. Others were instructed to curtail shipments.

The spokesman for the corporation said that the order was made necessary primarily by a shortage of glass caused by a strike in the plate glass industry, although the possibility of further strikes in General Motors plants also was a factor.

Continuation of the glass strike for two weeks more might cause widespread shutdowns of General Motors plants, the corporation spokesman explained.

Two major producers which supply about 90 per cent of flat glass to the automobile industry are now closed by strikes. They comprise plants of the Libbey-Owens-Ford Glass Company and the Pittsburgh Plate Glass Company.

Because there may not be enough glass to maintain schedules, General Motors officials decided to authorize purchasing agents to prevent heavy stocks of other parts from accumulating.

As far as can be learned, every General Motors plant has at least two weeks' supply of glass on hand. Under the stop-order, plants with only a two weeks' glass supply were authorized to cut orders for other supplies to cover a like period.

General Motors has more than ten plants throughout the country, with most of them devoted to automobile production.

Firms manufacturing tires, batteries, radios, hardware, light bulbs, safety glass, speedometers, instrument panel equipment, oil filters and hundreds of other parts are affected by the stop order issued by the corporation today.

December 31, 1936

AT THE MOTOR STRIKE STORM CENTER

James Dewey (left), representative of the Secretary of Labor, and Governor Murphy of Michigan

DATES AND EVENTS IN MOTORS STRIKE

The First 'Sit-Down' Was Begun by Fisher Body Workers at Atlanta Nov. 18

By The Associated Press.

Here are the important dates and events in the dispute between the United Automobile Workers of America and the General Motors Corporation:

1936

Nov. 18—The first "sit-down" strike was called by U. A. W. A. in the Fisher Body plant at Atlanta, Ga., followed a week later by strikes at Kansas City.

Dec. 21—Homer Martin, the union president, asked General Motors to confer on collective bargaining.

Dec. 22—William S. Knudsen, the corporation's executive vice president, told Mr. Martin that grievances should be taken up with individual plant managers.

Dec. 31—As the "sit-down" strikes increased, Mr. Knudsen called the strikers "trespassers" and advised them to leave the plants.

1937

Jan. 2—Circuit Judge Edward D. Black at Flint, Mich., which had become the strike "capital," issued a broad injunction against the strikers, ordering them to leave; Sheriff Thomas Wolcott ordered the evacuation in "half an hour," but took no action.

Jan. 3—The union "strategy board" was formed at a Flint conference and was empowered to call strikes in all General Motors plants.

Jan. 7—Governor Frank Murphy joined in the efforts to conciliate the strike as the plant shut-downs increased.

Jan. 11—The first serious violence occurred at Flint, with twenty-seven persons injured in a street battle.

Jan. 12—Governor Murphy ordered 2,300 National Guardsmen to Flint and asked General Motors and union leaders to confer with him at Lansing.

Jan. 15—A truce pending a fifteen-day period allotted to negotiations was reached in a seventeen-hour conference at Lansing; it provided for evacuation of the plants.

Jan. 17—Evacuation was halted at Flint on the union's charge that General Motors broke faith by agreeing to confer with the Flint Alliance, an anti-strike group.

Jan. 18—Conferees met but dispersed after five minutes, and all negotiations were abandoned; Governor Murphy went to Washington.

Jan. 20—Conferences at Washington between Secretary Perkins and Governor Murphy and opposing leaders in the strike opened, but were abandoned after three days without any notable progress.

Jan. 25—General Motors disclosed a plan to give at least part-time work to 95,000 of 135,000 idle wage-earners.

Jan. 30—Governor Murphy made a new effort to bring the disputants together as the first month of the "sit-down" at Flint ended.

Feb. 1—A dozen persons were injured in a renewal of violence at Flint.

Feb. 2—Judge Paul V. Gadola at Flint issued a new injunction, giving the strikers twenty-four hours to leave under $15,000,000 penalty; picketing was barred.

Feb. 3—The new conference of General Motors and union representatives opened in Detroit; evacuation deadline passed at Flint, with the strikers holding their positions.

Feb. 5—Sheriff Wolcott received the eviction order, but no action was taken against the "stay-in" strikers as the Detroit conference continued.

Feb. 6—Governor Murphy announced that the parley was deadlocked over the union demand for recognition as the sole bargaining agency in twenty strike-bound General Motors plants; the conference continued.

Feb. 11—Governor Murphy announced at 2:40 A. M.: "An agreement has been reached." The end came after more than fifty hours of conference over a nine-day period.

February 12, 1937

Glossary of the Terms Used in Labor Espionage

Special to THE NEW YORK TIMES.

WASHINGTON, Dec. 21.—A glossary of the terms used in labor espionage was appended to the report of the La Follette civil liberties subcommittee of the Senate Labor Committee, made public today, for the convenience of students of the report. This glossary is as follows:

CORRESPONDENT — A labor spy. See hooked man, informant, and stool pigeon.

COVER—The fiction employed by a hooker or roper or an ordinary operative to conceal his detective agency connection. See pretext.

DATEWOOD—Pinkerton's code designation for E. S. Clark, superintendent of the Cleveland division of the agency.

EDUCATION—Used by Corporations Auxiliary Company to denote "hooking" in Wisconsin to circumvent the State requirement of registration of employes of detective agencies.

ENTERTAINMENT — Designation used in bills and accounts by Corporations Auxiliary Company and other agencies to conceal expenditures for union dues of the spies.

FINK—One who makes a career of taking employment in struck plants, or of acting as a strikebreaker, strike guard, or slugger.

GENERAL OP—A labor spy who holds influential position in labor union and reports on labor conditions in an entire city or area.

GOOD—Pinkerton's code word for the ribbon copy of a labor spy report.

GUARD—A fink serving on guard duty during a strike. Often armed.

HOOKING—To entrap an employe into spying on fellow employes. Usually accomplished by approaching the prospective hooked man under a pretext and engaging him to write reports.

HOOKER—Detective agency official who induces workers to become spies.

HOOKED MAN—An employe engaged in industrial espionage without knowledge that he is reporting to a detective agency, or that his reports are going to the employer.

HUMAN ENGINEERING—Used by the Corporations Auxiliary Company and other agencies as an alternative term for its labor espionage service.

INSIDE MAN—A spy placed in a plant as an employe. See hooked man, stool pigeon, missionary, outside man.

INSPECTOR—Euphemism used to refer to spies in accounts, correspondence, etc.

JOURNAL SHEET—The detective agency record of orders and operations on a specific client who is purchasing labor espionage service.

MDABY—Pinkerton's code designation for General Motors Corporation.

MDEIC—Pinkerton's code word for Chevrolet Motor Division of General Motors Corporation.

MHUPO—Pinkerton's code word for Alfred Marshall, personnel director for Chevrolet Motor Division of General Motors Corporation.

MISSIONARY — A spy whose work it is to spread anti-union or anti-strike propaganda in the general neighborhood of a plant and particularly among the wives of workers. Is not employed in the plant.

NOBLE—A lieutenant of strike operations usually in charge of a detachment of guards, sluggers and finks.

OP — See operative.

OPERATIVE — A spy employed by an agency. Usually has a secret designation. An operative may be a hooked man or professional spy.

OUTSIDE MAN — A spy under a cover, but not masquerading as an employe of a plant. See missionary.

PEGWOOD — Pinkerton's code designation for Robert Peterson, assistant superintendent of the Detroit office.

POOR — Pinkerton's code word for a carbon copy of a labor spy report.

PRETEXT—A "cover." (Qv.)

ROPING — Securing information by striking up acquaintance or friendship with union men.

ROUGH SHADOW — To keep a man under surveillance in such a manner that he knows that he is being followed and is intimidated.

SCO SERVICE — National Metal Trades Association term to denote labor espionage. Special contract operative service.

SHADOWING — The operation of keeping a person under secret surveillance.

SLUGGER—A specialized type of fink used to attack, assault and beat up strikers or union leaders. Generally armed. See fink, guard.

STRIKE-BREAKER — One whose trade it is to take employment in struck plants. Distinguishable from "scab," who is a workman. May pretend to work in the plant or act as a guard. A fink.

TMEHY—Pinkerton's code designation for the International Association of Machinists.

VENDOR SURVEY—Special service rendered by Corporations Auxiliary Company for the Chrysler Corporation of placing labor spies in the plants of companies supplying the corporation with parts used in manufacturing its product in order to check their labor relations. A similar service was rendered by the Pinkerton Agency for the General Motors Corporation.

December 22, 1937

LABOR WILL DRIVE FOR A NEW POWER

Federation and C. I. O. Expect to Share Large Gains in Membership

MISS PERKINS IS PLEASED

Chief Strike Cause Held Gone —Lewis Assails 'Caprice,' Compares Guffey Ruling

By LOUIS STARK

Special to THE NEW YORK TIMES.

WASHINGTON, April 12.—Jubilant over the Supreme Court's decisions, leaders of organized labor were confident today that the opportunity was at hand to build, within a year, the most powerful labor movement in the world.

In labor circles it was freely predicted that the effect of the opinions upholding the Wagner act would be to release a vast wave of sentiment favoring unionization.

The American Federation of Labor and the Committee for Industrial Organization are both expected to share in the large accretions to union ranks in the next year.

The C. I. O. campaign is among the millions of employes in the basic industries (such as steel, oil, textiles and automobiles), while the A. F. of L. is pressing for action in other industries.

The decision, awarding as much jurisdiction to the National Labor Relations Board as it had asked, gratified Chairman J. Warren Madden and his associates, Edwin M. Smith and Donald Wakefield Smith. Mr. Madden said:

"This means industrial peace."

Conferences to Begin Soon

Secretary Perkins said that the Supreme Court "has done away with the principal cause of industrial unrest in America," and then announced that on April 20 she would hold the first of a series of conferences here to discuss how labor and management could cooperate in utilization of effective techniques of conciliation and mediation in collective bargaining under the Wagner act.

William Green, president of the A. F. of L., said:

"The decisions are fraught with deep significance and will prove to be of tremendous importance. Labor will now be free to organize without fear of discrimination and persecution. A new impetus will be given the organized labor movement. It means the end of company unions."

John L. Lewis, president of the United Mine Workers of America and head of the C. I. O., called it "an astounding judgment."

"The quibblers of ancient Greece were intellectual sluggards as compared with our Supreme Court," he said. "Apparently, the destiny of our Republic and the well-being of its population depend upon the legalistic whims and caprices of one man.

"Yesterday the Guffey Coal Stabilization Act was struck down. Today the Wagner Labor Relations Act is sustained. If today the Court is right, then yesterday, forsooth, the Court was wrong.

"The Court is as variable as the winds, and the people wonder how long they are to be the victims of its instability. Obviously the situation needs change. The President's court plan is the immediate answer."

Major George L. Berry, president of Labor's Non-Partisan League, said:

"Naturally, I am delighted with the decisions upholding the National Labor Relations Act. They are a tribute to this man (Senator Wagner) who fought for a principle, and a victory for labor unequaled in the nation's history."

Expect Rush at Labor Board

As the Labor Board has been putting off consideration of many types of complaints in view of the imminence of the court rulings, it is now expected that unions will press for action. Accordingly it is probable that the board will be occupied for some time with the disposition of these matters.

Labor economists and others who view the possibility of a quick rise in labor union membership are aware also that this movement will carry with it demand for more comprehensive legislation, particularly governing mediation of labor disputes. The present Wagner act does not empower the board to mediate cases.

It is expected that in the next year a more articulate demand will be made for legislation similar to the Railway Labor Act and its comprehensive system of conferences, mediation, conciliation, voluntary arbitration and fact-finding. A bill embodying such a proposal has already been presented in the Pennsylvania Legislature.

Expect Drive to Amend Act

In some labor quarters the effects of the series of sit-down strikes—caused, as many of them are said to have been, by employers refusing to grant recognition to unions—are credited with having had a part in the Supreme Court reversal today on labor relations in manufacturing.

At the same time, now that union recognition in manufacturing industry is legalized, the number of sit-down strikes is expected to diminish.

Labor leaders feel that the next line of attack by employers will be to seek amendments to the Wagner act to provide for the incorporation and registration of trade unions and to call upon both sides to refrain from coercion in industrial disputes.

Mr. Madden, the chairman of the Labor Board, said that the court had apparently drawn a boundary line "at about the right place, where there is a substantial flow of goods in interstate commerce, a considerable proportion of which is manufactured or processed by particular enterprises."

Asked whether the decisions would hasten industrial peace, he said that if employers obeyed the law, the number of strikes for union recognition and against discrimination on account of union membership would diminish.

In this connection David Saposs, economist for the board, pointed out that the largest single cause of strikes was the demand for recognition. He said that Labor Department figures showed that 47.8 per cent of strikes last year were for the right to organize and the figure for 1935 was 47.3 per cent and for 1934 about 46 per cent.

The Labor Board will now seek rehearings in some cases, Mr. Madden said, ask for reconsideration of some in the light of the court decisions, and take steps to dismiss injunctions still in existence against the board.

Some eighty-two injunctions have been issued against it, of which thirteen or fourteen are still outstanding, Charles Fahy, general counsel, said. Most of these suits are pending in the Eighth Circuit.

Mr. Madden then said that fifty-seven employes were involved in the five cases today, twenty-two in the bus case, ten in Jones & Laughlin, eighteen in Friedman-Harry Marks,

one in The Associated Press and six in Freuhauf Trailer Company.

"Where does the Supreme Court action leave Henry Ford?" Mr. Madden was asked.

"Subject to the law," he replied.

"When you consider the decisions handed down today and the decision in the Virginian Railway case, you will see that all points in the Wagner act are covered," he added.

"Do you expect increased business by the board as a result of the decision?" he was asked.

"No, the reverse," he said. "Our regional directors will be able to adjust matters very well."

The "economic briefs" prepared under the direction of Mr. Saposs and referred to by Mr. Hughes in the Jones & Laughlin case were credited with having opened up before the court the wide social and economic implications of the labor-employer relations and their effect on interstate commerce.

Miss Perkins's View of Effects

In her statement today Secretary Perkins said that more strikes had centered around union organization than from all other causes combined.

"Of the 1,015 strikes reported during the six months' period ending Feb. 1, 1937, 524 were for union

organization and 491 for other causes," she said.

"These decisions mean that employers in the basic interstate industries will now recognize the established right of their employes to bargain collectively and not interfere with the attempt of their workers to organize for this purpose.

"These decisions mean that the legal machinery which the Federal Government has provided for the protection of this right is now available. In recent months when lower court injunctions had created grave doubts as to the validity of this machinery and greatly impaired its effectiveness there has been a tendency on the part of both employers and employes to ignore the Labor Relations Act.

"The action of the court removes all doubt that peaceful labor relations in manufacturing and other industries are vital to the orderly flow of interstate commerce, and therefore are a proper subject of Congressional concern.

"The decisions, therefore, in the manufacturing cases are of great significance. They illustrate conclusively that the Constitution is indeed broad enough to give Congress power to deal with our most pressing social and industrial problems when the court is willing to recognize the statutory technique."

April 13, 1937

C. I. O. CHIEFS DECIDE ON PERMANENT BODY

Lewis Attacks Democrats for 'Broken Promises'—Congressmen Are Warned

By LOUIS STARK
Special to THE NEW YORK TIMES.

WASHINGTON, April 13.—The chiefs of thirty-eight international unions affiliated with the Committee for Industrial Organization decided today to form a permanent organization.

By unanimous vote of those who took part in the voting, but with the abstention of Julius Hochman of the International Ladies Garment Workers Union, the international union spokesmen decided to hold a constitutional convention, to formulate rules and by-laws and to set up a permanent staff of officials.

The details, such as fixing the time and place of the convention, were turned over to a committee comprised of Philip Murray of the Steel Workers Organizing Committee and Sidney Hillman of the Amalgamated Clothing Workers of

America. The convention will be held in September or October.

The decision to form a permanent organization as a rival to the American Federation of Labor was the high light of the two days' meeting which adopted a score of resolutions on relief and unemployment, wage and hour legislation, the labor policies of the United States Maritime Commission and other subjects. Reports were made by John Brophy, a director, on the present status of the C. I. O., and by Ralph Hetzel Jr., unemployment director, on unemployment activities.

Hochman Unable to Vote

During the discussion on the formation of a permanent organization, Mr. Hochman explained that he was not authorized to vote and he would have to report to his union's general executive board. The board, he said, would decide or the union's policy. David Dubinsky, president of the union, has been reported to be confident that his group would not "go along" with the C. I. O.'s decision to form a permanent organization.

Discussion of the motion to take another step which widens the rift between the C. I. O. and the A. F. L. brought out arguments for this action based upon two lines of reasoning.

The chiefs of the younger unions which have had slight or no contacts with the A. F. L. favored the step because, they argued, they had

been met with unsparing opposition by the Federation when they sought to organize. These speakers asserted that they owed nothing to the A. F. L. except attempts to break up their unions and to divide them among existing craft organizations. They hoped that the C. I. O. would steer as wide a course as possible from the A. F. L.

The heads of the older unions maintained that the stronger the C. I. O. became, the larger its membership and influence and the more permanent its status, the more likely would it be in the end to have a united labor movement. But such unity, it was maintained, would be on the basis of equals, with the A. F. L. making the vital concessions to industrial unionism necessary to really unite all groups in the most formidable labor movement the nation has ever seen.

These speakers did not close the door to an eventual peace between the A. F. L. and the C. I. O., but they emphasized that, in their opinion, the federation was still unwilling to make those compromises which would assure the future of the industrial union idea.

As another step in the direction of strengthening its organization, the C. I. O. spokesmen agreed to form an industrial council for the New York metropolitan area, a step that has lagged for some months since the A. F. L. Central Trades and Labor Council purged itself of C. I. O. delegates.

After the meeting had adopted a resolution favoring the pending wage and hours bill, Mr. Lewis called upon the Administration and

the Democratic party to carry out its campaign pledges by fulfilling their promises for such legislation.

"It's a sad commentary that the pledges have not been liquidated by now," he said.

While the meeting was aware of the imperfections in the Ramspeck bill, Mr. Lewis said it was favored so that the principle of wage and hours legislation might be enacted into law.

Congressmen Warned

The resolution on the wage and hour proposal declared that "It will be considered by the 4,000,000 members of the C. I. O. as an unfriendly act to the workers of this country on the part of any Congressman striving to prevent the enactment of such legislation and to vote in opposition."

In relation to a resolution favoring enactment of the Wagner bill which would allow the National Labor Relations Board to cancel government contracts of those violating the labor law, Mr. Lewis alleged that Federal Government agencies were subsidizing violation of the Wagner Labor Relations Act. In this category he placed the Procurement Division of the Treasury, the RFC and the War and Navy Departments, which, he maintained, insisted on dealing with firms adjudged to be violating the Wagner act.

He declared that 80 per cent of WPA material was purchased from firms unfair to labor. At the WPA offices it was said that materials were purchased for it by the Procurement Division.

Mr. Lewis during the meeting rebuked Albert Stonkus, chairman of the Utility Workers Organization Committee, for the "stay-in" strike of Consumers Power Company employes in Michigan two weeks ago. While Mr. Stonkus was making his report Mr. Lewis inquired whether the decision to take possession of the plants and oust supervisors had been referred to C. I. O. officials, and Mr. Stonkus said that this had not been done.

Mr. Lewis said that before taking such an important step, which might affect the prestige of the C. I. O., it would have been well had communication been arranged with the C. I. O., so that an attempt might have been made to settle the dispute by other means. Last year the dispute was settled following exchanges between Wendell Willkie, head of the Commonwealth and Southern, holding company for the Michigan plants, and Mr. Lewis.

The conference supported a resolution opposing compulsory mediation and arbitration legislation for the maritime industry, now pending in Congress, and urged Congress to allow the maritime unions to bargain collectively with their employers before further legislation is enacted.

The Maritime Commission was accused of adopting practices that were aimed to destroy the unions. It was alleged that the commission refused to permit collective bargaining on government-owned and privately operated ships; that it arbitrarily fixed wages, hours and working conditions on ships other than those owned by the commission, and that it was attempting to eliminate hiring halls "which are the sole protection of the maritime unions against constant attack from the maritime employers."

Congress, in another resolution, was requested not to adjourn before the enactment of legislation for relief, housing, minimum wages and the extension of collective bargaining to government contracts.

In his report on the development of the C. I. O. since the previous meeting in December, Mr. Brophy said that seven national unions had been added in the last five months.

EARLY LABOR PEACE BARRED BY MURRAY AS NEW C. I. O. HEAD

By LOUIS STARK
Special to THE NEW YORK TIMES.

ATLANTIC CITY, N. J., Nov. 22—Philip Murray accepted the gavel of the presidency of the Congress of Industrial Organizations from the hands of John L. Lewis today and immediately cautioned the Roosevelt Administration not "to force shotgun agreements between the C. I. O. and the American Federation of Labor."

With grim earnestness the newly elected president of the C. I. O. announced his agreement with the policies of Mr. Lewis, who slammed the door to labor peace last Tuesday. In effect Mr. Murray locked the tightly closed door and intimated that there could be little hope for peace until the C. I. O. had made more progress in organizing the defense industries in which it already has many contracts and over which it claims "complete jurisdiction."

Mr. Murray emphasized that the kind of unity the nation was interested in was unity between management and labor, which as a result of collective bargaining would lead to greater efficiency, greater production and greater practical security "than any will-o'-the-wisp methods suggested by the leaders of the A. F. of L."

Whirlwind Campaign Seen

As a result of this speech the C. I. O. is expected to turn "full steam ahead," concentrate at once on a whirlwind campaign in the aircraft, automobile (Ford), chemicals, munitions, "little steel," shipbuilding and other defense industries. Then, if that job is consummated with success, it will turn toward the idea of peace with the A. F. of L.

And so, despite what he called a "mild protest," Mr. Murray in effect plainly urged the Administration not to call a White House labor peace parley at this time or to expect early resumption of unity talks between committees of the two labor organizations. His words were also intended to discourage rumors of the possible appointment of a Presidential commission to study the problem of ending the five-year factional struggle between the warring wings of organized labor.

Concentration on the immediate task ahead, organization of the defense and other industries, was the keynote of addresses and resolutions by officers and delegates.

Lewis Intends to Be Active

Mr. Lewis, in nominating Mr. Murray, strongly intimated that he expected to be a power to be reckoned with in the future when he brushed aside talk that he was "a dying gladiator or even sorely wounded."

After unanimously electing Mr. Murray, who had no opposition candidate, the convention re-elected James B. Carey of the United Radio, Electrical and Machine Workers as secretary.

The delegates then re-elected four of the six vice presidents: Emil Rieve, Textile Workers Union; S. H. Dalrymple, United Rubber Workers of America; R. J. Thomas, United Automobile Workers of America, and Reid Robinson, International Union, Mine, Mill and Smelter Workers.

A surprise was sprung on the delegates by the nomination and election of Joseph Curran of the National Maritime Union to the vice presidency. Mr. Curran came within an ace of being named to his post at the last convention. He was nominated by Michael Quill of the Transport Workers Union. Both Mr. Curran and Mr. Quill are outstanding left-wing leaders in their unions.

Frank Rosenblum of the Amalgamated Clothing Workers of America was elected to the vice presidency made vacant by the retirement of Sidney Hillman, labor member of the National Defense Advisory Commission. This vacancy and the one made by the retirement of Mr. Lewis were filled by the two new members.

Election of officers was preceded by the report of the constitution committee, headed by John Owens of the United Mine Workers. The convention approved amendments to the constitution requiring a two-thirds vote for suspending or expelling affiliates and providing for the filling of vacancies on the executive board by nominations from the union entitled to the vacancy. Each union has an officer on the board.

Mr. Lewis nominated his old colleague, the vice president of the United Mine Workers of America, in a twenty-minute speech in which he praised his achievements as chairman of the Steel Workers Organizing Committee, as a warm personal friend, as "a scholar, a profound student of economics, a natural leader, an administrator, a family man and a God-fearing man."

Recalling Mr. Murray's assistance to other C. I. O. organizations, Mr. Lewis also praised him for his success in adjusting important internal relationships of the C. I. O.

As he closed with the name of Mr. Murray on his lips the audience broke into prolonged applause. A band of kilted Scottish pipers paraded through the hall and to the platform as the delegates cheered, whistled, rang cowbells and used other noisemaking devices.

After the demonstration died down Mr. Hillman seconded the nomination, saying that the election of Mr. Murray would give leadership not only to the labor movement but to the nation as well. Other seconding speeches were made by Vice Presidents Robinson, Thomas and Dalrymple.

Mr. Murray was then elected by acclamation to the accompaniment of another enthusiastic demonstration. Mr. Lewis presented the new president with a gavel that had been presented to him by his mining union associates and termed the gift a symbol of his election.

The new president then told the delegates that he expected them to demonstrate their loyalty to him not by resolutions but by their accomplishments in the field of organization.

"Deeds count," he declared. "Hard work is needed. Petty bickering must stop. The tongue of the slandermonger must be stilled."

Then he launched into a discussion of labor unity. It was his view that when people thought of unity they thought of it in terms of a unity "that comprehends greater efficiency and more continuity in the production of machinery of American industry."

Mr. Murray emphasized that he did not wish to be misunderstood on the question of unity because he stood exactly where Mr. Lewis stood in his report to the convention.

Political Resolution Criticized

Thomas F. Burns of the United Rubber Workers Union criticized a resolution that referred to the need for labor organizing its political activities by interpreting it as a proposal for a "united front" of all groups with the Communists. Thomas Kennedy, chairman of the resolutions committee, insisted that this construction could not be placed on the resolution saying it merely sought to bring together those forces that believe in the C. I. O. program. The resolution was adopted.

A resolution was adopted upon suggestion of the Transport Workers Union condemning the New York City Board of Transportation "for its anti-labor conduct" and urging Mayor La Guardia to take measures to insure safe and uninterrupted service on the city's transport system "by enforcing the principle and practice of collective bargaining."

Another resolution called upon the Department of Justice to prosecute alleged violations of constitutional rights of employes by the Ford Motor Company. The department also was urged to investigate employment by the company "of known Nazi agents and of the relationships between officers of the Ford Motor Company and German industrial combines."

David McDonald, secretary of the Steel Workers Organizing Committee, on behalf of the delegates, presented a scroll to Mr. Lewis thanking him for his achievements in helping organize the unorganized.

April 14, 1938

November 23, 1940

148

HEALTH INSURANCE WON IN UNION PACT

Philadelphia Dress Factories Accept Obligation Said to Create a Precedent

Special to THE NEW YORK TIMES.

PHILADELPHIA, Aug. 25—An agreement imposing on the employer the obligation to provide health insurance for his workers was adopted today by the International Ladies Garment Workers Union and the Philadelphia Waist and Dress Manufacturers Association. It was the first time such a clause had been written into a labor contract, union officials said.

Immediate and future wage increases and a reduction in weekly working hours were also embodied in the contract, which was praised by David Dubinsky, president of the union, as "a progressive step in employer-employe relations in our industry and the result of mutual understanding between our union and an association of employers ripe with the experience of many years."

The health clause will apply to 10,000 workers in Philadelphia plants making cotton dresses and blouses.

It calls for an assessment each week of 3½ per cent of the payrolls of the members of the employers' association. One per cent will go into a fund to provide vacations with pay and 2½ per cent will be used to establish a system of weekly sick benefits and a medical clinic to supervise the health of the workers.

The agreement is for twenty-nine months and becomes effective immediately to supplant an agreement scheduled to expire Feb. 1.

An immediate wage increase of 7 per cent was provided, and, in view of the increasing cost of living, a 5 per cent increase on Feb. 1. Wage benefits to the workers under the contract will be about $2,500,000 a year, Mr. Dubinsky stated.

Working hours were reduced from forty to thirty-seven and one-half hours a week for all shops producing garments wholesaling at more than $15.75 a dozen.

ORGANIZED LABOR GAIN ADDS RESPONSIBILITIES

The Nation Takes Stock of Its Unions, Now Claiming 11,000,000 Members

By LOUIS STARK

WASHINGTON, June 21—The combined total of recent events on the labor front has prompted the unions as well as the general public to take stock of the whole union labor situation.

Organized labor claims a membership of approximately 11,000,000 out of a total of 50,000,000 workers. The American Federation of Labor figure for members whose dues were paid up was set at 4,247,443 last August, with about 750,000 whose dues were unpaid, making 5,000,000 in all. The Congress of Industrial Organizations claims 5,000,000 members, but does not insist that all of them are paying dues. About 1,000,000 men are in independent unions.

In the last thirty years the membership of trade unions has ebbed and flowed. Dr. Leo Wolman of Columbia University points out that in 1910 there were only 2,052,402 trade union members, or 8.6 per cent of the 23,809,904 employes eligible for membership. In 1920 the organized workers numbered 4,795,100, or 17.5 per cent of 27,359,-600 eligible employes. But by 1930 the union membership had dropped to 3,073,200, or 9.3 per cent of 33,-217,886 employes.

From 1910 until the formation of the C. I. O. in 1935 the main lines of growth of trade union membership were in the mining, construction, transportation, printing, textile, shoe and service industries and in the entertainment field. In the last six years organization has been extended to such basic industries as steel, metal mining, rubber, automobiles, aluminum, electrical manufacturing, chemicals and aircraft.

The backbone of the A. F. of L. is the compact bloc of twenty-one building trades unions, with about 1,000,000 members. The most strategic of the A. F. of L. unions is the teamsters' organization, whose 500,000 members spread fanwise over the nation's construction activities as well as over every industrial plant which sends or receives supplies by truck. A general strike of teamsters could cripple the nation's business.

In the railroad industry, with 1,000,000 union members, there are fifteen standard railway unions affiliated with the A. F. of L. and four independent brotherhoods.

In the theatrical field, three A. F. of L. unions dominate the musical, stage and motion picture industries

FOUNDED THE C. I. O.

Meriwether

John L. Lewis

so completely that at a word from the chiefs of these three unions every theatre in the United States could be darkened and the motion-picture industry could be paralyzed.

The A. F. of L. carpenters, with 300,000 members, have a vertical industrial union that extends from the woods to the furniture factories and carries with it large segments of the building trades and construction workers. And in the past seven years the A. Γ. of L. electrical union has added some 70,000 new members to its rolls, and the hotel and restaurant workers have increased by about 150,000.

In addition the A. F. of L. is predominant in printing, entertainment, service industries, certain apparel trades — excluding men's clothing — and in the food, liquor and tobacco trades.

The C. I. O., on the other hand, now stands pre-eminent in the coal, rubber and steel fabricating industries, in machine manufacture, in the radio and rubber industries, in men's clothing, textiles and the newspaper fields.

The C. I. O. miners' union—which includes chemical workers—claims a membership of 600,000. Five years ago scarcely a handful of union men with contracts could be found in the nation's vast electrical and machine manufacturing industry. Today the General Electric and Westinghouse, the Radio Corporation of America and scores of electric manufacturing plants are enrolled under the C. I. O. banner, to the number of 250,000.

The C. I. O. automotive union, five years ago an infant with possibly 30,000 members, now claims some 500,000 members with strong local unions in the "big three" manufacturing plants (Ford, General Motors and Chrysler) and in many scores of accessories plants.

Both the A. F. of L. and the C. I. O. have been making heavy inroads into industries which, until recently, resisted unionization. The phenomenal growth of the defense industries, including aviation, shipbuilding, machine tool and electrical manufacturing, has spurred the unions to extraordinary activity. In the last three or four months the C. I. O. has organized some 50,000 aircraft workers, a field which the A. F. of L. began to cultivate much earlier.

Intense rivalry between the A. F. of L. and the C. I. O. may be found in the shipbuilding, maritime and communications, lumber, longshore, warehouse, electric manufacture, shoe manufacturing and aluminum industries. But as yet labor's principal organization efforts have scarcely touched the telephone and utilities industries, the distributive trades or the agricultural and cannery workers.

For the workers, the spread of organization has meant a better bargaining position from which they have won wage increases, shorter hours and better working conditions. For the employers, it has meant higher wage outlays and a consequent concentration on more efficient production methods, including a tendency to introduce more labor-saving machinery.

But the unions have their weakness in their lack of trained leadership, which has not increased in proportion to membership growth. As a result, extreme rank-and-fileism, with its attendent irresponsibility, embarrasses both responsible unions and employers.

Legislation in the past few years has solidified labor's position. Trade union members are no longer frustrated by ex-parte federal injunctions. The Wagner Act and the National Labor Relations Board protect them from hostile practices by employers and from company-dominated unions. They are rapidly winning an equal place in American institutional life and becoming part of industrial government.

But there is little doubt that if the unions abuse their rights they will lay themselves open to government regulation. The law that gives those representing a majority the right to speak for all employes in a plant or company will presumably protect the minority in their normal rights. If unions oust dissenters they may expect a public reaction. The powers conferred on unions by law, the enhancing of their authority, prestige and power, will mean public scrutiny of their acts, according to all precedent.

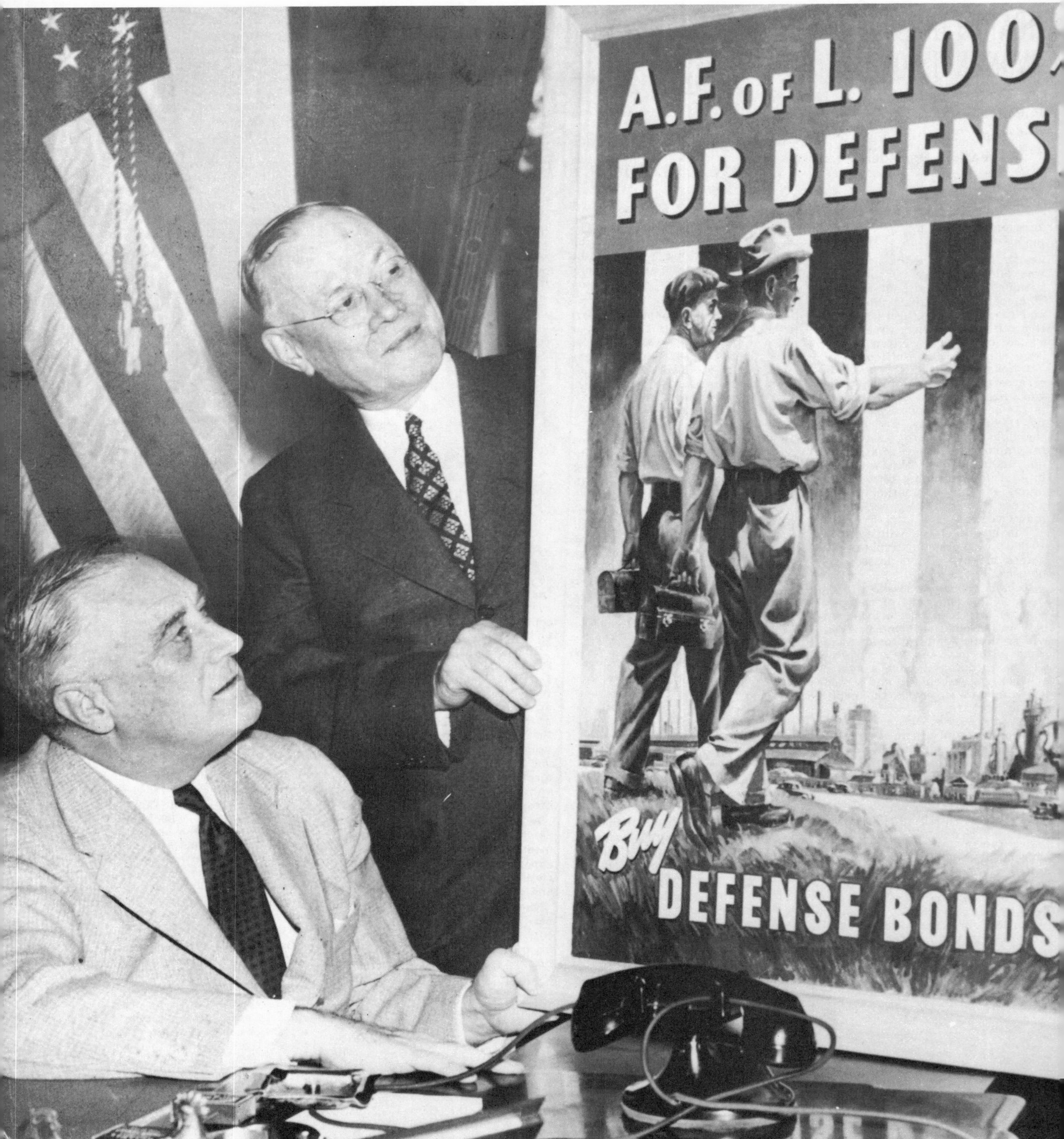
A.F. OF L. 100
FOR DEFENS
Buy
DEFENSE BONDS

William Green of the A.F. of L.
supporting the war effort.
The New York Times.

CHAPTER **4**
Again War

6,000,000 NEW JOBS SEEN

Government Statisticians, Labor Leaders Make 1941 Forecast

WASHINGTON, Jan. 1 (P)—The prospect of millions of new jobs as a direct or indirect result of the nation's defense program was foreseen for 1941 by government statisticians and labor leaders.

Government experts said about 4,000,000 probably would receive employment in connection with the manufacture of ships, aircraft, arms, ammunition and supplies needed for national defense and for aid to Britain.

Payroll expansion was expected to cause an upturn in mercantile and other non-defense lines, adding possibly another 2,000,000 new jobs.

11-MAN LABOR BOARD NAMED

Dykstra Heads Agency to Avert Strikes in Defense Industries

President Chooses 3 Members for Public, 4 Each for Employes and Employers— Murray and Meany in Labor Panel

By LOUIS STARK

WASHINGTON, March 19—President Roosevelt today created an eleven-man National Defense Mediation Board "to assure that all work necessary for national defense shall proceed without interruption and with all possible speed."

With Clarence A. Dykstra, director of Selective Service, as chairman and also as one of the three public representatives, the board consists of the following, by groups:

PUBLIC
Mr. Dykstra.

William Hammatt Davis of New York—A patent attorney and chairman of the New York State Mediation Board.

Dr. Frank P. Graham—President, University of North Carolina.

EMPLOYES
George Meany of New York—Secretary-treasurer, American Federation of Labor.

George M. Harrison of Cincinnati—Grand president, Brotherhood of Railway and Steamship Clerks.

Philip Murray of Pittsburgh—President, Congress of Industrial Organizations.

Thomas Kennedy of Hazleton, Pa.—Secretary-treasurer, United Mine Workers of America.

EMPLOYERS
Walter C. Teagle of Port Chester, Conn.—Chairman, Standard Oil Company of New Jersey.

Roger D. Lapham of San Francisco—President, Hawaiian-American Steamship Company.

Eugene Meyer of Washington, D. C.—Publisher, The Washington Post.

Cyrus Ching of New York—Vice president, United States Rubber Company.

According to the executive order, the board's jurisdiction will begin whenever the "Secretary of Labor certifies to it that a controversy (excluding any dispute under the Railway Labor Act) cannot be adjusted by the Department of Labor's conciliators."

When the board receives such certified disputes, the chairman will name a panel of three, one each representing the public, labor and employers, to adjust the dispute.

The panel will be authorized, according to the order, to make every effort at adjustment by assisting the parties to negotiate arrangements, to afford them means for voluntary arbitration; to designate arbitrators when requested by both parties; to assist in seeking methods to avoid or resolve future controversies; to conduct hearings, take testimony and make findings of fact and formulate recommendations for settlement of disputes, and to make these findings public; and to ask the National Labor Relations Board to expedite disputes over representation.

First Meeting Planned Soon

The first meeting of the board will be held in a few days on the return of Mr. Dykstra, who was out of town today.

The Allis-Chalmers dispute which has been unsuccessfully handled by Federal, State and Office of Production Management mediators, is likely to be the first case to go before the new board. This is a C. I. O. dispute involving a demand for the equivalent of the closed shop.

Modelled somewhat after the National War Labor Board created during the World War, and the National Labor Board headed by Senator Robert F. Wagner, set up during the administration of the National Industrial Recovery Act, the new mediation board partakes of the "pressure" aspect of the other two boards.

Efforts were made to make the new board simply a mediatory body comprising public representatives solely. Those who argued for such a set-up said that to place spokesmen for labor and management on the board would transfer to the board itself the disputes submitted to it. Thus, it was said, the labor and employer members probably would feel constrained to uphold the respective points of view of the litigants.

The Dykstra Board, like the two previous Federal labor boards, is set up principally to mediate and conciliate disputes, to help voluntary arbitration, and to make findings of fact and recommendations. In the main, the previous boards did little conciliation work, but became agencies which handed down awards that were quasi arbitral.

War Labor Board's Experience

The War Labor Board's report stated:

"Although the board was constituted both a conciliatory agency and an arbitration tribunal, in practice it seldom acted in a conciliatory capacity."

The report of the old War Labor Board also stated that the appointment of labor and management spokesmen as investigators "operated rather to accentuate the original differences as to which complaints were made and it was therefore discontinued."

Designation of the board was received here with mixed feelings. William S. Knudsen, Director General of the OPM, expressed the hope that it would obviate the necessity for legislation dealing with strikes, but he added: "We can't have this thing going on all the time."

Senator Byrd of Virginia declared that a mediation board "without power to act, as now proposed," will not put down strikes in defense industries.

"Under conditions confronting this country today, strikes in vital war industries must be dealt with sternly and firmly in the interest of our national welfare," he said.

William Green, president of the A. F. L., said:

"By the creation of the new National Defense Mediation Board, President Roosevelt has taken an important and constructive step toward the promotion of uninterrupted production in defense industries.

"The President has appointed distinguished men to serve on this board, men of long training and experience in the field of industrial-labor relations. I believe that the personnel of this board is a guarantee to the public of effective service.

"The American Federation of Labor, which favored the creation of the National Defense Mediation Board from the outset, pledges to it the full cooperation of its entire organization in the furtherance of industrial peace and stability."

Waited on C. I. O. Decision

Delay in announcing the names of the members was caused partly by the awaiting of word from C. I. O. officials. Announcement in New York that Messrs. Murray and Kennedy were to be the C. I. O. nominees was followed by official announcement of the new set-up at the White House. Decision of the C. I. O. to have these two ranking officers as members was regarded as significant in view of Mr. Murray's opposition and his charge that the board would be concerned largely with maintaining the "status quo" while the C. I. O. was intent on complete organization of the defense industries.

No progress was made toward settlement of the strike of 400 A. F. L. building mechanics on the Wright Airfield, Dayton, Ohio. The dispute arose over the employment of five C. I. O. electrical workers. The War Department is understood to have extended for twenty-four hours the time limit for drastic action in taking over the work of the eight contractors employing A. F. L. labor.

The strike was discussed at a conference attended by Secretary Stimson, Under-Secretary Patterson and Edward F. McGrady, Assistant to the Secretary of War.

Joseph Keenan, OPM mediator, continued his efforts to work out an agreement with the A. F. L. spokesmen, but without result. It was understood that the International Brotherhood of Electrical Workers (A. F. L.) refused to recede from its stand against working on a job where C. I. O. men were employed.

Mr. Keenan said a truce had been arranged in the dispute threatening a strike of operating engineers at three St. Louis power plants.

Frank A. Fitzgerald, secretary-treasurer of the International Union of Operating Engineers, said members of his union would not strike pending an inquiry by the OPM into a charge that the Union Electric Company of East St. Louis had discharged union men and replaced them by non-union men.

Knudsen "A Little Premature"

At a press conference Mr. Knudsen complimented Sidney Hillman, his associate, for work he was doing in trying to settle strikes.

"But it seems that every time we get one settled here, another one breaks out over there," he remarked.

Mr. Knudsen said he was "a little premature" in his statement to a Congressional committee recently that labor troubles in defense industries were minor.

"We've had plenty since," he added.

The production director expressed belief that the finding and publication of all the facts about strikes would tend to reduce the number.

"The more facts the less strikes," he said.

Most of the walkouts so far have been over organization and jurisdictional questions, Mr. Knudsen added.

A knowledge of the facts as to their nature would have prevented some and settled others, he believed, but pressure had been so great on the OPM that its officers did not have time to develop the facts properly.

"I plead guilty to our ability or our lack of time in getting at the facts," Mr. Knudsen said. "Our job was to get production going and we may have put too little emphasis on this strike problem at the outset."

Mr. Knudsen said he would favor legislation, or any other means, to provide a "cooling-off" period between the time a labor dispute arose and a strike is called. He preferred to have it done some other way than by legislation, and, most important of all, thought the new mediation board should decide the policy to be followed.

"I favor legislation to make cooling-off periods mandatory if it cannot be done by agreement," he said.

The National Mediation Board which functions for the railroad and air transportation industries conferred separately with spokesmen for the railroads and the fourteen standard unions involved in a dispute over the union demand for vacations with pay. The mediatory meetings will continue.

March 20, 1941

War Labor Board Created; Davis Heads 12-Man Body

By W. H. LAWRENCE
Special to THE NEW YORK TIMES.

WASHINGTON, Jan. 12—Declaring that "the national interest demands that there shall be no interruption of any work which contributes to the effective prosecution of the war," President Roosevelt created by executive order today a twelve-member National War Labor Board and appointed as chairman William H. Davis, a New York patent lawyer and head of the National Defense Mediation Board, which was abolished at the same time.

Mr. Roosevelt gave to the new board broad powers to adjust all kinds of labor disputes, including union demands for a closed shop, and, in so doing, he overruled a plea from industrial management that the union shop issue be ruled out as a proper grievance for government mediation and arbitration during the war.

Mr. Davis was selected as chairman of the new board despite a campaign by some labor leaders and representatives of industry to remove him from the key industrial-relations post in the war effort.

George W. Taylor of Philadelphia, a University of Pennsylvania economics professor and impartial umpire under the collective bargaining contract between the General Motors Corporation and the C. I. O.'s United Automobile Workers, was named vice chairman of the new board.

The board's members, equally divided among representatives of the public, employers and employes, were named as follows:

PUBLIC — Messrs. Davis and Taylor, Dean Wayne L. Morse, University of Oregon Law School; Dr. Frank P. Graham, president of the University of North Carolina.

EMPLOYERS — Albert W. Hawkes of Montclair, N. J., president of the Chamber of Commerce of the United States and president of Congoleum-Nairn, Inc.; Roger D. Lapham of San Francisco, chairman of the board of American-Hawaiian Steamship Company; E. J. McMillan of Knoxville, Tenn., president of Standard Knitting Mills, Inc., and Walter C. Teagle of New York, chairman of the board of the Standard Oil Company of New Jersey.

LABOR—Thomas Kennedy of Hazleton, Pa., secretary-treasurer of the C. I. O.'s United Mine Workers of America; George Meany of New York, secretary-treasurer of the American Federation of Labor; R. J. Thomas of Detroit, president of the C. I. O.'s United Automobile Workers of America, and Matthew Woll of New York, vice president of the A. F. L.

Half of the new board's members were taken from the Mediation Board, which ceased to function effectively in November after the C. I. O.'s representatives resigned in protest against the board's refusal to grant the union-shop demand of the mine workers union in the "captive" coal mines owned by steel corporations. This decision subsequently was reversed by a special Presidential arbitration board, headed by Dr .John R. Steelman.

The new board was set up to carry out the labor policy promulgated by President Roosevelt on Dec. 23, which provides that there shall be no strikes or lockouts for the duration of the war and that "all labor disputes shall be settled by peaceful means." This policy, the President said, represented the "general points of agreement" by industry and labor conferees who had reached a deadlock on the question of permitting the board to act on union-shop disputes.

Connally Insists on a Law

Although creation of the board under a no-strike, no-lockout policy might be expected to head off enactment of anti-strike legislation on Capitol Hill, particularly the Smith bill which the House passed by a large majority and over the opposition of Administration leaders, Senator Connally of Texas served notice today that it was his intention to ask the Senate within a few days to take up his bill providing for government seizure of any struck mines, mills or smelters.

In naming a board of twelve "special commissioners," who will receive $25 a day when engaged in official business, the President made it plain that he expected the four public members to devote full time to the board work. He did not provide for alternate public members, although he named four alternates each for the employer and labor members, as follows:

LABOR—Martin P. Durkin, secretary-treasurer of the A. F. L.'s United Association of Plumbers and Steamfitters of the United States and Canada; C. S. Golden, regional director of the C. I. O.'s Steel Workers Organizing Committee; Emil Rieve, president of the C. I. O.'s Textile Workers Union of America, and Robert J. Watt, A. F. L. international representative.

EMPLOYERS—L. N. Bent, vice president, Hercules Powder Company; R. R. Deupree, president, Procter & Gamble Company; James W. Hook, president, the Geometric Tool Company, and H. B. Horton, Chicago Bridge and Iron Corporation.

The President's order established the following procedure for adjustment of labor disputes:

1. Direct negotiations between employers and employes.
2. Conciliation efforts by Labor Department commissioners of conciliation.
3. Consideration by the War Labor Board, after certification by the Secretary of Labor, or direct intervention by the board itself.

"After it takes jurisdiction, the board shall finally determine the dispute, and for this purpose may use mediation, voluntary arbitration, or arbitration under rules established by the board," Mr. Roosevelt stated.

The wording of this section made it clear that the President expects both labor and industry to abide by decisions of the board. He gave to the board the power to require arbitration of disputes, even if the parties previously have refused voluntary arbitration.

The A. F. of L. and C. I. O. each were permitted to pick two members of the board, and to nominate labor alternates. Secretary of Commerce Jones selected the employer representatives. President and Secretary Perkins picked the public members.

After appointment of the board had been announced Mr. Davis made the following statement:

"We now have a nation-wide agreement by management and labor to keep war production rolling and to settle all disputes by peaceful means. In setting up the National War Labor Board, the President provided the peaceful means. The board has been given the power to finally settle all such disputes.

"Worker and employer morale will play a large part in determining our output of guns, planes, ships and tanks. The board will do its best to contribute to this morale by disposing of all questions which may become before it promptly, fearlessly and fairly.

"The board will meet and go to work just as soon as the members can convene."

January 13, 1942

WLB ORDER KEEPS MEMBERS IN UNION

Harvester Decision by 8 to 4 Calls for Maintenance if the Workers Vote Contract

EMPLOYERS DISSENTING

Board Is Unanimous on Wage Increases and End of Bonus on Sundays and Holidays

By LOUIS STARK
Special to THE NEW YORK TIMES.

WASHINGTON, April 15—The National War Labor Board ordered the International Harvester Company to sign a maintenance of union membership provision in its union contract if a majority of union members in each of eight plants favored such a provision at a secret referendum ordered by the board.

The decision split the board eight to four, the labor members concurring with the public members, while the employer members dissented. This was said to be the first occasion on which a government body, of its own volition, took upon itself to adjudicate an intra-union problem.

The opinion of the majority, prepared by Dean Wayne L. Morse of the University of Oregon Law School, said that the labor members of the board approved the plan in the interest of promoting maximum production in war industries, but that in peace they would vigorously oppose such an effort as "an unjustifiable government encroachment upon internal union affairs."

Dissenting Opinion by Lapham

Roger D. Lapham, who wrote the dissenting opinion on behalf of the employers, declared that according to the majority decision a minority of 1,400 in a plant comprising 3,000 workers would be bound to remain in the union even if they voted against the provision, assuming that 1,600 favored it.

"We emphasize in this order that each union worker is denied the right to decide individually whether he wants to retain or not retain his union status for a stated period," Mr. Lapham wrote.

The employers proposed this alternative:

"If the contract provided the worker must remain a union member as a condition of employment, then within ten days after the execution of the contract each union worker would be given the opportunity to resign from the union. Failing to resign within those ten days, he would be required to stay a union member for the contract period."

Issues on which the board was unanimous were:

1. Union members who are employes shall not lose pay during time spent handling grievances in the plant.

2. A wage increase of 4.5 cents an hour as of Jan. 15, 1942; increase of starting rate 4.5 cents an hour as of Jan. 15, 1942, and review of wages six months from Jan. 15, 1942, and each three months thereafter upon notice.

3. No overtime is to be paid for Saturdays, Sundays or holidays as such, but time and a half shall be paid beyond eight hours a day or forty hours a week.

Fowler McCormick, president of the International Harvester Company, eight of whose plants with 25,000 employes were involved, said the order would have to be taken up by the company's directors.

William H. Davis, chairman of the NWLB, explained at a press conference today that the secret balloting will take place in the eight plants as soon as possible after the unions and the company sign a contract. If any union members desire to give up their memberships, he said, they may do so between now and the elections, subject to the union constitutions.

The majority opinion urged that for the duration of the war the following basic principles should be considered as minimum guarantees in any wage issue considered by the board:

"First, all workmen shall receive wages sufficiently high to enable them to maintain a standard of living compatible with health and decency.

"Second, the real wage levels which have been previously arrived at through the channels of collective bargaining and which do not impede maximum production of war materials shall be reasonably protected.

"Third, to the extent that it can be done without inflationary effects, labor should be encouraged to negotiate through the processes of collective bargaining for fair and reasonable upward wage adjustments as an offset against increases in the cost of living. Labor should not be put in an economic strait-jacket during the war without redress to some such agency as the War Labor Board, which has authority to grant fair and deserved wage adjustments."

The majority signing the order, besides Dean Morse, were Chairman Davis, Dr. Frank P. Graham and George W. Taylor, representing the public, and the following labor members: George Meany, R. J. Thomas, Martin P. Durkin and Thomas Kennedy.

The dissenting opinion was signed by Mr. Lapham, George H. Mead, Walter Teagle and Horace B. Horton.

April 16, 1942

NWLB TIES WAGES TO PRICES; JAN. '41 TO MAY '42 THE BASIS; RISE OF 15% SHOWN IN PERIOD

FORMULA IS SET UP

By LOUIS STARK
Special to THE NEW YORK TIMES.

WASHINGTON, July 16 — The National War Labor Board promulgated today a national wage stabilization policy according to which wage earners are entitled to maintain their peacetime purchasing power standards as of Jan. 1, 1941.

In announcing a wage increase of 5.5 cents an hour to 157,000 "Little Steel" workers, the board took the period between Jan. 1, 1941, and May, 1942, as the yardstick. Since the cost of living rose 15 per cent in that period, it ruled, wage earners are entitled to a 15 per cent advance in hourly earnings.

A five-point policy enunciated by Dr. George W. Taylor, vice chairman of the board, will, according to Chairman William H. Davis, "lead to a 'terminal' for the tragic race between wages and prices."

Dr. Taylor pointed out that use of the five guiding principles for evaluating claims for wage increases in the steel case "is not to be construed as establishing an inflexible pattern to be regularly followed if that would necessarily lead to injustice."

In this connection he indicated that even if in some cases 15 per cent wage increases had been made since Jan. 1, 1941, this would not be a bar to a further upward adjustment if wages were still substandard.

Labor Members Dissent

The four labor members dissented from the wage ruling approved by the eight public and industry members. They maintained that the dollar a day wage increase demanded by the union should have been granted and held that the wage ruling of the majority "struck a serious blow at the foundations of the collective bargaining process."

154

Dr. Taylor's five principles are as follows:

"(1) For the period from Jan. 1, 1941, to May, 1942, which followed a long period of relative stability, the cost of living increased by about 15 per cent. If any group of workers averaged less than a 15 per cent increase in hourly wage rates during or immediately preceding or following this period, their established peacetime standards have been broken. If any group of workers averaged a 15 per cent wage increase or more, their established peacetime standards have been preserved.

"(2) Any claim for wage adjustments for the groups whose peacetime standards have been preserved can only be considered in terms of the inequalities or of the sub-standard conditions specifically referred to in the President's message of April 27, 1942.

Inequalities to Be Considered

"(3). Those groups whose peacetime standards have been broken are entitled to have these standards re-established as a stabilization factor.

"(4). The board, as directed by the President in his April 27 message, will continue to 'give due consideration to inequalities and the elimination of substandards of living.'

"(5). Approximately twenty wage disputes, still pending before the board, were certified prior to the stabilization date of April 27. The question arises in these cases whether wage rates being paid on April 27, 1942, can or cannot be considered as 'existing rates' within the meaning of the President's message, or whether they then had the tentative character of disputed rates. Due regard must be given to any factors of equity which would be arbitrarily swept away by 'a change of rules in the middle of the game.'"

Thomas Kennedy, Secretary-Treasurer of the United Mine Workers, at the press conference where the board's decision was made public, declared that the wage decision "stymies collective bargaining and restricts it to the employer's interpretation of this formula."

He also said he had raised the question in the board as to whether the wage directive did not go beyond the terms of the labor-industry-government conference which created the WLB following Pearl Harbor. To this Lyman Morse, Dean of the University of Oregon Law School, public member, quickly replied that the agreement creating the board was made "for the duration of the war."

Earlier in the day the question of wage stabilization with particular reference to the role of the Office of Price Administration in wage fixing, was understood to have been the subject of an animated discussion at a luncheon conference between President Roosevelt and Philip Murray, president of the C. I. O.

Mr. Murray, who is also president of the United Steel Workers

of America, was obviously distressed by the WLB's ruling, and the recent pronouncements of an agent of Leon Henderson, OPA chief, at the West Coast aircraft stabilization conference, and it was indicated that he had expressed his feelings to the President.

The luncheon was private, and Mr. Murray slipped out of a side door of the White House, as he entered it, and then started for Pittsburgh.

The question of a referendum on the wage provision will come before the steel union's policy committee tomorrow, and it will be decided what form a referendum of the members will be taken. To clear up the dispute on wage policy which arose at the West Coast aircraft meeting, Donald M. Nelson, Director of the War Production Board, under whose auspices the meeting was being held, decided to recess it for the present. Paul Porter, chairman of the conference and chief of the wage stabilization branch of the WPB's labor production division, announced that "no doors have been closed to wage adjustments."

The announcement was intended to allay the fears of organized labor that the aircraft case had been prejudged and that any negotiated way adjustment would be limited to the formula advanced by the WIB today.

While it was made clear by the WIB that today's decision was the board's own ruling and did not affect any wage adjustment which might be voluntarily made between employers and employes, it was the opinion of the labor members that such conferences would be likely to seek adjustments on the basis of the steel case.

Other Adjustments Expected

Wage adjustments similar to those made today are likely to be followed soon by "Big Steel" and the other steel companies not dealt with directly by the current case which was limited to employes of the Bethlehem Steel Company, Inland Steel Corporation, Republic Steel Corporation and Youngstown Sheet and Tube Company.

There are also pending before the board wage increase demands for $1 a day by more than 300,000 employes of Ford, Chrysler and General Motors.

The entire question of wage stabilization will be taken up by governmental agencies on the return of the aircraft conference member from the West Coast. It was reported today that legislation dealing with the creation of wage adjustment boards would be one of the topics to be considered when spokesmen for the WPB, the Labor Department, the Manpower Commission, the WLB and other Federal agencies meet again.

In its decision today the board ordered the four steel companies to include a maintenance of membership and check-off clause in what will be their first contract with a national steel union. This was ordered as a "wartime" measure. The employer members dissented on the union security provi-

sion. Those employes who do not wish to be bound by the union security and check-off provisions will have fifteen days during which they can resign from the union if they wish.

A wage demand which was first made by steel workers twenty-four years ago was granted by the board when it directed the companies to guarantee their employes a daily minimum wage rather than a daily guarantee averaged over a week or a two weeks' pay period. This was adopted by all three groups, public, labor and industry members.

Increase to Be Retroactive

The 44 cents a day wage increase will be retroactive to the date of certification of each case. The cases were certified between Feb. 6 and 10.

Dr. Taylor said that the directive order calls directly upon the steel workers and indirectly upon all labor to accept their share of the sacrifices "under the national program for adjusting our war economy to the needs of total war." He added:

"By accepting its responsibilities labor will have the opportunity for leadership in the fight against economic instability. For with labor meeting its obligations, it has a right to insist that vigorous steps be taken to effectuate every point to the seven-point program. This is a time when labor statesmanship can serve the country well.

"The time is now. On the domestic front the dangers of instability have fortunately been perceived before they are overwhelmingly upon us. We can act now to avoid future dangers. The President has set forth, in his seven-point program, a plan of action to prevent domestic economic instability. It can be carried out now if every citizen stands up to his responsibility. Those seven points chart the road to economic stability in war time. We will fail to achieve that goal, however, unless all civilian interests accept fully the restraints and the sacrifices which constitute their share of the program. A meeting of the clearly defined needs of this hour will avoid any possibility of the charge of failure on the domestic front because of action 'too little and too late.'"

Reasons for Decision Given

In his opinion Dr. Taylor pointed out that the board arrived at the 5½ cent increase by applying the guiding principles in the following fashion:

"1. The steel workers had secured a wage increase of 11.8 per cent between Jan. 1, 1941, and May 1, 1942, as compared with a 15 per cent increase in the cost of living index during this period. Thus, they had suffered a loss of 3.2 per cent in their peacetime standards.

Therefore, Dr. Taylor pointed out, they were entitled to an hourly increase of 3.2 cents in order to re-establish their peacetime standard, since the average hourly wage rate in the steel industry is $1.

"2. Since the dispute was certified to the board more than two and one-half months prior to the

President's message to Congress of April 27, outlining the National Economic Policy, the steel workers were caught by 'a change of the rules in the middle of the game.' Dr. Taylor pointed out that in view of this factor, and the greater cost of living change in steel towns as compared with the national average, the board had decided that the workers in this case had an additional equity which entitled them to a further increase of 2.3 cents an hour.

"'There is no mathematical exactness in the fraction of a cent which is specified,' he said. 'Exact fraction was supplied in order to insure a total rate practical for payroll purposes.'

Problem of Inflation Cited

"Labor's sacrifice, necessary for the stabilization of our domestic economy, has been clearly set forth. For the duration of the war organized labor is expected to forego its quest for an increasing share of the national income. These considerations are also to guide the National War Labor Board in deciding cases which come before it.

"It is also recognized by the President that in considering wage equities the National War Labor Board should give 'due consideration to inequalities and the elimination of substandards of living.' Such wage adjustments as may be necessary to account for these factors do add to the purchasing power pool. They do not, however, have a vital bearing upon the vast problem of inflation, since such additions to purchasing power make but an insignificant change in the total problem. Such adjustments can and should be made by the National War Labor Board, in cases before it, when equitable considerations are served. Equally clear, however, is the responsibility of the board to avoid the starting of another round of general wage increases all over the country."

Fair Yardsticks, Says Davis

William H. Davis, board chairman, in a separate concurring opinion summarizing the case as a whole, ended his comments on the wage issue as follows:

"We are convinced that the yardsticks of wage stabilization thus applied are fair and equitable and at the same time sufficient to prevent the cost of living from spiraling upward because of wage adjustments. We think they lend to a 'terminal' for the tragic race between wages and prices.

"On this basis labor will have made its move of self-restraint in the seven-point program. If all other groups likewise do their part we may expect to get and hold for the duration of the war stability of standards, and the freedom from apprehension that goes with such stability.

"When the war is over we may expect, with our feet on the ground in a free world, to go forward together, with a renewed determination to improve the standard of living of wage earners, and indeed of all groups of our people."

Mr. Davis pointed out that the board recognized that all citizens who had a decent standard of living would be called upon to surrender many things they have become accustomed to, but that this common sacrifice should come not "in wage determinations by the War Labor Board addressed to workers alone but in taxation by Congress, where all our citizens are represented, and where taxes can be so measured that the imposed reduction of income will fall equitably upon all groups according to their financial ability to contribute to the national purpose and to the preservation of the things for which we fight."

Dissenters Are Sharp

The dissenting opinion of the labor members on the wage issue, signed by Robert J. Watt, Thomas Kennedy, George Meany and R. J. Thomas, concluded, in part, as follows:

"The conclusion is inescapable that the majority carried on its deliberations with a fixed intention not to grant more than a token adjustment, selecting those facts which would fit that pattern and rejecting a multitude of facts and cogent arguments which call for a more substantial adjustment.

"Substituting rhetoric for analysis, it has gone all-out for the inflation thesis, a thesis compounded of conjectures and prophecies, fears and hysteria. It has, in effect, accepted the contention, advanced, among others, by government agencies which are not charged with the duty of adjusting wage disputes, that there shall be no substantial wage adjustments, no matter how meritorious the case may be, and no matter if that increase can be made in a manner that is concededly not inflationary.

"The National War Labor Board has a very strict responsibility to the people of this nation. This responsibility cannot be discharged by substituting theoretical discourses for consideration of the justice of specific demands of the workers. We concluded that the demand of the union for a dollar a day wage adjustment should be granted."

The dissent quoted from the panel's report that "all four companies are able to pay the requested wage increase of $1 a day."

On the question of inflation, the dissenting opinion pointed to the estimate of Inland Steel that the 1942 national income will exceed that of 1941 by 21 per cent and, assuming constant wage rates, 1942 payrolls will exceed 1941 by only 11 per cent.

Inflation Danger Disputed

The dissent then noted that th labor members of the board firs presented a motion that $1 a day be awarded in the form of war bonds and, after this was voted down, that 56 cents be paid in war bonds and 44 cents in cash, which was likewise voted down.

"The majority insists," the dissent stated, "that a wage adjustment of $1 per day in cash would be dangerously inflationary and must therefore be refused. But inasmuch as the majority does not, and cannot, contend that granting the wage adjustment of $1 per day in the form of war bonds would be inflationary, its whole argument collapses."

In concurring with the public members on the wage increase the employer group, comprising Messrs. Roger D. Lapham, George H. Mead, E. J. McMilland and H. B. Horton, said that "there should be some central body set up to stabilize all wages, not only in the event of all disputes but also where no disputes exist."

"Government should define a national wage policy and lay down rules to make its policy really effective," the employers' concurring opinion declared. "We should prevent voluntary general wage increases, which all tend to upset the anti-inflation program."

The employers also noted that any wage stabilization program, to be effective, must go hand in hand with a price fixing program, a price fixing of all commodities including farm products.

Employers Point to Ceilings

"Industry has already accepted price ceilings imposed on its products," they added. "Labor must likewise accept a wage ceiling."

Mr. Lapham filed a separate statement in which he made some general observations. One was that management "has plenty to learn" in dealing with labor, while labor leaders "must learn that their high, wide and fancy decade is over and that the world war we are now engaged in is really going on."

"Labor leaders still demand privileges and favors because they have given up the right to strike," added Mr. Lapham. "This is plain bunk with a capital 'B'. What citizen has a right to strike in a war for his country's existence? Yet stoppages and slowdowns appear to be on the increase and the overworked members of this National War Labor Board are still compelled to take time out because of AFL-CIO jurisdictional disputes."

Wayne Lyman Morse, the public member, who wrote the section on the board's jurisdiction, rejected the contention of the steel employers that the board had no jurisdiction to deal with union security and check-off and held that it derived its authority from the war powers of the President.

Beside Mr. Morse the public members who joined with the employer members in approving the 5.5 cents an hour wage increase were Dr. Frank P. Graham, Mr. Davis and Dr. Taylor.

July 17, 1942

ROOSEVELT ORDER FREEZES WAGES AND PRICES

ACTS ON INFLATION

INFLATION CURB IS AIM

By W. H. LAWRENCE
Special to THE NEW YORK TIMES.
WASHINGTON, April 8—President Roosevelt strengthened the anti-inflation program today with a sweeping executive order forbidding wage increases above the level of the "Little Steel" formula and restricting future price rises to the minimum extent required by law.

To implement what he called a "hold-the-line order," the President authorized Paul V. McNutt, War Manpower Commission chairman, to issue regulations which would prevent employes from shifting to a job at a higher rate of pay unless the change would aid in the prosecution of the war.

He called upon Congress to impose higher taxes in order to reduce and hold in check excess purchasing power and to pass no new legislation which would require further price increases.

"The only way to hold the line is to stop trying to find justifications for not holding it here or not holding it there," the President said in an accompanying statement. "No one straw may break a camel's back, but there is always a last straw. We cannot afford to take further chances in relaxing the line. We already have taken too many."

The order appeared certain to bring a showdown between the

Administration and John L. Lewis, president of the United Mine Workers of America, who is demanding a $2-a-day wage increase for 450,000 bituminous coal miners and 90,000 anthracite coal miners.

On wages, the President specifically directed the National War Labor Board, the Commissioner of Internal Revenue and other agencies administering wage or salary controls "to authorize no further increases in wages or salaries except such as are clearly necessary to correct substandards of living" and except in accordance with the "Little Steel" formula, which limits general wage rises to a total of 15 per cent since Jan. 1, 1941, in order to compensate for increased living costs between January, 1941, and May, 1942.

Merit Increases Permitted

The wage control agencies also will be permitted, under general policies laid down by James F. Byrnes, Economic Stabilization Director, to authorize "reasonable adjustments of wages and salaries in case of promotions, reclassifications, merit increases, incentive wages or the like, provided that such adjustments do not increase the level of production costs appreciably or furnish the basis either to increase prices or to resist otherwise justifiable reduction in prices."

Bituminous miners would be entitled to no general increase under the "Little Steel" formula, and anthracite miners would be entitled to only a small general rise.

Late tonight the full War Labor Board met and, after studying the President's order, sent this telegram to all regional boards, commissions and other agencies to which authority has been delegated by the agency:

"First, continue to prepare as heretofore all your cases.

"Secondly, approve no further wage increases whatever except those that clearly come within the 15 per cent limitation of the 'Little Steel' formula.

"Thirdly, all final wage decisions or rulings which you have made up to 7:30 P. M., Eastern wartime, April 8, which do not require pre-review may be validly issued to the parties and those which do require prereview should be sent us as heretofore.

"Further instructions will come in a few days."

The board has already asked its regional boards for details of substandard wages in each region.

The President's order came as a surprise to most of Washington. It followed by twenty-four hours the Senate's 62-to-23 vote to send back to the Agriculture Committee the Bankhead bill, which the President had vetoed as "inflationary."

The President indicated a firm determination to hold the cost of living at its present level and, if possible, to reduce some prices.

More Ceiling Prices Ordered

He directed Prentiss M. Brown, the Price Administrator, and Chester C. Davis, the Food Administrator, to take immediate steps to put ceiling prices on all commodities affecting the cost of living and "to authorize no further increases in ceiling prices except to the minimum extent required by law."

"E ch of them is further directed immediately to use all discretionary powers vested in them by law to prevent further price increases direct or indirect to prevent profiteering and to reduce prices which are excessively high, unfair and inequitable," the order continued.

The order would permit the Price and Food Administrators to authorize "readjustments in price relationships appropriate for various commodities, or classes, qualities or grades thereof or seasonal variations or for various marketing areas."

It would also allow them to authorize "such support prices, subsidies or other inducements as may be authorized by law and deemed necessary to maintain or increase production provided that such action does not increase the cost of living."

Striking at another element which affects living costs, the President appealed to all utility rate regulating agencies to disapprove rate increases and effect rate reductions wherever possible in accordance with State and Federal law.

Because employers often have complained that they were losing men to higher-paid factories because of governmental restrictions on pay increases, the order includes authorization for the manpower agency "to forbid the employment by any employer of any new employe or the acceptance of employment by a new employe except as authorized in accordance with regulations which may be issued by the chairman of the WMC, with the approval of the Economic Stabilization Director, for the purpose of preventing such employment at a wage or salary higher than that received by such new employe in his last employment unless the change of employment would aid in the effective prosecution of the war."

The President at the same time delegated to Mr. Byrnes all the authority granted to him by Congress in the Emergency Stabilization Act and authorized him "to take such action and to issue such directives under the authority of that act as he deems necessary to stabilize the national economy, to maintain and increase production and to aid in the effective prosecution of the war."

In his statement the President appealed to the country, and especially to Congress, to cooperate in preserving the economic stabilization program.

"Some groups have been urging increased prices for farmers on the ground that wage earners have unduly profited," he said. "Other groups have been urging increased wages on the ground that farmers have unduly profited. A continuance of this conflict will not only cause inflation but will breed disunity at a time when unity is essential."

Under the Emergency Economic Stabilization Act approved last October, the President said, the progress of inflation "has been slowed up," but, he said, "now we must stop it."

The statement declared that "to hold the line we cannot tolerate further increases in prices affecting the cost of living or further increases in general wage or salary rates except where clearly necessary to correct substandard living conditions."

The President said that today's action had been indicated for some time "because of the continued pressure for increased wages and increased prices," but that he had waited because of the controversy over whether subsidy payments to farmers legally could be included in deciding whether a price had reached the parity level. The Bankhead bill, vetoed by the President, forbade such inclusion.

Inferentially, the President was critical of the Senate for not giving a clear-cut decision on his veto when it decided, instead, to send the bill back to committee.

The President said that it might be weeks or months before the Bankhead bill came up again, but that because of the price situation he could not wait to see whether it again was reported. He said that he had been advised that never in the history of Congress has a vetoed bill become law after being recommitted.

ROOSEVELT SEIZES ALL STRUCK COAL MINES

ICKES IN CONTROL

President Orders Him to Run Mines in Interests of 'Nation at War'

By LOUIS STARK
Special to THE NEW YORK TIMES.

WASHINGTON, May 1—President Roosevelt today ordered Secretary Ickes, as Solid Fuels Administrator for War, to take over all the bituminous and anthracite properties because "the national interest is in grave peril as a result of almost complete cessation of operations of 450,000 soft-coal and 80,000 hard-coal miners."

Secretary Ickes complied immediately, taking over 3,400 bituminous properties, and the hard-coal workings as well, and ordering the flag of the United States to fly from all tipples.

Acting swiftly and firmly, the President, by executive order based on his constitutional powers and his authority as Chief Executive and Commander in Chief of the Army and Navy, directed the Secretary of War to give protection to those who might wish to work, if this were requested by Secretary Ickes.

In a public statement the President called upon all miners "who may have abandoned their work to return immediately to the mines and work for their government."

Stresses the Country's Need

"Their country needs their services as much as those of the members of the armed forces," he declared. "I am confident that they do not wish to retard the war effort; that they are as patriotic as any other Americans and that they will promptly answer this call to perform this essential war service."

The President announced that he would "talk over the radio to the miners of the nation" at 10 P. M. tomorrow. His address will be carried on all networks.

Mr. Roosevelt's action today was based upon the continued refusal of John L. Lewis, president of the United Mine Workers, and his associates to submit their dispute with the Appalachian operators to the determination of the WLB.

The miners have maintained for many weeks that the board would not give them an unprejudiced hearing, that Chairman William H. Davis and his associates had prejudged their case and that, in any event, the "Little Steel" formula and the President's "Hold-the-Line" Executive Order of April 8 precluded any fair and judicial determination of the miners' equities in the case.

Seizure of the coal properties, while unpalatable for the operators, was greeted with something like a sigh of relief. They indicated that, in their opinion, the President had no other recourse in view of the circumstances. However, they were not quite clear as to the next moves of the government, but said that they would stand by and carry out the orders of "our new boss, Secretary Ickes."

The use of troops as an immediate possibility appeared to be in the background today, but such action, it was stated, would depend on what happened in the far-flung coal fields of twenty-six States in the next few days.

That the government has no desire to use the military to put down a coal strike was apparent in the President's executive order authorizing Secretary Ickes to act in accordance with the civil and organizational liberties of the miners.

In addition to directing him to "maintain customary working conditions in the mines" as well as the "customary procedure for the adjustment of workers' grievances," he also told the Secretary to "recognize the right of the workers to continue their membership in any labor organization, to bargain collectively through representatives of their own choosing, and to engage in concerted activities for the purpose of collective bargaining or other mutual aid or protection, provided that such concerted activities do not interfere with the operations of the mines."

The first inkling of what the President would do came at 10:30 this morning, half an hour after Mr. Roosevelt's ultimatum of last Thursday to President Lewis and Secretary Thomas Kennedy of the miners union had expired.

Early Reveals Radio Plan

Stephen T. Early, White House Secretary, called newsmen and announced that the President would go on the air at 10 P. M. tomorrow with a brief but important statement. The speech, he said, would be carried by all networks.

"It is a safe surmise that it will deal largely with the question of the need of coal to win the war," he added.

He was asked whether it would be "a safe surmise" that no action would be taken before the speech tomorrow night.

"I can't tell.' he replied. "That may be safe for you but not for me."

About an hour later Mr. Early sent for the newsmen and outlined to them the gist of the Executive Order taking over the coal mines and enrolling every employe as an employe of the government. The ink was hardly dry from the President's signature on the document which he had in front of him as the secretary dictated its substance to the reporters.

Workers of the Rail and River Corporation Mine at Bellaire, Ohio, came out of the pits as the time was reached.

The White House seethed with press activity as the reporters rushed to the telephones to flash their newspapers and a little later the text of the Executive Order and of the President's own statement were given out.

Almost the entire force of the order was centered on the office of Secretary Ickes, who was in conference with his aides. As a result of their talks the messages went forth to the operators and Mr. Ickes said that "all of us in the coal-mining business are now working for Uncle Sam."

Action No Surprise to Capital

The President's seizure of the mines did not come as a great surprise to official Washington. It was regarded as an inevitable step in the "showdown" between Mr. Roosevelt and Mr. Lewis.

Government agencies, upon issuance of the Executive Order, swung promptly into line. Donald M. Nelson, WPB Administrator, issued an order extending control of coal in transit to the anthracite tonnage now en route and permitted diversion of hard coal to

those industrial users who had less than five days of fuel stocks on hand.

Proclamation posters, apparently printed in advance, were issued and sent to the mine fields for display at mine shafts and company property. The posters showed the American flag in colors and proclaimed the mines to be United States property.

In his statement, the President recalled his telegram of last Thursday to Messrs. Lewis and Kennedy, pointing out that the rising tide of coal strikes which preceded the expiration of. the extended bituminous agreement last midnight were "a direct interference with the prosecution of the war, and challenged the governmental machinery set up for the orderly and peaceful settlement of labor disputes, and the power of the government to carry on the war."

He recalled also that he sad said that continuance of the strikes would be the equivalent of "a crippling defeat in the war," and that he had appealed to the miners to put their case before the WLB.

If work were not resumed by 10 A. M. today, Mr. Roosevelt continued, he had advised the miners that he would use all his powers "to protect the national interest and to prevent further interference with the successful prosecution of the war."

President Repeats Promise

After saying that "the national interest is in grave peril," the President then announced that he had asked Mr. Ickes to take possession of the mines and operate them for the government.

He repeated his promise that an nvestigation into living costs would be made and was now under way in the mining areas, and that orice violators would be prose-:uted.

"Whenever the miners submit their case to the WLB, it will be determined promptly, fairly and in accordance with the procedure and law applicable in all labor disputes," he went on.

The President then underscored his determination to carry on the fight for coal so that the war ef-

fort might not suffer, by adding the following as a separate paragraph:

"The production of coal shall and must continue."

The Executive order, which was titled "Possession and Operation of Coal Mines," began by pointing to widespread stoppages as "threatening to obstruct the effective prosecution of the war" by curtailing vitally needed production in the coal mines directly affecting "the countless war industries and transportation systems dependent upon such mines."

The order then went on to say that inasmuch as the officers of the miners' union "have refused to submit to the machinery established for the peaceful settlement of labor disputes in violation of the agreement on the part of labor and industry that there shall be no strikes or lockouts for the duration of the war," it had become necessary for the government to take over the mines "in order to protect the interests of the nation at war and the rights of the workers to continue at work."

The order then gave Secretary Ickes complete and summary jurisdiction over all mines "together with any or real and personal property, franchises, rights, facilities, funds and other assets used" in connection with the operation of the properties.

William Green, president of the American Federation of Labor, announced that Lloyd A. Thrush, president of the Progressive Miners of America, an A. F. L. affiliate, had telegraphed him that his union was extending its present agreement for another thirty-day period for the second time in order to permit negotiations to continue with the operators employing its members.

"The Progressive miners represent approximately 40,000 miners in Kentucky, Illinois and Virginia," said Mr. Green.

Mr. Green, accompanied by R. J. Thomas, president of the United Automobile Workers of America, C. I. O.; David B. Robertson, president of the Brotherhood of Enginemen and Firemen, and Mrs. Anna Rosenberg, New York war manpower regional director, conferred with the President today.

After the meeting, Mr. Thomas said that Mr. Roosevelt had informed his visitors that troops would not be used in the coal areas unless absolutely necessary.

"I told the President that troops would raise chaos, that labor could not stand up under it," said Mr. Thomas. "I also said you cannot force a man to work with a bayonet and the President agreed with me."

The President, he added, had promised to have his advisers look into labor's complaint that the WLB was exceeding its authority in refusing to consider "inequalities" in wage rates when adjusting a wage dispute.

They turned in their equipment shortly after emerging from the mine

Associated Press Wirephotos

ROOSEVELT ORDERS STRIKERS IN AKRON TO RETURN BY NOON OR HE WILL ACT FOR NATION

SAYS U. S. IS DEFIED

President in a Telegram Calls Rubber Tie-Up Blow to War Effort

LEADERS ACT AT ONCE

Order a Resumption of Work in the Crippled Plants at 6 This Morning

Special to THE NEW YORK TIMES.

WASHINGTON, May 26—President Roosevelt tonight ordered the 52,000 striking Akron rubber workers to return to their jobs by noon tomorrow.

[The United Press reported that after receiving the ultimatum from President Roosevelt last night the striking rubber workers received a joint order by the locals of the United Rubber Workers (C. I. O.) and the international executive board of the union instructing them to resume operations by 6 A. M. today.]

The ultimatum, served in telegrams to Sherman H. Dalrymple, president of the C. I. O. United Rubber Workers, and heads of three Akron local unions, followed by less than two hours an announcement by the War Labor Board that it had asked the President to intervene in the strike.

Strike Held 'Inexcusable'

The text of the President's telegram follows:

"The National War Labor Board has reported to me concerning the serious strikes existing in several rubber plants in Akron, Ohio. From the point of view of the nation these strikes are inexcusable and must therefore be accepted by the country and by your government for what they basically are: namely, a defiance of the WLB, a challenge to government by law, and a blow against the effective prosecution of the war.

"Further, these strikes constitute a flagrant violation of the no-strike pledge. They must not be permitted to continue any longer. In the midst of a war calling for the supreme sacrifice of many in the ranks of our armed forces, it is shocking to the nation to discover that any group within our citizenry would impede for a single moment the production of materials of war needed for our war effort.

"Economic sacrifices, whether real or not, do not justify the strike action taken by the members of your union. The WLB has already called your attention to the fact that orderly procedures exist for a review of your grievances, but those procedures cannot be made available to you in the face of a strike against the security of this nation. As I have stated before, the decisions of the WLB are binding on all employers and all employes, and a defiance of the board cannot be permitted.

Orders Return by Noon

"Therefore, as Commander-in-Chief of the Army and Navy, I direct all picketing to cease and all employes now out on strike at the rubber plants to return to work at once. If this strike is not ended by 12 o'clock noon Thursday, May 27, 1943, your government will take the necessary steps to protect the interest of the nation, the legal rights and properties of the companies involved and the rights of the patriotic workers who desire to work. I hereby request and delegate you to notify the members of your union accordingly and make clear that each and every one of them now out on strike should consider that this telegram is also addressed to the individual strikers."

CONGRESS OVERRIDES VETO OF ANTI-STRIKE BILL

CONGRESS REBELS

President Is Defeated by 56 to 25 in Senate, 244–108 in House

SWIFT VOTE TAKEN

Criminal Penalties Are Made Law, but 30-Day Strike Vote Is Set

By W. H. LAWRENCE
Special to THE NEW YORK TIMES.

WASHINGTON, June 25—A rebellious Congress, angered by three coal strikes and other sporadic interruptions of war production, quickly overrode President Roosevelt's veto today and enacted into law the Smith-Connally anti-strike bill requiring thirty days' notice in advance of strike votes and providing criminal penalties for those who instigate, direct or aid strikes in government-operated plants or mines.

The Senate voted 56 to 25 to make the bill law despite the Chief Executive's disapproval. The House voted 244 to 108 immediately afterward. Both votes were well over the constitutional requirement of a two-thirds majority to override a veto.

Both Houses acted not only quickly, but with a minimum of discussion to reject the President's warning that the measure would stimulate labor unrest, give governmental sanction to strike agitation, and foment slow-downs and strikes.

How the Parties Divided

In the Senate, twenty-nine Democrats, including the acting Majority Leader, Senator Lister Hill of Alabama, and twenty-seven Repub-

licans voted to override the President's veto, and nineteen Democrats, five Republicans and one Progressive voted to sustain it.

Of the Senators who voted after the veto message had been read and who had been recorded on the conference committee report, not one changed his vote as a result of Presidential disapproval of the measure. Senator Joseph Ball, Republican, of Minnesota, who had been paired for the bill but did not vote at the time the conference committee report was taken up, voted to sustain the veto.

In the House 130 Republicans and 114 Democrats voted against the President. Of those who voted to sustain the veto, sixty-seven were Democrats, thirty-seven were Republicans, two Progressives, one Farmer-Laborite and one member of the American Labor party. Advocates of the bill gained twenty-five votes between approval of the conference committee report and the veto action, while opponents of the measure lost twenty-one supporters.

Law Goes Into Effect at Once

The measure, which had been bitterly opposed by all organized labor, is effective immediately and until six months after the conclusion of the war, and contains these provisions:

The President receives authority to take immediate possession of plants, mines or other production facilities affected by a strike or other labor disturbance.

Wages and other working conditions in effect at the time a plant is taken over by the Government shall be maintained by the Government unless changed by the National War Labor Board at the request of the Government agency or a majority of the employees in the plant.

Persons who coerce, instigate, induce, conspire with or encourage any person to interfere by lockout, strike, slowdown or other interruption with the operation of plants in possession of the Government, or who direct such interruptions or provide funds for continuing them shall be subject to a fine

of not more than $5,000, or to imprisonment for not more than one year, or both. The penalty clause does not apply to those who merely cease work or refuse employment.

Subpoena Power for WLB

The NWLB receives subpoena power to require attendance of parties to labor disputes, but NWLB members are forbidden to participate in any decision in which the member has a direct interest as an officer, employe or representative of either party to the dispute.

Employes of war contractors must give to the Secretary of Labor, the NWLB and the National Labor Relations Board notice of any labor dispute which threatens seriously to interrupt war production and the NLRB is required on the thirtieth day after notice is given to take a secret ballot of the employes on the question of whether they will strike.

Labor organizations, as well as national banks and corporations organized by authority of Federal law, are forbidden to make political contributions in any election involving officials of the National Government, with the organization subject to a fine of not more than $5,000 for violating the act and the officers subject to a fine of not more than $1,000 or imprisonment for not more than one year, or both.

The President waited the full ten days of the constitutional period before vetoing the measure which was sent to him by a 219-to-129 House vote and 55-to-22 Senate vote. At 3:13 P. M. his veto message was read to the Senate, and by 5:28 P. M. the measure was law.

Senate Is First to Act

The Senate acted first, with Senator Connally of Texas taking the floor to say:

"I am sorely disappointed. The Senate is sorely disappointed. The House, I am sure, is disappointed. The people of the United States by an overwhelming majority are disappointed. The soldiers and sailors wherever they may be, on land, on the sea, in the air, all over this globe are disappointed.

"The section of the bill to which the President objected was in the House provisions.

"The President has a right to veto legislation. The Senate has a right to pass a bill over the veto.

"I hope that the Senate now will exercise its constitutional privilege."

Senator Carl Hatch, Democrat of New Mexico, seconded the motion, and the roll-call began.

When the vote was announced as 56 to 25 to override, there was applause from the galleries, led by men in uniform.

The large House majority in favor of overriding was apparent as soon as word of the Senate action reached it. A Commodity Credit Corporation extension and modification bill was up for consideration and members immediately began to move that this either be laid aside or that debate close and immediate action be taken on it, thus to clear the way for consideration of the veto.

Appeal for Action Cheered

Representative Clifton Woodrum, Democrat, of Virginia, received repeated applause and cheers for his plea for "action, not tomorrow, not Monday, but today, so that we can send the message to our boys in the foxholes that the American people are behind them."

Chairman Andrew J. May of the House Military Affairs Committee, which brought out the original draft of changes in the Senate bill to which the President objected so vigorously, repeated the same thought, bringing objections that he was out of order and "trying to create a lynching spirit in the House." The latter assertion came from Representative Vito Marcantonio, American Labor, of New York.

Apparently sensing the House insistence on action today, Representative John W. McCormack of Massachusetts, the majority leader, quickly promised that the veto message would be taken up as soon as the pending bill was disposed of. Delaying tactics by other Administration supporters in seeking record votes on amendments to the CCC bill failed to find sufficient House support to be effective and a motion made at 4:50 that the House adjourn was overwhelmingly shouted down. The veto message was then read, and the vote taken immediately.

Says Strikes Won't Be Tolerated

The President's veto message firmly declared that the Executive would not countenance strikes in wartime and was conciliatory in its approach to Congress.

Declaring it was the will of the people that for the duration of the war all labor disputes shall be settled by orderly, legally established procedures, and that no war work shall be interrupted by strike or lockout, the President said that the no-strike, no-lockout pledge given by labor and industry after Pearl Harbor "has been well kept except in the case of the leaders of the United Mine Workers." During 1942, he said, the time lost by strikes averaged only 5/100ths of 1 per cent of the total man-hours worked, a record which he declared had never before been equalled in this country and which was as good or better than the record of any of our allies in the war.

He conceded that laws often are necessary "to make a very small minority of people live up to the standards that the great majority of the people follow" and in this connection he cited the recent coal strike.

Favors First Seven Sections

Analyzing the bill, section by section, he said that the first seven sections, "broadly speaking," incorporate into statute the existing machinery for settling labor disputes and provide criminal penalties for those who instigate, direct or aid a strike in a government-operated plant or mine. Had the bill been limited to this subject matter, he said that he would have signed it.

His principal objection was to the eighth section, which, he said, would foment slow-downs and strikes. That section provides a thirty-day notice before a vote to strike can be taken under supervision of the National Labor Relations Board, and, while Congressional sponsors called this a "cooling off" period, Mr. Roosevelt contended that it "might well become a boiling period" during which workers would devote their thoughts and energies to getting pro-strike votes instead of turning out war matériel.

"In wartime we cannot sanction strikes with or without notice," he declared. "Section 8 ignores completely labor's 'no-strike' pledge and provides, in effect, for strike notices and strike ballots. Far from discouraging strikes, these provisions would stimulate labor unrest and give government sanction to strike agitations."

Draft Change Recommended

The President was highly critical also of Section 9, which prohibits, during the war, political contributions by labor organiza-

tions. This section, he remarked, "obviously has no relevancy" to an anti-strike bill. If the prohibition on trade union political contributions has merit, he expressed the belief that it should not be confined to the war. Congress, he added, might also give careful consideration to extending the ban to other non-profit organizations.

The President reiterated his recommendation that the Selective Service Act be amended to provide noncombat military service for persons up to the age of 65, declaring that "this will enable us to induct into military service all persons who engage in strikes or stoppages or other interruptions of work in plants in the possession of the United States."

"This direct approach is necessary to insure the continuity of war work," he said. "The only alternative would be to extend the principle of selective service and make it universal in character."

Whether enactment of the bill would cause the withdrawal of labor representatives from NWLB was an open question. Many persons in Washington thought that it would, but no responsible leader of

labor would commit himself on this question tonight.

After Congress, by overriding the veto, had enacted into law the section banning contributions by labor organizations to which the President had objected, Senator Hatch introduced a measure forbidding similar political contributions by associations of employers.

It was the eighth time that Congress had overridden President Roosevelt by a veto during the more than ten years he has been in office, and it was the most important measure on which the Congress acted independent of the Executive since payment of the soldiers' bonus was authorized, January 27, 1937.

Observers on Capitol Hill believed that the continued absence from work of a large number of coal miners, despite the back-to-work order of the UMW policy committee, and the lukewarm reception by Congress to the President's draft proposal, played a major role in the decisive votes. There was a roar of protest on the floor of the House when the President reiterated his proposal to increase the draft age to 65 to deal with strikers.

June 26, 1943

ARMY SEIZES RAILROADS ON PRESIDENT'S ORDER

WAR IS PUT FIRST

Roosevelt Says He Must Make Sure Troops Get Goods Without Halt

---

By LOUIS STARK
Special to THE NEW YORK TIMES.
WASHINGTON, Dec. 27—President Roosevelt ordered Secretary

of War Henry L. Stimson at 6 P. M. today to take over all railroads in the continental United States at 7 P. M., despite assurances at 5 P. M. that the fifteen nonoperating unions were cancelling their notices for a strike Dec. 30 and were ready to have him arbitrate the amount they were to receive for overtime pay.

The President, however, declared that he could not wait "until the last moment to take action to see that the supplies to our fighting men are not interrupted."

He said that he was taking over the railroads because the nonoperating employes, numbering 1,100,000, did not agree with the carriers "upon the scope of the issues to be arbitrated by the President." Strike orders of three operating brotherhoods, the firemen, conductors and switchmen, were still in force.

Lieut. Gen. Brehon B. Somervell, commanding the Army Service Forces, was designated by Secretary Stimson to take over the railroads in conformity with the Presidential order.

Operating Chief Named

Directly responsible for operating the roads under General Somervell will be Maj. Gen. C. P. Gross, Chief of Transportation, Army Service Forces.

Mr. Stimson also announced that the Army officials would have the advice of Martin W. Clement, president of the Pennsylvania Railroad, as well as the staff of the Association of American Railroads.

An offer to act as labor consultants is being made by Mr. Stimson to A. F. Whitney, president of the Brotherhood of Railroad Trainmen, and Alvanley Johnston, president of the Brotherhood of Locomotive Engineers. These two brotherhoods accepted President Roosevelt's wage arbitration offer last week and canceled their strike orders.

The President's arbitration award was announced today. It granted to the trainmen and engineers 5 cents an hour for work in excess of forty hours a week, or in lieu of claims for expenses while away from home.

Increase Is 9 Cents an Hour

Added to the 4 cents an hour previously awarded to the operating unions by a Presidential board, the President's award makes a total wage increase of 9 cents an hour, which gives to the trainmen and engineers increases aggregating $81,000,000 a year.

The President also ruled that these two unions were entitled to a vacation of one week a year with pay at the basic hourly rate of employment. The wage increases, according to the Presidential announcement, shall remain in effect until the end of the war.

Seizure of the railroads appeared to have been averted when the fifteen nonoperating unions sent a letter to the President advising him they were ready to abandon their repeated refusal to accept a sliding scale of wage increases of 4 to 10 cents an hour and were willing to have him arbitrate what they were entitled to for overtime after forty hours a week.

The President had stated on June 16 at a press conference and had repeated several times that

there was no justification for railroad workers not being paid time and a half after forty hours.

The heads of the brotherhoods of firemen, conductors and switchmen, who rejected the Presidential arbitration proposal last week, announced tonight that they would reconsider their attitude tomorrow. It was expected that they would follow the lead of the seventeen other unions and accept Presidential arbitration.

Informed Federal sources expressed the opinion tonight that Government operation would be brief, with Presidential arbitration awards covering all the wage disputes and enabling return of the roads to private management.

It is estimated in management circles that if the overtime award is extended to the other three operating unions the total wage advance for the operating unions would be about $100,000,000. The four-to-ten cents sliding scale increase for the nonoperating unions was estimated at $182,000,000. An award of five cents for overtime would cost an additional $125,000,-000.

In signing the executive order taking over the railroads, the President said:

"Railroad strikes by three brotherhoods have been ordered for next Thursday. I cannot wait until the last moment to take action to see that the supplies to our fighting men are not interrupted. I am, accordingly, obliged to take over at once temporary possession and control of the railroads to ensure their continued operation.

"The Government will expect every railroad man to continue at his post of duty. The major military offensives now planned must not be delayed by the interruption

of vital transportation facilities. If any employes of the railroads now strike, they will be striking against the Government of the United States."

Non-Operating Group's Letter

The text of the letter from the non-operating unions was as follows:

"Dear Mr. President:

"On Nov. 4, Hon. Fred M. Vinson, Director of Economic Stabilization, approved a sliding scale of wage adjustments for the non-operating group and provided these increases should become effective on Nov. 19. We protested against these increases because we did not feel they were sufficient to meet the problem.

"We have now concluded to abandon any further objections to Judge Vinson's order making these increases effective retroactive to Feb. 1, 1943.

"However, in view of recent offers by the railroads to grant to the operating group the benefits of the Fair Labor Standards Act in respect to overtime for the sixth day in any work week, we feel that the equities of the situation require that this consideration be extended to the nonoperating group.

"While we prefer the benefits of this overtime be distributed in a pro rata amount to all employes, if that is not agreeable to you we will accept the literal application of the Fair Labor Standards Act provisions on overtime.

"Therefore, there is no longer any dispute over the amount of wage increase to be granted to our group. The only remaining question in dispute is 'shall the nonoperating group receive the benefits of overtime after forty hours per week offered to the operating group.' We agree to leave decision on this single question in dispute to the President of the United States and agree to accept the decision.

"Having, with your assistance, accommodated our immediate difficulties, we are withdrawing approval heretofore granted to the employes to stop work at 6 A. M. on Dec. 30, 1943.

"We thank you for your assistance in this disposition of our difficulties."

Signers for the Unions

Signers were George M. Harrison, J. J. Duffy, J. A. Franklin, Felix H. Knight, V. O. Gardner, S. J. Hogan, James J. Delaney, George Wright, Roy Horn, E. E. Milliman, A. E. Lyon, Edward Flore, I. M. Wicklein, Joseph P. Ryan, H. J. Carr and B. M. Jewell, chairman.

In the executive order taking over possession and operation of the railroads, the Secretary of War was authorized to terminate operation "as soon as he determines that such possession, control and operation are no longer required to prevent interruption of transportation service."

Secretary Stimson was not authorized to make a contract with the railroad labor organizations. In this respect, the order differed from the one which the President signed in the most recent seizure of the soft-coal mines as the result of a strike by the United Mine Workers. On that occasion, he authorized Secretary of the Interior Harold L. Ickes to make an agreement with the union.

In today's order, however, the Secretary of War was authorized to prescribe compensation of employes subject to any approval which may be required by law, by executive orders or by regulations relating to economic stabilization.

The Secretary was also authorized to recognize the right of employes to continue their membership in labor organizations and to bargain collectively with the representatives of the carriers' owners, subject to existing statutes and executive orders.

CHAPTER 5

Reconversion

An unhappy John L. Lewis orders
the United Mine Workers back to work.

Courtesy Wide World Photos.

Labor Lexicon

By A. H. RASKIN

CONGRESS has been spending much time debating labor issues. In the process, members of both houses are bandying about terms that are not always clear to the public and perhaps not even clear to the Congressmen. Here are a few such terms and their meanings:

Arbitration — The process whereby a union and an employer voluntarily agree to let an umpire decide their quarrel. Both sides present their arguments to the arbitrator, and his decision is binding.

Closed Shop—A shop in which all employes, old and new, must belong to the union. This applies to workers being hired, as well as those already on the payroll.

Closed Union—A union that accepts no new members or that establishes prohibitively high entrance standards. Such unions are found primarily in industries having the closed shop.

Compulsory Arbitration —A Government-imposed requirement that all disputes that cannot be settled through direct negotiation be resolved through arbitration.

Conciliation—Introduction of a third party, usually a Government representative, into direct negotiations between management and labor. The conciliator tries to help the parties to reach an agreement but has no power to compel a settlement or to set forth terms binding on either side.

Fact-Finding—An attempt by an outside board of citizens or Government representatives to determine the basic facts underlying a labor-management controversy. Their findings, usually accompanied by recommendations for settlement, are published for the guidance of the public and the parties. Acceptance of the recommendations is not mandatory unless both sides have signified in advance their willingness to be bound by the panel's report.

Impartial Chairman—An arbitrator selected by labor and management, usually on a permanent basis, to assist in administering a contract. His role as arbitrator is almost always limited to disputes arising out of the contract.

When the contract expires, he has no authority to decide what should go into a new agreement.

Industry-wide Bargaining—The carrying on of union-employer negotiations simultaneously for all companies and all workers in an industry. In some cases, such as coal and men's clothing, all employers are directly represented in the negotiations. In others, like steel, separate negotiations are held with each company, but all are expected to conform to a single master pattern, usually set in negotiations with the largest unit in the industry.

Jurisdictional Strike—A strike growing out of a row between two or more unions, each of which claims the right to do a particular type of work.

Maintenance of Membership—A contract provision requiring that workers who belong to the union on a certain date must stay in good standing to hold their jobs. Employes who do not belong to the union or who withdraw from membership before the specified date are not required to join. New employes are similarly free to join or stay out of the union.

Mediation—This is essentially the same as conciliation. The mediator may nag, bluster or cajole in the effort to produce an accord, but he cannot force acceptance of his own ideas on how the dispute should be settled.

Open Shop—A shop in which no worker is obliged to belong to the union as a condition of employment.

Secondary Boycott — Refusal of workers in other plants to handle or work on products made by an employer who has a labor dispute in his plant or who is involved in jurisdictional difficulties.

Sympathy Strike—A walkout by workers in other crafts or industries to help a striking union win its demands.

Union Shop—A shop in which non-union workers may be hired with the proviso that they must join the union within a stated period. All regular employes must belong to the union.

Union Security—Any contract provision establishing protection for the union against loss of members. This would include maintenance of membership, union shop and closed shop.

April 20, 1947

Proposed Management=Labor Code
By The Associated Press

WASHINGTON, March 28—*Following is the text of the "New Charter for Labor and Management" announced today by President William Green of the AFL, Philip Murray of the CIO and President Eric Johnston of the Chamber of Commerce of the United States:*

We in management and labor firmly believe that the end of this war will bring the unfolding of a new era based upon a vastly expanding economy and unlimited opportunities for every American.

This peacetime goal can only be attained through the united effort of all our people. Today we are united in national defense. Tomorrow we must be united equally in the national interest.

Management-labor unity, so effective in lifting war production to unprecedented heights, must be continued in the post-war period. To this end, we dedicate our joint efforts for a practical partnership within the framework of this code of principles:

1. Increased prosperity for all involves the highest degree of production and employment at wages assuring a steadily advancing standard of living. Improved productive efficiency and technological advancement must, therefore, be constantly encouraged.

2. The rights of private property and free choice of action, under a system of private competitive capitalism, must continue to be the foundation of our nation's peaceful and prosperous expanding economy. Free competition and free men are the strength of our free society.

3. The inherent right and responsibility of management to direct the operations of an enterprise shall be recognized and preserved. So that enterprise may develop and expand and earn a reasonable profit, management must be free as well from unnecessary governmental interference or burdensome restrictions.

4. The fundamental rights of labor to organize and to engage in collective bargaining with management shall be recognized and preserved, free from legislative enactments which would interfere with or discourage these objectives. Through the acceptance of collective bargaining agreements, differences between management and labor can be disposed of between the parties through peaceful means, thereby discouraging avoidable strife through strikes and lockouts.

5. The independence and dignity of the individual and the enjoyment of his democratic rights are inherent in our free American society. Our purpose is to cooperate in building an economic system for the nation which will protect the individual against the hazards of unemployment, old age and physical impairments beyond his control.

6. An expanding economy at home will be stimulated by a vastly increased foreign trade. Arrangements must therefore be perfected to afford the devastated or undeveloped nations reasonable assistance to encourage the rebuilding and development of sound economic systems. International trade cannot expand through subsidized competition among the nations for diminishing markets, but can be achieved only through expanding world markets and the elimination of any arbitrary and unreasonable practices.

7. An enduring peace must be secured. This calls for the establishment of an international security organization, with full participation by all the United Nations, capable of preventing aggression and assuring lasting peace.

We in management and labor agree that our primary duty is to win complete victory over Nazism and Japanese militarism. We also agree that we have a common joint duty, in cooperation with other elements of our national life and with Government, to prepare and work for a prosperous and sustained peace.

In this spirit we agree to create a national committee, composed of representatives of business and labor organizations. This committee will seek to promote an understanding and sympathetic acceptance of this code of principles and will propose such national policies as will advance the best interests of our nation.

March 29, 1945

WAGE POLICY IS STUDIED FOR CONVERSION PERIOD

AFL, CIO Unite in Drive to Modify Government's 'Little Steel' Formula

By LOUIS STARK

WASHINGTON, June 16—On the judicial front this week labor scored one gain and lost one objective, while on the economic front it renewed its effort to modify the wage stabilization policy and to win acceptance for its reconversion policy program.

The Supreme Court is apparently with organized labor in its fight against State laws compelling the licensing of union business agents and the filing of certain data by the unions. Although the court's split decision—5 to 4—was a narrow squeak, nevertheless it was held that the Florida legislation, which was in question, interfered with the Wagner Act respecting the freedom of workers to choose their own bargaining agents.

Closed Shop Decision

This does not mean that labor will have clear sailing in its attempts to invalidate the rapidly mounting number of State restrictive laws. New cases will be presented to the high court from time to time, and each one will be adjudicated on an individual basis.

On the same day that the Supreme Court acted on the Florida licensing case, a Federal court in Tampa, by the unanimous vote of three members, upheld Florida's constitutional amendment banning the closed shop. This case will go to the Supreme Court next fall. In view of organized labor's long fight for the closed shop and its progress toward that end during the war, the reasoning of the Supreme Court on the issue will be awaited with great interest.

On the economic front the American Federation of Labor and the Congress of Industrial Organizations pressed their plans for modification of the Little Steel formula and for adoption of Federal policies looking toward "full employment."

William Green, AFL president, after requesting President Truman to modify the Little Steel formula to permit a 20 per cent wage in-

"WON'T GIVE UP."

The Philadelphia Inquirer

crease, came away with the impression that Lewis B. Schwellenbach, the new Secretary of Labor, would play a part in investigating the problem for the President.

AFL, CIO Agreed

The AFL and CIO, whatever their other differences, see eye to eye on the need for changing the wage stabilization yardstick. Philip Murray, the CIO chief, had preceded Mr. Green to the White House in support of similar demands.

The rapidity of reconversion from war to civilian goods as a result of cutbacks has made discussion of the possible change in wage stabilization policy no longer theoretical.

According to Chairman George W. Taylor of the War Labor Board, several problems relating to a change in policy are now being discussed with regional boards.

This is unlikely to gain the acceptance of Government agencies.

Dr. Taylor says frankly that "payment of the present take-home pay for a much shorter work week on civilian goods would create such an irresistible pressure on the price structure as possibly to bring about the runaway inflation which has so far been held in check at great sacrifice."

He does not shrink from recognizing, however, that there is a need to correct any new equitable wage relationships which may develop during reconversion.

Labor Policy Aspects

On the other hand, the AFL, in its petition to the President, insists that wage rates can be increased without danger of inflation since the higher rates would only make up losses because of the elimination of overtime. The AFL also maintains that manpower bottlenecks in industries like textiles and lumber are due to low wages. The remedy proposed is collective bargaining negotiations for wage increases with price adjustments recommended if necessary.

The broader aspect of labor's post-war policy on wages also covers the planning of large-scale housing developments, road building, public works and rural electrification.

The vice presidents of the CIO, meeting a few days ago drew up a "must" program which included Presidential revision of the national wage policy. Mr. Truman was called on to give the WLB authority to make wage adjustments if required to aid in the prosecution of the war, to eliminate substandard wages and to assure a continued high level of purchasing power for the maintenance of full production and full employment.

Recalling that the WLB had reported to President Roosevelt that average straight time hourly earnings constituted a proper yardstick for wages, Dr. Taylor now raises the question as to the possible downward effect on wages induced by the pressure of reconversion.

Would Stop Inequities

In other words, will the pressure for lower wage rates in civilian industries so reduce average straight time hourly earnings that a new inequity between wages and prices will appear? If wage-earners lose shift premiums, promotion pay and overtime earnings, then their average straight time hourly earnings will be below present rates. Dr. Taylor, the author of the Little Steel formula, feels that

the WLB must be ready to recognize the need for correcting any new inequitable wage relationships which may develop during the strains and stresses of reconversion.

James Byrnes, former War Mobilization Director, in his report on April 1 said that there were a few industries in which hourly wage rates had increased less than the cost of living, so that any sharp decline in hours worked a week would seriously affect the living standards in these industries. As a result of this report, the WLB and William H. Davis, Economic Stabilization Director, are trying to determine what wage adjustments can be made in the industries referred to by Mr. Byrnes.

Up to this moment the thinking on this problem centers around the possibility of formulating a new type of exception to the rule against general wage increases. For example, discussion is under way as to the possibility of making industry-wide adjustments rather than adjustments in individual companies or plants. It is quite possible that the meat packing industry may be the "guinea pig" for the new type of wage adjustment.

At the present time, the WLB, dealing with dispute cases, holds that payment of less than 55 cents an hour is substandard. Discussions now revolve about the possibility of raising this substandard whether by the board or by action of Congress. Such a change would, no doubt, also be accompanied by a proposal to raise the 40 cents an hour minimum provided by the Fair Labor Standards Act.

Fear Employer Competition

Another possible approach to the wage problem now being considered by Federal officials is the lifting of control by the WLB over voluntary wage increases made by employers provided such adjustments do not affect prices. It is not expected, however, that this change will be made while there are shortages in manpower and in civilian goods. It is felt that to lift the voluntary wage adjustment ban at this time would merely mean competition among employers for workers and among consumers for the present limited supply of civilian goods.

Organized labor hopes for adjustment of wages in the reconversion period which would provide the same pay for forty hours work as now paid for forty-eight hours.

TRUMAN EASES WAGE CURBS

NEW LABOR POLICY

President Asks Increase in Pay to Correct Inequalities

FOR TERMINATION OF WLB

Renewal of No-Strike Pledg Urged Pending Meeting With Management

By JOSEPH A. LOFTUS

WASHINGTON, Aug. 16—President Truman announced today a relaxation of wage controls subject to the restraint of existing price ceilings, and appealed to employers and unions to continue to accept War Labor Board decisions and renew their no-strike, no-lockout pledges until a management-labor conference, which he will convene, finds a substitute for the WLB disputes machinery.

President Truman's statement, which is to be complemented by an Executive order soon, did not specifically write off the Little Steel Wage Formula, but it was thought in some quarters that this was the beginning of the end. Employers and unions can negotiate and effectuate any wage adjustments which do not affect prices. In case of a dispute which goes to the WLB, the board will be empowered to deal more liberally with wage rates that have lagged behind living costs or below the wage levels paid by other employers in the industry, whether they are in the immediate area of the dispute or not.

With the ending of war production, the President's statement said, "there is no longer any threat of an inflationary bidding up of wage rates by competition in a short labor market."

"I am therefore authorizing the WLB," he went on, "to release proposed voluntary wage increases from the necessity of approval upon condition that they will not be used in whole or in part as the basis for seeking an increase in price ceilings."

Proposed wage increases requiring price relief must continue to be passed upon by the board and by the director of economic stabilization.

New Powers Indicated

Indicating the broad, new stabilization authority which the WLB will have during the transition period, the President said that agency should have power to deal with maladjustments and inequities in wage rates "which will tend to interfere with the effective transition to a peacetime economy." And whose "scope and nature cannot be clearly foreseen."

The term "maladjustments" in stabilization language commonly means a disparity between straight-time hourly earnings and the cost of living. This is the sole relation with which the Little Steel formula dealt, and not inequalities or inequities growing out of differences in wages within plants and areas.

The announcement did not deal in specific terms with control of wage reductions. The stabilization law provides for such control, in general, and the WLB is reported to feel that restraints should be mposed.

Declared Emergency Agency

President Truman's statement noted on the matter of disputes that the foundation of wartime industrial relations was an agreement to forego strikes and lockouts for the duration of the war on condition that a WLB was established to settle disputes peacefully. He added:

"The board is an emergency agency. Its effectiveness has been rooted in the wartime agreemen' which led to its establishment. As a result of that agreement industry and labor, with but very few exceptions, have voluntarily accepted the board's decisions in the disputes which have been certified to it as affecting the war effort. A new industry-labor agreement to minimize interruption of production by labor disputes during the reconversion period ahead of us is imperatively needed."

Pending the completion of new disputes machinery, the President went on:

"I call upon the representatives of organized labor and industry to renew their no-strike and no-lockout pledges, and I shall expect both industry and labor in that period to continue to comply voluntarily, as they have in the past, with the directive orders of the WLB."

The President said the WLB should be ended "as soon after the conclusion of the forthcoming industry-labor conference as the orderly disposition of the work of the board, and the provisions of the War Labor Disputes Act permit, and after facilities have been provided to take care of the wage stabilization functions" provided by law.

Unified Agencies Planned

Finally, the President said that the Secretary of Labor was planning unified Federal labor agencies, with particular stress on the upbuilding of the United States Conciliation Service. The President referred to "voluntary" arbitration as the desirable final step in the peacetime system of labor relations.

The announced policy for dealing with disputes left many questions unanswered. Dr. George W. Taylor, WLB chairman, said he would try to clarify some of these at a news conference tomorrow. One question is whether a "voluntary" agreement to raise wages, under pressure of a strike, will be approved.

President Philip Murray of the Congress of Idustrial Organizations indicated at a news conference his organization's willingness to comply with such a program, but said he hoped the management-labor conference would not confine itself to a no-strike proposition.

He added that it was reasonable to assume that CIO unions would now avail themselves of the wage reopening clause which the WLB wrote into its decisions when it refused increases in excess of the Little Steel formula.

The CIO Executive Board, in a resolution today, declared it to be the "unshakeable policy of the CIO and its affiliated organizations to adhere to their contractual obligations in letter and in spirit." The resolution pointed out that collective bargaining agreements customarily provide that during their life there shall be no stoppages and that all grievances shall be adjusted under the machinery provided by the contract.

Employers' Caution Asked

The resolution called upon employers who have such agreements to "equally adhere to their contractual obligations and not endeavor in any way to provoke their employes by violating their agreements and thereby hope to encourage strikes and stoppages."

Mr. Murray continued:

"It should not be understood that it is, or was, the purpose of the organization in executing these agreements to either encourage or foment strikes as a result of disputes that grew out of negotiations which follow the institution of a new wage policy.

'I know of no better and more effective way to avert strikes than through the universal restoration of collective bargaining throughout American industry, with proper incorporation of machinery for settlement of disputes."

The CIO chief said he did not know how noncompliance with WLB decisions could be dealt with in the interim period, but that it should not be serious if management and labor accept the WLB as the adjudicator for a while. He made clear that he understood that the new stabilization policy, in settling wage disputes, would permit the Government to take into account not merely living costs and inequalities but the drop in workers' total earnings, because of loss of overtime, and the profit situation of employers.

Asked what the policy would be in a case where an employer conditioned a wage increase on price relief, and the OPA refused, Mr. Murray said that would be left "largely in the hands of negotiating committees of the unions."

The American Federation of Labor executive board, which just ended a meeting in Chicago, indicated its expectation that the WLB would continue in existence for a while and that the AFL would participate in a management-labor conference.

President William Green stated that although labor was not strictly bound by the no-strike pledge, the AFL membership would be urged to exercise restraint.

Propose Series of Steps

The executive board, with a warning that "expressions of pious hopes proved disastrously insufficient in 1929," proposed a series of steps which it said was imperatively required to avoid economy chaos.

These included: Basic wage increases, increase of the 40-cent hourly minimum to 65 cents, effective price control, increased unemployment compensation, a permanent Fair Employment Practices Committee, enactment of a broader social security program and a full employment bill, amendment of the GI Bill of Rights to provide increased mustering out pay and better education and business advantages, and drastic revision of tax legislation.

August 17, 1945

STRIKES SEEM HEADED FOR NEW HIGH RECORD

Labor Adjustment Machinery Proves Inadequate in the Emergency

By LOUIS STARK

WASHINGTON, Sept. 29— Mounting strikes in the oil, lumber, coal, automobile and other industries appear to be headed for record proportions in the reconversion period.

The strike of CIO oil workers in seven States has already reduced to a trickle oil and gasoline supplies in some communities. Threat of a general oil workers' strike hangs over the conciliation conference arranged by the Government. The conference was deadlocked from Tuesday to Thursday, but was resumed in this city today under direction of Secretary of Labor Schwellenbach.

The oil workers' union, even though it has not fully organized the oil industry, hopes to achieve an industry-wide agreement. The oil companies, however, are vigorously resisting this demand as well as the one for a 30 per cent wage increase. Mr. Schwellenbach has said that he would not force industry-wide bargaining.

In the Pacific Northwest, 40,000 AFL lumber workers are on strike for a wage agreement and an industry-wide contract. If the threat of CIO lumber workers to join the strikers is carried out, the great Northwest lumber industry will be entirely shut down.

The United States Conciliation Service labored in vain to forestall the lumber strike, but the employers were willing to go no farther than to negotiate on an area basis.

Grave Ramifications

The gravity of the lumber dispute, coming at a time when plans are being made for post-war construction, need not be stressed.

Among the other concomitants of this dispute is the effect it may have on the shipment of crops, especially fruit. The lumber shutdown is depriving the farmers of fruit crates, which are already in short supply.

Steel blast furnaces at Cleveland and Youngstown have been closed down because of the strike of coal mine foremen and supervisors, affiliated with District 50 of the United Mine Workers of America. In another week this situation threatens to be extremely critical unless prompt action is taken to end the walkout.

The strike of coal-mine foremen is a repetition of a similar movement last year. Mr. Lewis wants a showdown, but the operators, ready to fight it out, insist he must order the strikers back to work before they will meet with him.

The National Labor Relations Board is directly involved in this dispute. Its present policy is opposed to certification of foremen's unions when they are affiliated with production workers' organizations. The board will only go so far as to say that an independent foremen's union is a proper unit for collective bargaining.

Although the building service strikers in New York City number only about 15,000, it is estimated that 1,500,000 workers are indirectly involved by being forced into idleness or otherwise affected.

Motor Makers' Reprieve

Large-scale strikes among the "Big Three" automobile manufacturers are not likely for another month, if then—when the NLRB-supervised strike plebiscites are completed under provisions of the War Labor Disputes Act.

The current strikes and labor disputes have caught the Government unprepared with a policy, though ample warning had been given that the wartime no-strike pledge would be "out of the window" on V-J Day. The public had hoped that the Administration would have had some plan ready to replace the War Labor Board set-up by the end of the war.

But whatever teeth the WLB had had to enforce its quasi-compulsion policy, its power and authority fell off with the end of hostilities.

Organized labor had been straining at the leash for a long time before V-J Day. Its hostility to what it considered a wage freeze, embodied in the "Little Steel" formula, led to the demand for "a return to real collective bargaining."

The public and industry members of the WLB, aided by the AFL members, adopted a policy which they felt would mean a return to direct labor-industry negotiations and free collective bargaining, unhampered by Government intervention.

CIO Stand

The CIO members of the WLB, however, while also wishing for a return to free collective bargaining, were not in agreement with the majority policy, which took the form of refusal to accept cases unless the parties agreed in advance to accept and to be bound by the board's findings. Yet the anomalous situation exists that the current disputes in the oil, automobile and steel industries, now in the forefront of public attention, are CIO movements.

At a time when new machinery to adjust disputes should be operating full blast the WLB is confining itself solely to winding up a backlog of 2,000 cases and planning with Mr. Schwellenbach on new machinery as a substitute for handling wage stabilization policy entrusted to it.

Under Presidential order the Secretary is required to certify all disputes which his department cannot settle to the WLB. But the board's present policy prevents acceptance of disputes unless the parties agree in advance to accept the board's findings. Thus there is a stalemate which is softened only by a general agreement between the Secretary and the board to consider each case on its merits.

The overnight return to free collective bargaining, coupled with a lack of interim adjustment machinery, has resulted in the wave of strikes which seem likely to increase. The Labor Department is hoping that a "reorganized" conciliation service may cope with the situation. However, aside from a new chief at the helm of the conciliation machinery, Edward L. Warren, no real steps have been taken to strengthen the service and no overnight "miracles" can be expected to take the department off the "hot spot" in which it now finds itself.

The labor-industry conference, to be convened on Nov. 5 at the request of President Truman, will discuss the entire problem of collective bargaining, labor and management responsibility, and machinery for peaceful adjudication of disputes. This conference, however, is still too far off to have any effect on the present situation. The price that the country is now paying for the present turmoil is due partly to the tardiness of the Government in calling the labor-industry conference. Proposals for such a meeting were made as far back as two years ago, but went unheeded.

Not Under One Roof

Mr. Schwellenbach's plan for integration of all Government labor functions under one roof have not been fulfilled. Last week the President granted him a small measure of the authority he had requested on Aug. 10. This included putting the WLB and the War Manpower Commission, two organizations now being liquidated, into the Labor Department, which also was handed the United States Employment Service; but this also is temporary, since the Senate has already voted to restore the service to the States, and similar House action is expected.

The Administration is compelled to carry out its labor adjustment work with its old-line machinery, namely, the conciliation service, the dying WLB, the National Labor Relations Board and the National Mediation Board. The latter adjusts disputes in the railroad labor industry.

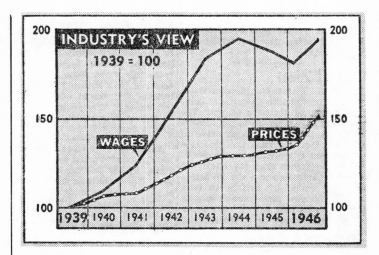

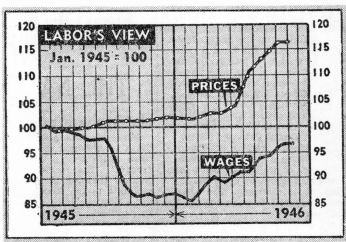

December 22, 1946

AUTO WORKERS STRIKE AT GM TODAY; 350,000 ARE QUITTING SIMULTANEOUSLY; LABOR-INDUSTRY CONFERENCE SPLIT

UAW BOARD ACTS

Hits 'Stalling' as Note From Company Defers Arbitration Reply

30% PAY DEMAND IS CRUX

But Linking of Wages and Profits Is an Added Issue— Strike Spread Possible

By LOUIS STARK

DETROIT, Nov. 20—The long-threatened strike against the General Motors Corporation was ordered this evening by the United Automobile Workers, CIO, and will start tomorrow morning at the far-flung plants of the world's largest industrial company.

The "zero hour" was staggered by time zones to make it country-wide at the same instant. In the Eastern Standard zone it is 11 A. M., in the Central Standard zone 10 A. M., in the Mountain States 9 A. M. and on the Pacific Coast 8 A. M.

Telegrams were being sent out tonight to confirm for the 350,000 General Motors employes a decision known to most of them through the press and radio, that the battle was on, and to convey to the members of the union the "zero hour."

Acting swiftly upon the announcement by the corporation at 2 P. M. today that it would not answer until Friday the demand made by the union yesterday that the wage dispute be submitted to voluntary arbitration, 200 delegates from more than 100 UAW locals in the General Motors system voted unanimously to urge the union's strike strategy committee to call the strike.

The union had set a deadline of 4 P. M. today for the corporation to accede to the demand for arbitration.

Decision Is Made Public

The strike strategy committee, comprising the six top officials of the world's largest union, met in the presence of the delegates to conform to the strike plea and at 5:07 P. M. the decision was announced in the press room established at the Barlum Hotel, where the union meetings are being held.

For the first time since before Pearl Harbor the UAW had authorized a major strike.

It was a solemn moment in the history of industry and the union movement in the United States, and if it needed accentuation it got it when, from behind the doors of the room where the union had hurled its challenge, there poured out through the corridors of the mezzanine of the hotel the lusty voices of the union delegates as they joined in a roaring chorus of "Solidarity Forever."

Led by R. J. Thomas, husky-voiced international president of the union, and Walter P. Reuther, international vice president and head of the union's General Motors department, the four attending

members of the strategy committee walked into the press room to make their announcement. They had obtained assenting votes by proxy from the absent members of the committee.

Says Action Was "Forced"

"This action," Mr. Thomas said, "would have been postponed if we had had even an indication from the company that it would consider arbitration."

He paused to clear his throat, then went on:

"The General Motors Corporation has at this moment forced upon us a tremendous strike. It is a sin against the workers, the public and the stockholders of the company."

He referred reporters to hastily prepared copies of a long statement expressing the union's reasons for the action.

This statement charged that the word received today from General Motors on the question of arbitration was "a stall, pure and simple." It added:

"The corporation management has heard from Wall Street and Wilmington, Del., and has made its choice. It has stated its decision."

The reference to Wilmington obviously had its basis in the circumstance that members of the du Pont family and affiliated du Pont interests control 23 per cent of the voting stock of General Motors.

Note Sent by Anderson

The tumultuous events of the late hours of the day came after the corporation, under the signature of Harry W. Anderson, its vice president in charge of labor relations, had sent the following note to the UAW delegates:

"We are in receipt of your letter of Nov. 19, 1945, demanding an answer to the proposal contained therein in twenty-four hours. Our reply to this communication will be delivered to you on or before Nov. 23, 1945. (Signed) H. W. Anderson."

This referred not alone to the request of the union for arbitration, but to the qualifications appended to or made a part of the request, agreement to which would have, on the part of the corporation, constituted a full concession to demands it has consistently opposed.

These qualifications had in a sense, greater importance even than the ostensible central issue of the dispute, whether the union was to gain a blanket increase in wages of 30 per cent to compensate for an alleged drop in wages resulting from the end of the forty-eight hour work week of wartime and return to the standard forty-hour peacetime week required by wages-and-hours legislation.

Access to Books Involved

To have agreed to the arbitration proposal as made by the union the company would have had to agree that the arbitrators would have the right of access to the books and records and other data of either side, that the hearings be held in public, that a finding against a price increase to compensate for a wage increase would be ground for a recommendation by the Board of Arbitration that General Motors prices be cut and that any wage increase would be retroactive to Aug. 18, 1945, the date the wage demand was first made, and would extend to next Aug. 18.

Over and above the implicit importance in each of these concessions would have been a surrender by the corporation upon the vital point of whether price and cost data were proper subjects in wage negotiations, and, bearing still further upon the future economic picture in the United States, whether wages could be hitched to profits.

These are some of the reasons why the struggle beginning with this strike, and possibly to spread not only through the motor industry but to steel and other basic industries, takes on a stature overshadowing any industrial dispute in many years.

There appeared to be no immediate danger that the strike would spread to the other members of the "Big Three," the Ford Motor Company and the Chrysler Corporation.

Negotiations between Ford and the union began today, with the union also asking a 30 per cent wage rise and the company pressing its thirty-one demands designed to provide it with "security." These negotiations were held quietly at the Book-Cadillac Hotel, a few blocks from the more momentous events occurring at the Barlum.

Chrysler Talks Continue

At Chrysler headquarters, in Highland Park, negotiations between the two parties continued. Here, Chrysler, too, was making demands and the union was asking the 30 per cent increase and making other demands.

The strike order culminated a ninety-seven day argument. It was Aug. 18, two days after President Truman restated the national labor policy in view of the ending of the war against Japan, that Mr. Reuther wrote to C. E. Wilson, president of General Motors, making demand for the 30 per cent increase.

It was not, however, until early October that actual negotiations got under way. From the start it was obvious, with the union adhering strictly to its original demands and the company making several counter-proposals, that it would take extreme diplomacy by both sides to avoid a strike.

Among other things, the company proposed an extension of the forty-hour week to forty-five, with an increase in hourly wage rates of 6 per cent, and, more recently, a cost-of-living increase. Both proposals were flatly rejected by the union, as was a final offer by the company to grant a flat increase of 10 per cent to hourly workers.

To all of these proposals the union reply was the same, in substance: "Show us you can't pay 30 per cent and still not raise prices and we'll scale down our demand."

November 21, 1945

INDUSTRY-LABOR END PARLEY, DIVIDED ON BASIC SUBJECTS; EACH SIDE FILES REPORTS

HOPE PUT IN FUTURE

But 3 of 6 Committees Are Unable to Agree on Problems Before Them

WAGE PROPOSALS BEATEN

By LOUIS STARK

WASHINGTON, Nov. 30—President Truman's Labor-Management Conference, which opened here on Nov. 5, ended deliberations this evening with disagreement upon the issues handled by three of the six committees, but with general expressions that the session had advanced as far as could have been accomplished under the circumstances, and with the expressed hope that another conference might add to the area of agreement reported yesterday by three committees.

Those who had expected or hoped to see a completely new and integrated machinery for minimizing disputes were disappointed. However, the feeling tonight was that the main progress which had been made had come from the fact that the delegates had come to know each other, that they had provided for further meetings and that they had agreed upon the following:

"Arbitration should be invoked to settle all disputes under contracts which have no-strike, no-lockout clauses; negotiations for new contracts should use every means at hand including mediation and voluntary arbitration before strikes be permitted; the United States Conciliation Service should be strengthened; no discrimination in employment due to race, color, creed or sex."

Main Items of Disagreement

The main items of failure were provisions for terminal points when the parties disagreed and the eschewing of fact-finding committees to make recommendations; legislation to "equalize" labor and industry; inability to agree on specific functions of management; disagreement on unionization of foremen and supervisors, and wage increases.

The three committees which submitted separate labor and industry reports today, none of which was adopted, were the committees on collective bargaining, on management's right to manage and on representation and jurisdictional questions.

Three separate resolutions on wages were also defeated owing to the rule that any action, to be the expression of the meeting, had to be unanimous.

At the three-hour concluding session this afternoon the emphasis was upon the spirit that had animated the conferees in spite of their differences of viewpoint.

Industry Asks Clarification

The accomplishments of the meeting, according to neutral observers, went beyond the results of President Wilson's labor-management meeting which collapsed in 1919 on collective bargaining and on the question of arbitration of the steel strike then under way. The industry side in 1919 had wished to define collective bargaining as allowing room for "company unions."

Although there was disagreement today on a definition of collective bargaining, the industry group made no attempt to diminish the right of employes to form their own unions as they saw fit. Expressing the belief, however, that collective bargaining in practice had resulted in a critical situation at the present time, the industry group said that before industrial peace could be attained the term must be more specifically defined and clarified.

The labor report on collective bargaining veered away from any discussion of any definition of labor responsibilities according to the terms set forth by the industry group, which had called for a measure of government control of unions in such a way as to assure labor and industry "equality of status before the law."

Although the industry group had requested that bonds be posted or some other form of guarantee be offered by both sides for fulfillment on contracts, it modified this demand somewhat and finally recommended in general terms that each contract "provide for appropriate guarantees to insure complete and effective compliance with provisions prohibiting strikes, lockouts or boycotts."

Differences on Bargaining

The Committee on Collective Bargaining agreed unanimously that contracts must include provisions permitting management to discipline any employes but subject to their right of appeal through the grievance machinery. It was also unanimously agreed that management and unions must encourage their respective officials from engaging in contract violations.

No agreement could be reached on management's request that labor endorse the principle that bargaining must be conducted in an atmosphere free from force.

Labor, on the other hand, proposed that management agree to a declaration that "union security, protected by collective bargaining, strengthen the process of collective bargaining." Management objected to anything that could be construed as enforced union membership.

Labor members on the Committee on Management's Right to Manage were unwilling to specify and classify functions and responsibilities of management. Because of management's insistence on this point unanimous agreement on a joint report was impossible.

The labor report on this subject stated that "it would be extremely unwise to build a fence around the rights and responsibilities of management on the one hand and unions on the other" as years of growth had shown that "the responsibilities of one of the parties today may well become the joint responsibility of both parties tomorrow."

The labor report added:

"We cannot have one sharply delimited area designated as management prerogatives and another equally sharply defined area of union prerogatives without either side constantly attempting to invade the forbidden territory, thus creating much unnecessary strife."

The management members of this committee reported that since labor had refused to list specific management functions, "the labor members are convinced that the field of collective bargaining will, in all probability, continue to expand into the field of management."

"The only possible end of such a philosophy would be joint management of enterprise," the management report states.

"To this the management members cannot naturally agree. Management has functions that must not and cannot be compromised in the public interest."

If labor disputes were to be minimized by genuine collective bargaining, the industry group insisted that labor must agree "that certain specific functions and responsibilities of management are not subject to collective bargaining."

Almost the entire conference this afternoon was devoted to the wage resolutions. Philip Murray, president of the Congress of Industrial Organizations, offered one calling for "the imperative need of granting substantial wage increases."

William Green, president of the American Federation of Labor, who had earlier opposed the discussion of wages, offered an amendment favoring "general wage increases" and Ira Mosher, president of the National Association of Manufacturers, proposed one pledging "sincere collective bargaining on wages," but recommending such discussions to the individual groups of employers and employes.

None of the resolutions was adopted because of the rule of unanimity. However, the wage proposals furnished a long battle of statistics which ranged over a wide area covering corporation profits and wage rates and changes in living costs.

Daniel J. Tobin, president of the International Brotherhood of Teamsters, regretted that greater achievements had not been attained, but he emphasized, as did others, the fact that the parties had been thrown closely together for four weeks and that this had enabled them to observe each other's viewpoints.

Striking the only light note of a solemn occasion, the chief of the teamsters' organizations prefaced his remarks by announcing that "whoever took my overcoat in the noon recess please bring it back; it is a 100 per cent union coat."

John Stephens, vice president of the United States Steel Corporation, disclaimed having purloined Mr. Tobin's overcoat, but volunteered to bargain collectively with his associates to buy a new one for the victim.

Eric Johnston, president of the Chamber of Commerce of the United States, felt that the tangible results of the meeting included the agreement to have an informal committee explore, from time to time, how industrial relations could be improved, the proposal on how to better the conciliation service, and the agreement on use of voluntary arbitration under contracts.

On the intangible side he said that the delegates learned to know each other better. While the results of the meeting, he said, might be disappointing to some, it did not mean "that we shall stop going forward."

Mr. Mosher, in his concluding address, said that despite the area of disagreement, industry, more than ever before, believed in collective bargaining. He summed up the areas of agreement and disagreement at the meeting and his associates gave out a copy of industry's integrated program after the session.

John L. Lewis, the final speaker, paid a compliment to the management group for their skill in handling their side of the conference business but, referring to the labor delegation's division into four groups, he urged them to harmonize their differences since "labor has a job to do in its own household."

The task of bringing harmony to labor's household, according to Mr. Lewis, was not that of government or of the public. He called upon labor to "stop its eternal caviling" so that it could be "in the proud position" of saying to industry that it was able to manage its own affairs.

Judge Walter P. Stacy of the Supreme Court of North Carolina, the chairman, concluded the meeting by thanking the conference on behalf of the Government for "the privilege of having been your servants."

TRUMAN ASKS LAW TO CURB STRIKES, PATTERNED ON RAILROAD LABOR ACT; TO NAME FACT-FINDING BOARD ON GM

NOTE TO CONGRESS

Plan Would Apply to Major Firms, Depend on Public Opinion

30-DAY 'COOL-OFF' URGED

Proposal Wins Favorable but Qualified Support at Capitol —Union Chiefs Oppose It

By LOUIS STARK

WASHINGTON, Dec. 3—President Truman offered today his pattern for settling major industrial disputes. He requested Congress to enact legislation similar to the Railway Labor Act and at the same time announced that he was naming fact-finding boards to make recommendations for settlement of the strike of General Motors Corporation employes and the dispute which threatens a walkout of United States Steel Corporation workers.

Acting with the utmost speed following the ending of his labor-management conference Friday, the President asserted in his message to Congress that the conference had failed to recommend a plan to avert work stoppages when collective bargaining and mediation failed.

Peril to Reconversion Cited

Therefore, since "strikes already in effect may possibly cripple our reconversion program," he proposed that for major industries a law be enacted following the railway act procedure, namely:

On certification of the Secretary of Labor that a dispute would vitally affect the public interest the President be authorized to appoint a fact-finding board within five days of the certification.

It shall be unlawful to call a strike or lockout during the five days following the Secretary of Labor's certification.

The board, consisting of three outstanding citizens, should make a thorough investigation of all the facts, with power to subpoena individuals and records, and should make its report within twenty days.

While the board is deliberating and for five days after its report is made it shall be unlawful to call for a strike or lockout.

Labor Opposes Proposals

These proposals came with something of a surprise and a shock to labor and industry. Labor leaders immediately declared their opposition, especially to the thirty-day cooling-off period. Employers, while endorsing the idea of fact finding in principle, avoided reference to the opening of books and records. This aspect of the recommendations will probably be opposed by industry.

By his message the President virtually challenged labor to oppose what his aides called a non-punitive measure strictly limited to industries like steel, automobile, aviation, mining, oil, utilities and communications.

No penalty but the force of public opinion is provided in case employers or employes fail to abide by the provisions of the proposed law.

In Congress, the program was received with considerable interest, with most of the views expressed being favorable but somewhat qualified, and there was a feeling that the proposal might not be as efficacious as expected by the President.

The idea of legislation was reported to be a last resort by the President who had warned the labor-management conference on Nov. 5 that Congress might act if the delegates failed to agree on labor disputes machinery.

Until the closing hours of the conference Friday, Mr. Truman is understood to have felt there was hope for something approximating what he had requested to come out

of the meeting. When this did not happen, he and his advisers hurriedly outlined what they had been considering tentatively and over the week-end it was put into shape. Judge Samuel Rosenman is credited with having drafted the message.

Telegrams in which the President appealed to the patriotism of the leaders of the unions and employers in the motor and steel industries, were sent to Charles E. Wilson, president of General Motors; R. J. Thomas, president of the United Automobile Workers, CIO; Walter P. Reuther, UAW vice president; Philip Murray, president of the United Steel Workers of America, CIO, and Benjamin Fairless, president of the United States Steel Corporation.

End of GM Strike Asked

The Chief Executive asked the striking General Motors employes to return to work at once and the corporation to proceed energetically with full production.

He appealed to the steel workers to remain at work pending the inquiry by the fact-finding board. The personnel of the two boards was not announced.

William Green, president of the American Federation of Labor, was the only labor official who made a statement on the President's proposal. He said:

"In my judgment the recommendation of the President will be unacceptable to labor. The principles and policies of the Railway Labor Act are in no way suited to private industry as a whole. The plan proposed for fact finding will operate disadvantageously to both employers and workers in many cases. The AFL cannot approve this legislation."

Mr. Murray remained silent. Associates indicated that his attitude, when announced, would be negative, but that he would not be in a hurry to make a statement because of the grave implications in the proposal.

John L. Lewis, president of the United Mine Workers, who like Messrs. Green and Murray, attended the labor-management conference, was not available for comment. Mining union officials indicated that in their opinion the Truman procedure would slow down collective bargaining.

Eric Johnston, president of the Chamber of Commerce of the

United States, discussed the Presidential message with his associates, then issued the following statement:

"Impartial fact-finding is a relatively new approach to the settlement of industrial disputes. The American people are entitled to know the facts in a dispute which vitally affects their interests.

"In large scale industrial strife, with both sides issuing conflicting statements, it is extremely difficult for the public to determine what the real facts and issues are. An impartial fact-finding panel should examine into the facts and then report to the public.

"I heartily endorse the principle of impartial fact-finding as I did frequently at the labor-management conference and as I have in other public utterances. I must, however, reserve judgment on any specific proposals until I find what form and scope legislation might assume."

In his message Mr. Truman recalled that he had advised the Labor-Management Conference that the meeting would be solely one for labor and industry to make their decisions without Government intervention as "the time has come for labor and management to handle their own affairs in the traditional American, democratic way."

While some agreements on general principles were reached at the conference, the Chief Executive said that "on the all-important question of how to avoid work stoppages" when other expedients failed "the conference arrived at no accord."

"Failing in that, the conference was unable to attain the objective most necessary to successful reconversion," he asserted, adding:

"If industrial strife continues, the quick reconversion which has been planned, and which is now proceeding on schedule or even ahead of schedule on many fronts, will fail.

"In that event we shall face a period of low production, low consumption and widespread unemployment—instead of high production, high employment, good markets and good wages that are within our grasp."

In key industries where industrial strife may affect the whole reconversion process, he said that when labor and management could not compose their differences "the public through the Federal Government has a duty to speak and act."

Good labor relations, he asserted, should be based on "justice and not on tests of strength."

Pointing out that "the American people have been patient," Mr. Truman said that they had waited long for labor and industry to agree.

Now that it is apparent they have no done so, he added, "it becomes the duty of the Government to act on its own initiative."

He then explained his plan to Congress. In doing so he stressed the idea that in proposing that the principles of the Railway Labor Act be followed, the general pattern of the act was not applicable to small industries or to small, local disputes in large industries. He did not think that local, inconsequential strikes, even within the industries he named, should be included under the fact-finding formula.

He hoped that Congress would act as quickly as possible "and certainly before the Christmas recess."

Many Praise the Proposal

Representative Smith of Virginia, who sponsored the War Labor Disputes Act, told the House that "the President's action was courageous." He believed "it will meet with the approval of 90 per cent of the American people. I congratulate him."

Senator Taft recalled that in December, 1941, he and Senator Ball had proposed fact-finding machinery which "was blocked by this Administration."

Declaring that he was gratified that President Truman had "reversed this procedure," Mr. Taft added:

"However desirable fact-finding machinery may be, the people should know that it will not prevent strikes or violence. Furthermore, it must be worked out in a sound way or it will do more harm than good. It must be on a company basis and not on an industry-wide basis. It should be truly impartial and confined to fact-finding, not dominated by the economic fallacies so prevalent in New Deal bureaus today."

Senator Ball, who, with Senators Hatch and Burton, offered a bill last year which embodied Railway Labor Act procedure, said that the President's message "is the most hopeful word I have seen on this particular front for a long time."

"So far so good," was Senator Vandenberg's comment. He felt, however, that Mr. Truman had "ignored the necessity of finding some way in which to guarantee mutual responsibility in collective bargaining contracts."

Senator George called the message "a partial approach." Senator Hickenlooper hoped it would help bring relief to "inexcusable chaos."

Senator Gurney urged Congress to act quickly on the message. Senator Wherry hoped the President's suggestion would result in remedial legislation.

Secretary Schwellenbach, who conferred with President Truman on the message this morning, later told a conference of State labor department officials that no single conference of labor and management could solve the basic issues of industrial disputes.

December 4, 1945

Summary of Strikes

Strikes and prospective strikes involving upward of 2,000,000 employes of the telephone, telegraph, meat packing, steel, electrical and other industries clouded the nation's peace-time horizon last night. Government officials were striving to conciliate workers and employers and hopes were held that some of the industrial gloom could be dispelled. In some localities precautions were being taken against possible disorders.

Three thousand members of the American Communications Association voted unanimously last night to go on strike next Tuesday in New York City, thereby severely crippling Western Union operations here.

In the New York metropolitan area, a strike by 17,400 workers in twenty-one plants of the Western Electric Company was scheduled for 11 A. M. today after last-minute efforts by Federal officials had failed to bring about a basis for agreement between the company and the Western Electric Employes Association. J. A. Beirne, head of the National Federation of Telephone Workers, whose membership of 263,000 represents about half the total employes of the Bell System throughout the country, said he had asked the support of the forty-eight unions of telephone workers in the federation to aid the Western Electric Employes demands.

The United Packinghouse Workers of America threatened to go on strike Jan. 16, thereby affecting 200,000 members across the country. There were indications the walkout could be averted by an immediate $17\frac{1}{2}$ cents hourly wage increase, with provisions being made for negotiating the remainder of the workers' demands.

On the eve of important Congress of Industrial Organizations "strategy" councils with regard to steel, automobiles and electrical industries, it was disclosed that the Government's efforts to avert strikes in Westinghouse, General Electric and the electrical division of General Motors had failed so far. The Government's chief conciliator did not reveal the next move.

Meanwhile, President Truman appointed a fact-finding board to investigate the steel industry, in which union workers have voted to strike Jan. 14. Such a stoppage would affect 700,000 workers.

In Connecticut from 10,000 to 15,000 workers threatened a general strike—the first of its kind in the State's history— at noon today in protest against the use of State police in breaking up picket lines of machinists at the Yale & Towne lock plant.

January 3, 1946

Strikers to Total 1,657,000 Today

With the strike of 750,000 steel workers and 30,000 farm implement workers set for today, the number of the country's strikers, including those who were already out, will reach 1,657,000.

According to Federal statistics, the year 1919 showed the largest number of workers idle due to strikes, 4,160,000 or 20.8 per cent of the working population. This was the all-time record.

A preliminary survey for 1945 by the Bureau of Labor Statistics indicates that the number of workers involved in strikes for that year was 3,250,000, the highest since 1919.

January 21, 1946

TRUMAN ANNOUNCES HIGHER WAGE-PRICE POLICY

STATEMENT IS BRIEF

New Formula Limits Pay Rises, Ends 6 Months' Wait on Price Aid

STABILITY IS URGED

Worker Gains Most When 'Line Is Held,' the President Asserts

Special to THE NEW YORK TIMES.

WASHINGTON, Feb. 14—President Truman modified tonight the national wage-price policy "to permit wage increases within certain limits and to permit any industry placed in a hardship position by an approved increase to seek price adjustments without waiting until the end of a six-month period."

At the same time, the President announced a shake-up in personnel, re-establishing the Office of Economic Stabilization with Chester Bowles as its director, and transferring Paul A. Porter, Federal Communications Commission chairman, to the post of OPA Administrator.

Charles E. Denny Jr. was made acting chairman of the FCC. He is now a member of the commission.

Steel Price Rise Is Due

The President's executive order cleared the way for announcement Tomorrow by John C. Collet, retiring stabilization director, of an increase of $5 a ton "across the board" in steel prices. This is expected to lead to an early end of the strike of 750,000 steel workers now in its fourth week.

The exact authority accorded to Mr. Bowles was in doubt tonight because the Office of Economic Stabilization, which is re-established as it was under William H. Davis but with greatly enlarged powers, is still lodged in the Office of War Mobilization and Reconversion.

The long battle between John W. Snyder, OWMR Chief, and Mr. Bowles on the authority over prices, while settled apparently to Mr. Bowles' satisfaction, also gives some authority to Mr. Snyder.

Collet Acted as "Mediator"

A compromise in this struggle was arranged by Mr. Collet who acted as mediator. Mr. Bowles had previously served an "ultimatum" on the President through Mr. Porter. This "ultimatum" was in the form of a draft of a proposed executive order stripping Mr. Snyder and John D. Small, civilian production administrator, of all authority over prices.

In explaining the modified wage-price policy, President Truman emphasized that if the general price level was to remain stable in the next few critical months, "the immediate price relief in such cases must be conservatively appraised."

However, the President immediately qualified this by assuring that the price relief must be sufficient to assure profitable operations in industry.

Taking recognition of the "general pattern" of wage increases since V-J Day, the President authorized the National Wage Stabilization Board to approve any wage increases consistent with that pattern.

Generally speaking, this pattern is between 15 and 20 per cent, or hourly from 15 to 22 cents.

Without mentioning these specific increases, the President explained that where there was no general pattern, his order provided for approval of increases found necessary as hitherto to eliminate gross inequities between related industries, plants or job justifications, or to correct substandards of living, or to correct disparities between the increase in wage rates since January, 1941, and the increase in living costs between that date and September, 1945.

Thus, the President explained, his order takes into account thousands of wage agreements reached before and after V-J Day. He warned, however, that the program was "not to be interpreted as permitting indiscriminate wage increases."

The executive order, he continued, provides that the Stabilization Administrator shall determine those classes of cases in which a wage increase may be put into effect without requiring prior approval of the Wage Stabilization Board and without any waiver of any rights to ask for price relief.

"The change now being made in our wage and pricing standards," Mr. Truman said, "can succeed only with the support of business, labor, Congress all the agencies of the Administration, and the rank and file of the American people."

Defending the partial retreat of the "hold the line" order of April, 1943, Mr. Truman declared that "increases outside and beyond this general policy cannot be approved without subjecting the workers and the public to the danger of inflation."

"It is to the best advantage of the American worker, above all other groups, that the price line be held," he added.

The President called on Congress for swift action to extend the stabilization statute without amendment, to continue the subsidy program for another year, to enact the Patman bill controlling housing prices and to extend the Second War Powers Act.

It was only by such measures, he asserted, that the country could "hope to retain our controls as a people over our own economic future."

Mr. Truman urged the public to support the economic stabilization program, and he called on labor and management to proceed with production, which he called "the basis of high wages and profits and high standards of living for us all."

The new Executive Order provides, by amending Executive Order 9599 of last Aug. 18, a method of adjusting price ceilings. The Price Administrator is permitted in case of an industry which is in a position of hardship as a result of approved wage increases to make certain adjustments in ceiling prices.

The adjustment is to be made when the administrator finds that the industry's ceiling prices will leave it an over-all loss position.

The adjustment to be provided should be such that it would permit the industry for twelve months, unless operating at a temporary low volume, to earn an average rate of profit equal to the rate of return on net worth earned by the industry in the peacetime base period applicable to that industry.

The Price Administrator is required to develop standards of price adjustment to be applied to industries operating at temporary low volume.

The order, under which the steel price increase will be provided tomorrow, states that in cases in which price regulations called for adjustment of ceiling prices on an individual firm basis the administrator shall establish such standards of adjustment as he may deem workable.

The order also establishes some elasticity in wage adjustments by authorizing the Wage Stabilization Board, "or other designated agency" with the stabilization chief's approval, "to establish special standards for approval of wage or salary increases, differing from the foregoing general standards, to be applied in particular industries or classes of cases if it finds that such action is necessary to effectuate the purposes of this order."

The foregoing provision is likely to cause considerable pulling and hauling since labor and industry will probably each seek to use it, the former to justify wage increases not provided for directly by the order, and the latter to resist such demands as unjustifiable.

The order also contains a drastic provision permitting the stabilization administrator to deem unlawful any wage or salary increase "unless made with the prior approval of the board or other designated agency, if in his (the stabilization administrator) judgment such action is necessary to prevent wage or salary increases inconsistent with the purposes of the stabilization laws."

In the final hectic hours of the conference leading to the completion of the program which began several weeks ago, Mr. Collet played what insiders said was the most constructive part in mediating between Mr. Bowles and Mr. Snyder.

Twenty-four hours ago, just as the solution of the tangled steel wage-price formula was in sight, Mr. Bowles presented to the President his "ultimatum" and upset all calculations.

Mr. Truman was understood to have stiffened and asserted that he was still President.

Today the President, resentful and angry, told Congressional visitors of the incident, even though they called in connection with other matters, principally the naming of a man to take the place of Secretary Ickes.

There was, however, a final peaceful meeting at Mr. Snyder's office late this afternoon and early evening. Present were Messrs. Bowles, Snyder, Collet, Porter and Secretary Schwellenbach and their counsel and technicians.

At this meeting, the language proposed by Mr. Bowles, which Messrs. Snyder and Small (but not Mr. Collet) strongly objected to as humiliating, was toned down.

Recalling to Mr. Snyder that Mr. Bowles was identified in the public mind with the Administration's anti-inflation policy, Mr. Collet mollified the reconversion chief. Gradually he brought the two men to an agreement.

February 15, 1946

STEEL STRIKE IS SETTLED WITH 18.5C PAY RISE; COMPANIES GET PRICE INCREASE OF $5 A TON

DECISION IS SUDDEN

U. S. Steel, Union End Retroactivity Issue by 'Splitting Difference'

WORKERS GET 9¼c

Agreement Covers 125,000 Who Will Return to Job Monday

By JOSEPH A. LOFTUS
Special to THE NEW YORK TIMES.

WASHINGTON, Feb. 15—A four-week strike at the mills of the United States Steel Corporation will end at midnight Sunday, and the rest of the industry is expected to return to production soon thereafter on the basis of a wage increase of 18½ cents an hour and a price rise of $5 a ton on steel.

"Big Steel," whose five producing subsidiaries employ more than 125,000, and the United Steel Workers, CIO, reached an agreement tonight which the principals said assured a year of peace for the concern.

John W. Snyder, director of War Mobilization and Reconversion, announced the settlement to reporters in a hotel suite in the presence of Secretary Schwellenbach, John Steelman, special assistant to President Truman, Charles Ross, White House press secretary, and the conferees of the corporation and the union.

Truman Suggestion Is Accepted

The 18½ cents was the figure suggested by Mr. Truman several days before the strike began.

The retroactivity issue, which kept the parties apart for the last several days, was resolved by "splitting the difference." The President suggested the increase be made effective as of Jan. 1, three weeks before the strike began.

The company said that it could not accept the principle of retroactivity, but agreed to a clause whereby an increase of 9¼ cents would be paid for all work performed between Jan. 1 and Feb. 17 when the strike ends. Beginning Monday, the 18½-cent increase will go into effect.

Philip Murray, union president, said that work would not be resumed at the plants of other steel companies until contracts were agreed on, but he added that he expected that would be accomplished quickly. Now that the pattern has been set, negotiations for the most part will be handled by local or regional union committees.

High Production Pledged

John Stephens, vice president of the United States Steel Corporation in charge of industrial relations, who reached the agreement with Mr. Murray, said that the existing contract, which would have expired in October, was extended to Feb. 15, 1947, and that the union subscribed to a new clause providing for cooperation in maintaining high productivity. The contract also contains a non-strike clause.

Mr. Stephens said that all employes would be reinstated without discrimination, and that the union agreed not to discriminate against any employes who did not cooperate in the strike.

The corporation also said that this was the highest single wage rise in the history of the industry. Increases also will be given to many of the salaried employes. The concern estimated that all the increases would cost about $100,000,000 during the life of the contract in excess of the realization from the $5 a ton price rise.

The application of the price increase to all kinds of steel will be worked out by the Office of Price Administration in consultation with its industry advisory committee.

The increase of $5 a ton is estimated at 8 to 9 per cent. The wage increase, which figures about 17½ per cent, raises the basic labor rate from 78 cents to 96½ cents.

The corporation said that straight time hourly earnings in the industry previously averaged $1.14, which is somewhat higher than the Bureau of Labor Statistics figure because it includes shift premiums and vacation pay. It does not include overtime premium pay. The increase would raise this average to $1.32½.

The steel producing subsidiaries covered under the United Steel contract are Carnegie-Illinois Steel Corporation, American Steel and Wire, National Tube, Columbia Steel and Tennessee Coal, Iron and Railroad Companies.

Mr. Snyder said that he was announcing the strike settlement on behalf of the President, and that Mr. Truman had expressed his appreciation to Benjamin F. Fairless, United States Steel president, and Mr. Murray, for their cooperation. Mr. Fairless participated in a phase of the negotiations which were conducted at the White House just before the strike.

Asked whether the strike might not drag on for several weeks at the independent company plants, Mr. Murray said:

"That is hardly conceivable."

He added that "we hope we can get around to the perfection of agreements no later than the beginning of the week."

Mr. Truman announced the $5 a ton price offer at his news conference. He did not say how it would be applied, but Mr. Snyder, sitting near by, asserted that it would affect both carbon and alloy steel. Mr. Truman added the whole thing would be fully explained at the proper time.

The American Iron and Steel Institute said today that even after the strike ended, it would take a few days to a few weeks to get all departments of the industry functioning on a pre-strike basis.

The institute estimated that the strike has resulted in the loss of about 1,500,000 tons of steel ingots a week and a weekly loss of about $20,000,000 in wages.

"Operations cannot be expected to return immediately to the 80-85 per cent of capacity level that prevailed prior to the strike," the institute said in a statement, adding: "Steel making is a complicated business of interrelated operations, in which certain processes go on continuously under normal conditions. The output of primary production units must be re-established before finished steel flows out in a large and uninterrupted volume.

"Restoration of high level operations may be delayed by the necessity of repairing equipment which was not properly shut off, due to the fact that a few workers quit the plants precipitately or due to the fact that maintenance crews could not get across picket lines at certain plants."

In the case of blast furnaces, the institute said that under the ideal conditions three to four days were required to get them into operation to make pig iron. Open hearths may require from two or three days to two or three weeks to resume capacity operations.

Furnaces which have been adequately heated during the strike and are otherwise in first-class shape, the institute said, and have plenty of fuel and raw materials, might begin producing twelve hours after charging.

Coke ovens under ideal conditions, it was stated, can produce coke in quantity one week after the resumption of operations. Soaking pits, where ingots are heated before rolling, must be warmed slowly. In some cases two to three weeks might be required to get back to full operations, the statement said.

Electric furnaces under the best conditions probably could produce steel in twelve hours after being charged, it added, and rolling mills can probably resume operations quickly.

February 16, 1946

STRIKES END AT GM AND GE WITH PAY RISE

PEACE ON 113TH DAY

UAW Accepts Increase of 18½c an Hour, but Cites Other Gains

LOCAL UNIONS MUST AGREE

But This Is Believed a Formality — Company Denies Giving Up Any Secret Data

By WALTER W. RUCH

DETROIT, March 13—The General Motors Corporation and the United Automobile Workers-CIO, the mightiest industrial and labor giants in the world, came to terms today on a proposition for settlement of the longest and most costly strike in the history of the automotive industry.

Despite the almost hysterical glee with which the news was greeted on the picket lines surrounding hundreds of plants in eighteen States scattered from coast to coast, the strike had not been ended, although there was little doubt that the prerequisite of ratification by local leaders and the rank and file would prove to be a mere formality.

It was at 2:40 P. M., after seventeen consecutive hours of negotiations which had worn on through last night, that James F. Dewey, special Federal mediator assigned to the strike, walked briskly into a press room to read an announcement which heralded the speedy ending of the 113-day strike.

Almost immediately the union claimed a major victory, although it was apparent that the wage increase of 18½ cents an hour and other concessions fell short of the original demand for almost twice as much in the form of a pay advance.

Hourly Pay Will Pass $1.30

The wage increase will lift from about $1.12 an hour the national average pay of hourly-rated General Motors workers to about $1.30½ an hour. It will mean, however, that the net take-home pay of the average worker, operating on a 40-hour week, will be less than it was at the old rate during the war, when he worked forty-eight hours, with eight hours at time-and-one-half.

Taking an employe with two dependents, the figures disclosed, the take-home pay in 1944 for forty-eight hours, after deductions, was $53.38. For the forty-hour week this year, he will take home $50.04, or $3.34 less a week than at the longer week during the war.

R. J. Thomas, president; George F. Addes, secretary-treasurer, and Walter P. Reuther, vice president of the union, issued a statement in which they said that "we and the top negotiating committee shall heartily recommend acceptance of the settlement to the National UAW - CIO conference," adding that the conference would be convened on Friday.

They hailed the proposal as "a victory for the whole American people because the GM strikers have fought and won their price battle," stating that the strikers had started their walkout "on the promise of wage increases without price increases."

Truman Figure Met, UAW Says

"They have held to that position," said the statement. "Under the present wage-price policy of the Government, a price increase in General Motors products cannot be justified on the basis of the flat increase won in hourly rates and other economic gains included in the proposed strike settlement."

The three leaders asserted that "the 18½-cent wage increase, plus the agreement to remove inequities in wage rates, meets the 19½-cent increase recommended by President Truman (through his fact-finding board)."

"In addition to those provisions," they said, "there are other economic clauses—improved vacation pay, which alone amounts to approximately $5,000,000 a year; improved overtime rates for seven-day continuous operations and equal pay for women—which bring the total average to well above 19½ cents. The corporation also agreed to grant the general wage increase and other economic gains to all the miscellaneous units of employes in GM represented by the UAW-CIO."

The union leaders then went on to give details of other "gains," contending that the proposed new contract would include all those won by the UAW through directives of the National War Labor Board, disclose "a tremendous step forward" with respect to the clause governing transfers and promotions, and show that the union had won "a new union-security provision which amounts to a long step forward toward the union shop."

The company issued no formal statement, but the scores of reporters covering the climax were invited to a press conference at which Harry W. Anderson, vice president, said that at no time had the corporation made available to the UAW any information not contained in the annual reports to stockholders or in reports to the Securities and Exchange Commission.

Anderson Deplores Losses

Mr. Anderson, after deploring such a "long and costly strike, both to the employe and the company," said that the new contract would extend for two years, with the union having no right to reopen the question of wages for one year—both of these provisions being innovations.

As to retroactivity, which was one of the final stumbling blocks to settlement, Mr. Anderson said that all employes who had worked between the period from Nov. 7 to Nov. 21, the day the strike began, would receive an increase in wages for that time at the rate of 13½ cents an hour. The company offered such an increase on Nov. 7 in an attempt to avoid the strike.

He said that the wage provisions were identical with those granted to the United Electrical Radio and Machine Workers, CIO. They matched also the pay increase granted by the Chrysler Corporation and bettered by one-half cent an hour the advance given the UAW by the Ford Motor Company, he added. Neither Ford nor Chrysler, however, suffered a strike.

Mr. Anderson insisted that the corporation had not yielded an inch regarding any prerogative which it considered was its own.

Reopenings Will Take Days

Mr. Anderson said it was his understanding that full ratification of the new agreement could be won by the union by March 18 or 20, but stressed that it would be some time thereafter before the various strike-bound plants could be put back in operation.

In an aside, Harry B. Coen, director of labor relations for the company, was heard to mention April first as the probable date for normal resumption of operations.

Mr. Anderson said that he assumed the company would proceed with its production schedule for 1946 models of its various automotive products, adding, however, that some plants still faced reconversion problems and others had not started producing models.

It was considered unlikely, according to some sources, that very many 1946 models would reach the market.

Mr. Anderson said that Mr. Dewey, who had come through with his 3,210th labor dispute settlement against nary a failure, had done "a good job" in keeping the parties together since the mediator's appearance in the strike picture on Jan. 30.

Mr. Dewey, who was sitting beside Mr. Anderson, arose to say: "Gentlemen, I'd like to make a brief statement. On behalf of the Government of the United States, I should like to state our appreciation of the courtesy displayed throughout these proceedings by both parties.

"On behalf of the President of the United States, I wish to state the appreciation of the Government. I thank you."

Mr. Dewey, who seemed to have endured the long siege better than any of the negotiators, nodded his appreciation of the chorus of "thank you's" which arose from the reporters, to whom he had been unfailingly courteous and helpful.

He ran a hand through his white, wavy haid, heaved a sigh, and said, "Well, gentlemen, that's that." With that remark, he turned to take his exit from a building where for forty-three days he had been seeking the settlement he had brought about this day.

It had been a grueling final session, one which started yesterday afternoon and had continued throughout the night with only a two-hour interlude for dinner. Of the last twenty-four hours, more than twenty had been spent in conference.

From the start of the night session, however, it was obvious that the strike was hourly approaching a conclusion. As the night wore on, with dozens of reporters groaning their disappointment with the passing of each additional deadline, members of the negotiating groups would from time to time drop into the press room to make cheerful quips which made it plain that all of the rancor marking previous sessions had disappeared.

Then, at 4 A. M., Mr. Anderson said that he would stay until noon or longer to reach an agreement, adding that the issue of an increase of 18½ cents an hour, as offered by the company, as opposed to the union demand for one cent more, had been fully settled at the lower rate.

It was too early to appraise the proposed settlement from the standpoint of intra-union politics. The agreement was reached at a time when forces were gathering to advance the candidacy of Mr. Reuther to succeed Mr. Thomas as president of the union when the UAW meets in international convention in Atlantic City on March 23.

There will be a meeting of the National General Motors Conference in Detroit Friday, after which, assuming approval of the terms, the document will go to the various locals for action over the week-end by the rank and file.

March 14, 1946

400,000 SOFT COAL WORKERS STAY AWAY FROM THE PITS; NO HOPE OF EARLY ACCORD

Special to THE NEW YORK TIMES.

PITTSBURGH, Monday, April 1 —The country's 400,000 soft coal miners formally went on strike at 12:01 A. M. today over a series of deadlocked issues principally involving health and welfare programs and wages.

Since today is a holiday in honor of John Mitchell, late president of the union who increased its membership from 33,000 to 263,000, and in observance of winning the eight-hour day in 1898, the miners will not actually refuse to go to work until tomorrow.

This is the second largest single strike in the country since the end of the war, outranked in size only by the four weeks' walkout of 800,000 steel workers who in February won a wage increase of 18½ cents hourly.

The strike threatened a new paralysis of the steel industry by choking off bituminous coal necessary for coke, a principal ingredient in steel-making. At the same time thousands of workers in industries reliant on coal faced lay-offs.

Arrangement for Reopening

Many celebrations have been arranged for John Mitchell Day with the largest at Uniontown and New Kensington, Pa. None will be attended by John L. Lewis, president of the United Mine Workers, AFL, who is renewing talks with the operators at Washington in the afternoon.

With the miners agreeing that there should be no picketing during the strike, it has been agreed that two to ten supervisory and maintenance workers, including pumpers and fan operators, will be assigned to each of the mines to keep them in condition for a return to work as soon as the walkout ends.

Under an agreement with the miners' union about 60,000 members of the United Clerical, Technical and Supervisory Employes of District 50, UMW, will continue on their jobs, particularly for inspection of mines before maintenance crews enter them.

Curtailment in Making Steel

As miners do not work on Sunday, coal digging ceased Saturday night for the duration of the walkout, which marks another handicap in the country's reconversion program. One of the first industries to feel the effect will be steel, which has just got back on its feet after an industry-wide strike.

Steel companies have made curtailment plans, which may be put in operation Tuesday.

The Carnegie-Illinois Steel Corporation, largest operating subsidiary of the United States Steel Corporation, had planned to begin closing down "almost immediately," but a spokesman said that the curtailment might be delayed on "an outside chance" that the walkout might be called off soon.

Steel men generally felt that the strike would be short, although they admitted that they had no concrete basis for their belief.

Carnegie-Illinois expects to close down twenty of its thirty-eight blast furnaces in the Pittsburgh district by the end of the week and then to taper off gradually.

The coke work at Clairton, Pa., which uses 30,000 tons of coal daily and is rated as the largest in the world, will taper off sharply at once. Carnegie-Illinois has an estimated twelve days' supply of coal on the ground here and a three weeks' supply in the Chicago district.

The Jones & Laughlin Steel Corporation, the country's fourth largest steel producer, has scheduled 100 per cent operation this week, with an estimated twenty-five to thirty days' supply of coal at hand, it expects to begin curtailing operations next week.

West Virginia and Pennsylvania and the twenty-three soft-coal producing States, with about 175,000 miners in the former and about 100,000 in the latter. Other principal bituminous sources are Kentucky, Ohio, Illinois, Virginia and Alabama.

The power-generating companies have been assured of emergency supplies of coal through rationing and an offer by the mine union to dig coal for emergency use.

Utilities in the Pittsburgh area have ample stockpiles, sixty days for the Duquesne Light Company and four to six weeks for the West Penn Power Company.

About 170 District 50 supervisory workers at four J. & L. mines, the Vesta 4, 5 and 6 in Washington County and the Shannopin in Greene County, are to vote on John Mitchell Day, on bargaining rights under a recent ruling of the National Labor Relations Board permitting them to join a rank-and-file union.

In a dispute over this issue at the four mines in September, the supervisors struck, precipitating a walkout by nearly 200,000 miners in the country.

April 1, 1946

GOVERNMENT SEIZES COAL MINES, UNIONS SILENT ON RESUMING WORK

KRUG TAKES OVER

Lewis Is Said to Put Decision to Work for U. S. Up to the Individuals

BUT HIS SUPPORT IS ASKED

Truman Empowers Secretary to Negotiate With Union on Pay, Other Concessions

By LOUIS STARK
Special to THE NEW YORK TIMES.

WASHINGTON, May 21—President Truman ordered Secretary J. A. Krug today to seize the country's soft coal mines and to arrange with spokesmen for the United Mine Workers "appropriate changes in the terms and conditions of employment for the period of the operation of the mines by the Government."

Some Administration forces felt confident that mining operations would continue after the two-week truce ends Saturday, but union officials would not comment. The operators stated in a letter to Mr. Truman that they would cooperate with the Government.

Saying that he would take over the coal properties at 12:01 o'clock tonight, Mr. Krug named Vice Admiral Ben Moreell to be his operating chief.

Mr. Krug acted rapidly soon after the President's order was issued. He conferred with John L. Lewis, UMW chieftain, and John O'Leary, union vice president. The Secretary later talked with Charles O'Neill, operators' spokesman, and the latter's associates.

At a press conference tonight Mr. Krug was asked whether Mr. Lewis had agreed to his request that the miners remain at work when the truce expires.

Parley Set for Today

The Secretary replied that Mr. Lewis made it clear that under the Smith-Connally law the union officials had no alternative but to stay out of the affairs of the workers, and that it was up to the miners as individuals to act as they saw fit.

"We asked his support to keep the mine workers on the job," Mr. Krug said. "He has that matter under consideration and we will discuss it further tomorrow."

Asked whether Mr. Lewis indicated that the union policy committee would meet to consider the situation, Mr. Krug quoted the UMW president as saying that "there was some question as to whether the policy committee could operate in view of the Smith-Connally Act."

The Secretary asserted that Mr. Lewis made no promises and had not pledged to give his answer at tomorrow's conference.

The Smith-Connally law makes it a crime to induce or to aid a strike when a plant or mine is in Federal possession. Thus the policy committee could, if it met, legally have but one decision, which would be to order the miners to continue at work after Saturday.

Saying that he would keep the public informed of developments, the Secretary, as Coal Mines Administrator, told reporters that talks with operators and miners showed that neither side felt that direct conferences would result in an agreement.

Problem Is Called Unusual

Therefore, he said, the Government would have to work out the principles of a new contract. He referred to the unusual problem before the Federal officials by recalling that some new features, such as a health and welfare fund and safety provisions, furnished part of the controversy.

Meanwhile, from New York came a report that a health and welfare fund arrangement had been decided on, calling for a payroll assessment of between 1½ per cent and 3 per cent and tripartite administration by Government, miners and operators. The union asked for a 7 per cent fund to be administered solely by it.

Union and operator sources professed to have no knowledge of the welfare fund decision. However, it is known that this proposal has been discussed in high Administration quarters. Confidence was expressed that these officials favored such a fund in principle and that at the proper time the proposal would be sent to Mr. Krug and furnish the basis for his conferences with operators and miners.

The New York report put the fund at between $17,500,000 and $35,000,000 annually, based on an output of 600,000,000 tons and an annual payroll of a billion dollars.

That the operators, as of today, are still strongly opposed to the creation of such a fund, was apparent, however, in their letter to Mr. Truman in which they promised to cooperate with the Government.

In directing seizure of the mines, the President ordered all Federal agencies to cooperate with Mr. Krug, who, in turn, was told to make employment available and provide protection to all employes at the mines.

On request of Mr. Krug, the Secretary of War was directed to "take such action, if any, as he may deem necessary or desirable, to provide protection to all such persons and mines."

Return of the mines to the operators is to be arranged as soon as practicable, according to the order, but in no event more than sixty days after the restoration of productive efficiency.

In issuing his appeal to the operators and miners for full production during Government operation, Mr. Krug said that except for the two weeks' truce, which began May 13, the mines were idle since April 1. He added:

"In the meantime irreparable damage has been done to the national economy, the reconversion program disastrously retarded and widespread unemployment because of the lack of coal has resulted.

"The coal produced during the first six days of the truce while far below normal production of 12,000,000 tons per week, staved off temporarily further and more serious disruptions in the life of the nation.

"Suspension of mining if it occurs at the end of the truce will be disastrous. I believe that the miners in agreeing to the twelve-day truce realize that without coal the United States will suffer a staggering blow from which it may take years to recover.

"I believe also that the miners and their leaders realize that unless the mines continue to operate, bankruptcy and ruin, and loss of markets to competing fuels will be the inevitable result of a further shutdown."

"With these serious considerations before them, I am asking the leaders of the miners to meet with me immediately to work out a plan to assure continued operation of the mines under government supervision until an agreement compatible with wage and price stabilization policies is determined."

Mr. Lewis avoided reporters after his conference with Mr. Krug and had no comment.

In their letter to Mr. Truman, the operators asserted that their committee would recommend full cooperation with the Government in the expectation that the seizure order would be the same as that issued Nov. 1, 1943, when the Government acted to take over the properties.

If the Government negotiated an agreement to remain in effect for the period of Government operation, the operators asked that they be afforded full opportunity to state their views; further that the OPA would increase ceiling prices for coal to compensate for any wage increases and other rises in costs because of the new agreement.

May 22, 1946

LEWIS SIGNS SOFT COAL TERMS WITH U. S.

LONG STRIKE ENDS

Truman Sees Agreement Reached on $1.85 Daily Rise, Welfare Fund

WORK TODAY IS ORDERED

Terms Cause Consternation Among Operators—35 to 50c a Ton Price Increase Seen

By LOUIS STARK
Special to The New York Times

WASHINGTON, May 29 — The forty-five-day coal strike ended today at the White House, where in the presence of President Truman, John L. Lewis signed a contract with the Government which gave him his major demands. Secretary J. A. Krug, who signed for the Government, arranged the contract.

The agreement, which will govern during Federal operation, grants the union an 18½-cent-an-hour wage rise—which, with overtime means a daily increase of $1.85—and a welfare and retirement fund, financed by payment of 5 cents a ton by the operators.

This fund will be managed by three trustees, one named by the United Mine Workers, another by management and a third chosen by them jointly. Mr. Lewis had asked sole control of the fund, to be financed by a 7 per cent levy on payrolls.

90 Million Tons of Coal Lost

Other terms of the agreement, which ended the walkout that cost 90,000,000 tons of coal and an estimated 18,000,000 tons of steel, were as follows:

Sole union control of the medical and hospital fund now paid by the miners through checkoff to the operators who provide such services.

Mandatory compliance with a Federal Mining Safety Code.

Permission of safety committees, consisting of miners to remove men to safe areas "unless and until" the Federal Coal Administrator modifies or cancels the miners' authority.

Wage provisions retroactive to May 22, when the Government took over the mines.

A vacation period from June 29 to July 8, with the vacation payment raised to $100 from the present $75.

Agreement that the Coal Mines Administrator will be guided, in considering the union demand for inclusion of foremen, by the decisions and procedure of the National Labor Relations Board.

This means that foremen may join the union along lines laid down by the NLRB in the Jones & Laughlin case. It also means that where there is a dispute over representation the NLRB will hold an election and if the UMW wins it will have control over the supervisory employes so far as contract-making goes.

The miners policy committee, which ratified the pact after several hours' discussion, hailed it as a smashing union victory.

Operator Spokesman "Amazed"

Operators were thrown into consternation by the terms of the agreement, and an unofficial spokesman said that he was "amazed," that what they had feared had happened, despite their appeal to Mr. Krug to face the possibilities raised by making such sweeping concessions to the union.

He said that Mr. Krug failed to disclose to the operators any but the "general principles" of the agreement. Many marginal mines will remain under Government control a long time unless immediate price relief is granted, the spokesman predicted.

John D. Battle, executive secretary of the National Coal Association, comprising the bituminous coal producers, said:

"The public must understand that the coal contract executed at the White House today is a contract between the United States Government and John L. Lewis.

"It is a victory for Lewis over the Government and a defeat for the American people, who must foot the bill."

The operators said that the agreement would require a price increase of 35 to 50 cents a ton, or between $200,000,000 and $300,000,000 annually.

The bituminous operators negotiating committee later authorized the following statement:

"The full text of the Government contract with the United Mine Workers was not shown to the coal operators until late today.

"Until full opportunity has been had for an analysis of all that is involved in this contract, the committee will reserve comment as to its effect on the industry."

The statement bore out earlier warnings by some operators that unless their negotiating committee was permitted to know the specific terms of the proposed agreement with the miners, they would be unable to save the Government from making "errors" or agreeing to terms which would require constant interpretation and which "in the end would mean more and more concessions from the operators and the public."

The agreement was signed at 4:07 P. M., Charles Ross, White House secretary, said. Mr. Krug, at the President's left, signed with his own pen, and Mr. Lewis, next to him, used the President's pen.

There was little conversation, and the President was "naturally gratified at the settlement," but had nothing further to say, Mr. Ross added.

Telegrams were sent over the country at once by the UMW directing the 400,000 miners to return to work tomorrow. Mr. Lewis said that full production would be attained by Monday.

News of the imminence of the strike's end came soon after noon when the union policy committee was reported to have approved the proposed terms. At 12:30 Mr. Lewis telephoned from his office and announced the decision to the Government officials waiting in the Interior Department.

A little before 4 P. M., Mr. Lewis, unshaven and appearing worn, arrived at the White House. He was accompanied by John J. O'Leary, UMW vice president, and John Owens, president of the UMW Ohio District.

"I can't say," Mr. Lewis replied when he was asked if a contract had been completed.

A few minutes later Mr. Krug, accompanied by Vice Admiral Ben Moreell, Deputy Mines Administrator, George Lamb of the Bureau of Mines, and Carlton Skinner, Information Chief of the Interior Department, arrived.

Asked the same question as that put to Mr. Lewis, Mr. Krug replied with a smile:

"Not quite."

Ten minutes later cameramen rushed pell mell from the President's office, shouting "They have signed."

"Signed what?" asked reporters.

"Something, a piece of paper," was the reply.

Mr. Krug was the first of the principals to leave the executive offices a few minutes later. He made the official announcement, and summaries of the terms were handed out by Mr. Skinner.

Mr. Lewis, who by this time reached Mr. Krug's side, said that telegrams were being sent out at once ordering the miners back to work. He added that the men would be instructed to work tomorrow, though it is a holiday. However, it would take some time to prepare the pits, and they might not be ready for work in large numbers until Friday.

Admiral Moreell, who was asked how the operators felt about the contract, said:

"The operators' feelings are hard to diagnose. From the questions they asked they are not too unhappy."

He conferred with the operators' committee, led by Charles O'Neill, earlier in the day.

Coal Assured, Lewis Says

The entire group then stepped out to the portico, where Mr.

Lewis, for the benefit of the news reels, said:

"A contract has just been executed in the White House covering the bituminous mines.

"This settles for the period of Government operation of the mines, all questions and issues.

"Instructions have been issued to the men to return to work immediately.

"This action will assure an ample supply of coal for essential needs of the country."

Secretary Krug added:

"I am sure Mr. Lewis will agree that the contract is fair to the operators and the men alike. It's too bad we didn't have it two months ago."

The miners were particularly pleased with the provision calling for Mr. Krug to direct each operating manager to provide employes with protection of workmen's compensation and occupational disease benefits, even in those States where such laws are elective and not mandatory on the employers.

The wage increase of 18½ cents an hour was what had been generally expected. It followed the general pattern of other increases.

The present nine-hour day, portal to portal, is retained. The five-day week remains with sixth-day work optional. Overtime, as previously, is paid after thirty-five hours.

On this basis, the daily take home pay of a rate worker who now earns $10 a day (the basic rate since 1943) will amount to $11.85, or an increase of $1.85.

On a weekly basis this means a miner will be paid $59.25 for five days of work and $75.25 for six days' work, as compared with the present wage payment of $50 for five days and $63.50 for six days.

The Federal Mines Administrator agreed to survey hospital and medical facilities and sanitary and housing conditions. The union charged that medical services by company doctors were poor, and that sanitary conditions in some coal mining areas were "disgraceful."

Following the signing of the coal agreement, the Office of Defense Transportation cancelled its order requiring a reduction of 25 per cent in the use of coal by railroads.

May 30, 1946

RAIL STRIKE ENDS AS TRUMAN DEMANDS LAWS, INCLUDING DRAFT, TO STOP ACTION AGAINST U. S.

ON TRUMAN TERMS

Unions Accept 18½ Cents, Part in Lieu of New Work Rules

'IN PUBLIC INTEREST'

Whitney Admits Defeat, Calls President Unfair, Asks Caution on Laws

By JOSEPH A. LOFTUS
Special to THE NEW YORK TIMES.

WASHINGTON, May 25—The railroad strike, which had paralyzed America's commerce, was settled today on President Truman's terms forty-eight hours after it had begun.

The chiefs of the two striking brotherhoods signed the memorandum of agreement in a hotel room as Mr. Truman was about to begin his address to a joint session of Congress. Dr. John R. Steelman, the President's consultant, witnessed the signing and telephoned the news to the Capitol in time for the President to make an extemporaneous announcement of the settlement to the legislators.

Within an hour after the announcement, strikers were "marking up" for duty. The Association of American Railroads forecast a restoration of normal operations by tomorrow afternoon.

18 Other Unions Accept

The basis of the settlement, which the two union chiefs had formally rejected the day the strike began, is an increase of 18½ cents an hour, of which 2½ cents is in lieu of changes in working rules for one year. The eighteen other railroad unions signed earlier in the day an agreement covering those terms.

A. F. Whitney, president of the Brotherhood of Railroad Trainmen, and Alvanley Johnston, chief of the Brotherhood of Locomotive Engineers, said they had ended the strike "in the interest of the public." They called President Truman's address last night "very unfair."

Mr. Whitney in a broadcast a short time later acknowledged the loss of the fight to change the working rules, condemned government interference and uttered a prayer that Congress would "cool off" before acting on labor legislation.

Several hours earlier the two union chiefs had dispatched a letter to President Truman indicating a willingness to backtrack. Mr. Truman, letting the letter lie on his desk while he went ahead with preparations for his speech to Congress, permitted the inference that he was demanding unconditional surrender.

Accord Is Read Amid Din

A minute or two after 4 P. M., Dr. Steelman emerged from a hotel room, followed by members of the carriers' negotiating committee and Mr. Whitney and Mr. Johnston. They went to press and radio headquarters. Dr. Steelman read the memorandum of agreement, shouting to make himself heard above the din made by reporters trying to complete telephone connections to their offices and by photographers who howled for poses.

The agreement was signed at 3:57 P. M. Mr. Whitney said that he had telephoned his union headquarters in Cleveland at 3:58. Mr. Johnston had sent word to the engineers' headquarters some time earlier, before the formal signing.

The code word used by the trainmen to authenticate their telegrams was "Cahill," which Mr. Whitney said was the name of one of the members. The engineers used the word "Division."

Mr. Whitney's statement to newsmen follows:

"We took this course in the interest of the public, realizing that the strike could not continue indefinitely because of the need of food and many other provisions required in our economy.

"We regard the President's statement of last evening as very unfair to our respective groups. However, it had but little effect upon the morale of the men we represent."

Fight for Rules Predicted

Mr. Whitney then stepped into the "dining room" of the hotel suite and spoke extemporaneously on the radio. Addressing principally the members of the two brotherhoods, he said, "We confess that we lost our case." He was speaking chiefly of the rules demands, which he said the brotherhoods would prosecute later and hope to win.

PRESIDENT LEARNS OF RAIL STRIKE SETTLEMENT

Leslie L. Biffle, Secretary of the Senate, hands a note to the Chief Executive during his address before the joint session of Congress.

Associated Press Wirephoto

The first in a series of swift developments came with a 10:30 A. M. statement by Presidential Press Secretary Charles G. Ross that, on orders of the President, the Government had withdrawn its mediation efforts as far as they concerned the striking engineers and firemen. For the future, he said, negotiations would be confined to the eighteen other brotherhoods and the carriers.

The Ross statement read:

"By direction of the President, the Government's efforts to mediate the dispute between the carriers on the one hand and the Brotherhood of Locomotive Engineers and the Brotherhood of Railroad Trainmen on the other have been discontinued.

"Mr. Steelman has called a meeting between the representatives of the carriers and the eighteen other unions at the Statler Hotel. The meeting will begin this morning at 11 o'clock. The purpose is to complete an agreement between these unions and the carriers in keeping with the President's recommendation.

"It should be understood that the carriers accepted the President's recommendation on the understanding that it would be accepted by all the twenty unions involved. Since two unions did not accept, it now becomes necessary to work out an agreement between the carriers and the eighteen unions.

"Manifestly, these eighteen unions should not be penalized for the failure of the two unions to accept the compromise proposal."

Truman Found Determined

While Mr. Ross was speaking at his usual morning press conference, Messrs. Whitney and Johnston were closeted with Secretary of State Byrnes. That the President was in no compromising mood was indicated by Senator Barkley, Majority Leader, the first and virtually the only White House caller of the day, who said on leaving the Executive Office that Mr. Truman was thinking of asking Congress for strike-curbing legislation.

Mr. Ross told reporters, in answer to questions, that the Government had made only one compromise proposal for settlement, that mentioned by the President in last night's address involving an 18½-cent wage increase in lieu of working rules changes.

"A categorical 'no'" was the only answer Mr. Ross said he could make to a question whether a compromise other than that mentioned by the Government had been suggested. He said there had been "various conversations" but that the Government had not proposed acceptance of the working rules changes recommended by the emergency board in addition to the wage increase put forth by the President.

Explains Separate Accords

All efforts of the carriers and the two striking brotherhoods having failed, Mr. Ross said, the only thing left to do was to complete an agreement with the switchmen, conductors and firemen and the fifteen "non-operating" brotherhoods, which had previously accepted the President's compromise.

After the settlement Dr. Steelman was asked to explain his further participation in the case after the President's order. He said that "at the request of both parties I have been working with them on a personal basis. I have been working with the permission of the President."

From Mr. Byrnes' office the two union chiefs returned to their suite in a hotel. A short time later they made public their letter to President Truman. The greeting, "Dear Mr. President," was in contrast to the plain "Sir" with which they had opened their letter of rejection to Mr. Truman on Thursday.

Today's message said that the members of the two unions "are patriotic men and they wish to cooperate with you in every possible way in the maintenance of rail service in the country. We know, however, that you want to be fair to our men and that you will be fair to our men. We know that you would not ask us to surrender our deep convictions that the carriers have not given our people the consideration they deserve.

"But we regret deeply the impression that our men are not willing to work for the Government. We will work for the Government."

They then referred to a conversation last night with Secretary Byrnes and Secretary Schwellenbach at which "it was suggested" that the Government enter a temporary agreement with the engineers and trainmen providing for an increase of 18½ cents and the rules changes recommended by the emergency board, and "the further proviso that we would be willing to arbitrate such other rules as we are unable to settle through negotiation with the railroads."

Then, seemingly as an alternative, the letter said:

"Our men await only your word that they can return to work for the Government on the basis of the award of your emergency board, that is the seven rules changes, with appropriate interpretations, and 16 cents an hour wage increase, to be effective Jan. 1, 1946, if you, Mr. President, will allow us to negotiate with you further concerning any other fair wage increases."

White House Receives Letter

The next development was the announcement at the hotel that the eighteen unions and the carriers had signed an agreement on the terms proposed by the President.

Then came the White House acknowledgment of the receipt of the Whitney-Johnston letter. Mr. Ross said it "is on the President's desk. He has not had a chance to look at it and certainly there won't be any comment on it today."

Dr. Steelman returned to the White House to report the signing. He made a telephone call and munched a sandwich while there. In fifteen minutes he was off again, this time to the final meeting of the two striking unions and the carriers.

Sixteen cents of the increase is retroactive to Jan. 1. Two and one-half cents of the increase will be paid for all work that began May 22.

May 26, 1946

The Worker's Point of View

Sketches from a reporter's notebook which throw light upon the motives of the strikers.

By A. H. RASKIN

WHAT is the mood of labor? What are the dissatisfactions that have led labor to strike in almost all the nation's basic industries?

When you ask the men and women on strike these questions you get an insight into the emotional and economic drives that underlie post-war labor conflict. There is nothing objective about the answers the strikers give. They are partisans, animated by a burning sense of the rightness of their position.

Go to their employers and you will get a different story. This, however, is the workers' story as they tell it. Here, taken from a reporter's notebook, are what some of the little people involved in big strikes think about some phases of the struggle between management and labor. The statements were gathered over a period of months, but the fundamental theme is the same today as it was last January.

* * *

"YOU'D see a lot less strikes if a dollar was still worth a dollar," the steel worker said. He huddled closer to the fire in the iron ash barrel and champed his feet on the snowy ground.

"I was overseas for three years and I read a lot about how much the workers were making. Now I'm back and I'm making it, but it don't seem like much when you take it to the store. I could make $50 a month stretch farther in the Army than I can $50 a week here. I picked up a wife when I got back. Like everybody, we got no place to live. We're living with her folks and I have to club them to make them take any dough for rent. Even so we can't make out. No matter how little you need you can't live on what you make in a mill."

* * *

THE strike headquarters for the trainmen was over a bar near a ferry terminal. It was a big mirrored room and it usually danced with light and merriment. Now it was dark and the men and women who filled the chairs around the wall were solid, sober people, not the kind you would look for in a bar.

"When I see the kids looking at me I know it's a holy thing, this strike," said the man with the tired eyes. "We've got four of them and they're all we care about. Every time prices go up those kids get paler and paler and my pocketbook gets thinner and thinner. We're eating potato soup five nights a week. Just keeping the kids in shoes is more than we can afford. I've always been a patient man and worked hard. But sometimes you've got to stop working before people will realize you've got to have enough to bring a little warmth and cheer into a home."

THE telephone girl put on her coat and prepared to leave her switchboard as the strike deadline neared.

"Was a time," she said, "when people never thought we'd strike. We've got a union now and we're telling the company we're not part of the switchboard any more. We're people and we've got to be treated like people. A lot of us are married, a lot aren't. But married or not, it costs us all more to live. A girl has to look nice, and that costs money. She has to eat right, and that costs money. She has to have a decent place to live, and that costs money. The company's got it. Why not us?"

HE was the head of a union whose members had climbed out of the sweatshop. He had made the organization's name one of the most respected in American labor. A normally cheerful man, he was not cheerful now.

"Our members are not like the youngsters in the unions that sprang up in the mass production industries almost overnight. They are seasoned people. Unionism is in their blood. And they have learned responsibility. They know they can't take out of the industry more than the industry can afford to pay.

"But today they are surrendering to the same fever as everybody else. Their wages are already probably the highest in the city and most of them are making as much overtime as they want to work. Still they are not satisfied. Our business agents go into the shops and fix the piece rates. The workers tell the boss: 'We can get more some place else.' The boss says: 'Stay. I'll pay you more.'

"When we go to the members and tell them they will end by killing the industry they shrug and say: 'The boss is making money so fast he can't give it away. Why shouldn't we get ours?' If anybody knows the answer to that one, I wish he'd tell me."

* * *

THE man with the Army field jacket and the teamsters' union button on his cap threw down the newspaper he had been waving. He started running across the vacant lot toward the break in the fence. He pointed at the two men carrying bundles of leaflets. It was the leaflets that gave them away. A hundred other striking truck drivers began moving toward them.

It was a movement full of quiet hatred. No one said anything. No one raised a fist. But the men with the leaflets sensed trouble right away. They turned round and started back through the fence. They weren't fast enough. The first of the drivers snatched the circulars from their arms. He looked at the signature, "New York State Communist party." He pulled out a match and set fire to one bundle. A moment later the second was in flames.

One of the Communists said: "Wait a minute, fellows, you've got us wrong. All we want to do is help you."

"We don't want your help," said the man with the field jacket. "Beat it before we toss you over the fence."

He came back to the reporter and picked up the newspaper. The headline shrieked: "Reds Rule Truck Strike, Mayor Charges." The man shook his head.

"Who's feeding the Mayor that line of poison?" he asked. "He's got more Communists in his own City Council than we have in our whole union."

He pulled out his union book and turned it open to a section that said no Communist could hold membership.

"That isn't there for fun," he said. "We don't like Reds and we don't let any of them stay around. Sure, they try to chisel in, like the two guys you just saw, but look how far they got."

* * *

THE reporter walked three blocks west to the harbor and asked the seaman with the CIO picket sign what he thought about communism.

"Listen, mister," he replied, "in our union we don't ask a man is he a Communist. We ask is he a good union man. If he is, he can be part Siberian wolfhound and nobody'll care. Never a day goes by I don't pick up a newspaper somewhere and see someone putting the burn on our officers for being Reds. Why are they doing that? I ask myself. Is it because they want to help our union? No, it's because they want to bust our union. If our officers were selling us out, no one would be saying a thing against them—except us, and they'd call us Reds because we were squawking. All I know is nobody was asking were we Reds when we rode those tubs through the wolf pack at the start of the war and we never knew when we hit the sack whether we'd wake up in our bunk or in the drink. The way I see it, anybody is a Red if he wants more money and that makes everybody in our union a Red—or maybe I should just say everybody everywhere."

* * *

THE banner in the union hall carried a big picture of Franklin D. Roosevelt.

"The way I see it," said the machinist, "there is no one left the working man can trust. Take Truman. He's a nice guy and loves his mother. But is that enough to be President? We've got a lot of guys here in this union could be President if that was all it takes.

"Roosevelt was a man you could respect, a big man in a big job. And nobody was pushing him around. He knew what the workers and the farmers and the little people needed, and the bosses never got away with a thing. Now they're down in Washington pulling all the strings. Congress does exactly what they say. That's why you have price control falling to pieces. They keep the clamps on wages, but nobody worries about profits. Everything for the big employers, nothing for the workers. That's the slogan now.

"Well, we've had a belly full of that kind of government. We're going to show the politicians that the people still run this country. And if we can't get any satisfaction from the Democratic or Republican parties, we'll start a party of our own to do it."

* * *

THE union organizer put the paper full of statistics back in his pocket.

"I'm not going to kid you," he said. "I've got a lot of figures to show our people are producing more now than they ever did. I use them every time the boss complains our people aren't putting in a fair day's work. But I don't believe them myself. I'm ready to admit our people could get a lot more done without really extending themselves.

"But why should they? They'll never do it as long as they believe that the boss, not the workers, will get the benefit from their working harder. You can talk yourself blue in the face about how prosperity for everybody depends on high production. You'll never make it real to the worker in the shop unless he feels that he is a partner in the business. And when I say partner, I mean partner.

"That's not just something in an annual report or a Christmas message from the front office. Partnership is something that affects the whole running of the plant. You've got to give the workers

LABOR'S GROWTH

The American trade union movement began with the organization of the Philadelphia shoemakers in 1792. The figures below give the estimated total number of organized workers in the United States in the years since.

1870:	300,000
1886:	1,000,000
1914:	2,687,100
1920:	5,047,800
1930:	3,392,800
1940:	9,000,000
1946:	14-15,000,000

a voice in how things are done and how the profits are divided. Maybe that's socialism or communism, but there are an awful lot of real Americans in our union who are going to keep on looking dumb when people talk about stepping up production until we make some progress in that direction."

* * *

THE girl in the blue slack suit snorted. "Don't talk to me about strikes holding back production," she said. "Everybody knows the manufacturers are holding stuff in warehouses waiting for higher prices. They could take care of all the people who want radios and refrigerators and washing machines—yes, and even automobiles—if they really wanted to."

The reporter showed her a clipping that said the Government had investigated charges that manufacturers were keeping finished goods off the market and found the charges completely unfounded.

"Who do you think makes those investigations?" she asked, unconvinced. "The bosses have their people in all those Government agencies covering up for them. We make electrical parts in our factory and we've turned out so many since the war that you could cover half of Africa with them. Nobody is going to tell me we're not doing our part. Sure, we could do more, but who would appreciate it? The boss would get richer, and what do you think he'd do for us? Why, he'd figure the work must be getting too easy and he'd cut our piece rates. No, thanks, no speed-up for little Jessie."

Waiting for jobs—Members of the National Maritime Union at a hiring hall.

LEWIS ENDS COAL CONTRACT, MEN QUIT WORK WEDNESDAY; CHALLENGE TO GOVERNMENT

CAPITAL MAY ACT

Considers Invoking War Labor Law Carrying Prison Penalties

LEWIS STEP HELD ILLEGAL

Act Bars Breach in Agreement, Says Clark as Truman and Krug Plead in Vain

By LOUIS STARK

WASHINGTON, Nov. 15—John L. Lewis challenged the Government today to prosecute him under the terms of the War Labor Disputes Act, which bars strikes against Government-seized facilities.

He did this by formally advising the Government that the contract he made with Julius A. Krug, Secretary of the Interior, on May 29 last would terminate at midnight Wednesday, Nov. 20.

Secretary Krug replied emphatically that the head of the United Mine Workers had no power, by unilateral action, to terminate the agreement which "covers for the period of Government possession the terms and conditions of employment."

The Government is apparently intent on meeting the Lewis challenge. Under the terms of the War Labor Disputes Act (Smith-Connally act) it may proceed to enjoin the miners from acting in concert to leave their work. Conviction would mean a fine of $5,000 and imprisonment for one year. The injunction, if one is sought, would also seek to tie up the union's treasury of several million dollars.

No Immediate Step Indicated

There were no direct indications that the Government would file a suit under the Smith-Connally act immediately. It was reported that a waiting period for events to develop would precede such action, which, in any case, would not be taken before next Wednesday and possibly much later.

If the Government proceeds against the miners' union it will be the first major test of the Smith-Connally act. Several minor soft coal union officials were found guilty last year of encouraging miners to walk out during the dispute over unionization of supervisors.

Mr. Krug's letter to Mr. Lewis, his second since yesterday, was one of a series of statements and letter exchanges that began with an announcement by President Truman. The Chief Executive stated at 2:15 P. M., after a Cabinet meeting and after a talk with Mr. Krug, that Attorney General Tom Clark had advised him that the Krug-Lewis agreement was "clearly applicable for the full period of Government operation."

Clark Cites Act's Provisions

Attorney General Clark's opinion, siding with Mr. Krug, that the contract could not be reopened because it applied for duration of government operation of the mines, was based on these grounds:

1. The contract statement that it applied for duration of government operation actually amended the reference that the agreement carried over previous contracts unless otherwise amended. Mr. Krug had claimed that the new agreement amended the operators-miners contract of 1945 Mr. Lewis insisted that the provision of the 1945 contract allowing either side to give it up on due notice was carried forward by the Krug-Lewis document.

2. The War Labor Disputes Act, under which the mines were seized, contemplates that the properties shall continue in government operation without interruption such as would be caused by termination of the contract.

President Truman, in his statement, pointed out that Mr. Krug had made a proposal to miners and operators which had been accepted by the latter, and urged Mr. Lewis to reconsider the Krug plan. He felt it to be "fair and equitable."

At the same time the President made public a letter from Mr. Krug to Mr. Lewis, dated yesterday, explaining the Government's proposal for a sixty-day truce. This letter advised the union chieftain that the Krug-Lewis agreement could not be modified except by mutual consent or by petition under Section 5 of the Smith-Connally act. Mr. Lewis' office then made public his reply to Mr. Krug, dated today, and his formal renunciation of the Krug-Lewis agreement. Mr. Lewis, in his letter to the Secretary defended his right to give five days' notice of the termination of the Krug-Lewis agreement.

He charged that Mr. Krug had only given three hours and fifty-eight minutes of his time to the negotiations for a new contract since Nov. 11. Mr. Lewis said he had received no reply to his request to Mr. Krug on Sept. 23, 1946, that he modify the miners' "brutal" fifty-four-working-hour week underground "until receipt of your ukase of yesterday."

The miners' president called what he termed the attempt by Mr. Krug to "supersede" the Krug-Lewis conference "sheer folly, empty platitude."

"We do not propose to be driven like dumb beasts to the slaughter of slow strangulation envisioned by your proposal and the operators' well-known and long-used tactics of evasion and delay," said Mr. Lewis in conclusion, rejecting the Krug truce proposal.

The correspondence was concluded by Mr. Krug with a second appeal to Mr. Lewis to reconsider the position he had taken.

In this letter he stated that since his letter of yesterday in which he spoke of an informal opinion on reopening the contract, received from Mr. Clark, he had received a "formal opinion that you are without power to terminate this contract with the Government."

In the meantime the bituminous coal operators limited their comment to this sentence:

"The statements of the President of the United States and the Secretary of the Interior have outlined clearly the position of the bituminous coal operators negotiating committee."

Several of the operators left town tonight. Chairman Ezra Van Horn of the Negotiating Committee remained to watch developments.

It was disclosed today definitely for the first time that Mr. Lewis had asked Mr. Krug for a 40-hour week to replace the present 54-hour week without a reduction in pay. This would mean a five-day week of eight hours each to replace the six-day week of nine hours.

The union also made the following demands:

That the work week begin on Monday so that if an operator began his work week on Tuesday, Saturday work, even though it fell on the fifth day, would bring overtime pay.

That the five-cents a ton royalty payment into the welfare fund be on the basis of tipple measurement and not railroad weights.

That a 30-minute lunch period replace the 15-minute lunch period.

Cessation of the issuance by the Coal Mines Administrator of "unilateral" interpretations of the Krug-Lewis contract.

Enforcement of the provision of the Krug-Lewis agreement for the naming of a trustee for the welfare fund.

Enforcement of the arbitration award on vacations made in Illinois.

The union argued that Secretary Krug's proposal meant that the miners would return to the status quo of April 1, before the Krug-Lewis agreement granted important concessions.

Operators Balk at Terms

Mr. Lewis insisted that before he would go into conference with the operators they would have to accept the terms of the Lewis-Krug contract as the starting point. The operators demurred, particularly the Southern group, led by former Senator Edward R. Burke.

Mr. Burke's associates balked at accepting the welfare fund, the Coal Mines Administrator's decision to enforce Federal safety regulations and the Administrator's ruling on unionization of foremen.

Mr. Lewis' letter to Mr. Krug and his denunciation of the Krug-Lewis contract was sent to the Interior Department at 10:30 this morning.

Mr. Krug then hurried to the White House where he conferred with the President. Reconversion Director John R. Steelman was present part of the time. The Cabinet then met and Mr. Krug remained with the President for more than half an hour.

Mr. Truman had planned to leave at 12:30 P. M., for the Washington Navy Yard to board the Williamsburg which, with steam up, was waiting to take him to Annapolis for tomorrow's Navy-Penn State football game. It was nearly 1:15 before the President left the Executive office and an hour later his statement and that of Mr. Krug were made public.

In his statement Mr. Truman recalled that on Nov. 9 he had directed abandonment of control over wages and prices. This, he said, required immediate resumption of collective bargaining between management and labor without government substitution for either party.

The nation, said Mr. Truman, has not yet recovered "from the long and costly coal strike of last spring."

Discussing the Krug-Lewis conferences in the light of this situation, Mr. Truman announced that the Attorney General had advised him that the contract was only for the duration of Government operation of the mines.

The Government, the President insisted, could not replace private management as the bargaining agent without interfering with true collective bargaining between management and labor.

After expressing the view that the Krug proposal was fair he said that its acceptance by the union "will satisfy the desire of 140,000,-000 Americans for industrial peace and continued production in the soft coal mines, and in all our great industries which are so dependent upon coal."

Mr. Lewis' letter to Mr. Krug, which he signed below the signatures of the negotiating committee, United Mine Workers, said that while the union had, under its interpretation of the Krug-Lewis agreement, served ten days' notice of the desire to confer, Mr. Krug had waited until Nov. 14 (yesterday), to make his sixty-day truce proposal.

"You, cavalierly now, propose a sixty-day freeze of the existing conditions on terms which you have first negotiated with the operators, who are strangers to the Krug-Lewis agreement," the letter added.

"You arbitrarily assert the right to designate that sixty-day period to begin on Nov. 16 and prescribe the method of conducting a conference between the mine workers and operators during that period. You likewise assert that the Krug-Lewis agreement can be 'modified by mutual consent.'

"Then, sir, where do you find the legal or moral right to deny to the mine workers their plain contractual right to reopen the contract as we respectfully requested on Oct. 21?

The sixty-day truce proposed by Mr. Krug would have continued Government operation of the mines for that period. During the first month, while operators and miners were conferring, the situation as to retroactive wages and higher prices would have remained in status quo. If no agreement were reached in the first month price limitations would have been removed and increased wages, if agreed upon, would be retroactive to Dec. 16, 1946.

If no agreement were reached by Jan. 16, 1947, the end of the two months' period, the mines would have been returned to private possession "and the normal operation of economic forces would then prevail in the coal industry." In the latter event the Government would have been out of the picture if the proceedings by Jan. 16 had terminated without result and a strike had ensued.

Congressional comment on a coal strike was that it would be a "catastrophe." Representative Clarence J. Brown, Republican, of Ohio, said it was "just another example of New Deal chickens coming home to roost."

Representative Earl C. Michener, Republican, of Michigan, said:

"Mr. Lewis may have the technical right to call his workers off the job but he has no moral right, with the winter approaching."

November 16, 1946

TEXT OF COURT JUDGMENT

Holds UMW Committed Both Civil and Criminal Contempt

WASHINGTON, Dec. 4 (U.P.)—Following is the text of the formal judgment and sentence on the United Mine Workers and John L. Lewis signed by Justice Goldsborough:

"This cause came on to be heard on the petition of the United States of America for a rule to show cause as to why the defendants should not be punished as and for contempts of this court, and on the rule which issued, and the defendnats having pleaded not guilty, and the court being fully advised in the premises and a full and complete trial having been held and the court having found beyond a reasonable doubt that the defendant, United Mine Workers of America, has committed a civil contempt and has committed and is guilty of a criminal contempt, and having made and signed findings of fact and conclusions of law, it, is, by the court this fourth day of December, 1946,

"Adjudged, ordered and decreed:

"That the defendant, United Mine Workers of America, be, and it hereby is, ordered to pay a fine in the sum of $3,500,000.

"That the defendant, John L. Lewis, be, and hereby is, ordered to pay a fine in the sum of $10,000."

December 5, 1946

LEWIS ENDS STRIKE, MINES OPEN TOMORROW

CAPITAL SURPRISED

By JOSEPH A. LOFTUS
Special to THE NEW YORK TIMES.

WASHINGTON, Dec. 7—John L. Lewis, president of the United Mine Workers of America, AFL, unexpectedly called off the country-wide soft coal strike today and directed all members to return to their jobs immediately.

He ordered the miners to continue working until April 1 at the wages and under the conditions existing before the stoppage.

With a bow to the United States Supreme Court and an acknowledgment of an economic crisis, the leader of nearly all the men who mine coal in the United States read to reporters at a suddenly called conference his letter of capitulation, directed to all UMW members and local unions in the bituminous districts.

He gave a virtual warranty of uninterrupted production at least until April 1, at the same time serving notice that the union would enforce the existing terms of employment at each mine.

Truman Cancels Address

The surprising announcement, on the fifth anniversary of the Pearl Harbor disaster and the seventeenth day of the strike, caught most of official Washington unprepared.

Within an hour President Truman canceled a radio address he was writing for tomorrow night. Revocation of the restrictions on transportation and coal consumption came later. Indeed, the Government at the time of Mr. Lewis' announcement was working on even more rigorous coal-conservation measures.

Mr. Lewis called his news conference for 2 P. M., a few hours after his lawyers and Government counsel conferred with Chief Justice Fred M. Vinson on the Government petition to the Supreme Court to take immediate jurisdiction of the contempt conviction and $3,510,000 fines levied against the union and its president.

It was learned that the United Mine Workers joined in the Government's petition to by-pass argument in the intermediate court of appeals. Lawyers left the Chief Justice with the impression that the court would accept the case immediately.

Court Argument May Be Delayed

The subsequent termination of the strike may alter that, however, perhaps to the extent of delaying argument for a few weeks. The national hardship factor has been eliminated by the strike termination, it was pointed out, even though the legal importance of the case remains.

Mr. Lewis' letter referred to the Administration's injunction as a "yellow dog" writ, which he said had "reached the Supreme Court." He called the Court "the protector of American liberties" and said the issues before it were "fateful for our republic."

"These weighty considerations," the letter continued, "and the fitting respect due the dignity of this high tribunal imperatively required that, during its period of deliberation, the Court be free from public pressure superinduced by the hysteria and frenzy of an economic crisis. In addition, public necessity requires the quantitative production of coal during such period."

Mr. Lewis said that in the meantime he would be willing to negotiate a new wage agreement "with such parties as may demonstrate their authority so to do."

He urged his men to return unhesitatingly, declaring "complete unity of action is our sole source of strength."

"We will, as always, act together and await the rendition of legal and economic justice," he went on, and concluded:

"I salute you, beside whom I have been privileged to fight."

With warnings of impending economic disaster and an Administration apparently buckling down to a finish fight, Mr. Lewis surrendered in circumstances analogous to those of another post-war coal strike in 1919, when he declared:

"We will comply with the mandate of the court. We do it under protest. We are Americans. We cannot fight our Government. That is all."

A dramatist, Mr. Lewis carried himself with an almost casual air as he faced sixty or more reporters in the basement room of the United Mine Workers' building. The reporters were already seated when he entered the doorway at the back of the room. Instead of going to the platform directly opposite the doorway, he strode around the fringe of the gathering and paused to give a friendly handshake to his sister-in-law, Mrs. A. D. Lewis.

UMW Chief Speaks Quietly

Then he ascended the dais and remarked quietly, "Gentlemen, how are you?" He took a seat at the long, polished table, with John O'Leary, UMW vice president, at his left. The backdrop effects were American and Canadian flags and a collection of framed cartoons and newspaper pages in which Mr. Lewis was the central character. Photographers were poised in front of the table and newsreel lights blazed at him.

He put aside an unlighted cigar and held a folded copy of the letter in one hand. He appeared freshly groomed and relaxed. Neither the extremes of cheerfulness nor of frustration were evident in his mien as he delivered a few prefatory remarks:

"I have a few words to say," he began slowly, "and they may be of something a little more than local interest. And afterward I would like the press to remain until I complete the statement. The statement will be self-explanatory and self-interpretive.

"It will require no questions after it is read to you," he warned.

"This statement is wholly mine," he emphasized. "It is a poor thing, but 'tis mine own." He said the statement was in the form of a letter from his office to the members.

"I will read it to you with meticulous precision," he went on, "and copies will be immediately furnished to you, after which the press conference will be terminated. I wish to read it to you myself so you will be assured it is my own.

Sentinels at Doors

"Questions as to the motive will be purely speculative. Some philosopher has said the pursuit of motives is the most elusive task in all the world. I think perhaps the ladies and gentlemen of the press will bear witness to that."

K. C. Adams, the UMW publicity representative, called on the reporters to restrain themselves and not to "break any doors" when the statement was completed.

Mr. Lewis intervened to say, "I'll see the doors are not opened." This was notice to the self-appointed sentinels to be firm at their posts. Then Mr. Lewis asked the photographers to pause in their work.

"Gentlemen," he said, "you have been extended your courtesies." He said he was "prepared to enforce" his wish.

Mr. Lewis put on his spectacles and read the letter with slow, measured intonation. He concluded his reading with "sincerely," and added parenthetically in a low voice: "Signed by this speaker."

"Sit down, gentlemen," he directed, as there was a stir in the room. Mr. Adams passed out copies of the letter and then Mr. Lewis called out, "All right, open the doors. Let them out." Some of the union officials at the door did not hear him and they were swept aside by the reporters rushing to telephone. Mr. Lewis remained behind to re-read portions of the letter for the newsreels.

The strike revocation order was the high point of an epic in American labor history. The economic effects and emotions engendered by the coal shutdown seemed even more intense than those which accompanied the wartime coal strikes and the much longer strike last spring.

The motives for Mr. Lewis' decision, as he said, were left to speculation. None doubted that public opinion was a powerful factor. Another was the Administration's evident determination not to yield this time. A hope of averting extreme measures by the new Congress was a possible consideration. Finally, by continuing the strike Mr. Lewis was courting further court fines at the rate of $250,000 a day. This would have drained the

UMW treasury in less than two months.

There was no valid evidence to indicate that the miners' chief had won concessions or commitments. All reports indicated the contrary. The promise of continued work at least until April 1 seemed to minimize the probability that a "deal" was in the making.

Whatever the motives, they evidently were strong enough to overcome the motives which impelled him to declare the Krug-Lewis agreement terminated. One of these motives probably was a wish to lead the parade in the "second round" of wage increases and set the pattern for American labor unions. That campaign collapsed today and industrial unions, at least, will now look to steel for leadership.

Some oil industry wage increases already have been agreed to, but they are confined to cost-of-living adjustments. The objective of the major unions is expected to be substantial increases in basic wage rates which will not be trimmed automatically by a decline in living costs.

Relief Felt on Capitol Hill

Public opinion against the coal strike was rising daily as the freight embargo and diminishing coal piles threw thousands out of employment, besides the miners, and dimmed lights across the country.

The mood of members of Congress was full of forebodings for organized labor. The reaction on Capitol Hill to the strike revocation was one of relief, but more than one member reaffirmed his determination to amend the labor laws of the land.

The strike's repercussions were far-reaching but, even so, the shutdown was not quite complete. In the week ended Nov. 30, the first full week of the strike, soft coal production totaled 2,050,000 tons.

This was a decrease of 83.5 per cent from the comparable period a year ago.

The National Coal Association reported that production was increasing. The association said 8,700 carloads were produced in Pennsylvania during the week, 8,300 in West Virginia, 4,500 in Kentucky, 3,800 in Illinois, several hundred in Indiana, and several thousand west of the Mississippi River.

Operators believe the strike worsened their competitive position because it accelerated the search for and use of other fuels, such as natural gas and oil, and weakened confidence in the steadiness of soft-coal supplies in the future. On top of that, according to industry spokesmen, the Interstate Commerce Commission's freight rate decision will add 18 to 20 cents per ton to the consumers' cost of the part of the coal output which moves by rail.

The total increased cost was estimated roughly at $70,000,000 a year on the basis of 1945 production figures.

Legal Issues Remain

Cessation of the strike permits the District Court to lift the temporary injunction, but its right to issue it in the first place remains a live issue.

The original restraining order, replaced by the injunction, directed Mr. Lewis to cease giving effect to his notice terminating the Krug-Lewis agreement.

He complied with that in substance today by ordering the resumption of mining, although only by indirection did he say that the Krug-Lewis agreement is still a valid instrument.

His approach to this was a statement that the status quo ante would be enforced.

The Government's petition for a declaratory judgment is still before the clerk of the District Court. If there is a trial and the Government's position is sustained, the UMW would be barred even on April 1 from terminating the Krug-Lewis agreement unless by that time the Government has relinquished possession of the mines.

The immediate issue, however, is the conviction and fining of Mr. Lewis and the union for refusing to obey the restraining order. A Supreme Court decision sustaining the District Could would not necessarily determine the question whether the termination of the contract is legal. Only the trial of the declaratory judgment would determine that.

December 8, 1946

LEWIS CONVICTION FOR CONTEMPT UPHELD BY HIGHEST COURT, 7 TO 2

By LEWIS WOOD

WASHINGTON, March 6—The Supreme Court by 7 to 2 upheld today the contempt conviction of John L. Lewis and the United Mine Workers, sustained the $10,000 fine against Mr. Lewis and ordered the $3,500,000 fine levied against the union cut down to $700,000.

But it was only by the margin of 5 to 4 that the tribunal ruled that the Norris-La Guardia Act did not outlaw the injunction issued against Mr. Lewis and the UMW by Federal Justice T. Alan Goldsborough.

The decision was announced in dramatic and almost unprecedented circumstances. When the tribunal met at noon Chief Justice Fred M. Vinson suddenly stated that he would read the majority opinion. This was a stunning surprise. Five decision days had passed with no reference to the issue. Almost fifteen years had passed since a decision was revealed except on Monday.

UMW Gets Court Order

Upholding the convictions were Chief Justice Vinson, author of the majority opinion, and Associate Justices Hugo L. Black, Stanley F. Reed, Felix Frankenfurter, William O. Douglas, Robert H. Jackson and Harold H. Burton. Opposed were Associate Justices Frank Murphy and Wiley B. Rutledge.

Voting that the Norris-La Guardia Act did not set up a barrier were Chief Justice Vinson and Associate Justices Black, Reed, Douglas and Burton. Voting that the act did apply were Justices Frankfurter, Murphy, Jackson and Rutledge.

In reducing the $3,500,000 fine assessed by Justice Goldsborough in the District Court for the District of Columbia, the Supreme Court commanded the United Mine Workers to withdraw the notice of termination of its contract with the Government that brought on the country-wide soft coal strike last fall.

Failure to do this within five days after the high court issues its mandate would force payment of the additional $2,800,000. Mandates are usually issued twenty-five days following a decision, so the miners would have thirty days to comply.

Court Divides on Fine

In addition to its other splits, the court divided on the $700,000 fine, Messrs. Vinson, Reed, Douglas, Burton and Jackson supported it, while Justices Murphy and Rutledge opposed it, and Justices Black and Douglas considered it "excessive."

The Supreme Court's unexpected action seemed to head off the threat of another strike April 1, when the truce set by Mr. Lewis expires. It appeared also to prevent further work stoppage so long as the mines were in Government possession. The Government, however, must give back the mines to private owners by June 30, under President Truman's executive order proclaiming the end of hostilities.

The decision, was a complete victory for the Government and for Justice Goldsborough except as to the amount of the UMW fine. President Truman had set his face against any compromise with Mr. Lewis and the union. Secretary of the Interior Julius A. Krug demanded a "fight to the finish" with the powerful mine union leader, after Mr. Lewis, last fall, told the Government in effect to reopen its wage contract with the miners or face a strike.

With the suddenness of the important decision astounding UMW officials as much as everyone else, there was no statement from Mr. Lewis, who recently returned from a Florida trip. He will testify tomorrow before the Senate committee considering labor legislation, and may announce his future course at that time.

Mr. Lewis was denounced by Chief Justice Vinson as the "aggressive leader in the studied and deliberate non-compliance" with Justice Goldsborough's orders. Moreover, the Chief Justice said that "immediately following the finding of guilty, defendant Lewis stated openly in court that defendants would adhere to their policy of defiance."

"This policy," Mr. Vinson continued, "was the germ center of an economic paralysis which was rapidly extending itself from the bituminous coal mines into practically every other major industry of the United States. It was an attempt to repudiate and override the instrument of lawful government.

"The course taken by the union carried with it a serious threat to orderly constitutional government and to the economic and social welfare of the nation."

The momentous ruling of the court required five documents to outline the positions of the various justices. In all there were about 56,000 words. There was the majority opinion by Chief Justice Vinson, to which Justice Jackson appended a four-line notice that the Norris-La Guardia act did not apply. Justice Rutledge presented a forty-four-page dissent. Justices Black and Douglas partly dissented and partly concurred. Justice Murphy dissented, and Justice Frankfurter concurred.

Argued Jan. 14, or nearly six weeks ago, the Lewis-UMW case was obviously a hard nut for the Supreme Court Justices to crack. This was evident in the diversity of their conclusions, which, naturally revolved chiefly around whether the Norris-La Guardia Act outlawed injunctions in cases where the Government was party. Justice Goldsborough had issued an injunction directing Lewis, president of the United Mine Workers and the union itself, to withdraw its notice of the contract termination.

All the Justices agreed that such restraining orders would be impossible in cases of a private arrangement. But they divided on whether this was a "private" case, the majority holding that the miners became Federal employes when the Government took over the mines.

Reasoning of Justices

Cut down to essentials, the reasoning of the nine high jurists was:

Chief Justice Vinson and Associate Justices Reed and Burton— The Government and the miners in this case stood in an employer-employe relationship; and the Gov-

ernment as a sovereign power was not subject to the prohibitions of the Norris-La Guardia Act. Even if it were true that the district court lacked jurisdiction under the Norris-La Guardia Act to issue an injunction, the lower court had power to compel Mr. Lewis's obedience until that question was finally determined by orderly judicial procedure.

Associate Justices Frankfurter and Jackson—The Norris-La Guardia Act deprived the district court of jurisdiction to issue the injunction. But they upheld the convictions on the doctrine that Mr. Lewis and the unions should have obeyed the court order until the jurisdictional issue was peacefully decided.

Associate Justices Black and Douglas—The Government was not barred from obtaining the injunction. The miners were Government employes in this case. The $700,000 fine against the UMW is excessive. This and the $10,000 fine against Mr. Lewis should be entirely conditional upon obedience to the injunction and withdrawal of the contract termination notice.

Associate Justice Rutledge and Murphy—The Norris-La Guardia Act bars issuance of the injunction. Since the injunction was jurisdictionally invalid when issued, violation of it does not give sufficient cause for sustaining a contempt conviction.

In his majority opinion, Chief Justice Vinson said "we must conclude that Congress in passing the Norris-La Guardia Act, did not intend to withdraw the Government's existing rights to injunctive relief against its own employes." The incidents of the relationship between the Government and the miners he described as "those of Governmental employer and employe," and thus, the act "does not apply."

Justice Goldsborough, said Mr. Vinson, had power to preserve existing conditions while his court was determining its authority to issue injunctive relief. Mr. Lewis and the United Mine Workers, the Chief Justice added, "in making their private determination of the law, acted at their peril. Their disobedience is punishable as criminal contempt."

As to the UMW fine reduction, Mr. Vinson held that courts could consider "the character and magnitude of the harm threatened by continued contumacy," and the probable effect of coercion.

The court could also, he stated, consider the financial burden to the defendant. The majority, he went on, found that the record of the case "clearly warrants" the $10,000 fine against John L. Lewis. But, he added that the majority did not believe the "unconditional" fine of $3,500,000 against the union was warranted.

And, he proceeded, the majority considered the $3,500,000 excessive; therefore the fine was modified to $700,000, with the proviso that the further $2,800,000 must be paid "unless the defendant union, within five days after the issuance of the mandate" com-

plies with the Goldsborough restraining orders.

Vinson Rebukes Miners

The union, he said, could comply "only by withdrawing unconditionally" the notice signed by Mr. Lewis, and sent to Mr. Krug terminating the Krug-Lewis agreement Nov. 20 last. The union must also notify its members and withdraw appropriate other notices.

At this point, the Chief Justice sharply criticized the striking miners.

"Loyalty in responding to the orders of their leaders may in some minds," he stated, "minimize the gravity of the miners' conduct. But we cannot ignore the effect of their action upon the rights of other citizens, or the effect of their action upon our system of government.

"The gains, social and economic, which the miners and other citizens have realized in the past, are ultimately due to the fact that they enjoy the rights of free men under our system of government. Upon the maintenance of that system depends all future progress to which they may justly aspire.

"In our complex society, there is a great variety of limited loyalties, but the overriding loyalty of all is to our country and to the institutions under which a particular interest may be pursued."

The conduct of Mr. Lewis and the United Mine Workers before Justice Goldsborough "showed a total lack of respect for the judicial process," Chief Justice Vinson wrote.

Justice Jackson joined the Vinson opinion, except as to the Norris-La Guardia Act "which he thinks relieved the courts of jurisdiction to issue injunctions in this class of case."

Justice Rutledge, one of the dissenters, said that to construe the Norris-La Guardia Act "as permitting what Congress so explicitly refused to allow is to go beyond our function and intrude upon that of Congress."

"This we have no power or right to do," he added.

He also said that since the injunction was invalid, the violation by Mr. Lewis and the UMW "gave no sufficient cause for sustaining the conviction for contempt."

He said also that he did not believe the Constitution "contemplated that there should be in any case an admixture of civil and criminal proceedings in one."

Justice Rutledge said it was in regard to the flat criminal fine of $700,000 that the Supreme Court's "disregard of the constitutional and other standards is most apparent."

"By what measuring rod this sum has been arrived at as the appropriate and lawful amount, I am unable to say," he continued. "Never has a criminal fine of such magnitude been heretofore laid and sustained, so far as I am able to discover. And only for treason, with one other possible exception, has Congress authorized one so large."

If, Mr. Rutledge stated, Congress has forbidden the use of labor injunctions in such cases, this is the "end" of the Supreme Court "function" in such matters.

Justice Murphy in his dissent insisted that the miners remained "private employes despite the temporary gloss of Government possession and operation of the mines."

Congress, he maintained, has decreed that strikes and labor disturbances are to be dealt with by other means than Federal court restraining orders and injunctions, and there is no exception where the public interest is at stake or the Government has seized private properties.

Even if the actions of the defendants had threatened orderly constitutional government, the Supreme Court lacked power to ignore "the plain mandate of Congress and to impose vindictive fines," Mr. Murphy held.

"A judicial disregard of what Congress has decreed," he added, "may seem justified for the moment in view of the crisis which gave birth to this case. But such a disregard may ultimately have more disastrous and lasting effects upon the economy of the nation than any action of an aggressive labor leader in disobeying a void court order."

Messrs. Black and Douglas had "no doubt" that the miners became Government employes when the mine seizure occurred. They agreed that the Norris-La Guardia Act would not interfere with the restraining order.

But they deemed the $700,000 union fine excessive, and urged holding up both this and the $10,000 penalty against Mr. Lewis. Fine payment should be made, "only in the event" that "full and unconditional obedience," including withdrawal of the termination notice, was not forthcoming.

Justice Frankfurter, in his concurrence, argued that the Norris-La Guardia Act barred issuance of the injunction. However, he said Justice Goldsborough had power to "make appropriate orders so as to afford the necessary time for fair consideration and decision while existing conditions were observed." He said that meanwhile, the authority of the district court must not be "flouted."

"The text, context, content and historical setting of the Norris-La Guardia Act," said Mr. Frankfurter, "all converge to indicate the unrestricted withdrawal by Congress from the Federal district courts of the power to issue injunctions in labor disputes, excepting only under circumstances explicitly defined and not here present."

Pointing to past injunctions in the Eugene Debs and other cases, obtained under "claim of compelling public emergency," he said these restraining orders gave "the most powerful momentum" to passage of the Norris-La Guardia law.

March 7, 1947

TRUMAN ENDS CONTROL ON WAGES

By JAY WALS

THE EXECUTIVE ORDER

An Executive Order accompanying the President's statement terminated all wage and salary controls under the Stabilization Act of 1942, including controls over decreases. It read as follows:

By virtue of the authority vested in me by the Constitution and statutes of the United States, and particularly by the Stabilization Act of 1942, as amended, and for the purpose of further effecting an orderly transition from war to a peace-time economy, it is hereby ordered as follows:

All controls heretofore in effect stabilizing wages and salaries pursuant to the provisions of the Stabilization Act of 1942, as amended, including any Executive Order or regulation issued thereunder, are hereby terminated; except that as to offenses committed, or rights or liabilities incurred, prior to the date hereof, the provisions of such Executive Orders and regulations shall be treated as still remaining in force for the purpose of sustaining any proper suit, action, or prosecution with respect to any such right, liability, or offense.

HARRY S. TRUMAN.
The White House,
November 9, 1946.

November 10, 1946

STRIKES DURING 1946 TO SET NEW RECORD

WASHINGTON, Nov. 29 (AP)—A Government report showed tonight that the number of 1946 strikes will establish a new record—eclipsing the existing mark set in 1919.

The Bureau of Labor Statistics announced that 4,095,000 workers were involved in strikes for the ten-month period through October of this year.

Add to this the 400,000 members of the AFL United Mine Workers now engaged in the crippling coal strike and the total already far exceeds the 4,160,000 striker record of 1919.

The bureau estimated man-days lost due to strike idleness through October this year were 102,525,000, or 1.6 per cent of the total available working time of the country's workers.

The full 1946 total of man-days lost may be close to triple the previous record of 38,025,000 man-days lost due to strike idleness in 1945.

The man-day lost figure was not kept in the prior banner strike year of 1919, when a coal strike lead by John L. Lewis then, too, figured prominently in the strike statistics.

November 30, 1946

General Strike of 100,000 Ties Up Oakland Industry

By LAWRENCE E. DAVIES
Special to THE NEW YORK TIMES.

OAKLAND, Calif., Dec. 3—More than 100,000 members of 142 American Federation of Labor locals in the Oakland metropolitan area went on a general strike today, paralyzing public transportation, closing newspapers, industrial plants and restaurants and disrupting normal life in the whole of Alameda County, with its 735,000 residents.

Called as a protest against importation of "strike breakers and trouble makers" from Los Angeles to drive merchandise trucks through department store picket lines with police escort, it was the first general strike the West Coast had experienced since 1934, when San Francisco was gripped for four days in a violent walkout originating on the waterfront. Seattle also had had a brief general strike.

Forecasting continuance of the walkout, Mayor Herbert L. Beach tonight summoned city councilmen to a special session tomorrow morning and informed citizens that he would ask the council to proclaim a state of emergency.

He described the general strike as "an attempt to push aside the government created by all the people," as "an attempt to substitute the physical force of mobs for that of government," and as "a physical assault upon the right of more than half a million people—men, women and children, young and old, to live their daily lives in a normal way."

"No community can exist in anarchy," his statement went on. "If one law can be broken openly, flagrantly, repeatedly, all laws can be broken. The city of Oakland is not going back to the jungle."

A short time before the Mayor made his statement, a spokesman for labor said that the strike would continue tomorrow.

Statements from union leaders indicated that labor's fight was directed mainly against the Oakland City Administration and its Police Department, but the strike was not confined to the limits of the nation's seventeenth largest city, with its estimated population of 408,000. Berkeley, Alameda and all other communities within the county, the third largest in California, felt its effects.

At 5 A. M., the key system buses and trains, which carry 120,000 commuters over the San Francisco-Oakland Bay bridge to their jobs in San Francisco, came to a halt. Picket lines were thrown around newspaper plants and none in Alameda County attempted publication. Many restaurants opened for business as usual but virtually all were closed by 8 A. M., following visits by union representatives. Here and there one was permitted to operate for the exclusive patronage of pickets, who showed their union cards as tickets of admission.

At shipyards, the Moore Drydock Company and Bethlehem, several hundred workers milled about outside the gates until business agents appeared to tell them of the strike order and ask them to leave.

Thousands of pickets massed during the morning about Kahn's Department Store and the nearby Hastings men's clothing establishment, where picket lines had been set up more than a month before to enforce the department store clerk's demand for a union shop. It was to these stores on Sunday that drivers for the "Veterans Trucking Company" of Los Angeles had delivered merchandise under police escort.

Union leaders took precautions to keep violence at a minimum, although there were occasional altercations and some hair-pulling and shoving as a few customers sought to enter the doors of the picketed stores. One person was treated at a hospital for cuts received when pushed through a store window, and a half dozen others, including a policeman, had

minor hurts from being struck or jostled.

New City Manager Takes Office

The Oakland City Council swiftly stepped into the strike situation when, at a special meeting, it gave an emergency appointment as City Manager to John F. Hassler. He already had been chosen for the managership but was not to take office until next Monday. Mayor Beach said that "governmental and civic groups" forming a "citizens strategy committee" had requested that Mr. Hassler be assigned immediately to take over and try to end the strike.

Upon taking office the new City Manager summoned representatives of labor and of the retail merchants' association into session to seek a peace formula.

Some of the conferees, when the session broke up after more than four hours, indicated the two sides had been brought somewhat closer together, but later statements by Mayor Beach and a union spokesman erased some of the optimism.

The Mayor, asserting that the right had been denied to Oakland residents "to get food, to travel in any form of public transportation, to send their children to school where there are distances to be traveled, to have a daily paper", went on to say it was not the function of the City Government to take sides in disputes between employers and employes.

"Management and workers," he stated, "must stand on an equal footing before an impartial Government. But the so-called 'general strike' is not a labor dispute."

"I am a believer in and a supporter of the organization of workers and of collective bargaining," he added. "I shall continue to be.

But as Mayor of your city, when unions are doing wrong, when they for a minor provocation are attempting to strike the whole city prostrate, I should and I shall oppose their wrong conduct to the limit of the city powers.

"The people of Oakland have a thousand things in common and only a few in conflict. Let us not destroy one another in disputing over the few."

Throughout the day special squads of police armed with tear gas and protected by gas masks waited at City Hall, a block from the center of the mass picketing for any call to action. Once police were summoned to "rescue" a special officer who was being roughly handled, but whenever violence was threatened, union leaders themselves rushed into the breach with loud speakers borrowed from the Police Department and pleaded with strikers to "behave."

The most noticeable early effect of the strike was a traffic jam on the Bay Ridge. Cars crept along for miles, bumper to bumper as the commuters took their automobiles or hitch hiked to work. Downtown Oakland soon became glutted with automobiles.

"Essential Services" Manned

In accordance with union plans to man "essential services," drugstores stayed open. Milk was delivered and hospitals were served. There was no interference with communications or with power and light.

The strike even reached across the bay to San Francisco and delayed for one day the murder trial of three Alcatraz convicts. Raymond G. Willis, a juror, telephoned to Federal Judge Louis E. Good-

man that he had no means of transportation from his home in Oakland.

James F. Galliano, attorney for the AFL clerks and their official spokesman, asserted in a formal statement that labor had acted "only after careful weighing of the responsibilities involved." He said the public would realize "the justness of this move and the necessity for making it" when it learned "the facts."

He made these demands, which, he asserted, were in the interest of labor peace:

"1. Return to Los Angeles the imported strikebreakers and trouble-makers masquerading under the name of 'GI' or 'Veterans Trucking Company,' since these men do not represent a legitimate non-union business but to the contrary are here for the sole purpose of creating barriers to any settlement.

"2. Assurance by responsible city officials and civic leaders that the City Council under pressure of influential employer groups will not use the Police Department as the tool of these groups and thus to give the citizens of Oakland assurance that their civil rights will be equally protected with employers' property rights."

Some 15,000 of the strikers overflowed the arena of the Oakland Auditorium tonight to hear union leaders call for "a fight to the finish," with predictions that the strike might go on for a week or ten days. No vote was taken, but Robert Ash, secretary of the Alameda County Labor Council, ended the meeting with a call for every man and women "out on this holiday" to report for picket duty in the morning.

PRESIDENT VETOES CASE BILL; DENIES IT WOULD END STRIFE; HOUSE FAILS TO REPASS IT

Vote to Override Is 255 to 135, With 260 Majority Required

BASIC STUDY AGAIN URGED

By C. P. TRUSSELL

WASHINGTON, June 11—President Truman vetoed the Case labor disputes bill today, condemning the long-controverted measure as one that hit at symptoms and ignored underlying causes of industrial strife, that would not stop strikes and would force men to work under compulsion for private employers in a peacetime economy.

The House at once sustained the Presidential action when 135 members supported Mr. Truman, and 255, with 260 needed for a two-third majority, voted to pass the bill over the veto. It was not necessary for the Senate to go on record in this contest, but it appeared that the result there would have been the same.

On the voting, the House divided as follows:

To override: 159 Republicans and ninety-six Democrats, with eighty of the latter from Southern States who were joined by sixteen from Maryland, Kentucky, Missouri, Oklahoma and California.

To sustain: 118 Democrats, fifteen Republicans and two minor party members.

Truman Again Asks Delay

In his veto message Mr. Truman again asked that passage of permanent labor control legislation await a half-year's study for a reorientation of basic causes of disputes.

The President stated that the Case bill would defeat its objectives for curbing strikes and lockouts and cause them to increase.

Further, he said, it would encourage, by its sixty-day "cooling off" period, a resort to "quickie" strikes.

Under the measure, he argued, employes would face penalties more severe than those for employers, and by its terms, he added, it would make workers feel free to strike, once the waiting period was over, "with the sanction of the Congress."

The proposed Federal Mediation Board, Mr. Truman said, could take jurisdiction "to outlaw" strikes under prescribed circumstances, then wind up with "the anti-climax of nothing."

"Not one of the major disputes which have caused such great public concern during the past months," he asserted, "would have been affected in any way by this bill had it been the law at the time."

The Mediation Board, he argued, would be inconsistent with the principles of good administration and would take on responsibilities which should be reserved for Cabinet members who in turn are responsible to the President.

Provisions of the measure which would authorize Presidential appointment of emergency commissions, Mr. Truman said, would permit the extension of cooling off periods to ninety-five days with an additional thirty days on the approval of the parties.

He criticized the application of fact-finding to disputes involving public utilities while omitting other industries.

While he was in full accord with the objective of the anti-racketeering provisions of the bill, the President asserted it was lacking the safeguard of the original anti-racketeering act against impairment of the rights of bona fide labor organizations lawfully to carry out their "legitimate" objectives. It also does not make clear in expressed terms that it would not be a felony to strike and picket peacefully, he added.

Expressing accord with the principle that a union should be held responsible for a violation of its contract, Mr. Truman said that the Case bill went much further than that and largely repealed the Norris-La Guardia Act.

The President asserted that a way "must be found" to prevent the jurisdictional strike, but not, he added, through the anti-trust laws.

A comprehensive study of the problems which Congress sought to meet with the Case bill, Mr. Truman asserted, should be made and "based on a realization that labor is now rapidly 'coming of age' and that it should take its place before the bar of public opinion on an equality with management."

Cheers and Boos in House

The veto and the House's action, though expected, caused immediate and apparently lasting repercussions. In the lower chamber, Speaker Rayburn's announcement of the vote was greeted with cheers, applause and a long barrage of boos, mostly from the Republican side.

Meanwhile, Joseph Curran, president of the National Maritime Union, CIO, said that the veto was a "victory for democracy" and added that the President had averted "what might well have been a national catastrophe." He did not elaborate on that statement or say whether the maritime strike threatened for Friday night was on or off.

William Green, president of the American Federation of Labor, issued a statement asserting that the President's action "reflects a high standard of statesmanship and courage."

Philip Murray, head of the Congress of Industrial Organizations withheld comment, while Senator Ball, Republican, of Minnesota, a leader of the fight for the Case bill, saw in the President's message a "paraphrasing" of "the biased and distorted arguments" made by Lee Pressman, CIO General Counsel, in the analysis of the measure Mr. Murray sent to Mr. Truman last week. Mr. Ball's view was echoed in many Capitol discussions.

Much of Congress did not receive well Mr. Truman's renewed proposal that there be created a Congressional joint committee to study, for perhaps six months, the fundamentals of labor-management discord, meanwhile passing immediately the emergency strike control bill he recommended on May 25, which many viewed as being much more stringent than the target of his veto.

A House Rules Committee, having a majority in favor of maneuvering the Case bill into a position where the President might "have to take it yet," prepared to provide a rule tomorrow through which the vetoed measure could be attached to the emergency bill, giving the Chief Executive a choice between approving it and vetoing his own program.

Signs appeared quickly, however, that this "all or nothing" plan might lead to nothing. Indications came from the House pro-labor group that its members would like very much to see this tried.

"The President would veto that too," prophesied Representative Marcantonio, American Labor party, of New York, leader of the group, "and we'd come out of this session of Congress with only the Petrillo bill and the courts will take care of that."

Proposed fast action gave way before the day ended to a tentative decision reached at a hurriedly called bipartisan meeting of sixteen Senators and Representatives to let the President's bill continue to rest on the Speaker's table in the House pending further developments.

Attending the strategy session were five members of the House Rules Committee, Representatives Smith of Virginia, Cox of Georgia and Slaughter of Missouri, Democrats; and Halleck of Indiana, chairman of the Republican Congressional campaign committee, and Brown of Ohio, Republican.

Others were Representatives Arends, the minority whip, and Case of South Dakota, author of the vetoed bill. Senators were Byrd and Burch of Virginia, George of Georgia, Hatch of New Mexico and Ellender of Louisiana, Democrats; and Taft of Ohio, Ball, Hawkes of New Jersey and Knowland of California, Republicans.

Although the conferees were in accord on objectives, some wanted to await "reaction from the country" before stepping farther. Others wanted to observe developments in the threatened maritime and other strikes, with some interested especially in the labor-management situation among the meat packers.

The situation accentuated the bitterness in many quarters. Senator Byrd viewed the veto as being "little short of a national tragedy," and pronounced the President's action, in the light of his emergency control recommendations for power to draft strikers, as "inconsistent, to say the least."

June 12, 1946

HOUSE LABOR BLOC NEARLY DESTROYED

Leading Advocates Riddled at Polls, With Few Surviving, and Senate Loss Is Heavy

By JOSEPH A. LOFTUS
Special to THE NEW YORK TIMES.

WASHINGTON, Nov. 6—Labor leaders conceded today, privately if not publicly, a blow to their political prestige in Tuesday's election, but would not concede that important labor law reform would necessarily follow.

Few labor stalwarts survived the fights for seats in the House, where agitation for labor legislation probably will be greater. Five or more Senators considered virtually "hundred percenters" by labor were defeated. Moreover, in three States where anti-closed shop constitutional amendments were considered they were apparently approved by the voters. A fourth State approved a proposal requiring unions to make public financial reports.

The forces which almost succeeded in the last session in enacting legislation fought by labor thus appeared to be strengthened considerably. In pro-labor circles, nevertheless, the opinion was expressed that the Republican leadership was not anxious to antagonize labor and might court its support in the 1948 election.

It was admitted, however, that a series of strikes in basic industry this winter probably would touch off extremely restrictive labor legislation. This recognition of the threat may act as a deterrent to labor unions which might otherwise be disposed to strike.

Casualties Are Heavy

The band of House members who generally took the lead in supporting organized labor's cause was almost destroyed. They included Representatives Hugh DeLacy of Washington, Frank E. Hook of Michigan, Michael J. Bradley of Pennsylvania, Andrew J. Biemiller of Wisconsin, James P. Geelan of Connecticut, C. M. Bailey of West Virginia, John E. Sheridan of Pennsylvania, John M. Coffee of Washington and Matthew M. Neely of West Virginia.

A few who were consistent and articulate in support of labor's views will return. They include Representatives Vito Marcantonio and Adam C. Powell of New York, Helen Gahagan Douglas of California and Augustine B. Kelley of Pennsylvania.

In the Senate, five members whose records are almost without blemish, from labor's viewpoint, will not sit in the next Congress. They are Senators Joseph F. Guffey of Pennsylvania, Hugh G. Mitchell of Washington, James M. Tunnell of Delaware, Abe Murdock of Utah, and James M. Mead of New York.

Comfort in Kilgore Survival

One face-saving result, from the CIO viewpoint, was the apparent success of Senator Harley M. Kilgore in West Virginia despite the opposition of the leadership of the United Mine Workers, AFL.

Labor leaders took a look at the committee chairmanships which will result from Republican control of Congress and found some reason to be cheerful. Senator George D. Aiken of Vermont will head the committee on labor and public welfare and Representative Richard J. Welch of California, presumably will be chairman of the Committee on Education and Labor. Both are friendly to the labor movement. At least one of the new Senators, Irving M. Ives of New York, is regarded by labor as friendly.

William Green, president of the American Federation of Labor, said, "I am not surprised at the results," but would not comment further.

James B. Carey, secretary-treasurer of the CIO, joined Jack Kroll, CIO-PAC director, in saying, "Labor political action is here to stay."

Mr. Carey was one of those who thought that the Republican leadership would see some political wisdom in courting labor's favor. "After all," he said, "the Republican party is a lot different now than it was ten years ago. It supports a great many things now that it once opposed."

Truman's Labor Program

By The Associated Press.

WASHINGTON, Jan. 6—President Truman offered in his message a four-point program for reducing labor strife.

Summarized, these points were:

(A) Legislation preventing such "unjustifiable" practices as jurisdictional strikes. (B) Extension of Federal facilities for assisting collective bargaining. (C) Broadening social security legislation. (D) Naming a commission to investigate labor-management relations.

More specifically, the President proposed regarding labor:

1. Enactment of legislation outlawing the jurisdictional strike as "indefensible."

2. Prohibition of secondary boycotts which involve "unjustifiable objectives."

3. Provision for machinery whereby unsettled disputes over existing collective bargaining agreements may be referred "by either party to final and binding arbitration."

4. Congressional action to set up a temporary joint commission to inquire into the entire field of labor-management relations, with legislative recommendations not later than March 15.

The President also stated:

"It is up to industry not only to hold the line on existing prices, but to make reductions whenever profits justify such action.

"It is up to labor to refrain from pressing for unjustified wage increases that will force increases in the price level."

CIO SEEN AVOIDING BIG STRIKES IN '47

Extension of Steel Wage Pact Interpreted as Evidence of Murray's Determination

Extension for two and one-half months of the wage agreement between the United States Steel Corporation and the United Steel Workers, CIO, was interpreted in labor circles yesterday as evidence of Philip Murray's determination to avoid big CIO strikes this year.

"If the manufacturers will meet us half-way, we can wind up 1947 without a single major strike," was the way one high CIO official summed up the outlook.

The contrast between this year's strike record and the 1946 situation was emphasized by a look at newspaper files for last year. On Jan. 27, 1946, 800,000 steel workers were on strike, along with 200,000 electrical workers, 175,000 General Motors workers, 200,000 meat packers and at least 50,000 workers in many smaller industries. Today there are no national strikes and few local strikes of importance anywhere in the country.

Coal Deadline March 31

The biggest cloud on the current labor-management horizon is the March 31 strike deadline set by John L. Lewis when he ordered 400,000 soft-coal miners back to work Dec. 7. The Southern operators are still reluctant to grant the terms Mr. Lewis won from the Government last May, much less the additional concessions the union now seeks.

The Northern operators, who have indicated their desire to negotiate a new agreement with Mr. Lewis, have not had any word from him as to whether he will meet with the Northern group alone or insist that all the owners bargain together. Mr. Lewis is now in Florida and is not expected to return to Washington before the middle of February.

The Government is still in possession of the mines, but its control must end by June 30. Northern operators say they have had clear indications of the Government's wish to be relieved of the necessity for further meetings with Mr. Lewis on new contract terms. Whether the Government will continue to take the position in March that the old contract must remain in force without change for the full period of Government possession is not known.

The United Automobile Workers, CIO, have already agreed to a thirty-day extension of their contract with the Chrysler Corporation. Walter P. Reuther, UAW president, attended the Pittsburgh session Friday at which Mr. Murray informed his union associates of the U. S. Steel extension, and it was expected that the spirit of conciliation would be carried forward in the automobile, as well as the steel, wage talks. However, the bitter factional strife within the union and the "tough" attitude shown by some Detroit industrialists in pre-negotiation speeches made some labor observers doubtful that amity would prevail in all automobile pay conferences.

UNIONS FORCED TO FIGHT ON MANY STATE FRONTS

By C. TRUSSELL

WASHINGTON, Feb. 22—While interest in labor legislation generally appears to be focused on Congress, organized labor actually is fighting defensive battles in most of the States, too.

The closed shop has been, or is about to be, outlawed in eight States. There are limitations on it in three others. Most of this has happened since the end of the war. Four States have enacted other union regulations since war's end. With forty-five Legislatures in session this year, more of this appears to be on the way.

Labor Was Forewarned

Organized labor was forewarned some months ago of the tremendous lobbying job it had on its hands. At the convention of the Congress of Industrial Organizations in November, the union's counsel, Lee Pressman, sounded the tocsin:

"Let's not make the mistake of solely concentrating our attention on Congress, because our enemies are not resting with Congress. There will be plenty of fights in Congress, but at the same time let us mobilize our forces in the various States to carry on the fight before the State Legislatures."

Unions experienced a wave of "anti-labor" legislation in 1943. Joseph A. Padway, counsel to the American Federation of Labor, said twelve States that year passed some form of union regulation covering such phases as registration, limitation on dues, public accounting, incorporation and disciplinary action.

Both the AFL and CIO started suits across the land. Mr. Padway said the litigation was "very successful" from the unions' standpoint. Practically all regulations except registration and financial accounting were beaten, and even those were able to be defeated in Florida.

Constitutional Method

Now, however, the unions will have constitutional amendments as well as statutes to contend with. Since 1943 constitutional amendments outlawing the closed shop have been approved in Florida, Arkansas, Nebraska, Arizona and South Dakota. Virginia joined the list at a special session of the Legislature last month, and Tennessee yesterday completed similar action.

The Florida constitutional amendment is the only one of these amendments which has reached the Supreme Court of the United States. In that case the high court ruled that the State courts must first rule on the merits of the

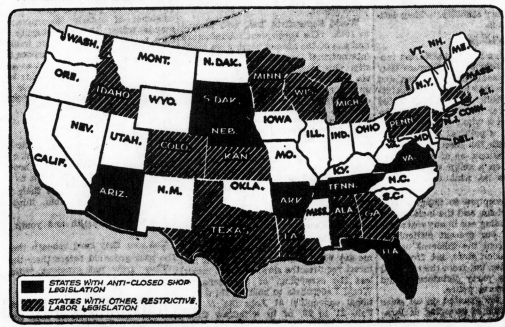

WHERE 'LABOR-RESTRICTIVE' LAWS HAVE BEEN PASSED

■ STATES WITH ANTI-CLOSED SHOP LEGISLATION

▨ STATES WITH OTHER RESTRICTIVE LABOR LEGISLATION

The "restrictive" legislation referred to above includes such State laws as those requiring unions to file financial statements, to give strike notice, to limit contributions to political parties and to elect officers at stated intervals.

amendment after application in specific instances.

The AFL, which was testing the Florida provision, complained of undue delay in the courts there and started a test in Arizona.

These amendments, with the exception of that of Arizona, provide that the right of persons to work shall not be denied or abridged on account of membership or non-membership in any labor union or labor organization. In Arizona, the amendment forbids denial of employment because of non-membership, permitting by implication denial of employment because of membership.

Colorado, Kansas and Wisconsin regulate closed-shop contracts. In the Colorado Peace Act of 1943, for example, any agreement requiring all employes to be union members is prohibited unless voted for by three-fourths or more of the employes in a secret ballot conducted by the State Industrial Commission.

"Right to work" constitutional amendments, which generally mean a prohibition on the closed shop, have been proposed in Colorado, Massachusetts, Minnesota and Utah. Bills in that category have been proposed in Indiana, Iowa, South Carolina and Washington.

Last year, only four states approved union regulatory provisions — New Jersey, Virginia, Massachusetts and Louisiana.

The New Jersey law is limited to public utilities. The Governor is authorized to seize a plant or property whenever an interruption of service is threatened.

Virginia's 1946 labor law prohibits interference or attempted interference by any person with the right of another to work, and the use of threats or intimidation, or insulting or threatening language to induce or attempt to induce any person to quit his job or to refrain from seeking employment.

Under Louisiana's 1946 law, certain types of picketing are prohibited. Unions are forbidden under the act to join with employers or other nonlabor groups to fix prices, eliminate competition, or otherwise act in restraint of trade.

A Massachusetts regulation approved in a referendum last November requires every labor organization to file a statement showing the salaries of officers, dues and assessments, and a financial report carrying the names of every person who received funds from the union.

Indicative of the climate, no doubt, is the fact that thirty-three Governors in messages to Legis-

latures up to Feb. 15 dealt specifically with some phase of proposed labor legislation.

Bills requiring financial statements or reports by unions have been proposed in Arizona, Michigan and Wisconsin. In Maryland a bill would prohibit the picketing of the residence of an employe. Michigan bills would prohibit a strike unless ratified by a majority vote of employes.

A Massachusetts bill would prohibit political contributions of any sum exceeding $1,000 by labor unions. Bills in Connecticut, Massachusetts and Pennsylvania would regulate labor relations in public utilities.

Secondary boycotts would be made unlawful by bills proposed in Indiana, Iowa and Michigan. A South Carolina measure would prohibit the check-off of dues.

In fighting labor legislation in the courts, Mr. Padway said the unions had relied mainly on three amendments to the United States Constitution, and kindred provisions in State Constitutions. These are the First, guaranteeing freedom of speech and press, the Thirteenth, forbidding involuntary servitude, and the Fourteenth, forbidding seizure of property without due process of law.

February 23, 1947

UNIONS AND STRIKES FROM WAGNER ACT TO TAFT BILL

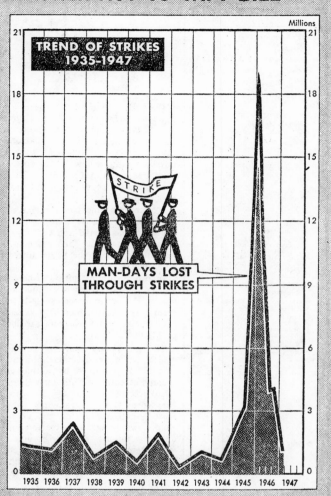

Senate Vote Voiding Veto of Labor Bill

By The Associated Press.

WASHINGTON, June 23 — The vote by which the Senate today overrode President Truman's veto of the Taft-Hartley labor bill (two-thirds majority being required to override):

FOR OVERRIDING—68

Republicans—48

Aiken	Dworshak	Reed
Baldwin	Ecton	Revercomb
Ball	Ferguson	Robertson(Wyo)
Brewster	Flanders	Saltonstall
Bricker	Gurney	Smith
Bridges	Hawkes	Taft
Brooks	Hickenlooper	Thye
Buck	Ives	Tobey
Bushfield	Jenner	Vandenberg
Butler	Kem	Watkins
Cain	Knowland	Wherry
Capehart	Lodge	White
Capper	McCarthy	Wiley
Cooper	Martin	Williams
Cordon	Millikin	Wilson
Donnell	Moore	Young

Democrats—20

Byrd	Hoey	Overton
Connally	Holland	Robertson (Va.)
Eastland	Maybank	Russell
Ellender	McClellan	Stewart
Fulbright	McKellar	Tydings
George	O'Conor	Umstead
Hatch	O'Daniel	

AGAINST OVERRIDING—25

Republicans—3

Langer	Malone	Morse

Democrats—22

Barkley	Kilgore	Myers
Chavez	Lucas	O'Mahoney
Downey	Magnuson	Pepper
Green	McCarran	Sparkman
Hayden	McFarland	Taylor
Hill	McGrath	Thomas (Okla.)
Johnson (Col.)	McMahon	
Johnston (S.C.)	Murray	

Not voting but announced against overriding: Thomas (Utah) and Wagner, both Democrats.

Labor Act Analysis Shows New Era for Industry

By LOUIS STARK

WASHINGTON, June 23 — The "Labor Management Relations Act, 1947," is the first amendment to the National Labor Relations (Wagner) Act of 1935. It adds a new story and a new façade to the earlier law in an effort to "equalize the relations between employers and employes."

By removing most of the administrative work of the National Labor Relations Board and vesting it in a new statutory general counsel, the act turns the board into a labor court.

In order to cope with the backlog of cases which continue to mount, the act increases the NLRB from three to five members. Their salaries are increased from $10,000 to $12,000 a year.

The provisions applying to the NLRB, the general counsel and unfair labor practices by employes become effective within sixty days. Also deferred for that period are the provisions outlawing the closed shop, regulating the union shop, requiring registration of data by unions, depriving unions with Communist officers of their rights under the law and forbidding foremen a recognition by law.

The other sections become effective at once. They include the following subjects:

Creation of a new statutory Federal mediation service to replace the present Conciliation Service in the Department of Labor; emergency machinery for handling "national-paralysis" disputes or strikes which "imperil the national health or safety"; stability of unions; regulation of welfare funds and check-off; banning of strikes by government workers; appointment of a joint Congressional committee to study labor-management re-lations and to observe the workings of the new law.

In shifting administrative responsibilities from the new NLRB's shoulders elsewhere, the law abolished the review section, comprising about fifty lawyers. This section had "predigested" all records for NLRB members but had been attacked as unduly "influencing" its chiefs.

The task of reviewing each case will now be vested with the board members who may be expected to increase their own legal staffs.

This step, it has been argued, will slow up administration and impair board efficiency but proponents of the law maintained that it would expedite the board's work.

President to Name Counsel

The new statutory General Counsel will be named by the President, subject to Senate confirmation. His salary will be $12,000 a year. The duties provided in the law give him general supervision over all lawyers employed by the board (except Trial Examiners and legal assistants to board members) and over all employes in regional offices.

Hitherto the NLRB's field director from Washington had supervision over all field agents in the various regions while the regional lawyers reported to the General Counsel. All this activity is now centered in the latter office, the chief field official taking his place under the counsel.

The closed shop-union shop section affects some 7,000,000 employes.

The closed shop (in which an employe must be a union member to obtain a job) is outlawed, while the union shop (in which an individual may be employed even if he is not a union member but must become one after a trial period) is hedged about with certain restrictions.

In order to qualify for the union shop a labor organization must be the representative of the majority of the employes. It must also be certified by the NLRB that the employes, by a majority of those eligible, have signified their desire to have the union shop. Then the union may ask for it.

But if the employer agrees to this request the union will be unable to dismiss anybody for any reason other than for failure to keep up dues payments.

Union Disciplines Limited

Thus, in the eyes of the bill's opponents, the usual reasons for the union shop (the union's right to discipline recalcitrants, "spies," provocateurs, etc., would be excluded.

This section was framed for the frank purpose of depriving union leaders of their prerogatives regarding the disciplining of union members, on the ground that the leaders had abused this power in many instances and had unduly deprived employes of jobs.

One of the most important sections of the new law deals with unfair labor practices by employes. This is a new provision which evoked heated debate during the consideration of the bill.

In addition to retaining the old Wagner Act sections prohibiting employers from discriminating against employes because of union activity, the law now provides for the following six "unfair" labor practices by labor organizations:

1. Restraining or coercing employes in the exercise of their guaranteed rights or employers in the selection of their bargaining agency; (intended to prevent unionization by force and to stop unions from compelling employers to bargain either as individuals or as members of larger units);

2. Persuading or attempting to persuade employers to discriminate against an employe, unless in accordance with the law; (the limited union-shop action);

3. Refusing to bargain collectively; (to stop unions from serving ultimata on employers);

4. Conducting strikes or boycotts for various purposes which are stated in some length; (aimed to lessen jurisdictional disputes and secondary boycotts and strikes against NLRB certification);

5. Requiring initiation fees which the NLRB finds "excessive or discriminatory"; (to meet the charge

that unions keep out qualified workers by excessive charges);

6. Causing or attempting to cause an employer to pay money for services which "are not performed or are not to be performed"; (to offset "featherbedding" practices).

These labor practices furnish the "heart" of the first section of the new law and may change the entire course of industrial relations.

The NLRB would be empowered to obtain injunctions against jurisdictional strikes and secondary boycotts. The board itself would also have the power to decide which employes should do the task over which they are fighting. The board, however, would not be permitted to name an arbitrator to take this problem off its hands.

Courts May Set Damages

Unions would also be subject to suits for unfair labor practices and the courts may now provide damages against them resulting from jurisdictional strikes and secondary boycotts.

Charges of unfair strikes or boycotts will receive priority over all other disputes and if preliminary inquiry shows there is reason to believe the charges are true, the NLRB is required to seek "appropriate injunctive relief." This section modified the Norris-La Guardia Anti-Injunction Act of 1932 which rigidly prescribed procedure for suits in the Federal courts against unions.

Employers receive more leeway in a "free-speech" section which states that expression of any views "shall not constitute or be evidence of an unfair labor practice if such expression contains no threat of reprisal or force or promise of benefit."

Supervisory employes are excluded from the protection of the law although they may, if they wish, form unions and employers may deal with them. Hitherto the NLRB has ruled in favor of permitting foremen and supervisors to join unions and gain protection under the Wagner Act.

Professional employes cannot be combined with non-professional employes in one unit unless they vote for such inclusion.

Guards cannot combine with other employes in a single bargaining unit.

The board receives the duty of voting craft units when application is made for such votes, a section which would enable small skilled groups to split off from larger industrial units.

The NLRB is not allowed to act upon any labor petition unless the union has previously filed with the Department of Labor data which includes the following: names, titles and compensation and allowances of its three principal officers if they aggregate over $5,-000; the manner in which the officers were elected; initiation fees for new members and dues for regular members; detailed statements regarding the constitution and by-laws, showing procedure in election of officers, calling of meetings, imposition of fines, disbursement of funds, audit of financial transactions, participation in insurance or other benefit plans and expulsion of members and grounds therefore.

This section permits unions which do not go to the NLRB to refrain from filing the registration data.

The NLRB is not permitted to investigate any union complaint unless there is on file with the NLRB an affidavit by each labor union official stating "that he is not a member of the Communist party" or affiliated therewith, "and that he does not believe in, and is not a member of or supports any organization that believes in or teaches the overthrow of the United States Government by force or by any illegal or unconstitutional methods."

The foregoing would deprive all members of a union of their rights under the act if their officers failed to sign the anti-Communist affidavits.

Another section permits Communists or others to be employed under union-shop contracts so long as they pay dues.

Title two of the law provides for (1) conciliation in ordinary disputes affecting interstate commerce and (2) national emergencies such as coal strikes, etc.

This section opens with the creation of the new Federal Mediation and Conciliation Service with a director at $12,000 a year whose duty it will be to offer his services in any dispute affecting interstate commerce or to intervene upon request. It provides for setting up certain procedures hitherto unavailable in the act creating the Department of Labor.

By making this service statutory and raising its chief to the dignity of a $12,000 position, it is hoped to place the new service on a plane with the NLRB. It was created de novo and its duties were taken from the Department of Labor because of the insistence by industry spokesmen that the present Conciliation Service was "partial" to labor, a charge that was denied by the older organization.

In an earlier section of the law, the procedure under which the new conciliation service would act requires the parties to "exert every reasonable effort to make and maintain agreements" including provisions for "adequate notice of any proposed change" in the agreement.

This section parallels a similar provision in the Railway Labor Act and it also provides that either party shall give the other a sixty-day notice of proposed termination of a contract or its modification.

Within thirty days of the expiration of the contract, the Federal Mediation Service is to be notified and then the parties would have to retain the "status quo" for sixty days.

Curb on Strikes, Lockouts

This would exclude employes from striking or employers from locking them out. In the event of a strike in this period employes would lose their rights under the act. An employer violating this section would be subject to a cease and desist order of the NLRB.

A labor-management panel, which now advises the present chief of the United States Conciliation Service, is made statutory. Its twelve members are divided evenly between labor and employers. They are to receive $25 a day and expenses when on government business.

The national emergency section concludes Title Two of the law.

This section would permit the government to obtain an eighty-day injunction to restrain strikes such as a coal mine stoppage while the Federal officers tried to settle the dispute.

Secretary of the Interior J. A. Krug, who is in charge of the coal mines, argued with President Truman that this section would not, as written, stop a possible coal strike on July 1 because the mines would revert to their private owners and the miners would not have an employer unless they made a contract in the meantime.

The government has not taken any action to stop the coal dispute from leading to a strike but took steps last November to enforce the contract between the union and the Secretary of the Interior.

At the end of the 80-day injunctive period provided in the law the employes would be permitted to strike. The last provision calls upon the President to submit a full report to Congress of the findings by a Board of Inquiry and the votes of the union members on whether they desired acceptance of the employers' final offer.

Title Three of the law deals with suits against labor organizations, restrictions on payments to employes and boycotts and other unlawful combinations, and restrictions on political contributions by unions.

While labor unions may be sued now in state courts of about three-fourths of the states, the law now makes it easier to sue unions in Federal courts by abandoning requirements concerning the amount in controversy and the requirement for diversity of citizenship.

Automatic and universal check-off of union dues is made illegal unless employes specifically authorize such deductions for a period of not more than one year.

Contributions to welfare funds are made illegal unless they are administered jointly by employers and employes and by a neutral, specifying the benefits derived from the fund, which must be audited annually. This would ban funds administered solely by unions and established since Jan. 1, 1946.

Political Fund Use Barred

The Federal Corrupt Practices Act is amended so as to prevent unions from making a "contribution" or "expenditure" from union funds "in connection with" any election to any political office. This section would stop a union from issuing a statement or publication criticizing or supporting a candidate if the money for the publication came out of union funds. If the paper were supported by subscriptions the ban would not hold.

The final provision in Title Three requires the discharge of Federal employes who go on strike.

Title Four calls for a joint Congressional committee assisted by an advisory body comprising labor and management, to study the field of labor relations. The committee would have extensive powers of inquiry and could subpoena witnesses and employ experts. Senator Joseph Ball of Minnesota may be named as chairman of this committee, which will consist of seven members of the Senate Committee on Labor and Public Welfare and seven members of the House Labor Committee, to be named by the presiding officers of each house.

A Tempering of Strife

President Truman seizes the steel mills.

Courtesy Wide World Photos.

GM RAISES WAGES 11C AN HOUR, TIES PAY TO LIVING COST

Walkout Friday Is Averted by New Formula, Which May Set Pattern for the Industry

CHRYSLER PEACE IS SEEN

Company and UAW to Meet Today—Tender of 6c Rise Preceded Strike May 12

By The Associated Press.

DETROIT, May 25—The General Motors Corporation reached a unique cost-of-living agreement today with the United Automobile Workers, CIO, to raise the wages of 225,000 employes. The contract is to run two years.

This, the largest company of its kind in the world, gave a flat 11-cent-an-hour rise to avert a strike set for Friday. The rate will be adjusted later to the cost of living.

General Motors did not reveal whether the wage adjustment would lead to another increase in its car prices.

This third round of post-war wage increases set a pattern for the 1,000,000-man auto industry. There were indications that the pattern might find favor also in other large industries in the United States.

Industry Studies Formula

There was little comment immediately from big business. But industrialists were studying the history-making wage formula closely.

General Motors offered the same terms to its 40,000 employes who are members of the United Electrical Workers, CIO. They were studying the formula.

General Motors called its sliding wage scale "the new approach to the living cost problem." Officials said it would add about $75,000,000 a year to the payroll. It will raise the average wage to about $1.61 an hour.

The UAW-CIO said that, if the rest of the industry followed the GM pattern, it would put an extra $220,000,000 a year in the pockets of the country's automobile workers.

The UAW-CIO contended that General Motors was not as generous as it might have been. However, union leaders hailed the agreement as proof that the company accepted "the principle that prices and profits are a concern of labor."

"This is progress," declared the big auto union.

Emil Mazey, acting president of the UAW-CIO, predicted that the General Motors formula would bring a quick end to a fourteen-day strike of 75,000 workers of the Chrysler Corporation.

Chrysler is scheduled to reopen negotiations with the union tomorrow. Its best offer was six cents an hour, made before its employes walked out May 12. The company later withdrew it.

The UAW-CIO demanded 25 cents an hour from GM and 30 cents from Chrysler and Ford. In 1946 the union got 18 to 18½ cents and in 1947 15 cents.

Ford has asked the UAW-CIO to accept a pay cut. However, negotiations between them have not begun yet.

How GM Formula Works

Here is how the new General Motors formula is to work:

As of May 29, wages go up 11 cents an hour. That raises the average from $1.50 to $1.61 an hour.

Next Sept. 1 and each quarter of a year thereafter, the two sides will take a look at the consumer price index put out by the Federal Bureau of Labor Statistics.

If this shows that living costs have gone up, then the union automatically gets another wage increase at the rate of one cent an hour for every 1.14 points of the rise. There is no limit on this wage escalator. It goes up as high as the index. [The BLS Consumer price index, based on 100.2 for 1940, stood at 169.3 for April, 1948.]

If the cost of living goes down, then the employes take a cut of one cent for every 1.14 points the index drops. But in no case can the corporation cut wages more than five cents and hour between now and 1950.

Moreover, a year from now wages automatically go up three cents an hour regardless of what happens to the cost of living.

Thus the worst that can happen to a GM worker making $1.50 an hour today is that his wage can be cut from $1.61 to $1.56 next Sept. 1. But it automatically goes back up to $1.59 next May.

The plan will be placed before UAW-CIO representatives from ninety General Motors plants Friday. Leaders of the union will ask them to approve it. Normally, they get what they ask.

May 26, 1948

RAIL DISPUTE ENDS AS UNIONS ACCEPT COMPROMISE OFFER

15½C AN HOUR RISE

Little Difference Is Seen in Pact and One Board Urged in March

By LOUIS STARK
Special to THE NEW YORK TIMES.

WASHINGTON, July 8—The White House announced today that an agreement had been reached in the long standing dispute between the class one railroads and the unions of engineers, firemen and switchmen.

The unions accepted a wage increase of 15½ cents an hour and some rule changes that will mean additional pay.

Charles G. Ross, the President's press secretary, told reporters that the carriers, which have been under Government control, would be turned back to their legal owners as soon as the necessary papers were drafted. That will probably be in a day or two.

The basis for the settlement was a compromise proposal made to the parties last night by Dr. John R. Steelman, assistant to the President. They advised him of their acceptance at 5 P. M. today and signed a preliminary memorandum on agreement half an hour later. Soon afterward the two committees were escorted to President Truman's office.

Truman Lauds Negotiators

"I want to congratulate you gentlemen on this settlement," Mr. Truman said. "It is great for our country. I wanted to see this thing settled as it should be done, by bargaining and not in any other way. You did this on your own hook, and I feel very good about it. I congratulate all of you on it.

"I am satisfied that you would like to have this publicly known as a settlement on your own hook, and I am going to ask you gentlemen to go out of here and tell the press exactly what happened and what the agreement is. Again I want to congratulate you."

Neither Daniel P. Loomis of the railroad committee nor Alvanley Johnston of the union group was able to estimate the difference in dollars and cents between the settlement and the one recommended by the President's emergency board, which the unions had rejected.

It was stated unofficially that there was little difference, however. The unions accepted the 15½-cent-an-hour increase, which the board, headed by Dr. W. M. Leiserson, had recommended. They also accepted most of the rule changes the board proposed, but they "swapped" one of these proposals for another suggested by Dr. Steelman. The unions agreed to waive the minimum guarantee rule proposed by the board and accepted instead a rule governing payment for initial terminal delay.

Pay Rise Retroactive to Nov. 1

The wage rise agreed on is retroactive to Nov. 1, 1947, as proposed by the emergency board. Other increases involved are effective as of Jan 1. Under the settlement, the switchmen were granted an additional 15 cents on their daily rate.

The Leiserson recommendations, it was estimated last March, would mean an addition to railroad pay of about $80,000,000 annually. The new agreement may run slightly above that figure, but how much could not be ascertained at once.

Dr. Steelman's proposal for settlement contained eight points. The final one stated that if the two sides failed to work out their agreement in written form in the next few days, any remaining unsettled issues would be referred to him as arbiter.

The final stages of the negotiations were completed by a committee which, for the carriers, was headed by Mr. Loomis and included H. A. Enochs and C. D. Mackey. The unions were represented by Mr. Johnston for the

engineers, D. B. Robertson for the firemen and A. J. Glover for the switchmen.

Although the settlement was not "nailed down" in a formal contract, the President, according to Mr. Ross, indicated to the two committees that he would lose no time in setting in motion the machinery to return the railroads to private management.

"I know you gentlemen and your word is good enough for me," the President said when they advised him of their agreement.

Mr. Steelman, who spent more than 300 hours with the two committees, appeared tired, but said that he was happy the dispute was settled.

The emergency board's report was made to the President on

March 27. It completed the unions' "second round" of wage increases but during the current meetings they asked for an additional 16 cents an hour. This request they justified on the ground of the long delay in settling the dispute which began last year.

The settlement today, however, made no concession in that direction, and the unions will seek a new wage rise as a "third round" inasmuch as the trainmen and conductors have served such demands.

The fact that the unions had originally asked for a 30 per cent increase (the 15½ cents an hour represented a rise of slightly more than 11 per cent) was not entirely lost sight of in the agreement.

The operators permitted the original demand to stand on the

books, making it unnecessary for the unions to serve new notice for the "third round." This concession gave the engineers, firemen and switchmen equal advantage with the trainmen and conductors in efforts to obtain another increase.

The railroads have been in the hands of Secretary of the Army Kenneth C. Royall since May 10 when the President seized the roads to halt a strike. An injunction order, signed by Associate Justice T. Alan Goldsborough, was issued to avert the walkout set for 6 P. M. May 11. On July 1, the Court turned the temporary injunction into a permanent writ against the unions.

The settlement affects 125,000 employes.

July 9, 1948

PACIFIC COAST DOCK STRIKE SETTLED; ATLANTIC MEN EXPECTED TO RATIFY TERMS OF AGREEMENT HERE TOMORROW

NEW ERA FORESEEN

Longshoremen of West and Owners Lay Pact to 'Complete Good Faith'

3-YEAR CONTRACT IS SET

Pay Rise of 15c an Hour Given —Other Striking Unions Continue Negotiations

Special to THE NEW YORK TIMES.
SAN FRANCISCO, Nov. 25— The CIO longshoremen and the Waterfront Employers Association have come to terms.

Announcement of the settlement was made through a joint statement tonight in the eighty-fifth day of the Pacific Coast waterfront strike.

The settlement depends, however, on ratification by the membership of both the International Longshoremen's and Warehousemen's Union and the WEA. It does not mean a full end to the tie-up, as negotiations are still in progress between the Pacific American Steamship Association and other maritime unions.

The Pacific association has booked a meeting tomorrow with the CIO Marine Cooks and Stewards.

The P.A.S.A. still must settle with the Marine Cooks, the Independent Marine Firemen and the CIO radio operators. Several obstructions to negotiations have been cleared, however. It was expected that full-dress negotiations would be in full operation by the first of next week.

Among terms of the longshore settlement are a non-retroactive wage increase of 15 cents an hour and a three-year contract lasting to 1951.

"Negotiating committees for I.L.W.U. and the W.E.A. agreed today to settlement terms which they will recommend to their respective memberships," the joint statement declared.

Look to a Long-Range Peace

Terming the new pact "one based on complete good faith," union and employer spokesmen joined in the prediction: "This contract and this new spirit can mean a new era for West Coast shipping."

Operations under the long-range peace plan, the three-year contract to 1951, CIO contract underwriting, improved grievance machinery, plus the new spirit of friendly cooperation which pervaded all meetings, formed the basis for the joint predictions of waterfront peace in the years ahead.

The longshore agreement is conditioned only on ratification by the memberships.

Even if no hitches developed, the most optimistic predictions were that it would be about a week before the unloading and loading of ships could be resumed.

Agreement came at 6:15 P. M. today, and was the result of compromise on both sides in the fifteen days of negotiations and subcommittee sessions since Nov. 11.

The 15-cent wage increase, effective upon the resumption of work, and increased vacation benefits topped the list of economic issues settled in the new pact.

New vacation rules provide for one week for men working 800 hours in the previous year, and two weeks for those with 1,344 hours to their credit.

Previous requirements of one or two years of service in the industry were dropped.

Overtime Arrangement Made

A designated day off each week

and the nine-hour maximum shift, agreed to in principle before the strike, were written into the new contract. Another hours provision, providing for an 8 A. M. starting time, was part of the new contract.

Two major points which consumed weeks of meetings before the strike were resolved in the back-to-work agreement. The complicated statutory overtime set-up (overtime-on-overtime) was solved by agreeing to an alternative provision in the wage-hour law.

Longshoremen will work not more than 1,000 hours in any consecutive twenty-six weeks, or more than twelve hours a day, or fifty-six hours a week, thus avoiding a pyramiding of overtime a recent Supreme Court decision, and avoiding limitation on work opportunity.

The highly controversial hiring-hall problem was resolved by both sides agreeing to continuation of present practices unless a court decision or Congressional action makes them illegal. In that event, the contract gives the parties 120 days to agree upon a change.

The major accomplishment was the promise of long-term stability in waterfront labor relations, offered by these items:

1. Agreement to operate under the long-range peace plan.
2. National CIO underwriting of contracts.
3. Improved grievance machinery, including express language ruling out work stoppages.
4. The three-year contract to June, 1951.

Bridges and Employers Sign

The biggest contribution to long-range peace, both sides agreed, was the new spirit of good faith and friendly cooperation which has run through all negotiation meetings.

This new factor was stressed in the joint statement subscribed to by I. L. W. U. head, Harry Bridges; Dwight C. Steele, W. E. A. negotiator and president of the Hawaii Employers Council; R. J. Thomas, national CIO representative, and Colonel John Kilpatrick, W. E. A.'s negotiating chairman.

Their statement read:

"We have come to an agreement which we believe to be fair to all. It meets the economic needs and several problems of both sides and was reached in a true spirit of compromise.

"The agreement is based on complete good faith, and the union and employers are pledged to continue that spirit into the future. In our opinion this contract and this new spirit can mean a new era for West Coast shipping, with more cargoes and more jobs for all of our ports."

Grievance Set-Up Changed

The all-important grievance machinery was improved to reduce the possibility of work stoppages.

Area arbitrators, in addition to the coast arbitrator, are created by the new contract for each major port area. The new area men will have assigned to them exclusively several fields of dispute, and there will be no appeal from their decisions on such items.

Increased speed and effectiveness in handling is expected from this arrangement. Other improvements are designed to end disputes at the job level, avoiding the friction and formality of committees.

Other important features of the new contract are:

1. Business agents will notify employers before going on ships and wharves.
2. Non-members of W. E. A. will have to pay proportionately for use of the jointly maintained longshore hiring halls.
3. A minimum of four hours of work will be provided when reporting for a job.
4. Clarification of "skill rates" of pay and load limits.

The longshore contract will be submitted, by yes or no ballot, to longshore locals at all coast ports. Steamship operators will vote upon it at a direct meeting.

The strike, the second longest in local maritime history, has cost the city, directly and indirectly, an aggregate of $4,000,000 a day, operators estimate.

About 265 ships, including about seventy in San Francisco, are presently tied up by the strike.

November 26, 1948

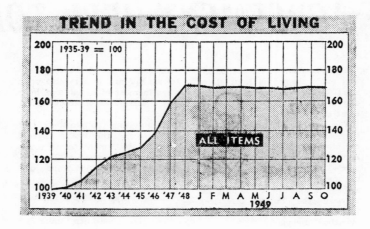

December 4, 1949

FOUNDRY—The gate to the plant where Henry Mikula (second from right) works: "Ever since the gate went up in 1942, Amity Street has pretty much lived up to its name."

'Not Today's Wage, Tomorrow's Security'

The steelworker, who has come a long way, believes it is time for another advance.

By DAVID DEMPSEY

HOMESTEAD, Pa.

THE main entrance to the enormous Carnegie-Illinois steel works in Homestead is at Amity Street, and Henry J. Mikula is one of 14,000 workers for whom, in a city freighted with a

DAVID DEMPSEY is a free lance who has written for The Times Magazine on many subjects. He spent a week in the Pennsylvania steel town of Homestead gathering facts for this article.

legacy of strife and bloodshed, it symbolizes a new era in peaceful labor relations. Ever since the gate went up in 1942, when the plant was expanded for war production, Amity Street has pretty much lived up to its name. Except for a three-week strike in 1946, steel and labor have worked in harmony: the open hearths, slabbing mills, structural works and the big blast furnaces across the river in

Pittsburgh have operated without interruption and at record capacity.

A few weeks ago labor called the second industry-wide strike in the history of steel. Narrowly averted at the last minute, the dispute is now in the hands of a three-man fact-finding board which will report its conclusions and recommendations to President Truman. If management or labor fails to go along, the gate at Amity Street will be closed.

Henry Mikula doesn't want to see this .appen. To him—to most of the 940,000 steelworkers across the nation—a strike means a belt-tightening that would be costly and unpleasant. Yet the belt has been tightened before, Henry says; as a union man, he believes that labor has gained in the end. His attitude is especially significant in view of the fact that the present dispute is not primarily over wages—which are reasonably good for a non-craft industry—but the less immediate factors of better pensions, more sick benefits, and other aspects of social security.

To find out just how pressing this issue is, I spent several days with Henry Mikula and his shop buddies at the Homestead plant. For, as a worker who is in most aspects typical of the men who make up this largest of CIO unions, Henry is the keystone in the Amity Street arch. What kind of person is he, how does he feel about his job, why is he willing to strike if necessary for a cause that will chiefly benefit men thirty years his senior? These are simple questions, but in a complex situation such as this they do not admit of simple answers.

On the plantward side of the big Amity Street gate is emblazoned the slogan: "Steel Is Permanent." Henry sees this sign on his way home and he says it reminds him—at a time of day when he is all too conscious of the irony—that although steel is permanent, men are not. And this is the crux of Henry's dispute with the company. If he goes on strike, it will not be out of hunger or desperation, but for the new principle of welfare that has been added to labor's arsenal of demands, now that the basic wage-hours fight has been largely won.

To know Henry—to understand even the most ordinary facts about his life—you have to visualize Homestead, which might fittingly be called Steeltown, U. S. A. Although its sprawling mills gushing clouds of smoke that settle over the city in a hazy smog, make up but a fraction of the plants that stretch for twenty-two miles along this industrial river valley, they dominate life in Homestead. Visible from almost every point in the city, which leans its way up the steep bluffs of the Monongahela River, they are the only major industries here, and nearly all of the wage earners work in them.

Henry has been employed in the Carnegie-Illinois plant—a subsidiary of United States Steel—for twenty of his thirty-six years. Most of his fellow-workers also started at 16, although the minimum age is now 18. Most of them will work until they are 65, the compulsory retirement age. Most of them—like Henry—have fathers who worked in the mills and the great majority have children who are already helping to "cook" steel, or soon will be. Henry's stepfather, for example, is still a millhand; his oldest son, Jack, 14, will "probably" follow in the tradition. In Homestead, people talk, think, make,

WORKER

A tractor operator, Henry averages about $56

a week in take-home pay.

and "breathe" steel. Steel is the hard, pervasive fact of their existence, the image of their future, and the substance of their memories.

MEMORIES here are long, and go back fifty-seven years to the great Homestead steel strike of 1892. To this city's steelworkers and their families, the

"strike" is symbolically as important as is the Easter Week rebellion to an Irishman. Oldtimers vividly recall the pitched battle between "Pinkertons" and workers. A plaque on one of Homestead's main streets commemorates the seven union men who were killed. The incident is still good timber with which to fire up a mass meeting or a memorial service.

Henry was born here in Homestead, and thus grew up in

the strongly labor-conscious tradition of its people. Not only his immediate family but his five brothers-in-law are employed in the mill. It would be strange if he were not biased in favor of the wage-earner. Yet, in a significant sense, Henry Mikula's bias is not born out of a feeling of exploitation or a sense of hopeless injustice. When his stepfather went on strike in 1919 it was in an effort to organize.

TODAY, after fifteen years of legally protected unionism and a company policy of harmonious labor relations, Henry is motivated by different reasons. It is security that has become the touchstone of Henry's world.

Nothing symbolizes so strikingly the gap between two generations of workers than this preoccupation with the intangible, or "fringe," benefits of the job. Until recent years most union demands centered on a fuller lunch pail. Today they are being extended to include the concept of a fuller life. To put it another way, in a phrase peculiar to steel, emphasis has been shifted from the hearth to the hearthside.

And as a result of this evolution in tactics, Henry now finds himself a sort of industrial guinea pig. No longer merely employe No. 45,118, a tractor operator in a slabbing mill, he is the subject of university research projects, Government surveys, newspaper interviews, fact-finding boards and a bewildering amount of solicitude on the part of both management and union.

And no longer is he an industrial Caliban, bumping his head against the lintel of an outdated system. Two wars, a New Deal and a Fair Deal have indoctrinated him with a new sense of importance in society. And thanks to a never-ending flow of union literature, he has grown amazingly articulate. Curious phrases like "unilateral action" have crept into his vocabulary. Statistics on the cost of living, company profits and wages are at hand to buttress his arguments.

EVEN the end product of Henry's labor has become more meaningful to him. During the war much of his time went into the production of armor plate and other necessary implements of battle. Right now the plant where Henry works is turning out steel for the United Nations headquarters in New York. The significance of this is not lost on him. He has bridged the barriers of his own small world to help build the physical core of a new one. All of this has given him, as an industrial worker, a new dimension largely unthinkable a generation ago.

Having learned to make new demands on the industrial system, Henry nevertheless no longer thinks of a strike as the only way of getting them. "We were relieved when the truce went in," he says. "Striking is no fun, especially when it's for something you won't get the main benefit from until you're an old man. We'd like a raise, of course, but this pension thing is more important. As long as the cost of living kept going up, pensions had to wait. Now seems like a good time to get started on them. We hope the whole thing can be settled without a showdown."

If Henry does go out, the placard that he will carry as a publicity weapon will be secondary to the heavy artillery which union brass have already moved into defiladed areas well to the rear of the company gates—the bulky reports on company earnings and workers' needs that have been prepared for them by private research organizations.

ALTHOUGH Henry and his buddies will be on the picket line, if necessary, they know that the real fighting will take place in Washington or New York, around the committee table, in the newspapers, and on the radio. That the statesmen of the nation, including the President, should make a special effort to solve their problems is something relatively new to the workers in this industry, where violence and bitterness were the order in years gone by. It is one more factor that has convinced Henry he counts for something in America.

Although Henry Mikula is a composite of all the steelworkers in this mill town—a symbol of the industrial wage-earner of 1949—he is also an individual, with a wife and three boys, and this, too, bears on the present period of tension. In what way?

First of all, Henry earns a wage that no one would call excessive—$1.45 an hour, or about $255 a month. From this, about $8 is deducted for taxes, group insurance and union dues, leaving him a net of $247, or roughly $56 a week. Henry's pay is less than the industry average of $1.69 an hour, but it is substantially higher than the Government's enforced minimum of $1.23 for steel mills holding United States contracts, and it compares favorably with the national average for all industrial wage-earners of approximately $1.31.

BY meticulous budgeting, making many of the children's clothes, keeping a garden, and "making out the grocery order with a pruning knife," the Mikulas have been able to get by and still have a little left for an occasional trip to the movies or a ball game. But there is nothing for savings and the war bonds which Henry bought regularly during the flush period when the mill worked overtime have long since been cashed in. Recently Henry bought a new furnace, and incurred a dental bill of $165. Both of these debts are being paid off in installments.

What might seem like a small miracle to the hard-pressed city worker—living on $55 a week—is explained in part by the fact that the Mikulas own their home, a four-room bungalow purchased eleven years ago, which is now entirely paid for.

FAMILY HEAD—With his family at supper. Henry's wages leave little for "extras."

Taxes run $175 a year, fuel about $125. Maintenance is nil, since Henry does all his own repairs. Furnishings include a 13-year-old washing machine, and the house is surrounded by a good-sized yard in which the Mikulas have planted shrubs, hybrid roses and a blue spruce tree. Aside from the house, their only other major possession is a 1935 car, which Henry bought last year for $50.

AS a home owner, Henry is no exception among workers here. Management long ago divested itself of company-owned houses and stores, and union officials estimate that half of the steel-mill employes with families own the homes they live in. Homestead is largely free of tenements, and the city's worst slums were razed during the war to make room for a new plant.

Replacing them is a low-cost housing development in which a family can rent a four-room apartment, complete with heat and utilities. for $35 a month. And despite the smoke, Homestead is surprisingly clean, bearing little resemblance to the mining towns close by. Nor does the district appear to be company dominated. In one borough the Burgess (Mayor) and ten out of sixteen public officials—all holding part-time offices—are steelworkers.

Two years ago Henry Mikula ran for the council in his own borough and was defeated by less than 200 votes. This year he's running again, and thinks he has a good chance of being elected. A Democrat (registration is about three to one Democratic in this area), he supports President Truman's Fair Deal. As a second generation American, he has no particular feeling of inferiority and casts no longing glances at the "new democracies," which do not seem to have improved the "old order" that his parents left when they emigrated to this country. Henry is a Roman Catholic and the head trustee of his local church. In the union he is assistant grievance chairman of his shop.

BUT the most important thing about Henry Mikula is the conviction that what is to him a fairly decent way of life can be made even better.

He has seen it happen with the older generation. Moreover, things have improved a lot in his own lifetime. When he went to work in the mill twenty years ago he made $2.28 a day operating the door

HOME OWNER—Henry, father-in-law and son, Jack, on the porch of the Mikulas' bungalow.

on an open-hearth furnace. Since then the plant's increased productivity, the general rise in industrial wages and the union's astute bargaining tactics have brought him a long way. It is a measure of his progress– not his poverty—that he wants to go further.

Which brings him once more to the issue of security. In some respects, Henry gets what he calls "a pretty good deal." If he should be killed, or die from any cause whatsoever while in the company's employ, his family would receive $4,000 from a group insurance policy that costs him $1.93 a month. In the event of illness, he and his family are covered by a company medical plan that takes care of hospital costs and pays sick benefits of $15 a week up to thirteen weeks. Henry's share of the cost of this plan is $2.81 a month. In addition, he carries $1,000 worth of life insurance on himself, $1,000 on his wife, and $1,250 on each child. His premiums, including hospitalization and his group insurance, total $203.32 a year, or not quite one-fourteenth of his earnings. Henry works about

three and a half weeks a year to pay for his "security."

The union is asking that a greater proportion of this insurance burden be shifted onto the company, and Henry makes no bones about the fact that such a plan would ease the economic squeeze for him.

Men earning the industry average of $68 a week, and the more highly paid $80-$90 a week employes, he says, can absorb these payments with less hardship. For the lower-bracket workers, both the high cost of "security" and its apparent inadequacy loom large. In this sense, Henry is a typical paradox among the industrial wage-earners: the man who needs security the most, yet who can least afford to provide for it.

ALTHOUGH it will be another twenty-nine years before he retires, the problem of "what to live on" is brought home by the fact that his father-in-law, who retired last year after forty-seven years in the plant, receives a combined pension-social security income of slightly less than $100 a

month. And this is considerably above the average.

"We're asking for $150 a month, although I suppose we'll take less if we have to," Henry says. "What really burns us up, though, is that the company subtracts the amount of the Federal social security benefits from the pension they pay. Instead of getting social security plus the pension, the men only get the amount of the pension, with social security figured in as part of it."

This is not the case with some steel companies, but it is true in the plant where Henry works and remains a rankling grievance which the union has effectively exploited. And since an ever greater proportion of steel's labor force is approaching the retirement age, the men are becoming pension conscious.

A union study of 722 pensioners, who averaged thirty-four and a half years of service, forms the basis for indoctrinating the rank and file with the "facts" in the current dispute. According to this survey, the average monthly pension for the group studied is

UNION MAN

Over lunch pails, Henry and some associates talk organization policies.

spokesman said, "is proof that our men are pretty well satisfied. Our company was the first to recognize the union and when Andrew Carnegie was still living it was the first to institute pensions. We anticipated a lot of social security years before the Government or most industries got around to it."

HENRY agrees that his personal relations with management always were cordial. He had no trouble getting transferred from his old job at a blast furnace to his present job when he requested it two years ago. Safety conditions are good and the company has been fair in settling grievances, he says, but when it comes to boosting wages, pensions, and other security benefits—the total "package" comes to thirty cents an hour per man—management declares that existing prices will not support the rise.

"Our salesmen are fighting for every order they get," an industrial relations representative told me. "Steel is not a sellers' market. Our present cost structure won't stand a thirty - cents - an - hour hike without a substantial rise in price of the finished product and we don't think this is the time to raise prices."

IT is along this front that the battle lines are drawn. "When a man gives forty or fifty years of his life to a job," Henry says, "he should be able to retire in comfort—a little comfort, anyway." Thirty years ago, in Homestead at least, this attitude would have been considered an impertinence by many. Today, to a generation of workers that has grown up in the midst of an increasing drive toward the "welfare state," Henry's point of view strikes him as anything but revolutionary.

He has, moreover, seen the company give way on three previous demands for higher wages — demands on which both union and management made concessions to avoid a strike—and he hopes for a similar solution this time.

But if it's fumbled, Amity Street will become enmity street; the big gate will be a barrier rather than a bridge, and Henry Mikula will be on the picket line. "It may be tough going," he says, "but if it will help these old guys get a better break, it'll be worth it. After all, I'm going to be in their shoes myself some day."

$6 which is paid by the company, and $31.83 under social security, or a total of $37.83.

A random check made by this writer of a much smaller —and perhaps not so representative — cross-section uncovered a high of $60.90 paid by the company, and a low of 62 cents, with the average amounting to $28.34. Social security benefits, which were in addition to company pensions, ranged from $40 a month down to $31.64, and averaged $36.05. About half of those interviewed had taken outside jobs in laundries, parks, etc., and earned another $3 to $6 a day. Thirty-eight out of fifty-six employes of

the borough of near-by North Braddock, the union says, are retired steelworkers who must supplement their pensions with outside income.

REGARDLESS of the sum now paid, Henry believes, it is not enough to dispel the fear of insecurity. And when union economists argue that the company can afford pensions of $125 a month, a pay rise and other fringe benefits at a rise in labor costs of 11 cents an hour per man, the plan seems feasible to him. Admittedly he is prejudiced in favor of the union's surveys. "But then, they haven't gone off half cocked on this thing," he says. "We're not asking for the impossible."

Management disagrees, and it is worth pointing out that the company regards Henry as a valued employe whose welfare is a matter of concern, since stability of employment —with consequent economy in labor costs—is a significant achievement in the steel industry.

"The fact that we have such a high proportion of men who stay here long enough to earn pensions," a company

BETHLEHEM SIGNS WITH UNION FOR PENSIONS, WELFARE PLAN; U. S. STEEL SEEKS NEW TALKS

FIRST STRIKE BREAK

Retirement at Minimum of $100 a Month at 65 Given After 25 Years

INSURANCE SHARED 50-50

Company and Worker Each to Pay 2½c an Hour—Return to Eleven Plants Begins

By LOUIS STARK
Special to THE NEW YORK TIMES.

CLEVELAND, Oct. 31—Philip Murray, president of the United Steelworkers of America, tonight announced an agreement with the Bethlehem Steel Corporation that provided noncontributory pensions of a minimum of $100 a month for employes reaching age 65 and having twenty-five years of service.

The pensions, which are to include amounts payable under Social Security, will be adjusted downward for employes reaching 65 but with a shorter service record.

The company and the employes will share equally in maintaining a social insurance program, each paying 2½ cents an hour. This supplants the present welfare plan, financed wholly by the workers.

The signing of the Bethlehem agreement was the first break in the month-old steel strike, in which 500,000 members of the Murray union took part and which has made many thousands of other workers idle.

Telegrams went out at once to all Bethlehem Steel locals to end at midnight tonight the strike of 77,000 workers in this, the country's second largest steel company.

Several Days Are Needed

At Bethlehem's eleven plants the men were being called in at once to start up the furnaces. A union spokesman said it would take two or three days before the mills would be going full blast.

PEACE COMES TO ONE STEEL COMPANY

Joseph Larkin (left), vice president of Bethlehem Steel, and Philip Murray, United Steelworkers head, signing agreement in Cleveland last night.

Associated Press Wirephoto

Company representatives, however, said a week or more would be needed before finished steel could be turned out again.

The Bethlehem plants are at Lackawanna, N. Y.; Bethlehem, Johnstown, Steelton, Lebanon, Williamsport and Pottstown, Pa.; Sparrows Point, Md.; Los Angeles, San Francisco and Seattle.

Confidence was expressed by Mr. Murray that this break in the solid ranks of the steel industry, where precedents have usually been set by the giant United States Steel Corporation, would be followed by an even more liberal pension agreement by the latter.

The union president, who is also head of the Congress of Industrial Organizations, emphasized at a large press conference in a hotel ballroom this evening that the Bethlehem agreement had been reached by voluntary collective bargaining and without benefit of Government. He hailed this pension plan as the most outstanding achievement of its kind attained by any union through collective bargaining in this or any other country.

The contract signed today by Mr. Murray and Joseph Larkin, vice president of Bethlehem, appeared to be more liberal than the proposal made by the President's fact-finding panel.

Old Pension Plan Liberalized

While the board recommended a noncontributory pension plan of 6 cents an hour and a social security arrangement of 4 cents an hour, the Bethlehem agreement, according to Mr. Murray, means that the company will pay for pensions alone close to 12 cents an hour. Part of this, however, is offset by the union's agreement to share equally the 5 cents an hour for social insurance.

Mr. Larkin, who has been negotiating the pension plan with the union for several weeks, walked into the Hotel Statler ballroom arm in arm with Mr. Murray a little before 8 o'clock this evening. They had just signed the agreement. The faces of both men were flushed. There had been a delay of two and a half hours in the announcement while reporters kept wires open to flash their offices.

Mr. Larkin read a brief announcement and then left the room, after which Mr. Murray explained the new contract.

The company statement was that the company's twenty-six-year-old noncontributory pension plan would be continued "with amendments" and that the agreement provided a "contributory social insurance program" for death, sickness and accident and hospitalization benefits.

The Larkin statement was that the principal amendment to the pension plan, which would be submitted to the stockholders for approval, would provide that the present minimum pension of $50 a month would be increased to $100 a month for pension granted to employes with twenty-five years or more of service at age 65 or over.

Pensions payable under the plan are reduced by amounts payable under Federal Social Security, the corporation statement added. The agreement runs to Dec. 31, 1951, with a reopening on wage rates provided after Dec. 31, 1950.

The deferment of the next wage reopening until the end of next year meant that the union, which renounced its demand for a fourth-round wage increase in compliance with the recommendations of the President's fact-finding board, would also forego any demand for a fifth-round pay rise during 1950.

Mr. Murray stressed that the $100 pension for employes at the age of 65 after twenty-five years of service was the minimum.

"There is no maximum set," he said. "The $100 pension begins for the lowest hourly rated employe, and for the higher rated employes the pension goes up to $250 or more."

The social insurance plan will end the company's present welfare plan, which the employes have paid for entirely. It amounted to 3 cents for each hour worked.

Union Position "Vindicated"

"I regard this new contract with Bethlehem Steel as a vindication of the union's position that there is a social responsibility in industry to take care of the aged and their families," said Mr. Murray. "I sincerely hope this will bring about a settlement with the rest of the steel industry."

Mr. Murray told the press conference that this was the first time in the long history of steel wage labor negotiations that any company other than United States Steel Corporation had set the pattern for a settlement.

The "break" in the thirty-one-day strike, which had begun to close mills, factories and curtail railroad and manufacturing operations all over the country, came at the end of protracted negotiations.

Mr. Murray and Arthur J. Goldberg, general counsel of the CIO, resumed conferences with Mr. Larkin in New York a week ago yesterday.

Mr. Murray went to New York last Thursday, and he and his counsel again conferred with the Bethlehem vice president in charge of industrial relations. When it seemed that an agreement was possible on Saturday, the union called in Murray Latimer, its pension expert. But Mr. Murray's presence was required here at the CIO convention, which opened to-

day. Therefore, he called the negotiating group to Cleveland, and yesterday the details of the agreement were explained to the union negotiating committee. The committee approved the terms and authorized Mr. Murray and David McDonald, secretary-treasurer of the union, to sign the document.

The delay this evening in making the announcement was "due to the lawyers and their language," Mr. Murray remarked with a smile.

The board of directors of the Bethlehem Steel Corporation met in New York to pass on the agreement.

When the company statement was made by Mr. Larkin there was a wild scramble for the copies. Mr. Larkin was flabbergasted as reporters grabbed them from his hands.

Mr. Murray then took over. He said that for employes with fifteen years of service a minimum pension of $65 would be paid at the age of 65; the minimum would be $80 for employes with twenty years of service.

The plan will be supervised by a joint pension committee of ten, divided equally between the union

and management.

The meetings of the committee will be held once or twice a year.

The agreement contemplates that the pension plan may go into effect on Jan. 1, next. Mr. Murray explained that there were some technicalities which would have to be straightened out first, but that in any event the pensions would begin to be paid not later than March 1, 1950.

The social insurance phase of the agreement will definitely go into effect on the first of the year.

When the pension plan becomes effective some 1,500 elderly former workers, who now get an average of $12 weekly under the present plan, will receive pensions of $100 monthly, according to the union leader.

It was estimated that about 5,000 Bethlehem workers in all would benefit from the pension plan as soon as it became effective.

The new agreement provides a minimum of $2,100 life insurance which will run as high as $4,500, with an average of $3,000.

This life insurance provision alone, said Mr. Murray, was the

largest life insurance agreement of this type ever negotiated in the history of collective bargaining in the United States. It offers benefits larger than any other similar plan, he added.

Other provisions are:

An average paid-up life insurance policy of $1,250 to $1,500 at retirement; $26 a week for sickness for twenty-six weeks; a Blue Cross contract or its equivalent for employes, wives and dependent children up to 19 years of age, with hospitalization up to seventy days.

"This is the first national Blue Cross plan covering workers from California to the Atlantic which has ever been negotiated by a labor union," Mr. Murray told reporters.

"Now, gentlemen, if you will excuse me, I will go to a steel strike meeting, for you know there is still a strike on against other companies," said the union chief, smilingly. James G. Thimmes, vice president of the union, took his arm and they hurried to a waiting cab which speeded them to a rank-and-file strike meeting.

November 1, 1949

THE COAL WAR: 'GEN.' LEWIS' STRATEGY

In Five Engagements
The Miners' Leader
Has Made No Gain

By A. H. RASKIN

No man in American history has been more successful in pushing the nation's blood pressure up and its steam pressure down than John L. Lewis. Undisputed ruler of the economic destinies of half a million coal miners in the bituminous and anthracite fields, his power rests on a record of almost legendary accomplishment in the quest for higher wages, a shorter work-week, pension and welfare benefits and other improvements in the lot of his members.

This year Mr. Lewis' interruptions of the coal supply have won him his usual harvest of public denunciation, but nothing in the way of gains for his members. Isolated from the rest of the labor movement and with no friends left in high public office, Mr. Lewis has functioned as his own board of strategy. Here are the situations he has been up against in his current battle with the operators; the way he has deployed his faithful army of coal diggers to meet each situation and what has come of each Lewis maneuver.

I. THREE-DAY WEEK

THE SITUATION: Thirty years of bargaining with the operators have convinced Mr. Lewis that his strongest weapon in raising wages and working conditions is a brisk demand for coal. When consumption is low and stockpiles high, the operators have little to fear in the way of lost profits if a strike occurs. In the early months of this year, the slump in industrial activity and the mild winter combined to knock the props from under the coal market. Prices started skidding and many mines cut their work schedules to two or three days a week. If Mr. Lewis was to exert any leverage in contract negotiations, he had to reduce the supply of coal.

THE PLAY: The first Lewis move was to order a two-week "memorial" stoppage in March. He described the "suspension of mining" as a token of the union's opposition to appointment of Dr. James Boyd as director of the Federal Bureau of Mines. The Sen-

ate, which had stalled on Dr. Boyd's confirmation for two years, promptly paid its respects to Mr. Lewis by voting overwhelmingly to confirm Dr. Boyd. In June, two weeks before the miners' old contract was scheduled to expire, Mr. Lewis ordered a one-week work stoppage. This time he described it frankly is a "stabilizing period of inaction" intended to prevent coal from glutting the market. When the contract ran out June 30, Mr. Lewis chose to ignore his historic "no contract, no work" rule. Instead, he instructed the miners to work three days a week during negotiations for a new contract.

THE RESULT: No gain for the Lewis team. The two work stoppages failed to make any sizable dent in the huge coal piles held by steel mills, utilities, railroads and other big users. The three-day week proved sufficient to satisfy the full demand in the slack summer months and few consumers had to reduce their reserve stocks. When the miners went on a full-fledged strike, there was enough coal above ground to meet the

country's requirements for at least two months.

II. APPEAL FOR ALLIES

THE SITUATION: With the operators under little economic pressure to settle with the union, Mr. Lewis needed friends outside his own ranks. As founder and first president of the Congress of Industrial Organizations, he had once been the symbol of labor's forward march in the mass-production industries. Now he had no supporters in the CIO, except in its Communist fringe, and their support would be a kiss of death in the eyes of the public. That left the American Federation of Labor as Mr. Lewis' one hope for a tie that would bring him back into the mainstream of American labor. The United Mine Workers president was no stranger to the AFL. He had been in and out twice before. By resuming a position of influence within its ranks, Mr. Lewis could not only count on its active help in his fight with the mine owners but could join forces with

209

it in fighting for repeal of the Taft-Hartley Act, which is the Government's most obvious weapon against a Lewis-ordered strike.

THE PLAY: Mr. Lewis had a private luncheon with William Green, AFL president, in Washington one bright May day. The AFL executive council was scheduled to meet a week later in Cleveland. Mr. Lewis asked Mr. Green to tell the council that the miners would come back into the federation if the AFL leaders would endorse Mr. Lewis' policy of boycotting the National Labor Relations Board under the Taft-Hartley Act. He maintained that the federation could make its most effective contribution toward wiping the law off the books by refusing to have anything to do with the NLRB or any other agency set up under the provisions of the Taft-Hartley Act.

THE RESULT: No gain for the Lewis team. The AFL executive council unanimously spurned the terms set by Mr. Lewis for reaffiliation. The federation leaders recalled that Mr. Lewis' last withdrawal from the AFL in December, 1947, had come over exactly the same issue. He had sought unsuccessfully to persuade the AFL convention in that year to instruct its officers not to sign non-Communist affidavits and had pulled out when the convention voted down his advice. The AFL executive council stood by the earlier decision, thus slamming the door in Mr. Lewis' face.

III. THE WALKOUT

THE SITUATION. Rebuffed in his search for outside allies, Mr. Lewis found little to encourage him on any front. The drive for Taft-Hartley repeal was put in cold storage by the Administration forces in Congress. The market for coal was sapped by the prospect of a strike in steel. The mine owners were standing fast against any contract that would involve a rise in labor costs. Mr. Lewis needed an issue that would appeal to his own members and the public at large as providing a valid basis for action against the operators.

THE PLAY: In mid-September Mr. Lewis sent a letter to James D. Francis, president of one of the largest of the Southern coal companies, denouncing him for failing to continue royalty payments to the United Mine Workers welfare fund and warning that the fund faced bankruptcy unless the payments were resumed. Mr. Lewis accused Mr. Francis and other defaulting operators of a "mad and vengeful attack" intended to bleed the fund white. Three days after

the first letter, Mr. Lewis, as chairman of the fund's trustees, announced that the fund was nearly broke and would have to suspend payments to aged and sick miners.

'GOOD OLD JOHN'

Morris in The Rochester Democrat

THE RESULT: Rallying around the slogan of "no welfare, no work," 480,000 miners throughout the country left the mines that week-end. They stayed out despite charges by the operators that Mr. Lewis' "profligate" spending, and not the withholding of royalty payments by "a small segment" of the industry, was the real cause for the exhaustion of the welfare fund. Mr. Lewis made the walkout official on Sept. 22 by declaring that the miners were on a "no-day work week" until the owners met the union's demands for a seven-hour work day, an increase in daily wages and a higher welfare royalty.

IV. WAR-CHEST MOVE

THE SITUATION: With the strike nearly four weeks old, the operators showed no sign of yielding to the union. They ruled out any rise in costs and asked revisions in the old contract to limit Mr. Lewis' authority over the welfare fund and to curb his freedom to halt coal production under the "able and willing" clause of the expired agreement. The UMW chieftain boasted that the miners could

whip the operators if the Government stayed out. The only kind of governmental intervention that appeared to Mr. Lewis was outright seizure of the mines, with the Government operating for its own account and signing a contract with the UMW. President Truman lost no time in letting it be known that he had no such plan in mind. Mr. Lewis still had to conjure up a rabbit in the form of outside help.

THE PLAY: On Oct. 14 Mr. Lewis proposed that nine AFL unions and his own UMW pour $2,500,000 a week into a war chest to win Mr. Murray's steel strike. He made his bid for labor unity through the medium of a letter to William Green, but he was careful to make his own contribution of $250,000 a week contingent on concurrence in the project by the major AFL groups. Mr. Lewis envisaged monumental benefits from adoption of the plan. In urging Mr. Green to make the steel strike the uncompromising fight of all American labor, Mr. Lewis assured the AFL president:

"If you will do so you will crown yourself with distinction."

THE RESULT: Mr. Green gave the boot to the proposal by informing Mr. Lewis that the pooling of labor's resources was "impossible and impracticable" until organic unity had been established. Mr. Lewis bowed out of the unity league with a charge that Mr. Green was following his "well-known policy of anxious inertia."

V. BACK TO WORK

THE SITUATION: The strike was seven and a half weeks old. Reports of restlessness began to circulate in the mine fields. With Thanksgiving and Christmas approaching, many miners were grumbling over their prolonged idleness. A few mines reopened on a non-union basis. The nation's railroads, with steam passenger service already cut 25 per cent, faced further cuts for lack of coal. Midwestern states rationed coal for household and hospital use. Industrial stockpiles were nearly exhausted. The Government scheduled a final mediation effort preliminary to invocation of the Taft-Hartley Law or establishment of a special fact-finding board with power to make recommendations for a settlement. Opposed to both forms of Federal intervention, Mr. Lewis sought vainly for a soft spot in the employer front. Illinois and Indiana operators turned down moves for separate peace talks. Key operators in other sections were equally resistant to Mr. Lewis' private approaches. The deadline for a Presidential crackdown appeared near.

THE PLAY: On Nov. 9 Mr. Lewis sent his miners back to work without a contract under a truce that was to prevail until midnight Nov. 30. He described the action as "an act of good faith designed to contribute to the public convenience" and "enhance the remote possibility" of an agreement with the operators. He castigated the owners as "arrogant and brutal" men with a "sordid and mercenary appetite" who had conspired to destroy the welfare fund through "deceitful stratagems" and who sought to conceal "enormous profits" wrung from the blood and backs of the miners. He advised public institutions and home owners to take advantage of the truce to refill their coal bins against the possibility of a renewal of the mine tie-up.

THE RESULT: It is too early to tell what Mr. Lewis has accomplished by his latest maneuver beyond assuring a three-week addition to the country's coal pile. President Truman has made it plain that he will employ the eighty-day injunction provisions of the Taft-Hartley Act against the UMW when and if he feels the country is confronted with an emergency. The operators have shown no eagerness to get back into negotiations with Mr. Lewis and he has shown an equal reluctance to accept their proposal for renewal of the main clauses of the old contract. The settlement of the steel strike and the consequent need for a dependable coal supply both in steel and steel-dependent industries adds urgency to the search for a peace formula in coal. But the knowledge that the President will eventually turn to Taft-Hartley diminishes the likelihood that the operators will hold out the olive branch to Mr. Lewis.

* * *

There is a wide disposition to believe that Mr. Lewis is at the end of his rope. With his seventieth birthday less than three months off and with his health shaken by a heart ailment, many observers are ready to count the UMW president out as a continuing force in American labor. But Mr. Lewis has been counted out before, only to rise stronger than ever. If Mr. Truman does get an injunction, it will merely defer the inevitable showdown between Mr. Lewis and the operators. It will not eliminate it. At the end of eighty days the union will be free to renew its strike without any avenue of further interference open to the Government. Mr. Lewis's "wink or nod" will still govern what the miners do. Win, lose or draw, he remains their champion and there is no sign that they are prepared to strip him of his title.

LEWIS AND OWNERS REACH COAL ACCORD AFTER TRUMAN ASKS SEIZURE POWERS; MEN WIN 70C A DAY MORE, WELFARE RISE

STRIKE END IN VIEW

Contract Signing Today Predicted With Miners Back in Pits Monday

ROYALTY TO RISE 10C A TON

8-Hour Shift Stands With Pay Increased to $14.75—'Able' Clause Is Abandoned

By LOUIS STARK
Special to The New York Times.

WASHINGTON, March 3—John L. Lewis, president of the United Mine Workers of America, and representatives of the Northern, Western and "captive" coal mine operators tonight agreed on a new contract to end their nine-month struggle.

Persons close to the contract parleys felt certain that the contract would be signed tomorrow and that the strike of 372,000 miners in the nation's soft coal fields would formally be called off by Mr. Lewis. This would mean that the miners would be back in the pits on Monday.

The agreement came only a few hours after President Truman had asked Congress for authority to seize the strike-shut mines. The terms of the new accord, which the Southern operators are expected to ratify soon, are:

1. A wage increase of 70 cents a day. Mr. Lewis had asked for 95 cents. The new basic rate will be $14.75 a day.

2. An increase of 10 cents a ton in operators' payments to the miners' welfare fund. Mr. Lewis had asked for 15 cents. The new total will be 30 cents a ton.

3. Continuance of the eight-hour day. Mr. Lewis had asked for a seven-hour day.

4. Elimination of the "able and willing" clause that permitted Mr. Lewis to call stoppages at will. Instead there is substituted the "good faith" clause of the anthracite agreement.

5. Limitation of "memorial periods" in mine disasters to five days in any one year. Longer stoppages have been called by the union under this clause.

6. Continuance of the agreement until July 1, 1952, with the provision that it may be reopened at the request of either party on thirty days' notice after April 1, 1951.

New Trustee Chosen

The operators abandoned their plan to have former Judge Charles I. Dawson of Kentucky as their trustee on the three-member board administering the welfare fund. They chose instead Harry M. Moses of the H. C. Frick Coke Company, a United States Steel Corporation subsidiary. Mr. Moses has been on friendly terms with Mr. Lewis for many years. His father and Mr. Lewis also were friends.

Thomas Kennedy, vice president of the United Mine Workers, will be the union spokesman on the board, replacing Mr. Lewis. Miss Josephine Roche, director of the welfare fund, becomes the neutral trustee. She is a former Colorado coal operator and has been a friend of Mr. Lewis and the union for many years.

The Taft-Hartley Act ban against granting the union shop unless the miners complied with the law's requirements was handled by referring this section to counsel.

Formal announcement of an agreement on "fundamental principles" was made tonight by David L. Cole, chairman of the Presidential fact-finding board, after reporting by telephone to the White House. His report covered the terms of the understanding that had been conveyed to him shortly before by Mr. Lewis, George H. Love, for the Western and Northern operators, and Harry M. Moses for the "captive" mine operators.

Details, mainly of a legal nature, will be worked out tomorrow, said Mr. Cole. He explained that the agreement had been made by the union with operators "producing a preponderance of the tonnage of the industry."

The Love-Moses group represents 350,000,000 tons annual production out of 500,000,000.

The meeting was held for the purpose of ascertaining the positions on both sides so that the board might report to the President. He chatted for a few minutes with Mr. Cole and Federal Mediation Director Cyrus S. Ching, and then withdrew.

The Moody group, which covers one-third of the nation's soft coal operations, indicated it was opposed to the welfare fund set-up. Specifically, its opposition was based on having Miss Roche as the neutral trustee.

The only question remaining open was how soon the Southern group would follow their Northern associates. The Dixie coal operators adjourned their sessions this evening for the night.

A joint drafting committee of union and Northern and "captive" mine spokesmen will work out details of the contract tomorrow. The formal signing is expected to take place shortly afterwards.

In asking Congress for power to seize and operate the mines temporarily, President Truman said the prolonged strike left him "no alternative."

Cabinet Meeting Is Tense

The Chief Executive sent the special message to the House of Representatives and to the Senate this afternoon after a tense Cabinet meeting. Accompanying the message was the President's draft of a seizure bill. It proposed that:

1. Two Presidential boards, one to fix wages, and the other to determine fair compensation to mine owners, be established.

2. The Government not be permitted to make a contract with the United Mine Workers on wages and working conditions, as has been the practice in previous seizures.

3. Properties be returned to employers when they and employes reach an agreement.

4. A Congressional commission of inquiry be set up to study the "sick [coal] industry."

Secret negotiations to speed a settlement of the dispute that has cut the nation's coal supply to the lowest in many years began shortly after the President decided to ask for seizure authority.

That the President would do so was virtually certain from the demeanor of the Government's observers at the wage conferences yesterday when they pressed the parties to speed an agreement.

In his message to Congress the President expressed hope that operators and miners would reach an agreement to end the nine-months controversy "before it actually becomes necessary for the Government to take possession of the mines."

Injunction Seen Nullified

The President's plan to ask Congress for seizure authority nullified the effects of an eighty-day injunction obtained by the Government today under the Taft-Hartley Act.

The national emergency section of the Labor Relations Law calls for the action Mr. Truman took today, but only after the conclusion of the eighty-day period. However, the President, noting that the strike still was going on, said: "We can wait no longer."

Mr. Truman's action was regarded as the second victory in two days for Mr. Lewis. Yesterday Federal Judge Richmond B. Keech ruled that the union had not been proved guilty of civil or criminal contempt of his back-to-work order of Feb. 11.

Today the President did what the miners had been hoping he would do for some time—ask for seizure powers. This gave Mr. Lewis a new and stronger handle in collective bargaining negotiations.

Operators Irate Over Proposal

Coal operators, irate on learning the terms of the President's proposal, charged that it went far beyond the needs of the occasion. Noting that the President had asked not only for authority to take over the mines, the operators said he had included also control of "real or personal property, franchise, right, fund or other asset * * * pertaining to or used in connection with the operation of any or all such plants, mines * * *".

The operators also held that the President's request for power over wages was "too sweeping."

The President's emergency powers would end June 30, 1951. The operators maintained that Mr. Lewis could compel Government retention of the properties until then unless the operators met the terms fixed by the President's recommended commission on wages. This "gimmick" they asserted, nullified the section that barred the President from making a contract with the union.

The wage aspect of the President's proposed bill meant "compulsory arbitration," according to operators' spokesmen.

Events moved rapidly today. The first intimation of the President's plan came when an announcement was made by Eben A. Ayers, assistant White House secretary, at 11 A. M., that the President had canceled his appointment list. By this time, too, the Cabinet meeting that had begun at 10 o'clock had been completed.

It was learned that the President had discussed the "inherent powers" that some persons held he possessed to intervene in the dispute.

Mr. Truman previously announced he definitely had discarded the idea.

To those present at the Cabinet meeting the President divulged his plans, which had been drawn up under the direction of Attorney General J. Howard McGrath.

An hour later another meeting was held in the Cabinet Room, presided over by the President.

Shortly before 1 P. M. White House Secretary Charles G. Ross called in reporters and informed them that the President would send his coal message to Congress at 3 P. M.

March 4, 1950

'BOOTLEG' UNION PACTS REPORTED ON THE RISE

WASHINGTON, March 20 (UP) —Government officials disclosed today that an increasing number of closed-shop and union-shop contracts were being "bootlegged" in violation of the Taft-Hartley Act and state labor laws.

Furthermore, these officials predicted, the practice might become even more widespread during the vital spring contract negotiating season because many unions and employers were looking to Congress to legalize "union security" arrangements.

A "bootleg" contract is defined as a hushed-up private agreement between labor and management that a firm will employ only union members. Most of them were simply verbal understandings, it was said, although some were written pacts which never reached official attention because neither party challenged their legality.

The Taft-Hartley law flatly outlaws the closed shop, under which only union members can be hired. It permits the union shop, under which all new employes must join the union within thirty days, only if that arrangement is approved in a Government-sponsored election by 51 per cent of the workers.

In thirteen states there are more stringent local laws regulating the union shop.

Meanwhile, the CIO tonight accused employers and their "highly paid lobbyists" of joining the country's press in a propaganda drive aimed at keeping the Taft-Hartley law on the books.

The accusation was included in a preview of a statement which the CIO general counsel, Arthur J. Goldberg, will make tomorrow before a House labor committee considering repeal of the Taft-Hartley law.

'Agency Shop' Urged For New Labor Law

By The United Press.

WASHINGTON, April 3— Government labor experts said today they believed they had found an almost perfect solution in the dispute over the Taft-Hartley's law closed-shop prohibition and union-shop restrictions.

They suggested legalizing the "agency shop," which does not force a worker to join a union but does require him to pay his fair share of the cost of negotiating and policing union contracts.

Proponents of the "agency shop" say it meets union demands for a job-security clause eliminating "free riders," and at the same time overcomes objections of employers who do not want their employes to have to join a union to hold their jobs.

Neither House nor Senate has taken up the Administration's new labor bill, which would repeal the Taft-Hartley law and revive the old Wagner Act with some changes.

INDUSTRY BARGAINING A MENACE, SAYS NAM

WASHINGTON, Aug. 8 (UP)— The National Association of Manufacturers recommended today that labor unions be made subject to the anti-trust laws and that industry-wide bargaining be prohibited.

The proposals were submitted in a statement to the Senate Banking and Currency Committee, which is investigating labor relations in the coal industry and the alleged "monopolistic" practices of the United Mine Workers.

If the trend toward industry-wide bargaining continues, the association said:

"It is our belief it will not only destroy collective bargaining itself, but will inevitably result in the control and direction by Government of production, prices, profits, the conduct of business operations and of labor unions themselves.

"This belief is founded upon the proposition that the Federal Government is the only agency powerful enough to deal with the combined might either of industry-wide unions or industry-wide employers or both."

Because of this situation, the association said, it believes "that employers and labor unions should be equally subject to the anti-trust laws."

The association contended that "long range public interest demands that all trade restraints be outlawed, whether they be imposed by management or by organized labor."

Its statement said that labor was the biggest single item in the cost of production and that industry-wide bargaining was aimed at removing that element from competition.

3,500,000 WORKERS IN WELFARE PLANS

Rise to 5,000,000 in Summer Sought by Union Leaders Negotiating Contracts

EMPLOYERS PAYING COSTS

Industry Is Divided on Theory, Finds Bankruptcy Possible —AMA Approves Projects

By A. H. RASKIN

Three and a half million workers now enjoy the protection of union-sponsored health, welfare or retirement plans, with their employers paying all or most of the bill.

Union leaders hope they can push the number of workers under welfare plans past the 5,000,000 mark this summer. Liberalization of existing benefits and increased employer contributions are also part of the union program in forthcoming collective bargaining negotiations.

A survey by THE NEW YORK TIMES indicated that union officers and members were generally enthusiastic about the operation of welfare plans now in effect, while employer reaction varied from approval of the basic idea to belief that the whole problem should more properly be met through governmental action on social security.

In no case was there any suggestion that the huge sums being collected for welfare purposes were being dishonestly administered or that unions were using them as war chests. However, many employers expressed fear that rivalry among union leaders might touch off a competitive race in the welfare field of such dimensions as to bankrupt industry.

The survey also disclosed that the American Medical Association, which opposes governmental steps toward compulsory health insurance, was well pleased with the way union health programs were working. Dr. James McVay of Kansas City, Mo., chairman of the association's council on medical service, said none of the plans now in operation ran afoul of its concept of what a sound medical program should contain.

United Mine Workers Lead

Biggest and best-known of the present plans are the two United Mine Workers welfare and retirement funds, which are taking in $120,000,000 a year in soft-coal royalties and $12,000,000 a year more in hard-coal royalties. Both funds are spending the money almost as fast as it is collected and are still far from providing the full list of benefits John L. Lewis feels the funds must supply.

The International Ladies Garment Workers Union, AFL, and the Amalgamated Clothing Workers, CIO, which were in the welfare field even before Mr. Lewis, have piled up nearly $110,000,000 in reserves in their welfare funds. The ILGWU, which includes a pooled vacation fund in its welfare program, expects to distribute more than $20,000,000 in benefits this year. The Amalgamated will pay out about $6,000,000 on the basis of current estimates.

Hundreds of thousands of truck drivers, longshoremen, millinery workers, building craftsmen, utility employes and workers in scores of other industries receive protection through group insurance or pension systems, but there is a wide deviation in the range of welfare services provided and in the percentage of employer contribution.

Retirement benefits vary from a straight dollar-for-dollar matching of Federal Social Security payments, which currently average about $26 a month, to the Lewis figure of $100 a month, in addition to Social Security. On the health side there is little uniformity of benefits. A few programs protect workers, and sometimes their families as well, by providing full insurance against medical, surgical and hospital bills. Most have fixed limits on the cost and duration of benefits.

Employer Contributions

Employer contributions usually take the form of allocation of a specified percentage of payroll or a certain number of cents an hour for welfare purposes. Most employer-financed funds run from 2 to 5 per cent of payrolls, with a few even higher. In the Philadelphia garment industry employer contributions total 8 per cent, but 3½ per cent of this goes into a unique "fair income" fund intended to safeguard workers against some of the hazards of seasonal unemployment.

The United Mine Workers funds derive their income from a royalty of 20 cents a ton on all coal mined in the bituminous and anthracite fields. With the aid of new high-speed mining machinery, the average soft-coal miner accounts for a production of six and one-half tons a day. This brings the royalty collection to about 8 per cent if measured on a payroll basis. In anthracite, where mining conditions make the per-man yield much lower, the royalty amounts to 3 per cent of payroll.

In steel, automobiles, electrical manufacturing, rubber and other industries, in which union welfare funds are still rare, several factors have combined to make unions feel that 1949 is the year to make the "big push" for expanded health and pension programs.

Chief among these is the adverse impact of the declining cost of living on union demands for fourth-round wage increases. Even though labor leaders argue that higher wages are necessary to promote a higher standard of living and to fortify purchasing power, they expect to win more popular support on the welfare front than on the wage front this year.

Another factor has been the demonstrated effect of existing welfare funds in building up union morale and membership loyalty. Under most programs workers lose benefits when they leave the industry or quit the union. From both standpoints the existence of insurance and pension provisions operates as a stabilizing element. This may become a particularly important factor if industrial conditions become worse.

Recent decisions by the National Labor Relations Board requiring employers to bargain collectively on pension and other welfare programs have strengthened the union position in this year's negotiations. In past years many employers have declined to accept the view that such matters were proper subjects for bargaining. The new NLRB rulings are being contested in the courts, but unions do not intend to put off their demands until final rulings are handed down.

Employers faced with new welfare demands take the view that any assumption of new labor costs, whether in the form of higher wages or of welfare payments, will force prices up at a time when consumers are refusing to buy because they feel prices are already too high.

Another frequent employer argument is that the plans of the Truman Administration for liberalizing and broadening the Federal social security program will entail a substantial rise in payroll taxes. With social security taxes likely to reach a combined employer-employe level of at least 8 per cent if all phases of the Truman program are approved, many industrialists contend that allocation of further funds for union welfare programs would undermine the national economy.

Union spokesmen retort with a double-barreled argument. In the first place they see little basis in the record of the Eighty-first Congress to expect favorable action on any substantial part of the Truman social security recommendations. In the second place they maintain that there will continue to be need for auxiliary programs to supplement and reinforce benefits available through social security.

Some major welfare agreements include provisions for reconsideration of employer contributions and employe benefits if social security taxes are increased or Federal services liberalized. Others are subject to change only when new basic wage contracts come up for negotiation.

The 3,500,000 workers now under welfare plans represent a little less than one-quarter of the country's organized workers. Most of the plans are jointly administered by union and employer representatives, but some of the pre-Taft-Hartley programs are exclusively in union hands.

In most cases the employers are content to exercise an advisory function in fund operations. Their main concern is that the fund be applied honestly and economically. There ahve been virtually no complaints of dereliction on either of these counts. The employers are also concerned that there be no undertaking of functions that would necessitate expanded financial contributions on their part.

One fund recently negotiated by the United Automobile Workers, CIO, in a Muskegon, Mich., foundry calls for an employer contribution of 7 cents an hour, with a proviso that the union and its members are to be responsible for making up any shortage that may develop in meeting the cost of providing agreed-upon health and welfare services for the workers.

With the business outlook uncertain, such clauses may be widely demanded by employers this year. If plants introduce short work-weeks, it may become necessary to provide welfare services to an equal number of workers with only half the money originally expected. Income in some funds has already dropped 10 to 20 per cent since the beginning of the year.

Union layoff policies will probably be influenced to some extent by welfare considerations. Where there is a choice between laying off some employes entirely or putting all on a reduced work schedule, the need for protecting the welfar fund may induce a decision to favor layoffs so that the reduced payroll contributions will be adequate to cover the smaller number of workers left in the program.

When the Kaiser-Frazer Corporation, which pays 5 cents an hour into a UAW welfare fund, cut back operations in January, the union gave its support to a program of layoffs instead of a reduction in the work-week. As a result, there are now some 3,500 fewer workers eligible for insurance protection and there has been no need to scale down benefits for those still on the payroll.

However, the determining factor in the Kaiser-Frazer decision was not the welfare fund but the fact that under the Michigan unemployment insurance law there is no provision for unemployment compensation to persons who are not totally idle. In New York and other states days of unemployment are taken into consideration, but in Michigan the workers would have drawn no benefits from the state unless some were laid off entirely.

The AMA's views on union health and medical programs was set forth by Dr. McVay in a telephone interview last week. He gave special praise to the program provided by the ILGWU through its Union Health Center in this city.

Dr. McVay said he favored the general approach being taken by Dr. Warren F. Draper, medical director of the UMW welfare and retirement funds, in setting up a comprehensive medical program for miners. In general, Dr. McVay remarked, the union welfare programs were successfully avoiding the objections the AMA has directed against "socialized medicine."

"We are interested in encouraging the development of any program that will provide a high standard of service to the patient, safeguard the traditional patient-doctor relationship and meet the other requirements of the AMA," Dr. McVay declared. "Thus far our study of the various plans established under collective bargaining leads us to believe that they are functioning satisfactorily in all respects."

March 28, 1949

213

EMPLOYER RIGHTS BIG LABOR PROBLEM

Wide Differences by Unions and Management Over Area of Collective Bargaining

SURVEY FINDS CONFLICTS

Rows Over Boundaries Result in Ford and Singer Strikes— Leaders' Views Outlined

By A. H. RASKIN

The battle to define and protect management's "prerogatives" seems likely to prove as stubborn a source of conflict between employers and unions as the original fight to establish labor's right to bargain collectively.

The inability of management and labor to agree on mutually acceptable boundary lines for collective bargaining is finding expression in picket lines at the Ford Motor Company, the Singer Manufacturing Company and a half-dozen smaller companies in various parts of the country.

More such strikes are in prospect as leaders of major industries proclaim their determination to defend "management's right to manage" in the face of union contentions that labor should have a "voice" in all phases of business operation.

Difference of Opinion Persists

A survey by THE NEW YORK TIMES indicated that there still was as much difference of opinion by employers and unions on what constituted the "proper" area for collective bargaining as there had been when President Truman's labor - management conference grappled unsuccessfully with the problem in Washington just after the war.

The survey also indicated that there were almost as wide differences within the ranks of labor and management as there were between the two groups. Labor leaders generally disclaimed any desire to "take over" the responsibilities of management, but contended that it was both "impractical and undesirable" to attempt to put a fence around bargaining practices.

Many management representatives agreed that labor's interest in business problems should extend legitimately beyond wages, working conditions and other subjects recognized as falling within the sphere of collective bargaining, but contended that a type of "creeping socialism" was introduced when management attempted to share responsibility with labor in solving these problems.

"The road to labor-management cooperation through collective bargaining is a dead-end street," was the way Carroll E. French, director of industrial relations for the National Association of Manufacturers, summed up this feeling.

The quarrel between employers and unions is less over the basic theory of bargaining collectively than it is over what should be included in the bargaining process.

Some industrialists insist that any division of management's control over production and pricing policies lessens the organization's efficiency, and strips it of the power to make quick decisions. Others feel that it is desirable to give to unionized workers an advisory role in the determination of plant policies, especially those dealing with quality control, spoilage and absenteeism, provided final right to make decisions rests with management.

Still others have set up joint committees empowered to establish production standards, to administer plant discipline or to pass on promotions. In these cases responsibility is shared by management and the union, and does not rest exclusively with either.

The labor argument for an expanding field of pooled responsibility rests on the contention that the security of the workers and their earning power depends on how the business is run and how much work is expected in return for the workers' pay. On that basis, union leaders contend, the fixing of production standards is "a logical extension" of collective bargaining over wages and hours.

The National Labor Relations Board, with the backing of the courts, has taken some part in the effort to set up guideposts for bargaining by holding that unions are entitled legally to insist that employers bargain on two issues that often have been held to be exclusively within the province of management discretion.

One was pensions and the other was merit wage increases. In both cases the board ruled that employers were obliged to bargain with unions on these subjects. Both rulings were affirmed in the Circuit Court of Appeals and the Supreme Court refused to review the lower court decisions, thus giving them the effect of law.

In many cases unions have found themselves obliged to take stands on matters in which they had no desire to become involved as a means of safeguarding the interests of their members. Thus, the Transport Workers Union, CIO, joined the city administration and the private bus lines in campaigning for higher transit fares on the ground that such action was necessary to insure higher pay for its members.

Similarly the Utility Workers Union, CIO, has intervened in rate cases before the State Public Service Commission, with a view to guaranteeing that authorized electric and gas rates will be high enough to support adequate wages for utility employes.

Members of Local 202 of the International Brotherhood of Teamsters, AFL, who deliver fruit and vegetables to local markets, are aligned with produce merchants in resistance to an Interstate Commerce Commission order imposing an additional charge on produce unloaded in this city.

John L. Lewis has indicated that one of his principal points of pressure in the immediate future will be enforcement of a "share the work" plan under which available work would be divided equally among members of the United Mine Workers in all soft-coal mines. Such a plan is operating in the hard-coal mines by joint agreement of the union, the anthracite operators and the Commonwealth of Pennsylvania.

Another union program aimed at pushing outward the boundaries of collective bargaining came recently from Julius Hochman, manager of the Dress Joint Board of the International Ladies Garment Workers Union, AFL. He suggested that the union take steps to institute a system of "compulsory saving" by dress manufacturers, under which they would put aside part of their profits in periods of prosperity as a business reserve intended to keep their factories running in slack periods.

Mr. Hochman is author of a plan adopted before the war under which the union and the manufacturers contribute to a joint promotion fund designed to increase the market for dresses made in this city. The United Hatters, Cap and Millinery Workers, AFL, and the millinery manufacturers are partners in a similar fund in the New York hat industry.

Murray's Planning Program

Philip Murray, president of the Congress of Industrial Organizations, is sponsor for what probably is the most ambitious program for union participation in basic industrial problems. It is supported officially by the CIO. The program calls for the setting up of industry councils, made up of representatives of employers, unions and the Government, to carry on industrial planning in all basic industries.

These councils, according to the CIO blueprint, would deal with such matters as production levels, employment levels, the rate and nature of capital investment, price ceilings, wage floors, guaranteed annual wages, foreign trade, the size and location of plants and the utilization and conservation of natural resources.

The NAM viewpoint, as set forth by Mr. French, is that labor and management can cooperate most effectively if unions will confine themselves to recognized spheres of collective bargaining and not attempt to undermine management's right to make decisions in other areas.

He emphasized his belief, based on experience, that it was possible for union and management to hold fruitful discussions on sales problems, quality control and wage incentives, provided there was no invasion of the basic rights of management.

The American Management Association, in a study supervised by Ernest Dale, a member of the graduate faculty at Yale and Columbia Universities, reported last month that formal plans for labor-management cooperation outside the sphere of collective bargaining had proved beneficial in many instances but had proved fruitless in others.

The Labor and Management Center at Yale has published two studies—one by its director, Prof. E. Wight Bakke, and the other by Prof. Neil W. Chamberlain—on the attitudes of employers and unions toward the scope of bargaining. Both tend to the conclusion that unions will press for an increasingly broad definition of collective bargaining.

May 27, 1949

Impartial Chairman System For Labor Peace Is Gaining

By A. H. Raskin

Styles in labor relations, as well as in coats, suits and dresses, are being set by the city's multimillion dollar garment industry. Other industries throughout the country are copying the impartial chairman system of arbitration that has kept the garment industry free of major strikes for many years.

The private bus lines in this city have been the latest to designate an impartial chairman. The general trucking industry is expected to follow within a few weeks. The National Maritime Union, CIO, is seeking employer agreement to a similar arbitration set-up for Atlantic and Gulf shipping lines.

The machinery that has made the New York needle trades a model of industrial harmony was the fruit of a series of strikes and lockouts that rank among the most bitter and costly in American labor history. Even the introduction of the arbitration principle provided no automatic key to peace. It took twenty-five years of development to produce the program that has proved successful in adjusting disputes between workers and employers without interruptions of production.

Despite the "growing pains" experienced by the garment industry in evolving its machinery, there is unanimous conviction among union and management leaders in the industry and among the men directly charged with the responsibility for deciding disputes that the main elements of the impartial chairman system can be readily applied in any industry in which both sides are prepared to commit themselves to abide by the arbitrator's decisions.

Under the contracts between the International Ladies Garment Workers Union, AFL, and the employer associations in the dress and the coat and suit branches of the industry, the impartial chairmen have the final voice in settling any disputes that arise under the terms of the agreement. Strikes or lockouts are prohibited during the life of the contract.

When the agreement expires, it is up to the parties to write a new contract. The impartial chairman has no authority over disputes that develop in the course of contract negotiations and either party is free to break off the talks and halt production if no agreement is reached.

Although there have been no major conflicts in the coat and suit industry since 1926 and in the dress industry since 1933, both sides feel it is important that the function of the impartial chairman be limited to deciding what the contract requires and not extended to deciding what should go into it.

This belief in the importance of preserving the right of the parties to do their own legislating, rather than allow the impartial chairman to become both law-maker and judge, has not prevented the union and the associations from referring some unresolved issues in contract negotiations to the impartial chairman for final determination.

For instance, Sol A. Rosenblatt, the present impartial chairman in the coat and suit industry, is scheduled to rule June 13 on a point left in dispute a year ago when the union and the employers signed a new three-year agreement. It will be his job to work out a percentage formula for applying three post-war wage increases totaling $15 a week to the system of piece rates that prevails for many of the industry's workers.

Employer Hailed as Arbiter

The impartial chairman in the dress industry, Harry Uviller, was executive director of an employer association in the coat and suit industry for fifteen years before he was selected by the dress manufacturers and the union to preside over their arbitration machinery in 1936. The union has never regretted its choice of an employer to serve as impartial chairman in this branch of the industry. It is as enthusiastic as are the manufacturers in praising Mr. Uviller's administration of his office.

What has become known in ILGWU history as "the great revolt" of 50,000 cloakmakers in 1910 provided the impetus for introduction of the arbitration principle into the industry. A commission headed by Louis D. Brandeis, later Associate Justice of the United States Supreme Court, drafted a historic "protocol of peace" to settle the two-month strike.

It established a four-man committee on grievances, made up of two representatives of the union and two of the employers, and a three-man board of arbitration, made up of Justice Brandeis as representative of the public, Dr. Hamilton Holt as representative of the employers and Morris Hillquit as representative of the union.

The arbitrators confined themselves to dealing with industry-wide problems. Individual cases were left to the committee on grievances. Complaints piled up and shop strikes became increasingly frequent. A fourteen-week lockout in 1916 signaled the collapse of the peace machinery set up in the protocol.

In its place came a panel of thirty-six arbitrators, mostly judges and civic leaders, who were called on to preside over the settlement of controversies. In 1924 a new general strike was threatened just as the Democrats were preparing to meet in national convention.

The convention was scheduled to meet in old Madison Square Garden, then in the heart of the garment area. Gov. Alfred E. Smith a leading candidate for the Presidential nomination, appointed a commission to investigate conditions in the industry and obtained a pledge from both sides that there would be no strike or lockout before the convention.

The commission, under the chairmanship of George Gordon Battle decided a permanent impartial chairman would be better than a panel of busy men, none of whom was familiar with the distinctive problems of the garment trade. Raymond V. Ingersoll, secretary of the City Club, became the first chairman.

In 1926, when the Battle commission submitted its final report, a twenty-six-week strike rocked the industry and split the union into irreconcilable right and left-wing factions. After the strike, the question rose as to which union faction was entitled to administer the contract and bring cases before the impartial chairman. Mr. Ingersoll ruled in favor of the anti-Communist group. David Dubinsky, president of the ILGWU, refers to this ruling as the turning point in the fight to wipe out Communist influence in the garment union.

Mr. Ingersoll served until 1931, when he was succeeded by George W. Alger. In 1935 Mr. Rosenblatt, whose first acquaintance with the garment industry was gained as regional code administrator for the National Recovery Administration, took over the post. In 1940 he was replaced by former Mayor James J. Walker.

After five years Mr. Walker retired in favor of Harry L. Hopkins, whose term was cut short by his death in January, 1946. Former Gov. Charles Poletti served for a year and a half, after which Mr. Rosenblatt resumed the chairmanship.

The first impartial chairman in the dress field was appointed in 1931. He was Dr. N. I. Stone, economist. He was followed by Adolph Feldblum, an attorney, who gave way to Mr. Uviller in 1936. The arbitration compact in the dress industry now covers 80,-000 workers and 2,200 employers. Forty-five thousand workers and 1,550 manufacturers are subject to the rulings of the impartial chairman in the coat and suit industry.

Under the contracts in both industries, every case that comes before the chairman must be treated as a new case. Precedents set in other cases cannot be cited to justify dismissal of new complaints. As a matter of working practice, however, neither the union nor the employers press cases in which there is a clear-cut pattern of prior decisions.

Relatively few disputes ever reach the chairman. If they cannot be settled by the shop chairman and the employer, the union and the employer association attempt to reach an amicable adjustment.

If they fail, they ask the impartial chairman to schedule a hearing. Most of these cases are disposed of before they get to the hearing. Others are settled by voluntary agreement in the course of hearing. Still others are composed before the decision is issued.

Over the years, the number of complaints requiring action by the chairman has dropped sharply, but all the parties agree that the very knowledge that there is a court of last resort is a potent element in this process of reaching direct agreement.

The key power vested in the impartial chairman is his right to insist that a strike or lockout be terminated within twenty-four hours, regardless of cause. The penalty for non-compliance may be an order that the workers involved be replaced or that the employer forfeit all his privileges under the collective agreement.

Decisions Come Quickly

That this requirement may not operate unjustly where genuine grievances exist, Mr. Uviller has made it a practice to schedule hearings within twenty-four hours where work stoppages are involved. Emergency cases are decided the same day. Most other cases are disposed of within a week.

Mr. Uviller feels there are three important ingredients to a successful impartial chairmanship. These are an all-inclusive agreement that leaves no loopholes in the arbitrator's authority to decide cases growing out of the contract, a fast-moving administrative machinery and a respect on the part of both sides for the decisions that are rendered.

Mr. Rosenblatt's office is also geared for speed. In addition to disposing of cases involving the union and the employers, he passes on disputes between jobbers and contractors. Mr. Uviller exercises a similar function in the dress field.

In the fixing of piece rates for dress shops, deputies attached to Mr. Uviller's staff determine the rates when union and employer representative cannot agree. If the parties are not satisfied, an appeal may be taken to the chief deputy and from him to the impartial chairman. In Mr. Rosenblatt's office, this price-fixing machinery functions on a semi-autonomous basis, with the parties retaining the right to take a final appeal to the impartial chairman.

Both Mr. Uviller and Mr. Rosenblatt feel that the type of machinery over which they preside can be employed to the benefit of all in other industries. They believe the operating problems in other industries would be substantially less, because few industries have as many complexities of corporate structure or wage practice to cope with.

The head of the union, Mr. Dubinsky, gives primary credit to the arbitration system for the elimination of illegal strikes and the creation of a cordial employer-employe relationship in the industry. He commends it to other unions and other industries as a tested method for achieving industrial stability.

On the employer side, Samuel Klein, executive director of the Industrial Council of Cloak, Suit and Skirt Manufacturers, praised the system for introducing "a basic respect for law and order" into the industry's labor-management relations.

J. Louis Dubow, managing director of the Merchants Ladies' Garment Association, agreed that the chances for arriving at an independent compromise were much greater when the parties knew they could appeal any disagreement to the impartial chairman.

"It is never good for an employer to win a case before an impartial chairman," he commented. "I would rather get much less from the union than more from the impartial chairman. Otherwise, I may lose much more later on. That is why we take as few cases as we have to before the impartial chairman. But our ability to go to him to get workers back at once when there is an illegal stoppage is a great virtue from the standpoint of the employers."

Truman Signs Pay Rise Bill; Drive for $1 Minimum Starts

By ANTHONY LEVIERO
Special to THE NEW YORK TIMES.

WASHINGTON, Oct. 26—The new minimum wage of 75 cents an hour became law in a White House ceremony today, and immediately the textile workers started a campaign for a new national minimum of $1 an hour.

Officials of the Labor Department and unions, as well as members of Congress, were on hand this morning when President Truman signed the bill raising the minimum from forty cents. Mr. Truman gave them souvenir pens used in signing the bill. The new law becomes effective in ninety days.

"The enactment of the Fair Labor Standards Amendments of 1949 is a major victory in our fight to promote the general welfare of the people of the United States," Mr. Truman said, in a statement in which he reviewed the main provisions in seven points.

He expressed regret that some workers previously covered by the minimum wage law were deprived of protection under the new law, and that other groups were not added. Improvements under the new bill, however, said Mr. Truman, would go far to assure minimum standards needed for the general well-being of workers.

About 1,500,000 workers are expected to benefit from the increase, which on a national basis is expected to cost employers about $300,000,000 annually. About half of this sum will go to employes in the South and the Southwest, according to William R. McComb, administrator of the Wage and Hour Division in the Labor Department. He also estimated that the average increase would be between 5 and 15 cents an hour.

Mr. Truman said in his statement that a provision of the new law would "result in the virtual elimination" of child labor evils. He also saw in the law a sign of progress toward an annual wage.

Among those present at the signing were Maurice J. Tobin, Secretary of Labor; Senator Elbert D. Thomas, Democrat, of Utah, chairman of the Senate Labor and Public Welfare Committee; William Green, president of the American Federation of Labor, and Jacob Potofsky and Emil Rieve of the Congress of Industrial Organizations, representing Philip Murray,

President of the CIO, who was in Cleveland.

Others at the ceremony were Michael J. Galvin, Under-Secretary of Labor; Mr. McComb; William S. Tyson, Solicitor of the Labor Department; James Green, president of the Shipbuilders Union; Albert J. Hayes, president of the International Association of Machinists, and W. D. Johnston, vice president of the Order of Railway Conductors.

Move for $1 Minimum Renewed

It was Mr. Rieve, president of the Textile Workers Union of America, CIO, which asserts that it has 450,000 members, who gave new impetus to a movement seeking the $1 minimum.

"Already the passage of the act," he said, "has reduced industrial strife in substandard industries, as employers have agreed to workers' demands for wage increases which the act would have called for. We can expect this trend to continue.

"It is extremely unfortunate that Congress, when raising the minimum, reduced the coverage of the law, removing from its protection some of those workers who needed it most. The labor movement cannot accept this as a final action and must continue to fight for the restoration of the law's coverage to those who have been removed, and its further extension to seamen, some types of food processing and industrial farming.

"At the same time we must renew our campaign for an increase in the Federal minimum to $1 an hour. Even that figure can barely provide a subsistence standard of living."

G. M. AUTO WORKERS REACH 5-YEAR PACT ON PENSIONS, WAGES

Workers, 65, Having 25 Years With Corporation Will Receive $100 to $117.50 a Month

---

BOTH SIDES HAIL ACCORD

---

4 Cents an Hour to Be Added to Basic Pay Rate Yearly— Health Cost to Be Shared

---

By WALTER W. RUCH
Special to THE NEW YORK TIMES.

DETROIT, May 23—The General Motors Corporation and the United Automobile Workers, C. I. O., agreed today to a five-year contract providing for annual wage increases, pensions and health insurance, and a form of union security.

Both sides hailed the terms of the contract as they were announced in an atmosphere of goodwill at a joint news conference following a final session of twenty-eight consecutive hours of secret negotiations.

The contract, longest in duration that has been written in the industry, assures the company of five years of uninterrupted production as it may not be reopened for any reason until its expiration in May of 1955.

Chief Gains Are Listed

The economic gains listed by the union include:

1. A jointly-administered pension plan providing $100 a month, including Social Security, for workers at the age of 65 with twenty-five years service. The maximum monthly payment will become $117.50 a month if congress grants Social Security increases as is expected.

2. A guaranteed annual wage increase of 4 cents an hour, described by the union as a reward for increased productivity, and to be added to the basic wage rate.

3. A continuation of the cost-of-living escalator clause, providing for wage adjustments in accordance with the price index of the Bureau of Labor Statistics, unlimited upward but lim-

ited downward to a point no lower than the basic wage rate.

4. A hospital-medical plan with the company paying half the cost of Blue Cross and Blue Shield protection for worker and family.

5. An improved insurance program, including accident and sickness weekly benefit, ranging from $31.50 to $45.50.

Chief among more than thirty non-economic concessions to the union is a modified union shop, requiring new employes to join the U. A. W. but giving them the option of withdrawing from the union after one year.

19-Cent "Package" Seen

The U. A. W. estimated that the contract would provide an estimated "package" increase of 19 cents an hour now, and 35 cents an hour in the fifth year.

[Wall Street circles credited a report of an agreement for a slight spurt in trading near the close of the Stock Exchange.]

Walter P. Reuther, international president of the union, said that the total gains for the workers during the life of the agreement would exceed $1,000,000,000 and in the fifth year alone would add $700 to the income of the average G. M. worker's family.

Mr. Reuther said it was "an historic agreement" regarded by the union "as the most significant development in labor relations since the mass production industries were organized in 1936-37."

C. E. Wilson, president of General Motors, said the contract "is unprecedented in labor-management relations."

"It is expected," Mr. Wilson said, "that it will have a stabilizing influence not only on our busi-

ness but on the economy of the whole country. We believe that removing the fear or possibility of a strike for five years is a tremendously constructive achievement for our employes and their families, our business, our dealers, our suppliers and the general public.

"The settlement should mean that all concerned can face the future with added confidence," Mr. Wilson added.

Philip Murray, president of the Congress of Industrial Organizations, told Mr. Reuther in Pittsburgh yesterday, upon being informed of the details of the impending agreement, that the step was "an amazing and very wholesome development."

The agreement, reached one week before the expiration of the current two-year contract, covers between 270,000 and 280,000 G. M. workers, Mr. Reuther said. Its terms are expected to be extended

CELEBRATING THE GENERAL MOTORS LABOR CONTRACT

Union and management officials shaking hands following surprise announcement of agreement. Left to right are Walter P. Reuther, president of the United Auto Workers; T. A. Johnstone, head of the General Motors division of the union; Harry W. Anderson, General Motors vice president in charge of personnel, and Louis G. Seaton, General Motors Labor Relations Director.

Associated Press Wirephoto

shortly, he added, to about 35,000 members of the International Union of Electrical Workers, C. I. O., having contracts with G. M.

The agreement, already approved by the International Executive Board and the national G. M. negotiating committee of the U. A. W., will be presented to the national G. M. council of the U. A. W. on Thursday, and to the various locals for ratification starting next week.

"Tremendous Gains" Cited

"The G. M. workers have made tremendous gains in this new agreement, both economic and non-economic," the U. A. W. said, adding:

"The economic gains won in this new contract when applied to the total General Motors payroll will give G. M. workers a total gain of $144,000,000 during the first year and will increase by $32,000,000 a year."

The company withheld comment on the union estimates and offered none of its own.

The G. M. pattern becomes one for the industry in 1950, Mr. Reuther told reporters, contrasting with the agreements reached with the Ford Motor Company last fall and on May 4 with the Chrysler Corporation, the latter only after a 100-day strike.

The union broke down its estimate of the 19-cent "package" this year in this way: seven cents for pensions, five cents for hospital-medical insurance, four cents for the flat wage increase, one and one-half cents for improved vacation pay, six-tenths of a cent to meet an additional five-cents-an-hour wage increase granted to about 30,000 skilled workers, and nine-tenths of a cent for other economic gains, including a special increase of five-and-one-half cents an hour for all apprentices.

Basic Wage Rate to Rise

The union noted that the present wage increases and the additional 16 cents in increases over the next four years would be added to the basic wage rate, establishing a rising platform beneath which cost-of-living adjustments downward may not go.

The cost-of-living allowance resulting from the operation of the 1948 agreement at present amounts to three cents. Thus, three cents represents the maximum downward revision of wages possible, since that is the difference between the current wage rate and the basic rate, the latter not being variable.

"Recent increases in prices point to a strong possibility that the three cents an hour cost of living allowance will be increased

as of Sept. 1 by at least one cent an hour," Mr. Reuther said.

"The union and the G. M. workers hope for a decline in living costs. Since the contract provides a floor below which wages may not be reduced, a sufficient decline in the cost of living means increased purchasing power for G. M. workers. At the same time, G. M. workers are protected against increased living costs, so that the total gains in this contract represent actual gains in purchasing power," the union said.

With the G. M. contract in hand, the U. A. W. proclaimed a "breakthrough" on the $100-a-month pension ceiling.

Pension Funds Pledged

The payment of the G.M. portion of all pensions will be not less than $1.50 per month for each year of service under the present or any future agreement or any future social security law during the life of the contract.

Normal retirement age will be 65, but an employe at his own option, provided he is capable of doing his job, may continue to work until the automatic retirement age of 68. At the option of the company, an employe with "unusual skill" and good health may continue beyond age 68.

There will be no compulsory retirements until Jan. 1, 1952. The plan will be effective for those retiring after Jan. 1, 1950, with payments beginning about Oct. 1, 1950.

Another feature of the pension plan provides that any employe who has had at least fifteen years of service and who becomes totally and permanently disabled after the age of 50 shall receive a disability pension ranging from $50 to $90 monthly, depending upon his length of service. This continues until he is 65, when he comes under the regular pension.

Pointing to the contrast between the Chrysler strike and the General Motors negotiations, Mr. Reuther said it was "tragic that two big corporations, neighbors in the same industry, have demonstrated two completely different approaches to the same problem."

"General Motors decided to live with our union. It is our considered opinion that Chrysler has not. Chrysler is still living under some delusion that by some miracle it can get rid of the union," Mr. Reuther said.

Among the non-economic gains listed by the U. A. W. were improved grievance procedure and revisions in the apprentice and skilled trades section of the agreement.

TRUMAN SEIZES RAILROADS; UNIONS 'GLADLY' VOID STRIKE; CHRYSLER RAISES ALL WAGES

ARMY TO TAKE OVER

Action Tomorrow Is Vital to Guard Security, President Says

WAGE DISPUTE LEFT OPEN

Government Will Not Negotiate Settlement, or Call Heads of Carriers for Talks

By LOUIS STARK

WASHINGTON, Aug. 25—President Truman announced today that the Government would take over and operate the nation's railroads Sunday at 4 P. M., Eastern standard time.

This step, the President said, was made necessary to protect the nation's security, defense and health because of the strike scheduled by 300,000 trainmen and conductors for 6 A. M. Monday.

Half an hour after the seizure announcement the unions postponed the strike indefinitely and announced that their men would "gladly" operate the roads for the Government "until this dispute can be settled on its merits through mediation."

President Truman's executive order turned the transportation system over to Frank Pace Jr., Secretary of the Army. Mr. Pace immediately directed Karl R. Bendetsen, Assistant Secretary of the Army, to act for him.

U. S. Will Not Negotiate

Charles G. Ross, White House press secretary who handed out the President's announcement, told reporters that neither the President nor Secretary Pace would negotiate an agreement with W. P. Kennedy, head of the Brotherhood of Railroad Trainmen, and R. O. Hughes, head of the Order of Railway Conductors.

Mr. Ross also blasted the hope of the union chieftains that Mr. Truman would call in railroad presidents to supplant the present three-member negotiating team named by the carriers.

The President's executive order provides that railroads shall be managed under the same conditions as were in effect on Aug. 20. This means there can be no change in wages or working conditions until the Government is assured by the unions and managements that they have reached an agreement.

In his brief statement, coupled to the seizure announcement, the President called upon "every railroad worker to cooperate with the Government by remaining on duty."

He asked the officers of the unions "to take appropriate action to keep their members at work."

The unions promptly sent notices by wire to their general chairmen postponing the strike indefinitely.

Union Refusal Cited

In his formal public statement the President pointed out that the trainmen and conductors had rejected the recommendations of an emergency board, named under the Railway Labor Act.

"In the strike situation thus confronting us, governmental seizure is imperative for the protection of our citizens," the Chief Executive added.

The carriers' committee, headed by Daniel P. Loomis, was as little surprised as were the union heads by the seizure announcement. They had no statement for publication but indicated that obviously it was to their and the nation's interest for them to cooperate to assure uninterrupted transportation.

Plans for government seizure had been prepared several days ago. All that remained was to take them off the shelf, fill in the dates and have the President append his signature.

The Army is expected to tap for top place in managing the railroad system Maj. Gen. Frank A. Heileman of St. Louis. He is a veteran Army engineer. His chief aid is expected to be Brig. Gen. Andrew F. McIntyre of Philadelphia, a veteran railroad operating man, now on leave from the Pennsylvania lines.

Management of the roads will remain in the hands of the present operating chiefs.

Call of Rail Heads Denied

A report tonight stated that the President has summoned heads of the railroads to Washington so they may be sworn in as Army officers for the duration of Government operation.

However, a high Administration official denied that, as in a previous wartime seizure, railroad presidents would be named as Army colonels.

The dispute that resulted in today's Presidential action began seventeen months ago when the trainmen and conductors asked for the forty-hour week at forty-eight hours' pay for 85,000 yardmen and certain rules changes for an additional 215,000 men.

A Presidential emergency board granted the forty-hour week and an 18-cents-an-hour wage adjustment to the yardmen to partially compensate them for the loss of the sixth day's pay. The rules changes urged on behalf of the other men were denied.

Last Saturday, at the suggestion of Dr. John R. Steelman, assistant to the President, the management committee offered to raise the ante to 23 cents for the yardmen plus 5 cents an hour for the others. This was rejected by the unions.

Pace to Inform Public

Secretary of the Army Pace announced this afternoon that it would be his policy "to see that the public is fully and swiftly informed on all matters affecting the operation of these carriers while under the control of the Department of the Army." He added:

"* * * I earnestly request all Americans to give their help in avoiding any dislocation of the national economy during this period of critical world conditions."

Headlines in the morning newspapers today reporting President Truman's belief that the trainmen and conductors had acted in bad faith in calling the general strike for Monday without notice stirred Mr. Kennedy and Mr. Hughes to immediate reply. They dispatched the following telegram to the President:

"We wish to personally advise you that at the concluding conference presided over by Dr. Steelman in the East Wing of the White House from 3 to 4 P. M., Wednesday, Aug. 23, 1950, no mention whatsoever was made regarding the calling of any nation-wide strike, and therefore any statement to the effect that we had broken our pledge is one hundred per cent false. Respectfully."

Mr. Kennedy assured a reporter that the decision to call the nation-wide strike had not been made when the parties left the deadlocked conference at 4 P. M. last Wednesday.

At that time they said that they had merely told Mr. Steelman that they would call off the five "token" strikes and call no more of that nature.

Notations made by the three carriers' spokesmen in the White House after the deadlocked meeting Wednesday were available today. The memorandum of Daniel P. Loomis included this phrase: "No other strikes scheduled."

Mackay Memo Quoted

C. D. Mackay and J. W. Oram, the other two management spokesmen, made similar notes. Mr. Mackay's was as follows: "Mr. Steelman asked Mr. Kennedy about other strikes and Mr. Kennedy stated that no strikes were in contemplation now, but, of course, he did not mean forever."

On this point Mr. Oram's note stated: "Dr. Steelman then asked whether there were any other strikes in contemplation. Mr. Kennedy replied that there are no other strikes contemplated but that did not mean forever."

Within less than an hour of the conclusion of this meeting (last Wednesday) the unions issued the nation-wide strike order.

The union officers concluded today that if they cannot deal with a new committee of railroad presidents the only thing they will get out of Government seizure is the "satisfaction" that comes to them from the belief that seizure means an end of possible "wildcat" strikes.

Mr. Kennedy said he had to go to New York last Friday to plead with his members on the New York, New Haven and Hartford Railroad not to go off on an unauthorized strike.

It is the general belief in Government and railroad circles that the flag will fly for a long time over the roads before they are turned back to private operation. This is based on the following:

Mr. Kennedy, who temporarily took over the post of president of the trainmen several months ago on the death of Alexander F. Whitney, is up for election to a four-year term. His union meets in quadrennial convention on Sept. 20 at Miami Beach. The convention will last six weeks.

It is unlikely that Mr. Kennedy will be able to leave his convention for Washington. Further conferences with the carriers between now and Sept. 20 may be held but seem likely to be abortive, in the opinion of Government observers.

Both the railroads and the unions approved the seizure.

Senate reaction to President Truman's announcement was one of general approval with an adverse comment here and there.

The Senate Labor and Public Welfare Committee voted down an attempt by Senator Forrest C. Donnell, Republican of Missouri, to obtain favorable action for his bill providing compulsory arbitration of railway disputes. Senator Donnell said he would seek to bring up his bill in the Senate. Senator Elbert Thomas, Democrat of Utah, chairman of the Senate Labor Committee, told reporters that the President had taken the only action open to him.

"I think that's the only thing he could do," was the comment by Senator Paul Douglas, Democrat of Illinois.

"The railroads have to continue to operate, don't they?" commented Senator Brien McMahon, Democrat of Connecticut.

Senate Majority Leader Scott Lucas of Illinois, said:

"The railroads must run in this emergency and it is apparent that the only thing the President could do was to seize them," he said.

Senator Karl Mundt, Republican of South Dakota, said that it was "deplorable that the President has been forced by the railway labor dispute to burden the Army with operating a transportation system at home during a critical period when its full time and talent are required to win the war in Korea."

Senator Wayne L. Morse, Republican of Oregon, was the most outspoken critic of the President's action in the Senate.

Timetable of Railroad Dispute

The following timetable covers the main developments in the dispute that led to yesterday's railroad strike:

1949

NOV. 1—Brotherhood of Locomotive Firemen and Enginemen asked for a forty-hour week with no cut in pay for firemen in yard, transfer and belt-line service.

DEC. 15—Order of Railway Conductors and Brotherhood of Railroad Trainmen started taking a strike vote after negotiations with the carriers had broken down over union demands for a forty-hour week for yard service employes and wage increases for road employes.

1950

FEB. 14—National Mediation Board proposed arbitration. Union rejected proposal; carriers accepted it.

FEB. 25—President Truman appointed three-man emergency board to head off strike set for Feb. 27. Unions canceled strike call.

JUNE 15—Emergency board recommended forty-hour week, plus 18-cent rise in old hourly pay rates for 75,000 yard workers. No change in pay for conductors and trainmen on road service.

JUNE 21—Conductors and trainmen threatened strike in protest against emergency board's recommendations. Unions complained take-home pay would be cut under board's plan. Outbreak of Korean war caused unions to defer strike plans and to urge President to take over railroads.

AUG. 21—Yardmen began "token" strikes in Cleveland, St. Paul and Louisville. Unions scheduled national walkout of trainmen and conductors for Aug. 28.

AUG. 24—President Truman criticized union strike call. He said he had been informed that the token strikes would end and that no new strikes would start pending additional White House mediation efforts.

AUG. 25—President ordered seizure of the nation's railroads by the Army, effective at 4 P. M. Aug. 27. He stressed that the Army was not to negotiate any agreements with the unions involved but to leave that to the carriers. Unions immediately directed their members to stay at work.

DEC. 13—"Sick" strike of switchmen in Chicago hit fifteen railroads. Strike spread to other centers, despite issuance of no-strike injunctions by Federal judges in three cities.

DEC. 16—Strikers returned after President called on them to end their "unlawful" interference with national defense. New White House talks began immediately after back-to-work movement.

DEC. 21—White House announced agreement on terms that would give higher pay to 300,000 engineers, firemen, conductors and trainmen. Pact called for three-year moratorium on further wage or rule changes. It provided 25-cent hourly pay rise for 120,000 yardmen and 10-cent increase for 180,000 road employes. A cost-of-living escalator was included to cover future changes in price levels. The forty-hour week was accepted in principle for yardmen, but its application was delayed.

1951

JAN. 5—Union officers, meeting in Cleveland, voted to reject the White House agreement, even though top officers had signed it two weeks before. Unions demanded immediate installation of forty-hour week, plus 31-cent pay rise; 35 cents an hour for road employes and other gains.

JAN. 24—Carriers demanded that unions live up to White House pact; unions denied that pact existed. National Mediation Board failed in peace efforts.

JAN. 31—Switchmen, members of Brotherhood of Railroad Trainmen, began new sick strike. This lasted until Feb. 8, when Army issued work-or-be-discharged ultimatum on instructions from President. Federal judges in Washington and Chicago imposed $100,000 in contempt of court fines on union for striking in face of injunctions.

MAY 25—Trainmen reached settlement for 150,000 members. Agreement provided 33-cent increase for yard employes and 18½ cents for those on road service, cost-of-living escalator and moratorium on rules changes till Oct. 1, 1953. Forty-hour week was accepted in principle for yardmen, but its application was deferred.

JULY 25—Engineers, firemen and conductors proposed that their continuing dispute go to arbitration, with forty-hour week as a chief issue. Carriers maintained that principles of Dec. 21 agreement had to apply.

NOV. 6—President named emergency board to avert firemen's strike called for Nov. 8. Union put walkout off "indefinitely."

1952

JAN. 26—Board recommended that firemen accept terms paralleling those already in effect for trainmen and nonoperating unions. This would involve wage increase of 38 cents an hour for yard employes and 23½ cents for road service employes. Board also proposed that yard men get 4 cents an hour when hours were cut to forty a week.

JAN. 28—Firemen, who had objected to board's personnel, rejected recommendations as effort to make union "swallow" proposals Truman Administration had been trying to have accepted for many months.

FEB. 28—Engineers announced "overwhelming" vote by 60,000 members in favor of strike.

RAILROADS ACCEPT WHITE HOUSE PLAN TO END LONG STRIFE

By JOSEPH A. LOFTUS
Special to The New York Times.

WASHINGTON, May 19—The nation's railroads accepted tonight a proposal of Dr. John R. Steelman, the Assistant to the President, for settling their three-year dispute with three major operating unions—the engineers, firemen and conductors.

The unions, with a combined membership of 150,000, replied that they would not be able to give their answer until tomorrow. If they accept, the Government will end its nominal possession of the roads, which President Truman seized in August, 1950, to head off a strike. Seizure authority under a 1916 statute is due to end on June 1 unless Congress grants an extension.

Dr. Steelman, who is the acting Defense Mobilizer and chief labor adviser to the President, had presented his settlement proposal to both sides today.

The plan provides for wage increases for road men of 12½ cents an hour, plus 10 cents for increases in the cost of living, for a total of 22½ cents an hour. Increases for men who work in railroad yards would be 27 cents an hour, plus 10 cents for cost of living increases, or 37 cents an hour.

Same Pay Proposal as in 1950

No change was proposed actually in the direct pay rates that have been available to the three unions since Dec. 21, 1950, when their presidents and management committees signed a memorandum of agreement at the White House. The unions later refused to ratify the agreement.

A fourth union, the Brotherhood of Railroad Trainmen, stood with the three others until May, 1951, then broke ranks and accepted the Dec. 21 plan.

Apparently the only change of consequence in the latest White House proposal was the elimination of arbitration on one working rule in controversy, known as the interdivisional run rule. The elimination of the provision for a binding decision by a referee was regarded by the railroads as an important concession to the unions.

The employes represented by the

trainmen's union have been receiving the increased pay for a year. The other employes would receive the increase retroactively, dating back in part to October, 1950, and in part to Jan. 1, 1951. Back pay would range from $600 to $1,100 for each employe, depending on his job and the amount of time he had worked.

The Army, which has been in nominal charge of the lines, permitted part of the proposed higher pay rates to go into effect in February, 1951, or the back pay pool would have been much higher.

If the yard men's working week is reduced from forty-eight hours to forty hours, thereby cutting their weekly take-home pay, rates will be raised 4 cents an hour more to offset that reduction in part. The holdout unions have been insisting on a 9-cent increase in case of conversion to a short week, but failed to win any concession on that item.

The yard workers now average $1.45 to $1.65 an hour while road men receive $1.95. The unions, all independent, are the Brotherhood of Locomotive Firemen and Enginemen, the Order of Railway Conductors and the Brotherhood of Locomotive Engineers.

The management demand for changes in the interdivisional run rule has been one of the important obstructions to settling the dispute. The changes demanded would permit management to run trains through terminals, from one division to another, without changing crews.

Recommendations Not Binding

The companies contended the rule was a relic of a past railroad age when trains were slower and it was necessary to change steam locomotives. The unions contended the proposed changes would uproot road men from their communities, require them to give up their homes and result in financial loss.

Under the Dec. 21 memorandum, disagreements between a carrier and a union on this issue were to be referred to a referee or arbitrator for a binding decision. The new plan accepted by the railroads provides that as a final step in negotiating changes in the rule, the dispute shall go to a board of arbitration, the neutral chairman to be named by the National Mediation Board.

The proviso then states:

"While the recommendations of the chairman are not to be compulsory or binding as an arbitration award, yet the parties hereto affirm their good intentions of arranging through the above procedure for the final disposition of all such disputes on a fair and reasonable basis."

Arbitration on Job Variations

The working rule known as "more than one class of road service" would go to arbitration under the White House plan, the arbitrator to be named by the President. This rule involves the question of pay for an individual who works on jobs with different rates of pay in the same eight-hour period.

May 20, 1952

Installment Buying Is Curbed On Autos, Home Appliances

One-Third Down, 21-Month Limit Decreed for Cars—Restrictions Effective Sept. 18 —Truman Signs Controls Bill

By CHARLES E. EGAN

WASHINGTON, Sept. 8—President Truman today signed the Defense Production Act of 1950 giving him emergency powers to control credit, production and distribution of materials and, if necessary, to set ceilings on wages and prices and to ration consumer goods.

Minutes later, the Federal Reserve Board announced restrictions on installment buying, effective Sept. 18.

The new curbs fix minimum down payments of one-third on time-payment purchases of automobiles, 15 per cent on such items as radio and television sets, mechanical refrigerators, washing machines and other household appliances and 10 per cent for household furniture.

Payments must be completed on automobiles within twenty-one months and on other articles within eighteen months.

A special provision covering down payments on residential repairs, alterations or improvements specifies a minimum of 10 per cent, with repayment to be completed within thirty months.

Charge accounts maintained in stores and single-payment loans—loans under which the borrower promises to repay in a lump sum at a given date—are not covered in the present regulation. Officials said they would be included later if conditions warranted such checks.

The new law is intended to curb inflation as well as spur defense production. It carries many discretionary powers, including authority to fix ceilings on prices, freeze wages and ration goods, when the President feels such steps are justified.

Mr. Truman is not expected to invoke the general rationing or wage and price-freeze powers for the time being. He did not ask for such authority and has said frequently that he does not believe general action along that line is necessary. He may, however, use the price and wage powers on a selective basis in industries where he feels prices are out of line.

Whatever his intentions, the President will explain the act and the actions he will take under it to the public tomorrow night when he goes on the air at 10:30 Eastern daylight time for a televised talk.

President Truman is expected over the week-end to draw up the necessary directives delegating powers of allocating materials and issuing priority orders to Government departments. The new law also provides for Government loans and loan guarantees to expand production and the requisitioning of plants and equipment for defense production, and the President also will issue orders covering these subjects.

The Federal Reserve Board received power to move against installment buying as one of several steps to be taken to curb inflation growing out of the defense production program. In announcing the restrictions today board officials said:

"Consumer credit has undergone an unprecedented expansion particularly in recent months. Under present conditions continued excessive growth of consumer installment credit adds materially to inflationary pressures.

"The regulation of consumer credit is one of the fiscal, monetary and credit measures designed to restrain the inflationary pressures that result in higher prices and to facilitate diversion of critical material and manpower to production of defense needs as such diversion is required."

First in Effect in 1941

Following the past policy of placing fewer restrictions on small credits, the new Regulation W does not contain down-payment requirements for articles costing less than $100, although such purchases will be subject to the payment-period limit applicable to the type of goods involved. Also, the rules provide that installment loans for the purchase of any article included in the list carry the same limitations that apply to the installment sale of the article. Other installment loans are limited to a maximum maturity of eighteen months.

Regulation W as a credit curb was first instituted in September, 1941. It remained in force until Nov. 1, 1947, was reactivated on Sept. 20, 1948, during the inflationary post-war spending splurge, and expired on June 30, 1949.

Officials said one of the major virtues of the regulation was its flexibility. It can be altered quickly to take care of any changes in the conditions it was created

to meet. If, as is expected, President Truman delegates to the board his powers over real estate credits, the board can amend the present regulation to include that field also.

Officials said today that in drawing up the regulation the board took into account prevailing practices and terms in the fields affected. There has been a material relaxation of installment credit terms during the last year or more, and the requirements of the regulation are substantially tighter than the terms now widely offered.

In the automobile field, it was added, most recent installment sales of new cars and late model used cars were reported made on substantially easier terms than permitted by the new order.

"Similarly," officials said, "many installment sales of appliances and furniture are reported as having been made with down payments of 10 per cent or less; in many cases only token or no down payments have been required. Maturities of twenty-four months on installment sales of such articles have been reported as widely prevalent, with longer maturities offered in some cases."

Those in businesses affected by the order are required to register with the Federal Reserve Bank, or one of its branches, within sixty days.

Penalties for violation of the regulation range up to fines of $5,000 and a year in jail.

Specifically exempt from the regulation were credits over $2,500 not involving automobiles; business or agricultural loans; credit to dealers and certain salesmen; credit to governmental agencies and religious, educational, charitable institutions; loans to pay fire and casualty insurance premiums; credit for purchasing securities; real estate credit; loans to meet educational, medical or funeral expenses; credit to finance repair or replacement of property damaged or lost by disaster, and certain loans on savings shares or accounts.

In setting up the regulation, the Reserve Board divided the various items affected into groups. Automobiles, meaning "passenger cars designed for the purpose of transporting less than ten passengers, including taxicabs," make up Group A.

Group B, on which 15 per cent minimum down payments and a maximum maturity of eighteen months apply, is made up of the following items "designed for

221

household use": cooking stoves and ranges; mechanical dishwashers, ironers; mechanical refrigerators and food freezers; washing machines or clothes drying machines; or combination units incorporating any of the listed articles named; sewing machines and suction cleaners.

In addition this group includes air conditioners, in room size units, dehumidifiers, radio or television receiving sets and phonographs or combinations.

Group C, embraces household furniture, including ice refrigerators, bed springs, mattresses and lamps, and soft-surface floor coverings. In this category a 10 per cent down payment and an eighteen-month' payment limit is set.

Group D covers residential repairs, alterations or improvements and applies to "materials, articles, and services in connection with repairs, alterations, or improvements upon urban, suburban, or rural real property in connection with existing structures. This does not relate to structures, or distinct parts thereof, which as so repaired, altered, or improved are designed exclusively for non-residential use."

Group D also requires a 10 per cent minimum down payment, but the time allowed to complete payments is thirty months.

Truman Establishes Agency To Bar Inflation as U.S. Arms

By JOSEPH A. LOFTUS

WASHINGTON, Sept. 9—President Truman prescribed tonight a regime of moderate controls, production stimulants, heavy taxes, and a big dose of self-denial to maintain this country's economic well-being in a war-menaced world.

In a speech to the nation over radio and television networks at 10:30 P. M., Eastern daylight saving time, Mr. Truman announced the creation of an Economic Stabilization Agency with price and wage powers he hoped to avoid using. He issued two executive orders to implement his program.

The President imposed no price or wage controls but warned that should milder measures fail the Government would not hesitate to employ them.

Other controls to be used promptly will assure the military services top priority in the allocation of scarce materials and restrict the use of credit for the purchase of houses and consumer goods.

He appointed W. Stuart Symington, chairman of the National Security Resources Board, to coordinate the administration of powers granted by the Defense Production Act he signed yesterday.

His speech was notice to the world that this country intended to extend its leadership in production without destroying the value of its currency through inflation.

That will mean, Mr. Truman declared, harder work, longer hours and fewer material things. He called for an end to "business as usual"—for the consumer, the business man and the wage-earner.

"We can and must submerge petty differences in the common task of preserving freedom in the world," the President said.

"Spurred by the world-wide menace of Communist imperialism, we can surpass every previous record. I am certain that the American people, working together, can build the strength needed to establish peace in the world."

He said the Government had been spending about $15,000,000,000 a year for defense; that present plans would bring that up to a rate of at least $30,000,00,000 by next June, and in the year after that we would probably have to spend much more than that.

The Stabilization Administrator still to be named, will have under him a Director of Price Stabilization and a Wage Stabilization Board. This board will be composed of representatives of labor, management, and the public.

The stabilization agency's job at first will be to check the danger spots and consult management and labor and try to work out necessary safeguards without compulsion.

Mr. Truman made it clear, however, that if this voluntary course failed, ceilings on prices and wages would be imposed.

Orders Records Preserved

One of his executive orders today required business men to preserve records of their prices and costs during the period of May 24 to June 24. That means, he said, that information will be available to set ceilings at fair levels, and to identify the sellers who have taken advantage of the present emergency.

The President expressed some misgivings about the selective procedure required by law in imposing ceilings. He said he was not sure that would work and "as a result we might have to resort to general controls before they are really necessary. This may prove to be a serious defect in the law which will require correction."

Mr. Truman also said present rent-control legislation was not adequate.

The major executive order of the day delegated most of Mr. Truman's power to allocate scarce materials to Secretary of Commerce Charles Sawyer, but he and other Administrators of war powers will have to defer to Mr. Symington on policy questions.

Mr. Symington will resolve interagency issues that otherwise would require the attention of the President; prescribe policy and program directives having the approval of the President; obtain reports and information on the status of work in the various agencies; advise the President on the progress of the defense production program.

Functions to Be Coordinated

In addition to Mr. Sawyer, priority and allocations powers, to be coordinated by Mr. Symington, were delegated as follows:

The Secretary of the Interior Oscar L. Chapman, for gas, solid fuels, and electric power.

The Secretary of Agriculture Charles F. Brannan, with respect to food, the domestic distribution of farm equipment and commercial fertilizer.

The Interstate Commerce Commission responsible for the supervision of the Bureau of Service, with respect to domestic transportation, storage, and port facilities, or their use, but excluding air transport, coastwise, intercoastal, and overseas shipping.

The Board of Governors of the Federal Reserve System exercises controls over financing.

The armed forces and other agencies were authorized to guarantee loans to war contractors for plant expansion and the financing of war contracts.

The Reconstruction Finance Corporation was directed to make loans for plant expansion and for stimulating production of important metals and minerals. The General Services Administrator was authorized to buy needed materials.

Guiding Principles Given

The order directed the Secretary of Labor, Maurice J. Tobin, to use the functions now vested in him to meet the labor needs of defense industry effectively. He and other appropriate officials will "develop policies applicable to the induction and deferment of personnel for the armed services, except for civilian personnel in the Reserves."

The order did not provide for any emergency manpower controls.

The President's speech laid down guiding principles for consumers, business men, and wage earners.

To the consumer, he said: "Buy only what you really need and cannot do without."

To the business men: "Do not pile up inventories; hold your prices down."

To the wage earner: "Do not ask for wage increases beyond what is needed to meet the rise in the cost of living."

The President committed himself to a "pay as we go" policy. That means heavier taxes for everybody, he said, and warned that inflation would hurt more in the long run than higher taxes now.

"Inflation would benefit the few, and hurt the many," he said. "Taxation—just and equitable taxation—is the way to distribute the cost of defense fairly."

Looks to Second Tax Bill

Recognizing that taxation was up to Congress, Mr. Truman asked the people to support their Representatives in Congress in enacting tax legislation. He said he regarded the tax bill that is about to be passed as the "first installment." It would raise an estimated $4,508,000,000 in new taxes.

He asked for still another bill that should include "a just and fair excess profits tax, which will recapture excess profits made since the start of the Communist aggression in Korea."

He simplified the inflation problem this way: "The defense program means that more men and women will be at work, at good pay. At the same time, the supply of civilian goods will not keep pace with the growth in civilian incomes. In short, people will have more money to spend, and there will be relatively fewer things for them to buy. This inevitably means higher prices, unless we do something about it. Higher prices would lead to higher wages which, in turn, would lead to still higher prices. Then we would be started on the deadly spiral of inflation."

Increased Living Costs and Taxes Eat Up Much of Workers' Pay Rises

By A. H. RASKIN

Unionized workers in the nation's principal industries won more than $2,000,000,000 a year in wage increases during 1950, but rising living costs and taxes ate up much of labor's gains in purchasing power.

The war-stimulated race between wages and prices, coming after twenty months of relative stability on both economic fronts, took the spotlight away from signs of increased maturity in the relationship between management and labor. The improved relationship reflected itself in the signing of an increased number of contracts barring strikes for periods of three to five years and putting wage adjustments on a more scientific basis than in past years.

The scope of employer-financed pension and welfare funds spread during the year, but the Korean war, record industrial profits and the expanded market for consumer goods caused unions to shift the bulk of their collective bargaining emphasis from welfare demands to higher wages.

Employers, worried about their ability to hold skilled labor in the face of growing manpower shortages, were not inclined to resist union demands too energetically. In most basic industries agreement was reached on larger pay envelopes even before contracts were scheduled for negotiation.

The ante went up to 25 cents an hour in a contract negotiated at the White House for 120,000 railroad yardmen. A day after this contract was signed Dec. 21, the government indicated that the end of the road for additional pay increases was near by freezing wages in the automobile industry until March 1.

The extent to which wage increases were nullified by inflation and increased taxes was indicated in figures compiled by the Federal Bureau of Labor Statistics.

These showed that the average weekly earnings of workers in manufacturing industries went up from $56.29 in January, 1950, to $61.99 in October, a total rise of $5.70 a week. However, when allowance was made for higher income taxes and price rises, the average single worker had only 51 cents a week more spendable income in October than he had in January, 1950, according to the bureau's figures.

January 2, 1951

PRICES AND WAGES FROZEN

PAY TALKS HALTED

Mine Increase of $1.60 a Day, Set for Feb. 1, Blocked by Order

RELIEF IN INEQUITIES

Stabilization Policy Due Next Week to Provide Wage Flexibility

By JOSEPH A. LOFTUS
Special to The New York Times.

WASHINGTON, Jan. 26—The Government froze wages, salaries and other compensation of employes today for the second time in less than nine years. The rates of the freeze are those paid yesterday and those rates may not be increased without Government approval.

Temporarily the freeze is absolute, but the Wage Stabilization Board expects to have ready by Monday or Tuesday a policy whereby inequities of various kinds may be adjusted.

The effect of the order is to bring to a standstill hundreds of collective bargaining negotiations throughout the country. Even wage increases already negotiated but not in effect are blocked by the order. These include the $1.60-a-day increase won by more than 400,000 bituminous and anthracite mine workers. These increases were to go into effect Feb. 1.

Violations are punishable under the Defense Production Act, with penalties ranging up to a fine of $10,000 or a year's imprisonment, or both.

Basic Provision of Order

The basic provision of the order reads:

"No employer shall pay any employe and no employe shall receive 'wages, salaries and other compensation' at a rate in excess of the rate at which such employe was compensated on Jan. 25, 1951, without the prior approval or authority of the Wage Stabilization Board.

"New employes shall not be compensated at rates higher than those in effect on Jan. 25, 1951, for the jobs for which they are hired."

Eric Johnston, Economic Stabilization Administrator, authorized the wage freeze order despite the refusal of some members of the Wage Stabilization Board to sign it. Mr. Johnston did not appear at the news conference where the announcement was made. Cyrus S. Ching, chairman of the W. S. B., read the order, which, he said, had been handed to him a few minutes earlier.

The authority given to the board by the order is extraordinarily broad. It says:

"This regulation may be modified, amended or superseded by orders or regulations hereafter issued by the Wage Stabilization Board."

Mr. Ching told reporters:

"I just received this order. We have a responsibility to stabilize wages. We are quite conscious of the responsibility of stabilizing relationships and making a contribution to production. All those factors will be taken into consideration."

He said that he had a crew of experts at work tailoring formulas to fit the diverse problems resulting from the Government's intervention in free collective bargaining.

The formulas will permit wage increases in some circumstances. The law does not deal with wage controls in terms of a freeze or ceilings. It says that wages shall be "stabilized."

One part of the stabilization policy, for example, probably will cover cost-of-living increases, as the Little Steel formula did in World War II. It will take care of those workers whose wages or salaries have lagged.

There also will be provisions to correct "in-plant" inequities so that merit increases, length-of-service increases, promotions, reclassifications and so on may proceed normally. Inter-plant inequities and substandards also will be covered, it is expected, and perhaps some provision will be made for adjustments necessary to divert labor to the most essential defense plants.

Whether the stabilization policy will dispose of the "escalator" problem was not definite tonight. "Escalator" clauses in union contracts provide for automatic wage adjustments geared to the Federal Consumers Price Index. The major contracts containing escalator clauses, such as those in the automobile industry, do not provide for any further adjustments before March 1.

The order provides relief for employes who may be caught by unusually low wage rates for seasonal or other causes. It says that nothing shall be construed to require the stabilization of rates below those paid during the period from May 24, 1950, to June 24, 1950. That is the period immediately preceding the Korean fighting.

Some parts of the stabilization policy probably will be self-interpreting, but thousands of petitions for approval of adjustments probably will start pouring into the board. Regional boards of labor, industry and public members will be set up to interpret and apply the policy.

A large number of disputes is regarded as inevitable. How long the Federal Mediation and Conciliation Service will continue to handle labor-management disputes involving wage stabilization problems remains to be determined.

The Wage Stabilization Board is geared to act only on wage adjustments where there is agreement by the employer and employe.

January 27, 1951

WAGE BOARD VOTES 10% RISE FORMULA; LABOR GROUP QUITS

Stabilization Unit Sets Policy on Pay — Increases Allowed From Jan. 15, '50, Base Date

APPROVAL UP TO JOHNSTON

Agency's Future Held in Doub —Union Leaders Assail Plan as 'a Great Injustice'

By JOSEPH A. LOFTUS
Special to THE NEW YORK TIMES.

WASHINGTON, Friday, Feb. 16 —The Wage Stabilization Board, by a vote of 6 to 3, early today adopted a basic pay policy for the nation's work force and employers, and the three labor members withdrew from the board in protest.

The policy, which is subject to the approval of Eric Johnston, Economic Stabilization Administrator, permits general increases in wage and salary levels of 10 per cent from a base date of Jan. 15, 1950.

The 10 per cent would not include "fringe" benefits like pensions and welfare funds, previously put into effect, but would include any such benefits begun from now on.

The policy also provided for reexamination in May in the light of changes in cost of living in the meantime. That implied a further adjustment above the 10 per cent then, but the amount and the timing were not specifically set forth in the formula adopted early today.

"Escalator" Clauses Restricted

The policy permits the operation of cost-of-living "escalator" clauses only to the extent that they stay within the 10 per cent ceiling. According to authoritative estimates the 10 per cent probably would permit the full adjustment due General Motors employes under their contract on March 1, but might limit adjustments under other "escalator" clauses to something less than the full amount indicated by the consumers price index.

Whether the Wage Stabilization Board can continue to exist was a question no one could answer with certainty today. It is possible, of course, that the three labor members who resigned will be replaced by other union officials, but that will be determined by the United Labor Policy Committee, which will meet at 11 A. M. today "to consider further appropriate steps."

When the wage board meeting broke up early today, the three labor members issued the following statement, which had been prepared even before the board's session last night began:

"We have tonight withdrawn from the Wage Stabilization Board in protest against an attempt to do a great injustice to all Americans who work for wages and salaries. We are acting on the instructions of the United Labor Policy Committee, representing the American Federation of Labor, the Congress of Industrial Organizations, the Railway Labor Executives Association and the International Association of Machinists, organizations with a combined membership of 15,000,000 Americans.

"As their representatives, we cannot give our approval or be a party to the unfair and unworkable formula adapted by the industry and public members of this board.

"This is the immediate reason for our action. The United Labor Policy Committee will meet again at 11 A. M. tomorrow (Friday) to consider further appropriate steps. At the conclusion of that meeting, a full statement will be issued."

Cyrus S. Ching, chairman of the wage board, said:

"I regret very much the labor members' retiring because I am firmly convinced that the tripartite system is the only sound and democratic way to do this job."

Clark Kerr, also a public member, made this comment:

"We are fully convinced this is a very fair and equitable policy. It matches the highest figure that could be called a pattern and it exceeds the increase in the cost of living."

The third public member of the board is John T. Dunlop.

The labor members who withdrew are Emil Rieve of the C. I. O. Textile Workers; John Murphy, who was sitting for Harry Bates, of the A. F. L. brick layers, and Elmer E. Walker of the International Association of Machinists.

The industry members are Ward Keener, Henry B. Arthur, and Reuben Robertson Jr. Mr. Keener, for the industry group, said:

"I think the order on the whole is equitable."

He said the industry members had moved upward from their original proposal of an 8 per cent formula. He noted that the 10 per cent was permissive and not mandatory and that collective bargaining could go on as before under that ceiling.

The formula is known as Regulation Number 6. The central paragraph reads: "If general increases in wage and salary levels in an appropriate employe unit have been less than 10 per cent since the base pay period, future increases in wages, salaries, and other compensations may be permitted in amounts up to but not in excess of the difference between such past increases, if any, and the permissible 10 per cent."

13% PAY RISES SEEN AS POLICY WAVERS AFTER 3 KEY DENTS

Major Increases Now in Force Outside Framework of 10% 'Ceiling' Are Vital Factors

SALARY PROGRAM DRAFTED

Executives Warned New Board Will Take a Firm Stand on Approving Increases

By JOSEPH A. LOFTUS
Special to THE NEW YORK TIMES.

WASHINGTON, June 17—The Wage Stabilization Board, fighting a holding action against pressures for higher pay, is about to fall back to a new line.

Allowable general increases in basic labor costs over the base period of January, 1950, probably will be raised to 13 per cent, instead of the present 10 per cent, although the bases of the two figures are not precisely comparable.

The 13 per cent figure would be composed of two factors: 10.5 per cent, a wage rate increase equivalent to the rise in retail prices since the base period, and 2.5 per cent, an extra fund that the parties could use as they saw fit but that is intended to close out all claims to such "fringe" items as annual improvement (productivity) factors, holidays and shift differentials.

The 10.5 per cent factor would be permitted to rise each quarter if the retail price index rose. No significant drop in the index is ex-

February 16, 1951

pected soon. The 2.5 per cent would be a fixed standard.

These are not final figures, because there has been no agreement. They describe generally the area most recently explored in board meetings and private conferences.

Salary Revisions Speeded

Meanwhile, the staff of the Salary Stabilization Board reported that it was drafting procedures to expedite salary adjustments by enabling business men to act without prior approval under Government regulations.

Salaries that are exempt from the wage and hour law are under the jurisdiction of the Salary Stabilization Board. Members of the board have not yet been appointed. but a staff is being assembled by Joseph D. Cooper, Executive Director.

Mr. Cooper announced that his board would be as firm in approving wage increases for executives as the Government was in considering wage rises for workers. He said the new board's central objective would be "to afford equal treatment under law for employes under its jurisdiction as compared with those under jurisdiction of the Wage Stabilization Board."

"This was considered to be in the best American tradition, just as the draft law subjects the sons of bankers and bakers to the same impartial standards of selection and rejection," Mr. Cooper said.

Mr. Cooper cited procedures under income tax laws, "which place responsibility for making determinations on the filer of a return."

"In some cases," he said, "the employer would keep a record of action, in others he would act and file a report for review. The cases where prior approval is required should be kept at an absolute minimum."

Mr. Cooper said approximately 750 cases were awaiting attention. There are three dents in the present wage line—increases that have been approved without refer-

ence to any of the twelve wage regulations established by the board.

The first was the case of the nonoperating railroad employes. Eric Johnston, Economic Stabilization Administrator, put that wage rise into effect himself virtually by direction of the White House. The reconstituted Wage Board had not begun to function at that time.

The rail increase could have been tied to the board policy covering "base pay period abnormalities." That is one of the exceptions to the 10 per cent formula for situations where the January, 1950, base is obviously unfair. Technically the order did not make that connection. To that extent, the rail case is a nonpolicy precedent, but since railroad wages are regarded as a separate problem, it is not believed the case will cause too much trouble in wage stabilization generally.

The second dent was the meat case. There a majority of the board approved a cost-of-living increase from the date of the last contract (August, 1950), instead of from January, 1950. The 10 per cent was exceeded without justification under any regulation.

The majority's explanation in the meat case was that this decision was headed in the direction of a new policy. Since then, Mr. Johnston has blocked the evolvement of such a policy. Some research has indicated that a policy based on the meat case would permit a great many 5 per cent increases on top of the present 10 per cent allowance. Mr. Johnston said that was excessive. It seems probable at this point that the meat case will be isolated from the general policy.

The third dent in the line is the improvement factor of four cents an hour, which the board approved unanimously in the automobile contracts and a few others. Four cents is a little more than 2 per cent for automobile production workers.

Employer members of the wage board do not regard the improvement factor as a "productivity" increase because, they contend, there is no actual measurement of productivity. They regard it more as a morale factor, or peace factor, and do not believe it can be limited to a few employers and union groups.

Hence, it is likely that this 2 per cent plus will become a general standard. The employer (and employes, where they are organized) would be permitted to use the money to iron out the wrinkles peculiar to their own situation.

In several other cases the board approved increases amounting to more than 10 per cent. That does not mean these cases "punched holes in the ceiling." There is no absolute ceiling on wages or on prices. There are various standards. Base period abnormalities is one. Shipyard increases of 15 per cent were approved under that standard. Manpower shortages in critical industric is another standard. An increase for Republic Aviation was approved last week on that basis.

General Electric Workers represented by one union got a nine-cent increase last week to bring them abreast of another union group in the same company. That was justified by what the board calls "tandem" policy.

These are case-by-case exceptions outside the 10 per cent formula but within general policy. If the self-administering 10 per cent formula should go to 13 per cent, or any other per cent, there will still be wage problems subject to other policy standards.

Only when the board approves an increase without relating it to any of its promulgated standards and regulations does it punch holes. It amounts to policy by precedent. The Wage Board's approval of the coal miners' increase last February, in the guise of a general regulation, is the cause of the greatest general pressure on the wage level right now, with union rivalries and politics what they are.

The meat case will continue to be a problem until it is adopted as policy or the board openly disowns it as a precedent. The improvement factor of 2 per cent plus is more likely to stick. The problem there is price relief.

Another issue blocking the way to adoption of a new wage policy is whether the formula should include pensions and health and welfare insurance. Labor members of the board insist these should be separate and extra.

Still another issue is whether to formalize new policy at all, or let it evolve decision by decision.

In the meantime, the board is working out new procedures to dispose of cases more rapidly.

NEW WAGE POLICY TIED TO LIVING COST DRAFTED BY BOARD

Plan Would Extend to Millions Negotiated Rises as Provided Under Escalator Clauses

JOHNSTON MUST APPROVE

Unanimous Action of 18 Labor, Industry and Public Members Called 'Major Achievement'

By LOUIS STARK
Special to THE NEW YORK TIMES.

WASHINGTON, Aug. 3—A major change in policy under which all wage earners in the jurisdiction of the Wage Stabilization Board would be allowed to obtain cost-of-living increases voluntarily negotiated was proposed by the board today.

Hitherto, cost-of-living increases tied to so-called escalator clauses for some 3,000,000 to 4,000,000 employes have been approved. That left millions of other wage earners at a disadvantage, because they did not have such contract provisions.

To make up for this inequity, the board has proposed the change to Eric Johnston, Director of Economic Stabilization. If he approves, a regulation will be adopted by the board to make the policy effective.

Mr. Johnston modified the Government's policy on March 1 to permit cost-of-living increases under escalator clauses signed before Jan. 25, the date of the wage freeze. The ceiling of 10 per cent on general wage increases, permitted without wage board approval, was not a bar. As a result, wage increases above 10 per cent were approved.

Price Index the Gauge

The usual type of escalator clause, such as that written into the General Motors contract with the United Automobile Workers, C. I. O., is geared to the consumers price index of the Bureau of Labor Statistics. Every three months, it is checked and wages are adjusted upward or downward one cent an hour for each 1.14 point change in the index.

The wage board, according to its

June 18, 1951

chairman, Dr. George W. Taylor, discussed the situation created by escalator clauses and the lack of them, and finally arrived at a unanimous recommendation.

"We feel that this is a major achievement of the board," said Dr. Taylor. "It is an exceedingly important plank in the wage stabilization program. It illustrates the strength of our tripartite (labor, management, public) treatment of wage matters.

"It is a better document than if the public members had worked out the policy themselves. All of us on the board are proud of this achievement."

The Wage Stabilization Board's jurisdiction covers wage earners paid by the hour or who are represented by unions. It cannot authorize wage increases but may say how large an increase may be made within stabilization policy.

Scope of Board Action

By its action today, the board takes into account three types of contracts:

1. Those with escalator clauses in effect prior to Jan. 25, the wage-freeze date. These clauses had been extended to July 1 and are now further extended.

2. Those who now wish to include escalator clauses in contracts. The board will approve those which make provision for the increase in living costs but no more.

3. Those who may wish to relate wages to living costs but who prefer not to have escalator clauses. This covers contracts where employers and unions have reopening clauses which allow wage rates to catch up to living cost advances but without being committed to automatic rises and drops.

Under the proposed regulation the board would permit living cost advances to begin from the date of the last contract instead of the Jan. 15, 1950, date of the previous regulations.

Dr. Taylor said that this would tend to preserve the relationship between wages and living costs that existed at the time the last contract was made. He added that there was no change in Regulation Six, which gave automatic approval to 10 per cent increases above those of January, 1950.

The board had no figures on how many employes might be affected by the proposed policy. Dr. Taylor's guess was that about 25 per cent of the country's wage earners had not received a 10 per cent increase over pay of January, 1950.

Dr. Taylor declined to predict what action Mr. Johnston would take on the board proposal, but he stressed that it had been endorsed by all eighteen members.

"If prices are stabilized there will be very little movement in wage rates under our cost-of-living resolution," Dr. Taylor explained at a news conference. "On the other hand if prices are not stabilized wages will move up also under the action taken by the board.

Dr. Taylor did not make public the specific resolution adopted by the board because it had some references meant only for the eyes of Mr. Johnston. He said, however, that the resolution specified the kind of cost-of-living clauses the board would approve.

August 4, 1951

KEY ISSUES IN THE STEEL CASE

By A. H. RASKIN

The big question on the inflation front now is: What will happen in steel? Since World War II steel has set the wage pattern for other large industries, and the fear now is that a pay raise in steel might lead to raises elsewhere and ultimately to price increases throughout the economy. For the past month Philip Murray's United Steelworkers of America, C. I. O., has been telling a special Wage Stabilization Board panel why the union feels its 650,000 members in the basic steel industry should get a wage increase of 18½ cents an hour and other concessions. The steel companies have been setting forth their reasons for believing that no wage increase is in order. Here are summaries of the union and industry arguments on four key issues.

WAGES AND PRICES

UNION SAYS: Higher living costs and the increased amount of steel the average worker produces justify an increase in the present basic wage of $1.82 an hour. When allowance is made for the bite that rising prices and rising taxes take out of pay envelopes, the average steel worker is only 5.3 per cent better off today than he was five years ago. Sixty per cent of the union members earn less than the $79.46 a week considered necessary by the Labor Department to finance a "modest but adequate" budget for a family of four. The average for all steel workers is $4.50 short of the Government figure (see chart). Even though the union members draw higher pay than workers in most other industries, they have been losing ground to other groups in relative wage standing in the war and post-war period. The increases sought by the union are consistent with the rules and interpretations of the Wage Stabilization Board. They would not stimulate inflation unless the companies prevail upon the Office of Price Stabilization to authorize an "unwarranted" rise in steel prices.

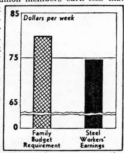

INDUSTRY SAYS: Any rise in steel wages would touch off a new round of increases in wages and prices that would spread throughout the economy, with inflationary results harmful to everyone. Steel workers have no legitimate basis for complaint about the adequacy of their present wages, whether measured on an hourly or weekly basis. Their pay has gone up considerably faster than the cost of living since 1939 (see chart) and has far outstripped the gain in individual output. The 16-cent hourly increase in wages which they got in December, 1950, took care of most or all of the rise in living costs that has occurred since then. Steel workers are among the highest-paid industrial workers in the country and are pulling further ahead. The union's estimate that steel workers are not up to the Labor Department's "modest but adequate" budget level is based on inflation of the average family size. Using a family of three, rather than four, as the standard, the average steel wage is $7 above the Government standard. It would destroy the entire stabilization effort to grant the union's demands.

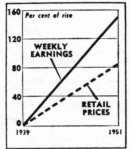

PRODUCTIVITY

UNION SAYS: The steel industry has not been passing on to its workers their proportionate share of the benefits resulting from rising individual output. The amount of steel produced for each man-hour of work went up 12.8 per cent in the three years from the middle of 1948 until the middle of last year. If the workers got their rightful share of this improvement, their "real" wages—the amount their pay envelopes would buy after allowance had been made for the impact of higher prices (but not counting higher taxes)—would have gone up 12.8 per cent. Instead, the increase in "real" earnings over the three-year period was 6.6 per cent, or only slightly more than half the rise in productivity (see chart). Steel prices have gone up more sharply than other prices in the post-war period so the industry cannot contend that it is sharing the benefits of increased productivity with the general public in terms of price reductions. The union has always made a major contribution to the industry's increased productivity.

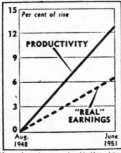

INDUSTRY SAYS: Steel wages have gone up six times as much as individual output in the last ten years. Productivity rose 17 per cent between 1941 and 1951; average hourly earnings soared 103 per cent in the same period (see chart). The gap between wages and output would become even greater if allowance were made for pensions, insurance and other "fringe" benefits steel workers received in the last decade. Allowing payrolls to outrun productivity in this fashion is the road to inflation. This is especially true in a defense period when the Government siphons off most of the fruits of increased productivity to meet military costs. With the total supply of civilian goods declining, workers cannot translate higher wages into higher levels of living, except at the expense of other groups in the economy. What is worse, the union has accompanied its pay demands with proposals for limitations on management's rights that would end further progress toward industrial efficiency.

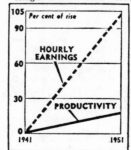

PROFITS

UNION SAYS: The steel industry's profits are big enough to enable it to raise wages without raising prices or depriving its stockholders of a fair return on their investment. The industry's profits, whether measured before or after taxes, have shown a "gargantuan growth" since the war. Profits before taxes went up 394 per cent in the last five years; profits after taxes went up 140 per cent (see chart). In determining steel's ability to absorb a wage increase, profits before taxes are the relevant measure because payroll costs are part of the cost of doing business and come out of a company's earnings before it figures how much it owes Uncle Sam.

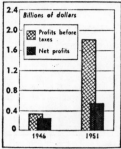

Studies made by the Office of Price Stabilization indicate that the industry could give as much as $1.2 billion a year in wage and "fringe" benefits without qualifying for price relief under existing O. P. S. rules. This is far in excess of all the gains the union seeks. The industry could pay the whole cost out of profits and still carry forward its plant expansion program.

INDUSTRY SAYS: Steel profits are low and getting lower. In 1950, after post-war expenditures of nearly $4 billion on new plant and equipment, steel stood twenty-seventh among the country's forty-five leading manufacturing industries in relative profits. In the whole period since V-J Day the rate of profits after taxes in steel has lagged behind the average for all manufacturing, even when the return is calculated on the basis of how much money is invested in the industry rather than how much steel it sells (see chart). This low rate of return is now falling rapidly under the pressure of increased taxes. In the first nine months of last year, steel

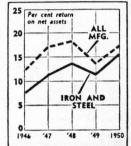

profits after taxes went down one-fifth at a time when steel sales were going up one-quarter. Granting all the union demands would mean a rise in direct labor costs of nearly 60 cents an hour and an equivalent rise in the price the industry would have to pay for goods and services it buys from others. To meet this without higher prices would prevent the industry from expanding to do its defense job.

TAXES

UNION SAYS: There is no factual warrant for industry forecasts that Federal tax revenues will drop $11 billion a year if the steel companies give the union everything it wants without raising prices and the same pattern spreads through all other industries. The steel workers will not be blazing a trail if their wages go up now; they will simply be catching up with workers in automobiles, electrical manufacturing, copper, textiles, rubber and other industries that have already given higher wages. What happens in steel will have no substantial effect on corporate taxes in these industries. Moreover, past experience indicates that

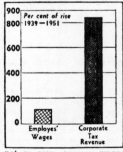

Federal taxes do not go down because wages go up. Last year, using 1939 dollars as a constant standard, corporations paid the Government more than eight times as much in taxes as they did in 1939, even though their total payrolls doubled (see chart). The industry's argument boils down to a suggestion that the Government should try to channel the national income into the hands of the wealthy since they pay taxes at the highest rates. The War Labor Board rejected a similar argument in 1942. The industry has always taken advantage of "each and every loophole" in the tax structure, and there is no sincerity in its present stand.

INDUSTRY SAYS: If the Government's decision gives the union what it asks and rules out any increase in prices, nearly 80 per cent of the cost of the wage rise will come out of the taxes the companies would otherwise pay Uncle Sam. For the steel industry alone, this would mean that the Government would collect $525,000,000 less in taxes than it is counting on. If the same loss ratio fanned out into all branches of industry, the total drop in corporate tax revenue would be $15 billion, or well over half of all the money President Truman hopes to collect from corporations this year (see chart). About $4 billion of this would probably be reclaimed as a re-

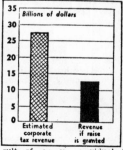

sult of higher individual tax payments by workers with fatter pay envelopes, but the net result would still be to throw the Government $11 billion deeper into the red. This would mean more inflation at the source of all inflation. To maintain its own income, the Government will have to lift the lid on prices sooner or later. Then the taxpayers will be called on to pick up a substantial part of the tab for higher wages in the prices the Government pays for the tanks, guns, planes and other weapons it buys. The country's best interests will be served by keeping both prices and wages where they are.

February 17, 1952

TRUMAN SEIZES STEEL; STRIKE OFF

PRESIDENT IN PLEA

Address on Air Charges Industry With Greed for High Profits

SAWYER WILL RUN MILLS

Washington Judge Signs Order Setting Hearing for Today on Legality of Action

By CHARLES E. EGAN
Special to The New York Times.

WASHINGTON, April 8—President Truman tonight ordered seizure of the steel mills to avert a strike of their 600,000 workers. An order directing that the Government take over the mills was issued effective at midnight, one minute before the scheduled strike was to take place.

Under the terms of tonight's order, which the President said had been issued "in the public interest," Charles Sawyer, Secretary of Commerce, will take over the operation of the steel mills.

In moving against the giant of American industries the President was believed to have touched off one of the sharpest legal battles in a generation. The steel mill owners are insistent that the President does not have power, under the Constitution or under his emergency grants of authority, to take possession of the mills. Counsel for steel mills were prepared to challenge the President's action in a half dozen Federal district courts in the country tomorrow, according to reports.

[Federal Judge Walter M. Bastian signed an order early Wednesday in Washington calling a hearing for 11:30 A. M. on suits filed by two of the major steel companies—Republic and Youngstown Sheet and Tube—challenging the Government's seizure, The Associated Press reported.]

Steelman Sets Meeting

In compliance with the President's request, Dr. John R. Steel-man, Acting Director of Defense Mobilization, telephoned representatives of the six big steel companies and Philip Murray, president of the United Steelworkers of America, C. I. O. Dr. Steelman asked the operators and Mr. Murray to come to Washington for a meeting with him at 3 P. M. tomorrow.

In addition, Dr. Steelman talked by telephone with Nathan Feinsinger, chairman of the Wage Stabilization Board, who has been in New York seeking to effect an agreement. Mr. Feinsinger will meet with Dr. Steelman at noon to give the Defense Mobilizer a complete report on the discussions that have been in progress in New York.

Also in response to the President's orders, Secretary Sawyer immediately designated the presidents of the steel companies as "operating managers" on behalf of the United States.

In a statement issued after the President's broadcast Mr. Sawyer said that he "neither requested nor wanted this job, but when our men at the front are taking orders in the face of great danger those of us farther back can do no less."

He indicated that he would not act on the wage question that brought about the strike threat until both labor and management arrived at an agreement.

The President announced his intention of seizing the mills to the public in a combined radio and television broadcast delivered over all major networks at 10:30 P. M.

The President in his speech called steel "our key industry."

"It is vital to our defense efforts," he declared. "It is vital to peace."

Mr. Truman castigated the steel industry, placing on the operators the blame for the present impasse in negotiations. Despite current profits which give them more than a comfortable return, the President said, the "companies are now saying they ought to have a price increase."

"That's about the most outrageous thing I ever heard of," he declared. "They not only want to raise their prices to cover any wage increase; they want to double their money on the deal."

He explained that he was taking the measures because they were the only way to prevent a shutdown.

"As President of the United States it is my plain duty to keep this from happening," Mr. Truman declared. He said the steel companies were "recklessly forcing a shutdown of the steel mills."

"They are trying to get special, preferred treatment, not available to any other industries," the President continued, "and they are apparently willing to stop steel production to get it."

Mr. Truman reviewed the activities of the Wage Stabilization Board in endeavoring to reach a fair settlement of wage claims of the steel workers. He said the recommendations that were made to the steel industry on March 20 provided "a fair and reasonable basis for reaching a settlement on a new management-labor contract —a settlement that is consistent with our present stabilization program."

"Steel industry profits are now running at the rate of about $2,500,000,000 a year," the President continued. "The steel companies are now making a profit of about $19.50 on every ton of steel they produce. On top of that they can get a price increase of close to $3 a ton under the Capehart Amendment to the Price Control Law. They don't need this, but we are going to have to give it to them because the Capehart Amendment requires it.

"Now add to this the $19.50 a ton they are already making and you have profits of better than $22 a ton."

Taft-Hartley Procedure

The President insisted that the settlement offered by the Wage Board was fair to both parties and to the public interest.

"What's more, I think the steel companies know it," he declared.

The President went on to explain that a big rise in steel prices would increase the prices of other things all up and down the line. Sooner or later, prices of all the products that use steel would go up—tanks and trucks and buildings, automobiles and vacuum cleaners and refrigerators right on down to canned goods and egg beaters, he said.

He conceded that many had been asking why he did not rely on procedures of the Taft-Hartley Act to deal with the emergency.

"This has not been done because the so-called emergency provisions of the Taft-Hartley Act would be of no help in meeting the situation that confronts us tonight," he declared.

"That act provides that before anything else is done the President must first set up a board of inquiry to find the facts on the dispute and report to him as to what they are. We would have to sit around for a week or two for this board to report before we could take the next step. And meanwhile the steel plants would be shut down."

Mr. Truman explained that the Taft-Hartley procedure could not prevent a steel shutdown of at least a week or two.

"The way we want to get steel production—the only way to get it in the long run—is for manage-ment and labor to sit down and settle their dispute," he said. "Sooner or later that's what will have to be done. So it might just as well be done now.

"At midnight the Government will take over the steel plants. Both management and labor will then be working for the Government. And they will have a clear duty to heat up their furnaces again and go on making steel.

"When management and labor meet down here in Washington, they will have a chance to go back to bargaining and settle their dispute. As soon as they do that, we can turn the steel plants back to their private owners with the assurance that production will continue.

"It is my earnest hope that the parties will settle without delay— tomorrow if possible. I don't want to see the Government running the steel plants a moment longer than is absolutely necessary to prevent a shutdown.

"There is no excuse for the present impasse in negotiations. Everyone concerned knows what ought to be done. A settlement should be reached between the steel companies and the union. And the companies should then apply to the Office of Price Stabilization for whatever price increase they are entitled to under the law.

"That is what is called for in the national interest.

"On behalf of the whole country, I ask the steel companies and the steelworkers' unions to compose their differences in the American spirit of fair play and obedience to the law of the land."

The Executive Order Cited

In his Executive Order the President said that to assure the continued availability of steel and steel products during the existing emergency, the Secretary of Commerce was directed:

¶To take possession of all plants, facilities, and other properties of more than eighty-eight companies.

¶To act through with the aid of public or private instrumentalities or persons as he may designate. All Federal agencies were directed to cooperate to the fullest extent possible.

¶To determine and prescribe terms and conditions of employment under which the plants of which the Government takes possession shall be operated, recognizing the rights of workers "to bargain collectively through representatives of their own choosing and to engage in concerted activities for the purpose of collective bargaining, adjustment of grievances, or other mutual aid or protection, provided that such activities do not interfere with the operation of such plants, facilities, and other properties."

¶To see that management of the plants continue their functions, including the collection and disbursement of funds in the usual and ordinary course of business in the names of their respective companies.

¶To keep existing rights and obligations of the companies in full force and effect. "There may be made, in due course, payments of dividends on stocks and of principal, interest, sinking funds; and all other distributions upon bonds, debentures, and other obligations end expenditures may be made for other ordinary corporate or business purposes.

¶To return the possession and operation of the plant to the private owner whenever the Secretary decides that the operation of a plant or other property is no longer necessary or expedient in the interest of national defense.

¶To issue such regulations and orders as deemed necessary for carrying out the purposes of the order and to delegate and authorize subdelegations of such of his functions under the order as he deems desirable.

Senators Fear Crisis

The decision that seizure of the mills was the only way out for the Government was reached at a three-hour conference of top governmental officials with Dr. Steelman this afternoon.

Dr. Steelman and Secretary Sawyer later called on the President and advised a direct explanation to the public. They are understood to have told him that the talk should include a sharp criticism of the steel mill owners for their failure to accept wage and other recommendations made last month by the Wage Stabilization Board.

The President has been charged with "playing politics" with the steel strike threat because he has not invoked the Taft-Hartley Law. In the Senate today, Senator John W. Bricker, Republican of Ohio, called on the President to use the provisions of the Taft-Hartley Act and asserted that the seizure of the mills "would be a perversion, a distortion of the law."

The Ohio Senator and Senator Harry P. Cain, Republican of Washington, voiced the belief that seizure of the plants would lead to nationalization of the steel industry.

"I believe there is a determination to break down private enterprise and move into heavy industry," Senator Bricker told the Senate. He called such a move "basic" to the plans of socialism, "which is in the minds of many of the planners and those who believe in centralized Government."

The steel deadlock developed when producers balked at accepting recommendations of the Wage Stabilization Board for a wage contract increasing the hourly wage of steel workers by 17½ cents an hour and allowing fringe benefits that would bring the total to slightly more than 26 cents an hour over a period of eighteen months. Wages in the industry now average $1.88 an hour.

Industry representatives insisted that the wage recommendations could not be accepted unless compensating increases in the price of finished steel were allowed by the Government. The industry maintained that a price advance of $12 a ton was essential while Government spokesmen maintained that an advance of $2 to $3 a ton was all the industry could expect.

JONES & LAUGHLIN STEEL CORPORATION

THIRD AVENUE & ROSS STREET

PITTSBURGH 30, PA.

April 17, 1952

TO OUR SHAREHOLDERS, EMPLOYES, CUSTOMERS, AND SUPPLIERS:

The steel companies, including Jones & Laughlin Steel Corporation, are in the hands of the government, seized by the order of President Truman on April 8, 1952. This seizure is being contested in the courts by a number of steel companies, including this Company. It is unlikely that we can expect an early conclusive answer from the courts.

The President has based his unprecedented action upon what he apparently claims to be powers inherent in his office. If such inherent powers can be upheld in the office of the President of the United States, we shall have lost the protection against dictatorship for which we have looked to our Constitution since the beginnings of this nation.

No law passed by Congress has given the President the power to make this seizure of the steel industry. This fact has not deterred the President. The Fifth Amendment to our Constitution—one of those Amendments included in our Bill of Rights—prohibits seizure of property except as provided by law.

The President has had a legal and proper remedy open to him in the present steel wage dispute. Article II of our Constitution states that the President "shall take care that the laws be faithfully executed". The President has refused to make use of a specific law dealing with this particular kind of a crisis.

A clear purpose of the Labor Management Relations Act of 1947 (Taft-Hartley Act) was to provide the President with the means for dealing with a labor dispute of importance to the national welfare. Neither the pleasure nor the desire of the union or the companies gives justification to the President for neglect of his obligation to execute this law. The President has deliberately chosen an illegal and dictatorial seizure instead of this lawful remedy.

The issue now raised is basic to our whole American life. It is the question of whether or not we will permit the continuance of dictatorship, brought about and governed by irresponsible and distorted motives, in this country.

The issue extends far beyond the action of the President to seize the steel companies. It cuts across the entire meaning of our Constitution and of our laws. It threatens not only the existence of one industry, but also the security of all personal rights.

The President's act, if permitted to stand, transforms our government into one in which a president has the power to take any and all private property at will without law—our homes, our savings, our means of livelihood, our free newspapers, and even the unions which may now seem to have a temporary benefit.

The salvation of American liberties depends upon informed public opinion and the will of thoughtful people.

Our own duty in J&L to our country and to our shareholders is clear. We will continue to do everything we rightfully can to maintain the production of steel. We will oppose in every proper way this effort to substitute irresponsible government force for fair collective bargaining; to impose union membership on our employes by edict; and to confiscate the property of our shareholders.

President

Ben Morell
Chairman of the Board of Directors

MANY CASES OF SEIZURE, FEW JUDICIAL DECISIONS

American Courts Have Never Clearly Defined Limits of Executive Power

By LUTHER A. HUSTON

WASHINGTON, May 3—Presidents have resorted to seizure of private property on many occasions and under divers circumstances, and their acts have been challenged frequently, but few of the challenges have produced actual litigation that was carried to a conclusion in the nation's courts.

The voluminous briefs filed by the Department of Justice and by lawyers for the steel companies in the steel seizure case are well sprinkled with citations of court cases. All have some bearing, or at least the lawyers think they have, on the broad question of the President's implied powers.

Citations of History

The brief of attorneys for the steel companies delves into history to show that resistance to seizure isn't a new idea among the Anglo-Saxons. It relates the case of so-called ship money, back in the reign of Charles I of England.

Charles was afraid that his realm was threatened with invasion and regarded his naval force as inadequate to repel it. He ordered the various counties of his domain to provide ships for the common defense.

John Hampden, citizen, resisted the order. The courts of the day sustained the King, and some judges who ventured to dissent were removed. Later, however, Parliament took a hand, and some of the judges who voted for the King were impeached and an act of Parliament canceled the judgment.

Royal Prerogatives

The framers of our Constitution had in mind the attempted use of royal prerogatives to control the property and freedom of subjects when they drafted the clauses that are being cited, by both sides, in the current controversy.

Four United States Presidents have used the power of seizure to deal with exigencies confronting them. They were Presidents Abraham Lincoln, Woodrow Wilson, Franklin D. Roosevelt and Harry Truman.

Lawyers consulted this week, however, could recall only four cases of actual seizure that were finally adjudicated.

The first were the so-called prize cases growing out of President Lincoln's blockade of the Southern ports and the seizure of ships found in them. There had been no actual declaration of war, but the courts held that Mr. Lincoln had exercised powers implicit in his responsibility to deal with an impending crisis and did not need special legislative authority for his act.

President Lincoln also ordered his Secretary of War to seize the railroad and telegraph lines between Washington and Annapolis but there was no court test of this case.

Seizure by Wilson

President Woodrow Wilson seized the Smith & Wesson arms plant when its management refused to abide by a decision of the War Labor Board. This seizure is cited in the briefs filed in the steel seizure case as supporting the powers of the President but no legal test of the President's action ever was adjudicated.

The champion "seizer" was President Roosevelt. Prior to the enactment of the War Labor Disputes Act, Mr. Roosevelt resorted to seizure of industrial concerns by Executive order on twelve occasions. The companies involved in these instances and the dates of seizure follow:

The North American aviation plant, June 9, 1941.

The Federal Shipbuilding and Drydock Company, Aug. 23, 1941

Air Associates, Inc., Oct. 30, 1941.

The Grand River Dam Project, Nov. 19, 1941.

Toledo, Peoria and Western Railway Company, March 21, 1942.

Brewster Aeronautical Corporation, April 18, 1942.

General Cable Company, Aug. 13, 1942.

S. A. Woods Machine Company, Aug. 19, 1942.

Triumph Explosives, Inc., Oct. 12, 1942.

The coal mines, May 1, 1943.

The American Railroad Company of Puerto Rico, May 13, 1943.

Howarth Pivoted Bearings Company, June 14, 1943.

All were known as non-statutory seizures, and involved labor disputes. The passage of the War Labor Disputes Act gave statutory authority for similar actions taken subsequently by President Roosevelt.

Mine Seizure Upheld

None of these seizure cases by President Roosevelt reached final adjudication in the courts except the coal mine seizure. This taking over was directed against the United Mine Workers' Union, and not the employers—the reverse of the situation in the current steel seizure case.

The lower courts and eventually the Supreme Court sustained the action by the President. On March 17, 1947, the high court affirmed an Appeals Court ruling, but it reduced to $710,000 the fine of $3,500,000 that Judge T. Alan Goldsborough had imposed on John L. Lewis and the miners union.

After the passage of the War Labor Disputes Act, President Roosevelt ordered the Office of Defense Transportation to take over several Midwest trucking lines known as the Employers Group of Motor Freight Carriers, Inc.

The Court of Appeals for the District of Columbia upheld the legality of the seizure, but ruled that the truckers were entitled to damages for any losses while their properties were operated by the Government. Congress set up a commission to adjust these claims and it is still sitting in Kansas City, endeavoring to settle claims that totaled approximately $11,000,000.

President Roosevelt's seizure of the plant of Montgomery Ward and Company during World War II also was challenged as not justified under his powers as Commander in Chief because the plants taken over were "outside the theatre of war" and a lower court sustained the challenge.

This ruling was reversed, however, by a higher court, which held that seizure was justified under the provisions of the War Labor Disputes Act and that under certain circumstances the Continental United States could be considered within the theatre of war, although no actual fighting was taking place on its soil.

Another Noted Case

President Lincoln's Emancipation Proclamation was called a

seizure of private property without due process as guaranteed by the Constitution. No court action to set it aside was brought, however, and where it has been advanced as an argument in support of non-statutory action by a President it has been justified on the grounds of the state of insurrection then prevailing.

One of the noted cases cited in briefs filed in the steel seizure case did not involve seizure but did center around a labor dispute. It is the so-called Debs case, which arose in 1894 when President Grover Cleveland sent troops into Illinois after rioting had broken out in a labor dispute between the American Railway Union and the Pullman Company.

The violence had resulted in obstruction of the rails and interference with interstate commerce. An injunction restraining the strike was issued by a United States District Court.

Opposition and Test

President Cleveland's action in sending troops was strongly opposed by Gov. John Altgeld of Illinois, and the injunction was tested in the courts.

The Supreme Court upheld the validity of the injunction and said that "the entire strength of the nation may be used to enforce in any part of the land the full and free exercise of all national powers."

There have been some cases of seizure where court action was contemplated or reached preliminary stages but which became moot through settlement before a final adjudication.

SUPREME COURT VOIDS STEEL SEIZURE, 6 TO 3

BLACK GIVES RULING

President Cannot Make Law in Good or Bad Times, Majority Says

VINSON IS DISSENTER

Rejects Idea Executive Is 'Messenger Boy' in Crisis—Steel Curbed

By JOSEPH A. LOFTUS

WASHINGTON, June 2—The Supreme Court of the United States ruled, 6 to 3, today that President Truman's seizure of the steel industry to avert a strike violated the Constitution by usurping the legislative powers reserved to Congress.

The President bowed promptly by directing Secretary of Commerce Charles Sawyer to release the properties to their private owners, and the United Steelworkers of America, C. I. O., went on strike.

As a result of the walkout the Government ordered a halt in deliveries of steel from retail warehouses to consumer goods producers in an effort to conserve steel for defense needs.

Authorities said the action was directed at preventing a drain on warehouses by buyers who usually got their steel at the mills. Manufacturers who ordinarily receive steel from warehouses will continue to do so, they added. No order was issued against steel exports.

The Supreme Court justices who voted to uphold District Judge David A. Pine's order dispossessing the Government were: Hugo L. Black, Felix Frankfurter, William O. Douglas, Robert H. Jackson, Harold H. Burton and Tom C. Clark.

Dissenting were: Chief Justice Fred M. Vinson and Justices Stanley F. Reed and Sherman Minton.

Founding Fathers' Action Cited

The court ruled in effect that when the President seized the steel mills he seized the lawmaking power, because only Congress could authorize the taking of private property for public use.

"The Constitution did not subject this law-making power of Congress to Presidential or military supervision or control," said the opinion of the court, written by Justice Black.

"The founders of this nation entrusted the lawmaking power to the Congress alone in both good and bad times," it added. "It would do no good to recall the historical events, the fears of power and the hopes for freedom that lay behind their choice. Such a review would but confirm our holding that this seizure order cannot stand."

Chief Justice Vinson, writing a vigorous dissent, declared that the President's action to keep steel flowing was warranted by the world emergency.

"History bears out the genius of the founding fathers, who created a Government subject to law but not left subject to inertia when vigor and initiative are required," the Chief Justice wrote.

Vinson Criticizes Majority

"As the district judge stated, this is no time for 'timorous' judicial action," he declared. "But neither is this a time for timorous executive action."

Chief Justice Vinson said the majority of the court, not the minority, was seeking to amend the Constitution. He declared:

"The broad Executive power granted by Article II to an officer on duty 365 days a year cannot, it is said, be invoked to avert disaster.

"Instead, the President must confine himself to sending a message to Congress recommending action. Under this messenger-boy concept of the office, the President cannot even act to preserve legislative programs from destruction so that Congress will have something left to act upon."

The court, contrary to a widely held expectation among lawyers, grasped the Constitutional issue firmly and interpreted it without equivocal language. It might have disposed of the case without reaching the ultimate question; indeed, it is the practice of the judiciary to do so whenever possible.

The court acted with unusual speed. Legal controversies often take years in their course through the three levels of the Federal judiciary. This decision came less than eight weeks after the President seized the steel mills.

The seizure took effect on April 9. The district court granted the steel companies' injunction against seizure on April 29. The Circuit Court of Appeals stayed the injunction the next day. The Supreme Court accepted the case the same week and heard oral argument on May 12.

In the three-week interval since argument was heard, the justices wrote more than 50,000 words in opinions in the steel case alone. Each of the six justices in the majority wrote concurring opinions. Only Justices Reed and Minton refrained from writing.

The history-making case hereafter will be known to law students and lawyers as Youngstown Co. v. Sawyer.

Opinions Take 2½ Hours

Delivery of the opinions took two hours and thirty-five minutes. The court convened at noon and Chief Justice Vinson announced that, contrary to custom, the admissions of attorneys to practice before the Supreme Court would be deferred until later. Usually that is the first order of business.

Justice Black started reading the opinion of the court at 12:01. It was comparatively brief, and he finished about 12:15. Justice Frankfurter followed with his concurring opinion. He spoke for thirty minutes and scarcely referred to the printed page, except near the end of his opinion.

He did not follow the precise language of his opinion. He used the expression once, "almost a suckling knows that," but the context was not clear.

At another point Justice Frankfurter appeared to be taking issue with Chief Justice Vinson, whose dissent quoted at length from a 1914 brief of John W. Davis as Solicitor General of the United States. Mr. Davis had argued for the steel companies in this case, and Chief Justice Vinson turned his 1914 phrases against him.

Justice Frankfurter said "I don't understand the relevance of quoting the brief of a lawyer in a case * * * with the well-known astigmatism of advocates."

Positions in Past Recalled

Chief Justice Vinson also cited the positions taken by Justices Jackson and Clark with respect to the President's powers when they were Attorneys General. Referring extemporaneously to Justice Jackson in what was taken to be friendly sarcasm, the Chief Justice remarked that changing one's mind is "evidence of strength."

At that point Justice Black turned and caught Justice Jackson's eye two seats away and grinned at him. Justice Jackson reciprocated.

The Chief Justice continued to refer to Justice Jackson's position as Attorney General in the seizure of the North American plant in June, 1941, when Mr. Jackson was Attorney General. He said that Mr. Jackson stated his opinion in support of seizure then as vigorously and as forcefully "as he ordinarily does now." The lawyers caught the inflection on "ordinarily" and there was a spontaneous burst of laughter. Justice Jackson joined in it.

Chief Justice Vinson was delivering his opinion when the court's regular luncheon hour of 2 o'clock arrived. He continued until he finished at 2:35 and the court then recessed for thirty minutes.

Clark in Different Approach

The differences among the six majority opinions were mainly differences in emphasis, except Justice Clark's. He said he concurred in the judgment, but not the opinion, of the court. He used a different approach to the same conclusion, declaring that the President's reservoir of nonstatutory powers was not available to him when Congress had provided statutory procedures.

Justice Clark referred particularly to the plant seizure provision of the Selective Service Act. He expressed skepticism of the Administration's contention that it had complied in substance with the intent of the Taft-Hartley law's eighty-day injunction provision by persuading the union to withhold its strike voluntarily for ninety-nine days.

Justice Burton, who was most interested during the argument in the President's nonuse of the Taft-Hartley injunction, came to no conclusion on that point. He grounded his position on the non-existence of statutory support for the seizure.

Justice Jackson's Views

Justice Jackson saw a tendency of Congress to abdicate its powers. He wrote:

"But I have no illusion that any decision by this court can keep power in the hands of Congress if it is not wise and timely in meeting its problems. A crisis that challenges the President equally, or perhaps primarily, challenges Congress.

"If not good law, there was wordly wisdom in the maxim attributed to Napoleon that 'the tools belong to the man who can use them.' We may say that power to legislate for emergencies belongs in the hands of Congress, but only Congress itself can prevent power from slipping through its fingers."

Justice Douglas, too, referred to Congress, though not so pointedly. "The Congress, as well as the President, is trustee of the national welfare," he said.

Justice Frankfurter declared that Congress had consciously withheld seizure power from the President.

Here and there in the opinions reversing the President there were friendly expressions directed to Mr. Truman the man, and the justices seemed to be saying that this was a decision for the ages and must be viewed impersonally.

Justice Frankfurter, for example, said: "It is absurd to see a dictator in a representative product of the sturdy democratic traditions of the Mississippi Valley. The accretion of dangerous power does not come in a day. It does come, however slowly, from the generative forces of unchecked disregard of the restrictions that fence in even the most disinterested assertion of authority."

Again, in concluding, Justice Frankfurter said, "It is not a pleasant judicial duty to find that the President has exceeded his powers and still less so when his purposes were dictated by concern for the nation's well-being, in the assured conviction that he acted to avert danger."

Justice Douglas remarked: "We pay a price for our system of checks and balances, for the distribution of power among the three branches of government. It is a price that today may seem exorbitant to many. Today a kindly President uses the seizure power to effect a wage increase and to keep the steel furnaces in production. Yet tomorrow another President might use the same power to prevent a wage increase, to curb trade unionists, to regiment labor as oppressively as industry thinks it has been regimented by this seizure."

Justice Jackson said: "I am not alarmed that it would plunge us straightway into dictatorship, but it is at least a step in that wrong direction."

Chief Justice Vinson stressed the emergency aspect of the seizure. "One is not here called upon even to consider the possibility of Executive seizure of a farm, a corner grocery store or even a single industrial plant," he said. "Such considerations arise only when one ignores the central fact of this case—that the nation's entire basic steel production would have shut down completely if there had been no Government seizure."

The Chief Justice recounted the seizures made by Presidents, beginning with President Lincoln through World War II. He dwelt extensively on the Midwest oil seizure cases, which Mr. Davis, the steel companies' present chief counsel, argued effectively for the Government in 1914, and on the North American Company seizure without statutory support before the Pearl Harbor attack.

"The Attorney General (Jackson) vigorously proclaimed that the President had the moral duty to keep this nation's defense effort a 'going concern,'" the Chief Justice wrote. "His ringing moral justification was coupled with a legal justification equally well stated * * *." He quoted at length from Attorney General Jackson's opinion at the time.

1949 Clark Letter Cited

The Chief Justice also referred in a footnote to a letter written by Attorney General Clark, now Justice Clark, informing the Senate Labor Committee in 1949 that in his opinion the emergency powers of the President were "exceedingly great."

Justice Jackson met the North American issue in a footnote, declaring that the labor action that stopped aircraft production in that case was a Communist insurrection, that the plant was under direct contact with the Government to supply defense items, that management acquiesced in the seizure, and that many of the employes were at the gates trying to work.

Justice Jackson observed: "The North American seizure was regarded as an execution of Congressional policy. I do not regard it as a precedent for this, but, even if I did, I should not bind present judicial judgment by earlier partisan advocacy."

Arthur Goldberg, counsel of the steel workers union, in a statement after the decision emphasized that the court had ruled only on seizure, on which the union had taken no position in the argument. He added:

"The court did not decide, as the steel companies had urged it to do, that the President should have used a Taft-Hartley injunction against the union. The United Steelworkers of America believes that the union's contention before the court and the public that the President should not use a Taft-Hartley injunction in this situation has been vindicated by the failure of any one of the justices of the Supreme Court to accept the companies' Taft-Hartley argument."

Steel Strike Is Settled With Increases in Pay and Prices

MILL OPENING SPED

Union and Industry End Dispute After Truman Says: Agree, 'Or Else'

$5.20 RISE A TON SET

16-Cent Increase in Pay and Modified Union Shop Are Provided

By A. H. RASKIN
Special to THE NEW YORK TIMES.

WASHINGTON, July 24 — The steel strike that has been choking the national economy for fifty-three days was settled at the White House today. The settlement came less than seven hours after President Truman had warned union and industry leaders to end the tie-up within twenty-four hours, "or else."

Orders to the 600,000 striking workers to return to the steel mills will go out tomorrow afternoon after the 175-member Wage Policy Committee of the United Steelworkers of America, C. I. O., meets here to ratify the proposed agreement. Two or three days more will be needed to get steel flowing to metal-starved factories producing military and civilian goods.

The settlement, which was announced personally by the President at 4:55 P. M., was hammered out in face-to-face talks between Benjamin F. Fairless, president and chairman of the United States Steel Corporation, and Philip Murray, president of the union and the Congress of Industrial Organizations. Dr. John R. Steelman, acting Director of Defense Mobilization, served as mediator in the White House session.

Bethlehem Plan Modified

The agreement follows the basic pattern of the so-called Bethlehem formula, worked out five weeks ago in secret talks between the union and the Bethlehem Steel Company. The accord was vetoed at that time by the rest of the "big six" steel companies, but subsequent modifications made it acceptable to all the parties.

Smaller steel companies indicated that they would follow the lead of the industry leaders in signing the agreement as soon as it had been approved by the union's Policy Committee.

The agreement provides for a wage increase of 16 cents an hour, "fringe" benefits that would cost another 5.4 cents an hour and a compromise form of the union shop. Pre-strike wages averaged $1.88 an hour. A novel feature of the understanding is an agreement that Mr. Fairless and Mr. Murray will make a joint speaking tour to promote improved labor-management relations in United States Steel plants.

At the same time that the union and industry leaders were initialing the memorandum of understanding at the White House, Dr. Steelman put his signature on an order for an increase of $5.20 a ton in the price of carbon steel.

The steel companies had been entitled to a price rise of $2.84 a ton under the Capehart Amendment to the Defense Production Act, but had declared that they could not undertake the higher labor costs involved in the proposed agreement without additional price relief.

17 Million Tons of Steel Lost

The pact will clear the way for reopening of the iron ore mines in the Mesabi Range of Minnesota and in other parts of the country, which had been closed by a parallel strike of 23,000 members of the Murray union.

Steel producers had warned that failure to resume maximum shipment of ore while the Great Lakes were open would have necessitated a new shutdown of the steel mills for lack of metal when the lakes froze next winter.

The settlement brought to an end a dispute that, in the words of Robert A. Lovett, Secretary of Defense, had inflicted greater damage on the defense effort than the worst enemy bombing raid could have done.

Canners and farm groups had feared that continuation of the tie-up would compel wholesale destruction of August crops of fruits and vegetables because tin cans would not be available.

The walkout caused a loss of roughly 17,000,000 tons of steel and more than $350,000,000 in wages. This did not count the wage loss to more than 1,000,000 workers who had been forced into joblessness in industries dependent on steel.

Management spokesmen said that many more workers would have to be laid off before the pipeline of steel supply refilled sufficiently to assure continuous factory operation. Some warned that the "worst effects" of the steel shutdown were still ahead because of the time required to get steel from mills to consumers.

The settlement came on the eve of Mr. Truman's departure for the Democratic National Convention, and his staff expressed particular gratification that it had been possible to work out an agreement without acting on Congressional suggestions that he use the Taft-Hartley Act.

Both houses of Congress had urged the President to get an injunction under that law after the Supreme Court had invalidated his earlier seizure of the steel mills to forestall a walkout. The strike began as soon as the mills reverted to private control June 2.

President "Poured It On"

The President, still looking drawn and sounding hoarse from the virus infection he suffered last week, met with Mr. Fairless and Mr. Murray at 10 A. M. He talked to them for only ten minutes, but, authoritative sources said, he "really poured it on in that time."

He stressed the urgency of restoring steel production in terms of the national welfare, and he warned that he would have some suggestions of his own to make if no settlement were reached by 10 A. M. tomorrow.

Mr. Truman never made plain what his alternative proposals would have been, but it was reported that he planned to insist that any unresolved issues be submitted to binding arbitration. Aides discounted speculation that he might have called Congress back into session or proceeded with tentative plans to seize a few key mills under the Selective Service Act.

Mr. Murray and Mr. Fairless spent an hour and twenty minutes in private session after the President finished his talk. Dr. Steelman moved in and out to make certain that the two men were talking and not glowering, but he left them largely to their own devices.

When the union president and the head of the country's largest steel company left the White House at 11:30 A. M., Mr. Fairless smilingly read a joint statement announcing that they planned to meet with their respective bargaining committees and come back to the President's office at 2:30 P. M.

The company executive gave Mr. Murray a ride to the C. I. O. office a block from the White House, then went to his own suite at the Carlton Hotel.

Key Associates Called

The two chief negotiators came back together and told reporters they had spent part of the recess in joint conference. An hour after they started talking again at the White House, they sent for key associates on both sides. By the time they got there, the agreement was virtually completed.

The union conferees were Arthur J. Goldberg, general counsel; James G. Thimmes, vice president, and David J. McDonald, secretary-treasurer.

For the companies, Mr. Fairless called John A. Stephens, vice-president in charge of industrial relations for United States Steel; Roger Blough, vice chairman of the corporation's board of directors; Joseph M. Larkin, vice president of Bethlehem Steel, and John H. Morse, Bethlehem's counsel. Mr. Larkin and Mr. Morse had been co-authors of the "Bethlehem formula" in talks in New York more than a month ago.

At 4:55 P. M., the President called reporters to his office. He was wearing a dark suit and a dark, figured tie. Mr. Murray, in a blue suit with a maroon tie, stood at the President's right, and Mr. Fairless, in a grey cord suit and bright red tie, stood at his left. Mr. Truman held a brief statement in his hand, but showed no visible elation.

"How are you feeling, Mr. President?" a reporter asked while the press gathered.

Mr. Truman grinned for the first time.

"I'll tell you in a minute," he said.

Statement by President

He read the statement in a low tone, after warning reporters that he would read it only once, and that no questions would be answered by anyone after he finished. This is what he read:

"Mr. Murray and Mr. Fairless have just advised me that six major steel companies and the United Steelworkers of America, C. I. O., have reached agreement on important basic issues. The union is calling its national Wage

ANNOUNCING AGREEMENT IN STEEL DISPUTE

Policy Committee to meet in Washington tomorrow [at 2 P. M. at the Mayflower Hotel] for the purpose of ratifying the agreement. This should lead to a speedy resumption of steel production."

The six companies, in addition to United States Steel and Bethlehem, are Republic, Jones & Laughlin, Inland and Youngstown Sheet and Tube. The "big six" represent more than two-thirds of the country's steel-making capacity, and they have been negotiating with the union as a bloc on the basic wage and union shop issues.

Mr. Fairless and Mr. Murray, who had been calling one another Ben and Phil all day, went out on the White House steps to pose for cameramen. Neither would amplify the President's announcement, but when the union president was asked whether he was satisfied with the terms he replied:

"I wouldn't be recommending them if I wasn't."

Both leaders stressed their hope that the bitterness of the long strike would speedily be forgotten.

"I am very happy that this disastrous steel strike is nearing an end," Mr. Fairless asserted. "I hope that our relationships in the future will prevent a recurrence of what we have just gone through."

"I echo what Mr. Fairless has just said," Mr. Murray declared. "I hope and I really believe that we will be able to develop a more friendly and cooperative relationship in the days that lie ahead."

News Sent to Convention

The two leaders shook hands warmly as they went off to report the agreement to associates in their respective field headquarters. Meanwhile, word of the pact was flashed to Democratic leaders in Chicago. It was received during a demonstration for Averell Harriman, and it took several minutes for Speaker Sam Rayburn, chairman of the convention, to restore order sufficiently to read the good news. He got it slightly confused, substituting the words "mine workers" for "steel workers," but every one understood right away and responded with cheers. The Democrats had feared that prolongation of the tie-up would provide fertile campaign material for the Republicans.

Secretary Lovett, who had given a grim account yesterday of the strike's impact on the arms program, was among the happiest men in Washington when he learned of the settlement.

"Gosh, that's wonderful," he said. "Now let's pull up our socks and get going full speed ahead."

Henry H. Fowler, head of the Defense Production Administration and the National Production Authority, let it be known that he would have an announcement Monday on plans for allocating the flow of new steel to users in greatest need of metal.

"It is too early yet to assess the full extent of the damage to our defense effort and the civilian economy caused by the steel strike," Mr. Fowler said. "Much more of the damage will become clear in the weeks ahead.

"We have made out plans, including the use of the Controlled

The New York Times (by Bruce Hoertel)

President Truman at his White House desk reading a statement telling of strike settlement while he is flanked by Philip Murray, left, head of the United Steelworkers union and Benjamin F. Fairless, president and chairman of the United States Steel Corporation.

Materials Plan, as to what we would do when the strike was settled. On Monday we will announce those plans."

Industry Backs Strong Union

The Fairless-Murray decision to undertake a joint speaking tour of United States Steel plants was expected to set a pattern for union and company leaders in other steel companies. The joint talks are intended to counteract any suggestion that the industry's unyielding resistance to "compulsory unionism" was prompted by a desire to undermine the union.

The industry has argued that it was as desirous as Mr. Murray of having a strong, healthy union in its plants. The presence of company and union executives on the same platform will help foster the concept that workers and employers have more in common than in conflict.

Four top industry executives made a dramatic appearance last Monday at a Pittsburgh meeting of the union's wage policy committee. Even though they were unsuccessful in swaying the committee from a decision to demand all the wage and union shop benefits recommended last March by the Wage Stabilization Board, the industrialists did moderate the

temper of the session to an extent that helped bring about today's agreement.

If Mr. Murray had stood fast on the committee's announced determination to get everything the wage board proposed, no agreement would have been possible, industry sources said. The board had called for a wage increase of 12½ cents an hour retroactive to last Jan. 1, a further increase of 2½ cents, effective July 1, and a third increase of 2½ cents next Jan. 1.

In addition, the board had called for fringe benefits that would cost another 8.9 cents an hour. The controversy engendered by the board's ruling led to a Congressional decision last month to reconstitute the Wage Board and strip it of most of its disputes functions.

Wage Rise Retroactive

The new pact was reported to call for a wage increase of 16 cents an hour, retroactive to March 1. This would give the average worker about $90 in back pay, or about $13 more than the best offer the industry had made in the Pittsburgh talks last week.

The agreement also provides for six paid holidays, with double time to be paid any worker who

has to work on a holiday, and an increase in the pay premiums, or differentials, for the afternoon and night shifts from the present 4 and 6 cents an hour to 6 and 9 cents an hour.

The accord further provides for three weeks' vacation after fifteen years of employment, effective as of last Jan. 1, and a cut in the Southern wage differential from the present 10 cents an hour to 5 cents. United States Steel and Republic are the only companies directly affected by the last provision.

The total direct value of all the fringe benefits was estimated at 5.4 cents an hour. The gains were identical with those proposed by the Wage Board, except that the board also had recommended time and one-quarter for Sunday work, beginning next Jan. 1. This would have cost an additional 3.5 cents an hour. The fringe benefits to which the union agreed had been available since the beginning of the strike.

The big point of contention was the form of the union shop compromise. The union insisted on a union shop, and the companies demanded that there be no "compulsory unionism." Under the proposed pact, old workers who are not in the union will not have to join.

New employes will have to sign a union membership application at the time they are hired, but the membership will not take effect if they send the company a letter during the last fifteen days of their first month on the job saying that they do not want to be in the union. The companies will turn copies of such letters over to the union.

This differs from the conventional union shop under which all employes, old and new, are required to join the union as a condition of holding their jobs. In the recent talks at Pittsburgh, the main ingredients of the compromise plan had been agreed on. The sole point at issue when Mr. Fairless and Mr. Murray got to the White House was whether the new contract should contain a fifteen-day "escape" period for workers now in the union who might want to get out.

Usually such an "escape" period comes at the beginning of a new contract, but the union argued that it was not necessary in the present agreement because more than six and one-half months had passed since the "maintenance of membership" provisions of the old contract expired. Workers could leave the union without penalty during the interim period.

The companies agreed that no "escape" period was needed now, but they protested against dropping the clause altogether. As a compromise, the escape period will be moved to the end of the contract. This would be June 30, 1954. The contract will be reopenable next June 30 on wages only. The precise language of the escape clause was still being worked out late tonight by company and union lawyers.

Fear that the return to work in United States Steel might be held up by disagreement over company demands for changes in contract clauses affecting management rights, incentive pay scales and local work practices were eased by the harmonious meeting between Mr. Fairless and Mr. Murray. Union officials, who had predicted that United States Steel would remain shut for weeks after every other company resumed operations, said they expected little difficulty now.

Price Rise Held Consistent

The rise of $5.20 a ton in the price of carbon steel had been tentatively agreed on twelve days ago when Dr. Steelman received private assurances from Mr. Fairless that a wage settlement was at hand. White House aides said that the agreement was consistent with a proposal Dr. Steelman had made before the President seized the steel mills April 8.

At that time, Dr. Steelman had promised the industry a price rise of $4.50 a ton, of which $2.84 would have been the amount allowable under the Capehart Amendment. This permits producers to pass on all increases in costs from the start of the Korean war to July 26, 1951. To the $4.50 offered at that time, Dr. Steelman added 70 cents a ton to cover the cost of a freight increase made effective by the Interstate Commerce Commission last May 2.

No Comment by O. P. S.

The Presidential assistant sent his order for higher steel prices to Roger L. Putnam, Economic Stabilization Administrator, with instructions that it be put into effect to "effectuate a settlement of the steel strike."

Mr. Putnam is expected to issue a detailed implementing order tomorrow. Because of the diversity in steel prices, some types of steel will go up more than $5.20 a ton and some less. Price officials said that they expected the average rise would be about $5.65 a ton. The present average price is $110 a ton.

Dr. Steelman said that his action was necessary "because of the position of the steel industry that it was unable to absorb increases involved in the settlement and because of the dire need for steel products for defense and for our civilian industries."

Ellis G. Arnall, Director of Price Stabilization, who had continued up to last week "to oppose any price rise that exceeded the sum mandatory under the Capehart Amendment, was at the Democratic convention and his office had no immediate comment on the Steelman order.

Special to The New York Times.

WASHINGTON, July 24—Following is a chronology of events in the steel dispute that was settled today at the White House:

Nov. 1, 1951—The United States Steelworkers of America, C. I. O., notified the industry it wished to bargain for a wage increase of 18½ cents an hour and other benefits that would have cost at least as much more, to become effective Dec. 31, expiration date of its working contract.

Dec. 17—Philip Murray, president of the union, announced a strike for Dec. 31.

Dec. 23—President Truman referred the case to the Wage Stabilization Board, and the union set a new strike deadline for Jan. 3.

Jan. 3, 1952—The union postponed the strike deadline.

Jan. 10-Feb. 16 — The Wage Board held hearings in New York and Washington.

March 20—The board, in a decision made by its public and labor members, with industry dissenting, recommended a wage increase of 26.4 cents an hour in three installments over eighteen months. The union accepted and postponed the strike until April 8. Management rejected the recommendations, but agreed to further negotiations.

April 8—President Truman seized the steel industry to prevent the scheduled country-wide walkout.

April 9—Seven major steel companies tried unsuccessfully to get a temporary restraining order in Federal District Court to nullify the seizure.

April 24-25—Federal District Court Judge David A. Pine heard arguments for a preliminary injunction to nullify the seizure and restore the mills to the industry.

April 29—Judge Pine ruled that the seizure was unconstitutional and ordered the return of the mills to private ownership. The union immediately began to walk out.

April 30—The United States Court of Appeals stayed the effect of Judge Pine's ruling, enabling the Government to appeal the ruling to the Supreme Court.

May 2—The strike was called off at the President's request.

May 3—Company and union repre-

July 25, 1952

sentatives met at the White House where Mr. Truman warned that he would raise wages if no settlement were reached. Later that day the Supreme Court agreed to review the case and forbade a wage increase pending its decision.

May 4—White House conferences broke down.

May 12-13—Industry and Government lawyers argued before the Supreme Court.

June 2—The Supreme Court ruled that the seizure of the steel industry was unconstitutional. Associate Justice Hugo Black wrote the majority opinion, which said that "this seizure order cannot stand." The union called another strike.

June 9—Union-management negotiations again collapsed.

June 10—President Truman went before a joint session of Congress and asked for a law permitting seizure of the steel industry. The Senate rejected the proposal and requested instead use of the Taft-Hartley Law's eighty-day no-strike injunction provision.

June 27—A break in the dispute occurred as the Pittsburgh Steel Company, the country's fourteenth largest steel producer, reached an agreement with its steel workers substantially on the union's terms.

July 10—Industry and labor representatives resumed talks in Pittsburgh.

July 12—Steel executives called at White House to meet with Dr. John R. Steelman, Presidential negotiator in steel strike.

July 14—The Chrysler Corporation shut down all its Michigan automobile and truck assembly lines because of the impact of steel strike.

July 18—Government officials disclosed that unless settlement was soon reached, President Truman would seize certain defense plants under provisions of the Selective Service Act.

July 22—Steel shortages forced the Army to shut down its largest shell-making plant at St. Louis.

July 23—President Truman summoned Benjamin F. Fairless, head of the United States Steel Corporation, and Mr. Murray to the White House.

July 24 — President Truman announced settlement of the dispute after conferring with Messrs. Fairless and Murray.

WHITE HOUSE ENDS ALL WAGE CONTROL, MANY PRICE CURBS

Actions in Force Immediately —11,000 Petitions on Pay Enabled to Take Effect

MEATS, FURNITURE FREED

Ceilings Also Go Off Long List of Department Store Items —Reuther Hails Step

By JOSEPH A. LOFTUS

WASHINGTON, Feb. 6—President Eisenhower suspended all Government controls on wages and salaries today and decontrolled a long list of consumer goods, including meat, furniture, clothing, nearly all the items normally sold in department stores and meals and drinks sold in restaurants and bars.

The actions were taken under Executive order and are effective immediately.

The order on wages means that employers and unions are back in the full collective bargaining business after two years of Federal restraint. Anything they agree on, they can put into effect, including retroactive payments. In the absence of an employe bargaining organization, the employer is free to make any adjustment by himself.

The impact of the President's action is a matter of conjecture. The wage and salary agencies had on their dockets at least 11,000 petitions for approval of higher pay or other benefits. Such increases may go into effect immediately, as far as the Federal Government is concerned.

Whether these increases would have a mild effect on other bargaining relationships or set off a new round of demands, no one could foretell. A great deal depends on what happens to prices.

Many Goods Affected

Many consumer goods now will be free to find their own price levels. These include children's wear, toys, yard goods, leather goods, small appliances, sporting items, towels and sheets, as well as the broader categories of meat, meals and furniture. Some prices had already been taken off the controls list temporarily, or "suspended"; today's decontrol order, covering many of these and other items, is a final action.

The President declared that supply and demand in the national economy were "approaching a practicable balance" and that "the earliest possible return to freedom of collective bargaining in the determination of wages will serve to strengthen the national economy and thereby the national security."

Labor leaders in general have felt the time had come to take off wage controls and have contended that wages had been more restricted than prices.

Walter P. Reuther, president of the Congress of Industrial Organizations, commented that he had told President Eisenhower today that the removal of pay controls was "a constructive step." He and David J. McDonald, president of the United Steelworkers of America, C. I. O., reported that they had had "a very pleasant conference" with the President.

Asked whether he thought the end of pay controls would touch off a fresh round of demands, Mr. Reuther said that that was a matter of interest for each individual union.

Some labor leaders thought there would be a period of unrest as unions sought to reopen their contracts—some contracts specifically provide for a reopening on the termination of wage controls. Still others provide for improvements of certain kinds immediately upon the end of controls. It has been illegal, however, for an employer to agree to set aside funds to pay out later what had previously been forbidden.

Permissive in Nature

One labor leader thought that some of the pending wage agreements had been made by employers in the hope that they would be disapproved in whole or in part, and that these employers now might try to hedge on their offers. Where this happens, it is considered a private dispute. The Executive Order does not compel anybody to live up to any agreement; it is permissive in nature.

There are some cases where the wage board already had disapproved part of a wage increase agreed to by an employer and a union. The union cannot, as a matter of legal right, claim the disapproved part now on the ground that wage controls have ended, unless the contract provides for the beginning of such payments automatically when controls end.

On the other hand, if the contract has a reopening clause, or if the employer is willing to reopen it, there is nothing to prevent a union demand, or union-management agreement, to pay now what had been illegal until today.

Charles C. Killingsworth, chairman of the Wage Stabilization Committee, said today that the automatic "clearance" of petitions for wage adjustments applied to all pending cases, including appeals from prior decisions at the national or regional level.

Wage controls have been administered by the committee since the industry members withdrew from the Wage Board several months ago in a protest. Harry S. Truman, then the President, had overridden the board in its modification of a soft-coal wage agreement.

DURKIN QUITS CABINET POST; CHARGES BREACH OF ACCORD TO SEEK TAFT LAW CHANGES

LABOR CHIEF IS OUT

President Expresses His Regret, but Does Not Comment on Issues

By JOSEPH A. LOFTUS
Special to The New York Times.

WASHINGTON, Sept. 10—Martin P. Durkin resigned as Secretary of Labor today, protesting that the White House had backed down on an agreement to send to Congress nineteen proposed amendments to the Taft-Hartley Law.

Mr. Durkin said that the agreement had been made with members of the President's staff, and that he had believed they had power to represent President Eisenhower and that the President was being kept informed.

President Eisenhower, after conferring with Mr. Durkin for half an hour, accepted the resignation, effective immediately. The President's letter to the first departing member of his Cabinet was one of warm, personal friendliness. It expressed his regret but did not touch on the issues raised by the Secretary.

Mr. Durkin's letter, which was made public later at the President's vacation headquarters in Denver, was friendly, too, and did not mention any dispute. He said that words failed him in attempting to thank the President for appointing him.

Mr. Durkin wrote that he was resigning because it was "necessary" for him to return to his post as president of the United Association of Journeymen and Apprentices of the Plumbing and Pipe Fitting Industry, A. F. L.

Two Issues Are Stressed

He told a news conference that his desire to return to his union post was one of the reasons for his resigning, but the emphasis was put on two other reasons: the White House refusal to honor the agreement that he said had been made, and the failure of the Administration to take any position on Taft-Hartley Law amendments.

Mr. Durkin said that he had written his letter in longhand at home on Aug. 31 and had consulted no one about it. The Taft-Hartley Law message was to have been sent to Congress on July 31, but it was dropped after advance copies had been shown to the chairmen of the Senate and House Labor Committees, Senator H. Alexander Smith of New Jersey and Representative Samuel K. McConnell Jr. of Pennsylvania, both Republicans, and to Sinclair Weeks, Secretary of Commerce.

The draft was attacked as too pro-labor and politically unwise. Vice President Richard M. Nixon, who was a member of the House Labor Committee in 1947 when the Taft-Hartley Act was written, was chiefly instrumental in killing the proposed message, but he had help from others, including the committee chairmen.

Criticism of Draft Voiced

The critics of the draft said that it undermined two fundamentals of the labor law: the bans on the closed shop and on the secondary boycott. A White House spokesman, commenting on a draft that got into print at the time, insisted that work on the message was nowhere near complete.

Mr. Durkin said that the President, at their meeting today, asked him to remain as Secretary. He did not say that he appealed to President Eisenhower on the proposed amendments, and he would not quote the President at all.

However, he was asked this question:

"If he had changed his position this morning, would you have been able to continue as Secretary?"

"I'd say so," Mr. Durkin replied.

Mr. Durkin's answer to the question in that form indicated the President had backed up his assistants in withholding the message draft on which Mr. Durkin said there had been agreement.

The Secretary said further that he had known the nineteen proposed amendments would not be recommended to Congress because he had been "told so," but he would not say who told him.

He would not identify the White House staff members involved in his accusation, but at one point he mentioned the names of a number of persons who had sat in on meetings for the purpose of reaching an agreement on Taft-Hartley Law amendments. The White House staff members who attended were Bernard M. Shanley, special counsel to the President, and Gerald D. Morgan, a special assistant.

"Did they have full power to represent the President?" Mr. Durkin was asked.

"I wasn't informed to the contrary," he replied.

President Eisenhower attended one of the meetings, and Mr. Durkin said:

"It was our belief that the President was being kept informed. We believed he had agreed to them [the amendments]."

The draft of a message prepared for the President to send to Congress just before adjournment was weighted heavily with concessions to labor. The draft did not contain the major changes urged by management spokesmen.

The main proposals in the draft were:

¶The National Labor Relations Board would not be required, as now, to ask the courts for injunctions in secondary boycotts, which are strikes against one employer to put pressure on the primary employer in a dispute. Some secondary boycott activities would be legalized.

¶Unions and employers in the building construction, maritime and entertainment industries would be permitted to make agreements before any employes were hired and the agreement could require the employes to join a union after seven days, instead of after thirty days as provided in the union shop section that is now applicable to industry generally.

¶Supervisors whose duties consisted only of giving directions to employes or assigning work to them would be treated as employes subject to the law, but front-line management supervisors would remain exempt.

¶Unions would be subject to the common law definition of an "agent" so that they would not be held responsible for the acts of an individual member solely because of membership.

¶Unions could expel a member and demand his discharge if he disclosed confidential information of the union or if there was reasonable cause to believe he had subversive intentions against the United States. The present union shop clause permits a union to cause an employe's discharge only if he refuses to pay his dues.

¶The injunction provisions in the law, including the national emergency section, would remain, modified only to the extent that the injunction would be discretionary, not mandatory, in boycotts.

Another factor may have figured in Mr. Durkin's resignation, but to what extent could not be determined. He had objected to the proposed nomination of L. E. Gooding to be a member of the National Labor Relations Board on the basis of opposition from organized labor in Wisconsin. Mr. Gooding is chairman of the Wisconsin Employment Relations Board.

If the President intended, nevertheless, to appoint Mr. Gooding to the N. L. R. B., it would have been a blow to Mr. Durkin, who as recently as Aug. 11 had defended the Administration and had said that he occupied a more "realistic position" as Secretary of Labor than any of his predecessors because he was consulted on all proposed appointments having to do with labor in the Government, and not just those in the Labor Department.

G.M. Lifts Pay, Rewrites Pact Though It Had 2 Years to Run

DETROIT, May 22—The General Motors Corporation consented today to rewrite the wage provisions of its five-year escalator agreement with the United Automobile Workers, C.I.O., although the original contract had two years yet to run.

About 350,000 General Motors employes will benefit from the improved wage formula, which is expected to set a pattern for the rest of the automobile industry. More than 1,000,000 U.A.W. members are covered by escalator agreements.

The new terms, reached without a strike threat, provide that General Motors will:

¶Transfer 19 cents an hour of a 24-cent cost-of-living allowance to the base wage, so that rates cannot drop more than 5 cents an hour, regardless of how much the cost of living goes down.

¶Increase the annual improvement or "productivity" factor from 4 to 5 cents an hour. Base wages will go up by 5 cents on May 29 and again on the same date of next year.

¶Increase the rates of 40,000 skilled tradesmen by 10 cents an hour on June 1.

The parties also worked out a formula for gearing the auto wage escalator to the new Consumer Price Index, rather than the "old series" index, which is soon to be abandoned by the Bureau of Labor Statistics.

The agreement, announced at a joint union-management press conference this morning, amounted to acceptance by General Motors of the union contention that long-term contracts must be "living documents," subject to revision when abnormal economic conditions raised unforeseen problems.

Other automobile manufacturers will be asked to meet the new wage standard. Walter P. Reuther, president of the U. A. W. and of the Congress of Industrial Organizations, made that clear at the press conference.

The Ford Motor Company and the Chrysler Corporation were expected to be next in line. While the General Motors agreement did not involve the union's demand for improvements in the existing pension scale of $125 a month, Mr. Reuther emphasized that the union "had not forgotten" the pension matter.

"Other corporations should assume the moral obligation of pioneering on pensions," he said.

Ford appeared to be the immediate target because its pension scale was slightly lower than those of other manufacturers.

For General Motors, the new agreement means about $30,000,000 over the next two years in additional labor costs. It also was taken as evidence of the corporation's apparent belief that the United States economy will continue at a high level of activity, despite fears of a recession among some automobile builders.

The union, having signed a binding five-year contract that does not expire until 1955, was not in a position to back its demands for wage improvements with strike action. However, John W. Livingston, vice president of the union and director of its General Motors department, had warned that unless the contract was improved by June 1 the union would refuse to sign long-term agreements in the future.

G. M. Head Hails Accord

General Motors, which pioneered the escalator type of agreement, has enjoyed virtually continuous production free of labor disputes since the original contract was signed and evidently wanted to maintain that condition.

Harlow H. Curtice, president of General Motors, hailed the agreement as "a practical solution to problems created by the Korean war with its resulting inflationary impact and the reinstitution of Government controls."

He noted that the 1950 contract had had a stabilizing influence in labor-management relations and added: "We expect the understanding reached today will contribute even more to stabilizing relations among our employes for the remaining two years of the contract."

Under terms of the original General Motors contract, negotiated in 1948 and extended for a five-year period in May of 1950, wages moved up or down 1 cent an hour at three-month intervals when the "old series" index rose or fell 1.14 points.

The new arrangement, beginning June 1, provides that wages will be adjusted 1 cent an hour for each quarterly change of 0.68 point in the new Federal index so long as the fluctuations are within the 5-cent escalation range. However, if prices rise above the present level, a change of 0.6 index point will alter the wage rate by 1 cent an hour.

Allowance Unchanged

The new index, which represents a wider sampling of consumer purchases than the old one, is considered a more accurate yardstick.

With the announcement today of the new index for April 15 at 113.7, the General Motors cost-of-living allowance will remain unchanged for the next three months. No cut was forthcoming because the agreed formula for shifting from the old to the new index was based on the relationship between the two as of last December.

Since then, the old index, which reflects changes in food prices more rapidly than the new one, has dropped more sharply. A union official hinted that had the arithmetical calculations been based on their relationship of last March, a 2-cent wage cut would have been likely.

The 5-cent productivity increase due June 1 will increase the average hourly wage of General Motors employes to approximately $2.05, the highest in the history of the automobile industry.

FORD AND UNION REACH 3-YEAR PACT INCLUDING MODIFIED ANNUAL WAGE; PATTERN SET FOR GENERAL MOTORS

COMPANY PRAISED

Reuther Applauds Its Courage, Puts Benefit at 20 Cents an Hour

By DAMON STETSON

DETROIT, June 6—The Ford Motor Company and the United Automobile Workers, C. I. O., reached a historic three-year agreement today providing cash benefits for laid-off workers and other contract improvements.

The pact thus established a new principle of company responsibility in industrial relations. It is expected to set a pattern for a settlement with the General Motors Corporation and to have a widespread impact elsewhere on the American scene.

[News of the Ford accord enlivened what had been a quiet session on the New York Stock Exchange. Active buying of basic issues lifted the industrial index to historic highs.]

Walter P. Reuther, president of the union, said the economic package contained in the agreement was the largest the union had ever negotiated. He estimated that it was in excess of 20 cents an hour.

He said the Ford Motor Company was entitled to a "great deal of credit" for having the courage to pioneer in finding a way to provide workers and their families greater security against the hardships of unemployment.

Mr. Reuther said he would resume bargaining with General Motors tomorrow. The General Motors contract expires tomorrow night.

Cost Limit Is Fixed

John S. Bugas, vice president of industrial relations for Ford, said the Ford plan for supplemental unemployment benefits would provide a large measure of security during unemployment for Ford workers. But he emphasized also that the plan had a definitely predictable cost and a fixed and limited company liability.

Mr. Bugas called the new principle "supplementary unemployment benefits." Mr. Reuther referred to it as a "guaranteed annual wage."

The agreement was announced at 11:45 A. M. today when Mr. Reuther burst out of the Silver Room in the Detroit Leland Hotel, where negotiations have been going on.

The red-haired union leader, who is president of the Congress of Industrial Organizations as well as of the 1,500,000-member auto union, was grinning.

"We've got an agreement, boys," he said. He and Mr. Bugas quickly went into a nearby room and explained details of what both agreed was the most significant pact they had ever signed.

The settlement ended the threat of a major walkout by 140,000 Ford employes throughout the country. The union had authorized a strike for today, however, and, according to a Ford estimate, 114,000 employes failed to appear for the day shift in forty-three manufacturing plants and twenty-six parts depots.

In addition, most of the 23,-000 day shift workers employed at the company's Rouge plant in Dearborn attended a mass meeting at noon to hear news of the agreement and did not go back to work this afternoon, the company said. But union leaders gave assurances that all local unions would be notified promptly of the new pact and also urged to get their members back on the job.

The agreement was reached after nearly twenty-six hours of continuous bargaining, interspersed with recesses, conferences and company and union caucuses. The negotiators had sat down together at 10:15 A. M. Sunday and had been working toward an agreement, either together or apart, on a continuous basis since then.

Rule of Reason

Although negotiations during the last several weeks were conducted in secret for the most part, the period was marked by perseverance and the rule of reason at the bargaining table. Except for company and union outbursts in the face of threatening disagreement Saturday night, the bargaining sessions were conducted without public recriminations.

Because of the complicated nature of the union's guaranteed annual wage, demands proposing supplementary unemployment compensation benefits, and the involved plan put forward by the company, statisticians and researchers dominated many of the most serious phases of the bargaining.

These technicians and experts came up with some different answers on how the $55,000,000 the company was willing to spend should be used. But in the end adjustments were made that satisfied the union's demands for more adequate benefits, particularly for some low-wage geographical areas.

The New Contract

Besides the plan for supplementary unemployment benefits, the new contract provides:

¶An increase in the annual improvement factor (based on greater productivity) that will automatically increase all base pay rises each of the next three years, starting this month, by 6 cents an hour or 2½ per cent of base pay, whichever is greater. Average straight time pay rates for Ford workers have been about $2.10 an hour, although overtime and fringe benefits have raised the over-all average to about $2.30.

¶A liberal pension plan that means that retirement benefits will be figured at the rate of $2.25 for each year of credited service instead of $1.75 as in the past. The company said this would increase maximum retirement benefits from $161 a month, including primary. Social Security under the present plan, to $188.50 for a forty-year employe.

¶Better vacations so that employes with ten to fifteen years of service will be entitled to two and one-half weeks vacation with pay instead of two weeks as in the past.

¶An improvement in the cost-of-living escalator clause so that the cost-of-living allowance will go up 1 cent an hour every time the cost-of-living index rises one-half of a point, whenever the allowance is higher than 6 cents an hour. In the past, the allowance increased 1 cent an hour every time the index went up three-fifths of a point.

¶A seventh straight holiday in the form of a half holiday Christmas Eve and a half holiday New Year's eve.

¶Triple pay for holiday work by most employes, wage increases for workers in certain skilled classifications and improvement in insurance, including workers' wives and children, for the first time, in in-hospital medical benefits.

The Cash Benefits

The major feature of the new contract, subject to membership ratification, is what the company called "the Ford supplemental unemployment benefit plan." It provides for cash benefits, ranging up to $25 a week, to supplement the unemployment compensation to which a laid-off worker may be entitled.

The benefit payments, when combined with unemployment compensation, would bring the worker's income to a maximum of 65 per cent of his weekly take-home pay for the first four weeks of lay-offs after a waiting

LOCAL UNION REACTION: Members of United Auto Workers, C. I. O., at Ford's Edgewater, N. J., plant fling their picketing signs away upon learning of contract settlement.

week. Under the agreement benefit payments would not begin until a year from now.

After the four-week period the benefit, when combined with unemployment compensation, would be the equivalent of 60 per cent of the worker's take-home pay. The benefits would continue for a maximum of twenty-six weeks.

To finance the plan, the company will make contributions to two separate trust funds, which, based on current levels of employment, could amount ultimately to $55,000,000. All benefits would be paid from these funds. The funds would be built up by company contributions of 5 cents for every hour for which an employe received pay during the three-year period.

Here is the way the plan would work in actual practice:

Take as an example a Buffalo man, with a wife and child, who earns $84.80 a week in straight-time earnings. After taxes he would have take-home

pay of $74.70 a week. If he were laid off he would be entitled to receive $36 a week in unemployment benefits.

The special benefit, 65 per cent of his take-home pay, for the first four weeks would be $12.56, or a total of $48.56. His regular benefit (60 per cent of take home) would be $8.82, or a total of $44.82 when combined with unemployment compensation.

Or take the case of a New Jersey man with a wife and three children who earned $81.80 in straight-time pay. After taxes, he would have $77.10. His unemployment benefit (as expected under pending legislation, according to Ford) would be $35 a week. His special benefit from the company for the first four weeks would be $15.12, giving him a total weekly income of $50.12, including unemployment compensation. The regular benefit would be $11.26, giving him

a total of $46.26 after the first four weeks.

In discussing the plan, Mr. Bugas said that for the first time a major corporation had devised a "sound, workable plan" for paying such benefits.

"In proposing our plan to the union and in pressing for its acceptance," he said, "we have assumed a grave responsibility. We are undertaking this responsibility with complete confidence. We have full faith in the ability of our company to progress and prospect in the competitive atmosphere of a free and vigorous economy."

The Benefit Plan

In working out the plan, Mr. Bugas said, the company was concerned about getting into the situation of unlimited liability and unpredicted costs. He noted that a tight plan would have re-

quired cash outlays when the company could least afford to make them—at a time of recession or unemployment.

Mr. Bugas said that it was only after a tremendous amount of research and internal analysis that the Ford company came to the conclusion that the one important road to improved security of its employes was the supplemental benefit plan.

"We think it is significant," Mr. Bugas said. "We think it offers additional security to our employes and particularly in the automotive industry where historically you have layoffs."

In the press conference of Mr. Bugas and Mr. Reuther, they were asked whether or not state laws might prohibit payment of unemployment compensation to workers who received supplementary benefits from the company.

Mr. Bugas replied that the plan had been written so as to offer the greatest inducement to the parties to achieve integration of the two. Mr. Reuther said that he doubted that there would be any difficulty although, he said, in a few states integration might pose a problem. But he said he had complete confidence that the problem could be licked before benefit payments would begin on June 1, 1956.

It was also brought out in the press conference that the stock participation plan originally offered by Ford was not included in the agreement reached today.

The success of Mr. Reuther in achieving in the Ford negotiations the essential elements of the guaranteed annual wage he demanded was expected to increase his stature in the labor field and in the nation. A long and costly strike might have done just the reverse.

He was asked today whether the guaranteed annual wage principle established through the Ford contract would provide a pattern not only for the auto industry but for other industries as well.

"Well," Mr. Reuther replied, "I think that there is a growing awareness in industry circles in America that we need to do more and more to achieve economic stability of our economy, that unnecessary lay-offs are a great economic waste. And I believe that the G. A. W. (guaranteed annual wage) is going to be the kind of constructive incentive, and I think more and more and more will be applied to a broader and broader section of American industry."

CAN UNION WINS WAGE GUARANTEE FOR A FULL YEAR

Nation's First Major 52-Week Contract Will Start Oct. 1— U. A. W.'s Limited to 26

By STANLEY LEVEY

The United Steelworkers, C. I. O., won yesterday the first major plan in American industry for a full year of supplementary unemployment benefits.

The program—often referred to as the Guaranteed Annual Wage—was contained in a two-year contract signed with the American and Continental Can companies. The union put the total cost of the package, which also provided for an average hourly wage rise of 13 cents, at 21½ cents an hour. The pacts go into effect on Oct. 1.

David I. McDonald, union president, making little effort to suppress his jubilation, lost no time in serving notice on the entire steel industry that his organization expected to seek and win a similiar guaranteed wage plan in negotiations next spring. The union represents 650,000 workers in basic steel.

Mr. McDonald also made it clear that he regarded the plan negotiated with the can companies as infinitely superior to the one worked out last spring between the United Automobile Workers, a sister C.I.O. group, and the Ford Motor Company and the General Motors Corporation.

Difference in Plans

The automobile industry plan provides for cash benefits ranging up to $25 a week to supplement state jobless compensation for a maximum of twenty-six weeks. For the first four weeks of idleness, after a waiting period of one week, the payments would amount to 65 per cent of the worker's take-home pay. For the next twenty-two weeks they would come to 60 per cent.

Under the plan made public yesterday, supplemental benefits would continue for fifty-two weeks. They would be the equivalent of 65 per cent of take-home pay, including state jobless compensation, and would go to workers with three years or more of seniority.

August 14, 1955

AID FOR SEAMEN EFFECTIVE TODAY

Benefits of Supplementary Unemployment Insurance Will Cover 40,000

Seamen stranded "on the beach" between shipping jobs become eligible today for benefits under the first industry-wide supplementary unemployment insurance plan in the United States.

The plan was set up last year in collective bargaining by the National Maritime Union and eighty-four steamship companies. Its implementation was held up until now to permit the accumulation of a reserve fund.

Under the plan an N. M. U. seaman who is out of work because of lay-off or a personal emergency or who is waiting for his ship after a vacation can receive $30 a week for from three to five weeks. These payments apply if he is not entitled to any state unemployment pay.

If the seaman begins to receive state unemployment insurance during the period he is covered by the industry security program, his benefits under the new plan drop to $15 a week for the remainder of his eligibility. In states where the receipt of any outside income is a bar to unemployment compensation, seamen will not be eligible for payments under the industry program.

In addition, if a seaman is disabled and does not receive benefits under any other union or company plan, he will be entitled to a maximum of thirteen weeks of compensation at $30 a week while he is unable to work. He will also receive five weeks' pay at the same rate after he recovers while waiting for a ship.

The plan is supported by employer contributions of 25 cents a day for each unlicensed crew member employed. The fund, which is jointly administered by the companies and the union, now totals approximately $1,800,-000. About 40,000 men are covered.

The arrangement is unique on several grounds:

¶It is the first supplementary unemployment pay arrangement to be established for a major segment of any American industry. Similar plans set up by the steel and automobile unions have been with individual employers.

¶It will provide benefits during the first week of unemployment.

¶It is specifically designed to meet needs peculiar to seamen, and will provide benefits in some cases to men unemployed for reasons that would not qualify them for compensation under most state laws.

In the last category are payments to seamen who leave a vessel because their presence ashore is required to provide for an ailing wife or to participate in legal proceedings. These men will received $30 a week for two weeks during the emergency period and the same amount for three weeks while waiting to re-ship.

Another problem of seamen that will be eased under the arrangement is the frequently long wait for a ship after a vacation ashore. Payments of $30 a week for four weeks will be made in such cases.

Men who are out of work because of the lay-up, transfer, loss or sale of their ship or the reduction of its complement will be entitled to $30 a week for three weeks.

The plan provides that seamen are eligible for benefits only when they are actively seeking shipboard employment, except while disabled or during the specified personal emergency period.

Although the plan becomes effective today, and any benefits will be payable from today, it was understood yesterday that actual payments may be delayed for several weeks.

At least one obstacle to the beginning of payments was the employer proviso that the entire plan would be contingent upon a Treasury Department ruling that contributions to the plan may be deducted as business expenses for income tax purposes.

A union spokesman said that while the Treasury has not yet ruled on this phase of the plan, such a decision would be a "routine formality." He said that similar contributions in the automobile and steel industries have been approved as tax deductions.

June 16, 1956

EISENHOWER SIGNS $1 MINIMUM PAY

Special to The New York Times.
WASHINGTON, Aug. 12— President Eisenhower signed into law today a bill to increase the legal minimum wage from 75 cents to $1 an hour.

He had recommended a rise to 90 cents. However, he did not protest the Congressional decision that overrode his proposal.

The wage measure was among forty-six bills the President signed today. He vetoed relatively minor bills. He has yet to act on three measures approved by Congress before it adjourned.

Among those on which he deferred action was a bill designed to end the streetcar and bus strike that has left the capital without public transportation since July 1. This measure would cancel the franchise of the Capital Transit Company, which operates the streetcars and bus system.

Labor in South Most Affected

The new minimum-wage increase, following periodic jumps from the 25-cent-an-hour minimum set in 1938, will affect directly more than 2,000,000 workers, largely in the South. It was expected to affect many more millions whose bigger wages have been based on concessions made above the legal minimum.

The $1 minimum for those covered will become effective next March 1.

At present about one-half of the workers sought originally to be included in the minimum wage program are covered. Still uncovered are workers in the retail trades, in service industries, in agriculture and in the construction industries.

President Eisenhower proposed that studies be made looking to their inclusion. This was not done by Congress.

Efforts were made in Congress to raise the minimum wage to as high as $1.35 an hour. Congress compromised, with votes overwhelming the Presidential proposal for a 90-cent minimum, at $1. Republicans joined Democrats strongly to go above the White House recommendation.

This had been the first such rise since 1950, when the then 40-cents-an-hour standard was increased to 75 cents.

The measure signed by the President does not raise minimum wages in Puerto Rico or the Virgin Islands. The Senate had voted to include their workers in the 25-cent rise, at least for a trial period of two and a half years. The House did not approve this and the provision was eliminated when the bill went to conference for adjustment of differences for final ratification.

August 13, 1955

RECORD LABOR FORCE MAKES INDUSTRY HUM

How 65 Million Workers, One-Third Of Them Women, Earn a Living

By CHARLES E. EGAN
Special to The New York Times.

WASHINGTON, Aug. 20—Never before in this country's history have so many as 65,000,000 people been gainfully employed.

This astonishing figure was made available to the public recently after experts in the Departments of Labor and Commerce had completed their computations on job-holding in July.

Joined with the experts' figures was the equally impressive statement that women and teen-age girls at work last month reached 20,204,000. This was, by far, the highest number of female workers ever employed in this country.

Back in the days when war plants were begging for female help to turn out fighter aircraft and when "Rosie the Riveter" was a popular musical bow to the patriotic devotion of women in war industries, there were only 18,850,000 women at work in factories and on farms.

In listing the July record of jobs for both men and women, the Departments of Commerce and Labor were able to show that employment had picked up by 1,000,000 compared with the month before, and by 3,000,000 compared with the corresponding month a year ago.

Experts and statisticians in both agencies found that the employment figures had raised questions they found of interest but very difficult to answer.

Who Is Typical?

For instance, they explained, there are 65,000,000 workers holding jobs, but many people would be hard put to it to describe what a "typical" American worker looks like. How old is he or she? What is the average pay? Is the average worker, male or female, a good workman? What are the living conditions of the average employed person?

No statistician, either at the Bureau of the Census in the Commerce Department, or the Bureau of Labor Statistics in the Labor Department, will give a firm answer. They will speculate, however. And they eventually come up with the following "off-the-record" descriptions of the average worker:

If a man, he is in his late thirties and most likely on a factory payroll, where he is earning $1.88 an hour operating a machine or tool of some sort, for an average of 40.3 hours a week. Compared with a year ago his hourly wage is one cent an hour higher and his work-week one hour longer.

If the subject is a female worker the chances are she is employed as a clerk in some retail store, earns slightly more than $30 a week, is married and is either in her late teens or early twenties, or is well into her forties.

The wide age range works out to an average of somewhere in the mid-thirties. The age spread is caused by the fact that many of the women workers disappear from the labor force during their child-bearing and rearing years. They return again after the family is grown.

Job Rolls Rise

The average male worker is a family man with a wife and two children. If he lives in the city his family lives in a rented apartment. If his work permits him to live in a suburb or a small town he owns his own home. In either case he has a car, a telephone and a television set.

With about 65,000,000 employed and 2,471,000 out of work, Administration spokesmen maintain that employment can grow in a peacetime economy. They point to the fact that in 1950, when the Korean war was under way, there were 3,142,000 idle in this country and 59,957,000 at work.

Back in 1944, when war production was hitting its stride, there were 53,960,000 men and women at work in the country, and a total of 670,000 without employment. The unemployed figure, according to the experts, was equal to the number of what they called "unemployables" at that time.

Of those at work today, slightly more than one out of every four holds a job in manufacturing. Next to production workers come those engaged in distribution.

Trade Group

Those in the wholesale and retail trades amount to nearly 19 per cent of the employed group. Behind the factory workers and the wholesale and retail distribution groups come those who toil on farms. Farm hands now constitute 12.44 per cent of the force currently at work.

Professional people, doctors, lawyers, dentists, etc., make up better than 8 per cent of the working ranks. Entertainers, including those in motion pictures, television, radio and the legitimate theatre, are only 0.98 per cent of the employed total.

While the make-up of the working force probably will follow the same proportions over future years (with minor variations as to agricultural and industrial workers), the consensus among experts is that by 1960 the number holding jobs in this country will reach the 70,000,000 mark.

A study completed last year by Congress' Joint Committee on the President's Economic Report was bold enough to project employment ratios into 1965.

The Congressional committee forecast a labor force of 76,000,000 by 1965, with 73,000,000 holding jobs and 3,000,000 (including the unemployable) idle.

August 21, 1955

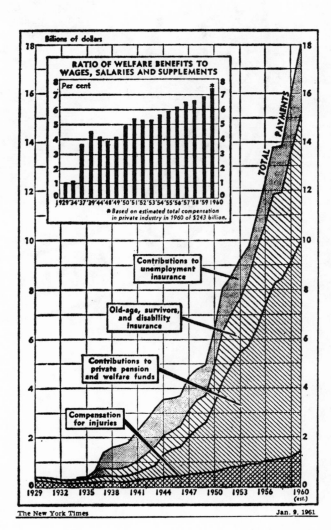

RATIO OF WELFARE BENEFITS TO WAGES, SALARIES AND SUPPLEMENTS

* Based on estimated total compensation in private industry in 1960 of $243 billion.

The New York Times   Jan. 9, 1961

January 9, 1961

The Protagonists Transformed

Labor unites.

AFL, RAIL UNIONISTS FROWN ON CIO-PAC

If Roosevelt Loses as Labor-Backed Man Where Will Labor Be? It Is Asked

SEE IT AS POLITICAL PARTY

By LOUIS STARK

WASHINGTON, Aug. 1—The fundamental policies of the CIO-Political Action Committee, as they relate to the raising of campaign funds and its methods of operation, are meeting increasingly with stern resistance from some important elements in the American Federation of Labor and the independent railroad brotherhoods. A split in labor has begun to develop.

The principal complaint of those AFL leaders who oppose Sidney Hillman's organization is that it has perverted the sense and meaning of labor's old-time nonpartisan political policy of "rewarding our friends and punishing our enemies."

In going beyond this policy, it is contended, the CIO group has formed what is virtually a political party, despite its disclaimers of any such intention.

The AFL has always opposed endorsement of either of the dominant political parties or the candidates for the two chief offices. It has supported pro-labor candidates down below, for Congress and other offices, both in the primaries and at the elections.

AFL Committee Non-Partisan

At the top the AFL has a nonpartisan political committee headed by President William Green. It is not an "action" committee, has no funds to speak of and is limited to collecting data on labor records of members of Congress and forwarding them to the AFL sub-leaders out in the country.

It issues no detailed analyses, or any kind of analyses for that matter, of candidates' records for publication. Its reports go to local AFL groups which usually work through the existing dominant parties. The latter do not, as a rule, form political action committees of their own.

Neither the top AFL committee nor the sub-leaders raise funds for political campaigns.

The AFL opponents to the CIO-PAC committee say:

"If Roosevelt loses and he is the labor-endorsed candidate, where will labor stand in the new Administration?

"But if we can return a Congress sympathetic to labor then at least we have the groundwork for labor progress."

Not publicly, but whisperingly, the AFL also says:

"If Roosevelt wins and the CIO-PAC gets a major part of the credit, the CIO will be favored by the Administration as it has been in the past and where will we be?"

Attitude of Railway Unions

The significance of the stand taken by "Labor," organ of nineteen standard railway unions, cannot be minimized. This publication, edited by Edward Keating, a former member of Congress and a sometime violent critic of the President and the New Deal, says that in twenty-five years the railway unions have not spent a half of 1 per cent of the amount of money that the CIO-PAC apparently has as its fund-collecting "goal" in 1944.

The CIO-PAC's tests for candidates, according to "Labor," are not always trade-union tests, and some candidates having favorable labor records do not always see eye to eye with the President's policies.

It is held that the Communist party alliances of the CIO-PAC in New York State and elsewhere will turn voters away from the Democratic party candidates.

It is recalled that Mr. Hillman took an active part in the intra-party fight which bedeviled the American Labor party in New York State. Although himself not a Communist and with a record of having incurred the enmity of the Communists, Mr. Hillman brought the wrath of the ALP right wingers down on his head by offering a unity proposal which the latter contended was a Communist project and meant that Mr. Hillman was throwing his weight on the side of the Communists. This split the American Labor party. Mr. Hillman became head of the ALP and the opposition formed the Liberal Labor party. As predicted at the time, the Communist issue is now rising to plague the CIO-PAC.

Strong Reaction Is Feared

In short, the more conservative American Federation of Labor and railroad labor leaders fear that the effect of the raising of large funds for political work will bring about a strong reaction in which it will be charged that labor is seeking to "buy the election," and this will bring demands for union regulation, while "the pot of gold" will attract "all sorts of crackpots, theorists and even grafters like those who were attracted by the Non-Partisan League of North Dakota."

The railway unions argue that their more "limited" nonpartisan policy has been attended by excellent results, including these:

1. An excellent railroad pension system,
2. An unemployment compensation system that is giving good results.
3. The Railway Labor Act, sometimes called "the magna charta" of rail labor.

Railroad labor legislation, it is also pointed out, has been enacted without roll-calls for it was evident that the vast majority of Congress favored the measures.

What effect the attacks of the more conservative labor leaders on the Hillman program may mean it is too early to say.

The Vote Of Labor

THE C.I.O. AND THE DEMOCRATIC PARTY. By Fay Calkins. 162 pp. Chicago: University of Chicago Press. $4.

By DANIEL BELL

WHETHER labor can "deliver" the union member's vote is a question that many politicians would like an immediate answer to. More generally, since political parties have today become congeries of diverse pressure groups the study of labor's role in the Democratic party has an important bearing on the future of politics in the United States.

Fay Calkins, a research assistant in the National C. I. O. Political Action Committee, has undertaken a more limited survey than the title of her book suggests. She presents five case studies of local P. A. C. groups in the 1950 elections and their type of relationship with the Democratic party. In Michigan the P. A. C., in coalition with liberal elements, captured the state machinery. In Ohio, operating independently of the Democratic party, it was the chief resource of Joe Ferguson in his campaign against Senator Taft. The cases include three local instances: in Chicago the P. A. C. unsuccessfully bucked the machine for a state Senate district nomination; in Steubenville, Ohio, it played ball with the local machine; in Rockford, Ill., in alliance with an Italian

August 2, 1944

political club, it won the county machinery.

MISS CALKINS provides simple and straightforward descriptions of these situations. Unfortunately, her vignettes stand as isolated pictures, since she fails inexplicably to discuss the over-all questions of the relationship between the national C. I. O. and the Democratic party, or even the organizational and disciplinary ties between the national P. A. C. and the local and state units. Internal union politics are treated gingerly. The relation between P. A. C. and local ethnic groups receives surface consideration. The crucial question of why the C. I. O. in Detroit was unable to elect a U. A. W. member, George Edwards, as Mayor in 1949 (apparently union members were swayed more by ethnic and racial feeling rather than union loyalty) is strangely omitted.

So far—to judge from evidence on hand—the P. A. C. has been unable to stimulate union members to the same degree of enthusiasm and work for political ends as for economic ends. This, however, is largely an organizational deficiency. Workers will still vote Democratic, but largely for the same reason that minority groups and even farmers do — the Democratic party, with the aura of the New Deal, is regarded as working for their benefit, while the Republican party is not.

Mr. Bell is labor editor of Fortune Magazine.

TWO LEFTIST UNIONS EXPELLED BY C. I. O.; 10 MORE FACE PURGE

By LOUIS STARK
Special to THE NEW YORK TIMES.

CLEVELAND, Nov. 2—In a series of lightning moves today the convention of the Congress of Industrial Organizations expelled the International Union of Electrical, Radio and Machine Workers of America and the Farm Equipment Workers and laid the basis for the purge of ten other unions commanded by left-wing, pro-Communist leaders.

The charter of the electrical union was turned over within an hour of its expulsion to an administrative committee of twelve right-wing leaders. Within minutes this committee issued a call for a re-organization convention in Philadelphia on Nov. 28.

James B. Carey, CIO secretary-treasurer, one of the leaders in the fight against the pro-Communist leadership of the electrical union, is in line for the presidency of the new group. This is to be called the International Electrical Radio and Machine Workers of America, CIO.

Mr. Carey, who has canceled his trip to London for the founding meeting of a new World Labor Federation next month, confidently proclaimed that loyal CIO supporters among UE locals all over the nation were "hitting 200,000." The ousted union, of which Albert J. Fitzgerald is president, says it has a membership of 450,000, with contracts covering 600,000 employes.

Recalls CIO Ouster by AFL

Today's action by the CIO convention was compared in some respects with the momentous decision of the American Federation of Labor in 1936 when it suspended ten unions for forming the Committee for Industrial Organizations.

Neither Mr. Carey nor his opponents, who now use the initials UE for their union without the CIO suffix, minimize the civil war that faces them.

The fight is already on for the funds and properties of the UE all over the nation. Right and left wing adherents in Schenectady, Syracuse, Pittsburgh, St. Louis and elsewhere have sequestered local funds. Court actions are under way.

Mr. Carey admitted that the civil war among electrical workers would be carried to the plants where contracts would be claimed by both sides. Some of the main agreements are in General Electric, Westinghouse, General Motors and the Radio Corporation of America.

In these plants Mr. Carey asserted that practically 100 per cent of the membership was with his organization.

The fight, said Mr. Carey, will also be carried on before the National Labor Relations Board, where election contests will be requested to determine the legal possession of contracts. It is also expected that as in similar labor wars the contests will extend to picket lines where bloody clashes in such affrays are a matter of course.

Significantly it was Joseph Curran, president of the National Maritime Union, who himself broke with the Communists and ousted them from his own union, who read the expulsion resolutions.

In preparation for all eventualities in the CIO's civil war with the Communist-led organizations the delegates granted extraordinary power to the executive board to prevent the use of the CIO's name by those whose policies favored the Communist party or any Fascist or other totalitarian movement.

This was taken to mean that the board would be able to expel any other left-led unions and to unseat their officers from the executive board.

With these extraordinarily swift manoeuvers went convention approval of a proposal to raise the present per capita tax 2 cents a month per member. This would mean an additional million dollars a year to replace the loss of taxes from severance of ties of dissident unions.

So well prepared were the right wing UE leaders for today's events that Mr. Carey was able to reveal to a large press conference after today's CIO convention session that his organization already had offices at 734 Fifteenth Street, N. W., Washington. It has a telephone, Executive 9060.

Replying to questions aimed to bring out whether employers would not be "in the middle" in the internecine struggle of the two electrical unions. Mr. Carey said that his adherents were already notifying the employers "plant by plant" that its group was the "official" union.

His group, he added, has even gone to the extent of beginning to file non-Communist affidavits with the NLRB to qualify for its services. The Fitzgerald-led UE officers filed such affidavits recently. It is understood that they are being investigated by the Department of Justice.

Mr. Carey is chairman of the UE-CIO administrative committee and William Snoots of Dayton, Ohio, is secretary.

The other members are Fred Kelly of Lynn, Mass.; Michael Fitzpatrick of Pittsburgh, Pa.; John Dillon of New York; Harry Block of Philadelphia; Dallas Smith of Fort Wayne, Ind.; Anthony Cimino of Springfield, Mass.; John Callahan of Pittsfield, Mass.; E. J. Kraft and Robert Elsner, both of Dayton, Ohio, and Joseph Hawkins of Mansfield, Ohio.

The climax of the debate on the expulsion resolutions came when the CIO president, Philip Murray, dramatically disclosed what he indicated was "inside information" of Communist party meetings in

New York attended by James Matles, director of organization, and Julius Emspak, secretary-treasurer of the expelled U.E.

These meetings, according to Mr. Murray, were held in the hall of the International Workers Order after the CIO convention in Boston in 1947. Their purpose, he said, was "formulating policy and directing the political destinies of the CIO for the year 1948."

Among those present, Mr. Murray asserted, were W. Z. Foster, Eugene Dennis and "a Mr. Williamson," Communist party leaders. They invited Michael Quill of the Transport Workers Union to attend, Mr. Murray continued. He had further testimony as to those present, he asserted, from Mr. Quill, "a delegate to this convention."

Parenthetically Mr. Murray interjected the remark that "our good friend Harry Bridges (president of the International Longshoremen's and Warehousemen's Union) attended a couple of meetings over in New York after that time with the same people."

Then, referring again to the Communist party meeting in the hall of the International Workers Order, Mr. Murray declared that these meetings evolved plans, drafted ideas and "gave a sense of political direction, so they claimed, to the CIO."

Then, he continued, the same group met again in the same place in January, 1948, and out of this conference "there evolved plans and policies to corrupt and destroy, if possible, the trade union movement of America."

The CIO leader then quoted from The New Times, a Moscow publication which stated in an issue last month that "The UE may leave the CIO and lead a movement for the formation of a third trade union center of the United States."

George Baldanzi, vice president of the Textile Workers Union, said that the convention was not ousting the UE "since that decision was made long ago by the Cominform and I am in favor of accommodating them."

He said the Communist leaders worked hard in their unions, "but only to gain control in order to sell out anybody in the interests of Russia."

BRIDGES PIER UNION EXPELLED BY C. I. O.

National Board Also Ousts Marine Cooks to Complete Clean-Out of Pro-Reds

Special to THE NEW YORK TIMES.

WASHINGTON, Aug. 29—The executive board of the Congress of Industrial Organizations expelled today Harry Bridges' International Longshoremen's and Warehousemen's Union and the Marine Cooks and Stewards Union.

These unions were found guilty of following Communist policy rather than the policies of the C. I. O.

Hugh Bryson, president of the Marine Cooks and Stewards, announced that he would appeal the action to the C. I. O. convention in November. In a statement he charged that the C. I. O. excluded his union "because it cannot allow any opposition to its program of rubber-stamping everything the Truman Administration says and does."

Mr. Bridges was not at today's meeting. He was represented by J. W. Robertson, the union's vice president. The latter and Mr. Bryson cast the two negative votes as 41 votes were cast in favor of expulsion of the Bridges' union.

After Mr. Robertson had left the meeting the Cooks and Stewards Union was ousted. The one negative vote was cast by Mr. Bryson.

Philip Murray, C. I. O. president, told a news conference he was confident that the bulk of the membership of the two expelled unions would decide to remain loyal to the C. I. O.

New Charter Possible

He indicated expectation that either a new charter would be issued to longshoremen loyal to the C. I. O. or they would upset Mr. Bridges and return the union to the C. I. O.

Mr. Murray stated that the expulsions today included the Fishermen's Union, which affiliated with the Bridges union several months ago.

The executive board, he declared, completed today its task of dealing with twelve left wing unions originally scheduled for trial.

Of the twelve, he said, two were expelled at the C. I. O. convention last November. These were the United Electrical, Radio and Machine Workers and the Farm Equipment Workers. Nine unions had been expelled since November, he added, and charges against one union, the Furniture Workers, had been withdrawn.

A large proportion of the members of the expelled unions had decided to cast their lot with the C. I. O., Mr. Murray asserted. For example, he said, the electrical and radio union had 400,000 members, and 281,000 had already joined the C. I. O.'s electrical and radio affiliate.

Of the 100,000 smelter workers whose union was expelled, he added, 60,000 were already back in the C. I. O. fold.

Mr. Murray expressed some doubt concerning the future of the longshore union contracts with employers, since these agreements were countersigned and guaranteed by representatives of the C. I. O. at the request of the employers and the union. The status of the contracts now was a legal question that would have to be examined, Mr. Murray said.

Interpretation of Contracts

Arthur J. Goldberg, C. I. O. general counsel, suggested that if a substantial number of longshoremen switched their affiliation from the Bridges' union to the C. I. O. they could take over the role of bargaining agent under the contracts.

The longshore union is estimated to have 75,000 members and the Cooks and Stewards about 5,000.

The investigating committee which reported to the executive board on the longshore union said that Communist party functionaries had decided what resolutions should be brought into the union's resolutions committee and assigned the speakers on each subject.

"This was all done secretly and conspiratorially," the report stated, "and was concealed from the C. I. O."

The support of Communist party policies by Mr. Bridges, the report said, was likewise concealed from the rank and file.

In conclusion the trial committee, headed by O. A. Knight of the Oil Workers Union, declared:

"The I. L. W. U. leadership has made its own choice between the C. I. O. and the Communist party and has chosen the Communist party."

U. S. RED EXPERTS URGED BY SENATOR

Humphrey Asks Training Course to Distinguish a Militant Unionist From Communist

Special to THE NEW YORK TIMES.

WASHINGTON, Aug. 26—Senator Hubert H. Humphrey, the Minnesota Democrat who last year headed a subcommittee investigating Communist domination of some trade unions, urged the Administration today to start early training of specialists how to tell "a bona fide militant unionist from a Communist agent."

In the background were expulsions of numerous unions from their parent bodies on the ground of Communist domination. Senator Humphrey's subcommittee indicated in a report filed last March that the expulsions had been justified.

However, Mr. Humphrey's subcommittee maintained, there could be "just a hairline of judgment separating the attitude of the patriotic, militant trade-union leader and the Communist party-line follower."

In a letter to Joseph M. Dodge, Director of the Bureau of the Budget, the Senator stated that he was "delighted" by word that the Administration had decided to follow a subcommittee recommendation that policies and activities relating to Communist activity scented in some trade unions would be coordinated.

Senator Humphrey also said he welcomed the news that Herbert Brownell, the Attorney General, had "now assumed the responsibility for that coordination."

Sharp Line Sought

However, Mr. Humphrey complained that thus far there appeared to have been no recommended establishment of in-service courses within such key security agencies as the Atomic Energy Commission, the Federal Bureau of Investigation and others, to train specialists how to draw the line between Communists and militant but patriotic union leaders.

The investigating subcommittee, a unit of the Senate Committee on Labor and Public Welfare, had emphasized in its March report that even the unions found by thorough investigation to have been dominated by Communists—it emphasized that the zeal and parliamentary skill of only a handful of Reds could attain control—were populated overwhelmingly by patriotic Americans who had been made dupes.

November 3, 1949

August 30, 1950

August 27, 1953

Union of Unions?

America's "house of labor" has been a house divided since 1936, when John L. Lewis led a secession from the A. F. L. to form the C. I. O. Since then there have been occasional efforts to achieve labor unity. The efforts have failed because of deep-seated rivalries between the two labor bodies.

The larger A. F. L. (now nearly 8,000,000 members) has insisted that the first step be "organic unity"—a "return to the fold" by the C. I. O. The smaller C. I. O. (now more than 6,000,000 members) has been leery of such unity because it would be outnumbered. It has insisted that the first step be "functional unity"—cooperation on common economic legislative and political problems. Behind these differences there are personal antagonisms between the C. I. O. and A. F. L. leaderships, and fear by some union leaders that they would be merged out of their jobs. For his part, Mr. Lewis has broken with the C. I. O., rejoined the A. F. L., and, in 1947, "disaffiliated" from it.

Last week the C. I. O. made a new gesture toward unity. President Philip Murray, with the approval of nine C. I. O. vice presidents, sent letters to A. F. L. President William Green, Mr. Lewis, A. J. Hayes, head of the International Association of Machinists, and leaders of the independent railroad brotherhoods. The letters proposed the creation of a joint committee which would work first for "functional unity" then for "organic unity" of unions representing the nation's 16,000,000 organized workers.

Reaction in Labor

The first responses to the proposal seemed to be favorable. Mr. Green expressed interest in it. On Thursday Mr. Lewis wrote Mr. Murray that he was forwarding the proposal to the mine workers' executive board with a recommendation of acceptance. Mr. Hayes also accepted.

Among labor observers the feeling is that the chances for labor unity are better than at any time in fourteen years. The feeling arises from these factors: (1) a general decline in labor's organizing momentum, with less conflict among the unions over jurisdiction in new fields; (2) increased political action by the A. F. L., paralleling that of the C. I. O. in favor of the Fair Deal; (3) the C. I. O.'s "purge" of its left wing, which has been a major obstacle to cooperation with the A. F. L.; (4) joint action by the major American labor groups last December in helping to form the new International Confederation of Free Trade Unions as an organ of anti-Communist labor throughout the world.

Nevertheless, big problems will have to be solved before labor unity can be achieved—particularly the problems of personal antipathies and of leaders' vested interest in their jobs. Specifically, there is the problem of John L. Lewis, whom other leaders fear and distrust but who does not readily accept a subordinate role.

April 9, 1950

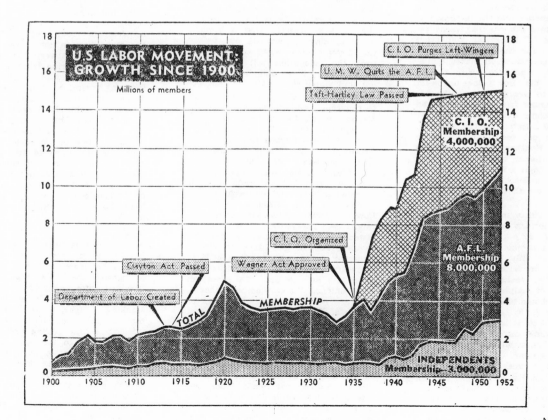

November 16, 1952

The New Labor Leaders— A Dual Portrait

Meany of the A. F. L. and Reuther of the C. I. O. are a study in contrasts but their goals are alike—unity and public responsibility.

By A. H. RASKIN

WHEN the country decided it was "time for a change," organized labor did not suspect it was in for the biggest and quickest change of all. Within a month after the voters canceled the Democratic lease on the White House and ended an era in which unions had made their most spectacular gains, the deaths of William Green and Philip Murray compelled both major branches of American labor to pick new leaders. The transfer of command put forceful new personalities at the head of the American Federation of Labor and the Congress of Industrial Organizations. More important, it set both union groups traveling along roads that may carry them to a new frontier of public responsibility—one in which the old "bread-and-butter" goals yield precedence to the idea that unions can succeed only when they put the interests of the whole population ahead of those of their own members.

This may seem an improbable horizon at a time when crippling strikes in key industries, the crack-up of wage and price controls and the incursion of racketeers into labor-management relations foster a depressing conviction that concern for the general welfare is the last consideration either industry or labor wants to bring to the bargaining table. But it does not seem improbable to George Meany, the 58-year-old plumber from the Bronx, who has just become chief spokesman for the 8,100,000 members of the A. F. L., and it does not seem improbable to Walter P. Reuther, the 45-year-old tool-and-die maker, whose nimble mind carried him from a Detroit automobile factory to leadership over 4,200,000 unionists in the C. I. O.

WHAT kind of men are these new pilots of American unionism, and what do they believe?

They get along so well together that it took them only thirty seconds of face-to-face conversation in a New York hotel two weeks ago to toss aside the morass of "Alphonse and Gaston" red tape that had blocked merger talks between the A. F. L. and C. I. O. for two years. Yet, it is hard to imagine two men more different in physical appearance, personal habits and ideological background.

Meany is a cross between a bulldog and a bull. He weighs 220 pounds, but his bulk bespeaks toughness and solidity. There is nothing flabby about him. Diplomatic double-talk has no place in his vocabulary. He says what he means, shunning the windy platitudes that make most labor speeches as dreary as a Rotary luncheon address. His frankness found expression at a conference with President Truman in April of last year. Labor was "on strike" against the defense agencies because it felt the Administration had stripped union officials of any real voice in the conduct of the preparedness program. The President called A. F. L. and C. I. O. leaders to the White House and sought to appease them by assurances that he was labor's best friend.

HE urged the unionists to resume the posts they had left and to rely on him to see to it that they got adequate representation in all facets of the defense effort. Most of the members of the labor delegation mumbled polite assent, but not Meany. "That doesn't take care of it, Mr. President," he declared. He reviewed in painstaking detail the incidents that made labor feel it had got the run-around in its past efforts to obtain representation, and he insisted that a specific understanding be worked out before the boycott was called off. By the time the delegation left the White House, everything had been spelled out and amity restored.

An admiring C. I. O. official, used to the rough and tumble of debate in his own union, turned to an A. F. L. colleague as they walked out the gate. "I never heard anyone talk up to the President of the United States like that," he said. "That Meany's sure got guts." Meany was equally blunt when a titled British trade unionist objected to receiving letters from subordinate A. F. L. officials, no matter how responsible or well-informed they might be. The British labor man insisted that the niceties of protocol required that he get letters only from Green or Meany, who was then A. F. L. secretary-treasurer. Meany's reply gave him no comfort. "In American trade unions," the ex-plumber declared, "we are not concerned with titles or epaulets. We deal with problems, and there is no such thing as rank when it comes to getting them solved."

Born at 125th Street and Madison Avenue and brought up in the Bronx, Meany became an expert on international affairs by the sheer force of his conviction that world labor was the only dependable bulwark against Soviet imperialism. In 1945, in a prophetic speech at Blackpool, England, he warned that Russia was trying to use the World Federation of Trade Unions as a fifth column to undermine the democratic nations. It took the C. I. O., the British and the French unions nearly four years to acknowledge the rightness of his judgment. When they withdrew from the Communist-dominated group, Meany joined with them in forming the International Confederation of Free Trade Unions to provide a constructive alternative to communism in all parts of the world.

AN ardent Catholic, he has opposed the efforts of European trade unionists to organize unions on denominational lines. When a leader of the Catholic trade unions in Belgium sought to convince him that ideological differences between the Catholics and the Socialists made separate labor movements necessary, Meany did not wait for the interpreter. "Ideology is baloney," he blurted. "There can be no ideological differences among real trade unionists."

His test of a real trade union is its freedom from state control. He has stood firm in his refusal to sanction relations between the A. F. L. and any totalitarian labor movement, whether it be that of Franco's Spain, Perón's Argentina, Stalin's Russia or Tito's Yugoslavia. No amount of Government or church pressure has sufficed to sway him on any of these. "The secret of his effectiveness in any situation," one of his close associates says, "is his appetite for acquiring every bit of relevant information. He can give you as detailed an analysis of something that is going on in Italy or Czechoslovakia as he can about a Teamster's Union dispute in Sheboygan."

HIS one weakness is a penchant for pearl-gray or cocoa-brown vests. In every other respect, his taste in clothes is conservative. He wears double-breasted suits and seldom bothers to button the jacket. When he is not smoking a cigar, he is usually chewing on the dead butt. He is the A. F. L.'s first golfing president and the first one to feel as happy in a plane as a train. A hard worker, he knows how to relax when the pressure is off. He likes an occasional Scotch and soda and enjoys a game of poker or gin rummy with his associates in the Federation Executive Council. Two or three times a year, he gets away from the office for some duck shooting. The rest of the time, he spends his idle hours playing golf or tending the grass on his three acres in Bethesda, just across the Maryland line from the capital. His heart still belongs to New York. For seven years, after he left the presidency of the State Federation of Labor to become the A. F. L.'s second in command in 1939, he commuted every week-end from Washington to the Bronx. Finally, he gave up the unequal struggle and moved his wife and three daughters to Bethesda. The eldest daughter is married now, the second works in Meany's office and the third is graduating from parochial school.

WHAT about Meany's opposite number on the C.I.O. side? Fifteen years have gone by since the first General Motors sit-down strikes pushed Walter Reuther into national prominence, but he still looks more like a stand-in for Van Johnson or some other movie prototype of clean-cut American young manhood than he does a labor leader. No touch of gray dulls his red hair, no lines crowd his gray-blue eyes. The right arm that the doctors despaired of saving after a thug's bullet pierced it nearly four years ago is slowly returning to normal usefulness. The arm is in such good shape that Reuther is able to putter around his basement carpentry shop again with hammer, saw and plane. A rare afternoon of fishing is his only outdoor exercise but he still has an athlete's build—square shoulders, barrel chest and taut stomach. He walks with a bounce and those who walk with him sometimes have to run to keep up. He bought a television set during the Presidential campaign, but his wife and two small daughters have not had much opportunity to watch it with him yet.

A sandwich and milk at his office desk is lunch. He never drinks, smokes or plays cards. His enemies in the free-wheeling United Automobile Workers, the C. I. O.'s biggest union, assumed that such an absence of conviviality would make Reuther poison to the union's hard-boiled rank and file. He proved they were wrong by winning the union presidency in 1946. He proved it again earlier this month by his victory in the C. I. O.

THE thing that won for Reuther on both occasions was not his good looks, or his multiplicity of copybook virtues, or even the political machine he was able to muster in his own support. Reuther's magic carpet was his ability to do an effective job on the wages-and-hours front and, at the same time, fire the imagination of his members with challenging new ideas for economic, social and political progress. He is as articulate as he is energetic, and he never forgets that a man who tosses off "Reuther Plans" with the profusion of sparks from an open hearth must chain his restless mind to solid accomplishment as well as idealistic visions.

Reuther started his union career with strong Socialist leanings, but his observations of the corrupting influence of power on Socialists in other countries, and his confidence in the potentialities of the American economic system, have made him distrustful of programs that would centralize all authority in Government's hands and remove initiative from the hands of the people. That still leaves him well to the left of the National Association of Manufacturers, but employers who have had intimate contact with him in the last ten years praise him for his success in overcoming the wildcat strikes that used to plague the motor industry and for adhering to his commitments.

THE man who led a 113-day strike against General Motors just after the war is now a party to a five-year peace pact that goes farther toward getting science into collective bargaining than any prior contract in other major industries. It is not a final answer to the problem of what constitutes a fair wage. No slide-rule formula, however intelligently conceived, will ever provide a final answer, but it does give the workers a share in the increasing productivity of our ever-expanding economy and it guarantees the stability of their pay envelope against inflation.

IN his new post as Philip Murray's successor, Reuther will have an even more potent role in setting the bargaining patterns that will shape wage contracts in the mass-production industries. "The preservation of a free society," Reuther says, "depends on the voluntary assumption of responsibility by free labor and free industry. It is up to us to work out machinery through which we can settle our problems on the basis of the economic facts and in the interest of the whole community. Our first job is to find out what the facts are. Our second job is to see to it that the facts get better and better each year because the bigger the economic pie we have to divide, the more chance there is to avoid conflict over how it is to be divided."

Reuther feels there can be no real collective bargaining if labor is deprived of its right to strike, but he recognizes that annual strikes in steel, coal, shipping and other vital industries eat away the nation's ability to support a higher standard of living. He sees nothing constructive, however, about a process in which strong unions and strong employers avoid strikes by ganging up to gouge the defenseless consumer. "I do not want to be part of a mechanism under which monopoly unions and monopoly employers put the squeeze on the consumer," he says. "If I thought my job was to get the most I could for a selfish economic pressure group, without concern for the public welfare, I would get on the other side where I could get more for my services. My interests simply do not lie in that direction."

EVEN by union standards, Reuther's salary of $11,250 a year is low. Meany draws $25,000 as head of the A. F. L., and Reuther's predecessor, Murray, earned $40,000 as president of the United Steelworkers. Some A. F. L. salaries run as high as $75,000. Men who sit opposite Reuther on the industry side of the table make as much in a month as he does in a year.

What facts are relevant in determining wage rates is bound to stir up controversy, just as they did in 1945 when Reuther first publicized his "look-at-the-book" demand. What conclusions the facts justify will also stir controversy. But Reuther is confident that these difficulties can be overcome if both sides start with a sincere desire to resolve their problems on a factual basis.

His touchstone of industrial peace is the establishment of an economy of abundance, in which improved technology provides a larger and larger pie to cut, and in which the interests of labor and management are identified with those of the entire community. Skeptics say Reuther has not always shown a single-minded devotion to the best interests of the community when they appeared to get in the way of the short-range interests of his own union. They point to his opposition to consumer credit controls and defense metal allocation policies when these cut automobile employment at the start of the Korean war, but Reuther does not feel either instance is a valid case in point. He says his objection was to Governmental bungling that caused waste of manpower, materials and facilities and not to legitimate sacrifices.

THE decentralized structure of the A. F. L. gives Meany a much less direct influence in collective bargaining than Reuther has in the mass-production industries. That does not keep Meany from having emphatic ideas about the importance of more active involvement of unions in the betterment of the community. He is determined to intensify the federation's efforts to expand and improve the public school system, to liberalize old-age and unemployment insurance, to institute health insurance and to wipe out racial and religious discrimination. Meany is no gymnasium fighter in the civil rights field. When A. Philip Randolph and Milton P. Webster, officers of the All-Negro Brotherhood of Sleeping Car Porters, were barred from the Houston hotel in which the A. F. L. was holding its 1949 convention, Meany marched into the lobby, with Randolph on one arm and Webster on the other. "Either they get in or we all get out," Meany told the manager. They got in.

Meany joins Reuther in pledging that America's unions will dedicate themselves to the common good. "Through our union organizations," he says, "we can and we shall make an ever-increasing contribution to the realization of a better and richer life by all the American people and to the preservation of our free way of life."

HOW well labor fulfills this commitment is the major test facing the two new leaders, but they have plenty of other tests to worry about. Meany has a problem of moss removal. Old men and old ideas still play too big a part in the federation's thinking. He has a problem of cancer removal, too. Gangsters are increasingly assertive in some A. F. L.

unions, a fact made clear in the State Crime Commission's investigation of the New York waterfront.

Reuther has to patch up the wounds left in the C. I. O. by the convention battle over his selection. Already he has made substantial headway toward conciliating the little unions that banded together against him. Now he is trying to achieve similar success in the much more crucial task of establishing cordial relations with the steel union.

ONCE the C. I. O. restores unity in its own ranks, the way will be clear for a fresh try at unity with the A. F. L. In the past, months were eaten up in fencing over who should write the letter calling for merger talks. Meany and Reuther disposed of that dilemma in their half-minute conversation. They decided not to have a letter. That took care of the preliminaries, but neither is kidding himself that the process of negotiating a merger will be as swift or harmonious.

You can get odds in both camps that unity will not come in the next year. Even if all the questions of jurisdiction and organizational structure could be hammered out satisfactorily, there would still be the problem of fitting all the officers, organizers and other assorted "pork-choppers" on the payroll of the fused organization. That is the problem no one likes to talk about. It may be the most stubborn one to solve unless the new group is to be turned into a super-W. P. A. with a Townsend Plan of its own to take care of those who are too old or weary to work for their union pay.

Politics will get more attention, rather than less, in the months and years ahead. Both Meany and Reuther hope General Eisenhower will adhere to his pledge to be "fair and friendly." but they are prepared to holler if the new President or the Republican Congress do things they don't like. Neither has any intention of going into the storm cellar because of labor's setback at the polls. The only moral they draw from the election results is that they still have a tremendous job to do in finding the common denominators that will identify labor's economic, social and political programs with the aims and aspirations of the great mass of the American people. That is the search to which both have dedicated themselves.

December 21, 1952

A.F.L., C.I.O. in No-Raiding Pact; Accord Held First Step to Merger

By JOSEPH A. LOFTUS

WASHINGTON, June 2—Leaders of the American Federation of Labor and the Congress of Industrial Organizations agreed today on a way to get rid of union raiding.

The compact was described as the first step organic unity of the two organizations. It will release staff energies for organizing the unorganized.

Subject to certain ratifications in the meantime, the agreement will go into effect Jan. 1 and run for two years. Ratifications are expected not only by the executive bodies and the conventions of the two federations, but by each national and international union.

Disputes over interpreting and applying the agreement will go to an impartial umpire if they fail to yield to negotiation. The umpire's decision will be final. However, no formal disciplinary measures are provided for noncompliance.

The agreement deals only with raiding—that is, the transfer, or attempt to transfer, a recognized unit of employes from one federation to another. A unit of employes is considered to be the nontransferable property of a union if it has a contract with an employer or is certified by the National Labor Relations Board.

A union that receives a unit of employes from the other federation, even though it has made no overtures, will be guilty of raiding. Therefore, if a group of employes is dissatisfied with its representation, it cannot go over to a union in the other federation without negotiating its release. It can, of course, cut all ties and become independent.

The agreement does not deal with jurisdictional disputes or rival claims to units of unorganized employes.

A jurisdictional dispute, in its common form, is a fight between unions over the right to perform certain work.

A. F. L. unions do raid each other, apart from any jurisdictional disputes, but the agreement does not deal with that. That is a problem strictly for the federation itself. The recent Executive Council meeting set up a three-member committee to do something about it.

Raiding within the C. I. O. is insignificant. Conflicts between C. I. O. unions over organizing unorganized plants was a serious problem, but the C. I. O. has virtually solved that by setting up impartial umpire procedures.

George Meany, president of the A. F. L., and Walter Reuther, president of the C. I. O., announced at a joint news conference they had agreed on the essentials of a no-raiding agreement. It has to be rewritten, but they were so confident of mutual understanding that the job was left entirely to sub-committees.

Mr. Meany said "it is just a question of language and details that Walter and I are going to work out."

The rewritten instrument will be ready in time for the August meeting of the A. F. L. Executive Council and for a C. I. O. executive meeting about the same time. Both federations will hold conventions in the fall.

Asked what would happen if some affiliate refuse to sign the agreement, Mr. Meaney said "if some union doesn't go along, it's outside the agreement. But we are convinced from experience it can't profit them."

"Maybe we'll let them try it," he concluded with a grin.

The union leaders' research into raiding statistics showed that only 17 per cent of the raids were successful; that out of 1,245 cases, involving 350,000 workers in the last two years, the net gain was 8,000 employes. The A. F. L. was on the gainful side, owning largely to a schism in the C. I. O. textile workers, which the A. F. L. United Textile Workers exploited.

The agreement will not prevent an A. F. L. and a C. I. O. national or international union from negotiating a merger. Such negotiations have been going on intermittently between the Amalgamated Meat Cutters, A. F. L., and the Packinghouse Workers, C. I. O.

Meantime, talks looking to complete unity of the two labor federations will go on. Mr. Reuther said today's agrement "will have a very good effect on the prospects of organic unity." He said that although the no-raiding agreement would not go into effect until Jan. 1 he expected that the attitude shown by both sides now would be reflected immediately in the day-to-day organizing of the two federations.

June 3, 1953

252

A.F.L. AND C.I.O. WILL MERGE, ENDING 20-YEAR LABOR SPLIT; MEANY WILL HEAD NEW BODY

15 MILLION UNITING

Formula Creates Place for Industrial Unions —Raiding Ban Set

By A. H. RASKIN

Special to The New York Times.

MIAMI BEACH, Feb. 9—A detailed formula for labor unity was approved today after twenty years of civil war.

The pact made it certain that the 15,000,000 members of the American Federation of Labor and the Congress of Industrial Organizations would come under one banner by the end of this year.

Every problem that could block a merger was overcome in the unity plan. Even the question of who would head the pooled organization was settled. He will be George Meany, now president of the A. F. L.

His opposite number in the C. I. O., Walter P. Reuther, announced that he would be happy to step aside in Mr. Meany's favor. William F. Schnitzler, secretary-treasurer of the A. F. L., will occupy the same post in the new group.

There was no formal name given as yet to the merged organizations. But the thirty-four unions now in the C. I. O. will go into it as a special department to be known as a Council of Industrial Organizations.

To Preserve Initials

This will enable the group to preserve the initials that were used in the unionization of steel, automobile, rubber and other mass production industries in the early years of the split.

The ticklish issue of interunion raiding was settled through adoption of a joint declaration that the integrity of every A. F. L. and C. I. O. union would be preserved after the merger.

The new organization's constitution will contain a specific declaration that affiliated unions are to respect the established bargaining relationship of sister unions. It will call on all unions to avoid stealing members from one another.

The precise machinery for enforcing this anti-raiding provision was not specified. However, both sides agreed that "appropriate machinery" was to be established. Its nature was left to the committees charged with drafting a constitution.

In the meantime both groups will seek to get more unions to subscribe on a voluntary basis to the existing no-raid agreements between the A. F. L. and C. I. O. Seventy-seven of the 111 unions in the federation already have bound themselves to eschew poaching. On the C. I. O. side thirty out of thirty-four have signed.

These pacts are scheduled to expire at the end of this year. Part of the merger understanding is that the voluntary ban on raiding would be extended for two years. This would provide more time for implementation of the constitutional declaration against raids.

The A. F. L. will control the executive council of the merged organization by a margin of nearly two to one. In addition to the two chief officers, it will have seventeen vice presidents in the new body. The C. I. O. will have ten vice presidents.

The ratio roughly reflects the present membership strength of the two existing bodies. The A. F. L. claims 10,300,000 members. The C. I. O. reports membership fluctuating between 4,500,000 and 5,000,000.

The Federation, which now has fifteen vice presidents will have to choose two more to fill its unity quota. The C. I. O. now has nine vice presidents, plus its president and secretary-treasurer. It is expected that Mr. Reuther and James B. Carey, secretary-treasurer of the C. I. O., will serve as vice presidents of the merged group, along with all but one of the present C. I. O. vice presidents.

Much of the authority now exercised by the A. F. L. Executive Council will pass to a nearly completed executive committee. This will consist of Mr. Meany, Mr. Schnitzler and six vice presidents —three from the A. F. L. and three from the C. I. O. Conventions of the new organization will be held every two years.

Twenty A. F. L. and C. I. O. executives signed the unity agreement at the Roney Plaza Hotel here this afternoon. They said its ratification would "materially benefit the entire nation" and add to the strength and effectiveness of the labor movement.

The A. F. L. Executive Council is scheduled to give its blessing to the pact here tomorrow. The C. I. O. executive board will take similar action at a meeting in Washington Feb. 24.

After this clearance, the same unity committees that drafted today's peace plan will work out full constitutional language. When the proposed constitution has been approved by the leaders on both sides, it will be submitted to separate conventions of each group. Then a joint convention will be held to finalize the merger.

No convention timetable was fixed. However, it was believed probable that both groups would seek to have all arrangements complete for a joint convention in the latter part of September.

The A. F. L. is scheduled to hold its regular convention in Chicago Sept. 15. The C. I. O., now set to meet in Buffalo Oct. 17, may shift its plans to mesh with those of the Federation on both city and date. This would make it easy to hold a joint ratification session without the expense of special conventions for both groups.

The amalgamation plan would protect the jobs of all persons now on the headquarters and field staffs of the two organizations. Overlapping state and city central bodies would be merged on a gradual basis over a two-year period.

Compulsion Ruled Out

The same gradualness would characterize the merging of individual unions now having similar jurisdictions. The pact provided that there was to be no compulsion on unions to get together. Where conflicts between unions exist, the new parent body would encourage — but not force — an effort to try to work out merger arrangements.

The charter recognized that industrial and craft unions were "appropriate, equal and necessary as methods of trade union organization."

It was this issue that touched off the original division in 1935. At that time the A. F. L. was dedicated to the protection of craft rights. Now, the principle of industrial organization has gained such wide acceptance within the federation that this presented no real hurdle in the unity negotiations.

An industrial union is often described as a vertical union. Its members are in one industry, from top to bottom. In this sense a craft union is described as horizontal. Its members are in the same skill stratum extending through several kinds of industry.

Separate Funds Planned

The new industrial department will have the right to maintain a separate treasury to finance organizing drives in such industries as chemicals. However, the bulk of the funds now held by the C. I. O. will be turned over to the merged group as part of a common central treasury.

The A. F. L. comes into the merger with $3,500,000 in cash, bonds and real estate. The C. I. O. is to put up roughly half as much, in recognition of its smaller membership. This will take virtually all of the $1,800,000 now held by the C. I. O.

However, the industrial group will have an opportunity to pile up additional funds for organizing by continuing to collect a per capita tax of ten cents a month. Under the merger, the central organization will get a payment of four cents a month for each member. This is the present A. F. L. rate. The difference between this and ten cents would stay with the industrial department.

CRAFT UNIONS DECLINE

Survey Finds 67% of Labor in Industrial Set-Ups

The growth of industrial unions is shown in an analysis of union membership made public yesterday by the National Industrial Conference Board.

Sixty-seven per cent of the membership of the new labor federation being formed by the merger of the American Federation of Labor and the Congress of Industrial Organizations belong to unions that are either industrially organized or that combine craft and industrial unionism, the survey found. The remaining 33 per cent are strictly craft organizations.

The board's analysis covers 123 A. F. L. and thirty C. I. O. unions—the entire 16,026,880 claimed membership of the unions in the new federation.

Labor Agrees to Arbitrate Disputes Between Unions

By A. H. RASKIN

SAN FRANCISCO, Sept. 22—The merged labor federation cleared the way today for establishment of compulsory machinery for arbitrating inter-union disputes. The decision marked a major break with the tradition of union autonomy. It reflected a recognition by warring craft and industrial unionists of the necessity for subordinating their internal feuds in the light of mounting employer resistance and the impact of the new labor law.

The refusal of the craft group in the old American Federation of Labor to go along with a mandatory arbitration procedure almost torpedoed the merger with the Congress of Industrial Organizations four years ago. Since then the combined group has repeatedly come to the brink of collapse as the result of unresolved jurisdictional disputes and raiding charges.

Today the federation's executive council unanimously decided that its biennial convention approve a plan for final and binding decisions on all inter-union conflicts by an impartial arbitration board. The plan was promised support by all factions in the federation and was scheduled for formal ratification tomorrow.

Under the formula authorized by the representatives of 13,-000,000 unionists, a special committee of the council was directed to develop a detailed program for creation of a panel of "prominent and well-qualified persons" to serve as arbitrators. Where the unions directly involved in a dispute fail to settle it voluntarily, the rulings of the arbitrators would be controlling. Their authority would extend to controversies over rating, inter-union boycotts and jurisdictional differences between the industrial unions in the mass production field and the craft unions in the building and metal trades.

Also covered would be complaints over organizing efforts in campaigns involving competition between rival unions and other provisions in union agreements prohibiting contracting out of work to companies employing members of other unions. Disputes of this kind have caused particular bitterness in recent months.

The entire procedure represented such a fundamental departure from past practice that the delegates instructed the federation's high command to call a special convention as soon as the mechanics of the plan had been completed. Its purpose would be to authorize any changes in the federation's constitution that might be necessary to make the arbitration procedure mandatory.

The new formula was drawn up by the same special committee that will develop the detailed machinery. It was headed by Al J. Hayes, president of the International Association of Machinists. The achievement added to his standing as a bridge between the feuding factions and labor. His 1,000,000-member union was in the old

A. F. L., but it embraces both craft and industrial locals.

The acceptance of arbitration as the last step in jurisdictional disputes represented almost as revolutionary a departure from historic concepts of the freedom of unions to run their own affairs in their own way as the assumption by the A. F. L. in 1953 of power to act against corruption in its affiliated organizations.

to be referred to the Executive Council for action.

The one sop to traditionalists in today's resolution was a declaration that the arbitration procedure would apply solely to the settlement of disputes and would not include the fixing of jurisdictional boundaries. This means that each case will be handled on an individual basis.

In another sign of internal harmony, six unions joined today in a mutual-aid alliance in the air transport field. Their aim was to offset the united front formed by the airlines last year by coordinated union activity.

Mr. Hayes was a prime mover in formation of the coordinating committee.

In addition to the machinists, the alliance will include the Transport Workers Union, the Airline Pilots Association, the Flight Engineers International Association, the Brotherhood of Railway Clerks and the Airline Dispatchers Association. The pilots and the flight engineers have been conducting a bitter feud over the manning of jet planes.

Mr. Haye's co-authors of the arbitration program were:

Walter P. Reuther, president of the United Auto Workers of America; Peter T. Schoemann, president of the United Association of Plumbers and Pipefitters; William F. Schnitzler, secretary-treasurer of the federation, and Joseph A. Beirne, president of the Communications Workers of America.

UNION MEMBERSHIP DROPPED IN 1956-58

WASHINGTON, Feb. 3 (UPI)—Union membership declined from 1956 through 1958, reversing a twenty-year trend. the Labor Department reported today. The proportion of union members to the total labor force remained unchanged.

The report showed that 18,100,000 men and women belonged to unions at the end of 1958, about 400,000 fewer than two years earlier. The total included about 1,200,000 members outside the country, most of them in Canada.

One out of four workers belonged to unions at the end of 1958, however, the same as in 1956. And one of every three non-farm workers was a member.

The figures were the result of a comprehensive survey of dues-paying membership in national and international unions having headquarters in the United States. The report was published in the current issue of the labor department's monthly Labor Review.

About 15,000,000 persons belonged to affiliates of the American Federation of Labor and Congress of Industrial Organizations, the others to unaffiliated unions.

The publication said that slightly fewer than 17,000,000 persons belonged to one or another of the bigger unions at the end of 1958, compared to a postwar peak of 17,500,000 in 1956.

LAG IN UNIONIZING WORRYING LABOR

17 Million Total Unchanged Since 1955, Federation Told—Drives Urged

By A. H. RASKIN
Special to The New York Times.

BAL HARBOUR, Fla., Feb. 9 —Labor's high command learned today that a smaller proportion of the work force was unionized now than when the American Federation of Labor and Congress of Industrial Organizations merged in 1955.

John W. Livingston, the federation's organizing director, said "ferocious attacks" by employer groups and labor's inability to overcome internal feuds had caused the decline.

His report to the executive council indicated that the enrollment of union members in and out of the federation had remained at 17,000,000 despite an increase of 2,000,000 workers in the non-farm force.

Mr. Livingston said there were 27,000,000 unorganized workers in chemicals, textiles, white-collar industries, civil service and other fields susceptible to unionization. This compared with 25,000,00 at the merger.

The unionized sector represents 39 per cent of the potential, against 40 per cent in 1955.

The report brought demands for stepped-up activity from heads of industrial and craft unions. One suggestion was that the millions contributed to help the steel workers in their recent strike be used as a "kitty" for organizing purposes.

Another was that all unions donate $1 for each member to finance a large-scale recruiting effort. However, no specific agreement was reached on how to approach the task of bringing more workers into the union fold.

Labor's failure to match the growth in the work force focused new attention on the handicaps it has created for itself by its inability to work out dependable machinery for interunion cooperation.

The federation's central organizing staff is unable to tackle any situation in which international unions, with nominal jurisdiction over the field, fail to agree on who shall get the workers after they are signed up.

Such agreements have proven so hard to attain that the federation has cut its organizing staff from 339 to 160. Only about half of those who are left are available for recruiting assignments.

PHILADELPHIA UNION OPENS HEALTH CENTER

ILGWU Dedicates Medical Project as Example to Labor

Special to The New York Times

PHILADELPHIA, March 4 — The International Ladies Garment Workers Union dedicated today its union medical center, believed to be the first project of its kind in the country.

The center, which occupies a four-story building and has the latest medical and surgical equipment, was hailed by David Dubinsky, national president of the ILGWU, as a milestone in the history of labor and as an example that should be followed by other labor organizations.

A similar view was expressed by James S. McDevitt, president of the Pennsylvania Federation of Labor, who said that the center would meet a need for medical service when Philadelphia was facing its greatest emergency.

The project was made possible by the joint cooperation of union members and employers, members of the Philadelphia Dress and Waist Joint Board of Trade.

The 15,000 members of the union in this area will receive free medical examinations and treatment from a staff of physicians headed by Dr. Joseph A. Landbord. A dental department is also planned.

More than 4,000 union members attended the opening ceremonies at the center, which will be directed by Isidor Melamed, a former union official here.

March 5, 1944

Signs of the Times

Labor union fund managers are coming to Wall Street to obtain professional "know-how" and improve the investment return on monies entrusted to their care. They are turning to mutual investment companies in some instances to gain professional guidance and consulting with brokers, investment counselors and investment bankers in an effort to make a success of their investment objectives.

Arthur Wiesenberger, senior partner in the investment firm bearing his name, and author of "Investment Companies — 1952," feels that it is of great significance that labor leaders realize that stock investments are the most effective means of improving the earnings and growth of labor funds.

"This view of labor fund managers represents a realistic approach to the problem of how to keep pace with rising costs and offset the prospect that beneficiaries will collect dollars with lower purchasing value sometime in the future," says Mr. Wiesenberger.

"Up to recently," he adds, "managers of union funds had been fearful of the responsibility of investing the funds entrusted to their care, and for the most part shifted the burden by investing in Government bonds." Such a decision, he holds, wiped out a major investment advantage which union funds enjoy because of their non-taxable status. Further, it failed to provide a means of protection against the steady decline of the dollar.

After all these years, union leaders and Wall Street seem to have found a happy meeting ground.

October 26, 1952

UNION'S AGED TO GET $5,000,000 VILLAGE

A. F. L. Upholsterers to Build 500 Cottages 12 Miles North of West Palm Beach, Fla.

NURSING HOME FIRST UNIT

Organized labor struck off in a new social welfare direction yesterday with an announcement by the Upholsterers International Union, A. F. L., of plans for a $5,000,000 village in Florida for retiring members.

The union's program calls for a self-contained community of 500 low-rent residential units for workers over 65 years old. Unlike most union benefit systems, it will be paid for by the 55,000-member upholsterers' group, not by employers.

The proposal for the retirement village has been under study for six months. Yesterday it was submitted to delegates at the union's twenty-seventh convention at the Commodore Hotel and was approved by all except five members from California.

The village, according to Sal B. Hoffman, president of the union, will be built on a 614-acre tract twelve miles north of West Palm Beach. It will front on lagoons and the intercoastal waterway near Jupiter light on Florida's east coast.

Site Already Bought

The site already has been purchased by the union. After land clearing and road building, work will commence on the first project —a convalescent and nursing home for insured workers.

Eventually the village will include a community center, recreation sections, a man-made lake, service areas if the surrounding centers cannot provide facilities, and vacation cottages that may be rented to other labor and liberal organizations, Mr. Hoffman said.

Rental for cottages occupied by pensioners will be between $42 and $50 a month. Under an industry-wide pension plan, recently negotiated by the union and effective July 1, retired workers will receive pensions of about $120 a month.

The pension plan, which will cover 13,000 members at first, will be financed by employer contributions amounting to 2 per cent of payrolls. Several hundred members will be eligible for retirement by July 1, 1954. Retirement is optional at 65 and compulsory at 68.

In the next year the union plans to spend about $1,250,000. It will provide central utilities and will seek tax exemption as a nonprofit organization.

Cottages generally will be of a concrete block type. Each one-story unit will contain one or two bedrooms, a kitchen and a living-dining room.

Consultants on the project included the Florida State Improvement Commission; the Older Workers Project of the University of Chicago; Ernst Burgess, sociologist of the university; Dr. Cletus Krag, United States Public Health Service; Dr. Robert Monroe, Harvard Medical School, and Newman Biller, director of the New York Hebrew Home.

June 11, 1953

DRESS UNION SETS ITS SIGHTS ANEW

Sportswear Local Focuses on Closer Ties to Varied Membership Pattern

By A. H. RASKIN

How does a community-minded union keep alive its ties to its rank and file when far-reaching changes in the racial and national pattern of employment in its industry occur?

The Skirt and Sportswear Union, Local 23 of the International Ladies' Garment Workers Union, is a good place to go to find the answer.

When the union was formed fifty-seven years ago its membership was made up almost entirely of Jewish immigrants from eastern Europe. It was, in the words of its manager, Shelley Appleton, a "ghetto" union. Its members lived and worked in a few crowded blocks on New York's lower East Side.

The union headquarters was their cultural center. They flocked there to learn English, talk politics and adjust themselves to the ways of their new homeland. As they became acclimated, they moved to Brooklyn and the Bronx and eventually to the suburbs. Their children went to college and made careers in other industries or the professions.

Migrants Enter Picture

With the shift of garment manufacture to Seventh Avenue and the sharp rise in the popularity of sportswear, the union found itself drifting farther and farther from its rank and file. Nearly half of its 9,000 members are now Spanish-speaking—the great bulk of them women from Puerto Rico and other Caribbean islands.

Its only remaining stronghold on the East Side is in Chinatown, where it has nearly 900 members working in sportswear factories established since World War II.

The rest of its membership is drawn from many lands and races. Ten to 15 per cent are Negroes born in the United States. Roughly the same number are carry-overs from the early Jewish bloc. The others include workers of Italian, Syrian, Turkish and dozens of other extractions.

The union followed its members to the garment center, but its cultural and community activities became increasingly the private preserve of a few old-timers.

When Mr. Appleton became manager last year at the age of 39, he decided it was time to modernize. He moved the headquarters to the tenth floor of the skyscraper that houses the I. L. G. W. U. Health Center at 275 Seventh Avenue.

Educating and Protecting

Huge photo-murals, pastel tints, highly stylized furniture and a general air of light and space make the new headquarters of Local 23 a match for the executive offices of any corporation. A library and an auditorium equipped with sound motion-picture facilities await the members.

The union will start on Feb. 8 a joint venture with the Bureau of Community Education of the Board of Education to help its Spanish-speaking members learn English in schools near their homes or their shops. The classes will deal with such practical topics as family budget-making, bank deposits and insurance and how to make the food dollar stretch.

In addition, the local is organizing a task force of 100 executive board members, shop chairwomen and other rank-and-file leaders to visit members in their homes and help guard them against exploitation by landlords or installment salesmen.

January 24, 1960

Union to Give Course In Planning Retirement

A seven-week course in preparing for retirement will begin today for union members approaching retirement and local union officials in charge of retirement programs.

The classes, directed by the Community Services Committee of the City Central Labor Council, will be held weekly at the auditorium of Local 32-B of the Building Service Employes Union, 1 East Thirty-fifth Street.

Geriatrics specialists will give talks under a program drawn up with the cooperation of the School of Industrial and Labor Relations at Cornell University.

The course will be aimed at showing retired persons how to adjust to retirement and channel their new leisure time into fields of interest.

STEEL UNION MAPS A LABOR COLLEGE

Accredited Program Opens in 1963 at Indiana U.

Special to The New York Times.

PITTSBURGH, July 21—The United Steelworkers Union has joined with Indiana University to establish the first labor college with full academic standing in America. The project is scheduled to begin in September, 1963.

Dr. Herman B. Wells, the university's president, and university trustees voted recently to accept a formal proposal by the union to establish a residential labor education program on the campus at Bloomington.

Although the first session will be limited to one semester, the ultimate goal is to offer a new degree in trade union affairs. The program, it was said, will pioneer many others that the steel union hopes to develop at other universities in coming years.

The project was hailed by David J. McDonald, United Steelworkers president, as a "giant step forward in the development of trade union education in the United States."

He pointed out that it would permit union members to attend the university, receive credits for their work and apply them toward a degree.

Locals Contribute Funds

The plan was drawn up by James Robb, director of the union's District 30 in Indiana, trustees of the district's education fund and the union's department of education, which is headed by Emery F. Bacon of Pittsburgh.

To finance the program, trustees of the district education fund have allocated $10,000 from funds raised by the eighty-five locals in the Indiana area. District 30 headquarters has offered $1,000 more and the university has agreed to assist in providing professional instruction.

Four basic aims of the program will be to provide opportunities for union executive development; to improve the quality of labor leadership; to encourage individual development; and to insure opportunities for able men to advance themselves.

For the first two years the program will be considered as a pilot project confined for the most part to steel workers selected by the district office. At the end of the trial period, if it proves successful, the program will be opened to any union member or staff representative in the United States and Canada.

Faculty to Tutor Students

A course covering thirteen hours a week will deal with trade union studies. Four hours of this course will be devoted to the humanities and five hours will be tutorial, with a full-time faculty member directing the studies of each student in any field offered on the campus.

The steelworkers union has been sponsoring labor education activities throughout most of the twenty six years since it was founded. Early in World War II it undertook an experiment in co-operation with the Federal Government in defense work training.

After the war it shifted the emphasis of the program to the state universities and land grant colleges by starting the first programs of their kind dealing with labor education and using university facilities and faculties.

The program, begun in 1946, has been expanded to include twenty-five universities. It offers both non-credit residential work during the year and extension courses. There are now 75,000 union members taking part in these programs each year.

UNION SUPPLEMENT TO MEDICARE BEGUN

CLEVELAND, Jan. 13 (AP) —For slightly less than $7 a month a person, retired members of the Brotherhood of Locomotive Firemen and Enginemen and their dependents will be able to supplement Medicare with "virtually complete hospital and medical protection," the union said today.

The brotherhood said it had begun signing up subscribers this week to its Retired-Members' Health Plan, which it believes is the first supplemental plan of its kind to be made available by a union or employer.

The new plan is underwritten by the Travelers Insurance Company, which now insures about 5,300 retired members and their dependents at a monthly cost of $13.86 for an individual and $27.72 for a family.

More than 10,000 other retired members are covered by Blue Cross and other plans. These also are being enrolled in the new plan.

A feature of the program is a major-medical coverage provision paying 80 per cent of all covered expenses not paid for by either Medicare or other portions of the policy, up to a total of $10,000. Any used portion of the $10,000 maximum is renewable at a rate of $1,000 a year.

The union's program will become effective next July 1. Those subscribing will have to sign up first for Medicare and the $3-a-month medical benefits coverage under the federal plan.

THE CHANGING ROLE OF MANAGEMENT

"INDUSTRIAL PSYCHOLOGIST" TO PREVENT LABOR TROUBLES

By Edward Marshall.

COMES into being, at the call of new industrial conditions, another profession.

The "business doctor," new not long ago, is now a common and an indispensable member of industrial society, with his study of physical conditions in the individual store or plant, from the viewpoint of one who knows the ins and outs, the wrongs and rights, the cans and can'ts of many other stores and plants, and from his knowledge finds himself in a position to suggest improvements bettering product, eliminating waste, increasing capacity.

He has become the surgeon, the physical physician of our modern industry.

Now we have the man who may be called industrial psychologist—a sort of business alienist, whose efforts are to be directed to prevention and cure of those conditions which lead frequently to the sort of business mania producing dissatisfaction and strikes.

Robert Grosvenor Valentine is this field's pioneer. Until September of last year he was Commissioner of Indian Affairs. Before he took charge of the Nation's red-skinned wards he had taught English in the Massachusetts Institute of Technology, served with the National City Bank of this city and with the Farmers' Loan and Trust Company, supervisor of Indian schools, and had been private secretary of Francis E. Leupp, his predecessor as Commissioner.

"The one object of my new work," he told me Wednesday, "is to secure, if possible, an increased stability in labor conditions. It is as essential that the personal relations between employer and employed should now and then be audited as it is that the shop account books should be.

"An audit of this sort must point out concretely specific sources of irritation, consider the more general factors affecting labor conditions within the business, show the effect of labor conditions at large upon the labor problems of that particular business, existing or probable labor legislation, the local community, the consumer, and public opinion.

"The moral issues in industry are fundamental. They must now be met broadly in order to provide the only efficient social basis for the still more troublesome economic problems with which we are confronted as to wages, profits, and prices.

"Stability in our industrial relations can only come through mutual understanding and the aim of the new profession must be to attain this understanding in an organized and effective way.

"Psychology has as much to do with business efficiency as physiology, as represented, for example, by lunchrooms and baths, or material arrangement such as a proper sequence of machine processes. Let me illustrate that:

"One of the principles of scientific management is that the workers shall have everything at hand, being forced to no false motions. This means, for instance, that the girl at the X. Y. Z. press shall, the moment she is ready for it, find material already rolled up to her elbow on a table running on rubber-tired wheels.

Too Sudden Change.

"This very thing, although it was the right thing, made trouble in one shop.

One of the workers complained that this system did away with a change which had formerly been refreshing. After finishing a certain stint of work it had been recreative to go to the source of the supply and get a new outfit of material.

"This may seem like a small matter; it is not. A change from the old and inefficient method to the new, efficient method worked great dissatisfaction in that plant.

"It was right to make the change, but, after it was made, investigation proved it to be necessary to substitute for the old-time break in work intervals of new and constructive recreation and rest. As soon as these had been supplied, the shop worked well again—better, indeed, than it ever had before. But time was wasted in the interim.

"Another example of the detail of the work: A man on piecework in a hat factory must, because of rents, live at such a distance from the factory that he is forced to come in by car. One car gets him to his work ten minutes early, the next gets him there five minutes late.

"The fifteen minutes in the morning means a lot to wife and family, for reasons that no father of a family needs to have enlarged. Incidentally, the man attends night school, thus growing in efficiency.

"Query: May that man be permitted to regularly arrive five minutes late? Would this interfere with shop discipline? Might not regular irregularity which means personal accommodation be tolerated in many of our giant systems of employment?

"I most emphatically contend that modern conditions do not make it necessary to lose as much of personal contact and personal adaptation as many managers think. I am convinced that careful study of such matters is essential to our National well-being. We seem to have arrived at a definitely crucial period in our industrial life. A little of this sort of adaptation would ease the entire situation.

"I wonder often if the 'efficiency engineers' of which we have of late heard so much have not gone too far with their idea of continually 'speeding up.' Such problems as the two which I have cited quite at random help to indicate the reason for my wondering. Theoretically rest periods are as much a part of good efficiency plans as, for example, proper store distribution; practically it does not generally work out that way. Rest is given scant attention; speeding up is given overmuch attention. Such details as I have suggested are given no attention whatsoever.

"I have traveled about 200,000 miles in the United States, and whenever I have had an opportunity I have studied factories, stores, and what not. I have gradually become convinced, with all due respect to both the employers and the workmen, that about 50 per cent. of the dissatisfaction on both sides is due to absolutely needless and usually almost inexcusable misunderstanding.

"Many employes are working under absolutely unnecessary conditions so bad that the employers, if put in their places, would not endure them for an hour; employes not infrequently make demands which they would never make if they but understood the difficulties under which their employers are straining every nerve. Both sides frequently need to be dynamited loose from old ideas.

"It is the terrifically complicated problem of relationship, not to any wilful wrong any intentional unreasonableness or selfishness on either side, which makes quite half the trouble. The more I study the more I am convinced that this is true.

"If we ever really solve our great industrial problem the beginning will come through wiping out the blurs, so that both sides can see straight. I have no ultimate remedy to suggest, but I have gone far enough to be convinced that there are many practical things at hand which might be done.

"Some believe the conflict between capital and labor to be irreconcilable, others think a real community of interest exists all along the line. I am of the latter school. My theory is that if a strong hydraulic stream of real desire for understanding is turned on to wash away the surface gravel of what everybody knows, we shall begin to get down to pay dust. At present surface dirt hides the real issues.

"I have become convinced that there has been too much theorizing and generalizing about this thing and too little deep, digging investigation of particular, individual problems. There has been a vast amount of deductive reasoning on both sides. We need some inductive reasoning.

"I am sure that we can profitably turn attention for awhile to immediate practical things. When we get the mass of facts together we shall have a basis for our theories. We have been producing theories and trying to fit facts to them. That it is reverse reasoning. It confuses.

"There is an enormous mass of material available to draw from. For some years I have been studying it and I am constantly astonished by results. Labor commissions, surveys, and other public efforts have produced much of it, much has been provided by intelligent individuals.

Conditions Must Be Studied.

"This, in order to be made effective, must all be viewed from the standpoint of each particular business. Each great industrial group has built up conditions peculiar to itself, both for employer and employed. The steel mills have their definite conditions, which are very different from those existing in the silk mills. And within every group each particular employer and group of employes has a definite individual problem to consider.

"The world of industry, taken as a whole, represents a circle, it is true, but inside that is an infinite number of circles which are complete, even though they may be small, and in the middle of each one is the man who has to earn a profit or else stop.

"If the relations between each of these to all the others and society at large are sound, we are progressing. Out of the concreteness of the definite, particular problem, plus the indefiniteness of the general situation has come the puzzle which has so intensely bothered us that it has sometimes seemed as if it stumped us. There arises, then, the need for investigation.

"Having investigated and obtained the facts the next step is to analyze them, put them together properly in their newly discovered relationships and thus learn what will build success where failure has existed theretofore.

"No man, neither the employer nor the employe, wants a strike. We all know that. But the only machinery which we have so far devised for their avoidance has been arbitration, which comes along too late. To arbitrate is to lock the stable door after the team of horses, peace and profit, has been stolen, and, presently, after an expensive process, to substitute for the lost span another, coercion and dislike, which will never take the place, completely, of that which has been lost.

"In other words, the very trouble which we all seek to avoid is the only force at present known by means of which a pressure can be put upon the button which will start machinery at work to bring about a right solution of the difficulties.

"With certain exceptions the interests of employers and employes are fundamentally the same. The object of the new profession is to furnish men to take their stand squarely on the middle ground between them. I have not named the new profession. Here are some of the things it is not: Scientific engineering, production engineering, industrial engineering, accounting, economy, psychology, ethical consulting, political science, philosophy, history, cultural anthropology, religion, law, medicine, education, statistics, efficiency engineering, or social work. Make your choice of such other names as may occur to you.

"The point is that both employer and employe must wish to make their capital and work produce as much as possible. Only a large product gives large profits to be shared, and, after all, the relations between capital and labor are fundamentally those of profit sharers. It is to the interest of every person in the world that his own work and that of every other person in the world shall count for as much as possible. The more valuable and numerous the product the more prosperous the world and all its individual citizens.

"The only real issue which should ever arise between employer and employed is that of what the share of profit going to each one shall be. To restrict wealth creation is sheer madness, obviously. You and I and every one should understand this and preach it everywhere. Production must not be hampered either by employer or employed. That should be the golden rule of industry.

"One of the biggest sticks of dynamite in the whole industrial situation seems to be that many labor leaders, as well as many large employers, fail to recognize this great, basic truth. What I hope is intellectual honesty compels me to express my thought that both are about equally prone to go wrong in this matter.

"I have talked with many workingmen, and I must admit that they seem oftener to see this light than their employers do, but it must be admitted that the average human being, be he workman or employer, is reasonably fair-minded. If this were not true the world could not have built up a society even as imperfect as that which now exists.

About 70 per cent. of the strength of the I. W. W., the working people's organization which is worrying so many these days, is the fact that working people have not always been treated fairly; this counts much more than any inherent righteousness in the I. W. W.'s platform or processes of action. Surely not more than 30 per cent. of its theories and methods are justified or sound. Most of the real anarchistic dangers have

their original foundation in the fact that some man has been really ill-treated. In other words the I. W. W. is an unnecessary and inefficient but perhaps inevitable outgrowth of perfectly remediable industrial errors.

"It must be reckoned with, and the only way to reckon with it is to recognize it as one of the really big movements on the firing line of industry and to rob its soldiers of their patriotism for it by applying remedies to the actual wrongs which do exist. If the real wrongs are remedied the fancied wrongs will be forgotten and industrial peace will come again.

"In my opinion conditions leading to industrial uprisings are particularly inexcusable under our form of government, which was especially devised to avoid them. We must learn to be democratic throughout, in industry as well as in political and social life. When we do there will be no general tendency to join such organizations.

"One of the biggest errors we have ever drifted into has been the substitution of a piece rate for a day's wage

when there was any likelihood of a necessity for cutting piece work prices. Our employers have sometimes been extremely wasteful in a way which many of them seem never to have thought of—they have 'scrapped' men. It is safe and often necessary to 'scrap' an old machine. To work upon a system which will use up men, as any system uses up machines, and to then throw the men away, as old machines must be cast out, is quite another matter. Men. We are all that, and none of us is more than that.

"When a manufacturer 'scraps' a machine he gets room in which to substitute a new, improved machine. Unfortunately new and improved men cannot be ordered from a factory, free on board the factory town. 'Scrap' a man and you have done your share toward making the employes of the next generation so less efficient.

"A concern should keep as careful records of the human beings which it uses in its business as it does of the machines it uses. A set of books in

R. G. Valentine.

which account is made of human brains and bodies will waste no bookkeeper's time. Such books, cast up and balanced, will yield totals of greater value often than those which show the volume of the business or the debts of creditors.

"Clients of the new profession, obviously, may be either employers or employed; truly both should make investigations. The man who digs for facts must tell the exact truth as he finds it or fail of usefulness. Already I have found it necessary to give some disagreeable deductions to those who have engaged my services. To drop into the vernacular for a descriptive phrase, my position must be that of one who doesn't care a whoop what may develop, but is searching for the facts, whatever they may be.

Employer and Employed.

"If employes wish to take a certain stand toward their employer, and I find that that demand will be unsound, I must tell them so and show them why. Not always in the past have the investigations preceding employes' demands been sufficiently profound. If an employer's attitude toward his men is bringing trouble to him, I must learn and show him why. I must not care whether a client ever comes back to me, or not; but it has been my experience that they will come back for more truth even when the truth which they have had has not been agreeable.

"The one detail in which the interests of employer and employed are not identical is the wage question. This is the sharing of the products of labor—the National dividend; but most of the social doctors who suggest their remedies forget that we shall have this with us, no matter what our industrial organization may be. No workingman, nor no employer, ever has suggested any plan which would entirely do away with it.

"A great deal of cant is written and preached about the differences between employer and employed. What we all are after is contentment, happiness. By no means all the locomotive engineers whose engines haul stringed sleepers, parlor cars, or even private cars, envy the passengers and magnates who may ride behind them. There are even those who pity them, or feel a real contempt for their soft lives, as long as they, themselves, are geting what they think a fair share of the earnings of the company they work for.

"No workingman will get a large share of the profits of a dissatisfied employer, any more than any employer will get the best of service from a discontented workingman. The real truth of the matter is that as regards hours, speed of work, rest periods and all other conditions of labor in factories, workshops, stores, mines and upon railroads, etc., what is best for the men is best for the owner and vice versa.

"It is as necessary for one as for the other to be well informed about the labor situation at large, about existing or probable labor legislation, about the attitude of the community in general and, especially, the particular consumer of their joint product, toward what they may be doing. No group of men, be it made up of employers or employed, can for any length of time successfully go counter to general public opinion.

"Nothing is more inefficient than lack of consideration for those among one's fellowmen with whom one is in close association. Too long working hours are evidence of inefficiency on the employer's part; a demand for too short working hours is evidence of inefficiency upon the workers' part.

"It is interesting to note the fact that German industrial publications are now expressing fear that in certain continuous industries, wherein German manufacturers compete with ours, we may substitute the eight-hour for the twelve-hour shift. They know that just as soon as we do this we shall increase efficiency, augmenting our own output till their market with us will be seriously constricted. They have studied these things far more carefully than we have.

"It is necessary, for both employers and employed, that records shall be kept of all these things. In Boston recently trouble has been brewing between the telephone girls and the company. What the girls are really fighting for is the mildest form of industrial democracy. They have asked for a permanent adjustment board, consisting of three representatives of the company and three of the operatives. Similar plans have been put into invariably successful operation in the mining industry, among longshoremen on the great lakes, and especially in the cloakmakers' industry in New York City. If books had been kept their profit would be generally known.

"In such things, doubtless, we see the beginning of the Magna Charta of industry. It will be put up to the industrial barons just as the Magna Charta was put up to old King John. It must be adopted, and the effect on both sides will be admirable—as admirable as the effect of that historic document was upon the British nation. Every one will gain. An enormous advance toward National efficiency will inevitably occur.

"I cannot but believe that our labor situation, although full of worrisome details, has begun to show some signs more hopeful than the best which it has ever shown before. We are now in just about the situation as regards our industries that we were as regarded medicine at the time of the discovery of the circulation of the blood. Industry has been very largely a monarchical proposition. Just so far as it remains so it is now behind the times.

"Therefore is there ample room for the new profession. Two quite different sets of activities occupy the investigative field in reference to relations between employer and employed. One includes all the Government activities, bureaus of labor, industrial commissions, the Children's Bureau, and all regular or temporary investigative activities of government, whether National or State; the other includes charitable, semi-charitable and philanthropic organizations, such as the Consumers' League, the Housewives' League, the women's trade unions leagues, women's industrial and educational unions, the Russell Sage Foundation, the people of the "survey," and college and social workers generally."

April 27, 1913

GIVES $10,000,000 TO 26,000 EMPLOYES

Ford to Run Automobile Plant 24 Hours Daily on Profit-Sharing Plan.

MINIMUM WAGE $5 A DAY

No Employe to be Discharged Except for Unfaithfulness or Hopeless Inefficiency.

Special to The New York Times.

DETROIT, Mich., Jan. 5.—Henry Ford, head of the Ford Motor Company, announced to-day one of the most remarkable business moves of his entire remarkable career. In brief it is:

To give to the employes of the company $10,000,000 of the profits of the 1914 business, the payments to be made semi-monthly and added to the pay checks.

To run the factory continuously instead of only eighteen hours a day, giving employment to several thousand more men by employing three shifts of eight hours each, instead of only two nine-hour shifts, as at present.

To establish a minimum wage scale of $5 per day. Even the boy who sweeps up the floors will get that much.

Before any man in any department of the company who does not seem to be doing good work shall be discharged, an opportunity will be given to him to try to make good in every other department. No man shall be discharged except for proved unfaithfulness or irremediable inefficiency.

The Ford Company's financial statement of Sept. 20, 1912, showed assets of $20,815,785.63, and surplus of $14,-745,095.57. One year later it showed assets of $35,033,919.86 and surplus of $28,124,173.68. Dividends paid out during the year, it is understood, aggregated $10,000,000. The indicated profits for the year, therefore, were about $37,597,-312. The company's capital stock, authorized and outstanding, is $2,000,000. There is no bond issue.

About 10 per cent. of the employes, boys and women, will not be affected by the profit sharing, but all will have the benefit of the $5 minimum wage. Those among them who are supporting families, however, will have a share similar to the men of more than 22 years of age.

In all, about 26,000 employes will be affected. Fifteen thousand now are at work in the Detroit factories. Four thousand more will be added by the institution of the eight-hour shift. The other seven thousand employes are scattered all over the world, in the Ford branches. They will share the same as the Detroit employes.

Personal statements were made by Henry Ford and James Couzens, Treasurer of the company, regarding the move.

"It is our belief," said Mr. Couzens, "that social justice begins at home. We want those who have helped us to produce this great institution and are helping to maintain it to share our prosperity. We want them to have present profits and future prospects. Thrift and good service and sobriety, all will be enforced and recognized.

"Believing as we do, that a division of our earnings between capital and labor is unequal, we have sought a plan of relief suitable for our business. We do not feel sure that it is the best, but we have felt impelled to make a start, and make it now. We do not agree with those employers who declare, as did a recent writer in a magazine in excusing himself for not practicing what he preached, that 'movement toward the bettering of society must be universal.' We think that one concern can make a start and create an example for other employers. That is our chief object."

"If we are obliged," said Mr. Ford, "to lay men off for want of sufficient work at any season we purpose to so plan our year's work that the lay-off shall be in the harvest time, July, August, and September, not in the Winter. We hope in such case to induce our men to respond to the calls of the farmers for harvest hands, and not to lie idle and dissipate their savings. We shall make it our business to get in touch with the farmers and to induce our employes to answer calls for harvest help.

"No man will be discharged if we can help it, except for unfaithfulness or inefficiency. No foreman in the Ford Company has the power to discharge a man. He may send him out of his department if he does not make good. The man is then sent to our 'clearing house,' covering all the departments, and is tried repeatedly in other work, until we find the job he is suited for, provided he is honestly trying to render good service."

January 6, 1914

WHAT IS BEING DONE TO MAKE EMPLOYES CONTENTED

IN these days of labor unrest, when Bolshevism, bred on hunger, stalks through Eastern Europe and is reflected by an increase of radicalism even in our own prosperous country, what are the real conditions of the workingmen of America? What are the relations between employer and employe?

Inquiries among representative corporations and their workers, among various industrial plants and larger business houses elicit illuminating information in reply to these questions. The inquirer learns about the new "industrial representation," profit sharing, employes' savings funds, pensions, disability benefits, death benefits, sanitation, housing, education, and health programs of industrial plants and decides that the labor problem in America is at least in a fair way toward finding a satisfactory solution.

The idea of industrial representation has been a much mooted question. How far could the employer go toward giving the employe a voice in the running of his plant and to what extent could the employe be trusted to exert his responsibility? These have been hypothetical questions that have been discussed at great length. They were the subject of discussion at the recent labor conference in England. The only thing settled at that time was the formation of a committee consisting of thirty laborites and thirty capitalists whose purpose was to make a thorough investigation into the questions of hours, wages, general conditions of work, unemployment, and its prevention, and the best means for promoting the relations between capital and labor.

Our own employers, too, have been thinking and developing the new ideas, conscious of the way the wind was blowing and anxious to come to some sort of understanding with the men in their plants, they have already done much and are planning still more to bring about happy working conditions.

Spread of Industrial Representation.

Industrial representation of one sort or another has become frequent. Men in different departments of a plant were chosen in the beginning by the managers of the plant to act as go-betweens between the managers and the workers. This, however, has not worked out in the way that was intended. The men were either jealous of the group representative and refused to trust him, or they felt he was acting as a spy upon their movements. Often he was. Far from being the entering wedge through which the employe might force his grievances through to the attention of those in a position to apply a remedy, he was the tool used to suppress any dissatisfaction that might arise on the part of the employes. Naturally he is by no means a popular individual in the shops.

Appreciative of this and desirous of getting into closer touch with their employes, a few of the larger corporations in this country have inaugurated a plan for industrial representation that is as nearly representative as such bodies can be. The Standard Oil Company has been in the vanguard of this movement. Early last year its Directors issued a statement to the effect that an election would be held in all the plants for the purpose of choosing representatives to sit in with the officers, superintendents, and foremen of the shops. The ballots were secret. The election was held on the general basis of one representative for every 150 men, with at least two men representing each division. Altogether there were about forty representatives. These met, and a form of constitution was adopted, insuring the working man a fair hearing at the board and a fair chance to prove his value to the firm.

Special rules for the engaging and discharge of help were formulated so that no man might go without work if he could show that there was no good reason for not taking him on and no man could be summarily discharged through pique on the part of the foreman. All such matters as the right of appeal, wage adjustments and hour adjustments are provided for in the agreement, and are taken up by the joint conferences held between the company representatives and the employes' representatives.

The system is still in its experimental stage, but thus far the results have been highly satisfactory to both employers and employes, and there is every indication that it will soon be taken up by a greater number of organizations. There are, however, other angles of labor interest or labor welfare work which are common to a large number of plants in the country.

Profit-Sharing Plans.

Not the least interesting of these are the profit-sharing plans which have been incorporated into many firms. The N. O. Nelson Manufacturing Company, makers of plumbers' supplies, inaugurated its system of profit sharing as far back as 1886. Under this plan all employes get a percentage of their year's wages, depending upon the profits of the business for the year after the payment of regular cash wages at the prevailing market rates and 6 per cent. on the capital stock of the company. The profit-sharing dividend is paid in stock in the company. Ever since the stock was organized in 1878 it has been paying a 6 per cent. dividend to the shareholders. The reason for paying the profit-sharing dividend in shares of stock in the company is one of business efficiency. Once a man has a definite interest in the growth of a firm he is obviously less likely to leave it on a hit-and-miss venture for something better.

A man must be employed six months in this company's shops or offices before he participates in the profit-sharing plan. The certificates of stock are not issued to him before he completes three years of service. Until the certificates are given to him, he gets 6 per cent. cash interest on his profit-sharing dividend. After stock certificates are issued they become the personal property of the employe, the same as any other stock. To insure against speculation with the stock, no employe who sells his shares may remain with the company. Once he severs his connection, however, he is free to dispose of his stock in any way he chooses.

Swift & Co., meat packers, have a stock purchasing plan of a different kind. Although they offer their employes no such stock as a bonus for length of service, they allow them to invest their savings in the stock of the company. Certificates are sold on easy terms. Thousands of the employes have taken advantage of the opportunity. This plan has been adopted by many other large corporations.

Unique among the plans of profit-sharing is the one of Sears, Roebuck & Co., wherein the employe is urged to put a part of his wages into a fund to which the company contributes 5 per cent. of its net earnings. This fund is invested in the shares of the company and draws its dividends in the same manner as the rest of the shares do.

In the Metropolitan Life Insurance Company's savings fund, for every dollar subscribed by any of its employes, the company deposits for him 50 cents extra. No employe may deposit more than 5 per cent. of his earnings, and no employe making more than $3,000 a year is allowed to be a member of the fund. In order to get full credit of the deposits made by him and for him, an employe must wait until he has completed twenty years of service before he can draw his money. Should he for any reason desire to draw it out before the term of service elapses, he can do so, but he forfeits the company's contribution to his fund. His forfeiture does not go back into the coffers of the company. It stays with the savings fund and is divided among the members as additional interest. There have been years when the interest on savings has gone up as high as 8 and 10 per cent. The twenty-year service clause is subject to changes in case of death or disability.

Shares in the Earnings.

Many companies which have profit-sharing plans have given the employes a share in the earnings of the firm in form of bonuses. The General Electric Company is one of these. In 1917 not only did the employes get the usual 10 per cent. bonus on their yearly earnings, but an additional 5 per cent. went to those who had been with the company more than five years. This system of bonuses has been inaugurated in a great number of plants throughout the country.

Whether pension funds, disability funds, and death benefits can be considered in the light of profit sharing is questionable. Nevertheless they make the employe feel that his connection with the firm will mean something more to him than his mere weekly wage or salary. All of the pension plans are based on term of service. This term varies from twenty to twenty-five years. There is an age limit set for retirement. This, too, varies with different organizations. The average retirement age for women runs from 55 to 65 years, and for men from 60 to 70 years. This does not mean that the man or woman coming into a firm in middle life and working for the required period of twenty to twenty-five years comes into the same pension allotment as the man or woman who has started working for the organization in early youth. There is a definite proportion between the number of years of service and the range of the pensions.

The formula upon which the pension allotment is figured is fixed. The yearly pension is arrived at by multiplying the average annual wage or salary for the last ten years of service by the percentage on which the pension is reckoned and then multiplying this result by the number of years of service. For instance, the General Electric Company's rate of pension is 1½ per cent. Taking a hypothetical case of a man at the retirement age of 70, who has worked for twenty-eight years with the company, having earned an average wage of $1,500 in the last ten years of service, the pension allotment would be $630. This is arrived at by taking 1½ per cent. of $1,500 and multiplying it by 28.

Retirement Provisions.

There are instances, of course, where the true word of the ruling is not followed, and where a man or woman is retired before reaching the required age. The Standard Oil Company has formulated a definite system to meet such cases. The company's basis of computation is 2 per cent. of the annual earnings. Under the hypothetical conditions mentioned above, a man in their employ would be entitled to a yearly pension of $840. Several companies have a percentage basis as low as 1 per cent. Again taking the above illustration, the pension allowed would amount to only $420.

Swift & Co. have a plan that is the simplest. After a man or woman has been with the firm for twenty-five years and has reached the age of 60 to 65 for the former and 50 to 55 for the latter, he or she can be retired on half pay. Corresponding provision is made for retirement because of disability at any age after fifteen years of service.

Akin to this system of pension funds are the disability funds, which have come to be a part of the welfare system of the large business organization. In most cases disability allowances are given for all cases of illness, irrespective of whether the illness was caused by conditions under which the employe was working or not. These allowances vary in different organizations. The American Telephone and Telegraph Company has organized this branch of the welfare work as follows:

"If term of employment has been ten years or more—full pay thirteen weeks, half pay thirty-nine weeks.

"If term of employment has been five to ten years—full pay twelve weeks, half pay for thirteen weeks.

"If term of employment has been two to five years—full pay four weeks, half pay nine weeks."

The Standard Oil pays its employes half salaries for periods varying from six weeks to one year, according to the length of service. In almost every large organization some plan has been formu-

lated to insure the care of the employe during the period of his disability.

In this field are the plans for death benefits which some organizations have completed. Most of the larger firms make some allotment to the bereaved wife or children of the deceased, but it is curious to note that few have as yet come to the point where they have a definite rule of procedure by which they are guided. Foremost among the companies that have inaugurated a system of this sort is the American Telephone and Telegraph Company. It has a definite sliding scale of allotments based on the number of years of service, varying from six months' pay to the family of the man who has been employed for less than ten years, to one year's pay, provided it is not more than $2,000, to the beneficiaries of the man who has been employed for more than ten years.

Watching the Worker's Health.

Much of the above has special reference to what is done for the employe after a definite period of service. In taking up this question of the relation between the employer and the employe, it is interesting to note what is done for him to make his life more comfortable, more happy, and more efficient while in service.

In January of this year the National Industrial Conference Board, whose membership is made up of national organizations of various industries, published a report made after a careful investigation of the need of rest periods for industrial workers. This report takes up in detail the effect of properly apportioned rest periods on fatigue, output, and discipline. The findings of 388 employers who had inaugurated the plan into their industrial system was used as the basis of the report. The first element arising in the discussion of the need of rest periods is not the efficiency of the plant but the welfare of the worker. The following will serve to indicate the attitude of the employer:

"At the beginning of the fatigue-eliminating campaign provide rest periods for those who seem to need them most. There are two offhand, quick methods of determining which workers these are. One is the appearance of the workers at various times of the day and at the end of the day. The other is the amount of output and the rate that output is turned out by the worker during the day and during the various parts of the day. In some organizations it has been the standard practice to take no chances when the worker looks or feels tired. They provide rest periods immediately, long enough to allow him to recover and go back to work with zest.

"This is, of course, the immediate reply: 'Provide the rest period first. Discuss its efficiency later.' This first aid plan has worked splendidly for a long time among women workers in such industries as the dry goods trades. The typical welfare work may be unscientific from the standpoint of those familiar with highly organized methods, but it has sensed the trouble keenly and quickly, and provided at least a temporary remedy without delay. 'Time to rest when one needs it.' This is the first slogan of the campaign for eliminating the evils of over-fatigue.'"

Efforts to Eliminate Fatigue.

Different organizations have tried different ways of eliminating the element of fatigue. A frequent substitute for rest periods is an arrangement of work which enforces change of position at regular intervals. On this principle it has long been the custom in some factories to prescribe a cleaning up period

in the middle of the forenoon and afternoon. This method has been tried out in several of our large industrial plants. The following are specific instances:

"According to the report of a telephone company which covers the chief cities of the country, the operators, numbering 110,000, in addition to being allowed two rest periods a day stand at their work several times during the day. During this time all operators push their chairs away from the board and stand while working. Supervisors who are on their feet their entire working time are given a fatigue relief by exchanging places with an operator in their division for a half hour twice daily, morning and afternoon. During this time they sit at the board and the operator stands.

"In some factories operations are planned so that the workers may alternate between sitting and standing positions. Similar arrangements have been elaborately developed where work is arranged on the task system. For instance, in a clothing shop the manager reported:

"'Our work is arranged so that our operators, the majority of whom are women, must leave their work tables on an average of four times an hour for the purpose of having time slips checked, procuring new and finished work. This amounts to about thirty minutes in an eight-hour day.'

"'In some establishments, where work is of a peculiarly trying character, employes are shifted for part of the day to a different task. For instance, in a chain manufacturing plant, employes operating kickers change with measurers every hour.'"

In a New England Factory.

What these changes mean to the workers in added efficiency is shown by the following example reported by a New England cloth finishing house:

"The first process at which women are employed is that of keeping cloth running evenly through a tentering machine. The machine holds on tenter hooks—the hooks of the metaphorical reference—the damp cloth brought from the process of bleaching and rolls it through evenly into a drier, where it slips off. There are two kinds of tentering machines. At one kind two girls sit, each watching an edge of the cloth and keeping it straight on the tenter hooks so it will feed evenly. The newer machines run in such a manner that one girl who may either stand or sit can watch both edges.

"The tentering machines used to run slowly. This slowness enhanced the natural monotony and wearisomeness of the work. The girls used to receive wages of $6 a week. They used to rest three-quarters of an hour in the afternoon, with the same period for dinner at noon in the middle of a ten-and-one-half-hour day. After scientific management was introduced the girls sat at the machine only an hour and twenty minutes at a time. They then had a twenty-minute rest, and these intervals of work and rest were continued throughout the day by an arrangement of spelling with 'spare hands.' The machines were run at a more rapid rate than before. The girl's task was watching 32,000 yards in a day, and if she achieved the bonus, as she did without any difficulty, she could earn $9 a week. The output of the tentering machines was increased about 60 per cent.

"The prevailing practice among establishments reporting for this investigation, the report goes on to say, was to provide one rest period in the forenoon and one in the afternoon. Ten minutes for each was the most frequent time allowance, although in a very considerable number of cases it was fifteen minutes. Longer pauses appeared to be exceptional. In some cases shorter but more frequent pauses were employed. Where only one pause a day was allowed it was usually in the morning and intended as a lunch period.

"In determining the length of rest pauses it is essential that they be long enough to secure real recuperation from fatigue and at the same time short enough not to reduce the speed attained by practice. In the field of education investigations have established the superority of a ten to fifteen minute recess, since a longer pause appears to lower the efficiency of work immediately following; in industry the practice has generally favored a pause of from five to fifteen minutes, which forms a regular break in the forenoon and afternoon spell."

To how great an extent this subject has been gone into is shown by a report made by Frank B. Gilbreth, who has made an intensive study of the subject of fatigue. It is given in illustration of an arrangement introduced by some employers where the rest periods are of shorter duration, but come at more frequent intervals. The work under observation was that of folding handkerchiefs.

Plan for Rest Periods.

"Each hour was divided into ten periods," he writes. "The work was placed on a work table of the proper height. The handkerchiefs already folded, those being folded, and those to be folded were arranged in the most convenient and efficient manner. All variables of the work had been studied, and the results of the study standardized. The first four periods, that is, the first twenty-four minutes, the girl remained seated. She worked five minutes and rested one; again worked five minutes and rested one. That is to say, she had four minutes rest out of the twenty-four, and spent this rest seated so that she might lose no time in getting back to the work.

"The next two periods, that is for twelve minutes, the girl was standing. Again she worked five minutes and rested one minute, and for the second time worked five minutes and rested one minute. That is, she rested two out of the twelve minutes in the same position in which she worked. The third group, a space of eighteen minutes, she spent either sitting or standing, as she pleased. Here also she worked five minutes, rested one minute; worked five minutes and rested one minute; worked five minutes and rested one minute, in the position, either standing or sitting, which she herself had chosen. The last period, which consisted also of six minutes, was spent by the girl walking about and talking, or amusing herself as she otherwise chose. With this might be combined the last rest minute, or period No. 9, which thus gave her seven consecutive minutes for unrestricted rest activity.

"This was the schedule for all hours of the day except the hour before noon and the hour before closing time at night. In these hours the first nine periods resembled the first nine periods of the other hours; but the tenth period was spent in work, as a long rest period was to follow.

"At the end of the day's work under these conditions the girls accomplished more than three times the amount of their previous best work, with a greater amount of interest and with no more fatigue. It may be stated here that the primary aim in this investigation was not to eliminate fatigue, but to increase the wages of the girls by raising the

output. The operators had not seemed overfatigued at the start. They maintained that they were less tired at the close of the day when using the new method, and certainly the amount of fatigue caused by producing an amount of output such as was made under the old method was reduced to an enormous extent."

The question of rest periods has become such an established feature in the large majority of industrial and commercial organizations that their rest rooms serve in a fair way to give the employes an idea of how a room can be made beautifully comfortable. In every rest room visited a conscious attempt could be seen to provide the place with eye and nerve resting furniture and decorations.

Supervision by Doctors.

In many instances the rest room is an offshoot of the medical department of an organization. It is no unusual thing these days to have a staff of doctors and nurses attached to a working plant of any kind. Most of the service rendered is free of charge to the employe; occasionally a nominal sum is charged for medicines. The Metropolitan Life Insurance Company, for instance, has its employes undergo a physical examination every year. Its purpose is fourfold—to detect a disease in its incipient stage, to correct ascertained minor defects, to encourage treatment, and to prevent disease. Separate rooms fitted up with the latest surgical appliances are provided for men and women.

The General Electric Company has stated the case for the medical clinics succinctly:

"We are all appreciating more every year that the better suited we are to our work, the more suited we will be with our work. Now that these examinations have been started, we see that their object is not to keep men out of employment, but to direct men away from the kind of employment which may damage their health.

"If a man had weak eyesight the modern industrial company would never give him work near rapidly moving machinery; or if his lungs were weak he would not be permitted to do any work of a dusty nature which would soon aggravate the condition of his lungs."

In addition to the regular medical examining rooms and wards connected with these clinics, a good many establishments have found it expedient to add an optical and a dental clinic. Here, too, the service is without charge. Where payment of any kind is made it is for the actual cost of lenses or material used in the treatment of teeth.

Together with the medical service given directly on the premises of the organization, a good many of the plants maintain staffs of visiting doctors and visiting nurses. The latter are of special benefit in smaller communities, where the life of the people centres about the factory. The United States Steel Corporation has enlarged this branch of service to such a degree that it takes in most of the smaller towns where the corporation has any work going on. The service of the nurse is offered free of charge to the employees and their families. There is a unique feature attached to her visiting. Her attention is not forced upon the people. A nurse is not permitted to visit the homes of the employes upon any occasion unless she is requested to do so by a member of the family. Her work follows three distinct courses: she attends the sick, she gives instruction in personal and domestic hygiene and science, and

she helps families deal with financial, physical, and domestic troubles.

The subject of tuberculosis deserves special mention. That seems to be the one disease that the men and women in industry have been least able to combat. Some industrial heads, appreciative of this, have in a good many cases gone a step further than just giving instruction as to prevention and care, and have opened sanitaria for the treatment of their employes.

Early in the history of welfare work for employes the subject of restaurants was taken up. Today there is hardly a corporation of any size which has not inaugurated a system of luncheon service for its employes. In those cases where the plants are at some distance from the homes of the men and women working, this innovation has been of particular value. In all cases it has meant a great saving in money spent for the noonday meal and a great gain in value of food purchased. It can be readily understood that where an organization buys food for thousands of people the price per unit will be vastly lower than when an individual does his own purchasing. The average price of a lunch is about 20 cents. In most of the organization restaurants the cafeteria has been substituted for the waitress system.

The Metropolitan Life Insurance Company takes a unique position in reference to this luncheon question. It carries the work one point further along the path of welfare work, and serves luncheons free of charge to all employes who wish to take advantage of them. About 4,000 men and women take their places every day at the tables. The fact that the department heads are among the people who make use of the service speaks well for the kind of food that is served.

The subject of accidents, of course, has received special attention from the large employers of labor. The United States Steel Corporation has a committee whose sole object is the instruction of the employes in safety measures and the need of observing them. A feature in their plan is the use of moving picture reels in showing the reason for accidents and the methods by which they can be prevented. Several hospitals have been built in those steel communities where the work is most hazardous and the occurrence of accidents through carelessness of the workers most probable. The General Electric Company also has organized its accident service work to a high degree.

"All of us are human and there is one characteristic which is particularly noticeable in us all—namely, our willingness to assume risks if we can save a little time," says the head of the latter concern's welfare work. "This trait is in daily evidence at all our busy street corners, where pedestrians disregard the warnings and rules of traffic officers and persist in crossing the street or railway tracks at unsafe moments, being willing to risk injury for the saving of a fraction of a minute. In the same way it has been found that workmen in the shops will frequently assume risks in order to save a second or two; and therefore we shall always have accidents and the larger the number of employes the larger the number of accidents.

"One of the strange facts developed from a study of these records is: Nearly 64 per cent. of the major accidents of the year take place in the six warm months, May to October, inclusive. Medical men and executives and statisticians are all baffled by this mystery. Not one has been able to explain satisfactorily why 64 per cent. of the accidents occur in warm weather and only 36 per cent. in cold weather, year after year.

"There is another mystery: Why do most of the major accidents take place either early in the morning or late in the afternoon? No one knows.

"These two facts are undeniably true. They are medical history, and right here in these two unexplained facts lie some of the problems on which high type executives, engineers, and surgeons are devoting serious thought. They will clear up these mysteries in time and their solution will probably result in some special instructions for us to follow at the beginning and the close of the day; and we shall be glad to do so, for all of us are anxious to avoid even a scratch."

Schools for Workers.

Continuation schools, departmental schools, and general educational facilities open to the ambitious men and women employes are provided in almost every large corporation. Where the need is purely elementary, that is, where the boy or girl has not completed the public school course offered by the community, special arrangements have been made with the public school authorities to send one of their teachers to give an hour's instruction in the course of the working day. That plan is being extended to some of the smaller commercial organizations.

The larger plants have gone several steps further. Some of them have planned regular courses for boys eighteen to twenty. Many of these boys are high school graduates, but through some handicap or other have failed to get a college education. The companies are glad of getting good material while it is still young and pliable. They take these boys and give them an education in the theory and practice of the specialized work in which they show marked aptitude. The courses range from six months to two years, the boy being paid through the entire period.

Some of the plants make a differentiation between the departmental school and what is known as the apprentice school. The first is organized for the training of skilled engineers, the second for the training of skilled mechanics. Both have their place in the work of the organization. The apprentice school is usually of special benefit to the boy having nothing but the grammar school education. He is taught a valuable trade and is assured of the power to find himself economically. The school rooms in most of the large plants maintaining schools of this sort are entirely apart from the shops. Special rooms, with special machinery under skilled teachers, are maintained. The theories of the classrooms are worked out in practice in the shops and the relation between algebra and geometry to the

working out of mechanical problems that can be illustrated to the boy in some concrete form is made clear to him. At the end of the course in the machinist's trade, for instance, the boy with nothing but a grammar school education is turned out a full-fledged journeyman, fully competent to operate the machinery found in the ordinary machine shop.

The brief which the manager of one of the General Electric plants holds for the apprentice school has special appeal in these days of specialized training.

"It is quite probable," he says, "that among one hundred average men, many of them never thoroughly learn any one trade; some of them probably learn a trade which will become obsolete, such as truck driving, a trade which is being displaced by the automobile; or the operation of steam pumps, a trade being rendered obsolete by the general use of electricity. Among other obsolescent trades are horse shoeing, the trade of the cobbler, and the trades connected with kerosene, gasoline, and gas lighting. It is dangerous for the future of a young man to learn a trade which will practically cease to exist during his lifetime.

Indispensable Mechanic.

"If the horse, the steam engine, and the steam locomotive were to vanish from the face of the earth, we could rest assured that some kind of machinery would do the work of transportation for the world—and it is not dangerous to prophesy that machinery in one form or another will not only carry on our transportation but will be used more and more in industry, commerce, and in the home. For this reason the boy who becomes a mechanic or engineer, whether electrical or mechanical, can rest assured that his trade will not become obsolete during his lifetime."

Several of the New York department stores teach buying and selling. They know that the future buyers and salespeople will grow out of the ranks of young boys and girls now holding minor jobs. What they are doing is to train and educate these people to take on the new work at the earliest possible moment. Classes in salesmanship, buying, finance, advertising, and similar subjects are held in the store schools during the regular working hours of the day. The only thing that binds a man or woman to attending these courses is his or her interest in the work. The poor and indifferent material is sifted out and those who show a marked ability get the opportunity for promotion.

The housing question is a big one for those corporations whose plants are established in undeveloped areas. The mining, steel, and oil industries come under this category. Appreciative of

the fact that the best results, gauged from the employe's point of view as well as from the employer's, can be obtained only under healthful sanitary and social conditions, the companies have gone into actual building of towns around or near their works. Unlike the larger towns of the country which have grown up of their own volition, these housing towns are products of short intensified work that has been planned to meet the needs of the situation.

Building a Town to Order.

As soon as a corporation takes over a parcel of land to be developed along the special line in which it is interested, advance surveyors and engineers are sent ahead to map out the district and plan for the building of the town. The size of the town depends upon the number of employes expected to work in the plants. Nearness to a railroad station and nearness to the works of the organization are two of the first considerations borne in mind. Streets are laid out and the numbers and types of houses drafted. In all instances the comfort of the families of the employes, the sanitation of the homes, the educational and religious opportunities, the recreation and the civic life are taken into consideration. The houses are of different designs and vary in size from three to ten rooms, in order to meet the needs of different families. The most modern of these houses are equipped with electric light and running water. Facilities are provided to keep the town in a healthful state. Sewerage systems are built, and the garbage taken care of. In many a town of this sort one of the first buildings is the hospital. Schools and churches find their place in the plan and in locations easily accessible.

Where a town is greatly separated from the next town within reach of it, the companies build places of amusement and recreation to meet the needs of population. Clubs, moving picture theatres, athletic fields, all are included. The houses are let out to the employes at a reasonable price, or are sold at easy installment rates. The result in social and industrial growth of the communities has in many instances been amazing.

There are numerous other details in which the welfare of the employe had developed rapidly in recent years. Clubs of all sorts built by the corporations, swimming pools, lecture rooms, libraries, boarding houses, vegetable cellars—these are found on the roster of things done by the American employer of large groups of men. What with the trend toward greater representation on the part of the employe in the affairs of the organization, the scope of future developments along similar lines seems boundless.

Harsh Boss Found Mental Hazard to Worker; Fear of Scolding Said to Impair Efficiency

Experiments in the elimination of "the boss," at least as that individual has been traditionally regarded by the industrial worker, carried out at the Hawthorne plant of the Western Electric Company, have convinced officials of the company that the traditional relationship of the individual worker to his or her immediate superior has been the greatest single obstacle in the way of increasing the welfare both of the worker and of the corporation. Reports on experiments which have already been conducted for two years at the plant were made yesterday at the Personal Research Federation Conference at the Engineering Societies Building by G. A. Pennock and M. L. Putnam of the company and Professor Elton Mayo of the Harvard School of Business Administration.

The experiments started out to discover the relative influence of various tangible factors on the character of work done by shop employes. The emotional upset and consequent loss of efficiency resulting from fear of a "bawling out" was first discovered largely by accident. It has now resulted in a revolutionary change in methods of training subordinate supervisors throughout the plant, which employs 40,000 men and women.

Mr. Pennock described experiments made with small groups of workers whose attitude and production were carefully checked, while their personal feelings and health were likewise carefully charted. Both their happiness at work and their efficiency of performance, the tests indicate, are far more influenced by mental hazards than by all the physical factors involved. The tests also indicated that a short rest period, both morning and afternoon, tended to more than compensate in increased efficiency for the time consumed by the rests.

Mr. Putnam described in detail the "supervisory training methods" that have been evolved in consequence of the conclusions reached in the tests. A staff of "interviewers," selected from the rank and file of the employes, is devoted to discussing their problems with the individual workers. The results, anonymously presented, are used in conferences with the "supervisors." In addition, it is planned to recruit future supervisors from the ranks of the interviewers.

Dr. Mayo in his address declared that the work being done by the Western Electric Company was of the greatest significance. Particularly, he declared that it would be difficult to realize today what the potentialities of the interviewing system might be in the field of public health and in increasing the happiness and welfare of workers in industry.

November 16, 1929

Advertising News

A new field for the advertising man and the profession as a whole can be opened up in the post-war period if management can be persuaded that a satisfied employe is just as vital to successful business operations as a satisfied customer, according to E. W. Falcon, manager of the advertising department of the Warner & Swasey Company, machine tool builders, Cleveland, Ohio.

The employer who takes the pains to inform employes about what goes on in their company, he states, goes a long way toward promoting a better understanding since an employe's sense of importance is recognized in this way and he gets his information direct instead of through rumors. Future advertising budgets, Mr. Falcon says, should include appropriations to keep employes sold on the company. The advertising man, he adds, is the individual best equipped to do the job.

August 23, 1944

SUGGESTION SYSTEM WINS WIDE ADOPTION

NAM Says Inquiries Are Piling Up Because of Savings and Better Labor Relations

By ALFRED R. ZIPSER JR.

Many business organizations throughout the nation which failed to install scientific employe suggestion systems during the war have been so impressed by their wartime performance both in effecting savings in production costs and improving industrial relations that widespread adoption of such systems has been effected since V-J Day, with an increasing number of concerns now engaged in setting them up, it was learned yesterday.

The National Association of Manufacturers has disclosed that inquiries as to the procedure for establishing suggestion systems are increasing daily and recent requests for information have been received from such diversified organizations as General Textile Mills, Inc., R. G. Le Tourneau, Inc., producers of roadbuilding equipment and Sheffield Farms.

Other concerns actively participating in installation of suggestion systems include the Air Reduction Company, Inc., producers of welding equipment, Canada Dry Ginger Ale, Inc., The Great Atlantic and Pacific Tea Company, Inc., Gristede Brothers, the American Express Company, the Mutual Life Insurance Company and General Mills, Inc. The Pennsylvania & Lake Erie Line of the New York Central System has recently completed experimental installations and is expected to adopt a plan permanently.

Crux of new suggestion systems is emphasis on scientific administration as opposed to the haphazard suggestion box system or the discredited practice of advancing suggestions to immediate superiors. In practice, the lack of personal contact discouraged employes in the former case, and, in the latter, appropriation of suggestions as their own by supervisors as well as definite psychological disadvantages made it unworkable.

The modern method of installation comprises the organization of a specific suggestions department within a business organiation at which representative supervisors, not necessarily top-flight executives, can receive suggestions and are in a position to determine whether acceptance will benefit over-all operations of the company. Compensation for accepted suggestions will vary with each enterprise adopting a formal system but

265

in many cases, it consists of 10 per cent of saved costs resulting from approved suggestions over a stipulated period of time. The Stromberg-Carlson Company, for example, paid an average of $55.28 to employes for suggestions during 1943.

Industry is coming to realize that the man on the job is often the expert most qualified to improve production methods in his particular niche and that ways and means must be sought to make his knowledge available to management. It is a foregone conclusion that the corporation president or board chairman with the "my door is always open to everyone" declarations does not reach employes since waiting for admittance by secretaries and other impeding maneuvers nearly always kill enthusiasm engendered in workers with valid suggestions.

Another feature of the suggestions system is the proved improvement in industrial relations demonstrated by numerous concerns throughout the war. According to business leaders, aside from the dollars and cents incentives which should not be discounted, the suggestions system gives labor the feeling that it is a definite partner of management and is working with the latter for the benefit of both.

NEW HELP IN FIELD OF SOCIAL STUDIES

Scientists, Educators Offer Aid to Industry, Business in Research Problems

PEACE IN LABOR IS SOUGHT

By RUSSELL PORTER

Since attention was directed recently to the growing interest being shown by business and industry during the reconversion period in research on human relations in the search for solutions of labor-management problems, letters and telephone calls from educators and scientists have made it clear that they also are deeply concerned with this subject and are anxious to do their utmost to help bring about industrial peace.

They feel that the application of modern scientific methods can do much to relieve this and other stresses and strains of twentieth-century civilization, such as the problem of racial relations and other group hostilities, if the effort is organized properly and supported over a sustained period of time.

It is conceded that there are many difficulties. The world has lagged in the development of the social sciences, the field in which such projects fall. Billions of dollars have been spent on the physical and biological sciences, and the results have been spectacular and dramatic in the way of atom bombs, radar, sulfa drugs, penicillin and the like.

The rewards of remuneration and prestige in these fields have attracted many skilled practitioners. But the social sciences, by their very nature offering more uncertainties in the vagaries of human nature, are still in the pioneering stage. On one hand, they must seek financial support and personnel, and on the other, fend off the cranks, quacks and do-gooders who seem to be attracted to this kind of activity.

Human Mass Reactions

Nevertheless, although it may not be well known to the general public, considerable progress has been made. This was stimulated by the war, when the social scientists were called in by the military authorities to answer some of the perplexing questions of human behavior posed by the hasty mobilization of millions of soldiers and sailors. Much of this wartime research, it is pointed out, is directly or indirectly applicable to postwar relationships.

Leaders in the field believe that they are now able in some cases to make fairly accurate predictions of how large masses of persons will conduct themselves under certain circumstances, not as individuals but en masse, and that the scope of this activity will steadily increase. They hold this is the important factor in dealing with problems of mass production, distribution and consumption.

If certain tests made at the time industrial workers were being selected and hired, for example, could spot those of a type particularly likely to become victims of accidents on the job and divert them into some other kind of employment, the advantages obviously would be enormous from the viewpoint of both efficiency and humanitarianism.

Leaders in the social sciences welcome the increased interest of business because they expect it will stimulate both research and practical application. They consider it logical for business to seek further understanding of human relations now, when it has demonstrated its ability to solve the physical problems of production but is confronted with the necessity of industrial peace and high labor productivity so that production can continue without interruption and at maximum efficiency.

One of the problems is to carry on research in such a manner as to make its findings acceptable to both labor and management. Therefore, it must not only be impartial, but be recognized as such. Research activity is being promoted in more than twenty universities throughout the country, some of them private and others State institutions, as well as in private industry. Representatives of the great labor organizations have been invited to participate in some. Some believe that labor and industry should be asked to finance some of this work together on a basis of equality.

Some of the university research groups have just completed a conference at the University of Minnesota, held under the joint auspices of that institution and the Committee on Labor Market Research of the Social Science Research Council, which has its headquarters in this city.

The council, of which Dr. Donald Young is executive director, and which is financed by the Rockefeller Foundation, the Carnegie Corporation and similar organizations, is acting as a sort of clearing house and coordinating agency for this type of research.

The chief function of the council's labor research committee is to encourage this type of research and integrate its results. It is concerned primarily with the identification and development of basic research regarding the nature and behavior of the human resources which constitute the labor market of the nation, and of particular industries, occupations and communities. This involves research in problems of employment, wages, institutional impacts upon the labor market; the characteristics of labor supplies and demands, and human characteristics, relationships and motivations which affect the ways in which individuals seek a livelihood or provide opportunities for employment.

DRAMA GIVEN NEW TWIST

Office Executives to Act Out Dealings With Employes

Typical situations calling for skill in dealing with employes will be acted out by office executives at the meeting of the office management division of the American Management Association Oct. 20-21, it was announced yesterday.

The demonstrations will be conducted by Alexander Bavelas, assistant professor of psychology, Massachusetts Institute of Technology. He uses the role-playing techniques in his teachings. Typical problems are those based on friction between employes and between employes and supervisors.

RESEARCH SPREADS IN INDUSTRIAL FIELD

25 Big Companies Have Set Up Full-Time Programs to Study Personnel Problems

More than twenty-five leading "blue-chip" companies have set up industrial relations research as a full-time, permanent phase of personnel administration. This was revealed last week by Ernest Dale, assistant professor of industrial relations, Graduate School of Business Administration, Columbia University.

Findings in the annual seminar on public relations at Columbia, which is conducted by Professor Dale, indicate that industrial relations research is growing. He said, last year at this time only ten companies had any organized activity in the field. The seminar ended last week.

Professor Dale, who also is research associate at the American Management Association, said the core of industrial relations research is a study of value schemes of employe-employer relationship. These include improvement in human relations and making employes aware of benefits other than compensation offered by management.

Practical achievements of industrial relations research lie in policy-making aid to making managerial decisions, according to Professor Dale. Specific improvements resulting from the relatively new activity are new types of psychological tests. Validation of such tests, new types of merit rating, use of seniority to improve performance and improvement of incentive plans.

As an indication of the segment of industry which has permanently adopted industrial relations research, Professor Dale cited a few companies now using it. They are Standard Oil Company (N. J.), Procter & Gamble, Armstrong Cork Company and Minnesota Mining and Manufacturing Company.

SIDEWALK CAFE AT NIGHT
Kröller-Müller State Museum, Otterlo
Painted 1888, Arles. 31 x 24½"

Western Electric
BOOKLET RACK SERVICE FOR EMPLOYEES

CALVARY
by Veronese (1528-1588)
Painted about 1570, Oil on canvas, Venetian

PUBLISHED FOR GM MEN AND WOMEN
INFORMATION RACK SERVICE
General Motors Personnel Staff

58-1   LITHO IN U.S.A.

ART FOR INDUSTRY'S SAKE: These booklets containing reproductions of great art are being distributed by the companies to their employes. The publishing firm of Harry N. Abrams, Inc., reports it is "overwhelmed" by demand for them from industry.

December 15, 1957

INDUSTRY SPURS EMPLOYE THRIFT

Cooperative Savings Plans Showing Steady Advance

By J. E. McMAHON

Thrift is playing a growing role in industry, a steady rise in establishment of savings plans by industrial corporations in recent years indicates.

Under these savings plans, in which employes and employers join in making contributions, both benefit in varying degrees. The employee gains a nest egg and often becomes a stockholder in the company having the plan. Employers benefit by the thrift of their employees, when new incentive to earn and save results. Employe morale is enhanced and the labor turnover of the organization is reduced.

The Great Atlantic and Pacific Tea Company, Inc., will soon be among the big companies having savings plans. Stockholders approved A. & P.'s

plan on June 21, and on July 22 the company filed a registration statement with the Securities and Exchange Commission covering 60,290 shares of the company's common stock to be offered to employes pursuant to its employes' thrift plan.

The plan is expected to start on Oct. 1, or soon after, following consideration by the Internal Revenue Service as to its qualification for favorable tax treatment. It will also become operative when the S. E. C. gives its approval to the stock offering.

In the proxy statement about the thrift plan, A. & P. said that "savings and investment plans, which many companies include among their employe benefit programs, are designed to help employes accumulate savings by means of regular, voluntary payroll deductions. The plans also recognize and provide a means for effectuating the desire of many employes to invest a part of their savings in common stock of the company."

Under the A. & P. thrift plan, an employe can contribute up to 4 per cent of his regular compensation, according to the

proxy statement. "The participants' savings will be invested in obligations issued or fully guaranteed by the United States of America, or, if the participant so elects, 75 per cent in such obligations and 25 per cent in the company's common stock," it was stated.

Contributions by the company from its current or accumulated earnings or profits will amount to 25 per cent of the amount saved by participants under the plan. The company's contributions will be invested in the company's common stock.

There are various forms of thrift or savings plans and many of them are coupled with other welfare plans, mostly with profit-sharing and stock-purchasing programs. Rates of contributions will often depend on the size of the company and the number of employes eligible to participate under the program.

Tax Benefits

Benefits under thrift plans are not considered taxable income until distributed or made available to a participant in the plan. When such funds are withdrawn while the worker is in service, his contribution is not taxed, but that part of the payment made to him from the plan furnished by the employer is taxed under ordinary income tax rates. Where payment is made to the employe or his beneficiary in one lump sum, because of retirement, resignation or death, the excess over an employe's contribution is taxed on a long-term capital gains basis.

One of the most successful and oldest savings programs in this country is the Sears, Roebuck & Co. Employes Savings and Profit Sharing Pension Fund. Established in 1916, the fund at the end of 1959 held 20,266,432 shares of Sears stock. This represented 26.9 per cent of the company's outstanding stock. The holding also represented 77 per cent of the fund's assets. There are 144,049 employes in the plan.

Each participant in the Sears' savings plan deposits a percentage of his salary a year in the fund and the company contributes a percentage of profits a year. The participation in the company's contributions vary under four service periods. In Group A, where the employe's service is less than five years, his share in the company's contribution is equal in units to the amount of his deposit. Under Group B, where the service period is five years or more but less than ten years, he shares in the company contributions by two units for each dollar that he has deposited in the year.

Group C covers ten or more years of service, but excludes employes who are more than 50 years of age and have more than 15 years of service. It entitles the employe covered in this group to participate on the basis of three units of the employer's contribution for each of his deposits. The employe over 50 years of age and with more than 15 years of service participates to the extent of four units of the employer's contributions for each of his deposits. A unit is a pro-rated amount of the company distribution and because the company's profits will vary, the dollar amount alternates.

G. E., Other Plans

Savings plans are to be found in many of the nation's leading industrial companies. They are prominent in the petroleum, chemical, retail, soap, paper, steel and electrical equipment fields.

Employes of the General Electric Company can save from 75 cents to $10 a week under their Employe Savings and Stock Bonus Plan, in effect since 1948. Their contributions to the plan are invested in Government bonds, which under the employe's authorization are held by the company for five years. At the end of each year, the company pays into the fund a bonus equal to 15 per cent of the value of the Government bonds acquired by the employe during that year. Half of G. E.'s employes are eligible for this plan.

G. E. has another savings and securities program, started in 1959, covering the rest of its labor force, in which the worker can save up to 6 per cent of his earnings, of which one-half can be invested in G. E. stock. The company contribution equals 50 per cent of his savings.

MUSIC IS SHOWN TO RAISE OUTPUT

17% Increase Is Found in Tests of Students

By ROBERT K. PLUMB

Background music, to which 55,000,000 Americans now listen at some time of day, does appear to improve individual performance of simple, monotonous tasks.

This was reported here yesterday at the Human Factors Society annual meeting by Stephan Konz of the department of mechanical and industrial engineering of the University of Illinois in Urbana.

The meeting is a gathering of engineers, psychologists and others who work for optimum design of tools, machines and other devices through which man interacts with his environment. Subjects covered during the two-day meeting ranged from medical electronics to design of space vehicles and the mechanization of mail-handling for the post office.

20,000 Use Music

Mr. Konz estimated that 20,-000 companies, including nine of the 12 rated as "best managed," used background music.

Despite this wide use of background music, he said, the amount of unbiased, impartial, experimental investigation of the effects of such music is very meager.

So Mr. Konz set up an experiment in which freshman students, men and women, were put to monotonous mental tasks (comparing groups of nonsense letters) and monotonous manual tasks (assembling and disassembling three washers and putting a nut on a bolt).

Background music, which started with "Stardust" and worked up as the monotonous tasks continued to "The Stars and Stripes Forever" was played at steady volume at intervals while the students worked.

Mr. Konz found that both men and women were affected by the background music. Their output for the manual task increased 17 per cent when music was played over their output without music and by 18 per cent for the mental task. The number of errors made during the test periods was not affected by the music.

The background music was played about one-third of the time, as is usual in industrial practice with music.

Despite his findings, Mr. Konz reported that he had some misgivings. He had expected that women, who do better than men do at monotonous tasks, would react better to the music, but he found no evidence of this.

An additional study will be performed to investigate the possibility that background music helps people in general but hinders a few.

NATION'S EXECUTIVES: CHANGES IN BACKGROUND AND EDUCATION

FAMILY BACKGROUND

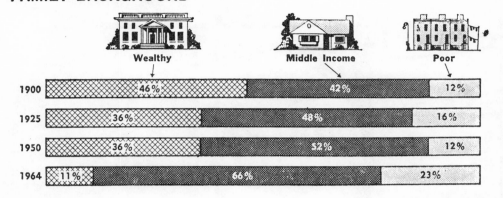

	Wealthy	Middle Income	Poor
1900	46%	42%	12%
1925	36%	48%	16%
1950	36%	52%	12%
1964	11%	66%	23%

EDUCATION

More college graduates

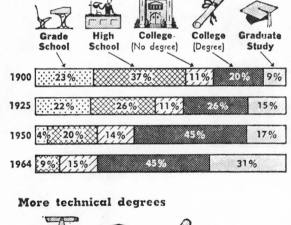

	Grade School	High School	College (No degree)	College (Degree)	Graduate Study
1900	23%	37%	11%	20%	9%
1925	22%	26%	11%	26%	15%
1950	4%	20%	14%	45%	17%
1964		9%	15%	45%	31%

More technical degrees

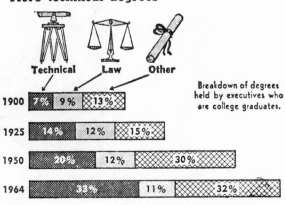

	Technical	Law	Other
1900	7%	9%	13%
1925	14%	12%	15%
1950	20%	12%	30%
1964	33%	11%	32%

Breakdown of degrees held by executives who are college graduates.

Beyond the Profits: Business Reaches for a Social Role

COMPANIES STEER AWAY FROM CLASH

Seek to Harmonize Student Revolt, Technology, Civil Rights and Economics

By ROBERT A. WRIGHT

"I foresee problems outside the limits of our industry having a growing effect on its character and the way we mold it. What I am talking about are the social problems which arouse more concern every day."

The speaker was Edmund F. Martin, a tall, sturdily built man of 63 who has spent his entire career in what many have long regarded as the ultra-conservative steel industry.

The chairman of the Bethlehem Steel Corporation, who only last December became a central figure in a price row with the Johnson Administration, stood behind the speaker's lectern in the Grand Ballroom of the Waldorf-Astoria Hotel and told May's annual meeting of the American Iron and Steel Institute that its members should work to improve Government - industry relations. More than that, he described a new vision of business responsibility.

Public affairs, or what might be termed business beyond the profit motive, increasingly have captured the attention of executives.

In speech after speech in recent months executives have urged their colleagues to take a more active role in politics and civic affairs, to join the war against poverty, to improve relations with government, academic circles and students.

The social responsibility theme seems suddenly to have gathered a steamroller momentum. A new generation of corporate managers — many of them self-critical of past performances — envisions a wider role for business than has been traditional.

New attitudes in the business community, which many observers believe are belated, appear to be designed to avoid what could be a collision course between the forces created by the vast postwar technological advances, the new economics, the expanding role of govern- and the campus revolt.

One complaint frequently made by businessmen is that their problems are not understood by laymen ignorant of economics. Another is that the changed stance of business in regard to other segments of society is not recognized.

In an attempt to provide a basis for a dialogue, The New York Times asked 52 leading executives to express their views on these matters.

The sampling found every executive who replied emphatic in expressing his belief that business had a social responsibility beyond providing quality goods and services to consumers. The respondents saw little or no conflict between the profit motive and other social goals.

Activities Listed

Most businessmen cited charitable contributions—to educational institutions and programs and community welfare organizations — the encouragement of employes to participate in civic affairs, and a long list of other activities. But some executives offered strikingly individual definitions of business' role.

George S. Moore, president of the First National City Bank, New York, believes that the subject of business' social responsibility is generally misunderstood and widely misinterpreted as a euphemism for corporate do-goodism.

"Social responsibility," he says, "is not an attitude that a business organization adopts in a fit of benevolence like a decision to hold a company picnic. Its social responsibility is, instead, inseparable from its response to the kind of world in which we live. For today's institutions—banking or business, public or private—cannot exist in modern society without reacting constructively to (1) the goals of society, and (2) the economic, technological, social and political forces that mold that society." He adds:

"No Other Alternative"

"In short, modern businessmen and bankers, of necessity, are environmentalists. And social responsibility, so-called, is, in fact, an indispensable act of profitable growth from which the American public has benefited incomparably. It consists of enriching society today so that the interacting interests of both business and society will endure tomorrow. Indeed, the public will not permit any other alternative."

Mr. Martin quoted Abraham Lincoln in his recent speech entitled "Challenges of Modern Management":

"The dogmas of the quiet past are inadequate to the stormy present. . . . As our case is new, so we must think anew and act anew."

Touching on the problem of air and water pollution caused by industry, Mr. Martin declared:

"Many of us neglected that part of the growing problem over which we had a measure of direct control. Some of us also kicked about rising taxes when people in our communities tried to deal effectively with such nonindustrial wastes as sewage." Then he went on to describe three things business had to do "intensively":

"We must participate more actively in politics. Only then will we better understand government problems and expand our influence in their solution.

"We must direct more of our attention and research to such matters as urban renewal, disposal of wastes and transportation.

"We must increase our contacts and assistance to schools and colleges—not just in money but in the realm of ideas as well."

Mr. Martin asserted that business could make great contributions to society. "We cannot, in our own interest, sit back and rest on our past accomplishments. To rest is to rust. We will be neither good businessmen nor good citizens if we leave the solution of our social problems entirely to government."

Profit Held Vital

Many of the executives agreed with the view of Dudley Dowell, president of the New York Life Insurance Company, that "self-interest, if nothing more, dictates the acceptance of such responsibilities when they offer the opportunity to assist important sectors of the environment which supports our operations.

"At the same time, however, we recognize that each company must strike its own delicate balance between its social responsibilities and its primary responsibilities to its stockholders."

J. E. Swearingen, chairman of the Standard Oil Company (Indiana) believes that "social responsibility begins with being successful—earning a profit, although this fact is not understood by enough people.

"Beyond providing goods and services for customers, the profitable company provides income for stockholders, jobs for employes, sales for suppliers, and taxes for Federal, state and community purposes. When these obligations are met, broader responsibilities can be undertaken, and should be undertaken."

Thomas J. Watson Jr., chairman of the International Business Machines Corporation, says that the fundamental question is "how far a company can go toward meeting its social responsibility if this effort detracts from or runs counter to what must be its primary mission — being successful and thereby providing jobs, goods or services and profits.

"There can be no general answer, for there is a wide range of choice between genuine self-interest and a concern for social responsibilities.

"Ultimately, however, a businessman simply cannot ignore for long his primary mission to conduct a successful business enterprise. If he does, he will fail and end up serving no one."

Mr. Watson notes that in the last decade business has supported a host of major movements such as "regional planning, urban renewal, balance of payments, employment of the handicapped, equal opportunity, financial support of colleges and voluntary price and wage restraints. . . . There is still a long way to go, but we are miles and miles ahead of where we were before World War II."

As for business' self-interest, Mr. Martin of Bethlehem Steel noted: "Solving these problems offers great business opportunities as well as the satisfaction of improving our society. Just think of what traffic jams cost our own companies. Or, consider what happens to our taxes when large areas in the cities where we have plants are allowed to become slums. How much of the present labor shortage results from inadequate education? Or, looking at the other side of the coin, how much business will be generated by improving urban transportation, housing and schools? The possibilities are immense."

Handling the Help

THE PEOPLE SPECIALISTS. An Examination of Realities and Fantasies in the Corporation's View of People, and the Plain and Fancy Specialties and Specialists That Arise Therefrom. By Stanley M. Herman. 320 pp. New York: Alfred A. Knopf. $6.95.

By JOHN BROOKS

SINCE "The People Specialists" is a serious, rather scholarly study of industrial personnel management history and practices by an industrial personnel man, I ought to state immediately that I am one whose eyes usually glaze over upon encountering the word "personnel," and who finds the book's title slightly nauseating. Stanley M. Herman would surely not be bothered by my prejudices. Clearly, he is addressing not me but other personnel men, and the corporate folk in whose destinies they deal. Nevertheless, I have found fun and enlightenment in eavesdropping on him, because what he has produced is a book about a durable and reliable comic theme, human folly within bureaucracy.

Like most comedy, his is based on a moral principle—that you can't have your cake and eat it, or anyway, shouldn't. Personnel management as practiced in American corporations gives him a field day, since, as he shows, such ideology as it has is uneasily based on the hope that you can. Historically, to begin with, personnel dogma is rooted in moral schizophrenia. Its grandfather, according to Herman, was Scientific Management (*floruit circa* 1900), an analytical method for the systematic observation of men at work, intended for no purpose but to determine how their material output could be increased and their masters accordingly enriched. Its grandmother, on the other hand, was Social Welfare, coming into its own at almost the same time and personified by the "social secretary," pure in heart and female in sex, who invaded the dark Satanic mill bent on improving the worker's conditions and uplifting his soul. To make workers more productive, then, or to make them happier—which?

The history of personnel theory, Herman argues, is its evolution toward the comfortable and handy notion that to do one is to do the other. Unfortunately (or for the Protestant ethic, fortunately), "there is no clear evidence to support any direct relationship between high morale and high productivity." Rather, there is contrary evidence. For example, in society at large psychic maturity is a generally prized quality; "in most corporations, however, maturity is not a prized quality. On the contrary, the infantile qualities—passivity, dependence, submissiveness—seem to be hallmarks of 'good employees.'" And as to the bosses, the whole history of capitalism from robber barons to wheeler-dealers is of leaders whose most incisive business traits—aggressiveness, ruthlessness, determination—were the very ones that made them forbidding to general society when they were not actually destructive of it.

A cruel dilemma, then, and one that, over the years, personnel men have blanketed with a whole panoply of obfuscations and rationalizations. There was something called the "human relations movement," for example, dating back, Herman says, to the 1920's and Elton Mayo of the Harvard Business School, marked by the introduction of social scientists into factories. Although it was addicted to big words, its motto, says Mr. Herman, might well have been, "Say please, but carry a big stick."

MORE recently, psychologists have followed the social scientists into the plants, and the inevitable result has been a much-discussed personnel philosophy called "permissive management." The idea here was to "depersonalize the giving of orders" —cause them to arise spontaneously out of the ambiance, so to speak, rather than issuing from the stern mouth of a particular boss, so that the question of someone ordering and someone else being ordered just doesn't come up. What next—finger painting? The emergence of this theory gave executives from coast to coast a chill of horror. "But," remarks Mr. Herman, "if anyone actually tried . . . permissive management [in any plant in the United States] . . . his valor went unnoticed and his name is lost forever to the roll of heroes."

Do personnel men do anything useful, then? Yes; they recruit employes, interview them, administer their wages and salaries, keep records, process insurance claims—useful, nononsense functions all. They also, of recent years, arrange for and conduct executive group-therapy sessions called T-groups. These take place at pleasant spots like Arden House, N.Y., Bethel, Me., and Palm Beach, and consist of several days of free-form discussion at which executives escape their inhibitions under conditions sometimes so hypnotic that the leader of one group, Mr. Herman relates, pulled out a pocketful of nickels and asked for competitive bids on them, and soon had the nabobs around the table so worked up that they were bidding seven, ten, and even twenty-five cents per nickel. Mr. Herman believes T-groups are frequently useful.

Personnel men, he says, numerous and influential as they may be, are generally underpaid and passed over for promotion—the ironical trouble being that hard-headed directors and top managers, in contradiction to their bland public philosophies, secretly suspect the awful truth that personnel men's humanizing efforts add nothing to profits. Full circle, then—and, potentially, the stage set for a return to the managerial philosophy of 1902, when George F. Baer, president of the Philadelphia & Reading Railway Company, magnificently said, "The rights and interests of the laboring man will be protected and cared for . . . by the Christian men to whom God in His infinite wisdom has given the control of the property interests in this country." The survival and salvation of personnel men, Mr. Herman believes, lie in their facing, even proclaiming, that their humanizing activities do not necessarily increase profits and ought to be continued for their own sake.

A Spartan creed. And a funny, engaging book, full of what an outsider can only suspect is purest heresy. Mr. Herman is described as currently serving as personnel director of one of the nation's major corporations. Unless heresy is the latest fashion in personnel ideology, he is a brave man, and I salute him. I salute him again for writing a whole book about people in corporations without once (so far as I recall) referring to anyone as an "individual," a usage that is a reliable sign of low respect for individualism.

More U.S. Companies Reducing Boredom of Workers

McDonald's Raises Output by Making Jobs Enjoyable

By ANDREW H. MALCOLM
Special to The New York Times

OAK BROOK, Ill.—Sharon Bush threw on an old blouse, slacks and loafers to go to work at the headquarters here of the McDonald's hamburger chain.

Other McDonald's office workers in this western Chicago suburb wore red denims, hot pants and very short skirts, while many men wore brightly colored golfing slacks, shirts and sweaters. The only men in ties and coats, it seemed, were rather surprised visiting salesmen.

But to those in the company the display of obvious casualness was not unusual. At McDonald's every summer Friday employes may wear anything that suits them, "as long as it won't get them arrested for indecency," said Tom Watterson, a company official.

For McDonald's is an example of a growing number of employers across the country who are adapting their job routines, regulations and conditions to make work more pleasant and, not incidentally, more efficient and profitable.

Also, on summer Fridays at McDonald's, all work ends at 1 P.M., to give employes an extra afternoon. Furthermore they receive free coffee, and nickel soft-drinks are available to all McDonald's employes.

The company's eight-story building, with its wall-less interior, has become a tourist attraction. Even the building's air circulation system is regulated to produce a bustle hiss—loud enough to cover normal conversation and avoid the total silence that disturbs some people but quiet enough not be noticeable.

"The whole thing is just ultra-fantastic," said the 23-year-old Mrs. Bush, who like all employes here reports to work 30 minutes early each summer weekday. "All winter we look forward to this," she continued, "on Fridays everyone is in such a happy mood. It helps you relate to the company." By 1:01 P.M. Friday she was on the way to a golf driving range.

Besides being pleasant for the workers, McDonald's methods have resulted in greater efficiency and productivity, lower employe turnover, improved morale, less Friday absenteeism and a bigger selection of job applicants.

The same attributes have prompted more than 1,400 concerns in all 50 states to adopt some form of the 35- or 40-hour three- or four-day work week.

So far, the four-day week has proved most attractive where 200 or fewer employes are affected, according to Mrs. Riva Poor, a Cambridge, Mass., publisher who has studied in the trend.

Sealtest has put some truck drivers on the shorter schedule, she said, as have a number of major oil companies. Lipton Tea has three plants on condensed week, while Samsonite and General Foods are trying it for some workers.

"It's a major decision to make," said Mr. Poor, "and it takes the larger companies longer to study all the ramifications."

Many companies have for years offered workers in-service training, financial aid for formal education, employe stock plans, company picnics and other benefits. Many see this as adequate and plan no further experiments.

But other firms are becoming increasingly disturbed over worker morale and the boredom that accompanies many repetitive tasks.

Slowly and with little fanfare many companies, such as McDonald's, have taken a variety of steps, some of them minor, to improve the situation. "It's all part of the better milk from contented cows philosophy," said one executive.

Many of the Social Security Administration's 18,-000 employes in Woodlawn, Md., a western suburb of Baltimore, perform monotonous filing chores. In an attempt to break the boredom, music is piped throughout the buildings with occasional interruptions for announcements on the weather, union meetings, features at the cafeteria.

Professional counselors are on hand to help with educational, employment or even personal problems. "Our self-interest is involved here," said Mrs. Charlotte Crenson, a spokesman. "if a person is distracted by his personal problems, he is simply less efficient on the job."

Officers also help employes find housing and day care centers or form chess clubs or modern dance groups.

McCormick & Co., the spice manufacturer, installed six-man middle-management boards of directors with junior, middle-management and hourly personnel. They wrestle with management problems, and every six months evaluate each other, dropping the poorest performer.

"They not only produce some good new ideas," said one officer, "but they become more directly involved with the company, and we can spot the good workers quickly."

In Baltimore the Kennecott Refining Corporation repainted its drab gray plant vats and machinery in psychedelic colors.

In New York City, Merrill Lynch, Pierce, Fenner & Smith began allowing clerks to perform a number of steps in clearing a stock purchase, instead of doing the same task time after time on an assembly-line basis.

In Pittsburgh Blue Cross plans employe birthday parties, while Kentown Corporation's apparel factory in Barnardsville, N. C., reported higher production after a disk jockey began spinning records over plant loudspeakers on Fridays, splicing the country music with dedications to units and individuals outproducing others.

"It makes us feel kind of special—like the plant really cares about us," said one worker, Mrs. Pat Feeder. And women, who are paid by the piece, are taking home about $20 more a week.

In Bensenville, Ill., next to O'Hare International Airport, the Flick-Reedy Corporation, makers of air and hydraulic cylinders, needed a large emergency water supply.

A water tower would have cost $120,000. But an indoor swimming pool could be built for about $70,000 and still store the water. So the pool was built and opened to employes and community groups.

Other water is stored in three stocked lagoons, which employes and their families use for fishing and canoeing. The company also shows noon movies for the machine workers, who incidentally must wear white shirts for a traditional "blue collar" job.

The machinists, it was found, are more careful about dirtying their white clothes on the machinery, a move that drastically improved the plant safety record. And that meant less insurance, less lost work time and fewer personal injuries.

"The philosophy is: If you do something right for the employe," said Art Conrad, a spokees man, "it's by definition right for the company."

GROUP TO PROMOTE PEACE IN INDUSTRY

'Scientific Practices' Will Be Introduced by Collective Bargaining Associates

TO CODIFY AGREEMENTS

32 Federal Officials, Economists and Engineers List Aims in Society's Charter

To promote peaceful relations between employers and employes by introducing "scientific practices" into collective bargaining, thirty-two government officials, economists and industrial engineers joined yesterday in the formation of a nonprofit membership society called Collective Bargaining Associates.

Members of the new organization include Solicitor General Francis Biddle, John M. Carmody, Administrator of the Federal Works Agency; William M. Leiserson, member of the National Labor Relations Board; Otto S. Beyer, chairman of the Railway Mediation Board; Robert W. Bruere, chairman of the Maritime Labor Board; Ordway Tead, chairman of the Board of Higher Education, and Morris L. Cooke, former Rural Electrification Administrator.

Defining the group's objectives at a press conference in the Hotel Chatham, Mr. Cooke said it was intended to implement the Wagner act by codifying "the best practices" of collective bargaining and suggesting improvements where possible. He observed that the rules governing collective agreements had "grown like Topsy" and that a scientific society was necessary to bring them together and to set them forth in a way that would produce the fullest cooperation between management and labor.

Mr. Cooke said he did not believe collective bargaining could ever be made to work if it was limited to wages, hours and working conditions. Labor must be given an opportunity to have its voice heard in the determination of production standards and all other matters affecting industry, he said.

Temporary headquarters have been established in the Graybar Building.

Methods Are Outlined

The principal aim of the organization, as defined in its charter, is the promotion and extension of the field of collective bargaining to be accomplished in the following manner:

"By a study of current practice and otherwise to outline a basic and adaptable technique of collective bargaining.

"By encouraging the creation in each industry of those organizations, both of employers and employes, required for the orderly practice of collective bargaining.

"By fostering comity and collaboration between the organized workers and management.

"By publicizing successful instances of collective bargaining.

"By assembling different types of model agreements between organized labor groups and management that will protect and give operative effect to the advancement of every common interest.

"By making pertinent information and data available to those negotiating or revising agreements.

"By developing methods for the joint determination of production standards and wages so as to safeguard the common interest through high productivity, low costs, reasonable wages and adequate profits.

"By working toward the increase of production through the joint formulation of methods for unleashing creative attitudes and performance at all levels, both in management and among the workers.

"By maintaining lists of experts, by function and by geographical location, who can be suggested for special service in facilitating the operation of collective bargaining.

"By seeking the establishment in educational institutions of agencies for exploring this field (research) and to encourage the teaching of the appropriate points of view and technique."

EDUCATION IN REVIEW

New York First State to Have Labor School, But Many Colleges Offer Labor Courses

By BENJAMIN FINE

With the signing of the Ives bill providing $200,000 for the establishment of the first School of Industrial and Labor Relations in the country, New York State has embarked upon a far-reaching program in the field of higher education. Members of labor and industry will work closely together to analyze the problems that are found in the economic world.

To be located at Cornell University, the school, which is to open next fall, is designed to fill an educational need in the labor field. Stress will be given to the history and principles of sound industrial and labor relations, the rights and obligations of employers and employes, the history and development of industrial practices, and other phases of industrial, labor and public relations of employers and employes tending to promote unity and the welfare of the people generally.

Three types of instruction will be available: a regular resident four-year curriculum for resident students; an extension program and short on-campus courses. A library of fact and opinion on industrial and labor relation problems will be provided; a continuing program of research in labor and management fields is also planned under the legislation.

Subjects for Study

Rules governing admission to the school will be flexible. If the applicant does not have the usual academic credits necessary for admission, but does have significant experience in the field of labor or management, he may be admitted. The fields of education, government, labor and management are being combed for a dean and for faculty members qualified to assume responsible positions.

Stressing the importance of this school, President Edmund E. Day declared that its basic function is to effect a broad increase of knowledge and understanding among those who engage in collective bargaining. Its purposes, he added, look away from continuing warfare between the parties in modern industrial enterprise and toward increasing cooperation.

Although New York is the first State to establish a labor school, many colleges and universities throughout the United States are now offering courses in this field, a survey conducted by this department discloses. In many instances the labor representatives sit together with leaders in industry to

February 24, 1940

discuss common problems. Controversial issues are brought out into the open.

Courses Offered

Several typical programs are here listed:

University of North Carolina—Six labor courses are offered, dealing with labor and social control, labor economics, human relations in industry and personnel problems. In normal times 300 students attend these courses. The objective is to acquaint students with the field of labor and to prepare those who are going into any part of this field. Plans are under way for an extension program of worker education for labor groups and workers generally.

Rutgers University — Economists, educators, labor and management representatives from all parts of the world participate in the Rutgers Labor Institute. Through these annual institutes more than 1,000 labor leaders in New Jersey have been able to spend a week discussing the problems of labor. Under the Engineering, Science, Management War Training Program, Rutgers has given 800 short courses which come under the general heading of labor education.

Temple University—Labor courses are offered in the undergraduate college and in the non-degree-granting evening school. A course in labor relations explores the relationships between capital and labor, reasons for strikes and general problems in this area. Guest lecturers, representing capital, labor and Government meet with the classes.

University of Virginia—Subjects such as history of the labor movement, industrial revolution, elementary economics, news analysis and public speaking are offered to workers' classes in three industrial centers. Informal weekend institutes for workers and labor leaders have been held at the university for five summers, with increasing attendance each year.

University of Minnesota—Three teaching techniques are employed: evening classes especially for labor union workers, institutes in the center for continuation study dealing with labor matters and conducted in cooperation with labor, and the traditional courses in the School of Business Administration dealing with labor problems, labor movements and legislation.

Courses at Chicago

University of Chicago—Various labor courses on the undergraduate and graduate level are offered. An Industrial Relations Center, recently opened, provides university-wide service in industrial relations for management executives, union leaders, Government officials, faculty members and students. The center integrates and expands the work touching on industrial relations in the various schools.

University of California—At present eight labor courses are offered on the Berkeley campus, ten at Los Angeles. More are scheduled for the future, with the expected establishment of a school or institute of labor and management relations. A bill is now pending in the Legislature to make an institute possible. The new school will train students to become skilled in labor-management problems.

University of Michigan — Labor courses are popular here. After the war a greatly expanded program is planned. Last year the university launched an educational program under the direction of the Workers Education Service of the Extension Service. The most popular courses have included social security, compensation, collective bargaining, safety laws and occupational diseases. An advisory committee of CIO, AFL, laymen and faculty members direct the work.

Appropriation Measure

Pennsylvania State College—The workers' education program, inaugurated in 1941, has now reached a total of thirty-two formal class units, with a larger body of union members receiving various types of informal instruction. A bill is now pending in the Legislature to appropriate to the college $100,000 outright, and $50,000 additional if that sum is matched by other sources such as labor or industry, to establish a labor division. This bill, patterned to some extent on the New York legislation, will permit the extension services to conduct labor and management education of all types.

Harvard University—Trade union leaders enter as special Labor Fellows, a project financed jointly by the university and the unions, designed to create a better relationship between labor and management. Labor Fellows are chosen by their own unions and are not required to meet definite scholastic standards, such as completion of a high school education. Nearly all students have been men with a record of successful experience as shop committeemen, local union officers, or national representatives.

It is evident that the American colleges and universities are planning to place greater emphasis upon labor education. As Mark Starr, educational director of the International Ladies Garment Workers Union, observed in a recent article, "cap and gown meets overalls." Educators and labor leaders are cooperating in this highly important area. Perhaps the campus and classroom can play a significant role in helping to iron out many of the problems of the post-war days.

April 8, 1945

WEIGH LABOR RELATIONS

New Cornell Review's Writers Are Industrialists, Unionists

ITHACA, N. Y., Oct. 23—The Industrial and Labor Relations Review, described as the first journal in its field, made its initial appearance today.

The quarterly, published for the New York State School of Industrial and Labor Relations at Cornell University, is edited by Prof. Milton R. Knovitz of the school's staff.

In a foreword, Edmund E. Day, president of Cornell, called the publication "a logical extension of the function which higher education is assuming in the area of labor-management relations."

The first issue includes a discussion of "Labor and American Foreign Policy," by David A. Morse, Under-Secretary of Labor, and contributions from such others in the industrial and labor relations fields as D. C. Prince, vice president of General Motors, Charles Luckman, president of Lever Brothers and William Gomberg, director of the management engineering department, International Ladies' Garment Workers Union, AFL.

October 24, 1947

I. L. G. W. U. TO OPEN OWN LABOR SCHOOL

A novel experiment in union education will get under way today when the International Ladies Garment Workers Union, A. F. L., opens a training institute for forty young men and women who want to make a career of union service.

The students will spend the next twelve months in the classroom and in union field assignments, receiving instruction in all phases of union affairs. Not all of what they learn will come from union "professors." Employer associations in the garment industry will designate lecturers to visit the institute and present employer viewpoints to the students.

The institute will occupy the sixth floor of the union headquarters at 1710 Broadway. A formal opening ceremony will be held this afternoon in the offices of the union's president, David Dubinsky.

Mr. Dubinsky said last night that the aim of the school would be to provide young persons with information and technical training that would equip them to serve competently as union staff members or officers. He stressed that the school was not intended to turn out an "elite corps," on which the union would draw for its future leadership, but rather to supply basic instruction for those who wanted a chance to prove their capacities within the union.

May 1, 1950

N.L.R.B. Condones Lies, But, Please, Little Ones

WASHINGTON, June 11 (UP)—The National Labor Relations Board said today it was permissable for unions or employers to lie to workers in trying to convince them to vote for or against a union.

In a unanimous opinion, Republican and Democratic members of the five-man board agreed that:

"Exaggerations, inaccuracies, partial truths, name - calling and falsehoods, while not condoned, may be excused as legitimate propaganda" before a union representation election.

But, the board said, such "propaganda" should not be so misleading as to prevent the exercise of a free choice by employes in the election of their bargaining representative."

The board's opinion was contained in a decision voiding an election last November at the Gummed Products Company of Troy, Ohio, where the workers voted to join the Paper Workers Union, C. I. O.

The board said the union had made "false statements" that "exceeded the limits of legitimate propaganda."

ARBITRATION RISE IN DISPUTES NOTED

By MILDRED MURPHY

Theatregoers, especially those accustomed to the frequently opinionated roles taken by Boris Karloff, would have been astonished at the impartial part he assumed yesterday.

Seated in one of the six tastefully decorated hearing rooms of the American Arbitration Association, 477 Madison Avenue, the impersonator of monsters and evil men listened impassively to testimony regarding an actress' salary claim. As a representative of the Actors Association, he was serving on a panel of three arbitrators whose ruling after the hearing will have the legal force of a court judgment.

A half-dozen students from a White Plains high school sat at adjoining tables, listening intently to the evidence presented by an Actors Equity representative and by one for the theatrical producer in question.

The case is a relatively simple one among the thousands handled annually by the association for persons wishing to settle disputes without going through the intricacies, expenses and delays of litigation.

Public Opinion Reversal

But the presence of the students indicated a fairly complete reversal in public opinion. At the time of the association's establishment thirty years ago, such opinion leaned heavily toward dubiousness on the part of management, labor, corporations and especially professional lawyers.

J. Noble Braden, executive vice persident of the association and one of its prime movers, described the change this way:

Arbitration is not new and, in fact, goes back to the Romans. But a few decades ago, especial of dispute by arbitration bore, ly in this country, the settling in the minds of most individuals, the suspicious marks of short cuts and inefficient methods. The supremacy of the courts of law was being jeopardized, some people thought.

But along with the growth in labor-management relations, the term of settlement by arbitration, with its obvious attractions, spread. Now, 95 per cent of labor-management disputes are settled by arbitration, Mr. Braden declared.

There are 4,000 organizations and corporations in the United States whose contracts contain an arbitration clause. In all states in the country, the ruling of arbitration is enforced by common law.

Mediators Find Their Role Is Gruelling but Challenging Art

By MARK HAWTHORNE

The men in the middle of strikes, such as the current airline and New York newspaper disputes — the mediators—pursue an art that is Gruelling because of the long hours and constant strain; gentle because they have no power.

"Our lack of authority is one of our strongest weapons," says John A. Burke, assistant regional director of the Federal Mediation and Conciliation Service. "It means we can't resolve disputes ourselves. The parties have to, and we can only help them."

He is quite unlike an arbitrator, who dictates a settlement after hearing both sides. Thus a mediator's effectiveness hinges on the parties' willingness to accept him as a middle man at each step of the negotiations.

In the national airlines strike the mediation job has fallen almost entirely on James J. Reynolds, the 59-year-old Assistant Secretary of Labor.

Mr. Reynolds entered the airline mechanics' dispute after the rigid framework of Federal mediation had collapsed. Airline and railroad strikes are governed by the National Railway Labor Act. In these disputes mediators from the Federal Mediation Board sit in on the bargaining until, as in this instance, an impasse is reached. This brought in Mr. Reynolds.

Federal, state, city and private mediators have been participating in the newspaper talks, behind the blue doors of the Publishers Association headquarters at 220 East 42d Street.

500 Mediators in U.S.

There are only about 500 labor mediators in the country —260 with the Federal Mediation Service, and most of the rest with state agencies.

Federal mediators are paid an average of $15,000 a year, state mediators somewhat less. The few private mediators depend on arbitration work for most of their income. "Unless you work for a government agency, mediation is not a living," says Theodore W. Kheel, a private mediator who participated in the early stages of the newspaper talks.

Although he estimates he spent 100 days of work in the last four New York newspaper strikes, he was paid no fees. "I look at it as a public service," he says.

The difficulties of Federal mediation were demonstrated in the airlines strike. When it was obvious a stand-off had been reached, the mediators asked both sides if they would be amenable to a binding decision to be made by the mediators. The mechanics union refused and the mediators were out.

Then, in accordance with the law, a 30-day period had to elapse before a strike could be called. In addition, the President used his right to call another 30-day cooling-off period and to appoint a special emergency board. After the second 30-day period had expired without a solution, the union struck. This left mediation up to Mr. Reynolds.

Though mediators do not have the official weight of Mr. Reynolds's sub-cabinet post, their efforts are frequently successful.

Each mediator has his own way of operating to end a dispute, but most begin by hearing each side's case, often in a joint session. Then they deal with each side separately, probing, clarifying, focusing discussion on the crucial points of disagreement.

Alertness Pays

"Often the real issues or feelings about them have not been mentioned," says Morris Tarshis, the city's Director of Franchises and an experienced mediator who represented Mayor Lindsay early in the newspaper dispute. "You have to be alert for them. A nod, someone bristling, someone suddenly taking notes, all these things can be signals."

"The job of a mediator," says Vincent D. McDonnell, chairman of the New York State Board of Mediation, "is to find out what the problem is."

"It's the art of asking the right question," says Miss Eva Robins, a state mediator and one of the few women in the field.

To Mr. Kheel, mediation is a "form of creative expression" and much more challenging than arbitration. "Arbitration is like drafting," he says. "Mediation is like painting."

"There is something philosophical about mediation," says David L. Cole, chief mediator of the newspaper talks. "Its success depends on bringing reason into the collective-bargaining process. Unfortunately there has been more muscle than reason in this dispute."

Questioning, listening, nudging, meeting with whole committees or individuals, sometimes tackling key issues, sometimes minor ones, the mediator helps the parties move toward an agreement.

A sense of timing, most mediators agree, is critical—knowing when to make a proposal, to reveal one party's concession, to call a meeting, take a break. Timing, the confidence of the parties in the mediator's fairness, and optimism — all are needed.

Cooperation Among Mediators

"If you're not an optimist, get out," says Mr. Burke.

The effectiveness of mediators is reflected in statistics. Although mediators are not involved in every one of the 125,-000 labor disputes in the United States each year, work stoppages occur in only about 3,500.

Federal mediators may step in if the dispute threatens interstate commerce or Government contracts. State mediators handle disputes in most other areas.

When the public welfare or a large number of employes is affected, as in the newspaper strike, mediators from more than one source often work together.

Although mediators have differing ideas of their role, they have similar complaints.

Expenses, for example. Unlike most union and management negotiators, mediators generally have meager expense allowances.

"I usually eat in Automats or inexpensive restaurants," says Robert E. Kennedy, one of four Federal mediators in the newspaper talks. "I live in Philadelphia, but since I am assigned to this region, I don't get any expenses."

Mr. Tarshis said recently that in previous negotiations he had often paid $20 for a dinner for himself and someone else, of which the city reimbursed him $2, its maximum meal allowance.

Impartial Dining

The necessity for impartiality also complicates the choice of a restaurant. "I generally go about 10 blocks away to eat," Mr. Tarshis says. "If they see you eating with anyone, they say you're playing favorites. Then if it's a good restaurant, they say you're a lush—and if it's a cheap one, you're a bum."

Mediators sometimes get around expense-account limitations on hotel rooms by listing them as "conference rooms."

Like the negotiators, mediators also face the culinary rigors of long sessions.

"The tendency when you get tired is to eat and drink more, and that in turn can throw your judgment off," says Mr. Kheel. "I try to eat light foods and avoid starches, like pastries or sandwiches," he says.

"Weight is a big problem in negotiations," says Mr. Tarshis. "You find yourself eating five or six meals a day but never feel satisfied. And, of course, you're always drinking coffee."

BARGAINING STUDY DIVIDES 2 EXPERTS

Kerr Disagrees That Labor Device Is Obsolete

Special to The New York Times

WASHINGTON, June 16 — The staff director of a massive study of unions said today that collective bargaining was obsolete. However, his boss, one of the most respected experts on industrial relations, disagreed.

Collective bargaining's obituary was written by Paul Jacobs, staff director of the trade-union project of the Center for the Study of Democratic Institutions at Santa Barbara, Calif. Mr. Jacobs is also on the staff of the Institute of Industrial Relations of the University of California at Berkeley.

Dr. Clark Kerr, president of the university, disputed Mr. Jacobs's conclusion in an introduction to the latter's pamphlet, published by the center today.

The pamphlet's title is "Old Before Its Time: Collective Bargaining at 28." In Mr. Jacobs's view, "the collective bargaining system is collapsing, and with its collapse the unions that have been so integral a part of it face a dim and uncertain future."

Dr. Kerr, a member of President Kennedy's Advisory Committee on Labor-Management policy, commented:

"I do not agree with his conclusions that the present system of collective bargaining is obsolete and needs replacing, although I do think we have entered a new stage in the relationships among labor, management and the Government.

"When this stage has been completed, collective bargaining in America will no longer have participating in it two major protagonists — management and labor—with the Government acting only as referee.

"Instead, the Government will be a third force, consciously exerting its influence upon the two other groups, and consciously attempting to solve problems that are beyond the capabilities of management and labor alone.

"As the role of this new governmental force increases, the complexeties of industrial society will have increased, too, raising new problems. But I am not so pessimistic about the future, as I take Paul Jacobs to be, nor am I as convinced as he is that some of the contradictions in public policy that he discusses cannot be resolved by the exercise of prudence and good judgment."

According to Mr. Jacobs, a lack of social vision by unions, a change in the work force that has put more and more workers outside the bargaining system and problems engendered by automation in a stagnant economy have caused a "breakdown" in collective bargaining.

Lack of public understanding of the unions' role in a technological society and the past economic success of unions, which have led them to rely on economic tools when political goals were called for, are also factors in the "present failure" of bargaining, he said.

Institute Is Formed Here for Improving Bargaining Process

The Institute of Collective Bargaining and Group Relations, which is aimed at improving and promoting the process of bargaining, was formally established here yesterday by a group of labor and management leaders.

E. T. Klassen, president of the American Can Company, was elected chairman of the board of the new institute.

Other officers elected are: vice chairman, P. L. Siemiller, president of the International Association of Machinists; president, Lane Kirkland, executive assistant to George Meany who is president of the A. F. L.-C. I. O., and vice president, Victor Borella, labor adviser of Governor Rockefeller and former executive vice president of Rockefeller Center, Inc.

At a luncheon at the Waldorf-Astoria Hotel, Theodore W. Kheel, mediator and president of the American Foundation on Automation and Employment, explained that the institute was based on the premise that in a democratic society there is no alternative to collective bargaining.

The institute, a nonprofit organization, was brought into existence by the foundation and will utilize as an educational resource the New York State School of Industrial and Labor Relations of Cornell University. Although the program of the institute has not been set, it is expected to foster seminars and discussions on collective bargaining problems.

The board of directors of the new institute was announced at the luncheon also. They are:

Joseph A. Beirne, president of the Communications Workers of America.
Frank L. Gallucci, vice president of the Essex Wire Corporation.
Walter K. Graham, director of Industrial relations for The Daily News.
Max Greenberg, president of the Retail, Wholesale and Department Store Union.
Ralph Gross, president of the Commerce and Industry Association of New York.
Efrem A. Kahn, president of E. A. Kahn & Co.
John H. Lyons, president of the International Association of Iron Workers.
Joseph E. O'Grady, former chairman of the New York City Transit Authority.
Bertram A. Powers, president of New York Typographical Union 6.
Harry Van Arsdale Jr., president of the New York City Central Labor Council.

Corruption

Worst Invasion by Gangsters Since '33 Vexes Unions Here

By A. H. RASKIN

A rash of racketeer-infested unions has cropped up in the metropolitan area in recent months, causing intense concern to the bona fide labor movement, employers and Government law-enforcement agencies.

Responsible union leaders said yesterday the invasion of the labor field by gangsters was the worst since the repeal of the Prohibition Act sent hordes of hoodlums swarming into unions nineteen years ago. Spokesmen for the American Federation of Labor and the Congress of Industrial Organizations promised full cooperation with the public prosecutors in efforts to clean out the corrupt elements.

Evidences of racket control have become so flagrant in certain unions that Charles T. Douds, regional director of the National Labor Relations Board, has asked his superiors in Washington for advice as to whether there is a legal basis on which the board might deny certification to unions that are vehicles for extortion.

Mr. Douds decided to act after a dozen employers had filed affidavits with the board testifying to shakedown attempts by men with long criminal records, operating under the cloak of newly issued union charters.

In some cases, the same men would function as representatives of two locals. One would present to the employer demand for higher wages, and establish picket lines when these were refused. Almost immediately the second union would appear and offer to sign a contract providing no gain for the workers—on condition that the company "remember" the union heads at Christmas time.

Investigations by the New York City Anti-Crime Committee, under the leadership of Spruille Braden, former Assistant Secretary of State, have indicated a close tie between many of the gang-controlled locals and the multi-million-dollar garment trucking racket here. Men who for years "protected" non-union dress and coat manufacturers are now running unions of their own.

The garment racket is so well-entrenched that it has defied all efforts at eradication. David Dubinsky, president of the International Ladies Garment Workers Union, A. F. L., and a life-long foe of union corruption, has sought vainly to stamp out racketeering in the industry, but his attempts have been retarded by a fear that the union representatives he assigns to the task are receiving a "death sentence" if they should defy the gangsters.

That this fear is not visionary was demonstrated by the fatal stabbing three years ago of William Lurye, a special organized for the union, who was engager in a drive against the non-union shops. His killers have escaped conviction, partly because of the refusal of Mr. Lurye's associates in the organizing drive to give evidence. Six of the organizers are operating non-union garment shops and one is reputed to have banked $4,000 in the course of the drive.

Aim at Vulnerable Concerns

The new unions in which racket influence is strong function with little regard for jurisdictional lines. Some hold charters from A. F.-L. unions, others are independent. They attempt to make agreements with small manufacturers, shopkeepers and other little business men who are especially vulnerable to a picket line.

Most of these new locals operate out of expensively appointed offices. Their leaders wear custom-tailored clothes and monogrammed shirts. They drive costly automobiles, although one explained that when he went into the union he "gave up" his Cadillac to avoid unfavorable comment on his affluence.

Asked why he was investing heavily of his own funds to help start a union in which his only on-the-record interest is a $100-a-week job, one prison alumnus replied blandly:

"Some people might say I am an idealist."

There are two theories among investigators and legitimate union officials on the sudden influx of hoodlums into the union field.

One is that organization of a union provides a "respectable front" for men who have made huge sums out of rackets and who have no valid basis for explaining what they do for a living. According to this theory, such men can afford to spend two or three years laying the foundation for what could prove a lucrative racket in its own right.

Another theory, less widely held, is that many of the recent converts to trade unionism have been driven out of their former rackets by the Kefauver investigation, the Federal gambling tax and other Government curbs. The prevailing opinion among crime experts is that there are some such "displaced persons" among the disciples of the new unionism, but that most are still actively in flourishing rackets outside the labor movement.

A bookmaker turned union labor leader told associates he had decided to enter the labor field because his son was growing up and asking questions about the source of his father's income. Another group of eight racketeers openly boasted they obtained a New York A. F. of L. charter as a reward for arranging a prize fight in Detroit.

Both wings of organized labor here regard the gang infiltration a a menace to unionism. Morris Iushewitz, secretary-treasurer of the New York City C. I. O. Council, warned that mobsters would "overrun everything" if steps were not taken promptly to drive them out of the labor field.

"For the first time since they were driven out ten and fifteen years ago, these gangsters are flooding back in," Mr. Iushewitz said. "They are not interested in legitimate contracts. They specialize in 'back-door' agreements, extortion, phony picketing and intimidation.

"Unscrupulous employers may welcome them, but we in organized labor intend to fight them with every weapon at our command. We will cooperate wholeheartedly with the District Attorney and all other Government agencies in stamping them out."

Tactics "Very Objectionable"

Martin T. Lacey, president of the Central Trades and Labor Council, A. F. L., said the tactics of some of the new locals, as reported to him, were "very objectionable."

"We are against them 100 per cent," he declared. "There are sufficient charters already issued in this area to provide for all legitimate organizing without granting overlapping charters to new groups."

The national C. I. O. at its convention here last November gave the national body power to oust racketeers from affiliated unions if the unions failed to show diligence in cleaning house. The president of one C. I. O. international union recently resigned under pressure from the parent organization. Another union forced the resignation of one of its vice presidents after a shortage in union funds had been discovered.

The A. F. L. has less authority to clean up its constituent unions. Each international has autonomy under the A. F. L. constitution and the only action open to the federation is to oust the entire international if it tolerates corruption.

The head of one A. F. L. affiliate that has been issuing charters with a free hand to men who are more familiar in police stations than in union halls said at his Midwestern office that he felt the newly chartered locals were "doing a good job." He said the recommendations for new charters were being made by the organization's regional director here, a man who has been jailed for extortion and who still owns a garment trucking concern.

Crime prevention agencies are close by watching the new labor developments. It was learned that United States Attorney Myles J. Lane had asked the National Labor Relations Board to provide all available data indicating a tie-up between organized labor and organized crime. The office of District Attorney Frank S. Hogan is understood also to be collecting evidence. Neither agency would comment officially.

Mr. Douds, the labor board's regional director, made no effort to conceal his concern over the influx of racketeers into unions. The board is obliged under the law to certify unions that have filed non-Communist affidavits and have complied with the other registration requirements of the Taft-Hartley Act. These certifications are granted when a union demonstrates it has the support of a majority of the workers in a particular enterprise.

"It is easy for men with criminal records to set themselves up under the guise of a union and get a majority in some small shop," Mr. Douds observed. "When they get a certfication from us, they are able to go out and say to other employers: 'See, we have a certification from the Government, that proves we are a real union.' Our action puts them in a position to claim they are a legitimate labor organization when they are a bunch of damn racketeers."

The difficulty about denying certification to a union on the ground of racket control is that it puts the N. L. R. B. in the unhappy spot of having to decide whether organizations are legitimate. This is the same problem the board has had in connection with deciding whether unions were Communist-controlled political conspiracies, rather than bona fide labor groups. The board has held it could not legally undertake this responsibility.

Court Action Favored

Keith Lorenz, chairman of the State Labor Relations Board, said he felt problems of this type were best handled by the courts. He said labor boards did not have staffs to investigate or pass on questions of gangster influence or political control, or to impose penalties on men who abused their rights as union officers.

However, some employers, when confronted with demands from unions they consider illegitimate, intend to insist that both the national and state boards hear evidence on the past criminal records and organizational tactics of the union leaders. Their hope is to force a definitive decision by the boards or the courts on whether racket-infested unions are entitled to the privileges of bona fide unions.

In one case, on which the national labor board has an affidavit, an employer testified that a union leader offered to discontinue his organizing activities in return for $10,000. When this proposal was turned down the same unionist came back with a representative of another local who offered to sign a contract on the employer's terms if he would be "taken care of at Christmas time."

The amount of the "remembrance" was to be proportionate to the sum the employer saved by not giving a pay increase to his workers. The affidavit said the unionist gave the employer a list of companies with whom the union had "played ball," together with the names of persons the employer could communicate with for corroboration of the union's "cooperation."

In another case the officers of an A. F. L. union who expected to lose their charter because of the presence of ex-convicts on their payroll set up a "dummy" independent union with the same local number and filed registration papers with the N. L. R. B. When the ouster threat blew over after a brief suspension, the officers told the board to forget about the new local.

In still another case, A. F. L.-C. I. O. cooperation frustrated a back-to-work movement organised by shady unionists in a C. I. O. strike. The walkout involved a small Brooklyn steel plant. Two thugs from another union went to the president of the striking local at his home and threatened to beat up the official's wife and children if he interfered with their plan to send strikebreakers into the plant the next day.

The strike leader asked the Seafarers International Union, A. F. L., for help in repelling the raid. When a carload of strong-arm men drove up to the plant and fell on the C. I. O. pickets, A. F. L. seamen sprang out of hiding and routed the invaders. That ended the back-to-work effort, and the plant signed an agreement.

April 24, 1952

NEW YORK'S PORT: 'RULE BY RACKETS'

By IRA HENRY FREEMAN

It is five minutes to eight any morning on West Street. A hundred and fifty men in worn workclothes stand in a semi-circle in front of one of the piers lining the seaward side of the dirty, cobbled street. Many lands have contributed to the group: Sicily, the depressed counties of Ireland, the Negro shantytowns of the South, also Poland, Hungary.

A rough, burly man in a leather jacket shouts above the din from the West Side Highway overhead and the bumping of trucks over the cobblestones:

"Number One deck gang, Number One dock gang, Number One hold gang! Just my regular men this time."

This is the "shape-up" of longshoremen which takes place at each working pier fringing the vast Port of New York—the "shape-up" or hiring method, heart and symbol of the crime that grips the waterfront. For more than a generation, the way of life on the longshore has been a complex of extortion, theft, fraud, graft, usury, violence, even murder.

Governors Take Action

Repeated attempts—all unsuccessful—have been made to clean up the mess. Last week, Governor Dewey of New York and Gov. Alfred Driscoll of New Jersey joined forces to "crack the nut that has defied every effort" of the authorities in the last fifty years. Governor Dewey promised $500,000 to the New York State Crime Commission for the job, while Governor Driscoll pledged all funds and manpower necessary. The situation now, they said, was worse than ever.

Nature made the Port of New York one of the finest in the world, with wide, deep channels to the sea, and numerous harbors close to, but fully protected from, the ocean. Shipping has always been one of the major industries of New York; the magnificent port was primarily responsible for the development of the greatest city of the New World.

Along the miles of ugly, filthy littoral, at 200 deep-water piers and 1,600 other docks, 11,000 ships are berthed annually to load and discharge passengers and cargo. Goods shipped each year through the port are estimated to be worth $7,000,000,000. But now there are complaints that the port is losing business to more "progressive" and "efficient" places like Baltimore and New Orleans, that New York got 25 per cent of all United States shipping business in 1931 but only 15 per cent this year.

What is the nature of this crime that has fastened upon the waterfront, and why has it been tolerated for half a century? Every investigator has produced the same answer: It is a labor racket which exploits the 36,000 day laborers who are the longshoremen, dockside truck loaders and railroad freight handlers. It also exploits the consumer by adding to the price of all goods shipped through the port millions of dollars unnecessarily paid out as graft and extortion, in payroll padding and featherbedding, and for shipments stolen. Many investigators also

UNION PRESIDENT

The New York Times
Joseph P. Ryan

conclude that the racket could not survive if the highly competitive shipping industry would unite to kill it.

One Meeting in 28 Years

The International Longshoremen's Association, A. F. of L., enjoys the nearest thing the Taft-Hartley law allows to a closed shop of longshore labor in this and most other East Coast ports. Its president, Joseph P. Ryan, holds office for life. The union convention occurs only once in four years. Some locals never meet. (Local 1181 has not met in twenty-eight years.) The members often get no chance to ballot on vital matters. The Staten Island locals, for example, did not vote on the new wage contract, dissatisfaction with which provoked the long, costly pier strike two months ago, but

their "acceptance" of it was telephoned to headquarters by Alex Di Brizzi, union boss in Richmond.

The I. L. A. in the New York Port is organized into locals of 500 to 1,000 workers, each local serving one to nine piers. Each local has its organizer and business agents, and each pier has its "shaping" or hiring boss, all appointed by Ryan, with patronage shared by other officers in the hierarchy.

These local bosses are, very often, plug-uglies with criminal records. Danny St. John, shaping boss of Pier 84, has been arrested nineteen times, three times for murder. Toddy O'Rourke, boss of Pier 88, was twice convicted of grand larceny. Ed McGrath, an organizer since 1937 and Sing Sing alumnus, has been arrested thirteen times. Cockeye Dunn, late boss of the "public loaders" division of the union, was put to death in Sing Sing in 1949 for murder.

Double Interest

Sometimes these union leaders are also part owners of the stevedoring companies who employ the longshoremen, like Ed Florio, New Jersey organizer for I. L. A. and also a proprietor of a Hoboken stevedoring concern. In collective bargaining, Mr. Florio has thus an interest in both sides.

There is not enough work for all longshoremen. The New York Shipping Association reported 15,000 of the 36,000 work only 200 hours a year or less. Only 1,900 men get a full forty hours work a week, fifty weeks a year.

Who works is determined by the pier boss at the shape-ups at 7:50 every morning. The men selected are expected to kick-back to the pier boss $2 or $3 out of the $16.80 they earn for eight hours of back-breaking, often dangerous toil. To be picked regularly costs more.

Demanding official action to clean up the port, Spruille Braden, chairman of the New York City Anti-Crime Committee, told Governor Dewey on Oct. 29:

"The unfair and brutal shape-up system of hiring spawns mobster control of large segments of the port. This results in all manner of criminal activity, from kickbacks and loan sharking through organized larceny and narcotics smuggling up to murder."

In 1946, a Citizens' Waterfront Committee declared "every ill and social waste on the docks sustains itself through the shape-up * * * the crucial factor nourishing the whole system." And as early as 1916, Mayor John Purroy Mitchel's Committee on Employment similarly condemned the shape-up.

The "Short Gang"

The normal work gang is twenty-two men and a foreman, but the shaping boss often picks a "short gang" of fifteen or eighteen men. Putting in fictitious pay vouchers for the men who were not there, he divides the loot with his henchmen. It is the job of the foreman to speed up his "short gang" to perform the work of twenty-two men.

At the end of a day's work, the longshoreman gets a brass check redeemable on Fridays for cash. If he can't wait until payday, a loan shark will buy the check from him at 10 to 20 per cent discount. Of course, the lender pays the pier boss for the concession. Numbers and horse bookies are on hand, also, to tempt the longshoreman with the possibility of a living wage, and these operators too pay rent to the boss.

It is no wonder, under these conditions, that personal finance companies refuse loans to longshoremen, and that low-rent housing projects reject longshoremen as tenants.

Strike Over "Sell-Out"

When longshoremen's demands for more pay became irresistible last fall, Mr. Ryan negotiated a 10-cent-an-hour rise with the New York Shipping Association, representing 175 ship lines and employer stevedores. A spontaneous strike against this "sell-out" by five locals tied up the port for twenty-five days in October and November and cost the industry many millions of dollars.

Thievery is quite a problem, too. Sometimes, a whole export shipment will disappear mysteriously. The truckman delivers the goods to a pier and gets a receipt. Weeks later, the foreign consignee protests the shipment never reached him. Investigation reveals the pier receipt was signed with a fictitious name, and nobody knows anything about the goods. Insurance companies report such thefts totaling as high as $60,000,000 a year since the war, and have consequently raised rates 25 per cent in the last ten years. Two shipping companies solved the problem by paying their pier bosses to "reduce" pilferage.

Competition Bars Unity

Waterfront racketeers escape prosecution, for one thing, because the I. L. A., in alliance with its brother teamsters' union, is a power in local politics. Mr. Ryan has been a leading Democratic politician for decades. Again, potential witnesses are mortally afraid of violent revenge by mobsters.

Besides, despite all pious wailing, the "companies tend to look the other way in exchange for the promise of the hiring boss to keep the longshoremen in line, increase productivity and curb pilferage," as Fortune Magazine says. Frank A. Nolan, president of Jarka Corporation, the largest New Jersey stevedoring concern, told the Kefauver Committee last spring that Anthony Anastasia of the notorious gangster family was a satisfactory hiring boss because he "preserved discipline" and "got out the work."

Certainly the shipping companies would not prefer a longshoremen's union like Harry Bridges' on the West Coast, which is led not by gangsters but allegedly by Communists.

The industry also remembers that when Joseph Curran organized a new seamen's union in this port fifteen years ago out of material and that of the I. L. A. today, the companies were rid of labor gangsters, but their labor costs became greater in the end.

The trucking companies' biggest complaint is what they call the loading racket. By contract between the I. L. A. and the Motor Carriers Association, all imported goods must be loaded from the pier onto trucks by I. L. A. men at a cost of 5½ to 10 cents per hundredweight. These services, which truckers assert are frequently unnecessary, cost $15,000,000 a year. The actual workers, of course, get only regular longshore pay, while handsome profits are pocketed by the employer-loaders, who are, paradoxically, I. L. A. members and sometimes officials.

Inadequate piers and traffic congestion on the shorefront often keep trucks idly waiting for hours. It is possible to arrange with the pier loading boss, however, to move to the head of the line.

December 9, 1951

ANTI-RED 'CRUSADE' BEGUN BY ANASTASIA

Anthony Anastasia, boss stevedore of six piers in South Brooklyn, began a "crusade against communism on the waterfront" in his territory yesterday.

Anastasia had taken the day off to preside at the opening of the clubhouse of the new "Longshoremen's, Checkers and Clerks Social Club." He showed visitors over the two-story brick building rented for the club at 371 Court Street.

On the street floor, Anastasia and his aides signed up members and took initiation fees of $5 plus the first month's dues of $1. The pier boss said he had been drafted as "acting president" at a mass meeting of longshoremen held ten days ago on Pier 1 at Columbia Street, Brooklyn. The club had 175 charter members, he said, adding that "several hundred" more longshoremen had joined yesterday.

Anastasia said the purpose of the social club would be to educate longshoremen to the menace of Communist machinations among them. He repeated his previous charge that Communists in the International Longshoremen's Association, A. F. L., were trying to "take over" the Port of New York.

Membership blanks, to be signed by the applicant, included the statement that "I am not and never have been a member of the Communist party or in sympathy with any of its principles."

Anastasia began his crusade while awaiting trial in an assault case. He had been arrested on similar charges in 1945 and 1946 and on a homicide charge in 1925, but he has never been convicted.

February 10, 1952

Dockland: Ships, Men, Machines

BROOKLYN'S ten-mile waterfront—from the throbbing Army terminal in Bay Ridge northward to the sugar docks and Greenpoint—offers one of the longest unbroken general cargo ranges in the world. Its sixty major piers handle an estimated 23 per cent of the Port of New York's foreign commerce, which in turn is about 40 per cent of the nation's total. They move fully half of all the high quality, high cost, packaged merchandise—"general cargo" in salt water parlance—for which New York is famed as a world shipping center. Six million tons of this valuable general cargo moved over Brooklyn docks last year—as much as in Manhattan, Staten Island and New Jersey put together.

It is this teeming rough-and-tumble gold coast

LONGSHOREMEN on one of sixty piers along the crowded Brooklyn waterfront await call to unload a Danish freighter inbound from the Far East with a cargo of rubber, copra (dried coconuts) and porcelain.

HOIST TRUCK, here moving bags of lima beans from dock to van, speeds handling of packaged cargo. The operator earns a slight specialist's premium over ordinary stevedores.

SHAPE-UP begins when hiring foreman (pointing, at left) blows his whistle and picks men to work the pier. Those chosen get $2.10 an hour base pay, as long as the job lasts; shape-up is repeated daily.

HAND TRUCK is used to trundle bags of naphthalene from pier to railroad lighter. Cargo is ferried across the bay and unloaded again at a plant on the New Jersey shore.

that is now the subject of what promises to be the first intensive official inquiry into a plaguing question: "How much does crime afflict the waterfront of the nation's premier port?" The Kings County Grand Jury and a Crime Commission named by Governor Dewey are both expected to dig into waterfront racketeering (kickbacks and loan sharks), union strife which recently tied up most of the docks, and dockside pilferings (estimates of losses run from $1,000,000 to $50,000,000 a year).

The pictures on these pages set the scene for these imminent investigations along the Brooklyn piers. They also show the role of the rugged longshoremen who work this loading platform for ships from every quarter of the globe. —G. H.

DOCK WALLOPERS, piling huge rosewood logs shipped from Brazil, work four hours at a stretch. Other longshoremen move cargo from the depths of the ship's hold.

CARGO NET, powered by deck winches (above), swings cartons of Hawaiian pineapple out of the hold. Longshoremen handle complete operation.

LUNCH BREAK in a typical waterfront tavern (left) lasts an hour. These men then return to the piers for another rugged four-hour stint.

NEW YORK TIMES photographs by SAM FALK

December 2, 1951

HIRING OF GANGSTERS TO BUY PIER PEACE ADMITTED BY SHIP, STEVEDORE FIRMS; PILFERAGE DROVE U. S. LINES FROM DOCK

UNION NAMED MEN

Some Chosen While in Prison—'Phantom' Got $25,000 From Grace

NEWSPRINT TRUCKER PAID

Gave $100-a-Shipload 'Bonus' —10 Tons of Steel at One Time Among the Thefts

By MEYER BERGER

A picture of multimillion dollar steamship and stevedore corporations meekly accepting union-designated ex-convict pistol-toters as their pier bosses rather than risk work stoppage came out of yesterday's State Crime Commission hearing in the County Court Building.

The picture was many-sided. It disclosed payment by the Grace Line of more than $25,000 in the last seven years to Tim O'Mara, a boss loader, who did no actual work on the Grace Line piers but whose presence "made for labor peace."

It showed the great United States Lines, owner of the record-holding United States and other famous ships, retreating from one of its Hudson River piers after only six months' occupancy because of mass pilferage, including the theft of ten tons of steel at one time.

It showed T. Hogan & Sons, a major stevedoring concern, hiring ex-convicts for United States Lines pier jobs before they had left state's prison; the eventual return of one of those ex-convicts to the Sing Sing Prison death house for murder of a hiring foreman.

Had to Rehire Thief

The same canvas held the picture of T. Hogan & Sons compelled to re-hire James Connors, a pistol-carrying hoodlum, after he had pilfered property from a North River dock, because "we might have trouble with the men on the pier."

The testimony, with accompanying records, disclosed that the Jules S. Sottnek Company, Inc., a stevedoring concern, had paid to officials and delegates of the International Longshoremen's Association a total of $14,402 in gratuities from 1947 to 1951. Paul W. Sottnek, the company's president, testified regarding cash withdrawals listed in an accountant's report but not recorded on the concern's books.

Michael Castellana, a vice president of the Sottnek concern, admittedly a social acquaintance of Michael Clemente, secretary of Local 856, I. L. A., on the East River waterfront, told of a "loan" of $10,902 in 1951 to help Clemente arrange a private wedding for his daughter in the Biltmore Hotel.

Vincent Carpenter, secretary-treasurer of Davie Transport Company, Inc., and half-owner of the business, admitted that he paid $100 a shipload above the normal handling price for the right to truck newsprint from the East River piers.

He testified that the money was split between Clemente and Thomas May, a member of Clemente's local—$60 a shipload to Clemente; $40 a load to May. May is under indictment on charges of extorting the money. Payments were in cash in sealed envelopes and ran to about $15,000.

Mr. Carpenter admitted that neither Clemente nor May performed any service for the payments; that the money was passed to prevent possible strikes or work stoppage that would hold up newsprint delivery.

The commission put in evidence a summary showing that the Jarka Corporation, one of the world's largest stevedoring concerns, had paid out at least $58,585 to officials and delegates of the I. L. A. between 1947 and 1951. Payments ranged from $50 to minor officials to $8,000 to international organizers. A separate payment of $16,635 went to someone listed as "unidentified."

Union Agent Got $1,400 Gifts

Frank Russo, a wide-eyed illiterate giant who is business agent of Local 327, I. L. A., in Brooklyn, stumblingly admitted on the stand that he received, in addition to his union wages and $200 a month for distributing the I. L. A. News, a union publication, $1,400 in gifts from various stevedore companies.

He has been the local's business agent only three years. When Theodore Kiendl, special counsel for the commission, pressed him on denials of having received money other than his union wages, Russo maintained he had misunderstood the question when he testified at private commission hearings.

The payments, the witness conceded, had come in varying amounts from Daniels & Kennedy, Inc., from the Sottnek Company, from Marra Brothers, from Universal Stevedoring, from William Spencer & Son, from A. H. Bull & Co, from Cosmopolitan Shipping Company and from Turner & Blanchard, from Pellegrino & Son, among others. Most of them are stevedoring concerns.

The witness went foggy when Mr. Kiendl tried to force him to explain why the companies had chosen him to receive their cash gifts.

"Some money on vacation we got," bumbled Mr. Russo.

"What do you mean by that."

"Well, I went on vacation one year, and Kennedy give me $100."

At another point the witness said, "Universal gave us vacation —gave me vacation money"; so, he testified, did Turner & Blanchard.

"Did they owe you vacation money?" Mr. Kiendl asked. The giant stared back, shook his head and said, "No."

"Just going on your vacation and they handed you some cash so you could enjoy yourself?" Scorn edged the words.

Russo nodded eagerly. "That's right. I didn't go to ask for it."

Hard-prodded as to whether he had ever discussed these "vacation gifts," the witness floundered.

"You did say a word about it, didn't you?" Mr. Kiendl pressed, smoothly. "You thanked them?"

"Well, I went down to the pier and I said, 'Thanks for the envelope.'"

Russo could not remember that he went with Gerry Anastasia, a union business agent in Brooklyn, to ask $100 a week for each of them from an official of Turner & Blanchard in 1951; nor that Anastasia, a member of the notorious Anastasia family in Brooklyn, told Capt. P. B. Blanchard, head of the company, "others are paying us."

The pilferage that drove the United States Lines from Pier 46 was related by Jones F. Devlin, general manager of the company, a portly white-haired gentleman, Boston-born but equipped with ripe British accent.

The disappearance of loads of cameras and clocks, and then of the ten tons of steel went into the record, with Mr. Devlin hoarsely remarking of the steel theft, "'Twas the most remarkable case of pilferage, really."

Laughter swept the chamber and Mr. Devlin harrumphed into the microphone.

The decision to abandon the pier he testified, was quietly arranged "to—ah—avoid any trouble—that is, stopping of work." He confessed that Joseph P. Ryan, lifetime president of the I. L. A., had heard about it anyway.

"He tried to persuade you to stay?" asked Mr. Kiendl.

"Yes," said Mr. Devlin, heavily, "he would have liked us very much to stay."

"Did you tell him it was because of the existence of extended pilferage you decided to move?"

Mr. Devlin chewed a moment on that. Then, audibly breathing into the microphone at the witness stand, he said: "No, sir. I told him we didn't need the space any more, which was right."

Thomas Maher, a red-faced stevedore superintendent for the Huron Stevedoring Company, subsidiary of the Grace Line and a second-generation West Side dock figure forty years in the business, made a blunt and refreshing witness. He is still a member of Local 791, I. L. A.

Questioned by Leslie H. Arps, assistant chief counsel for the Crime Commission, Mr. Maher testified that the "Edward Joseph Ross" carried on the Grace Line payroll was actually the boss loader Tim O'Mara, an ex-convict with a burglary and robbery record, who operated on Piers 61, 62, 73 and 74, North River.

"You know what we mean by a phantom?" asked Mr. Arps.

"Somebody on your payroll not by their real name," the witness answered cheerfully.

He said he had inherited O'Mara as the phantom Ross when he took over his present job with Grace Line; that O'Mara's status had been made clear to him by a Grace Line official.

O'Mara, it developed, drew "a standard $50 a week" that grew between 1945 and the end of 1951 to more than $25,000. He had been a phantom on the line's payroll before that, too, but for how many years the testimony did not show.

'What does O'Mara do to earn all this money?" asked Mr. Arps.

"Well," said Mr. Maher, "O'Mara was to keep labor—that they wouldn't be going out on strike—that was my understanding."

"He was to prevent strikes?"

"Prevent strikes, that's right."

The witness testified that O'Mara was not a union official but was a kind of strike deterrent kept around the piers.

Former Supreme Court Justice Joseph M. Proskauer, commission chairman, asked, "What was O'Mara?" and Mr. Arps undertook the explanation.

"O'Mara was just a boss loader on these piers; never did any work. He's a phantom and the purpose of paying him, as I understand it, Mr. Commissioner, is that he would help make labor peace. He settled strikes. You heard Mr. Maher so state."

Mr. Maher testified that payments to O'Mara as phantom ended last April 18, on orders from Capt. Richard E. Pendleton, Grace Line marine terminal superintendent.

A bit of mystery crept in here. Stoppage of phantom payments at the Grace line ended on that date, apparently because of something connected with the murder of Thomas Plunkett, a longshoreman who had worked on the Grace Line piers but was murdered on April 18 in MacGregor's Bar and Grill at 68 Gansevoort Street, Greenwich Village waterfront.

Why the killing should have ended O'Mara's payment did not seem at all clear from the testimony.

"Isn't it a fact," asked Mr. Arps, "that shortly after the Plunkett murder Captain Pendleton asked you whether there were any phantoms on the Grace Line payroll?

"He asked me that question," said Mr. Maher. "That's right."

"And what did you say?"

"I said there was—there were two of them."

"Well," said Mr. Arps, "we are going to confine our attention solely to the Ross checks."

Mr. Arps then explained to the commissioners that he was purposely avoiding questions about the second "phantom" because "that matter is under investigation and I believe that the other phantom has already been indicted by the New York County Grand Jury. It is being handled by Mr. Hogan's office."

Before Mr. Maher was called, John C. Hilly, former assistant United States Attorney now in charge of the Security Bureau, Inc., a police force organized by the shipping industry in 1946, had testified about John Scanlan, a longshoreman with a long criminal record, having been caught in an attempt at theft on Pier 56, North River, in September, 1950.

Prosecution Dropped

Mr. Hilly testified that when action for prosecuting Scanlan was started, all other longshoremen on Pier 56 walked off the job; that at end of three days with the Britannic tied up, unloaded, officials of Jarka Corporation reluctantly yielded.

They told Mr. Hilly that they had discussed the case with Mr. Ryan and had agreed to drop the Scanlan prosecution on condition that he could not work on that pier again, nor on any other Cunard Line pier. A lawyer for Scanlan even got formal releases to shield his client from prosecution.

The Scanlan question came up again in the questioning of Mr. Maher. He had been hired by the Grace Line after the affair at the Cunard Pier.

Commissioner Ignatius Wilkinson asked:

"The net result of this finagling is that he was discharged by the Cunard Line and thrust on the Grace Line?"

Mr. Arps said: "That's right."

"By orders of Fourteenth Street?"

"That's right."

"Meaning thereby Mr. Ryan?"

"That's right."

The union's headquarters, it had come out earlier, are in Fourteenth Street.

Commissioner Proskauer wondered what would happen if a steamship line refused to accept a union designee with a criminal record.

"When you open a pier," Mr. Maher told him, "what hiring man is there you take, whether you like it or don't."

"And if the company refuses to take the union's designee for hiring foreman or hiring stevedores what happens then?"

"What would happen?" asked Mr. Maher. "I don't think you would open up that pier. You would have a strike on your hands."

Watchmen, Mr. Maher testified, never make arrests on the piers. He could recall no such arrest in his long experience. Mr. Hilly had testified that his own men, not affiliated with the watchmen nor with any other union, had obtained 225 waterfront convictions with the help of the city police, the Federal Bureau of Investigation and through the United States Customs Service.

Hearing on a motion by the Jarka Corporation to stay the commission from interrogating Jarka officials at the public sessions was set yesterday in Federal Court for next Friday. At the same time the commission was restrained pending the outcome of the hearing from making public testimony taken in private.

James McNay and James O'Rourke, hiring bosses on the North River, were to have been witnesses at the hearing today, but they have sought a Supreme Court order to have their subpoenas vacated. The commission agreed at a hearing yesterday that it would resubpoena the men for next Monday instead, to allow time for a ruling in their case.

THE SHAPEUP—At the early-morning call, the hiring boss (left) picks four or five gangs of about 20 men each from the 200-250 men who shape themselves into an informal horseshoe around him. On being given the nod, dockers are issued work tabs which they present later to a pay office to draw their wages. Under this system each day means finding a new job.

Joe Docks, Forgotten Man of the Waterfront

Behind the current investigation into longshore racketeering is a plain guy whose hands perform one of the city's toughest jobs. By BUDD SCHULBERG

WE all know the big names of the current investigation into crime and corruption on New York's waterfront. The headlines are hogged by Anastasia, Joe Ryan, Mike Clemente, "Big" Bill McCormack, the polished executives of the great shipping lines and influential stevedores. But there is a forgotten man on the waterfront. His voice is lost among the gravel-throated alibis of high-bracket hoodlums, the oily explanations of labor politicians and the suavely martyred inflections of the shippers.

You whiz by him on the West Side Highway but you don't see him. You hurry past him as you board ship for Europe or a winter cruise through the Caribbean, and never notice his face. But his muscles move your groceries and your steel; he carries your baggage on his back. From his pocket comes the notorious kickback you've been reading about. He's the one who has to show up every morning for the "shapeup" you've been hearing about. He is the human material with which racketeers, masquerading as union officials, pull flash strikes to shake down shipping companies and force the em-

ployment of such key personnel as boss loader and hiring boss. He is the man who performs the most dangerous work in America, according to the statistics on labor injury and death.

He's the longshoreman, the dock walloper, the little man who isn't there at investigations; the forgotten man in the great city of New York, the forgotten man of American labor. Miners, railroad men, even sailors were fighting fifty years ago against the kind of medievalism that passes for work conditions on the docks this very morning. In a day when social security and old age pensions are accepted as economic facts of life by both major parties, the longshoreman hasn't got job security from one day to the next.

If he's the forgotten man of the current investigation, here's the forgotten fact: it is this basic insecurity —breeding fear, dependence, shiftlessness, demoralization—that feeds the power of the mob. The weaker, more frightened and divided are the dock workers; the stronger and more brazen are the Anastasias, Bowers, Florios and Clementes who manipulate them.

WHO are these longshoremen? What kind of lives do they lead? What do they think of these investigations? What are they after?

I went down to the waterfront two years ago for what I thought would be a few days' research for a film about the docks. Long after I had enough material for a dozen waterfront pictures I kept going back, drawn by these forgotten men performing a rugged, thankless job in a jungle of vice and violence where law and constitutional safeguards have never existed.

In the past few weeks I returned to watch the shapeup. I talked with dock wallopers in the bars from the Village to the mob hangouts along the midtown docks. I went to the homes of longshoremen who talked to me frankly (over cases of beer) about their lives, their fears and their hopes for a decent set-up on the piers. I talked to the defeated who shrug off every investigation as just one more political maneuver and who are resigned to grabbing a few crumbs from the gorillas who rule them. I talked to "insoigents" —as they call themselves—who think the time finally is at hand when honest unionism can remove the killers, grafters and seller-outers, and institute regular and honest employment on the docks.

About 35,000 men are paid longshoremen's wages in the course of a year. Of these, about half are regular longshoremen, men who depend on this work for their livelihood. The rest are what you might call casuals, now-and-theners who drift in to pick up an occasional extra check. Many of these are city employes, policemen and firemen who like to grab off the overtime money on nights and week-ends. Some 50 per cent, for instance, earn less than $1,000 a year. Another 10 per cent earn less than $2,000. About a third of all the longshoremen, fifteen thousand at most, earn from $2,000 to $4,000 a year. These are the regulars, the ones who have to hustle every day to keep meat and potatoes on the table for the wife and kids. An upper crust of favored workers averages more than $75 a week on a yearly basis. The base pay of $2.27 per hour sounds all right. It's the irregularity and mob intimidation that make longshoremen the most harassed workmen in America.

NINE out of ten are Catholic—if not Irish Catholic, then Italian or Austrian. This accounts for the influence of certain waterfront priests who have championed the dock workers, in a few dramatic cases going so far as to challenge known hoodlums face to face on the piers. You'll find the Irish on the West Side and in Brooklyn, some 6,000 of them, but they are now outnumbered by the Italians, which explains the growing influence of the Italian underworld that controls the Brooklyn waterfront, as well as the Jersey, Staten Island and East River docks. Irish longshoremen are devout. Before the 7:55 A. M. shape, you will see them going to Mass at St. Bernard's, St. Veronica's or St. Joseph's. Italians follow the Latin tradition of letting the wife handle the church responsibilities.

THE Irish longshoremen, while kept in line by strongarm boys and plagued by an inhuman hiring system, have a better deal than their fellow Italians, who in turn are a niche above the Negroes, who work in traveling gangs picking up the extra work when they can get it and are often relegated to the hold, the job nobody wants. The Irish are hardly ever asked to kick back any more. In other words, when the hiring boss picks his four or five gangs of twenty men each from the 200-250 men who shape themselves into an informal horseshoe around him, the Irish no longer return part of their day's pay to him in order to assure themselves of a job. But the Italians and Negroes systematically kick back as

WATERFRONT PRIEST—Father John Corridan is a "kind of one-man brain trust of union rank-and-filers."

much as $5 per man per day. With seven or eight thousand men kicking back, this quickly becomes big business, some $30,000 or $40,000 a day in illegal fees being passed up from the hiring boss to his superiors as part of the $350,-000,000 illegal take from the New York harbor each year.

"It's a stinkin' feelin' standin' there in the shape every mornin' while some thievin' hirin' boss looks you over like you were so much meat," one of the Irish dockers was telling me the other day. "But once in a while an Italian gang is brought into work with us and that really looks like something you've heard about in Europe, not America. They work in a short gang—sixteen instead of twenty—so the cowboys c'n pick up the extra checks for themselves. But they've got to do the work of twenty—or else. If they squawk, the boys work 'em over—or they don't get no more work. I've actually seen 'em beaten like cattle for a question.

"So the rules take a beatin'," my Irish friend went on. "In the first place, 90 per cent never read the contract. In the second place, it's just a piece of paper if the shop steward and the delegate are part of the mob. Jerry Anas-

tasia, for instance, he's a delegate. A lotta help you get from a stiff like that. Half them I-talians are ship-jumpers, which leaves 'em at the mercy of the trigger boys. They ain't citizens and they can't even apply for unemployment insurance. The way I see it we got it lousy and they got it double lousy."

TODAY most of the Irish workers are picked up by gangs—in this case a legitimate work group, not the Mickey Bowers type. Each gang has its own leader and when the hiring boss points to him it means his whole crew works that day. But the Italians, Austrians and Negroes are still hired on an individual basis by gang carriers, exactly as Henry Mayhew described it in his book, "London Labor and London's Poor" a century ago:

He who wishes to behold one of the most extraordinary and least-known scenes of his metropolis should wend his way to the docks at half past seven in the morning. * * * [When] the "calling foremen" have made their appearance, there begins the scuffling and scrambling forth of countless hands high in the air, to catch the eye of him whose voice may give them

work. * * * It is a sight to sadden the most callous to see thousands of men struggling for only one day's work, the scuffle made fiercer by the knowledge that hundreds out of the number must be left to idle the day out in want. * * * For weeks many have gone there, and gone through the same struggle, the same cries; and have gone away, after all, without the work they had screamed for.

NOT a word need be changed in this description to apply it to hiring methods in New York Harbor a hundred years later. Now, as then, two or three times as many men as will be needed loiter near the dock entrance waiting for the hiring boss to blow his whistle when a ship is ready to be loaded or unloaded. Now, as then, he will pick them out according to his own whim and preference. But on too many docks in the great harbor of New York, the nod is given to the man who plays ball, kicks back, buys the ticket for the benefit he will not be expected to attend or signs up for haircuts in a barber shop where all the seats are filled by labor racketeers. Too often the numbered metal tag which a dockworker gets from the hiring boss, his admission card to a four- or eight-hour shift on the pier, is a badge of compliance, an acceptance of inferior status on the waterfront.

Thousands of longshoremen are wondering why a modern metropolis insists on maintaining a practice so barbarous that it was outlawed in England sixty years ago and is now abandoned in nearly all American coastal cities but not in the great Port of New York.

WORK is slow right now and even the longshoreman who stands in with his hiring boss is lucky to pick up three split days a week. How does he make ends meet? "Ya live f' t'day—ya never put nuttin' away—if ya need money ya borry it," I was told. Borrowing comes easy on the docks and is deeply imbedded in the system. The men passed over in the shape must have eating money and they get it from the loan sharks who are part of the mob.

If you "borry" four dollars you pay back five and the interest keeps mounting each week. A rap of 30 per cent isn't unusual. Nor is it unusual for a longshoreman getting the nod in a shape to turn over his work tab to the loan shark who collects the debtor's check directly from the pay office. So our longshoreman winds up a day's work by borrowing again.

"I was born in hock and I'll die in hock," a longshoreman told me in a Chelsea saloon. In some locals a longshoreman who wants to be hired has to go the route—come up with a bill for spurious "relief" drives and play the numbers and the horses with books belonging to the syndicate. In Brooklyn Albert Anastasia had everything for six blocks in from the river. Longshoremen have to buy their wine from the groceries and their meat.

Unquestionably their incomes are supplemented by regular filching of meat and liquor from the supplies flowing through the piers. Even the insurgents who are doing their best to buck the graft and large-scale pilferage are no different in this respect. Their ethics may be questionable but they stem from a deeply ingrained cynicism that is easy to understand. For years they have watched the fantastic loading racket make off with whole shipments of valuables. The pilferage of ten tons of steel reported to the Crime Commission by a shipping executive may have been front-page headlines to the general public but it was hardly news to the dock workers. "If 5 per cent of everything moving in and out is systematically siphoned off by the mob, why shouldn't I take a few steaks home for the wife and kids," a longshoreman figures.

"TAKIN' what you need for your own table is never considered pilferage," it was explained to me rather solemnly. Shortly before Thanksgiving a longshoreman who could double for Jackie Gleason noticed barrels of turkeys being unloaded from a truck. He was not working that day but he simply got in line and waited for a barrel to be lowered onto his back. Everybody in his tenement got a free turkey.

Another longshoreman, known for his moxie in standing up to the goons of a pistol local ("one of them locals where you vote every four years with a gun in your back"), told me he was starved out on the docks for sixty straight days. "I stand there lookin' the crummy hirin' boss right in the eye but he never sees me." In a whole year he made less than

$1,500 and he had kids to feed. "We couldn't 've made out if I hadn't scrounged the groceries on the dock," he said.

WHAT are their politics? Traditionally Democratic, as befits good New York Irish and Italians, but you might say their universal party is cynicism. Because so many mobsters were aligned with the Democratic city machine, some longshoremen took to wearing Ike buttons on the docks as a sign of defiance and undoubtedly the President-elect was well supported. Like the majority of voters nationally, they hope our political change will break the ties between racketeers and the office holders who have been protecting them.

But longshoremen have a feeling of being political orphans inevitably betrayed by the people for whom they vote. They'll tell you their cause has been ignored by the politicians, the police and even the press. Still, they aren't fooled by communism. Despite periodic outcries against subversive influences on the docks —unfortunately used as a cover-up for various forms of racketeering, communism is as unpopular among longshoremen as among stock brokers, farmers or railroad workers. The insurgents who led the harbor-wide wildcat strike a year ago have a hatred for Joe Stalin and his slave labor system that burns just as fiercely as their feeling for Mickey Bowers, Mike Clemente and the whole waterfront system that keeps union racketeering in power.

MEN in the Chelsea area are still bitter at the editorials calling their strike Communist-inspired. The local involved, 791, is made up of staunch Irish Catholics, many of them under the influence of the waterfront priest Father John Corridan, and are so rabidly anti-Communist that they have been refusing for years to load war materials headed for Russia or China. It is safer to call these men Communists in print than to deliver that opinion face to face.

"I belt guys for less 'n that," said an embattled member of 791, identified with opposition to Joe Ryan, to strong-arm methods, and to chronic insecurity on the docks. "Anastasia—that great patriot—he calls us Commies. Florio and Di Brizzi—to those bums we're Communists.

Strange breed o'Commies who never miss Mass in the morning and who'll give up a day's pay before they'll work a Russian ship. But I'll tell you one thing, if we don't clean this mess up ourselves, the Commies'll have a nice fat issue all ready to take over."

FATHER CORRIDAN, of the Xavier Labor School on the Lower West Side, who has become a kind of one-man brain trust of the rank-and-file, sums up the Communist angle this way:

"In '45 the Communists did move in and try to take credit for the leaderless, rank-and-file strike. But right now their influence is nil, no matter what the I. L. A. brass says. The men down here—almost without exception—are loyal, God-fearing Americans. The way to fight Communism in the labor movement is to accentuate the positive — in other words find out what the men really need in order to live healthy, happy, dignified lives and then fight for it."

What longshoremen want has nothing to do with ideologies and millenniums. Their aims are so modest as to be taken for granted by some sixty million American wage earners. What they want most is an assurance that the job they're lucky enough to have today is the same one they'll have tomorrow—and next week—and next month. They don't want to keep wandering from pier to pier like a lot of miserable strays, begging for work.

An old man with forty years on the docks compared his status—or lack of it—with a railroad engineer's. "Look at him, he goes to work every morning knowing he's got a place in the world. The more time he's got behind him the more secure he feels. That's seniority. He knows if he does his job well his pay'll increase, his position improves and he'll finally retire with a good pension. He's got dignity, that's what he's got. Now take me. All my life on the dock. And I know my job. I know how to handle copper in the rain and how to get my fingers into a bag of flour. I c'n work fast. I like to take pride in my work. But what kind of pride can I feel when some punk comes out of the can and starts makin' five times as much as I am for doin' nothin' except pushin' us around?"

The old man insisted on buying me another drink. It may have been loan-shark

money, but longshoremen are proud and open-handed and fine drinking companions when they feel they can trust you.

"After forty years I get up t'morra mornin' an' stan' over there on the dock like an orphan. I'll be lucky if I bring home twenty-five bucks this week. Is the hearings gonna change it? Well, lad, I'll tell ya one thing, it can't make it any worse. I just hope it goes all the way."

THIS hope is echoed all up and down the waterfront. Joe Docks, bottled up in his cramped cold-water flat or his waterfront bar, doesn't get much chance to tell us about his life. But he doesn't like it. Hard - drinking, two - fisted, high-strung, a rabid sports fan, an all-out friend, a dangerous enemy, he's also a loyal, religious, hard-working, responsible family man concerned with getting his kids through school and seeing them get a better break than their old man. He lives for the day when his job will be systematized through some plan of work rotation based on an adequate annual wage. He'd like some advance notice of where and when he's going to work. Today there is not even a central information service on shipping traffic, and the men pick up their information as to job chances in the same haphazard, chaotic way they did a hundred years ago.

Joe Docks thinks he deserves something better than the hopelessly outmoded hiring system that delivers him into the hands of hardened criminals. He's hoping, but not counting on the hearings, which are the most thorough ever held on the problem, to rescue him from underworld bondage and raise him to a level of dignity and security enjoyed by other American workers.

He's too solid and useful a citizen to be left to stew in his own bitterness and bewilderment in the waterfront bars. Anti-hoodlum, anti-corruption, anti-Communist, anti-uncertainty and anti-hunger, he is the real forgotten man of American labor.

THE other morning a little fellow who sounded enough like Barry Fitzgerald to make the Ed Sullivan TV show was left standing on the dock by an ex-Sing Sing hiring boss for the fourth consecutive jobless day. "In Liverpool back in 1912 they knocked out this kinda hiring," he was saying.

"I could tell them judges on the Crime Commission a thing or two about this stinkin' set-up." Even now, early in the morning with another jobless day ahead and the Good Lord only knew what tomorrow, there was a twinkle in his eye. These are indestructible men (until a strong-arm man, a St. John or an Ackalitis, has the last word) and laughter comes easy to them for all their grief and frustration. "When those high mucky-mucks get all through and there's a zillion words of testimony all nicely bound, they'll know what we knew in the first place—down here it's really time for a change."

He gave his cap a jaunty poke, stuck his hands into his battered wind-breaker, pushed his chest out in a gesture of general defiance and crossed Forty-fourth Street to Mc-Ginty's Bar and Grill.

AS you read this over Sunday breakast or in the paper-littered parlor, Joe Docks may be in church, or playing with his kids, or lying in bed reading about the basketball games. He'll be back on the docks tomorrow morning around half past seven. If he's passed over he'll be over at McGinty's or some other place, looking for the loan shark, drinking a little beer, worrying about the wife and kids, playing a number, wondering if the Crime Commission can really get those gorillas off his neck, and waiting for the general public to respond to a golden challenge: "If you do it to the least of mine, you do it to me. . . ."

December 28, 1952

BI-STATE PIER PACT APPROVED BY HOUSE

Measure to Set Up Commission to Curb Port Crime Here Now Goes to the President

Special to THE NEW YORK TIMES.

WASHINGTON, July 30—A bill authorizing New York and New Jersey to establish a bi-state commission to curb crime and racketeering on the New York waterfront was passed by the House of Representatives today and sent to President Eisenhower for his signature. The Senate passed the bill on July 16, two days after it was introduced.

The House approved the bill by unanimous consent. Senate action also was taken without a dissenting vote.

The speed and unanimity with which the measure swept through the national legislature followed the pattern set by the two states that will be parties to the compact. Both houses of the New York Legislature approved unanimously a bill establishing the commission and a similar proposal passed the New Jersey Legislature with only one dissenting vote.

Congressional approval is required of all compacts between the states.

Several Withhold Votes

Representative Kenneth B. Keating, Republican of upstate New York, as chairman of the Judiciary Subcommittee that had reported out the bill, urged its passage when the measure came up on the consent calendar. He said that the New York waterfront was "infested with gangsters, mobsters, racketeers, thieves and unsavory characters with lengthy criminal records," and that "political graft and corruption are closely linked with waterfront activities."

Although no votes were cast against the measure, several Representatives said that they withheld such votes only so as not to delay the adjournment of Congress. Mr. Keating thanked them for this consideration.

Representative Edward J. Hart, Democrat of New Jersey, called the bill a "big patronage grab on the part of the Governors of two states," and Representative Alfred D. Sieminski, Democrat of New Jersey, said that there were several features of the plan that were objectionable and deserved further investigation.

The bill sent to the President today would establish a two-man commission—one from New York and one from New Jersey—which would be employed to license pier superintendents, hiring agents, stevedores and port watchmen. Conviction of a crime would be grounds for refusing a license. Longshoremen would have to be registered and would have the right to register unless they had been convicted of a crime or had engaged in subversive or other activities that would endanger public safety.

Under the bill, public loading and the shape-up would be abolished. Public loading is an extra operation under which longshoremen transfer cargo from piers to trucks but not from ships to piers or piers to ships. This practice had been described as a wasteful and obnoxious racketeering device.

Hiring System Assailed

The shape-up is a system of hiring controlled by union leaders which the Senate Commerce Committee called "wasteful and unworthy." The bill replaces it with regional employment exchanges for licensed port watchmen and registered longshoremen.

The American Federation of Labor opposed the compact bill at Congressional hearings. Passage of the measure came as the federation was engaged in a fight to drive out of the International Longshoremen's Association its life-time president, Joseph P. Ryan, or bring about the designation of an administrator to clean up the racket-infested organization.

Governor Dewey of New York had urged enactment of the Federal legislation "to stamp out the evil conditions which have blighted the port, terrorized honest workmen and subjected a multi-million dollar industry to a system of organized piracy."

Gov. Alfred E. Driscoll of New Jersey likewise had advocated Federal legislation to drive criminal and corrupt elements out of waterfront labor organizations.

July 31, 1953

RYAN'S DOCK UNION EXPELLED BY A.F.L.; VIOLENCE FORESEEN

I.L.A. Leader's Receivership Bid Rejected 72,362-765 in Favor of New Pier Labor Group

By A. H. RASKIN
Special to THE NEW YORK TIMES.

ST. LOUIS, Sept. 22 — The racket-riddled International Longshoremen's Association was expelled today from the ranks of legitimate trade unions. By an overwhelming vote, the American Federation of Labor convention revoked the pier union's charter and authorized the establishment of a new union to drive it from the docks.

The action ended the sixty-year-old tie between the I. L. A. and the federation. Joseph P. Ryan, the union's lifetime president, made a futile plea to the delegates to put his organization under A. F. L. receivership empowered to rid it of criminal elements.

The convention heard his plea in icy silence. When the roll-call vote was taken the only opposition to expulsion came from the dock union itself, the tiny Masters, Mates and Pilots Union and individual delegates from Galveston, Tex., and Lake Charles, La. The official vote was 72,362 for ouster and 765 against. Each vote represents 100 union members.

The decision to go forward at once in setting up a rival union raised the possibility of strikes and violence in ports along the Atlantic and Gulf Coasts, with New York the principal battleground.

Ryan, who is under indictment on charges of stealing union funds, led the six members of his delegation out of the convention immediately after the vote. They were silent and shaken, even though there had never been any doubt of the outcome.

Big Locals to Switch

The Ryan group lacked any specific plans on what to do next. Consideration was being given to the calling of a special convention of I. L. A. locals to decide union policy. However, there was no question that the union intended to fight on a port-by-port and, if necessary, a pier-to-pier basis to hold its ranks against the A. F. L. challenge.

Seven I. L. A. vice presidents from districts outside New York, where the underworld has its tightest grip, were expected to swing their locals into the new union as soon as the new charter is issued.

The pro-A. F. L. group says it will have the allegiance of half the union's total membership of 64,200. However, the I. L. A. contends that the revolt is confined to the Great Lakes and Mississippi River ports and does not embrace more than 6,000 longshoremen.

The cancellation of the I. L. A. charter represented the first time since its founding in 1881 that the federation had expelled a union for corruption.

Nearly eight months ago the A. F. L. executive council warned the Ryan organization that it must clean house or face ouster. The intervening months brought repeated pledges of reform but virtually no accomplishment.

The original warning to the I. L. A. was prompted by the New York State Crime Commission's disclosure that union members on the New York and New Jersey docks were being victimized through systematic shakedowns and discrimination and that many I. L. A. officers were partners in waterfront rackets.

Meany Condemns I. L. A.

Summing up the Crime Commission record in a convention speech today, George Meany, A. F. L. president, said there was "nothing that resembled legitimate trade union activity" in the testimony given by the local and international officers of the pier union.

The expulsion of the I. L. A. presents an immediate problem to shipping employers in New York and other ports along the North Atlantic coast from Portland, Me., to Newport News, Va. These employers are negotiating with the I. L. A. for new contracts to become effective Oct. 1. If they sign new agreements, the A. F. L. will find it hard to break the I. L. A. grip on the Eastern Seaboard in the next year. If no agreements are signed by midnight Sept. 30, the East Coast faces the prospect of a crippling strike.

Officers of seven of the seventy-one I. L. A. locals in the Port of New York have signified interest in joining the new union, and the A. F. L. expects to make substantial headway in such other ports as Philadelphia, Baltimore, Norfolk and Hampton Roads.

The new union will operate under the supervision of five trustees to be appointed by the A. F. L. executive council. They will direct its affairs for six months to a year, after which the members of the union will elect their own officers.

Mr. Meany is to head the committee and the key operating responsibility will rest on Dave Beck, president of the International Brotherhood of Teamsters, and Paul Hall, secretary-treasurer of the Atlantic and Gulf District of the Seafarers International Union.

The Beck and Hall unions are the two most powerful A. F. L. organizations on the waterfront and are in a position to exert leverage over the longshoremen by their control of truck and ship movements to and from piers.

The trustees of the new union are expected to cooperate actively with the bi-state waterfront commission set up by Gov. Thomas E. Dewey of New York and Gov. Alfred C. Driscoll of New Jersey. The commission's goal is the elimination of criminal rule of the docks. After Dec. 1 all dock workers will have to register for jobs through state employment centers, stevedoring companies and pier watchmen will need licenses, and the commission will be empowered to bar anyone it feels will jeopardize law and order on the docks.

Not One Delegate Applauds

At the end of his rambling discourse, he repeated the proposal he had made to the A. F. L. resolutions committee yesterday for appointment of trustees to run the I. L. A. without stripping it of its charter. As he slumped into his chair, no delegate applauded.

"We want to find a home in the A. F. L. for the longshoremen that is consistent with the moral standards of this organization," Mr. Meany said. Then he added:

"But we have an obligation to keep this organization abreast of its responsibilities as an important part of the social and economic strength of our country. We have a duty to the longshoremen and to the other members of the A. F. L. to bring into being a new union in which the longshoremen can hold their heads high and face the world. It is a difficult task, but it must be done."

Ryan left for New York less than an hour after the vote, but other I. L. A. officers stayed in St. Louis. There were unconfirmed reports that some of the Ryan associates intended to oust him as president and move to replace him with Capt. William V. Bradley, now an I. L. A. vice president and head of the local representing tugboat employes in New York Harbor.

PRESIDENT INVOKES TAFT ACT IN MOVE TO END PIER STRIKE; MEN DUE BACK NEXT WEEK

BAN TO RUN 80 DAYS

Dewey Urges Shippers to Aid Clean-Up by Not Accepting Old Union

By A. H. RASKIN

President Eisenhower invoked the national emergency provisions of the Taft-Hartley Act yesterday to halt the coast-wide dock strike, and leaders of the crime-spattered International Longshoremen's Association promised that they would send the 50,000 strikers back to work as soon as a formal no-strike order was issued next Monday or Tuesday.

The delay necessitated by the fact-finding requirements of the labor law made it certain that the great Port of New York and smaller harbors from Portland, Me., to Newport News, Va., would remain shut to commerce over the weekend, but the economic loss will be held down by the virtual certainty that the tie-up will end in a few days.

When the injunction is issued, it will compel the pier workers to stay on the job for eighty days. If the tangled waterfront situation has not been unraveled by the end of that truce period, the men would be free to start a new strike about Christmas.

President Acts At Noon

The President acted just twelve hours after a midnight walkout had halted all loading and unloading operations, except on military troopships. Two giant luxury liners, maneuvering without the aid of tugs, nosed safely into North River piers just before sunrise, but passengers had to trundle their own baggage with such help as they could get from white-collar employes doubling as longshoremen.

Thousands of policemen patrolled the docks all along the Eastern Seaboard, alert for clashes between rival unionists,

but there was less trouble on the waterfront than on a normal Sunday.

The setting for the President's injunction move, the first he has made since he entered the White House eight months ago, was radically different from that attending any previous Federal intervention in a critical labor situation.

The usual aim of a Federal injunction is to give Government mediators time to bring about a peaceful agreement between management and union representatives. In the case of the crippling waterfront strike, high officials make no secret of their conviction that it would not be in the public interest for the shipping companies to enter into any new contract with the I. L. A., which was expelled from the American Federation of Labor and made the chief target of laws adopted by New York and New Jersey and approved by Congress to drive racketeers from the waterfront.

Governor Dewey Gives Views

This feeling was put into words officially for the first time yesterday by Governor Dewey as he arrived here to confer with heads of the new union the A. F. L. has chartered to wipe out the old I. L. A. The Governor, who played a prominent part in the President's decision to press for a no-strike order, said he would be "shocked" if the employers signed a new contract with the old union.

"I am greatly interested that the shipowners do not sign up with the old, racket-controlled union," the Governor asserted. "It would make our job much more difficult; our job is to clean out the gangsters and racketeers from the waterfront. It's a big, tough and complicated job and one that will take time. It will make it much harder if the steamship companies sign up with the old I. L. A."

The Governor's statement drew an angry retort from Patrick J. (Packy) Connolly, executive vice president of the striking union.

"The Governor is talking out of both sides of his face," Mr. Connolly declared. "Only last week he had a man from the State

Mediation Board sitting in on our negotiations trying to get us to settle; now he tells the employers never to settle with us. I don't think it is right for the Governor to butt into a union's affairs. What does he want us to do—stay on strike for six months while the National Labor Relations Board tries to decide which union the men want, if it ever gets around to holding elections?"

Mr. Connolly challenged the new union, which operates under the same name of the old union, to prove that it had the support of 30 per cent of the dock workers in New York or other major ports, the minimum percentage required to back up a petition for new elections. He estimated that the A. F. L. could not muster the signatures of 2 per cent of the dock workers at this time.

A contrary view of the A. F. L.'s chances of dislodging the old union was taken by Dave Beck, president of the International Brotherhood of Teamsters and a member of the five-man trusteeship committee set up by the federation to run the new union until it gets on its own feet.

After he and Paul Hall, secretary-treasurer of the Atlantic and Gulf District of the Seafarers International Union, had met with the Governor and M. S. Pitzele, chairman of the State Mediation Board, Mr. Beck said the old union was "rotten to the core" and would "fall of its own weight" when an election was held.

Mr. Beck conceded that the eighty-day cooling-off period would give the new union more time to get its story across to the dock workers and would relieve it of the necessity for seeking to organize in the face of a strike.

"The A. F. L. is in this situation to help the longshoremen help themselves," Mr. Beck declared. "We desire nothing from this but a clean, strong union run by the longshoremen themselves and not operated as an instrument of exploitation by racketeers and musclemen."

The A. L. F. group pledged its cooperation with the Bi-State Waterfront Commission appointed to enforce the new waterfront reform laws. The old I. L. A. has begun a court suit to have the laws declared unconstitutional and thus prohibit the commission from carrying out its assignment of eliminating corruption on the docks.

Mr. Beck and Mr. Hall will meet, perhaps today, with the two members of the commission—Lieut.

Gen. George P. Hays of New York and Maj. Gen. Edward C. Rose of New Jersey — to coordinate the clean-up efforts of the bi-state agency and the A. F. L.

Registrations Pour In

One indication that the I. L. A.'s grip on its membership was slipping was in a report by the commission that it had received a first-day response of 2,350 signed application forms from longshoremen wanting to register for pier employment. After Dec. 1 no longshoreman may legally work on the docks unless he has registered, but the I. L. A. has advised its members not to sign the application forms. The A. F. L. union has asked the commission for 10,000 forms to be distributed among its members on the piers.

In Philadelphia, two I. L. A. leaders announced that they had swung over to the A. F. L. group. One was Joseph F. Trainor, president of the district council representing all I. L. A. locals in the port, and the other was Jack Banks, president of Local 1291.

The strike offered no test of strength between the rival unions in New York or other centers because the A. F. L. made it plain before the walkout that it would make no attempt to cross picket lines or work piers during the tie-up.

There was some tension yesterday morning at docks under A. F. L. control, but this evaporated as soon as the I. L. A. pickets learned that there would be no work calls.

A swarm of fifty pickets invaded the West Forty-fourth Street pier as the American Export liner Constitution came in unescorted. They were incensed by the help the ship's passengers were getting from office employes of the line in carting off their baggage. However, the men went away quietly after the police warned them that mob tactics would not be tolerated.

The Association of American Railroads imposed an embargo on export freight, except for items that could be loaded without the aid of longshoremen, and truck operators imposed a similar ban on deliveries to and from the docks during the strike. The I. L. A. considered ordering a sympathy walkout by its members in waterfront warehouses, but decided against this course. Towboat employes, who belong to the I. L. A., did refuse to work, and their employers started legal proceedings to force them back to work.

The President's invocation of the Taft-Hartley Act took the form of appointment of a board of inquiry, consisting of David L. Cole, former director of the Federal Mediation and Conciliation Service; Dr. Harry J. Carman, dean emeritus of Columbia College, and the Rev. Dennis J. Comey, Philadelphia "waterfront priest."

The board, which will hold its first hearing at the Governor Clinton Hotel here tomorrow morning, must report to the President not later than midnight Monday. On the basis of its report, he is expected to ask Attorney General Herbert Brownell to apply for an eighty-day injunction. The order would be signed by a Federal judge and would be effective as soon as signed.

Speaking for the I. L. A., Mr. Connolly said it would order its members back to their jobs when the injunction became effective. He turned down a request from Clyde M. Mills, deputy director of the Federal Mediation Service, that the men be asked to return without waiting for the intermediate steps required by the law.

The New York Shipping Association, which had urged the President to act, called the invocation of the injunctive machinery "a great forward step toward rendering a tremendous public service."

The association's conference committee will meet this morning and may have something to say about the Governor's demand that it sign no new agreement with the I. L. A.

Strike Ostensibly Over Pay

The ostensible cause of the strike was a deadlock over wages and other contract terms. The I. L. A. had asked, in its "final" demand, for an increase of 10 cents in the old basic wage of $2.27 an hour,

plus an additional employer payment of 3 cents an hour for workers. The employers had refused to go beyond 8½ cents an hour in wage and welfare improvements.

Originally the union had been seeking 50 cents an hour in wages and 10 cents in welfare, but it scaled its total demand down to 10 cents last week, just twenty-four hours after it had been ousted from the A. F. L.

The strike went into effect with Joseph P. Ryan, lifetime president of the old union, still a patient in French Hospital, where he is under observation for a liver ailment. Well-supported reports continued to circulate that Ryan, who is under indictment on charges of looting the union treasury, would never return to active leadership of the organization. Capt. William V. Bradley, an I. L. A. vice president and head of the towboat division, is expected to succeed him.

THE PRESIDENT'S ORDER

Whereas there exist certain labor disputes between employers (or associations by which such employers are represented in collective bargaining conferences) who are (1) steamship companies or who are engaged as operators or agents for ships engaged in service from or to North Atlantic ports from Hampton Roads, Va., to Portland, Me., or from or to other ports of the United States or its territories or possessions, (2) contracting stevedores, (3) contracting marine carpenters, or (4) other employers engaged in related or associated pier activities, and certain of their employes represented by the International Longshoremen's Association; and

Whereas in my opinion such disputes have resulted in a strike affecting a substantial part of

the maritime industry, an industry engaged in trade, commerce, transportation, transmission or communication among the several states with foreign nations, which strike, if permitted to continue will imperil the national health and safety:

Now, therefore, by virtue of the authority vested in me by Section 206 of the Labor-Management Relations Act, 1947, (public law 101, Eightieth Congress) I hereby create a board of inquiry, consisting of such members as I shall appoint, to inquire into the issues involved in such disputes.

The board shall have powers and duties as set forth in Title II of the said Act. The board shall report to the President in accordance with the provisions of Section 206 of the said Act on or before Oct. 5, 1953.

Upon the submission of its report, the board shall continue in existence to perform such other functions as may be required under the said Act until the board is terminated by the President.

October 2, 1953

A. F. L. ENDS FIGHT ON DOCK ELECTION

Drops Protest, Shuts Offices —Ranks Returning to I.L.A.

By A. H. RASKIN

The American Federation of Labor's dock union scrapped last night its announced plan to protest last week's indecisive waterfront election.

This action came as the federation closed its special longshore headquarters here and prepared to put its pier union on a skeleton footing for the next two years.

The federation did not concede that it had lost the National Labor Relations Board poll, but the dismantling of its campaign

organization made it plain that it had virtually abandoned hope of keeping the old International Longshoremen's Association from being certified as sole bargaining agent for 25,000 workers in the Port of New York.

Some of the men who left the old union to become paid organizers for the new one did not wait for their lay-off notices. They informed Capt. William V. Bradley, president of the I. L. A., that they wanted to return and bring their following with them.

Heading the group was Willie DeNoble, the new union's chief organizer in New Jersey and vice president of its port committee. Mr. DeNoble, who had received $150 a week and expenses for his work with the federation, said 98 per cent of the A. F. L. members in Jersey City and Hoboken were ready to return to the old union.

"They see the handwriting on the wall," he declared. "They say the I. L. A. has won two elections and they want no more of this bickering. The rank-and-file longshoreman is the real sufferer from all these contests. All he wants is one strong union and a chance to work."

His views were echoed by five other former A. F. L. organizers from Jersey City and Hoboken— his brother, Ernest DeNoble; John Romano, Nicholas Napolitano, Leonard Ladagona and Nunzi Molfetti.

Captain Bradley gave assurances that all rank-and-file dock workers would be welcomed back into the I. L. A. without discrimination in job or welfare benefits. He extended a similar welcome to the DeNoble brothers and their associates, but drew the line at any return by former I. L. A. officials who had bolted to the new union.

Specifically blacklisted by Captain Bradley were John Dwyer, port chairman of the A. F. L. group; Vincent and John Erato, Sigmund (Whitey) Brovarski, Frank Nawrocki and John J. (Gene) Sampson. The I. L. A. leader said all the former officials in the list had "failed to produce" for either union.

"Regardless of what the N. L. R. B. or Governor Dewey intend to do, the rank and file of longshoremen are going to stick to the I. L. A.," Captain Bradley said. "With a little cooperation from the press and public, we can build a good, honorable organization in this port."

The federation's detailed pro-

gram for scaling down its waterfront organization here will be worked out at a meeting of the new union's trustees in Washington today. Ace M. Keeney, executive director of the group, has closed his offices in the Plymouth Hotel and is expected to return to his former duties with the International Association of Machinists.

The decision not to file objections to last week's election was made on instructions from the A. F. L. in Washington. One high federation official said his group was certain that the I. L. A. would win the right to sign a new two-year contract with the shipping employers.

What the A. F. L. expects is that the old union will discredit itself by reverting to all the malpractices exposed by the State Crime Commission, thus giving the federation a chance to win control two years hence. By dropping its plan to try to upset the election, the federation lessened the chances of strikes and labor unrest here this year.

In last week's balloting, the I. L. A. received 9,110 votes to 8,791 for the A. F. L., with 1,752 ballots challenged. No victor will be certified until the board has passed on the challenges, a process that will begin today.

June 4, 1954

293

I.L.A. REINSTATED BY MERGED LABOR

Prodigal Pier Union Gets a Charter, and Is Placed on Two Years' Probation

By JACQUES NEVARD

The International Longshoremen's Association was welcomed back into the House of Labor yesterday, ending an exile of six years, one month and twenty-seven days.

George Meany, president of the American Federation of Labor and Congress of Industrial Organizations, presented a charter of affiliation to Capt. William V. Bradley, president of the pier union.

Mr. Meany was president of the old American Federation of Labor when that organization voted on Sept. 22, 1953, to revoke the sixty-year-old charter of the I. L. A. after public disclosures of crime and corruption on the New York waterfront. The ouster was voted after the I. L. A. had ignored repeated warnings to clean its house.

Standing by Mr. Meany during yesterday's brief ceremony at the Commodore Hotel were the four high officials of the merged labor movement who ruled last summer that the orphaned pier union had cleansed itself sufficiently to warrant another chance.

They were Richard F. Walsh, president of the International Alliance of Theatrical Stage Employes; David Dubinsky, president of the International Ladies Garment Workers Union; Joseph Curran, president of the National Maritime Union, and Jacob S. Potofsky, president of the Amalgamated Clothing Workers of America.

The four-man committee, headed by Mr. Walsh, reported to the A. F. L.-C. I. O. executive council on Aug. 17 that the pier union was "in substantial compliance" with the 1953 housecleaning directives and that further compliance could best be attained by allowing the I. L. A. to enter the merged movement.

The executive council endorsed the committee's recommendation, and on Sept. 22, at its annual convention in San Francisco, the labor movement authorized the admission of the pier union on a two-year probationary basis.

Two Unions Merge

The I. L. A. had already completed a referendum in which its members voted to accept admission, if it should be offered. The only remaining obstacle to affiliation—the existence of the International Brotherhood of Longshoremen—was cleared on Oct. 31, when that union voted to merge with the I. L. A.

The brotherhood, most of whose 14,000 members work at Great Lakes ports, was set up by the old A. F. L. in 1953 in a vain effort to win the coastal port members away from the exiled pier union.

Another man on hand for yesterday's ceremony was Peter M. McGavin, Mr. Meany's assistant, who will supervise the 75,000-member I. L. A. during its probationary period.

In a press conference that followed the formal presentation of the charter Mr. Meany said that while he had the right for the next two years to send Mr. McGavin to I. L. A. executive board meetings, he did not now plan to do so.

Instead, he said, Mr. McGavin will rely on I. L. A. officials for his information, unless there are specific problems to be looked into.

Mr. Meany told reporters that there were still "two or three items" to be cleared up by the I. L. A., but he refused to say what they were.

Later in the day the I. L. A. resumed negotiations on a new contract with waterfront employers here. At the end of the day no progress was reported, and the two sides were expected to meet again early next week.

The dockers are working at piers along the East and Gulf Coasts under a Taft-Hartley Act injunction that halted an eight-day strike last month. The injunction will expire Dec. 27.

November 19, 1959

BILL BANNING UNION RACKETS IS SIGNED BY THE PRESIDENT; INTERSTATE EVILS OUTLAWED

HOBBS BILL IS LAW

Truman Says Measure Does Not Infringe on Labor's Rights

'GREAT SAFEGUARDS' HOLD

President Cites Railway Act, Norris-La Guardia, Wagner and Parts of Clayton Laws

By WALTER H. WAGGONER
Special to THE NEW YORK TIMES.

WASHINGTON, July 3—President Truman signed today the so-called Hobbs bill aimed at curbing "racketeering" by labor unions by making it a felony, carrying a fine up to $10,000 or imprisonment for as long as twenty years, or both, for any person to commit robbery or extortion which in any way "obstructs, delays or affects" interstate commerce.

In a special message to Congress delivered just before he left for an extended holiday, the President explained that he felt justified in approving the measure, H. R. 32, which has had a long and controversial record, he having been advised that the act in no way denied to labor organizations their rights "in carrying out their legitimate objectives."

Major Labor Laws Stand

Mr. Truman asserted also that he had been advised by Tom C. Clark, Attorney General, that nothing in the bill could be construed "to repeal, modify or affect" provisions or protective features of such other major pieces of labor legislation as the Railway Labor Act, the Norris-La Guardia Act, the Wagner Act, and some sections of the Clayton Act.

Mr. Truman described these measures as "the great legislative safeguards which the Congress has established for the protection of labor in the exercise of its fundamental rights."

Attorney General Clark also informed him, continued the President, that the bill was not intended to deprive labor of any of its recognized rights, "including the right to strike and to picket, and to take other legitimate and peaceful concerted action."

Case Bill Veto Recalled

Mr. Truman declared that he approved the terms of the bill only after they had been separated from the Case Bill which he vetoed on June 11. He stated then of Section 7, which contained the provisions of the Hobbs Bill, that he was "in full accord" with those specific terms.

"Section 11 of the Case Bill," the President added, "seriously weakened the protection afforded to labor by the Norris-La Guardia Act and correspondingly crippled the exceptions contained in Section 7 of the Case Bill. The present Act, standing alone, is not subject to this objection."

The bill as it was made into law this afternoon by the President's signature has the general purpose of preventing interference with interstate commerce by robbery or extortion. Representative Sam Hobbs of Alabama, author of the bill, reported on Feb. 27, 1945, that the measure also aimed at preventing interference "during the war" with transportation of troops war supplies or mail in interstate or foreign commerce.

The bill is a successor to H. R 6872, of the Seventy-seventh Congress in 1944, on which hearings were held by the Committee on the Judiciary to H. R. 7067, which was favorably reported by the committee in that year, and to H. R. 653 of the Seventy-eighth Congress. The last was favorably reported by the committee and passed in the House, but was not acted upon in the Senate.

Statement by Department

Attorney General Clark told reporters this morning that he had discussed the bill with Mr Truman about a week ago. The Department of Justice issued a statement late this afternoon which said:

"The Attorney General informed the President that Title III and the bill as a whole must be construed in the light of interpretative statemens made during the Congressional debate or the measure. These statements, he said, indicated "a clear legislative intent that the bill should not apply to legitimate union activity and the exercise of any of labor's fundamental rights."

Among the statements cited by Mr. Hobbs, who sated that Title II "exempts from the operation of the law any conduct under the anti-trust statutes, under the NIRE act, under the Norris-La Guardia statute, the Railway Labor Act, the Big Four that have been termed the Magna Carta of Labor.

Complaint Against Teamsters

The origins of the Hobbs bill are found in practices by members of the teamsters' union who were reported to have committed acts of violence against truckers crossing from New Jersey to New York, for the purpose of exacting fees from the drivers said to correspond to a day's wage under the union scale.

A suit was filed on the basis of an anti-racketeering bill enacted in 1934. That statute came under the scrutiny of the United States Supreme Court in October, 1941, in the case United States v. Local 807. In a decision handed down on March 2, 1942, the court ruled 6 to 1, with the late Chief Justice Harlan F. Stone dissenting, that the union was exempt from the 1934 statute.

Mr. Truman's statement to Congress approving the Hobbs bill was as follows:

"I have today approved H.R. 32 the so-called Hobbs bill. This measure makes it a felony for any person to commit robbery or extortion which in any way obstructs, delays or affects interstate commerce or the movement of any article or commodity in interstate commerce.

"This bill corresponds in terms to Section 7 of H.R. 4908, the Case bill, which I returned on June 11, 1946, without my approval. In my message of June 11 I stated that I was in full accord with the objectives of Section 7 of the Case bill. I added that 'some question may arise from the fact that Section 7 omits from the original act the provision that it was not to be construed so as to "impair, diminish" or in any manner affect the rights of bona fide labor organizations in lawfully carrying out the legitimate objects thereof." '

"The measure now comes before me as a separate enactment, rather than as one provision of the Case bill.

"Section 11 of the Case bill seriously weakened the protection afforded to labor by the Norris-La Guardia act and correspondingly crippled the specific exceptions contained in Section 7 of the Case bill. The present act, standing alone, is not subject to this objection.

Attorney General's Views

"The Attorney General advises me that the present bill does not in any way interfere with the rights of unions in carrying out their legitimate objectives. He bases this conclusion upon the language of the bill, as a separate measure, and upon the legislative history.

"He makes reference in particular to Title II of the bill. That title provides that nothing in the bill shall be construed to repeal, modify, or affect the Railway Labor Act, the Norris-La Guardia act, the Wagner act, and specified sections of the Clayton act, i. e., the great legislative safeguards which the Congress has established for the protection of labor in the exercise of its fundamental rights.

"The Attorney General also advises that the legislative history shows that the bill is not intended to deprive labor of any of its recognized rights, including the right to strike and to picket, and to take other legitimate and peaceful concerted action.

"Under this understanding I am approving the bill."

July 4, 1946

RACKETS DETECTED IN UNION AID FUNDS

Insurance Agents Linked to the Underworld Found Getting Excessive Commissions

By A. H. RASKIN

Concerned over reports that insurance agents with underworld ties are siphoning off hundreds of thousands of dollars a year in excess commissions and service fees, District Attorney Frank S. Hogan is preparing to crack down on rackets in the administration of union-management welfare funds.

Other public and private law-enforcement organizations also are directing their attention to the elimination of abuses that have crept into the operation of funds set up to provide workers and their families with adequate insurance against the financial hazards of sickness, accident and death.

A survey by THE NEW YORK TIMES indicated that the giant welfare funds in such mass industries as steel, automobiles, mining and men's and women's clothing were untouched by any suggestion of racketeering, but the suspicion of kickbacks, payroll-padding and favoritism in the placement of insurance contracts existed in an increasing number of small funds in various parts of the country.

The volume of tainted welfare insurance is microscopic when considered against the total of $2,591,-000,000 in premiums paid for all forms of group insurance last year. Yet even a surface check indicates that several million dollars each year in employer-financed welfare contributions are being expended in ways that make no visible contribution to the security of the workers they are supposed to protect.

The New York City Anti-Crime Committee, headed by former Assistant Secretary of State Spruille Braden, has spent more than a year looking into some phases of welfare rackets. Its conclusion is that gangsters and their henchmen in union ranks are finding a safer and more lucrative field for their acquisitive instincts in welfare funds than in shakedowns of employers or workers.

The Case of One Agency

Support for this theory comes from the example of one insurance agency, which handles the placement of welfare premiums for twenty-two comparatively small unions in the metropolitan area. This agency reportedly received nearly $300,000 in fees last year on an annual business of slightly over $2,000,000 in employer-financed welfare payments.

The books of this agency already have been subpoenaed by the District Attorney, and his rackets bureau is trying to discover why so much business went to the agency when other brokers could have supplied the same service without skimming so much of the cream off for themselves.

The District Attorney also wants to know whether anyone was sharing in the "take" besides the men licensed to write insurance in the agency. Under the State Insurance Law, it is illegal for agents to split their commissions with persons who bring them the business, but the "business expenses" listed by the agency are so big that a number of invisible partners could have lived well on them.

The disparity between the fees some funds pay and those others consider adequate is indicated by comparing the amounts collected by the agency that is under the District Attorney's scrutiny with those charged by one of the largest and most reputable union-management consultants, Martin E. Segal & Co.

The Segal company, which places $60,000,000 a year in welfare premiums, retains about 1 per cent of that amount, as against the nearly 15 per cent kept by the investigated agency.

On the New York milk industry fund, which involves premiums of $1,800,000 a year, the fee collected by the Segal agency is $11,000. The largest fund handled by the other agency involves $1,400,000 in annual premiums, the agency getting $150,000 of that amount.

State Insurance Head Acts

Alfred J. Bohlinger, State Superintendent of Insurance, has been keeping a watchful eye on the development of the welfare business, which has had a mushroom growth in the last five years. As part of his effort to wipe out the possibilities for "bleeding" the funds through excessive charges, he has called all New York companies involved in the writing of group insurance to a conference July 16 to discuss the establishing of tighter rules on service fees. The meeting will be held at 2 P. M. in his office, 61 Broadway.

The call went out after the Insurance Department had informed one large company that it felt the company was being too open-handed with the policyholders' money in paying a blanket agency commission of 10 per cent on welfare premiums and rebating an additional 5 per cent to be used by the administrators of the funds to pay for "services that would otherwise have to be performed in the company's home offices."

The company agreed to notify its agent that the 5 per cent service fee would have to be eliminated, and it is expected that the new contracts will provide for a corresponding reduction in the premium rate paid by the funds. The department has no power to force a cut in commissions. However, it often succeeds in persuading companies to adjust these and other charges when it is convinced that they are out of line with proper protection for the policyholder.

The conference in Superintendent Bohlinger's office next week will be concerned specifically with the rewriting or cancellation of a ruling issued by the department a year ago under which companies were authorized to make allowances for services they would otherwise have to perform themselves.

But the discussion is expected to encompass all other phases of group insurance operation with a view to closing the door against rackets of the type Mr. Hogan and the New York City Anti-Crime Committee have been looking into.

The general philosophy of the Insurance Department was summed up by Mr. Bohlinger in these words:

"In connection with group coverages, this department is alert to possible abuses and seeks to correct them at all times to the end that the policyholder gets the maximum benefit consistent with sound business operation. Whenever we have detected irregularities, immediate steps have been taken to correct them.

"The vast majority of insurance carriers show a sincere interest in conducting their business in such a way that the public interest and the welfare of the policyholder will both be protected."

Employers Usually Stand Aside

Most welfare funds operate under joint employer-union trusteeship, but in many funds the employer representatives are content to exercise a passive role for fear of incurring union illwill.

The study by the Anti-Crime Committee indicated that abuses were most prevalent in unions that had close connections with the underworld. The committee expressed hope that the efforts of the top leadership of the American Federation of Labor and the Congress of Industrial Organizations to drive corrupt elements out of positions of union influence would of itself do much to prevent the victimizing of welfare funds from spreading.

The committee asserted that certain unions in this area, controlling more than $2,000,000 a year in premiums, were placing all their insurance through an agency dominated by Abner (Longie) Zwillman, New Jersey racketeer. The committee also charged that a Chicago unionist, often linked to gangster elements, had been responsible for funneling $10,000,000 a year in welfare premiums into an agency headed by his son.

According to the anti-crime group's study, some unionists were helping racketeers get new union charters on the promise that their welfare business, would be channeled to favored agents. The committee said kick-backs from insurance fees were "the biggest source of graft" now open in the union field.

One insurance company head reported that his organization had lost a welfare account because a competitor agreed to put two union officers on the company payroll at salaries of $12,000 to $15,000 a year.

Graft on Eyeglasses

Even on such comparatively small items as the purchase of eyeglasses with welfare funds, opportunities for graft present themselves and are being seized by a few union leaders. Companies offering payoffs have been able to win over several New York locals, even though the per capita cost of their service is almost triple that charged by the original contract supplier.

In contrast to the record made by such groups, most unions have taken pains to keep their welfare funds from turning into gravy trains and have been concerned solely with getting the most substantial benefits possible for their members. The result of their stewardship and the vast rise in the volume of employer-financed welfare programs has been a steady expansion in the area of protection and a steady cut in the cost of coverage.

A survey by the Life Insurance Association of America showed that group life insurance now covers 22,873,000 workers and 573,-000 dependents for a total of $62,-889,200,000. The premiums on this insurance came to $727,500,000 last year, a growth of 80 per cent in five years.

Group accident and health coverage showed an even more meteoric growth. The combined premiums for such protection came to more than $1,000,000,000 last year, against $306,200,000 in 1947. Experts in the field report that premium rates and the percentage of the premium dollar retained by the insurance companies has dropped sharply in the same period.

Many funds now operate on the basis of a total retention by the insurance company of 3 to 7 per cent. Out of its share the company must take care of taxes, commissions and overhead. In other funds, however, the retention rate runs as high as 20 per cent.

U.S., Canadian Union Dues Exceed Half Billion a Year

By A. H. RASKIN

Unions in this country and Canada have a combined income of more than $500,000,000 a year, a research study disclosed yesterday. The year-long survey, compiled by the National Industrial Conference Board, represented the most comprehensive analysis ever made of union constitutions and dues structures. Only three unions, all racket-tainted, refused to cooperate with the private research agency in its study.

The board reported that a total of 194 unions with a membership of 17,500,000 collected a minimum of $457,000,000 annually in dues payments. No specific tabulation was made on how much more the unions received in initiation fees and assessments. However, James J. Bambrick, director of the study, said these payments would bring the total "well above the half-billion mark."

The report indicated that dues collections were divided almost evenly between the locals and their parent unions. The board estimated that per capita taxes to the internationals cost the locals $228,000,000 a year. This left the locals $229,000,000 with which to meet their own obligations.

The average dues payment for the individual union member was put at $26.14 a year. This compared with an average current factory wage of $78.69 a week. In some cases dues were as low as $1 a month. The highest scale reported was $25 a month for airline pilots earning more than $19,000 a year.

Initation fees varied from 65 cents to $250, with the top entrance charges enforced in the skilled trades. Seven unions were found to have constitutional prohibitions against initiation fees, and most were in the $2 to $5 range.

The survey covered 139 unions affiliated with the merged American Federation of Labor and Congress of Industrial Organizations, plus fifty-five independent unions. The groups have 16,000,000 members in the United States, or 98 per cent of the national total. Their 1,000,000 Canadian members represent three-quarters of the organized workers there.

Among the highlights of the 120-page report were these:

¶Unions with 10,500,000 members have constitutions requiring a membership vote before a strike. Unions with 6,000,000 members require that the strike vote be taken by secret ballot.

¶Most unions compel locals to obtain authorization from the international office before a strike can be called. Thirteen unions, representing Government workers, have a constitutional ban on strikes.

¶More than one-third of the union members belong to unions that exclude Communists or other subversives. The constitution of John L. Lewis' United Mine Workers also bars members of the United States Chamber of Commerce, the Ku-Klux Klan and the Industrial Workers of the World.

¶Thirty-five unions with 3,000,000 members bar supervisors, employers and others who have the power to hire or fire. A few constitutions exclude stockholders in a company from union membership, but with the spread of employe stock ownership these provisions are becoming dead letters.

¶Only five unions with 442,000 members still have constitutional clauses barring workers on racial grounds. These include four independent railroad unions and an association of postal transport workers. Thirty-nine unions have specific guarantees that all qualified workers will be let in without regard for race or national origin.

The report contains an extended analysis of union disciplinary and election procedures. The board refrained from making any judgments or conclusions of its own.

The three unions that refused even to supply copies of their constitutions were the International Longshoremen's Association, the Hod Carriers, Building and Common Laborers International Union, and the Distillery, Rectifying and Wine Workers Union.

The pier union was expelled from the A. F. L. two years ago on charges of racket domination. The others, both affiliates of the unified labor movement, have frequently been critcized by official bodies.

The bulk of the 3,400 subscribers to the studies made by the National Industrial Conference Board are business and financial organizations. However, the board includes thirty-five unions among its subscribers and a large number of colleges.

Assisting Mr. Bambrick in the study was George H. Haas. Mr. Bambrick is the board's labor relations specialist and Mr. Haas is his aide.

December 21, 1955

RACKETS AND CRIME LINKED IN RIESEL CASE

By STANLEY LEVEY

The case involving the blinding last April 5 of labor columnist Victor Riesel has focused attention on the rackets in New York's garment industry. What follows is a description of the industry, the rackets fastened upon it, and the theories now advanced as to how these rackets might have brought about the Riesel crime.

Is it any wonder that the eyes of a racketeer glitter when he thinks of New York's fabulous garment industry? It is the biggest in city and state, employing 300,000 persons, producing three-quarters of the garments worn by American women. It is composed of 4,000 fiercely competitive manufacturers. The wholesale value of its product comes to $4,000,000,000 a year.

Most of the plants are organized by the International Ladies Garment Workers Union, a substantial and forward-looking group with 200,000 members in New York. But there are clusters of nonunion shops in Manhattan, Brooklyn, New Jersey and Pennsylvania.

Because of its scattered form of organization, the garment industry is heavily dependent on trucking. A dress pattern may be cut in a jobber's loft, trucked to a contractor or manufacturer for finishing and returned to the jobber for sale to the retailer. In New York, garment truck workers belong to Local 102 of the I. L. G. W. U.

The garment industry and the garment union have benefited from good relations for many years. Strikes are few and production is efficient. But costs are high. The union has improved wage levels over the years and it has won health and welfare benefits that are paid entirely by the employers.

Some manufacturers would obviously prefer not to go along with these union conditions. Some do not. A few have fled to the hinterland and the union has pursued them and forced them to fall into line. But a number has remained outside the union fold both in New York and out of it.

This state of affairs is tailor-made for racketeering. Let's take an imaginary jobber in New York—unionized or not. He would like to cut his costs and increase his profits. So he decides to send his material for manufacturing to a non-union contractor or manufacturer (the terms are generally interchangeable). He may even own all or a part of the non-union plant.

The link between the jobber and the contractor is obviously the trucker. Now things get really complicated. The trucker may own a piece of the jobber, the contractor or both. In some cases the jobber may not know —and probably doesn't want to know—where his goods are going and the contractor may not know whose patterns he is assembling.

The racketeer linking the two sections of the garment industry by means of his trucks thus has two main objectives. One is to keep either or both ends of the manufacturing process non-union. The second is to maintain iron control over the trucking unions to which his drivers belong.

Avoiding Unions

There are two ways to keep a union out of a plant. One is to strongarm it out with help of goons and hoodlums. Racketeers have ample manpower on which to draw for this technique. The other is to set up a "kept" or dummy union, subservient to the racketeer.

But to form a dummy union and to give it a reasonably accurate relationship to the real article, a racketeer must be less muscular and more cerebral. So, he either captures a legitimate union or gets someone to issue him a charter in a going and recognized organization. With either of these types of unions a racketeer can sell protection to an employer who wishes either to avoid organization or to rid himself of a decent labor group. The going rate for this kind of service is high.

This pattern of illegality has been known generally for many years. So have the identities of most of those who implement it and profit from it. Many considerations—political power, reluctance of many business men to "blow the whistle" on anyone and simple fear—have accumulated to maintain the status quo.

Then last spring there was a stirring. Both District Attorney Frank S. Hogan and United States Attorney Paul W. Williams began to warn that the underworld was seeking to fasten its hold on the garment and trucking industries. Two New York County grand juries and two Federal panels went to work

Renewed Effort

The acid blinding of labor columnist Victor Riesel, a hard-hitting foe of Communists and labor racketeers, and the subsequent arrest of John Dioguardi, alias Johnny Dio, an ex-convict with links to both the garment and trucking rackets, appear to be at once the cause and result of this renewed effort to wipe out the mobsters.

The Federal charge against Dio and his six alleged accomplices is that they conspired to obstruct justice by preventing Mr. Riesel from appearing before the grand jury and telling the panel what he knew of the rackets. Word that the columnist would testify was made public last March. The acid attack occurred April 5.

Big New York Garment Industry
A Rich Field for the Underworld

Johnny Dio (left), with lawyer Noah Braunstein,

Abraham Telvi

Victor Riesel

How much Mr. Riesel knew that he had not already used in his columns is, of course, a matter of conjecture. But there is another way of looking at the case. Perhaps his blinding was a premeditated signal from the underworld to any and all witnesses—newspaper men, garment manufacturers, truckers, union officials et al—that a word to the wise was sufficient and that a word from the unwise would be fatal.

This interpretation perhaps means also that the various inquiries were producing important data, that the rackets were being hit in the pocketbook because of the fuss and that the

underworld had decided to act before things went too far.

The list of persons summoned for questioning by the Federal grand jury included men from all sections of the garment and trucking industries. Some were labor leaders, some graduates of the Louis (Lepke) Buchalter-Jacob (Gurrah) Shapiro-Murder Inc. school of garment racketeering, some manufacturers, some reputed gangsters. Some would have been harmed by a vigorous and relentless investigation into the rackets. Others would not have been affected.

Johnny Dio was one of the names on the list of those to be questioned. He had good cre-

dentials for being on it. He spent three years in Sing Sing from 1937 to 1940 for garment and trucking extortion. He was a mobster in his teens, a big shot in his twenties. He was a skilled man in his trade, a master of the threat, a technician with the acid bottle, a marvel at disabling trucks of uncooperative employers. He was a triple-threat, all-underworld performer at shakedown, extortion and kickback.

Trucking Union

He had other credentials no less imposing. Chief among them was his relationship to the trucking unions and the leaders of those groups. In 1950, after a decade of circumspection, Dio turned up with charters for six locals in the old United Automobile Workers Union, A. F. L. (The name of the organization has since been changed to the Allied Industrial Workers. It has no connection with Walter Reuther's auto workers union.)

Dio has always insisted that he was "legit" as a labor leader; he even spent a large sum of his own money trying to organize taxicab workers here. Ultimately he lost the auto locals, but not for long. They turned up next — hastily chartered — at a time when a major battle was under way for control of the powerful Teamsters Joint Council here.

Dio is an old and respected friend of John J. O'Rourke, president of Local 282 of the Teamsters, who was seeking to unseat Martin T. Lacey as president of the council. He is also a friend of James R. Hoffa, vice president and Midwest boss of the Teamsters, who has sought to take over the union organization in the East and who was generally credited with being the power behind Mr. O'Rourke.

Stacking Attempt

The six Dio locals, it was alleged by the Lacey forces, were to be the means by which the O'Rourke camp hoped to stack the council election and control Teamster activities in the metropolitan area.

Last June Dio and a lieutenant of one of the old auto (now Teamster) locals were indicted for trying to sell labor peace for a price, by using the dummy local to free a dissatisfied employer from the organization that had represented his workers for some years.

Further adding to Dio's credentials was alleged ownership of a number of out-of-town non-union garment shops. Mr. Hogan spoke of him as "one of the most powerful underworld figures in the field of labor."

The credentials of the six other men arrested with Dio for the conspiracy against Mr. Riesel are not so impressive, but in general they form a pattern. This is what U. S. Attorney Williams says about them:

Thomas Dioguardi, alias Tommy Dio, younger brother of Johnny Dio, is an executive of a cotton goods firm. He was arrested for assault and robbery in 1931 but the charges were dismissed.

Charles Tuso was employed by the Women's Apparel Shoulder Pad Association, which supplies shoulder pads to garment manufacturers. He has a conviction for robbery and went to Sing Sing for the same crime.

Dominico Bando, alias Nick Bando, a bakery worker, has an arrest record and a prison sentence for violating the narcotics law.

Charles Carlino, alias Charlie Woppie, has a record going back to 1933 for felonious assault and attempted robbery. He was described as the payoff man in the Riesel case.

Hired Hoodlum

Joseph Peter Carlino, not related to Charles Carlino, was described by the United States Attorney as a longtime member of the garment rackets. He was the contact man who hired Abraham Telvi, a smalltime East Side hoodlum, to throw the acid at Mr. Riesel. Telvi's body was found on July 28 with a bullet in the head.

Gondolfo Miranti was the fingerman who pointed out Mr. Riesel to Telvi. He has four arrests, one for possession of burglar tools, and one conviction.

There are still many questions to be asked and answered in the Riesel case. Why did Dio take the risk of ordering an acid attack on a newspaper man? Will the incident prevent witnesses from talking? How deeply will the United States Attorney be able to dig into the garment and trucking rackets? Can the case against Dio and Company be made to stick? What are the chances of a trial in the state courts for the actual acid throwing—and possibly murder?

A few years ago, the murder of Tommy Lewis, Bronx boss of the Building Service Employes International Union, blew the lid off rackets in welfare funds and harness racing. It led to a broad inquiry that had profound political overtones. It is conceivable that the Riesel case may finally expose to public view—and conviction—the human termites that have infested the garment and trucking industries.

September 2, 1956

Labor Council Tells Unions To Oust Chiefs Using Fifth

By A. H. RASKIN
Special to The New York Times.

MIAMI BEACH, Jan. 28—The united labor movement officially decreed today that union leaders who invoked the Fifth Amendment in Government investigations into racketeering had no right to hold their jobs.

The decision was a sweeping rebuke to the International Brotherhood of Teamsters, largest and most powerful affiliate of the merged federation. The 1,400,000-member truck union had notified its officers and members that they would not be subject to union discipline for exercising their constitutional privilege against self-incrimination.

Dave Beck, president of the teamsters, was the only member of the Executive Council of the American Federation of Labor and Congress of Industrial Organizations to vote against the ouster policy at the opening of the council's midwinter meeting here.

Beck Plans No Change

He told reporters afterward that his organization would not curb the right of its officials to plead the Fifth Amendment even if its stand resulted in its suspension from the parent federation.

He said Government inquiries into labor abuses often turned into "inquisitions" and he warned that the A. F. L.-C. I. O. was embarking on a program full of danger for "the whole democratic way of life."

The declaration that unions should bar officials who dodged questions about corruption was a personal victory for George Meany, president of the united movement. He decided to press for general adoption of his stand when he read dispatches from Washington two weeks ago about teamster defiance of the Senate Permanent Subcommittee on Investigations.

26 Support Meany

Twenty-six of the twenty-seven council members voted for the policy statement in precisely the form in which it had been drafted by Mr. Meany. The statement now becomes an official guide for the federation's 140 international unions and its 900 directly affiliated locals. These unions have a combined membership of 15,000,000.

The international unions, which are self-governing under their charters of affiliation with the parent organization, are not compelled to adhere to the new policy. However, if they fail to do so, the federation has the right to expel them from membership. In the case of the directly affiliated locals and the federation's own subsidiary departments and councils, the rule becomes effective on a mandatory basis.

The statement was approved by the federation high command after a two-hour debate, in which Mr. Meany and Mr. Beck clashed sharply on the standards of conduct that should be required of persons in positions of union trust.

Walter P. Reuther of the United Automobile Workers, Al J. Hayes of the International Association of Machinists and Joseph A. Beirne of the Communication Workers of America, gave vigorous support to Mr. Meany.

Problem for Woll

The cleavage between the teamsters and the federation on the Fifth Amendment presents a problem for Albert J. Woll, who serves as general counsel to both organizations. Mr. Beck said his union had taken its stand on the basis of advice given by a group of fourteen attorneys, headed by Mr. Woll.

Mr. Meany has repeatedly warned his general counsel in past clashes between the parent organization and its giant affiliate that he would eventually have to decide where his loyalties lay. In the past Mr. Woll has indicated that he would prefer to stay with the federation. But A. F. L.-C. I. O. leaders said his stand in the present controversy made it unlikely that he could continue to do so.

The federation's resolution pledged full cooperation with "all proper legislative committees, law enforcement agencies and other public bodies seeking fairly and objectively to keep the labor movement or any other segment of our society free from any and all corrupt influences."

This meant, the declaration said, that all union officials should "freely and without reservation" answer all relevant questions asked by such Government agencies. The A.F.L.-C.I.O. council conceded that any person was entitled, in the exercise of his individual conscience, to the protections afforded by the Fifth Amendment.

See Peril to Unions

The union disavowed any intent to weaken this constitutional safeguard. However, it warned that tolerance in office of any leader who refused to answer questions dealing with abuse of union responsibilities might create the impression that labor sanctioned use of the amendment as "a shield against proper scrutiny into corrupt influences in the labor movement."

Mr. Meany declined to be drawn into a discussion of the propriety of the charges made by the teamsters that the Senate investigations subcommittee lacked authority to look into labor matters. The A.F.L.-C.I.O. head said it was up to the Senate to decide that issue.

He added that there could be no doubt that the special eight-man committee now being set up in the Senate through a fusion of the investigations subcommittee and the Labor Committee would be entitled to make a full study with labor cooperation.

Mr. Beck was less inclined to give unequivocal endorsement to the new committee. He said he believed the federation should have insisted that the task be assigned to the Senate Labor Committee. However, he added that the teamsters would go along with the new group unless their attorneys informed the union that it was usurping powers reserved by law to the Labor Committee.

No Blank Check

The teamster chief said his union did not intend to give a blank check to persons accused of wrongdoing. He acknowledged that there might be a few dishonest men in the truck union, but he insisted they were "a wee, small, little minority."

He declared that the teamsters did not feel it was in the interest of labor or the nation to jettison constitutional rights under the pressure of "hysteria, emotion and the desire for a good press."

"I object to crucifying our people, no matter what price I or our organization may have to pay," Mr. Beck declared. "Bad publicity doesn't mean anything to me. I've been having it for forty years, and our organization is bigger and stronger than ever."

He challenged the American Bar Association to expel lawyers who advised witnesses to take the Fifth Amendment. He said he could see no reason why unionists should be thrown out of office for exercising their constitutional rights if the bar took no action against the attorneys who suggested such action to them.

"I think the Fifth Amendment is indivisible," he declared. "You can't circumscribe the constitutional right. If it isn't right, then take the Fifth Amendment out of the Constitution."

Beck's Statement

Mr. Beck issued a statement that said:

"The policy of the International Brotherhood of Teamsters with respect to investigations by legislative committees, law-enforcement agencies and other public bodies has long been and will continue to be:

"1. Any officer or member of our organization shall have the same right as any other American citizen to invoke the privilege of the Bill of Rights without, by such act alone, subjecting himself automatically to trial or disciplinary action by our union. The action taken by the Executive Council of the A. F. L.-C. I. O. with respect to these matters does not in any way alter our position.

2. The charter grant under which the International Brotherhood operates guarantees us autonomous rights in the conduct of our internal affairs. Those rights we shall continue to exercise and defend."

Mr. Beck, in noting the autonomy guaranteed to his union by the federation's constitution, said:

"They can review what we do if they don't think we are right. They can't tell us what to do, but they can suspend us. If the A. F. L.-C. I. O. doesn't want us in, we don't want to be in."

The precise procedure to be used by other unions in enforcing the Executive Council's policy was not speeled out. However, Mr. Meany indicated that each union would be expected to set up review machinery to guard against unfairness in application of the policy.

What top unionists envisaged is a possibility that officials will be interrogated about strike payments, violence or other acts performed in the service of their organization. They feel that the ban on invocation of the Fifth Amendment is intended to cover efforts to escape personal punishment for betrayal of union trust, not to deprive unionists of protection in the conduct of strikes or other normal duties.

Local unions would be expected to pass on any use of the Fifth Amendment in individual cases, one A. F. L.-C. I. O. vice president said. If the international union is not satisfied that the policy is being carried out by the locals, it then becomes its responsibility to check. The A. F. L.-C. I. O. will be the final arbiter of enforcement.

A federation spokesman said that the announcement by the teamsters that they would not penalize officials for invoking the Fifth Amendment would bring no action against the truck union at this time. The spokesman said the federation was concerned with "actions, not words." He said that Mr. Meany and the A. F. L.-C. I. O. high command would not consider that the teamsters were in defiance until such time as a specific case presented itself.

The Teamsters Executive Board affirmed the policy laid down by Mr. Beck.

LABOR VOTES CODE TO CURB RACKETS

Council Adopts Rules Against 'Crooks' and Communists, and Graft In Aid Funds

By A. H. RASKIN
Special to The New York Times.

MIAMI BEACH, Jan. 31— Stringent codes designed to bar all forms of union racketeering were approved today for the 15,-000,000-member united labor movement.

The Executive Council of the American Federation of Labor and Congress of Industrial Organizations adopted rules for eliminating convicts and men "commonly known to be crooks or racketeers" from union office.

The codes also forbade union officials from maintaining compromising business ties and laid down rigid standards to guard against graft in welfare funds. The rules were drafted by the federation's Ethical Practices Committee, official watchdog of union morality.

The council endorsed the codes by unanimous vote. However, the head of the union that has been getting top attention in Congressional investigations into labor abuses was not present when the vote was taken.

Beck Takes a Drive

He is Dave Beck of the International Brotherhood of Teamsters. Aides said his wife, Dorothy, was not feeling well and he had decided to take her out for a drive.

Mr. Beck was the sole dissenter Monday when the council decreed that union chiefs who invoked the Fifth Amendment in Government inquiries on corruption should leave their jobs.

James R. Hoffa, vice president of the Teamsters and a dominant figure in its affairs, derided the codes in an impromptu news conference this afternoon.

Mr. Hoffa said he knew of no one in the truck union who would be affected by the new rules. He added that it would take lawyers at least two weeks to figure out what the codes meant.

Mr. Hoffa said he thought a meeting of the Teamsters' general executive board would be called to decide its official position on the yardstick established by the parent organization.

The union already has announced its intention of standing behind officials who invoke the constitutional privilege against self-incrimination in Congressional investigation, under the Fifth Amendment.

George Meany, president of the merged federation, made it plain that the rules would have the same force as the union group's basic constitution. Affiliates that defy the code or fail to crack down on violations by their locals will be subject to suspension or expulsion under this interpretation.

Mr. Meany said his own office would superintend the enforcement task. He emphasized that he would not have to wait for complaints from union members or any other source, but could initiate action if he felt the federation's mandate was being flouted.

"These codes are drafted in very, very good English," Mr. Meany declared. "They should not be hard to understand."

A rule of reason will be applied in defining racketeers under the new ban. Mr. Meany said there was no intent to oust men who were conducting themselves honorably simply because they had been convicted of a crime twenty or thirty years ago.

On the other hand, men who never had been found guilty in a legal proceeding will find themselves liable to removal under the labor commandments. Mr. Meany said unions would be expected to look into officials with racket connections, whether or not they had criminal records.

The codes are equally strict in banning Communists, Fascists and other adherents of totalitarianism. Unionists who are consistent supporters or active participants in such movements are on the prohibited list, even though they do not hold party cards.

Concern about the vagueness of the language used in the ban on "crooks and racketeers" was voiced at the council session by J. Albert Woll, general counsel for both the federation and the truck union.

A. F. L.-C. I. O. executives quoted him as expressing doubt that courts would uphold the removal of an official on the charge that he was "commonly known to be a crook or racketeer preying on the labor movement and its good name for corrupt purposes."

Mr. Meany replied that the codes were not meant for enforcement by courts of law, but by unions intent on maintaining high standards of morality for the protection of their members. The codes themselves emphasized that no inflexible standards could be established to tell who was a racketeer, and called on each union to apply common sense in enforcing the rule.

BECK USES 5TH AMENDMENT TO BALK SENATE QUESTIONS ABOUT TEAMSTERS' $322,000

4TH ALSO INVOKED

Labor Leader Ignores Subpoena — Won't Yield His Files

By JOSEPH A. LOFTUS
Special to The New York Times.

WASHINGTON, March 26— Dave Beck refused to tell a Senate committee today about his financial relations with the union he heads.

The president of the International Brotherhood of Teamsters repeatedly invoked the Fifth Amendent to the Constitution as the committee pressed him to say whether he had taken $322,-448.80 from the union treasury for his own use.

"I refuse to give testimony against myself," he declared again and again. He had been advised, he said, "of proposed criminal actions against me" for alleged income tax evasions.

In standing on the Fifth Amendment scores of times and refusing to talk, Mr. Beck was protecting himself both against such criminal actions and against possible prosecution for contempt of the Senate. If he had refused to answer questions without invoking his constitutional rights, he would have exposed himself to contempt charges.

McClellan States Case

Senator John L. McClellan, Democrat of Arkansas, chairman of the Select Committee on Improper Activities in the Labor or Management Field, stated the burden of the case against Mr. Beck at the outset. Evidence had been developed, he said, "that clearly indicates that from the years 1949 through the first three months of 1953, Mr. Beck took more than $320,000 from the Teamsters Union treasury in Seattle."

Associated Press Wirephoto

INVOKES FIFTH AMENDMENT: Dave Beck, head of International Brotherhood of Teamsters, at Senate hearing.

Mr. Beck was asked again and again about the total and a breakdown of it, but each time he fell back on his constitutional rights, relying specifically on the first three articles of the Constitution and on the Fourth and Fifth Amendments.

The Fifth Amendment protects a citizen in many areas, such as deprivation of life, liberty or property without due process of law, the seizure of private property without just compensation, and double jeopardy for the same offense. However, Mr. Beck relied specifically on the provision that no person "shall be compelled in any criminal case to be a witness against himself."

The Fourth Amendment is a protection against unreasonable searches and seizures. He brought his personal papers as requested, he said, but he refused to turn them over, even after Senator McClellan signed a subpoena in his presence calling for these papers. He relied on the two amendments and the first three articles to protect him from possible contempt action.

The first three articles detail the separation of powers among the Executive, Legislative and Judicial branches.

The union he heads is the largest in the country, possibly even in the world. Its membership ranges between 1,400,000 and 1,600,000. Three of its vice presidents are under indictment and a fourth has been convicted of illegally accepting payments from an employer.

Mr. Beck avowed his intention to continue as president of the union and to run for re-election at the September convention. He further declared he would not resign as a vice president of the A. F. L.-C. I. O. He said he did not feel bound by that body's policy statement that although the Fifth Amendment should be preserved, its invocation was not compatible with holding union office.

The portly, florid, bald, 62-year-old president of the Teamsters was in the witness chair fifteen minutes before hearing time. Hundreds of would-be spectators were already lined up

301

outside the caucus room. He was accompanied by several lawyers. One of them, Arthur C. Condon, sat at Mr. Beck's side at the witness table.

Mr. Beck identified former Senator James H. Duff, Pennsylvania Republican, as his "chief counsel." Mr. Duff was not present.

"I am following the advice of my chief counsel, former Senator Duff," the witness intoned repeatedly. Finally the audience broke into laughter at Mr. Beck's expostulations.

Senator Pat McNamara, Democrat of Michigan, told Mr. Beck at one point:

"I am not a bit impressed by the fact that your counsel is ex-Senator Duff."

Later, Senator Joseph R. McCarthy, Republican of Wisconsin, said he was "tired of that routine" and that "Duff is a defeated Senator who hasn't practiced law in twenty-five years."

Thereafter Mr. Beck omitted the former Senator's name from his pleadings but Senator McCarthy himself raised the issue later by demanding to know why Mr. Duff was not present. Mr. Beck said he did not know.

On March 14, Senator Duff said he had agreed to serve as legal counsel for Mr. Beck—but not in Mr. Beck's appearance before the Senate committee.

The all-day hearing, however, turned largely on the remark in Senator McClellan's opening statement that the president of "the largest and most powerful union in our country may have misappropriated over $320,000 of union funds."

Mr. Beck in a television show ten days ago acknowledged that he had obtained interest-free "loans" from the union but had paid back the money.

Mr. Beck told Robert F. Kennedy, committee counsel, he was paying his counsel from his own pocket and that he could well afford it.

The Teamsters' president often has said he did not rely on his $50,000 union salary for a living. He has announced that his last income tax payment was $91,000, which indicates an income of $180,000 to $200,000.

Beck Opposed to Code

Senator John F. Kennedy, Democrat of Massachusetts, questioned the witness about the A. F. L.-C. I. O. code. Mr. Beck's reply was:

"I certainly do not agree with the code and I opposed the code because in my personal judgment it is a violation of the constitutional rights of the citizens and I am unalterably opposed to any violation of any rights of the citizens which in my judgment far transcends the rights of labor or any other group."

Mr. Kennedy, the committee counsel, questioned the witness about a breakdown of the $322,-448. The largest item was $196,-516. Mr. Kennedy asked whether Mr. Beck took that amount to pay John Lindsay "for work that was done on Mr. Beck's home and on homes that were on Mr. Beck's property."

The witness invoked the Fifth Amendment. The question referred to the house that Mr. Beck later persuaded the Teamsters Union to purchase for $163,000, though permitting him to continue living in it.

Mr. Kennedy said some $85,-000 of union money had been used to pay personal bills, and that it had been channeled through Nathan Shefferman, long-time friend of Mr. Beck and a management consultant on union problems.

Mr. Shefferman himself testified toward the end of the day's session and said he had paid Mr. Beck $24,500 in 1949 and 1950. That money, he said, was in payment for business that Mr. Beck was able to get for him.

UNION ORGANIZING HURT BY HEARINGS

Some Who Are Asked to Join Reply With Taunts About Beck and Teamsters

By JOSEPH A. LOFTUS

Special to The New York Times.

WASHINGTON, April 6—Senate hearings on labor racketeering have dealt a stunning blow to union organizing programs, informed sources disclosed today.

One union official described resistance to unionism in the South in recent weeks as the worst in twenty years. Some of the employes whose membership is solicited taunt organizers with references to Dave Beck, president of the teamster' union.

Mr. Beck refused to tell the Select Committee on Improper Activities in the Labor or Management Field of his financial affairs on the ground that the answers might tend to incriminate him.

Case in South Cited

As an example of the prevailing atmosphere, a union official cited a mid-South factory owned by a concern well known for its resistance to unionism.

This company suddenly dropped its resistance and agreed without delay to a National Labor Relations Board election to determine whether the employes wanted a union.

"No doubt they knew that the climate would be most favorable to securing a 'no' vote," the union official concluded. The union withdrew its election petition a week ago and no election will be held there at this time.

The organizing problem had been a difficult one even before the Senate hearings. John W. Livingston, director of organization of the American Federation of Labor and Congress of Industrial Organizations, started with 340 organizers in January, 1956. He has lost about sixty-five, some by death, others by transfer back to their original unions.

A few months ago the A. F. L.-C. I. O. undertook an ambitious campaign to organize "white-collar" workers—teachers, office workers, and so forth. Mr. Livingston had expected to hire forty new organizers—young people familiar with the "white-collar" problem. None has been hired and the prospect now is that none will be.

A few representation elections among "white collar" workers have been held and won, but the collapse of plans for additional organizers—for policy or financial reasons beyond Mr. Livingston's control—plus the climate created by the hearing, have put the organizing campaign behind schedule.

Reports from the field in the last week have shown by hard examples the impact of the hearings.

Beck Appearance a Climax

The climate of resistance was building slowly from the day the hearings began and reached a climax with the appearance before the Senate inquiry of Mr. Beck, and his refusal to answer questions.

Organizers had expected this, to a degree, so that in most cases they report a determination to ride out the blow.

A confidential letter from the official of one union to A. F. L.-C. I. O. headquarters here under date of April 3 said:

"There could be no question that the wide publicity given these hearings is seriously hampering our efforts to organize. The publicity is furnishing the anti-union employer and other enemies of labor additional ammunition with which to fight the union.

"The atmosphere throughout the Southeastern States for successful organizing campaigns is in my opinion worse than it ever has been during the last twenty years. There have been very few union victories in Labor Board elections during the past few weeks while election losses continue to mount.

"This, however, as you know, is not altogether attributable to the Senate investigation of labor racketeering, but also to many other factors with which you are familiar.

Employers Shift Tactics

"Where petitions for elections have been filed the employer is now more likely to consent, thus taking advantage of the anti-union atmosphere enhanced by the committee's hearings rather than to stall by going to a hearing before the N. L. R. B."

March 27, 1957

April 7, 1957

302

UNION SUSPENDED BY THE A.F.L.-C.I.O.; 2 OTHERS WARNED

Laundry Workers Are Slated for December Expulsion in Misuse of Welfare Fund

COUNCIL APPROVES CODE

Lists Democratic Standards for Affiliates—Deplores Rank-and-File Apathy

By JOSEPH A. LOFTUS
Special to The New York Times.

WASHINGTON, May 23— Organized labor suspended the Laundry Workers' International Union today and marked it for expulsion in December.

Two other unions were given a choice of suspension or of probation under a monitor. They were the Allied Industrial Workers and the Distillery Workers International Union.

All are charged with ethical practices abuses. All had been given a trial and an opportunity to clean up by the Executive Council of the American Federation of Labor and Congress of Industrial Organizations.

The Laundry Workers Union has about 85,000 members; the Allied about 75,000, and the Distillery Workers Union between 30,000 and 35,000.

Principles Defined

The executive council also adopted a code of democratic processes for the guidance of all affiliates. Minimum democratic standards were defined and the rank and file was exhorted to exercise the rights of union democracy.

In the case of the laundry workers, the Executive Council found that the union "has not in good faith complied with [its] directives." The council directed that the union "shall stand suspended from the A. F. L.-C. I. O. and face expulsion from the A. F. L.-C. I. O. at its forthcoming convention." The con-

vention is set for Dec. 5 at Miami Beach.

All three unions had been cited by a Senate subcommittee headed by Senator Paul H. Douglas, Democrat of Illinois, for misuse of welfare funds. The committee's report said Eugene C. James, who was the laundry workers' secretary-treasurer at the time, had failed to account for more than $900,000.

Continued Union Role

George Meany, A. F. L.-C. I. O. president, said that Mr. James ostensibly retired from the union executive board last February. However, he said that Mr. James later had attended board meetings during the union's convention and that the meetings had been held in his hotel suite.

Mr. Meany also cited the resignation of Sam J. Byers as president of the Laundry Workers. Mr. Byers quit after disclosing that he once had served time for a felony under another name. He changed his name legally.

Mr. Meany said there probably would have been no objection to retiring Mr. Byers on pension, in view of his age and health, but the union had honored him with a title of president emeritus at full salary.

Mr. Meany said it was not an "act of good faith to retire with an honorary title and high honors a man who at least tolerated some of these apparently corrupt conditions."

Official 'Hand-Picked'

The federation chief said Mr. Byers' successor, Ralph T. Fagan of Chicago, was vice president of Mr. James' own local and apparently had been hand-picked by Mr. James for the presidency.

Finally, Mr. Meany said, the union has not filed suit against Mr. James for an accounting of the missing $900,000 although Mr. Meany had advised such legal action.

An Executive Council statement said the two other unions had partly corrected abuses reported by the federation's Ethical Practices Committee but had not "satisfactorily cleaned house."

The council directed that the two unions "shall stand suspended from the A. F. L.-C. I. O. unless these organizations agree forthwith to be placed under probation status in the A. F. L.-C. I. O. for a period of one year and further agree that the president of the A. F. L.-C. I. O. shall

appoint a special representative to inspect the operations of each of these organizations during this period and to report to each meeting of the Executive Council the further actions taken to insure full compliance with the report of the Ethical Practices Committee and the directives of the Executive Council."

Mr. Meany's word for the representative he would assign was "monitor." He said the monitor would have access to all the records of the unions so there would be "no finagling."

Veterans in the labor movement could not recall any precedent for this proposed supervision of an autonomous union's affairs by the federation.

In the case of the Allied Industrial Workers — formerly known as the United Auto Workers, A. F. L.—Mr. Meany said the officers had offered to hold a special convention and take a chance there on re-election, although their terms still had a long time to run.

He also said they had removed from membership the secretary-treasurer, Anthony Doria. A financial settlement was made with Mr. Doria by the union. Mr. Meany said the officers had agreed to disclose the details of this at the convention.

The distillery workers, he said, changed secretary-treasurers and put their welfare funds in good shape.

These corrections, he explained, saved them from an expulsion recommendation. He declined to specify what further actions they must take to satisfy the federation.

House Hearings Slated

In this connection, Representative Graham A. Barden, Democrat of North Carolina, chairman of the Education and Labor Committee of the House of Representatives, announced that his committee would open formal hearings next week to seek ways to prevent the "pillaging" of union funds.

The democratic processes code, adopted today said that "a few unions do not adequately, in their constitutions, provide for these basic elements of democratic practice. A few unions do not practice or implement the principles set forth in their constitutions.

"Finally, while the overwhelming majority of American unions both preach and practice the principles of democracy, in all too many instances the membership by apathy and indifference have forfeited their rights of union citizenship. * * * Just as eternal vigilance is the price of liberty, so is the constant exercise of the rights of union citizenship the price of union democracy."

The council will hold its next meeting on Aug. 12 in Chicago.

TEAMSTER STUDY IS 3 MONTHS OLD

Select Group Was Created by Senate After Beck's Challenge of Authority

It was just three months ago that the Senate Select Committee on Improper Activities in the Labor or Management Field began public hearings on the Teamsters' Union.

Dave Beck announced yesterday that he would not seek re-election as president of the International Brotherhood of Teamsters.

The inquiry started with an attack on the original investigation by the teamster official. Mr. Beck contended in January that the Senate Permanent Subcommittee on Investigations did not have specific authority to investigate labor racketeering and corruption in labor-management relations.

Rather than take a chance with legal complications or face protracted debate, the Senate promptly created the committee that started its public hearings in Washington on Feb. 25.

The highlight of that opening session was testimony that the teamsters, directed from union headquarters in Seattle, Wash., had combined with underworld elements to dominate law enforcement in Portland, Ore., and its county government. The testimony also pointed to the use of union funds for non-union purposes. It also linked Mr. Beck with personal loans.

Both the Permanent Subcommittee on Investigations and the select committee, are headed by Senator John L. McClellan, Democrat of Arkansas. The gathering of evidence, its analysis and preparation for use in hearings have been under the general direction of Robert F. Kennedy, committee counsel. He is a brother of Senator John F. Kennedy, Democrat of Massachusetts.

From the outset, Mr. Beck denied any misuse of his official position or of union funds. However, officials of the Teamsters Union refused to answer questions of the subcommittee in January.

When the special subcommittee was formed, Mr. Beck quietly left the country. He had been nominated by the American Federation of Labor and Congress of Industrial Organizations to be one of two delegates to an International Labor Organization meeting in Germany from March 11 to 23.

May 24, 1957

The select Senate committee had been trying to serve Mr. Beck with a subpoena, but his departure averted service. But James P. Mitchell, Secretary of Labor, refused to approve the Teamster chief as a delegate because he had kept out of the way of the inquiry.

Then things began to happen quickly. Mr. Beck returned from Europe. James R. Hoffa, vice president of the Teamsters Union, was arrested in connection with an alleged plot to bribe an aide of the Senate committee

staff for advance information on the nature of the investigation.

The next day the McClellan committee requested Mr. Beck to present his personal financial books and records from 1949 through 1945. Mr. Beck said he would do so "if my attorneys want me to." On March 17, four days later, Mr. Beck stated on a television program from Tacoma, Wash., that he had borrowed $300,000 to $400,000 in Teamster Union funds over ten years. He said he had paid no interest and that "every bit has been repaid."

During his several appearances before the inquiry, Mr. Beck refused to answer some 200 times, citing the Fifth Amendment in every case. Most of the time, the rank and file of the Union and most of the Teamsters officials had expressed solid support for their chief.

It was not until last month, however, that the special subcommittee heard evidence that struck a vital blow at Mr. Beck's hold on his union. At the May 10 hearing, Don Hedlund, a Seattle mortgage expert and one

of Mr. Beck's business partners, admitted he had shared with Mr. Beck in a deal through which the two had contributed to a charity fund for the widow of Mr. Beck's "best friend" and then had reaped a profit from it.

From that moment, Mr. Beck's star sank. Leader after leader, local after local deserted him. Demands for his resignation grew louder and more insistent. Evidently, Mr. Beck felt he could no longer resist the demand when he issued his statement yesterday.

May 26, 1957

Text of M'Clellan Statement on Hoffa and Transcript of Hoffa-Dio Call

Special to The New York Times.

WASHINGTON, Aug. 23— *Following is the text of a statement by Senator John L. McClellan, chairman of the Select Committee on Improper Activities in the Labor or Management Field, and the transcript of a wiretapped telephone conversation between James R. Hoffa in Detroit and Johnny Dio (John Dioguardi) in New York on June 16, 1953. Senator McClellan's statement charged Hoffa with forty-eight points of "conflict of interest and questionable actions." In the telephone conversation, preliminary remarks made while operators were trying to connect the two men have been deleted. Deletions of profanity, as indicated in the text, were made by the Senate committee.*

McClellan Statement

1. James R. Hoffa borrowed $5,000 in cash from Jack (Babe) Bushkin, a labor relations adviser who represents a number of employers with whom the teamsters have contracts.

2. James R. Hoffa borrowed $5,000 in cash from J. L. Keeshin, a truck owner who had contracts with the Teamsters Union.

3. James R. Hoffa borrowed $25,000 in cash from Henry Lower, a real estate promoter whose Florida development, Sun Valley, is being sponsored by the Teamsters Union. Hoffa made this loan shortly after he urged a Detroit bank (where the teamsters had large deposits) to loan $75,000 to Lower at 4 per cent interest. Hoffa paid Lower no interest.

4. James R. Hoffa sent Teamsters Union business agents to Florida at union expense to assist the Sun Valley project and had Teamsters Union business agents sell lots in the project. He did this despite the fact he had an option to buy property in the development, the success of which depended on the number of teamsters' purchasing lots.

Dealings with Union Auditors

5. James R. Hoffa borrowed $25,000 in cash from Harold Mark, an accountant and auditor whose firm reviewed the records of the Central States Southeast-Southwest Welfare Fund. In addition, Hoffa obtained the loan soon after Locals 299 and 337 of Detroit made loans to Mark in excess of $100,000 at 6 per cent interest. When Mark loaned Hoffa back $25,000, he charged no interest.

6. James R. Hoffa borrowed $11,500 in cash from Herbert L. Grosberg, the accountant for teamster organizations in Detroit, who holds his job at the pleasure of James R. Hoffa.

7. James R. Hoffa borrowed $18,000 in cash from a group of teamster business agents in Detroit whose jobs depend on the good will of James R. Hoffa.

Union Funds

8. Local 337 of the Teamsters Union loaned $30,000 to the Northville Downs racetrack, a trotting horse track in Michigan, where the long-

time associate of James R. Hoffa, Owen Brennan, a Teamster Union official, raced part of his string of harness horses.

9. James R. Hoffa's home Local 299 and Local 337 in Detroit, Mich., purchased the home of Paul (The Waiter) Ricca, notorious mobster of the Capone gang who has been ordered deported from this country.

10. James R. Hoffa's home Local 299 and Local 337 in Detroit, Michigan, lent $75,000 to the Marberry Construction Company, owned by Herbert Grosberg, accountant for the Teamsters Union, and George Fitzgerald, attorney for the Teamsters Union. This is about the same time that Hoffa obtained loans of $11,500 from Herbert Grosberg.

11. James R. Hoffa donated $5,000 of dues money paid by Michigan teamsters to the re-election campaign of one Edward Crumback who was running for the post of president of Local 107 in Philadelphia, Pa., against another teamster. Hoffa added he would not hesitate to use union dues money for his own re-election if he felt it necessary.

12. James R. Hoffa made arrangements for the donation of $3,000 to the Wholesale Produce Buyers Association of Detroit which had been charged by the Federal Government for violation of the antitrust laws. Hoffa admitted that the members had not been consulted on whether or not they wished to make this contribution.

Conflicts of Interest and Business Transactions

13. James R. Hoffa set up a trucking company which leased its equipment to the Baker Driveaway Company owned by William Bridge, a truck owner who had contracts with the Teamsters union. The stock of this company, the J. and H. Sales Company, was put in the name of Hoffa's friend, James Montante, and then transferred to the names of Josephine Poszywak and Alice Johnson, maiden names of the wives of James Hoffa and Owen Brennan.

14. J. and H. Sales became National Equipment Company owned by Josephine Poszywak and Alice Johnson, maiden names of Mrs. James Hoffa and Mrs. Owen Brennan. National Equipment leased equipment to Baker Driveaway Company, at that time owned by William Bridge and Carney Matheson, the Detroit lawyer who negotiated and negotiates with the Teamsters Union on behalf of the Driveaway and Haulaway truck employers.

15. The National Equipment Company owned by Mrs. James Hoffa and Mrs. Owen Brennan in their maiden names, ultimately sold its equipment to the Convertible Equipment Leasing Company, owned by William Bridge, a truck owner who had contracts with the Teamsters Union, and Carney Matheson, Detroit lawyer who negotiates contracts with the Teamsters Union.

16. Following the solution of labor problems in Flint, Mich., with the intercession of James R. Hoffa, Commercial Carriers, Inc., a trucking company with contracts with the Teamsters Union, played a part in setting up the Test Fleet Corporation. The general counsel of Commercial Carriers, Mr. James Wrape, incorporated the Test Fleet Corporation in Tennessee under his name. Elliott Beidler, accountant for Commercial Carriers, kept the books and records of Test Fleet for four years at no salary. Commercial Carriers' owner, Bert Beveridge, signed a $50,000 note for equipment for Test was set up the stock was quietly transferred into the names of Josephine Poszywak and Alice Johnson, the maiden names of Mrs. James Hoffa and Mrs. Owen Brennan.

17. Commercial Carriers Corporation handed Test fleet. After the company Fleet Corporation lush contracts for the transportation of Cadillacs. The result: on an original investment of $4,000, Mrs. Hoffa and Mrs. Brennan received a net profit of $125,000 in the period from Jan. 1949 to Dec. 31, 1956.

18. James R. Hoffa set up a company to make investment loans with Carney Matheson, the Detroit attorney who negotiated contracts with Mr. Hoffa and the Teamsters Union.

19. Mr. Hoffa joined with Mr. Allen Dorfman, general agent of the Union Casualty Company, and Mrs. Rose Dorfman, a partner in the Union Casualty Company, to purchase the Jack O'Lantern Lodge, known as Joll Properties. Mr. Hoffa entered this business relationship despite the fact that he was the trustee for the Central States Conference Welfare Fund, and the Dorfmans were representatives and collected large premiums for the handling of this insurance fund.

20. Joll Properties in which James R. Hoffa had a financial interest received $11,000 loan from the insurance company which handled the multi-million dollar business of the Central States Conference of Teamsters.

21. James R. Hoffa and Dr. Leo Perlman, a majority stock owner in the Union Casualty Company, went into business in North Dakota under the name of Northwest Oil Company.

22. Mr. Hoffa joined Mr. Carney Matheson, the attorney who negotiates contracts for a segment of the trucking industry, in an investment in the Terminal Realty Company in Detroit, Mich.

23. Mrs. James Hoffa acquired an interest in a trucking company in Detroit,

Mich., which had contracts with Local 299 of the teamsters union, of which Mr. James R. Hoffa is president. Another stockholder in this company was Dale Patrick, nephew of Frank Fitzsimmons, a business agent of Local 299.

Conflicts of Interest in Stock

24. James R. Hoffa purchased 400 shares of stock in the A. C. F. Wrigley Company, a Michigan supermarket firm with whom the Teamsters Union has contracts. Labor relations director of the A. C. F. Wrigley Company is Mr. Jack (Babe) Bushkin from whom Hoffa borrowed $5,000 in cash in 1952 or 1953.

25. James R. Hoffa purchased 600 shares in McLean Industries, a company whose trucking division had contracts with the Teamsters Union.

26. James R. Hoffa purchased $25,000 in stock of the Fruehauf Trucking Company with whom the Central States Conference of Teamsters, of which he is the head, has contracts.

Close Associates of James R. Hoffa

27. James R. Hoffa placed Eugene C. (Jimmie) James as head of juke box Local 985 in Detroit, Mich. James was accused by the Douglas-Ives Committee of stealing some $900,000 from the Laundry Workers International Union Welfare Fund.

28. James R. Hoffa and Owen Brennan, president of Local 337 in Detroit lent James $2,000 or $2,500 to start the operations of Local 985. James repaid Hoffa and Brennan by placing their wives on the union payroll under their maiden names, Josephine Poszywak and Alice Johnson. He had repaid almost three times the original investment when the matter came to light before a Michigan grand jury.

29. James R. Hoffa assisted Samuel (Shorty) Feldman, Philadelphia ex-convict, in obtaining a charter for friends in the Hotel and Restaurant Workers Union.

30. James R. Hoffa imported Robert (Barney) Baker to work for him as an organizer in the Central States Conference of Teamsters. Baker, a New York "tough" with a prison record for throwing stink bombs and injury to property, is referred to in the records of the New York State Crime Commission as a collector for the "service collective agency," a front through which large sums of money were obtained from the public loading racket.

31. James R. Hoffa has had a long and continued association

with Johnny Dio, three times convicted labor extortionist, who has served time in Sing Sing Prison.

32. James R. Hoffa maintained Gerald Connelly, a Minneapolis organizer, in his job after he had been convicted of taking a bribe from an employer in Minneapolis, Minn. Connelly had come to Minneapolis after leaving Florida "under a cloud" after participation in an organizational drive of the Laundry Workers International Union in which he was associated with two gunmen, Solly Isaac and Dave Cominsky, who were convicted for attempted murder.

33. Chicago Taxicab Local 777, a part of the Central States Conference of Teamsters, of which Hoffa is chairman, has maintained the services of trustee Joseph Glimco. Glimco has been indicted twice on charges of murder and convicted on charges of larceny. He is a close associate of Capone mobsters, including Tony Accardo and the late Frank Nitti.

34. James R. Hoffa played a part in the speedy ascent of William Presser to the chairmanship of the Ohio Conference of Teamsters. Presser has been convicted of violation of the Federal antitrust laws and has taken the Fifth Amendment before Congressional committees in relation to his financial affairs. Also, testimony in Toledo showed Presser had accepted a payment of $2,500 for the setting up of an employers juke box association which was negotiating a contract with his own union.

35. James R. Hoffa played a part in organizing a testimonial banquet for Louis (Babe) Triscaro, head of the excavating drivers local in Cleveland, Ohio, who spent time in the Ohio State Reformatory.

36. James R. Hoffa has a long and continued association with Lou Farrell, a Des Moines, Iowa, racket figure who is also involved in the labor relations business. Reports of the Kefauver Committee identified him as a Capone mobster operating in Iowa.

37. Local 299, Joint Council 43, the Michigan Conference of Teamsters and the Central States Conference of Teamsters, all of which are headed by James R. Hoffa, employed persons as business agents and organizers, despite the fact that they had been accused of armed robbery, kidnapping, larceny, bookmaking, throwing stench bombs, impersonating government officers, felonious assault, and carrying concealed weapons.

38. James R. Hoffa set up an alliance with the International Longshoremen's As-

sociation after it had been thrown out of the A.F.L.-C.I.O. for racket control. He also attempted to loan $490,-000 to this organization.

39. James R. Hoffa has a long and continuing association with Angelo Meli, a Detroit prohibition hoodlum who has twice been accused of murder.

Questionable Expenses

40. More than $5,000 in union funds were paid to the Woodner Hotel in Washington, D. C., for the lodging of friends and associates of James R. Hoffa during his trial on bribery-conspiracy charges. This money came from union dues of teamster members in Chicago, Detroit and St. Louis.

Paper Locals

41. James R. Hoffa masterminded and played a key role in the chartering of seven paper locals in New York City, knowing these locals to be racket-controlled and devoid of membership. Hoffa did this to effect the election of his friend, John O'Rourke, who took the Fifth Amendment before this committee as head of Joint Council No. 16 in New York City.

Trusteeships

42. James R. Hoffa was named trustee of Local 614 in Pontiac, Mich., after top officers of that local were indicted for extortion in a Michigan highway paving scandal. Hoffa then appointed two of the indicted officials as business agents to run the affairs of this local. They were both subsequently convicted of extortion.

43. James R. Hoffa was named trustee of Local 823 in Joplin, Mo., after the local's president, Floyd C. Webb, had been accused of spending thousands of dollars in union funds for his own personal benefit and after union members had complained that Webb had threatened their lives for complaining about the way he was running the union. After being named trustee, Hoffa named Webb to run the union under the trusteeship.

Union Members

44. James R. Hoffa, who arranged for the loans of almost $250,000 in union funds to friends and acquaintances, sent a Detroit teamster who wanted to borrow $500 to the bank.

45. James R. Hoffa, who has repeatedly labeled himself as the champion of workingmen, attempted to put 30,000 taxicab drivers in New York under the leadership of Johnny Dio, a convicted labor extortionist. He did this only a month after New York newspaper had published the fact that Dio had accepted more than $11,000 to keep

certain dress firms in Allentown, Pa., non-union.

Teamsters Union

46. James R. Hoffa, the ninth vice president of the International Brotherhood of Teamsters, supported the cause of labor racketeer Johnny Dio in relation to a New York taxicab charter while he knew that his own union was attempting to organize taxicabs under the direction of Teamsters Union third vice president, Thomas L. Hickey.

47. James R. Hoffa, and others under his direction, joined with labor racketeer Johnny Dio in conspiring to obtain derogatory information which could be used for the purpose of blackening the character of a fellow teamster, vice president Thomas L. Hickey, and thus permit Dio, a convicted extortionist, to operate the taxicab locals in the teamsters.

Questions
Answers to Committee

48. While Teamster General President Dave Beck took the Fifth Amendment 140 times during one session, James R. Hoffa either avoided or equivocated the answers to 111 questions at Thursday's session. Today, though we adjourned early, I think he broke that record.

Hoffa-Dio Call

JIMMY HOFFA—Hello.
DIO—Hello, James.
HOFFA—Johnny; how are you?
DIO—Aw, J——, I've been worried about you; I've been following you up every day in the newspapers.
HOFFA — Yeah. Well, I didn't call beca——
DIO—I know, but I was d——all I wanted to know was how were things; that's about all. I finally called Dave yesterday. I tried because I saw his name in the papers too, so I though maybe he'd know and he said everything so far so good. I tried to contact you in Cleveland.
HOFFA—Yeah; I run out of there early—
DIO—I know, and—I know I saw, I read in the papers where you give whatshisname a nice verbal lashing. When you are ready on the election let me know; I'll come up and be a picket.
HOFFA—[Much laughter]

Dio's Men in Detroit

DIO—Did my man get there all right?

HOFFA—Yes, he was here last week.
DIO—Yeah.
HOFFA—He—he was to see you over the week-end that's why I thought he would tell you the whole story.
DIO—Yes, well, I didn't see him because I was busy.
HOFFA—I see. He was back here again this week—two of them.
DIO—Well, he'll be back.
HOFFA—He's here now.
DIO—Is he there now?
HOFFA—And they are doing that work.
DIO—Uhuh.
HOFFA—Uhuh—He had to have thirteen last week for supplies.
DIO—Huh?
HOFFA—He wanted——
DIO—Well, I gave him a few hundred when he left.
HOFFA—He wanted $500 for [inaudible] supplies.
DIO—Uhuh, I'll a——
HOFFA—Now, ah—insofar as work is concerned you better have him call you before he starts.
DIO—Yeah, but look Jim, you remember you do all your discussing there with him because if you don't like anything tell me. You know what I mean?

'We Got a Grand Jury'

HOFFA—Well, he's doing all right.
DIO—Well, I'm going to tell you this. Those are the best——
HOFFA—Yeah, you're doing a wonderful job.
DIO—They are the best; they work for the U. N. and everything else, now—and whenever you want to need 'em any part of the country if you want to find out they're your people you let me know. You know what I mean?
HOFFA—Yup.
DIO — Otherwise, how's things Jim?
HOFFA—All right, John. We got a grand jury.
DIO—They do have one?
HOFFA—Grand jury started this morning.
DIO—Uhuh.
HOFFA—Apparently they are going to try to indict everybody in sight.
DIO—Uhuh.
HOFFA—However, I don't know what in the h— they gonna indict people on; there don't seem to be nothing here; primarily it's Buffalino they are after.
DIO—Yeah. Bad publicity too.
HOFFA—And now they have put it into the parking lots——

DIO—Uhuh.
HOFFA — Ahah, bowling alleys——

Pledges Help to Hoffa

DIO—Uhuh.
HOFFA—Right.
DIO—Uhuh.
HOFFA — Laundries and linen.
DIO—Uhuh. Hello?
HOFFA—I'm not talking from my office so it don't make any difference.
DIO—Yeah. Well—I'm only—all I'm interested in is that I hope everything works out fine and that's all I'm interested and if I can be of any help Jim in any way; I know politically there I can't help you.
DIO—My case, incidentally, I went to court this morning and they postponed it till October the Fifth.
HOFFA—Ah, just what you said—political.
DIO—Well, that's—that's what—but it was important for me to get it postponed, Jim, because nominations are this month, y'know.
HOFFA—Yeah.
DIO—And we'll see.
HOFFA—But I feel sure it's going to be a long drawn-out affair, I'm afraid.
DIO—Ah, for C——'s sake.
HOFFA — I don't think they'll make it in a hurry; I think they'll drag it along and make a lot of publicity and bad headlines——

'I Feel For You'

DIO—Yeah, uhuh—
HOFFA—And a lot of that stuff.
DIO—Well, d— it, boy; I feel for you. I know what I've been going through.
HOFFA—Well, I've had—this is the third trip I've had with them.
DIO—Well, I won't discourage you but I can only—only say one thing I want to tell you, not that I want to do anything about it, but I want to tell you. One thing I wanted to read if you don't mind a minute.
HOFFA—Go ahead, Johnny.
DIO—A statement from Thomas L. Hickey, International Vice President: "The recent action of the Executive Council of the A. F. L. in removing Local 102 from the New York City taxi scene has cleared the way for New York City cab drivers to organize under the jurisdiction of the largest union in the A. F. of L." and then the rest of the bull——. After I send them that telegram and everything.

HOFFA—That stupid son of a —.
DIO—Well, I just wanted you to know. Don't do nothing about it. Take care of your own troubles right now—
HOFFA—After all, what luck is he having?
DIO—What did you say?
HOFFA—What luck does he have?
DIO—Oh, you know he ain't going to have no luck. Son of a —; God alone is going to pun—punish him. He ain't got no luck. For c—'s sake, guys are walking away left and right. But, we won't worry about that Jim; you know, you said once, "don't rock the boat."
HOFFA—Right.
DIO—Yeah, well listen, we're here to stay, we're not going to die tomorrow—we hope—and—a—we're not that old.
HOFFA—Ah, I think it'll work out.
DIO—You know we're only a couple of four-year-olders; you know.
HOFFA—These old has—will all be dead.
DIO—What?
HOFFA—These old has—will all be dead.
DIO—Well, Jim, you ju—ah, I'm glad I spoke to you; I didn't want anything other than I wanted to know if my guys were doing a job—
HOFFA—Very good.
DIO—And please call me at anytime, Jim if I can be of any help.
HOFFA—Right, Johnny.
DIO—And one of these weeks maybe I'll run in on you for a day—
HOFFA—Okay.

Plan to Keep in Touch

DIO—And give my regards at home and to Bert and everybody else.
HOFFA—Right, Jack.
DIO—Well, I'll call you now and then—it will only be just like to find out what's what.
HOFFA — I'm tickled to death to talk anytime; I'll call you to keep you informed, too.
DIO—All right, Jim.
HOFFA—Right.
DIO—I been buying the Detroit papers every day—
HOFFA—Ha, ha, ha—
DIO—You know, we got 'em here, you know, on Forty-second Street.
HOFFA—Yeah, yeah.
DIO—So I've been following them up.
HOFFA—Yeah.
DIO—All right, Jim, take it easy.
HOFFA—Okay, Johnny.
DIO—Right. Bye.

HOFFA IS ELECTED TEAMSTERS' HEAD; WARNS OF BATTLE

Defeats Two Foes 3 to 1 —Says Union Will Fight 'With Every Ounce'

By A. H. RASKIN
Special to The New York Times.

MIAMI BEACH, Oct. 4—The scandal - scarred International Brotherhood of Teamsters elected James R. Hoffa as its president today.

He won by a margin of nearly 3 to 1 over the combined vote of two rivals who campaigned on pledges to clean up the nation's biggest union.

Senate rackets investigators and Hoffa critics in the union rank-and-file immediately opened actions to strip the 44-year-old former warehouseman from Detroit of his election victory.

A jubilant Hoffa exhibited, however, greater concern over the possibility that his union might be ousted from the American Federation of Labor and Congress of Industrial Organizations. He appealed for time to prove that he could make the teamsters "a model of trade unionism."

The parent organization has ordered the 1,400,000-member Teamsters Union to get rid of corrupt leadership by Oct. 24 or face suspension. Hoffa said he felt actions by the union at its week-long convention here should satisfy the federation.

Warns Union Will Fight

He made it plain to the 1,700 cheering delegates that he did not intend to go before the convention in the role of suppliant. He said expulsion would not destroy the teamsters. He warned that the union would fight "with every ounce of strength we possess" if it found itself outside.

In such a civil war the teamsters would start with a warchest of $38,000,000 in the hands of the international union and much more at the disposal of its locals. The teamsters also could count on their strategic power over other unions through their control of trucks and warehouses.

The Hoffa victory brought warnings of repressive legislation from James P. Mitchell, Secretary of Labor, and Senator John L. McClellan, Democrat of Arkansas. The Senator heads the Select Committee on Improper Activities in the Labor or Management Field, which has accused Hoffa of gangster associations and questionable financial practices.

Winner on First Ballot

A three-hour roll-call gave Hoffa the $50,000-a-year union presidency on the first ballot. His machine, in full command of the convention since it opened Monday, registered 1,208 votes for Hoffa.

William A. Lee of Chicago, the union's seventh vice president, was second with 313 votes. Thomas J. Haggerty of Chicago, secretary - treasurer of Milk Wagon Drivers Union, Local 753, trailed with 140 votes.

The Hoffa forces then began providing the new leader a rubber stamp board. It elected five of thirteen vice presidents and would have elected the rest today if time had permitted completion of the cumbersome balloting procedure.

Hoffa repeatedly indicated his irritation that some of the old vice presidents marked for elimination had refused to give up without the formality of a roll-call.

Even before the voting, the McClellan committee subpoenaed the full records of the convention's credentials committee. A United States marshal served the subpoena this morning on Joseph Konowe of New York, the committee secretary. He was directed to turn over all credentials and committee minutes "forthwith."

Gerard Treanor, counsel for the union, said the material would be made available but that it would take a week to get it to Washington. The Senators have charged that the convention was "packed" with Hoffa supporters not qualified to vote under the union constitution.

In New York, Godfrey P. Schmidt, counsel for thirteen rank-and-file teamsters, announced that he would press for a quick Federal Court trial on charges that the convention had been "rigged" in Hoffa's favor.

Mr. Schmidt admitted, however, that he had no hope of preventing Mr. Hoffa from assuming office when the retiring president, Dave Beck, steps down Oct. 15. The lawyer said it would take at least a month before the case came to trial.

Credentials Weeded Out

Hoffa's own legal aides expressed certainty that the election would never be upset. They said care had been taken to weed out credentials that were in clear violation of the constitution.

Hoffa faces still another threat to his tenure. He is under Federal indictments charging illegal wiretapping and perjury. He is scheduled to appear in New York to answer both charges on the day set for his inauguration.

If he gets past all the legal roadblocks, he will serve for five years under a new constitution that gives him and the executive board vastly expanded authority for centralized control over strikes, wages, contracts and welfare funds.

If he goes to jail, the union's probable custodian will be Harold J. Gibbons of St. Louis, one of the new vice presidents.

Everything went Hoffa's way at today's convention session. When the voting was over, it was evident he was so far ahead that the delegates did not wait for the official tally before unleashing a thirty-minute demonstration.

In speeches after the vote, Mr. Lee and Mr. Haggerty said they intended to continue their fight for clean unionism within the teamsters. They expressed hope that the union would stay united and stay in the federation.

There were signs, however, that the friction created by the internal battle would result in the splitting off of many locals in the New York metropolitan area and in the Far East if the A. F. L.-C. I. O. did oust the teamsters.

Frank W. Brewster of Seattle, a Lee supporter, was purged as a vice president. Hoffa congratulated him dropping his fight.

The battle is likely to be renewed if Mr. Hoffa decides to oust the Seattle leader as chairman of the Western Conference of Teamsters.

Mr. Brewster will be replaced by George E. Mock, international organizer in Sacramento. Mr. Brennan will make way for Gordon R. Conklin, president of the St. Paul Joint Council. The other vice president elected today were John J. Conlin of Hoboken, a holdover; John T. O'Brien of Chicago, another veteran, and Mr. Gibbons. Mr. English was re-elected secretary-treasurer. The eight other Hoffa choices, all certain of election, are Joseph J. Diviny, San Francisco; Einar O. Mohn, Los Angeles; Harry Tevis, Pittsburgh; John J. O'Rourke, New York; Owen Bert Brennan, Detroit; Thomas E. Flynn, Chicago; John B Bachus, Philadelphia; Murray W. Miller, Dallas.

The elections will continue tomorrow night after a twenty-four-hour recess to permit Jewish delegates to observe Yom Kippur.

A.F.L.-C.I.O. OUSTS TEAMSTERS UNION BY VOTE OF 5 TO 1

DRAMA AT SESSION

A Last-Minute Peace Move Collapses— Hoffa Defiant

By A. H. RASKIN
Special to The New York Times.

ATLANTIC CITY, Dec. 6— The giant International Brotherhood of Teamsters was expelled from the merged labor federation today on charges of domination by corrupt elements.

The victory for George Meany and other leaders of the clean-union forces in the American Federation of Labor and Congress of Industrial Organizations came by a margin of nearly five to one at the federation's second biennial convention.

It followed the collapse last midnight of cloak-and-dagger moves to arrange a peace meeting at which James R. Hoffa, the chief target of the federation's charges, was to have stepped down as president-elect of the 1,333,000-member truck union. The federation refused to hold off the ouster vote until Monday to give Hoffa a final chance to abdicate.

Lewis Fight Recalled

The convention session was the most dramatic held by a labor organization since John L. Lewis punched William L. Hutcheson of the Carpenters Union in the nose at the start of the split between the old A. F. L. and C. I. O. twenty-two years ago.

Both the teamsters and the federation pledged themselves to seek to avoid a new civil war as an aftermath of the ouster. However, the bitterness of the debate made an increase in interunion raids, strikes and economic conflict appear inescapable.

The actual vote to eliminate the scandal-stained teamsters from the mainstream of organized labor was 10,458,598 to 9,266,497. It was based on the membership strength of the unions that voted for and against the ouster.

Roll-Call Vote Taken

The teamsters were drummed out through a roll-call vote. Fewer than 1,000 delegates were able to cast the total of 12,275,-095 votes, because the due-paying strength of their union determined how many ballots each group was entitled to. Thus, in the case of the huge auto union, each delegate was recorded as having 35,275 votes. In smaller organizations, delegates cast as few as twenty-five votes each.

The teamsters mustered the support of twenty-one international unions, four others split their votes and eight indicated their lack of sympathy for the orphaning of the country's largest and most powerful union by staying away from the meeting.

Ninety-five unions voted to expel the teamsters. Included were the only two others in the million-member class — Walter P. Reuther's United Automobile Workers and David J. McDonald's United Steelworkers of America. Mr. McDonald made no secret of his personal unhappiness at voting against the Teamsters. He twice went over to a corner of the Convention Hall, where thirty teamsters were sitting in what looked like an improvised mourners' bench, to express his grief at the action.

In New York, where Hoffa is on trial on a Federal indictment accusing him of illegal wiretapping, the 44-year-old Detroiter sneered at the A. F. L.-C. I. O. exile order. He asserted that the federation "didn't build us; they won't weaken us."

He again denied that he had any thought of quitting as top man of the Teamsters, even though a high Teamster official had told Mr. Meany by telephone at 11:40 P. M. yesterday that Hoffa was ready to jump into a car and race over icy roads to this seaside resort to make a pre-dawn surrender move.

Senate Group Attacked

The ouster made the Teamsters the second union in the history of organized labor to be dropped for racket penetration. The first was the crime-infested International Longshoremen's Association, expelled from the old A. F. L. four years ago. Almost no one rose to the pier union's defense when the ouster vote was taken. Today the federation's high command found itself under much sharper floor attack than the Teamsters.

Dictatorship and hypocrisy were charged against the A. F. L.-C. I. O. chiefs. They were accused of seeking to "appease" the Senate Select Committee on Improper Activities in the Labor or Management Field in the hope of warding off restrictive legislation. A half d. en speakers denounced the committee and charged that its principal aim was to undermine unions through its inquiry into labor racketeering.

If the truck union had been able to count on its own votes and those of four other unions accused of corruption, it would have had an additional 1,605,000 votes. This would have put it within hailing distance of the one-third total necessary to block expulsion.

However, the Teamsters were barred from voting. So were the 132,000-member Bakery and Confectionery Workers International Union, the 75,000-member Laundry Workers International Union, the 40,000-member United Textile Workers and the 25,000-member Distillery, Rectifying and Wine Workers International Union.

The Bakers, Laundry Workers and Distillers are slated for expulsion from the federation next week. The Textile Union is under suspension for financial irregularities. The convention is expected to authorize the A. F. L.-C. I. O. executive council to expel the union if it fails to set its affairs in order quickly.

All of the backing for the Teamsters came from the ranks of the old A. F. L. Every union from the old C. I. O. supported the federation's nine-man appeals committee in its decision that the truck union must go because of "the dishonest, corrupt, unethical practices of the few who betrayed their trust and who have apparently looked upon the trade union movement primarily as a means to advance their own selfish purposes."

Hoffa Also Accused

Hoffa himself was found guilty of having "associated with, sponsored and promoted the interests of notorious racketeers." Along with Dave Beck, the union's retiring president, he was condemned for having used his union position for personal enrichment.

The federation voiced hope that the members of the union would take speedy action to clean house and thus clear the way for a return to the A. F. L.-C. I. O. The parent group does not intend to charter a rival union to conduct a finish fight against the teamsters. Federation supporters inside the truck union will be encouraged to stay in and seek to oust the Beck-Hoffa leadership.

As a further safeguard against jurisdictional warfare, the federation seems disposed to put off a decision on whether to order cancellation of mutual assistance pacts now in effect between the Teamsters and a half-dozen federation affiliates. Maintenance of such pacts with an expelled union violates the A. F. L.-C. I. O. constitution. But officials said formal action to end them would not come at once.

Einar O. Mohn, administrative vice president of the Teamsters, said it intended to maintain the group's cordial working relations with friendly unions and that it would not refuse to respect the picket lines of A. F. L.-C. I. O. units engaged in strikes or organizing campaigns.

"We're going to continue doing business pretty normally," Mr. Mohn said after the ouster. "We have no chips on our shoulders, but we are not going to play dead just because somebody doesn't like us."

A more truculent tone was taken by the Teamsters' secretary-treasurer, John F. English. He said the union's enemies could all "go straight to hell." He expressed doubt that five unions in the federation could meet the "acid test" of probity that was being applied to the Teamsters. And he warned that many of the Teamsters' critics would find themselves the object of unwelcome attention from the Senate investigators and the federation leadership.

While Mr. English was delivering his lament, the union and its leaders were under fire in three courts a continent apart. In Washington Federal Judge F. Dickinson Letts was considering whether to make permanent an injunction barring Hoffa and a hand-picked executive board from taking office.

Hoffa himself was on trial in New York, with a second indictment accusing him of perjury still to be tried. Federal tax authorities in Detroit were studying his income tax returns to determine whether he had made full payments on transactions involving hundreds of thousands of dollars in cash. In Seattle Mr. Beck was being tried in a county court on charges of grand larceny, with an income tax indictment awaiting trial after that.

The accent in the expulsion report submitted to the convention by the appeals committee, through its chairman, Alex Rose of the United Hatters,

Cap and Millinery Workers International Union, was that the members of the truck union were the principal victims of the corruption at the top.

"We hope that out of the efforts of the A. F. L.-C. I. O. to keep its own house in order the members of the Teamsters Union will be encouraged to take the necessary steps to bring them back into the brotherhood of honest trade unionism," the report said.

Mr. Meany, the only other speaker to take the floor in favor of the expulsion call, also voiced hope that the Teamsters would soon be back within the federation. He said his door always would be open for any move by the truck union to bring itself into compliance with the clean-up directives.

The support for the teamsters came from a wide range of unions, including some with outstanding records for internal democracy and high ethical standards. Among those who opposed expulsion were Woodruff Randolph, president of the International Typographical Union, which has long prided itself on a two-party system without parallel in any other union.

Another foe of expulsion was Sal B. Hoffman, president of the Upholsterers International Union. This was the first union in the country to set up an independent appeals board of prominent citizens to protect its members against unjust acts by the union leadership.

The biggest union to vote to keep the Teamsters in was the 750,000-member United Brotherhood of Carpenters and Joiners, now headed by Maurice A. Hutcheson, son of the man whose battle with Mr. Lewis was the symbolic start of the twenty-year war between the A. F. L. and C. I. O. The Carpenters' books have been subpoenaed by the Senate rackets investigators.

The most tantalizing part of the discussion was the official disclosure of the behind-the-scenes steps the last month to try to arrange a meeting between Mr. Meany and Hoffa. The intermediary in these unsuccessful efforts was Patrick E. Gorman, secretary-treasurer of the meat cutters' union.

Mr. Gorman said he had got into the situation because cooperation between his union and the teamsters had helped the meat cutters add 20,000 members to their rolls in the last two years.

He said Mr. Meany had been "most cooperative" in the attempts to arrange a meeting but that nothing had come of the attempts till last night. According to Mr. Gorman, Hoffa told him by phone that he did not want to hurt either his own union or the merged federation. However, Hoffa reportedly said the court trial made it impossible for him to come to Atlantic City until tomorrow or Sunday.

Mr. Meany then filled in some blanks in the story for the delegates. He said he had made it clear he could meet Hoffa at any time but that Hoffa always had some excuse for being unable to come. This continued up to last night, Mr. Meany said, even though "I cooperated, I stood on my head, I did everything possible under the sun."

December 7, 1957

Why They Cheer for Hoffa

The boss of the teamsters has emerged from the attacks upon him stronger than ever, bolstered by the principle that anything goes so long as he delivers the benefits.

By A. H. RASKIN

DETROIT.

THE wail of a bagpipe cut through the shop steward's report that everything was O. K. at the barn of the Merchants Motor Freight. A chunky little man with the shoulders of a heavyweight boxer plowed past the six-footers in the overflow crowd at the rear of the union hall. Two truck drivers lifted him off his feet and bore him down the aisle. A thousand others leaped from their seats and cheered. Jimmy Hoffa was back with "the guys that made me."

Everyone wore a button with the slogan, "Hoffa—The Teamster's Teamster." Some wore two or three. This was the rank and file of Local 299 of the International Brotherhood of Teamsters—the local that started a tough, cheeky kid named James Riddle Hoffa on his climb from the loading platform of a grocery warehouse to the presidency of the country's biggest and strongest union.

And this was their answer to two years of effort by Senate rackets investigators to convince them that their union was being turned into a hoodlum empire by a faithless leader. Every instrument of mass communication—newspapers, magazines, television, radio and newsreels—had brought them the sordid record of union despoliation uncovered by the McClellan Committee.

They knew of the testimony that Hoffa had treated the union's money as his own, entered into subterranean relations with employers, suppressed the democratic rights of members by brute force and allied himself with the underworld. They knew of the Senators' charge that he had used his vast power in ways "tragic for the Teamsters Union and dangerous for the country at large." They knew of the merged labor federation's decision that their failure to cast out Hoffa made them pariahs unfit to live inside labor's house. All this they knew—and they let Hoffa know it made no difference. He was still their boy.

When he rose to speak, they were on their feet again, whistling, shouting, stomping. He waved them down with a quick gesture. He spoke in a flat tone —confident, insistent, bare of oratorical adornment. There was none of the platform magic of a John L. Lewis or a Walter Reuther.

YET the sensation that came across was of relentless, elemental strength. The 45-year-old Hoffa exuded it, from the glossy hair that bristled away from his scalp like a porcupine's quills, past the chill, hooded eyes, to the rocklike hands. He teetered a little on the balls of his feet in the manner of a fighter about to throw a punch. His navy blue suit strained across his thick chest and heavily muscled arms. Here was no Dave Beck softened by easy living. For all his Cadillacs, his $50,000-a-year salary, his limitless expense account and his free hand with the union's millions, Beck's successor still looks, talks and acts like a truck driver.

No note of apology marked Hoffa's report on his stewardship. Everything was black or white, with all the black on the side of his critics. He had taunts for Senator McClellan ("he's back in Arkansas now trying to straighten out Faubus, I guess"); the newspapers ("they propagandize the teamsters for only one reason—because of the size and strength and militancy of the Teamsters Union"); college professors and other longhairs with proposals for laws to clean up labor ("they only talk that way after they have had four long glasses of booze").

That still left Hoffa with a few jibes to fling at the two union chiefs he considers principally responsible for the Teamsters' expulsion from the A. F. L.-C. I. O.—George Meany ("he always hid in his office as a bookkeeper—he has yet to negotiate his first contract or meet his first scab on a picket line") and Walter Reuther ("here we talk a language the teamsters understand, not a language to change the United States into a socialist country or to worry about what politician is elected").

He had a simple explanation for the charges that the union had become a homing ground for jailbirds: "All this hocus-pocus about racketeers and crooks is a smokescreen to carry you back to the days when they could drop you in the scrap heap like they do a worn-out truck." The teamsters applauded dutifully.

They kept applauding as he told them how much other unions owed them and how much they owed their union. He reminded them of the days when they worked seventy or eighty hours for $18 a week, without vacations, pensions, welfare, pay for breakdown time or seniority protection. "There are men here who used to pull Toledo for 75 cents or Chicago for $1.50; now the scale to Toledo is $17 and $34 or $36 to Chicago," he declared.

Always he was the teamster talking to teamsters: "You know me since I'm 17—the kid, you called me. They say I've got a police record. Sure, I've got a record and you know where I got it. It's no secret. There's not one thing there outside the labor movement. And I tell you Hoffa will have it again if they start kicking the truck driver around."

He warned them that the next five years would be "the five toughest years we ever saw in this union business," and this provided the jumping-off point for another slap at his detractors. "They even criticize me for calling this a business," he complained. "Well, what do you hire us for, if not to sell your labor at the highest buck we can get?"

THERE was much more, all designed to get across the point that "what we have had we can lose overnight, if we are foolish enough to become divided." And then it was time for the main business of the evening, a vote on whether Local 299 wanted to strip Hoffa and his executive board of their control over the union's finances and internal affairs.

"You are here for one purpose," Hoffa declaimed, "to show the solidarity and strength of this organization

The Hoffa Record

James R. Hoffa has been accused of eighty-two specific acts of betrayal of his union obligations by the Senate Select Committee on Improper Activities in the Labor or Management Field.

These include granting union charters to men with long criminal records, keeping jailed teamster officials on the union payroll, manipulating hundreds of thousands of union dollars for his personal benefit, making millions more available to his friends without membership approval, profiting from conflict-of-interest business arrangements set up for him and his wife by employers dependent on the union's goodwill, using strong-arm tactics to maintain and extend one-man rule and conspiring with racketeers to defeat his own union's organizing efforts in the New York taxicab field.

The committee also charged that Hoffa's announced intention to weld all transportation unions —land, sea and air—into a single front would make him more powerful than the Government itself.

Much of the Senate testimony dealt with financial abuses in Local 299, of which Hoffa has been and continues to be president. According to the committee, he arranged to transfer $500,000 of the local's money to a Florida bank in connection with a loan by the bank to a real estate development project in which Hoffa and Owen Bert Brennan, president of Local 337, held an option to buy a 45 per cent interest.

The Hoffa and Brennan locals also were accused of supplying $150,000 to buy a home for "Paul the Waiter" Ricca, Chicago mobster. The committee estimated that the joint welfare fund maintained by Local 299 and other Michigan teamster units had been mulcted of $700,000 as a result of dubious real estate investments in Detroit. Censure also was expressed of a $1,-200,000 loan of welfare funds to a Minneapolis department store, now in bankruptcy. The owner, a Hoffa pal, who paid only $14,000 to get the store, disappeared with $100,000 of its assets.

Hoffa has been in and out of courtrooms often, but he has been convicted only three times. In 1937 he paid a $10 fine for assault and battery. Three years later he pleaded nolo contendere to a Federal charge of monopoly conspiracy and was fined $500. In 1947 he received two years' probation and a $500 fine on a charge of attempted extortion under Michigan law. In the last two years he has been acquitted on Federal charges of bribery and illegal wiretapping.

Hoffa has emphasized that he intends to stay on as head of Local 299, despite his duties in the No. 1 spot in Washington. He still draws his $15,000-a-year salary from the local, on top of his $50,000 from the parent union, but he says he plans to give the local its money back as soon as his lawyers get pension and tax problems straightened out.

to those who think the teamster is a coward, that he can't find his way into his union hall or that he is the victim of a business agent who is a racketeer, a bum or a hoodlum. You and only you have established the rules of this organization, and only you—not the propaganda of the press and McClellan — will change the rules."

He waved a thick bundle of bills at the crowd. They represented all the local's obligations for the preceding month. He told the members they could insist on having each bill submitted to them for approval if they did not want to leave blanket authority in the officers' hands. "Send 'em to McClellan," was the bull-voiced suggestion of one rank-and-filer. The others shouted that they wanted the executive board to keep on using its judgment about how to spend the union's money.

The story was the same when Hoffa mentioned charges that the welfare and pension funds had been "stole blind" by investments he had made for his own profit or to help out his cronies. He lauded the funds' accomplishments, and he asked where his critics— "the great saviors of the workers"—had been when the union was battling to get the benefit programs set up. He contrasted the pension payments of $135 a month at age 60 with the lower standards in force in "many so-called progressive, clean unions."

When he got through and asked whether they wanted the union to change its way of doing business, there was a mass roar of "no, no, no." He was not satisfied with that. "Let's do this in an orderly way," he said, "so no one can charge I stole the vote." He called for a standing vote on whether the executive board should continue to have a blank

check on the handling of union funds, the designation of convention delegates, the calling of strikes and all other matters of internal administration. Everybody stood up.

When the "nays" were called everybody sat down—except one brother, who had apparently had one beer too many on the way to the hall. When the crowd laughed, he slumped into his seat. That made it unanimous.

HOW significant was the whole performance? Should it be dismissed as the obeisance of cowed and servile men to a master armed with life-and-death power over their jobs? Did fear of physical violence against themselves or their families chain the members of Local 299 to the Hoffa truck? Was their vote an expression of insensate mass adoration akin to that extended to their fuehrers by the brain-washed populace of totalitarian lands?

None of these possible explanations seemed adequate for an observer who had spent three days before the meeting in individual contact with many of the drivers, talking to them privately in the terminals and on the loading docks.

ONLY two out of nearly 200 said they felt that the union was in a mess and that the membership was powerless to do anything about it. The others declared, with every indication of sincerity, that they felt Hoffa had done a standout job on wages, welfare, grievances and every other phase of union service. They brushed aside the accusations of gangsterism and racketeering as part of an attempt by outside forces to cut Hoffa down to size because he was doing too good a job in defense of the rank and file.

Their words added up to a hymn of contentment. Listen to Chad Virdin, an over-the-road driver, who shuttles the mail between Detroit and Jackson, Mich., on a night run: "So far as I'm concerned, the union is 100 per cent. Every year that old raise is there, and it has been ever since Hoffa took over." Or hear Robert E. Jones, a 345-pounder, who drives for the New York Central: "I think Jimmy Hoffa did more for the truck driver than anyone else who ever lived." Or these words from Clyde Miles, a loader on the dock at the Union Truck Company: "I'm only sorry there can't be more 299 locals and two Jimmy Hoffas. Where they get all that stuff in Washington, I don't know."

Some put their accent on the improvement in wages, from 65 cents an hour less than twenty years ago to $2.72 an hour now. Others enthuse about children delivered or operations performed at the expense of the welfare fund. Still others say that the thing they liked best was that Jimmy's office door was always open, that he was never too busy to listen to their gripes. Even now when he is in Washington, he will take a long-distance call collect if a member has an urgent problem.

HE drives his staff harder than his members drive their trucks. A giant picture of Hoffa stares down, with the intensity of Big Brother, from the wall of the room in which the business agents have their desks. The headquarters contains a steam bath and massage table for their use, but they get little chance to luxuriate under the masseur's

fingers. Hoffa's partner, Owen Bert Brennan, whose standing with the McClellan Committee is no higher than Jimmy's own, laments that Hoffa never asks "how are you" or "how do you feel" when he telephones from the capital. His only query is, "What are you doing, and why the hell aren't you doing it right now?"

BUT even a casual visitor to the union offices is swiftly reminded that there is another side to the organization's affairs—the side that has caused the Senate investigators to bear down so heavily on underworld influence in the teamsters. The day that Hoffa was due back in town to attend the membership meeting, Philip Weiss, an industrialist with strong racket ties, strolled into the headquarters for a conference with Hoffa's aides.

Weiss was convicted two years ago of conspiring to steal $100,000 in auto parts, but his five-year jail sentence was set aside on a technicality. He is awaiting retrial in Detroit. When Hoffa was asked that night what Weiss was doing in the union, he shrugged indifferently. "He probably just dropped in to say hello; he does business with a lot of truck employers." And that was that.

The two union members who

confided that they felt there was much that needed correcting in the local made it clear that they did not believe it would be healthy for them to try to do the correcting. "They have a way of eliminating you if you make trouble," said a car haulaway driver with twenty-two years in the organization. "What can one man do?" asked a platform loader. "Someone else is going to have to clean it up."

AND what of the top-heavy majority who do not rebel because they see nothing to rebel

against, whose fealty to Hoffa is so great that they are prepared to disregard or disbelieve all the venality disclosed at the Washington hearings? An observer comes away with no sense that these are callous, calculating men, sunk in cynicism or allergic to considerations of conventional morality. Many are churchgoers, heads of families, war veterans. They seem to differ little from workers in auto plants or steel mills or other industries in the urges and satisfactions to which they respond.

If they lack polish, that is hardly a surprise. As Joseph McDonald, a moon-faced, barrel-bellied movie driver, who has been a member of the local since it was born, puts it: "We didn't build our union in this tough industry in a town this size with feather pillows."

It is precisely because the rank and file of Local 299 has so much resemblance to most teamsters and most workers that the enthusiasm with which they embrace the Hoffa brand of leadership is in many ways more disquieting than Hoffa's own long record of moral delinquency. For it tends to lend substance to the creed by which Hoffa lives, namely, that anything goes so long as the union keeps delivering fatter pay envelopes, bigger pensions and better conditions to its members. He summed up his prescription for keeping workers' loyalty in one of his wiretapped conversations with extortionist Johnny Dio. It was: "Treat 'em right, and you don't have to worry."

This is the philosophy of the slot machine, with the gamble eliminated. The wheel is set for a payoff on every spin and while the dollar signs keep coming up no one is disposed to check too carefully on what is happening in the back room. The teamsters hold no monopoly on this attitude; it pervades much of our economic, social and political life. We admire the man who can deliver—how he delivers is much less important.

THIS is a concept that holds dismal implications for those who look to increased democracy in unions as the answer to corruption. For it is distressingly apparent that Hoffa has emerged from all the attacks on him much more solidly entrenched than ever—not only in the allegiance of his home local but in every section of the 1,600,000-member brotherhood.

Votes of confidence have been piling up around him like confetti as he pilots his out-

cast teamsters uphill in wages and membership at a far faster clip than unions which proudly wear the Good Housekeeping seal of the A. F. L.-C. I. O. Against this backdrop of bread-and-butter gains, he has been mobilizing support for his

fight to jettison his court-appointed monitors and win full control of the union at a new convention next March.

If the convention is held, the peppery little Detroiter seems sure to come out on top, and this time he will need none of the rigging tactics that cast so much shadow over his victory in Miami Beach a year ago. If Hoffa is stopped, it will be by the courts or other outside forces, not by any prohibitions from the rank and file.

No piling up of legislative safeguards for the exercise of democratic rights within the union seems likely to alter that fact in the near future. Unless Hoffa loses the energy and skill he has displayed as a delivery man for ever-expanding benefits for his members, there is every reason to believe he can count on their backing for an indefinite period.

Only as we achieve loftier moral standards not only in labor but in business, politics and every other branch of our society can we hope for a real transformation. This is a road on which progress is sometimes agonizingly difficult, but it is an effort that must be made unless we are ready to concede that democracy itself is a failure.

November 9, 1958

Text of Taft-Hartley Amendments of Labor Reform Bill Agreed to by Conferees

Special to The New York Times.

WASHINGTON, Sept. 3—Following is the text of Title VII (Taft-Hartley Act amendments) of the labor reform bill agreed to by a Senate-House conference committee. The Labor-Management Relations Act, commonly known as the Taft-Hartley Act, is an amendment to the National Labor Relations Act, which was known as the Wagner Act.

TITLE VII
Amendments to the Labor Management Relations Act, 1947, as Amended

Federal-State Jurisdiction

Sec. 701. Section 14 of the National Labor Relations Act, as amended, is amended by adding at the end thereof the following new subsection:

"(C) (1) The board, in its discretion, may, by rule of decision or by published rules adopted pursuant to the administrative procedure act, decline to assert jurisdiction over any labor dispute involving any class or category of employes, where, in the opinion of the board, the effect of such labor dispute on commerce is not sufficiently substantial to warrant the exercise of its jurisdiction: Provided, that the board shall not decline to assert jurisdiction over any labor dispute over which it would assert jurisdiction under the standards prevailing upon Aug. 1, 1959.

"(2) Nothing in this act shall be deemed to prevent or bar any agency of the courts of any state or territory (including the Commonwealth of Puerto Rico, Guam, and the Virgin Islands) from assuming and asserting jurisdiction over labor disputes over which the board declines, pursuant to paragraph (1) of this subsection, to assert jurisdiction."

(B) Section 3 (B) of such act is amended to read as follows:

"(B) The board is authorized to delegate to any group of three or more members any or all of the powers which it may itself exercise. The board is also authorized to delegate to its regional directors its powers under Section 9 to determine the unit appropriate for the purpose of collective bargaining, to investigate and provide for hearings, and determine whether a question of representation exists, and to direct an election or take a secret ballot under subsection (C) or (E) of Section 9 and certify the results thereof, except that upon the filing of a request therefor with the board by any interested person, the board may review any action of a regional director delegated to him under this paragraph, but such a review shall not, unless specifically ordered by the board, operate as a stay of action taken by the regional director. A vacancy in the board shall not impair the right of the remaining members to exercise all of the powers of the board, and three members of the board shall, at all times, constitute a quorum of the board, except that two members shall constitute a quorum of any group designated pursuant to the first sentence hereof.

"The board shall have an official seal which shall be judicially noticed."

Economic Strikers

Sec. 702. Section 9(C)(3) of the National Labor Relations Act, as amended, is amended by amending the second sentence thereof to read as follows: "Employes engaged in an economic strike who are not entitled to reinstatement shall be eligible to vote under such regulations as the board shall find are consistent with the purposes and provisions of this act in any election conducted within twelve months after the commencement of the strike."

Vacancy in Office of General Counsel

Sec. 703. Section 3(D) of the National Labor Relations Act, as amended, is amended by adding after the period at the end thereof the following: "In case of a vacancy in the office of the general counsel the President is authorized to designate the officer or employe who shall act as general counsel during such vacancy, but no person or persons so designated shall so act (1) for more than forty days when the Congress is in session unless a nomination to fill such vacancy shall have been submitted to the Senate, or (2) after the adjournment sine die of the session of the Senate in which such nomination was submitted."

Boycotts and Recognition Picketing

Sec. 704. (A) Section 8(B) (4) of the National Labor Relations Act, as amended, is amended to read as follows:

"(4)(I) to engage in, or to induce or encourage any individual employed by any person engaged in commerce or in an industry affecting commerce to engage in, a strike or a refusal in the course of his employment to use, manufacture, process, transport, or otherwise handle or work on any goods, articles, materials, or commodities or to perform any services; or (II) to threaten, coerce, or restrain any person engaged in commerce or in an industry affecting commerce, where in either case an object therof is:

"(A) Forcing or requiring any employer or self-employed person to join any labor or employer organization or to enter into any agreement which is prohibited by section 8(E);

"(B) Forcing or requiring any person to cease using, selling, handling, transporting, or otherwise dealing in the products of any other producer, processor, or manufacturer, or to cease doing business with any other person, or forcing or requiring any other employer to recognize or bargain with a labor organization as the representative of his employes unless such labor organization has been certified as the representative of such employes under the provisions of Section 9; provided that nothing contained in this clause (B) shall be construed to make unlawful, where not otherwise unlawful, any primary strike, or primary picketing;

"(C) forcing or requiring any employer to recognize or bargain with a particular labor organization as the representative of his employes if another labor organization has been certified as the representative of such employes under the provisions of Section 9;

"(D) Forcing or requiring any employer to assign particular work to employes in a particular labor organization or in a particular trade, craft, or class rather than to employes in another labor organization or in another trade, craft, or class, unless such employer is failing to conform to an order or certification of the board determining the bargaining representative for employes performing such work;

"Provided, that nothing contained in this subsection (B) shall be construed to make unlawful a refusal by any person to enter upon the premises of any employer (other than his own employer), if the employes of such employer are engaged in a strike ratified or approved by a representative of such employes whom such employer is required to recognize under this act: provided further, that for the purposes of this paragraph (4) only, nothing contained in such paragraph shall be construed to prohibit publicity, other than picketing, for the purpose of truthfully advising the public, including consumers and members of a labor organization, that a product or products are produced by an employer with whom the labor organization has a primary dispute and are distributed by another employer, as long as such publicity does not have an effect of inducing any individual employed by any person other than the primary employer in the course of his employment to refuse to pick up, deliver, or transport any goods, or not to perform any services, at the establishment of the employer engaged in such distribution";

New Subsection Added

(B) Section 8 of the National Labor Relations Act, as amended, is amended by adding at the end thereof the following new subsection:

"(E) It shall be an unfair labor practice for any labor organization and any employer to enter into any contract or agreement, express or implied, whereby such employer ceases or refrains or agrees to cease or refrain from handling, using, selling, transporting or otherwise dealing in any of the products of any other employer, or to cease doing business with any other person, and any contract or agreement entered into heretofore or hereafter containing such an agreement shall be to such extent unenforcible and void: provided, that nothing in this subsection (E) shall apply to an agreement between a labor organization and an employer in the construction industry relating to the contracting or subcontracting of work to be done at the site of the construction, alteration, painting, or repair of a building, structure, or other work: provided further, that for the purposes of this subsection (E) and section 8(B) (4) (B) the terms 'any employer,' 'any person engaged in commerce or an industry affecting commerce,' and 'any person' when used in relation to the terms 'any other producer, processor, or manufacturer,' 'any other employer,' or 'any other person' shall not include persons in the relation of a jobber, manufacturer, contractor, or subcontractor working on the goods or premises of the jobber or manufacturer or performing parts of an integrated process of production in the apparel and clothing industry: provided further, that nothing in this act shall prohibit the enforcement of any agreement which is within the foregoing exception."

"(C) Section 8(B) of the National Labor Relations Act, as amended, is amended by striking out the word "and" at the end of paragraph (5), striking out the period at the end of paragraph (6), and inserting in lieu thereof a semicolon and the word "and," and adding a new paragraph as follows:

"(7) To picket or cause to be picketed, or threaten to picket or cause to be picketed, any employer where an object thereof is forcing or requiring an employer to recognize or bargain with a labor organization as the representative of his employes, or forcing or requiring the employes of an employer to accept or select such labor organization as their collective bargaining representative, unless such labor organization is currently certified as the representative of such employes:

Limitations Listed

"(A) Where the employer has lawfully recognized in accordance with this act any other labor organization and a question concerning representation may not appropriately be raised under Section 9(C) of this act,

"(B) Where within the preceding twelve months a valid election under Section 9(C) of this act has been conducted, or

"(C) Where such picketing has been conducted without a petition under Section 9(C) being filed within a reasonable period of time not to exceed thirty days from the commencement of such picketing: provided, that when such a petition has been filed the board shall forthwith, without regard to the provisions of Section 8(C)(1) or the absence of a showing of a substantial interest on the part of the labor organization, direct an election in such unit as the board finds to be appropriate and shall certify the results thereof: provided further, that nothing in this subparagraph (C) shall be construed to prohibit any picketing or other publicity for the purpose of truthfully

advising the public (including consumers) that an employer does not employ members of, or have a contract with, a labor organization, unless an effect of such picketing is to induce any individual employed by any other person in the course of his employment, not to pick up, deliver or transport any goods or not to perform any services.

"Nothing in this paragraph (7) shall be construed to permit any act which would otherwise be an unfair labor practice under this section (8) (B)."

"(D) Section 10 (L) of the National Labor Relations Act, as amended, is amended by adding after the words "Section 8 (B)," the words "or Section 8 (E) or Section 8 (B) (7)," and by striking out the period at the end of the third sentence and inserting in lieu thereof a colon and the following: "Provided further, that such officer or regional attorney shall not apply for any restraining order under Section 8 (B) (7) if a charge against the employer under 8 (A) (2) has been filed and after the preliminary investigation, he has reasonable cause to believe that such charge is true and that a complaint should issue."

"(E) Section 303 (A) of the Labor Management Relations Act, 1947, is amended to read as follows:

"(A) It shall be unlawful, for the purpose of this section only, in an industry or activity affecting commerce, for any labor organization to engage in any activity or conduct defined as an unfair labor practice in Section 8 (B) (4) of the National Labor Relations Act, as amended."

Building and Construction Industry

Sec. 705, (A) Section 8 of the National Labor Relations Act, as amended by Section 704 (B) of this act, is amended by adding at the end thereof the following new subsection:

"(F) It shall not be an unfair labor practice under subsections (A) and (B) of this section for an employer engaged primarily in the building and construction industry to make an agreement covering employes engaged (or who, upon their employment, will be engaged) in the building and construction industry with a labor organization of which building and construction employes are members (not established, maintained, or assisted by any action defined in Section 8 (A) of this

act as an unfair labor practice) because (1) the majority status of such labor organization has not been established under the provision of Section 9 of this act prior to the making of such agreement, or (2) such agreement requires as a condition of employment, membership in such labor organization after the seventh day following the beginning of such employment or the effective date of the agreement, whichever is later, or (3) such agreement requires the employer to notify such labor organization an opportunity to refer qualified applicants for such employment, or (4) such agreement specifies minimum training or experience qualifications for employment or provides for priority in opportunities for employment based upon length of service with such employer in the industry or in the particular geographical area: provided, that nothing in this subsection shall set aside the final proviso to Section 8 (A) (3) of this act: provided further, that any agreement which would be invalid but for clause (1) of this subsection, shall not be a bar to a petition filed pursuant to Section 9 (C) or 9 (E)."

"(B) Nothing contained in the amendment made by subsection (A) shall be construed as authorizing the execution or application of agreements requiring membership in a labor organization as a condition of employment in any state or territory in which such execution or application is prohibited by state or territorial law.

Priority in Case Handling

Sec. 706. Section 10 of the National Labor Relations Act, as amended, is amended by adding at the end therof a new subsection as follows:

"(M) Whenever it is charged that any person has engaged in an unfair labor practice within the meaning of subsection (A) (3) or (B) (2) of Section 8, such charge shall be given priority over all other cases except cases of like character in the office where it is filed or to which it is referred and cases given priority under subsection (L)."

Effective Date of Amendments

Sec. 707. The amendments made by this title shall take effect sixty days after the date of the enactment of this act and no provision of this title shall be deemed to make an unfair labor practice, any act which is performed prior to such effective date which did not constitute an unfair labor practice prior thereto.

September 4, 1958

UNIONS' DUES FOUND MODERATE IN STUDY

WASHINGTON, Oct. 29 (AP) —With some exceptions, labor union membership costs are generally moderate.

The first comprehensive study of union dues and fees ever made shows that some workers pay as high as $1,400 to join a union. But this is a rare case. The initiation fee usually is a fairly modest sum. Similarly, some monthly dues exceed $25 but most are below $4.

Full data have become available because labor organizations now are required to submit sworn statements of dues and fees to the Labor Department. More than 50,000 such reports are on file.

The department's Bureau of Labor - Management Reports says this is what they show:

More than half the unions have monthly dues rates below $4. Three out of ten charge $5 or more. About one in a hundred charges $10 or more.

One in four charges $5 or less for initiation. Two in five charge more than $10. One in ten charges $100 or more.

Less than 12 per cent of the unions charge transfer fees. They are collected when a member switches from one local to another in the same national union.

October 30, 1960

Yablonski of U.M.W. Slain With Wife and Daughter

CLARKSVILLE, Pa., Jan. 5—Joseph A. Yablonski, whose unsuccessful challenge last year for the presidency of the United Mine Workers of America touched off the bitterest election campaign in the union's 79-year history, was found shot to death today, with his wife and daughter, in their secluded home here.

The state police said that all three had been murdered.

The police said that the body of the chunky, 59-year-old, gravel-voiced union leader had been found sprawled on the floor of a bedroom.

On the bed, also in night-clothes, lay the body of his wife, the former Margaret Rita Wasicek, 57, a playwright. In another bedroom of the family's two-story fieldstone home, hidden by hedges from a country road, was found the body of their daughter, Charlotte, 25.

The young woman, a social worker, had left her post in a clinic in Centerville last year to work in her father's campaign.

Capt. Joseph Snyder of the state police told newsmen: "The decomposition of the bodies indicates they have been dead for several days."

Mr. Yablonski had been shot once in the back of the head. His wife and daughter had also been shot.

The bodies, on the upper floor of the recently refurbished home where signs of Christmas—a wreath on the door and cards in the windows—were still visible, were discovered by a son, Kenneth Yablonski, a lawyer who had been unable to reach the family by telephone.

Captain Snyder said telephone lines in the home had been cut.

The tiny community where the triple slaying took place is situated in soft-coal country near the Monongahela River, about 55 miles from Pittsburgh in the southwestern part of Pennsylvania.

The population of less than 1,200 is mainly composed of miners, many of whom are employed in the Robena mine, owned by the United States Steel Corporation.

Another Son Is Bitter

In Washington, another Yablonski son, Joseph Jr., known as Chip, expressed bitterness about the slaying, telling a reporter: "You guys just didn't believe how rotten this union was." Mr. Yablonski, a lawyer, was asked if he thought the union had anything to do with the death of his parents and sister.

"I'm convinced of it without even knowing," he said.

At United Mine Workers' headquarters in Washington, a statement on the deaths was issued through a spokesman by W. A. (Tony) Boyle, who defeated Mr. Yablonski in the balloting Dec. 9.

The spokesman said that Mr. Boyle was shocked at the news. The spokesman expressed assurance that the slayings had no connection with the union or last month's election.

Mr. Boyle's statement said, in part: "I do not know at this time what caused the deaths of Brother Yablonski, his wife and his daughter, but whatever the cause, the violent deaths of three members of the Yablonski family can only be called a tragedy."

The New York Times
Joseph A. Yablonski

He added, "As president of the United Mine Workers, I offer the fullest cooperation to the authorities of all facilities of our organization to try to resolve the cause of these deaths."

Mr. Yablonski's announcement last May 29 of his candidacy took union leaders by surprise. Standing in the Mayflower Hotel in Washington, the bushy-browed Mr. Yablonski, whose nickname was Jock, charged Mr. Boyle, the incumbent president, with "shocking ineptitude and passivity" in not pressing more vigorously for mine safety reforms and accused him of adopting an "abject, follow-the-leader posture toward the coal industry."

In the room at the time were Ralph Nader, the automobile safety and consumer advocate, who had recently criticized the leadership of the United Mine Workers for what he termed its lack of militancy on miner health and safety reforms.

Mr. Yablonski also charged that Mr. Boyle was running a "dictatorial" and "decaying" administration that was "riddled with fear."

Aid in West Virginia

Mr. Yablonski's campaign, in the days that followed, also drew the support of John D. Rockefeller 4th, the Democratic Secretary of State of West Virginia, and Representative Ken Hechler a Democrat from West Virginia who is a bitter critic of Mr. Boyle's leadership.

Today after learning of Mr. Yablonski's death Mr. Rockefeller said: "I was very strongly moved by his intensity and commitment to making the life of the coal miner better. And if the life of the coal miner does get better—and I think it will—Jock Yablonski will deserve a lot of the credit."

Mr. Hechler termed the slayings a "tragedy" and said:

"His candidacy helped spur a number of policy changes at the United Mine Workers headquarters and forced the top leadership to get behind the stronger coal mine health and safety legislation and other reforms at least prior to the Dec. 9 election.

"Coal miners throughout the nation owe Joseph Yablonski a lasting debt for his courage in speaking out for the rights of the rank and file coal miners to be represented by a a clean and strong union."

The challenge posed to Mr. Boyle by Joseph Albert Yablonski was the first real one raised within the union since 1926, when John Brophy unsuccessfully opposed John L. Lewis, the union's fiery, long-time president who died last June 11 at the age of 89.

Mr. Boyle, who had held the presidency since 1963, was the head of a union with 110,000 active members and about 40,000 retired but voting members in more than 1,300 locals in 23 states and four Canadian provinces.

He had been groomed for the job by Mr. Lewis. However, although successful in negotiating larger wage increases in recent years, he found that his constituency was ahead of its leadership in demanding more bargaining emphasis on working conditions.

Among the rank and file demands were improved mine safety, a guaranteed wage that would compel operators to end the method under which miners can be called to work with little notice and receive pay for anywhere from one to six days a week.

New 5-Year Term

In the balloting, Mr. Boyle was returned to office for another five-year term by a vote of 81,056 to 45,872 for Mr. Yablonski.

Mr. Yablonski, whose father was killed in a mine accident in 1933, was born in Pittsburgh on March 3, 1910. He began working in the mines in 1925, when he was 15 years old, turning his earnings over to his family.

After serving as a picket and union organizer, he was elected president of a local in 1934. Then he was elected to represent 15,000 workers on the executive board of District 5. He was a workers' representative in Washington from 1934 to 1942.

In the latter year he was elected to the international executive board, representing 35,000 miners from District 5, in a post that he has held continuously through seven elections.

In 1958, Mr. Yablonski was also elected president of District 5, but was forced out by Mr. Boyle in 1966. He said several times during last year's campaign that his decision to oppose Mr. Boyle for the union presidency was made at that time. Mr. Yablonski had run without authorization from headquarters for the vice-presidency in 1964.

Over the years, Mr. Yablonski earned a reputation as a fair and effective trouble shooter.

His campaign against Mr. Boyle was marked by a series of lawsuits alleging unfair tactics and by an attack on Mr. Yablonski in a hotel in Springfield, Ill., where he was knocked unconscious by a karate blow to the neck.

The Nation

U.M.W.:

The Heavy Shadow Of a Murder

WASHINGTON — The events that battered the once-mighty United Mine Workers of America last week were described by some in the Bible Belt Appalachian coalfields as acts of a God "exceeding wroth." But that explanation left out the shade of Jock Yablonski—by week's end, his vengeance seemed almost complete.

Three years ago, Joseph A. Yablonski was an ex-convict and an ex-coalminer who for 20 years had truckled to the autocratic U.M.W. hierarchy. With a natural talent on the stump, he had been its gravel-voiced orator and apologist, invariably a keynote speaker, lionizing the aging, nepotistic union leaders.

Then in May, 1969, secure at the age of 59 in a $30,000-a-year sinecure, Mr. Yablonski risked all, as a reform candidate for the union presidency. Since the late John L. Lewis put himself at the center of the miners' and the American labor universe in 1925, opposition in the U.M.W. had been systematically stifled.

Treasonably, in the eyes of Mr. Lewis's annoined heir, W. A. (Tony) Boyle, to whom Lewis had passed the presidency in 1963, Mr. Yablonski accused the 66-year-old Boyle of conducting a corrupt and ruinous "reign of terror" over the 190,000-member union. At his announcement news conference here, Mr. Yablonski found it prudent to deploy bodyguards. And for the next seven months the U.M.W. insurgent lived in fear.

Scoffed at by the Boyle regime; sneered at by the rest of the labor movement (the A.F.L.-C.I.O.'s George Meany called Mr. Yablonski "just one of the boys in the kitchen trying to move into the living room"); ignored by the Labor Department (it rejected repeated Yablonski pleas for a pre-election investigation)—Mr. Yablonski predictably lost the Dec. 9 election.

It was known, however, that the Yablonski faction intended to go down fighting. One lawsuit seeking redress through the courts was filed; others were pending. On the night of Dec. 30, hired gunmen murdered the Yablonski family—father, mother and daughter.

Boyle denied any union connection with the slayings—union spokesmen actually hinted at possible Yablonski connection with drugs or with the underworld—and the U.M.W. offered a $50,000 reward for the killers. But the fate of Mr. Yablonski had a checking effect on the remnants of the Boyle opposition in the rank-and-file.

Then last week, in United States District Court here, and in a dingy Washington County Common Pleas Courtroom not far from the Yablonski's Clarksville, Pa., home, the union leadership was struck two heavy blows.

● In Washington County, there was a courtroom confession that accused two U.M.W. officials—Albert Pass, a Boyle ally on the International Executive Board, and a Pass staff man, William J. Prater—of conspiracy in the murder. The confession also implicated others higher up in the hierarchy here, unnamed for the moment. Silous Huddleston, a Tennessee U.M.W. local president and one of the original five murder suspects, admitted that he had been the middleman who had passed $15,000 from U.M.W. headquarters here, received from Pass, to the hired killers. Under arrest, Pass and Prater face murder charges in Pennsylvania. There was a prospect of further arrests. And there was no comment, no denial from the U.M.W.

● In Washington, D. C., a United States District Court judge, set aside the election of Boyle as union president. In a 33-page decision, Judge William B. Bryant found that the evidence of wrongdoing by Boyle and other incumbents in the 1969 election was "too strong to resist." He ordered the Department of Justice to prepare a formal order by tomorrow declaring the election results void.

The week's events did not stand alone. Mr. Yablonski's 1969 exposure of the Lewis legacy in the U.M.W. (collusion with coal management, rewards to the favored with members' dues, violence to dissenters) had already brought the union low.

Moreover, the union last year lost a Yablonski-inspired rank-and-file damage suit that accused the U.M.W. welfare and pension fund of bizarre irregularities with the union-owned bank here. More than $8-million of the membership's money has had to be paid out to non-union coalmine operators, who have won a series of treble-damage antitrust suits against the union's practice of using unionized companies to penalize the non-union holdouts.

And Boyle has been convicted of violating the Federal prohibition against labor political contributions by giving $30,000 in union funds to the 1968 Presidential campaign of Hubert H. Humphrey. If the conviction stands on appeal, he will be barred as a felon from holding any union office for five years.

Whether Boyle and his cohorts will be thrown out earlier by the miners in the coming rerun of the 1969 election is less certain. If Boyle chooses to run again, the scattered remnants of the Yablonski opposition among the rank-and-file—men who know coalmining better than politics and administration—may have difficulty finding a candidate. Mr. Yablonski's sons, Chip and Kenneth, who have carried on their father's fight, are barred by a U.M.W. requirement of five years in the mines. Both are lawyers.

The Yablonski sons and their father's lawyer, Joseph L. Rauh Jr., are to convene a dissidents' policy committee meeting today in Charleston, W. Va. There is certain to be an anti-Boyle U.M.W. convention to make nominations. And Mr. Rauh said he would be in court here tomorrow, possibly to ask for the immediate removal of Boyle under a court-ordered Federal trusteeship.

But the outlook for the U.M.W.—the originator of industrial unionism in this country and the father of the C.I.O.—has never been less certain. Boyle may step aside for a candidate from within his own satrapy. Thousands of miners, convinced by U.M.W. propaganda that Mr. Yablonski was perhaps a Communist, or at least was ruled by "outsiders," will remain loyal to Boyle.

—BEN A. FRANKLIN

CHAPTER 9

New Horizons

Albert Shanker and Harry Van Arsdale
after conferring with Mayor Lindsay on one
of New York City's numerous labor problems.
The New York Times.

1 IN 8 CLERKS IN UNIONS

Study Shows Clerical Workers Resist Organization

Of the nation's 7,950,000 clerical workers, only one out of eight is unionized, according to a survey of management contracts with unions representing office workers, as distinguished from sales, editorial and professional personnel, announced yesterday by the American Management Association.

The analysis was based on a survey of 1,029 unionized companies and the study of 300 existing contracts covering more than 250,000 employes in representative industries in thirty-seven states, Canada and Hawaii.

The association said the study, which will be published under the title of "Collective Bargaining in the Office" for association members, was undertaken to establish the type of contracts now being written. The report pointed out that, contrary to general belief, a great majority of white collar workers remained unorganized and unions still were "encountering resistance from this highly individualistic group."

February 7, 1948

TREND TO UNIONS SEEN FOR OFFICES

'White Collar' Organization Only Matter of Time, Professor Predicts

The unionization of office employes is almost inevitable in the future, C. Wright Mills, Associate Professor of Sociology, Columbia University, declared yesterday. He spoke before concluding sessions of the American Management Association's two-day office management conference in the New Yorker Hotel.

Professor Mills said white collar employes have watched their former advantages over factory and production workers disappear one by one. He noted that factory workers now had paid vacations, sick leave and other non-monetary advantages once peculiar to office employes. Much of the white collar employe's prestige has faded as more and more benefits have been extended to production personnel, Professor Mills told more than 800 office executives attending the conference.

In addition, he emphasized, in the last ten years the white collar average income has been only slightly above the average income of various production groups. In several important instances, Professor Mills said, white collar employes earn less than production workers.

"All of these trends," he declared, "affect the white collar people with whom you deal in your offices. They are also back of the tensions and the problems that are manifested by the drive for unions. That is why it is only a question of time and of the greater and more intelligent effort of unions before your office forces are significantly organized."

James E. McCabe, secretary of Merck & Co., Inc., said more scientific methods are needed in office management. Particular needs, he continued, are for scientific measurement of office work, development of work standards, creation of incentives and improvement of the sense of satisfaction that office employes "should have."

"The field of electronics," Mr. McCabe declared, "may reveal amazing opportunities for eliminating drudgery and for lightening the growing burden of paper work."

October 18, 1952

Labor to Push Organizing Of White-Collar Workers

By A. H. RASKIN
Special to The New York Times.

MIAMI BEACH, Feb. 6—The united labor movement gave the green light today for its first large-scale organizing campaign—an effort to lure 13,000,000 unorganized white-collar workers into union ranks. The go-ahead signal was given at the closing session of the mid-winter meeting of the Executive Council of the American Federation of Labor and Congress of Industrial Organizations.

A total of 120 organizers will be assigned by the parent body to work with a score of international unions in trying to "crack" the white-collar field.

George Meany, the federation's president, expressed confidence that the drive would not be held back by jurisdictional conflicts. Such fights between unions over which group should get any workers who might be organized have blocked recruiting plans among industrial workers in the fourteen months since the labor merger.

New Union Feud Flares

Meanwhile, a new union feud broke out here when the Sheet Metal International Association threatened a libel suit against the International Union of Electrical Workers.

The threat grew out of a formal charge by the electrical union that its sister organization in the merged labor federation had made a "reprehensible, collusive deal" with a Long Island manufacturer.

Labor's plan for an organizing drive was warmly received by John W. Livingston, director of organization for the combined union. He said the results of isolated attempts to sign up white-collar employes in various areas had convinced him there was "greater receptivity to unionization" among such workers now than ever before.

However, there was little outward indication that the council members shared his optimism that any substantial increase in the present estimated total of 3,000,000 union white collar workers would be recorded in the near future.

Even though four workers are still unorganized for every union member in banks, insurance companeis, retail stores, offices, Government agencies and other white-collar enterprises, most top unionists appear to believe the chances for an immediate break-through of major proportions were slight.

No action was taken on a standing offer by the old C. I. O. unions in automobiles, steel, electrical manufacturing and clothing to put a combined total of $4,000,000 into a central organizing fund provided other large unions made comparable contributions.

The whole subject of new organization was put off until the tail end of the council's agenda, and Mr. Livingston was obliged to rush his report to keep the federation leaders from missing their planes and trains.

Mr. Meany characterized the report as "pretty routine." However, he made it plain that the federation did hope to give help to every union interested in organizing white-collar workers without being stopped by jurisdictional roadblocks.

The two principal unions now active among white-collar workers are the Office Employes International Union and the American Federation of State, County and Municipal Employes. There are also two unions organizing insurance workers and several groups active among Federal postal workers. The federation has two affiliates in the merchandising field and a scattering of small unions in other white-collar occupations.

In addition, industrial unions in the mass production industries have made substantial headway in bringing the office employes in their companies into the same union as hourly-rated workers. Mr. Meany said the A. F. L.-C. I. O. would cooperate impartially with all groups in organizing within their jurisdictional spheres.

Mr. Livingston, a former international vice president of the United Automobile Workers, said he intended to hire thirty-five or forty young men and women for the new drive. He said all would be white-collar workers themselves and that many would have college degrees.

The federation also will detail eighty or eighty-five members of its present 275-man organizing staff to work in the campaign. Mr. Livingston said specific assignment plans would be worked out in Washington in the next few weeks.

February 7, 1957

GOODS PRODUCERS NOW U.S. MINORITY

Service Force Takes Lead as Machines Raise the Level of Output

By EDWIN L. DALE Jr.
Special to The New York Times.

WASHINGTON, March 30— Last year, almost without notice, the United States economy passed a major milestone.

For the first time in the nation's history the number of people employed in the production of goods was fewer than the number employed in everything else—government, trade, services, finance, utilities, transportation.

This was revealed by data on the working force now becoming available.

The passage of the milestone was inevitable because of the trend in the way Americans have been earning their living. Economists here agree that this trend has important implications. It may mean that the economy is more "depression-proof" than has been generally realized.

Meanwhile, exactly what has been happening to the labor force in the past decade?

People who produce things include all those working in manufacturing, farming, mining and construction. Their output has risen about 45 per cent since 1947.

This huge outpouring of goods has occurred with only a small increase in the number of people producing them.

There are considerably fewer farmers and miners today than ten years ago. The number of workers in all of the nation's factories has risen by only 1,600,000 to a present total of about 17,000,000. This total represents only about one fourth of all the Americans who are gainfully employed.

Construction workers have been the only category of goods-producers to increase substantially. They have risen by a half to a present total of 3,000,000.

On balance, these goods-producers, turning out today almost half again as much as in 1947, have increased by only 825,000, or a little over 3 per cent.

The reason for the rise in output is productivity. New machines enable each worker to turn out more each year than he did the year before.

But what about the "non-goods" producers? The picture is dramatic:

¶Government workers (Federal state and local) up 1,700,000 or 31 per cent.

¶Retail shop clerks and others employed in trade—up 1,950,000 or 21 per cent.

¶Bank tellers, stock brokers, insurance salesmen and others employed in finance—up 628,000 or 38 per cent.

¶Auto mechanics, laundry workers, barbers, bellhops and others employed in a multitude of services—up 1,220,000 or 26 per cent.

¶Domestic servants—up 700,000 or 40 per cent.

Only two categories of "non-goods" producers have failed to show a rise in employment in the past decade. They are transportation and utilities, and the self-employed, such as shopkeepers, lawyers and family doctors. In both categories, employment today is almost exactly the same as ten years ago.

Autos Give Example

The significance of the relative decline in the importance of manufacturing and other goods-production in supplying a living for the nation's workers can be illustrated by something that happened in the state of Michigan last spring.

From January to June of last year, employment in the auto industry in Michigan dropped from 479,000 to 375,000, or nearly one-fourth. Total employment in the state dropped by about the same absolute amount. But the percentage of unemployment amounted to only 5 per cent.

But people in other lines held their jobs. The following table shows the percentage change in department store sales for the United States as a whole, Detroit, and Flint as compared with the year before:

	Total U.S.	Detroit.	Flint.
Jan.	+ 3	+ 5	— 2
Feb.	+ 9	+ 8	— 1
March	+11	+11	+ 7
April	— 6	— 9	—25
May	+ 8	+ 5	—19
June	+ 9	+ 8	—10

The April decline across the country was caused by an early Easter last year. The figures show that Detroit suffered scarcely at all from the auto slump. Flint did suffer—but the Flints of the nation are becoming exceptions.

The effect of the shift in the work force can be illustrated also by what happened to some key economic indicators in the mild 1953-54 recession.

This was primarily a recession in manufacturing. From the peak in 1953 to the bottom of the recession in 1954, manufacturing output throughout the nation fell off by nearly 11 per cent—a substantial drop.

The number of workers in manufacturing fell off by about the same amount—1,800,000 or 10 per cent.

But the movement of indicators that describe the total economy was considerably different. These were the changes from the high quarter in 1953 to the low quarter in 1954:

Gross national product (the total output of goods and services)—down less than 3 per cent.

Total personal income (the basis of purchasing power)—down just under 1 per cent.

Disposable income (income after taxes)—down less than one half of one per cent.

Obviously, the slump in manufacturing left vast sectors of the economy untouched. Thousands of establishments in trade and service probably did a little less business, but the falling off was not nearly enough to cause them to discharge workers.

Over-all, the number of people at work has grown since the war by about 7,300,000. Of this, almost 90 per cent has been employment in the "non-goods" areas.

A nation with relatively more and more workers employed in producing "non-goods" probably has a more stable economy for a reason that is obvious.

If a factory loses orders, it rather quickly has to lay off production workers. If a department store loses the same proportionate amount of sales, or a restaurant the same proportionate amount of patrons, they may not lay off any workers at all—certainly not nearly as quickly.

What is more, that huge segment of modern employment, the government workers, would, if anything, increase.

FEDERAL EMPLOYES GIVEN UNION RIGHTS

WASHINGTON, Jan. 17 (AP)—President Kennedy put into effect today Government regulations recognizing the right of Federal employes to join unions and negotiate agreements on their working conditions.

Mr. Kennedy signed two Executive Orders that he said would enable Federal workers "to participate in improving personnel policies and working conditions not specifically fixed by the Congress."

Congress sets pay scales for most of the Government's 2,300,000 civilian employes.

Members of a task force that recommended the employe-management program witnessed the signing in the President's office. Also present were Secretary of Labor Arthur J. Goldberg, other Government office-workers.

One Executive Order sets forth procedures for recognizing and dealing with employe organizations. It provides that such organizations be given the chance to speak at discussions on grievances, personnel policies and practices or other matters affecting working conditions.

The second order calls for the Civil Service Commission to issue regulations by April 1 creating a system of appeals from actions taken against any Government employe. The regulations would provide for hearings.

MUNICIPAL UNION PLANS TO EXPAND

Wurf, Newly Elected Head, Seeks a Million Members

Special to The New York Times

WASHINGTON, May 4—Jerry Wurf took over today as head of what is potentially one of the nation's most important labor unions after ousting the incumbent president in a bitter convention battle.

Mr. Wurf, the executive director of the New York District Council of the American Federation of State, County and Municipal Employes, narrowly defeated Arnold S. Zander for the presidency of the national union in an election at its convention last week in Denver.

Mr. Zander, who is 62 years old, had been the only president in the union's 28-year history. He is thought to be the only national union head in the country to hold a Ph.D. degree.

Mr. Wurf moved into his new post at the union's headquarters here today full of plans to put some steam in the union's organizing effort.

The union has about 250,000 members out of a potential of about two million. Moreover, state and local government employment is one of the country's most rapidly expanding job categories.

Mr. Wurf's immediate aim is to reach a membership of one million, but he would not set a time limit for the achievement of this goal.

'A Revolutionary Era'

Mr. Wurf said that the union was entering "a revolutionary era" insofar as its organizing possibilities were concerned. The voluntary check-off of union dues by state and local governments is expanding, he said, giving the union greater financial stability.

In addition, he said, the old concept of government sovereignty, under which many units of government refused to bargain with unions, is being modified to permit exclusive representation rights and negotiations.

The 44-year-old union president said that he would move first to bolster his union's locals where they have organized only a minority of their potential. Next, he said, the union will move through its established locals and district councils to organize new territory, with the national union supplying funds and technical assistance.

White Collar Study Planned

Mr. Wurf pointed out that his union was predominantly blue collar in its membership. He said that he plans to undertake research to determine why clerical workers have shunned it.

He also said he planned to ask independent government employe associations, which have thousands of members in state and local government, to affiliate with his union. This would reverse a Zander policy, which was to battle these groups or ignore them.

The convention that ousted Mr. Zander also elected 11 of 12 executive board members from Mr. Wurf's slate, giving him firm control.

The convention made Mr. Zander president emeritus. He will receive $21,000 a year until he retires at the age of 65.

Mr. Wurf did not dismiss any of the union's staff today, but he was expected to begin later in the week.

May 5, 1964

The New York Times

ASSUMES UNION POST: Jerry Wurf, new president of American Federation of State, County and Municipal Employes, speaking at a meeting here yesterday.

600,000 Federal Workers Affected by Labor Pacts

WASHINGTON, Feb. 13 (AP)—The Labor Department said today that the Federal Government had negotiated collective bargaining agreements with groups representing nearly 600,000 of its 2.5 million civilian employes in the last three years.

Secretary of Labor W. Willard Wirtz said this clearly indicated that "the philosophy of good labor-management relations is being effectively and extensively implemented within the Federal Government."

The department issued a report covering 205 agreements with Federal agencies since a 1962 Presidential executive order designed to encourage Government employes to bargain collectively.

Unlike other labor union members, however, Government employes do not have the right to strike. They are prohibited by law, as well as by the executive order.

February 14, 1965

---

17 Unions Join in White Collar Council

By DAVID R. JONES
Special to The New York Times

WASHINGTON, March 15—Seventeen labor unions began organizing a new council today to promote the interests of white collar workers and spur their unionization.

Charles Cogen, president of the American Federation of Teachers, said at the opening session of the council's founding convention that labor was "not organizing a snob department." He said one aim of the group would be to organize professional workers "who now think snobbishly they are too good to take part in the labor movement."

The new organization was named the Council of American Federation of Labor and Congress of Industrial Organizations Unions for Scientific, Professional and Cultural Employes.

The constitution said the organization's objectives would be to promote cooperation among member unions, to encourage such workers to share fully in organized labor's programs, and to engage in legislative and public relations activities in behalf of such workers.

Mr. Cogen said the council would seek to counteract the "very sad conception" that it was "unprofessional" to join a labor union. The official had said late last year that such a body was needed to "overcome this false image."

Joseph A. Beirne, president of the Communications Workers of America, said in a speech that the A.F.L.-C.I.O.'s support of the council meant it was making "an important pledge" that "American trade unions cannot stand still" in relation to the total work force.

The union official noted Government estimates that the number of white collar jobs would grow by 11 million by 1975 while the number of blue collar jobs would grow by only four million. By 1975, he said, these estimates show that half of all workers will be in white collar jobs.

Asks Unions at All Levels

"For this new group of workers—for these so-called middle class people from the professional, scientific and cultural communities—we're going to have to bring out a more attractive, thoroughly modern union" with "the sweet smell of high status," Mr. Beirne said.

"What was right for grandpa when he was 'working on the railroad' or swinging a pick in a coal mine isn't good enough for the man or woman in the classroom, in the laboratory or in the studio," he said. "And why should it be?"

"We are saying that in every part of the country, at every level of economic condition, there must be an effective union for wage and salary earners," Mr. Beirne said.

The 17 unions taking part in the founding convention are:

The Actors' Equity Association.
The American Guild of Musical Artists.
The Journeymen Barbers and Hairdressers Union.
The National Association of Broadcast Employes and Technicians.
The Communications Workers of America.
The International Union of Electrical Workers.
The International Brotherhood of Electrical Workers.
The Insurance Workers International.
The American Federation of Musicians.
The Office and Professional Employes Union.
The International Union of Operating Engineers.
The Retail Clerks International Association.
The Seafarers International Union.
The International Alliance of Theatrical Stage Employes Union.
The American Federation of State, County and Municipal Employes.
The American Federation of Teachers.
The American Federation of Technical Engineers.

March 16, 1967

Union Militancy of Nation's 10.5 Million Public Employes Is Found Increasing

By DAVID R. JONES
Special to The New York Times

WASHINGTON, April 1 — The Pacatello public schools were shut down for one day last week when angry teachers stayed home to protest the Idaho Legislature's use of tax money.

More than 100 Kansas City firemen suddenly got "sick" the other day and did not show up for work. And in a Cleveland suburb, 200 placard-bearing pickets have been tramping for five weeks outside the county-owned Sunny Acres Hospital.

This turmoil is part of a pattern of unrest that is raging these days among the nation's 10.5 million public employes. The once docile public servant has begun increasingly to rely on strikes and unionization to resolve his complaints about lagging wages and arbitrary bosses.

The trend has broad implications for the American taxpayer, who eventually must shoulder the cost of the union demands. It is already having an impact on civil service systems and public managers, who are facing new challenges to their authority.

And it offers fresh hope of growth for organized labor, whose share of the work force has slipped in recent years.

'Decade of Public Employe'

"All over the country there's a greater interest among public employes in collective bargaining and unions," observed Herbert Haber, New York City's labor relations director. He foresees even more union activity in the months ahead, and says "any manager that ignores that is burying his head."

"The nineteen-sixties have already earned the right to go down in labor relations history as the decade of the public employe," says Jack Stieber, director of Michigan State University's School of Labor and Industrial Relations. The rise of these unions "is the most significant development in the industrial relations field in the last 30 years," he adds.

"Militant unionism has become one of the hottest issues in public administration today," remarks W. V. Gill, the Civil Service Commission's labor relations director. "It's been a rare day this past year that you could pick up a paper without seeing a public employe strike or work stoppage somewhere in the country."

Union membership among public workers has soared by about 60 per cent over the last decade to around 1.5 million.

Some of this reflects the fact that public employment is the fastest growing segment of the labor force. Even so, labor unions have increased their share of the public jobs from 13 per cent to around 15 per cent since 1956.

The American Federation of State, County and Municipal Employees has grown from 99,-000 to around 350,000 since 1955, for example. The American Federation of Teachers has climbed from 46,500 to about 135,000 during that time, while the American Federation of Government Employees has risen from 51,600 to 234,000 among Federal workers.

This growth is crucial for the labor movement if it hopes to reverse the decline that has cut its share of the nonfarm labor force to 21.9 per cent from 28.9 per cent since 1953.

James J. Reynolds, Under Secretary of Labor, calls public employment "a tremendous untapped area—like opening a new oil field for them."

"Government employes who join unions could change the image of the labor movement to make it more acceptable to white collar employes and technicians in private industry," says Mr. Stieber of Michigan State. "If the teachers of the United States join unions in large numbers," he adds, "youngsters may re-evaluate the role of labor in society."

State Bargaining Laws

Some of the growth of public unionism stems from increased organizing efforts, but labor experts attribute more of it to worker discontent over lagging wages and poor personnel management.

Perhaps the biggest single factor, however, was President Kennedy's 1962 executive order that provided for collective bargaining in the Federal service.

That set the pace for similar developments in states and cities. Scores of localities are now bargaining with unions for the first time, and 11 states have enacted various forms of collective bargaining laws. Federal managers have signed about 600 union contracts covering over 900,000 workers.

The vast majority of states still provide no negotiating procedures, and even states with laws run into problems on their application. Michigan modernized its labor law in 1965, for instance, but still had 23 stoppages in 1966, mostly in education.

Although public employe strikes have traditionally been declared illegal—by statute, court decision, and common law—such walkouts are on a sharp upswing. The number of strikes rose from 28 in 1962 to 42 in 1965, and authorities believe 125 to 150 occurred in 1966.

Within the last few months, for instance, there had been strikes by hospital employes in Providence, firemen in Atlanta and garbage collectors in St. Louis.

Among the most militant public employes are teachers, who have struck lately in such cities as Woodbridge, N. J., and Youngstown, Ohio.

"I think we're going through what the unions in private industry went through in the thirties," says Jerome Wurf, the State, County, Municipal Employes' president.

"We have strikes simply because public employers are still finding it difficult to deal with the concept of unions," he explained. "After we get past that, things will settle down."

Most labor authorities believe it will be a long time, however, before most public managers agree to share decision-making with workers. Even if that occurs, these experts say, there are unusual structural problems in public employment that will affect negotiations.

Some experts believe that many public managers have failed to adjust honest worker grievances simply because there was a law to prevent any strike. Others contend that public officials have too often lacked the political courage to seek higher taxes to pay their workers adequately.

"School boards and local governments have been saying for years, 'We'd like to do something for you, but the taxpayer just won't stand for an increase,'" remarks Malcom L. Denise, the Ford Motor Company's labor relations vice president. "In a sense, they've asked for organization, and they've got it."

"There's no question that in the public service, at all levels, the employes have not got a fair shake," says Kenneth O. Warner, executive director of the Public Personnel Association in Chicago, an organization of 800 government personnel agencies.

"The final decisions on how you are going to treat the employe are made by the legislative body, and they've been pretty chintzy," he adds.

Lower Earnings Cited

Union men say that public employes often earn from 10 per cent to 30 per cent less than workers in private industry.

Mr. Wurf's union says, for instance, that a Boston city laborer averages $737 a year less than a manufacturing laborer, while a Detroit city stock clerk averages $1,085 a year less than auto company stock clerks.

The unions have made some impressive gains. Mr. Wurf's organization recently moved into a nonunion refuse strike in Montgomery County, Md., signed up the workers, got employer recognition, and negotiated wage increases of 15 to 31 cents an hour—all in one day.

The union also won an $11.50 a week raise for garbage truck drivers after a month-long strike in York, Pa.

Labor leaders often schedule such negotiations with an eye toward budgetary deadlines. But it is not always possible to do that, and such agreements frequently play hob with government budgets.

Mr. Warner, of the Public Personnel Association, says officials "are going to have to develop brand new notions about the ability of an agency to pay."

New York City officials say the government has already overspent by nearly $20-million its budget for improving benefits for its 300,000 employes this year. The city hopes to make up for the added cost by putting a freeze on jobs, but that offers no permanent solution.

Lack of Funds Disputed

Union leaders, contending that public employes for years have subsidized the mounting cost of government through low wages, are in no mood these days to hear officials plead a lack of funds.

"When they have to, they find it," snaps Victor Gotbaum, executive director of the state-county union's Joint Council 37 in New York.

Some labor experts are worried that elected public officials, anxious to prevent damaging strikes, will shell out big settlements to militant unions, unnecessarily forcing up government costs. They also fear that stronger unions will intrude unduly into the right of officials to manage the public business and win concessions that will spread to private industry.

"I'm terribly worried about the introduction of collective bargaining in public employment," remarks one of the nation's most highly regarded labor experts.

"Public managers are inexperienced, and they're going to allow work rules that are so wild and woolly they will cause trouble for everyone down the road," he adds.

This expert says the 1965 agreement between New York City and the Social Service Employes Union, which sets a limit on the number of cases a worker can handle, is the type of thing that could cause trouble later.

He also believes recent teacher contracts, limiting the number of students in a class, may prove to be too restrictive as new education techniques are developed.

Mr. Haber, New York City's labor relations director, believes some unions "have moved too far into policy decisions." He cites the welfare union's effort to obtain a voice in the location of welfare centers and the amount of money to be given to clients as examples.

In another case, the police and firemen sought to bargain over the number of men to be assigned to patrol cars and fire engines.

Public employe unions, who believe these are perfectly legitimate demands, have not pursued them fully in the past partly because of laws prohibiting strikes. Those laws still exist, but the increased militancy among workers is pressuring union leaders to use strikes as a weapon.

The laws prohibiting public employe strikes are rooted in the concept of governmental sovereignty. Eighteen states have no-strike statutes, and courts have ruled against public employe strikes in at least 12 others. The Federal Government requires its workers to promise not to strike.

Most of those supporting the no-strike policy subordinate the vague "sovereignty" argument in favor of a claim that important differences between public and private employment justify the ban.

These experts note that government is a monopoly created to perform essential public services and is not subject to the normal market pressures that exist in industry.

Government cannot lock out strikers, or go out of business, if the union demands are exhorbitant, they observe. And they say financial decisions are often made by legislatures, which are representatives of the public that cannot bargain with unions.

Objectionable Strikes

Many union leaders accept this argument, but an increasing number are rejecting it. Mr. Gotbaum, for instance, only objects to strikes by policemen, firemen and prison guards because "we don't have the right to bring about death."

If other strikes cause acute public inconvenience, he argues, that is the price of democracy.

Although 77 per cent of the public queried in a recent Louis Harris poll said they believed in the right to strike, only 48 per cent said they would accept strikes against the Government.

Some authorities believe this showed a remarkably high tolerance of public strikes. But most labor experts doubt they

ever will be legalized in the United States.

Even so, legal bans against public employe strikes are proving ineffective because the penalties are so severe they are unrealistic.

The Condon-Wadlin Act in New York, which prohibits wage increases for any public striker for three years, has been invoked in only eight of 20 possible times since 1947, and in the 1966 transit strike its penalties were not applied.

George H. Hildebrand, a Cornell University labor relations professor, notes that the act has been invoked almost entirely in upstate New York, where labor is not politically powerful.

"Where public officials are vulnerable to reprisal, there is a strong probability that they will not enforce such a measure despite their sworn oath of office," he adds.

Procedural Means Sought

Many labor experts say that too much time is being spent arguing over the legality of strikes and not enough on developing machinery to prevent them. "The important thing is that the law is unenforceable," says Mr. Wurf. "So let's start getting procedures for resolving these disputes without relying on brute force."

Some authorities question whether it is possible to transfer the bargaining methods of private industry to the unique

political and legislative arena of public employment.

Eli Rock, a Philadelphia arbitrator, notes that private bargaining is based on negotiations between two parties that can make a deal. But in public employment, he says, the source of money to pay for the deal is often not even involved in the talks.

"One of the questions that is most puzzling is the question of who is the employer in the public sector," says Theodore W. Kheel, a New York labor authority. "Is the employer the Mayor, the Governor, the head of the department, the authority or the legislature which appropriates the money?"

"What happens to your precepts of representative government if the legislature has to conform to collective bargaining?" Asks George W. Taylor, the University of Pennsylvania's noted labor relations expert. "These are terrific problems. I don't think you can solve them simply with muscle, and by being kinetic," he adds.

Some labor authorities believe that traditional bargaining concepts have already become so mixed into the public employment field, however, that a fresh approach now is out of the question.

"A whole new set of concepts has to be worked out," Mr. Taylor says firmly. And then he adds weakly: "It won't be, you know. It's going to be a mess for generations."

April 2, 1967

Teachers' Strikes Loom Across Nation

Rising Militancy Noted in Public Employes

By JOSEPH A. LOFTUS
Special to The New York Times

WASHINGTON, Sept. 2 — Thousands of public school districts start a new year this week with the prospect that it will be a year of great teacher discontent.

Officials of the National Education Association, the larger and more conservative of two national teacher organizations, foresee as many as 300 to 400 teacher strikes in the next six to eight months.

St. Louis, with 4,000 teachers, is on the brink of its first recorded strike, on Wednesday, when the schools are scheduled

to open. East St. Louis, Ill., with 900 teachers, was struck at its opening last week. The same thing happened in Madison, also in southern Illinois, and in Bradley-Bourbonnais, Ill., south of Chicago.

Thirty districts near Detroit are in teacher trouble. Other possible trouble spots are Philadelphia, Pittsburgh, Toledo, Ohio, and Duluth, Minn., as well as New York City.

Massachusetts, Connecticut and Florida report trouble spots in a few districts.

Statewide problems loom in New Hampshire, Colorado, Oklahoma and Idaho.

"It's going to be a very tumultuous year," said Charles Cogen, retiring president of the American Federation of Teachers, the other national teacher organization. It is an affiliate

of the American Federation of Labor and Congress of Industrial Organizations.

David Selden, elected 10 days ago to succeed Mr. Cogen, does not rule out the possibility of a nationwide strike "to bring about the vast improvement in schools that we need."

The surge of teacher militancy is part of a broader manifestation of discontent among public employes generally.

Sam Zagoria, a member of the National Labor Relations Board, says public employe unions are growing at the rate of 1,000 members every working day.

Three unions of public employes in recent days voted to delete a no-strike policy clause from their constitutions. These are the International Association of Fire Fighters, the United Federation of Postal Clerks and the National Postal Union.

The first two are A.F.L.-C.I.O. affiliates.

Another affiliate, the National Association of Letter Carriers, took a step in the same direction by voting an investigation of the legal and legislative technicalities of the ban on Federal employe strikes.

psychologists are viewed in union circles as being some of the most frustrated and strike-minded groups in the country.

Thirty to 35 years ago private industry and labor experienced the turmoil that derived from the organizing of the Congress of Industrial Organizations. With the subsequent acceptance of industrial unionism, collective bargaining became systematized and calmer.

The dynamism of the sixties is found in the public employe ranks.

There is no single, simple cause for this development. Like so many social phenomena, much of the explanation can be found in a historical context.

Jerry Wurf, president of the American Federation of State, County and Municipal Employes, recalls that in the Depression days before the defense buildup and World War II, public employes were the "aristocrats" of the working class because of their job security.

While private employers furloughed millions of workers, and millions more worried whether their next payday would be their last, the teacher, the policeman, the fireman and the sanitation worker enjoyed the dignity of security along with paychecks that were regular and more valuable as prices dropped.

During the war, industrial employment expanded and the unions dug in. The National War Labor Board, while restraining wage rates, sanctioned fringe benefits, such as pensions, holidays at premium rates, seniority and grievance protection machinery.

Indeed, many employers lobbied Washington in those days for permission to be more generous, so they could hold their work forces against raiding rival employers. Unions and their members grew in strength and security.

After the war, industrial wages shot up. Mr. Wurf notes that public employes did not share fully in these gains. The relationship between elected officials and their employes was sluggish.

The lag in pay, fringe benefits and security persisted in public employment. Therein, said Mr. Wurf in an interview, could be found the stimulus to unionism.

What is going on now, he said, is "a struggle for dignity." He said the public employe wanted not only the pay and conditions of a first-class citizen, he wanted also to escape from the capricious boss who makes the rules as he goes along.

He said that teachers, social workers and psychologists, for example, "find Uncle Louie, who never went to college, coming home with pay of $5 an hour, and they feel frustrated."

Sam Lambert, executive secretary of the National Education Association, said, "The average teacher is 39 years old and is making $7,300 a year. That's not a lot of money. If a person is going to be getting anywhere professionally, he should be getting there by 38 or 39."

Teacher spokesmen say teachers are angry about large classes and dilapidated and half-tended plants.

They say, too, that a society that purports to believe education is the cure for most of its ills pays teachers below the level of the average budget of a four-person, middle-class city family.

There are other stimuli to discontent. The big N.E.A. and the American Federation of Teachers are competing for members. The organization that can win recognition or a better settlement in a community looks more attractive to discontented teachers in other communities. Hence the demands and successes of each organization are stimulants to militancy.

In St. Louis, the federation is said to have enrolled only a fourth of the 4,000 teachers. It has been forbidden by court order to strike but is taking a strike vote tomorrow night. The local expectation is that those teachers will disregard the court order.

The St. Louis School Board says it is prevented by law from bargaining. The Teachers' Association, an affiliate of the N.E.A., has gone to court for a declaratory judgment on that point.

A Tide of Militancy

The N.E.A., which had prided itself on conservative "professionalism" and shrank from even the word "strike," has found itself in many instances scooped up and reluctantly borne along on a tide of grass-roots militancy. It lost members to the smaller teachers' union in some of the major metropolitan areas.

The increasing number of men on the faculties of public schools is believed to have contributed to the rising militancy.

Some of the complaints reported by teacher spokesmen, besides pay, are remoteness from policy making in the school system and a sense of repression that prevents teachers from telling the public about their working conditions.

Public employes at all levels run into problems that organized employes in private industry have overcome or never encountered. The new group seeking recognition and improved pay and conditions has had little experience in collective bargaining, and their employers have probably had less. Mediation skills are scarce.

Public employers tend to rely on laws, or official opinions and court judgments forbidding public strikes, although laws have become less and less effective.

In public employment, usually the money to meet a pay rise demand is not readily available, and the politician is loath to sponsor a tax increase to produce the money.

Between 1945 and 1965 there were about 100 strikes of public school teachers. There were 30 such strikes in 1966 alone. The number more than trebled in 1967. Now another trebling is foreseen.

"The politicians don't believe the teachers mean business," said an N.E.A. staff man, "so you have to fight."

September 3, 1968

Uncle Sam Learns About Living With Labor

By A. H. RASKIN

Uncle Sam's relations with his 2.7 million civil servants will never be the same. The landmark settlement negotiated by the Nixon Administration and the A.F.L.-C.I.O. after the nation's first postal strike marks the end of a sleepytime era in which the leaders of most Federal unions were closer to Congress than to their own rank and file.

From now on governmental collective bargaining will correspond much more to the industrial pattern than it ever did under the pioneering Executive Order President Kennedy promulgated in 1962 or even under the liberalized version President Nixon signed, to labor's delight, less than six months ago.

Wages, traditionally the province of Capitol Hill and the White House, have been brought into the orbit of direct negotiation. To be sure, the settlement speeds emancipation of the postal service from Federal operating control, but this fact will not keep workers in every other agency from clamoring for the same right to voice and veto over pay that the postal employes dragooned the Government into granting.

That prospect is heightened by the assurance written into the pact that the postmen will have the best of both worlds. They will retain all the established benefits, preferences and protections of the civil service, plus as much more as they can get through bargaining in vacations, holidays, health and life insurance, seniority and promotion procedures. And, of course, in pay.

Not surprisingly, the accomplishments already recorded on the postal wage front have brought hints from other Federal unions of "me too" demands.

Spur to Chain Reaction

The Administration hoped that it could head off a chain reaction by voluntarily including all Federal civilian and military personnel in the first-round postal pay increase of 6 per cent, retroactive to last Dec. 27. Under the President's original budget, such an across-the-board increase would not have become effective until next Jan. 1 and, even then, it would have averaged only 5.75 per cent.

On the basis of that $2-billion pot-sweetener, some White House officials were optimistic that they could confine the promised second-round postal pay raise of 8 per cent to mailmen alone. That increase will not go into effect until Congress okays the postal reform plan.

The 8 per cent was a major incentive for labor's decision to abandon its long resistance to the whole reorganization idea—a resistance that had effectively blocked the plan on Capitol Hill. Indeed, the union switch came only after the Administration upped its second-round offer from 6 per cent, thus putting another $130 million into postmen's pockets.

But these special factors in the mail negotiations are unlikely to slake the appetites of other unionized Federal employes. Their wages have always moved up in rough tandem with those in the postal service, and their family budgets are just as pinched by the current upsurge in living costs.

Most important, they have had their first object lesson that strikes in vital governmental agencies do pay off, even when troops are called in to end them. That lesson may have more carryover impact than the President's warning in his postal message to Congress last week that "the people of this nation cannot and will not submit to the coercion of strikes by employes of the Federal Government."

The recognition of this danger in Washington is coupled with the evidence given by the air traffic controllers' "sick-out"

as well as the postal strike that laws calling for mandatory dismissal and even jail terms for strikers are unenforceable.

One safeguard against the potentially catastrophic interaction of these realities would be to extend into the wage area all the instruments of negotiation, mediation and even arbitration provided under the October Executive order for other phases of employe relations. George Meany and the postal union chiefs have agreed to binding arbitration as the end point for settling all contract disputes in the new postal establishment.

That involved a 180-degree shift away from tradition for them, as it did for the Government.

In the Face of Tradition

If Congress buys this approach for mailmen — and the indications are strong it will — there is every good reason to make the same techniques applicable as a safety valve throughout the Federal Government. That may upset traditionalists, but it offers promise of heading off confrontations that undermine respect for all law.

Tradition already has taken a long flight out the window when

the President of the United States and the president of the A.F.L.-C.I.O. negotiate not only on wages but on basic governmental policy on how to deliver the mails.

"We never could have got this settlement with a pro-union Administration in the White House," said one union spokesman after the pact. "The President would have been scared silly of being accused of selling out to the unions."

The test for both sides from here on out is to prove there was nothing to be scared about.

April 20, 1970

TEACHER STRIKES OPPOSED IN POLL

Walkouts by Policemen and Firemen Also Not Backed

Special to The New York Times
PRINCETON, N. J., Jan. 11—Americans support the right of teachers, policemen and firemen to organize for collective bargaining but draw the line when it comes to strikes, according to the Gallup Poll.

A recent Gallup survey shows that six persons in every 10 interviewed across the country believe that teachers, policemen and firemen should be permitted to join unions, but the same proportion also believe they should not be permitted to strike.

The Nixon Administration seems committed to an early search for ways to head off strikes by public employes.

Throughout the Presidential campaign, Mr. Nixon said his Secretary of Labor would hold a conference on the subject of strikes by public workers. He added that the meeting, to be held "early in the next Admin-

istration," would include labor leaders, public officials and representatives of public employes.

George P. Shultz, the incoming Labor Secretary, said on Dec. 13 that he would make a "careful study" of this problem.

Many Teacher Strikes

The seriousness of the teacher-strike problem is revealed by figures recently released by the National Education Association. They show that some 163,000 teachers in 21 states and the District of Columbia went on strike in the 1967-68 school year.

Policemen and firemen in many United States cities were also restive last year over wage demands. No full-scale strikes were reported, but numerous "slowdowns" occurred.

To gauge the public's views on this problem, four questions were put to a representative national sample of 1,501 adults between Dec. 6 and 8.

On the question, "Should public school teachers be permitted to join unions, or not?" the results were:

Yes 61%
No 30
No opinion 9

The sampling was then asked, "Should public school

teachers be permitted to strike, or not?" The results were:

Yes 35%
No 60
No opinion 5

On the question, "Should police and firemen be permitted to join unions, or not?" the results were:

Yes 60%
No 32
No opinion 8

Finally, on the question, "Should police and firemen be permitted to strike, or not?" the results were:

Yes 30%
No 65
No opinion 5

Seven in 10 persons in nonunion families opposed walkouts by firemen and policemen, while the comparable figure for union people was 54 per cent.

Two in three in the nonunion group said that teachers should not be permitted to strike.

The results of another question show that Americans are pessimistic about the prospects for peace on the labor front during the coming year. Two in every three predicted that 1969 would be marked by industrial problems and strikes, with union and nonunion people equally pessimistic.

The question asked was:

"Looking ahead to 1969, which of these do you think

is likely to be true of 1969—a year of strikes and industrial disputes or a year of industrial peace?"

The results were:

A year of strikes 65%
A year of labor peace . . 24
No opinion 11

The idea of compulsory arbitration as a solution to labor disputes has never been popular with either management or labor leadership. But in the absence of any other acceptable formula, many students of labor problems believe that some type of arbitration is needed to protect the public's interests.

One plan that wins widespread support, with both union and nonunion people, was presented to a cross section of adults in these terms:

"It has been suggested that no strike be permitted to go on for more than 21 days. If after 21 days, the union and the employer cannot reach an agreement, the courts would appoint a committee that would decide the issue and both be compelled to accept the terms. Would you favor or oppose this idea?"

The results were:

Favor 67%
Oppose 25
No opinion 8

January 12, 1969

Teachers And Power

The Story of the American Federation of Teachers. By Robert J. Braun. 287 pp. New York: Simon & Schuster. $7.95.

By MARIO D. FANTINI

"The American Federation of Teachers — led by its strongest affiliate, Local 2, United Federation of Teachers (who have made "U.F.T." a household term to most New Yorkers) — is determined to control the public schools of America by waging an all-out war against any of its enemies, whether they be parents, students, school boards, politicians or minority communities, all in the name of education. Modeling itself after the American Medical Association and the American Bar Association, the teachers' union is after a strong, disciplined national organization that will negotiate contracts escalating teachers' demands without genuine responsibility to any one, certainly not the public." This is the warning of Robert J. Braun, education editor of the Newark Star-Ledger, in his fascinating account of "Teachers and Power." Since he first covered a teacher strike in Perth Amboy, N. J., in 1965, Braun has become an intimately involved observer of teacher strikes, including the two prolonged affairs in New York City (1968, the Ocean Hill-Brownsville crisis) and Newark (1970), which he skillfully recounts and analyzes.

Braun points out that after the U.F.T.'s awesome display of power in the 36-day New York strike in 1968, few could doubt that a real political war was being waged in our schools. Alarmed, outraged, the author hopes that this book will jolt those "who believe that education is too important to be left to educators, who believe that the battles should be not for control over the schools, but to rid them finally of any form of control by special interests, who believe that popular control, while often illusory, is yet desirable." To the author, the innocent victims of this political war are the educational consumers themselves: students and parents.

Since he is dealing with a national institution second only to defense in expense, and involving 50 million people, Braun pulls no punches in his indictments:

"Because it is a union first and foremost, its organization is geared to war, to servicing strikes, to collecting new members, to protecting teachers — whether or not they deserve protection — never considering the possibility that teachers, as surrogate parents, should really derive their true protection from the pure love they provide for their children and the respect they earn in a community, a neighborhood or a town. A.F.T. leadership behaves like the leadership of any other established union — that is, with an eye to staying in power as long as possible. Although it pays considerable lip service to local autonomy and union democracy, the national trains its reps to mold opinion, to exploit fears, if necessary, to promote paranoia and hysteria and even racism among its teachers, for the war must be won."

Braun maintains that "educationally the A.F.T. has produced little beyond the M.E.S. (More Effective Schools) — a collection of the most generally agreed-upon and, until late, unchallengable educational improvements — small classes, extensive psychological care, team teaching, and so on." It is not surprising that he also argues that "the union hardly has displayed a depth of understanding of either the political or the educational process which would motivate a community willingly to turn over its schools to its kindly command. And there is little in the history, its present operations or its leadership, to indicate that the A.F.T.

would know what to do with the public schools of the nation should it manage to assume control through contract — beyond, of course, increasing salaries, decreasing workloads, picking up more members and strengthening leadership control at the top."

While these may be startling revelations to many citizens, they represent concerns some of us have had for a number of years, especially those who have been close to the urban action. Braun is essentially correct in his assessments: teacher organizations do appear to be on a collision course with the public.

The struggle for teachers' rights started in Chicago in the 1890's. It was led by Margaret Haley, whose incessant criticism of the failure of big corporations to pay school taxes won her a reputation as "the lady assistant mayor," that "opinionated, nasty, unladylike woman" and more. It took time to overcome the chronic timidity of female teachers, but in 1897 the "hard-driving Miss Haley finally convinced them to form the Chicago Federation of Teachers." Haley and her raiders wanted and ultimately achieved a salary of $900.

Among the heroes of the early days of the movement for teachers' rights was John Dewey, one of the first members of the teachers' union in New York City. Dewey gave the New York Chapter a strong philosophical base; he envisioned a strong teacher organization committed to responsive community service and dedicated to the principles of democracy. The American Teacher, which became the official voice of the teachers' union, carries the slogan "Democracy in Education: Education for Democracy."

By the time the Depression rolled around, Chicago was again the scene of teacher unrest and, in 1933, John M. Fewkes led a group of teachers in raids on the city's largest banks. Teachers' salaries were being held back, and in their place scrip was doled out to be redeemed once large corporations paid municipal taxes. There was an eruptive episode, and it served to highlight the differences between the National Education Association — which was company-aligned, ruled by school administrators, and encouraged teachers to return their salaries to keep school systems from bankruptcy — and the teachers' union, whose members would sooner break bank windows than continue to starve.

Divisive elements posed severe strains on the union during the thirties: a Midwest-New York split, an A.F. of L.-C.I.O. split, the Communists vs. the non-Communists. It remained for George Counts, prominent educational philosopher and author of "Dare the Schools Change the Social Order," to try to pull the union together. He received assistance from the theologian, Reinhold Niebuhr. (Other notables in the story of the A.F.T. include Samuel Gompers, Walter Reuther, John L. Lewis, Mike Mansfield, Paul Douglas, Hubert Humphrey, Albert Einstein.)

The modern era of teacher unionism belongs to Dave Seldon, president of the A.F.T., Charles Cogen, first U.F.T. president, and Albert Shanker, president of U.F.T. Under these men, the A.F.T. has grown — begun to build strong locals in some of our major cities (the A.F.T. is considered city-oriented) and pressed national teacher unification. For the past few years the A.F.T. (with about 950 locals) and its larger national rival, the National Education Association (N.E.A.), with nearly 9,000 affiliated locals, have been talking merger. In the last decade the dominant power in the N.E.A. has shifted from school administrators to classroom teachers. This change fits neatly into the projected aspirations of the A.F.T., which is almost completely teacher-oriented. (A recent event not included in the book gives further credence to Braun's thesis that the A.F.T. is after a professional-teacher monopoly. In April, 1972, a potentially prototypic

merger was announced in New York State between the 85,000 member U.F.T. and the 105,000 member New York State Teachers Association.)

Yet, since Braun's verdict that the A.F.T. is guilty of growing misuse of power is final, in all fairness to the A.F.T. the reader should keep certain factors in mind. He should note that this is a se-

tive story and not a *definitive* history of the American Federation of Teachers. Braun's purposes are more to expose than to instruct. For instance, we may be left with the mistaken impression that increased teacher militancy, including strikes, is an exclusive A.F.T. strategy. But the number of strikes, work stoppages and interruptions in service reported by the rival N.E.A. in 1961-62 was merely one, while in 1969-70, it reported 181.

There are various inconsistencies in Braun's argument. For him the A.F.T. today is somehow both "bankrupt" and "potent." And while Braun does note that teachers were an oppressed group, he moves almost too quickly into making them oppressors. He seems to want to make sure that we all realize that power, even in the hands of schooled professionals, inevitably corrupts, and is used for selfish not public interests.

As Braun is making his telling and alarming points, it is difficult to understand why he did not strengthen his case by spending some time on the institutional causes of increased teacher power. No book that deals with public-school teachers can escape the cold fact that they work in an institution forged in the 19th century, with a hierarchal, monolithic structure. Teachers, no less than students and parents, are imprisoned by this outmoded institution. It was never meant to deal with an urbanized, technologically advanced, pluralistic society groping toward universal education for survival. The author, as a journalist, an outside observer looking in, cannot completely sense what the teacher's life is like inside the school. Teachers are forced to behave in certain ways by the institution. If we accuse teachers of outdated behavior, it is also, in part, the result of their outdated institution.

Furthermore, when teachers are isolated every day in egg-crate school rooms — trying to cope with human and cultural diversity that they were never adequately prepared to deal with and sensing the increased public demand for accountability — they are pressed to respond largely in ways that make sense within the institution itself. Their suggestions for improvement usually include smaller classes, remedial services, special classes for the non-adjusters — in brief, more of the same old measures. (These measures not only cost more money, but are being increasingly criticized as to their value.) This does not make the teachers' actions right; it only partially explains them. But the basic problem lies not so much with the teacher, the student or parent, but with the institution, which is in urgent need of reform. This fundamental point is difficult to glean from the book. To be sure, we have expected and not received from professional educators the statesmanlike leadership necessary for this reform, but we must also realize that few of us can rise above the environment that shapes us. Ironically, for the teachers to achieve control of a dying institution is a futile feat indeed, if their control is not directed at its renewal.

It's also important to note that teachers unify not only to increase their political and economic power but also to protect themselves against unfair pressures and demands. Repressive school administrators and get-tough-on-education legislatures unite teachers. Desperation attempts at educational reform — such as community control, a voucher plan that obviates public schools, performance-contracting with private firms, no schools at all — are also threatening to people who are trying to play by the ground rules of an established, albeit debilitating institution that finds it necessary to contract for police-guard protection.

It would be a serious mistake to blame individual teachers, either for the general crisis in American education or for the behavior of professional organizations. That would be a simple answer to a complex problem. There are thousands of individual teachers dedicated to child growth and leading a national struggle for reform through educational alternatives within the framework of public schools — with or without the support of A.F.T. or N.E.A. affiliates. Teachers' unions are not the same as teachers. Braun expresses the deep disappointment many of us have felt in what the A.F.T. could have done for school reform:

"Sadly for an organization which has the muscle and skill to join with students, parents and others concerned with significant reform of education, the A.F.T. has all but betrayed its founding principles, including those articulated by its most prized member, John Dewey. . . .

"As a protest organization, and not the educational establishment it aspires to be, the teachers' union might have become the central organizing force for all the diverse elements which, within the public schools, are demanding change. Oriented to local concerns, allied with what should be their natural allies — parents and students — organized teachers might have been able to provoke reform, even through mass action like strikes, while still maintaining a sound enough base among the local gentry to ensure competitive salaries and tolerable working conditions, something that every worker deserves."

Braun's story of the American Federation of Teachers is a courageous and hard-hitting report. He has given us much that was hidden from the public. He has dared to say the emperor wears no clothes. While there will undoubtedly be disagreement with Braun's assessments, it is difficult to criticize his attempt to deal openly with the intricate and controversial politics of the teacher-power movement in America. ∎

UNIONIZING SLOW IN OFFICE STAFFS

White-Collar Membership Is Put at 14% of Potential by an N.I.C.B. Survey

By DOUGLAS W. CRAY

White-collar unionization is widely regarded to be on the upswing. But a survey just completed by the National Industrial Conference Board indicates that the pace is well short of breathtaking.

The N.I.C.B. reported that as of 1968, white-collar union membership totaled a little under 3.2 million workers, or about 16 per cent of all union members.

There were, however, an estimated 23.3 million white-collar employes in 1968 who were eligible for union affiliation.

The 3.2 million white-collar employes who were already organized at this point represented about 14 per cent of the total potential.

Membership Advanced

According to the study, white-collar union membership has climbed from 2.1 million in 1958 to 3.2 million in 1968.

The 2.1 million membership in 1958 represented 10.9 per cent of the nonmanagerial white-collar work force and the 3.2 million membership in 1968 represented 11.4 per cent of the nonmanagerial white-collar work force (including all professional and technical employes).

Despite the relatively modest net gains in membership being shown by the unions active in white-collar organizing, there is no question about the gains in the number of bargaining elections being held annually. In 1961 there were 395 elections and by 1968 the total had reached 808.

Moreover, the N.I.C.B. study, entitled "White-collar Unionization" and released over the weekend, showed increases in the annual number of elections won by unions and in the number of employes in elections won by the unions.

As the report notes: "Overall, between 1961 and 1969, the unions won 58 per cent of the white-collar elections and lost 42 per cent of them."

On the basis of results of bargaining elections of white-collar workers held from 1961 through the first nine months of 1969 the average size of units won by the unions was 25.9 employes. The units that the unions lost averaged 46.1 employes.

For the Office and Professional Employees International Union, the average unit won had 26 employes, while the average unit lost had 61 employes.

Eleven unions active in white-collar organizing cooperated with the N.I.C.B. in its study.

Based on a close look at 140 white-collar organizing campaigns—in which the union won certification in 67 or 48 per cent of the total and lost in 73 or 52 per cent of the total—the N.I.C.B. study suggested that the following factors were found more often in those elections the union lost than in those the union won:

¶Large election unit;
¶Above average salaries;
¶Formal grievance procedure;
¶Absence of another union at the location;
¶Use of both personal and written campaign communications by company;
¶Company learned of drive from employes.

Conversely, where the union won the election the following factors were found:

¶Small election unit;
¶Below average salaries;
¶Lack of personal communications between employer and employes during the campaign;
¶Same union represented plant employes;
¶Company learned of union activity from union or National Labor Relations Board.

FEDERAL COURT BARS LEGAL STRIKE RIGHTS

WASHINGTON, April 1 (AP) —A three-judge Federal court ruled today that there was no constitutional right to strike and that Government workers could be barred from striking.

The court said private employes did not have such a constitutional right but had been given the freedom to strike by the National Labor Relations Act.

The ruling involved specifically the United Federation of Postal Clerks. But court sources said it would affect all Federal employes and could be interpreted as applying also to municipal employes. They said this included teachers, who in several cities in recent years have gone out on strike.

One judge, J. Skelly Wright, in a concurring opinion, said he questioned whether a flat ban on strikes by public employes could be made but suggested that it was a question the Supreme Court should decide.

The union, in its suit against Postmaster General Winton M. Blount, contended that the right to strike was fundamental and protected by the Constitution. It said public employes who were barred from striking were denied equal protection under the law.

PRISONERS' UNION FORMED UPSTATE

Green Haven Inmates Seek to Negotiate on Wages, Hours and Work Rules

By EMANUEL PERLMUTTER

The formation of the first prisoners' union in the country —by inmates of Green Haven Prison at Stormville, N.Y.—was announced here yesterday.

The organization, called the Prisoners Labor Union at Green Haven, has notified State Correction Commissioner Russell G. Oswald that it wants to be recognized as exclusive bargaining agent for the inmates of the Hudson Valley prison.

A similar request has been sent by the union to John L. Zelker, Superintendent of Green Haven. The letters, sent yesterday, also ask that a meeting be set up for negotiations on wages, hours and working conditions for the inmates.

At the request of inmate leaders of the union, the executive committee of District 65, Distributive Workers of America, has agreed to accept the prison group as an affiliate. The 30,000 members of District 65, an independent union, as well as the prisoners of Green Haven will soon be asked to vote on the proposed affiliation.

The constitution of the prison labor union and its aims were outlined at a news conference in the offices of the New York Urban Coalition, 55 Fifth Avenue.

Although the union was started by the prisoners last fall, most of the legal work has been done by the Prisoners Rights Project of the Legal Aid Society.

William E. Hillerstein, the lawyer in charge of the Legal Aid project, said at the news conference that more than half the 1,800 prisoners at Green Haven had signed membership petitions in the union.

He said some of the funds for the organization of the union had been provided by a Federal grant to Mayor Lindsay's Criminal Justice Coordinating Council under the Law Enforcement Assistance Act and the rest by the Legal Aid Society.

Eugene Eisner, a labor lawyer of 351 Broadway, who has been retained as legal counsel to the prison union, said that since the inmates performed work for the state, they were entitled to collective bargaining rights under the Public Employers Fair Employment Act—the Taylor Law.

The Taylor Law contains in part the following definition:

"The term public employe means any person holding a position by appointment or employment in the service of a public employer except that such term shall not include persons holding positions by appointment or employment in the organized militia of the state.

An 'Unusual' Subject

In answer to a query about the legitimacy of the prisoners' union as "public employes," Deputy Chairman Jerome Lefkowitz of the Public Employment Relations Board said. "It is certainly an unusual subject," and added, "There is nothing in the Taylor Law that specifically exempts prisoners."

"However, if the union made an application to us for certification, we would have to determine whether they are public employes within the meaning of the Taylor Law," he added.

A spokesman for Commissioner Oswald said he would have no comment on the letter to him until he had received it.

The prisoners at Green Haven earn an average of 35 cents a day. They make hospital gowns and bathrobes for men, women and children, slips, sheets, pillowcases, baby bibs and United States flags, all destined for state institutions. Other jobs performed are as maintenance workers, porters, tailors, barbers and agriculture workers at Green Haven.

Mr. Eisner said that there was a prisoners' union in Los Angeles, but that it was not an exclusively inmates union since it included their families as well as other civilians.

Representative Herman Badillo of the Bronx, one of the sponsors of the union at the news conference said that it would provide a responsible bargaining unit for the inmates and could lead to improved prison conditions.

Eugene S. Callender, another sponsor and president of the New York Urban Coalition, said that the project was "a historic development in the labor movement." He said that because the men were prisoners "does not mean they are not entitled to constitutional rights."

Public Support Sought

David Livingston, president of District 65, said that if the prisoners affiliated with his union an organizer would be assigned to them and that his union would try to mobilize public support for their efforts. The organizer would have to ask permission of prison authorities to talk to the men.

Mr. Livingston said that the idea for forming the union had come last summer from Earl Smoake Jr., a former member of District 65 who is an inmate at Green Haven. He said that if the union affiliated with District 65, nominal dues would be collected.

The constitution of the prisoners' union states that they will seek "through peaceful and lawful means" to equalize to the fullest extent possible "the rights, privileges and protections of prison labor with those of free labor everywhere." Also to "advance the economic, political, social and cultural interests" of the prisoners at Green Haven.

February 8, 1972

ENGINEERS EYING HELP FROM UNIONS

Layoffs Lead to Study of Affiliation for Protection

By AGIS SALPUKAS
Special to The New York Times

ATLANTIC CITY, April 29—Many engineers and other well paid professionals buffeted by massive layoffs in the aerospace industry are beginning to look to unions for protection.

Many have swallowed their professional pride and are looking for ways to affiliate with unions such as the United Automobile Workers so they can get some of the same protection as production workers.

Engineers, often a small élite group within a company only a decade ago, now sometimes outnumber production workers in companies working on complex government projects.

The engineers, jammed in huge rooms before long rows of drawing boards, are often laid off without benefits. Now it is becoming harder and harder for them to be convinced that they are closer to management than to the workers in the shops.

To take advantage of this new fertile soil, the U.A.W. put out its welcome mat to the engineers at its convention this week.

Delegates to the 23rd annual convention here approved a change in the union's constitution allowing its international executive board to negotiate with professional groups for affiliation and to intensify efforts to organize professionals.

The most fertile ground is on the West Coast, where thousands of engineers in the aerospace industry have been laid off, have taken salary cuts of up to 25 per cent and reductions in benefits to keep their jobs, and have had to retrain to get jobs in other fields.

A crucial test of whether engineers want to join unions, which they have traditionally held as being beneath their professional dignity, will come at the five divisions of the North American Rockwell Corporation in Los Angeles.

There a group called the National Engineers and Professional Association, affiliated with the large U.A.W. Local 877, have signed up 3,000 of 8,000 engineers who favor holding an election to determine if they should form a collective bargaining unit.

The National Labor Relations Board is expected to decide within three months whether an election can be held.

The potential election is being watched by other associations of engineers, including the Seattle Professional Engineering Employment Association at Boeing with 9,000 members; the Engineers and Scientists Guild at Lockheed in Burbank, Calif., with 4,000 members, and the Southern California Professional Engineering Association of McDonnell Douglas, with 5,000.

All three groups have expressed interest in the U.A.W. effort at North American Rockwell and have sent letters supporting the organizing drive.

Bob Leventhal, executive secretary of the association at McDonnell Douglas, said in an interview that an underlying reason why engineers were thinking of joining unions was that they were increasingly facing the insecurity of being laid off, the same as production workers, except that they usually have no benefits.

"It's harder for them to consider themselves part of management," Mr. Leventhal said "when you look into the bull pen of a company and see 600 engineers, elbow to elbow, sitting at drawing desks and getting laid off at the end of the project."

He said that one major issue was that when engineers were laid off, their health and life insurance was no longer paid by the company. The engineer must be back on a job for 30 days before the company pays it again. A production worker who belongs to the U.A.W. gets his life and health insurance paid during a layoff and will also receive 95 per cent of his pay if he has worked in a plant a year.

A. R. McKinstry, an organizer for the National Engineers and Professional Association, said that the recession was also a major factor.

"It's become a matter of survival," he said. "A lot of guys thought that when they finished their training they had it made for life. Then they get laid off without being able to say anything and without other jobs in sight."

At North American Rockwell the work force at one division has declined from 32,000 three years ago to 11,000 now. The space division, which makes the Apollo rocket, has dropped from 22,000 to 6,500.

Another issue is that benefits such as pensions cannot be transferred in a field where projects usually last from three to five years. Engineers then often have to go to another company to find new work. Many of them have reached their forties and have no pensions as a result.

While the professionals want to affiliate with the unions, they do not want to be assimilated with rank-and-file production workers. As part of the condition to affiliate with the U.A.W., the National Engineers and Professional Association wants almost complete autonomy from the union's executive board.

May 1, 1972

Unionism's New Frontier

By A. H. RASKIN

After a full generation of stagnation in unionism's traditional blue-collar strongholds, labor organization is suddenly racing ahead in fields where Samuel Gompers never would have dreamed of finding a union button.

The State Department's Foreign Service, once an "old-boy club" of career diplomats whose class identifications matched their work clothes of striped trousers and cutaways, is preparing for its first union election. Another group unused to overalls—Wall Street stockbrokers—proclaim themselves "fed up with being under the thumb of a feudal overlord, the New York Stock Exchange," and plan to turn their association into a collective bargaining instrument at a meeting tomorrow.

Hospital internes and staff doctors, engineers, chemists and a dozen other varieties of industrial scientists, college professors, lawyers, architects, museum curators, even a few artists and sculptors are following big league baseball and football stars toward unionization. To be sure, not all these groups are rushing headlong into the embrace of the A.F.L.-C.I.O. or other established labor bodies. But even the most mossbound of professional associations find themselves under intense internal pressure, especially from their younger members, to take on economic concerns in dealing with giant corporations, universities and that biggest boss of all—government.

Thus the annual meeting of the American Chemical Society in Boston last month authorized a new department to study salary scales and draw up a model code of employment standards. The American Association of University Professors, after years of shunning direct involvement in bread and butter matters, has just voted overwhelmingly to seek bargaining rights on campuses all over the country. The New York State affiliates of the National Education Association and the American Federation of Teachers are urging their 190,000 members to approve a merger of these once legendary enemies—a merger that may eventually unite the two parent organizations and make the fused group the biggest union in the A.F.L.-C.I.O.

The militant forward push of teacher unionism in the last decade and the substantial advances it has brought both in salaries and in union voice in determining educational policies are major elements in the current surge toward union-type activity in the erstwhile bastions of professional elitism.

The second big spur to professional unionism is the heavy shakeout of engineers and other holders of scientific degrees as a result of cutbacks in defense and space and in government-financed research projects. Jack Golodner, executive director of SPACE, the central council the A.F.L.-C.I.O. set up four years ago to coordinate recruiting efforts among scientific, professional and cultural employes, puts it this way: "The balloon has popped. What with the economic depression in the technical professions, these people suddenly feel very naked. The old fear that unionization meant you'd have some Teamster telling you what to do is long gone. Now there is a great sense of their own impotence, a worry about whether they will have enough clout even if they do join a union."

Unionism's advent to the Foreign Service has brought anguished wails from some old stalwarts. Even before the American Foreign Association filed a formal election petition last week, Ellis O. Briggs, a retired career ambassador, resigned complaining that the organization was turning into a "Foggy Bottom local of the Amalgamated Bureaucrats of the Potomac," dedicated to letting drones take over under the watchword, "Mechanics of the motor pool, unite: let the ambassador put on his own damned chains."

But William C. Harrop, chairman of the association's board, who has had sixteen years in foreign service posts in Europe and Africa and is currently attached to the State Department planning staff, feels confident that the organization can play a vigorous economic role while maintaining its concern for high professional standards. That is why the association helped negotiate the text of a special Executive order signed by President Nixon last December to govern labor-management relations in the Foreign Service, as distinct from those in the rest of the sprawling Federal establishment.

The association's election rival will be the American Federation of Government Employees, whose unit chairman, Don Kienzle, says unreservedly: "We feel we can develop more clout in the economic and legislative process by having formal links to the 15-million workers in the A.F.L.-C.I.O."

For Wall Street tomorrow's scheduled vote by the Association of Investment Brokers on amending its bylaws to include collective bargaining on compensation, working conditions and grievance procedures is an even more startling departure than the moves toward unionizing the diplomatic service. Indeed, it may be a jolt for the high command of organized labor if later on the association decides it wants to apply for a union charter.

May 22, 1972

STRIKES OUTLAWED IN PUBLIC SERVICE TO CURB 'ANARCHY'

DEWEY SIGNS BILL

He Ignores AFL and CIO as the Condon-Wadlin Plan Is Made a Law

By LEO EGAN
Special to THE NEW YORK TIMES.

ALBANY, March 27—Governor Dewey signed today the Condon-Wadlin bill which outlaws strikes by public employes and fixes dismissal as a penalty for violations. In doing so he declared that such strikes could paralyze government and produce anarchy.

Senator William F. Condon of Yonkers and Assemblyman John F. Wadlin of Highland, both Republicans, who were co-sponsors of the legislation, witnessed the signing in the Governor's office. Later they received the pens he used to make the bill a law.

At the time Mr. Dewey approved the law he had before him briefs filed by both the State Federation of Labor and the State Congress of Industrial Organizations asking that he veto the measure, one of the most controversial to come before the recent session of the Legislature.

In a memorandum filed in connection with his approval, the Governor took cognizance of the arguments advanced by the labor unions, Mayor William O'Dwyer of New York City and the Democratic members of the Legislature in opposition to the bill.

Arguments of Opponents

They had contended that the measure was unnecessary, since strikes by public employes had been held unlawful by the courts, and that it would fail to accomplish its purpose of preventing such strikes. They argued, too, that it was drawn so loosely that the penalties it provided could be invoked against non-strikers as well as strikers and that the harshness of the penalties would destroy the morale of public employes.

Mr. Dewey, in approving the bill, ignored completely the requests that had been made by CIO unions and others for a public hearing on the bill before it was signed. It was pointed out by members of the staff that Mr. Dewey had never held a public hearing on legislation pending before him since he took office.

The bill was introduced in the Legislature following a week-long strike by Buffalo public school teachers for improved pay, but its sponsors said it had been under consideration before that time, possibly since a group of Rochester municipal employes went out on strike last autumn.

It applies with equal force to teachers, employes of the New York City transit system and all other employes of governmental agencies under the control of New York State.

GOVERNOR'S MEMORANDUM

Following is the text of Governor Dewey's memorandum filed in connection with his approval of the bill:

"Strikes against Government are wholly unlawful. This bill places upon our statutes a clear statement of the principles involved and provides effective penalties in case of violation.

"The bill declares that a public employe who strikes loses his Civil Service protection, and if re-employed does not regain it for five years. To remove any possibility of profit from his wrongful act, his compensation may not be increased for three years.

"The bill carefully preserves every right enjoyed by public employes to express their views, complaints and grievances, privately or publicly.

"The conditions of public and private employment are entirely different. The special characteristics of public employment are as follows:

"1. Public service is a public trust not only for elected officials but to all employes. It is a trust in behalf of all the people. A trustee cannot strike or falter in the performance of his duties.

"People the Employer"

"2. A public employe has as his employer all the people. The people cannot tolerate an attack upon themselves.

"3. The public employe has no employer who may profit from depressed conditions of employment.

"4. The conditions of public employment, the rules governing it, and the revenues available to pay for it are all matters of public record.

"5. Public employes have the right to improve their conditions through arguments before all the people, before legislative bodies, to administrative officials and, of course, by their own ballots on election day. These rights are so effective that among all the types of employment over the years public employment has been rated as having the best and most desirabl conditions.

"Public employes by virtue of their rights or otherwise enjoy a highly beneficial pension system, supported in large part by government; unprecedented security and stability of employment, and compensation through bad times as well as good, and machinery for correction of individual grievances before administrative officials before Civil Service commissions, and even in the courts.

"The duty of public employes is to the whole of society. A strike of firemen could overnight permit the destruction of a whole city. A strike of policemen could endanger the safety of millions of people and of all their possessions.

"A strike of sanitation workers could almost overnight produce an epidemic threatening the lives of other millions of people. A strike in the mental hospitals of the State could cause the deaths of thousands of patients by starvation or by the violence of other disturbed patients.

"Government is not an end in itself. It exists solely to serve the people. The very right of private employes to strike depends on the protection of constitutional government under law. Every liberty enjoyed in this nation exists because it is protected by government which functions uninterruptedly. The paralysis of any portion of government could quickly lead to the paralysis of all society.

"Paralysis of government is anarchy and in anarchy liberties become useless. A strike against government would be successful only if it could produce paralysis of government. This no people can permit and survive.

"The penalties in this bill are moderate but firm. By their clear terms they will protect loyal employes and what is more important will protect the interests of all the people.

"The bill is approved."

March 28, 1947

CITY WORKERS GET RIGHT TO ORGANIZE IN UNION OF CHOICE

Police, Schools and Transit Employes Excepted Under Code Signed by Mayor

By A. H. RASKIN

A "Little Wagner Act" granting city employes many of the same bargaining rights as workers in private industry was signed yesterday by Mayor Wagner.

The new labor code took the form of an executive order guaranteeing Civil Service workers the right to join unions of their own choosing. Organizations designated by a majority of the employes in their bargaining units are to receive exclusive recognition in negotiations on wages and other grievances.

The signing came after months of behind-the-scenes conflict at City Hall over the political and budgetary consequences of the proposed order.

Increased Pressure Seen

Some of the Mayor's aides took the view that strengthening Civil Service unions would lead to increased pressure for higher wages and other rises in operating costs.

Others contended that the establishment of orderly machinery for the presentation of labor problems would bring stability to municipal agencies and promote higher efficiency.

Observers felt that the Mayor's decision to act now was influenced by a desire to conciliate major union groups on the eve of the publication of the executive budget for the fiscal year beginning next July 1.

It is no secret that the budget, to be submitted to the Board of Estimate this morning, calls for no across-the-board pay rise for the city's 200,000 employes.

Some Rises Slated

The only cheer for them in the Mayor's message will be that provided by mandatory rises for certain workers under automatic pay schedules.

The bargaining order will apply initially to nearly 100,000 workers in departments directly responsible to the Mayor.

However, the Borough President's offices and other municipal agencies will be invited to adopt identical procedures.

Firemen will be covered by the code, but the uniformed police force will be outside "pending further study and possible public hearings on the special problems in this area."

Most firemen already belong to the Uniformed Firemen's Association, an affiliate of the merged labor federation. Unionization of policemen has been a subject of political controversy for many years.

The plan's principal sponsor is Labor Commissioner Harold A. Felix, whose office will ascertain the appropriate bargaining units, conduct representation elections and intervene in disputes that are not settled directly by unions and agency heads.

Also exempt from the Wagner program will be employes of the Board of Education and the Transit Authority, which establish their own labor policies under state law.

The executive order was drafted by Miss Ida Klaus, counsel to the Labor Department and former solicitor of the National Labor Relations Board. The order extends into the Civil Service field key features of the original Wagner Act of 1935, which labor hailed then as its "Magna Charta." The act was drawn up by the Mayor's father, the late Senator Robert F. Wagner Sr.

Union Hails Step

The Mayor's signing of the new code was described as "a monumental forward step" by Jerry Wurf, regional director of the American Federation of State, County and Municipal Employes. This union only last week was threatening a strike of its 25,000 members in city departments.

Mr. Wurf said his organization would move for recognition at once in a half-dozen agencies. He predicted that the union's membership would double by the end of this year. Similar expressions of jubilation were expected from most other unions of municipal employes.

However, there was one conspicuous exception. Fred Q. Wendt, president of the Civil Service Forum, an independent organization with members in many departments, called the new order a "Wagner Slave Labor Act."

He accused the Mayor of reneging on a pledge he had made before the November elections to hold a public hearing before he issued the order.

Mr. Wendt said the sole effect of the code would be to "put caviar on the table of money-hungry union leaders."

The Mayor expressed confidence that his program would lead to "more harmonious, mature and responsible relations between the city and its employees."

He added that it would also provide a vehicle for testing the

worth of "new and untried concepts and principles" before they were embodied in permanent legislation.

The order rules out any form of compulsory union membership for employes unwilling to join.

Its provisions for exclusive bargaining rights for majority unions are tailored to bypass some of the headaches the Transit Authority has encountered in its extension of sole recognition to Michael J. Quill's Transport Workers Union on the city-owned subways.

Minority Rights Explained

The authority's refusal to give any hearing to so-called splinter unions was a pivotal point in the pre-Christmas walkout of subway motormen and members of other craft groups.

Under the Wagner plan, minority unions will retain the right to present to city officials the views and requests of their members. Bargaining on all issues, including the adjustment of grievances, will be restricted to the majority spokesman.

No fixed procedure was set up for the peaceful settlement of disputes that could not be resolved through direct negotiations. Commissioner Felix was vested with authority to "take such steps as he may deem expedient to effect an expeditious adjustment."

Under the Condon-Wadlin Law state and city employes are subject to dismissal if they strike.

April 1, 1958

The $92 Schoolteacher

In New York City a public schoolteacher gets a minimum annual salary of $4,800, which on the basis of a fifty-two-week year comes out to $92 a week. To qualify for this starting salary, a bachelor's degree representing four years of college is required. After thirteen years the salary can rise to $9,450, or $182 a week, but regardless of how many Ph. D.'s are earned or how long the teacher stays on the classroom job, that's as high as the salary can go.

Why would anyone want to be a teacher, with all the grief that goes with it, when he could be an electrician, who receives $161 for a 30-hour week, and is almost sure to get an extra hour daily of premium overtime to make it $198 a week and maybe if he works a full 8-hour day like most other people he gets $236 a week!

But think of the prestige and community admiration the teachers enjoy. They'd better not write any checks on that part of the salary, however.

January 20, 1962

PICKING UP PIECES IS CHIEF AIM NOW

Business Hopes to Recoup Some of Its Huge Loss

By ROBERT ALDEN

New York began to pick up the pieces yesterday after the staggering blow dealt by the transit strike.

The garment center planned to embark on a period of night and weekend work in an effort to fill a large backlog of seasonal orders that must be shipped in the next 21 days.

Department stores started large advertising campaigns to move merchandise from their shelves. Customer traffic in the stores was still thin yesterday as the people continued to be concerned, in the main, with essential travel to and from work. Moreover, many wallets were empty because of missed paychecks.

The strike had paralyzed the economic life of the city. New York's business tempo was at its lowest ebb since the dismal says of the Depression in the early nineteen thirties.

Dollar estimates of the total lss ranged from "upwards of $500 million" by Mayor Lindsay to a "conservative estimate" of $800 million by the Commerce and Industry Association of New York.

Sales Off 41 Pct. Here

Figures released by the Federal Reserve Bank of New York this morning showed department store sales were down 41 per cent in the New York area, while in other parts of the country sales were up sharply.

"The shellacking we have taken is like a nightmare," Michael B. Grosso, vice president of the Fifth Avenue Association, declared. "We can never recover from it."

Some of the hundreds of millions of dollars lost during the strike will be recovered by increased post-strike sales of merchandise, but many more millions have been permanently lost by employes who were unable to get to work and did not receive pay.

"A lot of business was taken out of the city and is gone for good," Neil H. Anderson, executive vice president of the New York Board of Trade contended. "It's going to take a lot of elbow grease to restore the shining bright armor of our city."

Walter F. Pease, president of the New York Chamber of Commerce, said, "the strike dealt particularly savage blows to those least able to withstand them—to small business and to unskilled labor."

To aid the small businessmen, whose sales loss has been estimated at 25 to 80 per cent, the Federal Small Business Administration informed commercial banks yesterday that it would guarantee 90 cents of every dollar of loans made by the banks to those businessmen.

"This should facilitate the loan process," Charles H. Kriger, area administrator for the Federal agency, said.

So far his own office has distributed 4,000 applications for the loans, which have a limit of $15,000 each. Mr. Kriger said it would take his agency at least a week to process applications and distribute checks. The banks, he said, could do it in three days.

Large New York retailers resumed their late Thursday hours last night. Gimbel's, Macy's, Bloomingdale's, Stern's and Ohrbach's were open until 9 o'clock and Alexander's was open until 10.

Ohrbach's will be open again tonight until 9 o'clock, and Abraham & Straus, open until 9 last night, will remain open until 9 P.M. on Monday.

Some Recovery Foreseen

William Tobey, vice president for sales promotions at A. & S., said his store would re-initiate promotions that had been cancelled as soon as it had decided on the strategy to adopt.

"Some of the business we lost is recoverable," Mr. Tobey said, "but it will take a little time to assess the situation to detemine what can be done."

Yesterday department stores were manned by 70 per cent of the sales persons normally present. In the early days of the strike attendance was about 35 per cent.

Business traffic in the stores increased compared with the strike period, but no great rush was apparent. Business in all the stores was heaviest in the winter clothing departments, with customers buying gloves, sweaters and accessories. There was also some buying of white goods on sale.

Newspaper advertising also increased.

Advertising for the remainder of the week and for Sunday is expected to be at least 20 per cent above what it would usually be at this season. In particular, retail and classified advertising will be above expected levels.

There were some checkouts from midtown hotels last night, as people who had been staying near their places of work moved back to their homes. But the city at this time of the year has such a heavy traffic in out-of-town buyers and persons attending business conventions, that the rooms used by the strikebound guests were immediately filled by those who had been staying in less centrally located hotels.

In the garment industry, the largest in the city, production was improving. Those hardest hit by the strike in the garment district were manufacturers of low and medium-price winter coats who found they could not meet their commitments for orders because a large proportion of employes could not get to work.

Spring merchandise should be shipped by the end of January, but it is expected in the industry that shipments can be delayed until the first week of February without substantial cancellations of orders.

With overtime schedules now being negotiated with the labor unions involved, it is hoped by the industry that an early February deadline can be met.

"I expect that manufacturers will do very well this season despite the transit strike," Henoch Mendelsohn, manager of the Joint Board, Cloak, Suit and Reefer Makers Union, I.L.G.W.U., said. "A small segment of the industry will suffer irretrievable losses. But I predict that the spring season on which most manufacturers are working, will be a good one."

Printing Industry Assesses Loss

The second largest industry in the city—the printing trades—lost in excess of $25-million as a result of the strike, Paul L. Noble, president of the Printing Industries of Metropolitan New York, Inc., reported.

Mr. Nobel said that some sales were deferred and probably would not be lost, but that the need to pay overtime to get this work done would result in a dollar loss to the companies doing the work.

The printing industry, as well as some other industries, will suffer, Mr. Noble contended, because customers were coming to think of New York as not a reliable city in which to place orders. To counteract this view, he said, the industry's advertising program would be enlarged.

The end of the strike is expected to bring immediate relief to New York's hard pressed amusement business.

However, Sol Hurok reported a loss of $20,000 in the first week of the run of "Antonio Ballets de Madrid" at the City Center. Business is off for the second week as well and the Hurok office feels that the end of the strike has come too late in the two-week run to be of much help.

But Carnegie Hall, where business had been off 10 per cent, except for top attractions, expects a quick return to normal.

Columbia Artists Management reported a 50 per cent dip in the advance sale for the Hungarian Ballet opening at the City Center next Wednesday. But Columbia expects sales to pick up now with only losses on the first few performances.

Suspended Shows to Resume

Two off-Broadway shows, "Medea," at the Martinique Theater and "Bugs" and "Veronica" at the Pocket Theater, which had suspended performances on Jan. 4, will resume their engagements tonight.

A third, "An Evening's Frost," at the Theater de Lys, will reopen tomorrow night.

Summing up the situation, Ralph C. Gross, executive vice president of the Commerce and Industry Association, called the strike "a calamity of huge proportions."

"It may be weeks before complete figures are known, but it is already abundantly clear that the city's economy was struck harder than at any time since the Great Depression," Mr. Gross said.

NEW STRIKE CURB ON PUBLIC AIDES VOTED IN ALBANY

UNIONS FACE FINES

Penalty for Employes Eased in Substitute for Condon-Wadlin

By SYDNEY H. SCHANBERG
Special to The New York Times

ALBANY, April 2—The Legislature replaced the 20-year-old Condon-Wadlin Law today. The new statute applies penalties for the first time against public employe unions that go on strike, and softens the previous penalties against union members.

Under the new law, unions can be fined up to $10,000 for each day they are on strike. A system of flexible penalties replaces the old provision of mandatory dismissal for individual strikers.

Bipartisan agreement on a substitute for the ineffective Condon-Wadlin Law was reached after three years of see-saw negotiations between the Republicans and Democrats.

The compromise measure, pieced together in long, tortuous bargaining by Governor Rockefeller and the legislative leaders in the final days of the session, was passed in the last hours before adjournment early this morning.

Would Fine Unions

The accord marked the first time in recent memory that the Democrats had broken with organized labor on a major issue.

Labor's most serious objection was to the imposition of fines — $10,000 or one week's dues, whichever is less, for each day on strike. Representatives of the state A.F.L.-C.I.O. did not stop lobbying against the measure until the final vote was taken in the Assembly at 6:05 A.M.

The tally, which followed two and a half hours of debate, was 93 to 51. All the nays were cast by Democrats.

The Senate had passed it nearly three hours earlier after a shorter debate. That vote was 38 to 18. The opposition came entirely from Democrats.

Special Session Loomed

The two-party negotiations this year were even more delicate and volatile than in the past. Time and again in the last few months there were reports that an agreement was imminent, but the discussions each time collapsed.

What apparently brought them to success at the last minute was the threat of picketing and work slowdowns by New York City policemen and firemen, who are involved in contract fights with the city.

All of the participants in the talks here—the Governor, Assembly Speaker Anthony J. Travia and the Senate majority leader, Earl W. Brydges—were said to be extremely worried that the firemen might strike, thereby precipitating a crisis in the city.

In such an event, the Governor, it was reported, would have immediately called a special session of the Legislature to try to solve the public-employe strike problem.

The specter of that was particularly unpleasant to both Speaker Travia, who is the Legislature's top Democrat, and Senator Brydges, his Republican counterpart. They are the leading officers of the constitutional convention that opens Tuesday, and a special session might have come in the middle of the convention's work.

Mr. Travia is the convention president-elect, and Mr. Brydges is the minority leader.

The compromise bill passed this morning, which will be signed soon by Mr. Rockefeller and will go into effect Sept. 1, represents concessions by both parties. But it will be probably be best remembered as a coup for Mr. Rockefeller, because it generally followed the recommendations of a committee he named last year after New York City's crippling transit strike.

The major provisions of the new legislation include the following:

¶A guarantee of union organizing rights and collective bargaining rights to all 600,000 state, county and municipal employes in the state. New York City employes now have such rights, but state employes and public employes in many municipalities do not.

The creation of a state Public Employment Relations Board to solve union representational disputes and provide mediation and fact-finding help in breaking contract deadlocks between public employes and public employers. New York City already has a similar program, and it would be exempt from the jurisdiction of the state board.

¶A fine of $10,000 or one week's dues, whichever is less, against any public employe union for every day it stays on strike.

¶A penalty depriving a striking union of its dues check-off privileges for a maximum of 18 months after the strike. Under the check-off system, which was won after years of fighting by union labor, the member's dues are deducted from his pay by the employer and turned over to the union.

¶A flexible system of nonmandatory penalties against individual strikers, under which each striker could receive anything from a simple reprimand to dismissal. The individual penalties in the present Condon-Wadlin law are mandatory — any public employe who goes on strike must be automatically dismissed. He can be rehired, but must remain on probation for five years and cannot receive a raise for at least three years.

The Governor, who had listened to some of the Assembly debate, was taking a nap when the final vote was announced. He returned to the Assembly, an aide said, to "thank all his friends."

For the vote, Speaker Travia had rounded up about a score of Democrats necessary to pass the bill in the Democratic-controlled Assembly. Even Mr. Travia voted, which he rarely does unless his is the deciding ballot or the issue is very important to him.

There was no trouble at all in the Republican-dominated Senate. The Democratic leader, Senator Joseph Zaretzki of Manhattan also voted for the measure, declaring this is not a union busting bill. This is a public protection bill."

After passage, the Governor issued a statement terming the new legislation "a landmark of sound progress in a highly complex and controversial field." Mr. Travia's statement called it "a major achievement of this session."

A spokesman for the United Federation of Teachers said it had vigorously opposed the measure and would now study its terms. "Penalties aren't the answer by any means," he said.

Victor Gotbaum, president of District 37, State County and Municipal Employes Union, said in New York, "You can't have collective bargaining and take away the right to strike. It's a tragedy. He [the Governor] is not going to have peace—we're going to give him war."

As an adjunct to passage of the Condon-Wadlin substitute, the Legislature also approved, in the final hours of the session, two amnesty bills wiping out the old Condon-Wadlin penalties against Welfare Department and Housing Authority employes who struck in New York City earlier this year. Mr. Rockefeller's signature was considered a certainty.

CITY ESTABLISHES BARGAINING UNIT

Seven-Man Board to Work on Averting Strikes Here

By JOHN P. CALLAHAN

Mayor Lindsay signed a measure yesterday setting up a permanent City Office of Collective Bargaining.

Amid cheers from labor leaders, who hailed it as "a model piece of legislation," Mr. Lindsay said the new law "is the first of its kind in municipal government."

The law provides for a broad and continuing program in which the city, labor and impartial mediators work together to avert strikes by city employes

A seven-man board will meet at least six times a year to consider grievance procedures, review fact-finding machinery and urge solutions in case of contract talk stalemates.

Harry Van Arsdale, the president of the New York City Central Labor Council, which represents 1,200,000 workers, congratulated the Mayor in behalf of the membership.

Nevertheless some labor leaders in the lobby of City Hall after the signing indicated they felt that the measure "has no force."

One union official said labor "doesn't have to bind itself to the findings." Another said that without penalties the law "just sounds good."

The names of the members of the collective bargaining office are not expected to be announced until late next month. A spokesman for Mayor Lindsay said the new law will not become effective until Sept. 1 and that "there will be no announcement of names or salaries until shortly before then."

Two of the seven members will be appointed by the Mayor, and two others on the recommendations of unions that negotiate with the city. Three impartial members will be chosen by the first four, who will also select the chairman from the impartial members.

Herbert L. Haber, City Director of Labor Relations, described the new machinery as "exciting and gratifying." He said that if it had been set up earlier, "situations such as the current dispute in the Department of Welfare could not have occurred."

Judith Mage, president of the Social Service Employes Union, whose members are involved in a tie-up in the Welfare Department, declined to attend the bill-signing ceremony yesterday. She said that "in view of the city's obvious determination to break the union, it is inappropriate that we attend this ceremony."

Other labor leaders who previously had expressed opposition to the new law were also absent yesterday. These included John J. Delury, president of the Uniformed Sanitationmen's Association, and officials of the International Brotherhood of Teamsters.

Paul Hall, president of the Seafarers International Union, which represents many workers in allied maritime jobs, said: "Recognition of the workers' needs—as the new law shows—is a meaningful gesture for better living."

Other labor observers said that while the new city law carried no fines, the state law scheduled to replace the Condon-Wadlin antistrike law on Sept. 1, contained stiff penalties for unions that went on strike. The new measure, conceived by Governor Rockefeller, will impose a maximum fine of $10,000 a day against a striking union.

July 15, 1967

TEACHERS RATIFY SCHOOL CONTRACT; CLASSES ON TODAY

Giardino Calls for Tolerance After Delay of 14 Days in Start of New Term

5 - TO - 1 VOTE FOR PACT

Loss in State Aid Offset by Savings on Pay—Negroes' Animosity Stirs Concern

By LEONARD BUDER

The city's teachers voted overwhelmingly yesterday at Madison Square Garden to ratify the new school contract and end the 14-day walkout that had disrupted education for more than a million public school pupils.

The approval by a better than 5-to-1 margin was announced shortly after 2 P.M., too late for teachers to return to work yesterday, but the city's 900 public schools will be in full operation today.

Albert Shanker, the president of the United Federation of Teachers, said, "All teachers will be back Friday."

Alfred A. Giardino, president of the Board of Education, declared:

"We expect every child back in the classroom tomorrow morning, bright and early.

"We expect that every school will be operating with normalcy, with understanding and with tolerance of other people's points of view. It is up to everyone to focus full attention on the children."

Vote Is 18,171 to 3,442

The vote to accept the contract was 18,171 to 3,442. These figures include votes of teachers and other school employes, such as secretaries, psychologists and social workers, who are also represented by the 50,000-member union.

The pact, put into final form on Tuesday after weeks of bitter negotiations, will give teachers $135.4-million in salary increases and other benefits over a 26-month period. It also mandates certain improvements in working and school conditions.

Even as the city system prepared to move into high gear this morning, school officials continued yesterday to assess the impact of the walkout that started on Sept. 11, the first day of the fall term.

Estimates of the Cost

Officials estimated that the sharp drop in pupil attendance because of the stoppage could cost the system between $10-million and $12-million in lost state aid. Only 141,612 pupils, about 14 per cent of the total enrollment, showed up for makeshift classes on Wednesday, and some days attendance was even poorer.

But on the other hand, it was noted, the system did not spend over $18-million that it normally would have spent for teachers' salaries. Between 47,000 and 48,000 of the system's nearly 59,500 teachers stayed out each day of the stoppage.

The end of the walkout did not end uncertainty about what the school system would do to make up for lost instruction time. The Board of Education has said it will reach a decision next week.

Some suggestions that have been made include extending the school year into July or holding make-up classes on non-religious holidays and during the Easter vacation.

But the problem that is causing perhaps the most concern at board headquarters and within the teachers union is the growing animosity between ghetto communities and teachers serving in those areas. Some Negro parent and community leaders, who had opposed the disruption of education, are warning that they will not permit teachers who stayed out to return to their posts.

Also of major concern to the union is the disposition of the criminal contempt charges that have been brought in State Supreme Court against Mr. Shanker and two other union officers. They have been accused by the board of disobeying a court injunction banning the walkout. A decision is pending.

The three, if found guilty, could be sent to jail for up to 30 days and fined $250 each. The union also could be fined up to $10,000 for each day of the walkout for violating the state's new Taylor law, which prohibits strikes by public employes.

Pickets Vanish

Picket lines were outside many schools yesterday morning, but they soon vanished as the union teachers left to cast their votes. Only members of the union were eligible to vote.

The actual vote for the contract among classroom teachers was 17,234 to 3,345. The most one-sided vote came from guidance counselors: 372 in favor of the contract, 2 against.

The results of the voting were announced by George J. Abrams, executive director of the Honest Ballot Association. Mr. Abrams, who oversees some 80 or 90 elections yearly throughout the country, observed: "The teachers behaved beautifully."

Basic Pay to Rise

The new contract will raise the basic annual starting salary of teachers, previously $5,400, by $800 as of last Sept. 1, and $550 next Sept. 1. Other teachers would receive increases of $400 and $800 on these dates. The pre-walkout offer for next Sept. 1 was $150 less.

Teachers with 30 graduate credit hours beyond the master's degree will receive $750 more than the extra sum now paid. This also is $150 more than the amount offered before the stoppage. The extra $150 will take effect March 1, 1969. This will then give the system a maximum salary of $13,900.

The contract also provides for a reduction of some class sizes, new procedures for handling disruptive pupils and a $10-million fund next year for school-improvement experiments.

Some teachers who waited outside their schools or at home for news of the results entered the school buildings when word of the contract's approval was received.

"Oh my, this is really something," said Mrs. Rose Feldman when she spied the huge pile of board circulars, schedules and other materials that had been accumulating at Public School 40, 319 East 19th Street.

"But it's really wonderful to be back," the middle-aged kindergarten teacher said. She went to her classroom to get it ready for this morning.

Not on the Marquee

Yesterday's main event at the Garden, the school contract vote, was not listed on the Eighth Avenue marquee. It proclaimed:

TONITE—BOXING
SHEA STADIUM
BENVENUTI V/S GRIFFITH
TOM'W—HOCKEY
RANGERS V/S MONTREAL

About 2,000 teachers were waiting when the doors were opened at 7:40 A.M. First on line was Louis O. Thompson, a fifth-grade teacher at Public School 156 in Brooklyn.

"It's a good contract," Mr. Thompson said. "It's not everything many teachers had hoped for, but it has good possibilities."

As the union members streamed into the Garden, passing under advertisements for the forthcoming "Moscow Circus," uniformed guards announced, "Voting in the basement" and "Teacher voting on your left downstairs."

The polls opened at 7:45 A.M. —15 minutes ahead of schedule. Some teachers voted at once. They gave their personnel file numbers to one of the 80 "agents" or registrars who were hired for the occasion by the Honest Ballot Association. The numbers were matched against I.B.M. cards by the agents who then gave the voters official ballots.

Ballots in Different Hues

The ballot, slightly larger than a standard-size index card, came in different colors according to membership category. Classroom teachers received yellow cards. All ballots asked:

"Do you accept the contract offered by the Board of Education of the City of New York?"

There were boxes for a "yes" or "no" response.

Some teachers dropped their ballots in the padlocked steel boxes provided for this purpose and headed for their schools.

A union official, speaking over a public address system, told teachers: "Don't go back to work until all the results have been announced."

Other teachers, before they voted, took seats in the bunting-draped main arena, facing the ice hockey rink prepared for yesterday's Rangers practice session and today's exhibition match. The New York team had obligingly delayed its practice session to accommodate the teachers.

Mr. Shanker arrived at the Garden at 8:22 P.M.

An elderly woman ran up to him, kissed him on the cheek and said, "God bless you."

The union president, standing on wooden planks placed on the ice, spoke to the teachers in the arena.

Notes Clash in Union

He announced the voting procedures and noted that there had been some differences of opinion among members of the executive board and the delegate assembly.

On Wednesday morning, the executive board voted 34 to 13 in favor of the contract. That night, the delegates also voted in favor of the contract, 1,303 to 621.

Mr. Shanker, his hands clasped around a stand-up microphone, said of the opposition:

"There's nothing wrong with that—that's what makes our organization great."

The teachers applauded.

When he announced that there would be no general discussion, there were some quick, short-lived murmurs of disappointment. But no one protested then. Afterward, some complaints were heard.

A bearded teacher, his green shirt open at the collar, told a small group of teachers gathered at a corner outside the Garden: "Shanker's got this union sewed up tight. He's power-hungry. He wants to move up. There's no democracy here."

A union official said that there was no discussion because this had come at the delegate assembly meeting, the teachers all had the contract terms for a day and most important, he added, had already made up their minds how they would vote.

Officials Continue Split

Mr. Shanker then went down stairs to the pink-walled exhibit hall that is used for side-shows during circus time. He gave his file number — 183-066 — to a registrar, who wore a large identification button.

The union president received his ballot and voted "yes."

George Altomare, the vice president for academic high schools, said he voted "no."

Mr. Altomare was one of the three union officers who strongly opposed the contract on Wednesday. The others were John O'Neill, vice president for junior high schools, and Richard Parrish, the assistant treasurer.

Mr. Parrish, one of six Negroes on the 50-member executive board, is also a vice president of the local's parent body, the American Federation of Teachers.

At 10 A.M., as middleweight fighters Nino Benvenuti and Emile Griffith arrived for weighing-in ceremonies at the garden, the line of union members waiting outside to vote stretched from Eighth to Ninth Avenue on 49th Street.

Vote at 4,000-an-Hour Rate

A woman elementary teacher walked along the line, saying: "We were sold out. The new contract stinks. Don't be a bunch of sheep. Reject it."

The votes were cast at a rate of more than 4,000 an hour. The turnout of voters, nearly 7,000 higher than at the Singer Bowl meeting on Sept. 10 when the previous contract offer was rejected, kept the pools open until 1 P.M., an hour later than planned.

Most of the teachers were "dressed" for school. But some men wore sport shirts without ties and several women wore bell-bottom slacks. A middle-aged woman wore knee-length shorts. They did not plan to return to school yesterday.

As they waited for the votes to be tallied, the union members continued to debate the contract.

"We got bupkis," a teacher was overheard to remark. He was using the Yiddish word for "beans."

But another teacher said: "We got as much as we could. It's a very good deal."

Mr. Shanker was back to the hall when the vote was announced. He was surrounded by a throng of well-wishers. Someone asked him if he was really satisfied with the contract.

"The terms of the contract don't represent final answers," he said. "They represent open doors."

GARBAGE STRIKE IS ENDED ON ROCKEFELLER'S TERMS; MAYOR 'SHOCKED' BY MOVE

MEN BACK ON JOB

Governor Asks State to Run Department for Time Being

By DAMON STETSON

The nine-day sanitationmen's strike here ended last night under a plan by Governor Rockefeller to have the state take over temporary operation of the city's Sanitation Department.

Sanitationmen began moving the nearly 100,000 tons of accumulated garbage and trash at 8:30, about two and a half hours after the Governor broadcast the dramatic announcement of the agreement.

He said he would ask the Legislature in a special message tomorrow to authorize the state to take over responsibility for Sanitation Department functions under health regulations.

Explaining his move, the Governor said:

"There's enough suffering on the part of the people, and I do not want to add to it or take the responsibility."

Contract Still Needed

While the state is in control of the department, he said, the men will be paid at the rate a special mediation board recommended early Friday—$425 a year over their current wages.

Even though Mayor Lindsay had rejected the rate proposed by the mediation board, which was set up by the Governor, the city will have to pay it under Mr. Rockefeller's plan.

This calls for the state to control sanitation operations as long as the State Health Commissioner finds that there is an emergency in the city. The city and the Uniformed Sanitationman's Association still must negotiate a contract.

Mayor Lindsay denounced the Governor's action as "capitulation" to a union that had gone on strike in defiance of a state law signed by the Governor that forbids walkouts by public employes.

Guard Call-up Refused

The Mayor had persistently urged the Governor to call out the National Guard to clean up the city, but Mr. Rockefeller refused. He said last night that such an action might cause "fighting in the streets."

While the Mayor referred to the union demands as extortionist, the Governor reported that he had sought to have the city and the sanitationmen submit their dispute to binding arbitration over a difference of $25 a year a man.

The city was willing to have binding arbitration with a ceiling of $375, he said; and the union binding arbitration with a floor of $400. That was the difference, he explained, and added that he had not been able to bridge the gap.

"The $25 is equal to 50 cents per week per man," he said. "That is what separates the two groups."

In view of the Mayor's refusal to accept the mediation panel's recommendation and his inability to establish a mutually agreeable basis for binding arbitration, the Governor said, he had worked out the other solution in which the state would take over the operation of the Sanitation Department for the duration of the health emergency.

The bill he will ask the Legislature to enact tomorrow would expand Section 1301 of the Public Health Law. This permits the State Commissioner of Health to take over a function of a municipality if he finds that the city is unable to abate a nuisance that endangers the public health.

Officials in the Governor's office said that such a step had never been taken before in the state.

They also cited Section 10 of the Executive Law, which gives the Governor general authority to urge legislation of this type. The cost of the services rendered under the state's operation, they said, would be borne by the city.

After the health emergency is ended, control of the Sanitation Department will return to the city.

Shortly after the Governor announced his proposal, two influential Democratic members of the Legislature said that while they did not have details of his plan they favored the idea.

Joseph Zaretzki of Manhattan, the Senate minority leader, said:

"I'd be in favor of it. I'm not playing games with the health of the eight million people in New York City. And the Legislature will go along."

Assemblyman Stanley Steingut of Brooklyn said:

"I think the Legislature certainly should cooperate in any manner to end the serious situation we have in New York City. I do not feel this is a sellout, and I think the word 'blackmail' in labor relations is not proper."

Mayor Lindsay had charged the union with "blackmail" in going on strike despite the state law that forbids walkouts by public employes.

Earl W. Brydges, the Republican majority leader of the Senate, said last night in Westbury, L. I., where he appeared at a party dinner, that he was calling a meeting of all Republican Senators for tomorrow morning in Albany. However, he said, he was withholding comment on the Governor's action until after hearing Mayor Lindsay's further reaction at his news conference today.

Threat of General Strike

In his statement, the Governor explained that he had not considered it feasible to call out the National Guard. He cited the difficulties of the work, the possible injuries that inexperienced guardsmen might suffer and the high cost involved.

Closely related to the Governor's reluctance to bring in the National Guard was a threat yesterday by the New York City Central Labor Council to call a general strike if the guard was used to collect garbage.

Harry Van Arsdale Jr., the president of the council and a long-time supporter of Governor Rockefeller, made public the council's threat after a closed meeting of the council's executive board at the Commodore Hotel.

"We will not tolerate the use of militia against any workers," the board warned.

A general strike, if participated in by the council's 1.2 million rank-and-file union members, would have involved people ranging from saleswomen, clerks and welfare workers to newspaper employes, hod-carriers and transport workers. Since labor has never staged a general strike here, there was no precedent for gauging how many workers might have stayed away from their jobs.

But Mr. Van Arsdale, who had been present in the Governor's offices at 22 West 55th Street during some of the negotiations, made it clear that the council's warning referred to the possibility of a general strike.

It was learned from participants at yesterday's meeting of the labor leaders that there was general condemnation of Mayor Lindsay. Speaker after speaker said that, if the Mayor were successful in "breaking the sanitation strike" it would be a blow to labor in general in the city.

At a labor dinner last night at the Commodore, Mr. Van Arsdale praised the Governor for "having the kind of guts a public official should have." He also assailed "the filthy press for their stand against labor in New York City."

Governor Rockefeller took cognizance of the dangers of calling up the guard in his statement.

"I would just like to say that having military men come in to collect garbage but also to break a strike in this city would have the most serious repercussions, be inflammatory, there could be fighting on the streets, and I think we've got trouble enough in this city," he explained.

The Governor appealed again to the Mayor to accept the recommendation of the mediation panel, but Mr. Lindsay showed no disposition toward changing his attitude in his brief comment last night.

Nevertheless, the problem of a contractual settlement between the city and the sanitationmen's union remains.

It was uncertain what the union would do if it was unable to reach a new agreement prior to the state's return of sanitation functions to the city. But if the city should then eliminate the new pay increase, the sanitationmen could be expected to resist.

Long Talks Held

Discussions aimed at finding a solution to the dispute went on all night Friday at the Governor's office here. They were recessed for only a few hours yesterday while participants showered, shaved and got a little sleep.

Mayor Lindsay, who remained at Gracie Mansion during the night, appeared briefly before newsmen late in the morning and said he was "standing firm" and had "nothing else to say."

Asked if he meant "standing firm" on his position that the city would not pay "blackmail," the Mayor said, in apparent anger, "Let's just leave it at that."

The situation was full of political overtones involving Governor Rockefeller and Mayor Lindsay, who are both Republicans and have been mentioned as possible political rivals for the White House.

Another element in the complicated situation was the close relationship between Governor Rockefeller and many of the city's top labor leaders, including Mr. Van Arsdale and John J. DeLury, president of the Uniformed Sanitationmen's Association.

Mr. DeLury is now serving a 15-day jail sentence for defying a court order enjoining the strike.

Both Mr. Van Arsdale and Mr. DeLury were strong supporters of Governor Rockefeller in his successful campaign for re-election two years ago. The council and labor leaders generally have been strongly opposed to the use of the National Guard, as Mayor Lindsay has asked.

The special mediation panel set up by Governor Rockefeller and agreed to by Mayor Lindsay last Thursday came up with a recommendation for a pay increase of $425 a year for the 10,000 sanitationmen, with the rise retroactive to July 1, 1967. It also urged a postponement of an additional city pension contribution from April 1, 1968, to July 1, 1968.

The sanitationmen now have a starting wage of $6,424 a year and get a maximum of $7,956 after three years.

These were the recommendations that the Mayor rejected and the union accepted.

Earlier, two of the mediators had proposed an annual increase of $300, retroactive to July 1, 1967, and an additional $100 retroactive to Jan. 1 of this year. The added pension contribution would have gone into effect April 1 and was valued at about $50 for the remaining three months of the year.

The city was reportedly prepared to accept the proposals of the two mediators, and so were the leaders of the union. But the membership voted it down at a raucous meeting in City Hall Park on Feb. 2, and the strike began.

Governor Rockefeller put the difference between the two proposals at $250,000 for the proposed one-year contract.

Union leaders said they could not understand Mayor Lindsay's refusal to agree to that relatively small pay increase. But city labor aides contended that increasing the settlement terms by that amount upset bargaining relationships with other unions and made it impossible to establish "sensible, coherent labor relations" in the city in the future.

City officials had also been disturbed by what they consider to be a pattern of defiance of laws prohibiting strikes by public employes.

Mayor Lindsay and his labor aides were known to feel that they had to draw the line somewhere if they were ever to avoid the leap-frogging efforts of one union group to outdo the others.

NEGRO UNIONISTS THREATEN REVOLT

Leaders of Minority Groups Protest Teachers' Strike

By EMANUEL PERLMUTTER

About 50 angry Negro and Puerto Rican union leaders warned the president of the New York City Central Labor Council last night that they would lead a racial revolt within the labor movement unless they were consulted in advance of strikes affecting their communities.

They gave the warning to Harry Van Arsdale Jr., head of the central labor body, at a heated meeting in the Prince George Hotel in which they demanded that he use his influence with the United Federation of Teachers to end the school strike.

"If we have to split the labor movement and go our own way, we will," Lester Roberts, chairman of the group, declared. Mr. Roberts is general organizer for District 65 of the Retail, Wholesale and Department Store Employes.

Thomas Mitchell, a vice president of Drug and Hospital Employes Union, Local 1199, said that "those of us who are black and Puerto Ricans and Hispanic will set up our own labor movement."

The Negro and Puerto Rican labor leaders charged Albert Shanker, president of the United Federation of Teachers, with racism and said his aim was to crush school decentralization.

They had gone to the Prince George Hotel after a five-hour sit-in at the headquarters of the central labor body, 386 Park Avenue South, where they demanded a conference with Mr. Van Arsdale about the school strike.

Shanker Defended

Mr. Van Arsdale defended Mr. Shanker by saying that the president of the teachers' union "has not been and is not racist." He added that the teachers' union "is not and has not been racist."

The New York Times

AGAINST THE TEACHERS' STRIKE: Negro and Puerto Rican union officials opposed to the New York Central Labor Council's support of the strike staging a sit-in at the council's office at 386 Park Avenue South. Later, Harry Van Arsdale Jr., head of the council, met with the officials. They urged him to use his influence to settle the strike.

He agreed with the business agents, organizers, vice presidents and other officers of the dozen unions who had insisted upon yesterday's meeting with him that "we would all be better off if we got this strike terminated immediately." But he characterized the situation as a difficult one, saying: "I don't have any more of a solution than you have."

He pointed out that the teachers union is an independent union and I cannot tell him [Mr. Shanker] to accept any settlement."

By this Mr. Van Arsdale meant that the United Federation of Teachers is an autonomous union within the Central Labor Council and the council has no authority to tell its members what to do.

When the meeting at the hotel ended at 8 P.M., Mr. Van Arsdale left to continue recessed private talks with leaders of unions having large Negro and Puerto Rican member-

ship. He had met with them earlier in the day.

Those with whom he met at an undisclosed place were Leon J. Davis, president of local 1199; David Iivingtston, President, and Cleveland Robinson, secretary-treasurer, of District 65, and Victor Gotbaum, executive director of District Council 37 of the American Federation of State, County and Municipal Employes.

Also present at the afternoon meeting was David Selden, president of the American Federation of Teachers, parent body of the striking union.

In making their demands upon Mr. Van Arsdale, the group at the hotel objected to the fact that labor council had endorsed the teacher's strike and had donated $50.000 to its support.

Declaring they were Negroes and Puerto Ricans first and trade unionists second, they said they would not support strikes against their communities.

Despite strong backing for the teachers among a majority of the New York unions, those with large minority membership have felt that the issue in the teachers' strike was the desire of the Negro and Puerto Rican communities to control their own schools.

This issue, the dissidents feel, transcends that of job security which arose in this case when the governing board of the Ocean Hill-Brownsville experimental district sought the "dismissal" or transfer of teachers that it considered undesirable.

In the early phases of the strike in September, some Negro trade union leaders sponsored an advertisement expressing support for the teachers' union.

Many of the leaders at the hotel meeting said that they had never broken strikes and that they had helped the teachers' union in the past. But they expressed the feeling that this strike was against the interests of the Negro and Puerto Rican communities.

STRIKE AT DRAWBRIDGES IN CITY CAUSES MASSIVE TRAFFIC JAMS; UNION DEMANDS PENSION ACTION

By LAWRENCE VAN GELDER

Hundreds of thousands of motorists were trapped in massive traffic jams on the hottest day of the year yesterday when municipal workers opened drawbridges in the city and abandoned trucks on major highways.

Angered by the failure of the State Legislature to approve a pension agreement negotiated last year with the city, the workers caught commuters by surprise in an unusual strike action that left 27 of the city's 29 movable bridges—many of them said to have been stripped by workers of critical parts —inaccessible to motorists throughout the day and into the night.

Army Crews Help

As the leader of the principal union involved threatened to broaden the strike, Mayor Lindsay said he had informed Governor Rockefeller that he was prepared to request National Guard assistance, if necessary, to insure public safety and maintain vital services.

In Albany, Mr. Rockefeller said the state stood ready to call out the National Guard but added that "we are not at that point yet."

Last night, after a request for assistance from the Mayor, the Army Corps of Engineers dispatched crews to act in "an advisory capacity only" to municipal personnel trying to close the bridges.

At 8:10 P.M., officials of the Transportation Administration, accompanied by the Army engineers, broke a window to gain access to the control tower of the Willis Avenue bridge and swung the span closed. The action re-established a vehicular route across the Harlem River between First Avenue in Manhattan and Willis Avenue in the Bronx.

Other Bridges Restored

At a news conference at City Hall early this morning, Mayor Lindsay reported that city and army engineers had opened seven other bridges to traffic. As the spans returned to operation, he added, they were being guarded by police units to prevent any further disabling action.

Mr. Lindsay urged commuters to use mass transit facilities this morning because of the uncertainty over how long it would take to restore operations to the other bridges and the threat of additional disruptive acts.

Earlier, the city had moved to halt the walkout, which left thousands of motorists frustrated and sweltering on the highways by obtaining restraining orders in State Supreme Court.

Union Leader Defiant

But Victor H. Gotbaum, head of the union that had negotiated the crucial pension agreement, scorned the legal action, won approval to enlarge the strike and expressed his willingness to go to jail.

Late last night Mr. Lindsay met at Gracie Mansion with Mr. Gotbaum and Barry Feinstein, president of Teamster Local 237, which represents the bridge tenders.

"They listened respectfully," the Mayor told newsmen later, "but there was no resolution."

Mr. Lindsay said that he had asked Mr. Gotbaum what his plans were for any escalation in job actions against the city, "but he wouldn't tell me."

Various city agencies have been instructed, Mr. Lindsay said, to keep personnel records on workers who do not report. This was an apparent allusion to the state's Taylor Law, which prohibits strike action by public employes.

Mayor Lindsay condemned the action as "immoral, illegal" and "outrageous" after road ways leading to and from Manhattan island were choked with automobiles during a chaotic morning rush hour.

Despite the strike and the prospect of escalation, Governor Rockefeller and Republican legislative leaders said there would be no action on the pension bill whose dim prospects had prompted two unions to plan their walkout last week and execute it yesterday.

The majority leader of the State Senate, Earl W. Brydges, condemned the strike and recommitted the pension bill, in effect killing it for this session.

Both in the morning and the evening, motorists were confronted not only by congested roadways but by engines that overheated in the sluggish traffic and steamy air. "It's not fair to the public," snapped one driver after an hour's delay in efforts to reach his home in Queens from Manhattan last night.

Late in the day, Mayor Lindsay said he had ordered an investigation of the walkout and was prepared to take administrative and legal action, where merited, against those involved.

Not long afterward, Mr. Gotbaum, executive director of the largest union involved, was authorized by its delegate assembly to extend and broaden the walkout.

Mr. Gotbaum, who heads the 90,000-member District Council 37 of the American Federation of State, County and Municipal Employes, declined to specify what form the escalation might take.

But he noted that the possibilities covered a wide spectrum. The union's jurisdiction covers 122,000 workers in such places as hospitals, welfare and sanitation offices and zoos and who perform such functions as driving ambulances and limousines, aiding nurses and serving as clerks.

Joining with Mr. Gotbaum's union in yesterday's strike action were members of Local 237 of the International Brotherhood of Teamsters. Under normal circumstances, 318 members of this local, which has 13,000 members, man the city's movable bridges. Another 500 members of Local 237 are repair and maintenance workers for the city's Department of Water Resources.

Yesterday, most of the bridge workers participated in a shutdown that affected 27 of the city's 29 movable bridges. The water workers set up picket lines or refused to work at various locations, and at one point yesterday morning, the water supply for West 48th Street, between Fifth Avenue and Avenue of the Americas, was shut down for about an hour.

But the trouble at the edge of the Rockefeller Center complex was the only strike-related incident of the day in the water system, according to Maurice M. Feldman, the Commissioner of Water Resources.

One hundred supervisory personnel and engineers moved in to replace the striking workers, and an unannounced number of policemen were assigned to guard critical points in the city's water supply system.

Mr. Feldman said he was constantly conscious of threats to the water system, but added that "in this case maybe I'm optimistic, but I'm not looking for sabotage."

"I can't visualize men working for this system ruining it," he said.

When the bridges were opened yesterday, some workers walked off with keys. Machinery handles, fuses and gears were also reported missing. In seeking a restraining order from Justice Samuel R. Rosenberg, Highways Commissioner Vincent J. Gibney said in an affidavit for the city, "No supervisory personnel have sufficient training and/or experience to safely operate the bridges in question."

NOT OPEN FOR BUSINESS: Movable sections of Bruckner Boulevard Bridge, left up as the strike got under way

Justice Rosenberg granted the city temporary restraining orders against District Council 37 and against both the water workers and the bridge operators of Local 237 and their officers. The three orders are returnable in State Supreme Court in Foley Square at 2 P.M. today.

Harry Van Arsdale, president of the New York City Central Labor Council, could not be reached yesterday for comment on the bridge operators' strike.

According to the city's Transportation Administration, the latest available figures show that the bridges affected by yesterday's walkout are used by slightly more than 900,000 automobiles, buses and trucks carrying nearly two million people every weekday.

Yesterday's strike did not affect the bridge linking Queens and Welfare Island and the little-used Nolins Avenue Bridge across Shell Bank Basin in Queens. The Broadway Bridge, crossing the Harlem River at 225th Street, was closed to automobile traffic by the dropping of barriers, but IRT subway traffic across the bridge was left unaffected.

In explaining why the Welfare Island bridge was not affected, Mr. Feinstein, the president of Local 237, said, "Unlike Rockefeller, we teamsters do not wage war on the sick and infirm." Bird S. Coler and Goldwater Memorial Hospitals are on Welfare Island.

In a statement, Mr. Feinstein expressed regret at the inconvenience the strike brought to commuters and other travelers but insisted that Local 237 had been left no alternative by the "arbitrary and capricious behavior of Governor Rockefeller and the Republican leadership in the Legislature."

"Governor Rockefeller needs to be reminded that we teamsters are made of sterner stuff than the peoples of Czechoslovakia and Austria who caved in so easily to Hitler three decades ago," Mr. Feinstein said.

He went on to say, in reference to the pension issue: "That which is good enough for white cops and firemen is good enough for black and Puerto Rican employes of New York City and the New York City Housing Authority."

He added: "It is apparent to our membership that their race and ethnic backgrounds, rather than the alleged fiscal crunch, motivates Rockefeller to refuse to permit the execution of the pension provision of the collective bargaining agreement we freely negotiated."

Mr. Feinstein said that blacks and Puerto Ricans composed half the membership of his local.

In discussing pensions, Mr. Gotbaum said yesterday that "old age and retirement in the United States are a disgrace—there are many retirees on relief."

He also attacked the editorial positions of The Daily News and The New York Times, declaring, "The campaign of the Governor, The Daily News and The New York Times from their vantage point is quite understandable. They are protecting interests of the private sector whose record on retirement is scandalous."

The pension program at issue was negotiated with the city by Mr. Gotbaum and would provide retirement at half pay after 20 years' service for the 122,000 municipal employes represented by the union. But legislative approval was needed before it could become operative.

Senate Majority Leader Brydges of Niagara Falls, a foe of the bill, said: "The Legisla-

Aerial view shows traffic jams in the Bronx. Penn Central train is in foreground. View looks west.

ture has not, and will not ratify this pension plan for a very good reason—because the people of the City and State of New York cannot afford it, and do not want it."

Steadfast opposition to the bill among Republican legislative leaders set the stage for yesterday's walkouts.

Motorists returning to the city from Long Island, West-chester and Connecticut after the weekend were greeted by open bridges, abandoned heavy trucks and long lines of traffic.

Police crews moved in to tow away the heavy vehicles, some of them laden with sand and left with flattened tires.

Mr. Gotbaum advised those inconvenienced by the walkouts to "get the man who really made the strike—Nelson Rockfeller."

The Commerce and Industry Association condemned the strike action, but said the impact on business was not serious. There was some tardiness, with many school teachers late for work. Some hotels reported some cancellations from individuals who had intended to spend the night in the city.

In preparation for the evening rush hour and the possibility of new abandonment of vehicles, the Police Department diverted trucks from illegal parking enforcement to standby alert for action on or near bridges.

The Fire Department ordered its men not to leave at the finish of the 9 A.M. to 6 P.M. tour unless relieved by incoming personnel. The order was designed to insure maintenance of an adequate force.

CHAPTER 10

Minorities Organize

*A. Philip Randolph of the Brotherhood
of Sleeping Car Porters at the
1963 March on Washington.*

The New York Times.

LABOR IN THE FAR SOUTH

HOW COLORED WORKMEN ARE DE-FRAUDED.

FACTS AND FIGURES PLAINLY STATED—SYS-TEMS DEVISED TO MAKE CHEATING SAFE AND EASY—INTEREST AT EIGHT-EEN PER CENT.—A SHORT-SIGHTED POL ICY AND WHAT THE RESULT MAY BE.

It has from time to time been fully proved in these columns that the colored men of the South were not regarded as equals before the law; that they were not permitted freely to exercise the rights of suffrage conferred upon them by the national Constitution, and that the Democratic State and local Governments gave them next to no opportunity of educating their children. But these are not the only wrongs of which the freedmen have to complain. From a number of facts which I obtained during a recent visit to the Gulf States—facts which will not be successfully disputed—it is evident that in every material relation the negroes are cheated and taken advantage of by the whites. From year's end to year's end they have been made to work for the profit of the land-owners, and each year they have found themselves growing poorer and poorer. Of course, there are isolated exceptions to this general rule. Here and there may be found a black man who, by dint of hard work and close economy, coupled with circumstances of a peculiarly fortuitious character, has gathered together enough money to buy a small farm, and who has a few thousand dollars in good securities. But such cases are very rare, so rare, in fact, that when one of them is discovered the Southern newspapers have much more to say about it than they would about half a dozen murders. In the great majority of cases the negroes are living actually from hand to mouth. They and their families are kept alive very much as they were in the days of slavery. That they are in any of their material relations more independent than they were during those days there is very little evidence. Since the results of the war made them free all sorts of means have been resorted to by the whites, who had and have all the money, to keep them from bettering their financial condition, and thereby placing themselves in a position to make more favorable terms with their former owners. One of the earliest of these devices was known as "the share system." Under its provisions the white capitalists supplied the land, provisions, seeds, and implements, the negroes, with their wives and children, gave their labor, and it was understood that at the end of the year the profits of the crops which were obtained should be divided between all those engaged in raising them. When the time for a division came, however, it was almost invariably found that all the money which had been made was by one means or another placed in the pockets of the land-owners, while the black laborers were declared to be in debt for extra supplies, to provide for which they were coolly required to give a lien on the share of the next year's crop which was supposed to be theirs. For a time this pretty little scheme worked admirably and to the very great advantage of the capitalists. But by degrees the negroes began to see that they were being systematically cheated out of their hard earnings, that, indeed, for all practical purposes, they might just as well be slaves as freemen. Knowing this, they ceased to take any interest in their work under "the share system" which never brought any "share" to them. They neglected the fields, and after a time convinced the land-owners that some new and less transparent means of defrauding them would have to be devised. To a very great extent the latter have succeeded.

In the far South, but particularly in Mississippi, the "share system" has now given place to what is known as the "lease system" and the "hire system." Under both of them the whites continue to get very much the best of the bargains which are made with the colored men. For instance, under the so-called hire plan the land-owner usually contracts to pay an able-bodied and experienced farm-hand, who is aided by a wife and perhaps by children, $16 a month, or a total of $192 a year. It is also understood that the negro is to be supplied with a "furnish," which consists of certain stipulated quantities of meal, pork, sugar, and coffee, and which is to be given at certain stated periods in the year. This "furnish" costs the capitalist $85. One mule and the farming implements necessary for the use of the negro, the ownership of which rests with the land proprietor, costs him about $200. The wear and tear of mule and implements, at a very liberal estimate, is $50 a year. These are the usual expenses which have to be borne by the land-owner under the "hire plan." It will be seen that they foot up a total of $327 a year; but, to be on the safe side, and to include a liberal sum on account of interest on the capital invested by the owner, let it be assumed that the total expense to him is $400 a year. On the other hand, what are his profits from the negro, the mule, the implements, and the land upon which he is supposed to expend this sum? It is always expected that the negro and mule will cultivate during the year 12 acres of ground. It is usual in Mississippi to plant nine acres of this in cotton and three in corn. In a reasonably good year nine acres of the rich bottom lands of the Mississippi, to which the figures given are applied, yield 12 bales, weighing 500 pounds each. At 10 cents a pound, the total derived from the sale of this product would be $600. From the corn land 60 bushels are usually expected from the acre. From three acres the yield at this rate would, of course, be 180 bushels, which, if sold at the average price of 70 cents a bushel, would bring $126. From these figures it will readily be seen that the total yield in money from the 12 acres would be $726. If the $400 which was allowed for expenses be deducted from this sum, it will be found that the land-owner has realized from his 12 acres the handsome profit of $326. And the majority of them are not content with these returns. By every conceivable trick, by extortionate charges for extra provisions which they may or may not have supplied to the negroes, they continue to evade payment of a large portion of the wages which it was agreed should be given to the laborer and the blacks in ninety-nine cases out of a hundred at the end of the year find themselves precisely where they commenced—that is to say, penniless and entirely dependent upon the white land-owner for the food which keeps them from starvation and the miserable cabin which gives them but scant protection from the elements.

STRIKING NEGRO KNIGHTS.

FEARS THAT THEY WILL REDRESS THEIR WRONGS BY FORCE.

LITTLE ROCK, Ark., July 8.—It was supposed that the trouble at the Tate plantation had ended, and that the striking negro Knights of Labor had become pacified and would return to work, their Master Workman having so advised. Just the reverse, however, seems now to be the condition of affairs, and many believe that this county is on the verge of one of the bloodiest race conflicts that has occurred since the war. Intelligence has arrived from the neighborhood of the late trouble that the striking negroes, reinforced by many sympathizers from the surrounding farms and plantations, numbering fully 1,000 in all, have made complete preparations for a general uprising; that, fully armed, they will attempt to redress their wrongs and grievances, directing their attention first to Sheriff Worthen, who recently subdued the strikers. They will next advance upon the farms of Morey and Fox, with the intention of burning their crops, barns, and houses. Others who have incurred their enmity will be visited and treated in a like manner. The negroes have been openly buying arms and ammunition within the past few days, and they state that if they are opposed in their campaign of revenge they will be freely used. Sheriff Worthen called a public meeting last night and stated these facts, at the same time requesting those who were willing to join his posse to hand him their names. About 100 men responded to his call and were sworn in as special deputies. At the first intimation of an outbreak among the blacks the posse will proceed to the scene of trouble and attempt to quell the disturbance, and bloodshed will doubtless follow. The Governor has been called upon to order out the militia, but he refuses to do so until some actual trouble shall have occurred. Some of the farmers in the vicinity of the Tate plantation have prepared to resist the negroes, while others have removed their families and valuables to places of safety.

The Knights of Labor are having a lively time at Richmond. After three days' session the convention is still unorganized. On the first day Mr. POWDERLY surrendered to the Home Club by packing the Committee on Credentials with its supporters, and this has aroused an antagonism which threatens to split the convention. In the meantime the zeal of District Assembly No. 49, from this city, in trying to break down the color line in the stronghold of race prejudice is doing far more harm than good. The taking of Delegate FARRELL to the Academy of Music on Tuesday night and seating him in the orchestra so excited the white population of Richmond that the purpose of taking him in a similar way to the Richmond Theatre last night would undoubtedly have produced a riot if it had not been abandoned. The disregard of local prejudices by the visiting Knights has had a disastrous effect upon the Richmond assembly already, and is likely to damage the order throughout the South. A little discretion would be useful even in a labor organization.

October 7, 1886

EXCITEMENT IN THE COKE REGION.

THOUSANDS OF LABORERS TO BE TAKEN FROM THE EAST.

PITTSBURG, May 3.—The expected sensation of the week is the promised importation of 7,000 workmen from different parts of the East. It is said that many of them will be negroes and Italians. The operators have little to say, except that they must run their plants somehow, while citizens generally are indignant that steady, skilled labor seems about to be driven from the field by this threatened invasion of ignorant and by no means desirable laborers. Money is rapidly coming into the miners' hands, and its effect was shown to-day at several mass meetings, which were attended by men from Jimtown and Kyle, who promised to come out in the morning on assurances of support. Some six hundred evictions will be made this week in order to make room for the new men coming into the region, but labor officials say they will be able to prevent the bulk of them from going to work. To-night the Rev. Father Lambing, a power among the Catholics of the region, stoutly denounced the labor leaders and Socialistic element from the pulpit. He also created a sensation by repeating his advice that the men return to work. At the Polish celebration in the Opera House he also reiterated these views.

May 4, 1891

SOUTHERN LABOR PROBLEM

Employment of Blacks in Cotton Mills a Probable Cause of Future Trouble.

WORK THE NEGROES PERFORM

A Future Time When the White Labor Must Become Short, and Recourse Will Probably Be Had to the Negroes.

COLUMBIA, S. C., Aug. 20.—Recent troubles in Atlanta, Ga., over the employment of negro labor in the cotton mills, coming upon the heels of newspaper discussion of that subject in this and other Southern States, bring to the surface a question which is likely to engender much feeling in this section as the mills multiply. Paradoxical as it may seem, the fact remains that less of race prejudice exists in those sections where negroes do most abound than where they are less numerous and the further fact that in all sections where they are in a numerical majority they are less aggressive and more deferential and polite to the whites than elsewhere.

It is also precisely in those sections, which, for want of a better name, are called black districts, that the negro vote is least potential and that they enjoy the broadest field of employment. Certain lines of work are monopolized by them in many parts of the South. In the cultivation and harvesting of rice, sugar, and, below latitude 32, of cotton, negroes do the work. The mining and manufacture of phosphates, the drayage, warehousing, and compressing of cotton, the gathering, distillation, and marketing of turpentine are done by them.

Labor of the Negroes.

From Norfolk all around the South Atlantic and Gulf coast to Galveston negro roustabouts load and unload ships, and some of the wealthiest of Southern corporations are these same longshoremen associations, which are universally conducted upon the co-operative plan. All, or nearly all, Southern hotels employ negro waiters, while the barber's trade is almost wholly in their hands. On the railway trains negro porters are usually found, but the engineers, firemen, and brakemen are all white. No negro telegraphers are employed by any of the lines, nor station masters, baggage masters, or express messengers, though they do occasionally find their way through competitive examinations into the mail cars, and frequently wear Uncle Sam's gray uniform as letter carriers in the cities of the South.

They furnish the bulk of household help, work side by side with white mechanics, machinists, masons, and farriers; sell in the markets and upon the streets, own shops, are preachers, doctors, occasionally lawyers, college Presidents and professors; while under license from white boards and paid by taxes collected from the property of the whites, they teach almost every negro school in the South. Thus it will appear that the field is broader and the restrictions " on account of race, color, and previous condition " are far less here than in some localities which might be named north of the Ohio.

No Interference with Whites.

Some things they do not do in the South. They do not intermarry with the whites; they do not send their children to the schools with white children; they do not mingle upon terms of equality with the whites in the hotels, theatres, or other places of entertainment. Thus far they have, as a rule, been debarred from the cotton mills, which by common consent employ only white labor, and are regarded as the one place where the laboring whites can obtain employment out of competition with the blacks. Cotton manufacturing in the South has passed the stage of experiment. The saving on transportation of raw material, the ability to run all the year round, the cheap cost of living, the adaptability of Southern whites to factory labor—all of these enable the Southern mills to earn dividends of from 8 to 20 per cent. per annum, while similar plants in the North are shutting down because of failure to declare dividends.

No scheme of protection, incidental or otherwise, can be devised which will not equally protect Southern products, and the inevitable result must be increase of cotton mills near the cotton fields. The time may come when, as in New England, the native whites will not be able to furnish all the factory labor, and then, as in New England, they looked across the St. Lawrence or the sea to supply the deficiency, the Southern spinner and weaver will look perhaps across the color line for his extra help. Meanwhile a few hardy adventurers may employ negro labor in the mills and demonstrate its utility; time will accustom the people to the usage, and when employment is plenty for all there will be no more objection to factories manned with negro labor than to schools filled with negro students or churches with negro worshippers. All of this, however, depends upon the absence of irritation resulting from unwise and premature agitation of the question. As an abstract proposition the Southern people care nothing for it so long as white families are not moved out and black ones moved into the factory houses, and so long as the negroes are not placed side by side with the whites in the factories.

Negroes May Be Used in Mills.

A mill company, with capital to erect its own plant and stock it from the beginning with negro labor, might possibly incur the ill-will of a certain class of whites and invite the criticism of a certain class of journals and politicians. But, beyond this, it would have nothing to fear. No planter would refuse a fair price for his cotton from such a mill, or, if he did, brokers and factors would speedily supply at market rates. State and Federal laws would protect the operatives; a strike in the mills employing white labor would only take the bread out of their own mouths, and not injure the mills employing blacks.

The Atlanta strike came of an unwise effort to employ mixed labor in the mills, just as similar trouble would have resulted from an effort to force negro children into white schools. The negro cannot take the initiative in this matter. He must wait until he is wanted, and should not be called upon until the supply of white labor is exhausted, and there is need for him in this new field.

Meanwhile it may suit the purposes of certain journals and politicians to inject this question into current politics, and to endeavor to stir up the dormant race prejudices of the whites and the ambition of the blacks for their own purposes. Such discussion is unwarranted and censurable, injurious alike to both races, and should be deprecated by the sensible and patriotic of all sections. The native whites should and will hold the field so long as they are able to fill it. When, if ever, the time shall come when there are not enough native whites to supply the demand for factory labor it will be better for all parties that the deficiency be supplied by native blacks. The negro is here, is acclimated, speaks the same language, is neither an Anarchist nor an agitator, is fully the equal in intelligence and capacity of the average foreign importation, is far less dangerous as a citizen and more effective and tractable as an operative.

August 21, 1897

Imported Negroes at Springfield.

SPRINGFIELD, Ill., Oct. 13.—The miners here held a mass meeting to-day at which it was declared by the union men that the imported negroes must be taken out of Springfield. Secretary Ryan says the United Mine Workers will not be responsible for them after to-day. A colored miner claiming to be one of those brought from the South yesterday for Virden was assaulted at the depot here to-day by white miners when they found he was on his way to Virden. Officers interfered. He was not badly hurt, but was surrounded again and taken possession of by the miners and taken to the hall of the miners' union, where he remained in the custody of the miners. A large crowd of miners surrounded the hall, but were not boisterous.

October 14, 1898

NEGRO LABORERS AND STRIKES.

To the Editor of The New York Times:

Thanks for your yesterday's editorial, "Building for the Future," to which I say amen. Argus-eyed sociologists who have studied the race troubles of the South and the alienation between labor and capital of the North see the adjustment of these conditions in the epoch-making movement inaugurated by the Newport News Shipbuilding Company and "contractors in Portsmouth," (Va.,) in the employment of negro labor, which "gave such satisfaction that more were asked for." If, indeed, the employers of labor would follow the "conspicuous example of Mr. C. P. Huntington," we believe that vested interest would be more secure from the lawless spirit that underlies the American strikes and periodic outbursts of labor against the hen that lays the golden egg. The special reasons why the collar manufacturing establishments, the mills, foundries, railroad and other corporations, factories, machine shops, and every avenue of industry should be thrown open to negro laborers on the same terms as other American citizens are cogent:

First—Because negro laborers are loyal to their employers, never becoming "particeps criminis" to movements that jeopardize the interests of their employers. This is their unsullied record for the consecutive period of 250 years. In all the avenues of industry where the colored laborers have been employed, they have done exactly what they are doing now, not only in the shipyards at Newport News, and with the contractors in Portsmouth, (Va.,) but elsewhere as well they have given "satisfaction." A recent public noteworthy example of the colored man's loyalty to his employer was seen out in Illinois, where, at Brush's coal mines, his (Superintendent Brush's) white miners went on a strike; but, says the report, "the negroes whom he had employed remained loyal to him."

Second—The negro laborers are not given to thrusting "demands" in their employer's face all the time. Although they, in common with their Caucasian brothers, are very fond of chicken, they cannot be made to kill the hen that lays the golden egg. The colored people know that invested capital is the source of the workingman's income, and they have the intelligence to appreciate that fact. Consequently the negro is not going to belittle his opportunity for making a livelihood. The negro laborer knows that when capital is "tied up," why, his chances to earn his bread and butter have diminished. The negroes' intelligence leads them to realize that the meal in their barrel and the oil in their cruse can only be replenished by the sweat of their brow. Hence, to cripple, destroy, or incapacitate in any manner his employer is suicidal to his and his neighbors' best interests. "Organized labor," says Dirie, (quoted by The Literary Digest, New York, of July 1, Page 8,) "as it exists to-day, is a menace to industry," and nowhere in the history of the race have the negro laborers allied themselves with lawlessness. The spirit of lawlessness that is now behind the strikes throughout the land is foreign to the colored laborer. Nowhere on the continent have they defied the "majority" of the Commonwealth or resorted to violence in any form to gain a point.

Third—Then the negro is a workman that needeth not be ashamed of himself. A recent Southern authority, in writing on this topic, says: "The negro is becoming skilled in the mechanical arts, and there is no possible hindrance to his efforts in that direction." Certain organizations may continue to draw the line on the colored mechanic, but when the Newport News Shipbuilding Company refuses to draw the color line among its employes, and when other large concerns go and do likewise, the deathknell to "riot's red hand" as a menace to industry will have been sounded. On this point a noted thinker, in The Literary Digest of June 19, 1899, Page 217, says: "The white man who would close the shop or factory against a black man seeking an opportunity to earn an honest living is but half free; the white man who withholds from his black brother any opportunity which he himself would possess, is but half free." So that it is to the best interests of capital and of profit to the labor field to see to it that the dusky sons of Ham play an important part in the drama of industry. In the shipyards of Newport News and in the watch case factory at Riverside, N. J., and elsewhere he is acting well his part. When employers in general do as Mr. Huntington and Mr. Zurbrug of Riverside, N. J., have done, the "labor problem" and "negro problem" will pass away as the mist before the rising sun or the stars before the dawn.   REV. JOS. BODDY.

Troy, N. Y., July 24, 1899.

July 26, 1899

NEGROES AND LABOR UNIONS.

To the Editor of The New York Times:

In view of President Roosevelt's invitation to the public to discuss the lynching evil which has of late assumed such alarming proportions and has spread to regions hitherto unaffected by this vestige of crudity and barbarism, and to suggest means of curbing its further propaganda, may I ask for the liberty of making a few remarks upon the subject? In my opinion the question to be discussed is not whether summary justice inflicted by a passionate mob is justifiable or not and, if justifiable, whether it is effective as a preventive of crime, but if we sincerely wish to remedy an existing evil, to probe to the bottom of the abuse and the conditions which produce it, and to discover the cause of the preponderance of crime among the negros which ultimately leads to the culprit's lynching, for in mental as well as physical ailments the knowledge of the cause of the affliction is already half of a cure. The answer might be startling to some, but is nevertheless true. It can be said without any hesitation that to the arrogant and belligerent attitude recently assumed by organized labor can be ascribed the present day shiftlessness, indolence, and crime of the negro. Almost all of the labor organizations refuse to enroll a negro as a member or to let him learn or work at any trade, no matter how competent and industrious he may be. Let any manufacturer with philanthropic inclination attempt to introduce a colored workingman into his shop and instantly there will be a panic. Tools will be thrown aside, benches and machines will be abandoned, and out will march the army of "outraged" workmen, leaving only the terrified negro and the employer to reflect; and presently the would-be industrious and docile negro will be informed of his discharge, and the rowdies will march triumphantly back and, flushed by victory, ready to plan new aggressions! The same applies to store or office.

"Idleness is the father of vice and poverty is the forerunner of crime." The negro has both the causes and effects. If you condemn a whole race irrespective of ability to render more useful service to be "hewers of wood and drawers of water; if the college bred negro, despite all his accomplishments, can expect only to eke out a miserable living by performing menial services for the meanest of the white men; if a whole race with but rare and insignificant exceptions must be porters and coachmen, blacken boots, and brush coats on the Pullman cars, or wash the windows and sweep the floors of our mercantile and residential establishments, services at once degrading and poorly paid for, how can you expect the colored man to possess any self-respect or civic pride and love for the institutions of a country which grinds him down and denies him the very means of existence?

Can you expect him to climb the lofty peak of virtue, the crown of human effort, when he is dehumanized and made the pack mule of the Nation? Let there be created a powerful public opinion which by its force will compel these demagogues to lift the unjust embargo, give the negro a chance to learn a useful vocation, and become a wealth-producing mechanic or laborer. Afford him the opportunity of developing the resources of his brain and muscle to the increase of his own and the country's wealth, and then when he will be convinced that virtue brings her reward and industry her blissful harvest of prosperity, when he will be self-supporting and self-respecting, with no prejudices to hamper him and no obstacles intentionally laid on his path of progress, then encouragement will lend more impetus to his ambition, while prosperity will bring in its wake intelligence, self-possession, civic pride, and patriotic devotion and adherence to the laws of the land to the diminution of crime and desperate deeds, and hence obviate the necessity of punishment.
                              HAROLD BERMAN.

Jersey City, N. J., Aug. 12, 1903.

August 16, 1903

NEGROES DESERTING SOUTH FOR NORTH

Considerable Discussion Caused by Migration of Laborers to Border Cities

INCREASE IS STRIKING

From 1900 to 1910 the Increase Was More Than Three Times That of the Total Negro Population.

New York, Oct. 28, 1916.

To the Editor of The New York Times:

The movement of negro laborers from the South in large numbers during the past few months has created considerable discussion in the public press, North and South, and not a little concern in parts of the South. A striking feature of most of this discussion is the absence of statements about the migration of negroes before the present movement. The migration of negroes northward in considerable numbers year by year for the last two or three decades has been quietly going on, although it may not have attracted much attention.

The indication of this movement since 1880 is shown by the percentage of increase of the negro population of the following nine Northern and border cities: Boston, Greater New York, Philadelphia, Chicago, Cincinnati, Evansville, and Indianapolis, Ind.; Pittsburgh, and St. Louis. The census figures for these nine cities showed that between 1880 and 1890 the negro population increased about 36.2 per cent.; from 1890 to 1900 it increased about 74.4 per cent.; and from 1900 to 1910 about 37.4 per cent. In the first decade the increase was more than three times the increase of the total negro population; in the second period it was more than four times as large and shows the influence of the economic disturbances of the period. In the last period the increase was nearly three times larger than the increase of the total negro population.

The rate of increase in the Southern cities has been large, although less than that of the Northern cities during the same period, indicating that similar causes were operating to draw negroes to Southern cities, although these causes were weaker than those operating in Northern cities. The percentage increase of negroes in fifteen Southern cities was, from 1880 to 1890, about 38.7; from 1890 to 1900, about 29.6; from 1900 to 1910, (sixteen cities with addition of Birmingham, Ala.,) 29.6 per cent. These percentages are based upon census figures for the following cities: Wilmington, Del.; Baltimore, Md.; Washington, D. C.; Norfolk and Richmond, Va.; Charleston, S. C.; Atlanta, Augusta, and Savannah, Ga.; Louisville, Ky.; Chattanooga, Memphis, and Nashville, Tenn.; Birmingham and Mobile, Ala., and New Orleans, La. It may be added in passing that from 1880 to 1910 the increase of white population in these Southern cities has been very similar to that of the negroes.

The causes of this movement during this longer period have been the same as those affecting the negro population in the last few months. The only difference has been the increase in the volume of the movement because of the increase in its influencing causes.

The newspaper discussion of the arrests, fines, and jail commitments, restlessness of the younger generation of negroes and political calculation may be given place as individual factors in the causes for such a movement. But a further sifting of the facts shows that at bottom the negro is reacting toward certain fundamental conditions in a similar manner to the response of other elements in our cosmopolitan population.

Economic, educational, and civic opportunities and conditions are having their influence. Among these forces economic conditions demand first consideration. The wages in all lines of occupations open to negroes in the North are considerably higher than those in the South. For instance, the writer found in New York City in 1910 that the majority of thirty-seven negro men who had recently come to the city had received weekly wages before they came of between $3 and $7, and after coming to the city the majority of the same group of men were receiving weekly wages of between $9 and $12 per week. Out of twenty-six women who had recently come to the city the majority, before coming, had received weekly wages ranging from below $3 to $5, and after coming to the city the majority had advanced in weekly wages so as to range between $5 and $8 per week.

Even if these facts are not conclusive, they are corroborated by the replies to a further question which was asked of negro wage earners in 1909 and 1910. In those years 365 wage earners were asked their reason for coming to New York City. Nearly half of the answers showed a decided economic reason; some gave reasons that were probably economic. The answers showed that probably three-fourths of these wage earners had been drawn to the city through economic motives.

It has been frequently stated and generally believed that the negro has no economic opportunity in the North. And it cannot be denied that heretofore he has been practically shut out of most of the highly paid employments. He has also been crowded into very limited fields and mostly into occupations where white men in large numbers did not care to compete. This has been mainly in domestic and personal service. What has not often always been considered is that in the Northern wage, in occupations where negroes might enter, coupled with board, lodging, and other perquisites, sometimes has been better than the wage in the more skilled occupations which negroes could enter in the South, to say nothing of the unskilled.

The writer has found many cases in the North of semi-skilled or skilled negro workmen who were crowded out of occupations to which they aspired either because of color discrimination or because of an efficiency lower than that of competing white workmen. Instead of returning to the South with its open field in their line, these men have become janitors in office buildings, messengers, Pullman porters, porters in stores, &c. They remain partly because in such jobs they receive better wages than they were getting as skilled workmen in the South. It should be borne in mind that the average workman does not consider the higher cost of living and the greater congestion of residence in the northern centre. He makes a comparison of wages in terms of dollars and cents and does not think of the economists' distinction between money wages and real wages.

The present labor demand in the opening of wider fields of employment for negroes, therefore, has simply accelerated a movement which has been under way for a long time. What should be emphasized both North and South in considering the matter in connection with the welfare of the negro and the nation is the negro's response to a fundamental economic call in a way similar to that of other groups. The migration cannot be stopped by ordinances or statutes and will probably continue as long as the conditions that create it persist.

There is another phase of the matter which has not seemed to find much expression in the public press. The settlement of large numbers of negroes in Northern towns and cities has been discussed from the point of view of its effect upon opinion concerning the so-called negro problem. Attention should also be directed to the adjustment of these newcomers to the life of the Northern communities in such a way that the political and economic forces which have attempted to exploit other elements of the communities may not use the negro in the same way. For example, the Northern communities need to see that proper houses, sanitary, and sewerage regulations are carefully provided in negro neighborhoods. Otherwise, the whole community may suffer from official neglect and landlord exploitation. "Loan shark" agents, company stores, and sweat-shop conditions may suck new life from the blood of these labor recruits. Ward heelers and local political bosses may gain a new grip on the community by posing as friends and champions of the new citizens.

Naturally, the question of the best steps to take in these larger community matters arises. Two or three suggestions may not be out of place:

First—Among the negroes in each of these communities may be found individuals of character and intelligence who are eager to do everything they can for the advancement of their people. Public-spirited white citizens may get in touch with these persons through personal contact.

Second—These white and colored citizens can then best help the adjustment of the colored people by coming together in some form of joint organization with a definite purpose to benefit in the main the colored population.

Third—This organized effort may look over the field and agree upon a definite program of active work along a few lines such as the community most seems to need. This program may include a careful study of the living and working conditions of the colored people, a plan of publicity, and a plan to keep check on the conduct of public officials wherever their duties touch negro life. It takes public attention to see that the police department, the housing, the sanitary, the health, and other departments of the community government adequately serve the colored neighborhoods. So fundamental is the question of work and wages that a special part of any community program should provide some employment, finding agency or agencies, should seek methods of touch with employers, and should aim to set negro workers thinking and acting collectively with their employers for their own interest.

GEORGE E. HAYNES,
Professor of Social Science, Fisk University; Executive Secretary of the National League on Urban Conditions Among Negroes.

RACE RIOTERS FIRE EAST ST. LOUIS AND SHOOT OR HANG MANY NEGROES; DEAD ESTIMATED AT FROM 20 TO 75

MANY BODIES IN THE RUINS

Mobs Rage Unchecked for 24 Hours Till Military Rule Is Established.

FLAMES ENDANGER CITY

Whole Business District Is Threatened—Loss So Far Is Put at $3,000,000.

GIRLS ACTIVE IN MOBS

Clash Caused by Influx of Blacks Brought from the South by Labor Agents.

Special to The New York Times.

EAST ST. LOUIS, Ill., July 2.—Many negroes have been killed in race riots which have been raging here since Sunday night. At a late hour most estimates of the dead range from twenty to seventy-five, of whom three were white men. The negroes were shot down by mobs as they fled from their homes, which the whites had set on fire. The disturbances arose out of the ill-feeling engendered by the importation of negro labor from the South.

State Attorney Schaumloeffel of St. Clair County, in which East St. Louis is situated, drove through the riot district tonight with Police Inspector Walsh of St. Louis, Mo. The State's Attorney estimated that the dead negroes would number 250, but all estimates are conjectural.

Thousands of persons were in the mobs. The rioting is a renewal of race troubles that occurred here a month ago, following the importation of large numbers of negro laborers from the South.

Military rule was proclaimed at 8 o'clock tonight, and at the same time 300 white men were arrested and locked up at Police Headquarters.

Nearly 500 negro men, women, and children are quartered in the City Hall and the police station. At frequent intervals all evening, and until late at night, trucks brought negro refugees from burning sections to augment the cowering groups at these refugee buildings, where a strong guard of troops was stationed. Terror spread among the black men and women at 10:30 P. M., when all the lights in both buildings suddenly went out, due to the destruction of electric wires in the downtown district.

Adjt. Gen. Frank S. Dickson of Illinois arrived and took charge of the situation late tonight. He went into conference immediately with military and civil authorities to outline a plan of procedure. In answer to a question as to why the troops on the ground when the trouble developed did not use force to put down the rioting, General Dickson said the purposes for which the soldiers were sent here had been gained without firing a shot, and that wholesale bloodshed would have been the result of any firing on the part of the troops.

"Five hundred rioters, the ringleaders of the largest mob, I am informed, are now under arrest," said General Dickson. "This was accomplished by surrounding the rioters and forcing them to submit without shooting or employing the bayonet."

General Dickson said after the 500 were taken into custody the disturbance at once took on a less serious aspect.

One of the fires which was started in the negro belt between Third Street and Railroad Avenue spread beyond the control of city firemen, and is threatening the business section of the city at a late hour. Another fire, started by part of the mob in Black Valley, a negro segregated district, between Fourth and Sixth Streets and Broadway and Railroad Avenue, spread until the firefighters admitted that it, too, was beyond their control.

Loss $3,000,000 Already.

The property loss so far is estimated by City Attorney Fekete at $3,000,000. At 11 P. M. another fire had broken out in the extreme northern portion of the city, where there is a negro section. This brought the burning sections to four, lighting the entire city with their glare.

Colonel Tripp, Assistant Adjutant General, stated shortly before midnight that the rioting crowds had for the most part dispersed.

When a report came to military authorities that negroes of Brooklyn, Ill., were moving on East St. Louis, a truck full of guardsmen was sent to the bridge to meet any attack that might be attempted. At the same time another truckload of soldiers was rushed to a corner near the Post Office, where negroes barricaded in upstairs quarters had been firing at soldiers standing guard in the street below.

The worst property damage was done along the tracks of the Southern Railroad Company, where the Southern's warehouse and between 100 and 150 cars, many of them loaded with merchandise, were consumed by flames. The damage there was estimated at between $400,000 and $500,000.

The Broadway Theatre, valued at $100,000, was destroyed. At night the flames were moving steadily along the tracks, almost unhindered by the feeble efforts of the firemen which were directed toward preventing the blaze from spreading to more important buildings.

Soldiers Ordered to Shoot.

All street railway traffic was suspended at 7 P. M., and theatres and saloons were ordered closed. At that hour, the militiamen were given instructions to shoot to kill in suppressing the white mobs. They at once started a tour of the city, rounding up the blood-mad men, who were out to avenge the death of Policeman Coppedge and William Kayser, a hardware merchant, two of the white men killed.

The third white man killed was Thomas Moore of Granite City. He was standing beside a soldier when a bullet struck him. The shot apparently was intended for the soldier.

Thirty-five houses in Black Valley were in flames within half an hour after the fire started. The blaze spread fast toward the centre of the business district. All fire apparatus in the city was assembled at Third Street and Broadway, where the firemen began a battle to save the town. When the flames reached Broadway a second general alarm was sounded, and apparatus from the St. Louis side of the river was rushed to East St. Louis.

It is estimated that 50,000 men and women were in the streets and that more than two-thirds of this number were armed. Small boys carried revolvers and were shooting at the blacks. Two hundred militiamen were on duty in the zone affected by the fire, but despite fixed bayonets they were unable to control the mob.

Every hospital on the east side is filled with blacks who are so severely injured that many will probably die. Police headquarters is packed with negroes badly beaten and shot. It is estimated that eighty negroes and ten white men have been injured.

One section of the mob gathered around a lone negro on Fourth Street, near Broadway. A rope was thrown around his neck and he was hoisted up a telephone pole, but the rope broke. Men and women in the mob shouted gleefully as the negro fell into the gutter, while half a dozen men riddled his body with bullets. Negroes are lying in the gutters every few feet in some places.

Girls Join the Mob.

Seized with the mob spirit, two young white girls climbed on a car at Broadway and Main Street about 4 P. M. and dragged a negro woman from her seat. As they pulled her through the door of the car to the street, there was a great cheer from men standing on the sidewalk. The negro woman attempted to break away from her assailants, and one of the girls pulled off her shoe and started to beat the victim over the head. The woman flinched under the blows, and was bleeding profusely when rescued by militiamen. The girls were not arrested, and walked away from the scene. There were blood stains on their clothes, and as they passed their friends they told about the part they had played in the riot.

Whenever a white man attempted to drag a negro from the street, intending to give him medical attention, the mob, with drawn pistols, forced him to desist. Several negroes who were killed were thrown into Cahokia Creek.

A mob of more than 100 men, led by ten or fifteen young girls about 18 years old, chased a negro woman at the Relay Depot about 5 o'clock. The girls were brandishing clubs and calling upon the men to kill the woman.

A lone negro man appeared in the railroad yards. The mob immediately gave up the chase of the woman and turned upon the man. He was shot to death.

Militiamen Fire a Volley.

About 8:30 o'clock a mob of more than 500 men, all heavily armed, charged into the negro district on Third Street and set fire to a number of houses. Before these men could start other fires two companies of militiamen, numbering more than 200, charged with fixed bayonets. A volley was fired over the heads of the mob, which then dispersed.

Charles Beach, an ambulance driver for the Deaconess Hospital, was shot and seriously wounded at Tenth and Bond Streets. He was accompanied on the ambulance by John Cange, who was not hit. Negroes congregated at Tenth and Duncan Streets and fired a fusilade into the ambulance. But for Cange's quick action it is likely the automobile would have crashed into a house and turned over. As Beach fell limp from the seat Cange took the wheel and drove with him to the hospital.

While straggling groups of soldiers and police looked on, a large crowd of white men gathered at Fourth Street and Broadway at 7:30 o'clock and captured two negroes who ran from the rear of a burning building. Placing a rope around their necks, the mob attempted to hang them to a telephone pole. The police and soldiers did not offer any interference. Finding the rope inadequate for the weight of the men, they were dragged screaming, to an alley, where many shots were fired into their bodies.

One of the negroes was dragged back to the pole and a new rope was tied around his neck. As two white men attempted to pull him into the air, the rope broke, throwing the white men on their backs, to the amusement of the mob. The negro fell to the ground, dead.

Three more negroes were seen by the mob as the terrorized blacks were trying to escape from a burning building. One of them was strung up to a telephone pole and the other two were shot. The bodies were left in the street.

Colonel Tripp early in the evening figured in the rescue of a negro who was being dragged down Broadway by a rope attached to his neck. The automobile bearing the Colonel and City Attorney Fekete appeared when a mob was in the act of stringing the negro to a telephone pole. Colonel Tripp leaped from the automobile and arguing with the white attackers to desist from their plan to kill the negro.

City Attorney Fekete later in the night saved the life of another young negro who was running from a crowd which had fired a number of shots at him while he was visible in the glare of burning buildings. Fekete placed the negro in his automobile, and, after arguing for ten minutes with the group of men, succeeded in gaining their consent to allow him to take the negro to the City Hall for protection.

Negroes Seized on Street Cars.

The whites began their attacks on street cars shortly before noon, and several negroes were taken from the cars and beaten or pelted with bricks. Eight negroes were injured in this manner before 1 o'clock.

At 1:30 o'clock a crowd of whites pulled the trolley from an Edwardsville car. A mob entered the car and dragged out all the negro passengers. One of them was kicked and beaten by the crowd and then shot. He died in an ambulance on the way to a hospital.

A Bellevue car appeared next. White women as well as men entered the car and pulled out the negroes. Women and girls seized terrified negro women, kicked and clubbed them, and sent them screaming down the street.

Shortly after 2 o'clock the mob pursued a negro down Collinsville Avenue. He was caught and severely beaten. A militiaman stood guard over him and tried to keep the crowd back, but was hustled aside. Fifteen other militiamen who ran to his aid were disarmed. Men in the mob fired the rifles and returned them to the soldiers.

One hundred white men met at Labor Temple Hall, 408 Collinsville Avenue, marched down the avenue, and at Broadway, the most important transfer point in the city, they encountered a negro on a street car. He attempted to run out the front end of the car, but was seized, knocked down, and repeatedly kicked. As he lay on the ground a white man in the mob standing over him fired six bullets into his body.

The mob then turned back down the street, at the mouth of Black Valley, where fifty negroes had assembled. The white men turned again, and in front of the Illmo Hotel came upon a lone negro. He ran, and the white mob hurled bricks at him. Some one fired two shots at the fleeing black, but he managed to escape.

At least 6,000 white men and women paraded through the downtown streets shortly after noon demanding that the authorities force every negro to leave town. Riot calls swept into Police Headquarters, and patrol wagons dashed about the city in what appeared to be a futile effort to stop the growing disregard of the mobs for law and order. In many instances the patrol wagons were bombarded with bricks and other missiles, and policemen were openly jeered.

Negroes Fire on Police.

The disorder began when a mob of 200 negroes fired on an automobile load of policemen last night, killing one. For several days there had been evidences of bad blood, and on Saturday night minor clashes between whites and blacks had occurred. These clashes apparently had alarmed the negro quarter of the city, or at least gave agitators a chance to organize the blacks for fighting. When word was telephoned to Police Headquarters that the ringing of a church bell had called armed negroes together, an automobile loaded with police left for the scene to disperse the crowd. The police were met with a volley. Detective Sergeant Coppedge was killed and three policemen were wounded.

C. W. Wallace, editor of a negro religious publication, said the firing on the police was due to a misunderstanding. According to Wallace's account, a negro minister, a negro physician, and himself were returning from St. Louis last night when they saw white "joy riders" ride down a block in Market Street inhabited by negroes and fire into the houses. The neighborhood was aroused and the negroes armed themselves. Wallace did not see the negro mob fire on an automobile filled with policemen, but he said a witness told him that the negroes thought when the police automobile stopped it was the joy riders returning. The shooting began, he was told, before this misunderstanding was removed. It was said that the policemen were in plain clothes.

Race troubles here began late in May as a result of the heavy influx of negro labor. Labor leaders then expressed a fear that the negro labor was being imported to break anticipated strikes during the Summer.

On May 28 a crowd of white men demanded of the City Council that the negro immigration be stopped. Mayor Mollman tried to calm the crowd, saying that an investigation would be ordered. After the meeting had adjourned, white mobs stopped street cars and dragged negroes off and beat them.

The next day State troops arrived. There was considerable disturbance the night of May 29, two white men and three negroes being shot. Within a day or two order was restored, and a few days later the troops were withdrawn.

An investigation by the State Council of Defense was made, and it reported that labor agents had induced negroes to come here from the South. This report was made public last Saturday. Up to that time there had been no serious indications of a renewal of the rioting.

TO ADMIT NEGRO UNIONS

Move Called by Gompers Most Important Labor Step In Years.

Special to The New York Times.

ATLANTIC CITY, N. J., June 13.— Addressing the convention of the American Federation of Labor to-day Secretary of Labor William B. Wilson made an attack on the I. W. W. and the Bolsheviki in the United States. The agitation of these two elements, he declared, did not exist to any great extent among the real wage workers of the community but existed principally among the "parlor coal diggers."

Mr. Wilson deprecated the movement which has for its object a general strike of all labor on behalf of Thomas Mooney, convicted in connection with the preparedness day explosions in San Francisco three years ago. A general strike, he said, would be a subversion of the American jury system. In passing he touched on the suggestion that labor enter politics as a separate party and asserted that conditions in this country were different from England. In expressing the appreciation of the delegates for his address, Samuel Gompers, President of the Federation, attacked the "enemies of organized labor in Congress who conspired to starve the Department of Labor."

Most of the day was spent in reading reports on resolutions referred to the Organization Committee. The delegates passed favorably on a resolution calling for the organization of the city policemen. Among the 211 resolutions which will come before the delegates for action the principal ones call for the 44-hour week, indorsement of the railway union's plan for Government ownership, the removal of Postmaster General Burleson, repeal of the Espionage act, sympathy with the aspirations of Ireland, the six-hour day, and withdrawal of American troops from Russia.

A committee consisting of C. L. Bain, E. H. McCarthy, and Martin F. Ryan will go to Washington tomorrow to take up with the Federal authorities the contemplated strike of telephone electrical workers scheduled for Monday.

The convention voted unanimously to permit the entrance of the 2,000,000 negro workers of the country into equal membership in the international unions. It was also decided that if any of the unions attempted to discriminate against negroes separate charters would be granted to negro organizations. In the opinion of many leaders in the convention the step was one of the most important that has been taken in many years by the federation.

John Lacy, a negro leader of Norfolk, made an appeal to the convention, not for social equality, but "for the opportunity to earn bread and butter on an equality with his white brother." It was after Lacy's speech that more than forty Presidents of international unions arose one after the other and declared that their unions would welcome negroes into their organizations.

The action removes every trace of class distinction in America, said Samuel Gompers after the meeting. He said that the action of the convention would mark a milestone in the history of the negroes' struggle for equal rights, as well as in the history of political and economic liberty of America. The discussion of the aspirations of the negroes in the labor movement came up when the Committee on Resolutions reported against the adoption of resolutions presented by the negro delegates asking for the right to organize international unions along color lines. The committee held that the economic interest of blacks and whites was one and that racial discrimination would doom the labor movement. It recommended the organization of negroes in international unions and the sending of organizers all over the country for this purpose. The report was adopted.

In his address Secretary Wilson declared that the philosophy which said that the worker was entitled to the full social value of his labor had its origin in socialism and was sound, but that the great difficulty was that no method has as yet been found to compute the social value of a person's labor. The poison of the I. W. W. scheme, he said, was in the belief that profits could be destroyed by the "strike on the job," by throwing sand into the machines. Closely allied to the I. W. W. in this country, he added, has been the Bolshevist agitation.

"I have no fear of a political revolution in the United States," he continued. "It may be possible that there are some parlorites who are misguided sufficiently to think in this way, but there is not one man in the ranks of labor, be he extreme radical or extreme conservative, who would stand for Bolshevism for a minute when he knows what Bolshevism stands for.

"They prate of the dictatorship of the proletariat," added the Secretary, "but we find that Marx by that phrase meant that the majority of the workers would impose their will on the balance of the people. But the workers of this country are not willing to bring that principle into play. They believe that every one who has to obey the laws of the country should have a voice in the determination of what the laws should be. The Bolsheviki do not even take that interpretation of the dictatorship of the proletariat. Lenin before the Moscow Soviet laid down the principle that the dictatorship of the proletariat meant the dictatorship of a self-selected advance guard, that the proletarian could not be trusted as he would waver. Therefore they resorted to obligatory labor. The military autocracy of Germany was built on the same idea.

"The American worker wants nothing of that kind of a dictatorship of the proletariat and nothing of the political and social conditions that existed and still exist in Russia. We are going to work out our own ideals, not by a self-selected advance guard, but by the workers themselves.

"The use of force to overthrow autocracy is the highest kind of patriotism, but the use of force to overthrow democracy is treason to the masses of the people. We have the ballot for the redress of grievances and those who cannot be depended on to vote right cannot be depended on to shoot straight."

Describing his work as a member of the President's commission to investigate the Mooney case, Secretary Wilson said that they could come to no other conclusion than that, as one of the principal witnesses had written to a friend in Illinois saying that he had seen the witness Oxman at a given point at a given time, and in view of the change in the evidence, the commission felt that Mooney ought to have a new trial so that his innocence or guilt might be established.

"At that time we had no fixed opinion as to his guilt or innocence," he continued. "With me it was only a question of securing a fair trial. Every effort of the Administration has been to get a new trial, and we are not through with it yet. There is a nation-wide agitation for a universal strike as a protest against the conviction of Mooney. Do you realize what this action means to the masses? Do you understand what struggles have taken place that trials may occur where the accused and the jurors and the accused and the witnesses meet face to face? That change in the establishment of the jury system was not brought about to protect men of great wealth. It was instituted to deal with poor devils like you and me. It may occasionally miscarry, but in the great bulk of cases justice is meted out and no one can undertake to try Mooney by the process of a strike. If he is to be tried, it should be by a jury that would digest the evidence bit by bit. None of us know very much about the case yet. It is proposed that every worker shall become a juror."

Mr. Wilson was received with enthusiasm.

Alfred Leavitt and Nathan Fine, of the Soldiers, Sailors and Marines Protective Association, addressed the convention on behalf of discharged service men, asking that the Federation support their movement for $360 pay to discharged soldiers and sailors.

Publication of a resolution concerning recognition of Soviet Russia aroused intense interest among the delegates, and was more discussed than any other. Indications were that when it comes up for discussion on the floor it is likely to precipitate a bitter controversy.

COMMUNISTS BORING INTO NEGRO LABOR

Taking Advantage of the New Moves Among Colored Workers Here to Stir Unrest.

NOT MUCH PROGRESS YET

Ten Young Negroes Are Sent to Moscow Under Soviet 'Scholarships' to Study Bolshevism.

'NUCLEI' SOUGHT IN UNIONS

Labor Federation and Older Leaders of the Race Seek Antidotes in Real Labor Unions.

A negro in shabby working clothes entered a newspaper office in the colored belt of Harlem and enrolled as a member of the embryonic Brotherhood of Sleeping Car Porters. He paid $5 initiation fee and agreed to pay $1 a month dues to support an organization which has promised him higher wages, shorter hours and better working conditions.

In Chicago a young, well-dressed, college-bred negro sat under a photograph of Lenin in a South Side newspaper office, reading "Russia Today," preparing pamphlets urging negro workers to unite with white workers in preparation for the "international proletarian revolution."

These two scenes were observed within the past few days by a reporter for THE NEW YORK TIMES. They visualize two new movements in the labor world which have grown out of the post-war migration of hundreds of thousands of negro workmen from the South to the big industrial centres of the North and West.

First, there is a growing demand among negroes for organization coupled with an increasing tendency in the American Federation of Labor to let down the bars which white unions have raised against negroes.

Second, there is an apparent attempt by the Communists, working through the Workers (Communist) Party of America and the newly formed American Negro Labor Congress, to influence the negro labor movement along radical lines and if possible to wrest control of it from the conservative organized labor movement in America.

This effort appears to be directed by the Communist Internationale in Moscow as part of its world-wide propaganda among backward and "oppressed" colored races. It bears the same "left wing" relationship to the negro labor movement as William Z. Foster's Trade Union Educational League bears to white labor in the United States.

Leaders Greatly Divided.

Negro leaders and the negro press throughout the country have been engaged for some weeks in a violent controversy regarding both movements. The National Association for Advancement of Colored People, which is one of the strongest negro groups, favors organization along conservative trade union lines. James Weldon Johnson and Dr. W. F. B. DuBois takes this stand. Dean Kelly Miller of Howard University, Washington, D. C., has come out against negro unionism, arguing that the best interests of negro workers would be served by standing with capital. (The breaking of several big strikes, notably the great steel strike in 1918, has been generally attributed to unorganized negro labor).

Many negro newspapers are attacking the present union movement on the ground that it is influenced by the American Federation of Labor, which they charge with gross discrimination against negroes. Only a small and comparatively uninfluential group is urging negro labor to line up with Communism.

See Trouble in New Propaganda.

Conservative negro leaders and white labor leaders regard the Communist propaganda among the negroes as a potential source of trouble. Hugh Frayne, general organizer of the American Federation of Labor in New York, takes this view, and says that the Federation will fight radicalism among negro workers as strongly as it has in white labor unions. Dr. Du Bois, negro editor of The Crisis, thinks it is up to the white people of America to treat the negroes better in order to keep them out of the Communist ranks.

"The American Negro Labor Congress is a straw that shows which way the wind blows," says Dr. Du Bois. "The Russian Communists have gone out of their way to express sympathy with negro and colored workers all over the world. On the other hand, such movements in the United States as the Ku Klux Klan and the Nordic supremacy propaganda have created a situation which certainly will make some negroes say: 'The Communists offer us relief, and we ought to train with our friends.'

"The Communist movement among American negroes has not made much progress yet, because the negro is very religious and is very conservative, except on the race problem, on which he is radical. But if colored people cannot get into white unions, if they cannot get decent places to live in, and if they cannot live in America without being subjected to constant insult, they are likely to be driven into the hands of revolutionary movements. If the American people want to keep negro labor out of Communism, let them give it the same right as white labor to organize. If you kick them out of the trade unions, you kick them into Communism."

Ex-City College Boy's Work.

Lovett Fort-Whiteman, a young negro Communist, is the head of the American Negro Labor Congress. He was dismissed from City College in New York, he says, because he was "too radical." After writing for negro newspapers in New York and Chicago for several years, he went to Russia and spent eight months studying the Soviet Government and the Communist Internationale, particularly with respect to their treatment of "oppressed" races. On his return he organized the American Negro Labor Congress with headquarters in Chicago and with "locals" in cities, including New York, which have large negro populations. William Green, President of the American Federation of Labor, and several negro leaders have charged that the Congress is financed directly by Moscow, but Fort-Whiteman denies this.

Fort-Whiteman admits that he is a Communist and a member of the Workers (Communist) Party of America, and that he and other Communists control the policies of the American Negro Labor Congress. He also admits that since his return from Russia he has sent ten young negro students to Moscow with Soviet "scholarships" to study in a Soviet university in preparation for careers in the Communist "diplomatic service." They will work for the Communist movement among backward colored races in various parts of the world, and will return to the United States for work among their own people "if they are needed here," he says.

Plans of the Communists.

About forty delegates, representing negro labor and farm organizations with a membership given as 18,000, attended what was announced as the first annual convention of the American Negro Labor Congress last October in Chicago. Public meetings drew audiences of about 500 whites and negroes. The gatherings took place under a picture of a negro laborer and a negro farmer clasping hands beneath the Communist symbol, crossed hammer and sickle.

Fort-Whiteman admits that his Communist "bloc" dominated the Congress in October and will continue to do so. The Congress, in its Constitution and resolutions, adopted a program consisting of Communist doctrine superimposed upon the negro's desire for racial equality. It hailed "the workers' and farmers' Government of Soviet Russia as the first to bring into being the full social, political and economic equality of all peoples, white and dark skinned." It denounced the present system of society in the United States as responsible for all the discriminations against the negro, and attacked the American Federation of Labor, whose anti-Communist position is well-known. It asserted that no negro owed "any respect or obedience" to any court which discriminated against him, and that a Government which discriminated against the negro had no right to conscript him for war. It called for "a solid front of the workers of both races against American capitalism." It declared for an international race conference to fight white imperialism among colored races in America, Africa and Asia.

Also, it demanded full social equality for the negro in America, with the abolition of laws forbidding the intermarriage of blacks and whites, the removal of barriers which force negroes to live in segregated districts in certain large cities, the repeal of all Jim Crow laws, and the admittance of negroes on equal terms with whites to all theatres, restaurants, hotels, railroad waiting rooms and other public places.

"Proletarian Revolution" Predicted.

The Daily Worker of Chicago, organ of the American Communists, and the Trade Union Educational League welcomed the American Negro Labor Congress enthusiastically. The Daily Worker, which boasts that the American Communists are "a real Bolshevik section of the Communist International, capable of leading the American working class to the victory of a proletarian revolution," said that the congress would enable the negroes "to play an effective part in the world mobilization of the oppressed colonial peoples against capitalism."

Fort-Whiteman publishes a monthly paper called The Negro Champion, an official organ of the American Negro Labor Congress. The first page of the January issue carries a large cartoon showing a burly, well-trained negro prize fighter, wearing a belt marked "Africa," dealing a knockout blow to the solar plexus of a paunchy, undersized white opponent, labeled "World Imperialism," with cheering black, yellow and white figures at the ringside representing India, China, Russia and "World Proletariat."

Because the average negro is normally little interested in radical political and economic theories, conservative white labor leaders and negro leaders see small immediate danger in the Communist agitation at present. They foresee, however, the possibility that the Communists will try to do the same thing in the negro unions that they have tried to do with white labor —that is, to establish small "Red" nuclei which will seek to "bore from within" to disrupt the unions with revolutionary propaganda. In the event of industrial depression and labor unrest, it is pointed out, serious trouble might ensue.

Labor Federation in Disfavor.

The situation is complicated by a widespread belief among negroes that the American Federation of Labor has discriminated against them in the past and will do so in the future. Of the 116 international unions in the Federation only three—the machinists, plumbers and electrical workers—bar the negro from membership. But negroes assert that even when allowed to join a union they are discriminated against by white officials and members. If the negroes' prejudice against the Federation continues, it is pointed out, they may form independent unions which, under certain circumstances, might prove more fertile fields for Communist propaganda than unions affiliated with the American Federation of Labor.

Pullman Porters the Target.

Within recent months the federation has shown a greatly increased interest in negro labor. It is actively supporting a new organization called the Trade Union Committee for Organizing Negro Workers, the purpose of which is to organize all the negro labor in New York City and to prevent the use of unorganized negroes to break strikes.

The federation is also supporting the new Brotherhood of Sleeping Car Porters, now being organized by A. Philip Randolph, a young negro Socialist who is editor of The Messenger, a negro monthly published in New York. He says that he has organized nearly 51 per cent. of the 12,000 porters employed by the Pullman Company. Under the rules of the Railroad Labor Board, a union composed of 51 per cent. of the employes is entitled to represent them before the board.

The porters' union demands that a porter's minimum wage on beginning work be increased from $67.50 to $155 a month, and that basis for the monthly wage be reduced from 11,000 miles (nearly 400 hours) to 240 hours' work. The chief grievance with respect to working conditions is that the porters are not paid extra when their trains are late, and are not paid for "preparatory time," the four hours before each trip they spend about ten times a month getting their cars ready for occupancy.

Against Old-Fashioned Negroes.

A porter's pay is greatly increased by tips, but the organizers say the union would be willing to do away with tips if the company paid "a living wage." The organizers are trying to eliminate what they call "slave psychology" among the porters. They say the service contains too many "Uncle Toms" and "Handkerchief Heads," meaning old-fashioned negroes who do not want to improve their positions.

The Pullman Company has been opposing the union on the ground that its plan of employes' representation fully protects the interests of the porters, and that most of the employes are satisfied with it. It points out that the porter's pay increases to a maximum of $125, that the average is $77 and that because of the tip system porters usually refuse better paid jobs in the Pullman Company's offices.

Conceding that the porters have a legitimate grievance in lack of pay for preparatory time and delayed arrival time, the company says it tried to remedy this situation at a conference with the men in 1924, when it suggested that this time be credited to porters at the rate of thirty miles an hour against the 11,000-mile monthly wage basis. According to the company, the men rejected the plan because it would have meant less money for porters on the fast trains, and asked for and received wage increases equal to the amount the change in working conditions would have cost.

Convention to Settle Matters.

The company issued a call last month for a conference with the porters, which will be held soon in Chicago to discuss wages, hours, working conditions and grievances. According to the company, union organizers tried to persuade the men not to vote, but at least 80 per cent. and probably 90 per cent. voted for delegates. The company believes that the conference will be followed by the collapse of the union movement.

PULLMAN PORTERS TO DEMAND PAY RISE

Organize Union in Harlem, Saying Reduced Tips Make Higher Wages Necessary.

200 JOIN THE NEW BODY

Ask Better Working Conditions and Abolition of Present Plan of Representation.

A movement to organize Pullman porters took definite form last night with the organization of Locals 1 and 2 of the Brotherhood of Sleeping Car Porters at a meeting in Harlem. Two hundred porters joined the new organization, which hopes ultimately to enlist 2,000 others in the metropolitan district and 12,000 throughout the country.

More pay and better working conditions are demanded by the men as well as the abolition of the present plan of employe representation, which the porters say keeps the men under the power of the Pullman Company.

The principal demands of the men include a fifty per cent increase in pay, payment on the basis of 240 hours work a month, pay for overtime, and for so-called preparation work, or making cars ready for occupancy. They assert that they now get $67.50 a month to start with and that the maximum is less than $90 a month. Recently there has been a marked decrease in tips from travelers, they say.

A. Philip Randolph, editor of the Messenger, a negro magazine, was the principal speaker, and urged a quiet organization of the men until they become strong enough to deal with the company openly.

NEGROES IN CODE PROTEST

Charge That Workers in the South Get Lower Wage Scale.

Negro workers in the South are being intimidated, on pain of dismissal, into accepting a lower wage scale than that provided in the NRA codes, it is charged in the annual report of the National Association for the Advancement of Colored People made public yesterday.

The report also noted that most of the codes, as submitted, provided for a differential wage of from 20 to 40 per cent less to the Negro worker than to the white man doing the same job. The association, as a member of the Joint Committee on National Recovery, has been fighting this tendency.

Another effect, according to the report, was "the displacement of many Negro workers throughout the South, where employers decided that if they had to pay the minimum wage of $12 a week they would not pay it to Negroes."

July 3, 1934

APPEAL FOR RACE EQUALITY.

Negroes Here Ask A. F. of L. to End 'Segregation of Workers.'

The National Association for the Advancement of Colored People yesterday sent a telegram to the American Federation of Labor, in convention in San Francisco, demanding abolition of the "segregation and discrimination in treatment of Negro workers," and warning that the American Federation of Labor can never win security for white labor as long as it permits the exclusion of black labor from unions." The telegram further said:

"The Federation's demand for a square deal for labor is meaningless hypocrisy as long as Federation itself denies equal opportunity to black workers who have borne their share of struggle throughout labor history for advancement of labor generally. Smash the color line in the unions before the unions are smashed by the color line. This association also urges Federation to pass resolution endorsing passage of Federal anti-lynching law to check mob murder, which is form of intimidation designed to continue separation of Negro and white labor and exploitation of both."

October 6, 1934

President Orders an Even Break For Minorities in Defense Jobs

He Issues an Order That Defense Contract Holders Not Allow Discrimination Against Negroes or Any Worker

Special to THE NEW YORK TIMES.

WASHINGTON, June 25—President Roosevelt took action today to prevent discrimination of defense jobs because of race, creed, color or national origin, asserting that "the democratic way of life within the nation can be defended successfully only with the help and support of all groups."

The President issued an executive order instructing official agencies to play their part in eliminating discrimination against Negroes and members of other minority groups and establishing a committee on fair employment practice in the Office of Production Management to deal with violations.

The Executive gave these instructions:

"All departments and agencies of the Government of the United States concerned with vocational and training programs for defense production shall take special measures appropriate to assure that such programs are administered without discrimination.

"All contracting agencies of the Government of the United States shall include in all defense contracts hereafter negotiated by them a provision obligating the contractor not to discriminate against any worker.

"There is established in the Office of Production Management a committee on fair employment practice, which shall consist of a chairman and four other members to be appointed by the President."

The order was issued principally because the government's attention had been called to cases of discrimination against Negroes in some defense industries and labor unions.

"There is evidence available that needed workers have been barred from industries engaged in defense production solely because of considerations of race, creed, color or national origin, to the detriment of workers' morale and of national unity," the President revealed. "It is the duty of employers and of labor organizations to provide for the full and equitable participation of all workers in the defense industries without discrimination."

The new unit of the OPM created to deal with the situation was instructed "to receive and investigate complaints of discrimination in violation of the provisions of this order" and to take "appropriate steps to redress grievances which it finds to be valid."

"The committee shall also recommend to the several departments and agencies of the government and to the President all measures which may be deemed necessary or proper to effectuate the provisions of this order," the President said.

June 26, 1941

NEW BOARD SET UP TO END HIRING BIAS

President Appoints Mgr. Haas Head of Committee on Fair Employment Practice

OLD GROUP IS SCRAPPED

Reopening of Hearing on Charges Railroads Barred Negroes Is Expected

Special to THE NEW YORK TIMES.

WASHINGTON, May 28—President Roosevelt issued an executive order today setting up a new Committee on Fair Employment Practice, with additional powers to prevent discrimination in war industry employment, and appointed Mgr. Francis J. Haas of Catholic University as chairman.

The action was designed to end widespread complaints among some groups, especially Negroes, that effective governmental action against discrimination had become impossible when the old committee was made a part of the War Manpower Commission, headed by Paul V. McNutt. Malcolm S. MacLean, president of Hampton Institute, resigned as committee chairman after Mr. McNutt ordered postponement of hearings into charges that railroads refused to employ Negroes for certain jobs.

The President has not yet appointed the new committee to serve with Mgr. Haas, but it is expected that one of its first official acts will be to reschedule the railroad hearing. Informed sources said that the committee probably would have six members, equally representative of industry and labor, in addition to the chairman.

The power given the new committee to carry out the President's policy forbidding discrimination in war industries because of race, creed, color or national origin consists of the authority to require not only war contractors but subcontractors to include a clause in their contract with the government forbidding such discrimination. The old committee could request inclusion of such a clause only in prime contracts.

May 29, 1943

FEPC'S LIFE ENDS WITH NO HOPE HELD FOR EARLY REVIVAL

WAR GAINS FADING RAPIDLY

By JAY WALZ
Special to THE NEW YORK TIMES.

WASHINGTON, Monday, July 1 —The controversial Fair Employment Practices Committee expired at midnight without hope that it will be revived by this Congress.

President Truman, accepting "with great regret" the resignations of Chairman Malcolm Ross and five other members, praised them for performing an important war service under a "continuous barrage of criticism and harassment."

The committee in a letter and final report told the President that wartime gains against discriminatory employment practices were today being rapidly dissipated. They emphasized that any national policy against such practices would require the force of legislation to be effective.

Enactment of such legislation could not be foreseen today, either by its supporters or its opponents. However, it was expected to be an issue when a new Congress convenes next year.

While bills to establish the agency on a permanent basis and give it broader scope are pending in both the House and Senate, it is not believed that they can be passed by this Congress in view of the pressure of other legislation and the desire of both houses for a midsummer adjournment.

Senator Dennis Chavez, Democrat, of New Mexico, who is author of the Senate bill, which precipitated a three week's filibuster early this year, said yesterday he had "no hope" for his measure.

"I expect it to be brought up in future Congresses, and I still feel it is sound legislation," he said.

Senator Richard B. Russell, Democrat, of Georgia, who led the fight against the FEPC, declared it would not pass this Congress. "It certainly won't if we adjourn July 20, because it would require more discussion than there is time left."

The same situation appears to prevail in the House, although Representative Marcantonio of New York expressed a belief that Congress would not adjourn "before Jan. 1," and said he hoped to get the House FEPC bill up before that time.

Committee's Affairs Wound Up

In addition to Mr. Ross, those turning in their resignation yesterday were Sarah Southall, Boris Shishkin, Milton P. Webster, Charles L. Horn and John Brophy.

Their work did not end abruptly, since for the past several months they had been winding up the committee's affairs on a $250,000 appropriation given to the FEPC by Congress for the purpose last July. The committee reported that its personnel of 128 had been cut to 31 by last December, and that since May 3 all employes had been on leave without pay status.

The committee presented President Truman with this summary of its activities and conclusions:

1. Wartime gains of Negro, Mexican-American and Jewish workers are being lost through an "unchecked revival" of discriminatory practices.

2. War veterans of these minority groups face far greater difficulties today than other veterans in obtaining training and finding work.

3. Government action was effective in reducing wartime discrimination, but the gains began to disappear as soon as wartime controls were relaxed.

4. Nothing short of Congressional action to end employment discrimination can prevent the freezing of American workers into fixed groups, with ability and hard work of no account to those of the "wrong" race or religion.

5. This denial of equal opportunity, if allowed to become permanent, cannot fail to create civic discord and to be a cause of embarrassment to the United States in its international relations.

6. Out of its experience, the committee said it had found that employers and workers abandoned discrimination in most cases where government intervened, and that "once the barriers were down" the workers of varying races and religions worked together efficiently and learned to accept each other without rancor.

The FEPC reported that in five years it had settled satisfactorily nearly 5,000 cases by peaceful negotiation. In the last year of the war it had docketed 3,485 cases, settling 1,191 of them.

The successful settlements, it was stated, were largely unpublicized, with the result that most people heard only about "the defiance of some recalcitrant employers and unions that developed in some fifteen cases requiring public hearings."

Most of the work, according to the report, was accomplished through "quiet persuasion" of committee personnel. But it was made clear that such efforts have their "limits" and were effective partly because of the wartime patriotism of both workers and employers.

Emphasizing the need for "final authority" to support any policy against discrimination, the report made note of the fact that the Government, itself, as an employer, was the source of 25 per cent of FEPC's complaints.

Negroes, it was stated, comprised the largest minority group and filed 80 per cent of FEPC complaints. The early defense period failed to help this group, the report pointed out, since unemployed whites were the first to receive training and jobs in the new war industries.

Negroes began entering war jobs in large numbers in 1942, and continued through 1945 to make gains, both in the number of industries entered and in the recognition of skills.

"Despite the advantages of Negroes beyond menial labor (greater than in World War I or ever before) the 'hard, hot and heavy' war jobs still fell largely to the lot of the Negroes," said the report. "This was true because white workers were first to rise above common labor, while Negroes newly entering the war labor market took the vacated common labor jobs.

"By dint of war need for skills, plus Government action against discrimination, a large proportion of Negroes did become skilled operators and foremen in war plants. Nevertheless, their basic concentration remained, and still remains, in common labor."

The chance to keep any job fell off for Negroes in 1945 much more rapidly than for white war workers, the report added. Generally, the opportunities for members of the race to rise into skilled professional and managerial categories "dwindled to a scant few." An exception, it was noted, was to be found in New York City.

The report devoted several paragraphs to prevalent discriminatory practices against returning service men of minority groups. It said that they were having trouble getting into school, getting GI loans and obtaining skilled jobs. These difficulties were being encountered not alone by Negroes but also by Jews, Mexican-Americans and Nisei, it was stated. There was a tendency to refer these minority veterans to menial jobs, and to advise them to file for unemployment insurance instead of skilled work, the report said.

"Given the alternative of accepting a menial job, requiring no skill or training, or of shifting for themselves, many former GI's have selected the latter," said the report. "In so doing some have discovered that barriers to employment can be broken down through adequate preparation and persistent effort. The others sign up for their $20 weekly readjustment pay allowance."

The report said a survey of job-seeking by Jews since V-J Day, conducted in fifteen cities, showed a marked rise of discrimination against all Jewish applicants and that "Jews who had fought for their country fared no better than those who had not."

According to this survey, discrimination in New York and New Jersey cities, where fair employment practice laws are effective, was lower than in cities where no attempts were being made to abolish discrimination.

July 1, 1946

353

TRUMAN ORDERS END OF BIAS IN FORCES AND FEDERAL JOBS;

PRESSES FOR RIGHTS

President Acts Despite Split in His Party Over the Chief Issue

LITTLE 'FEPC' IS CREATED

'Merit, Fitness' Set as U. S. Employment Guides—Military Equality Is Demanded

By ANTHONY LEVIERO
Special to The New York Times.

WASHINGTON, July 26—President Truman ordered today the end of discrimination in the armed forces "as rapidly as possible" and instituted a fair employment practices policy throughout the civil branch of the Federal Government.

On the eve of his appearance before Congress, the President issued two executive orders to carry out his sweeping aims. He said that men in uniform should have "equality of treatment and opportunity" without regard to race, color, religion or national origin.

Similarly, he decreed that "merit and fitness" should be the only application for a Government job, and that the head of each department "shall be personally responsible for an effective program to insure that fair employment policies are fully observed in all personnel actions within his department."

The two orders were expected to have a thunderbolt effect on the already highly charged political situation in the Deep South, a situation which is expected to be aggravated further tomorrow when Mr. Truman makes his omnibus call on Congress for action. The message, in one of its eleven major elements, is expected to go down the line for his ten-point civil rights program, which last February started the deep fissures in the Democratic party.

The Presidential orders, which require no Congressional sanction,

specified in detail the machinery that would be employed to monitor both anti-discrimination programs.

In the National Military Establishment, Mr. Truman created an advisory panel, called the President's Committee on Equality of Treatment and Opportunity in the Armed Services. It will consist of seven members, none of whom was named today.

It was said, however, that one man who probably would be recommended for membership is Dr. Frank Graham, president of the University of North Carolina. It was believed he would be acceptable to North and South, Negro and white.

The civilian employe order directed that a Fair Employment Board be formed from among members and employes of the Civil Service Commission. This, too, is to be a seven-member board, as yet unnamed.

The committee of the armed forces received the mission of determining how present practices might be altered to carry out the Presidential order. In stipulating rapid application of the policy, Mr. Truman said that it should be done with due regard to "the time required to effectuate any necessary changes without impairing efficiency or morale."

In the civil departments, the head of each was directed to designate an official as "Fair Employment Officer," who was charged with full operating responsibility for the non-discrimination program. Provision was made for hearings of complaints, appeals and disciplinary action.

As the top agency in this program, the Fair Employment Board in the Civil Service Commission received a six-point program providing for review of decisions, drafting of regulations, advice on problems to all departments, publication of information relating to the program, coordination of the policy in the departments and reports to the Commission and to the President.

While the orders did not so state, they implied that they were designed to deal with the Negro problem. Both orders have their roots in the President's civil rights program, and further, in the report of his Committee on Civil Rights,

which was issued late last year.

In recent months, Mr. Truman has been caught between two fires on the civil rights issue. The more extreme Southern Democrats, arguing that the program infringed on states rights, have named their own Presidential and Vice Presidential candidates. Their feelings, it was predicted, would become even more exacerbated by the executive orders.

On the other hand, the President has been under pressure by organizations with opposite views. For instance, A. Philip Randolph, president of the Brotherhood of Sleeping Car Porters, AFL, recently visited Mr. Truman with a disturbing report.

He told the President that there was a widespread feeling among Negroes that they would not obey the draft unless discrimination was ended in the armed forces. Mr. Truman asked him if they, too, were not Americans who should loyally serve their country.

More recently, Representative Leo Isacson, American Labor, of New York, demanded that Mr. Truman start his civil rights program in the Government, where he did not need the authority of Congress. Mr. Isacson is prominent in Henry Wallace's Progressive party, which put proposals similar to the President's in its platform.

A federal official interested in promoting the rights of Negroes said tonight that while the orders were a step in the right direction, they called for the end of "discrimination," but made no mention of ending "segregation." Proponents of the Negro cause declare that segregation is prima facie evidence of discrimination.

This official recalled that integration of Negroes in the Army went down to companies who served alongside of companies of white troops. He believed that the President's order on the armed forces, which was not specific on the degree of integration or mixing to be attained, might push the line down to platoon.

He did not believe that it would go down to the squad, the smallest unit, or twelve men, as that would involve white men and Negroes eating and sleeping in the same quarters. The official expressed the opinion that high officers would not for a long time carry integration lower than the platoon.

In the absence of a deadline for action in the military order and its omission of the question of segregation, the official saw "a pretty good political approach," which should not too greatly affront Southern Democrats.

July 27, 1948

COURT UPHOLDS NEGRO ON RAIL UNION'S BIAS

BALTIMORE, Oct. 22 (AP)—The United States Circuit Court of Appeals ruled in a decision reported today that a workman can recover damages from a union which fails to protect him from racial discrimination in collective bargaining.

Involved is the policy of Southern railroads against the employment of Negroes as locomotive engineers.

Judges John J. Parker, Morris A. Soper and Armistead M. Dobie also ruled that the Brotherhood of Locomotive Firemen and Enginemen has a bargaining responsibility to Negroes employed by the Southeastern railroads even though it does not accept them as union members.

They upheld the award of $1,000 damages by a lower court to Tom Tunstall, a fireman on the Norfolk & Southern Railway.

October 23, 1947

RAIL PACT LIMITING NEGRO JOBS VOIDED

CHARLOTTE, N. C., Jan. 3 (AP)—The United States Fourth Circuit Court of Appeals reversed today a lower court decision which permitted railroads to restrict the hiring of Negroes as firemen.

The opinion, delivered by Senior Judge John J. Parker, voided an agreement by railroads and railroad brotherhoods to restrict the hiring of Negroes to no more than 50 per cent of those employed as firemen.

The original suit, filed in United States District Court of Virginia by Willie J. Relax and others against the Atlantic Coast Line Railroad and various railroad brotherhoods, asked the court to void the agreement. The district judge dismissed the case, and Mr. Relax appealed.

Judge Parker's decision noted that the Brotherhood of Locomotive Firemen had urged that Negroes be excluded from employment as firemen because they were nonpromotable to engineers. The opinion noted also that "no railroad in the United States has ever employed a Negro as engineer."

"Because railroads do not permit Negroes to hold engineer's posts is no reason that the bargaining agent representing them should use bargaining power to deprive them of desirable positions as firemen which railroads permit them to hold," the opinion held.

In Cleveland a spokesman for the Brotherhood of Firemen and Enginemen said the union had no immediate comment.

January 4, 1951

PRESIDENT SETS UP GROUP TO BAR BIAS IN CONTRACT WORK

Creates Committee to Insure Compliance With U. S. Bans on Discrimination in Jobs

POWERS SHORT OF F.E.P.C.

By W. H. LAWRENCE
Special to THE NEW YORK TIMES.

KEY WEST, Fla., Dec. 3—President Truman created a new top level committee today to police compliance with clauses in Federal contracts against racial or religious discrimination in employment.

The contracts cover nearly a fifth of the nation's total economy.

By Executive Order, and without further reference to Congress, Mr. Truman established a Committee on Government Contract Compliance, but gave it much less power than was exercised by the old Fair Employment Practices Committee that operated during World War II but was starved to death by lack of funds when Congress refused further appropriations in 1946.

The President's action today represented another step in carrying out his controversial civil rights program, which has been stymied in Congress by Southern filibusters.

Although the power of the new committee is limited, its creation is certain to stir new political controversy in the South and may have an important effect upon the 1952 Presidential contest.

Spur to Southern Revolt Seen

It almost certainly will spur the efforts of those dissident Democrats who would like to put up a third party candidate or form a working alliance with Republicans in an effort to insure Mr. Truman's defeat if he decides to seek re-election next year.

The civil rights program was the underlying cause of the Southern Democratic revolt in 1948 that led to creation of the State's Rights party, whose Presidential and Vice Presidential candidates carried South Carolina, Mississippi, Alabama and Louisiana but were not able to block Mr. Truman's re-election or throw that contest into the House of Representatives for decision.

In the order issued today, Mr. Truman created a committee of eleven members, including six to be appointed by him in the near future, and five to be nominated by the Department of Defense, the Department of Labor, the Atomic Energy Commission, the General Services Administration, and the Defense Materials Procurement Agency.

Mr. Truman noted that for nearly ten years all Government contracts had included a clause specifically requiring contractors and subcontractors not to practice discrimination in employment because of race, creed, color or national origin.

Lack of Uniformity Cited

But, he added, compliance with this requirement has "not been secured by any system of uniform regulation, or inspection, common to all the contracting agencies of the Federal Government, and widely understood by contractors and their employes."

"The present order is designed to correct this deficiency," Mr. Truman said. "It places the primary responsibility for securing compliance with the nondiscrimination clause with the head of each contracting agency of the Federal Government.

"The committee will be expected to examine and study the compliance procedures now in use and to recommend to the department and agency heads changes that will strengthen them. As part of its functions, the committee may confer with interested persons. Recommendations of this committee are subject to review under certain conditions by the Director of Defense Mobilization, so that our efforts towards eliminating discrimination in employment will at all times aid in increasing defense production."

The Executive Order was made public at a news conference by Joseph Short, Presidential press secretary, and his explanations of it were supplemented by remarks of Philleo Nash, a Presidential staff member assigned to work with minority groups.

Powers of F. E. P. C. Recalled

Asked how the new agency compared with the old Fair Employment Practices Committee, which Congress refused to place on a statutory basis, Mr. Nash replied that the new committee dealt only with Government contractors and subcontractors. He said that the F. E. P. C. had powers to look into discrimination in the field of transportation, inside labor unions, and in many other economic activities that were not subject to supervision by the committee established today.

Mr. Short said the organization more properly should be compared with the Committee on Equality of Treatment and Opportunity in the Armed Services, headed by Judge Charles Fahy, which Mr. Truman said "pointed the way toward ending discrimination in our fighting forces."

Mr. Short said in response to questions, that the new committee would be concerned with compliance only on the question of nondiscriminatory employment practices, and would not police other fields of Government contract compliance such as wages, hours or quality of product.

The committee, Mr. Short said, will have no enforcement powers of its own, but Mr. Nash observed that the committee might decide to hold public hearings to point up important cases where discrimination was charged.

The Presidential press secretary said that members of the committee would not be subject to Senatorial confirmation, and that funds for the work of the group would be provided by the five Government agencies that also have representatives on the committee.

Curbs on Funds Held Possible

Asked if the matter would in any way be referred to Congress for approval, Mr. Short said it would not. In response to questions, however, he said it was possible that when appropriation bills were debated next year there might be an effort to attach restrictive amendments forbidding expenditures of any funds to defray the costs of the new anti-discrimination committee.

Asked if the order grew out of widespread failure of contractors to live up to the nondiscrimination clause, Mr. Nash said the lack of a general inspection system left the Government without knowledge as to how well the contract clauses were observed.

He said the White House had received some complaints of discrimination, but he offered no details. One of these, it was understood, involved alleged discrimination in the employment of personnel at the new hydrogen bomb plant being constructed by the Atomic Energy Commission on the Savannah River in South Carolina.

Right to Cancel Contract Noted

Mr. Short said the new Executive Order was related to two previous orders issued by President Roosevelt. The first was Executive Order No. 8802, issued Jan. 25, 1941, which forbade discriminatory employment practices by Government contractors, and No. 9346, which extended the ban to subcontractors as well. Under these two orders, Mr. Short said a typical contract clause inserted in Defense Department contracts read as follows:

"In connection with the performance of this contract, the contractor agrees not to discriminate against any employe or applicant for employment because of race, creed, color or national origin; and further agrees to insert the foregoing provision in all subcontracts hereunder except subcontracts for standard commercial supplies or for raw materials."

Mr. Short said that the Government had the right to cancel a contract and withhold payment when any provision of any contract was not observed, and that this would apply as well to the nondiscrimination clause as it would to a provision requiring that the product meet certain quality standards.

This, it seemed, constituted the main enforcement weapon, aside from publicity, available to the new committee and the Government in its effort to stamp out discrimination.

December 4, 1951

UNION COMMISSION TO FIGHT RACE BIAS

National Drive Led by Top Officers Is Announced at I.L.G.W.U. Convention

By A. H. RASKIN
Special to The New York Times.

ATLANTIC CITY, May 14—Top officials of the united labor movement will head a national campaign for union funds to fight anti-Negro discrimination and other violations of civil rights.

A. Philip Randolph, vice president of the American Federation of Labor and Congress of Industrial Organizations, announced here today that George Meany, the Federation president, would serve as chairman of the drive, and David Dubinsky as treasurer.

Mr. Randolph told the convention of Mr. Dubinsky's International Ladies Garment Workers Union that the committee would seek $2,000,000 in contributions from unions and members. However, Mr. Dubinsky said no decision had been made as yet on the specific goal or on how the money would be spent.

The garment union expects to start the drive this week with a gift of $10,000. Mr. Randolph said the 12,000 members of his own Brotherhood of Sleeping Car Porters would be asked to contribute one hour's wages each or a total of $18,000.

The fund-raising campaign comes at a time when many A. F. L.-C. I. O. unions in the South are threatening to secede in protest against the parent organization's support of the Supreme Court decision against school segregation.

The constitution of the merged movements commits it to fight racial bias, but some of the organization's leaders have been urging a "go-slow" policy to avert a southern bolt.

Mr. Meany indicated his own rejection of any foot-dragging approach in a speech to the garment workers last Friday. He told the 1,100 delegates that labor had to "go all the way" in defending civil rights.

At today's session Mr. Randolph, who is a Negro, said that the White Citizens Councils in the South had the double purpose of depriving negroes of "first-class citizenship" and of weakening unions.

In an interview after his talk, he expressed confidence that the establishment of the new committee would help check the secessionist movement among white unionists in the South. However, the purposes for which he thought the money should be used were in fields that have aroused intense opposition from unions identified with the Citizens Councils.

Mr. Randolph proposed that the funds go to the National Association for the Advancement of Colored People for court cases and general activities; to the sponsors of the bus boycott in Montgomery, Ala., and to negro farmers who found it hard to get bank loans in the South because they were considered out of sympathy with racial segregation.

Secretary of Labor James P. Mitchell told the convention that the blame for lack of progress on labor legislation lay with the Democratic-controlled Congress and not with the Eisenhower Administration. Most previous convention speakers have interests" in the Administration blocked improved labor laws.

Mr. Mitchell said Democratic committee chairmen in Congress had refused even to permit hearings on White House proposals for "completely noncontroversial" legislation. Under such conditions, he asked, what chance is there for amendments to the Taft-Hartley Act or broader coverage under the Wage-Hour Act?

Mr. Mitchell received a cordial greeting from the garment workers, even when he said he expected to have an opportunity to stay in the Cabinet four years more.

The union has been consistently critical of the Republican Administration, but Mr. Dubinsky made it plain that it considered Mr. Mitchell a friend.

Mr. Dubinsky also conceded that organized labor had been wrong when it fought the appointment of one of Mr. Mitchell's key aides. He referred to the designation last year of Newell Brown of New Hampshire as wage-hour administrator. Mr. Dubinsky said Mr. Brown had turned out to be "the right man in the right job."

The garment union chief said his organization recognized that there were "good" and "bad" candidates in both major parties. He emphasized that the union would exercise independence of judgment in passing on all nominees this fall.

A twenty-two-year-old feud between the Dubinsky union and the Amalgamated Clothing Workers of America was healed at the session. Jacob S. Potofsky, president of the Amalgamated, received a long ovation when he and purposes of the two unions.

May 15, 1956

WISCONSIN UPHOLDS NEGRO BAN BY UNION

Special to The New York Times.

MILWAUKEE, Wis., April 9—The Wisconsin Supreme Court ruled today that a union could bar Negroes from membership solely because of their race and color. The decision was 6 to 1.

The court said the State Fair Employment Practices Act was not compulsory.

"We grant it is cold comfort to the appellants but it is all the Legislature saw fit to provide."

The ruling was in the cases of Randolph Ross, a mason contractor, and James Harris, a mason who works for Mr. Ross. Both are Milwaukee Negroes.

Milwaukee Local 8 of the Bricklayers' Union refused to accept the two men in membership, contending that they had not followed union rules in applying for membership. The union denied that the men had been excluded because of their color, but said that even if they had, the men had no case in law against the union.

The court upheld the union. It said:

"Unions in the past and at present in this state are voluntary associations to which members may be admitted by mutual consent but into which applicants either by their own efforts or by the aid of courts cannot force themselves against the will of those already members.

"Racial discrimination in employment, so far, is not declared to be illegal [by Wisconsin statutes]."

April 10, 1957

RAIL BIAS RULE FOUGHT

CLEVELAND, June 4 (AP)—Fourteen Southern Negro railroad firemen have asked Federal Court here to invalidate a rule of the Brotherhood of Locomotive Firemen & Enginemen that in effect limits membership to whites.

In the suit against the union, its president, H. E. Gilbert, and its secretary - treasurer, Ray Scott, the Negroes contend they are not adequately represented in collective bargaining as provided in the Railway Labor Act because they have no voice in electing the negotiators.

Homer L. Ellis, vice president, told a reporter the brotherhood had no Negroes among its 100,000 members in the United States, Canada and Alaska, although its contracts covered about 1,100 nonmember Negroes. He said the brotherhood had pressed claims for nonmember Negroes before the National Railway Adjustment Board.

June 5, 1957

N.A.A.C.P. ACCUSES LABOR OF BIAS LAG

Action on Discrimination Doesn't Match Words, Association Charges

By A. H. RASKIN

The National Association for the Advancement of Colored People has accused organized labor of not doing enough to wipe out racial discrimination in unions.

In a memorandum to George Meany, president of the American Federation of Labor and Congress of Industrial Organizations, the association charges that many unions still exclude Negroes from membership or confine them to segregated locals.

It calls for more aggressive enforcement of the federation's constitutional pledge to abolish bias in labor.

The association's complaints will be brought into the open for the first time today at its annual meeting in Freedom House, 20 West Fortieth Street. In the past the association has steered away from public criticism of the federation because of its strong stand against all forms of discrimination.

A report will be presented at today's meeting by Herbert Hill, the association's labor secretary. It asserts that "all too often there is a significant disparity between the declared public policy of the national A. F. L.-C. I. O. and the day to day reality as experienced by the Negro wage earners in the North as well as in the South."

Construction Work Cited

The Hill report charges that Negro craftsmen are unable to get jobs on construction projects in many cities because of union practices.

"It is ironic to note," Mr. Hill says, "that because of the 'lily white' exclusion policies of Local 26 of the International Brotherhood of Electrical Workers and other building

trades unions in Washington, D. C., Negro mechanics were barred from employment in the construction [four years ago] of the A. F. L.-C. I. O. national headquarters building and today Negro workers are denied job opportunities in major public and private construction installations in the nation's capital."

Mr. Hill contends that some unions that have eliminated racial bars from their constitutions still exclude Negroes "by tacit consent."

Others enter into collective bargaining contracts limiting Negroes to menial jobs or depriving them of the same seniority and promotion rights white employes enjoy, the Hill report asserts.

"The leaders of some international unions operating in the South, in seeking to avoid conflict over racial issues, are permitting racist elements to gain control of local union operations," the report declares.

In White Citizens Councils

"Direct observation indicates that in many instances union shop stewards and business agents openly solicit funds and support for the White Citizens Council, and in Front Royal, Va., a local affiliated to the Textile Workers Union of America has provided space in the union's building for classes to be conducted by the private school corporation."

The report cites union bias in construction, railroads and other fields operating under the union shop as a factor in keeping unemployment among Negroes more than double the national rate.

Mr. Hill says that in March, near the low point of the recession, 14.4 per cent of the non-white work force was idle, as against 6.9 per cent of the white work force.

In a letter sent to Mr. Meany Dec. 19, Roy Wilkins, executive secretary of the association, recalled that his organization had cooperated with the federation in defeating "right to work" proposals in Ohio, California and other states.

Advocates of these measures to outlaw compulsory union membership had sought to win Negro support by arguing that the laws would combat "Jim Crow" practices in unions.

January 5, 1959

356

NEGRO APPRENTICE RARE, STUDY FINDS

U. S. and States, Employers and Unions Are Blamed in N.A.A.C.P. Report

By STANLEY LEVEY

Organized labor, management and state and Federal Governments share responsibility for the general exclusion of Negroes from the nation's apprenticeship training programs, a report to the Administration charges.

This is one of the main conclusions of a nation-wide study by the National Association for the Advancement of Colored People of the apprenticeship system for schooling skilled craftsmen.

The report, which was prepared by Herbert Hill, labor secretary of the association, will be presented to Vice President Nixon today by Roy Wilkins, the association's executive secretary, and Mr. Hill. Mr. Nixon is chairman of the President's Committee on Government Contracts.

Discrimination against Negro apprentices is not confined to the South, the report concludes. On the contrary, the report said, it extends throughout the country and largely prevents Negroes from obtaining apprenticeships as carpenters, electricians, machinists and tool makers, plumbers and pipe fitters and in the printing industry.

In the construction trades, the study discloses, less than 1 per cent of those admitted into apprenticeship training programs are Negroes.

For this condition the report holds craft unions of the American Federation of Labor and Congress of Industrial Organizations largely responsible because of their control over the training system.

"On the level of the small shop and local union," the report says, "the tradition of discrimination has often been deeply institutionalized. A form of caste psychology impels many workers to regard their own positions as 'white men's jobs,' to which no Negro should aspire.

"These workers and, often, their union leaders regard jobs in their industries as a kind of private privilege to be accorded and denied by them as they see fit. Often Negroes are not alone in being barred from such unions, which attempt to maintain an artificial labor shortage.

"This is especially true in the building and printing trades, which have much of the character of the medieval guild. On the local level the inertia which sustains discrimination is to be found among skilled workers in big industry as well as among craftsmen, and in the North almost as commonly as in the South."

Of management's role in racial discrimination in apprenticeship programs, the report says:

"No matter what the formal or informal hiring procedure, the ultimate authority to hire an apprentice resides with management. It follows that management is basically responsible for the rejection of Negro applicants when this occurs on the basis of their race or color."

Of Government's responsibility for the exclusion of Negroes from training projects, the report declares:

"The record clearly indicates that state and municipal anti-discrimination commissions as well as certain Federal agencies have not invoked the power provided whether by legislation or by administrative authority to eliminate the broad pattern of racial discrimination in apprenticeship training programs throughout the nation."

Cost Is Assessed

In an introduction to the report, after discussing the cost of discrimination to Negroes and to the economy as a whole, Mr. Wilkins says:

"The analysis indicates that given a continuation of present rates of advance it will take Negroes 138 years, or until the year 2094, to secure equal participation in skilled-craft training and employment. Surely this condition will not be accepted by Negroes and we hope it will not be countenanced by others."

Many state and Federal agencies are directly involved in the apprenticeship training program by providing subsidies and other forms of assistance. The report urges that such subsidies be withheld where the projects refuse to admit Negroes and other minority groups.

In presenting the report to Mr. Nixon, Mr. Wilkins and Mr. Hill are expected to propose that the full power of the President's Committee on Government Contracts be directly invoked to eliminate discriminatory practices.

Mr. Nixon's committee already is under fire from the A. F. L.-C. I. O. for alleged refusal to put pressure on a balky employer in Washington to use Negro workers as a means of smashing a capital union's ban on Negro members.

Among other recommendations made by the report are these:

¶That boards of education be required at once to withdraw all forms of support from discriminatory apprentice programs, including the use of public buildings.

¶That the labor federation immediately enforce all its anti-bias declarations and that its high command take direct action against recalcitrant affiliated unions that continue to discriminate.

¶That industrial management institute fair employment policies and procedures, resist discriminatory union or employe practices and fully comply with anti-bias laws.

¶That apprenticeship agencies withhold public monies from discriminating programs and that they establish an atmosphere of equality of opportunity.

¶That the full power of civil rights statutes be used against unions and employers responsible for the exclusion of Negroes from training plans.

Mr. Hill will leave soon on a country-wide tour to confer with the heads of state and municipal fair employment practices commissions to win support for the association's objectives.

January 25, 1960

A.F.L.-C.I.O. CHIEFS SCORE RANDOLPH

Say Civil Rights Views Split Labor and Negro Groups

By STANLEY LEVEY

The united labor movement yesterday censured A. Philip Randolph, its only Negro vice president. It charged that he had caused "the gap that has developed between organized labor and the Negro community."

The rebuke was voted by the executive council of the American Federation of Labor and Congress of Industrial Organizations at the closing session of its quarterly meeting at the Commodore Hotel. The only dissenter was Mr. Randolph, who is president of the Brotherhood of Sleeping Car Porters.

The censure was contained in a twenty-page report made to the council by a three-man subcommittee. The report disputed in almost every detail charges made last June by Mr. Randolph of discrimination and racism by several A.F.L.-C.I.O. affiliates and of laxity by George Meany, president of the federation, in fighting for civil and employment rights for Negroes.

The report did not stop with a denial of the allegations. It accused Mr. Randolph of engaging in discrimination himself, saying that his union employed only Negro staff members and that he had never attempted to negotiate a nondiscrimination clause in his contract with the Pullman Company.

Labor observers could not recall a federation report so blunt in language since the accusations made against the International Brotherhood of Teamsters when it was expelled four years ago on charges of being under corrupt domination. Yesterday's report accused Mr. Randolph of "incredible assertions," "false and gratuitous statements" and "unfair and untrue" allegations.

In announcing the council's action Mr. Meany was equally outspoken. He called the report "factual and constructive," and he appealed to Mr. Randolph to stop making it necessary for the federation to defend itself against "baseless charges."

"We can only get moving on civil rights if he comes over to our side and stops throwing bricks at us" Mr. Meany said. "I think we could do a lot with his cooperation. But it seems in the last two or three years he's gotten close to these militant groups and he's given up cooperation for propaganda."

Despite the report, Mr. Randolph did not change his views. In an interview he said the report was "designed to refute all the demands made in my memorandum."

"I feel it is distressing, innocuous, sterile and barren of any creative, bold, challenging ideas that can give strength and force to the civil rights movement in the A. F. L.-C. I. O. for the elimination of

Associated Press

CENSURED: A. Philip Randolph, head of Brotherhood of Sleeping Car Porters.

race bias," he declared.

"There's not a single proposal in the statement to meet the problem of the second-class citizenship of the black laboring masses in the American labor movement."

Mr. Randolph denied he had refused to cooperate with Mr. Meany. He said he resented "the policy of some A. F. L.-C. I. O. leaders in equating opposition to trade-union policies with opposition to the trade-union movement."

He contended the report would "create a sense of frustration and anger among Negro trade unionists and in the Negro community as a whole."

In his memorandum of last June Mr. Randolph had asked for a policy of strong penalties, including expulsion, against affiliates that did not end discriminatory hiring practices and other violations of employment rights by a target date. That proposal was found distasteful and "punitive" by the subcommittee.

"It is obvious," the report declared, "that expulsion as such does not cure the offending practices. Put outside the ranks of the federation, the offending organization is left free to carry on its discriminatory practices—probably more stubbornly than ever.

"And, what is most important, once outside the federation, the membership of such an organization is no longer accessible to corrective influences from the parent body through education and persuasion."

Mr. Meany was asked if that reasoning did not apply to the

teamsters and other affiliates that were expelled from the federation four years ago.

"It does not, it does not, it does not," he said. "I do not equate the problem of racial discrimination with the problem of corruption any more than I equate Hungary with Little Rock."

Mr. Meany said a new chairman had not been named for the federation's Committee on Civil Rights since Charles S. Zimmerman, manager of the Dress Joint Board of the International Ladies Garment Workers Union, resigned that post several months ago.

"No one is volunteering for the job these days," Mr. Meany explained. "We lost our last chairman — as good a friend of all minorities who ever lived — because he got tired of being hit over the head."

Mr. Randolph, in answering the charges of discrimination brought against his 8,000-member union, said that the organization employed a white lawyer and a white accountant and that it had a white economist on its staff. He acknowledged that there were no white railroad porters, but he said that the Pullman Company had a policy of hiring only Negroes for those jobs.

"I have never had a single complaint from the membership of any form of discrimination," he said.

The differences between Mr. Meany and Mr. Randolph go back several years. At the 1959 convention of the A.F.L.-C.I.O. in San Francisco, the Negro labor leader aroused Mr. Meany's anger by raising the subject of discrimination on the floor of the convention without first taking it up with the Executive Council.

"Who the hell appointed you spokesman for the whole Negro race?" the federation president asked at that time.

Yesterday Mr. Randolph said he would again carry his fight to the convention of the A.F.L.-C.I.O. The meeting is scheduled to begin in Bal Harbour, Fla., Dec. 7.

The members of the three-man subcommittee that brought in the report on Mr. Randolph's memorandum were George Harrison, president of the Brotherhood of Railway Clerks; Richard F. Walsh, head of the International Alliance of Theatrical State Employes, and Jacob S. Potofsky, president of the Amalgamated Clothing Workers.

Mr. Meany scotched rumors that he would retire as president of the federation. Asked if he would be a candidate to succeed himself, he said: "I sure will. Do I act like a guy who's getting ready to retire?"

RIGHTS UNIT ASKS CONGRESS TO END UNION RACE BARS

Also Urges President to Halt Segregation in National Guard and Reserves

REPORT CRITICIZES U. S.

Calls on Kennedy to Insure Equal Opportunities on Projects Getting Aid

By PETER BRAESTRUP
Special to The New York Times.

WASHINGTON, Oct. 13 — The Civil Rights Commission today urged Congress to pass legislation banning racial discrimination by labor unions.

The commission also asked President Kennedy to end segregation in the National Guard and to insure equal job opportunity for Negroes on all projects subsidized by Federal grants to states and cities.

These were the chief proposals in the commission's 246-page report on racial discrimination in Federal and "Government-connected" employment.

"The efforts of the Federal Government to achieve equality of opportunity in employment have been limited and sporadic," Berl I. Bernhard, the commission's staff director, said.

'Largely Ineffective'

Similarly, he contended, "the efforts of the A. F. L.-C. I. O. have proved to be largely ineffective" in curbing discrimination against Negroes by local unions, especially in some of the building trades.

The commission, headed by Dr. John A. Hannah, president of Michigan State University, submitted several broad recommendations for action to the President and Congress. They echoed, in part, proposals by the National Association for the Advancement of Colored People and other civil rights groups.

Commission officials predicted stout opposition from Southern legislators, some employer groups and labor leaders.

The commission urged Congress to amend the Labor-Management Reporting and Disclosure Act of 1959 (Landrum-Griffin Act) with a provision barring any union from segregating, expelling or refusing membership to "any person because of race, color, creed or national origin."

Some Are Praised

Yesterday the executive council of the American Federation of Labor and Congress of Industrial Organizations, meeting in New York, overwhelmingly rejected proposals by its only Negro member, A. Philip Randolph, for stiff penalties against unions failing to lower racial barriers.

The council contended that its current policy of "voluntary effort" would be more successful. Mr. Randolph is president of the Brotherhood of Sleeping Car Porters.

The commission said a few international unions had taken "forceful steps" to prevent locals from discriminating. It named the United Packinghouse Workers, United Automobile Workers and Textile Workers.

However, the commission found that, despite official policy statements, "most international unions have failed to exhibit any profound concern over civil rights problems."

The commission emphasized discrimination in the construction field. There, it was noted, union membership is practically a prerequisite to a job, since hiring is done by most contractors through the craft unions.

Yet Negroes have consistently been denied access to union locals and particularly to apprenticeship training programs that pave the way to better-paying work, the commission said.

The Negro American, it continued, is caught in a "vicious circle" of nation-wide discrimination by employers, unions, state employment services, and vocational and apprenticeship training programs. It went on:

"The Negro is denied, or fails to apply for, training in jobs * * * which * * * have traditionally been denied him; when jobs do become available, there are consequently few, if any, qualified Negroes available to fill them; and often, because of lack of knowledge of such newly opened opportunities, even the few who are qualified fail to apply * * *."

Increase of 50%

The number of Negroes in construction has increased 50 per cent since 1950, the commission said. But the Negro is still largely confined to semi-skilled and unskilled labor and the trowel trades—plastering, bricklaying and cement work. In many cases, even as a union member, he is held back in lower-paid jobs by union-management collusion, the commission said.

To date, it continued, only the Federal courts have acted to secure "fair representation" by unions of Negro members' interests. The National Labor Relations Board has not pushed the issue, it said. Neither the courts nor the board, the commission reported, have regarded a union's refusal to admit Negroes as failure to provide "fair representation."

On Oct. 5, the commission, in another report, urged President Kennedy to issue an Executive Order banning discrimination in federally subsidized housing and by federally supervised mortgage lenders.

The six-member Commission on Civil Rights was established by an act of Congress originally approved Sept. 9, 1957. Its duties include investigation of allegations of denial of voting rights and other discrimination because of race, color, religion or national origin.

It is charged with collecting and studying information on legal developments constituting a denial of equal protection of laws under the Constitution and with appraising law and policies of the Government in this field.

It reports to the President and Congress and has no enforcement authority.

In addition to asking Congress to take action against union discrimination, the commission called for action in the following areas of Government-related employment:

The President should issue an order banning segregation in the National Guard, reserve units and the Reserve Officers Training Corps. He should also order a survey of Negroes' status in both regular and reserve forces.

The commission said that, although President Harry S. Truman banned segregation in the armed forces in 1948, the order did not explicitly include reserves and the federally aided but state-controlled National Guard units.

Today, the commission reported, there are separate Negro and white guard military police battalions in the District of Columbia, and Negroes are either segregated or excluded by the National Guard and R. O. T. C. in most Southern states.

Currently 11.8 per cent of the Regular Army's enlisted men and 2.8 per cent of its officers are Negroes, the commission said. But the Army Reserve showed only a 6.4 per cent Negro enrollment, possibly, the commission indicated, because of whites' antipathy to Negro participation in reserve social functions.

No comparable figures were available for the Air Force, Navy and Marine Corps.

The President was asked to issue an Executive Order "making clear" that employment supported by Federal grant funds was subject to the same antidiscrimination rules applying to employers with Federal contracts since March.

During the year that ended last July 1, the commission declared, some $7,500,000,000 was distributed in Federal grants to state and local governments. These funds helped finance highways, airports, housing projects, urban renewal, operation of state employment services, research programs, child welfare clinics and public schools in areas hard hit by influxes of Federal employes.

The commission reported that the Federal agencies involved in these programs were willing to comply with a Government-wide anti-discrimination policy, but were reluctant to go it alone. At present, even where nondiscrimination employment policies are set for certain Federal grant programs, the commission reported, they are "often a closely guarded secret and hence inoperative."

Congress was asked to grant statutory authority to the newly created Presidential committee or "some similar agency" to enforce nondiscriminatory policies in federally assisted training and recruiting services, in all Federal or federally supported employment and by all unions involved in federally financed projects. Vice President Johnson heads the Presidential committee.

The committee's present potential, the commission said, is too limited since it has no direct jurisdiction over unions and no clear jurisdiction over employers in Federal grant programs.

The President was asked to direct the Secretary of Labor to grant administrative funds only to those state employment offices that "offer their services to all, on a nonsegregated basis, and which refuse to accept and or process discriminatory job orders."

The commission indicated that discrimination by the state offices, a key source of manpower for industry, was widespread, especially in the Deep South.

"Perhaps the greatest need for future Federal action, however, lies in the area of training," the commission said. It suggested that local federally aided vocational schools be required to give Negroes equal training with whites, instead of schooling Negroes for menial tasks only.

The commission urged Congressional passage of nondiscriminatory programs for expanded vocational and apprenticeship training, retraining of the unemployed and special programs for youth, as well as special job placement and information services for teen-agers.

October 14, 1961

UNIONS JOIN DRIVE ON JOB PREJUDICE

A.F.L.-C.I.O. Units Sign Oath on Racial Discrimination

By HEDRICK SMITH
Special to The New York Times

WASHINGTON, Nov. 15 — The American labor movement opened today a "positive and concerted" drive to wipe out racial discrimination in all its activities.

Top officials of 100 national trade unions met at the White House with President Kennedy to sign pledges "to eliminate discrimination and unfair practices wherever they exist" within labor's ranks.

Nineteen other national unions signed the pledges, but did not take part in the White House ceremonies.

In all, the unions represent nearly 90 per cent of the membership of the American Federation of Labor and Congress of Industrial Organizations.

President Kennedy commended the labor leaders on their action. He said that their fight against discrimination was appropriate because "the labor movement began as a union of those who were the least privileged in our society."

"So I ask you today," he added, "to join in an old cause and a new one, and that is to make sure that in the ranks of labor, labor itself practices what it preaches."

Parleys Preceded Pledges

The pledges were sponsored by the President's Committee on Equal Employment Opportunity. They were worked out during months of negotiations with labor leaders.

During the 25-minute ceremonies in the gold and white East Room of the White House, the pledges were signed by an official of each participating union and by Vice President Johnson, who heads the President's committee.

A gathering of about 200 persons heard brief remarks by the President; Mr. Johnson. Labor Secretary W. Willard Wirtz; George Meany, president of the A.F.L.-C.I.O., and Hobart Taylor Jr., the committee's executive vice chairman.

Mr. Meany recalled previous progress against racial discrimination by organized labor. However, he told the President:

"The new union programs for fair practices mark the beginning of a new, practical, posi-

tive, concerted effort by these unions and your committee to move forward at a firmer and faster pace toward our common goal of equal opportunity for all."

The committee has no direct authority over trade unions. Its prime function is to insure nondiscrimination by business concerns that hold Government contracts. Union support of the program has been voluntary.

Company Agreements Signed

The agreements signed today were patterned after "plans for progress" previously signed by 85 Government contractors. Another 20 to 30 business concerns are expected to sign similar pledges next month.

Vice President Johnson hailed the union pledges as a concrete step forward.

"These agreements I consider of prime importance," he said, "not just because they are a pledge of nondiscrimination, but because they give us something that we all need, agreed-upon guidelines for action."

The union agreements provide for several fairly specific actions against discrimination. These include provisions committing unions:

¶To accept all eligible applicants for membership without regard to race, creed, color or national origin.

¶To insure equal employment opportunities for all in the way of hiring, training, transfer and promotion.

¶To "make every possible effort" to abolish segregated local unions and not to charter any new ones.

¶To seek guarantees of nondiscrimination from management in any apprenticeship training programs run jointly by labor and management.

¶To seek abolishment of segregated facilities in all plants.

¶To try to write into "all collective bargaining contracts nondiscrimination clauses covering hire, tenure, terms, conditions of employment, work assignment and advancement," and provide for "effective administration and enforcement of such clauses."

The agreements were signed not only by 119 of the 131 national unions affiliated with the A.F.L.-C.I.O., but also by George Meany, the group's president, on behalf of 300 local unions directly affiliated with the labor federation.

The President's committee held a meeting following the ceremony. Three new committee members were sworn into office, bringing the committee membership to 30.

The new members are: Dr. Joaquin Gonzalez of San Antonio, Tex., a brother of Representative Henry B. Gonzalez, a Democrat; David A. Schulte, a New York philanthropist, and Mrs. D. H. Watson, the wife of State Senator James L. Watson of New York.

November 16, 1962

New U.S. Directives Bar Discrimination In Apprentice Plan

By JOHN D. POMFRET
Special to The New York Times

WASHINGTON, July 26 — Strict new regulations were issued today to prevent racial discrimination in union-management apprenticeship programs sponsored by the Government.

The regulations, issued by the Labor Department's Bureau of Apprenticeship and Training, will apply to about 9,000 joint programs with 150,000 apprentices.

Programs that do not adhere to the new standards will lose their Federal support.

The action provoked a storm among labor and management leaders in the construction industry. They asked Labor Secretary W. Willard Wirtz to suspend the plan until they could confer with him.

They said the regulation threatened the existence of the apprenticeship system.

Loss of Federal registration would stigmatize a program as discriminatory and, presumably, in the 24 states with fair employment practices laws, would make it vulnerable to legal attack.

In addition, under the Federal law specifying payment of prevailing wages on Federal construction, employers will not be allowed to pay apprentices in unregistered programs less than the regular journeymen's wage on Federal building work.

Apprentices customarily are paid a percentage of the journeymen's rate. The percentage rises as the apprentice's training advances. The practical effect of loss of registration of a program would be to deny apprentices in it work opportunities on Federal construction projects.

The opening up of opportunities for Negroes to enter these programs has been high on the agenda of civil rights groups.

Unskilled jobs are rapidly vanishing under the impact of automation and other forms of technological change. Negroes, with an unemployment rate that is twice as high as the general rate, face an economic crisis unless they can break into skilled jobs in greater numbers than they have in the past, Negro leaders believe.

Construction Program

Many apprenticeship programs are in the construction industry. However, there also are many in manufacturing and service industries.

The new standards provide that existing programs, to retain their Federal registration, must pick apprentices on the basis of merit alone, unless the selections made otherwise show equality of opportunity.

Programs that operate on a merit basis must provide for selection of apprentices, after full and fair opportunity for application, in accordance with objective standards that permit review.

This calls for determination of eligibility by specific requirements so that questions of discrimination in selection can be promptly adjudicated. It also calls for dissemination of information publicly about the availability of apprenticeship opportunities.

In situations where the programs sponsors do not wish to adopt a merit system based on objective standards that permit review, the regulations provide that their selections must include a "significant" number of members of minority groups or must provide a "significant" number of openings for members of minority groups and make a good-faith effort to fill them.

New Programs Curbed

The standards specify that programs applying for Federal registration in the future must adopt the merit approach.

They also specify that action must be taken to offset the effects of any previous practices under which discriminatory patterns of employment resulted.

Under this requirement, programs that have operated on a merit basis or have enrolled Negroes in significant numbers would not have to take action.

"Where these conditions are not met, application lists developed in the past must be disregarded to the extent necessary to provide opportunities for current selection of qualified members of racial and ethnic minority groups for a significant number of positions under one of the systems," the Apprenticeship Bureau said in an interpretation accompanying the regulations.

The standards also prohibit discrimination in apprenticeship training or employment during apprenticeship after selections have been made.

The Apprenticeship Bureau's field staff, under the supervision of its regional directors, are to enforce the standards.

Instructions are being prepared to cover this. They will be told to periodically survey apprenticeship programs in their areas to make sure of compliance. They also will be instructed to investigate complaints.

The circular issued today instructed the regional directors to make special efforts to secure qualified applicants for apprenticeship programs from among minority groups.

Construction unions and employers objected to the new standards mainly on the ground that they make the Government the final judge of who is qualified for apprenticeship.

They also argued that the new standards contained "a veiled quota system." They have consistently objected to any system that would require accepting a fixed percentage of Negroes.

A spokesman for the Building and Construction Trades Department of the American Federation of Labor and Congress of Industrial Organizations said:

"We want to conform and we have conformed to the need for eliminating discrimination. We are afraid that these regulations will completely destroy the voluntary apprenticeship system of many years standing."

EQUAL JOB LAWS EXIST IN 25 STATES

Federal Rights Bill Would Extend Provision to South

Special to The New York Times

WASHINGTON, June 6—One of the most hotly debated sections of the civil rights bill, Title VII dealing with fair employment practices, is already in force under state statutes in half the states of the Union where an estimated 41 per cent of the Negro population resides.

These state laws vary widely in their effectiveness. None exists in the South where opposition to the bill, and to this provision in particular, is most intense.

Passage of the Federal civil rights package would not, in all cases, impose stricter hiring regulations where state laws are in effect.

But it would strengthen enforcement in those states by providing automatic recourse to the Federal courts to correct a grievance. It would also, of course, introduce nondiscriminatory hiring, regulations into those 25 states that do not have them now.

In a state-by-state survey of such laws by Congressional Quarterly, it is noted that the first Federal efforts in this direction began in 1933, and that the first state fair employment law was enacted by New York in 1945.

Federal Action Limited

Attempts by the Federal Government to abolish racial and religious discrimination in hiring have been limited to Government agencies and to private companies working under Government contracts.

The sanction has derived chiefly from Executive orders rather than statutes. Orders extending the regulations have been issued by Presidents Roosevelt, Truman, Eisenhower and Kennedy.

Amendments to the House-passed civil rights bill now before the Senate provide, among other things, for state action to correct a grievance before the Federal Government steps in.

Civil rights supporters accepted this concession in the hope that it would satisfy the objections of legislators who favor the objectives of the bill

July 27, 1963

but feel that chief responsibility for its enforcement should be left with the states.

Negroes Assail Statutes

Spokesmen for the National Association for the Advancement of Colored People have argued, however, that state statutes that now exist have been "unable to cope with the problem of changing the Negro occupation pattern." State enforcement, they have said, has been left to "timid political appointees."

The 25 states that have such statues are spread generally through the East, the Middle West and the West. They include all the big industrial states.

The deepest penetration into the South is in the border state of Missouri, but three other states in this category—West Virginia, Kentucky and Oklahoma—have set up commissions to consider the adoption of anti-discrimination laws.

Similarities Are Noted

The proposed Federal law would be similar to many of those now in force in the states. For example, like the laws in 21 states, it would apply to labor unions and employment agencies.

As in 16 states, the Federal law would exempt such groups as nonprofit social, religious, charitable and educational organizations.

Title VII would establish a minimum number of employes —eventually 25 after the law has been in effect for four years —before an employer would come under its provisions. Only one state has a higher minimum, Missouri, where the level is set at 50.

The Federal law would differ most markedly from the majority of state laws in its enforcement procedure, which would be less stringent. Over half the states provide criminal penalties of varying severity for violations.

The Federal law would be enforced by civil court action, with employers who violated such orders being subject to contempt of court proceedings.

The states with laws prohibiting job discrimination are Alaska, California, Colorado, Connecticut, Delaware, Hawaii, Idaho, Illinois, Indiana, Iowa, Kansas, Massachusetts, Michigan, Minnesota, Missouri, New Jersey, New Mexico, New York, Ohio, Oregon, Pennsylvania, Rhode Island, Vermont, Washington and Wisconsin.

Union Race Discrimination Is Ruled an Unfair Practice

By JOHN D. POMFRET
Special to The New York Times

WASHINGTON, July 2— The National Labor Relations Board ruled today for the first time that racial discrimination by a labor union was an unfair labor practice prohibited by the Taft-Hartley Act. The board stripped the offending union of its official board certification as bargaining agent for employes at the Hughes Tool Company at Houston, Tex.

This was the first such action by the board, although it had made clear in earlier decisions that it was prepared to revoke the certifications of discriminating unions.

The board split 3 to 2 on a key element in the case: Whether Congress intended the unfair labor practices section of the Taft-Hartley Act to apply to cases of racial discrimination. The board majority held that racial discrimination was covered.

Counsel Hails Decision

Robert L. Carter, general counsel for the National Association for the Advancement of Colored People, called the decision "almost revolutionary."

The decision, Mr. Carter said at a news conference, "gives Negroes a new tool in their quest for equal opportunity."

Mr. Carter, who participated with N.L.R.B. lawyers in prosecuting the case and who initiated the request for decertification, indicated that in situations where the board's new doctrine would apply, he would prefer to process complaints of discrimination through the board rather than through the fair employment practices provisions of the Civil Rights Act of 1964.

The board's procedures, he said, will be quicker and less expensive. Further, he pointed out, the fair employment provisions of the Civil Rights Act do not go into effect for a year.

The case arose from the refusal of an all-white local at Hughes Tool to process a grievance filed by Ivory Davis, a Negro, against his elimination from a list of employes who had applied for apprenticeship openings.

The local was Local 1 of the Independent Metal Workers Union. Mr. Davis belonged to Local 2 of the same union, an all-Negro local.

The two locals had been certified jointly by the labor board as bargaining agent for the employes.

The board majority—Boyd Leedom, Gerald A. Brown and Howard Jenkins Jr.—and the minority—Chairman Frank W. McCulloch and John H. Fanning—agreed that the certification should be rescinded.

Opens Way for Raids

The effect of this action is to take away the union's immunity from raids by other labor unions. Ordinarily, certified unions are protected from raids during the life of their labor contract with a company if the term of the contract is more than three years.

In the present situation, the United Steelworkers of America is expected to try to take the Hughes Tool plant away from the Independent Metal Workers Union, which is not affiliated with the American Federation of Labor and Congress of Industrial Organizations.

In addition, a decertified union cannot file unfair labor practice charges with the labor board against its employer.

The threat of decertification will not mean anything to some unions, however, because they never have been certified in the first place. This is generally the case with building trades unions, which have frequently been accused of racial discrimination.

These unions generally rely on their own economic power in relationship to other unions and their employers rather than the protection afforded unions by the Taft-Hartley Act of 1947.

Enforcement Power

A potentially stronger remedy lies in the finding of the board that an unfair labor practice was committed. The board has authority, enforceable in the courts, to order that unfair labor practices be remedied.

In the present case the board approved the recommendation of Frederick U. Reel, its trial examiner in the case, that the white local stop refusing to process grievances filed by Negro workers and stop entering into or enforcing labor contracts with the company that provide greater benefits for white workers than for Negroes.

The board was unanimous in finding that the white local's refusal to process Mr. Davis's grievance was an unfair labor practice.

The minority, however, limited the grounds for its finding to the fact that the discrimination against Mr. Davis was based on his not belonging to the white local. Taft-Hartley makes illegal any discrimination by a union based on nonmembership.

The broader majority finding was that when a union, in its capacity as bargaining agent for all the employes, discriminates against some of them on racial lines, it commits an unfair labor practice.

The majority based its position on Supreme Court decisions holding that a union must fairly, without racial discrimination, represent all the employes in a bargaining unit.

NEGRO MILITANTS SCORED BY U.A.W.

Accused of Using 'Terror' in Detroit Auto Plants

Special to The New York Times

DETROIT, March 12 — The United Auto Workers accused a Negro extremist group today of trying "to spread terror" in Detroit auto plants.

The union made its charge in a four-page letter to 350,000 workers in area plants against a group that calls itself the League of Revolutionary Black Workers.

The U.A.W. warned that it "will not protect workers who resort to violence and intimidation with the conscious purpose of dividing our union along racial lines." It said that such men "put in jeopardy the jobs" of union members.

The Chrysler Corporation dismissed 25 persons connected with the movement after they put up a picket line at a Chrysler plant last month.

The extremists have been active in three Detroit area plants —Chrysler's Dodge Hamtramck assembly plant, Chrysler's Eldon axle plant and the Ford Motor Company's Dearborn plant. They have criticized the companies and the union with equal vigor and succeeded last year in closing the Dodge plant for a day.

The league recently accused the auto companies and the union of a conspiracy "which has reduced the black worker to a superexploited, supersubjugated beast of burden, with less rights than a common street dog."

The union said that four of six full-time officials and 56 per cent of the elected stewards at the Dodge union local were Negro, while at the Eldon plant local 65 per cent of all elected stewards and committeemen were black.

REVERSE LAYOFFS REJECTED BY FORD

Proposal to Help Hard-Core Jobless Held Impractical

By JERRY M. FLINT
Special to The New York Times

DETROIT, April 11 — The Ford Motor Company rejected today a union proposal to create a reverse seniority program to keep formerly hard-core unemployed persons at work while older workers voluntarily take layoffs.

The United Auto Workers made the proposal earlier in the year and Ford agreed to discuss it.

Malcolm Denise, Ford's labor relations vice president, said the discussions and Ford's own month-long study "have failed to reveal a practical approach to inverse seniority." He said that Ford's "commitment to the hard-core unemployed remains as broad and resolute as ever."

The U.A.W. had no formal comment on the rejection.

The automobile industry has been the leader in hiring the unemployed, partly because the traditionally heavy turnover at the plants opens each year tens of thousandsof jobs paying over $3 an hour.

Auto production has slowed a bit recently and there are some fears that sales and production might slacken even more. Traditionally the first persons laid off are the last hired, which means the hardcore unemployed.

Ford has not done much hiring recently and ended recruitment in Detroit's Negro area. But Mr. Denise said that "present market indications give us hope that within a short time we will be in a position again to accelerate these efforts."

It is also likely that Ford hesitated to begin a reverse seniority program for the hardcore unemployed because the unions might later use it as a wedge in getting such a program for all workers.

Negro Groups Step Up Militancy In Drive to Join Building Unions

Blacks, Dissatisfied With Slow Pace of Job Integration, Increase Picketing and Work Stoppage at Projects

"If black men don't work, nobody works."

That is the militant slogan being shouted on some of the picket lines at construction projects across the country.

Civil rights groups, long dissatisfied with the number of jobs Negroes are getting in the construction industry, are increasing their pressures through demonstrations and court actions to get minority group members admitted to building trades unions.

Developments in the long struggle of Negroes for a real foothold in the highly paid but restricted memberships of the construction trades are occurring on several fronts:

¶In Pittsburgh, a loosely organized coalition of Negro groups has been demonstrating this week, disrupting traffic and clashing with the police in a bid for jobs on $200-million worth of construction projects.

¶In Chicago, demonstrations over the last few weeks have halted $80-million worth of contracts on 20 different construction sites, mostly on the predominantly Negro South Side.

¶Negro activists warn of the possibility of more demonstrations soon in such cities as Milwaukee, Cleveland and Boston.

¶In Amherst, N. Y., a suburb of Buffalo, a dispute over the hiring of Negroes has delayed construction for months on the new $650-million campus of the State University.

¶Herbert Hill, labor director of the National Association for the Advancement of Colored People, said a series of suits in the Federal Courts would be announced next week in an effort to block discrimination on certain Federal construction pojects and in the Model Cities programs.

Ironically, the new push to overcome discriminatory practices in some of the skilled trades and to obtain jobs for Negroes in a construction industry that is expecting a period of startling growth comes at a time when labor leaders are boasting of new achievements in taking in minority group apprentices.

Donald Slaiman, civil rights director for the American Federation of Labor and Congress of Industrial Organizations, listed figures showing that craft unions and community action agencies had helped to enroll 1,537 minority youths in the Apprentice Outreach program during the first six months of 1969.

The number of minority youths placed as apprentices in programs registered with the Labor Department rose from 2,325 to 3,862 from Jan. 1 through June 30—an average of 256 a month.

The Apprenticeship Outreach program is conducted by local building and construction trade councils in 14 cities, by the Urban League in 21 cities, the Workers' Defense League in 10 cities and seven other groups in six cities.

To emphasize further what the A.F.L.-C.I.O. considers significant progress, Robert M. McGlotten, a Negro who is on the staff of the labor federation's civil rights department, cited over-all figures for last year that showed 16,200 nonwhites, or 7.2 per cent, among the 225,000 persons in registered apprenticeship programs.

Another measure of recent progress, he reported, is that 9.4 per cent of the 26,156 apprentices enrolled in the first half of 1968 came from minority groups. In 1950 minority participation in apprenticeship programs was 1.9 per cent, he said, and by 1960 had risen to 2.5 per cent.

The more recent increases, he said, reflect "a systematic and combined effort on the part of the labor movement, Government and private organizations to recruit and place more minority youths in skilled trades."

Called a 'Ruse'

In civil rights circles, however, there is a tendency to scoff at such reports of progress on the ground that it represents "mere tokenism" while literally billions of dollars in construction wages are going to white rather than to Negro workers—even when Government-sponsored projects are in Negro neighborhoods.

Mr. Hill, one of the sharpest critics of the building trades unions, characterized "concessions" on apprentices as a "ruse."

He said: "They come out of three or four year apprentice programs and are still not given membership in the unions or else they don't get referred to jobs. The fundamental issue is the question of taking in Negro journeymen. If the building trades were honest, they would open their doors and black workers would be there."

Labor federation officials say that Mr. Hill himself is not honest in his assessment of what the building trades are now doing to take in Negroes and other minority group members. They observe that it has long been the A. F. L.-C. I. O. policy to oppose discrimination in any form. They say that, over-all, the attitudes of building trades leaders are excellent in this area.

One federation official commented: "But there are thousands of locals, and you're dealing with people. There are some prejudices and also reactions to confrontations. And there are setbacks due to unrealistic confrontations and demands."

Demands such as the Coalition for United Community Action is making in Chicago are an example of what federationists and even some Negroes active in getting minority group members construction jobs in New York consider to be an unrealistic approach.

The coalition is demanding that 10,000 on-the-job training positions be made available to Negroes within 90 days, that Negroes with four years of construction experience be made foremen on construction in black communities, that construction in Negro areas be approved by the community and that the union hall referral system of assigning jobs be abolished.

Tradition of Unions

The building trades unions have traditionally limited their membership to insure that there will be work for members. With strict rules relating to qualifications, they have been selective, particularly in the skilled trades such as the plumbers, steamfitters, sheet metal workers, ironworkers and electrical workers.

When civil rights activists demand that Negroes be taken in directly as journeymen, building trades officials inquire, "Would you want your house wired by an amateur?"

They emphasize that qualified Negro journeymen can get into their unions but that the activists, when asked to provide qualified applicants usually fail to produce them in any sizable number.

"The apprentice route is the most solid way to get into the building trades," Mr. Slaiman said. "While there may be a relatively small number of highly skilled jobs, they are well paid and they are an important symbol for the black community."

Nevertheless, the process of qualification and the hiring hall arrangement by which contractors set their skilled artisans are under increasing attacks from the black community as construction jobs proliferate and in the face of the prospect for a bigger boom in the seventies as the nation's cities are rebuilt. They are demanding shares of the action and the wages that go with it.

In the immediate struggles ahead, it appears that civil rights groups will continue to use demonstrations and picket lines to force contractors and unions to accept increasing numbers of black workers—either as journeymen, if qualified, or to train on the job. The growing shortages of qualified artisans in many areas may speed up the process.

Ernest Greent, program director for the Workers Defense League, who has been active in training and placing Negro apprentices, does not think the pace of the present apprentice program will be able to fulfill the needs of the future.

He said: "Unless there are drastic adjustments, present apprentice programs won't fill the needs of the future. But the well-trained apprentices who become journeymen are more likely to become the supervisors and foremen. But with all the construction being planned for the years ahead, I think the industry will have to rely increasingly on Negro and Puerto Rican workers."

Johnson Order of 1965

Executive Order 11246, issued in 1965 by President Johnson and banning discrimination by Federal contractors, and more recent court decisions specifying that contractors have a responsibility for integrated workers are providing leverage for civil rights groups now pushing for greater Negro representation.

Although civil rights groups have been critical of the manner in which the Government enforced contract regulations relating to integration of work forces, the new Assistant Secretary of Labor Arthur A. Fletcher is firmly pledged to strict contract compliance enforcement.

Mr. Fletcher said recently: "The Office of Federal Contract Compliance stands at the gate, where Federal dollars flow to the contractor, and into the economy as a whole.

"It stands at the one point where the Government can affect the use of those dollars, where it can either close its eyes and let those dollars continue to support institutional racism, or whether — if it chooses—it can see that all groups in our society have full opportunity to share in their benefits, where the Federal dollars have a fair chance of supporting the black, Mexican American, and Puerto Rican economies, as well as the white one."

One of the first steps by the Administration to achieve compliance with the Executive Order was what is called the Philadelphia Plan to give Negroes a larger share of construction jobs.

The plan, Mr. Fletcher explained, would establish for the first time specific goals and timetables for minority group employment. It would apply to seven skilled trades in which, he said, there have been "clear patterns" of discrimination.

Under the plan, he said, all contractors in the five-county Philadelphia area working on Federally assisted projects would be expected to make every effort to hire members of minority groups in the seven trades.

Most of the trades, he said, have admitted that they had less than 1.5 per cent Negroes among their employes in a city whose racial composition is about 20 per cent black. He said, however, that if union and contractor representatives worked out a satisfactory action program of their own in place of the plan, then he would be willing to waive the Philadelphia proposal.

BUILDING UNIONS SPUR NEGRO JOBS

Defend Record in Hiring but Pledge Greater Effort— Reject Quota Plan

By DAMON STETSON
Special to The New York Times

ATLANTIC CITY, Sept. 22— The A.F.L.-C.I.O. building trades unions, smarting under charges of racial discrimination, defended their record in admitting blacks today and called for further steps to accelerate the process.

In a 3,800-word policy statement, the Executive Council of the Building and Construction Trades Department stressed the importance of taking experienced minority group members into their unions. This has been a sore point because civil rights organizations and other critics of the building trades have contended that few Negro journeymen could gain membership in unions.

[In Chicago, 4,000 Negroes and a few white supporters staged a rally to emphasize demands for skilled construction jobs. Page 56.]

"We make the flat and unqualified recommendation to local unions throughout the United States," the statement said, "that for a stated period of time they should invite the application of qualified minority journeymen for membership in their respective local unions and should accept all such qualified minority journeymen provided they meet the ordinary and equally administered requirements for membership."

The statement, which was approved unanimously by 400 delegates to the department's 55th convention here, also urged speeding up and extending the Outreach Program, which it said had been successful in recruiting minorities for apprenticeship training. Additionally, the statement recommended that local unions and councils "vigorously pursue training programs for the upgrading of minority workers who are not of apprenticable age."

New Emphasis

The building trades made a similar declaration of intent to take active steps to recruit Negroes for apprenticeships in February, 1968. But there was a new emphasis in today's statement on the entrance of qualified minority journeymen into the unions.

There appeared to be a time qualification implicit in the council's recommendation proposing that local unions invite applications for a "stated period." But a spokesman said that this was intended only to mean a "reasonable time."

While supporting positive steps to admit more Negroes into the building trades, the statement made it clear that the council did not favor capitulation by its local unions to "unreasonable" demands One group of Negro militants in Pittsburgh, the council said, had demanded 40 per cent black membership in each of several craft unions within two years.

The council also said that it was "unalterably opposed" to the quota system, in which contractors would be required to hire a specified percentage of minority group members. It was in this connection that the council and delegates made clear their opposition to the so-called "Philadelphia Plan" under which contractors on Federal projects there would have to make certain that the number of nonwhites employed was within certain specified ranges.

Media Criticized

Much of the emphasis on the first day of the construction department's three-day convention was focused on the record to date in admitting minority group members, but the Executive Council, in its statement, singled out the news media and the Government for particular criticism because of their attitudes toward the building unions.

"The Executive Council of the Building and Construction Trades Department," the statement said, "is of the considered view that the failure of the communications industry and the Government to maintain an objective attitude is inflammatory and prejudicial to the sound and proper solution of the racial issue in the building and construction industry and other segments of American life."

The statement charged that critics, including Arthur A. Fletcher, Assistant Secretary of Labor, used lesser ratios of Negroes participating in particular trades to prove that the industry was "lily white." Mr. Fletcher did this, the statement suggested, when he cited a figure of 1.6 per cent minority group membership in seven critical trades in the Philadelphia area, whereas a representative of the Building and Construction Trades Council of Philadelphia reported that more than 30 per cent of the members employed on unionized jobs within its jurisdiction were black.

Even with laborers removed, he said, the ratio of black participation among the remaining crafts was 12 per cent.

The council said that the same kind of charges made against the building trades could be made against other industries, citing the newspaper industry in particular.

Harassment Charged

In the keynote address on the convention's opening day, C. J. Haggerty, president of the department, said that the building trades were being "harassed" by so-called black coalitions in several cities and added that many of these areas of conflict were the result of the news media's failure to check the facts.

Since the Outreach Program began in 1967, he said, over 27,000 minority youths have been recruited, counselled and tested, and 3,862 have been indentured into apprenticeship programs.

"Now I want to say," Mr. Haggerty continued, "that we stand ready to give anyone, regardless of race, creed or color, an equal opportunity to enter our programs. Everyone on the same basis—favoring no one, minority or otherwise. I also believe we should make it perfectly clear that we are 100 per cent opposed to a quota system."

U.S. TO START PLAN GIVING MINORITIES JOBS IN BUILDING

Philadelphia Pilot Program Will Be Extended Later— Mitchell Terms It Legal

By JAMES M. NAUGHTON
Special to The New York Times

WASHINGTON, Sept. 23— The "Philadelphia plan" setting minority hiring guidelines for six skilled construction crafts working on federally assisted projects in Philadelphia was ordered into effect today by Secretary of Labor George P. Shultz.

At the same time, Attorney General John N. Mitchell issued an opinion declaring, contrary to an earlier ruling of the Controller General, that the plan was legal and did not violate terms of the Civil Rights Act of 1964.

Both announcements underscored the apparent decision by the Nixon Administration to concentrate its civil rights activity in the field of equal job opportunities—a decision that could have important political overtones.

Arthur A. Fletcher, an Assistant Secretary of Labor, said that it was time to "quit looking at the civil rights movement without looking at the unemployment rate."

Problem Termed Economic

"This is an economic problem and we can use the economic genius of this country to solve it," he said.

One White House source said that President Nixon believed such traditional civil rights activities as open housing and voting rights were less significant in the long run than efforts to open up the job market to minorities.

Mr. Shultz said that the Philadelphia plan was a pilot program that would be extended later to other cities.

Chicago, one of several cities that have been scenes in recent weeks of demonstrations by Negroes for more construction jobs, could be next to receive a Labor Department mandate date for more affirmative action on equal employment.

Under the plan set in motion today for Philadelphia, contractors working on federally assisted projects would be required to set specific goals, within the Federal guidelines for hiring members of minority groups.

Affected by the order are six skilled crafts — ironworkers, steamfitters, sheetmetal workers, electrical workers, elevator construction workers and plumbers and pipefitters. Employers would be expected to demonstrate "good faith efforts" at meeting minority hiring levels ranging from 4 per cent this year to 26 per cent in 1973.

The plan was first devised a year ago, but it has been blocked by rulings of the Controller General, Elmer B. Staats, who said that it would violate the Civil Rights Act of 1964 by setting racial hiring quotas.

Attorney General Mitchell's 20-page ruling today argued, however, that the plan was legal because it required affirmative action to meet goals rather than establishment of firm quotas.

Asked to explain the difference between goals and quotas,

Mr. Shultz said that a "quota is a system which keeps people out."

"What we are seeking," he said, "are objectives to get people in."

Demonstrations Recalled

Implementation of the plan in Philadelphia has national significance because of efforts by Negroes and other minority groups across the United States to secure construction jobs.

Pittsburgh and Chicago have been scenes of demonstrations by Negroes, and in Pittsburgh white craft union members have conducted counter-demonstrations.

The American Federation of Labor and Congress of Industrial Organizations building trades unions went on record yesterday in Atlantic City in opposition to the Philadelphia plan or any other quota system.

C. J. Haggerty, president of the construction and building trades department of the federation, told its convention, "We are 100 per cent opposed to a quota system, whether it be called the Philadelphia plan or whatever."

Mr. Fletcher estimated that between 30 and 50 per cent of the work force in the United States was employed by companies with Government contracts.

One high Administration official said in an interview that there might be "justifiable criticism of the Nixon Administration on school desegregation, but I'm confident we're going to go farther in this Administration than did any other on job equality."

He said that the decision to focus on job equality "to a great extent reflects the priority of black people."

"Look at what's happening now in Chicago, Pittsburgh, Boston and Philadelphia," he said. "The big thrust now is not schools, but jobs."

By adding Government impetus to this thrust, the Nixon Administration could well be risking political reaction.

During the demonstrations in Pittsburgh last month, white construction workers stood before City Hall and chanted, "Wallace, Wallace, Wallace"— a sign that they linked the issue to the political philosophy of George C. Wallace and his renewed quest of the Presidency.

Mr. Fletcher said in an interview that the Nixon Administration had come on the national scene at a time when there was "a need to analyze what has been happening in the last two decades."

Courtroom battles and social legislation have opened up opportunities for minorities to overcome previous discrimination, but the Nixon Administration has become aware that it must concentrate on developing economic opportunities, Mr. Fletcher said.

He said that the unemployment rate among nonwhites nationally "still lingers at the depression era levels." Faced with joblessness in the depression, the Federal Government acted to solve what was an economic problem, Mr. Fletcher said, and the same approach must now be made toward the economic problem of nonwhites.

"The dilemma has been that the rebuilding of the American cities is happening right under the black man's nose," he said. "Here he is saying, 'I won the right to go to the hotel, and I won the right to go to school, and I won the right to buy a house; now I need the money.'"

Asked if he believed that his views represented a policy decision by the Administration, Mr. Fletcher replied that Mr. Nixon stated on Aug. 13 that "there may be argument in this country on this whole problem of equality of opportunity, but there can be absolutely no compromise and no argument on that score."

The President's remark, made as he swore in John Wilks as Deputy Assistant Secretary of Labor for contract compliance, is "my license to do the job," Mr. Fletcher said.

Blacks Making Few Gains In the Construction Trades

By PHILIP SHABECOFF

WASHINGTON, June 26—The building of houses, offices and factories, of bridges and dams and highways is still largely white man's work in America.

Despite Government-imposed quotas and timetables, despite voluntary "home town solutions," despite "Outreach" programs to train inner-city youths and despite seemingly constant litigation, the number of black and other minority workers entering the construction industry remains a thin trickle.

There is some evidence that these efforts have forced open the door to employment in the construction trades at least a crack. The number of blacks now entering construction jobs is still insignificant in terms of their need for employment and higher income, but the foundation for future equal employment is perhaps in the process of being laid.

High Wages Paid

The findings on minority employment are based on visits to several major employment centers over a two-week period as well as reports submitted from a cross-section of cities around the country.

At stake are jobs for economically underprivileged minorities in the $90-billion-a-year building and construction industry, which pays the highest blue-collar wages and occupies a central position in the nation's economy.

The examination of the various programs to bring more members of minorities into the building trades indicates that the responsibility for the lack of rapid progress is widely shared.

Unions have opened their doors barely a crack, in some cases because of racial discrimination but more frequently to protect their select position in the job market.

The Pattern Varies

The Nixon Administration has not been as vigorous as it could have been in enforcing the law and in implementing its own programs, according to testimony by civil rights groups.

In addition, the Administration has presided over a sluggish economy that has created a poor climate in which to find jobs for blacks in the trades.

The black community itself, by the admission of some of its leaders, bears some of the responsibility for failing to recruit qualified workers vigorously enough and for not pressing minority rights in this area as strongly as it could.

The pattern of minority employment varies from trade to trade and from local to local across the country.

The laborers' union, the lowest-paying of the construction trades, has long been wide open to minorities. The carpenters, the bricklayers and other "trowel trades" have generally good records in employing blacks.

But many of the more highly paid skilled trades such as the sheet metal workers, the electricians, the plumbers and pipefitters and others still have a low percentage of minority members.

Examples of progress in integrating the building trades are easy to find, but examples of failure are even easier.

Project Shut Down

In Chicago, an equal number of black and white young men stand side by side, carefully troweling mortar on cement blocks in a pre-apprenticeship school operated by Local 21 of the bricklayers' union with funds provided by Chicago contractors. Now about a third of all apprentices in the local are black.

But in Pittsburg, Calif., white pickets recently shut down a housing project in a black neighborhood when the black contractor hired all his workers from the surrounding community.

Construction sites around the United States are becoming arenas of conflict for the construction trades, black communities and civil rights groups, and the Federal Government.

According to the Bureau of Labor Statistics, at the end of April there were 218,000 Negroes and members of other minority groups among the total of 2.9 million construction workers in the "skilled trades" —that is, excluding the laborers. This was about 8 per cent of the work force in the skilled trades.

In 1960, minorities accounted for 5.6 per cent of construction workers. In the total work force they account for about 15 per cent.

Leaders of the building trades unions say that great progress has been made in bringing minorities into the construction industry. If the number of blacks in the skilled trades is small, union leaders insist, it is because of economic factors and skill requirements, not because of discrimination.

Donald Slayman, director of civil rights for the American Federation of Labor and Congress of Industrial Organizations, declared it was a "myth" that the construction trades "are lily-white, or discriminate against blacks."

"Blacks have as many good-paying jobs in construction as in any other industry," he added. Where discrimination remains, it is being eliminated, he said.

In the Nixon Administration, attitudes toward the building trades vary, but the general position of the Labor Department is that the craft unions are not moving quickly enough to integrate and that programs to enforce the employment of blacks are necessary in many areas.

To many civil rights and black community leaders the problem is clear. The building trades, they contend, are excluding minorities on the basis of racial discrimination and the Government has provided little but lip service in the way of enforcing equal opportunity legislation.

Herbert Hill, national labor director for the National Association for the Advancement of Colored People, said in an interview:

"No organized group in America is more vigorously resistant to civil rights laws than the construction industry craft unions. They are currently conducting a rear-guard delaying action in the courts to prevent full implementation of Title VII of the Civil Rights Act and other civil rights laws."

A number of cases have been taken to court under Title VII of the Civil Rights Act of 1964, which prohibits racial discrimination in employment. But the chief thrust of Federal efforts to bring more minority workers into the construction trades has increasingly centered on mandatory programs of the "Philadelphia plan" type, which require companies bidding on federally funded construction projects to promise to hire a specific number of minority workers.

The Administration has been proclaiming the Philadelphia plan itself a resounding success.

Indeed, there are signs that the Administration will seek to use the plan as a symbol of its dedication to the cause of civil rights.

Meanwhile, the "Chicago plan," considered the bellwether of volunteer programs to bring more blacks into the construction trades, has been written off as a failure by the Nixon Administration. The Government recently decided to impose mandatory plans in Chicago and other cities that were working on voluntary programs.

Some Funds Vanish

Under the plan, Chicago area craft unions, contractors and minority community organizations agreed to work together and, with the help of Federal funds, recruit, train and find jobs for black and Spanish-American journeymen and apprentices. Although there is disagreement as to how many people were to be involved, there was talk about the program's affecting 4,000 minority workers and trainees.

In fact, the plan reached fewer than 1,000 people. Some of the Federal funds simply disappeared. And intense disputes and angry exchanges broke out among the groups that were supposed to cooperate in the plan.

Thomas J. Nayder, president of the Chicago Building Trades Council, attributed much of the plan's lack of success to the poor condition of the economy and to the refusal of the Federal Government to spend funds allocated for construction in the Chicago area.

Noah Robinson, head of Operation Breadbasket, a black community economic organization, said that the experience of the Chicago plan indicated that "we have to use threats and muscle."

Third Approach Is Tried

The third major approach to increasing minority participation in the construction trades is through "Outreach," "LEAP" (for labor education advancement program), "the Joint Apprenticeship Program" and other efforts to recruit and train minorities for entry into the apprenticeship system of the skilled trades.

Programs of the Outreach type are looked on with favor by the unions as a way to bring minorities into the trades without sacrificing skills and without disrupting job markets.

According to building trades officials, the number of members of minorities in federally registered apprenticeship programs has risen substantially in recent years. Minorities now account for about 10.4 per cent

Mill Told to Help Blacks Gain in Jobs

of all apprentices, according to union figures.

Goals Set by U.S.

But the Government, which recently published rules requiring specific goals and timetables for registered apprenticeship programs, is not convinced that Outreach programs are doing the necessary job. Civil rights groups and black community leaders are not convinced, either.

Asserting that most craft union members never had to go through a full apprenticeship program, Mr. Hill said that "the basic fallacy of Outreach is that, even if full racial integration of apprenticeship programs were achieved, there would be no substantial integration of the craft union jobs" because the flow of apprentices into the unions was only a trickle.

In Atlanta, Ed Couch, a Negro who is business agent of the cement masons local, which is 60 per cent black, disputed the contention of other craft leaders in the area that the chief problem was finding qualified blacks for apprenticeship programs.

'Don't Need High I.Q.'

"If they tell you that all doors are open, that's a lot of bull," Mr. Couch said. "The kids are there and anybody that says you can't teach them is lying. You don't need a high I.Q. to work in any of the building trades."

But there is also support for the contention of the building trades that the groundwork has been laid for the steady, if slow integration of construction industry employment.

Bayord Rustin, executive director of the E. Philip Randolph Foundation, who is a long-time civil rights leader, predicts that the building trades will be 50 per cent black within 25 years. At the top of the labor union leadership, he said, there is "a definite commitment to straighten things out."

Mr. Couch is a little less sanguine.

"Until the old people die off and the young generation takes over, we're not going to solve this problem," he said. "It seems, you just can't knock segregation out of the heads of older people."

By C. GERALD FRASER

The United States Court of Appeals yesterday ordered the Bethlehem Steel Company and the United Steelworkers of America to permit black employes to transfer from "hotter and dirtier" jobs in the plant to higher-paying and cleaner jobs with no loss in seniority or pay.

The decision is believed to be the first to outlaw transfer and seniority provisions that violate Title VII of the Civil Rights Act of 1964. Such violations are regarded as penalizing blacks who seek to change jobs within their plant.

The judges in the Second Circuit appeals court who participated in the unanimous ruling were J. Edward Lumbard, Wilfred Feinberg and T. Emmet Clarie. Judge Clarie is from the Federal Court in the Western District of New York. He served in the case by designation.

Judge Feinberg, who wrote the decision, called the Lackawanna, N. Y., plant of Bethlehem Steel—where the case arose—"a microcosm of classic job discrimination in the North."

The case was brought to the Court of Appeals by the Government. Although it won in the court for the Western New York District, where Chief Judge John O. Henderson held that the company and the union did indeed discriminate, the Government did not get a ruling that "would have made the exercise [of transfer rights] more attractive."

Judge Feinberg wrote:

"In hiring, jobs were made available to whites rather than to blacks in a number of ways. There were no fixed or reasonably objective standards and procedures for hiring.

"The aptitude test scores of some white applicants were fraudulently raised; some white applicants were hired without testing; and whites were given preference in summer employment.

"Job-assignment practices were even more reprehensible.

Over 80 per cent of black workers were placed in 11 departments, which contained the hotter and dirtier jobs in the plant. Blacks were excluded from higher-paying and cleaner jobs."

District Judge Henderson had found that the "transfer and seniority system negotiated" by the company and the union "operates in such a way as to tend to lock an employe into the department to which he has been assigned."

Judge Henderson ordered certain changes in hiring and promotion policies. He also told the company and the union to give employes in the "black" departments hired before Oct. 1, 1967, priority transfer rights.

But he did not order that future transferees should be paid in new jobs at a rate equal at least to the old jobs they held.

The three Circuit Court judges ruled that there would be no "bumping" of white employes, that transferees would have to be "qualified" and that there would be no "right to leapfrog" over intermediate spots to get a top job.

Top Federal Agency Urged For Migrant Farm Workers

By LOUIS STARK
Special to THE NEW YORK TIMES.

WASHINGTON, April 7—The President's Commission on Migratory Labor reported today that the industrialization of agriculture had brought with it all the social evils that accompanied the earlier industrial revolution. In an 80,000-word report to the White House the commission pointed out that while workers in industry had derived benefit from the rapid increase of productivity in mine, mill and factory, similar strides in production on the farm had, on the contrary, thrown the farm migratory workers backward.

The commission's principal suggestion for corrective action centered about its proposal for an entirely new Federal Committee on Migratory Farm Labor.

This group, as recommended in the report, would coordinate all Federal activities concerning itinerant farm workers. The body, to be named by the President, is not intended to be a permanent new agency, but rather a top functionary unit to unify all the efforts of Federal agencies that have to do with the itinerant problem. The ultimate goal of the new set-up would be complete elimination of farm labor migrancy, by gradual steps.

Current approaches to the problem, according to the commission's findings, have been to deprive the migrant of the benefits of farm mechanization and the advances in social legislation. Some of the migrants, it was stated, live in a state of "virtual peonage."

On receiving the report, President Truman issued a statement in which he said that it "makes an impressive contribution to a subject which should be of serious concern to us all."

Mr. Truman thanked the members of the commission for their efforts and said that "their contribution will assist greatly in developing fair and practical solutions to what is admittedly a complicated problem."

The chairman of the commission is Maurice T. Van Hecke, Professor of Law, University of North Carolina. The other members are Noble Clark, College of Agriculture, University of Wisconsin; William M. Leiserson, economist, Washington; the Most Rev. Robert E. Lucey, Archbishop of San Antonio, and Peter H. Odegard, Professor of Political Science, University of California, at Berkeley.

The report deals with the plight of 1,000,000 migratory farm workers, of whom half are domestic migrants. The other half is made up of 400,000 illegal Mexican "wetbacks" (persons who cross the border by swimming or wading or just walking) and 100,000 Mexicans legally here under contract, and a small number of British West Indians and Puerto Ricans.

Some of the evils which the commission says it found during its eight months' investigation were pinned on the large industrial growers, many of whom deal with so-called "contractor," and "crew leaders." These last-named bear no direct responsibility to the migratory workers.

The commission, too, discovered an anomaly in the employment conditions of migratory farm workers. Alien workers, such as those who come here from Mexico, for example, are, by intergovernmental treaty, guaranteed employment, minimum wages, workmen's compensation, medical care, housing and sanitation standards. But domestic migrants not only have no protection through collective bargaining but employers refuse to accord to them the guarantees they extend to imported alien farm workers.

This leads the commission to conclude that the importation of foreign contract labor be undertaken only on the basis of intergovernmental agreements which should be uniform for all foreign governments.

This recommendation is based partly on the fact that from some regions, notably the West Indies, alien farm workers arrive "on whatever terms these foreign governments were able to secure in negotiation with private employers of the United States." In these cases this country has "given no official scrutiny to the terms of the work contracts or their enforcement."

It was emphasized by the commission that the problems under study were not primarily those of "the poor little farmer," but were largely confined to conditions on about 125,000 farms which "amount to 2 per cent of the farms of the nation and produce crops equal to approximately seven per cent of the value of all farm products."

While governmental agencies do not escape criticism in the report, the commission finds that, primarily, the failure of Federal and state agencies to remedy conditions affecting migratory farm workers is traceable to the fact that virtually all social legislation exempts agricultural workers on the assumption that they are employed on small family farms.

The commission submitted a series of specific recommendations for raising the standards of life among the migrant farm workers. It is suggested that dependence on foreign labor for farm work be reduced until this source is no longer required. When it is necessary to import labor, first preference should be given to United States citizens from Puerto Rico and Hawaii.

The conclusion that it is not necessary to import aliens in large numbers during the present emergency is supported broadly by this argument:

Estimated farm output for 1951 is 3.6 per cent above 1949. If this additional output were to require an equal percentage increase in man-hours then we would need about 700,000,000 additional man-hours to produce the 1951 output. These additional man-hours could be supplied by the present domestic labor force, including farm family labor, if each worker put in 6½ more days per year. And, even at that, they would be working three days fewer per year than in 1945. The average hired farm worker who in 1949 was getting only ninety days of farm work—twenty-three fewer than in wartime—would be willing, if given the opportunity, to contribute this amount and more.

In a chapter on alien contract labor the report refers to the difficulty of negotiating the inter-governmental agreement for farm labor importation from Mexico.

Mexico and the United States do not approach the negotiations with equal freedom for bargaining, according to the commission. This is so because Mexico prescribes minimum standards for nationals leaving the country for employment abroad, while we prescribe no minimum standards for domestic farm workers.

Then, too, the commission notes, the State Department is handicapped in negotiating the treaty with Mexico by not being able to consult all interested groups. Farm employers who are well organized and articulate are consulted; but farm workers with virtually no organization, are not in a position to set forth their views.

The commission heard a sizeable volume of testimony which indicated that imported Mexican labor in the Southwest encroached on domestic labor, while illegal "wetbacks" and also the legalized worker of the same category further depressed already low standards.

So vast was the "wetback invasion" by Mexican nationals from 1947 onward, that the Republic south of the border opposed the recruitment of workers from its interior regions when large numbers of its nationals already were illegally in the United States.

To meet this condition, the United States agreed to legalize "wetbacks" in 1947, 1949 and 1950. These illegals received identification papers from the United States immigration service, after which they stepped over the border as a "token deportation," then stepped back and were permitted to become contract workers.

From 1947 to 1950, according to the commission, Texas, with a large supply of "wetback" and contract labor, reduced its wages 11 per cent; California, with little contract labor and a relatively smaller "wetback" saturation, raised its wages 15 per cent.

The conclusion is drawn from these and other figures that the Government agencies responsible for importing and contracting foreign labor have not protected domestic farm labor from detrimental effects of imported, contract alien labor.

The report describes what the commission considers the inadequacies in the method of ascertaining whether a farm labor shortage exists.

The farmers, it was pointed out, meet at the beginning of the season and decide unilaterally what the prevailing wage is to be. The rate is usually low before the season begins, and so, the report finds, it is possible that insufficient domestic labor is attracted. Therefore a "labor shortage" can be said to exist "at that price."

Since foreign workers cannot be imported until the United States Employment Service certifies that a shortage exists, this apparent lack of applicants becomes the basis for the necessary certification.

To safeguard the interests of domestic farm labor and to avoid, so far as possible, discrimination that favors imported alien contract labor, the Commission proposes that "no certification of shortage of domestic labor should be made unless and until continental domestic labor has been offered the same terms and conditions of employment as are offered to foreign workers."

The official vigilance during World War II that provided for temporary admission of alien farm workers was abandoned in the post-war years, the report points out.

Since then, responsible Government administrative agencies have ceased putting forth efforts to preserve national immigration policy, the report continues.

The Commission, in fact, found that the importation of alien farm workers since the war had been on a larger scale than during the war.

The result is that temporary foreign laborers have come to furnish "the very competition to American labor that it is the purpose of the immigration law to prevent."

The responsibility for organizing an orderly and expeditious movement of farm workers to successive jobs with minimum loss of time between work opportunities is the responsibility of the Farm Placement Division of the United States Employment Service. But the report offers the opinion that "hardly a dent has been made in the disorder that accompanies the migration of domestic farm workers across the country, and (that) the Farm Placement Service has made little progress towards its goal."

Smooth System Not Devised

While the normal procedure of public employment offices in placing industrial and commercial workers is to have employers file applications for the personnel they seek, the Commission notes that the Farm Placement Division believes it impractical to devise a system for taking employment applications from migratory workers and orders from employers for seasonal or migratory laborers.

But the Farm Placement Division, according to the Commission, is more successful in winning the confidence and cooperation of employers than of the migratory workers.

"This seems to be due to the fact that in practice the service places greater emphasis on its function as a recruiting agency for farm employers than it does on the equally important function of a work-finding agency for the migratory farm laborers," the Commission points out.

In some areas, migratory workers who apply at the public placement offices of the Farm Placement Division are actually referred to "crew leaders" and other types of labor solicitors, according to the report.

These practices "have convinced the Commission that the employment service conceives its functions as rather narrow and limited. Moreover its activities are marked by a certain one-sidedness in favor of corralling supplies of migratory farm workers to meet growers' labor demand regardless of the effect on the workers."

The general attitude of the Farm Placement Division which impressed the Commission as "one-sided" was that although Congress, in establishing the United States Employment Service, provided for a Federal Advisory Council representing workers, employers and the public, the Farm Placement Service (a part of the Federal Employment Service) has disregarded this tripartite principle. Instead, it has organized and depended for advice on a Special Farm Labor Committee, composed wholly of farm employers and their representatives.

The Commission, however, softened these strictures by absolving the Placement Service of sole responsibility for present unsatisfactory labor placement practices. It points out that while the Government has been responsible for two decades for labor placement, administrative transfers of the Employment Service to various Government departments in those years may have interferred with the development of a well-rounded placement program.

Only Two Labor Pacts Uncovered

Only two instances of farm employes being covered by collective bargaining contracts were found during the Commission's study.

The Commission said it was convinced that balanced organization and effective collective bargaining would be of great assistance not only to farm workers but that it woudl also contribute to more orderly management of labor. Adoption of the system would, for instance, eliminate the labor contractor and middleman and the "sweatshop conditions that are frequently associated with them," the report said.

As a result, it was recommended that the Taft-Hartley Act be amended to cover employes on farms having a specified minimum employment.

A widening inequity between wages paid to migratory farm workers in nonagricultural employment, was noted by the Commission.

Comparing the hourly earnings of farm laborers and factory workers the Commission reported that during 1910-1914, the period designated by Congress as the base for the farmparity price system, farm wages were two-thirds of factory wages. Today they are a little more than one-third.

Actual average hourly earnings of farm workers in 1950 was 55 cents and those of factory workers $1.45. In 1910-1914 the comparable figures were 14 and 21 cents.

Notwithstanding perquisites furnished by employers such as housing and transportation, the Commission finds that farm workers' annual earnings, compared with the pay of factory workers are even worse than is suggested by relative wage rates because factory employes get more work than farm employes.

Whereas average cash earnings of factory workers in 1949 were $2,600, average earnings for both migratory and nonmigratory farm workers were only slightly more than $500.

Farm Earnings Are Low

Thus, while average factory workers' wages were two and a half times the average pay on farms, the average annual factory earnings were five times the average farm earnings.

The Commission condemned most of the on-the-job housing offered to migratory farm workers as "below minimum standards of decency." As to the so-called "permanent" housing in which the migrants live for the six to eight months of the year when they are not working on the crops, the Commission characterizes them as "among the most deplorable in the nation."

The Government, according to the report, does not assume any responsibilities concerning conditions of work for which it recruits farm labor.

This was emphasized to the commission again and again by officials of the United States Employment Service.

The summary found, too, that migratory workers were more subject to sickness and had a higher death rate than most other segments of the population.

The diet of migrant farm laborers was described as insufficient to maintain health.

Also, the growing trend toward mechanization of agriculture, according to the report, has substantially increased the risk of injury in farm employment.

The use of tractors and other machines, of mechanized blades and other cutting tools, and of noxious gases in fumigation as well as the truck transportation of farm workers all have contributed to make the accident rate in agriculture one of the highest in the United States.

Safety Plan Is Urged

With this in view, the Commission proposes that the United States Departments of Labor and of Agriculture lay the foundation for a safety program in agriculture.

In this connection, it was pointed out that safety programs and workmen's compensation legislation have proved of benefit to employers and employes in industry and that no responsible spokesman for either group would question their value or seek their repeal. Most state workmen's compensation laws exclude farm workers, the report showed.

While child labor has all but disappeared from American industry, the Commission found, nevertheless, that it still was a serious problem in agriculture.

The Commission found evidence, too, that some employers had put pressure on school authorities to permit children to work in the fields.

Following the President's directive to inquire into the educational conditions among migratory workers, the Commission reports that "migrant children are among those with lowest educational attainments found in the United States. * * * Nor are they likely to get educational opportunities so long as they work during school hours and move from place to place with their parents in search of employment."

At the same time the Commission also found that children of migrants suffer from the discrimination and social stigma which excludes them from full participation in the community.

After describing a few educational experiments for migrant children in New Jersey, Michigan and California, the Commission proposes joint educational programs by the Federal and state governments for migrants and their children.

UNION A FAILURE, REFUSES TO QUIT

Leader of Farmhands' Group Is Still Hopeful Despite 25 Years of Few Gains

WASHINGTON, Dec. 15 (AP) —A quarter-century of effort to organize the nation's farmhands has failed on a big scale but the man behind it, Harry Mitchell, says he will not give up.

Mr. Mitchell, the son of a Tennessee tenant farmer, admits that he is tired and discouraged. But after devoting nearly a lifetime to an unsuccessful crusade, he says he cannot quit.

"I've got a bear by the tail and don't know how to turn it loose," Mr. Mitchell said in an interview. "Not that I'd want to. There's nothing else I know, or want to do."

Why this lack of success, he was asked, in view of the success of unions in organizing many other types of workers?

Most observers agree that a big handicap has been the lack of Government help and protection of the kind given other unions. Agriculture is exempt from practically every labor law, state and Federal.

Thus farm employers are not required by law to bargain with unions as are employers in other industries. Similarly, farm workers are exempt from laws on minimum wages, maximum hours, unemployment compensation, safety and various other labor laws.

These exemptions have been a matter of political compromise with powerful rural elements in Congress and state Legislatures.

Union on the Rocks

"But the results," Mr. Mitchell says sadly, "are that our farm workers in this land of plenty make up the largest group at the bottom of the nation's economic heap."

The truth is that Mr. Mitchell's union—the National Agricultural Workers Union—is on the rocks. Mr. Mitchell is president and his wife, Dorothy, is secretary-treasurer.

Mr. Mitchell says there are about 50,000 farm workers claiming membership in the union. But he says there are fewer than 5,000 dues-paying members. The dues are $1 a month.

Other labor unions used to help with occasional donations, but that is rare nowadays. His union exists, barely, on its few dues payers and on occasional donations from well-wishers.

Mr. Mitchell says "we've weathered worse times before" and that he will keep going somehow. But even his best

369

friends have their doubts this time.

Mr. Mitchell is frank about his union's drawbacks and troubles. One of the severest blows the union has had to face, he says, comes from the Government policy of importing thousands of farmhands from Mexico, Puerto Rico, and other areas each year.

"It's crazy," he said. "It doesn't make sense, when people work in Alabama for as little as 35 cents an hour, to bring in Japanese 5,000 miles or more to work for 75 cents an hour."

Another problem faced by his union is one of distance. Farm workers are scattered out in the fields and cannot be reached at a single place like factory workers can be reached at a plant gate.

Out of a hired farm population of approximately 2,000,000, some 400,000 workers are regularly employed by large corporation-type farms. This is the group Mr. Mitchell would like to organize and that has been the source of most of his members so far.

"We are about in the position most labor unions were in fifty years ago," said Mr. Mitchell. "We haven't gotten very far, but it's been a tough fight getting this far. Maybe we've accomplished a few things and stopped the situation from being worse."

As to salary, Mr. Mitchell says he is supposed to get $4,800 a year but, because of the union's bare treasury, he drew only $2,900 last year. His wife gets $2,200 as secretary-treasurer.

The N. A. W. U. was started in 1934 as the Southern Tenant Farmers Union. Mr. Mitchell and a small group of supporters felt sharecroppers were not getting enough of the Government payments to landowners for plowing up cotton.

"I may be an eternal optimist," he said. "You have to be to keep going. But I think we can do the job some day."

TV: 'Harvest of Shame'

Exploitation of U.S. Migratory Workers Is Documented on 'C.B.S. Reports'

By JACK GOULD

THE shocking degradation and exploitation of millions of human beings who pick the fruits and vegetables that are served on America's richly laden dinner table were shown last night on "C. B. S. Reports" over Channel 2.

"Harvest of Shame," narrated by Edward R. Murrow and produced by David Lowe, was uncompromising in its exposure of the filth, despair and grinding poverty that are the lot of the migratory workers who follow the sun from Florida to upstate New York and from Mexico to Oregon.

•

Mr. Murrow described the plight of the roaming laborers as "The grapes of wrath of 1960"; the program proved it.

Mr. Lowe, working under the over-all supervision of Fred W. Friendly, executive producer, spent months in following the fruit and vegetable pickers as they made their northward circuits. With his cameras he showed real-life scenes that could add up only to a terrifying blot on Democracy's escutcheon.

Humans were shown stacked vertically in trucks for trips of hours and hours while the products they picked were shipped in streamlined trains and refrigerated trucks. The hovels called homes, one-room shanties for large families working near Princeton, N. J., and Riverhead, L. I., were contrasted with the lush stables for race horses.

The faces of the migratory workers were their own eloquent editorial on a national disgrace. There were young women who looked like aged wretches; bright little children with no hope of a decent education; men and women, both white and Negro, with no apparent hope of experiencing minimum toilet facilities and youngsters waiting for the unspeakable meals that pass for nourishment.

"Harvest of Shame" stressed the role of "crew leaders" who recruit the migrant workers in the South and then truck them from state to state. But the chief blame was put on the so-called "farm lobby." The Secretary of Labor, James P. Mitchell, indicated that he had been powerless to push forward the steps necessary to protect the mobile labor force.

Charles B. Shuman, president of the American Farm Bureau Federation, did not help his position by complaining over the possibility of Federal interference. The indignities visited upon the pickers made his words sound as if they came out of the Dark Ages, especially after a viewer had heard a mother of fourteen children explain how she worked in the fields from 6 A. M. to 4 P. M. Her total pay for ten hours under the broiling sun was $1.

•

One aspect of the migratory labor situation was not too thoroughly developed, namely the influence of the large chain grocery stores. One farmer said the food chains ultimately call the tune in the economics of fruits and vegetables, but Secretary Mitchell indicated this was just an alibi by the farmers. The matter should have been pursued further.

The photography in "Harvest of Shame" was of exceptionally good quality; Mr. Lowe can be extremely proud of his accomplishment.

Mr. Murrow and "C. B. S. Reports" left no doubt of where they stood. The commentator concluded by asking viewers who benefited from the labors of the "excluded Americans" to raise their voice in Congress, something very likely to happen.

UNION ENDS DRIVE FOR COAST FARMS

By LAWRENCE E. DAVIES

SAN FRANCISCO, July 8— The latest effort to unionize California farm workers is about to become history.

The Agricultural Workers Organizing Committee, chartered by the American Federation of Labor and Congress of Industrial Organizations to undertake the task, is in its last months of operation.

Its death sentence was pronounced by the A. F. L.-C. I. O. Executive Council last week at Unity House, Pa. The move has been greeted with a variety of reactions in this rich agricultural state, where union after union has tried over several decades to bring California's hundreds of thousands of field hands into the house of organized labor.

Some employers say California agriculture, marked increasingly by big operations, now will avert unionization for many years. They contend that the migratory workers are not interested in belonging to a union.

Some union officials dispute this hotly. Among them is Norman Smith, director of the Organizing Committee, who will be closing up shop at Stockton in two or three months when the last of the committee's funds is exhausted. Mr. Smith is confident that with enough "education," the California farm worker can be organized.

Meanwhile, the State Department of Employment, without a labor dispute in sight this week on the farms, foresaw a drop in its work load now that the Organizing Committee is going out of business.

California farmers, however, did not drop their vigilance against labor organization. O. W. Fillerup, executive vice president of the Council of California Growers, made this comment:

"Agriculture is not tearing down its forts because one band of marauders has been wiped out. Agriculture knows that there are many more shadows lurking outside the door."

One of these shadows is that of the International Brotherhood of Teamsters. Early this year the Teamsters signed a union shop contract with Bud Antle, Inc., in the Salinas Valley. The Antle lettuce and carrot growing operations are immense.

Mr. Smith himself said that if George Meany, president of the A.F.L.-C.I.O., had been working for the Teamsters, "he could not have picked a more opportune time—just before the opening of the Teamsters Union conpension of our operations."

Day of Alien Labor Over, Wirtz Tells Coast Farmers

Growers Must Compete for Domestic Workers, He Says After Tour

By GLADWIN HILL
Special to The New York Times

LOS ANGELES, March 28—Secretary of Labor W. Willard Wirtz has proclaimed the advent of a new era in a major segment of American agriculture.

Mr. Wirtz declared this weekend, after making a four-day investigation of California's vast farming industry, that the day of a Government - sponsored "guaranteed and assured" farm labor supply, through the seasonal importation of cut-rate alien field hands, was over.

Henceforth, he said, agriculture will have to get its workers through direct wage competition in the domestic labor market.

He predicted that even major increases in farm wages would bring only insignificant increases in retail food prices.

To facilitate this far-reaching transition to domestic labor, Mr. Wirtz indicated that he was strongly inclined to press for two innovations lon considered radical in agricultural economics: a national minimum wage and unemployment insurance for farm workers.

Minimum Wage Studied

The Secretary is also considering the development, under Federal-state auspices, of a national network of trailer parks, with full community facilities, as bases from which migrant farm-worker families could follow the crop cycle and live decently.

Many of these families still live in battered automobiles or shacks on ditch-banks in the "Grapes of Wrath" fashion of the nineteen-thirties.

A score of states, mainly in the West, have made extensive use of alien labor, chiefly Mexican "braceros," imported annually by the hundreds of thosands on grounds of domestic labor shortages.

This importation was ended by law Dec. 31, Since thern

The New York Times
W. Willard Wirtz

there has been mounting clamor from farm quarters, and pressures on Congress and the Administration, to revive the traffic.

The system has long been opposed by organized labor and social welfare organizations as a wage-cutting device. The so-called shortages of domestic labor, in the face of large-scale unemployments, have been attributed to farm employers's refusal to offer enought pay as long as they could get dollar-an-hour alien labor.

Little Disruption Seen

Mr. Wirtz concluded that in California, the biggest agricultural state and the biggest user of braceros [Spanish idiom for manual laborers], the shift to domestic labor had been effected thus far with minimal disruption of farming, although there might be very limited and selective transitional needs for some aliens in this fall's harvest peak.

The Secretary presented his conclusions at an airport news conference last night as he headed back to Washington, his shoes daubed with mud from tramping through dozens of vegetable fields, fruit groves and labor camps during a thousand-mile tour of the state by plane and car.

In four 16-hour days, he talked with hundreds of workers, employers and officials. In collaboration with an entourage of Federal and state agricultural and labor experts, he probed farm economics down to fractions of a cent.

California's large-scale farm employers had hoped the visit would be an occasion for continuation of the long-simmering argument about the asserted indispensability of a "supplementary alien labor supply," which critics have likened to the garment industry's onetime dependence on a flow of immigrants from Europe.

But Mr. Wirtz, after his investigation, rejected this notion as a dead issue. He emphasized that in terminating Public Law 78, which authorized federally regulated importation of labor, Congress had expressed its will that this labor source be ended.

The only question now, he said, is how to achieve the transition to a stable, and economically and socially satisfactory, domestic supply.

The will of Congress, he added, likewise precluded reviving any large-scale admission of foreign labor under Section 414 of the McCarran-Walter Immigration Act, on which many farm employers have been pinning their hopes.

Under this provision, foreign labor can enter the United States temporarily to work in a certain area if the Labor Department agrees that the area has a labor shortage.

"Some people have felt that Section 414 would replace Public Law 78," Mr. Wirtz said. "It will not."

"I see the situation moving from the recriminations and absolutes of the last several months of discussions," he said, "into a period where we face squarely the fact that Public Law 78 has been terminated. What lies ahead is a longer-range challenge to meet the change-over in California's agriculture."

"A fully guaranteed, assured labor supply will no longer be the case," Mr. Wirtz said. "It will be up to employers, with the cooperation of public and private agencies, to provide adequate incentives. A basic decision implicit in the action of Congress was that labor should find its price on a competitive basis."

He declared, "There has been substantially no bargaining power between employes and employers over wages and working conditions. From here on there'll be a competitive factor in the situation."

"Under Public Law 78," he continued, "at least one-fifth of California agricultural work was performed by single individuals, from a foreign country, living apart from their families, in a network of bachelor labor camps. In the future this portion of the work will be performed by people of

this country who travel with their families."

"There will be problems of providing family housing, and such things as schools, churches and other community facilities. But it's clearly within the area of achievable accomplishment," he said.

"There is no question whatsoever," Mr. Wirtz said, "that we can end the anomaly, the paradox of there being 400,000 to 500,000 unemployed in California and there still being difficulty recruiting labor for farms."

The normal farm employment in California at this time of the year is around 275,000. Against this, Mr. Wirtz observed that there were pending only three emergency applications for supplementary alien labor—which he can still authorize under Section 414—totaling only about 8,000 workers.

These applications report shortages of 5,100 workers for lettuce harvesting around Salinas, 2,900 for tomatoes around Stockton and 250 for date-palm pollination at Indio.

Deartment of Labor officials and growers' representatives will discuss these areas this week in Washington.

Mr. Wirtz's tour took him from the asparagus ranches of Northern California to the citrus groves around Los Angeles and the various crops of the Imperial Valley, where lettuce alone brought in $39 million last year to a small number of ranches.

Hears Both Sides

From employers Mr. Wirtz heard countless explanations of why United States citizens could not do the "stoop labor" on farms, although a good deal of it admittedly has been done by them all along, and how the domestic labor supply was undependable.

From workers he heard equally numerous accounts of having been denied jobs, up to January, in favor of aliens, and of wages below the subsistence level.

"I observed that the most serious reports of labor turnover came from farm operations where conditions were bad," he commented, "and the fewest complaints from places that obviously were well operated."

A memorable vignette occurred as the Secretary surveyed asparagus harvesting in Northern California.

"Where are the toilets?" he asked.

The ranch owner blurted out in astonishment: "What toilets?"

March 29, 1965

RELIGION INSPIRES GRAPE MARCHERS

Coast Workers End Week of Their Walk to Sacramento

By LAWRENCE E. DAVIES
Special to The New York Times

PARLIER, Calif., March 24 —A colorful column, banners flying, moved along back highways in the San Joaquin Valley today, past pruned vineyards, tomato and cotton fields and rich plowed land.

In the vanguard trudged the proud bearer of a silk and velvet tapestry depicting Our Lady of Guadalupe, a national and religious symbol of Mexico. On either side fellow marchers carried United States and Mexican flags.

Behind them a dozen big red banners, each decorated with a black thunderbird in a white circle, were thrust high above the shoulders of a band of pilgrims on an unusual mission.

The thunderbird is the official symbol of the National Farm Workers Union, an unaffiliated family association. The paraders were 70 or so members of the union—men and women, fat and thin, mostly Mexican-Americans, but with a sprinkling of Negroes and whites.

Some wore red ponchos, with the thunderbird and the Spanish word "Huelga," meaning "strike," inscribed across the back. All, despite blistered and aching feet, were bent on reaching the state Capitol in Sacramento on Easter Sunday, April 10, for a rally after a 300-mile trek from Delano, center of a grape pickers' strike that began on Sept. 8.

Party is Relaxed

This was not a taut, emotional group of singers. It was a relaxed party, reflecting patience and determination, well-ordered, quiet for the most part but occasionally chanting "Viva la huelga" [long live the strike] to the time of a guitar or accordion. Accompanying state highway patrolmen and sheriff's deputies have had nothing to do except keep the sightseers moving on Sunday.

The workers' pilgrimage, dedicated to "seeking our basic, God-given rights as human beings," has heavy religious overtones.

The marchers are attempting to bring the hired hand on California farms into organized labor. Implicit in the strike, and in the organizational structure of the march, is the threat of a general farm labor strike, depending on the success of a contemplated one or two-day work stoppage in the central valley this spring or summer.

The big grape growers of the southern San Joaquin had labeled the Delano strike pure fiction eight days ago in testimony before a Senate investigating committee headed by Senator Harrison A. Williams, Democrat of New Jersey.

Criticized by a Grower

Only yesterday, when the striking column walked 17 miles from Cutler to Parlier, a leading Delano grower, Martin Zaninovich, told the California Grape and Tree Fruit League's annual meeting in San Francisco that the public had been "treated to a monumental snow job."

"The so-called strikes," he declared, "are pure myth, manufactured out of nothing by outside agitators who are more interested in creating trouble in the United States than in the welfare of the farm workers."

Today marked the end of the first week of the march, led out of Delano by Cesar Chavez, soft - spoken, self - assured, 38-year-old director of the National Farm Labor Union. Mr. Chavez, who has lived in Delano "off and on since 1937," led a hard core of what he says is 2,000 or so member families toward Sacramento on a pilgrimage of "penitence and revolution."

"This is different from former organizing efforts," Mr. Chavez explained over a picnic dinner of beans, potato salad, tortillas and chili peppers with soft drinks and coffee.

Limping badly from a pulled muscle that had sidelined him from the march for a few days, he talked in the city park at Cutler on Tuesday evening.

Previous Attempts Failed

"All attempts in the past have been made by outside organizers who tried to organize and strike at the same time," he went on. "This didn't work. We have an organized, dues-paying membership — monthly dues over $3.50 cover the whole family — and if we were to lose this strike, something I don't think will happen, we have got to be strong enough to survive."

The same theme had been picked up earlier on the march by Manuel Vasquez, a lean, thin-faced heavily sunburned Mexican - American, 32 years old, from Earlimart, near Delano.

"Many people," he said earnestly, "think this is like other strikes—on and off. When they see this strike is lasting seven months and they see us, they will have the courage to join. We're bringing it to the areas where people are afraid."

And Manuel Sanchez, 35, of Delano, the chubby, round-faced driver of a union truck who was prevented from marching by a stroke, told of his birth amid poverty and said of Mr. Chavez, with whom he grew up:
"I've known Cesar all my life. He will give up his life for the poor people. All the people believe in Cesar."

'Gentle, Religious Nature'

A similar feeling infects some of the accompanying clergymen supporting the strike and the march. One of those captivated by what he called "the gentle and religious nature" of Mr. Chavez, said to a reporter, "This country doesn't deserve men like Martin Luther King and Cesar Chavez heading minority movements."

The wife of a grape grower in this area who never had met or seen Mr. Chavez had a contrary view.

"What an awful man he must be," she said.

Here in Parlier last night, as in Cutler the night before — towns in a sun-warmed region dotted with post-office names like Selma, Dinuba and Reedley — a candlelight parade took the marchers through La Colonia, the Mexican-American workers' quarter. A meeting, combining education and entertainment, serious discussion and laughter, followed.

When a clergyman — so far a Protestant minister or Catholic priest — is along the rally opens with a prayer. The Teatro Campesino (Farm Workers Theatre) is a highlight of the evening. Louis Valdez, a Delano-born, former member of the San Francisco Mime troupe, has put together, with several of his colleagues, a series of skits, reflecting bitter social and political satire.

At the Cutler City park several hundred appreciative farm workers and city dwellers cheered a dialogue between a grower, wearing a pig-faced mask, and a Mexican-American strikebreaker.

An actor playing the role of Gov. Edmund G. Brown was brought into a skit in this election year along with the Digiorgo Corporation and Schenley Industries, two of the big employers in the Valley. The union has a nationwide boycott underway against Schenley.

A 6-Point Program

At every meeting a four-page, six-point Plan of Delano is read to the audience in Spanish.

"This is the beginning of a social movement in fact and not in pronouncements," it begins. "Because we have suffered — and are not afraid to suffer—in order to survive, we are ready to give up everything, even our lives, in our fight for social justice. We shall do it without violence because that is our destiny."

It pledges suffering "for the purpose of ending the poverty, the misery, and the injustice with the hope that our children will not be exploited as we have been."

It emphasizes religion and says the strikers "seek, and have, the support of the church in what we do; we ask the help and prayers of all religions."

The strike and the march have had the backing of the California Migrant Ministry, a largely Protestant group, headed by the Rev. Wayne C. Hartmire of Los Angeles. The Rev. Thomas Fry of San Jose, a Roman Catholic priest who spent several days with the marchers as one of the representatives of Archbishop Joseph T. McGucken of San Francisco, said:

"It's ironic that the Migrant Ministry is taking the lead in the frontline, full support of the Delano strike. We Catholics came in late but we're in to stay now."

A monthly contribution of $5,000 from the United Automobile Workers, headed by Walter Reuther, is divided equally between Mr. Chavez's union and the Agricultural Workers Organizing Committee of the American Federation of Labor and Congress of Industrial Organizations.

March 28, 1966

GRAPE UNION SIGNS PACT AT SCHENLEY

First Contract Provides for 35-Cent Pay Increase

LOS ANGELES, June 21 (AP) — A one-year contract involving about 450 grape pickers in the Delano vineyards was signed here today by Schenley Industries, Inc., and the National Farm Workers Association, an independent union.

The pact, the first since pickers in the Central California area struck last year, provides a 35-cent hourly wage increase, raising the minimum to $1.75 an hour.

Piece rates will be adjusted to correspond to the new basic wage, a spokesman said. These rates apply to those paid for the amount they gather rather than for the hours they work.

Cesar Chavez, director of the union, said, "This is a milestone in the history of U. S. agriculture."

Schenley also agreed to a union shop and a union hiring hall, making the association the prime source of labor for the company.

Under the agreement the company must give the union 72 hours' notice of a need for workers. Should the union fail to provide them within that period, the company is free to hire outsiders.

Settlement of fringe benefits was left for further discussion.

The contract, effective today, specifies that "in cases where inequities exist with respect to insurance, medical, hospitalization and vacations, the company and the union will meet to eliminate them."

The contract was signed after negotiation sessions at the offices of the Los Angeles County Federation of Labor.

Last April 6 Schenley became the first of 33 grape growers in Tulare and Kern Counties, north of here, to recognize the association as bargaining agent for some 5,000 pickers, who struck last Sept. 8. The strike against Schenley was called off when that company agreed to negotiate with the union.

A few days after recognition came from Schenley, the DiGiorgio Corporation, biggest employer in the Delano area, pledged it would negotiate with a union if its workers voted for it. Later DiGiorgio offered the association a contract if the union first would sign a no-strike clause and submit to arbitration. The union declined. Subsequently the Christian Brothers, another major wine and grape producer, recognized the union, but no contract has been negotiated.

June 22, 1966

Farm Union Pins Its Hopes on Victory in Coast Grape Strike

EARLIER SUCCESS SPURS U.S. DRIVE

Workers' Gains in Dispute With Processors Inspire Wide Organizing Effort

By DAVID R. JONES
Special to The New York Times

WASHINGTON, Oct. 1—The tattered Mexican-American pickets who tramp the macadam roads in the verdant vineyards in California's fertile San Joaquin Valley know how to wait.

More than 200 families have been on strike against 32 grape growers there for more than two years, and they say they are resigned to striking two more.

Their struggle is concentrated now against the Guimarra Vineyards Corporation, whose 6,000 acres of grapes point like a finger through the hot and rich valley, and the outcome of the strike may tell whether the farm workers can build a viable labor union.

"Guimarra is one of the biggest growers, and if we can crack Guimarra we can crack them all," says Dolores Huerta, the 37-year-old mother of seven who conducts the union's contract negotiations in Delano, Calif.

Contracts With Processors

The achievements of the strikers have been modest, but they have won several contracts with big companies that process grapes into wine.

This was the first success of any magnitude for farm workers in 30 years of sporadic organizing efforts, and it is encouraging workers elsewhere to seek unionization.

The Delano movement has spread into bleak Starr County, Tex., where it seeks to organize fruit and vegetable growers. Another union drive is under way among migrant workers in Florida's citrus belt.

There has also been some union success in Wisconsin, and there are reports of activity in Michigan, New York, Oregon and Arizona.

Those promoting unionization see it as the best way to ease the oppressive poverty of most of the nation's 1.8 million regular farm workers.

They earned an average of $1.23 for each hour worked last year, and those who worked 150 days or more averaged $2,300 for all employment in 1965.

This, however, would have been relative affluence for the migrant workers among them. There are about 400,000 migrants, and in 1965 they averaged $1,362 from all sources of income.

The migrants are generally unprotected by unemployment insurance or workmen's compensation, and it was only last February they were covered by the Federal minimum wage of $1 an hour. Their living conditions are generally substandard, and thousands of them live in quiet despair.

The United Farm Workers Organizing Committee is trying to change things for the California migrants. The contracts with the wine processors marked the first step, and now it is tackling the growers of fresh table grapes.

The union, an affiliate of the American Federation of Labor and Congress of Industrial Organizations, chose to concentrate on Guimarra now because this is the time of the grape harvest.

Most authorities agree it must win over Guimarra to maintain the momentum of its victories over the processors.

The key figure in organized labor's drive to improve the lives of farm workers, is César Chávez, a stocky, unassuming man who operates out of a spare office in a pink stucco house in Delano. Atop the house is a flag with a thunderbird, the symbol of the grape strike.

Mr. Chávez, who learned community organizing techniques from Saul Alinsky, the professional organizer of the poor, began to work among the Mexican-American grape pickers in 1962.

He wanted to build a union, and after three years his National Farm Workers Association joined a strike begun by Philippine-American workers of the Agricultural Workers Organizing Committee.

The strikers won unexpected support from church groups, civil rights workers and students. They also were aided by a Federal decision in 1964 to end the bracero program, under

LEADER: César Chávez led workers in their strike against the grape growers.

which growers were allowed to import Mexican workers, who could have broken the strike.

9 Companies Settle

The Mexican-Americans and the Philippine-Americans merged to form the United Farm Workers Organizing Committee, which in the last two years has won contracts covering about 5,500 workers at nine companies that process grapes into wine.

The contracts with the grape processors provided minimum hourly wages of $1.65 to $1.80 an hour, some benefits, and hiring halls through which the union can refer workers to the employes.

The union says the prevailing wage for grape pickers around Delano is $1.30 to $1.40 an hour. The growers say that with piece work the grape pickers can earn as much as $2.15 an hour, but the union disputes this.

Mrs. Huerta, meanwhile, sits in her cluttered office in slacks and sandals and explains the strike.

All the major agreements so far have been with big processors, and she rattles off their names: Schenley Industries, Di-

Associated Press Wirephoto

MARCHING: Striking grape pickers of the National Farm Workers Association passing through a vineyard near Malaga, Calif. More than 200 families have been on strike against 32 grape growers for more than two years.

Giorgio Fruit Corporation, E. and J. Gallo Winery, Almaden Vineyards, Novitiate of Los Gatos Winery, Christian Brothers Winery and A. Pirelli-Minetti and Sons.

Because they are big, she says, it is easy to seek a boycott of their products. But it is harder to boycott growers of fresh fruit, she says, because their names are unknown to consumers.

The Rev. James L. Drake of the United Church of Christ is Mr. Chávez's assistant. He estimates that several hundred workers have stayed away from Guimarra because of the picket lines, and he says the company has lost "close to $2-million on spoilage of grapes," picked by inexperienced help.

Boycott in 34 Cities

Mr. Drake says that the boycott of Guimarra is working better than the union had expected. The union, he says, has established a boycott of the grapes in 34 cities and that 15 store chains with 13,000 outlets have stopped selling them.

However, Philip Feick, Guimarra's labor relations counsel, says the strike has had "very little impact" on the harvest and that there is no labor shortage.

He also says "there is some truth" to union claims that the

company is shipping grapes under the labels of other growers because of the boycott.

But this, he says, is only "a precautionary measure" for buyers who "might be apprehensive" about the boycott. It does not mean the boycott has been effective, he says.

Most informed sources believe that the union operation here, which, Mr. Chávez says, costs about $50,000 a month, will survive. But there is a question of whether it will grow into a national union, and of how long this will take.

Mr. Chávez asserts that about 8,000 members pay the $3.50 monthly dues for at least nine months a year, but that the union pays a per capita tax to the A.F.L.-C.I.O. on an annual membership of only 1,700.

He estimates it may take 10 years to build a self-sustaining union, with thousands of members who pay year-round dues from all around the nation.

Extensive Preparations

Much of the union success here is attributed to the three years Mr. Chávez spent in community organizing before the strike began. It led to a small health clinic, a gas station and a 600-member credit union, all of which are run by the National Farm Workers Service Center.

The absence of preliminary spadework has handicapped organizing efforts in Texas and Florida.

The Texas strike began more than a year ago when a California organizer went to Rio Grande City and called a walkout.

The Texas strike is in the harsh Rio Grande Valley, which now is being swept by floods. The growers, with the support of the Texas Rangers, were able to ship the key melon crop last spring without significant trouble.

The union organizers, faced with a hostile community, have fallen back to emphasize community organizing. But the going is slow, the outlook bleak.

The outlook is only a little brighter in Florida, where Walter P. Reuther's A.F.L.-C.I.O. Industrial Union Department tried last year to organize fruit and vegetable pickers around Belle Glade. But a lack of resources, poor organizing, and the absence of indigenous leadership led to disaster.

Last March Mr. Reuther called in the United Packinghouse Workers, which decided to follow the Chávez formula of tackling an industry dominated by big processors with brand names that could easily be boycotted.

Consequently, it moved the effort about 115 miles north to the citrus groves around Winter Haven, Fla.

Vernon Thomas, a 39-year-old Negro organizer, says service centers on the Chávez pattern have been set up to aid

the predominantly Negro farm force in Winter Haven and Tampa and that a third will be established in Orlando.

He indicates that the union hopes to strike a processor in early 1968 for a contract that could be used as a wedge against other processors and fresh fruit growers.

The growers are uniformly opposed to the organizers in Florida, Texas and California.

They argue that the unions are irresponsible civil action groups, that the workers are happy, that unionization would produce unbearably higher costs, and that farmers cannot tolerate unions because they are peculiarly vulnerable to a strike at harvest time.

Mr. Feick of Guimarra agrees, saying the Chávez group is not a "responsible" union but "a socialist-civil rights movement."

Furthermore, he says, Mr. Chávez has enlisted the aid of "do-gooder elements, beatniks and socialistic-type groups," and that "they don't represent regular Guimarra employes."

Martin J. Zaninovich, a Delano grape grower, says the employers do not make big profits, cannot afford higher labor costs, and fear that a union would interfere with management.

"I think any employer is going to resist unionization because then you're taking on a partner in the management of the business," he says.

"The people in the citrus industry don't feel they run a sweatshop, and feel they pay the pickers adequately," says Thomas W. Osborne of Florida Citrus Mutual, an association of 14,500 growers.

"The average grower wouldn't see any need for a union, and would think the worker would be better off without one," he declares.

The strategy for cracking the growers' opposition, and building a national farm worker union is a major issue in the feud between Mr. Reuther, president of the United Automobile Workers union, and George Meany, president of the A.F.L.-C.I.O.

The Meany forces want to score a major victory in Delano as a foundation for a broader effort. But the Reuther forces, while saying they want to keep fighting in Delano, are eager to push quickly into new areas with a big burst of spending.

The A.F.L.-C.I.O. is spending $10,000 a month, not counting extensive staff time, in Delano. The Industrial Union Department is spending $17,500 a month in Delano, Texas and Florida. Mr. Reuther's auto union is spending $7,500 a month in Florida and Delano.

Mr. Reuther contends this is far too little, and he has called for a commitment of nearly $5-million a year.

But the Meany forces believe such an expenditure would be wasted unless Congress amended the National Labor Relations Act and gave collective bargaining rights to farm workers.

Mr. Chávaz admits he is torn between the two ideas. He says money alone will not organize farm workers, and that he is committed to sticking in Delano until he wins.

But he also says he needs more money, and that he would like to respond to "a large and increasing demand for organization from many places around the country."

"It's getting to be a very large movement," he says. "But we find that although it is very healthy, we have to be very careful that we don't spread ourselves so thin that we can't win any place."

"The hell of it is that we can't intensify the strike [in Delano] because we don't have the money to do so," he says. "We have to do a great balancing act. If we overspend, we're out of the game."

What is really needed, he says, is legislation to give collective bargaining rights to farm workers. Otherwise, he says, "It's going to be one death struggle after another. The growers are going to hold out to the very end."

October 2, 1967

Associated Press

LONG STRIKE NEARS END: Cesar Chavez, seated left, and John Giumarra Jr., of grape growers, preparing to sign contract in Delano, Calif., yesterday. The Most Rev. Joseph F. Donnelly of Hartford and Jerome Cohen, lawyer for the union, are with them.

26 Grape Growers Sign Union Accord; Boycott Nears End

By STEVEN V. ROBERTS
Special to The New York Times

DELANO, Calif., July 29 — Farm workers and table grape growers signed an agreement in this dusty rural town today that both sides said would bring a "new day" to American agriculture.

The agreement signified that after decades of struggle, some of it violent, farm workers were now well on their way to securing the rights and benefits long enjoyed by other workmen.

Twenty-six grape growers, representing 35 per cent of the industry, signed contracts with the United Farm Workers Organizing Committee, the first successful union in the history of agriculture.

This meant that 65 per cent of the growers were now unionized. The rest, centered in the area around Fresno, are expected to sign shortly.

When those growers do sign, the union will end its nationwide boycott of nonunion grapes. "Then all grapes will be sweet grapes again," said Cesar Chavez, the union leader.

The ceremony today marked the turning point in the efforts of Mr. Chavez and the union to organize the poor migrants, most of them Mexican-Americans, who pick the nation's fruits and vegetables.

Almost five years ago, the union first struck the vineyards of this area of the vast San Joaquin Valley, 140 miles northeast of Los Angeles. But the strikers, hampered by the opposition of local law enforcement agencies and their own poverty, made little impact.

Two years later, Mr. Chavez turned his major effort to a boycott of grapes. Eating grapes became a great cause for liberals throughout the country, and it was ultimately their power that brought the growers to the bargaining table

"We said from the beginning that we were not going to abandon the fight, that we would stay with the struggle if it took a lifetime, and we meant it," said Mr. Chavez, a slight, soft-spoken former farm worker who became a national figure during the campaign.

"I think that gave hope to people around the country who were supporting us."

John Giumarra Jr., a spokesman for the growers, acknowledged the power of the boycott.

"It was seriously affecting the market," he said today. "We were concerned that it would actually destroy a number of farmers, particularly the smaller ones."

Today's ceremony was a victory, above all for the campesinos, the farm workers, who suffered tremendous economic hardships during the five-year strike.

Hundreds of them today crowded the union's new headquarters, whose walls were covered with banners reading "Poor Men, They Do Penance They Do Penance Daily" and "First, Relieve the Needy."

They crowded in, faces burnished by the sun, hands roughened by the earth, backs bent by endless days of toil And their eyes, their proud dark eyes, filled with tears of joy.

As they waited for the ceremony to begin, they sang the songs of "La Causa," as they call their movement. "Nosotros venceremos," they sang, "We shall overcome." And then they shouted, Viva la huelga," Viva the strike, the strike that is almost over.

This spirit of conciliation extended to the growers, rough-hewn men in open-necked sportshirts who looked rather ill at ease among the people they had fought for so long. Mr. Giumarra was applauded when he was introduced. He is a young man whose father and uncles started as fruit peddlers in Los Angeles and built one of the largest farms in the valley.

"We are starting a new relationship here," he said, "a relationship that's going to be a very important one. Our businesses and your jobs depend on it. We have to work together and respect each other and go forward for a better life for everyone."

The hostility toward the growers was not completely submerged, however. "You're learning," one farmworker muttered at Mr. Giumarra's speech. Another said, "The great white father speaks."

In his speech Mr. Chavez paid tribute to the idea of nonviolence.

"When we see so much violence in our midst," he said "this event justifies the belief of millions that through the theory of nonviolent action social justice can be gotten. We are proving this here every day."

Then the two men signed a contract calling for a wage of 1.80 an hour plus 20 cents for each box picked. Before the strike began, workers were receiving about $1.10 an hour, but in recent years union pressures moved wages up to $1.65 an hour.

Health Plan Gets Aid

In addition growers will contribute 10 cents an hour to the union's health plan and 2 cents for each box to an economic development project. The contract also includes stringent safety requirements on the use of pesticides.

The agreement was hammered out in two weeks of vigorous negotiations. As with previous contracts, in the industry, members of the Bishops Committee on farm labor helped to mediate between the two sides.

In a statement he read to the audience today, the Most Rev. Joseph F. Donnelly of Hartford, chairman of the committee, said:

"Still, this is really only a beginning. What is needed now is a thorough evaluation of the whole process of farm labor-management relations, spelling out the rights and duties of both sides. We need Federal legislation offering protection for both sides, but especially the farm worker, who has little or no protection as of now."

Even as the contracts were being signed, the union was getting involved in several other battles. Thirty farmers in the Salinas Valley, including such giants as the United Fruit Company and Purex, signed contracts earlier this week with the teamsters union.

The farm workers' union charged that they are "sweetheart" contracts, which do not call for any wage increase, and announced that it would file a suit against the teamsters.

Jerome Cohen, the farm union's lawyer, said that the teamsters did not represent the workers. Moreover, he said, the teamsters signed an agreement with Mr. Chavez several years ago, in which they promised not to organize farm workers.

"We will make it so miserable for those growers that they will have to do something," Mr. Chavez vowed. The Salinas farmers grow mainly lettuce, celery and strawberries.

While concentrating on table grapes in recent years, the farm workers union has also won contracts covering workers in such crops as melons, plums and peaches.

Farm Workers Accepted As Union by A.F.L.-C.I.O.

MIAMI BEACH, Fla., Feb. 21 George Meany announced today that the United Farm Workers Organizing Committee, headed by Cesar Chavez, had been accepted into the American Federation of Labor and Congress of Industrial Relations as a full-fledged union.

The farm workers, numbering some 30,000 members, have had the status of organizing committee for the last several years since first being formed.

Mr. Meany, the A.F.L.-C.I.O. president, said that the Chavez union would probably be renamed the United Farm Workers National Union.

Chavez Signs Florida's First Farm Pact

Special to The New York Times

MIAMI, Feb. 29—The first labor contract for migrant agricultural workers in Florida was signed today between Cesar Chavez's United Farmworkers of California and the Coca-Cola Company's Foods Division.

Announcing the signing of the three-year contract, Mr. Chavez said at a news conference here this morning that the agreement was a "precedent-breaking, important and tremendous" event.

"It will not only drastically change the lives of the 1,200 workers for whom we have been negotiating," he said, "but as in California, it will benefit all agricultural workers in the state."

Mr. Chavez said it was the first such agreement in the Southeast.

"It was accomplished without a strike or violence," Mr. Chavez said. He praised Coca-Cola officials as being "very enlightened and fair." "We hope that other companies will follow the lead of Coca-Cola," he added.

The Coca-Cola Foods Division markets Minute Maid orange juice.

The union, which established

Associated Press

Cesar Chavez, left, and Manuel Chavez, a cousin, at news session in Miami yesterday about the labor agreement.

itself in California and other Western states after years of sometimes bitter struggle, has gained an important foothold in Florida only six months after it started its organizational drive here.

The Coca-Cola contract covers full-time and seasonal employes working in orange groves in central and south Florida. The former will receive a 25-cent-an-hour increase, with the new hourly rate ranging from $2.25 to $3.70.

The harvesting piece rate paid to employes would increase 5 cents a box for most fruit. The average payment has been 35 cents a box.

Regular employes, who number about 300, will receive nine paid holidays annually, 10 paid sick days and two to four weeks of vacation. They would continue to receive life and medical insurance coverage, pensions and other benefits.

The benefit package for seasonal workers who work at least 100 days is approximately half of that of regular employes.

Minute Maid workers selected the United Farmworkers as their bargaining agent in December, and negotiations began in January. Mr. Chavez's organization received support from the American Federation of Labor and Congress of Industrial Organizations and the archdiocese of Miami.

Small food growers may be less likely to succumb to pressure.

In a statement issued today in Lakeland, Fla., Fred Atkinson, president of the Citrus Industrial Council, an organization of growers, termed the Cola-Cola contract "an individual action" by a conglomerate company.

Mr. Atkinson, who described the United Farmworkers as a "union with no roots in the area in which it is operating," said that he "doubted" that the contract would become a "guide-line for either the harvesting hands or harvesting companies."

Mr. Chavez said that his organizers were active in several agricultral areas of Florida.

"The problem is struggle or peace," Mr. Chavez said today. "We want to negotiate. We are not interested in strike, but we are here to stay. We are not going away, and I hope the companies will realize that."

March 1, 1972

HOSPITAL STRIKE ENDS IN 46TH DAY AS PACT IS VOTED

1,100 Union Members Roar 'Aye' to Plan Their Chief Calls a 'Partial Victory'

7 PICKET LINES HALTED

All 81 Voluntary Institutions Asked to Ratify Terms— Wide Acceptance Seen

By HOMER BIGART

Hospital strikers roared approval yesterday to an agreement ending the bitter forty-six-day strike at voluntary institutions.

Eleven hundred nurses' aides, cooks, orderlies, porters and housekeeping workers squeezed into the ballroom of the Diplomat Hotel and shouted "Aye" when proposals described as a "partial victory" were read to them. A loud but solitary "No" was also heard.

Leon J. Davis, president of the striking union, Local 1199 of the Retail Drug Employes Union, said that the agreement provided only "backdoor recognition" for his union. But he added: "We'll be in the front door before long."

Mayor Gets Statement

The agreement, arranged by Mayor Wagner after weeks of negotiation, was embodied in a statement of policy by the hospitals. John V. Connorton, president of the Greater New York Hospital Association, handed it to the Mayor late yesterday.

Mr. Connorton denied that the agreement provided for union recognition. Neither, he said, did it provide for a union structure within the hospitals.

The policy declaration will apply to those of the association's eighty-one member hospitals that ratify the document.

The seven hospitals that were struck were members of the association.

Mayor Wagner predicted that the majority would go along, since most of the association members had participated in the negotiations. He said he was "delighted" by the ending of the strike and hoped that the peace would last for years.

Decisions to Be Prompt

He said that he understood that the declaration would be considered promptly by the boards of all the voluntary hospitals. "Am I right, John?" he asked Mr. Connorton. Mr. Connorton nodded affirmatively.

The provisions for grievance machinery and wage reviews were couched in such terms that both Mr. Connorton and Mr. Davis appeared correct in their conflicting interpretations.

In the mediation of grievances, workers may be represented by anyone they designate. The union considers this "foot-in-the-door recognition" because there is nothing to prevent a worker from choosing a union official.

Wage levels would be reviewed annually by a twelve-man "permanent administrative committee" composed of six hospital trustees, to be named by the hospital association, and six public figures to be designated by the chief judge of the Court of Appeals.

The agreement calls for a minimum hourly wage of $1 an hour with a wage boost of at least $2 a week to every employe whose weekly wage is not increased by $2 through the lifting of the hourly rate. The struck hospitals put this wage rate into effect several weeks ago.

The hospitals promised not to discriminate against employes who joined or remained members of any union. They also promised to drop all legal action against the union except an appeal from a decision by Justice Henry Epstein in State Supreme Court.

Justice Epstein ruled on June 12 that the strike was a "bona fide labor dispute" and refused to punish the union's leaders for contempt of a no-strike injunction. He contended that voluntary hospitals were subject to a section of the Civil Practices Act that makes injunctions difficult to obtain.

Both sides agreed that an important matter of law was involved and that the appeal should be continued but with the understanding that no punishment would be sought by the hospitals.

Picket Lines Withdrawn

Picket lines were withdrawn from the hospitals yesterday and Mr. Davis said the strikers would start drifting back to their jobs today.

The hospitals are not obligated to take all of them back at once. But they have promised to reinstate them "as quickly as practical and feasible, unless guilty of violence."

Mount Sinai, the largest of the struck hospitals, said it would mail reinstatement cards to all workers who had not reported by 11 A. M. today except for thirty-five employes charged with violence.

The vote to end the strike came at a meeting that was relaxed and jubilant, with no more tension than a clambake.

Mr. Davis made no attempt to explain the fine points of the agreement, and other officials said that one point—the classification of nonprofessional employes—was still in dispute.

The hall was stifling. Men sat around in T-shirts, fanning themselves with newspapers. Many of the women brought their children and the din was terrific.

Mr. Davis cautioned the strikers, most of them Negroes and Puerto Ricans with no prior union experience: "Be patient. Don't create imaginary things. Don't make it more difficult. Don't be offensive. Don't be provocative. Act like organized workers."

After the vote, the strikers met in groups to elect their representatives. Mr. Davis said these representatives were, in effect, shop stewards although the term was offensive to the hospitals.

He also said that the six public members of the wage-review committee would be selected by the chief judge of the Court of Appeals from a slate nominated by the union. This statement was challenged by a hospital association spokesman who denied that such a procedure was part of the agreement.

Mr. Davis announced that the drug union was setting up an "independent" division for the hospital workers.

Meanwhile the hospital association approved its policy declaration at a general membership meeting. Then Mr. Connorton took it to the Mayor.

At City Hall Mr. Connorton said:

"Unpleasant as the strike has been for all concerned it will have accomplished a great deal for both the hospitals and their employes if it has dramatized to the public the urgent need for hospitals funds from increased Blue Cross income, from the city and from the public."

The city's first major hospital strike began May 8 at Mount Sinai, Lenox Hill, Beth David, Beth Israel, Bronx and Brooklyn Jewish Hospitals and spread June 5 to Flower and Fifth Avenue Hospital.

Union recognition was the key issue. As private, nonprofit institutions, the hospitals contended that they were exempt from provisions of the State Labor Relations Act and were not obliged to engage in collective bargaining with any union.

Their adamant refusal to recognize Local 1199 fanned a confused and intensely bitter labor dispute. The support and prestige of the entire labor movement in the city was committed to Local 1199. The struck hospitals were strongly backed by the Greater New York Hospital Association, which represents eighty-one voluntary institutions.

There were undertones, too, of racial tension. Most of the strikers were Negroes and Puerto Ricans. The charge of racial exploitation was raised by labor leaders, who said that the hospitals were taking unfair advantage of the pool of cheap labor from the slums.

Despite this explosive element, there was only one major outbreak of violence. It came June 9 when street fighting broke out between pickets and the police near Flower and Fifth Avenue Hospital. Seven pickets were arrested in the fifteen-minute clash.

On the same day, Mayor Wagner released a peace formula devised by his special three-man mediation board. This board consisted of William Hammatt Davis, chairman; Aaron Horvitz and Joseph P. McMurray.

Neither labor nor management was entirely happy with the Davis formula. But Mayor Wagner approved it as a basis for settlement and summoned both sides to all-night meetings in City Hall.

HOSPITAL ACCORD LIFTS PAY TO $100

2-Year Pact Covering 17 Institutions Expected to Raise Room Costs $20

By PETER MILLONES

Agreement was reached here yesterday on a two-year contract that will give 17,000 nurse's aides, kitchen workers, porters and other hospital employes a minimum weekly wage of $100.

The accord between Local 1199 of the Drug and Hospital Union and 17 private, nonprofit hospitals came at about 7 A.M. after a night of negotiations at City Hall and after six hospitals had been struck for about an hour.

The gains in wages and benefits — said by the hospitals to total 30.7 per cent over the two years of the contract — are expected to have these major effects:

¶The cost of room and board at the 17 hospitals, now $70 to $85 a day, will increase by about $20 a day, the hospitals predicted.

¶Other unionized workers at the remaining 82 private and municipal hospitals — and workers in related areas—are expected to seek comparable increases when their contracts expire.

¶Local 1199. jubilant over its gains, will move rapidly to attempt to add hospital workers in other cities to its 35,000 members in New York, New Jersey and Connecticut.

In addition to increasing the minimum salary to $100 from the present $76, the new contract gives those already earning $100 a general wage increase, in two steps, of $24 to $30. Workers earnings more than $150 will get two increases of 8 per cent.

Local 1199, which first organized hospital workers here in 1959, when their average wage was $32 a week, gained a pension plan for the first time. Employer payments of 5 per cent of the gross payroll to a pension fund will begin Jan. 1, 1970.

William J. Abelow, executive director and counsel for the League of Voluntary Hospitals and Homes, described the agreement as "extremely costly."

He said the prediction that room and board rates would increase by about $20 was only a prediction that awaited complete analysis of the contract by financial experts. He said that the figure included the likely "ripple" effect on the contracts of other hospital workers.

Leon J. Davis, president of Local 1199, said of the agreement: "We are very happy."

Mayor Lindsay, his eyes red from the all-night negotiations, told newsmen: "It is a fair and equitable settlement for all concerned."

Some union, hospital and city officials had been concerned that the contract dispute might develop into a strike with racial conflicts.

The union, with a membership that is 70 per cent Negro and Puerto Rican, quietly spread the word during negotiations that a strike might take the form of sit-ins, and the hospitals formulated plans on when they might want to call the police.

City officials were sensitive to this possibility, and some people close to the negotiations believe the union in its efforts.

The 17,000 workers covered by the agreement work at the 17 voluntary hospitals and also at six municipal hospitals that have affiliation agreements with the voluntary institutions. Other employes at the six municipal hospitals are covered by other contracts.

Another 17 private, nonprofit hospitals, whose contracts have expired and were negotiating separately with Local 1199 are expected to follow the pattern set by yesterday's agreement, union officials said.

Hospitals That Were Struck

The six hospitals that were struck briefly between 6 A.M. and 7 A.M. were Beth Israel Medical Center and Mount Sinai Hospital in Manhattan; Montefiore Hospital in the Bronx; and Maimonides Medical Center, Kingsbrook Jewish Medical Center and Jewish Hospital, all Brooklyn.

Picketing was brief and there was no trouble or interruption of patient care, the hospitals said.

The other private hospitals covered by yesterday's agreement are: the Hospital for Joint Diseases, Jewish Memorial Hospital, Trafalgar Hospital, Bronx Lebanon Hospital Center, Albert Einstein College of Medicine, Lutheran Medical Center, St. John's Hospital, Lenox Hill Hospital, Long Island Jewish Hospital, and Neustadter Convalescent Center in Yonkers.

The six affiliated municipal hospitals with some workers covered by the agreement are: Coney Island Hospital, City Hospital Center in Elmhurst, Queens, Gouverneur Ambulatory Care Unit, Greenpoint Hospital, Morrisania Hospital and Queens General Hospital.

No sooner had pickets appeared at the struck hospitals than Mayor Lindsay, who had summoned the negotiators and mediators to City Hall late Sunday night, announced to newsmen that an agreement had been reached.

Harry Van Arsdale, president of the New York City Central Labor Council, and Vincent Borella, a labor aide to Governor Rockefeller, also assisted in the talks.

The employes will also receive improved medical care benefits, additional pay for night work, improved holiday and vacation benefits and severance pay for the first time.

The hospitals have also agreed, according to the union, to pay 1 per cent of gross employes' wages into a fund to pay workers while they train for better jobs. This will take effect in the second year of the contract, and the union estimated the cost at $52-a-year for each worker.

An issue that the hospitals were very concerned about—managerial prerogatives—was turned over by both sides to Deputy Mayor Timothy W. Costello and Vincent D. McDonnell, chairman of the State Mediation Board, for future arbitration.

This issue involves such areas as subcontracting by the hospitals, seniority and promotions, and changes the hospitals feel will reduce costs and improve efficiency.

Automation

Automation Puts Industry on Eve of Fantastic Robot Era

Its Effect on Workers Spurs Unions' Drive for Annual Wage

By A. H. RASKIN

The electron is doing more to revolutionize American industry than atomic energy. Automation—the harnessing of electronic brains to mechanical muscles—is making normal concepts of mass production obsolete.

So fantastic are the potentialities of new control devices that it is possible to visualize acres of factory or office space in which no worker is needed. Automated equipment can process raw materials, assemble them into finished goods, package them and load them into freight cars without direct human help.

That is not all. The automated machines can adjust to variable productive conditions, correct their own mistakes, inspect the finished product and even change their own parts when parts break or wear out. Little wonder that some engineers estimate that 70 per cent of all the machine tools now in use are outmoded.

Already automation is being used to refine oil, make artillery shells, put together television sets, bake cakes, process chemicals, generate electric power, mail out insurance bills, put through transcontinental telephone calls and build automobile engines.

In the automated operations a few engineers and a maintenance crew are all the work force required. They spend most of their time watching the flashing lights and checking the dials on the control panels; the machine does the rest, even to letting them know when it needs human attention.

Automated machines do not stop with telling other machines what to do; they even "breed" new automated equipment. With magical new calculators, design data for huge mechanical installations can be completed in one-fortieth the time formerly required.

Vending machines are being used to sell some of the goods automation produces, but the human touch is still necessary to do most of the sales job, to say

Engineer adjusts parts of an experimental transistor computer built by International Business Machines. Automation, which implies continuous-flow production with a minimum of human labor, requires technicians who are highly skilled.

nothing of the buying. Even here automation has its foot in the door. Electronic tabulating equipment is being used to do the market research that tells a company where its customers are.

How Automation Works

The heart of automation is the feedback principle embodied in every home thermostat. When you set the thermostat for 70 degrees, you can rely on it to turn the furnace on when the temperature drops too low and to turn it off when the temperature rises too high. The same self-correcting technique is involved in automation, except that the number of variable factors controlled by the electronic brain is infinitely more complex. Once you give the brain its instructions through a punch card or a recording tape, it will carry

them out with inhuman precision.

No precise boundary can be drawn between automation and mass production, and it is doubtful that one method will ever completely replace the other. What is more, the cost of automating all sections of industry and adapting all products to automation would involve so many billions of dollars that the change is bound to be gradual.

But the pace of technological progress and the pressure of business competition on large and small enterprises make it more expensive for many companies to dawdle than to accommodate themselves to the new technology. Automation is a process of today as well as tomorrow.

It opens up vistas of unparalleled abundance and comfort; at the same time it stirs fears of mass unemployment and frustration. It promises a vast expansion in goods and services,

sharp reductions in prices and increased opportunity for the enjoyment of leisure. It makes the three-day week-end a realizable goal; it offers emancipation from the drudgery of routine, repetitive tasks.

Retraining Plan Urged

But with these prospective blessings comes concern that liberation from drudgery also will mean liberation from any regular paycheck for large numbers of workers. Unions are demanding that the Federal Government take the lead in working out a retraining and adjustment program to prevent widespread hardship from attending the dawn of the new industrial era.

This same concern provides a powerful spur to union campaigns for a guaranteed annual wage. By assuring a worker a full year's pay after he loses his job, the wage guarantee would help a man pay his bills while he sought another job at the work he knew or trained himself for a new type of employment.

Industry is not so sure such absolute assurance of income will work out to anyone's benefit. Employers contend that pay guarantees will discourage companies from putting new workers on the payroll, impose a crushing financial obligation on industry and check the speed of technological change-over.

The basic fears aroused by automation are not new. A century and a half ago the advent of the industrial revolution stirred European workers to such excesses of anxiety that they hurled wooden shoes into automatic looms and smashed newly installed machinery with sledge hammers. The battle of men against machines was carried to this country. It was a major factor in the rise of American unions.

However, experience has taught labor leaders two things. One is that it is impossible to stop technological advances; the other is that it is contrary to the best interests of the workers themselves even to try. Over the long haul, labor shares with all other groups in the community the advantages of improved productive methods. This has been the root of higher wages, shorter working hours and better living standards for American workers.

More Jobs Foreseen

More to the point, the forward march of productivity has had the effect of creating more jobs than it has wiped out. New industries and new products come into being; people with more money to spend reach out for new services, attend more adequately to their medical and pro-

Operator checks flow charts on an automatic control panel in the Sun Oil Company plant at Chester, Pa. Self-regulating control, or feed-back, is a basic principle of automation, which is notably successful in petroleum processing.

The New York Times (by Ernest Sisto)

fessional needs, provide more schooling for their children.

Union leaders do not question that this general process of long-term improvement in living standards and expansion in job opportunities will accompany automation. What worries them is what happens along the road to the new economy of abundance. They note that the steel industry is turning out a third more steel than it did a year ago with no increase in the number of workers. The automobile industry is doing much the same.

Government statistics at the end of last year indicated that all manufacturing industries were producing as much as they had a year earlier, even though the number of factory workers had dropped by nearly a million. For each man-hour of human labor the average factory turned out 7 per cent more in February of this year than in the same month of 1954. And all this with automation in its self-diapering infancy.

Population experts insist that this upsweep in productivity, going forward at double or triple the rate that has prevailed over the last half-century, comes at a happy time for the United States. Without it, they fear that the nation's problem will not be

too many workers for the jobs available, but too few.

They foresee a shortage in the next ten or twenty years of qualified workers — partly because the working population will reflect the abnormally low birth rate of the depression years of the Thirties, partly because people start working later and retire earlier and partly because the work week is likely to keep getting shorter.

Skilled Workers Needed

The National Manpower Council is convinced that the next few years will see a jump in the need for technicians and highly skilled workers, while unskilled workers find fewer and fewer places to work. The council warns that electricians would have to learn electronics and pipefitters hydraulics if they wanted to keep in step with science. Even a hand trucker must be able to interpret charts to discover where supplies are needed.

It is this increasing call for highly developed labor skills that has prompted Secretary of Labor James P. Mitchell to tell the country that its survival is menaced by the decline in work skills. Colleges and universities are giving increased attention to the requirements of the new in-

dustrial technology. This attention is not limited, however, to the need for more specialists in engineering and other specialized spheres.

It also extends to preparing men and women in the humanities so that they will be better equipped to guide our complex industrial society along a constructive course, to think through industrial problems and to make effective use of the leisure time that will be opened up in the next decade.

Even for technicians automation will bring some jolts. With robots giving orders to other robots and telling one another when they are wrong, the most skilled workers are likely to find themselves made superfluous by machines unless they have the adaptability to move to other and radically different assignments.

At the General Electric plant in Utica, for instance, automatic testing equipment was designed recently to check the reliability of military electronic devices. One girl with no technical training is able to run the new equipment. It took seven technicians with a high degree of specialization and fourteen semi-skilled workers to do the same testing job before. All were put to work on other tasks in the Utica plant.

More Work Created

But even in this instance automation proved that it could be a job-builder as well as a job-destroyer. The company is considering establishment of a new product line to turn out testing equipment that could be used by military forces in the field. Thus automation would open up a new area of employment at the same time that it provided increased security for our armed services.

President Eisenhower has made it plain that he sees nothing but good stemming from automation. He is convinced that an expanding economy will find work for those displaced by automatic machines. As the nation finds ways to do more work with fewer men, there always springs up more work to do. That is the President's view.

But he has instructed his economic advisers to keep an eye on the situation. If they decide that there are things to worry about, he has committed himself to the establishment of a Presidential commission to advise on means of smoothing out the rough spots. Everyone agrees that the future holds incalculable promise of economic betterment for all Americans. The question is: Can we get there without dislocation and suffering?

April 8, 1955

AUTOMATION STIRS A FEAR OF WASTE

Industry Worried Lest Gains of Machines Be Erased by Union Featherbedding

By A. H. RASKIN

Automation and other radical changes in industrial technology have given a new dimension to management's old worries about union-enforced make-work rules.

Industrialists are fearful that labor demands for the assignment of unneeded workers — a practice known as featherbedding — will put a brake on the installation of equipment that could materially cut production costs.

Union spokesmen ridicule these fears. They insist that labor welcomes improved technology, provided adequate guarantees are given that its benefits will be equitably shared among workers, employers and the consuming public.

Few Cases at Present

The harnessing of electronic brains to mechanical muscles is still too new to permit any definitive judgment on the validity of industry's fears. Thus far only a few cases have come to public attention of situations in which slowdowns, excessive manpower requirements or artificial restrictions on output have canceled the savings permitted by technological progress in manufacturing.

Complaints about featherbedding still stem in far greater volume from the fields in which such practices have been a headache for a half-century or more — railroads, printing and publishing, the building trades, trucking and the entertainment industry.

Some factory executives contend that stretch-the-work procedures have resulted in a holdback of at least 15 per cent in the over-all productivity of manufacturing enterprises. This figure is disputed by many management engineers.

Measuring what men can reasonably be expected to produce, consistent with health and safety, remains a process in which the area of disagreement among experts often exceeds the estimated holdback. Union time-study specialists note that the productivity of American factory workers runs well above that of workers operating identical machinery in most foreign countries.

Government officials are hopeful that two factors will minimize the danger that the gains to be derived from automation will be neutralized by demands that new machines be overmanned or that their productive pace be made too slow.

Gradual Transition Seen

One safeguard is that the transition from present factory methods to the much more automatic techniques made possible by the use of machines to run other machines will not become general on an overnight basis. This will allow time to retrain displaced workers and prevent any mass unemployment as a result of the shift.

The second favorable factor, in the estimation of Federal labor specialists, is the expectation that total opportunities for employment will remain high. The prospect that the long-range manpower problem will be one of shortage, rather than surplus, is counted as insurance against a "depression" psychology that would intensify pressure for inflating job requirements.

Secretary of Labor James P. Mitchell is among those who feel that featherbedding is unlikely to become a serious drag on productivity outside of the industries in which it has been prevalent for many years. He is convinced that an expanding economy and an increasingly limited labor force will put the future focus on ways to produce more goods with fewer men.

Charges that make-work policies already in effect are forcing up costs by many millions of dollars a year have been included in the flood of letters received by the Senate Select Committee on Improper Activities in the Labor and Management Field.

However, the committee's present feeling is that its time can be spent more usefully in exploring other abuses. Robert F. Kennedy, the group's chief counsel, says it intends to continue concentrating on irregularities in the internal administration of some unions and on collusive relations between labor and employers in some industries.

Teamster Abuse Cited

Even within this orbit, the committee's spotlight touches on occasional instances of featherbedding. Thus, in its inquiry into racketeering in the building trades in Scranton, Pa., the committee turned up evidence that a Texas manufacturer had paid two unionists $175 a week to obtain a waiver of a rule by the International Brotherhood of Teamsters that required a second driver on each truck when it came from other districts into the "territory" of the Scranton local.

In 1946 and 1947 Congress passed three bills designed to limit payroll padding of this type. One was the Hobbs Anti-Racketeering Act, aimed at the teamsters. Another was the Lea Act, intended to hit at James C. Petrillo and his American Federation of Musicians for compelling radio stations to hire more musicians than they could use.

The third was the Taft-Hartley Act, which contained a clause making it an unfair labor practice for a union to "cause or attempt to cause an employer to pay or deliver or agree to pay or deliver any money or other thing of value, in the nature of an exaction, for services which are not performed or not to be performed."

Many employers hoped the Taft-Hartley provision would free them from the necessity for continuing, on pain of strikes, to employ workers they did not need or want. However, this hope evaporated when the Supreme Court interpreted the clause for the first time in two decisions handed down on March 9, 1953.

One case involved the setting of "bogus" type in newspaper composing rooms, a practice that began soon after the Civil War. At the heart of the practice is the insistence of the International Typographical Union that local advertisements coming into newspaper plants in the form of electrotype plates or "mats" suitable for direct use must be reset, locked into forms, corrected and scrapped.

Wasteful But Legal

In a 6-to-3 ruling, the high court held that the practice was wasteful but legal. The majority declared that agreements between the union and the publishers had made the reproduction rule "a recognized idiosyncrasy of the trade and a customary feature of the wage structure and work schedule of newspaper printers."

The second case went even further in upholding the legality of made work. It resulted in court sanction for a demand by the Musicians Union that an Akron theatre hire a local orchestra as a condition to permitting a touring "name band" to appear.

With three justices again dissenting, the court ruled that it did not matter whether the theatre actually used the services of the local musicians, so long as they were ready to play and not merely seeking payment on a stand-by basis.

On the strength of these decisions, the anti-featherbed clause of the Taft-Hartley Act has become something of a dead letter. John J. Cuneo, regional counsel of the National Labor Relations Board, reports that few cases are filed under the section. Those that are submitted are usually withdrawn after the complainant has familiarized himself with the court's view of the law's scope.

The National Association of Manufacturers and the United States Chamber of Commerce favor amendment of the law to put teeth in its provision against featherbedding.

Action Not Likely

One suggested change is that the act make it an unfair labor practice to "cause an employer to pay for the hiring of workers who, in his judgment, are not required or for the performance of services which, in his judgment, need not be performed." Another employer-sponsored idea is that strikes to enforce featherbedding or other work restrictions be subject to injunctive relief.

Labor is hostile to both proposals. With Congress giving priority in labor matters to measures aimed at the eradication of union racketeering, little likelihood of action at this session is seen by Washington observers. This means that court aid against union pressure for unwanted services and unneeded employes will be available almost exclusively in cases involving threats of force or violence.

Of the industries that have been the traditional strongholds of restrictive work rules, only one offers even a faint chance that a basic overhaul of archaic practices may come in the measurable future.

This dim possibility exists in the railroads, the industry often credited with giving featherbedding its name. According to legend, the term started early in the century when a local representative of the trainmen on the Rock Island brought in a grievance about the mattresses put in the road's cabooses for freight crews to sleep on when trains were at terminals away from home.

When the union agent complained that the mattresses were filled with corn cobs, shucks and cottonseed hulls, the trainmaster retorted:

"What do you damned brakemen want—feather beds?"

Most of the grumbling about excess labor costs in the railroads stems from the survival of rules that had some justification many years ago when the "iron horse" chugged along at ten or fifteen miles an hour. Railroad engineers and firemen still receive a full day's pay for a 100-mile run. This is a standard capable of achievement in a little more than an hour in the cab of a high-speed diesel locomotive.

Payroll Losses Cited

The so-called "full crew" laws in force in fifteen states are blamed by rail management for much of the fat in their payrolls. In New York alone the carriers estimate that $6,000,000 a year is spent on wages and other benefits for men hired solely to meet the technical requirements of the state law. The railroad brotherhoods defend the statutes as a safety aid, but the companies say they are ready to pay a reward to anyone who can cite a case in which the extra men served any worth-while function.

Some wasteful practices have been frozen into operating costs through strike threats, some through mismanagement and some through decisions of the National Railroad Adjustment Board. This is an arbitration agency set up as part of the labor peace machinery of the Railway Labor Act.

Last year, on the recommendation of a Presidential emer-

NOT ALARMED: Secretary of Labor James P. Mitchell, who feels featherbedding is not likely to become a serious drag on productivity.

gency fact-finding panel, Robert O. Boyd, chairman of the National Mediation Board, proposed that a national commission be established by the carriers and the unions to make a thorough evaluation of the industry's work rules and wage structure.

The railroads indicated their willingness to participate in such a move to bring their pay and manpower practices up to date. The brotherhoods, preparing to enter contract negotiations, objected to the timing of the proposal.

This led Mr. Boyd to put the idea in cold storage until completion of the wage talks. The unions representing engineers and conductors are still in negotiation, but it is expected that a new effort to win joint agreement to the plan will be made soon after all contracts are signed.

In the meantime the railroads are counting on a recent decision of the Supreme Court as a bulwark against a worsening of the featherbedding problem. The ruling forbade the brotherhoods from calling strikes over issues awaiting action by the adjustment board.

The companies contend that such use of economic muscle has been a major element in driving up costs unjustifiably. The unions are less happy about the court decision. They say the roads will be able to stall for years on grievances by throwing all disputes into the overloaded machinery of the Federal board

Resistance to the introduction of new techniques and curbs on how much work individuals may do are perennial charges against labor in the building trades. The most scientific appraisal of these charges was made in a survey completed last year by two manpower experts at the University of Michigan, Prof. William Haber and Prof. Harold M. Levinson.

They found much evidence that the efficiency of construction workers had declined in the last quarter century. Their reports showed that the worst dip had come from the mid-Thirties to the end of World War II. In that period the loss in productive efficiency was put at 20 to 30 per cent. After the war, things began to improve, but the efficiency rate stayed 10 to 20 per cent under the pre-war base, the educators said.

The survey emphasized that no relation appeared to exist between the lowered efficiency and the presence or absence of union control over the supply of building mechanics. In cities where unions were weak, the efficiency record was substantially the same as in cities where the construction trades were dominated by well-entrenched unions.

Building Unions Cleared

The two economists criticized some union policies for swelling labor requirements unduly, but, in general, they found that the record of the building crafts in permitting the use of new methods and in avoiding any calculated restrictions on productivity was better than commonly believed.

Other analysts have been more severe in their castigation of building unions for "dragging their feet" on the erection of prefabricated buildings, for using spray guns and rollers in painting and for adopting other labor-saving processes.

The principal conclusion of the Haber-Levinson study was that the best hope for liberalizing union attitudes toward higher productivity lay in greater assurance of steady employment in an industry long characterized by "feast or famine" job patterns.

The number of men needed to monitor automatic machines is currently a source of conflict in the printing and publishing field. At the convention of the American Newspaper Publishers Association in this city last month, William Dwight of Holyoke, Mass., the organization's president, asserted that some unions had put hobbles on the full utilization of new mechanical processes.

Other leaders in the newspaper industry said that greater productivity with such devices as the Teletypesetter and the phototypesetter would create more and better jobs by reducing publication costs. However, they warned that such benefits could not be achieved if unions insisted on overburdening the new equipment with men or on restricting their use.

Printers Deny Stalling

Francis G. Barrett, president of New York Typographical Union, No. 6, denied that there was any reluctance on the part of his organization to see changed techniques introduced. He noted that the training school run by the union, in cooperation with the printing trades' employers and the Board of Education, already was teaching printers how to operate Teletypesetters and other new machines.

Mr. Barrett said the union's sole concern was that arrangements be made to guarantee that its members would gain, not suffer, from technological advances. Under the union's contract with the Publishers Association of New York City, no Teletypesetting equipment can be installed in newspaper offices here unless agreement has been reached with the union on the number of machines one journeyman can attend.

Disputes over this issue are not subject to arbitration. Industry spokesmen feel it is practical for one man to tend four machines. The union contends that two machines is the maximum feasible for a single monitor. Its contract with The Wall Street Journal calls for one man to each machine, Mr. Barrett said. The actual work of setting type is done by the machine itself on the basis of impulses supplied from a perforated tape.

The make-believe world of the theatre has always been a spawning ground for expensive make-work practices. Stagehands often earn more than actors, singers or dancers. Unneeded workers abound in television, radio, opera and every other branch of entertainment.

Musicians are still paid for doing nothing. In the Broadway production of "Major Barbara," records provide the incidental music, but four union members stand by. In the short-lived rendition of "The Greatest Man on Earth," a recorded version of "Taps" was played. A union bugler was paid for listening.

However, Broadway producers appear less wont to complain about featherbedding rules than they did a few years ago. The unions themselves seem more self-conscious about such practices. The relative plentifulness of employment opportunities in every field except music has appeased some of the hungrier elements in the payroll-padding fringe of the theatre.

Mass Production Problem

The real interest in featherbedding these days is over the extent to which it will retard automation in the mass-production industries. If union assurances are any guide, the holdback will be negligible. But many employers accept these declarations of goodwill with reserve.

The establishment of work

standards on an individual or group basis has always been a ticklish business in manufacturing. Such unions as the United Automobile Workers grew out of resistance to the "speed up." Even today, with long-term no-strike agreements between the union and the auto companies, the union still has the right to walk out if it cannot agree with management on how fast the assembly line is to run or how many units a worker is to turn out.

The contracts further affirm the doctrine that "to produce more with the same amount of human effort is a sound economic and social objective."

What many authorities in both labor and management foresee is a basic change in the nature of work that will make featherbedding a minimal factor in the operation of the automated factory.

The machine will set its own pace, and the chief function of the men at the control panels will be to guard against breakdowns. Emphasis will be on maintenance and the avoidance of costly "down" time.

William Gomberg, who resigned last year as director of the management engineering department of the International Ladies Garment Workers Union to become Professor of Industrial Engineering at Washington University in St. Louis, sums up the altered situation this way:

"The factory worker will become a watchman whose job will be comparable in concept to that of an airline pilot. The pilot gets paid well primarily because of the responsibility he must undertake in taking off and landing. The rest of the time the automatic pilot does most of the work.

"In the automated factory, the worker will be paid for the critical periods when he is needed to prevent damage to the machine. The cost in lost production of the periods when the machine is unable to operate will be the paramount consideration. The worker will be there as insurance against 'down' time."

Many management officials are confident that the transition will be handled with minimum friction in plants that start with a good company-union relationship. They note that in different plants of the same company, making identical products with virtually identical equipment, the volume of output tends to vary with the quality of the supervision and the cordiality of the in-plant atmosphere.

The official labor view, as set forth by James B. Carey, president of the International Union of Electrical Workers, is that automation will mean a wholly new approach to wage rates as they are determined by established job evaluation systems.

Wages will have to be paid to workers because they are on

duty rather than because of the physical or mental effort required by their assignments as nursemaids to the machine. Mr. Carey says payments to the entire work force in the establishment "must be maintained at a high level," whether or not the individual is directly involved in production.

Along with this he foresees such developments as a shorter work week, longer vacations, earlier retirement, or a combination of all three. It is in these areas, rather than in debates over manning tables, that the future battles are most likely to be fought.

Management Guilty, Too

One wry note has been injected recently into the old concern over work-stretching practices. It took the form of a report by a big nonprofit foundation that management seemed to be about as guilty of featherbedding as labor.

The American Institute of Management said 90 per cent of all companies seemed to suffer from featherbedding at the executive level. As examples the institute cited a bank merger that left four vice presidents without specific responsibilities, and the "kicking upstairs" of a sales manager who could not get along with other department heads in his company.

Despite manpower waste at the top and the bottom, the economy is still setting records in corporate profits and employe earnings. If fears of unemployment can be permanently set at rest, real progress may eventually be made in squeezing some of the water out of our job system. Twelve years of postwar prosperity have provided a start toward such reassurance.

COSTS OF OUTPUT CUT BY RESEARCH

New Techniques Streamline Operations—Companies Cite Huge Savings

By WILLIAM M. FREEMAN

A scientific way to cut costs and speed output is gaining greater acceptance among business men.

The technique is used to solve business problems being handled in a certain way because they always were or because the man at the top is positive that he has devised the best way possible.

The method is called operations research. Many companies that have tried it report dramatic successes.

George W. Chane of Ernst & Ernst, management consultants, commended the technique last week to two dozen company presidents and chairmen attending a five-day management course for top executives.

"Many business men have an obsolete view of what internal cost improvement really involves," he said. "They have an equally obsolete view of how great the benefits are.

"Modern programs include far more than good plant layout, sound organization and a specific plan for business growth. Well-integrated inventory and production control, for example, could very quickly increase machine utilization from 10 to 25 per cent in many instances and reduce in-process inventory from 10 to 40 per cent. And this is only one phase of modern cost control."

Mr. Chane, who spoke at the American Management Association's Academy of Advanced Management at Saranac Lake, N. Y., cited three instances of how operations research was combined with automation to lower internal costs:

An airline cut the time needed to get a new work shift on the job from thirty-five to five minutes

A wire and cable company was able for the first time to measure accurately the effectiveness of new inventory procedures.

A big music publisher was able to use automation to tackle the job of determining royalty payments to composers of music played on radio and television.

A recent conference at the Case Institute of Technology, Cleveland, reviewed operations research advances linked to computers and management decisions generally.

The installation of an integrated process control system at the Cummins Engine Company of Columbus, Ind., was studied at the conference. The new system for receiving and processing orders was found to eliminate many steps that had caused delay and extra expense. The older method required sixteen working days and the new system took five and a half. Major changes in making the original orders more complete and accurate were credited with the saving.

Reorganized methods of material and production control also were studied. These changes created a need for a central point at which data could be processed. An electronic digital computer was bought to control data on 20,000 out of 25,000 parts and to make decisions on reordering. This permitted more efficient production planning.

The entire process of control, from raw materials to finished parts and engines, was broken down into several well-defined steps. Formulas were computed that permitted more economical control of each step.

Another study reported on at Case was on the use of electronic computers in the railroad industry to speed the distribution of empty freight cars. The computers were called on to process information on the cars, which produce no profit when they are idle. It has been estimated that 10,000 empty boxcars a day, which is not uncommon on the larger roads, can cost a railroad $10,000,000 a year.

Dr. David B. Hertz, manager of operations research of Arthur Andersen & Co., accounting concern of this city, said the method was being used more and more widely by business men.

He made the comment in reporting findings of an American Management Association survey of how widely the technique was being used. As recently as 1951, he said, there was "virtually no recognition or understanding of industrial operations research by American management," whereas today it is making rapid advances.

Of 631 companies questioned by the association, 324, or 51.3 per cent, are using the method. Of 307 not using it, 144 indicated that they were considering it. Not one of the companies using operations research said they intended to discontinue it.

The association said that of the 288 companies that offered evaluations of their operations research programs, fifty-five said they had realized appreciable savings. Considerable improvement in operations was reported by seventy-five companies, and 167 said it was too early to tell.

Improvements were reported by aircraft companies, utilities and transportation concerns more often than by companies in other industry categories.

Survey participants also were asked whether they could identify dollar savings, actual or future or both, attributable to operations research activities. The number of answers to the question was too small to be significant, but some of the amounts were impressive.

Seventeen companies reported savings of more than $100,000, and five cited savings of more than $1,000,000. A chemical company and a petroleum concern each noted a saving of more than $2,000,000. Twenty-three companies looked for savings of more than $100,000 and eighteen expected to save more than $300,000. Five expected to save more than $1,000,000.

Some of the replies emphasized that the dollar savings were a small part of the gains.

ARMOUR PACTS AID AUTOMATION GAIN

Company, Under New Union Accords, Finances Study of How to Save Jobs

By A. H. RASKIN

A joint study plan set up by Armour & Co. and representatives of its 14,000 unionized employes to deal with the problems of automation is arousing wide interest among industry and labor officials.

The plan calls for establishment of a $500,000 fund, to be financed through company contributions of 1 cent for every 100 pounds of meat slaughtered or packed in Armour's twenty-seven plants.

A labor-management committee, functioning under the direction of an impartial chairman, will use the fund to develop retraining and relocation programs for workers whose jobs have been wiped out by new technological processes.

The novel arrangement is attracting extra attention because it was proposed by the company at a time when many managements are pressing for the reduction of union contract clauses rather than being receptive to additional ones.

Others Adopt Idea

Six smaller meat packers have already followed the Armour lead and adopted the fund idea, but two of the industry's giants, Swift & Co. and Wilson & Co., are resisting it.

The industry has been undergoing a drastic overhauling of its systems of production, processing, marketing and distribution as a result of new automated equipment. The trend has resulted in the closing of major plants in Chicago, St. Louis and other stockyard centers and in the scrapping of thousands of jobs.

The Armour plan was designed to provide an alternative to demands for a shorter work week or a guaranteed annual employment program as presented by the two dominant unions in the field, the United Packinghouse Workers and the Amalgamated Meat Cutters and Butcher Workmen. The plan was originated by William Wood Prince, the company's president, and Frederick R. Livingston, its special labor relations counsel.

Attitude of Unions

It involves a contractual recognition by the two unions that Armour's modernization program is "vital to its ability to compete and grow successfully, thus providing a reasonable return on capital invested in the enterprise and providing the assurance of continued employment for the employes under fair standards of wages, benefits and working conditions."

The joint announcement noted that jobs with the company depended on its success in making its products desirable to customers in terms both of quality and price. To ease the effects from the introduction of cost-cutting equipment the study committee is instructed to recommend means of promoting new employment opportunities within the company for those displaced.

One step to be considered is the appointment of a training director in each Armour plant to upgrade workers for duty on the more complex machines used in the new processes.

The whole program is supplemental to a severance pay system under which the company already has distributed $10,000,000 to workers affected by plant shutdowns.

Company Comment

A company spokesman said last night that the entire approach was based on an appreciation by both sides that automation created troublesome problems that had to be solved if the full potential of new technology was to be realized and its benefits shared equitably among stockholders, workers and consumers.

In addition to the automation fund, contracts signed last week by Armour and the two unions call for a full union shop and wage increases.

The meat unions, which had been feuding bitterly only a few months ago, grew so friendly during the Armour negotiations that they have arranged to prepare a union label to cover both. The company will have the right to use the label on its products. It is expected to aid Armour sales, since most clerks in retail butcher shops are members of the Amalgamated.

The two unions called a strike of 17,000 workers against Swift Friday. They have threatened a walkout of 6,500 Wilson workers Saturday. Federal mediators will meet with union and management representatives in Chicago today.

Labor:

IN A STEEL MILL—"Labor and industry must give priority to the public."

THE strike tensions that have developed in steel and other key industries are somber tokens that we are moving into a new era of bad feeling in labor-management relations. After six years of peace so enduring that only one day in every 400 of available work time was lost through strikes, tests of economic muscle are becoming the rule in many pivotal sections of industry.

The President's truce plea that prevented a blackout of the blast furnaces last week reflected White House anxiety over the need for ways to check the rising tide of hostility. It came after the longest strikes in the history of the rubber industry, protracted shutdowns of three huge farm-equipment manufacturers, the grounding of four big air fleets and a bargaining siege in the Big Three auto companies of such bitterness that Walter P. Reuther called it the toughest in his twenty years of union leadership. A crippling tie-up of the nation's railroads seems virtually certain next winter or spring, and the Government's industrial police and firefighters—the National Labor Relations Board and the Federal Mediation and Conciliation Service—are answering more alarms than ever.

What makes all these conflagrations on the economic front particularly significant is that the biggest of them seem to stem from something more than the conventional "battle over the buck." It would be no surprise, in a period of swift upturn after a business slump, to find the mastodons of industry and labor squabbling to the point of strike over how fat a wage package should be. But this year's combat is rooted in a basic reassessment of relationships that may have more dramatic consequences for the total community than any development since the New Deal gave unions their original charter for growth.

IT is the employers who are on the march this year, taking the offensive after a quarter-century of what they consider undue subservience to "monopolistic" unions and their political allies. In the front rank of management's embattled forces are the billion-dollar corporations which were among the first to make their peace with unionism in the mass-production industries.

A. H. RASKIN has specialized in labor coverage for The New York Times for many years.

A New 'Era Of Bad Feeling'?

The steel situation raises the question whether labor and industry must again meet head-on.

By A. H. RASKIN

Some of the harshest sentiments toward unions these days come from companies which only a few years ago were wholeheartedly embracing the doctrines of fraternity. Indeed, the regularity with which each partner in this improbable marriage gave the other a hand up with wage and price increases caused many officials in Congress and the White House to wonder whether even their spats were not part of a cynical routine in which the public wound up paying all the bills. Strikes often seemed less an expression of rancor than a cooperative effort by the "warring" parties to empty overstuffed warehouses and thus create an improved setting for higher prices, higher wages and higher employment.

NOW a compound of politics, economics, sociology and psychology has generated a fresh outcropping of ill-will. It is of lower voltage than that involved in the sit-down strikes or the picket-line battles of the Thirties, and much of it is more appropriate for exploration on a psychoanalyst's couch than at the bargaining table. But it is serious enough to make moderates on both sides fear that a large measure of our capacity for economic improvement will go down the drain if some formula for accommodation is not found.

Management's feeling that it is time for a change stems, in part, from the McClellan committee's disclosures of gangster influence and monopoly tactics in labor. The moral that most employer associations have drawn from the hearings is that unions have grown too strong and that legislation is needed to cut them down to size. But in last November's voting on "right to work" laws and candidates pledged to fight "power-hungry union bosses," the electorate showed little sympathy for the idea that the way to make unions better was to make them weaker.

Employers have turned to an issue that is seemingly closer to the average citizen's heart—and is certainly closer to his pocketbook. This is the impact of wages upon prices. Industry's battle cry is that union-enforced increases in labor costs have been the chief culprit in inflation. The bitterest pill for the big unions in the big industries is that their very bigness makes them peculiarly vulnerable to this hold-the-line argument in wage negotiations.

WHEN a single bargaining decision controls the pay of a half-million workers and the price of a commodity as basic as steel, every phase of the negotiations is conducted in a publicity spotlight almost as bright as that focused on a summit conference. President Eisenhower publicly warns that the country will not stand for a settlement that pushes prices up. Congress hints at price controls and tighter anti-trust laws. All this fortifies the employers' no-increase position in the face of union efforts to prove that profits and productivity are high enough to enable the industry to give more without getting more.

No similar inhibitions beset unions which negotiate on a local or regional basis in fields that may have an even more direct in-

Can collective bargaining avert a steel strike and picket lines like the one above?

fluence on the trend of living costs than does steel. Thus unions in construction, trucking, baking, food products and many other fields continue to ring up substantial pay rises with no public outcry. And their employers translate increased operating costs into higher prices, usually without having to account to any public agency for their contribution to inflation.

The feeling of many leaders of the mass industries that they have ridden the wage-price tandem to the last stop is reinforced by a belief that their investments in friendly union relations have not paid off in heightened plant efficiency. On the contrary, many top industrialists complain that they have ceased to be bosses in their own enterprises. They accuse unions of devoting most of their effort to protecting "incompetents," frustrating attempts to cut down operating costs through maximum output per man-hour and insisting on the retention of archaic work practices. Arrogant is their word for the labor leader.

THE aim of the corporate rebellion is to restore management's initiative at the bargaining table and in the plant. This determination to climb back into the driver's seat was emphasized by the industry bargainers in the pre-truce negotiations in steel. "You've been pushing us around for eighteen years and we're going to stop it," was the blunt way one of them put it in a session with the union chiefs.

Such displays of toughness are becoming increasingly fashionable in management circles. Indeed, company officials make little secret of their disdain for colleagues who fail to put up a sufficiently resolute battle against union negotiators. The United

Auto Workers got a taste of this when it concluded a two-month strike with one farm-equipment maker and prepared to begin contract talks with another. The head of the union committee told the second company that everything ought to be simple since a pattern already had been set by the first manufacturer, the biggest in the field.

"Oh, we won't be influenced by their pattern," was the quick reply. "They go into negotiations armed to the teeth and vowing that they will fight to the last drop of blood. Then, at the first approach of the union, comes the command: 'Ready, aim—abandon ship!' "

IT took an eleven-week strike of 13,600 workers, over issues so abstruse no one on either side could explain them adequately, before the second company signed. The basic terms were the same as those in the first agreement, and the first was itself a direct but acrimonious carryover of terms originally incorporated in the settlement between the Reuther union and the auto Big Three.

In the negotiating chamber, companies are borrowing the tactics that unions originated. Instead of letting the union carry the ball, the employers form a united front against any "divide and conquer" maneuver; decide in advance what concessions, if any, they are prepared to give and what concessions they hope to get from the union; then dig in at the bargaining table or on the receiving end of a picket line.

Lemuel R. Boulware, the General Electric vice president who is the spiritual godfather of the new technique, calls it an effort on management's part to decide what is best for workers, stockholders, distributors and consumers and

to do it without yielding to pressure. He says it represents an application in the labor relations field of the same "gumption, honor, forthrightness and good sense" that industry uses in marketing its products.

Union heads have a less flattering estimate of the new approach, which they have christened "Boulwareism." They consider it a take-it-or-leave-it formula intended to destroy unions by stripping them of any effective voice in bargaining.

AT a recent conference in Philadelphia, most of the top leaders of the A. F. L.-C. I. O. spent two days bemoaning the trend as indicative of a desire by giant corporations to provoke class warfare along Marxist lines. David J. McDonald, president of the United Steelworkers, even conjured up visions of "Cossacks" riding up and down the streets of steel towns dealing out death and destruction to the families of steel workers.

Behind the extravagance of such oratory lies a genuine concern about the shift in bargaining philosophy in the mass industries. The unions contend there is no evidence in the company profit reports or efficiency records to indicate that unionization has hurt the employers or the public. Labor insists that, with corporate earnings setting new records and with productivity on the upgrade, there is much to support its position that strong, secure unions play a positive role in improving employe morale, preventing wildcat strikes and stimulating the mass purchasing power needed to provide an expanding market for industry's products. All these contribute to checking inflation, not promoting it, labor says.

WHAT makes the employer initiative particularly disturbing to the unions is the ocean of woes with which they are already surrounded. The recession hit the giant industrial unions hard; hundred of thousands of their members suffered months of unemployment. Automation may cause an even more drastic long-term shrinkage in their membership and influence; organizing is at a virtual standstill; efforts to penetrate the South are meeting with increasingly violent resistance; the A. F. L.-C. I. O. is racked with internal feuds.

The inevitable remoteness of the heads of mass unions from their rank and file makes it hard to establish any real rapport on such problems as technological displacement, dues schedules or collective bargaining. Local unions have been showing a growing unwillingness to bow to directives from their internationals. Even in the best-run unions, rebellious rank-and-filers have told protesting officials of the parent organization to "go home." At General Electric last fall strike plans had to be scrapped ignominiously because of the manifest reluctance of the union members to walk out.

The rise of employe stock ownership (1,335,000 unionists now are listed as participants in this aspect of people's capitalism); the influence of seniority and pension programs in anchoring workers to particular companies; the advances in educational levels, home ownership and involvement in community agencies, the increased assertiveness of employers in developing avenues of direct communication with workers and their families—all these tend to create pulls toward the company and toward identification with middle class mores, rather than with labor as a separate entity.

Perhaps most disquieting of all in the considerations making for an upsurge in strikes is the fantastic productivity of our industrial machine and our inability to find markets here and abroad for all we can produce. Our steel mills can fill in nine or ten months all our annual requirements for domestic or export use. We are similarly over-endowed with capacity to make automobiles, washing machines, refrigerators, lamps, television sets, ships, railroad cars and a thousand other items for which there is need in an under-endowed world—but too few buyers.

THIS is the kind of problem that requires the collective and cooperative best judgment of government, industry and labor for solution, not the use of strikes as a periodic device for draining inventories and thus keeping prices artificially high. Otherwise, as the miracles of pushbutton production open the way to a limitless expansion of living standards for ourselves and the world, we will turn instead to the type of calculated lunacy we already follow in maintaining artificial farm prices.

How prepared are management and unions to undertake such a joint mission in arming the United States for its economic competition with the Communist bloc? Not at all, if one accepts the gloomy assessment of the current state of industrial relations that has come from one of the country's best qualified observers.

He is Boyd Leedom, chairman of the National Labor Relations Board, an Eisenhower appointee and, by his own boast, "never a New Dealer."

He describes himself as heartsick at the hardening of attitudes he finds in both camps. He reports that many employers overreach legality to thwart their workers' efforts to organize, even when the union involved is untouched by scandal. Some carry their rancor so far, he declares, as to believe that "there is no such thing as a decent union unless it might be one dominated by their own companies."

A look at the labor side does little to cheer him. He concedes that many business men have reason to be provoked at union goon tactics, corruption and the indiscriminate use of labor's economic muscle.

Fortunately, not all union-management relations are conducted at this primordial level. In many industries powerful companies and powerful unions are comporting themselves in a civilized fashion that pays dividends for workers, employers and consumers alike. John L. Lewis, who used to be regularly accused of killing "King Coal," is now acclaimed by the mine operators as the industry's savior for his encouragement of mechanization and other measures to make coal more competitive with oil and natural gas.

The industry associations in the needle trades look to the heads of their unions—David Dubinsky of the International Ladies Garment Workers Union, Jacob S. Potofsky of the Amalgamated Clothing Workers and Alex Rose of the United Hatters—as the architects of stability in what otherwise would be an industrial jungle. The hat union has plowed $6,000,000 into measures intended to spur hat sales, increase jobs and revive faltering enterprises.

The building trades unions and the major associations of contractors have set up joint machinery to war on wasteful construction practices. Similar mutual-help projects are under way in other sizable industries.

What is needed in the general collective bargaining field is a comparable search for yardsticks that will bring some science into the process. Bargaining should not be a process of dictation by one side or the other and it certainly should not be a mechanism through which both sides gorge themselves at the expense of the general welfare. Thus far both groups have displayed much more ingenuity in devising slogans to make what is good for them sound good for the country than they have in applying themselves to socially constructive solutions.

ONE hopeful road to peaceful relations already is being explored on a limited scale. It is the calling in by labor and management of private consultants like David L. Cole, one of the country's most distinguished arbitrators, to survey what is wrong with their joint dealings and to make recommendations for a more fruitful partnership. Such a detached stocktaking can do much to elevate the bargaining process into a vehicle for enriching the entire community.

Charles E. Wilson, during his presidency at General Motors, left a useful heritage in the form of the annual improvement factor he introduced into the wage agreements between his company and the U. A. W. This provides a regular increase of 2½ per cent each year in a worker's buying power as his

share in the long-term growth of the economy—a concept to which Wilson gave the happy name of "progress sharing."

IN the current reorientation of management thinking about bargaining, this plan has come in for sharp attack. Its elimination would remove almost the only scientific method now in widespread use for determining what is a reasonable pay increase.

From the union side have come proposals for a conference of leaders in industry, labor and public affairs to seek a more harmonious climate. But the collapse of George Meany's attempts to work out a nonaggression pact with the National Association of Manufacturers after he became head of the merged labor federation in 1955, and of the post-war labor-management conference called by President Truman do not encourage optimism about the chances for anything but self-serving talk.

The trial separation now in effect between important segments of labor and industry may help convince both that their future relations must give priority to the public interest. But no lasting stability can be achieved if either side arrogates to itself such Olympian wisdom that the other's views are excluded from meaningful consideration. For one bargaining team to feel that it is omniscient enough to balance all the conflicting claims of owners, employes and buyers with no help from the other, is hardly fitting in a society that would rather make its mistakes democratically than have all the crucial decisions made by any power élite.

STEEL STRIKE BEGINS, MILLS SHUT; LENGTHY WALKOUT IS PREDICTED; TALKS SET ON PRESIDENT'S PLEA

SESSION ON TODAY

Two Sides Will Meet Here With Finnegan —500,000 Affected

By A. H. RASKIN

A half-million steel workers struck at 12:01 A. M. today. The walkout cut off production of 85 per cent of the country's basic industrial metal and threatened to slow the upsurge of the economy from last year's crippling recession.

Peace talks initiated by President Eisenhower collapsed at 3:15 P. M. yesterday, with each side blaming the other for the shutdown. The President immediately ordered the Federal Mediation and Conciliation Service to seek a speedy termination of the walkout.

Leaders of the United Steel workers of America and the twelve biggest steel producers arranged to hold separate meetings this afternoon with Joseph F. Finnegan, the director of the service. But the total inability of the parties to make any headway toward a settlement in ten weeks of bargaining made it unlikely that the Government peacemaker could bring about a quick accord.

Longest Strike Feared

Top union and management officials expressed fear privately that the shutdown would prove the longest in the industry's history. This would mean a stoppage more protracted and

more costly than the eight-week walkout in 1952.

The pouring of steel halted at most mills hours before the first pickets appeared. The stoppage cast a shadow over the aluminum industry, faced with a July 31 strike deadline by the same steel union. It brought gloom to Pittsburgh, Youngstown, Birmingham and other steel centers, enjoying their first touch of prosperity after months of business decline.

The blackout of the blast furnaces will spread a pattern of paralysis over tens of thousands of workers in other industries. The first layoffs will come within forty-eight hours in railroads, coal mines, trucking, river barges and other enterprises that serve the idle mills.

Steel stockpiles will delay the pinch in factories and construction projects, thus deferring for at least a month or six weeks any necessity for a decision by the President on whether to obtain an eighty-day no-strike injunction under the national emergency provisions of the Taft-Hartley Act.

Ironically, the worst tie-up in any industry since the five-week steel strike of 1956 got under way as the Labor Department reported that the number of Americans holding jobs had reached an all-time peak of 67,342,000 last month.

The breakdown of the steel contract negotiations came as an anti-climax after a week of frenzied talks, spurred by repeated pressure from the White House. The union made a last-minute attempt to skirt the most explosive bargaining issue —the companies' insistence on increased management authority to eliminate restrictive local work rules.

The industry rejected the proposal and declared that the strike had actually been on since Saturday when the first

steps in the complex process of shutting the mills were taken.

R. Conrad Cooper, executive vice president of the United States Steel Corporation, did not rule out the possibility that the companies might consider reopening the mills if the strike proved a long one.

He said the industry had been giving all its thoughts in recent weeks to ways of avoiding a strike. Now, he said, the companies will turn their thoughts to other matters. He said he had "no speculation" on whether operations in the face of the strike would be among such matters.

Violence in Thirties

The companies have not attempted to make steel in any of the five national steel strikes that have been called since the end of World War II. Any "back-to-work" drive under company sponsorship would touch off picket-line violence of a type that has been unknown in the steel industry since the strikes of twenty years ago.

The stalemate in this year's negotiations was marked by indications of unusual bitterness. In recent years the steel industry has been a front-runner in evidence of labor-management amity, with leaders on both sides joining in goodwill tours of the mills and exchanging pledges of "mutual trusteeship."

No note of friendliness brightened the final statements issued by the parties last night. The union's 171-man wage policy committee accused the company bargainers of a new look intended to restore "the days of industrial dictatorship" and turn the union into "an empty shell."

The industry charged that the settlement terms proposed by the union would necessitate "a complete surrender of all of the economic and other principles for which we stand." The companies said it was a "mockery" for the union to pretend that it was not blocking efficiency or promoting inflation.

'No Contract, No Work'

Industry plans for a mutual-aid program of inter-company strike payments to defeat any "divide and conquer" strategy of union walkouts proved academic. The union spurned any selective strike pattern in favor of its traditional "no contract, no work" policy.

This meant a suspension of work in all unionized mills, except for those of three relatively small companies. These producers had signed agreements under which any wage increases ultimately put into effect by the big companies would be given retroactively to their employes.

The union did not budge from its refusal to consider any over-all extension of its contracts with the industry's Big Twelve. A two-week truce arranged by the President expired at midnight, and the union resisted all appeals to grant a further armistice.

The three companies that were exempted from the walkout by their expressions of willingness to promise that any pay benefits would be retroactive account for a combined production of 3,200,000 tons of steel a year. The companies were the Detroit Steel Corporation of Portsmouth, Ohio; Granite City Steel of Granite City, Ill., and Jessop Steel of Washington, Pa., and Owensboro, Ky.

Also unstruck were companies that have contracts with other unions or that are unorganized. The biggest of these are the Weirton Steel Company of Weirton, W. Va.; plants of Armco Steel in Butler, Pa., and Middletown, Ohio; the steel mill of the Ford Motor Company at its giant River Rouge plant and Wisconsin steel-making facilities of the International Harvester Corporation.

The fundamental position of the coordinating committee that spoke for the major steel producers in the pre-strike talks was that it was necessary to hold the line on both wages and prices this year. The companies contended that any rise in

Associated Press Wirephoto

AS DEADLINE NEARED: Steelworker at United States Steel Corporation mill at Braddock, Pa., taps open hearth furnace before it is cooled in anticipation of steel strike.

KAISER GIVES 22.5C AN HOUR IN STEEL PACT

CONTRACT SIGNED

Work Rules Issue Is Put to Labor and Industry Panel

By JOSEPH A. LOFTUS
Special to The New York Times.

WASHINGTON, Oct. 26—The Kaiser Steel Corporation and the United Steelworkers of America signed a new contract today. It cracked the united front of major steel companies.

The contract gives the union a package that is worth up to 22½ cents an hour in the next twenty months. The company said it was too early to talk about the effect the contract would have on steel prices.

The twelve major companies, headed by the United States Steel Corporation, have bargained with the union through a 104-day strike. The Kaiser strike, affecting about 7,500 employes at Fontana, Calif., was terminated.

[Kaiser immediately began recalling workers to fire up furnaces at its Fontana Mill, but it is expected to take three or four weeks for the plant to get back into full production.

[In Pittsburgh, other steel producers informed the union and Government officials that the Kaiser settlement had made them more determined than ever to hold out.]

Kaiser and the union said they regarded the agreement as "a non-inflationary settlement."

Terms of Agreement

These were the principal terms:

---

wages and fringe benefits would have to be counterbalanced by increased plant efficiency through modification of local work rules.

The union shaved its original list of 250 demands down to a package proposal for the same average increase it had received in each year of the old three-year agreements. This meant a basic rise of slightly more than 15 cents an hour each year, plus continuation of a cost-of-living escalator clause. The operation of this clause had added 17 cents an hour to steel wages since 1956.

The companies said the only basis on which they would retreat from their original call for a one-year wage freeze was through union agreement to a change in clauses that protected "featherbedding and loafing" in the plants. The union denied that any of the existing clauses blocked efficiency. It was the impasse over this issue of management rights that prevented any progress toward an economic settlement.

David J. McDonald, president of the union, called the entire campaign to change the local work practices "as phoney as a $7 bill." In an effort to bypass the issue, he proposed the inclusion in all company agreements of a clause declaring that the section on plant rules was not intended to "prevent the company from continuing to make progress."

The suggested language was already included in the union's contract with Bethlehem Steel, second largest producer in the industry and one of the chief advocates of increased industry power to get rid of wasteful practices.

The industry asserted that the proposal for inclusion of the same words in all pacts would not bring any progress toward more efficient use of existing facilities. The companies conceded that the union did not oppose improvements resulting from automation or other costly technological developments.

Where the union was derelict, the industry contended, was in resisting progress toward greater efficiency where equipment remained the same but where change could be made by the "adoption of different methods, reassignment of duties and elimination of unjustifiable idle time."

This brought from Mr. McDonald a declaration that it was "simply inconceivable to the union that a local working

condition such as the great American custom of a 'coffee break' is preventing a settlement." It was on this note that the talks collapsed.

Mr. McDonald told the wage policy committee, which had been standing by since Monday, that the union had given the negotiations "the all-American try" but that the industry had been determined to provoke a shutdown. He said he would have been written off by the entire labor movement as "a real, complete sell-out artist" if he had agreed to the industry's terms.

Ready for Talks

After President Eisenhower had declared in Washington his disappointment at the failure of the contract talks, both sides communicated with Mr. Finnegan and assured the Federal mediation chief of their readiness to meet with him.

Mr. Finnegan will meet with the industry's four-man team at 4 P. M. at the Park Lane Hotel and with the union's team an hour and a half later at the Roosevelt Hotel.

Mr. McDonald left the Roosevelt at 8 P. M. to drive to Morrisville, Pa., to address workers coming out of the Fairless Works of United States Steel.

July 15, 1959

393

¶In the first year, which has been whittled down to about eight months by the strike, wage rates will not be increased but take-home pay will rise as the company takes over the payments that employes have been making on group insurance. Improvements in pensions and supplementary unemployment benefits will make the first-year cost of the package about 10 cents an hour.

¶In the second year, beginning July 1, 1960, wage rates will rise 7 cents an hour. A cost-of-living rise, if warranted, will add a maximum of 3 cents. The impact of these increases on incentive pay, a widening of the spread between job rate classifications, and minor fringe costs, will raise the cost of the second year package to about 12½ cents. Pre-strike earnings of the steel workers averaged $3.10 an hour.

¶The work-rules issue was referred to a labor-management committee with authority to resolve shop problems on the spot. This issue and the wage package had been the two major blocks to an agreement. The companies had been insisting on more freedom to change shop practices without consultation with the union.

¶A committee was set up to develop a long-range plan for the "equitable sharing of economic progress." The committee will include three outside experts. They will attempt to find a formula by July 1 so that by mutual agreement it may be substituted for the second-year terms of the contract.

Edgar F. Kaiser, board chairman of Kaiser Steel Corporation, said the impact of the contract on prices "depends on how successful we are in working with this committee [on the work rules] and on the long-range committee."

Mr. Kaiser said he regarded the long-range committee as the most important provision in the contract.

In terms of any added stimulus to inflation, the package does not contain quite as much new money as the total implies at first glance.

In the first place, the union traded its claim on a cost-of-living increase in the first year. An extension of the old escalator clause would give the union a rise of 3 cents an hour now.

Secondly, 3 cents of the 22½-cent total is payable in the second year only if living costs warrant it.

On the other hand, the employes will receive more than at first appears because of the effect of taxes. They had been paying income taxes on total earnings before withholding of the insurance payment. Now they will get their full earnings —the equivalent of a pay rise— without the increased income tax that normally would accompany a wage rate increase of the equivalent amount. There is no tax on the payments made by the company toward the insurance costs.

David J. McDonald, president of the steelworkers, in a joint news conference with Mr. Kaiser, and his associates, said:

"We hereby invite all other steel companies which are shut down to come forward immediately, sign this agreement and put 500,000 steel workers back at their jobs."

The Kaiser company is the ninth largest producer and accounts for about 2 per cent of the country's steel tonnage. Nearly 15 per cent of the country's capacity has been operating through the strike. Some of the mills are non-union, others have been operating under special contract extensions.

Mr. Kaiser was asked whether the cost of the contract to the Kaiser corporation was the same as it would be for other steel companies.

"I don't think I could answer for the other steel companies," he replied. He added, however, that "we question whether there has been as much difference" in costs as the other companies have claimed.

Two weeks ago the steel industry's chief bargainer, R. Conrad Cooper, put a 32-cent price on a package estimated by the union to be worth little more than 20 cents. That package was approximately the one signed by Mr. Kaiser today and estimated by him at 19½ cents without the cost-of-living item.

The joint announcement was made in the sub-lobby banquet room of the Sheraton Carlton Hotel after day-long meetings.

The work-rules problem is not an outgrowth of the new technology called automation. The old contract deals with automation satisfactorily to both sides. Where the basis of an operation is changed by the introduction of new equipment the company has the unilateral right to change the shop practices.

Other rules—such as the size of a crew required to perform a certain operation, unrelated to automation—are at issue. The companies have not identified the practices they would change if the contract authorized them to act unilaterally.

October 27, 1959

SUPREME COURT, 8 TO 1, UPHOLDS 80-DAY STEEL STRIKE INJUNCTION; FIRST WORKERS RETURN TO MILLS

DOUGLAS DISSENTS

He Doubts Necessity for Requiring All to End Walkout

By ANTHONY LEWIS
Special to The New York Times.

WASHINGTON, Nov. 7—The Supreme Court called a halt to the nation-wide steel strike today with a decision upholding a Taft-Hartley Act injunction against the walkout.

The vote was 8 to 1. The majority upheld the constitutionality of the Taft-Hartley emergency procedure and its application to the steel strike.

As a result, 500,000 workers on strike at eleven major producers, which turn out about 85 per cent of the nation's steel, will be forced to go back to work for eighty days.

The sole dissenter was Justice William O. Douglas, who would have sent the case back to the trial court to make the Government prove why it needed the whole industry instead of just a few plants re-opened for defense needs.

Union Acts Quickly

David J. McDonald, president of the United Steelworkers of America, said the union would comply with the injunction. He sent telegrams ordering union members "to resume work forthwith."

Just how quickly the mills will get back to production is uncertain. It takes days, in some cases weeks, to get the blast furnaces working again. Thus it may be some time before all the strikers are called back by the companies.

The strike was called to a halt on its 116th day. It was the longest nation-wide steel strike in the country's history.

The Government had moved for an injunction about three weeks ago. The Federal District Court in Pittsburgh issued the order, but its effect had been stayed during appeal.

Effective Immediately

The stay ended when the Supreme Court handed down its decision. At the Government's request, the court made its formal mandate effective immediately, instead of waiting for notification to go through the mails to the District Court in Pittsburgh.

Under the Taft-Hartley emergency provisions, the injunction is now good for a maximum of eighty days, counting today as the first day. The union is then free to strike again.

Sixty days from today, if the contract dispute is not settled, the Board of Inquiry appointed by President Eisenhower reports to him again on the position of the parties, including management's last offer. The board is headed by Dr. George W. Taylor of Pennsylvania.

During the following fifteen days the National Labor Relations Board must conduct a vote among the employes on the companies' last offer. In the twelve-year history of the Taft-Hartley Act no vote on a last offer has been favorable.

If the offer is rejected, the Attorney General must move within five days to end the injunction. If the strike resumes, it would be up to Congress to authorize any further Government action. The eighty days will end Jan. 26; Congress returns Jan. 6.

The law requires both sides to continue negotiating during the injunction.

The Director of the Federal Mediation and Conciliation Service, Joseph F. Finnegan, said he hoped to announce Monday when the next sessions would be held. Some sources thought bargaining might be postponed for some time because union and management will be preoccupied with reopening the plants.

Old Contract Prevails

Union members will go back to work under their old contract, under which wages average $3.10 an hour. A union demand for payment of any eventual wage increases retroactive to today will undoubtedly be an issue in the negotiations.

Arthur J. Goldberg, counsel for the union, was naturally disappointed in the outcome of the case. He said:

"The only appeal from the Supreme Court is an appeal to God."

The White House press secretary, James C. Hagerty, said President Eisenhower hoped that steel production would resume as soon as possible and that the parties would continue to negotiate and settle their differences.

The Supreme Court did not follow its usual custom of holding a formal session in the courtroom to announce the decision. Copies of the opinions

were passed out in the press room just after 9 A. M.

The majority opinion was a per curiam—an unsigned opinion for the whole court. Justices Felix Frankfurter and John Marshall Harlan noted at the end that they joined in the per curiam but intended to file "an amplification of our views" when time permitted.

The opinion dealt briefly and bluntly with each of the three main arguments made in the court last Tuesday by the union.

The first contention was that the District Court, even if satisfied that an injunction could be issued under the Taft-Hartley Law, should have withheld an injunction in this case because of a number of considerations.

Judicial Inquiries Opposed

One consideration advanced by the union was that the President could have taken other steps instead of seeking an injunction. Another was that an injunction might delay settlement by collective bargaining—the ground of the dissent by Judge William H. Hastie when the Third Circuit Court of Appeals affirmed the injunction, 2 to 1.

"We do not believe," the Supreme Court majority said today, "that Congress in passing the statute intended that the issuance of injunctions should depend upon judicial inquiries of this nature.

"Congress was not concerned with the merits of the parties' positions or the conduct of their negotiations. Its basic purpose seems to have been to see that vital production should be resumed or continued for a time while further efforts were made to settle the dispute."

The opinion went on to say that Congress had determined "the policy factors involved in the difficult problem of national emergency strikes." This determination, it added, "is of course binding on the courts."

Mr. Goldberg's second argument was that the Government had not proved, as required by the Taft-Hartley Law, that the strike, if continued, would "imperil the national health or safety."

As for "health," he said this word referred only to the physical health of the population, not to economic well-being. The Government, through Solicitor General J. Lee Rankin, scoffed at this narrow definition.

The majority today did not resolve this issue. It found no need to define "national health" because, it said, the injunction was justified in any event in terms of "safety."

The Government had said the country's safety was threatened because defense projects were being halted. To this the union replied that only 1 per cent of steel production went for defense, that non-struck plants were turning out 15 per cent of

normal production and that any effects on defense could be met by reopening only a few selected mills instead of all.

But the court said it could not construe the statute "to require that the United States either formulate a reorganization of the affected industry to satisfy its defense needs without the complete reopening of closed facilities, or demonstrate in court the unfeasibility of such a reorganization."

It went on:

"There is no room in the statute for this requirement which the petitioner seeks to impose on the Government."

Finally, the majority tersely rejected the union argument that the emergency provisions in the Taft-Hartley law were unconstitutional because they put nonjudicial duties on the courts. The opinion said the emergency in injunctive procedure was in keeping with the exercise of judicial power.

The decision thus settled whatever doubts there may have been about the constitutionality of the eighty-day injunction. It was the first Supreme Court ruling on the emergency provision since the enactment of the Taft-Hartley law in 1947.

Douglas' Reasoning

Justice Douglas, in his dis-

sent, did not reach the constitutional question.

He began by agreeing with Mr. Goldberg's narrow definition of "national health." He said Congress, when it used those words, "was safeguarding the heating of homes, the delivery of milk, the protection of hospitals and the like."

Surveying the legislative history, the dissent noted that Congress had dropped the word "interest," contained in the House bill. It said the Congressional debate had focused on strikes in the coal industry, "closely identified with physical health of people."

As for "safety", Justice Douglas said there was no way of knowing what was needed for defense because the Government had never produced the detailed facts.

"Will a selective re-opening of a few mills be adequate to meet defense needs?" he asked. "What mills are these? Would it be practical to re-open them solely for defense purposes or would they have to be reopened for all civilian purposes as well?

"This seems to me to be the type of inquiry that is necessary before a decree can be entered that will safeguard the rights of all the parties."

Justice Douglas emphasized the traditional flexibility of equity courts—those which issue injunctions—in fashioning their orders. He said there was

Associated Press Wirephoto

STEEL WORKER RESTOCKS LARDER: Joe Dudas, in Pittsburgh, with groceries he and his family bought yesterday, when Supreme Court ordered strikers back to jobs.

nothing to show that Congress had eliminated that judicial discretion in the Taft-Hartley emergency section.

"We cannot lightly assume," he said, "that Congress intended to make the Federal judiciary a rubber stamp for the President."

"If the Federal court is to be merely an automaton stamping the papers an Attorney General presents, the judicial function rises to no higher level than an I. B. M. machine," he said. "Those who grew up with equity and know its great history should never tolerate that mechanical conception.

"Equity decrees are not like the packaged goods this machine age produces. They are uniform only in that they seek to do equity in a given case."

More Details Urged

Justice Douglas made clear his view that ending the entire strike because of defense needs was prejudicial to the union side of the bargaining table.

"I cannot believe," he said, "that Congress intended the Federal courts to issue injunctions that bludgeon all workers merely because the labor of a few of them is needed in the interests of 'national safety.'"

Justice Douglas' conclusion was that the case should be sent back to the District Court for "particularized findings" as to how the strike imperils national safety and what plants actually had to be reopened.

The New York Times (by Meyer Liebowitz)

CLEARING A PATH FOR PRODUCTION: An employe at Fairless Works in Morrisville, Pa., removes seal from a blast furnace tap hole through which iron will flow.

November 8, 1959

STEEL SETTLEMENT IS REACHED; UNION VICTOR; PRICE RISE SEEN

ALL-NIGHT SESSION

Work Practices Issue Shelved—Cost Put at 41c an Hour

By JOSEPH A. LOFTUS
Special to The New York Times.

WASHINGTON, Jan. 4 — A historic labor - management struggle in steel ended today with a major victory for the United Steelworkers of America.

An agreement was announced shortly after 9 A. M. following an all-day and all-night bargaining session between the union and eleven major steel companies.

Industry calculations put the cost of the agreement as high as 41 cents an hour over thirty months, from last Jan. 1 to July 1, 1962.

The troublesome problem of local work practices was referred to committees for recommendations.

Secretary of Labor James P. Mitchell, who participated in the night-long session, announced the agreement.

"It is my belief the steel companies will not need to increase prices immediately," he said. "I can't forecast the future because a great many things go into prices other than wages."

Terms Recommended

The settlement was on terms recommended by Vice President Nixon and Secretary Mitchell. They had held eight or ten meetings with both sides in the last four weeks.

Actually, while the Vice President brought no "plan" to the negotiations he did recommend settlement on the basis of proposals that were evolved.

Secretary Mitchell had managed to scrape some of the stubble from his face before appearing at the early morning news conference. He managed a grin, too, but the effects of two nights without sleep were evident.

R. Conrad Cooper, chief spokesman for management negotiators, showed some of the same effects. The union's president, David J. McDonald, who

396

had not been up all night like the others, appeared refreshed. The union had been represented by a staff headed by Arthur J. Goldberg, general counsel.

It was a noisy, crowded scene in the banquet room of the Sheraton-Carlton Hotel, diagonally opposite the Solar Building, where the negotiations had been conducted in the offices of the Bethlehem Steel Company.

The negotiations for a new contract began last April. The union struck on July 15, and the men stayed out for 116 days. They went back to work after the Supreme Court sustained on Nov. 7 an injunction under Taft-Hartley Act that would have run until Jan. 26. In the meantime, they were scheduled to vote on Jan. 11-13 on whether they would accept the company's last offer.

In today's settlement the union won almost everything it had been demanding in recent months. The industry retreated on most of its demands. It was evident in retrospect that the industry could have settled more cheaply last fall.

Like Kaiser Agreement

Essentially, the agreement is like the one that the Kaiser Steel Corporation made with the union in October, with two qualifications. Costs to the steel industry for the same items will be higher than they are for Kaiser; the industry agreement is for thirty months, the Kaiser agreement for twenty.

Costs for identical items vary from company to company, depending on the composition of the work force. Pension costs, for example, run higher for an older work force.

Unofficially, the main terms of the steel agreement are:

¶The companies will pick up immediately the employes' share of the insurance costs, and insurance coverage will be increased. That means the employes' take-home pay will go up immediately, from 6 to 9 cents an hour, as these withholdings cease.

¶Wage rates will rise a minimum of 7 cents an hour on Dec. 1, 1960, and again on Oct. 1, 1961. Wages now average $3.10 an hour.

No Adjustment Now

The union agreed to a proposal on insurance costs that offsets to some extent the employes' cost-of-living protection as it continues in the new contract. That is, the employes will receive no cost-of-living adjustment now.

A simple extension of the old contract would have given

them 4 cents an hour. The union traded that and the next 3 cents that might be due them hereafter for the average 7 cents the companies are contributing on the total cost of insurance.

Hence, the cost-of-living escalator will not pay anything to the employes until after the 7-cent mark has been passed. Even then, a rise in insurance costs to the companies may further offset cost-of-living adjustments that would otherwise be due the employe.

A further limitation on cost-of-living payments to the employes is a 6-cent ceiling for the thirty-month period.

The cost-of-living clause represented the union's principal concession. When the 1956 contract was made, the industry bet on stable prices. Instead, it had to raise wages 17 cents over the three-year period to compensate for rises in the Government's Consumer Price index.

The new contract puts more concern about a rise in consumer prices on the union and its members. The employers' liability is protected.

The two 7-cent wage increases over the life of the contract are minimum increases that go to the lowest of thirty pay-rate classifications. There is in addition an increment of two-tenths of a cent to maintain the spacing of differentials between each pay group. That is, the second lowest wage group would get 7.2 cents, the third lowest, 7.4 cents, and so on.

The pension clause provides for a lump sum payment of $1,400 to $1,500 on retirement.

Insurance costs can only be estimated, but the companies have to make certain assumptions on the basis of available data.

Total costs are then translated into terms of cents-an-hour. The companies have not made public their breakdown of the costs of these items, but their total, not counting cost-of-living, is expected to show 39 to 41 cents an hour.

On Working Conditions

The companies clearly lost their big fight for a change in Section 2B, the local working conditions clause. They had charged that this was a hindrance in changing work practices, such as wash-up time and crew sizes. The companies have a right to make any changes when they change the base of the operation, such as machanizing, but arbitrary changes in established practices have been resisted successfully by the union in many cases.

The agreement provides for a joint committee, headed by a neutral chairman, to study the local working conditions provisions and their application and

to make recommendations by Nov. 30, 1960. The agreement provides only "for such action as the parties may mutually agree upon."

The union won its point on supplemental unemployment benefits, requiring the companies to restore to the record books millions of dollars in contingent liability and carrying this over into the new contract period. This is not cash but a liability that the employers may or may not be required to finance, depending on the unemployment burdens of the next three years.

Supplemental unemployment benefits are an employer-financed plan to supplement state unemployment insurance payments. The employer payments to the fund in behalf of each employe are based on the employe's service record.

The pressures on the companies were a welter of economic and political factors. The 4-cent cost-of-living item was a big element in the showdown.

This 4 cents was the amount due the employes by a simple extension of the old contract during the Taft-Hartley injunction that became effective Nov. 7. The Federal Court in Pittsburgh, however, reserved decision on that point when it issued the injunction.

Argument on that item had been set before the court for this morning. The union's chances of getting the 4 cents had been generally considered good.

Therefore, the companies were bargaining last night with a package that included that 4 cents, but in a matter of days they might have had to give up that 4 cents involuntarily. The union then could go back to bargaining for a rate base 4 cents higher than it was last night.

A Plane Stood By

The union's counsel, Mr. Goldberg, impressed on the management team that he was prepared to make his case in court this morning if there was no agreement. A chartered plane was kept standing by to make the point clear to the industry negotiators.

Vice President Nixon and Secretary Mitchell had also impressed on the companies the prospect that their "last offer" would be overwhelmingly rejected by the employes when they voted on Jan. 11-13. The Taft-Hartley Act procedure provides for a Government poll of employes on their employer's "last offer" of terms for an agreement.

The companies' "last offer," as filed with the President's Board of Inquiry last week, provided for benefits at a cost estimated by them to be more

than 30 cents an hour. That offer also provided for binding arbitration on the local work practices issue.

It may still be necessary to take that vote in a few places. The settlement early today covered only eleven of the ninety-five steel companies that had unsettled bargaining relationships with the union.

Unless the other companies reach their separate agreements in the meantime, the Government may have to go through with a statutory poll of the employes of these companies.

A Risk in Congress

Mr. Nixon and Mr. Mitchell also talked to the companies about the risks of throwing the issue into Congress, which would surely happen if there was no agreement by Jan. 26, when the Taft-Hartley injunction, would expire. A resumption of the 116-day strike would have been legal at that time.

The Administration, of course, had something at stake politically. Democratic leaders in Congress could be expected to make political capital of a failure by the Republican executive leaders to bring peace to the steel industry.

Secretary Mitchell said tonight that what had started as a "not-too-popular strike" among the steel workers themselves last July became a popular, solid movement after the companies had made their demand for changes in the local work practices clause and the union leadership had "translated it into a threat."

The Secretary said that while he and the Vice President had sought the basis for recommendations in a series of meetings with both sides, it was not proposed that these recommendations be made public. Such persuasion, or pressure, as was used was to stay within the confines of the conferences.

Secretary Mitchell, who had not been in bed since Saturday morning, told reporters late this afternoon that it seemed to him at the moment that the negotiations had taken a hundred years. He did not think the settlement could have been brought off any sooner, he said, because "it needed the passage of time, the crisis and the pressures."

So far as he is concerned personally, no recommendations will be made to Congress this year for changes in the emergency strike provisions of the Taft-Hartley law. He said that the problem required a great deal of serious study, aside from politics, and that 1960, a Presidential year, was not the time for a labor-management conflict over major legislation.

Chronology of Controversy Over New Steel Contract

PITTSBURGH, Jan. 4 (UPI) —Following is a chronology of the steel-contract dispute:

July 15—Strike begins. President Eisenhower adopts "hands-off" policy.

Aug. 18—President orders Labor Secretary to make public statistics on the strike.

Aug. 19—Secretary of Labor James P. Mitchell issues statistics showing steel wages and profits ahead of those in industry generally.

Sept. 8—The strike enters its fifty-sixth day and becomes longest strike since World War II. The 1952 walkout lasted fifty-five days. The President asks "intensive, uninterrupted, good-faith bargaining."

Oct. 2—Industry makes its first money proposal.

Oct. 5—Union's Wage Policy Committee rejects as "completely unacceptable" the steel industry's latest proposal. President Eisenhower expresses "keen disappointment" and implies he may invoke the Taft-Hartley Act.

Oct. 9—President Eisenhower invokes provisions of the Taft-Hartley Law in eighty-seven-day walkout. Orders three-man fact-finding board to investigate strike.

Oct. 19—The President orders Justice Department to seek eighty-day back-to-work injunction after his Board of Inquiry reports it found no likelihood of voluntary settlement.

Oct. 21—Federal Judge Herbert P. Sorg issues injunction, but union wins stay of the order by appealing.

Oct. 22—Third Circuit Court of Appeals in Philadelphia makes stay indefinite while appeal is reviewed.

Oct. 26—Kaiser Steel breaks industry's solid front by signing contract with union. Detroit Steel and Granite City Steel follow suit.

Oct. 27—Appeals Court in Philadelphia upholds District Court's back-to-work injunction but leaves way open for appeal to Supreme Court.

Nov. 7—Supreme Court upholds injunction directing workers back to mills for eighty-day cooling-off period.

Nov. 19—Union rejects new company proposal of 30 cents an hour over three-year period.

Nov. 23—Steel production approaches 90 per cent of capacity on sixteenth day of eighty-day cooling-off period.

Dec. 4—Management and union open third round of talks with Federal mediators in Washington but industry not hopeful of settlement.

Dec. 7—President Eisenhower in nation-wide TV address before an eleven-nation tour pleads with both sides to end steel strike.

Dec. 8—Union signs new wage contracts with can manufacturers.

Dec. 9—The big eleven steel companies reject Labor Secretary's proposal to have neutral party recommend settlement of steel strike.

Dec. 10—Union opens talks with aluminum industry.

Dec. 14—Federal mediators watch aluminum contract negotiations in Chicago for bargaining pattern that could end steel strike.

Dec. 19—Steelworkers and five major aluminum producers reach contract settlement estimated to be worth 30 cents an hour over a three-year span.

Dec. 21—Big eleven steel firms agree to company-by-company bargaining, long sought by union.

Dec. 27—Steel concerns reluctantly begin company-by-company negotiations with United Steelworkers.

Dec. 28—President Eisenhower's three-man fact-finding panel re-enters negotiations. Union said its "straw vote" showed steelworkers 95 per cent against accepting companies' last offer.

Dec. 29—President's Board of Inquiry ends hearings, says both sides further apart than when panel entered case two months earlier.

Dec. 31—Vice President Nixon says he and Labor Secretary Mitchell are conducting behind-the-scenes efforts to reach steel settlement.

Jan. 4—Agreement on new contract terms announced in Washington, removing threat of resumption of strike Jan. 26, the expiration date of eighty-day cooling-off period.

Steel Prices and Wages

PITTSBURGH, Jan. 4 (AP) —Here is a table showing the increases in steel workers wages and steel prices at the dates of successive contracts since the Steel Workers Organizing Committee—now the United Steelworkers of America—negotiated its first contract in 1937:

Year.	Strike Length.	Minimum Pay.	Hourly Increase.	Steel Price Increase Per Ton.
1937		.625	.10	. .
1941		.725	.10	11.00
1942		.78	.055	. .
1946	(Twenty-six Days)	.965	.185	5.00
1947		1.09	.16*	5.00
1948		1.185	.13*	9.34
1950		1.36	.16*	5.50
1952	(Fifty-nine Days)	1.435	.16*	5.00
1953		1.52	.085	4.00
1954		1.57	.05	3.00
1955	(Twelve Hours)	1.685	.15*	7.35
1956	(Thirty-four Days)	1.82	.105*	8.50
1957		1.89	.21	6.00
1958		1.96	.07	4.50
1959	(116 Days)†	. .	. .	. .
1960		2.03‡	.07‡	. .

*—Denotes hourly increase which was included in "package" spread over the various job classifications, and not exactly matched in the minimum pay rates.

†—The strike lasted from July 15 until Nov. 7, 1959 when workers returned to the mills under a Taft-Hartley injunction. But the labor settlement was not reached until Jan. 4, 1960.

‡—Includes reported but unannounced wage increase of 7 cents an hour effective Dec. 1, 1960.

Minimum pay and hourly increase figures do not include a total of 17 cents an hour that workers received between 1956 and 1959 in cost-of-living increases under the last contract signed in 1956. The cost-of-living increases brought the 1958 base pay to $2.13 an hour.

The composite price of steel was estimated at $150 a ton last June.

I. L. A. HERE VOTES TO BAR CARGO VANS

'Containerization' of Freight Is Opposed — Fight Also Planned on Automation

By JACQUES NEVARD

The leaders of New York's 25,000 longshoremen voted overwhelmingly yesterday for a showdown fight against the off-pier "containerization" of ship freight and what they call the automation of dockside cargo handling.

In a stormy two-hour meeting at the Cornish Arms Hotel, the New York District Council of the International Longshoremen's Association took ·the following action:

¶Endorsed unanimously a decision made last week to stop handling cargo in shipping vans or other outsized containers for any lines that did not use the huge boxes before Oct. 1, 1956.

¶Broadened the ban to include a lift-on, lift-off trailership service operated by the Pan-Atlantic Steamship Corporation, despite insistence by the concern that its sea-going fleet of truck-trailer carriers started operations before the cut-off date.

¶Petitioned Capt. William V. Bradley, I. L. A. president, to schedule a meeting in Washington, of the union's leaders from ports from Portland, Me., to Brownsville, Tex., "in the very near future" to establish industry-wide policy on automation and containerization.

Meeting to Be Called

Captain Bradley said after the session that he would issue the invitations for such a meeting shortly.

According to Fred R. Field Jr., president of the district council and chairman of yesterday's meeting, the council members came to no decision on his recommendation that they settle all future "beefs" at the pier level. They were urged to do this rather than submit them to the labor-management

grievance machinery established in the current contract with the New York Shopping Association.

The shipping association, through its chairman, Alexander P. Chopin, had warned over the week-end that it would fight any unilateral departure from the contract, which runs until next Sept. 30.

"We will take action through the National Labor Relations Board and the courts, if necessary, to enforce our contracts," he declared.

The solidification of the union's position on the question of handling containers was viewed by shipping observers yesterday as ruling out a return to the waterfront "era of good feelings" that marked the first two years of the existing three-year contracts.

The port has enjoyed one of its longest periods without a major pier tie-up. There also has been almost a complete absence of the so-called "quickie" strike—the traditional method of settling a grievance against one company.

New Gear an Issue

The present bitterness has been traced to the introduction by the Grace Line in its new liners Santa Rosa and Santa Paula of virtually automatic loading gear.

Efforts by the line to reduce sharply the number of men in the work gangs for the new ships touched off dockers' fears that their employment opportunities would be cut each time such "automation" was introduced.

Also contributing to the friction, according to the union, are moves by the Grace and United States Lines to increase the amount of freight handled in containers. The use of the huge boxes, which are loaded off the piers by men who are not members of the longshore union, is viewed as another threat to dock employment.

A test of the union's willingness to fight on the questions will come today. Burton B. Turkus, the impartial arbitrator of the waterfront, will resume proceedings in the Grace Line container dispute.

It is understood that the union will try to turn the hearing into a bargaining session, and is ready to walk out if Mr. Turkus insists on arbitrating the matter.

3-Year Pier Pact Reached; New Walkout Is Averted

East Coast Accord Includes a 41-Cent Package—Automation Issue Settled by Agreement on Gang Size

By JACQUES NEVARD

The International Longshoremen's Association and a major group of waterfront employers reached a basic agreement yesterday on three-year contracts.

The agreement virtually ruled out a new East and Gulf Coast pier tie-up when a Taft-Hartley Act injunction expires Dec. 27. The injunction stopped an eight-day strike that began when the old contracts lapsed Sept. 30.

Yesterday's agreement included a master contract covering wages, hours and employers' contributions to pensions and welfare funds for all dockers from Maine to Virginia, and a detailed accord for the 20,000 men who work in the Port of New York.

The key issue of automation on the docks, which had delayed the contract, was settled as the employers agreed not to reduce the size of work gangs.

Dockers here will vote on the agreement by Dec. 10. By then, it was expected yesterday, most of the other ports would have reached their own detailed contracts.

Union spokesmen said that they would recommend that the rank and file accept the proposed 'contract, which they called "a very good one."

Basically, the New York accord provides a 41-cent-an-hour package increase. Wages would rise immediately from $2.80 an hour to $2.92, and would reach $2.97 Oct. 1, 1960, and $3.02 Oct. 1, 1961.

Besides the 22 cents in direct wage increases, 7 cents is alloted to pensions, 4 cents to welfare, 3 cents to clinics and 5 cents to increased vacations and holidays.

Alexander P. Chopin, chairman of the New York Shipping Association, which represents Northern waterfront employers said that if the dockers accepted the new contract by Dec. 10, the 12-cent-an-hour wage increase would be made retroactive to Oct. 1.

There had been general, if tacit, agreement on the money items for nearly a week before the final settlement was reached. The major issue was automation, a term that is used by the union to describe the entire field of mechanized cargo handling and the use of huge shipping vans or containers to speed freight on and off ships.

The employers had demanded the right to institute such labor-saving devices at will, while the union opposed this on the ground that the devices would eliminate jobs. In yesterday's settlement, the employers agreed not to cut the existing twenty-man standard work gang, a key point in the automation fight.

The question of a fee or premium for the handling of lift-vans or large shipping containers that were not packed or unpacked on the piers by I. L. A. members was left for further negotiation.

If no agreement can be reached in the next ten days, the question will go to "final-and-binding" arbitration, with a decision required within thirty days of submission.

A three-man Presidential fact-finding board, which had been scheduled to hold hearings today and tomorrow in Washington, was expected to cancel the sessions.

The agreement obviated the need for New York dockers and employers to appear, while Gulf Coast representatives—who had reported progress in their own talks—asked for and were granted a delay until 5 P. M. Saturday.

December 21, 1958

December 2, 1959

399

UNION SANCTIONS DOCK AUTOMATION

West Coast Longshoremen Get Pay Guarantee and Fund of $27,500,000

By LAWRENCE E. DAVIES
Special to The New York Times.

SAN FRANCISCO, Oct. 19 —West Coast maritime employers have agreed to pay longshoremen $5,000,000 a year for work lost through gradual replacement of men with machines.

In return, the employers have won almost complete freedom to operate without work restrictions of the kind sometimes referred to as "featherbedding" and "make work." Such restrictions have been the subject of disputes for a quarter-century.

The agreement was hailed by both sides as "epochal." It was reached just before midnight last night by negotiating committees of the Pacific Maritime Association, representing the employers, and the International Longshoremen's and Warehousemen's Union (independent).

Accord Lasts Until 1966

J. Paul St. Sure, president of the association, and Harry R. Bridges, the union's international head, led the negotiating committees.

The agreement extends until June 30, 1966. Allowing time for ratification by union locals, it was calculated today that the association would contribute the $5,000,000 a year for about five and a half years, starting Jan. 1, for a total of $27,500,000.

This is on top of a $1,500,000 "automation" fund set up by the association last year after preliminary negotiations. That figure was "plucked out of the air" rather than being based on any serious study of the losses to the workers from increased mechanization and modernization.

The new agreement permits the employers to determine, in general, how to run the docks. They will decide how many longshore gangs are needed, the size of the gangs, the weight of the slingloads in the loading and unloading of ships, and the number of times cargo will be handled.

The longshoremen have a guarantee of no lay-offs stemming from mechanization and also a guarantee of minimum weekly earnings. They are protected against any "individual speed-up" and infringement of safety rules. The contract permits early retirement or a lump sum benefit at normal retirement. It provides increased death and disability benefits.

Hope for Better Service

Mr. St. Sure said that the employers "are gambling $5,-000,000 a year against the right this contract gives us to remove work restrictions, in the belief we can save that much or more in our payrolls, gain faster turnaround of ships and give better service to shippers."

Three years of informal talks on the effects of waterfront automation preceded the formal negotiations, which began five months ago.

The Teamsters Union had an observer present for part of the negotiations. The two unions have a cooperative program to solve jurisdictional problems.

The agreement recognized the obsolescence of many waterfront practices.

It has long been customary for eight longshoremen to be assigned to each hatch of a ship during loading and unloading. Four rest while the others work. Under the new agreement, four men will constitute the minimum gang, with the employer deciding whether more than that are necessary.

This and some other matters will still be subject to arbitration.

Weight Limit Lifted

Since 1937 there has been a weight limitation of 2,100 pounds on a slingload of a number of commodities. This limit will be continued where loads are "hand built" and manually moved, but the limit is removed where machinery is introduced. On commodities not specifically covered by load limits, the employers will decide how much can be lifted.

"Multiple handling" of cargo is outlawed by the agreement. This means, for example, that if a trucker delivers cargo to a dock on a pallet board, the cargo no longer has to be placed on the surface of the pier and put on another pallet before it can be loaded aboard a ship. If any intermediate handling is ordered by an employer, it is to be done only by longshoremen.

The agreement covers about 15,000 men.

The automation fund may be used if, as a result of mechanization, their pay drops below that guaranteed for a thirty-five-hour week of straight-time work at $2.82 an hour.

This does not apply if the decrease results from a business decline.

Mr. St. Sure said that a "considerable cushion" was present because the average longshoreman gets forty-two hours of work a week and 10 to 12 per cent of the total work is done by casuals, who are not registered longshoremen. He said he considered it unlikely that the fund for the weekly guarantee would be used soon.

Wage increases and other matters were dealt with under a wage opening of the longshore contract dating from June, 1959. That contract was to have expired next June. However, it is to continue in effect, with annual wage openings for the lifetime of the present "automation" contract and with a "no strike" provision.

DOCK PACT CALLS FOR 4-YEAR PEACE

80c Package Won in Return for Revised Work Rules

By JOHN P. CALLAHAN

Four years of waterfront labor peace were assured yesterday for the first time in the 92-year history of the International Longshoremen's Association.

Terms of a new contract were reached, narrowly averting a strike of 60,000 longshoremen from Maine to Texas next Sunday night. The new pact will add $94.5 million to steamship industry costs in the four years.

The dockers won substantial guarantees of work, wage increases, better fringe benefits, longer vacations and pensions for widows, embodied in an 80-cent-an-hour package.

The industry obtained a reluctant concession — reduction of the work gang in stages from 20 to 17 men by Oct. 1, 1967. Two men will be dropped April 1, 1966.

A second major concession on work rules resolved the cargo checker "featherbedding" issue, which had been a snag in contract talks. Sounding a note of amity in contrast to the enmity that had marked all negotiations since June 25, when the talks began, Alexander P. Chopin, chairman of the 145-member company New York Shipping Association, praised Thomas W. Gleason, president of the union. They shared the head of the table when agreement on the four-year contract was announced.

Off to the side, in the board room of the shipping association at 80 Broad Street, sat two union officials who, negotiators confirmed, did more to accomplish the first long-term contract in the history of the union "than any others of the 125-man wage scale committee of the union." They were John Bowers, a quiet, unassuming man in his early thirties who holds the post of executive vice president, and Anthony M. Scotto, the 30-year-old leader of the union's largest local, Local 1814, in Brooklyn, with 8,000 members.

Bowers and Scotto Lauded

The adamant opposition of Mr. Gleason and some of his supporters on the wage-scale committee against changes in many of the union's traditional work practices — "featherbedding," the companies called it —was finally overcome by the continuing efforts of Assistant Secretary of Labor James J. Reynolds, chairman of the mediative panel, and by Mr. Bowers and Mr. Scotto. A tribute by a member of the 14-man labor policy committee of the shipping association to the effectiveness of the three men drew a unanimous nod from both negotiating committees as they walked away from yesterday's session.

Theodore W. Kheel, New York lawyer and arbitrator, and Prof. James J. Healy of the Harvard School of Business Administration, who were Mr. Reynolds's colleagues on the panel, also were lauded.

The key checker "featherbedding" issue was resolved late last week when the union agreed to discontinue the specialist role of the tally men. No longer will certain checkers clear only, say, automobiles. Instead, the employer has the right to utilize the checker's service in the tallying of any type of cargo.

Mr. Chopin emphasized that the new contract applied only to the Port of New York, and that the old contract would continue in effect for 22 days in all of the other ports. However, he added, it was the master agreement, or pattern, for all ports from Searsport, Me., to Hampton Roads, Va., and for other ports along the Gulf Coast to Galveston, Tex.

Mr. Gleason agreed, adding, however, that he would inform union delegates in all ports today on both the Atlantic and Gulf coasts of the settlement.

In New Orleans, a union officer cast some doubt on the avoidance of a strike Sunday. Alfred Chittenden, a vice president of the I.L.A. and leader of Local 1418, said the New York agreement did not bind New Orleans longshoremen. He said that if the locals there did not obtain a contract by Sunday night, longshoremen in New York and other ports "are duty bound to go on strike with us."

Breakdown of Package

Impartial labor experts said that the size of the money package was "so attractive" that they felt certain it would be acceptable all along both coasts.

The new 80-cents-an-hour package calls for 36 cents an hour in wage increases through Sept. 30, 1968. Of that total, 10 cents an hour will be retroactive to Oct. 1, 1964, when the two-year contract expired. An additional 10 cents will be paid in the second year and 8 cents more will be added in each of the last two years. The present base hourly wage is $3.26.

Pensions will be increased from from $100 a month on April 1, 1, to $125. On Jan. 1, 1966, longshoremen who have worked 25 years and have reached their 65th birthday will be eligible for $175 a month. Widows of men with 25 years of service who died before retirement will receive $87.50 a month.

The union won assurance of 1,600 hours of work a year, which means, according to Mr. Gleason, that a longshoreman who has been available for work can expect $5,860 a year. Heretofore, the only guarantee was four hours of work each time a man signed up for a day's work.

Tied in closely with the guarantee and with the cut in the gang size was an agreement to seek closing of the register of longshoremen. The register is the list of men licensed by the Waterfront Commission to apply for work on the New York and New Jersey sides of the Hudson River.

By attrition — now estimated at 1,400 men a year—the available work force will be reduced, thus increasing work opportunities for the men left on the register.

Closing of the register requires approval of the new York and New Jersey legislatures.

The union also won a fourth week of paid vacation. Its leaders had demanded a fourth week after 10 years of service; the companies preferred 20 years. They settled on 12 years of service. The companies will contribute 6 cents to the vacation fund.

Three holidays — New Year's Day, Decoration Day and Election Day—were added, raising the total to 12, at a cost to the companies of 6 cents.

Union Realized Need

While Mr. Chopin hailed the agreement as the "most difficult ever achieved in the Port of New York," he also said that the "union has realized that something had to be done to get better utilization of our manpower."

When Secretary Reynolds, as chairman of the mediative panel, began work in August to avert a strike, the blueprint was a 54-page study of manpower utilization and job security on the waterfront, prepared by the Labor Department.

The study recommended that better utilization of manpower in an industry where mechanization was making steady inroads, could be accomplished by cutting the work gang in exchange for a guaranteed annual wage and job security.

The shipping association based its contract proposals on the recommendations, but the union fought the cut in gang size and elimination of "featherbedding" and struck all ports on the Atlantic and Gulf coasts on Sept. 30.

The strike was halted with imposition of an 80-day injunction, which would have expired next Sunday.

December 17, 1964

FEATHERBED FIGHT LOOMING IN RAILS

3-Year Truce Has Ended— Roads and Brotherhoods Prepare for Showdown

---

VIEWS ARE FAR APART

Mileage-Pay System Called 'Outrageous' by A. A. R., Proper by Labor

---

By ROBERT E. BEDINGFIELD

The mileage-pay system of recompensing railroad train service employes is an "outrageous" imposition on common sense, according to Daniel P. Loomis, president of the Association of American Railroads. He notes that it results in engineers on the 225-mile Washington-to-New York run earning two and one-quarter days' pay in four hours.

The railroad workers see it another way. They assert those pay segments aren't days' pay at all; they are units of pay and when compared with other rising wage scales they represent a "perfectly proper" incentive system. Authority for that rebuttal is G. E. Leighty, chairman of the Railway Labor Executives' Association.

Railroad management and railroad labor have held these 180-degree opposing views for a long time. For the last three years they have been stayed by agreement from doing anything about them. Before that, especially during the "fat" war years, railroad finances weren't hurting enough to provoke management to take a strike over the issue of technological advances that require less manpower for train operation.

After all, the dual pay system for recompensing operating employes effects only about 12 per cent of the nation's 800,000 railroad workers and 4.5 per cent of the industry's $5,000,000,000-a-year wage bill.

Showdown Looms

But now the railroads—and particularly those here in the industrial Northeast—are sorely ailing financially. They have served notice that they intend to fight out the issue of "featherbedding." This is a generic term that applies in the railroad industry to work paid for and not needed. The brotherhoods have expressed themselves as equally ready for a showdown. They want to keep things as they are.

The truce in this battle, a three-year moratorium on work rules changes, which was part of the price of the 1956 wage-contract negotiations between the railroads and the brotherhoods, expired last night at midnight.

The oblique fashion in which the issue is joined, with the employes asserting that there is no such thing as featherbedding, rather than showing an inclination to trade it for something else, promises a really bitter struggle once the intricate preliminaries to any rail labor walkout have been performed.

Under the Railway Labor Act, there can be no legal strike over work rules—the cardinal issue to the writing of a new contract — until several steps have been taken. First, each railroad in the industry must serve each of the various union locals in its area with the industry's proposals. That is expected to happen tomorrow.

After the local chairmen of the brotherhoods have been served, both sides decide whether their dispute is a regional or national matter. There is little doubt that it is the latter. Once it is decided the two sides then begin to negotiate, presumably.

(There is no fixed time for the length of these negotiations.) If the negotiations collapse, both management and labor then are free to enlist the services of the National Mediation Board.

If that body, after an appropriate review, is unable to bring the two sides together or to get them both to put their arguments to arbitration, the dispute then must be referred to the President of the United States. He is required by the Railway Labor Act to appoint an Emergency Board to look into the dispute.

Cooling-off Period

The board has thirty days to complete its fact-finding, although the thirty-day period can be extended, before making its report to the President. Once it submits the final report, however, there must be a thirty-day cooling-off period before a legal strike can be called by the brotherhoods.

This suggests that, if the carriers are prepared to stand their ground and the unions aren't willing to make concessions, a railroad strike isn't a probability much before late winter or early spring, even though the three-year wage contract agreements expired last night.

The work-rules, which the railroads insist are so heavy with featherbedding provisions, and which the unions insist aren't, are of ancient vintage. They were fixed during and immediately following the period of Government operations of the carriers in World War I.

Under the rules, the carriers pay employes who actually run the trains—mainly conductors, engineers, trainmen, brakemen and firemen—not by the hour or day, but according to the number of miles that the trains they operate run. In railroad freight service a minimum day's work is 100 miles or eight hours or less on duty, whichever yields the most pay; in passenger service it is 150 miles or eight hours.

This pay system, the railroads stress, was fixed back in 1919. Then the average speed of passenger trains was about 20 miles an hour and freight trains moved about 12½ miles an hour. But with modern day Diesel power, the marked reduction of steep grades and curves of the track and the establishment of modern signal and communications systems, the average train—both passenger and freight—speeds twice as fast as it did forty years ago.

"As long as most railroad operating employes continue to receive a basic day's pay for operating 100 miles or less," the railroads have appealed to the nation through hundreds of newspaper and magazine advertisements, "and as long as the average speed of trains continues to increase, thereby steadily reducing the number of hours necessary for operating employes to earn a basic day's pay, just so long will we continue to follow a policy that benefits no one, but is harmful to all."

"Don't be fooled by the railroads' propaganda," the brotherhoods have replied to the carriers advertisements. "Let's analyze the railroads complaint that engineers on the 225-mile Washington-to-New York run make '2¼ days' pay' in four chouse * * * The unit of pay (basic days') for these locomotive engineers is $19.65. The '2¼ days' pay' amounts to only $44."

The union acknowledges the management contention that it still works out to more than $10 an hour for the four-hour run. It notes, however, that the engineer had spent almost an hour's preparatory time before guiding his New York-bound train out of Washington Union Terminal. At Pennsylvania Station, it observes, the engineer had to spend almost another hour tying up the locomotive, making checks on it and filling out the trip report.

"Then the engineer has a layover at New York before returning to Washington," the union stresses. "On the return trip, he makes another $44. A total of seventeen hours have elapsed. That's about $5 an hour pay for the total period. Is an hourly rate of $5 excessive, when you consider that the New York-to-Washington run is a very choice assignment, held by only a handful of men with top seniority, highly developed skills and judgment? Is it even sufficient?" the union asks.

The National Association of Railroad and Utilities Commissioners, a group that is close to the railroad picture and largely neutral between employer and employe, has made these conclusions after listening to the arguments of both labor and management:

"It is obvious that the controversy can never be reconciled by the parties themselves alone, The situation is such that an investigation into the problem is demanded, both in the interest of the parties directly concerned and in the interest of the public which not only has a right to lower rates and better service if there can be eliminated the cost inflation now blamed on these rules and which would be the innocent loser in any nation-wide railroad strike which might result from the deadlock on the rules."

The railroads, earlier this year, did ask for a White House Commission to study the equities of the situation, but President Eisenhower refused to name one on the ground that it would be taking sides prematurely in a labor dispute.

RAILROADS UPHELD IN SUPREME COURT ON REDUCING JOBS

Right to Make Wide Changes Aimed at Featherbedding Is Affirmed 8 to 0

PARLEYS WILL RESUME

5 Unions and Carriers Will Meet March 13 in Effort to End Long Dispute

By JOHN D. POMFRET
Special to The New York Times.

WASHINGTON, March 4 — The Supreme Court upheld today the legal right of the nation's railroads to make sweeping changes in work rules to eliminate what they call are unnecessary jobs.

Immediately afterward, the five rail unions that represent 200,000 on-train employees announced in Cleveland that they would agree to a proposal by the carriers to resume negotiations March 13 in Chicago.

The Supreme Court's 8 to 0 decision affirmed an appeals court opinion rejecting union arguments that the rules changes the railroads want to make would violate the terms of the Railway Labor Act.

Although the court swept away a major legal obstacle that had blocked work rules changes by the railroads, its action does not mean that the four-year-old dispute is on the verge of a showdown.

Actions Are Foreseen

If no agreement is reached at next week's bargaining session, the railroads undoubtedly will set a date to put the new rules into effect. The unions will threaten a strike. President Kennedy then may appoint an emergency board to investigate and recommend settlement terms. This would delay action by both sides for at least 60 days.

J. E. Wolfe, chief railroad negotiator, said in Chicago that the carriers would not set a new date for the rules changes until the Supreme Court mandate was issued. This, he said, could take as long as 25 days.

The dispute between the unions and the carriers centers on work rules that the carriers complain force them to retain unneeded employees at a cost of $600,000,000 a year. The carriers call this "featherbedding." The unions contend that the men the railroads want to get rid of perform jobs necessary for safe and efficient operation.

Revisions Recommended

In February of last year, a special Presidential commission, after a year's study, recommended sweeping revision of both the work rules and the railroad pay structure.

The recommendations would have the effect of eliminating, over a period of years, about 65,000 railroad jobs, of which 40,000 are those of diesel firemen in freight and yard service. They would also raise the pay of about 150,000 employees.

The carriers have offered to accept the recommendations, but the unions so far have rejected them.

In a letter to the rail unions Thursday, Mr. Wolfe proposed that negotiations resume March 13 in an effort to dispose of the issue involving firemen. When that has been accomplished, Mr. Wolfe said, the carriers would be willing to proceed with discussions on other issues.

Goldberg Not Participating

Although Mr. Wolfe did not say so in his letter, he told a reporter by telephone that he intended that the discussions should resume Monday within the framework of the Presidential commission's report. The unions have consistently sought to give the talks broader scope, so the new negotiations — the first since June 22 — could break down quickly on this point.

Today's Supreme Court ruling was on a petition by the five operating rail unions asking that the court review a decision by the United States Court of Appeals in Chicago. The appeals court upheld the railroads' legal right to make the rules changes.

The Supreme Court granted the union's request for review,

then in a seven-page decision reaffirmed the appeals court decision.

The decision was issued in the name of the court with the notation that Associate Justice Arthur J. Goldberg had not participated. He had dealt with the rules dispute as Secretary of Labor.

The court found that the only question presented was whether the record sustained the findings of the appeals court and the United States District Court that the parties had exhausted the procedures provided by the Railway Labor Act for handling major disputes.

The court ruled that they had and thus were "relegated to self-help in adjusting this dispute" subject only to possible appointment by the President of an emergency board. Self-help would include imposition of new work rules by the carriers and a strike by the unions.

The unions had argued that the appeals court implied that the railroads somehow were entitled to impose the new rules as a penalty for the unions' failure to bargain in good faith. The Supreme Court said there was no evidence to indicate that either side acted in bad faith and disapproved any contrary implication in the appeals court's opinion.

Decision is Supported

The Supreme Court said the appeals court had correctly rejected the unions' contention that the work rules changes contained in the carriers' notices themselves violated the Railway Labor Act. It reiterated its earlier opinion that the act does not undertake governmental regulation of wages, hours and working conditions, but seeks to provide a means by which agreement may be reached with respect to them.

The court also disposed of a minor point of contention — the argument by the railroads that the 1960 agreement between them and the unions establishing the special Presidential commission provided that those proceedings should replace proceedings under the Railway Labor Act. The court said the terms of the agreement were inconsistent on this point, but in any case no private agreement could interfere with the duty of the National Mediation Board or the power the act confers on the President to appoint an emergency board.

The work rules disputes involved virtually all the nation's major railroads and the Brotherhood of Locomotive Engineers, The Brotherhood of Locomotive Firemen and Enginemen, the Order of Railway Conductors and Brakemen, the Brotherhood of Railroad Trainmen and the Switchmen's Union of North America.

KENNEDY SIGNS BILL AVERTING A RAIL STRIKE

PRECEDENT IS SET

Arbitration Imposed by Congress—Vote in House 286-66

By JOHN D. POMFRET
Special to The New York Times

WASHINGTON, Aug. 28 — Congress passed today a bill that prevented a national railroad strike scheduled for midnight. President Kennedy signed it immediately.

The House completed the Congressional action. It adopted by a standing vote of 286 to 66 the same joint resolution passed yesterday by the Senate. The measure provides for arbitration of the two principal issues in the railroad work rules dispute and bars a strike for 180 days.

The action was without Federal precedent. Never before in the history of peacetime labor relations has Congress imposed arbitration in a labor-management dispute.

The failure of the railroads and the five train operating unions to resolve their dispute, and the Congressional action this made necessary, is considered by many to represent a major failure for the collective bargaining system.

Many Are Reluctant

Even many Congressmen who voted for the measure, convinced that the economic consequences of a national railroad strike made action to head it off essential, did so with great reluctance. They said they feared that their action might set a precedent detrimental to collective bargaining.

An arbitration board was created by Congress to consider

the two key issues. These are whether diesel locomotive firemen are necessary in freight and yard service and the size of train-service crews.

Congress ordered negotiations on the remaining issues on the theory that with the two main issues disposed of, the presumably less important matters could be settled by traditional collective bargaining.

But some well-informed Government sources do not believe the remaining issues will be easily settled. These sources indicate that, in 180 days, the dispute will be back in the lap of Congress.

Representative Oren Harris, chairman of the House Commerce Committee, said on the floor of the House today that Congress would be "unhappy" if this happened. This should be notice on both sides to settle the remaining issues themselves the Arkansas Democrat said.

These issues involve the carriers' demands for extension of existing runs beyond present division lines, greater flexibility in using road crews for yard work, the manning requirements of self-propelled vehicles and revision of the complicated railroad pay structure based on a combination of time worked and miles traveled.

It took about four hours for Mr. Harris to shepherd the legislation through the House. He proposed amendments that were adopted to make the legislation proposed by his committee identical to the version passed by the Senate yesterday by a vote of 90 to 2.

Conference Avoided

This avoided the need for a time-consuming Senate-House conference to iron out differences and enabled the President to sign the joint resolution at 6:14 P.M., nearly six hours before the strike was scheduled to start.

Actually the railroads and the unions did not wait for the President's signature to call off the shutdown.

The strike would have been triggered by changes in work rules over union objections. When the House acted, the railroads announced that the changes in the rules, set for midnight, had been canceled. When they received word of this

the unions announced that there would be no strike.

In approving the joint resolution, President Kennedy said that free collective bargaining was not being eroded.

The President said in a statement that on Aug. 16 the carriers and the unions had agreed that the two central issues should be submitted to arbitration.

"Unfortunately, they were unable to agree on arbitration terms or the handling of other issues," Mr. Kennedy said. "Yet, incomplete as this agreement was, it has permitted the Congress to confine its action to implementing, in effect, what is essentially a private and voluntary decision."

The railroads praised Congress for "its timely and constructive handling of this crucial legislation."

Picking Board Members

The unions said in a statement that "the enactment of compulsory arbitration by the Congress of the United States can only be viewed as regrettable and a backward step in the preservation of the rights of workers."

"Only time will tell whether Congress has changed the course of labor-management relations," the union statement said.

The arbitration procedure provides for the naming within five days of the two members of the arbitration board by the carriers and two by the unions. These members, who will be the representatives of both sides on the board, are to pick three neutral members. If they cannot agree, the President will name the neutral members.

It is considered unlikely that the unions and the carriers will, in fact, be able to agree on who the three neutrals should be. Secretary of Labor W. Willard Wirtz has a large number of names under consideration.

No firm decisions have been made, but the indications were that a widely respected and well-known person would be named chairman and that the two other neutral board members would be persons with technical competence in the labor-management field.

The appointment of the board is to be completed in 10 days. It is to begin its deliberations

403

within 30 days after today, and to make its award in 60 days more. The award is to be effective 60 days after it is made and will hold for two years. The resolution will expire 180 days from its enactment today.

Court Action Provided

During the 180-day period, its ban on strikes or unilateral changes in conditions by the carriers is enforcible by Federal Court injunction on application by the Attorney General.

The two issues before the board have eluded a bargained solution by the carriers and the unions for nearly four years. the 32,000 firemen's jobs in freight and yard service and drastically reduce the number of train-service employes, principally brakemen and yard helpers.

The carriers involved in the dispute operate virtually all of the railway mileage in the country and have about 700,000 employes. The only major carrier not involved in the dispute is the Southern Railway, which bargains separately, but has not reached any agreement on the issues either.

ARBITERS ORDER GRADUAL CUTBACK IN RAIL FIREMEN

Panel Rules 90% of Such Jobs in Freight and Yard Service Unnecessary

By JOHN D. POMFRET
Special to The New York Times

WASHINGTON, Nov. 26 — An arbitration board set up by Congress ruled today that 90 per cent of the diesel locomotive firemen's jobs in freight and yard service were unnecessary and eventually could be eliminated.

The two unions representing firemen immediately announced that they would attack in United States District Court here the award and the legislation under which it was rendered.

Even if the award is sustained by the court, it does not mean that 90 per cent of the affected firemen will be laid off.

Effective for 2 Years

The board drew a sharp distinction between the jobs that it said could be eliminated and the men who occupy them. The great majority of the 40,000 men involved must be retained as firemen by the terms of the award until they quit, die, retire or are dismissed for cause, or are offered a comparable job by the railroad employing them.

The award is effective for only two years. This means that its terms will be subject to renegotiation long before the men who occupy most of the jobs are gone. Normally, attrition from

resignations, deaths, retirements and discharges runs about 5.5 per cent a year on the railroads.

Other Issue Remanded

The board sent the other issue before it, involving the number of trainmen needed in various train operations, back to the individual carriers and the unions involved for local negotiations.

Pending settlements, however, it prescribed an arbitration procedure to settle disputes over the size of some train crews and specified the crews subject to the procedure.

The arbitration was the first to be imposed by Congress in a peacetime labor dispute.

Congress acted Aug. 28, on the eve of a national railroad strike, to bar the walkout and to refer the two principal issues in the four-year-old railroad work rules dispute to the arbitration board it created.

The three neutral members of the board were joined in their award by the two members representing the railroads. Both union members dissented.

The three unions representing train crews have not decided whether to attack the award in court. Their presidents will make the determination Monday when they meet here with the presidents of the two engine-service unions to discuss the award and its implications.

Congress hoped that once the two key issues had been ruled on by the arbitration board, the secondary issues could be resolved through collective bargaining.

These involve the carriers' demands for extension of existing runs by train crews beyond present railroad division lines, greater flexibility in using road crews for yard work, the manning of self-propelled vehicles

and revision of the complicated railroad pay structure, which is based on a combination of time worked and miles traveled.

Negotiations on these questions will resume Dec. 4. If they are not resolved by Feb. 24, the unions will be free again to strike over the secondary issues. Both sides indicated today that they hoped the secondary issues could be resolved amicably. But informed sources indicated that a settlement was by no means certain and that the entire dispute might wind up in the lap of Congress again.

Members of Board

Today's award, unless it is set aside by the courts, will become effective Jan. 25. It will continue in effect for two years except in the unlikely event that it is amended by agreement between the railroads and the unions.

The three neutral members of the board were the chairman, Ralph T. Seward, of Washington a professional arbitrator; Benjamin Aaron, director of the Institute of Industrial Relations of the University of California at Los Angeles, and James J. Healy, professor of industrial relations at the Harvard University Graduate School of Business Administration.

The union members were H. E. Gilbert, president of the Brotherhood of Locomotive Firemen and Enginemen, and R. H. McDonald, vice president of the Brotherhood of Railroad Trainmen.

The engine service union involved in the dispute, in addition to Mr. Gilbert's, is the Brotherhood of Locomotive Engineers. The three train service unions are the B. R. T., the Order of Railway Conductors and Brakemen and the Switchmen's Union of North America. The five unions represent about 200,000 of the nation's 700,000 railroad workers.

The two management members of the board were J. E. Wolfe, chairman of the National Railway Labor Conference, and Guy W. Knight, vice president of the Pennsylvania Railroad.

The dispute formally began on Nov. 2, 1959, when most of

the nation's railroads served notice on the unions that they wanted sweeping changes in work rules to allow them to eliminate thousands of jobs that they contended were unneeded.

Result of Conversion

The railroads also opened a national publicity campaign to enlist public support in their fight against what they for years have called "featherbedding" — a term, infuriating to rail unions and workers, meaning a requirement that employers hire unneeded workers.

The dispute has become the classic modern example of the difficulty of adapting to technological change in the face of shrinking employment.

Although there have been many innovations in railroading, the principal one has been the conversion from coal-fired steam to diesel locomotives. The diesels can pull longer trains faster and need less maintenance.

Under the impact of the diesels, other new machines and dwindling business, railroad employment has been cut since the end of World War II from 1,-400,000 to 700,000.

The unions have vigorously resisted any contract changes that would result in the elimination of still more jobs.

The symbol of the fight is the diesel fireman in freight and yard service. The railroads have argued that he is not necessary; the engine-service unions, that he is. The board ruled for the railroads.

Neutrals' Reasoning

The neutral members, in a separate opinion accompanying the board majority's award, said that the lookout function now assigned to the fireman was performed by the head brakeman, who also sits in the cab with the engineer in road freight service, and by all members of the train crew in yard service. The railroads have never demanded that firemen on passenger trains, where there is no head brakeman in the cab with the engineer, be eliminated.

The neutral members also said that most of the mechanical duties now performed by the fireman were not absolutely essential to the safety and efficiency of road freight and yard operations. Such duties as are essential can be performed by the engineer while the locomotive is operating and by shop workers at other times, they said.

If the engineer is incapacitated while a freight train is moving, the head brakeman can take over, the neutral member said. Yard locomotives must be equipped with a dead-man control before they can operate without a fireman, the board decided.

The board conceded that there might be some cases where foremen might be needed on freight or yard crews for safe and efficient operation and to prevent an undue burden from falling on other workers.

Here is the procedure it set forth for the elimination of firemen's jobs:

Within a week from the date the board's award is effective, the railroads will hand the unions lists of engine crews on which the railroads say firemen are not needed. The unions will have the right to insist that firemen be retained on 10 per cent of these crews. They will indicate which ones within 30 days after getting the railroads' lists and their judgment will be final.

The process will be repeated every three months to allow for the fact that the total number of train crews on duty fluctuates according to the volume of rail business.

But the railroads will not immediately be able to stop assigning firemen to 90 per cent of the freight and yard crews.

The board said that working firemen with 10 or more years' service—an estimated total of 26,000 of the 40,000 firemen involved—must be provided with firemen's jobs until they quit, die, retire or are dismissed for cause.

Other Rulings Given

Those with more than two years' seniority, but less than 10 years, about 10,500 men, will continue as firemen unless offered comparable employment by the railroad on which they work. The offer of another job will carry with it relocation expenses, the continuation of accumulated seniority rights toward vacation and other fringe benefits and guaranteed annual earnings equal to the total earnings of the employe in the year prior to transfer. The pay guarantee applies for up to five years.

Several remaining groups, with less than two year's seniority or an irregular attachment to the industry, may be laid off permanently with severance pay of varying amounts. About 3,500 men are estimated to be in this group.

The board also ordered the carriers and the two engine-service unions to establish a joint board, with two members representing the unions and two the railroads, to make the continuing study of the experience under the award and to report to those they represent within three months before the award runs out.

With respect to train-service crews, the board ruled that they should stay the same size in road service, unless changed by mutual agreement, in cases where they are made up of one conductor and two aides, such as brakemen, flagmen or ticket collectors.

In branch line and yard service or in road service where other than three-man crews are being used, either side may propose changes. If they cannot agree, the issues will be decided by arbitration.

The board set forth certain guidelines, such as safety, avoidance of unreasonable burden and volume of rail traffic in the area, to guide the arbitrators.

Union estimates are that about 50,000 train-service jobs could be subject to review under these procedures. Even counting three-man crews, the railroads, never proposed eliminating more than 19,000 employes in this category and more recently cut the number to 12,000.

Even if the award is sustained by the courts, the railroads will not be able to eliminate jobs they otherwise might in 17 states that have so-called full-crew laws or regulations requiring crews of minimum sizes on trains that run inside their boundaries.

Battle in the State

One effect of today's award is expected to be to sharpen the battle over these laws at the state level, with the railroads trying to get rid of them where they exist and the unions trying to have them enacted where they do not.

The neutral members, in their opinion, expressed their regret that the railroads and the unions were not able to agree on resolving their differences.

Noting that never before in peacetime had Congress imposed arbitration in a labor dispute, the neutrals said:

"The great virtue of arbitration as it has developed in this country's labor relations has been the fact that it was a voluntary procedure, created and shaped by the disputing companies and unions themselves and thus responsive to their peculiar problems, values and needs.

"It is unfortunate that the parties in this case, though finally agreeing in principle to arbitration, failed to agree upon the terms and procedures of an arbitration agreement and thereby abandoned to Congress an opportunity and responsibility that should rightly have been theirs."

Little Effect in New York

The New York State Association of Railroads said yesterday that the arbitration award would probably have little effect in the state because of minimum crew laws enacted in 1913.

An association spokesman said the state laws required a fireman on freight trains and yard engines and on "trains other than freight trains of five cars or more." The state laws also require a fireman on all diesel locomotives.

5-YEAR RAIL DISPUTE ENDS; PRESIDENT WINS ACCORD HE TERMS 'JUST AND FAIR'

STRIKE IS AVERTED

Settlement Viewed as Personal Triumph for Johnson

By JOHN D. POMFRET

Special to The New York Times

WASHINGTON, April 22 — The five-year-old railroad work rules dispute was settled today, ending the threat of a nationwide rail strike at midnight Friday.

The agreement, which provides for a raise for about 100,000 workers along with other benefits and gives the railroads additional flexibility in assigning work crews, was announced by President Johnson over nationwide television about 6:45 P.M.

The President said the terms of the accord "are just and are fair."

The settlement was a great personal triumph for Mr. Johnson. He intervened forcefully in the dispute on April 9 to persuade the five operating rail unions and the railroads to call off a national rail shutdown set for midnight that day.

And Mr. Johnson clinched the settlement personally today by persuading the railroads to accept it.

Throughout the talks, the President had kept in close contact with the negotiators, dropping in on them almost daily.

Half to Get Raise

The agreement by itself appeared to be a victory for the unions. They won a pay raise for about half of the 200,000 employes they represent and got the carriers to drop several important demands.

The total settlement, however, including the earlier arbitration award covering the two main issues in the original dispute, represents a substantial gain for the railroads. This results from eliminating thousands of workers who the roads contend are no longer needed.

An informed source estimated that the railroads would save $317 million a year from the manpower reductions permitted by the arbitration award, once it is fully in effect. The cost to the railroads of today's settlement was put at $64 million. The eventual net saving to the railroads was thus estimated at $253 million a year.

That an agreement emerged at all in the protracted and bitter controversy was considered remarkable by nearly everyone involved.

Collective bargaining had collapsed. Those involved gave the President credit for breathing new life into it. They said that Mr. Johnson, at his April 9 meeting with union and railroad officials, had convinced them he would not accept any result other than a bargained settlement.

The President was obviously jubilant over the agreement.

When he learned that it would take more than an hour to set up the necessary equipment for a live television broadcast from the White House, he decided to go to the studios of the Columbia Broadcasting System in northwest Washington to make the announcement.

It was C.B.S.'s turn to act as the "pool" network for the other networks; C.B.S. fed the program to the other networks.

The President's motorcade made the four-mile trip from the White House through the city streets to the studio in nine minutes.

Mr. Johnson read his announcement from three-by-five-inch cards held in his hand. His audience in the studio consisted of 25 reporters and photographers and technicians.

Lauds Mediators

Mr. Johnson praised the mediators in the dispute, then added:

"But it was the railroad men, the company management and the union leadership who won this common victory for collective bargaining and for industrial democracy."

The President said the terms of the agreement took into account the need for modernization in order for the railroads to survive and prosper and the human needs and aspirations of those affected by technological progress.

"But most of all," the President said, "this agreement prevents—we hope for all time—a most crippling and disastrous strike in the railroad industry."

The strike, had it occurred Friday night as scheduled, would have put six million workers off their jobs, cut the gross national product by 13 per cent and forced a rise in prices throughout the country, the President said.

The mediators in the dispute indicated they felt the settlement had given both sides a renewed faith in collective bargaining in the railroad industry.

Prof. George W. Taylor of the Wharton School of Finance and Commerce of the University of Pennsylvania, one of the nation's senior mediators, likened today's developments to the basic turn toward harmony in labor relations that occurred in the coal industry in the early nineteen-fifties and in the steel industry in 1960.

Ratification Needed

The settlement is subject to ratification by the five unions. In the case of the Switchmen's Union of North America, this will require a membership referendum. Officers or committees are empowered to ratify in the case of the four other unions.

The agreement represents a distillation of the positions of both sides drawn up by the mediators from documents handed them by the railroads and the unions at a meeting that began at midnight Monday and continued for seven hours.

Only one copy—handwritten—of the mediators' blending of the positions was prepared. It was read to the parties. There was agreement in advance that if it did not prove to be the basis for settlement, it would be destroyed and forgotten.

This was necessary, presumably, because neither side wanted to jeopardize its position in the event a settlement failed to emerge and the dispute went before an arbitration board.

The unions agreed to the mediators' suggested settlement yesterday afternoon.

This morning at a private meeting at the White House, the President urged J. E. Wolfe, chief railroad negotiator, to accept. Mr. Wolfe met with the nine-man executive committee of the National Railway Labor Conference, of which he is chairman. Then he met with the mediators. This afternoon, he said the railroads would agree.

The railroads nearly balked at the last minute, because the proposed settlement gave them no concessions on the issue of interdivisional runs.

This involved a demand by the railroads that they be allowed to extend the distance some train crews travel before being relieved by other crews. It would allow the carriers to cut down on the number of crews.

The agreement refers the question to a national committee for further bargaining. It specifies that Professor Taylor and Theodore W. Kheel, New York lawyer and labor relations expert, who was brought into the mediation with Professor Taylor by the President, will help in the discussions.

Some carriers operating in states with so-called "full-crew" laws, which specify the minimum number of men that must man a train, believed that the earlier arbitration award was meaningless to them. They wanted concessions on interdivisional runs.

The arbitration award came as the result of Congressional action last Aug. 28 that barred a strike until Feb. 25 and referred the two main issues in the dispute to an arbitration panel.

The panel ruled that the railroads could eliminate 90 per cent of firemen's jobs in freight and yard service, largely as the occupants quit, died, retired or were offered comparable jobs.

The panel ruled that the other issue, involving the demand of the railroads that the size of some train crews be cut, be sent back to the individual carriers for negotiation and arbitration.

The unions are challenging the award in court. So far, it has been upheld in United States District Court and the Court of Appeals. The unions are asking the Supreme Court to review the rulings.

Today's settlement does not affect the litigation.

The question of interdivisional runs was the only issue left up in the air by today's settlement.

The other issues were settled in principle, with an agreement that if any dispute over interpretation arose, Mr. Kheel and Professor Taylor would decide it.

The unions won seven paid holidays for all hourly workers —about 65 per cent of the 200,000 involved.

They won a wage adjustment for yard employes that will raise the pay of foremen 12 cents an hour to $3.10 and that of helpers 8 cents to $2.90. With commensurate increases for other yard workers, about 100,000 employes will get a raise.

The agreement also provides that men away from home for more than four hours will be furnished lodging and given a $1.50 meal allowance.

The unions dropped demands for overtime pay and for premium pay for night work.

The railroads dropped a demand that the so-called mileage basis of pay be altered. For employes who man the trains, 100 miles is considered equal to a day's work. The railroads wanted the number of miles increased.

In return for this concession, the unions agreed that any wage increase paid up to Jan. 1, 1968, would apply only to the basic daily rates and not to the existing mileage rates. The effect will be to keep the disparity between the mileage and daily rates from increasing.

The agreement enlarges to a limited extent the right of the carriers to assign long-distance train crews to yard work. Where only one yard crew remains at a yard or on a shift, it may be eliminated.

The carriers also won a reduction in the number of crew members required to man self-propelled maintenance vehicles.

Experts said there was no way to estimate how many jobs would be eliminated by the combination of road and yard service and by reduction of men on self-propelled vehicles but that it would not be large.

Men who are displaced are guaranteed income protection, which will be negotiated, probably on the basis of 60 per cent

of their annual earnings for four years.

The major manpower cuts foreseen by the railroads were allowed by the arbitration award, which eventually may lead to elimination of some 50,000 jobs.

In his announcement of the settlement, President Johnson said the mediators deserved the "applause of the nation" for their efforts. In addition to Mr. Kheel and Mr. Taylor, the mediators were Secretary of Labor W. Willard Wirtz, Assistant Secretary James J. Reynolds and Francis A. O'Neill Jr., chairman of the National Mediation Board.

Roy E. Davidson, head of the Brotherhood of Locomotive Engineers, said the settlement fell short of the union's demands but "significant gains" had been made.

Mr. Davidson followed the President on television and, in turn, was followed by Mr. Wolfe.

Mr. Wolfe said the railroads had agreed to the settlement at the President's request. He said it "promises to restore the morale of our 700,000 employes

to its highest level and bring a rebirth of the spirit of cooperation between management and union leaders."

The President ended the television session with a typically homey anecdote.

He said a 7-year-old girl, Cathy May Baker of Park Forest, Ill., had written him asking him to keep the railroads running so her grandmother from New York could come to the child's first Holy Communion.

"Cathy May," the President said, "tonight I am pleased to tell you that the railroads are going to continue to run without interruption."

Whereupon Mr. Wolfe and Mr. Davidson went to have a drink together.

The 195 carrier and terminal and switching companies involved in the dispute include virtually every major railroad in the country.

The unions, in addition to the Switchmen and the Engineers, are the Brotherhood of Locomotive Firemen and Enginemen, the Brotherhood of Railroad Trainmen and the Order of Railway Conductors and Brakemen.

April 23, 1964

FACTORS IN THE AUTOMATION PICTURE AND THE EFFECTS ON THE AMERICAN ECONOMY

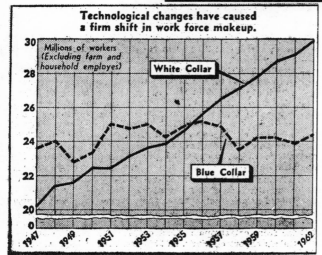

Technological changes have caused a firm shift in work force makeup.

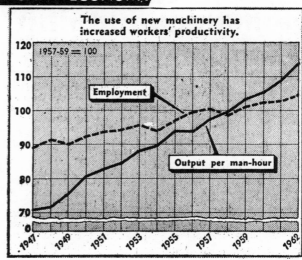

The use of new machinery has increased workers' productivity.

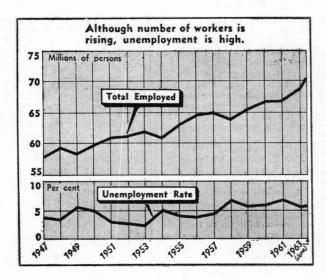

Although number of workers is rising, unemployment is high.

Millions of persons

75
70
65
60
55

Total Employed

10
5
0

Per cent

Unemployment Rate

1947 1949 1951 1953 1955 1957 1959 1961 1963 (June)

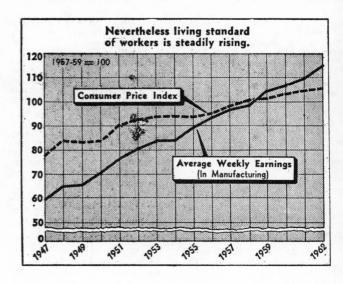

Nevertheless living standard of workers is steadily rising.

120
110
100
90
80
70
60
50

1957-59 = 100

Consumer Price Index

Average Weekly Earnings
(In Manufacturing)

1947 1949 1951 1953 1955 1957 1959 1962

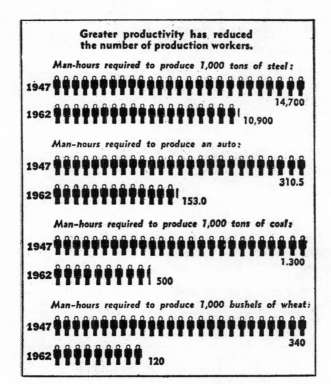

Greater productivity has reduced the number of production workers.

Man-hours required to produce 1,000 tons of steel:

1947   14,700
1962   10,900

Man-hours required to produce an auto:

1947   310.5
1962   153.0

Man-hours required to produce 1,000 tons of coal:

1947   1,300
1962   500

Man-hours required to produce 1,000 bushels of wheat:

1947   340
1962   120

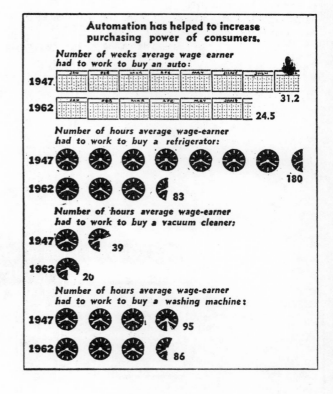

Automation has helped to increase purchasing power of consumers.

Number of weeks average wage earner had to work to buy an auto:

1947   31.2
1962   24.5

Number of hours average wage-earner had to work to buy a refrigerator:

1947   180
1962   83

Number of hours average wage-earner had to work to buy a vacuum cleaner:

1947   39
1962   20

Number of hours average wage-earner had to work to buy a washing machine:

1947   95
1962   86

July 14, 1963

Steel Strike Negotiations: An Exercise in Irrelevancy

By A. H. RASKIN

LORAIN, Ohio — The headlines are black with warnings of a strike next Saturday for higher pay, but the workers in this steel center are more worried about jobs than money.

Frank Caruso looks down a quarter-mile shed full of coiled sheet steel. "As of right now," he says, "there is no chance for a youngster in this mill. Jobs keep going down, even though we make more steel than we ever did."

Three Centuries in Steel

Frank Caruso knows a little about steel. His father worked in the huge Lorain plant of United States Steel from the time it opened in 1894 until he retired in 1938. Frank has worked in the mill 43 years himself. All five of his brothers work here, except for one who has just retired after 48 years. Their combined service comes to nearly three centuries.

The Lorain mill, the biggest producer of pipe in the world, has always been like that—a father-and-son mill, the economic mainspring of this community of 80,000. But now Frank Caruso's gloomy pronouncement reflects a worry widely held among the plant's 7,800 workers, the one a visitor hears expressed almost obsessively as he trudges through the endless acres of blast furnaces, open hearths and rolling mills or visits the men in their neat, well-tended homes.

This rank-and-file preoccupation with the dislocative effect of automation on jobs makes the wage dispute that threatens a national steel shutdown seem an exercise in irrelevancy. The top-level negotiators in Pittsburgh are arguing over how large a down payment the workers should get for extend-ing their union contract until the union is sure who will lead it for the next four years. This is an issue that leaves untouched any of the real problems that bother the men in the mills and their families.

"I have a grievance against the union," says Mrs. William E. Balogh, whose husband is a former chairman of the Lorain local's grievance committee. "The world is changing, but the unions aren't. This whole thing about negotiating on money is old hat. We have big problems of automation—people being automated out of jobs. The Government is sympathetic surely. Why don't the unions and the companies get together with the Government and do something?"

The worry about technological displacement extends into almost every department of the vast plant. This is probably the most modern pipe mill anywhere; yet it is a mill in transition, for pipe is among the steel products most sharply challenged by cheap imports from automated foreign producers and by the competitive onsurge of copper, aluminum and other materials.

When the country's first continuous line for making seamless pipe was installed here in 1949, it was so advanced that Yale assigned a research team to make a four-year study of the interaction of men and machines. In 1961 the company took an even longer step into the automation age by opening a continuous line for welded pipe. It runs at only half-capacity because so much of the market has been usurped by pipe from Japan, Germany and Belgium.

So the company is moving toward still greater efficiency by rushing completion of a $10 million electric mill for welded pipe. Now in the shakedown stage, it uses a fantastic array of manless methods to mold cold metal into tubing through the kind of instant heat treatment Howard Johnson employs to quick-cook a hot dog. All the automation at the two other new mills seems primordial alongside its high-frequency induction heaters, ultrasonic inspection devices and unmonitored controls.

One result of all these advances was a shrinkage in total employment at the Lorain works from a World War II peak of 12,000 to half that number a year ago. Until strike fears caused a big influx of stockpile orders early this year, the plant had hired no new workers since 1957. Even men whose seniority went back fifteen years found themselves laid off almost as much as they were on. Now the build-up of pre-strike backlogs, plus the unparalleled prosperity of the national economy, has brought renewed hiring and a present roster of 7,800 employes.

Worries About Jobs

Yet this transitory expansion has meant no surcease from anxiety about technological unemployment. The plant's twelve open-hearth furnaces, where iron ore, limestone and scrap are fused into raw steel, are about to be replaced by vastly more efficient oxygen furnaces. Many workers fear their skills will become as worthless as the scrap they feed into the inferno they now tend.

Ralph Welter, a second helper, whose father worked as a water boy when the Lorain mill was being built at the turn of the century, worries about how he will support his five small children after the change. What makes him especially apprehensive is the plight of skilled workers displaced when some of the old pipe mills became tombstones to progress. Those with no place to go in the new facilities were downgraded to laborers' jobs in the open hearth—at cuts in pay of $1 an hour or more.

Titan With a Cigar

Even the highest rated of Lorain's steelmakers are susceptible to such fears. Take Louis Hanko, a stooped titan with a well-chewed cigar, who sits on a thronelike swivel chair in an air-conditioned booth and uses two cranks to manipulate mammoth slabs of fiery steel until he pounds them to just the right size and shape. Hanko is a hot roller, a Paul Bunyan of the steel industry, so adept that he can fashion square or round billets with never a glance at the big illuminated dial before him or at the pillar of flame bouncing on the rollers below. Does he think automation can ever outmode a skill like his? The answer is swift: "When you can go up to the moon, anything can happen. There isn't anything that can't be done today."

This recognition of the meteoric pace of change and of the many ways in which it is changing their lives explains why the men of Lorain appear so detached from the wage debate in Pittsburgh. The local has a tradition of militancy; it voted heavily for the insurgent slate headed by I. W. Abel in the recent steel union election. Its members will strike if the union says strike; but the message they most want to hear is, no strike. Because nothing the negotiators are bickering about is genuinely important to them.

A. H. RASKIN is assistant editor of the editorial page of The Times.

Miners:
Dig They Won't

John L. Lewis, unlike many of his colleagues in the labor movement, was in the forefront of those who accepted mechanization and automation of industry.

"It's better to have a half million men working in the industry at good wages," he said, "than to have a million men working in the industry in poverty and degradation."

Mine working conditions improved under this Lewis policy. But problems remain for the workers. Last week mechanization of American coal mines was a principal factor behind the nation's biggest soft coal strike in 14 years.

Such turmoil had been common in the first three decades of Mr. Lewis's presidency of the United Mine Workers. After a 1949-1950 strike, Mr. Lewis became convinced that mechanization was necessary if the industry was to survive competition from gas and oil.

Thus when he stepped down in 1960 after 40 years as U.M.W. president, he was widely hailed for having raised his coal diggers to the level of the highest paid industrial workers, while at the same time saving the soft coal industry from extinction.

Mr. Lewis's policies not only increased the pay of miners, but made possible a sharp rise in the amount of coal each miner could dig. Yet, while coal output rose, mine employment declined sharply as a result of mechanization.

Rising unrest in the mine fields over job losses after Mr. Lewis's departure opened the way for opposition to Thomas Kennedy, his hand-picked heir. By the time little-known W. A. (Tony) Boyle ascended to the presidency upon Mr. Kennedy's death in 1963, the rebellion was building up steam.

Although Mr. Boyle senses the industry's need to remain competitive and has a philosophy toward mechanization that does not differ basically from Mr. Lewis's, he is responding to pressure from the rank-and-file to slow down the pace of mechanization through job and income protection devices.

This has been demonstrated in the current negotiations, where Mr. Boyle is pressing for wider seniority and added helpers on machines.

But he does not appear to be moving rapidly enough to soothe the dissidents. Last week's strike was prolonged in defiance of back-to-work orders by Mr. Boyle.

April 17, 1966

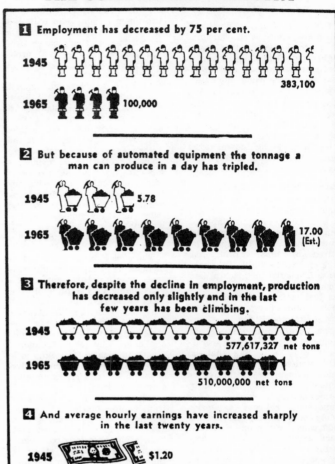

HOW AUTOMATION HAS CHANGED THE COAL MINING INDUSTRY

1 Employment has decreased by 75 per cent.

1945   383,100
1965   100,000

2 But because of automated equipment the tonnage a man can produce in a day has tripled.

1945   5.78
1965   17.00 (Est.)

3 Therefore, despite the decline in employment, production has decreased only slightly and in the last few years has been climbing.

1945   577,617,327 net tons
1965   510,000,000 net tons

4 And average hourly earnings have increased sharply in the last twenty years.

1945 $1.20
1965 $3.49

April 17, 1966

UNION CURBS UPHELD FOR OVERPRODUCERS

WASHINGTON, April 7 (AP) —The Supreme Court upheld today the right of unions to punish workers who go over production quotas set by their union.

Production beyond such quotas is a matter of internal policy not forbidden by Federal labor law, the Court said, 7 to 1.

The decision, given by Justice Byron R. White, dealt with quotas set by the United Automobile Workers Union at the Wisconsin Motor Corporation in Milwaukee. Four machine operators, tried by the union, were fined $50 to $100 and suspended from the union for a year for having exceeded the production ceiling for piece workers.

Half the production workers at the plant, which makes internal combustion engines, are paid on a piece work basis. The union rule, enforceable since 1944 by fines and expulsion, allows members to produce as much as they like each day but sets a ceiling rate for how much pay they may draw on any day. Their overproduction is "banked" by the company and the wages for it are paid to the worker on days when the production ceiling has not been reached.

The average piecework rate is recognized in the collective bargaining contract between the union and the company.

The company has regularly urged the union to abandon the ceiling.

April 2, 1969

HIGH COURT BACKS RIGHT TO STRIKE OVER AUTOMATION

Special to The New York Times

WASHINGTON, April 17 — The Supreme Court upheld today the legal right of labor unions to block the automation of their members' jobs by enforcing contract provisions against the use of prefabricated materials.

In two 5-to-4 decisions, the Court held that key Taft-Hartley and Landrum-Griffin amendments to the National Labor Relations Act had not been intended to deny workers the right to strike to keep their employers from subcontracting work to other companies that would do the work with machines.

"Before we say that Congress meant to strike from workers' hands the economic weapons traditionally used against their employers' efforts to abolish their jobs, that meaning should plainly appear," Justice William J. Brennan Jr. said in the majority opinion.

Allied to 'Hot Cargo'

He was joined by Chief Justice Earl Warren and Justices Abe Fortas, Byron R. White and John M. Harlan.

Justice Potter Stewart argued in a dissent that the Court "has substituted its own notions of sound labor policy for the words of Congress." His dissent was joined by Justices Hugo L. Black, William O. Douglas and Tom C. Clark.

The decisions had particular importance for the building construction industry, where the unions have traditionally bargained for contract clauses to prohibit the use of prefabricated materials.

The National Labor Relations Board has upheld the legality of these "work preservation agreements." They have acted as a brake to automation by barring the use of prefinished materials that would abolish work traditionally done by hand on the job.

However, some lower courts have held that these provisions amounted to "hot cargo" clauses that were outlawed in 1959 by the Landrum-Griffin Act. The "hot cargo" amendment to the national labor law prohibited agreements to "cease from handling the products of any other employer."

Strikes to enforce these provisions have also been held in some cases to be "secondary boycotts" prohibited by the Taft-Hartley Act of 1947.

Secondary boycotts are usually held to be a situation in which workers strike Employer A, with whom they have no dispute, to force him to cease doing business with Employer B, with whom there is a dispute.

The Court held that a strike to enforce a work preservation agreement is not a secondary boycott because the workers' dispute is not with the subcontractor, but with their own employer.

It held that the prefabricated materials are not "hot cargo," which is generally considered to be a material produced by nonunion shops or businesses engaged in disputes with their workers.

The two cases decided today involved a contract between carpenter unions and a group of building contractors in the Philadelphia area and an agreement between heating contractors and asbestos workers in Houston.

Justice Brennan's opinions concentrated on the carpenters' contract, in which the employers had agreed that no carpenter would have to work on prefabricated materials.

When three contractors inherited a job calling for prefabricated doors they ordered 3,600 such doors. The carpenters refused to hang them and, after the contractors sent the doors back, the door manufacturer contended that it had been a victim of a "hot cargo" contract.

The United States Court of Appeals for the Seventh Circuit agreed with the door manufacturer. It said the agreement against the use of prefabricated door amounted to a contract to "cease from handling the products of any other employer," which was prohibited in the "hot cargo" law of 1959.

The Supreme Court reversed that decision and affirmed the contrary decision of the Court of Appeals for the Fifth Circuit in the Houston asbestos case. The Fifth Circuit had upheld a contract provision under which the workers had refused to use prefabricated materials in placing insulation around pipes.

Charles B. Mahin of Chicago argued for the National Woodwork Manufacturing Association, which brought the case for the door manufacturer. Dominick L. Manoli, associate general counsel for the labor board, argued for the Government.

W. D. Deakins of Houston argued for the Insulation Contractors. Norton J. Come, assistant general counsel of the labor board, argued for the Government.

April 18, 1967

Container Revolution Hailed by Many, Feared by Others

By GEORGE HORNE

Winds of change are sweeping the trade lanes of the world, promising to alter the face of commerce, and impose radical and sometimes devastating transformations for existing ports.

It is the time of the container revolution, embodying the first genuine progress in cargo-handling methods in centuries. It is a real revolution and, like all revolutions, it is seized with enthusiasm and acceptance by many, and feared by others.

It all began with a box.

Just how far it will go, no one knows, but the idea of moving domestic and overseas cargo in the boxes or containers is swelling like a tidal wave.

But the wave means stormy seas, and they may engulf some of the industry: As it progresses, ports may lose out and some shipping lines are expected to go under, for the new trade calls for concentration. And the big question along the Atlantic Coast is posed in current labor negotiations now going on in New York, with a Sept. 30 deadline.

Vital Issue for I.L.A.

The crucial impact of the container business on the longshoremen is a vital issue, and the union has already said that if the deadline were passed without a contract it would work conventional cargo ships, but not containers or container carriers.

"We do not propose to be drowned in this wave," a ne-

Container ships, like Atlantic Span, handle cargo quickly

411

Hawaiian Monarch, a Matson ship, rounding Diamond Head. For its Pacific routes, Matson uses 24-foot containers.

gotiator for the International Longshoremen's Association said last week.

"It is an extension of our mass production techniques into the carrying of overseas trade, and it has to come," an operator replied.

Major steamship lines all over the world are building containerships and variations such as trailerships that haul their boxes on wheels. They are simply an extension across the ocean of the familiar over-the-road truck.

United States Lines, one of the nation's largest shipping operators, is plunging into the business so rapidly that in a few weeks it will have no conventional ships in its prime Atlantic trade.

Great Shaped Boxes

Other big lines, such as Moore-McCormack and American Export Isbrandtsen, also have the ships in being or on the ways. The vessels are great shaped boxes themselves, equipped with inner cells like phalanxes of cells similar to elevator shafts into which the boxes are securely fitted, one on top of the other. On the decks are tiers of more boxes.

Other companies on the Pa-

cific and Gulf Coasts are equally busy.

Some companies fear the concept and are waiting before they plunge, in the conviction that the business is moving too fast. Longshoremen, who have moved cargo by hand, by parcel in sling loads from hold to dock for decades, rightly view the new era as a threat to employment levels.

And since the container business depends on great volume and fast dispatch, with a minimum of time wasted along the coast, some ports will inevitably be bypassed.

But the economist and the accountant, once they have espoused the cause, find the profit possibilities entrancing even in the face of the excitingly dangerous capital expenditures involved.

How It Works

How does it work?

The XYZ Manufacturing Company in Great Bend has a consignment ready for shipment to Dusseldorf, Germany. A steamship line serving North European ports is notified, and a traffic man in New York starts three containers from a Chicago pool toward the XYZ loading platform.

When loaded and sealed, the containers move off truck or rail to the Port of New York. The containers, or trailer-vans, are picked up at dockside by $1-million shore-based cranes and deposited at the rate of one every three minutes into the cells of a containership.

The 25-knot ship unloads its cargo with the same kind of equipment in Rotterdam or Hamburg, and it is sped on from there to the inland destination.

The boxes have never been opened, they have been loaded aboard with a minimum of manpower, and at perhaps a tenth of the loading and unloading cost for conventional piece-by-piece cargo.

The ship that carried them is the answer to the worried operator who has always complained in the past that his costly freighter spent two-thirds of its time in port instead of at sea where the money is made.

Many More Voyages

The S.S. Container can make twice as many voyages back and forth across the Atlantic as her conventional sister. She carries more cargo; under ideal circumstances she can unload

and load and be off to sea in 36 to 48 hours instead of seven or eight days.

To achieve this tremendously greater carrying capacity the ship turns in only one additional expense item: fuel for the multiple voyages.

The boxes themselves are pretty much what the turnpike driver sees in droves all over the country, the trailer van hauled by a tractor. They are generally 8 feet high, 8 feet wide, and in a variety of lengths, usually 40 feet or 20 feet.

But there are other lengths. Sea-Land Service, Inc., which is credited with the bellwether role in starting the revolution, uses 35-foot containers. The Matson Navigation Company, which began in 1958, not far behind Sea-Land, sticks to its 24-footers as ideal for its particular Pacific Ocean uses. Internationally, as far as other companies are concerned, the metal or fabricated boxes in 40-foot or lesser 10-foot multiples will be virtually standard.

Domestic Style Packing

In effect, what the container operators are doing for the first time in history is to supply

American Lancer, a United States Lines vessel, handles both 20-foot and 40-foot containers, above and below decks

their customer shippers with packaging. Not only that, they deliver the package free of charge to the manufacturer's door for loading.

In the past he had to pay highly for special export packaging; now he can pack domestic style and depend on the box to protect his packages. Then he pays the transportation bill for getting his consignment to shipside in a coastal port, such as New York, as he always did.

A 40-foot container costs $3,000 to $4,000, depending on design and on variations and sophisticated refinements. They have an estimated life-span of five years. Sea-Land, for its growing fleet of ships in Puerto Rico, Europe and coastal areas, already has 24,000 containers, either owned or on long-term rental from leasing companies.

Moreover, it must have 16,-000 pieces of wheeled chassis equipment on which to deliver and retrieve the valuable boxes.

On the new United States Lines monster containerships of the American Lancer class, 1,200 20-foot containers, or the same equivalent in a mix of 20's and 40's, are stowed in the cells or on deck. The big containers hold an average of 20 to 22 tons, depending on cargo density.

But there is more. For each of the ships, there must be another 1,200 containers ashore in this country and another 1,200 ashore in North European ports.

Role for Computers

All of the tens of thousands of boxes must be kept track of, and with computers this is relatively simple, a factor of prime

importance in preventing the carriers from simply wandering off into limbo. Expensive as they are, the boxes must be utilized to the fullest, as must the ships.

"The object of the game is to facilitate the movement of cargo on a large scale," said John H. Griffith, general freight traffic manager of United States Lines.

Lyle King, director of marine terminals of the Port of New York Authority, also stressed the need for volume. This is why shipping lines that used to send their peripatetic general cargo freighters up and down the coast, making call at seven or eight ports each voyage, now plan to limit container calls to only two ports.

The Port Authority has poured millions of dollars into a tremendous containerport complex in the Newark-Elizabeth area, and further expansion is planned. New York City and private interests have built or will build container facilities on this side of the port. Whatever the extent of the swing from slings to boxes, this port will be ready.

More Cargo, More Trips

"Take a typical well-planned containership," Mr. King said. "She shows up here from the North Atlantic run every three weeks instead of every six weeks. She carries out 14,000 tons of cargo after unloading 14,000 tons. That's 28,000 tons for a round trip and she can make perhaps nine more round trips a year than her old predecessor.

"That is 252,000 tons more a year, with an average revenue of $40 or $50 a ton. She has

earned around $10-million extra."

Obviously the cost of loading and unloading is a major consideration, and this is what put the shipping operator on a collision course with the International Longshoremen's Association. A high Federal official has said it costs 10 times as much to load and unload parcel by parcel than it does by container.

According to Harrison R. Glennon, executive vice president of Moore-McCormack Lines, it costs $16 a ton to load conventional cargo, and $2 to $2.50 a ton for containerships.

An American Export Lines report shows an average of 15 tons an hour for each work gang on an old ship compared with 300 tons an hour with one gang at a containership hatch.

Fewer Men Needed

United States Lines reports this comparison: Ten 17-man gangs would load 1,000 tons of parcel cargo in a 10-hour operation, while one gang and one crane can now load 200 containers, each with about 22 tons, in the same time.

Actually, the lines agree that they do not need a full gang for each container hatch, but they use them.

There is a variation that means additional economy. At one stage in the unload-and-load process, the cranes have cleared enough space to permit loading and unloading in the same motion. The giant "spreaders" that hold the boxes simply drop one in its cell and pick up another one for off-loading.

But the union in a sense

views a successful container operation as a possible death sentence and is determined to take evasive action. The International Longshoremen's Association's president, Thomas W. Gleason, has said that in a few years the 23,000-man work force in this port could be reduced to 12,000 men.

Last year the industry in this port reported 40.7 million man-hours of work, down 3 million man-hours from the previous year. Mr. Gleason forecasts a reduction under the pressure of containers to 28 million man-hours a year.

Indemnity Established

Some years ago when the volume of container carrying was a relative trickle, an agreement with employers established an indemnity, or royalty payment, to the union of $1 a ton for all full container shipments. In the current negotiations with the New York Shipping Association, the I.L.A. demands on containers have not been officially reached. But the men may ask for an indemnity of $4 a ton.

They demand, and will likely be given, the right to strip and reload every container that represents consolidated shipments; that is, small loads that have been put together to make full box loads. Indeed, thousands of containers that move through the port now are being opened, unpacked, repacked and sealed, as make-work.

With the container menace in mind, the union is seeking, in addition to base pay increases, substantially improved pension rights, including early retirement and a work guarantee of 2,080 hours a year for regular men, a full 52 weeks of pay.

KEY ISSUE SETTLED IN DOCKER STRIKE

A Role for I.L.A. in Filling and Stripping Containers Clears Way for Pacts

By EDWARD A. MORROW

The major hurdle to a settlement of the 23-day-old waterfront strike was cleared late yesterday by negotiators for the New York Shipping Association and the International Longshoremen's Association. They reached an agreement on how container shipments would be handled.

David L. Cole, Presidential mediator, described the development as "the key breakthrough" in the negotiations. He expressed the hope that before the end of the week longshoremen would again be handling the more than 300 ships that have been tied up in Atlantic Coast ports and thus permit a resumption of oceanborne foreign trading.

Mr. Cole announced that the union committee, which re-presents longshoremen in ports from Maine to Virginia. had accepted unanimously a new clause in the master contract covering container shipments.

Union negotiators from other cities immediately started returning to their home ports to negotiate minor clauses, which are not covered in the master agreement.

The projected three-year contract provides a $1.60-an-hour package for wages, pensions, welfare, vacations and holidays.

It is the costliest package ever offered by the association, which represents 140 New York employers. Over the three-year period a longshoreman's wages will rise by 98 cents to $4.60 a hour.

Although this increase has been on the table for weeks, the union was unwilling to accept it until it obtained a safeguard against the loss of work opportunities resulting from the increased use of containers. The shipside handling of containers requires many fewer man-hours than do general cargo shipments because they have been loaded elsewhere and are taken by truck or rail to shipside.

This safeguard was provided by extending the I.L.A.'s jurisdiction over the stuffing and stripping of less-than-trailer-load containers, or containers with consolidated shipments within a 50-mile radius from any port. The jurisdictional clause was accompanied by 17 paragraphs of "rules" defining application of the clause.

Jobs for I.L.A. Guaranteed

The new master clause reads:

"Containers owned or leased by employer-members (including containers on wheels) containing LTL loads or consolidated full-container loads, which are destined for or come from, any person (including a consolidator who stuffs containers of outbound cargo or a distributor who strips containers of inbound cargo and including a forwarder, who is either a consolidator of out-cargo or a distributor of inbound cargo) who is not the beneficial owner of the cargo, and which either comes from or is destined to any point within a 50-mile radius from the center of any North Atlantic District port shall be stuffed and stripped by I.L.A. labor at longshore rates on a waterfront under the terms and conditions of the General Cargo Agreement."

Essentially, one union negotiator explained, the clause is designed to prevent the use of lower-cost, non-I.L.A. labor in filling or emptying containers by making such a practice uneconomical.

At the same time by giving each port its own radius, it partly stills the fears of outports that they might lose container traffic to New York.

Meeting Is Delayed

Although the union and management aggred to this clause, the New York association still did not have a contract. A joint meeting between the two parties, scheduled to begin at 10 A.M., did not take place until 7:15 P.M. because the checkers' local demanded special provisions for 300 of its 3,400 members.

Management negotiators were irked by the "last-minute monkey wrench" and caucused long enough for the more than 100 union negotiators to watch the New York Jets-Baltimore Colts football game on television.

Mr. Cole said he believed the checkers' demand, which would allow the 300 checkers to refuse permanent assignment to any pier, was a minor one that could easily be resolved, so that complete agreement could be reached on a contract covering New York Harbor.

Several union leaders admitted that the demand was a plot that would give the negotiators in other ports time to reach an agreement and thus not put New York longshoremen in a position of having to honor a contract while the outports were still negotiating their's.

The "master" agreement covers such basic items as wages, hours, the duration of the agreement and contributions, and in the past it has been accepted by Atlantic ports as far south as Hampton Roads, Va.

January 13, 1969

Panel in Rail Strike Urges New Diesel Job Category

By JAMES M. NAUGHTON

WASHINGTON, Aug. 6—A Presidential emergency board recommended today that the 33-year-old dispute over use of firemen in railroad locomotives be settled by creating a new job classification.

The three-member panel expressed optimism that the National Railway Labor Conference, which bargains for the railroads, and the United Transportation Union would agree to combine the duties of firemen and brakemen on diesel locomotives.

Under the board's recommendations, no newly hired workers would be classified as firemen, but the 17,500 firemen currently on the job would not be dismissed.

President Nixon, who created the panel July 7 while calling a 60-day halt to the union's strike against three major railroads, endorsed the recommendation.

Ronald L. Ziegler, the White House press secretary, said Mr. Nixon was "confident" both sides would accept the panel's findings before the cooling-off period expires on Sept. 6.

The optimism was not universal, however. It was known that Frederick R. Livingston, chairman of the Presidential panel, had sought unsuccessfully to win agreement on the key recommendation before submitting it to the White House.

John P. Hiltz Jr., chairman of the management conference, said tonight that the railroads were "anxious to resume negotiations" in a search for settlement of the dispute, but would make no comment on the issues involved.

In Cleveland, headquarters of the union, H. E. Gilbert, assistant president, declined to comment until he had had an opportunity to study details of the panel's report.

The board sided with man-agement in stating that it agreed unanimously that "there is no need for firemen on diesel locomotives." But it also said that the only hope for long-term stability was a "solution freely arrived at through collective bargaining."

Crux of Long Dispute

The dispute over having a third man in diesel locomotives —in addition to the engineer and brakeman—is the longest in the history of American collective bargaining.

Since the introduction of diesels in the nineteen-thirties, management and labor have sparred over whether firemen are essential to safe and efficient operation.

Congress ordered compulsory arbitration of the issue in 1964, but the arbiter's ruling—elimination of 90 per cent of firemen's jobs — expired in 1966.

The union has fought since for restoration of some 18,000 firemen's jobs.

Mr. Livingston was attempting to mediate a settlement in July, when the union struck the Baltimore & Ohio, Southern Pacific, and Louisville & Nashville Railroads. Mr. Nixon invoked the Railway Labor Act's provision for a 60-day cooling-off period to seek a solution.

The emergency board, whose other members are James C. Vadakin and Willoughby Abner, in its report to the President noted:

"The parties are on the very threshold of settlement. They need take only one small step to conclude a final and complete agreement, an agreement that is substantially their own."

Evolution of Concept

The White House emphasized that the concept of a dual job classification—combining duties of fireman and brakemen on road locomotives and those of firemen and yardmen on yard engines—was being evolved by the management and labor negotiators.

Men already holding seniority as firemen would have an opportunity on an agreed date—to be called Sadie Hawkins Day—to bid for the new jobs of firemen-brakemen or remaining firemen. The firemen classification would eventually be eliminated through natural attrition.

The report said the union should give its commitment that it would not oppose repeal of "full-crew laws" in states where firemen are now required.

At the same time, the panel said that carriers should share the savings realized by the introduction of the new job title and the gradual elimination of the fireman classification through wage increases.

One sticking point, which appeared to have blocked the earlier attempt at mediation, was the union's insistence on premium pay for members required to carry two-way radios and management's refusal to discuss the demand apart from the manning issue.

The Presidential panel said there was "no real merit" to the carriers' position on the radios.

"With potential solution so near at hand to the age-old fireman manning issue, that long-sought goal should not be ost" by linking it to the radio issue," the report said.

August 7, 1970

RAIL STRIKE ENDS WITH 42% PAY RISE

42-Month Contract Provides for Change in Work Rules and Binding Arbitration

By PHILIP SHABECOFF
Special to The New York Times

WASHINGTON, Aug. 2 — A damaging rail strike ended today with the signing of a contract that could usher in a new era of labor-management relations for the nation's long-troubled railroad industry.

Negotiators for the United Transportation Union and the railroads reached agreement this morning after almost continuous bargaining over the last three days.

The union withdrew its picket lines, some of which had been up for 18 days, at 12:01 P.M. in each time zone.

Rail officials said that the first passenger trains started to move soon after the pickets had been withdrawn and that the freight trains would begin rolling by midnight. The whole rail system, they said, will be operational by the weekend, although it will take some time until rail service is completely normal again.

The new contract establishes some of the work rule changes that the railroads have sought for many years—rules they insist are needed to make their operations economically viable.

The union also agreed for the first time to submit to binding arbitration involving what had heretofore been jealously guarded prerogatives.

In return, the railroads granted a 42 per cent wage increase over a 42-month period and agreed to provisions for job and income security.

At least five other rail unions also signed up for 42 per cent wage increases over 42 months.

Today's rail agreement capped what Secretary of Labor James D. Hodgson described at a WHhite House briefing as "a pretty good weekend on the industrial peace front."

Last night, the United Steelworkers of America and nine major steel companies reached a contract settlement just hours short of a threatened strike.

Today's rail agreement followed 20 months of bitter dispute between the U.T.U., which represents 190,000 brakemen, firemen, switchmen and other train operating crewmen, and the carriers.

The dispute was punctuated by intermittent bargaining, Government arbitration, court tests, a brief strike last December and, starting 18 days ago, "selective" strikes against specific lines.

At the time of the settlement, the Union had shut down 10 carriers, including five major railroads: the Union Pacific, the Southern, the Southern Pacific, the Norfolk & Western and the Santa Fe. The other five were smaller switching and steel carrying lines.

Charles Luna, president of the union, said that the settlement would go down in history as showing that "selective" strikes against certain railroads rather than the whole rail system could work in reaching a national agreement.

The contract must still be ratified by local leaders of the union, but Mr. Luna said that he expected no difficulties.

The new contract grants the railroads many of the work rules changes they said that they required to pay large wage increases and to run their lines efficiently and economically. However, some of the rules were modified to meet the objections of the union.

The most important of the changes granted the railroads the right to institute "interdivisional runs," or longer daily train runs for crews. In the past, daily runs were limited to traditional "seniority districts" that averaged 100 miles.

The carriers will not institute the interdivisional runs unilaterally, however. If the lengthening of a daily run eliminates home terminals of crew members, it must first be agreed upon by a standing labor-management committee.

If the committee fails to agree within 90 days, the proposal goes to a tripartite "task force" with union and railroad members and a "neutral" member appointed by the Federal Mediation Board. The decision of the task force would then be binding.

The pact gives those railroads that do not have it now the right to require workers to carry two-way radios as standard equipment. It also calls for the elimination of extra payments for use of radios, called "arbitraries," by Jan. 1, 1973.

Other important rules changes include the following:

❡Yard crews will be required to provide service to industrial plants built before 1951 if they are within four miles of the yard. Such service was limited to newer plants in the old rules.

❡Crews taking cars to other rail lines can be required to bring cars back with them if the railroads deem it necessary.

All of these changes have various interpretations and applications from carrier to carrier, and many details are still to be worked out.

Standing Committees

The agreement also calls for permanent standing labor-management committees to deal with economic and rules disputes on a continuing basis.

The contract provides for wage increases of 4 per cent effective April 1, 1971; 5 per cent Oct. 1, 1971; 5 per cent April 1, 1972, and 5 per cent Oct. 1, 1972, plus 15 cents an hour as of Jan. 1, 1973, and 19 cents an hour on April 1, 1973.

Union members are guaranteed higher compensation if they are laid off as a result of work rule changes and also may be given allowances if they are forced to relocate because of the changes.

The contract also guarantees that there will be no reprisals against striking workers. This had been one of the sore points blocking a settlement in recent weeks.

August 3, 1971

Auto Industry Struggling to Stop Lag in Productivity

Unimate manipulators flanking Chevrolet's assembly line for new Vega move lightweight spot-welding guns through complex routines. Robot machines make 95 per cent of the body welds on minicar, against 20 per cent on earlier cars.

G.M. Enlists Robots, Chrysler Presents Green Stamps

By JERRY M. FLINT
Special to The New York Times

DETROIT, Aug. 7 — At Chrysler's Mound Road engine plant here they are trying green stamps. At the General Motors plant in Lordstown, Ohio, they are trying robots. The aim is the same: To cut costs, improve quality and raise productivity.

Productivity has been lagging in Detroit, and when productivity does not go up as fast as pay, prices are likely to rise. And if foreign competitors are offering lower priced goods at the same time, sales are likely to fall. That is what has been happening to Detroit.

But rising costs and declining productivity growth are not just the problems of the auto industry. They are national in scope, and other industries will be watching as Detroit searches for solutions.

Over the last quarter century, the nation's productivity has risen by an average of 3.2 per cent a year. For a year and a half, however, the pace of the increase has slowed. In the first quarter of this year, output per manhour fell by more than 2 per cent.

A Key to Affluence

Productivity is just a measuring tool: How much output comes off the line per manhour worked. But producing more with less manpower is a key to creating a wealthier society.

"To produce more with the same amount of effort is a sound economic and social objective," General Motors and the United Auto Workers acknowledge in their labor contract. "A continuing improvement in the standard of living of employes depends upon technological progress, better tools, methods, processes and equipment and a cooperative attitude on the part of all parties in such progress."

Productivity goes down and up with production because em-

ployers do not layoff or hire as fast as volume shifts, and three has been a downturn in the car business as well as other industries.

The work force is changing. There are more younger workers and they may not be as hungry as their parents were and may skip a day or two from time to time. That can push up production costs. And the hiring of the poor and unskilled, considered an important social objective, may cause some inefficiency on the line or raise training costs.

Changes in Economy

The economy is changing, too, with more emphasis on services, where it is hard to increase, and less on factory production, where output can often be raised by simply adding new machinery.

According to Labor Department calculations, auto industry productivity rose at an average rate of 6.7 per cent from 1957 through 1962, but from then on the gain averaged 3.4 per cent a year to 1968. Jerome Mark, Assistant Com-

missioner for Productivity and Technology for the Bureau of Labor Statistics says figures for 1969 will show another drop in the productivity increase rate. He is certain this year's figures are falling off, too, and attributes the decline mainly to the lag in production in the auto industry.

"We don't put any great stock in that thing," Malcolm Denise, Ford Motor Company labor relations vice president, said of the Government figures.

The car makers say they do not try to measure their productivity. But labor costs, they agree, have been increasing by an average of 6.5 per cent a year over the last six years. And last fall James Roche, the General Motors chairman, said productivity gains were probably not 3 per cent a year at his company "and it's been declining."

Big Rise in Output Seen

The auto workers union complains that productivity gains of the past were not shared enough with the workers and the public — through higher wages and lower prices — and that the industry can absorb higher pay by trimming profits.

Leonard Woodcock, the union's president, agrees that productivity gains "probably slowed up, which is always true in a downturn period anyway," but predicts that Detroit is "on the threshold of a big burst of productivity."

Mr. Denise of Ford believes that part of the past productivity gains in Detroit came from automation breakthroughs. "In the fifties we were automating engine blocks," he said, "and we took a lot of work out of the engine machining with the transfer lines." (Tarnsfer lines move engine blocks from station to station automatically for automatic machining.)

"But then what do you do the next year?" he went on. "You can't come up with those quantum jumps regularly." Moreover, it takes years to spread such breakthroughs through the industrial system.

Breakthrough on the Vega

There may be a breakthrough coming in Lordstown, Ohio, where General Motors is building its new minicar, the Vega 2300. Some 4,800 workers on two shifts there are expected to build 100 cars an hour, against the 60 big cars an hour that the 4,800 men turned out in the past.

This quantum jump represents more than just automation or new machinery, although there is plenty of that. It represents a new type of team operation, with General

Motors engineers, stylists and production experts reportedly working together as never before to raise productivity by wringing costs out of the car design. Here are some examples:

¶The number of parts on the new Vega body was cut to 1,231 against 3,500 on a big Chevrolet body, with large subassemblies and panels substituted for the many small parts in conventional body building.

¶Robot welding machines called Unimates are lined up on each side of the Lordstown line, replacing men. These 26 robots are equipped to carry welding guns and "memorize" the motions they must go through on the job. Where 20 per cent of body welds were made automatically, in the old setup, 95 per cent of the 3,900 body welds on the Vega are made with automatic equipment. The body was designed to eliminate hard-to-reach weld points that a robot could not handle.

¶A precision-built window track is laid into the door, eliminating a time-consuming window adjustment job. Door hinges are atuomatically welded, not bolted, to the body, and doors are fitted and hung automatically, eliminating manual adjusting.

¶Machinery will fit front and rear windows into place automatically.

¶The assembly line itself raises the car 14 to 72 inches to allow workers and machines easy access as the car body winds around a mile-and-a-quarter track.

¶Interior trim, such as the side panels and the doors are almost all plastic and molded, eliminating many of the cut-and-sew operations, and a one-piece plastic headliner — that is, the car's ceiling — is used, eliminating cloth cutting and sewing. A foam bucket seat eliminates the layers of padding, insulators, and clips common in car seats.

¶Computers were used to determine in advance of production whether parts were difficult to install and parts such as the front bumper were modified when installation appeared cumbersome on the computer simulation.

Not all of the manufacturing techniques are new, but it is the first time that they have been combined to such an extent, General Motors officials say.

The Vega production techniques are aimed at outflanking problems that the carmakers say hurt productivity: the lack of technological breakthrough in recent years, the proliferation of car models, and the changing work force.

At some plants today most of the workers are under 30 years old, and at other plants there is an infusion of the poor and least skilled. There is some drug taking and some racial antagonism, and absenteeism has doubled in a decade. It is so high before or after weekends and holidays that quality falls sharply as men are switched into unfamiliar jobs.

At Chrysler's Mount Road engine plant in Detroit, trading stamps are being used to combat the costly absenteeism.

For one month on the job without absence, a worker gets 200 S & H green stamps, and he receives up to 3,200 for six months without absence.

Mr. Bramblett of General Motors says that "a good percentage of the work force has never seen anything but affluence," and blames this for some of the plant troubles. He calls for "cooperation, working together, so you don't have to do the job over." Some workers do not even bother to alert repairmen when they see errors in a car, he said.

Another auto executive said: "If workers are more careless, and the younger guys tend to be, it adds to costs. They may be keeping up with the job as far as the line speed goes, but if you have big numbers in repairs it costs."

The union, too, recognizes the problem, but says that today's younger, better educated worker will not be enthused by dull, repetitive and dirty work in car plants, and that the younger worker puts his personal life first and will not be treated as a part of the plant machinery.

Some of the thorniest issues in this summer's round of bargaining among the automakers and the U.A.W. will center on company attempts to toughen plant discipline to cut costs. But some auto industry men are not convinced that this is the entire answer.

A Ford executive said of the young secretaries in his department: "They want to participate. It's not so much what they make, if they don't feel they are participating."

Young Workers Disrupt Key G.M. Plant

A WORKER at the Lordstown, Ohio, plant of General Motors that builds Vega cars

By AGIS SALPUKAS

Special to The New York Times

LORDSTOWN, Ohio, Jan. 22 —Production on the world's fastest assembly line, on which the General Motors Corporation has pinned its hopes of being able to meet foreign competition, has been seriously disrupted by mostly young workers who say they are being asked to work too hard and too fast to be able to turn out quality automobiles.

The outcome of the labor dispute, in which the youngest local of the United Automobile Workers is confronting one of General Motors' toughest management teams, could have wide repercussions for United States industry.

The struggle has raised a wider issue of how management can deal with a young worker who is determined to have a say as to how a job should be performed and is not so easily moved by management threats that there are plenty of others waiting in line if he does not want to do the job.

It also comes at a time when the Nixon Administration is stressing rising productivity as the way to stop inflation and the influx of foreign goods.

The costly dispute centers on whether management has eliminated jobs and distributed extra work to the remaining men to the extent that they are unable to keep up with the assembly line in the Lordstown plant.

General Motors estimates that it has lost the production of 12,000 Vega automobiles and about 4,000 Chevrolet trucks worth about $45-million. Management has had to close down the assembly line repeatedly since last month after workers slowed their work and allowed cars to move down the line without performing all operations.

A. B. Anderson, the plant manager, said in an interview, "We've had engine blocks pass 40 men without them doing their work.

Management has also accused workers of sabotage, such as breaking windshields, breaking off rear-view mirrors, slashing upholstery, bending signal levers, putting washers in carburetors and breaking off ignition keys.

In the last four weeks a lot that holds about 2,000 cars has often been filled with Vegas that had to be taken back into the plant for repair work before they could be shipped to dealers. Sales of Vegas in the last two weeks have been cut about in half.

The union, which concedes that there may have been some sabotage by a few angry workers, maintains that the bulk of the problems with the cars were a result of cutbacks in numbers of workers in a drive by management to increase efficiency and cut costs.

According to the union, the remaining workers have had to absorb the extra work and cannot keep up with the assembly line. The result, the union men say, is improperly assembled cars.

The dispute is taking place in one of the most modern and sophisticated assembly plants in the world, built in 1966 on a farm field near Lordstown.

Through better design, a variety of new types of power tools and other automated devices, much of the heavy lifting and hard physical labor has been eliminated in the plant. Even the parking lots were planned in such a way that the long walk to one's car has been done away with.

Less Bending Required

Workers on the assembly line have easier access to the car body and do not have to do as much bending and crawling in and out as in the older plants in Detroit. The Vega also has 43 per cent fewer parts than a full-size car, making the assembly easier.

But, as the jobs become easier and simpler, the rate at which they can be done can be increased. On a regular assembly line, which runs at about 55 cars an hour, a worker takes about a minute to perform a task, while workers at the Lordstown plant need only about 40 seconds.

The wages are good. Workers start out on the line at $4.37 an hour, get a 10-cent-an-hour increase within 30 days and another 10 cents after 90 days. Benefits come to $2.50 more an hour.

The plant sits almost in the center of the heavy industrial triangle made up of Youngstown, with its steel plants; Akron, with its rubber industry, and Cleveland, a major center for heavy manufacturing.

The plant, which produces all the Vegas made by General Motors, draws its 7,700 workers, whose average age is 24 years, from areas that have felt the sting of foreign competition and where unemployment and layoffs have been heavy.

Many of the fathers of the young auto workers are employed in steel and rubber and have watched their jobs dwindle because foreign products have undercut their industries.

But the threat of unemployment and pressure from mothers and fathers, from the local press and public officials, have so far had little effect on the militant young workers who began their struggle with General Motors last October.

It was then that General Motors Assembly Division, a management team that has developed the reputation for toughness in cutting costs and bettering productivity, took over the operation of the Fisher Body Plant and Chevrolet assembly plant here and began to consolidate the operations.

From the point of view of management, the two plants had not been operating at their peak efficiency.

A major reorganization of work began. According to management it consisted mostly of changing jobs to make them more efficient, although management conceded that about 300 jobs had been eliminated and some workers had been given additional work.

Mr. Anderson explained that changes had to be made to bring the assembly line, which can turn out 100 Vegas in an hour, up to the potential it was designed for.

"If we are to remain competitive, we will have to take advantage of those sections of the contract on making the work more efficient," he said.

But across the Ohio Turnpike, Gary Bryner, the 29-year-old president of Local 1112, in an interview in his office in a modern brick union hall, said that about 700 jobs had been eliminated and that much of the extra work had been shifted to men who had no time to do it.

"That's the fastest line in the world," Mr. Bryner said. "A guy has about 40 seconds to do his job. The company does some figuring and they say, 'Look, we only added one thing to his job.' On paper it looks like he's got time."

Increase in Grievances

"But you've got 40 seconds to work with," he continued. "You add one more thing and it can kill you. The guy can't get the stuff done on time and a car goes by. The company then blames us for sabotage and shoddy work."

He said that before the new management team took over, there were about 100 grievances in the plant. Since then, he said, grievances have increased to 5,000—about 1,000 of which consist of protests of too much work added to a job.

Mr. Bryner, on whose desk sit a peace symbol and a little book of "Revolutionary Quotations by Great Americans," said that a decision by the workers to work at their old pace to protest the changes had come from the rank and file and not from the union leadership.

"These guys have become

The New York Times/Jan. 23, 1972

tigers," he said. "They've got guts. You used to not see them at union meetings. Now we've got them in the cafeteria singing 'Solidarity.' "

Both union and management concede that they were surprised by the depth of the resistance that has arisen among the work force whose average age on some assembly lines is about 22.

Management has attempted conciliation and has instituted sensitivity sessions with groups of workers to find out what the complaints are.

But the over-all management strategy so far has been one of toughness of hoping for results from the smaller pay checks that are issued when workers are sent home early when there is a slowdown and from foremen's disciplining workers by sending them home without pay.

When the workers went into the plant yesterday they found on the bulletin boards a notice saying that not only would work slowdowns be dealt with through disciplinary measures but also that workers could be dismissed.

Many young workers said in interviews that, the tougher the company became, the more they would stiffen their resistance, even though other jobs were scarce and many of them had recently been married and had families.

Nick Schecodonic Jr., 27, a repair spot welder, said, "In

some of the other plants where they did the same thing, the workers were older. They took some of this. But I've got 25 years ahead of me in that plant."

Mr. Schecodonic, who is married and has children, added, "I actually saw a woman in the plant running along the line to keep up with the work. I'm not going to run for anybody. There ain't anyone in that plant that is going to tell me to run."

Another worker who is worried about keeping his job said that he decided to support the union rank-and-file when he saw a gap between the body of a car and the instrument panel and brought it to the attention of the foreman.

The worker, who has a job as an inspector, said the foreman told him, "To hell with it. Ship it to the dealer." He said that after he refused to approve the car, the foreman signed the paper himself.

Mr. Bryner said that, at one meeting with the company, a management official said that in November there were about 6,000 complaints from Chevrolet dealers about the quality of the Vegas shipped to them, more than the combined complaints from the other assembly plants.

Andrew O'Keefe, public relations director at the plant, denied that any defective cars had been shipped and said that any foreman passing on a defective car would "be fired on the spot."

Mr. Anderson attributed part of the dispute to the attitude of the young worker. But he also laid much of the resistance to the fear that a worker's job would be changed. "We're getting problems in areas where we haven't changed a thing," he said.

He added that management faced a difficult task in getting workers "to take pride in our product—if a man drops a bolt and he doesn't pick it up and put it on, he's more apt to let it go the second time."

Union Strikes G.M. Facility In Work Methods Dispute

LORDSTOWN, Ohio, March 4 (UPI)—The United Automobile Workers struck the big complex of the General Motors Corporation here today, idling 10,000 employees and shutting down the only Chevrolet Vega assembly line in the nation.

Local 1112 of the union, by a 97 per cent vote, authorized the strike because of a long-smoldering dispute over production line methods. The line produces 100 of the small Vegas an hour.

Some of the workers took personal tools with them when the strike began at 2 A.M., indicating they expect a long walkout. About 50 pickets patrolled the plant gates or huddled around fires in frigid weather.

January 23, 1972

March 5, 1972

G.M. Plant in Ohio Is Producing Again

By AGIS SALPUKAS
Special to The New York Times

DETROIT, March 27—Vegas were rolling off the assembly line again at the General Motors plant in Lordstown, Ohio, today, but it was uncertain whether the labor strife at the plant had ended.

Members of Local 1112 of the United Automobile Workers approved a settlement yesterday after a 22-day strike that cut off all production of the Vega.

But the vote was light. Only about 3,000 of the 7,600 members turned out and about 30 per cent of those who voted turned down the settlement.

And while the production line at Lordstown was being restored, the General Motors Assembly Division, whose policies caused the strike at Lordstown, was being challenged by U.A.W. locals in three other plants around the country.

The struggle, which began at Lordstown, pits the U.A.W. against a tough G.M. management team that is determined to improve efficiency in many of its plants.

Locals at plants in Wilmington, Ded.; and Norwood, Ohio, and St. Louis have voted to strike or have given strike notices.

Strike Called in Ohio

Also, the U.A.W. announced today that it was sending a special team to aid in the negotiations at the plant in Norwood where Local 674, representing 4,000 workers, has voted to strike on April 7 if a settlement is not reached.

Irving Bluestone, the head of the G.M. section of the U.A.W., said in a statement that the assembly division was creating the same problems at Norwood as it had in Lordstown by "reducing manpower, disciplining workers in wholesale numbers" and taking away agreements previously negotiated.

In the settlement that was worked out last Friday, the union won some major concessions from G.M. Gary Bryner, the presidnt of the local, said today, "we're back where we started in October as far as jobs."

He said that 240 jobs had been restored and that 130 men would be laid off but most of these had less than 90 days on the job."

Mr. Bryner said that an important result of the struggle was that it had changed a young work force—the average age is 24—many of whose members wede indifferent to the union, into one strongly committed to the U.A.W. "They built more unionism than we ever could," he said.

March 28, 1972

Workers Increasingly Rebel Against Boredom on Assembly Line

By AGIS SALPUKAS
Special to The New York Times

DETROIT, April 1 — Mike Kingsley goes to the assembly plant about an hour before his shift every day and takes out his worn little Bible to read and meditate before he faces his job.

"You've got to prepare yourself mentally," he said as he paused by the Ford assembly plant at Wixom. After three and a half years in the plant assembling dashboards, he feels he has reached a dead end.

"I'm going back to school at the end of the summer," he said. "There's only three ways out of here. You either conform and become deader each day, or you rebel, or you quit."

Discipline Is Resisted

The feeling that there is no future, that the work is boring, that the only solution is to get out of the plant or wait for retirement has become widespread among many of the hourly workers who man the nation's industrial plants.

The problem, often referred to as the "blue collar blues," is not new. There have been complaints about the monotony of assembly line work from the beginning. But what is new is that, increasingly, a significant number of workers are starting to resist the discipline required by their jobs.

Nowhere is the difficulty more apparent than in the automobile industry, which prides itself on being the epitome of industrial mass production.

The problem has just been underscored at the General Motors Corporation's assembly plant in Lordstown, Ohio, where worker resistance to the discipline of a highly automated assembly line has led to sabotage and a 22-day strike. But union and management men say the troubles in Lordstown are merely an acute aspect of broader troubles.

Rise in Absenteeism

More workers are taking days off without excuses. Absenteeism among the big three auto makers — General Motors, the Ford Motor Company and the Chrysler Corporation—has doubled in the last seven years, from 2 to 3 per cent in 1965 to 5 to 6 per cent now.

Indeed, on Fridays and Mondays in many plants up to 15 per cent of the workers do not go in, causing severe production problems.

Turnover has also almost doubled. Chrysler reported in its 1970 negotiations that almost half its workers did not complete the first 90 days on the job in 1969.

An increasing number of workers are also asking the United Automobile Workers to press for early retirement, to change the jobs so that they are made more interesting, and to make overtime voluntary, issues that were rarely mentioned in the past.

There has been a slight decrease in absenteeism and turnover in the last year. But many in the industry believe this may be a temporary lull because of a scarcity of jobs caused by high unemployment and the little new hiring by the industry in the last two years.

The companies have begun to react. Each of the big three is looking into new ways to motivate workers.

The most far-reaching changes are being tried at Chrysler, where workers are being brought into management decisions and consulted on how new cars should be built and plants organized.

Corporate executives, union leaders, Government officials and labor experts are debating whether a new work force has emerged that will increasingly demand jobs that will fulfill creative needs as well as provide food and shelter.

There are some who believe that these problems have always existed and that no major modifications of work will be needed to keep the economy running.

There are others who believe that American industry is being confronted by a young, more highly educated worker who will demand major changes in the workplace.

The awareness that many workers are unhappy has reeached high levels of the Government. President Nixon, in his Labor Day address last

The New York Times/Frank Lodge

His Bible on the table, Mike Kingsley prays in lunchroom of Ford plant in Detroit

year, stressed that "the dignity of work, the value of achievement, the morality of self-reliance—none of these is going out of style."

But he added, "Let us also recognize that the work ethic in America is undergoing some changes."

He said, "We must make sure that technology does not dehumanize work but make it more creative and rewarding for the people who will operate the plants of the future."

There is much at stake on how the 30 million blue-collar workers view their jobs. It will affect productivity, which in the long run will determine if American industry can meet foreign competition and if inflation can be stopped.

Automation and new technology can still contribute to higher productivity.

Edward Cole, president of General Motors, said in a recent speech, "It is not machines but people on whom our future progress must depend."

Increased Monotony

Some industrial engineers also believe that American industry in some instances may have pushed technology too far by taking the last few bits of skill out of jobs, and that a point of human resistance has been reached.

At the General Motors Lordstown plant, many workers have said that, even though the hard jobs have been automated and made simpler, the process has led to increased monotony and has decreased their pride in the work.

There is also a wider issue of alienation. Some studies have shown that blue-collar workers who feel their skills are not used, have little chance for promotion, and cannot change jobs are least likely to vote and identify themselves with either major party.

Jerome M. Rosow, an Assistant Secretary of Labor, in the report on the blue-collar worker in 1970, said, "They feel like forgotten people, those for whom the Government and the society have limited, if any, direct concern and little visible action."

Peak Is Reached Early

According to the report, the average blue-collar worker earns $5,000 to $10,000 a year and reaches his peak earning power and chances for promotion early in life.

Unlike the white-collar worker, he earns wages that remain steady even though expenses at home mount as his children become ready for college or he has to support aging parents.

To keep up, he usually takes a second job, or has his wife work and hopes for big wage increases from his union. He feels inroads by minorities into his neighborhood and feels trapped because of a lack of mobility on his job and from his neighborhood.

Other research has found that the main cause of discontent of the blue-collar worker lies in the nature of his work.

A major study of 1,095 workers by the Institute of Social Research at the University of Michigan has found that one cannot isolate those with the "blues" simply in terms of age, sex, and income, although income does make a small difference.

A worker is satisfied, the survey found, if he has a chance to use his skills, be creative and learn new things, and if he works for a supervisor who knows the job and leaves him alone.

Although adequate pay, job security and comfort were important, the study concluded, "For the American worker in the 1970s these do not insure against the blues."

Many assembly line workers agree with these findings.

Willy Raines and two of his friends sat in an Oldsmobile on a parking lot outside the Wixom plant sipping Teachers Scotch from paper cups. It was 11 A.M. and this is the way they usually spend their half-hour lunch break.

Mr. Raines, on the assembly line for 17 years, had spent the morning glancing at a computer sheet that told him what kind of tires were needed for the Lincolns moving down the line.

His job is to take tires off a rack and hang them on hooks that move by at waist level. "I don't know what it is they can do, but they got to change these jobs," he said. "If you don't get a break off that line, you can go crazy."

Looks to Retirement

Like many older workers who have built up seniority and benefits and have limited education, he sees no choice but to keep his job. His hope is to put in his 30 years and retire at $500 a month in benefits at the age of 58.

For a younger worker, however, 30 years and retirement seem a long way off. Many feel the frustration of Dewey Burton, who started at the Wixom plant when he was 18 and full of optimism. He had hoped that he would either make enough money to set up his own body paint shop or become a foreman.

"Each year," he said, "I felt like I accomplished something. Suddenly I realized that I'm at a dead end and I'll probably be hacking on the line for 30 years."

He is satisfied with his pay of $4.67 an hour, which with benefits such as hospitalization and life insurance comes to about $7 an hour and brings in about $9,500 a year. It is enough to support his wife and child.

It has taken him seven years to get into the paint department, even though he has won numerous trophies for his custom paintwork on the outside.

He has passed his foreman's test but was denied promotion after he was disciplined for not wearing safety glasses. Now he sometimes puts down a quart of wine at lunch. "Why should I be in a dead end?" he asks. "There's got to be some changes."

Many young workers simply

quit. Three years ago, when the Wixom plant on the outskirts of Detroit was hiring some new people, about 8 per cent of the workers would quit each month. This meant that 4,800 workers had to be hired each year to maintain a work force of 5,000.

On Fridays, which is pay day, and on Mondays up to 500 workers did not go in. To keep the plant operating, a labor pool of about 200 college students was set up for those two days.

Heavy unemployment and layoffs have now stabilized the work force at the plant. But still foreman often have to fill in on Fridays and Monday. Special plans have to be made on the opening of the fishing and deer seasons.

There are small encouraging signs.

Absenteeism, which had risen each year since the nineteen-sixties, has leveled off and in some cases is beginning to decline. At Ford, for example, absenteeism was running at 5.8 per cent a year but went down to 5.2 per cent in 1971. General Motors has also seen a slight drop in absenteeism since last spring.

The level is still too high to be acceptable to the industry.

Ford estimated that just the fringe benefits of those out without excuses costs about $30-million a year. That does not count the much greater expense caused by losses of production.

Malcolm Denise, head of Ford's labor relations, is encouraged by the decline but is still cautious about the future.

The average age of the work force, he said, has fallen by four years in the last decade and will continue to fall. The younger employe, he said, is less willing to put up with the type of work and conditions encountered by the men who entered the plants before and after the Depression.

He is also pessimistic, as are most of the other top executives in the industry, that the jobs on the assembly line can be changed to make them more interesting.

"You can't stay in the auto business by throwing parts on the floor and saying to the guy, 'Make an automobile out of it,'" he said. "There are a lot of economic constraints."

Will Discuss Proposal

He has agreed to talk over a proposal made by Kenneth Bannon, head of the auto union's Ford department, that

in the 1973 negotiations, Ford consider having workers build cars in teams as an answer to monotony.

Eugene A. Cafiero, president of North American operations for Chrysler, recalled the early days in an interview: "People came off the boat and had no livelihood. They thought a job in the plants was heaven. My parents went through the sixth grade. I have two college degrees and that's what's happening in my generation all over the country."

According to the statistics of the Department of Labor, the educational level of young workers has gone up dramatically in the last 10 years and will continue to rise into 1980.

To Mr. Cafiero this means that the auto industry will have to make major changes.

Through his efforts, Chrysler has gone into an extensive program under which workers are taken into the planning of how a car is to be produced and what kind of machinery should be set up, and in some instances workers have set up minor assembly lines themselves.

But so far there has been little change in the actual jobs on the assembly line.

Proposals such as having teams of workers build one car or a large unit, or having workers follow one car along the assembly line are considered impractical by auto executives and even some union leaders.

Douglas Fraser, the head of the union's Chrysler department, said, "If you triple plant capacity and would be willing to pay $10,000 per car, then you could have teams build cars."

There is increasing evidence, however, that the job itself will have to be changed.

In the University of Michigan survey, for example, when workers were given 25 aspects of their job and asked to rank them in importance, interesting work was ranked first and pay second.

Paul F. Maine, a job design consultant at Case Western Reserve University, said in an interview, "We may have created too many dumb jobs for the number of dumb people to fill them."

He said that perhaps the high absenteeism, the turnover and the shoddy work may be a way to express a deep and growing resentment towards boring, unfulfilling work.

"The young guys may be saying, 'I don't have the guts to start a revolt in the plant, but I'll kick other ways,'" he said.

April 2, 1972

Auto Workers Are Given a Voice on Assembly Line

By AGIS SALPUKAS
Special to The New York Times

DETROIT, June 18—Since Henry Ford and his engineers put together the first car assembly line in 1914, the auto industry has been fitting the man to the line.

Today, faced with spreading absenteeism, high turnover and even sabotage among an increasingly dissatisfied work force, the industry is experimenting to see what can be done to make the line fit the man.

The Chrysler Corporation is the most deeply involved

of the Big Four auto producers in trying to make work not simply a penalty a worker feels he has to pay to survive but something that provides satisfaction in itself.

For the last year and a half, workers in many of Chrysler's 32 plants have been meeting with their foremen, engineers and production managers to exchange ideas, solve problems and make suggestions about their jobs.

Some plants are experimenting with letting workers supervise their own assembly

lines, letting them control the flow of material on the lines, and allowing them a choice of working on an assembly line or at tables where they can make whole components.

The program is still in its early stages. Its problems are complex, and any judgments would be premature. So far, it has often resulted in giving more responsibility to middle managers while reaching only a small part of the rank and file.

But many of those who have participated are enthusiastic. John Rand, a black assembly line worker

for three years at the Hamtramck plant, paused for a moment in his job and said: "Things were explained, now you feel like a part of things. Before it was: 'You do this. You do that.' And that's it."

During the last year he has met many times, on company time, with foremen, production supervisors and other workers who are responsible for assembling caster and camber parts, which are vital to steering and wheel alignment.

Before the meetings, he said, he did not know what the part was for and did not care. Often he would let the car body go by and grumble to himself about the pace of the line.

It was this kind of dissatisfaction and indifference that led Chrysler to begin its experiments.

Eugene A. Cafiero, group vice president of the Chrysler North American operations, said: "We've changed more in the past year and a half than in the last 12 years. This company has been through a small revolution."

Effects Hard to See

The effects are hard to see since almost no major changes have been made in the way workers scrape, wipe, lift, paint and assemble cars and none is expected in the near future.

What has been brought to many of the company's plants is a new atmosphere, a new team spirit. Workers are now often given a voice, for example, in deciding how to set up their assembly lines.

In many plants, workers are being given a chance to look over the '75 models. The parts are explained and the workers are asked to comment on how the line will be set up.

Mr. Cafiero, the prime mover behind the program, is continuing to visit the company's plants and prod managers to experiment. He has let it be known that the program does not have to show sudden gains in productivity.

At this point, he measures results mostly through re-

actions of workers and supervisors. A skilled trades worker, he recalled, recently came to him and said: "This is the first time in 16 years anyone has asked me to use my head and heart instead of my hands and feet."

Other Companies' Efforts

The effort is not unique to Chrysler. Other major companies such as Bell Telephone, Corning Glass and Texas Instruments are trying to change jobs not only of blue-collar workers but of white-collar workers as well.

General Motors and Ford also have programs, although none is on the scale of Chrysler's, which is a priority effort throughout the corporation.

Those in charge concede that there are major uncertainties on how it will come out. Although workers like Mr. Rand may feel better about their jobs, there is some question how long it will last—especially as they go on working with the same parts in the same way on the same line as before.

It is hard to try to change work on assembly lines. Even a seemingly simple change such as letting workers follow a car along and assemble a large part of it would mean a major cost increase.

Chrysler's management is also worried that frustrations may only be intensified if expectations are raised and workers are involved in decision making and then, for whatever reason, no important change results.

Only a few feet away from Mr. Rand, for example, another worker, Edward Walker, a 23-year-old Vietnam veteran, compared the plant now to when he left for the service two years ago.

"There's nothing easier and there ain't nothing harder," he said as he shoved one side of a car body to the line. "You're still under pressure. That line don't stop."

There is little possibility in the near future that assembly lines will change significantly in an industry where costs are figured to the penny and foreign competition is a major threat.

Douglas Fraser, a vice president of the United Automobile Workers Union and head of the union's Chrysler department, made a recent tour of plants in Japan.

In a report to the union's executive board, he said that in some plants Japanese workers put together cars at speeds that would not be tolerated by American workers.

Still, even with those uncertainties, there is optimism at Chrysler that major gains can be made in motivating workers without making major changes in the jobs themselves.

At the Hamtramck plant, for example, some workers are no longer punished for taking an unexcused day off.

Instead, large calendars have been put up in one part of the plant and workers are

asked to mark the day in advance when they want to take off.

Management can then juggle its schedules by knowing when a man will be absent, instead of having to scramble around at the last minute to fill in for absent workers.

For two months absenteeism dropped, but then it crept up again to near its old rate. One advantage has remained. Half of the men now notify the company ahead when they take a day off.

One foreman objected so vociferously to the program that he resigned. Older workers, who often have more skilled jobs and do them with ease, have objected to proposals such as letting men rotate in different jobs. And some supervisors fear that their jobs will be eliminated through the program.

At the Detroit Gear and Axle plant, workers are being allowed to control the flow of assembly lines. William White, a 44-year-old worker, sat on a stool in front of a line where gear assemblies moved past him. There was a pedal he could hit with his foot to stop the line if he wanted to get a drink of water or take a break.

He is still expected to turn out 1,000 units a day, but now has a choice of working ahead and then shutting off the line for a while. "It's better," he said. "You've got more control now."

CHAPTER **12**

Wages, Prices and Productivity

George Meany of the A.F. of L.—CIO react-
ing to President Nixon's wage-price freeze.

Courtesy Wide World Photos.

A Contrast in Unions

Difference in Garment and Steel Units Reflected in Wage and Price Structures

By A. H. RASKIN

Two powerful unions are in the labor news today. One is the one-million-member United Steelworkers of America, which is moving into the decisive stage of its pattern-setting wage negotiations with twelve big steel companies at the Roosevelt Hotel here. The other is the 443,000 - member International Ladies Garment Workers Union, opening its triennial convention in Miami Beach.

News Analysis

The records of these two unions and of the industries in which they operate offer some curious contrasts of consequence to the fight against inflation and to the future of labor-management relations. The most startling way to sum up these contrasts is also the simplest. It is by comparing what has happened to prices and wages in steel and in the manufacture of women's clothing since World War II.

Figures compiled by the Federal Bureau of Labor Statistics show that the general rise in living costs, as measured by the Consumer Price Index, has been 23.7 per cent since the 1947-49 base period.

Contrast in Price Rises

Steel prices have gone up 88.2 per cent in the same period, or nearly four times as fast. The price of women's and girls' clothing has not gone up at all. On the contrary, the index of retail prices in this field stands 1 per cent below the figure for the immediate post-war period. The wholesale price is down by about the same amount.

On the wage side the general level of factory earnings has risen from an average of $1.31 an hour in February, 1948, to $2.20 in February of this year. The average steel wage started at $1.51, or 20 cents above the factory level. It is now $3.06, or 86 cents above the factory average.

In the 1948 period the average pay for workers making dresses, coats, suits, skirts and other outer wear for women was almost the same as the steel average. The garment wage stood at $1.50 an hour. Now it is $1.73, or $1.33 less than the average mill hand earns in steel.

Part of this difference in wage progress stems from the fact that the nature of the garment industry has changed. There is more stress now on casual clothes, which involve less skilled craftsmanship. Part also lies in the fact that 80 per cent of the garment workers are women and thus not always the mainstay of financial support for their households.

Two Industries Different

But a more substantial explanation is to be found in the differing character of the two industries and the degree to which they do or do not regulate their business conduct by the conventional market considerations of supply and demand.

The garment union deals with two thousand employers in an industry so volatile that nearly one-fifth of the companies go out of business every year and are replaced by others willing to take the risk of survival in the dog-eat-dog competitiveness of Seventh Avenue.

The industry has an annual volume of $6,300,000,000, yet three-quarters of all garment shops have fewer than fifty employes.

This casts the union in the role of industrial policeman, constantly on guard against the incursion of racketeers and the return of the sweatshop.

The turnover of employes is so high that the union must run to stand still in its organizing activities. Nearly half its members drop out of the industry in the three years between conventions. This means that the union would soon be memberless if it failed to enroll the newcomers.

The steel industry is dominated by three giant companies— United States Steel, Bethlehem and Republic. These three account for 55 per cent of the country's steel capacity. Production is concentrated in mills that employ anywhere from 5,000 to 15,000 employes.

The uniformity of price movements in the industry has led to charges in Congress that the major companies "administer" their prices on a basis that permits increases divorced from usual considerations of competition or market demand.

The companies retort that higher labor costs have been the principal factor in pushing their prices up. The union says the industry has added $3 a ton to prices for every extra dollar it has given in wages.

A Scramble for Business

For the garment manufacturer competition is not merely a matter of trying to undersell the man in the next loft. It is also a scramble to keep a bigger share of the consumer's dollar from going into washing machines, television sets, toasters, refrigerators or other items that might shut out a new coat or dress.

The steel industry controls a basic metal, only slightly threatened thus far by copper, aluminum or other substitute materials or by the inroads of foreign steel producers. United States Steel reported a profit margin of 9.9 per cent on sales in its first quarter. Bethlehem's margin was 8 per cent.

The industry contends that such returns are too low to permit adequate investment in improved plants and equipment. In the garment industry the average profit is only ½ of 1 per cent.

It is a truism among students of labor history that the nature of the industry determines the nature of the union with which it deals. The steel union, near the top of the industrial income ladder, is pressing for a "substantial" new rise in wages, a four-day work week every fourth week, three months of paid vacation every five years and a host of other improvements.

The Cloak Joint Board, a pillar of the garment union, with 50,000 members in the New York district, has just signed a three-year labor contract. It calls for no general pay rise, but it does establish a severance pay system for workers whose jobs are ended when their employers quit the industry.

The quixotic aspect of all this is that it is the garment union and its employers who are now under antitrust attack by the Justice Department.

PRESIDENT NAMES WAGE-PRICE UNIT

21-Member Group Directed to Map Sound Policies— Goldberg Is First Head

By W. H. LAWRENCE
Special to The New York Times.

WASHINGTON, Feb. 16 — President Kennedy established today a twenty-one member Advisory Committee on Labor-Management Policy. He gave it the task of promoting sound wage and price policies.

The group consists of seven representatives of the public, including the Secretaries of Labor and Commerce, seven from management and seven from organized labor.

In his Executive Order setting up the panel, Mr. Kennedy directed the committee to report back to him on a wide range of economic problems.

Specifically he asked for suggestions on ways to advance "free and responsible" collective bargaining, insure industrial peace, raise standards of living and increase productivity.

Other subjects he directed study of were the benefits and problems of automation and competition of American products in world markets.

Secretary of Labor Arthur J. Goldberg and Secretary of Commerce Luther H. Hodges will rotate the chairmanship annually. Mr. Goldberg will be the first chairman.

Others On Committee

Others named to the committee were:

For the public—Ralph McGill, editor and publisher of The Atlanta Constitution; George W. Taylor, Professor of Labor Relations, Wharton School of Business at the University of Pennsylvania; Clark Kerr,

Chancellor of the University of California; Arthur F. Burns, chairman of the National Bureau of Economic Research at New York and former Chairman of President Eisenhower's Council of Economic Advisers, and David Cole of Paterson, N. J., arbitrator and former head of the Federal Conciliation and Mediation Service.

For labor—George Meany, president of the American Federation of Labor and Congress of Industrial Organizations; Walter P. Reuther, president of the United Automobile Workers; David Dubinsky, president of the International Ladies Garment Workers Union; George Harrison, president of the Brotherhood of Railway Clerks; Thomas Kennedy, president of the United Mine Workers; David J. McDonald, president of the United Steel Workers, and Joseph Keenan, secretary-treasurer of the Brotherhood of Electrical Workers.

For management — Thomas Watson Jr. of New York, president of International Business Machines Company; Joseph Block of Chicago, president of Inland Steel Corporation; Henry Ford 2d of Detroit, chairman of the board of the Ford Motor Company; J. Spencer Love of Greensboro, N. C., chairman of the board of Burlington Mills; John Franklin of New York, president of United States Lines; Richard S. Reynolds Jr. of Richmond, Va., president of Reynolds Aluminum Company, and Elliot Bell of New York, editor and publisher of Business Week Magazine.

President Kennedy himself telephoned many of the industrialists and union leaders to join the public member on the committee.

Pierre Salinger, the White House press secretary, said that Mr. Kennedy chose the committee members himself after lists of names had been submitted by Secretaries Goldberg and Hodges. He said he did not know whether the A. F. L.-C. I. O. or business groups such as the Chamber of Commerce or the National Association of Manufacturers had been asked to suggest committee members.

It is uncertain when the group will hold its first session, but it is expected to be soon.

CONGRESS PASSES MINIMUM PAY BILL; PRESIDENT WINS

Measure Setting $1.25 as the Standard Is Adopted— 3,624,000 Added to Rolls

HOUSE VOTE A SURPRISE

Compromise Version Gains 230-196 Tally—Harder Fight Was Predicted

By TOM WICKER
Special to The New York Times.

WASHINGTON, May 3 — President Kennedy's minimum wage bill received final Congressional approval today. It assures raises for 2,500,000 workers.

They should start collecting fatter pay checks about Labor Day. President Kennedy is expected to sign the measure immediately and the first-step increases it provides are to take effect four months after the bill becomes law.

In addition to those directly benefited by the minimum wage increase and the extension of a Federal minimum to about 3,624,000 workers not now protected, millions more could get additional wages from a so-called "balloon effect."

That is, employers forced to increase the pay of low-wage workers are expected to maintain wage differentials now in effect. That would mean subsequent raises for higher paid workers.

Raises Would Vary

Raises would vary for those workers, mostly in manufacturing, whose present $1-an-hour minimum would go to $1.15. About 1,900,000 will get raises up to 15 cents an hour.

Increases for newly covered workers, most of whom are in retail, service and construction industries, also would vary. About 663,000 earn less than $1

an hour now and in many cases their raises will be more than 15 cents an hour.

The wage bill, the second of the President's five top-priority legislative requests to be passed, moved through both houses with surprising ease.

The Senate, after some desultory opposition and a thunderous speech by the Republican leader, Everett McKinley Dirksen of Illinois, passed the measure by 64 to 28.

The House, where the Administration's original bill had been cast aside for a more restrictive version offered by a Republican-Southern Democratic coalition, then debated the bill for an hour and passed it by 230 to 196. A much closer vote had been predicted.

Both ballots were on a compromise bill worked out in a Senate-House conference. It was much nearer the Administration's requests than the coalition bill passed in the House by 216 to 203 on March 24.

Secretary of Labor Arthur J. Goldberg called the bill passed today "a great advance in our nation's social legislation." It affords, he said, "long overdue protection to a large group of underprivileged Americans who previously did not share fully in the benefits of our society."

For the 24,000,000 workers, mostly in manufacturing, who already had a $1-an-hour minimum wage, the bill provides increases in the minimum to $1.15 in four months and to $1.25 two years after that. Those who earn less than $1.15 will get raises about Labor Day; about 3,000,000 * more will get increases when the step to $1.25 is taken in September, 1963.

3,624,000 Newly Covered

The measure extends for the first time a $1-an-hour minimum to 3,624,000 workers, mainly by requiring the wage to be paid by retail establishments doing more than $1,000,000 in annual business and importing more than $250,-000 in goods for resale across state lines. Large gasoline stations, construction companies adn transit companies also must pay the minimum for the first time.

The newly covered would begin to earn overtime for more than a forty-four-hour week two years after the minimum took effect. One year after that their minimum would go to $1.15 and overtime would start at forty-two hours.

After four years from the effective date, their minimum

would rise to $1.25 and they would earn overtime after forty hours, putting them on a par with those now covered.

In addition to the 663,000 of the newly covered who would get raises in four months, 1,093,-000 would get increases at the $1.15 step and 1,330,000 more would be raised at the $1.25 step.

1964 Election Is Cited

Senator Winston L. Prouty, Republican of Vermont, who supported the bill, reminded the Senate somewhat sadly that the increases to $1.15 for the newly covered would come in September, 1964, only two months before the next Presidential election.

Passage of the bill in the House was made possible when thirty-three Republicans crossed the party line to vote with 197 Democrats. There were 138 Republicans in opposition.

Democratic leaders also succeeded, as they had planned, in attracting substantial Southern Democratic support. Fifty-eight Democrats, mostly Southerners, opposed the bill but that was far below the potential of ninety-odd votes.

The main bait for the Southerners was in the conference's elimination from the final bill of about 140,000 laundry workers, to whom the minimum would have been extended by the Senate version, and 15,000 cotton-gin employes who would have been covered by the House bill.

Over-all new coverage was reduced by about 400,000 from the 4,086,000 that would have been covered in the Senate measure. The bill first passed in the House would have brought only 1,200,000 new workers under minimum wage protection.

Both Senator Wayne Morse of Oregon, a Democratic supporter of the bill, and Representative William H. Ayres of Ohio, a Republican opponent, assailed the elimination of the laundry workers.

The main arguments against the bill were made by Senator Dirksen and Representative Charles A. Halleck of Indiana, the House Republican leader. Senator Dirksen contended that the exemptions left the measure "no philosophical unity."

"Shall the House of Representatives without firing a shot surrender its position? Mr. Halleck asked. "I say no!" he declared.

But it did about an hour later, thus wiping out the only major defeat President Kennedy had suffered on Capitol Hill— the earlier action of the House in adopting the coalition's minimum wage bill.

Labor Spurns Kennedy Bid To Restrict Pay Demands

Higher Wages and Shorter Hours Urged In Resolutions at A.F.L.-C.I.O. Parley —Reuther Replies to Administration

By STANLEY LEVEY
Special to The New York Times.

BAL HARBOUR, Fla., Dec. 12—Organized labor rejected today President Kennedy's plea for voluntary restraint in collective bargaining. It called instead for higher wages and shorter hours.

This position was set forth in two resolutions adopted unanimously by delegates to the convention here of the American Federation of Labor and Congress of Industrial Organizations.

It was underscored by Walter P. Reuther, president of the United Automobile Workers, in a speech to the delegates.

President Kennedy made his appeal in an address to the convention last week.

Secretary of Labor Arthur J. Goldberg sounded the same theme a day later, although he assured labor that there was still "plenty of room" for wage increases under a policy of gearing them to increases in productivity.

The resolutions adopted by the federation today made no mention of the Administration's plea. They pointed to continued hard-core, long-term unemployment and urged a constantly expanding economy. They specifically rejected a wage freeze and a balanced budget as solutions to the nation's economic problems.

A resolution on collective bargaining reached this general conclusion:

"In collective bargaining in the period ahead, A.F.L.-C.I.O. affiliated unions will press for wage advances as a vital means of increasing inadequate consumer purchasing power.

"Purchasing power must catch up and keep pace with fast rising national productive power so as to help stimulate and sustain an increased rate of national economic growth."

Objectives Listed

The federation urged its 132 affiliates, representing 12,500,-000 workers, to seek the following objectives in future sessions at the bargaining table:

¶Year-round income or employment and adequate benefits upon loss of jobs.

¶Improved health, welfare and pension programs.

¶Measures to minimize ill effects on workers of automation and plant relocation.

¶Shorter hours with no loss in pay and "substantially more paid vacations, holidays and other paid leisure time."

The last item is in direct conflict with the policies of the Kennedy Administration. Both the President and Secretary Goldberg have spoken against a cut in the work week.

They have said that it would have an adverse effect on this country's ability to meet its international commitments and on the economic system generally.

They fear that shorter hours will mean less productivity, and argue that the nation needs more productivity, not less.

Reuther Replies

Mr. Reuther made light today of the Administration's contention that this was not the time for a shorter work week. He said:

"We ought to say to them [the Administration] that we are prepared to work forty hours a week if you can give every American who wants a job a job forty hours a week, and if you cannot, then we ought to fight to reduce the level of the work week until every American who is willing and able to work has a job in the American economy."

A resolution adopted today on the national economy hit out at "some leaders of opinion who have been urging a wage freeze or a substantial reduction of wage increases and restrictive monetary policies."

This, the resolution said, would mean "weak consumer markets, rising unemployment and economic stagnation at home."

The resolution urged "an expansionary Federal budget policy," more Government spending and increased economic activity generally. It said a general reduction in taxes might have to be postponed temporarily if Federal spending was increased sufficiently in the next few months.

On the related subject of prices, organized labor contended that "most industries can afford to grant improvements of wages, salaries and fringe benefits without price increases."

Other industries could even cut prices, while still others, where productivity was standing still or falling, might have to raise them, the resolution held.

"The over-all price level, therefore, can remain reasonably stable," the resolution concluded, "if business would seek rising profits from low margins and an increasing volume of sales."

December 13, 1961

Advisers Offer an Outline Of Wage-Price Restraints

WASHINGTON, Jan. 22—President Kennedy's economic advisers pleaded again today for a common front in the fight against inflation. They supported their appeal by laying down general guidelines for restraint on wages and prices.

The Council of Economic Advisers said that the rate of increase in wages in any industry should not exceed the trend in the rate of productivity for industry generally.

For example, if productivity in industry generally is found to be rising 3 per cent a year, the council indicated, an industry with a 6 per cent productivity rise still should limit wage rate increases to 3 per cent and cut prices, unless there were sound reasons to the contrary.

Since the end of World War II, productivity generally has risen at the rate of 3 per cent a year. For some industries it has risen more, for some less. If the 3 per cent rule were applied generally, the high productivity industries would still limit wage increases to 3 per cent.

As a general guide to price adjustments, the council said that price reductions were in order if an industry's rate of productivity exceeded the overall rate, for this would mean declining labor costs in that industry. The guide would sanction an appropriate increase in price if the productivity rate of an industry failed to match a general rise in productivity.

There was no mention of wage reductions in the council's report.

The council emphasized that it was offering guides, not rules or mechanical formulas, and that the guides were general ones.

Even so, the report set out, in more detail perhaps than ever before in peacetime, what the Administration meant by a productivity guide in determining the size of wage increases.

President Eisenhower's Administration, and the Kennedy Administration until today, had urged productivity gains as the outer limits of wage gains. But they did not define clearly what was meant and did not recognize the many variables that enter into specific cases.

Productivity, as distinguished from production, means the rate of output rather than the volume of output. Generally this is measured on a man-per-hour basis.

This does not mean that the individual worker is the controlling factor in the rate of output. More and more, as mechanization progresses, the rate of output is determined by the employer's investment in capital machinery.

In the total private economy, the productivity trend has been on the rise since measurements began. However, the rate of rise has not been steady.

Thus, while productivity has risen at an average annual rate of 3 per cent since World War II, it has risen only 2.4 per cent since 1909 and only 2.6 per cent since 1954.

Members of the council, in a session with newsmen, indicated that the intermediate period, 1947-1960, was the logical base now for measuring productivity against wage-rate increases.

January 23, 1962

Goldberg Says Mediation Must Aid National Interest

Secretary Asserts U. S. Role in Labor Disputes Will Go Beyond an Attempt to Settle the Immediate Issues

By AUSTIN C. WEHRWEIN
Special to The New York Times.

CHICAGO, Feb. 23—Secretary of Labor Arthur J. Goldberg said today that the Government henceforth would define and assert the national interest when it moved into collective bargaining situations. It will not confine its role to mediating the immediate issues, he said.

The Secretary drew a distinction between previous policy and what he said would be Government influence of a new and greater kind in collective bargaining. In the past, he said, the only aim of Government officials was to obtain a settlement.

The Kennedy Administration, he said, has the "courage" to draw the economic "guidelines" to protect the national interest in a world in which domestic inflation, wages, profits and price levels can create international crises.

He said the issues in labor-management affairs had become "far too complex, far too potent, and far too influential on the rest of society to be resolved on the old testing ground of clash of selfish interest."

In a speech to the Executives' Club here that he called a "definitive" statement of the Kennedy Administration's labor-management philosophy, the Secretary said:

"I have the conviction that the plain fact is that our destiny as a free nation depends as never before in history on achievement of a greater sense of national unity. For the country that is the world's foremost industrial power, the building of a stronger and more durable industrial peace is clearly a precondition of national unity."

"The Government has got to give more help to the collective bargaining process," he said.

He denied that he wanted to force "cut and dried" settlements on labor and management. He said he opposed compulsory arbitration. He criticized wage and price controls.

The Government, he said, will produce better and more precise economic data—before bargaining begins, rather than as a "post-mortem inquest."

In sum, he said, the Government will assist settlements, not just analyze them.

The Secretary spoke to an overflow crowd of 1,500 persons at the Palmer House at a luncheon sponsored by the Executive's Club, a businessmen's forum group.

The audience, while hardly hostile, applauded only once, and mildly, during the speech. That was when Mr. Goldberg said:

"It is a universally shared and obvious truth that we cannot this year afford a repetition of the 1959 steel strike."

The Secretary departed from his text to make it clear that steel was only one of the industries he was watching closely.

The others, he said, are the airlines, the railroads and the space and missile industries.

Stresses Productivity

Among the goals he said the nation should achieve was an increase in productivity, to be shared by labor, management and the public.

He said both labor and management were "more responsible and less belligerent," and that last year was the greatest period of industrial peace in the United States since the end of World War II.

But he had warnings for both sides. He said both must "cooperate with change." Labor organizations setting wage and other policies must seek both to protect the immediate welfare of members and to look ahead "into the broad fields of modern economic realities," he said.

He advised unions to stop obstructing technological change.

Management, too, he went on, "must stop its blind resistance to change." He said management must face the fact that unions would resist change if they failed to receive offsetting job security.

He scolded management for having taken an "almost automatic stand" against proposals to improve the unemployment insurance system and to put medical care for the aged under Social Security. He said that if the unions did not get these benefits from Government, "you've got to expect them to be raised in the bargaining arena."

"The result may well be more expensive for management than an increase in the tax," he said.

In an interview Mr. Goldberg said a White House conference on national economic issues, to be attended late this spring by at least 100 labor, management and public representatives, would discuss collective bargaining as one of the major issues. He said the significance of this had been overlooked.

Cites Foreign Impact

This group will be an outgrowth of the President's Advisory Committee on Labor-Management Policy, the Secretary said. The committee, Mr. Goldberg said, is symptomatic of the change for the better since 1958. Then, he said, there was a "hardening of attitudes" and the next year "the cold war between management and labor erupted into conflict in the steel industry."

From that strike, he said, management learned that "despite loose talk" to the contrary, union members will stand by the union, while the union learned "the test of strength in a strike is not the best way to solve problems." He was the steel union's lawyer at the time.

Moreover, he went on, the recession made both sides "more responsible."

STEEL AND UNION AGREE ON TERMS; KENNEDY PLEASED

He Cites Stress on Security of Jobs and Pay and Says New Pact Aids Stability

NO PRICE RISE IS SEEN

But Industry Notes Increase in Cost of Production— More Work Expected

By JOHN D. POMFRET
Special to The New York Times.

PITTSBURGH, March 31 — The steel industry and the United Steelworkers of America announced agreement today on new contract terms.

President Kennedy said the terms were "obviously noninflationary and should provide a solid base for continued price stability."

The accord settles the nation's major collective bargaining problem of the year. It will provide a pattern for settlements covering thousands of workers in steel fabricating, aluminum making and can-manufacturing plants.

450,000 Workers Covered

The agreement approved here today by the union's thirty-four-member executive board and 170-member wage-policy committee, is designed to improve the job and income security of the union's 450,000 members.

The union said the new vacation benefits in the agreement would create job opportunities for "thousands" of workers.

The present contracts expire June 30. The settlement is the earliest in advance of deadline in the quarter-century relationship between the industry and the union.

President Kennedy had put pressure on the industry and union to prevent the economic disruption of a strike and the harmful economic effects of a build-up of steel inventories in expectation of a strike. It was feared that a build-up would be followed by a let-down as steel users worked off their stockpiles if no strike occurred.

Kennedy Telephones Union

The President, at his desk at the White House, telephoned his congratulations to the union and industry. The message was carried over a loudspeaker in the union's wage-policy committee meeting at the Penn-Sheraton Hotel here.

The settlement, Mr. Kennedy said, provides "new and imaginative benefits in areas most vital to employes—job and income security."

"I am sure that the nation will agree with me that the most notable aspect of this settlement is that it demonstrates that the national interest can be protected and the interests of the industry and of the employes forwarded through free and responsible collective bargaining," the President said.

After he spoke to the union meeting, Mr. Kennedy telephoned R. Conrad Cooper, chief industry negotiator, and extended his congratulations to the steel industry.

The President plainly believed that the settlement costs would not justify an increase in steel prices.

The Administration in general, considers any agreement that raises labor costs for employe by less than 3 per cent an hour to be not inflationary. It is felt that that figure does not exceed the average annual increase in output for man-hour during the post-war period. Steelworkers now make an average of $4.10 an hour, including fringe benefits.

An industry statement said the new benefits would increase employment costs by about 2½ per cent during the first year.

That, the statement said, compares with an average annual increase of from 3½ to 3¾ per cent under the contract negotiated in 1960 after a 116-day strike, and with 8 per cent a year in the period between 1940 and 1960.

The industry added, however, that the cost of settlement exceeded by about 50 per cent the average increase of 1.7 per cent in shipments of steel for man-hours worked. The industry considers this as its true productivity gain. The statement seemed to leave open the possibility for price increases.

Mr. Cooper, chief industry negotiator, said that the settlement cost did not fall wholly "within the limits of anticipated gains in productive efficiency."

But he added that the accord represented real progress in the development of voluntary collective bargaining in the steel industry.

David J. McDonald, president of the steel union, termed the settlement "noninflationary," but would not put a price tag on it. "I am interested in benefits, not costs," Mr. McDonald said.

Associated Press Wirephoto

STEEL UNION GROUP APPROVES PACT: Officials of the United Steelworkers of America at an executive board meeting yesterday in Pittsburgh. From the left are: I. W. Abel, secretary-treasurer; David J. McDonald, president; Howard R. Hague, vice president; David Feller and Eliot Bradhof, lawyers; Marvin Miller, aide to president.

Points in Settlement

The settlement includes these features:

¶No wage increase the first year.

¶A new savings and vacation plan to make available vacation and retirement benefits and expand job opportunities.

¶Protection against short work weeks.

¶Pension improvements.

¶Seniority plan changes to improve protection against layoffs for longtime employes.

The new contracts will go into effect July 1. They are for two years, but may be reopened on issues of wages, pensions, insurance and work practices on ninety days notice on May 1, 1963, or after.

The new vacation plan will be financed by a contribution by the companies of 3 cents for each hour worked by covered employes.

Under the plan workers would be credited with an extra week of vacation pay for each two years' continuous service after Jan. 1, 1961. They can either take it or bank it against the day they retire, are laid off or are disabled. If they ban kit, their credits will draw interest at a minimum of 3 per cent annually.

The plan also provides one week's extra vacation pay credit for each five years of continuous service before Jan. 1, 1961. This will be added to the thirteen weeks of vacation pay workers now get at retirement. It will be reduced by 10 per cent for each three-month period a worker stays on the job after he reaches 65 and is eligible for pension. The

aim of that provision is to encourage workers to retire.

To finance the improved supplemental unemployment benefits plan, the companies will raise their contribution from 5 cents to 9½ cents an hour for each hour worked. If any of the extra 4½ cents is left over after the benefits have been paid, the money will be added to the new vacation plan.

The maximum weekly benefit under the supplementary unemployment benefit plan was raised from $25 plus $2 for each dependent to $37.50 plus $1.50 for each dependent for workers receiving state unemployment compensation.

Short Work-Week Plan

For workers not covered by state unemployment compensation, it was raised from $47.50 plus $2 for each dependent to $60 plus $1.50 for each dependent. The gross amount collectable also was increased substantially.

The new short work-week benefit provides that an employe will receive the difference between the number of hours for which he was paid during a given week and thirty-two hours' pay.

A moving allowance will be provided under the plan for laid-off workers who take jobs under a new interregional preferential hiring program.

Pension eligibility rules were changed to allow more workers caught in a permanent plant shutdown or a permanent layoff, or who develop a disability, to receive pension benefits.

Employes with at least three years of service will get an extra week's vacation with an

extra half-week's pay. The companies already have been paying a man on vacation a half-week's pay more than the length of his vacation. The worker now will have to take his vacation unless the union's grievance man in his department agrees he does not.

Under the new agreement, the industry-union human relations committee will study the scheduling of overtime while employes are laid off or are working short weeks and what work should be done by foremen and other employes not covered by the union.

The committee also will study the scheduling of vacations and the question of training employes to permit them to perform new and more highly paid jobs.

The agreement announced today will be supplemented in negotiations between the union and company committees representing each of the eleven steel-producing concerns involved in the main negotiations.

Those talks start here Monday and are expected to be completed by Friday. After that, formal contracts will be signed.

The eleven companies, which represent about 80 per cent of the nation's steel production, are the United States Steel Corporation, Republic Steel Corporation, Bethlehem Steel Company, Armco Steel Corporation, Colorado Fuel and Iron Corporation, Great Lakes Steel Corporation, Inland Steel Corporation, Jones and Laughlin Steel Corporation, Pittsburgh Steel Company, Youngstown Sheet and Tube Company and the Wheeling Steel Corporation.

April 1, 1962

STEEL GIVES IN, RESCINDS RISES UNDER PRESSURE BY PRESIDENT

KENNEDY IS VICTOR

Uses His Full Powers for 72 Hours to Subdue Industry

By RICHARD E. MOONEY
Special to The New York Times.

WASHINGTON, April 13 — President Kennedy triumphed today over the titans of the steel industry.

Almost precisely seventy-two hours after the United States Steel Corporation's abrupt announcement of a price increase, the corporation backed down and rescinded the increase late this afternoon.

The action by United States Steel, the nation's largest steel producer, followed announcements by the Inland Steel Company and the Kaiser Steel Corporation that they would not increase their prices, and a statement by Bethlehem Steel Corporation, the nation's second largest producer, that it was canceling its rises.

By early evening seven of the eight companies that had raised their prices in the last three days had canceled them. The eighth, Wheeling Steel Corporation, said it would announce its decision tomorrow.

Many Forms of Pressure

For three days the great forces at the command of the President of the United States had been brought to bear on the steel industry.

Some of the effort was exerted in the open—the President's open denunciation of the companies, calculated to arouse public opinion against them; the opening of grand jury proceedings leading to possible anti-trust action, and the threat to divert orders to companies that had not raised prices.

But privately as well, the President and his advisers were bringing every form of persuasion to bear on the industry, trying to hold back the companies that had not yet raised prices and induce the others to roll back the price increase.

Kennedy's Statement

President Kennedy was informed of the actions by United States Steel and Bethlehem off Norfolk, Va., where he was aboard a cruiser observing naval maneuvers. He issued this statement:

"The people of the United States are most gratified by the announcements of Bethlehem and United States Steel Company that their proposed price increases are being rescinded.

"In taking the action at this time, they are serving the public interest and their actions will assist our common objective of strengthening our country and our economy."

Even during this dramatic day, as the steel industry started to weaken, the Administration pressed on with the actions that the price increase had started.

Secretary of Defense Robert S. McNamara announced that defense business would be channeled, if possible, to companies that had not raised steel prices. Grand jury subpoenas were served on some of the companies that had raised their prices. And the Labor Department issued a new set of statistics designed to prove the Administration's case that the price increase was not warranted.

Tonight it was evident that President Kennedy had scored a great personal success such as few Presidents had experienced in their relations with American industry.

He had strengthened his position for dealing with the business community. He had regained stature in the eyes of labor leaders. He had aroused a resounding chorus of popular support that would do his party no harm in next fall's elections.

The conflict between Government and the leading steel companies was set off Tuesday when United States Steel announced that it would raise the price of steel about $6 a ton.

White House Incensed

This announcement, which was quickly followed by similar announcements from seven other big companies, was received almost as a declaration of war at the White House.

Only a few weeks previously, the companies and the steel union had negotiated a new contract, to take effect July 1. The Administration had kept the two sides under pressure to reach an agreement that would not set off a new wage-price spiral, and it hailed the agreement, which contained no direct wage increase but only fringe-benefit improvements, as noninflationary.

President Keenedy was furious at the price increase, regarding it as a "double cross" of the Administration. Immediately he and the highest officials of the Administration set to work to counter the steel companies' move.

The objective of the Administration was to prevent the nation's third largest industry — its sales are exceeded only by those in autos and petroleum — from setting off an upward spiral of prices and wages.

The strategy was to divide and conquer. If two big companies could be persuaded to

Associated Press Wirephoto

CONFER ON STEEL PRICES: The President with Defense Secretary Robert S. McNamara yesterday at the White House. They discussed policy on Federal steel buying.

hold the line, the rest would have to retreat.

The key target in the strategy was Inland Steel, eighth largest in the industry. A secondary target was Armco Steel Corporation, the sixth largest.

Behind all the public declaiming and swinging of clubs, Administration officials were engaged in intense personal campaigns to persuade these two not to follow the lead of United States Steel, and to persuade other companies to retreat if possible.

By long-distance telephone the ranking powers of the Federal Government called the ranking powers of the steel industry—management, directors and stockholders. Edward Gudeman Jr., the Under Secretary of Commerce, was a central figure. He knew Inland Steel well as a lifetime Chicagoan, and he handled the dealings there.

President Kennedy turned to the long-distance telephone too.

This morning, in Chicago, the industry began to crumble. The Chicago Daily News published an interview with Joseph L. Block Inland's chairman, who is vacationing in Japan.

"We do not feel that an advance in steel prices at this time would be in the national interest." Mr. Block said.

Less than an hour after the paper hit the streets, Inland announced its position. It was made public by Philip D. Block, Jr., vice chairman of Inland, a cousin of Joseph Block.

President Kennedy heard the news on the steps of the White House as he bade farewell to Mohammed Riza Pahlevi, Shah of Iran. "Good, good," the President said. "Very good."

At 12:15 P. M. he held a final strategy conference with the officials who were working on the steel campaign in its many aspects.

An hour later, Secretary McNamara announced the Pentagon order on steel buying. He told a news conference that he

believed, both as a Cabinet officer and former president of a big business, the Ford Motor Company, that the price increase was not justified.

Forty-five minutes later, news bulletins said Kaiser Steel Corporation had announced that it, too, would hold the line.

Kaiser was the company that broke with the industry in the 1959 strike and was first to make peace with the United Steelworkers of America. Its action today was just as welcome to the White House.

The President, at Andrews Air Force Base preparing to take off for Norfolk, took a last-minute telephone call on board his plane from Dr. Walter W. Heller, his chief economic adviser.

He was airborne when the big news came. At 3:20, Bethlehem Steel retracted the price increase. The game was won, though the big one, United States Steel, had yet to make its concession of defeat.

At Norfolk, the President went straight to a motorcade and missed the Bethlehem development. Andrew T. Hatcher, his associate press secretary, caught up with the announcement by telephone from Washington about an hour after the event and passed a note to Mr. Kennedy.

Meanwhile, Secretary of Labor Arthur J. Goldberg had gone to New York City to talk to the men at 71 Broadway, headquarters of United States Steel, including the chairman, Roger M. Blough. About 5 P. M., word sped around Washington that the end was at hand. Mr. Hatcher was on the phone again with Washington, this time from dockside as the President prepared to sail.

United States Steel's announcement, according to one report, was to come from the White House. Another report said it would come from Mr. Kennedy himself. It came from 71 Broadway at 5:25 P. M.

The Administration rejoiced. The challenges of political battle had dominated the White House activity for three days, bringing back the intensity of the 1960 campaign, if not the joys. Outside the White House a guard heard what had happened.

"This'll get Kennedy reelected!" he said.

Minutes before Bethlehem's break, Senator Estes Kefauver, Democrat of Tennessee, announced that his Anti-Monopoly subcommittee would subpoena the major steel companies for cost figures in a few days. An aide said later that the price cancellations would not change the subcommittee's plans.

In Miami Beach, Representative Emanuel Celler, Democrat of Brooklyn, took a more lenient attitude. He said his House Antitrust subcommittee would not make the across-the-board investigation that it had scheduled to start early next month. "The penitent shall not be punished," he said.

He added, however, that the subcommittee would canvass the situation to see if antitrust laws needed change.

Attorney General Robert F. Kennedy said the Justice Department's plans for the grand jury investigation were unchanged.

Another official said that the investigation was not a club to bring the prices down. It is aimed, he said, at discovering whether there was a conspiracy in the quick succession of price increases following United States Steel's, and whether United States Steel was so strong that it constituted a monopoly.

At the White House, a Presidential aide said that the Administration had made "no deal" to get the price increase removed from the books.

The only plans that the Administration changed in the wake of its victory were plans

for a news conference tomorrow by Secretary of the Treasury Douglas Dillon, publication of a "white paper" on steel industry economics, and the Pentagon order on steel buying.

The order directed defense suppliers to buy steel from companies whose prices were lowest, if it was possible. There was some question that it would have shifted much business, but the return of all prices to the same level made it meaningless in any event.

United States Steel had justified the price increase on the ground that it was necessary to make the company competitive. Raising prices makes a company competitive, according to United States Steel, by providing profits out of which to finance plant modernization that permits more efficient, and therefore more competitive, production.

As Bethlehem brought its prices down this afternoon, competition was cited again as the reason. This time it was the competition of Inland's and Kaiser's lower prices.

Bethlehem, Inland and Armco represent more than one-quarter of the country's steel-making capacity.

Armco had not raised its prices, but neither had it issued a statement saying that it would not.

Inland was a natural target for the Administration's attention from the start because Joseph Block, its chairman, is a member of the President's Labor - Management Advisory Committee. His membership on the committee made him a vital cog in the early settlement of the steel industry's wage contract negotiations last month, too.

Officials of Inland have said that they were flabbergasted by United States Steel's move to raise prices just five days after the last contract was signed.

Chronology of Events Leading to Capitulation on Steel Rise

Following is a chronology of events leading to yesterday's action in the steel price situation:

FEB. 6

Acting on behalf of President Kennedy, Secretary of Labor Arthur J. Goldberg urged the steel industry and the United Steelworkers of America to start negotiations as soon as possible for a new contract effective July 1. He emphasized the importance of a noninflationary new steel contract to "vigorous economic recovery."

Mr. Goldberg said continued recovery required that there be no disruption by "abnormal expansion in the steel industry followed by a compensating contraction and that there be a peaceful settlement in steel."

Contract negotiations affected 430,000 basic-steel workers and 500,000 other union members in related fields. Both the industry and the union seemed anxious to prevent a repetition of the 116-day strike in 1959. The union appeared more interested this year in job security and shorter work schedules to combat automation. Latest Government statistics showed steel workers averaged $3.28 an hour.

FEB. 14

Negotiations began officially in Pittsburgh, the first time in the nearly twenty-six years' history of the union that bargaining had begun at such an early date. R. Conrad Cooper, executive vice president of the United States Steel Corporation, headed the management negotiating team representing eleven major steel companies. David J. McDonald, president of the United Steelworkers, headed its delegation.

FEB. 15

Both sides pledged cooperation and speedy action to reach an agreement.

FEB. 17

Secretary Goldberg told reporters in New York that he welcomed the "constructive attitude" taken by the industry and the union.

FEB. 19

Wages were discussed for the first time in the negotiations

Both sides expressed hope for an over-all economic settlement before March 1.

FEB. 24

The negotiations recessed.

FEB. 26

Union and management negotiators discounted reports that little progress had been made in the talks. But George Meany, president of the American Federation of Labor and Congress of Industrial Organizations, said in Bal Harbour, Fla., that the negotiations had "made no progress whatsoever."

MARCH 3

The negotiations collapsed in a stalemate over the size of the money costs of contracts to replace the agreements expiring June 30. The union suggested a resumption of talks on May 1. President Kennedy let it be known he wanted them resumed earlier.

Secretary Goldberg issued a statement that the President had asked him to urge both sides to resume talks after a suitable recess.

The industry was reported to have offered package terms worth 6 to 8 cents an hour. The union was reported to be holding out for about 10 cents.

An industry statement said it could not afford the employment security guarantees sought by the union.

MARCH 14

A speech by a top United States Steel official gave a preview of the attitude that resulted in the later attempt to raise prices. Speaking at the University of Chicago, Leslie B. Worthington, the company's president, asserted that American industry must obtain higher profits if the United States was to meet the challenge of world trade.

On the same date the steel talks resumed in Pittsburgh after a twelve-day respite.

APRIL 6

United States Steel and Bethlehem Steel, the nation's two largest producers, led the major companies into signing formal two-year contracts with the United Steelworkers of America.

The new contract for the basic steel industry will become

effective July 1. Under the agreement, steel workers will receive an average 10 cents an hour more. No immediate wage increase was included, but the contract can be reopened on wages and other issues on ninety days' notice after April 30, 1963.

President Kennedy described the contract as "noninflationary" and urged that both sides use restraint in wages and prices so that the American economy would remain stable and competitive with foreign industry.

Mr. McDonald hailed the agreement as one that could possibly "eliminate for all time basic steel strikes in America."

APRIL 10

United States Steel, bellwether of the industry, announced price increases averaging $6 a ton effective at midnight. It described the increase as a "catch-up" adjustment amounting to about three-tenths of a cent a pound in the first rise by the company since 1958.

Mr. Worthington said that since 1958 the level of steel prices had not increased but, if anything, had declined somewhat.

He said the company had "reluctantly concluded that a modest price adjustment can no longer be avoided in the light of production cost increases." The company's profits were being squeezed between rising costs and declining prices and were inadequate to provide facilities needed to compete with low-cost foreign mills, he said.

President Kennedy was infuriated by the price increase. He let it be known that he regarded it as an unjustified and deliberate affront to his Administration.

APRIL 11

Five major steel companies followed United States Steel's lead in raising prices. They were the Bethlehem Steel Corporation, Republic Steel Corporation, Jones and Laughlin Steel Corporation, Youngstown Sheet and Tube Company and Wheeling Steel Corporation.

President Kennedy at his news conference attacked the companies that had raised prices for "irresponsible defiance" of the public interest and "ruthless disregard" of their duty to the nation. He spoke in a tone of cold anger about the "utter contempt" of a "tiny handful" of steel executives toward the rest of the American people.

He said the whole purpose of his Administration's efforts for a peaceful labor-management settlement in steel had been to make any increase in prices unnecessary.

APRIL 12

Roger M. Blough, chairman of United States Steel, said in New York that company documents had been subpoenaed. Mr. Blough defended the increase as a move to strengthen the nation's industrial power.

The Justice Department announced that it was ordering a grand jury investigation of the price rises, in which other leading steel makers had followed United States Steel. This action was taken under the Sherman Antitrust Act.

Of the nation's top eight steel producers only two did not join the price increase—the Armco Steel Corporation and Inland Steel Company. Asked what would happen if they continued to hold out, Mr. Blough said: "It would definitely affect us and I don't know how much longer we could maintain our position."

APRIL 13

Inland Steel announced it would not increase prices at this time. The Kaiser Steel Corporation made a similar announcement. Then the Bethlehem Steel Corporation rescinded the increase it announced two days earlier.

Late in the afternoon United States Steel also rescinded its increase. Mr. Worthington said this was done "in the light of competitive developments today and all other current circumstances."

Other companies then followed suit.

May 2, 1962

PRESIDENT SIGNS MINIMUM PAY BILL

Hails Rise to $1.60 in '68 —Recalls 25-Cent Wage Gained by New Deal

By MAX FRANKEL
Special to The New York Times

WASHINGTON, Sept. 23— With evident personal and political satisfaction, President Johnson today signed a law that will raise the minimum wage to $1.60 an hour in 1968.

Recalling his own New Deal battles for the first minimum wage of 25 cents an hour in 1938, Mr. Johnson hailed the new law as a boon to eight million people who will be covered for the first time, including 390,000 farm workers.

For the nation's farm hands, the President promised, "that's just a starter."

"Our new minimum wage law, in my judgment, will bring a larger piece of this country's prosperity and a greater share of personal dignity to millions of our workers, their wives and their children," the President said. "And for me, frankly, that is what being President is all about."

Celebrating Victory

Mr. Johnson, addressing 75 leaders of organized labor and members of the Congress in the Cabinet Room of the White House, was also celebrating an important political victory.

Only a few months ago, he was in deep trouble with the unions because he had not obtained repeal of Section 14 (b) of the Taft-Hartley Act—which allows the states to prohibit the union shop—and because he was pressing labor to hold down wage demands. Then, to add to the injury, the House of Representatives voted to defer the $1.60 minimum until 1969.

It took a rigorous battle in both wings of Congress to retrieve the 1968 date.

The new law will raise the minimum wage from $1.25 to $1.40 an hour next Feb. 1, thus providing an increase for about 3.8 million workers of the 30 million now covered by minimum-wage laws. A year later, the same workers plus 2.1 million who already earn $1.40 will be raised to $1.60.

In addition, about eight million workers will be covered by the guaranteed minimum for the first time. These include employes of large farms, small retail establishments, hospitals and similar institutions, restaurants, hotels and motels, and laundries.

Of the newly covered workers, about a million will have to be raised to $1 an hour next Feb. 1. They and others will gain further gradual increases to $1.60 by 1971.

It has been estimated that while the increases will bring significant benefits to a sizable number of people, they will add only 1.1 per cent to the total wage bill of industries now covered by minimum-wage legislation and 0.9 per cent to the newly covered industries.

Minimum wage legislation helps business as well as workers, Mr. Johnson argued in rebutting the contention that some employers will be forced to eliminate jobs and discharge employes.

The President ticked off the nine increases since 1938 and said that after every rise "employment rose, rose, rose."

"The straight fact is that a fair minimum wage doesn't hurt business in any way," he insisted. Decent employers want to treat their employes decently, he added, leaving only a few exceptions who want to exploit labor and thus force other employers to compete "in their unholy dealings."

"If a businessman can't do well with this minimum wage in our booming economy that we have today, perhaps he might not be just a good businessman," Mr. Johnson said.

He gave special thanks to Senator Ralph W. Yarborough of Texas—whose liberal faction is having its troubles with the dominant Democratic forces in the President's native state— and to other members of the Senate Labor and Public Welfare Committee.

The President also acknowledged a debt to Representative Adam Clayton Powell, Democrat of New York, who was stripped yesterday of many of his powers as chairman of the House Education and Labor Committee, and to John H. Dent, Democrat of Pennsylvania, chairamn of a House Labor subcommitee.

Mr. Johnson gave tribute and warm handshakes to George Meany, President of the American Federation of Labor and Congress of Industrial Organizations and to David Dubinsky and Jacob Potofsky, the heads of garment industry unions, who were leaders in the minimum wage battles over the last quarter-century.

W. Willard Wirtz, the Secretary of Labor, also stood by to receive one of the three dozen pens with which the President, a stroke at a time, put his signature to the act.

As always, Mr. Johnson checked the date with one of the witnesses.

Thomas Jefferson called his days in the Presidency "a splendid misery," the President said. He declared that he sometimes agreed. "But today," he said, "is one of those splendid days."

September 24, 1966

JOHNSON DROPS GUIDEPOST OF 3.2% FOR RISE IN WAGES

RESTRAINT URGED

By EDWIN L. DALE Jr.
Special to The New York Times

WASHINGTON, Jan. 26 — President Johnson and his Council of Economic Advisers tacitly abandoned today the Government's fixed standard of 3.2 per cent for noninflationary wage increases, approving settlements somewhat higher.

They also called on industries with high profits to absorb wage increases this year without raising prices, thus reducing their margin of profit.

In general, the President urged business and labor to exercise "the utmost restraint and responsibility" in their wage and price decisions. He said price stability could not be fully restored this year, but he foresaw less inflation than last year.

These major developments in the Government's anti-inflation guidepost policy were disclosed in the President's Economic Report to Congress and the Economic Advisers' lengthier companion report.

Business and labor indicated satisfaction with the end of the guidelines.

Growth to Resume

The Economic Report projected a prosperous economy this year, with unemployment remaining at its current level of just under 4 per cent. However, it forecast some sluggishness in the economy in the first half of the year, with stronger growth resuming in the second half.

Following are other highlights of the economic message:

¶The President announced the formation of a new Cabinet-level Government group, headed by Gardner Ackley, chairman of the Council of Economic Advisers, to prepare for "quick adjustments in our economic policies" should the war in Vietnam end.

¶He said he would appoint a "commission of leading Americans" to make a two-year study of various proposals for "guaranteeing minimum incomes." Mr. Johnson called these plans

"almost surely beyond our means at this time."

¶The number of Americans in poverty was estimated to have declined by 5.5 million from 1961 to 1965 and probably by 1.2 million more last year.

"In purely material terms," the President said, "most Americans are better off than ever before."

The modified wage guidepost in the report of the Council of Economic Advisers accepts that wage settlements this year are likely to be larger than 3.2 per cent, which represents the average growth over the years of productivity, or output for each manhour. The reason is the recent rise in consumer prices, which was 3.3 per cent from December of 1965 to December of 1966.

But the council said settlements should be "substantially less" than the combined total of productivity and price increase, which would be 6.5 per cent.

'A Full Allowance'

"If the average wage increase in 1967," the report said, "were to include a full allowance for productivity plus an additional margin to 'compensate' for past increases in living costs, unit labor costs would rise at a rate which would require living costs to continue their rapid rise."

The council reiterated its opposition to "cost of living" escalator clauses in labor contracts under which wages automatically rise as the Consumer Price Index goes up. It said that if all unions, as well as "other groups in society," were to succeed in tying their incomes to price changes, "the arrangement would become a vast engine of inflation."

As for industry, the council suggested that last year's near-record profit margins were too high for a "stable" economy.

It continued:

"Firms in those industries in which market power, combined with strong demand, has pushed profit margins to record levels, have a special responsibility in price-making at this critical time.

"If, in 1967, firms with discretion as to their prices should follow pricing policies which even maintain present margins, the opportunity for a significantly improved price record will be compromised. It would speed up the rise in living costs, and it would again pose inviting targets for inflationary wage demands by unions.

"To assure steady movement toward price stability in 1967, the public interest requires that producers absorb cost increases to the maximum extent feasible, and take advantage of every opportunity to lower prices."

The President said in his message that the "more moderate pace of economic advance now under way, which the policies I am recommending are designed to maintain, should further diminish inflationary pressures."

Costs Still Spreading

He cautioned that "price stability cannot be restored overnight," partly because "we cannot rescind all of last year's increases in costs, some of which are still spreading through our structure of prices."

Restoring price stability rapidly, the President said, "could be done, if at all, only at the cost of mass unemployment, idle machines, and intolerable economic waste."

In the last year, the President said, "most businessmen who had a choice in setting prices and most trade unions that negotiated wage contracts acted responsibly."

The council's report identified a few price decisions that violated the guideposts, chiefly the failure to reduce automobile prices and the price increases for fabricated aluminum products.

It said "guidepost questions might be raised" about price increases for newsprint, gasoline, alloy and specialty steels, some chemicals and agricultural machinery.

In wages, the report singled out as "inflationary" most construction settlements, along with the New York transit and the national airlines agreements. It observed that recently negotiated settlements in the electrical and telephone industries were about 1.5 percentage points above the old 3.2 per cent guidepost.

Council Sees Companies

The report disclosed that the council had discussed prices with companies involved in "perhaps 50 product lines" and had succeeded in some cases in avoiding, deferring or reducing prospective price increases. In general, the report said, "the response on the part of the businesses involved has been extremely encouraging."

The report said, "This activity will be continued by the council."

Officials said they believed the new and more flexible wage guidepost might work better in achieving "moderate" settlements than the former rigid formula.

Although officials would not put any figure on settlements they would regard as acceptable, it is generally believed that the Government would consider the economy as fortunate if settlements averaged no more than 5 per cent.

A basic theme of the economic policy section of the report was that "excessive demand is not now a serious threat" as it was last year. The problem for the first half of the year, the report suggested, might be some decline in output as business works off the huge accumulation of inventories that occurred last year.

But, the report said, "The budget will be appropriately stimulative in the first half of 1967," with a deficit in the national income accounts budget at an annual rate of more than $5-billion.

"By midyear," the report continued, "construction should be recovering with the stimulus of monetary ease, and inventory investment should be leveling off at a moderate rate. In combination, these two sectors should significantly strengthen over-all private demand.

"A shift toward restraint in fiscal policy (through the President's proposed 6 per cent income tax surcharge) is appropriate at that time to assure that demand does not outrun capacity, that movement toward restoration of price stability is maintained, and that monetary policy does not have to be tightened again."

For the year as a whole the report projected a rise of 6.5 per cent in the gross national product, or total output of goods and services, to $787-billion. Of this, 4 per cent would be "real" growth and the rest would be higher prices, though prices are expected to rise less than last year.

The report said the outlook was for "healthy forward motion".

"Most important," it said, "the nation should continue to experience substantially full employment in 1967," with a jobless rate averaging 3.9 per cent of the labor force.

Another theme was, in the President's words, that "the brakes applied last year worked, but tight money worked painfully and inequitably."

The main impact was on housing construction, and the report projected a strong advance in housing after mid-1967 as a result of the current and prospective moves toward easier money.

WAGE CURB PLEA BY JOHNSON FAILS

Labor Also Rebuffs Okun in Second Private Meeting

By DAVID R. JONES
Special to The New York Times

WASHINGTON, May 14 — The Johnson Administration appealed without apparent success today to organized labor to restrain voluntarily its wage demands.

Authoritative sources said that President Johnson and Arthur M. Okun, chairman of the Council of Economic Advisers, addressed the anti-inflationary appeals to the A.F.L.-C.I.O. Executive Council in separate meetings here.

George Meany, president of the American Federation of Labor and Congress of Industrial Organizations, made it clear in advance that the labor movement would not respond.

The labor official said at a noon news conference that if the Administration asked for wage restraint the A.F.L.-C.I.O. "answer will be what it's been right along." This meant it would reject voluntary restraints.

Informed sources said later that it did so.

"Voluntary controls just don't work," Mr. Meany said. He indicated again that the A.F.L.-C.I.O. would abide by mandatory controls if they were applied "equitably" to prices, rents, dividends and other forms of compensation.

The Administration has appealed repeatedly to organized labor to hold down wage demands to help curb inflation. It has been rebuffed each time. Many past appeals have been made in public, but today's were made at private meetings and were not announced by the White House.

The wage restraint appeals today were no surprise because President Johnson and Mr. Okun both told the Business Council last weekend that business must share responsibility for holding down inflation and show price restraint. The council is an organization composed of leading business executives.

Mr. Okun said in his council speech that the responsibility for stopping inflation would rest primarily on business and unions once the pending tax increase took effect.

He said that neither business nor labor had gained by the current economic spiral, in which consumer prices are rising about 4 per cent a year.

The Council of Economic Advisers said recently that there was no hope of stopping inflation unless major wage settlements this year were appreciably lower than the 5.5. per cent average achieved in 1967. But major settlements lately have been running around 6 per cent a year or better.

The Council of Economic Advisers met with the A.F.L.-C.I.O. leaders at lunch, shortly after Mr. Meany made it clear that organization would not accept voluntary wage restraint. President Johnson met with the labor officials at the White House around 5 P.M.

Two-Way Pull in City's Wages

By A. H. RASKIN

The strike pressure through which New York City hospital employes already have won assurance of a minimum wage of $100 a week is part of a much broader drive—formless but insistent—to push up scales for unskilled workers performing grubby, unpleasant jobs essential to community safety or comfort.

The drive goes beyond the demand universal among workers in offices, factories and every other field for higher wages to offset the bite that higher prices and higher taxes are taking out of their pay envelopes.

Part of the spur for the special pressure of those at the foot of the wage ladder comes from the revolution the civil rights and antipoverty movements have brought in the attitudes and aspirations of many Negroes, Puerto Ricans, Mexican-Americans and others long excluded from equal opportunity.

The dead-end jobs as porters, dishwashers, emptiers of bed pans, haulers of trash, slop scrubbers, messengers and handymen that once represented the horizon of expectation for many such workers no longer hold much allure unless drudgery pays at rates well above the statutory wage floor of $1.60 an hour, or $64 for a standard forty-hour week.

A further spur in the same direction is that it literally does not pay to take a job at the legal minimum in a city like New York, with its relatively high welfare allowances. The basic relief stipend for a family of four now comes to $272.50 a month. This sum is about to be raised by 6 per cent to take account of the upsurge in living costs in the last year, and an additional raise is in prospect under a flat-grant system now awaiting a go-ahead from Washington.

More Money on Welfare

Even without these increases, however, a worker with a wife and two children earning $1.60 an hour would take home $12 a month less in wages than he could get simply by sitting home and waiting for his welfare checks. And that deficit would be made greater still by the cost of subway fare, work clothes, lunches and other job-related expenses. The bigger the worker's family (the regulator of how much he would get on relief), the bigger the financial sacrifice he would be making for the joy of working.

The incongruity of this reverse-incentive was a mainstay of the union case for a $100 pay floor for hospital orderlies, culinary workers and other aides without special skill or training. The hospitals gave in on the $100 figure well before last night's strike deadline; what is left of the wage dispute now revolves around whether it should become effective in two jumps over the next year or in three over the next 23 months. The real conflict is not over the money but over the union's unwillingness to go along with the hospitals' desire for more flexibility in contracting out work.

The upward trend in payment for the downtrodden is asserting itself strongly in both organized and unorganized fields. Businessmen cooperating with the city in its campaign to defuse ghetto tensions by finding jobs for the hard-core unemployed report that the Manpower and Career Development Agency gets few takers for jobs paying less than $100 a week. Porters and car sweepers in the municipal subway system earn $128.60 a week, sanitation workers $160.

One of the hallmarks of an affluent society is the multiplication of services designed to relieve people of the necessity of performing humdrum tasks for themselves. On that basis, those willing to take on such tasks are sure to keep insisting on getting some small handhold on affluence in their own right — not only in hospitals but everywhere else.

High Price of Egalitarianism

That opens up a whole new range of problems because it upsets historic wage relationships based on skill and training. Workers who were accustomed to think of themselves as labor's upper crust suddenly find they are down in the ruck in terms of earnings. The complications attendant on that discovery began asserting themselves a decade ago in the mass production industries, where the leveling effect of across-the-board wage increases had erased much of the pay superiority once enjoyed by toolmakers and other skilled machinists.

Resentment against this egalitarian trend touched off what amounted to an upper middle-class revolt within labor of such dimensions that even the United Auto Workers, a union built on equal treatment for everybody from janitor to patternmaker, had to start negotiating extra increases for its skilled craftsmen and to give them a veto over companywide agreements in General Motors, Ford and Chrysler.

In New York City, where the average factory wage is only $108.04 a week, the move toward an informal floor of $100 is obviously going to dislocate pay scales for everybody else. The answer unquestionably will be the usual one in labor: Keep the differentials by pushing all wages up. The only trouble with that solution is that prices will go up even faster than wages and the fight to preserve the buying power of the dollar will become impossible to win. The prospective increase of $20 to $25 a day in the cost of hospital care is merely the latest in an endless series of reminders that no one comes out ahead when wage increases are paid in what Walter P. Reuther calls "the wooden nickels of inflation."

A. H. RASKIN is assistant editor of the editorial page.

Nixon Asks Inflation Fight By Unions and Businesses

A Letter Sent to 2,200 Leaders Calls for 'Sense of Responsibility' in Their Decisions on Wages and Prices

By ROBERT B. SEMPLE Jr.
Special to The New York Times

WASHINGTON, Oct. 18— President Nixon called on labor and business today to join him in the fight on inflation.

In his first direct appeal to the leaders of corporations and unions, Mr. Nixon asked them to show a "sense of responsibility" in their price and wage decisions.

He declared that Federal fiscal and monetary policies had begun to slow the rate of inflation and warned that "price and wage decisions that anticipate inflation's continuing at or near present levels would be shortsighted, imprudent, and unprofitable."

Prices are currently rising at a rate of over 5 per cent a year, but in recent days Administration officials have been saying that the steady upward trend of the last five years has slowed and, in time, may be reversed.

The President's appeal was contained in a letter mailed this morning to 2,200 "major business and labor leaders," according to the White House press secretary, Ronald L. Ziegler.

The letter represented yet another stage in Mr. Nixon's accelerating effort to enlist public support for his anti-inflation policies.

On Thursday, his principal economic advisers pledged to continue the Government's strict fiscal and monetary policies, and yesterday, in a nationwide radio address, the President urged all Americans to exercise self-restraint in their purchasing decisions and thus ease demand.

At a White House briefing yesterday, Herbert Stein, a member of the Council of Economic Advisers, said the intent of the letter mailed today was to inform the private sector that there had been a "real change" in the economic climate and to warn private leaders that "for the sake of their own business and their own employment" they should pay close attention to the new trend.

The rate of inflation will continue to decline in each quarter of the 1970 calendar year, he said, adding:

"The point is that we are not giving them a precise standard of reference to which they should adhere, but that we are saying that they should observe the economy."

Asked whether labor was entitled to compensate for past inflation with large new wage demands, Mr. Stein replied indirectly: "They simply cannot act as if the rate of inflation is going to continue as it has in recent years. If they continue to act that way some of them are going to be unemployed."

Mr. Stein made no effort to give an official definition of

what the Administration considered a reasonable level of wage and price increases, and neither did the President.

Mr. Nixon has said that he regards as unworkable and ultimately unenforcable the wage-price "guidelines" for specific industries invoked during the Kennedy and Johnson Administration. He did not mention them in his letter today.

Self-Interested Cited

He appealed instead to the self-interest of the businessmen and labor leaders, arguing that businesses and unions that push prices and wages up too quickly will soon find themselves priced out of the market.

"It is in the interest of private business to consider pricing policies in the light of Government's determination to check inflation," the letter declared, adding:

"The business that commits errors in pricing on the up side, expecting to be bailed out by inflation, is going to find itself in a poor competitive position. Betting on ever-higher prices is a sure way of losing."

The President had this message for labor:

"It is in the interest of every union leader and workingman to avoid wage demands that will reduce the purchasing power of his dollar and reduce the number of job opportunities."

As he did in his radio address yesterday, Mr. Nixon listed in the letter the steps he has taken to reduce inflationary pressures, including reducing Federal spending by $7-billion, curtailing Federal construction commitments, urging extension of the surtax at a reduced level of 5 per cent until mid-1970, and promoting a restrictive moneaary policy.

"Economic policy needed backbone rather than jawbone," he wrote, "and backbone is exactly what our record shows. We have taken the unpopular road to earn back government's credibility in fiscal affairs, and by our actions we have shown that we mean what we say about cooling inflation."

Labor Report Calls for Revised World Trade Policy

By DAMON STETSON
Special to The New York Times

BAL HARBOUR, Fla., Feb. 21—The economic policy committee of the A.F.L.-C.I.O. said today that the United States' position in world trade had deteriorated in recent years and that as a result a thorough revision of Government policy was required in the interest of the American people.

The committee's report reflected growing concern by labor in such industries as glass, shoes, electronics, textiles and steel over the effects of increasing imports and competition.

The American Federation of Labor and Congress of Industrial Organizations has traditionally supported the expansion of international trade on a reciprocal basis in the national interest. But the report said that the federation's backing of the orderly expansion of trade did not include the "promotion of private greed at public expense or the undercutting of United States wages and labor standards."

The 40-page study of the nation's deteriorating trade position and its adverse impact on affected workers and their communities was made public today after being presented to the executive council of the federation, which is holding its winter session at the Americana Hotel here. The report was prepared by Nathaniel Goldfinger, the federation's director of research.

A Disappearing Surplus

In every year since 1894, the report said, the United States sold more to foreign nations than it bought. But by 1968 and 1969, it said, this surplus of merchandise exports over imports had almost disappeared.

Major causes of the deterioration of the United States' position in world trade, the report said, have been new developments in the postwar period that accelerated in the 1960's. Among these, it said, have been the spread of managed national economies, with direct and indirect Government barriers to imports and aid to exports; the internationalization of technology; the skyrocketing rise of investments by United States companies in foreign subsidiaries, and the spread of multinational corporations based in the United States.

"Such changes have made old 'free trade' concepts and their 'protectionist' opposites outdated and increasingly irrelevant," the report said. "Yet United States Government policy has failed, for the most part, to face up to these new developments. As a result, United States Government policy in the area of foreign trade is more applicable to the world of the late 1940's and 1950's than the 1970's."

The deterioration of this nation's foreign trade position, the report said, has had significant impact on jobs, on collective bargaining strength of unions, on wages and labor standards in adversely affected industries.

Although precise information on the job loss resulting from imports was not available, the report cited a Labor Department estimate that about 2.4 million jobs would have been required in the United States in 1968 to produce the equivalent value of the products imported into the United States that were competitive with products made in this country.

Diverse Attack Urged

For workers and trade unions, the report said, there is no one-shot panacea for the trade problem. Rather, it said, a battery of policies and mechanisms is needed to make it possible to get at the varied causes of the specific problems that affect different groups of workers in different industries.

The choice is not free trade vs. protectionism, the report said, but an effort should be made to face up to the need to move ahead for an orderly expansion of world trade, while emphasizing that trade is a two-way street, and to develop realistic policies to deal with foreign investment of United States firms and multinational corporations.

A statement on the national economy, which was approved by the federation's executive council, said that the United States was now confronted by both an economic slump and rapidly rising prices, after more than a year of the Administration's policy of severe economic restraint.

February 22, 1970

Strike Fever Speeds Up Wage-Price Spiral

The labor scene came apart in a big way last week, with more turbulence in more key sectors than the country had experienced in any single period since 1946. A few of the worst trouble spots had been smoothed out by week's end, but the price of peace was extremely high—so high that it threatened to give extra bounce to the upsurge in living costs that caused most of the strikes in the first place.

The first casualty of that inflationary push was President Nixon's precariously balanced budget. A union-White House wage agreement negotiated to settle the first strike in the history of the postal service carried with it retroactive pay increases for all of Uncle Sam's civilian and military personnel. That added $3-billion a year to Federal spending and obliged the President to propose tapping the pockets of most Americans to help pay the bill. The first installment was a message to Congress urging that the cost of mailing a first-class letter go up from 6 cents to a dime.

But few citizens needed the Nixon jolt to be aware that the settlement of a strike could be almost as painful as the strike itself. Every time a contract in private industry calls for a sizable wage increase, that industry's customers steel themselves for a pass-along in the form of higher prices, often a good deal higher than the jump in labor costs. Last week brought fresh evidence that, whatever the success of the Administration's anti-inflation efforts in other fields, the wage-price spiral was still whirling upward at a dizzy pace.

Since 1965 unions have been setting pay records each year in an effort to keep ahead of the rising cost of living. It has been a losing race for most workers. In the last four years, the gross weekly wage of the average factory employe went up by $22 to a $129 total, but he wound up nearly a dollar poorer in purchasing power after taxes and higher prices took their bite out of his take-home pay.

That melting away of wage envelopes in a period of high corporate profits and high interest rates has been a principal spur to the unrest that has rocked the industrial front this year and that threatens to spread to many additional enterprises in the weeks and months immediately ahead. Assurances by Administration spokesmen that an end of inflation is just around the corner gain no credence in union halls as each month shows another climb in the consumer price index.

On the contrary, many unionists take seriously the warnings of the American Federation of Labor and Congress of Industrial Organizations that the pro-business policies of the Nixon Administration insure a gilt-edged recession in which prices will stay high while millions of workers get the ax. The result is a widespread union conviction that the course of wisdom is to grab while the grabbing is good, even if long strikes are necessary to push up the settlement.

Increased Restlessness

To such economic factors is added the restlessness that pervades all institutions in these days of participatory democracy. The authority of union leaders no longer overawes the rank and file. One contract in every eight recommended by union negotiators is thrown back in their faces by dissident members. Usually the outcome is a bigger employer

Labor's Argument for Higher Pay

Auto Workers
Average Weekly Earnings

Gross Wages

Real Wages

$180
$160
$140
$120

Truck Drivers
Average Weekly Earnings

Gross Wages

Estimated

Real Wages

Estimated

$160
$145
$130
$115

Wholesale and Retail Workers
Average Weekly Earnings

Gross Wages

Real Wages

$90
$80
$70
$60

1965 '66 '67 '68 1969

Labor says that while contracts have provided for large raises in the past five years, the purchasing power of the dollar has fallen so that real wages have remained about steady or even fallen. Charts use Consumer Price Index base of 1957-59=100.

The New York Times (by Neal Boenzi)

offer the second time around, a practice that undermines the foundations of collective bargaining.

The truculence of the 1970 wearer of a union button got abundant expression in last week's discord. The stand-in head of the country's biggest union — Frank E. Fitzsimmons, caretaker of the International Brotherhood of Teamsters in the absence of the jailed James R. Hoffa—found himself powerless to wield his predecessor's whip.

A contract that would have given 450,000 truck drivers a package increase of better than 30 per cent over a three-year period failed to end local strikes in a half-dozen cities. Worse still, local barons in Chicago virtually consigned the pact to the scrap heap by telling Mr. Fitzsimmons to stay out of town while they negotiated a richer deal.

The story was much the same with fractious Federal air controllers, rail shopcraft employes and workers in other key fields. The mood was one of reliance on economic force, heedless of no-strike laws, court injunctions and admonitions from union leaders.

The delight of Administration officials over the postal accord was tempered by a knowledge that many letter carriers and clerks in New York, spearhead of the original revolt, remained unhappy — this despite the substantial gains the pact promised for mailmen and its enthusiastic endorsement by the entire labor high command, from George Meany down.

An even greater anxiety attended the signing of the pact. It was the awareness of everybody on both sides of the table that unions elsewhere in the Federal service would read a clear lesson from the $2.5-billion windfall their members will receive as a by-product of the postal settlement. It is the lesson that has caused so much grief in New York and other cities long familiar with strikes by unionized municipal employes: Walkouts pay off in higher wages and other benefits, law or no law.

The President made it plain in his private talks with Mr. Meany and the postal union chiefs after the postal agreement that he intended to counteract this feeling by trying to make sure that Federal employes never would have grievances so oppressive they would feel the need to quit work over them.

If the outlook remains troubled in government, it is even more so in the private sector. Rubber workers, meat packers and a million construction workers are all on the spring negotiating list. New York's apartment house employes are threatening to walk out April 20 in a row that links higher pay with a relaxation of rent controls. And midyear will see the opening of what could prove the toughest struggle of all, the triennial negotiations between Walter P. Reuther's United Auto Workers and the automotive "Big Three." The end of the spiral is nowhere in sight.

—A. H. RASKIN

April 5, 1970

For Tripartite Talks

To the Editor:

First it was the transportation workers, then the garbage collectors, thereafter the school teachers, the gravediggers and the mail carriers.

How long will it be before we have a civilized system of adjudicating management-labor disputes?

What is wrong with changing from bipartite to tripartite negotiating bodies, comprising equal representation from labor, management and the public (who, in the final analysis, pays the bill) with all parties pledged to accept the decision of the majority?

Thus we would end interminable deadlocks, avoid costly, crippling strikes and obtain agreements based on equity instead of power struggles and settlements determined by who is strongest.

HERMAN P. SCHARF
Bay Harbor Islands, Fla.
March 29, 1970

April 24, 1970

Chart at right shows sharp rise
in median wage increases in
construction industry in relation
to the rest of industry, particularly
since 1968. Index below shows
the steady over-all rise in
building costs in recent years.

June 14, 1970

Median Wage Increase in Cents Per Hour

70
60
50
40 — **Contract Construction Industry**
30
All Industry Excluding Construction
20
1u
Manufacturing
0

1958   '60   '62   '64   '66   '68 '69

Source: Bureau of National Affairs

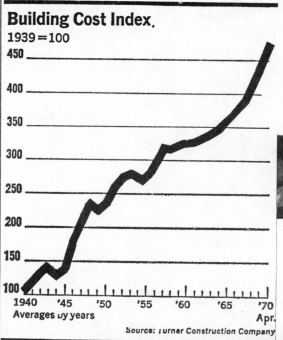

Building Cost Index

1939 = 100

450
400
350
300
250
200
150
100

1940   '45   '50   '55   '60   '65   '70
Averages by years   Apr.

Source: Turner Construction Company

NIXON ASKS FOR RESTRAINT ON WAGE-PRICE DEMANDS; BARS MANDATORY CONTROL

The New York Times (by Mike Lien)

POLICY UNCHANGED

But President Sets Up 'Inflation Alert' Plan and Output Panel

By ROBERT B. SEMPLE Jr.
Special to The New York Times

WASHINGTON, June 17 — President Nixon announced to the nation today that he was standing by his basic strategy against inflation and recession.

In a long-awaited television speech on the economy, he urged business and labor to support him in his efforts and to display "social responsibility" by moderating demands for price and wage increases.

Instead of outlining important departures from his basic economic strategy, the President sought to buttress his strategy by naming two new governmental bodies.

One, the National Commission on Productivity, will suggest ways of lowering prices through increased industrial productivity. The other, the Regulations and Purchasing Review Board, will examine the Government's contribution to inflation.

Wage-Price Controls Out

In addition, he said he would establish an "inflation alert" system to focus public attention on excessive wage-price settlements and called on Congress to shore up specific weaknesses in the economy.

Mr. Nixon rejected outright any direct wage-price controls as both a temporary expedient and a threat to individual freedom.

And while lecturing business and labor to "raise their sights by lowering their demands," he pledged that he would never single out specific industries or labor leaders for Presidential criticism.

"I believe this is the right program at the right time and for the right purpose," the President said. "There is no more important goal than to curb inflation without permitting severe disruption."

Then he added: "This is an activist Administration and should new developments call for new action in the future, I shall take the action needed to attain the goal."

None of the new devices announced by the President would involve "jawboning" as commonly understood—that is, the firm use of the moral authority of the Presidency to prevent excessive wage-price increases. Nor would they involve direct confrontations between Government, business or labor.

New 'Alert' System

Under the "inflation alert" system, the Council of Economic Advisers would study and make public "outstanding cases of price or wage increases"—but only after such increases had taken place.

The National Commission on Productivity — with six representatives each from labor, management and the public and five from Government—will not recommend the specific wage-price guideposts used in previous Administrations but will suggest ways of increasing output per man hour, thereby reducing pressures on business to raise prices to maintain profit margins.

And the Regulations and Purchasing Review Board will confine itself exclusively to a detailed examination of the impact of Federal purchasing and import policies on domestic price levels.

Of the three new devices, Government officials attached the greatest importance to the productivity commission. Productivity — usually defined as output per man hour—has declined during the recent economic slowdown. Increased productivity is regarded as the key to raising wages without causing inflation because it allows business to raise wages and improve profits without raising prices.

Congressional reaction to the speech divided along predictable but not necessarily partisan lines.

Republicans generally hailed it as a reasonable and responsible approach to orderly growth.

Senator Edward M. Kennedy, Democrat of Massachusetts, applauded Administration officials for "painting themselves out of their ideological corner on price and wage restraint."

Proponents of even firmer Government action, by contrast, criticized the President's remedies as too little, too late and too soft.

Assurances on Credit

"What the President proposes is to tell business and labor to drive slow," said Representative Henry Reuss, Democrat of Wisconsin, "without setting any speed limits."

Mr. Nixon said little about high interest rates—except to assure businessmen of sufficient credit and a steadily growing money supply—and this brought howls from advocates of easier money.

This criticism was muted somewhat when Wright Patman, chairman of the House Banking and Currency Committee, made public a letter from the President saying that he would use standby authority to control interest rates and credit if he decided it would serve the nation's economic objectives. But Mr. Nixon challenged Mr. Patman's assertion that such controls were needed now to avert a "mounting economic crisis."

Speaking slowly and in a low voice, Mr. Nixon said he was trying to manage the delicate transition from a wartime to a peacetime economy. Two major factors, he said, made the task especially difficult: the threat of a recession caused in part by reduced Federal spending on defense and the threat of continued inflation fueled by a decade "in which this nation lived far beyond its means."

During his tenure as President, he admitted, "unemployment has increased, the price index continues to rise, profits have gone down, the stock market has declined [and] interest rates are too high." He conceded, too, that some of his own remedies had been slow to take hold.

But he reaffirmed his faith in those remedies and predicted that the twin techniques of a stringent fiscal policy marked by reduced Federal spending and a flexible monetary policy assuring business plenty of credit would bring inflation under control without triggering a recession.

"I am convinced," he said, "that the basic economic road we have taken is the right road, the responsible road, the road that will curb the cost of living and lead us to orderly expansion."

Mr. Nixon returned time and again to the theme of preparing for a peacetime economy — a theme that his principal economic speechwriter, William Safire, had worked all yesterday and part of last night to refine and embellish.

To achieve economic security and progress, the President declared, "we need no artificial dependence on the production of the weapons of war."

On the contrary, he said, a well-run peacetime economy would mean greater benefits for all Americans, would "give us more room in the Federal budget to meet human needs at home," and would make possible, "a much more enduring prosperity."

However, he asserted, the transition period could bring dislocation and pain, and for that reason he promised to adhere to a flexible monetary policy. For that reason, too, he called on Congress to take eight steps "to help the people who need help most in a period of economic transition:"

¶Approve legislation submitted over a year ago to provide unemployment compensation for five million more workers.

¶Pass the Manpower Training Act, which provides an automatic increase in training funds in periods of high unemployment.

¶Approve a recent proposal —which the Administration did not write but supports—to provide insurance to investors in the stock market.

¶Approve his proposal to tie Social Security benefits to the cost of living to "keep the burden of the fight against inflation from falling on those least able to afford it."

¶Pass the Emergency Home Finance Act of 1970 to stimulate housing construction, which has passed the Senate but not the House.

¶Give greater authority to the Small Business Administration to stimulate banks and other lending institutions to make loans to small businesses at lower interest rates.

¶Approve new legislation, which Mr. Nixon promised to submit shortly, enabling the Department of Transportation to provide emergency help to financially troubled railroads.

¶Exercise restraint on spending to avoid a large budget deficit. The Administration is now estimating the deficit for fiscal year 1971, which begins July 1, at $1.3-billion, but Congress has before it several legislative items that could push the shortfall to $5-to $6-billion.

Blames Democrats

If the President placed much of the burden for a successful transition to peacetime on the Congress, he placed nearly all of the blame for his present difficulties on the Democrats.

While conceding that his own policies would require more time to work, he insisted that they would have been unnecessary in the first place had not his Democratic predecessors in the 1960's accumulated budget deficits totaling $57-billion over 10 years.

"He attempted to blame everyone but himself and his advisers," former Vice President Hubert H. Humphrey declared in a statement. Mr. Humphrey also criticized Mr. Nixon for failing to recommend specific wage-price guidelines and display "effective Presidential leadership."

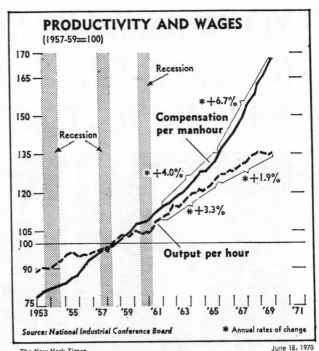

PRODUCTIVITY AND WAGES
(1957-59=100)

Source: National Industrial Conference Board   * Annual rates of change

The New York Times   June 18, 1970

NIXON AIDES ISSUE 'INFLATION ALERT' CITING PRICE RISES

But the Economic Advisers Avoid Placing Any Blame on Industry or Labor

By EDWIN L. DALE Jr.
Special to The New York Times

WASHINGTON, Aug. 7—The Nixon Administration's first "inflation alert," issued today, identified several recent price increases, some accompanied by large wage increases, that it said had been important in raising the price level. It pointed no finger of blame, however.

The report attributed the rise in prices this year to a wide variety of causes. Only some of the causes were associated with "concentrated" industries, those dominated by a few large corporations, and with wage increases won by unions.

The basic conclusion of the report was that inflation in the United States always eventually responds to Government policies curbing total spending in the economy. But the longer the duration of the inflation, the slower the response, the report found.

Increases Detailed

Solely because they were important recently, the report discussed in detail price increases for coal and electric power, rubber, cigarettes and trucking.

There was no effort to say whether wage bargains won by unions, or price increases made by the industries involved, were "justified," as was done in the Kennedy and Johnson Administrations.

For 1970 to date, the report mentioned price advances in a variety of sectors of the economy, all different in their causes—steel and construction, medical care and mortgage interest rates, copper and New York City subway fares.

Smaller Union Role

It also pointed out that only 7 per cent of the labor force would have its wages determined by union negotiations this year, although it noted that wage increases in the settlements negotiated so far "have not slowed down."

The most dramatic single price increase identified in the report was that for coal, up 35 per cent in the last year. The cause was a rapid rise in demand, not higher wages, the report found.

So far, electric power rates for consumers have been slow to rise despite the coal price increase and higher interest rates, another important utility cost, but the report made clear that many rate increases were on the way. The Tennessee Valley Authority, it noted, has just announced a 23 per cent increase in its wholesale price of power.

The report was compiled by the Council of Economic Advisers and, just before being made public, was submitted to the new National Commission on Productivity, which held its first meeting. The commission itself made no public statement. Its purpose is the longer-range one of trying to improve productivity, or output per manhour.

Rate Held Unconstant

President Nixon established the commision in June and announced that periodic "inflation alerts" would be issued purely as warnings to the public. The alerts were never intended as a "jawboning" device to force down wages or prices.

The report had a historical section on inflation in the United States since the early nineteen-fifties. It said, "The explanation of inflation cannot be found, or the blame for it assigned, by looking at the behavior of particular prices, or categories of prices."

It also emphasized that the rate of inflation in the United States had not been constant but rather had fluctuated "in response to economic conditions."

"Previous periods," it said, "also had their apprehensions, notably in 1957-58, that the then-current rate of inflation would persist forever or accelerate, but these were not justified."

The tone of the report was consistent with that of the Administration from the beginning. The President has persistently refused to try to influence private wage and price behavior by such devices as "guideposts" or criticism of individual company or union actions.

Easing of Prices Seen

...ussion of cigarette
...in the re-
...on that

PRESIDENT SIGNS BILL ON CONTROLS

Acts Reluctantly and Implies He Won't Use Powers

Special to The New York Times

WASHINGTON, Aug. 17—President Nixon reluctantly signed today a bill that authorizes him to freeze wages, prices and rents.

But the President made it clear, in a statement issued at the White House, that he objected to such controls and would not use the discretionary power provided in the bill extending the 20-year-old Defense Production Act.

"Were it not for the need to extend the basic law," he said, he would veto it.

Earlier today, in another skirmish with the Democratic-controlled Congress, the President accused it of lagging behind the Administration in efforts to save money by abolishing "sacred cow" programs. He said that Congress's refusal to adopt a variety of Administration cost-cutting proposals was costing the Government $2-million a day.

House Speaker John W. McCormack issued a statement accusing the President of playing "partisan political games" that were intended to disguise the failure of the Administration's economic policies.

Cites 'Saving' Last Year

Mr. McCormack said that, using the President's logic, Congress "last year saved the taxpayers $21-million a day which the President wanted to waste, by making cuts in his budget."

Mr. Nixon said that wage and price controls "simply do not fit the economic conditions which exist today." He cited, as support for his argument, a 1969 report of former President Johnson's economic advisers declaring that controls were "a last resort appropriate only in an extreme emergency such as all-out war."

The President said that if controls really were needed, Congress "should face up to its responsibilities and make such controls mandatory." His statement noted that the House voted 270 to 11 against a motion to make controls mandatory.

The suggestion was that Congress was less interested in establishing wage and price controls than in setting up an opportunity, during a Congressional campaign, to accuse the White House of failing to use the controls.

Other Objections

Mr. Nixon listed other objections to the bill. He said its provision setting up a Cost Accounting Standard Board outside the executive department to police defense procurement contracts was an incursion on the Administration's responsibility. He asked Congress to amend the legislation to put the new board in the executive branch.

And he said that a $20-million limit on the amount of permissible guarantees of defense production loans was "arbitrary" and could interfere with the effective conduct of defense production activities.

Earlier, Mr. Nixon chastised Congress for failing to join the Administration in efforts to trim spending on programs he described as "obsolete, low priority or inefficient." He said, "Congressional inaction is extremely expensive."

The White House sent Congress a message six months ago, pledging to cut spending on 42 such programs and asking the legislators to join in trimming 15 programs, including payments to individuals cured of tuberculosis, duplicate funeral benefits that veterans may receive and the abolition of Federal tea tasters.

The President said his efforts had saved $983-million but that Congress, by blocking some Administration cost-cutting efforts and not enacting others, would leave $707-million "unsaved" in the 1971 fiscal year.

NIXON'S 2D INFLATION ALERT SCORES WAGE-PRICE SPIRAL IN SEVERAL BIG INDUSTRIES

RESTRAINT URGED

Failure to Slow Rate of Pay Rises Held Chief Concern

Special to The New York Times

WASHINGTON, Dec. 1—The Nixon Administration's second "inflation alert" leveled specific criticism today at wage or price increases in several industries, including construction, oil and automobiles.

The report was the closest this Administration has come to what is known as "jaw-boning"—efforts by the Government to influence private price and wage decisions. But there was no sign of threats or action by the Government, except a possible future decision relating to oil that had already been disclosed.

A decision aimed at increasing oil supplies and thus exerting downward pressure on prices is under consideration and may be announced in a few days. One possible move would be to abandon all production restraints on federally leased offshore oil wells.

Issued by Council

The report, issued by the President's Council of Economic Advisers, had these main themes:

¶The chief current concern "is the failure of the average rate of wage increases to slow down." While a possible increase in business profit margins is "another cause for concern," profits for each unit of output now are some 20 per cent below their peak in 1966.

¶To the extent that the wage-price "spiral" does not moder-ate, the Government will be held back in its policies to expand the economy and reduce unemployment.

Conclusions of Report

The discussion of specific wage or price developments was limited to events that have occurred since midyear. These were the report's conclusions:

¶Construction industry wage increases averaging 17.5 per cent in the first nine months of this year went to some 504,000 workers, but 324,000 construction workers have no jobs. "Unquestionably the extremely large wage increases obtained this year and last year have contributed to this slack in the construction industry."

¶In the automobile field, the recent wage settlement at the General Motors Corporation, estimated at 7 per cent a year, "if generalized throughout the economy, would crowd further upward costs per unit of output and, therefore, the price level." A recent price increase for cars, the largest since 1952, will cost consumers some $2.5-billion a year and "will inevitably expose the domestic industry and its employes to increased competition from cars made overseas." (The Chrysler Corporation raised its 1971 prices today by an average of five-tenths of 1 per cent.)

¶A recent price increase for crude oil, followed by a 16 per cent increase in posted gasoline prices excluding taxes, came "when petroleum inventories are at a level higher than is normal for this time of year." This condition should normally exert downward pressure on prices. The price increase was made possible only through "direct actions to curtail production," mainly a decision by the state of Texas to reduce allowable output.

¶A railroad industry wage increase averaging 9 per cent a year proposed by a special Presidential emergency board cannot be fully evaluated in its implications for future freight rate increases because the proposed contract may also lead to less "featherbedding" and increased productivity. But the board's assumption that wage increases should allow for a 6 per cent rise in consumer prices each year "would saddle the industry with rising costs, and it would also be unfortunate for the larger cause of achieving a new stability for the price-cost level."

¶The airline industry is "another industry where employers have granted large wage increases and [as a result] has been especially affected in its profits."

¶The present price-setting system for copper has left United States producer prices "well above the world price." The report was written before the announcement of price reduction this week by Phelps Dodge.

¶Rising wages in the transit field have been a key element in a "vicious circle" in which fares go up and patronage goes down. "It is proving virtually impossible for fares to be increased fast enough to keep operating revenues abreast of rising operating costs," even though the price index for public transport rose more than 15 per cent in the 12 months up to last September.

Paul W. McCracken, chairman of the Council of Economic Advisers, termed today's report "a little sharper, a little more pointed" than the one issued Aug. 7. But the new report did not appear to signify any fundamental change in Administration policy, which has resisted direct intervention by the Government in wage or price decisions.

George Meany, president of the American Federation of Labor and Congress of Industrial Organizations, attacked the report. Noting that it cited wage increases as the "chief concern," he said, "I don't buy that, and American workers won't buy that."

"The fact is," said Mr. Meany, "that workers and wages did not cause this inflation and they have not profited by it."

In Toronto, Leonard Woodcock, president of the United Automobile Workers, said the automobile wage agreement "is not inflationary."

Associated Press
DISCUSSES NEW ALERT: Paul W. McCracken, head of Council of Economic Advisers, at news session at White House on inflation.

The report called third-quarter figures on wages "disappointing," noting that total employe compensation, union and nonunion, had risen at an annual rate of 7.8 per cent—"essentially the same as the previous high of 7.7 per cent in the third quarter of 1969."

Prices and Labor Costs

"One of the best-established facts about the American economy," the report continued, "is the long-run tendency for prices on the average to rise at about the same rate as unit labor costs on the average. Put another way, apart from temporary aberrations the general price level tends to rise by the excess of wage increases over productivity increases.

"Productivity cannot be counted on for long to rise more than about 3 per cent per year, although this rate will probably be exceeded in the next year. This means that a continuing rate of increase of employe compensation per hour of 7 per cent per year would commit the economy to a continuing inflation rate of about 4 per cent."

...report also made this
moment there are
...have recently
in

December 2, 1970

Unions Aim for Big Raises Despite Lagging Economy

By JERRY M. FLINT
Special to The New York Times

DETROIT, Dec. 24 — The Administration calls it wage inflation, but labor leaders and workers call if "catch-up." And despite a slow economy and high unemployment rates, some union men say they will keep on running after big raises until they have caught up.

"We're behind," said Charlie James, a steel worker getting his pay a the Great Lakes mill here. "Take a welder like me on the big pressure pipes. We're getting only half what a man outside gets for the same job, $8.95 an hour."

Earlier this month President Nixon said; "This is the critical moment, then, for business and labor to make a special effort to exercise restraint in price and wage decision." And Arthur Burns, Federal Reserve Board chairman, said that the current inflation was caused by "pressures on costs arising from excessive wage increases."

The Government reported today that consumer prices continued to rise in November, though at a slower rate than in the two previous months. Experts in Washington were pleased at the slackening in the upward spiral, but cautioned against drawing any conclusions from it.

Pace of Rise Unexpected

Government economists, counting on the slowing economy to hold back labor's demands, did not expect wages to climb as fast as they did in e-the last year.

In1958, a recession year, hourly earnings in the privaten nonfarm sector went up only six cents an hour to $1.95, a 3.2 per cent gain from the year before. In 1961, another bad year, wages went up only five cents an hour, 2.4 per cent, from the year before.

But average hourly pay this year climbed from $3.13 in January to $3.28 an hour in October, and with the 51 cent-an-hour increase for auto workers it is expected to be up 6 per cent-to-7 per cent over 1969 for the full year.

These increases have come at a time, moreover, of rising unemployment, a traditional brake on rising pay levels. November's 5.8 per cent jobless rate, though below the respective 6.8 per cent and 6.7 per cent rates of the 1958 and 1961 downturns, is nevertheless the highest in seven and a half

years and still seems not to have deterred wage demands.

At the Chrysler Corporation, for example, workers were being laid off this month because of slow sales, and yet the United Auto Workers were insisting that the company match the wage package given by bigger, richer manufacturers.

'Car Prices Up Twice'

"The prices will go up faster than we get it," said Frank Centala as he left the Chrysler assembly plant in Detroit. "Why, we haven't even gotten our raise yet and the car prices are up twice. We've got to get a big raise to keep up with the rest of the crowd."

There are some signs, however, that the size of pay increases could slow down in the next year, easing the inflationary pressure, and in line with the desires of the Administration. Pay increases of nonunionized workers seem to be slowing, perhaps to 3.4 to 4 per cent this year against 5 per cent increases last year.

In addition, productivity is rising. Over the long term productivity is calculated to be climbing at a rate of 3 per cent a year. But in 1969 it climbed only 0.7 per cent, and in the first quarter of this year it ·dropped 2.5 per cent. By the third quarter, however, it was climbing at a 4.6 per cent rate.

Unit labor costs, stable for years, were up 6.5 per cent in 1969 and 9.6 per cent in the first quarter. But by the third quarter the climb was down to 3 per cent, still moving up but at a slower rate.

President Nixon said this month that the rise in productivity and the slowing of the unit labor cost increase were creating "an opportunity to break the vicious cycle of wage-price escalation."

Government and bank economists say that the cost of living could be climbing at less than a 4 per cent-a-year rate by the end of next year against a 5-to-6 per cent rate this year Some theorize that without the current economic troubles wage increases might be even larger And workers themselves say they are tired of winning large increases only to see them eaten up by climbing costs.

But there is no guarantee that rising productivity will

slow price increases, says Nat Weinberg, the U.A.W.'s chief economist. And he believes that manufacturers, expecting better times, will keep raising prices to improve profit ratios, and that this will in turn keep demands for wage increases high.

It is generally agreed that rising productivity is tied to layoffs, with employers eliminating unneeded workers and taking back fewer workers as business picks up.

But despite these signs of a possible easing of inflationary pressures, union men approaching a new round of contract negotiations next year appear as determined as ever to win big-money settlements. The steel workers are a case in point.

The union's contract with the major steel producers, covering 400,000 workers, expires Aug. 1. It will be the big contract of 1971, although 4.8 million other unionized workers have contracts expiring next year covering metal working, coal, aerospace, communications and clothing workers.

'A Head-On Clash'

"It's all right for every one else to get wage increases but when the steel workers come it's time to stop," said Charles Younglove, district leader and chairman of the union's national steel committee. "The leadership, the rank-and-file aren't going to take it laying down. There's going to be a head-on clash."

"There'll be a revolt in the union if the leadership tries to water down the demands," the union leader said.

"The needs of our workers are important, not if it's inflationary or not," said Norman Pearlstine, a Wall Street Journal reporter who is director of the union representing Dow Jones & Company workers. If he called for restraint, he said, he would be promptly voted out of office and considered "a management shill."

Mr. Pearlstine wears a button reading "15-11-11." The figures stand fot the union's demands of raises of 15 per cent, 11 per cent and 11 per cent in three years, matching the settlement of other newspapers in New York this year. "Our holding back would make no difference," he said.

Government economists admit they were surprised when

wages continued rising as fast as they did despite the slowdown in the economy. Labor economists say the Government men have not been working in the real world.

"Unemployment and tight money didn't stop price increases," said Mr. Weinberg of the U.A.W. He insists that prices, not economic conditions, determine wages.

Economists Assailed

"No one is as ignorant about the economy as economists," he said. "The supply-demand market isn't relevant to the present. In the classical economy you can't have unemployment and inflation side by side" and today's conditions "show how far we are from a classical economy."

In the Great Depression of the nineteen-thirties, he noted, prices as well as wages fell.

As long as prices continue to climb, Mr. Weinberg figures that wages will go up too, and he insists that the workers are still behind. Government figures he said, show that real, spendable earnings of workers. adjusted for inflation, were $77.04 a week for a worker with three dependents in October against $79.35 a week in October of 1965.

Nathaniel Goldfinger, research director of the A.F.L.-C.I.O., said wages rose amid an apparent recession because "a large number of workers are willing to take strike action" and can win their demands despite the bad times.

The big money gains of the nineteen-sixties were taken by professionals, doctors, lawyers and bankers, he said, and "the average working man is on a treadmill for the last couple of years and fed up to the gills."

The economists who figured that pay would not go up fast "live in a textbook world," he said.

Mr. Weinberg even figures that the new Government moves to pump up the economy may well encourage expansion and increase inflationary pressure again.

'A Lot of Catching Up'

"We've got a lot of catching up to do even to have a substandard living wage," said Harold Crotty, president of the Brotherhood of Maintenance of Way employes, one of four rail unions that struck briefly this month and that reject the contract package raising their wages 37 per cent over three years.

"We have between 35,000 and 40,000 members whose wage scale, before the Congressional action this month, was $3 an hour or less," he said. "That's positive proof we're not contributing to in-

445

flation." He added, "Thirty-seven per cent of nothing is nothing."

Without a fair answer to the wage problems, "we'd have a revolution in the working class," the union leader said. He expects the rail dispute will not be solved by the bargainers but will be back in the hands of Congress next year.

The late Walter P. Reuther once warned his auto workers, "You can't build a New York skyscraper in Japan, but you can build a car in Japan." But the U.A.W. still registered increases in pay and fringe benefits expected to average 10 per cent a year in a new three-year contract.

"If we get a good solid wage increase we may not be working," said Joe Wilson, a steel worker who studied economics in college.

He said he was aware of the import problem but also noted that his new small Chevrolet Vega cost $2,500, or $200 more than he paid for a full-sized Ford in 1964.

He is a skilled crane operator at a Detroit mill and says he now earns 50 cents an hour less than an unskilled auto assembly line worker.

"I can't conceive of the men taking less than a decent pay increase," he said.

December 25, 1970

Wage Increases
Special to The New York Times

WASHINGTON, Feb. 23— *Following are figures from the Bureau of Labor Statistics on average hourly earnings, union and nonunion, in manufacturing and construction from 1965 to 1970 and on average union hourly wages in the nation's construction industry on Jan. 4, 1971:*

AVERAGE WAGES, 1965-1970

Year	Manufacturing	Contract Construction
1965	$2.61	$3.70
1966	2.72	3.89
1967	2.83	4.11
1968	3.01	4.41
1969	3.19	4.78
1970	3.36	5.22

AVERAGE WAGES, 1971

	Jan. 4, 1971	Changes between Jan. 2, 1970, and Jan. 4, 1971 per cent	cents
All trades	$6.39	11.9	66.3
Bricklayers	7.00	14.0	86.1
Building laborers	4.91	12.6	54.5
Carpenters	6.64	11.1	65.8
Electricians	7.20	12.5	79.3
Painters	6.11	10.1	54.4
Plasterers	6.56	11.0	64.4
Plumbers	7.20	12.9	81.8

February 24, 1971

NIXON ACTS TO CUT CONSTRUCTION PAY ON U.S. PROJECTS

He Suspends Requirement That Scales Must Match Prevailing Local Rates

UNIONS CRITICIZE MOVE

President Backs Extension of His Authority to Impose Wage-Price Controls

By ROBERT B. SEMPLE Jr.
Special to The New York Times

WASHINGTON, Feb. 23—In an effort to curb inflation in the construction industry, President Nixon suspended today provisions of a law requiring that union scale wages be paid to workers on Federal and federally assisted construction projects.

The action was far less severe than the wage-price freeze that had been urged upon the President by the contractors and some of his advisers.

But Mr. Nixon kept his options open for stiffer action in the future by endorsing—through Secretary of the Treasury John B. Connally Jr.—a bill extending beyond the end of March his stand-by authority to impose wage and price controls.

Negligible Effect Seen

Meanwhile, in Bal Harbour, Fla., leaders of building trades unions said the President's action would have a negligible effect on inflation but might adversely affect the pay of non-union workers.

The President suspended provisions of the Davis-Bacon Act of 1931 requiring contractors on Federal or federally assisted projects to pay "prevailing" wage rates. What this has meant, in practice, is that workers on such projects have been guaranteed wages not less than the top union scale locally.

"Wage rates on Federal projects have been artificially set by the law rather than by customary market forces," Mr. Nixon said. "Frequently, they have been set to match the highest wages paid on private projects. This means that many of the most inflationary local wage settlements in the construction industry have automatically been sanctioned and spread through Government contracts."

$25-Billion Involved

The action applies to wage negotiations in some $25-billion worth of federally assisted construction—a sizable portion of the $90-billion industry.

It is clearly Mr. Nixon's hope that with the prop of Davis-Bacon removed, these negotiations will henceforth be more responsive to market pressures and will yield lower wage settlements. But neither the President nor his advisers were prepared today to make any specific predictions.

The authority for Mr. Nixon's action is contained in the Davis-Bacon Act itself, which allows the President to suspend its wage provisions in an "emergency." The "emergency," Mr. Nixon argued, consists of these factors:

¶Wage settlements in the construction industry have been twice as high as in manufacturing generally. In 1970, the average contract settlement in the building trades called for first-year increases of 18.3 per cent, compared with 8.1 per cent for manufacturing workers.

¶At the same time, unemployment in the construction industry has shot upward, reaching 11.1 per cent in January, or double the national average.

Asked how long the suspension would last, James D. Hodgson, the Secretary of Labor, replied: "It will continue as long as the emergency exists."

Meeting With Hodgson

Mr. Nixon made up his mind to suspend Davis-Bacon, rather than impose a wage-price freeze, at about noon yesterday after a meeting with Mr. Hodgson, who reported that the unions and management had failed to devise voluntary methods to cut costs despite a Presidential request to do so Jan. 18.

Mr. Hodgson, briefing newsmen on the President's statement at the White House this afternoon, said that union leaders were "most upset at the prospect of being singled out for selective wage-price controls," and that this had persuaded the President to take a softer approach.

Both labor and management professed disappointment with the President's decision, especially labor.

Edward J. Carlough, head of the International Association of Sheetmetal Workers, charged in Miami that Mr. Nixon had suspended "the Magna Carta" of labor and had freed contractors to negotiate "antilabor" settlements.

"There will be 3.5 million angry people when this news gets out," he said.

Lobbyists for the builders, meanwhile, argued that the President had not gone far enough.

A statement issued here by William E. Dunn, executive director of the Associated General Contractors of America, called the action indecisive and said it would "not help in any way to stop the demand for huge wage increases with 1,368 construction agreements set to expire this year."

Mr. Nixon may still impose a wage-price freeze, which management groups want, under authority contained in a bill passed by Congress last year.

The bill gives him stand-by authority to order either selective freezes or, if he thinks it

446

necessary, nationwide mandatory controls over all prices, rents, wages and salaries at levels not less than those prevailing on May 25, 1970.

The Administration opposed the measure last year but reversed itself at hearings before the House Banking and Currency Committee this morning.

Mr. Connally said that the White House now supported an extension of the act, which expires March 31, but quickly added that the Administration continued to oppose general wage-price controls and that Mr. Nixon would not invoke them "short of an all-out national emergency."

Officials provided several illustrations to buttress their hopes that the President's action might at least slow the rapid rise in construction wage settlements.

Under Davis-Bacon, they said, it was the Labor Department's responsibility to make a "determination" on wages to be paid by contractors on all federally assisted projects.

As a rule, the department took the top union settlement on a private project in any given city and told the contractor for the Federal project to match it. In effect, therefore, the local wage ceiling on private contracts became the "floor" for wages on Federal contracts.

With the wage provisions of Davis-Bacon now suspended, these officials said, unions and management will bargain collectively for wage agreements on federally assisted projects without being required to meet the "prevailing" wage pattern.

Although a contractor might already have agreed to a wage level of, say, $6.50 an hour for a private project on one side of town, another contractor might be able to negotiate a lower settlement, especially if there was a plentiful supply of labor and intense competition for availble jobs, they said.

Similarly, these officials said, the suspension of Davis-Bacon will eliminate situations in which small-town contractors find themselves forced to pay big-city wages.

In one such instance, officials said, the Labor Department was unable to establish a "prevailing wage" for a federally assisted project in Quantico, Va. The department based its determination on the nearest major labor market, Washington, D. C., and the Quantico contractor found himself paying Washington wages.

PRESIDENT ORDERS WAGE-PRICE CURBS IN CONSTRUCTION

'Constraints' Aim at Holding Annual Pay Rises to 6%— Davis-Bacon Reinstated

By ROBERT B. SEMPLE Jr.
Special to The New York Times

SAN CLEMENTE, Calif. March 29 — President Nixon ordered into effect today what he described as a largely self-regulating system of "constraints" designed to halt the spiral of wages and prices in the construction industry.

Mr. Nixon signed an Executive order at the Western White House for the wage-price plan which was outlined in general terms last Friday by Secretary of Labor James D. Hodgson.

The President also reinstated the Davis-Bacon Act, which requires contractors in federally funded projects to pay union scale wages. He suspended these provisions Feb. 23 in a move deplored by the unions. Mr. Hodgson said the suspension had begun to exert downward pressures on wages.

Object of Move

According to Mr. Hodgson the object of the Executive order is to keep negotiated wage increases in the construction industry to an annual level of about 6 per cent. Wage increases in the industry for 3 million union members averaged between 15 and 18 per cent in 1970.

The action represents a considerable switch from Mr. Nixon's previous hands-off approach to wage negotiations. For while the judgment as to whether specific unions had exceeded the 6 per cent formula would rest with committees made up largely of union and industry representatives, the Government would be able to exercise some measure of control through sanctions and penalties.

Mechanism Set Up

The Executive order establishes a mechanism to monitor construction prices as well as to determine "acceptable" salaries, bonuses, stock options and other forms of compensation to salaried industry employes.

In an accompanying statement, Mr. Nixon said he had won support for the plan from contractors and labor leaders, who "indicated their willingness to cooperate with the Government in fair measures to achieve greater wage and price stability."

The order would seek to moderate wage and price demands through 16 to 18 "craft dispute boards." These boards would review all collective bargaining agreements in the construction industry after today, as well as wage agreements negotiated earlier but scheduled to take effect after today.

Each board would decide whether a wage settlement met criteria set forth in Section 6 of the order, which defines an acceptable settlement as one "not in excess of the average of median increases in wages and benefits over the life of the contract in major construction settlements in the period 1961 to 1968." These increases averaged about 6 per cent, Mr. Hodgson said.

The criteria would make certain allowances for trends in the cost of living, improvement in productivity and other factors.

If it found what it believed to be an unacceptable wage settlement, the craft dispute board would notify another new group to be known as the Construction Industry Stabilization Committee, which will be composed of 12 members appointed by the Secretary of Labor—four from labor, four from management and four from the public. The committee would have 15 days to decide whether the wage settlement violated the criteria.

Mr. Hodgson said the Government would have recourse to three sanctions against offenders.

The mildest would be to give national publicity to the fact that the criteria had been violated.

Second, the Secretary of Labor would be authorized to inform other Government agencies of the identity of the offender. The agencies in turn would be required to take a new look at Government construction contracts in the area and possibly suspend them.

Third, the Secretary of Labor would be authorized to take action that would effectively suspend the Davis-Bacon Act as it related to offending unions. This would be a "selective" suspension of the union found to be in violation of the order.

Mr. Hodgson gave a hypothetical illustration of a labor market where the union wage was $5.50 an hour. On Government projects, the workers would continue to be paid this amount though their unions might have negotiated—in violation of the criteria—a considerably higher settlement.

Thus, the Secretary of Labor, in making wage determinations on Federal projects under Davis-Bacon, would not accept as the area "prevailing wage" any contract negotiated at a level above that allowed by the criteria.

Mr. Nixon issued the Executive order under the Economic Stabilization Act of 1970 which gives the President standby authority to invoke either general or selective wage and price controls. The act was extended for 60 more days today by the House of Representatives. The Administration opposed the act when it was first debated in Congress but did not oppose its most recent extension.

The order indicated more clearly how the Government intended to deal with wages than it did prices, salaries, bonuses and stock options. Section 8 merely established an interagency committee on construction to develop "criteria for the determination of acceptable" price levels and salaries. The committee will be chosen by the Secretary of Housing and Urban Development, George Romney, and will include Government officers only.

Weapons Unclear

Even less clear were the weapons the Government would use against construction companies that violated the criteria. Presumably, Government agencies could refuse to award contracts to companies found to be in violation.

Administration oficials unanimously regarded today's action as a major victory for the President. They asserted that it vindicated his decision to suspend the provisions of Davis-Bacon in February, which persuaded labor and management to agree to a partly voluntary control mechanism.

Mr. Hodgson said that the Administration would consider other means to curb wages and prices if this mechanism failed.

ADMINISTRATION OPPOSES BIG RAISE IN STEEL INDUSTRY

Economic Advisers Caution on Harm to Companies and a Loss of Employment

UNION CHIEF IS DEFIANT

Abel, Replying to 'Inflation Alert,' Declares Demands Will Not Be Reduced

By EDWIN L. DALE Jr.
Special to The New York Times

WASHINGTON, April 13 — The Nixon Administration warned steel management and labor today that a big wage increase, such as the one the union recently won from the can industry, would only increase the steel industry's troubles and would probably mean higher unemployment.

The warning, in the third "inflation alert" of the President's Council of Economic Advisers, was promptly dismissed by I. W. Abel, president of the United Steelworkers of America. He said that the union would not change its demands in the contract negotiations, which are to begin shortly.

The union has never stated what it will demand, but it is widely believed that it will seek no less than workers in the can industry have won.

The inflation alert touched on recent price and wage developments in other industries besides steel, from oil to New York City taxicabs. But the remarks on steel drew the most attention because of impending wage negotiations.

Price Rises Moderating

As to the economy in general, the report found that the rise in prices has been "distinctly more moderate" in recent months but that there has been no comparable slackening in wage increases.

For example, it noted that the Consumer Price Index was rising at an annual rate of only 2.8 per cent in the first two months of this year, contrasted with 6.1 per cent in the first half of last year and 4.8 per cent in the last half.

The report said, "For the general economic expansion to translate into new job opportunities and rising output and real incomes, rates of increase in compensation per employe must move down to where they are more consistent with longer-run rates of improvement in productivity."

In discussing the steel problem, the alert put the increase won by the steelworkers in the can industry at 13 per cent the first year and an average of 9 per cent a year over the three-year life of the contract.

It called this "clearly in excess of any realistic assessment of long-term productivity growth prospects" and continued:

"If the terms of the settlement are extended to the basic metals industries, the competitive position of these industries and many of the metals-using industries will be further jeopardized. Our steel industry is faced with strong international competition and, if its competitive position is significantly eroded through large increases in wage costs, the result will be sharply reduced employment opportunities in the industry.

"Protection of the steel industry from the full consequences of a deteriorating position in international competition, on the other hand, would reduce the ability to meet foreign competition for industries which are major users of steel, with a consequent reduction in employment opportunities in those industries."

The reference was to the present "voluntary" limitation on steel imports from Europe and Japan, which expires at the end of this year. The Administration has left open the possibility of a refusal to renew the agreement as a means of keeping downward pressure on steel prices.

The report noted that, with the current high demand for steel in advance of a possible strike, the industry may have "considerable discretionary pricing power." But it added, "The long-term interests of the steel industry, its customers and its workers obviously dictate the need for prudence in pricing."

Paul W. McCracken, chairman of the Council of Economic Advisers, gave no hint in a press briefing of what the Government might do. But he said, "The financial performance of the steel industry is not strong," noting that by the middle of the last decade the return on investment "had fallen substantially below manufacturing generally and that deterioration has continued."

First Advance Comment

In discussing other specific industries the report recounted the recent events in the construction industry, which culminated in a system of semi-compulsory wage controls administered by a new stabilization board. There was no indication in the report, however, of any intention to use this device in steel. Construction wages have been rising far more rapidly than wages generally, while steel wages have not.

This was the first "inflation alert" to comment on a major wage negotiation in advance of the bargaining. Mr. McCracken declined to state, however, the size of the wage settlement that would be regarded as acceptable.

As in the two revious inflation alerts, the one today was in two main parts — a general review of developments on prices and wages, and a detailed examination of events in a few industries. Past reports, for example, assessed the automobile wage increase, though after the fact, and developments in construction and other industries.

Following are highlights of the report today dealing with industries other than steel:

¶For several reasons, the big increase in price of crude oil recently negotiated in the Middle East "should have no necessary effect on most U.S petroleum prices." The exception might be the price of heavy fuel oil, on which there are no import restrictions and whose price in the United States reflects the world price

¶In rail and truck freight rates, depsite regulation by the Government, "substantial" wage increases "have been accompanied by substantial increases in freight rates," far above increases in the general wholesale price level. Although the rate increases "were probably made inevitable by underlying cost increases, the lack of competition in many sectors of the transportation system may have aggravated the problem." The council said it is now studying proposals "for stimulating competition by gradual deregulation of the transportation industries."

¶Although prices of lumber and plywood have started rising again, supply conditions are such that there should be some restraint on further increases.

April 14, 1971

3-Year Steel Agreement Averts Strike; Wage Increase Is 30%; Price Rise Seen

By PHILIP SHABECOFF
Special to The New York Times

WASHINGTON, Aug. 1—The United Steelworkers of America overwhelmingly approved tonight a new three-year contract described as "the best ever" by union officials.

The agreement, reached earlier in the evening by union and industry negotiators, was accepted by the 600 local steel union presidents who form the steel industry conference. A strike of 350,000 workers, scheduled for midnight tonight, was called off.

The total wage package is estimated at somewhat more than 30 per cent over the three-year contract period, although the precise amount varies considerably from worker to worker.

Steel industry officials said that the size of the wage package meant that an increase in

448

steel prices was virtually certain.

Meanwhile, Government officials said tonight that a settlement was in sight in the long and bitter dispute between the nation's railroads and the United Transportation Union, the train crewmen's union that is now on strike against 10 rail lines.

Pact May Come Today

The officials said a settlement could come as early as tomorrow morning.

Earlier, Charles Luna, president of the striking United Transportation Union, said on the Columbia Broadcasting System's television program, "Face the Nation," that while he felt at midnight last night that a contract settlement was near, this morning "the carriers were very adamant, and now I doubt a contract will be made, and if a contract isn't made, more railroads will be struck."

John P. Fishwick, president of the Norfolk & Western Railway, said on the same program that he was optimistic that a settlement would be reached.

Steel mills across the country, which had been shut down in anticipation of a strike, will begin reopening tomorrow. It will take several days before they are back in full operation.

The contract, which is not subject to member ratification, provides a basic wage increase of 50 cents an hour in the first year and 12.5 cents an hour in each of the next two years.

With pay "increments" based on skill levels, Sunday pay and other extras, wage increases for skilled workers will reach more than $1 an hour over the life of the contract.

The contract provides a cost-of-living increase based on the Consumer Price Index. The steelworkers will be given a 1-cent increase for each rise of four-tenths of one per cent in the index.

There is also a guaranteed 12.5-cents-an-hour increase in the cost-of-living allowance in

Associated Press

Accord reached by R. Heath Larry of U.S. Steel, left, and I. W. Abel, union chief, will reopen the steel mills.

the last two years of the contract.

The pension for steelworkers, now $6.50 a month for each year of service, goes to $8 for each of the first 15 years of service, $9 for the next 15 years and $10 for all additional years.

Average Wage $3.50

The average standard wage in the basic steel industry under the old contract was $3.50 an hour.

The negotiators, headed by I. W. Abel, president of the union, and R. Heath Larry, vice chairman of the United States Steel Corporation, met in bargaining sessions late last night and into this afternoon.

A strike had been set for midnight Saturday but had been postponed 24 hours because both sides believed that differences could be resolved in a few hours more bargaining.

At a news conference with Mr. Abel at the Shoreham Hotel here after the union vote, Mr. Larry said that the contract was similar in pattern to the settlements reached in the can, aluminum and copper industries earlier this year.

Mr. Larry described the settlement as "certainly inflationary" and said it would cost the steel industry 15 per cent more in wage costs in the first year of the contract alone.

He asserted that the industry had reluctantly agreed to the large settlement "because it is

so important to the national economy that we not have a long and bitter strike at this time."

Concern Expressed

Mr. Larry and Mr. Abel expressed concern about the impact of foreign competition on the domestic steel industry. They announced that union and management would join together at the plant level to devise ways to improve productivity in their industry.

Productivity, or output per worker, has been static in the industry in recent years.

In a statement issued after the union vote, Secretary of Labor James D. Hodgson said, "to an Administration intensely concerned about industrial productivity, we are pleased that the new contract contains a special provision to encourage productivity. The new steel labor contract reflects this emphasis."

The nine steel companies that took part in the bargaining here are the United States Steel Corporation, the Bethlehem Steel Corporation, the Republic Steel Corporation, the National Steel Corporation, the Inland Steel Corporation, the Jones & Laughlin Steel Corporation, the Youngstown Sheet and Tube Company, the Armco Steel Corporation and Allegheny Ludlum Industries, Inc.

The rail negotiators again talked far into the night, but Government officials who have followed the contract impasse that has lasted some 20 months said that there seemed to be signs of real progress.

The United Transportation Union, which represents train operating crewmen other than engineers, is on strike against 10 railroads, including five major lines, and has threatened to shut down eight more carriers within the next 11 days.

The railroads shut down so far account for nearly half of all railroad track mileage in the United States and originate more than half of all the freight carried in this country.

The two sides have long since agreed on a wage settlement that will give the workers a 42 per cent increase over 42 months.

However, a full agreement is blocked by the dispute over new work rules that the railroads say they need for economic viability and that the union rejects because it says the rules will endanger the job security of its members or force them to relocate.

NIXON ORDERS 90-DAY WAGE-PRICE FREEZE

SPEAKS TO NATION

Urges Business Aid to Bolster Economy— Budget Slashed

By JAMES M. NAUGHTON

Special to The New York Times

WASHINGTON, Aug. 15 — President Nixon charted a new economic course tonight by ordering a 90-day freeze on wages and prices, requesting Federal tax cuts and making a broad range of domestic and international moves designed to strengthen the dollar.

In a 20-minute address, telecast and broadcast nationally, the President appealed to Americans to join him in creating new jobs, curtailing inflation and restoring confidence in the economy through "the most comprehensive new economic policy to be undertaken in this nation in four decades."

Some of the measures Mr. Nixon can impose temporarily himself and he asked for tolerance as he does. Others require Congressional approval and — although he proposed some policies that his critics on Capitol Hill have been' urging upon him—will doubtless face long scrutiny before they take effect.

2 Tax Reductions

Mr. Nixon imposed a ceiling on all prices, rents, wages and salaries — and asked corporations to do the same voluntarily on stockholder dividends — under authority granted to him last year by Congress but ignored by the White House until tonight.

The President asked Congress to speed up by one year the additional $50 personal income tax exemption scheduled to go into effect on Jan. 1, 1973, and to repeal, retroactive to today, the 7 per cent excise tax on automobile purchases.

He also asked for legislative authority to grant corporations a 10 per cent tax credit for investing in new American-made machinery and equipment and pledged to introduce in Congress next January other tax proposals that would stimulate the economy.

Combined with new cuts in Federal spending, the measures announced by Mr. Nixon tonight represented a major shift in his Administration's policy on the economy.

Cuts Ruled Out Earlier

Only seven weeks ago, after an intensive Cabinet-level study of economic policy, the President announced that he would not seek any tax cuts this year and would hew to his existing economic "game plan," confident of success.

Eleven days ago, Mr. Nixon reasserted his opposition to a wage and price review board—a less stringent method of holding down prices and wages than the freeze he ordered—and said only that he was more receptive to considering some new approach to curtailing inflation.

The program issued tonight at the White House thus came with an unaccustomed suddenness, reflecting both domestic political pressures on the President to improve the economy before the 1972 elections and growing international concern over the stability of the dollar.

The changes represented an internal policy victory for Paul W. McCracken, chairman of the Council of Economic Advisers, and Arthur F. Burns, chairman of the Federal Reserve Board, both of whom had pushed over a number of months for a wage-price curtailment. It marked the first major defeat for George P. Schultz, Mr. Nixon's director of management and budget, who has vigorously opposed such an incomes policy.

The President adopted the new tactics following a weekend of meetings at the Presidential retreat at Camp David, Md. With him there were Dr.

Burns, Mr. McCracken, Mr. Shultz and John B. Connally, the Secretary of the Treasury.

'Action on 3 Fronts'

"Prosperity without war requires action on three fronts," Mr. Nixon declared in explaining his new policies. "We must create more and better jobs; we must stop the rise in the cost of living; we must protect the dollar from the attacks of international money speculators.

"We are going to take that action—not timidly, not half-heartedly and not in piecemeal fashion," he said.

As a corollary to his tax cut proposals, the President announced that he would slash $4.7-billion from the current Federal budget to produce stability as well as stimulation. The budget cutback would come from a 5 per cent reduction in the number of Federal employees, a 10 per cent cut in the level of foreign aid and through postponement of the effective dates of two costly domestic programs — Federal revenue sharing with states and localities and reform of the Federal welfare system.

Mr. Nixon's sudden adoption of a wage and price freeze represented his most drastic reversal of form. He established an eight-member Cost of Living Council to monitor a program under which management and labor must keep wages and prices at the same levels that existed in the 30 days prior to tonight. Wage or price increases that had been scheduled to go into effect during the next 90 days, such as a 5 per cent raise for the nation's rail workers due to take effect on Oct. 1, must be postponed at least until the 90 days expire. But wage improvements that took effect before tonight, including the 50-cent-an-hour increase won by the steelworkers on Aug. 2, will not be affected.

The White House did not include interest rates in the freeze on the theory that they cannot properly be kept under a fixed ceiling. Although describing the freeze as "voluntary," officials noted there was a provision for court injunctions and fines as high as $5,000 for failure to adhere to the ceiling.

The freeze could be extended after 90 days if Mr. Nixon should decide it still is needed.

This authority to impose a ceiling will expire on April 30.

Political pressures for some form of an incomes policy have been building for weeks. Public opinion polls have certified concern over unemployment and prices as the No. 1 domestic issue. Democratic Presidential hopefuls have singled out the economy as the primary area for criticizing Mr. Nixon.

At a White House briefing just before the President's address, Secretary Connally said that the changes had been "long in the making." But he conceded in response to questions that he had left last week on vacation without any expectation that Mr. Nixon would put the program into effect tonight.

Why Strategy Changed

In explaining why the White House had shifted its economic strategy since he expressed confidence on June 30 that "we're on the right path," Mr. Connally cited tonight an "unacceptable" level of unemployment—currently running at an annual rate of 5.8 per cent—as well as continued inflation, a deteriorating balance of trade and an "unsatisfactory" balance of payments in dealings abroad.

Congress, which is in recess until after the Labor Day weekend, must approve the President's request for new consumer tax breaks and investment credits.

The individual income tax exemption, currently $650 for each member of a family, is scheduled to rise to $700 next Jan. 1, and to $750 a year later. Mr. Nixon asked that it go to $750 in one step next January.

"Every action I have taken tonight is designed to nurture and stimulate [the] competitive spirit, to help snap us out of the self-doubt, the self-disparagement that saps our energy and erodes our confidence in ourselves," the President said.

In calling for repeal of the tax on automobiles, the President said it would represent an average drop of about $200 in the price of a new car. "I shall insist that the American auto industry pass this tax reduction on to the nearly eight million customers who are buying automobiles this year," he emphasized, but did not say how he would keep that pledge.

The tax would continue to be collected until Congress acts to repeal it, with the provision for

450

rebates later to customers who do not wait to purchase a car.

Mr. Nixon's political advisers have been hoping to cast him as the President of peace and prosperity in a bid for re-election next year.

With every speech in recent weeks emphasizing his initiatives toward global peace — his forthcoming journey to Peking, disengagement from Vietnam and negotiations on arms, the Middle East and Berlin with the Soviet Union — Mr. Nixon has faced a pro-liferation in Democratic statements criticizing him for permitting continued unemployment and inflation.

Possible 1972 Theme

Mr. Nixon's address tonight contained the kernels of what could become, if his policies have the desired impact, the prosperity rhetoric of 1972.

"Today we hear the echoes of those voices preaching a gospel of gloom and defeat," he said.

"As we move into a generation of peace, as we blaze the trail toward the new prosperity," he added, "I say to every American—let us raise our spirits, let us raise our sights, let all of us contribute all we can to this great and good country that has contributed so much to the progress of mankind."

The Cost of Living Council, which will recommend to Mr. Nixon some form of "second-stage" of wage and price stabilization to follow the 90-day freeze, will be chaired by Mr. Connally and will also have Mr. McCracken and Mr. Shultz on it.

The other members are:

Clifford M. Hardin, Secretary of Agriculture.
Maurice H. Stans, Secretary of Commerce.
James D. Hodgson, Secretary of Labor.
George A. Lincoln, director of the Office of Emergency Preparedness.
Virginia H. Knauer, assistant to the President for consumer affairs.

Dr. Burns will serve as an adviser to the council.

August 16, 1971

UNIONS REJECT NO-STRIKE APPEAL

U.A.W. CHIEF IRATE

Labor Leader Warns Against Extension Beyond 90 Days

By DAMON STETSON

Striking unions in many sections of the nation defied yesterday the Nixon Administration's call for a return to work during the 90-day wage and price freeze imposed last Sunday.

Other unions, not on strike, warned against any extension of the freeze beyond Nov. 12, the end of the 90-day period. Labor leaders were almost uniformly critical of the Administration's sudden moves aimed at ending the inflationary spiral.

One of the strongest outcries came from Leonard Woodcock, president of the United Automobile Workers. He warned that his independent union would terminate its contracts with the auto companies if the wage-price freeze was extended and workers were not granted wage increases due them under the agreement.

United Press International
Leonard Woodcock, auto workers' leader, warns against extension of wage freeze.

Bridges Is Adamant

Another sharp attack came from Harry Bridges, president of the longshoremen's union on the West Coast. He announced that the 48-day dock strike there would continue "in full force."

"If this Administration thinks that just by issuing an edict, by the stroke of a pen, they can tear up contracts, they are saying to us they want war. If they want war, they can have war," Mr. Woodcock declared.

George Meany, president of the American Federation of Labor and Congress of Industrial Organizations, was reported seething with anger because of Secretary of Labor James D. Hodgson's comment Tuesday that "Mr. Meany appears to be sadly out of step with the needs and desires of America's working men and women."

Mr. Meany and his 35-member Executive Council are scheduled to meet with White House representatives in Washington today in what is expected to be an angry confrontation.

Phone Strike Continues

Among the fast-breaking developments in labor's fast-growing rebellion were the following:

¶Striking members of the Communications Workers of America, representing 38,500 plant employees of the New York Telephone Company, continued their strike here but agreed to meet with a Federal mediator and start a new round of bargaining with the company.

¶Striking Western Union employees, also represented by the Communications Workers of America, continued their strike in New York.

¶In California, an official of

the teamsters' union said that his union would not remove picket lines at this time and end a strike that has idled 50,000 workers and tied up most of Northern California construction.

The back-to-work plea had been issued by J. Curtis Counts, director of the Federal Mediation and Conciliation Service. Mr. Counts said Tuesday that the Administration was asking for a halt to all current strikes and a moratorium on new ones during the freeze, and he hinted that legal action might be used to bar walkouts.

Late yesterday, however, the Secretary of Labor, Mr. Hodgson, issued a statement in Washington saying "we intend to continue our policy of urging strikers to go back to work and negotiate, but we have no intention at the present time of using sanctions."

Administration officials said the Government had only limited authority to end strikes. If a strike causes a national emergency, the Government could invoke the Taft-Hartley Law with its 80-day cooling off period. Also, they said, the

Government could order a union to halt a strike if it was aimed at forcing an employer to violate the wage-price freeze.

Almost without exception, according to available reports, striking unions refused to go back to work, but leaders of some said that they were consulting their attorneys and seeking further information before making a final decision.

One plumbers union local in New Mexico reportedly went back to work without settling its strike, but the action was reported to have taken place before Mr. Counts issued the Government's appeal that all strikes be stopped.

Officials of unions still on strike acknowledged that any wage increase agreed upon could not be paid until the end of the 90-day freeze. They expressed concern that, even then, there was the prospect of an extension of the freeze or the imposition of some wage limitation by the President's Cost of Living Council.

And no one knows, they said, whether a negotiated wage increase could be made retroactive.

U.A.W. Raise Due Nov. 22

Mr. Woodcock, head of the 1.3-million-member auto union, said he did not know of any law that permitted the Government to say that a corporation "shall not pay money to its workers but instead put it in its own coffers."

About 750,000 auto workers are due to receive a pay increase of 3 per cent on Nov. 22, 10 days after the freeze ends. Mr. Woodcock said the U.A.W. would not necessarily strike if the freeze was extended and these workers were denied their increase, but he added that the union would then consider itself "free to take any action we want."

Some unions asked the White House for special exemptions from the wage-price freeze. One such union was the State, County and Municipal Employes, headed by Jerry Wurf.

"There is great doubt," Mr. Wurf said, "whether the Federal executive has the legal authority to impose freeze conditions on local and state government bodies."

But later in the day the Cost of Living Council decided that

state and local employes were subject to the freeze.

Edward J. Carlough, president of the Sheet Metal Workers, sent a telegram to President Nixon noting that construction workers were already subject to a previous wage stabilization program.

"Construction workers already wear one straitjacket," he said. "Must they wear another one?"

Under the stabilization plan for construction workers, wage increases have been permitted but an attempt has been made to limit the amount.

In San Francisco, where the American Federation of Teachers is holding its convention, David Selden, president, said that locals of the union were urged to continue negotiations on wages and working conditions. It is "inconceivable," he said, that negotiations be halted in big cities where some negotiations are "coming to a climax."

The 22-member executive council of the teachers federation criticized the wage freeze as "blatantly discriminatory" because it exempted profits, dividends and interest rates.

August 19, 1971

NIXON SETS UP ECONOMIC CONTROL SYSTEM TO CURB PRICES, PAY

NO TIME LIMIT SET

A Year's Extension of Stabilization Power To April '73 Asked

By ROBERT B. SEMPLE Jr.
Special to The New York Times

WASHINGTON, Oct. 7—President Nixon announced to night that the present wage-

price freeze would be followed by an indefinite period of close Government supervision of the economy to limit prices, wages and rent without direct controls on profits.

Addressing a nationwide television audience on Phase Two of his economic program, Mr. Nixon described new machinery — effective when the wage-price freeze expires Nov. 13—that would allow for some increases in wages and prices.

His broad objective would be to reduce the annual rise in consumer prices to 2 to 3 per cent by the end of 1972—or

about half the rate that prevailed before the freeze.

New Panels Urged

The new machinery would include boards to limit increases in wages, prices and rents.

Wage earners whose pay increases were blocked or businessmen whose price increases were negated by the 90-day freeze on wages and prices will not be able to regain the lost income, the White House said earlier today.

The President's authority to control wages and prices derives from the Economic Sta-

bilization Act of 1970. The act expires next April 30, but Mr. Nixon said that to insure victory in his fight against inflation he would ask Congress for a one-year extension.

"I am announcing tonight," the President said on TV, "that when the 90-day freeze is over on Nov. 13, we shall continue our program of wage and price restraint. We began this battle against inflation for the purpose of winning it. We are going to stay in it until we do win it."

No Specific Guidelines

The President's plan does not include any specific guidelines covering the amount by which wages will be permitted to rise.

Given the target of holding price increases to 2 or 3 per cent, it was possible, however, to calculate the average wage increase that might be permitted.

Wage increases averaging 5 or 6 per cent might be granted without creating any economic need for businesses to raise prices more than 2 or 3 per cent, Government economists acknowledged.

The difference between the percentage wage increases and the percentage price increases would be made by rising productivity, which has recently averaged 3 per cent a year. The profits of business would remain essentially unchanged and in some cases could rise.

Permitting wages to increase an average of 5 or 6 per cent would mean, of course, that some wages, for sake of equity, might be allowed to rise more than that and some to rise less.

Mr. Nixon stressed throughout his speech that the success of the wage-price freeze had been due to widespread voluntary cooperation by the American people and that the success of Phase Two would also rest on voluntary compliance.

But to create what his aides called the "framework for voluntary cooperation," the President announced his intention to establish expanded control machinery backed by legal sanctions to set wage and price standards, to review wage and price increases in the light of those standards and to punish offenders.

Various interest groups in the economy — including business and labor — will participate intimately in this machinery, Mr. Nixon declared. But ultimate authority for establishing long-range goals, coordinating wage and price standards and imposing penalties to insure compliance will rest with the Cost of Living Council.

The council, an all-Government body already in being, will continue to operate under the chairmanship of the Secretary of the Treasury, John B. Connally.

Mr. Nixon spoke at length tonight about the machinery that will develop wage-price standards and apply them to various segments of the economy, but he said nothing about the standards themselves except to announce his general objective.

According to his advisers, who met with newsmen and representatives of various interest groups throughout the day, the task of establishing durable and equitable guidelines for wages and prices that command widespread public support will be left to the Cost of Living Council and the men whom Mr. Nixon names to run the rest of the control apparatus. The three basic elements of the apparatus are these:

¶A semi-autonomous tripartite pay stabilization board made up of five representatives from labor, five from business and five from the public, and chaired by one of the public members on a full-time basis. This board will establish wage guidelines, examine labor settlements to see whether they comply with those guidelines, and review specific requests for adjustments.

¶A price commission made up of seven public members — "not beholden to any special interest group," in the President's words—to formulate and issue standards governing price and rent adjustments, and hear appeals for exemptions and exceptions.

The Cost of Living Council, which will exercise coordinating powers and review guidelines and procedures established by the other two groups. But it will not act as a final appeal board—a court of last resort—nor will it involve itself in the day-to-day administration of the post-freeze program.

The task of keeping an eye on corporate profits—a controversial subject throughout these last few weeks of planning for Phase Two—will be left to the price commission. The commission will attempt to identify what Mr. Nixon called "windfall" profits and force the offending company to pass along a share of its cost savings in the form of reduced prices for consumers.

"Windfall" profits can be defined as those that result directly from the constraints on wages imposed during Phase Two, not from other factors such as greater efficiency.

But as a general rule, Mr. Nixon made clear, he will not seek to restrain profits and he explicitly ruled out an excess profits tax.

"Let us recognize an unassailable fact of economic life," he said. "All Americans will benefit from more profits. More profits fuel the expansion that generates more jobs; it means more investment that will make our goods more competitive; it also means there will be more tax revenues to pay for programs that help people in need."

Similarly, a committee on interest and dividends, operating under the Cost of Living Council, would monitor increases in both areas in an effort to seek voluntary restraint.

Although Mr. Nixon did not explain many of the details of the program in his 15-minute talk, his aides made clear that while the entire economy would be covered in Phase Two, certain areas of the economy would be given special attention.

Certain economic units of critical importance to the economy, for example, will be required to notify either the pay board or the price commission in advance of proposed wage and price increases. Such increase may then be approved or disapproved or otherwise adjusted.

Other economic units, less strategic yet still important, will not be required to furnish advance notice but must promptly disclose their wage and price decisions afterwards. If these are found to be out of line with the guidelines, the companies involved may be forced to adjust them.

Spot Checking Planned

The behavior of prices and wages in the rest of the economy—thousands of small businesses and the like—will be monitored by spot-checking and by investigation of specific complaints.

Mr. Nixon assured his audience that Phase Two would not usher in a vast and cumbersome bureaucracy.

"Stabilization must be made to work not by an army of bureaucrats," he said, "but by an army of patriotic citizens in every walk of life."

He said the professional staffs attached to the various boards and commissions here would be small, and aides explained that the existing resources of the Internal Revenue Service would be used to help with the task of monitoring wages and prices in other parts of the country.

In addition to describing in general terms the machinery he intends to establish, Mr. Nixon's speech set forth three general themes.

One was his emphasis on the need for voluntary cooperation, another was his assertion that a major purpose of the program was not only to restrain specific prices and wages but also to create a whole new climate in the nation.

"We have lived too long in this country with an inflationary psychology," he declared. "Everybody just assumes the only direction for prices to go is up. The time has come for some price reduction psychology."

A third theme was his pledge not to continue the controls longer than necessary. He implied that to announce a deadline for Phase Two tonight would be a tactical mistake, and he warned that he would "continue price and wage restraints until inflationary pressures are brought under control." But he also added:

"We will not make controls a permanent feature of American life. When they are no longer needed we will get rid of them."

The speech was shorter than some persons here had expected. Mr. Nixon clearly wanted to keep his points simple and use the address as a vehicle for inspiration rather than explanation. He obviously conceived his task tonight to be one of summoning the nation to a common task: fighting inflation.

"What is best for all of us," he said, "is best for each of us."

As for details, he said he would leave these to Mr. Connally, who will make a television appearance of his own tomorrow at noon.

LABOR SUPPORTS PHASE 2 AFTER RECEIVING PLEDGE FROM PRESIDENT ON VETO

Associated Press

From left, at labor meeting in Washington, were George Meany, head of A.F.L.-C.I.O.; Frank Fitzsimmons, head of teamsters, and Leonard Woodcock, auto workers' head.

PAY UNIT DEFINED

Unionists to Serve on Panel but Discord on Policies Persists

By PHILIP SHABECOFF
Special to The New York Times

WASHINGTON, Oct. 12—Organized labor pledged its support today for President Nixon's program to fight inflation after the current 90-day wage-price freeze expires.

The pledge was made after the President sent top leaders personal assurances that decisions of the tripartite Pay Board, set up to control wages following the freeze, would not be subject to veto by the Cost of Living Council, the governmental agency supervising the current freeze. Mr. Nixon's note bore his handwritten initials and the letters "O.K."

Despite the pledge, labor leaders indicated that they still disagreed with some aspects of the President's program, raising the possibility of new difficulties between the Administration and organized labor.

Labor, management and the public each will have five representatives on the board.

George Meany, president of the American Federation of Labor and Congress of Industrial Organizations, said at a news conference that the federation would serve on the Pay Board and would try to help make the President's program work.

Leonard Woodcock, president of the United Automobile Workers, and Frank Fitzsimmons, president of the International Brotherhood of Teamsters, who had attended a meeting of the A.F.L.-C.I.O. Executive Council, also pledged their support at today's news conference. Neither the U.A.W. nor the teamsters is a member of the labor federation.

In a statement made shortly afterward at the White House, President Nixon welcomed the action of the labor leaders, saying, "They have acted in the best interest of their own members and of the country."

However, a possible new source of conflict between the Administration and organized labor arose today when Mr. Meany said at the news conference that the goal set by the Administration of reducing inflation to 2 to 3 per cent by the end of 1972 would be "a little too ambitious."

Mr. Meany said that a goal of 4 per cent would be reasonable and would make the stabilization program a success if achieved. A higher rate of allowable inflation would pre-sumably allow for a higher level of average wage raises.

Under 4 Per Cent Sought

Asked about Mr. Meany's comment at a White House briefing, George P. Shultz, director of the Office of Management and Budget, said that inflation was running at a rate of about 4 per cent right now and that the Administration was trying to reduce that rate.

Wage rates approved by the Pay Board would be a major influence on the inflation rate.

Mr. Meany tackled the thorny question of retroactive wage increases in the post-freeze period today, saying that after the freeze expires Nov. 13 contracts will be unfrozen and that he was sure that some deferred wage payments would be approved.

In a statement issued on behalf of the A.F.L.-C.I.O. Executive Council, Mr. Meany also said that "watchdog units" would be set up to monitor prices. He later added that he had "not much confidence" in the Internal Revenue Service to monitor price controls, as called for in the President's program.

The statement also declared that labor would continue to oppose the President's tax measures in Congress and would "continue our fight for full employment, which is the key answer to America's problems."

Mr. Meany indicated that the key to labor agreeing to support the President's program was the affirmation in the President's written statement today that the Cost of Living Council "will not approve, revise, veto, or revoke specific standards or criteria developed by the Pay Board and Price Commission."

He said that statements attributed to Administration officials last Thursday in explaining Phase Two of the President's economic plan had suggested to labor leaders that the Cost of Living Council would have veto powers over standards set up by the Pay Board to control wages.

Early Labor Stand

Labor leaders said from the beginning of the freeze period on Aug. 15 that they would cooperate in wage controls only if those controls were administered by a board of labor, management and public sector representatives operating free of Government interference.

The labor leaders have been withholding their support of the President's program while awaiting assurances that the Pay Board would in fact be autonomous.

Mr. Meany said that the President himself could have veto power over the program but only by eliminating the Pay Board and appointing a new one.

President Nixon said that the question would "inevitably arise" about who won the confrontation between the Administration and organized labor. "The answer is the country won," the President declared.

Mr. Nixon noted that wage and price controls tried in other countries without the support of labor "inevitably break down."

In his statement issued after the statement made by Mr. Meany, the President said:

"I welcome the participation of organized labor in the work of the Pay Board and in helping make the nation's efforts at price and wage stabilization succeed. Bringing the cost of living under control requires the public-spirited cooperation of all Americans, and in giving such cooperation, the leaders of organized labor have acted in the best interest of their own members and of the nation.

"I also reaffirm my concern that the economy expand and attain full employment. Prompt action in the Senate on my tax proposals, which will create over one-half million jobs, is essential to attainment of this objective."

Mr. Meany said that because of "personal reasons" he might not serve on the Pay Board. However, Mr. Woodcock and Mr. Fitzsimmons said that they were willing to act as labor members on the tripartite board.

The auto workers and the teamsters both have broken with the A.F.L.-C.I.O. Today's meeting to discuss whether to cooperate with the President's program marked the first time top leaders of the three organizations had met together since 1957.

Other labor leaders who reportedly will be named to the Pay Board are I. W. Abel, president of the United Steelworkers, and Floyd Smith, president of the International Association of Machinists.

The President's statement to the labor leaders explained that the Cost of Living Council, a Cabinet-level group, would serve as a "policy review group for the post-freeze program." It would assure that actions of the Pay Board and the Price Commission were "of such a pattern and impact as to achieve stated goals and objectives."

The council would also monitor, evaluate and coordinate the policy and conduct of the post-freeze agencies, provide them with budget, staff and quarters, recommend enforcement proceedings to the Department of Justice, and initially determine to what extent various elements of the economy were covered by controls —with the advice of the agencies.

Meanwhile it was learned that Neil H. Jacoby, professor of business economics and policy at the Graduate School of Management, University of California, Los Angeles, has been offered a position as a public member of the Pay Board.

Served Under Eisenhower

Dr. Jacoby, who declined to confirm the report, was a member of the Council of Economic Advisers under President Eisenhower and was formerly dean of the U.C.L.A. Graduate School of Business Administration.

Mr. Meany said today that no no-strike pledge had been made to the President and none had been requested. He said, moreover, that the pledge of support was not binding on member unions of the labor federation.

Asked whether the retroactive pay would be allowed for workers after the 90-day freeze, Mr. Meany said that the Pay Board would have to decide on a policy "My own position is that that money is coming to the workers and they should get it," he said.

The executive vice president of the United States Chamber of Commerce, Arch N. Booth, issued a statement this evening accusing Mr. Meany and other labor leaders of "sabotaging the fight against inflation and blackmailing the Government and public."

The strongly worded statement said that despite getting the independent tripartite wage board they demanded, Mr. Meany "and his cohorts among the union leaders" had issued another threat by "insisting on retroactive pay increases after the wage-freeze ends on Nov. 13 even if a majority of the board decided it would be inflationary."

October 13, 1971

PAY BOARD, WITH LABOR OPPOSED, VOTES 5.5% TOP ON WAGE INCREASES; BARS MOST RAISES LOST IN FREEZE

GUIDELINES ISSUED

Current Pacts Allowed Except When They Are Challenged

By WALTER RUGABER
Special to The New York Times

WASHINGTON, Nov. 8—The Pay Board overrode unanimous labor objections and voted 10 to 5 tonight to set a 5.5 per cent standard for wage increases during the Nixon Administration's economic stabilization program.

The board's guidelines for Phase Two of the anti-inflation effort ruled out retroactive payment of most of the raises that workers had lost during the Phase One freeze, which expires Saturday.

Wage increases scheduled under existing contracts to go into effect after the freeze will be allowed, the agency said, unless they are challenged by a "party at interest" or by at least five Pay Board members.

When such a challenge occurs, the deferred raises will be reviewed "to determine whether any increase is unreasonably inconsistent with the criteria established by this board," the board said in a policy statement.

Details to Be Worked Out

These were the general outlines of the controls that were approved tonight by all 10 of the public and business members of the tripartite Pay Board over the strong objections of all five labor members. American wage earners will have to live with the guidelines for an indefinite period beginning Sunday. The board said that it would meet Thursday to write more detailed regulations.

The provisions dealing with money lost in the freeze and scheduled raises were especially repugnant to organized labor, which had insisted from the start that all existing contracts be allowed.

George Meany, president of the American Federation of Labor and Congress of Industrial Organizations, said as he left the Pay Board meeting, "They have abrogated our contracts."

There has been concern in many quarters that the five labor members might walk out over the issue, but a spokesman for the labor federation said that a representative would be on hand for the session Thursday.

The A.F.L.-C.I.O. will decide whether to keep its representative on the board when Mr. Meany reports to the federation's executive council and to convention delegates in Miami next week, a spokesman said.

455

Labor sources made clear tonight their feeling that, despite some qualifications in the Pay Board's policy statement, frozen raises were barred.

George H. Boldt, chairman of the Pay Board, said during a news conference called to announce the Phase Two policy that he was confident that the organized labor members would not walk out as a result of the vote.

Mr. Meany, who had planned to leave tonight for Florida, where various labor conventions are scheduled, temporarily postponed his departure but was expected to go in a day, or two. His alternate on the board, Nathaniel Goldfinger, research director of the A.F.L.-C.I.O., will represent him at Thursday's meeting, a spokesman said.

The Pay Board would grant exceptions only on a case-by-case basis, the statement said, and it was clear that mainly the burden of proving that one of the qualifications applied would be up to the unions.

Recovery of lost money might be permitted if businesses had already raised prices "in anticipation of wage increases scheduled to occur during the freeze," the board said, or when retroactive payments were an established practice or agreed upon by both sides.

This was interpreted to mean that employes who worked during the freeze with a contract that had expired and who reached a new agreement on a raise during the 90-day period could get it retroactively.

Price Links Objected To

Labor spokesmen objected to the provision involving price increases, which appeared to be the only way that any substantial amount of money in prozen pay rises could be thawed, because some situations had little to do with prices.

For example, a labor official said, the railroads had agreed just before the freeze to give their employes a raise and while they did not raise prices —or rates—they did win important savings through the elimination of work rules.

The Pay Board statement indicated that the 5.5 per cent over-all standard would be "reviewed periodically, taking into account such factors as the long-term productivity trend of 3 per cent, cost-of-living trends, and the objective of reducing inflation."

The policy is intended to carry out President Nixon's objective of cutting the inflation rate in half, or lowering it to 2 or 3 per cent annually, by the end of next year.

If improvements in the productivity of workers continue

at the long-term rate of 3 per cent, the 5.5 per cent guideline would be expected to produce an inflationary trend of about 2.5 per cent a year.

Those who asked public members of the board at a news conference tonight whether the 5.5 per cent standard would include fringe benefits such as hospitalization plans were referred to one paragraph in the policy statement. It said:

"Provisions may be considered for vacation plans, in-plant adjustment of wages and salaries, in-grade and length of service increases, payments under compensation plans, transfers, and the like."

The statement's opening sentence seemed to imply that as a general principle fringe benefits would be included in applying the standard, a procedure business and public representatives are known to have backed.

The sentence said that "millions of workers" were seeking guidance on changes in wages, salaries, "various benefits and all other forms of employe total compensation"—and presumably 5.5 per cent is it.

There was no specific mention of merit pay rises, but the board made it clear its guidelines would cover all wages and said that when no union contract exists it would cover "existing pay practices."

The labor representatives on the board had proposed that existing contracts be honored unless they were "unreasonably inconsistent with the criteria established by the board" or more than 8 per cent.

This plan was defeated in the first vote of the session, 10 to 5.

There was a second vote on a proposal by the business members, which was defeated. The plan that won approval had been drafted by the public members. It was not entirely clear how the last two offerings differed.

Labor sources said that they had been essentially the same. Other sources close to the Pay Board said that there were differences, but these were not made known in any detail.

"For the past two weeks we have been working many hours every day to achieve a result as fair to all Americans, whatever their economic situation, as the complexities of the problems involved will permit," Judge Boldt said.

"Issues are involved which allow for wider ranges of judgment and opinion, and some of them arouse strong feelings," he continued. "I would be less than candid not to admit that viewpoints have been exchanged with considerable emphasis from time to time."

Labor Unit's Statement

Special to The New York Times

BAL HARBOUR, Fla., Nov. 18—Following is the text of a statement by the Executive Council of the American Federation of Labor and Congress of Industrial Organizations, including three recommendations for action by organized labor during President Nixon's economic program. The recommendations were approved by the labor federation's convention here today.

It is our duty to report to the membership of the A.F.L.-C.I.O. and to the working people of America that the wage control mechanism established by the President of the United States is being used as a device to destroy the basic American concept of free collective bargaining.

The trade union movement joined the Pay Board on the basis of a commitment from the President that it would be tripartite and independent and that the public members would be citizens of high repute, knowledgeability and neutrality. That commitment has not been kept.

We must now report that the public members, so called, are not independent but rather are handmaidens of the Administration. They are not neutral but have long ties either to industry or to Government. In fact, one is still on the Government payroll and another was a Government official until the day before his appointment to the Pay Board.

As one of its first acts, the Pay Board—by a 10-5 vote with the industry and the so-called public members acting in concert—nullified thousands of legal contracts covering millions of workers.

We flatly reject the concept that anyone—be it Pay Board or President—had the power to abrogate any legal collective bargaining agreement or any other contract voluntarily and legally entered into by American citizens or their representatives. If we were to take any other position, then every contract —mortgage, corporate bond

issue, sales contract or any other form of agreement voluntarily entered into by American citizens—would be subject to abrogation in similar fashion, a concept we reject without equivocation.

There is little hope that economic justice can be achieved by this board, the majority of whom are guided by the dictates of the Administration or the interests of big business.

Against this background, the A.F.L.-C.I.O Executive Council recommends to the convention:

1. That our representatives remain on the Pay Board only so long as a reasonable hope exists of securing recognition of the validity of contracts and of achieving justice for working people generally—including, most particularly, those with low or substandard incomes and those without the protection of strong bargaining representatives.

Until those objectives are assured, labor cannot associate itself with the actions of the board or encourage cooperation with their administration or enforcement.

2. That the unions of the A.F.L.-C.I.O insist at every level on the validity of their contracts in all their terms and in all their particulars, and that they take every lawful action at their command to insure that their contracts are honored.

3. That the A.F.L.-C.I.O. continue the legislative effort in the Congres to protect the validity of contracts.

We will not relax for a moment our fight to increase the standard of life and livelihood for those at the bottom of the economic ladder— those whom the majority of the Pay Board seem to have forgotten.

We repeat what we have said in the past:

The American labor movement will not permit itself to become the scapegoat for Administration policies which have brought this nation to the brink of economic disaster.

Militant Dock Leader

Harry Renton Bridges

By DAMON STETSON

Until recently Harry Bridges, the lean, hawk-faced, Australian-born agitator who plunged San Francisco into an agonizing general strike in 1934, seemed to have mellowed with the years.

But Mr. Bridges and the union he heads, the International Longshoremen's and Warehousemen's Union, demonstrated a renewed militancy last summer and fall in a strike that closed down West Coast ports for 100 days. On Monday, after bargaining talks had again failed to produce a settlement, 13,000 longshoremen at 24 West Coast ports resumed their strike, bringing a quick announcement from the White House that it was considering Congressional action to get the longshoremen back on the job.

Ironically, it was Mr. Bridge's metamorphosis from radical agitator to what some labor and management officials grudgingly called labor statesman that has been at least partly responsible for the current trouble on the West Coast docks.

Man in the News

Forward-Looking Contract

In 1960, Mr. Bridges signed a forward-looking contract in which the West Coast longshoremen agreed to eliminate antiquated work rules and to permit mechanized loading of cargo in huge prepacked containers. In return, the shipping companies granted assurances against job loss, early retirement

Otto Hagel

Mellower but not weak

provisions and other monetary premiums.

Subsequently, two additional long-term agreements between the longshoremen and the Pacific Maritime Association, the employers' group, contributed to the friendly relations between the union and the employers. But this cordiality, praised by so many, rankled militant rank-and-filers who suggested that Mr. Bridges—once the symbol of all that was revolutionary in organized labor—had become a "partner of the bosses."

The militant longshoremen contended that neglected local issues should be given priority in the negotiations. And Mr. Bridges, already involved in bitter internal conflict with ideologues in his own high command, found himself—at the age of 70—in danger of serious challenge by rebellious rank-and-filers. Rather than run the risk, he put the bargaining focus on clearing away all grievances, and the strike went on until stopped by a Taft-Hartley injunction last October.

Harry Bridges, whose first name is a nickname given him by American sailors, was born July 28, 1901, in a suburb of Melbourne, and named Alfred Bryant Renton Bridges. After completing his secondary education in 1917, he became a clerk in a retail stationery store. But the novels of Jack London had imbued him with an urge to go to sea and for the next five years he shipped on sailing vessels, touching many ports of the world and surviving two shipwrecks.

In 1920, Mr. Bridges entered the United States when the barkentine Ysabel, from the South Seas, docked in California. He drifted from San Francisco to Mexico, working in the oil fields and as a rigger, but later returned to the sea.

Picket Duty

In 1921, his ship arrived in New Orleans during a maritime strike. He reported for picket duty the next day and was in charge of a picket squad when the strike ended. The next year he became a longshoreman in San Francisco, continuing his union interests and demonstrating increasing militancy.

In 1933, a group Mr. Bridges headed began an organizing campaign and within six weeks most longshoremen had joined the new San Francisco local of the International Longshoremen's Association. The union demanded coast-wide recognition, wages higher than the prevailing $10.45 a week, and a 30-hour week. Mediation failed and the longshoremen struck in May, 1934.

On July 5, 1934, the police charged a picket line in which two persons were killed and a hundred injured. Martial law was declared and a general strike ensued, stopping all industry except gas, electricity, telephone and newspapers for three days.

Mr. Bridges led the union's Pacific locals out of the American Federation of Labor into the Committee of Industrial Organizations (later the Congress of Industrial Organizations) in 1937, reorganizing them as the International Longshoremen's and Warehousemen's Union.

As president of the I. L. W. U., Mr. Bridges received strong support through the years from his membership, even when the Federal Government tried unsuccessfully to deport him as a Communist in the nineteen-forties.

Mr. Bridges, twice divorced, has been married three times. He had a son by his first marriage, a son and daughter by his second, and a daughter by his third. He lives on Golden Gate Avenue in San Francisco.

There has been continuing antagonism between Mr. Bridges's union and the old I.L.A., with Mr. Bridges criticizing what he called "corrupt" I.L.A. dock-work practices and I.L.A. leaders denouncing what they described as the "Communist line" of the I.L.W.U.

But times have changed, and Mr. Bridges is now an advocate of a merger of the two longshoremen's unions.

DOCK TALKS REACH TENTATIVE ACCORD IN TIE-UP ON COAST

Negotiators for Shipowners and Longshoremen Settle All Economic Issues

STRIKE BAN THREATENED

Senate Adopts a Resolution Similar to Nixon Proposal to Force Arbitration

By United Press International

SAN FRANCISCO, Feb. 8—Negotiators reached a tentative agreement today in the 123-day West Coast dock strike —the longest port strike in United States history.

Representatives of the International Longshoremen's and Warehousemen's Union and the Pacific Maritime Association, representing the shipowners, announced they had settled all economic issues and would arbitrate the rest.

The agreement must be ratified by the I.L.W.U.'s 15,000 members. Harry Bridges, president of the union, said that he would recommend ratification to a 110-member I.L.W.U. group called the coast longshore caucus, which will meet at 10 A.M. this Saturday at the union's headquarters here.

The caucus, which represents locals in the 24 ports closed by the strike, will determine when the longshoremen will vote on the proposed agreement.

Intervention Threat

The agreement came under the threat of Congressional intervention and the criticism of Nixon Administration officials, who called the strike an economic catastrophe for the United States.

[In Washington, the Senate voted Tuesday to adopt a resolution similar to that asked by President Nixon under which the strike would be settled by compulsory arbitration.

[In the House, the Rules Committee adopted a rule under which three bills, including that passed by the Senate, may be considered Wednesday.]

Meanwhile, in Hawaii, where the I.L.W.U. represents workers in a wide range of industries and negotiates separately from the West Coast dockers, the threat of a new dock strike loomed.

May Set Wage Pattern

The union's Hawaiian dock contract expired last June 30 and has been extended repeatedly. The West Coast settlement may set the wage pattern for Hawaii, but I. L. W. U. members also are demanding improved fringe benefits that the employers have refused.

Longshoremen on the East and Gulf Coasts also were working without a contract, although members of the International Longshoremen's Association and shipowners have tentatively agreed on a wage package.

The West Coast settlement was known to include the following details:

¶A solution to a jurisdictional dispute between the I.L.W.U. and the International Brotherhood of Teamsters over containers, an insoluble problem on the docks for nearly 10 years.

¶A $5.2-million guaranteed annual wage based on a minimum work week of 36 hours.

¶Wage and pension increases.

¶Improvements in medical, hospital and other fringe benefits, including prepaid prescription drugs.

Edmund J. Flynn, president of the employers' association, said the shipowners were satisfied with the settlement.

A Costly Strike

If the settlement is ratified, it will end a strike that the Government estimates has cost the economy nearly a billion dollars and that Western agriculture and business leaders say may have caused irreparable damage to foreign trade.

It had been going on since last July 1, interrupted by a Taft-Hartley injunction on Oct. 6. But the 80-day cooling-off period imposed by the injunction expired Christmas day, and the dockers resumed the strike on Jan. 17.

The strike exceeded by a week the longest previous dock strike in United States history, a 116-day walkout on the Gulf and Atlantic Coasts in 1968 and 1969.

The negotiators bargained until 11 P.M. yesterday and showed up today at the association's headquarters, where the meetings were held, smiling broadly.

At 10:20 A.M., they held a six-minute meeting and then broke up into committee sessions for work on specific parts of the contract.

The settlement represented what could be a historic breakthrough in labor relations on the docks and settled dozens of issues, some of them insoluble for a decade.

Among them was a jurisdictional dispute between the longshoremen's union and the teamsters union about handling container cargo at locations off but adjacent to the docks.

Members of the teamsters union, who had been doing some of the work, were given continued jurisdiction but the shipowners agreed to pay a $1 a ton "tax" to the longshoremen's union for such cargo.

The contract also provided a guaranteed annual wage to longshoremen, and laid down specific rules for the employment of highly skilled "steady men" on the docks.

Agreement was reached last month on the salary issue. The agreement gave longshoremen an increase of 72 cents an hour, to $5 an hour, in the first year of the contract and an additional 44 0cents the second year. The union insisted that the raise be retroactive to last Nov. 14, when the wage freeze imposed by President Nixon last August expired.

The new contract would run to July 1, 1973.

Pay Board Reduces Raise For Coast Dock Workers

Rejects 20.9% Increase Over Dissent of Labor Members, Then Approves 14.9% Gain—Strike May Resume

By PHILIP SHABECOFF
Special to The New York Times

WASHINGTON, March 16— In a decision that may precipitate a new dock strike, the Pay Board voted today, 8 to 5, to reduce substantially the West Coast longshore contract settlement.

The board said that a revised computation showed the agreement between the International Longshoremen's and Warehousemen's Union and the Pacific Maritime Association amounted to a 20.9 per cent increase in wages and fringe benefits in the first year of a two-year contract. The board's guidelines permit general increases of not more than 5.5 per cent, with certain exceptions of up to 7 per cent.

After rejecting the contract, the board authorized approval of a settlement providing a total increase of 14.9 per cent, including a 10 per cent rise in pay and fringe benefits and 4.9 per cent increase in fringe benefits that are excluded from controls by law.

Harry Bridges, president of the West Coast union, who recently promised to shut down the waterfront again if the board reduced the wage settlement by as much as a penny, was not immediately available for comment.

One of Mr. Bridges's aides would say only that "he looked very unhappy" after hearing of the board's action.

Judge George H. Boldt, chairman of the Pay Board, said that the action was consistent with the goal of "winding down this stubborn inflation."

However, the five labor members of the board, who voted against the majority, bitterly assailed the decision as the product of an "unholy alliance between public members and employer members of the Pay Board."

A statement by the labor members asserted that the settlement ordered by the board would mean an average loss of $1,150 to each of 15,000 West Coast longshore employes over the next 18 months.

The labor members also charged that the board's action was a political move designed to force a strike that would lead Congress to adopt a law requiring compulsory arbitration of labor disputes in all transportation industries. The Senate is scheduled to hold hearings soon on such legislation.

The 14.9 per cent settlement that the board authorized is still considerably higher than its guidelines allowing exceptions to as high as 7 per cent for "catch-up wages."

A statement by the majority of the board who voted for the reduced settlement said that the 10 per cent rise in wages and fringe benefits reflected "a special exception" allowing 3 per cent additional to reflect productivity gains made through collective bargaining.

The majority said that it approved the full 4.9 per cent in "excludable fringes" because these payments were needed to provide the income security that had helped promote efficiency along the West Coast docks.

Productivity, or hourly output per worker, rose about 150 per cent along the West Coast docks over the last 10 years as labor and management cooperated in the mechanization of stevedoring operations.

One Pay Board member privately disclosed that there had been some effort to reduce the longshore settlement even more sharply. However, the prevailing feeling was that, even though the board does not have any responsibility for resolving labor disputes, it would be better to avoid precipitating a new strike if possible.

The majority also felt that the West Coast longshoremen should be given something for permitting productivity gains on the waterfront, as a good example for industrial relations throughout the economy.

The Justice Department declined to comment today on what action could be taken if the longshoremen, who struck for a total of 134 days last summer and earlier this year, threw up picket lines once again. However, Pay Board officials said that the board could ask the Justice Department to seek an injunction under the Economic Stabilization Act, the legal authorization for the system of wage and price controls.

Pressure on Bridges

A refusal to heed such an injunction could lead to contempt citations against union leaders.

The 70-year-old Mr. Bridges, who faces strong internal challenges to his leadership as well as external jurisdictional competition from the International Brotherhood of Teamsters, is considered to be under heavy pressure to defy the Pay Board's ruling.

Mr. Bridges has been quoted as saying that the International Longshoremen's Association of the East Coast would join his union in a walkout if the Pay Board reduced the wage agreement. The East Coast longshore settlement, higher than the West Coast agreement, is to be considered soon by the board.

Earlier this week the board's staff said that the West Coast settlement provided a 25.9 per cent increase in the first of two years, but this was reduced to 20.9 per cent today in a revised computation.

Basis for Revision

The computation was revised by adding to the wage base a 31-cent-an-hour payment made under a "modernization and mechanization" program. The program no longer exists as such but the board considered that the productivity payments had been passed along in other forms, including a guaranteed pay program.

Under this computation, the board said, the scheduled increase in total wages and fringe benefits, except for the "excludable" benefits, amounted to 16 per cent, which the board then cut to 10 per cent. This sum includes straight pay, overtime and guaranteed pay.

Labor members said that the board's action reduced the longshoremen's pay package by 42.5 cents an hour.

3 LABOR LEADERS QUIT PAY BOARD; WHITE HOUSE SAYS ACTS OF A 'FEW' CAN'T 'SABOTAGE' INFLATION FIGHT

MEANY IS AROUSED

Says 'Unfair' System Controls Wages but Benefits Profits

By PHILIP SHABECOFF
Special to The New York Times

WASHINGTON, March 22—Three A.F.L.-C.I.O. labor leaders quit the Pay Board today, declaring that the board offers labor "no hope for fairness, equity or justice."

The walkout provoked a sharp and immediate response from President Nixon, who declared through a spokesman that he would not allow "a few labor leaders to sabotage" his fight against inflation.

George Meany, president of the labor federation; I. W. Abel, president of the United Steelworkers of America, and Floyd Smith, president of the International Association of Machinists, announced their immediate resignation from the board this morning following a meeting of the federation's Executive Council.

"We will not be a part of the window dressing for this system of unfair and inequitable government control of wages for the benefit of business profits," Mr. Meany told a crowded news conference at the federation's headquarters.

Two Unionists Stay

The leaders of two unions unaffiliated with the A.F.L.-C.I.O. kept their seats on the board, at least for now.

The president of the International Brotherhood of Teamsters, Frank E. Fitzsimmons, announced later in the day that he would remain on the board to "work within the system."

The fifth labor member of the tripartite board, Leonard Woodcock, president of the United Automobile Workers, declined to disclose his plans pending a meeting tomorrow of his union's executive committee.

Judge George H. Boldt, chairman of the Pay Board, said that the work of the board would "go on" as far as he was concerned.

It was not immediately clear what action would be taken in the wake of labor's walkout or what impact the walkout would have on the functioning of the economic stabilization program as a whole.

Ronald L. Ziegler, the White House press secretary, said at a briefing today that the Administration was not sure what it would do in response to the three Pay Board resignations.

"You can be sure of one thing, the stabilization program will continue and wage-price controls will continue," Mr. Ziegler said.

"The President is not going to allow a few labor leaders to sabotage the fight against inflation," Mr. Ziegler said. He added that "the President cannot and will not allow any leader of labor or any leader of management, no matter how powerful, to put himself above the best interests of the American people."

Judge Boldt said at a hastily called news conference that the board would continue to conduct its routine business unless it was told otherwise by the Cost of Living Council, the Administration's umbrella organization for Phase Two of the economic stabilization program.

Phase Two, which succeeded the wage-price freeze imposed by the President, is now in its fifth month.

Under the board's rules, a quorum of 10 is required to conduct business. Even should Mr. Woodcock decide to resign, that quorum could still be assembled.

Some high officials of the auto workers union reportedly are concerned over the political repercussions that might follow if their independent union joined the labor federation's boycott. They and other labor leaders have expressed concern that President Nixon will attribute all failures of his stabilization program to organized labor.

The Administration's performance in dealing with the nation's economic problems is expected to be a significant issue in the forthcoming Presidential campaign.

At a news conference this morning Mr. Meany announced the unanimous vote of the American Federation of Labor and Congress of Industrial Organizations Executive Council to end participation on the Pay Board.

"I am sure they [the Administration] will use us as a scapegoat for the collapse of their policy," Mr. Meany said.

In giving the reasons for the withdrawal of the labor federation, Mr. Meany charged that the Administration had not kept its promises on the kind of mechanism the Pay Board would be. The board, he declared, is neither tripartite, independent nor autonomous.

Noting that most of the public members of the board had backgrounds in government or business, Mr. Meany declared: "The Pay Board represents Government control. It represents political and business interests.

"If the wage stabilization program is to be Government controlled, let it be so openly and clearly. Let the people who are exercising the power take the full responsibility for their decisions without the facade of labor representation and the pretense of tripartism."

Mr. Meany cited a list of particular grievances leading to the federation's decision, the most recent of which was the board's reduction of the West Coast longshore agreement.

Mr. Meany also charged that price controls were being laxly controlled while wage regulations were being rigidly enforced. He took the Cost of Living Council to task for exempting from controls only workers earning 1.90 an hour or less, which he said was below the subsistence level.

At his news conference, Judge Boldt defended the actions of the five public members saying, "We unequivocably reject the assertion that the public members have been concerned with any objective or consideration other than the goals of the stabilization program and the economic welfare of all Americans."

He insisted that there had been no attempt by the Administration to influence the votes of the public members. "We think we have reached the right decisions, but we know that we have reached them independently," he said in a statement on behalf of the public members.

Judge Boldt pointed to the Pay Board's record, which he said showed that there was no "sinister plot" against workers. He said that since the board went into operation last November the labor members had voted with the majority 36 times, in the minority 13 times and abstained four times. He added that in recent weeks the entire board had reached considerable harmony on the working level.

Public Found Ignored

"We believe," Mr. Boldt's statement concluded, "that the A.F.L.-C.I.O. action ignores the achievements of the Pay Board and shows little concern for fair play for the American public. For it is the American public and the American worker who will have to bear the costs of inflation if the economic stabilization program should fail."

In a related move, the labor representatives on the Construction Industry Stabilization Committee, which controls construction wages, said today that they would remain on the committee only if that panel was independent of the Pay Board.

The Construction Committee was formed last March, well before the economic stabilization program was inaugurated, but was placed under the Pay Board during Phase II.

The New York Times/Mike Lien

George Meany, president of A.F.L.-C.I.O., announcing resignation from Pay Board.

George H. Boldt, chairman of Pay Board, says he is prepared to continue its work.

Judge Boldt reiterated this afternoon that the committee was under the "aegis" of the Pay Board.

Construction accounts for the largest of the wage settlements in collective bargaining this year.

Mr. Fitzsimmons, in stating why the teamsters would remain on the board, conceded that he had not always been happy with its decisions. He said that the public and management members "are more concerned with their public image than they are with the proper recognition of the problems of American workers."

But he added, "I have maintained from the beginning that inflation must be checked, that the teamsters will participate in any effort to achieve that economic goal as long as the rights of workers are protected."

The Nixon Administration has been wooing the teamsters and its two million members assiduously for some time. Secretary of Labor James D. Hodgson spoke at the teamsters convention last year, the first time an Administration official had done so in many years.

Late last year the Justice Department acquiesced in the parole from prison of James Hoffa, former teamster president. Mr. Hoffa has since said that Mr. Nixon is the best candidate for President in 1972.

The teamsters, meanwhile, are seeking to block legislation proposed by the Administration that would give the President the right to halt crippling transportation strikes. The teamsters also have a deferred wage rise coming due in June that is higher than the board guidelines.

Mr. Meany indicated that labor was considering other ways to protest the economic stabilization program. He was not explicit, but other federation officials said that the possibility of supporting a strike of longshoremen on the East and West Coast had not been ruled out.

Another option being considered by labor is a lobbying effort to persuade Congress to amend the economic stabilization law in a way that will require the Administration to apply controls that labor considers fair.

But in the wake of today's walkout, the next move probably is up to the Administration. The President's executive order promulgating Phase Two requires that the Pay Board be tripartite. Whether the presence of one labor leader—or even two—on the board constitutes tripartitism is problematical.

A spokesman for the Cost of Living Council said that the Pay Board would just continue to function as is for a while.

But other Administration officials conceded that the President would have to appoint new members to the board or to reconstitute the board and perhaps the whole stabilization program.

March 23, 1972

461

The Nation

Pay Board Seems to Have Won The Big Test

"The big circus is over. From here on out it's all sideshows."

That relieved reaction came from a member of the storm-tossed Pay Board last week after longshoremen in Atlantic and Gulf ports stayed on the job in the face of a board order slicing 15 cents an hour off the fat wage settlement they had won with the help of a two-month strike.

Ever since the board's birth last November at the end of President Nixon's 90-day wage-price freeze, everyone in Washington had recognized that the sink-or-swim test for Administration efforts to check wage inflation would come on the waterfront. On all coasts powerful unions with long traditions of militancy were using their economic muscle to push through agreements calling for increases far above Pay Board guidelines.

The first showdown came in Pacific ports where Harry Bridges' International Longshoremen's and Warehousemen's Union emerged from eight months of strike, injunction and more strike with a pact that would jack up pay rates by 20.9 per cent in the first year, nearly four times the Pay Board norm of 5.5 per cent.

All pretense of labor-management discord evaporated when the waterfront employers joined with the union in a strong plea for Pay Board endorsement of the figure. They argued that the increased efficiency made possible by union cooperation in handling containerized cargo made the pact noninflationary, a contention the board found hard to reconcile with the simultaneous filing by the terminal operators of applications for big increases in loading charges.

In the teeth of a Bridges warning that any cut in the package might result in strike paralysis of all United States ports, the board's public and industry members teamed up in mid-March to trim 6 per cent from the settlement, still leaving it nearly triple the anti-inflation standard. George Meany led a protest walkout from the board of four of its five labor members (Frank Fitzsimmons of the Teamsters, the President's favorite labor leader, was the only one to stay).

But the walkout that the Administration and the country had really feared—a union-enforced shutdown of all deep-sea ports—did not materialize. The ally on which the Bridges union had counted most heavily—the International Longshoremen's Association, with control over the Atlantic and Gulf coasts—cooled the strike fever by making it clear that its members would keep working until the slimmed-down Pay Board took a look at the I.L.A.'s own strike settlements.

One reason for the unwonted restraint by the I.L.A., a union that holds the undisputed championship for striking with or without reason, was that its pacts called for package increases of 12.1 to 14.4 per cent, seemingly comfortably inside the productivity cushion the Pay Board had allowed the Bridges union.

A second incentive to slowness on the strike trigger was an I.L.A. expectation that the White House might put in a good word for it with the theoretically independent wage regulators. That expectation grew out of the eagerness of top Administration officials, engaged in negotiating a mutual trade pact with Moscow, to obtain union guarantees that Soviet ships would encounter no labor hang-ups in American ports.

Until now the I.L.A. has stood well to the right of the American Legion in its abhorrence of any traffic with the Communist world, but its cooperation with the Administration in recent weeks has been so complete that Thomas W. Gleason, the I.L.A. president, is among the guests invited by Secretary of Commerce Peter G. Peterson to a banquet for the Soviet trade delegation at Blair House tomorrow night.

None of this helped the dock union when the Pay Board got around to ruling on its case last week. Despite back-door signals from the White House that the last thing the country needed was another waterfront shutdown, the board voted 6 to 1, with the truck unionist, Mr. Fitzsimmons, the sole dissenter, to shave the I.L.A. increases by roughly the same amount of money that had come out of the Bridges pact. That left the Atlantic and Gulf dock workers with pay rises ranging from 9.8 to 12 per cent.

In other years, such an action would have turned all the I.L.A. strongholds into ghost ports within 24 hours, espec-

ially with Mr. Bridges in the same Washington hotel with Mr. Gleason urging that the two unions pool their economic strength for an all-coast tie-up. But to the board's considerable surprise, the only thing that happened was a decorous joint request by the I.L.A. and the employers for a reconsideration of the decision—a request plainly designed to defuse any runaway strike by hotheads in the Port of New York or other trouble centers.

The I.L.A. leaders got an unscheduled assist from President Nixon in keeping the lid on. His television speech announcing plans to mine the port of Haiphong was made just after the Pay Board trimmed the longshore pay increase.

"Can you imagine us blockading all United States ports at the very moment the President is blockading North Vietnam?" asked one dock union chief.

By way of underscoring their determination not to backtrack on the two longshore decisions, the wage czars wound up the week with a ruling barring West Coast moves to put the difference between what the employers had agreed to give and what the board had allowed into an escrow fund to be paid to workers whenever controls were lifted.

Neither longshore union has yet run up a surrender flag, but the tradition of the waterfront makes strikes unlikely if they do not occur right away.

—A. H. RASKIN

CHAPTER 13

Into the Seventies

The hard hat—symbol of the
increasingly affluent but unhappy worker.

The New York Times.

Cordiner Backs Work Law

ATLANTA, Oct. 9 (AP)—
"Right-to-work legislation very definitely is a factor in deciding where General Electric plants are built," Ralph J. Cordiner, board chairman, said today.

Mr. Cordiner and the giant concern's eighteen other directors are touring the Southeast. They will hold their annual meeting tomorrow.

"General Electric has a very firm stand in favor of right-to-work laws because we are interested in the rights of individuals," Mr. Cordiner said.

N. L. R. B. Backs a Device To Skirt Union-Shop Ban

Reverses Previous Stand—Rules That Indiana 'Right-to-Work' Law Does Not Forbid Payments in Lieu of Dues

By JOHN D. MORRIS
Special to The New York Times.

WASHINGTON, Sept. 29 — The National Labor Relations Board, in a reversal of policy, ruled today that the agency shop is legal in Indiana, a "right-to-work" state.

By a 4-to-1 vote, the board reconsidered and reversed a 3-to-2 decision of last Feb. 20 in a case involving the General Motors Corporation and the United Automobile Workers.

Under agency-shop agreements, nonunion employes must pay the union sums equal to union fees and dues to keep their jobs.

The agency shop is designed to ease the impact on labor unions of so-called "right-to-work" state laws, which bar union-shop agreements. Under the union shop, employes are required to join the union within a specified time to hold their jobs.

The new ruling had no direct effect on agency-shop agreements in eighteen other states with right-to-work laws. But it established the principle that such state laws, in the board's opinion, do not necessarily bar agency-shop agreements.

The decision left unanswered the question whether the agency shop would be legal in a state with a right-to-work law that specifically prohibits it. Nothing in the Indiana statute specifically deals with the agency-shop device.

The majority opinion was signed by two new board members appointed by President Kennedy and two holdover appointees from the Eisenhower Administration who had taken the same position in the decision on Feb. 20. The Kennedy appointees were Frank W. McCulloch, chairman, and Gerald A. Brown. Philip Ray Rodgers and John H. Fanning joined them in the decision. Boyd Leedom, a former chairman, dissented.

Based on Taft-Hartley

The ruling was based on a section of the Taft-Hartley Act of 1947 that allows union-shop agreements. It did not touch on another section, which permits states to outlaw union-shop agreements.

The contract at issue was proposed by the U. A. W. shortly after the Indiana Appellate Court ruled in a 1959 case that the state's right-to-work law did not bar an agency-shop agreement. The board cited the 1959 case in today's opinion without taking a position on it.

The board ordered General Motors to bargain with the U. A. W. on an agency-shop arrangement to cover 14,000 non-union employes in nine Indiana plants. The plants are in Anderson, Bedford, Kokomo, Indianapolis, Marion and Muncie.

One effect of the decision was to reaffirm previous N. L. R. B. rulings upholding the agency-shop principle in states that do not have right-to-work laws. This was the first case involving a state with a right-to-work law.

The majority members emphasized their belief that "an agency-shop agreement is a permissible form of union security" within the meaning of the Taft-Hartley Act.

It cited a 1954 Supreme Court decision in which the court said that Congress, in writing the Taft-Hartley Act, "intended to prevent utilization of union security agreements for any purpose other than to compel payment of union dues and fees."

"Thus," the court added, "Congress recognized the validity of unions' concern about 'free riders,' i. e., employes who receive the benefits of union representation but are unwilling to contribute their share of financial support to such union, and gave unions the power to contract to meet that problem."

Device Called 'Travesty'

In his dissent, Mr. Leedom contended that the agency shop for all practical purposes had the same effect as the compulsory-membership requirement of the union shop. He declared:

"The device of an agency shop, where 'membership' is unlawful, is such an impairment of an employe's freedom that, in my view, it is a travesty to condone the imposition of such device when the [Taft-Hartley] by act forbids the requirement of literal membership."

The N. L. R. B. decision is subject to court appeal. Both the corporation and the union, however, agreed in advance to accept the board's ruling.

The agency shop dates back to 1939, but it did not gain widespread use until recent years as more states enacted right-to-work laws. About 6 per cent of all current wage contracts contain agency-shop clauses.

HIGH COURT BACKS RIGHT TO STRIKE OVER AUTOMATION

Decides, 5-4, Unions May Enforce Contract Ban on Prefabricated Items

BUILDERS ARE AFFECTED

Justices Agree Law Allows Carpenters to Walk Out in Fight to Save Jobs

Special to The New York Times

WASHINGTON, April 17 — The Supreme Court upheld today the legal right of labor unions to block the automation of their members' jobs by enforcing contract provisions against the use of prefabricated materials.

In two 5-to-4 decisions, the Court held that key Taft-Hartley and Landrum-Griffin amendments to the National Labor Relations Act had not been intended to deny workers the right to strike to keep their employers from subcontracting work to other companies that would do the work with machines.

"Before we say that Congress meant to strike from workers' hands the economic weapons traditionally used against their employers' efforts to abolish their jobs, that meaning should plainly appear," Justice William J. Brennan Jr. said in the majority opinion.

Allied to 'Hot Cargo'

He was joined by Chief Justice Earl Warren and Justices Abe Fortas, Byron R. White and John M. Harlan.

Justice Potter Stewart argued in a dissent that the Court "has substituted its own notions of sound labor policy for the words of Congress." His dissent was joined by Justices Hugo L. Black, William O. Douglas and Tom C. Clark.

The decisions had particular importance for the building construction industry, where the unions have traditionally bargained for contract clauses to prohibit the use of prefabricated materials.

The National Labor Relations Board has upheld the legality of these "work preservation agreements." They have acted as a brake to automation by barring the use of prefinished materials that would abolish work traditionally done by hand on the job.

However, some lower courts have held that these provisions amounted to "hot cargo" clauses that were outlawed in 1959 by the Landrum-Griffin Act. The "hot cargo" amendment to the national labor law prohibited agreements to "cease from handling the products of any other employer."

Strikes to enforce these provisions have also been held in some cases to be "secondary boycotts" prohibited by the Taft-Hartley Act of 1947.

Secondary boycotts are usually held to be a situation in which workers strike Employer A, with whom they have no dispute, to force him to cease doing business with Employer B, with whom there is a dispute.

The Court held that a strike to enforce a work preservation agreement is not a secondary boycott because the workers' dispute is not with the subcontractor, but with their own employer.

It held that the prefabricated materials are not "hot cargo," which is generally considered to be a material produced by non-union shops or businesses engaged in disputes with their workers.

The two cases decided today involved a contract between carpenter unions and a group of building contractors in the Philadelphia area and an agreement between heating contractors and asbestos workers in Houston.

Justice Brennan's opinions concentrated on the carpenters' contract, in which the employers had agreed that no carpenter would have to work on prefabricated materials.

When three contractors inherited a job calling for prefabricated doors they ordered 3,600 such doors. The carpenters refused to hang them and, after the contractors sent the doors back, the door manufacturer contended that it had been a victim of a "hot cargo" contract.

Producer's View Upheld

The United States Court of Appeals for the Seventh Circuit agreed with the door manufacturer. It said the agreement against the use of prefabricated door amounted to a contract to "cease from handling the products of any other employer," which was prohibited in the "hot cargo" law of 1959.

The Supreme Court reversed that decision and affirmed the contrary decision of the Court of Appeals for the Fifth Circuit in the Houston asbestos case. The Fifth Circuit had upheld a contract provision under which the workers had refused to use prefabricated materials in placing insulation around pipes.

Charles B. Mahin of Chicago argued for the National Woodwork Manufacturing Association, which brought the case for the door manufacturer. Dominick L. Manoli, associate general counsel for the labor board, argued for the Government.

W. D. Deakins of Houston argued for the Insulation Contractors. Norton J. Come, assistant general counsel of the labor board, argued for the Government.

December 3, 1963

ATLANTA

Labor Reported Finding Problems in South

Special to The New York Times

The South is still a tough nut for labor unions to crack.

It is so tough, rapid industrial growth and lagging wage rates notwithstanding, that the Textile Workers Union of America last month urged the American Federation of Labor and Congress of Industrial Organizations executive council to unite in a crusade against an alleged "South-wide anti-union conspiracy."

The T.W.U.A. is particularly incensed over what it calls "the unbridled arrogance and growing intensity of this conspiracy." The textile industry, rarely vanquished by labor organizers, was a leader in last year's victorious counterattack on the union movement's massed effort to win Congressional repeal of Section 14b of the Taft-Hartley Law.

As a result, the South remains almost solidly the same "right-to-work-law" stronghold that since the start of this decade has increased its army of industrial and white-collar workers more rapidly than all the unions have been able to organize them.

In the last seven years, the National Labor Relations Board has conducted 6,252 representation elections in nine Southern states — Alabama, Arkansas, Florida, Georgia, Louisiana, Mississippi, North Carolina, South Carolina and Tennessee.

The unions have won barely half of them, 3,378, or 54 per cent. But only if they had won all of them, and thereby had organized all of the 546,875 employes who voted in them, only then would the unions have increased their membership in the South by roughly the same number by which Southern manufacturing employment grew during the same period.

Ironically, the union compiled their best 1960-66 won-lost record in the region's least industrialized state. Mississippi, where they captured 156, or 62 per cent, of the 252 N.L.R.B.-conducted elections. And the ratio of union wins rose from 52 per cent in 1960 to 65 per cent in 1966. But the total number of workers who voted in these elections was small, 27,063, and the total number organized even smaller.

In only two of the nine states did the unions fail to win half of the elections conducted in the last seven years. This was in North Carolina and South Carolina, which also happen to be the largest and second largest, respectively, textile producing states in the nation.

Organized labor's seven-year win ratios in the other Southern states were 57 per cent in Louisiana, 56 per cent in Alabama and Georgia, 55 per cent in Arkansas and Tennessee, and 53 per cent in Florida.

March 12, 1967

U.S. FINDS UNIONS GAINING MEMBERS, REVERSING TREND

An Increase of 283,000 to 16,586,000 in '62 Alters a Five-Year Pattern

FEDERAL AIDES ENROLL

But Factory Roster Is Down —Only a Slight Rise Noted in White-Collar Field

By JOHN D. POMFRET
Special to The New York Times

WASHINGTON, May 24—A Labor Department study suggested today that the downward trend in union membership since 1957 might have been reversed.

The Bureau of Labor Statistics survey covers the years 1961 and 1962.

Based largely on the reports of labor organizations, the bureau's biennial tabulation is considered the most reliable basis for appraising trends in union membership. It will be published in the next issue of The Monthly Labor Review.

After rising to a peak of 17,490,000 in 1956, the United States membership of national and international unions began dropping. With the exception of the period between 1958 and 1959, when a small gain of 88,000 members was posted, membership strength slipped steadily to a low of 16,303,000 in 1961 the survey shows.

However, between 1961 and 1962, membership rose by 283,000 to 16,586,000. With this gain "the downward trend seems to have been reversed," the study said.

Loss in Manufacturing

What has worried American labor leaders perhaps as much as the decline in absolute numbers has been the drop in union membership measured as a proportion of the total labor force.

Although the gain was slight, this rose between 1961 and 1962 for the first time since 1956. The proportion dropped from 24.8 per cent in 1956 to 22 per cent in 1961. In 1962, it rose to 22.2 per cent.

One of the principal factors in the increase in membership between 1961 and 1962 was a gain in the number of union members in Government service.

The unions lost 541,000 members in manufacturing and 86,000 in private nonmanufacturing sectors between 1960 and 1962. In Government, however, membership rose by 155,000.

This significant gain was largely in the Federal service and was attributed to the stimulation of President Kennedy's Executive Order of 1962 giving recognition to the right of Federal workers to organize.

Despite the gains shown in the report, the study indicates that labor's basic predicament — its failure to organize large numbers of white-collar workers who make up an increasingly large proportion of the work force—is unchanged.

The unions had 2,463,000 white-collar members in 1956, 2,184,000 in 1958, 2,192,000 in 1960 and 2,285,000 in 1962. Although there was a gain of 93,000 in the organized white-collar contingent between 1960 and 1962, the report points out that this must be viewed against an organizable potential of about 22 million such workers in various occupational groups.

"Moreover, about two-fifths of this gain is accounted for by two unions of Federal employes surveyed for the first time," the report said. "Thus, as in previous years, the evidence —rough as it is—points to a near standstill in union organization in the white-collar field."

Newcomers to the list of 44 unions reporting a membership of 100,000 or more in 1962 were the Fire Fighters, the American Federation of Government Employes and the Postal Clerks.

The Packinghouse Workers and the Mine, Mill and Smelter Workers dropped off the list.

Slight shifts took place in the order of the six largest unions. The International Brotherhood of Teamsters stayed at the top. The United Steelworkers of America fell to third place, while the United Automobile Workers of America, previously third, rose to second. Fourth place was still held by the International Association of Machinists. The International Brotherhood of Electrical Workers displaced the United Brotherhood of Carpenters as the nation's fifth largest union.

May 25, 1964

ORGANIZED LABOR—WHY IS ITS MEMBERSHIP DECLINING?

1. Membership is declining on a percentage basis while nation's work force is growing.

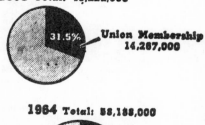

1950 Total: 45,222,000

31.5% Union Membership 14,267,000

1964 Total: 55,155,000

28.9% Union Membership 15,841,000

2. One reason is the shift from blue collar —traditionally unionized—to white collar jobs.

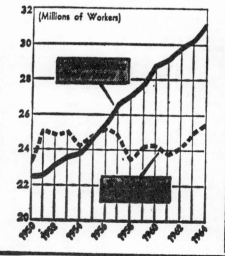

(Millions of Workers)

3. The second reason is automation, as the charts below on rise in productivity illustrate.

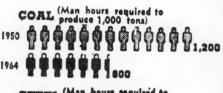

COAL (Man hours required to produce 1,000 tons)
1950 — 1,200
1964 — 800

STEEL (Man hours required to produce 1,000 tons)
1950 — 19,800
1964 — 15,700

AUTOS (Man hours required to produce an automobile)
1950 — 198.3
1964 — 160.9

December 19, 1965

A.F.L.-C.I.O. Drops Automobile Union For Dues Arrears

By JOSEPH A. LOFTUS
Special to The New York Times

WASHINGTON, May 16—The United Automobile Workers was suspended from the American Federation of Labor and Congress of Industrial Organization today because of its failure to pay dues.

The union owes per capita dues of about $90,000 a month for February, March and April. Its president, Walter P. Reuther, has long been in dispute with George Meany, the federation's president, and has demanded what he considers reforms in the A. F. L.-C. I. O.

It was the first major break in the labor front since the International Brotherhood of Teamsters was expelled from the federation in 1957.

What the future holds for the federation, established with high hopes 13 years ago, depends on the course Mr. Reuther pursues in his campaign for a more aggressive union policy.

The separation of Mr. Reuther and Mr. Meany, however, is not the dissolution of the bond that was established in 1955. Mr. Reuther brought C.I.O. unions with about 4 million members to that merger with the A.F.L.

He leaves with 1.6 million members of his own union, at most, and he had been paying per capita dues on fewer than that. He is not taking with him any of the 31 other unions that made up the Congress of Industrial Organizations at the time of the merger.

In fact, the original C.I.O. unions have demonstrated that they are not in sympathy with Mr. Reuther's course. These include the United Steelworkers of America, the International Union of Electrical Workers, the Amalgamated Clothing Workers and the Communications Workers of America.

John L. Lewis of the United Mine Workers, as founder and head of the original C.I.O., made history in organizing, in labor law creation and in collective bargaining. But after he broke with the rest of organized labor, he became a relatively lonely figure.

Federation Law Cited

Mr. Reuther set out on an organizing mission, he could possibly stimulate the bulk of the labor movement to more aggressive action.

If he succeeds, the break that was formalized today could find himself on the same lonely road that has taken Mr. Lewis into silent retirement.

Mr. Meany warned Monday that three months' delinquency was all the law of the federation allowed unless special waivers were asked.

When the mails today brought no check, he addressed a "Dear sir and brother" letter to Mr. Reuther. It cited the relevant sections of the federation constitution, including the provision that suspension means the auto union cannot be represented in any subordinate body, such as the Industrial Union Department and the federation's state and local bodies.

Mr. Meany has gone to a labor meeting in Brussels. Mr. Reuther is attending a meeting in Italy.

The federation has waived the automatic suspension pro

vision in cases where the reason for nonpayment was a shortage of funds. Mr. Reuther made no such plea.

The auto union, the federation's largest unit, had been paying per capita dues on about 1.3 million members. The federation has 14.3 million members.

A labor split could lead to certain disadvantages to labor generally in terms of legislation and favors from the White House. At this point, the division is so numerically lopsided that Mr. Meany will continue to be the recognized labor spokesman in governmental affairs.

Nevertheless, Mr. Ruether's lobbying will carry some impact, and that could mean a slowdown while friendly legislators grope for formulas that will not offend either labor group.

The auto union leadership has accused the federation of being too rigid in foreign policy, of failing to organize the unorganized and of being "the complacent custodian of the status quo." Mr. Meany's supporters have replied that Mr. Reuther was merely frustrated at his inability to succeed 73-year-old Mr. Meany as federation president.

May 17, 1968

U.A.W. and Teamsters Form Alliance

By DONALD JANSON
Special to The New York Times

CHICAGO, July 23 — The United Automobile Workers and the International Brotherhood of Teamsters announced the formation today of an alliance to organize unorganized workers and pursue social and political action projects.

The joint venture by the nation's two largest unions is neither a merger nor a federation, but offers a great potential for rivalry with the American Federation of Labor and Congress of Industrial Organizations for leadership in the labor movement. It marks the formative stage of a new labor power bloc that seeks to wield significant political influence.

"This is a most historic agreement," said Walter P. Reuther, U.A.W. president, at a news conference in the Palmer House.

Joining him in the announcement was Frank E. Fitzsimmons, acting president of the teamsters.

The new organization is called the Alliance for Labor Action. It starts with a membership of 1.9 million teamsters and 1.5 million auto workers.

In a statement, the alliance invited "all bona fide labor organizations" to join in its program.

Former Members

The unions forming the new alliance are both former members of the A.F.L.-C.I.O. The teamsters were ousted, on charges of corruption, in 1957. The auto workers disaffiliated July 1, following assertions by Mr. Reuther that the federation was not pursuing its organizing and bargaining goals with vigor and had failed to actively promote civil rights and other social welfare objectives.

Today Mr. Reuther said any union, including members of the federation, would be welcomed by the new alliance. He said that joining the alliance would not require disaffiliation from the larger federation.

The A.F.L.-C.I.O. represents nearly 13 million members of affiliated unions.

Mr. Reuther refused to speculate about which unions might join the alliance.

Formation of the alliance followed many preliminary meetings of representatives of the two unions and a two-day meeting here of the executive boards of the unions.

Ending their meeting today, the boards adopted a preliminary program with broad objectives. They pledged to contribute sufficient funds to finance specific projects to be decided upon later. A national conference of the alliance will be held early next year.

Aims of Program

The program of the alliance calls for projects to provide low-cost housing, jobs, a guaranteed income, a better education and adequate health care for the inner-city poor.

It envisages help for unorganized groups, such as farm workers, to build their own unions, and it calls for instituting more aggressive and effective collective bargaining procedures and helping the presently unorganized with bargaining.

The general program adopted by the alliance calls for support of state and Federal legislation and policies "responsive to the needs of the American people" in a changing society.

The alliance pledged itself to back candidates for public office on a nonpartisan basis "who are committed to such programs and policies."

It pledged itself to seek to "repair the alienation of the liberal-intellectual and academic community and the youth of our nation in order to build and strengthen a new alliance of progressive forces."

Mr. Reuther and Mr. Fitzsimmons said the unions had not yet agreed on support for specific candidates seeking state or Federal office this year but would endorse and work jointly for the election of any they do agree upon, now that the alliance has been formed.

Obstacle Removed

The assassination of Senator Robert F. Kennedy removed an obstacle to agreement at the Presidential-nomination level. The teamsters opposed him because of his long feud with James R. Hoffa, the teamster president.

Hoffa, who is still president of the teamsters, is in a Federal prison for tampering with a jury. Mr. Fitzsimmons said Hoffa had not been consulted about the alliance.

Ironically, Mr. Reuther was instrumental in the ouster of the teamsters from the A.F.L.-C.I.O. Asked how he could now align his union with the teamsters, he said:

"That was 11 years ago. There has been a great deal of water over the dam since. The teamsters union has demonstrated social responsibility and in interest in building the labor movement."

He noted that Mr. Fitzsimmons was one of the few labor leaders at the funeral of the Rev. Dr. Martin Luther King Jr. He said he was there because he wanted to be identified with the aspirations of the deprived.

4 Rail Operating Unions Merge; Seek Tie to Bus and Air Groups

Special to The New York Times

CHICAGO, Dec. 10—Four of the five railway operating unions will merge into a new United Transportation Union, effective Jan. 1.

The new union will be the largest affiliate of the American Federation of Labor and Congress of Industrial Organizations concerned solely with transportation. The merger, it was announced at a news conference here, was approved by a substantial margin in a mail poll of the four unions.

The new union will have about 220,000 members employed in the United States and Canada, most of them by railroads, and about 60,000 who have retired.

At the news conference union officials said that the new organization would seek to expand, primarily through further mergers with other unions in transportation, including bus and airline operations. They said they did not intend to foment jurisdictional disputes with the International Brotherhood of Teamsters or other unions.

The president of the new United Transportation Union will be Charles Luna, 62 years old, president of the Brotherhood of Railway Trainmen. This is the largest of the merging unions. It has about 185,000 members, including about 40,-000 who are retired.

Assistants Named

Presidents of the three other unions involved in the merger will become assistant presidents.

These men, their unions and approximate memberships of each are:

Clyde F. Lane, 53, Order of Railway Conductors and Brakemen, 13,700.

Neil P. Speirs, 55, Switchmen's Union of North America, 12,000.

H. E. Gilbert, 62, Brotherhood of Locomotive Firemen and Enginemen, 69,750.

John H. Shepherd of the Railway Trainmen's union, will be general secretary and treasurer.

All the officers will serve until the new union holds its first convention in 1971.

The union will have its headquarters in Cleveland, Ohio, now the headquarters of the Trainmen and the Locomotive Firemen and Enginemen.

The only other railway operating union is the Brotherhood of Locomotive Engineers, with about 70,000 members. It was invited to join in the merger, but declined.

There was speculation that friction would develop between the new union and the locomotive engineers union. Both have members among the engineers and firemen.

Hope was expressed by some involved in the merger that eventually all railroad unions, including 18 unions representing the 350,000 nonoperating employes, might be merged into one.

In a joint statement, the presidents of the four merging unions referred to the decline of the railroad industry, noting that employment had been steadily reduced largely because of automation and the shifting of much transportation to trucks, buses and air lines.

"This shrinking industry no longer makes it possible for the traditional individual unions to meet demands of the times," they wrote. "We have united to save our energy for constructive purposes—to end the battle of craft against craft; working man against working man."

He said many of the inner-city problems stemmed from poor transportation and "we hope to attack this problem through our proposed bill."

Mr. Luna said that the new union was preparing for the next Congress "a broad mass transportation bill aimed at the basic problems of transportation."

Mr. Luna said the new union wants innovation in the railroad industry, which has "followed the old ways too long."

The four merged unions range in age from 82 to 100 years old.

Ernst & Ernst, accounting concern that conducted and audited the voting, reported the unions approved the merger by these margins:

Firemen and Enginemen, 24,-988 to 937; Trainmen, 59,967 to 9,490; Conductors and Brakemen, 9,117 to 3,011, and Switchmen, 3,656 to 1,629.

Excerpts From Interview With Meaney on Status of Labor Movement

Following are excerpts from an interview with George Meany, president of the American Federation of Labor and Congress of Industrial Organizations, which was held last Thursday in his office in Washington:

Q. Would you say that the labor movement is in better or worse condition this Labor Day than all the others that you can recall?

A. I think the movement is in better condition than it ever was. When I look back, it is hard really to realize the progress that is being made when you are so close to it, but if you take a leap back a few years and try to think of what was going on then—for instance, this business of welfare funds and pension and holidays with pay—this was a dream at one time. This is now accepted as commonplace. People say, well, we have so many paid holidays, vacations with pay and we have got pensions and hospitalization and welfare. You say, so what, everybody has got it. But I remember a time when this was unthought about.

Q. The laboring man has become middle class, has advantages that he didn't have before, more conservative than he was. Some people think that labor people now —leaders—are out of tune with the generation.

Actually I think the labor leaders are out of tune with the people who feel that they know better than labor does what is best for labor. We have always had that type of people. We have people who are constantly worrying about the lack of militancy on the part of labor. Labor, to some extent, has become middle class. When you have no property, you don't have anything, you have nothing to lose by these radical actions. But when you become a person who has a home and has property, to some extent you become conservative. And, I would say to that extent, labor has become conservative. I don't think there is any question of that. But, at the same time, the programs of the trade-union movement —the things we lived for— there is nothing conservative about that. We still want to break through with new ideas.

Associated Press

LABOR UNREST IN PITTSBURGH: Demonstrators picketing U.S. Steel Building to demand more jobs for Negroes. According to George Meany, militants "want sort of instant solutions for all these problems. And, of course, they are not going to get it."

The Rank and File

Q. How do you assure that the rank and file—the man and woman in the home in the suburb—is behind the leadership as you look for new areas of . . .

A. I don't. I go by what happens in the organization. For instance, when you say the rank and file who owns a home—he might not have attended a union meeting for 10 years. So he is pretty hard to reach. But still you will find that from his union, from the local union level, these problems come into the movement and I am not looking over my shoulder to see if the rank and file is following. I am quite sure that if we are doing things the rank and file don't want, we will learn it in the very same way as we find out about the things that they do want.

Q. In other words, you are doing what you think is right and good for the labor movement.

A. Yes, and doing it on the basis of what we know about the labor movement. The heads of the trade union movement and the so-called liberals that were on the fringe of the movement, they didn't go off into a smoke-filled room, as you say, and come up with the idea that workmen's compensation is a good thing. That isn't the way it happened. Workmen's compensation came right out of the shop.

I don't think about what the rank and file wants because I know I will hear what they want. I don't go searching out and hold a referendum here and a referendum there because these things have a way of coming to the trade union structure.

Q. What is the answer, Mr. Meany, to bring in today's militant groups—the poor and the black and others —so that they own a house and they have a piece of the action and perhaps are less militant and stop creating the

same kind of disturbances that labor perhaps once had created.

A. What is the answer to bringing them in? I don't know what you mean.

No 'Instant Solutions'

Q. How do we face this particular problem?

A. We face it by doing what we have always done and we continue our constructive work. As far as the black militants are concerned, some of them I don't think want improvement. I think they want the issue. I think they want to be militant. I think they want to demonstrate. I don't know what I can do for them but as far as the black, non-white minority is concerned, there is no question that they still have a long way to go—but there is no question that they have come a long way.

They are going up. But the black militants don't want to hear about that. They don't want to know what happened yesterday or the day before, they want sort of instant solutions for all these problems. And, of course, they are not going to get it.

Q. There seems to be no doubt that a great many young people are either suspicious of the labor movement or downright openly hostile to it. How can the labor movement expect to have much of a future if that feeling is as wide as it seems to be?

A. I don't know and I don't spend any time worrying about it because I don't think there is any justification for it.

Q. You don't think there should be some special steps to awaken the interest of the young people in the labor movement?

A. No.

Q. Some labor statisticians of late have been proving that workers are on a treadmill, that they are not really getting any place. What do you think about the state of collective bargaining? Is it really working?

A. This doesn't represent a failure of collective bargaining at all. In fact, this shows that by the collective bargaining process, at least he is keeping pace with the treadmill. He is not gaining anything, maybe he is losing a little bit, but if he didn't have collective bargaining, where would he be?

Q. Secretary [of Labor George P.] Schultz has been making quite a case in recent public statements to the effect that unions should not make the basic assumption that inflation is a condition that is going to persist forever and that sooner or later there is going to be a downturn and if they continue to negotiate these high-cost contracts, they are going to be pricing the guy who they work for, out of the market and also their own labor out of the market. What do you think of that line of thinking?

A. I don't buy it. I think there is some logic to it. But let me say this. If Shultz was the head of a big steelworkers union and made those sort of observations to his members, he wouldn't be the head of that union next year. Now this is a very practical situation.

Q. What is the answer to inflation? How are we going to stop it? Controls on everything?

A. The only way you are going to stop it—and I am not advocating this, but you are asking me and I can only go by my experience and I don't pretend to be an expert but I do have some experience—the only way you are going to stop it is by controls.

Q. Legal controls?

A. Legal controls. And we will not accept legal controls unless they control all forms of income, prices, dividends, profits and everything else.

Q. Do you think it is coming to that, Mr. Meany?

A. I don't know. I hope not, but you ask how do I see the end. I don't see the end to this.

Q. That statement yesterover at Commerce [Assistant Secretary William H. Chartener] wasn't very encouraging, was it, George?

A. I don't see the end of this. You see, if Dave Kennedy is right and the President is right and Arthur Burns is right, we should be seeing the end to this within a few months. If they are right, I hope. I don't know. You see, this high interest rate and the squeeze, this is supposed to cut down the demand for money and it is supposed to cool the economy.

Q. Would the labor leader who is being pressed for bigger raises by his members been better off if the Nixon Administration kept a voluntary guide post on wages and prices as some argument to use against his own members?

A. I suppose so, but most of the people that go to the bargaining table try to think in terms of satisfying their members. I think this is only natural.

Q. Is there any voluntary way you can work it out between labor and industry to resume some restraint on wage settlement?

A. The fellows who have this responsibility directly—I don't have it directly—wouldn't buy wage controls unless it was a national emergency, unless the President said that our commitments overseas were such that we had to have this.

Q. Looking way ahead, philosophically, where is the labor movement going to end up?

A. The labor movement isn't going to end up. It is going to keep on whirling along.

Looking Back

Q. After all these years in the labor movement, are you able to look back and reflect and say if things had been different you would have preferred to do somtehing else other than what you have done?

A. No, if I look back, I don't know of anything else I would prefer doing. I don't know of anything that could ever possibly have given me the excitement, if you want to put it that way, the interest or the satisfaction.

Q. What stands out as you look back on the career of yours in the labor movement?

A. Five years as head of New York State Federation of Labor [1935-1939] when they put more legislation on the statute books of that state in favor of labor than had ever been put on in any period before or since by any other state union.

Q. How were you able to do that?

A. I worked hard but I was damn lucky. I was very lucky. I came in there at the Depression. It is an amazing thing how the attitude of a state legislature toward labor could be influenced by a depression. I put 72 new laws on the statute books in one year, 1935, out of a program of 112 bills. But I had a governor who was without parallel in my book in the field of public service Herbert Lehman.

Q. Which President do you think has done the most for the working man while you have been watching things?

A. Johnson.

Q. Are you including Roosevelt with this?

A. Yes. You are talking about quantity and quality of the two. Now, of course, Roosevelt couldn't possibly have done what Johnson has done because there were different times. Johnson couldn't have done what he did if there hadn't been a Roosevelt before him. It was a difference of 30 years.

Something for Everybody

Q. What about Nixon? Can you size that up yet?

A. Well, I have been trying and waiting and, up to the present time, I just can't size it up. He seems to come out with statements, he has a little bit for everybody. He has got some for people on each side. He has certainly done things to warm the cockles of Strom Thurmond's heart and, at the same time, he has been doing things that the civil rights people think are all right, too, in certain areas.

Q. You say something for everybody. What has he given labor?

A. Well, I think that some of the things on his tax position were favorable. I think as far as the common people, merely by opening up this welfare thing with the statement from the highest level, the White House, I think this was a great plus. That doesn't mean I agree with the remedies he proposes, but the mere fact that he said this business has got to be overhauled, it is out of date, it is bad and so forth, I think this will be helpful.

Q. Are you with him on Vietnam now?

A. I haven't changed my mind on Vietnam. I think that we made a commitment there. I think it is unfortunate the way we got into it. I don't see how we can get out of it unless we can, in some way, insure that this area is not going to fall over, one country after another, to the Communists. I can't see anything that changes my theory that, if they take Vietnam, they will keep going. They will take Laos, Cambodia and they will be knocking at the doors. I wasn't a critic of Johnson on this war and I certainly am not going to be a critic of what Nixon inherited. But I think Johnson inherited it. Now, frankly, I think Nixon would like to get out of this war.

I know Johnson would have done almost anything within his power to get out of this war except surrender and withdraw unilaterally. And I don't think Nixon will do that.

Q. Do you object to his present steps of kind of disengaging?

A. No. I do not. That part of the war I had better leave to the strategists. I am not a military strategist. I know something about international communism. I know that it has got to feed on this sort of thing.

Number of Problems

Q. What do you think labor's program, looking ahead, has got to be in the next few years? What are some of the major challenges that are confronting the A.F.L.-C.I.O. labor generally?

A. Any number of things. I think this inflation thing is a real problem. I think we have got a long way to go before we can say that the job is done in the field of civil rights. And I think something that we talk about more and more is becoming more and more important and that is the question of how do we live in this country, what happens to our air and our water. This is a tremendous threat.

Q. On a broader basis, Mr. Meany, what kind of a situation does the formation of the A.L.A. [Alliance for Labor Action] present? Does it indicate perhaps some splitting of the labor movement?

A. That's the purpose of it. Whether it succeeds or not, I don't know. I don't see signs of any great succcess. This is history repeating itself. We had this back in 1934 and 1935 [when John L. Lewis formed the rival Congress of Industrial Organizations].

Q: Would you carry the comparison to the next logical step and say that [Walter Reuther], like [John L.] Lewis, was interested only in splitting [labor by forming the A.L.A.]?

A. I think that he [Reuther] is interested only in being head of an organization. He would like it to be the whole thing, in other words as many as he can.

Q. Do you think Reuther could have done better if he stayed inside instead of going alone?

A. Oh yes. By far.

Q. Looking back, do you think the C.I.O. helped the labor movement by pepping things up?

A. Yes. The formation of the C.I.O.—and I don't think Lewis had this in mind, I don't think Lewis even thought about it—the formation of the C.I.O. was a shot in the arm to the labor movement.

An Active Organization

Q. The next question of course will the A.L.A. . . . .

A. We don't need a shot in the arm. No, you see this is not a decadent organization. This is an organization that is moving, moving all the time into everything. We are in more activities now than I ever thought would be part of the routine work of the trade union movement.

Q. How damaging is it, Mr. Meany, to have a split at this time with the social issues?

A. I don't know. It certainly isn't strengthening the organization. After all, if the A.L.A. believes in the things it believes in, they believe in a lot of the things we believe in and there shouldn't be any difference of opinion. There shouldn't be any difference of opinion, for instance, on legislation.

Q. Can you look ahead, since you have seen the cyclical nature of these things in the past, to the rejoining of this element at some distant date to the federation?

A. I don't know. It took 20 years the last time. I don't want to look ahead that far.

Q. What essentially beat [Vice President] Humphrey [in the 1968 Presidential election]?

A. Oh, I think what beat Humphrey really was the lack

of a party machine. He didn't have a party machine.

Q. You substituted for the party machine.

A. We substituted to whatever extent we could.

Q. What do you think about [Senator Edward M.] Kennedy?

A. I feel that this is a very unfortunate thing that happened up there. I don't know what the facts are and I am certainly not going to pass judgment on him, but looking at it from the point of view of the stark naked facts of political life, I think the thing has hurt him badly.

Q. For good?

A. Oh, I don't know. Who can say? As of now, I think it has hurt him very badly because I think what the average person feels is that no matter what happened, when it did happen, he sort of panicked. He practically says that himself.

Needs More Experience

Q. Aside from the merits of that, George, what do you

think about his qualifications for the presidency?

A. I think he is too young. I think he needs a good deal more experience. I was certainly a great admirer of John Kennedy but I don't think being the brother of a President is, in itself, any qualification at any time. I think Teddy works harder as Senator. I think he has done a good job for the people of Massachusetts. But I feel that he needs a whole lot more experience before he could convince me that he has the qualifications of President of the United States.

Q. What about [Senator Edmund S.] Muskie?

A. I think Muskie made a lot of progress and drew a lot of attention as the Vice Presidential candidate. I don't know. I think Muskie has great possibilities. I think Hubert would certainly welcome another shot.

Q. Would you welcome his welcoming another shot?

A. I don't know. I wouldn't want to make the decision on that. I surely was very much for him. If he was the candidate in 1972, I suppose he would get a lot of support from our people. But I think it is a little too early.

August 31, 1969

Woodcock Pledges   Goals Will Not Change

Associated Press

Leonard Woodcock, left, the new president of U.A.W., at G.M. stockholders' meeting

By JERRY M. FLINT
Special to The New York Times

DETROIT, May 22—Leonard Woodcock was elected president of the United Automobile Workers today. He is the fourth

president in the union's 34-year history, and he immediately pledged that the U.A.W.'s direction—for social causes and economic goals—would not change.

As evidence, he announced that he and other U.A.W. aides would fly to Atlanta and "march against repression" tomorrow in a protest against the shootings in Augusta, a march

that is sponsored by the Southern Christian Leadership Conference.

"Walter Reuther would have been there," Mr. Woodcock said, and his presence would "signify our alliance with progressive forces."

On the economic front he said the union would win a contract with the automobile industry "of which Walter Reuther would have been proud."

Mr. Woodcock's election as successor to Mr. Reuther, who died in a plane crash May 9, was assured yesterday when his one opponent, Douglas Fraser, withdrew. Both men were U.A.W. vice presidents. Mr. Fraser nominated Mr. Woodcock for the presidency at the union's executive board meeting this morning and he was elected by acclamation.

After the news conference, Mr. Woodcock left for the General Motors Corporation stockholders meeting, held in downtown Detroit this afternoon. He said he would speak for and vote the union's shares in General Motors for a proposal to put representatives of the public on the G.M. board. The U.A.W. owns seven G.M. shares.

May 23, 1970

Some Intellectuals and Some Unionists Seek to Restore Interest in Old Alliance

By PHILIP SHABECOFF
Special to The New York Times

WASHINGTON, Nov. 21—The political strategy and economic policies of the Nixon Administration are helping to revive interest in the shattered alliance between organized labor and the liberal academic community.

The intellectual and the working man, once bulwarks of the New Deal coalition assembled by Franklin D. Roosevelt, have drifted far apart over the last two decades. Their relationship has long been marked by bitterness and suspicion, and it remains distant for the most part.

But the Administration's withering partisan attacks on the universities in the election campaign are causing some teachers and students to look for support to the trade unions.

And some union leaders, worried about economic developments and convinced they will be the next targets of the Republican party's program to build a middle-American coalition, have indicated a new interest in working with the liberal academic community.

At the moment, the two sides seem to be approaching each other with extreme caution, like estranged lovers looking with both hope and skepticism for a remaining spark of passion.

The labor leaders are particularly wary because much of their rank-and-file membership has demonstrated hostility to the "radicals" and "progressives" on American campuses. And the leadership of many craft unions, particularly construction trades unions, have made no response at all to initiatives from the universities.

But recently there have nevertheless been indications of a desire for reconciliation, or at least recognition of benefits to be gained from renewed cooperation.

One indication was a meeting of union officials, teachers and students at Harvard University in the last week of October. The meeting, the second in a series, was called by Prof. George Wald, the Nobel Prize laureate in biology who has been an outspoken critic of the Vietnam War and a frequent ally of student activists.

Professor Wald was frank in stating why he had called for an alliance with workers.

"All of the Administration's forces of repression are turned against the schools," he declared. "We are isolated. We are in a completely defenseless position. If we need anything now it is a base in the outside community."

Fear Being Bypassed

Some of the union leaders at the meeting expressed the fear that the Nixon strategy was to appeal directly to blue collar workers to support his party and programs, bypassing the unions and the unions' leadership.

"Nixon's strategy is not Southern strategy but Southern and blue collar strategy," Nat Weinberg, director of special projects and economics of the United Auto Workers, told the faculty members and students. "Nixon hopes to split us off. If he succeeds, then democracy is in trouble. You are articulate. What you say commands respect. We have the numbers. Let's put our assets together to beat Nixon and Agnew."

The Cambridge meeting ended with the formation of a national committee of union, student and faculty members charged with the task of establishing local organizations in 10 or more metropolitan centers around the country.

Leonard Woodcock, president of the United Automobile Workers, and Jack Potofsky, president of the Amalgamated Clothing Workers, are the union representatives on the committee. The group avowedly will seek the broadest possible spectrum of union and academic membership.

There have been several other initiatives in labor-university cooperation recently. Mr. Weinberg recalled that earlier this year, for example, an anti-Vietnam advertisement published at the University of California was signed jointly by students, teachers and union members, including, Mr. Weinberg said, members of some building trades unions.

In addition, the American Federation of Labor and Congress of Industrial Organizations is helping to bring union members and scholars together at the Labor Study Center, which began operations here in Washington last January.

And the League for Industrial Democracy, a liberal, labor-oriented organization in New York, has been pushing for closer cooperation between the unions and the universities in support of democratic social change.

Both sides tacitly agree that a return to the close working relationship of the nineteen-thirties is not in the cards.

Daniel Bell, the sociologist and the author of "The End of Ideology," acknowledged in an interview that he no longer was as interested in the labor movement as he had been in the 'thirties and 'forties.

Professor Bell, now at Harvard University, reeled off a long list of reasons for his disenchantment with the unions:

"The degree of corruption in labor has become absolutely incredible . . . The pomposity of labor leaders has become unbearable . . . A lot of union leaders are corrupted by power . . . The labor movement has stagnated. Membership has reached the saturation point except in some white collar unions. Union leadership has grown old. Labor is no longer pushing up the kind of extraordinary leaders that it did in the 'thirties and who are emerging from the blacks today."

This sort of criticism from intellectuals infuriates many union leaders.

"The degree of hypocrisy among intellectuals is beyond belief,' said Nathaniel Goldfinger, director of research for the A.F.L.-C.I.O.

Mr. Goldfinger, who like Daniel Bell went to the City College of New York in the 'thirties, declared that the intellectuals had become "well-heeled and affluent" by working with governments, big business and foundations as consultants and experts.

"But the intellectuals go after the working class to bear the brunt of all the social, racial and urban adjustments now being made," Mr. Goldfinger went on. "There is much bitterness in the union movement over the shocking elitism and condesension with which the so-called intellectuals treat us."

Nevertheless, despite continuing mistrust and antagonism between labor and the academic community, a framework for renewed cooperation does seem to be developing.

The liberals, who had been openly skeptical of the political effectiveness of the trade unions, are now conceding that it was organized labor that took the lead in defeating the Haynsworth and Carswell Supreme Court nominations. They are also considering the role that labor played in nearly electing Hubert H. Humphrey in 1968 against long odds.

For organized labor, the incentives for cooperation with the liberal academic community are less pressing. One goal of the unions, pointed out by Hal Gibbon, vice president of the International Brotherhood of Teamsters, is to acquire for labor the same sort of pool of technical expertise that the universities now provide for Government and industry.

But as Derek C. Bok, dean of the Harvard Law School and an expert on labor affairs, pointed out in a recent interview, the priorities of what should be done for the country and the world differ sharply between intellectuals and unions.

Dean Bok echoed a refrain often voiced by union leaders—if the intellectuals want to cooperate with the unions, they must develop an interest in the problems of labor, in comprehensive health care, full employment, work environment, wages and prices.

Mr. Goldfinger of the A.F.L.-C.I.O. put it another way: "If the intellectuals want to work with us again, it will be on the basis of equality this time. We don't believe that God appointed them to be our leaders."

Meany Bids Labor Seek Alternatives To Strike Weapon

WASHINGTON, April 18 (UPI) —George Meany, head of the A.F.L.-C.I.O., said today that he had become disenchanted with strikes and had appointed a committee of labor leaders to search for an alternative weapon.

He said that the alternative would involve binding arbitration with labor and management voluntarily agreeing to submit .their differences to an outside third party.

"I don't believe in strikes," Mr. Meany told a Senate Labor subcommittee. "I don't believe they mean what they did years ago."

When he was growing up in the labor movement, he said, a union could afford to pay strikers 60 cents an hour in strike benefits. But now, he said, working people have children in college and mortgage payments to meet, and strike benefits arc too slight to help them.

At the same time, he said, he will oppose with all his strength the Administration's bill outlawing strikes in the transportation industry. The bill would let an arbitrator impose a settlement, choosing from the last final offer of both sides.

"When you take away a man's right of not working," Mr. Meany said, "you are taking not just the man's property but the man himself—his labor is himself, his hand, his mind."

Mr. Meany's solution to the transportation strike problem is a bill to permit selective strikes that could tie up no more than 40 per cent of the freight-carrying capacity of the railroads or the airlines.

April 19, 1972

U.A.W. Officials Deny a Shift From Social Activism of Reuther Era

By JERRY M. FLINT
Special to The New York Times

ATLANTIC CITY, April 26— The United Auto Workers are considering holding a convention in Miami Beach, and Paul Schrade, the West Coast regional director, has lost his high-ranking post within the union.

For union watchers, those two items are likely to symbolize a tilt in the U.A.W., a swing toward the center of the political spectrum.

Top union men at the auto workers' convention here deny there is such a tilt from the social activism espoused by the late Walter P. Reuther, who headed the union until his death in 1970.

Mr. Schrade, they say, lost his position as regional director and his seat on the union's executive board not because he was an outspoken liberal but because he did not pay enough attention to union affairs. And a move to Miami Beach, they say, may be triggered by scheduling problems at the big Convention Hall in Atlantic City.

But Mr. Reuther always pointed to a Miami Beach meeting place—and that city is the favorite meeting spot for unions affiliated with the American Federation of Labor and Congress of Industrial Organizations — as a symbol that unions were getting fat and soft and moving away from the cause of social justice.

Atlantic City remained the favorite meeting place of the U.A.W. as long as he headed it. Officials of the union conceded today that Miami Beach was being considered for the 1974 convention.

Mr. Schrade, who became widely known for his activist stands against the Vietnam war and his involvement with black and farm worker groups on the West Coast, was challenged in his re-election effort and defeated tonight in a vote of delegates from the West Coast.

Last night Mr. Schrade said that if he was defeated he would go back to work in a West Coast defense plant, and he said so again this evening after his defeat.

"I think this union is changing and I don't like some of the ways it's changing," he said.

Earlier, he had talked about going to work with Cesar Chavez, the farm union leader, if defeated. An aide said that Mr. Schrade had earlier turned down a post with the American Civil Liberties Union.

Mr. Schrade, who was wounded when Senator Robert F. Kennedy was assassinated, complained that some of the top leaders of the U.A.W., including Leonard Woodcock, the union president, had failed to give him their full support in his re-election effort.

"Walter Reuther never would have done that," he said.

After the loss he said, "I feel no bitterness." However, he said that he was not willing to forgive those that did not back him.

But other executives of the union said that they worked to save Mr. Schrade's job two years ago and would not do so again. They said that Mr. Reu-ther had warned Mr. Schrade, in writing, to pay more attention to union business.

The winner in the race for regional director on the West Coast was Jerry Whipple, president of Local 509 at Los Angeles. Despite Mr. Schrade's well-known support of black groups in the Watts area of Los Angeles and of Chicano farm workers, he was not endorsed by black and Chicano caucuses in his own district.

"I feel very strongly that our union has to get back to the problems of the people in the shop," Mr. Whipple said.

Mr. Woodcock, who succeeded Mr. Reuther as U.A.W. president in 1970, was elected to the union presidency today for a two-year term with only token opposition.

If there is any criticism of Mr. Woodcock here — and this is mild — it's that he pushed the union into an early political endorsement of Senator Edmund S. Muskie for the Democratic Presidential nomination.

April 27, 1972

Conciliator for Labor

Jacob Samuel Potofsky

By EMANUEL PERLMUTTER

Erect and vigorous-looking, despite his 77 years, Jacob Samuel Potofsky stood yesterday before a microphone at a journalism award luncheon in the Commodore Hotel and declared:

"The labor movement can only thrive and grow in a climate of freedom." This philosophy has guided his devotion to progressive causes since he joined the Amalgamated Clothing Workers of America at its founding in 1914 and from which he is about to retire after having served as its president since 1946.

Man in the News

Mr. Potofsky has long been considered a mediator between the right and left wings of the American Federation of Labor and Congress of Industrial Organizations. Nonetheless, as a senior member of the merged labor movement's 35-man executive council, he has not hesitated to differ with George Meany, the A.F.L.-C.I.O. president, on American involvement in the Vietnam war, which Mr. Meany and most of the council supports. But he and Mr. Meany have remained warm friends.

An Impeccable Dresser

Trimly bearded and a conservative, impeccable dresser,

The New York Times

Advocate of political involvement as well as the picket line.

Mr. Potofsky looks more like a State Department dignitary than a labor leader and onetime pants-pocket maker. In fact, he has been occasionally mistaken for a diplomat. One such occasion was in 1949 when he debarked from the Queen Mary in Cherbourg on a trade union mission and found himself the object of a welcoming address by a representative of the French Foreign Ministry.

The man from the Quay d'Orsay had mistaken him for Count Carlo Sforza, the Italian Foreign Minister, who was a passenger on the same ship.

Mr. Potofsky does not pound tables. He is a conciliator, as well as a leader, and other labor leaders often turn to him for advice in complicated situations. His prestige is enhanced, too, by the fact that he heads a union of 385,000 members.

For five decades, he has been an advocate of the concept that labor unions should affirm their needs through political involvement as well as on the picket line. In the days when garment workers were laboring in sweatshops, he would declare: "What you win at the bargaining tables can be taken away in the legislative halls."

Under his leadership and before that under the presidency of Sidney Hillman, the amalgamated has been innovative and socially conscious. It was the first to open health, housing and recreation centers for its members as well as the first to have lobbyists in Washington.

For one who began working as a 13-year-old, marking tags in a pants shop 54 hours a week at $3 a week, he developed into a self-educated

and cultured man with a polished wit.

On one occasion, at a dinner in New York, he jokingly reproached President Dwight D. Eisenhower for creating unemployment among clothing workers by wearing a dinner jacket that was several years old. When the President asked how he knew that, Mr. Potofsky said he could tell by the cut of the coat.

He is a restless sleeper and keeps a pad at his bedside in his apartment at 19 East 88th Street in New York. He will frequently switch on the light to jot down a note about some union problem. When he was a young man, he used to write poetry. He relaxes mainly at the 90-acre farm he owns near Flatbrookville, N. J., in the Delaware Water Gap.

Mr. Potofsky came to Chicago in 1908 with his parents from the Russian Ukraine. Two years later, he joined his father and two older brothers on a picket line that led to the formation of the amalgamated. He went to work for the union in 1914 as a business agent at $15 a week and successively moved up in its hierarchy.

His first wife, Callie Taylor, a one-time shirtmaker, died in 1946. Five years later, he married his present wife, Mrs. Blanche Lydia Zetland, widow of a Brazilian exporter. He has two daughters and three grandchildren

UNIONIST WARNS CHIEFS ON LUXURY

By A. H. RASKIN

The president of the State Congress of Industrial Organizations is cautioning his fellow labor leaders not to let high salaries and luxurious living make them too remote from their union rank and file.

The warning is being given by Louis Hollander, who doubles as C. I. O. head and manager of the New York joint board of the Amalgamated Clothing Workers. In a frank series of talks to the union's executive board members and shop chairmen, he has set forth some of the things that worry him about union conduct.

"In many unions," he complains, "there is little sign that the leaders are even trying to maintain contact with their membership. Some seem to feel that union-shop contracts and compulsory check-off of union dues have made it unnecessary for them to know what the members want or need. Too many such leaders live in a world apart—a world in which the badges of achievement are high salaries, expensive automobiles, membership in country clubs and the other appurtenances of wealth.

"It is not my purpose to suggest that any of these things is bad in and of itself. Nor is it my purpose to contend that the only true union leader is one who takes a monastic vow of poverty. What requires vigilance is that we in positions of leadership not succumb to the notion that power, public acclaim or good living are the important things. Each one of us derives his strength from the men and women in the shop; we have value only to the extent that we serve them faithfully and well."

Mr. Hollander feels that the merger of the American Federation of Labor and the C. I. O. has improved the chances for a basic re-evaluation of union practices, with accent on service to the membership and the community.

The state C. I. O. chief is confident that consolidation of his organization and the State Federation of Labor will promote the ideal of a labor movement "entirely responsive to the welfare of the community." Under the constitution of the parent federation, the state bodies must merge by Dec. 5.

However, the A. F.-L.-C. I. O. has set Aug. 15 as a deadline for voluntary action at the state level. If no progress has been recorded by that time, the national organization is under mandate to step in and speed unification. Mr. Hollander expressed hope that action could be completed here well before the deadline.

February 25, 1957

MEDIATOR WARNS OF A UNION TREND

By DAVID R. JONES

Special to The New York Times

WASHINGTON, Aug. 19—The nation's top Federal mediator has expressed a rising concern about the growing tendency of union members to reject contracts negotiated by their leaders.

William E. Simkin, director of the Federal Mediation and Conciliation Service, said the concern the agency had felt about the matter since 1962 had been increased by a recent study that showed a sharp rise in rejections over the last four years.

He said that a study of the 7,000 to 8,000 cases a year in which Federal mediators had led bargaining sessions showed a rise of more than 50 per cent in the proportion of contract rejections since the 1964 fiscal year.

The proportion of rejections rose from 8.7 per cent in 1964 to 10 per cent in 1965, to 11.7 per cent in 1966, and to 14.1 per cent in the fiscal year that ended last June 30.

Mr. Simkin disclosed the figures at the annual conference of the Association of Mediation Agencies in San Francisco this week.

He said that the proportion of rejections would be lower if all mediation cases were counted because the service normally was involved only in the most difficult negotiations.

But he said he still was disturbed to find that about one in seven of these selected cases ended up with a rejection that prolonged the dispute.

He said he believed there had been a rise in rejections because younger workers were more difficult to satisfy than older workers, because there was a gap between worker expectations and final settlement, and because strong employment puts strikers under less pressure to accept an agreement because they could find temporary jobs elsewhere.

Mr. Simkin said that union leaders must improve communications with members to bring expectations into line with the realistic prospects of settlement and to sell the contract.

He also suggested that Federal mediators should discuss the ratification problem openly with labor leaders and work out methods to assure membership approval.

Some labor-management experts believe that more and more union members have decided to reject contracts in the belief that their negotiators will return to the negotiating table and win a bigger agreement.

This has prompted some management negotiators to offer less than they could so they would have something left to add to the agreement if it was rejected.

Mr. Simkin said that the service's study indicated, however, that in most cases neither side benefited from a rejection because the second settlement was not sufficiently better to have justified a longer strike.

The official estimated that in perhaps 20 per cent of the cases the ultimate contract was the same as it would have been if the settlement had not been rejected.

In another sizable group of contracts, minor improvements were won after rejection. He said, and in a small percentage there was a substantial improvement after rejection.

August 20, 1967

Support for Wallace Is Found Among Union Members by Poll

Special to The New York Times

PRINCETON, N. J., Sept. 10—The fear of labor leaders that George C. Wallace is successfully raiding the traditionally Democratic ranks of organized labor is well founded, according to the Gallup Poll.

Mr. Wallace, running on the American Independent party ticket, is particularly strong with union families in the South, where his vote far surpasses that given either Richard M. Nixon or Vice President Humphrey.

Among nonunion people in the South, the vote is fairly evenly distributed between the three candidates.

Despite the fact that labor leadership is backing Mr. Humphrey, the union rank-and-file nationally does not give the Democratic candidate majority support for the first time since 1936.

To measure support for Mr. Wallace among union members, the following question was asked in two successive stages conducted during the last two months:

"Suppose the Presidential election were being held today. If Hubert Humphrey were the Democratic candidate, running against Richard Nixon, the Republican candidate, and George Wallace of Alabama, were the candidate of a third party, which would you like to see win?"

Here is the vote of registered voters—union and nonunion—in the South and outside the South:

SOUTH

	Union	Nonunion
Nixon	16%	33%
Humphrey	29	26
Wallace	50	35
Undecided	5	6

OUTSIDE SOUTH

	Union	Nonunion
Nixon	36%	51%
Humphrey	43	33
Wallace	12	10
Undecided	9	6

NATIONALLY

	Union	Nonunion
Nixon	35%	48%
Humphrey	42	31
Wallace	15	14
Undecided	8	7

The poll, taken July 20 to 23 and Aug. 8 to 11, involved interviews with 3,052 people, including 2,315 registered voters.

In Presidential elections from 1946 to 1948, the vote of union labor was consistently more than 70 per cent Democratic.

In 1952, however, the appeal of Dwight D. Eisenhower drew many union members into the G.O.P. column, and the Democratic percentage dropped to 61 per cent. In 1956 the per cent voting Democratic dropped still lower to a 20-year low of 57 per cent.

In the elections of 1960 and 1964 many union members returned to the fold with large majorities voting for the Democratic ticket.

This has been the trend of the Presidential vote of persons in union member families over the last 32 years as determined by Gallup Poll election checks:

	Dem.	Rep.
1936	80%	20%
1940	72	28
1944	72	28
1948	74*	26
1952	61	39
1956	57	43
1960	65	35
1964	73	27

*Including votes for Democratic, Progressive and States' Rights tickets.

September 11, 1968

Negro Members Are Challenging Union Leaders

By DAMON STETSON

A growing movement of Negro union members is increasingly challenging white leadership to eliminate discriminatory practices and invigorate complacent labor bureaucracies.

The drive, which is gaining in strength and militancy, promises to force sharp confrontations that could have strong impact on the future of both internal union affairs and broader black-and-white relationships.

Already the black-power advocates, organized in caucuses within unions, have begun a move to displace the Transport Workers Union as representative of city transit workers; forced the secession of District 65 of the Retail, Wholesale and Department Stores Workers from its parent international, and shut down the Ford Motor Company plant at Mahwah, N. J., for two nights with a wildcat strike.

In New York City, black caucuses are operating with varying strength and visibility in the transit, freight, utility, garment, hotel and restaurant, and construction fields.

One of those most active in coordinating and assisting the different groups has been James Haughton, the aggressive director of the Harlem Unemployment Center, 2035 Fifth Avenue.

"This city is in profound crisis," said Mr. Haughton, "and I see a greater thrust developing in the labor field— blacks and Puerto Ricans organizing more and more in these industries. First because they're black and Puerto Rican and second because they're victimized."

The black-caucus movement is difficult to measure, but it appears to be gaining momentum — particularly in unions with large numbers of blacks who feel that they have not been given adequate recognition or representation.

Herbert Hill, national labor director of the National Association for the Advancement of Colored People, said in a recent article in "Issues in Industrial Society" that through the caucuses "black power" had finally reached organized labor and was challenging the traditional systems of racial controls by whites over blacks.

Transit Union Criticized

"Black caucuses and independent Negro unions are creating a new sense of community among their members," Mr. Hill said, "and they are also forcing on the labor union bureaucracies the task of eliminating the discrepancies between their increasingly highglown rhetoric and their persistently sorry performance.

"This is being done not only with regard to the urgent issues of racial justice and equality, but also on the basic question of internal union democracy as well."

In New York City, different caucus groups are meeting regularly at the storefront headquarters in Harlem of the Harlem Unemployment Center. At these sessions, members are discussing problems and grievances, and making plans for a more aggressive role in achieving their goals in industry and within their unions.

One of the most active blackcaucus efforts now under way here is the drive by the rank and File Transit Workers for signatures on petitions for a representation election among employes of the Transit Authority.

This group, headed by Joseph Carnegie, a black subway conductor, is attempting to wrest the representation right from the long-established Transport Workers Union, headed formerly by the late Michael Quill and now by Matthew Guinan.

T.W.U. officials tend to scoff at Mr. Carnegie's assertions of strength, noting that he was defeated in an earlier bid for election as president of Local 100, the T.W.U. unit representing bus drivers and subway workers.

But the Rank and File leader is pressing forward and reported last week that he and his committee had collected more than 4,000 signatures among the 27,000 (an estimated 17,000 are black) employes of the Transit Authority. He said that the group needed 9,000 signatures to get a new representation election under New York labor law.

"We hope to have 10,000 signatures by Aug. 31," Mr. Carnegie said.

'Racist Power Structure'

In explaining the objectives of his group, Mr. Carnegie charged that the T.W.U. had failed black workers at the Transit Authority. He criticized the union particularly for its election procedures, contending that the manner in which the ballot is used has deprived workers of a real voice in the operation of the union.

He said also that in its negotiations the union had permitted the pay of transit workers to fall behind other comparable employes in the city. And he charged that the union had neglected to stress safety measures on the subways.

"For the first time," Mr. Carnegie said of his effort, "nearly 20,000 black transit workers have the opportunity to be involved in a struggle in which their numerical strength can decide whether transit workers will be represented by a union in which they have no real voice (no other workers do, for that matter) or whether we will be represented by an independent union that is not tied to management and the rotten, racist power structure of this city."

Some recent events have provided evidence of the growing impact of black workers in their unions. District 65 of the Retail, Wholesale and Department Store Workers seceded from its parent international in a dispute over organizational policies and a demand that its "lily-white" leadership be reconstructed to reflect the large Negro and Puerto Rican membership.

A few weeks ago a group of black workers, calling themselves the United Black Brothers, at the Mahwah, N. J., plant of the Ford Motor Company embarked on a wildcat strike on the grounds that a supervisor had shouted a racial slur at a black worker. The walkout, which had only limited effect, did, however, force the plant to shut down for two nights, gained support from Black Panther members from Newark and from Students for a Democratic Society at some New Jersey and New York City colleges.

U.A.W. Rejects Charges

The Brothers were also critical of the United Automobile Workers, arguing that leaders of the local and at the plant and the company had been working in collusion. The Brothers demanded that their group be established as spokesmen for black workers at the Mahwah plant.

The U.A.W., which represents workers at the plant, took strong exception to the allegations that it was not adequately representing the black workers in connection with grievances and other complaints. The union said that every legitimate issue listed by the Black Brothers had been part of an action program of the U.A.W.'s Mahwah Local 906.

In the building industry, black workers have picketed builders, conducted sit-ins at the Department of Development of the Housing and Development Administration, and applied other pressures in an effort to obtain construction jobs — and have had some success.

In April rank and file activists from many sections of the country, including representatives of the Dodge Revolutionary Union Movement in Detroit and other black caucuses, met at the Hotel Diplomat here to chart a course for a nationwide movement.

Servio Mello, who gave the keynote address, set the tone when he sharply criticized the trade unions as presently constituted, contending that they have lost the dynamic force that they used to have. He called for a revitalization of organized labor through black and white rank and file movements "based on the strength of workers, rather than the relationship between the individual leaders, opportunist politicians and the employers."

Mr. Haughton made a series of proposals which included: Establishment of workers' centers in key cities around the country, patterned after the Harlem Unemployment Center, to provide workers with an independent base; setting up a national "Fight Back" publication; regional conferences to involve additional rank and filers, and a national fund to facilitate travel by black rank and file leaders.

The four proposals were unanimously adopted by the conference delegates.

June 29, 1969

Topics: Workers and Students—Enemies or Allies?

By HARVEY SWADOS

Recently a number of dissident black militant unionists, picketing the Mahwah, N.J., assembly plant of the Ford Motor Company, where I myself used to work as a metal finisher, were joined by two groups of young people—Black Panthers and S.D.S.

Ignored by almost everyone else in a disorderly America, white factory workers have been expressing their frustration only in occasional wildcat walkouts, flirtations with racist politicians, and bumper stickers proclaiming bitterly: "I Fight Poverty—I Work." College kids who have been characterizing labor unionists as "Fascists" are living proof of the galling fact that for increasing numbers of Americans beyond the factory gates, hard unremitting labor is no longer a simple necessity.

But as we approach Labor Day, 1969, there are signs that some students (like their counterparts in France and Latin America) are ridding themselves of glib anti-union attitudes and coming to the factories in search of allies, rather than simply as hip leafleteers on another kind of trip. They are, to be sure, a minority of a minority, and the leftist students' summer work-in does not seem to have been particularly fruitful. It is the fact of the shift in attitude, however, that is of significance. The S.D.S. youths who turned up at Mahwah had in fact been invited by a substantial group of black workers, whose grievances, supported by numbers of white workers, have little to do with dollars and cents and much to do with self-respect.

Detroit's reaction to this kind of development would seem to be a mixture of confusion and uneasiness. "The auto industry has tried to meet its social responsibilities," a dispatch from Detroit notes plaintively. "More of the hard-core and black unemployed have been put to work by the Big Three than by any other industry. But racial trouble is erupting on the lines."

Dissent and Dropping Out

Such an ungrateful response (not unlike that of black students newly admitted to college campuses by administrators trying to "meet their social responsibilities") can only unsettle those in Washington who are determined to do good by rounding up the rootless and teaching them how to handle a few tools and punch a time clock. They are the ones who are now involved in "racial trouble" and are speaking in "Marxist-Leninist phraseology which calls for revolt."

For many assembly-line workers in America, being dumped into dead-end jobs deepens the gulf not so much between colors as between classes. Their racist bias has hardly diminished in recent months—but as some students have been discovering to their surprise—this does not preclude a passionate concern about the human condition, sometimes in concert with those with whom they are willing to work and unwilling to live.

In our bemusement with students dropping out of the hypocrisy machine like mercury slipping from a broken thermometer, not many of us have been paying attention to the parallel phenomenon of workers rebelling against the bureaucracies of both employers and unions. Delegates to recent U.A.W. conventions—among the highest-paid industrial workers in the country—have been holding up placards bearing two words: "Dignity Now."

Multi-Racial Society

As we stagger forward somehow from the post-industrial to the multi-racial society all too few are trying to confront the basic problems we are stuck with a generation sooner than anyone else in the world—on campuses and in factories, in suburbia and in slums.

In any of these places, "Dignity Now" means an end to mindless, senseless time-filling, whether it is labeled "education," "factory work," "office work," "military service" or "welfare." Everyone, not just the fly-now-pay-later swinger, is going to be demanding an escape route: if the stupefied student can drop out for a time, why not the worker? If universities are to be humanized, why not factories and offices?

Redefinition of Work

The statistics-obsessed in Detroit and Washington, computing the health of the state in terms of cars at home and kill ratios abroad, have all but done us in. In a society in which labor grows obsolescent and schooling is a recurrent necessity for everyone from the surgeon to the mechanic, "practical" men may well be cast aside in favor of those who speak for a whole new beginning.

That new beginning must include a redefinition of work—usually left undefined because most Americans either hate or are embarrassed by what they do for money—and of education—usually defined as something done to kids by older and wiser heads. If those holding power cannot perceive that work and learning, far from being antipathetic, are complementary to the point of being interchangeable, they must give way to others who are beginning to make the connection.

Harvey Swados, novelist and professor in the Literature faculty of Sarah Lawrence College, is the author of "On the Line," a fictional account of auto assembly workers.

Writing About Trade Unions

By IRVING KRISTOL

A few months ago, I attended a meeting of the editorial committee of a quarterly journal devoted to the study of America's social problems. The editors had it in mind to bring out a special issue on "Trade Unionism Today." The 15 learned men in attendance thought this an excellent idea — the subject, everyone agreed, had been sorely neglected of late. For a couple of hours we talked about the idea, with steadily diminishing animation—and, when we adjourned, the project was pigeonholed. It turned out that we simply could not come up with the names of 10 or so interesting writers who might contribute to such a special issue. As a matter of fact, we couldn't even come up with five.

There seems to be no doubt that trade unionism has become that most dangerous of social phenomena: a boring topic. One cannot help remembering that, back in the 1950's, the university was a similarly boring topic. Then, the study of higher education was an academic backwater. Now, it is trade unionism that bright young scholars tend to avoid instinctively. In every discipline — whether it be economics, history or sociology — the study of trade unions is regarded as a marginal affair, and an ambitious young man knows he will achieve relatively little scholarly recognition even if his work in this area is first rate.

To be sure, trade unions continue to figure in the news. But journalistic coverage has actually declined during the last decade, in both quantity and quality. The New York Times today has no one to carry on the great tradition of labor reportage established by Louis Stark and A. H. Raskin — apparently because none of the younger reporters is interested in spending so much time in the company of trade-union officials or in reading trade-union newspapers. Fortune magazine has discontinued its "Labor" department. Time and Newsweek report on trade unions only occasionally — and then in their "Business" section! TV will take notice of a trade union's existence only when it is engaged in a tumultuous strike or when some flagrant instance of corruption results in public prosecution.

This situation is not only undesirable: it is positively absurd. Trade unions in the United States today are major institutions. Their economic and political power is enormous. It is impossible to launch any significant social program today — whether it involves race relations, environmental betterment, housing, vocational education, or a war on poverty — which does not, at some point, have to ask itself: what will the unions say? And what the unions say is, if not always the final word, then very close to it.

At the same time, these powerful institutions are beginning to suffer the fate of all contemporary American institutions. They are slowly but inexorably being drained of meaning, and therefore of legitimacy. It is this process of drainage that exudes the odor of boredom. Within the institution itself, of course, other symptoms of impending trouble are to be discerned. The membership is restless and increasingly contemptuous of its leadership. The leaders are bewildered, insecure and increasingly contemptuous of the public. As for the public, it is beginning to wonder whether the institution of trade unionism itself is really "relevant" to the emerging American society of the 1970's. It is too early to say that trade unions are in crisis, in the sense that our universities and churches so obviously are. But it is as certain as anything can be that crisis is what they are headed for.

Very little of this critical state of affairs is reflected in recent books on trade unionism. The writing of trade-union history continues to be dominated by those who formed (or inherited) sentimental attachments to "the movement" back in the 1930's. Sometimes this results in excellent if conventional scholarship. Irving Bernstein's "Turbulent Years: A History of the American Worker, 1933-1941" (Houghton Mifflin, $14) is the second volume of what will surely be the standard history of American trade unionism to have been written before the deluge. Its 873 pages are immensely learned, lucidly written and impeccably fair-minded. It is a major work and one couldn't reasonably ask for better history — though one might, with some presumption, ask for a rather different kind of history.

Mr. Bernstein's basic perspective is a mildly progressive one — he is narrating the successful evolution, despite many vicissitudes, of a viable and well-established institution. I have the feeling that, in the not too distant future, the history of American trade unionism is going to be seen in a very different light. This feeling is perhaps unduly influenced by the fact that the book is dedicated to Clark Kerr, who — one recalls — gave us a most thoughtful explanation of the multiversity just before it collapsed.

Inevitably, the emergence of a new radical temper over the last decade has turned the attention of scholars toward a sympathetic exploration of past industrial conflict. Sidney Fine's "Sit-Down: The General Motors Strike of 1936-1937" (University of Michigan Press, $12.50) is, like Mr. Bernstein's larger work, an example of scrupulous, liberal scholarship at its best. Mr. Fine tends to give the United Auto Workers the benefit of most doubts; and though I am sure he would be among the first to deplore the strain of violence in American life, he is something less than censorious toward violence when it is committed by striking workers. Still, his book is doubtless as definitive as such a study can be, within the present context of labor history. It also makes for quite exciting reading.

More obviously enthusiastic about its subject is Melvyn Dubofsky's "We Shall Be All: A History of the I.W.W." (Quadrangle Books, $12.50). Mr. Dubofsky cannot seem to make up his mind whether "the Wobblies" are to be admired for being intransigent revolutionaries against the American capitalist system or whether the repressive governmental authorities are to be rebuked for taking their revolutionary intentions at face value. But he has done a fine job of research and his enthusiasm tends to be infectious. The Wobblies really were an extraordinarily colorful crew. They also constituted the only significant predecessor in American history for the varieties of anarcho-syndicalism that dominate the American left today. College students, for most of whom labor history is as inspiring as business history, will like this book.

And then, of course, there is the New Left, ably represented by Ronald Radosh's "The American Labor Movement and Foreign Policy" (Random $10). This is not labor history but what may be called antilabor history — more precisely, antitrade-union history — which, never having been written by the right (one wonders: why not?) is now apparently going to be written by the left. For Mr. Radosh, trade unions are a mechanism whereby an imperialistic welfare state implicates — through economic interest and political ideology—the working class in its maleficent designs. It is perfectly possible, given this perspective, to reconstruct a plausible history of the last half century of American foreign policy and of American trade-union politics; and Mr. Radosh does so, with passion and erudition. The question remains, however, whether this reconstruction is not only plausible but true.

Essentially, what is involved here is the assumption one makes as to what the political ideology of the working class would have been in the absence of trade unions. As a Marxist, Mr. Radosh thinks that a working class is by nature radical, and that if the American working class is clearly nothing of the sort, then the trade-union superstructure is to blame. On the other hand, it seems clear to me, as a non-Marxist, that working classes may by nature be either radical or conservative, depending on the national political tradition to which the working class is attached. In France where this tradition is radical—where rhetorical Jacobinism is the ordinary political language the working class is radical, and so are its trade unions. In the United States, where the political tradition is relatively conservative, the working class and its trade unions have this same coloration.

American workers, to be sure, may be extremely militant in defense of their interests, just as American businessmen, may be rapacious in defense of theirs. But militancy is not radicalism. And even a casual survey of public-opinion data over these past decades reveals that trade union "bureaucrats" are, far more often than not, more liberal—even more radical—than their membership in matters of both domestic and foreign policy. It is also evident that, on those occasions when the American working class gets momentarily "radicalized," it is far more likely to move to the radical right than to the radical left. Mr. Radosh's true quarrel is with America itself, and one surmises that in his vigorous "exposé" of trade-union complicity in American foreign policy he is indulging in a bit of scapegoating.

Whatever the limitations of trade-union history as now written, it is a flowering field when compared with the desert that surrounds the subject of the trade union in American society today. This is not to say that respectable work is not being done. A book like William Chernish's "Coalition Bargaining: A Study of Trade Union Tactics and Public Policy" (University of Pennsylvania Press, $7.95) is a valuable contribution to a subject which—despite the current, bitter General Electric strike—is not widely known or understood. And the readings collected in Robert E. Walsh's "Sorry . . . No Government Today: Unions vs. City Hall" (Beacon, $5.95) are earnest and thoughtful commentaries on collective bargaining in the public sector. But the extensive literature of this order is beginning to wear thin. It takes too much for granted about the role and structure of trade unions; it assumes too blandly that the "Era of Collective Bargaining" that began with the New Deal is destined to continue indefinitely.

Indeed, this whole matter of "collective bargaining" — of what it is, what sense it makes, what nonsense it perpetrates— is one that, I predict, will soon be on the agenda for urgent public discussion. As regards collective bargaining by public employes, there is already considerable disquiet. No one can imagine—it is in truth unimaginable — authentic collective bargaining that does not involve the right to strike. At the same time, no one can imagine that unionized policemen, or firemen, or sanitation men will ever be free to exercise that right as they, in their trade-union wisdom, see fit. At the moment, all of our experts on trade unionism are circling around this issue in the most delicate and obfuscating way. But at some point someone is going to have to take a new and candid look at the adversary procedures that define what we call "collective bargaining." At that point, a new era in American trade-union history will be opened.

Nor is it only in the public sector that "collective bargaining" is becoming an ever more questionable idea. In the private sector, too, it is running into all sorts of paradoxical dead ends. Thus, trade-union leaders are always pleased to point out how many fringe benefits—in pensions, sick pay, extended leaves—they have won for their workers over the past decade. What they fail to point out is that these benefits are financed, not only out of corporation profits, but even more out of the withheld earnings of workers who do not stay on the job long enough to enjoy the benefits. In an economy where the labor force is becoming more transient — where working wives and working students play an ever growing role—this state of affairs cannot be expected to endure without giving rise to a "backlash" of resentment and acrimony.

Or take the growing if subterranean antagonism that is developing between the unionized worker on the one hand and the welfare state on the other. Human nature being what it is, the worker—especially the young worker—looks at his "take home pay" and wonders where all those wonderful trade-union victories have gone. He is aware that the heavier taxes and Social Security payments deducted from that check are, in some large sense, for his ultimate benefit. But this awareness does not survive the shock of seeing, every week, a paycheck that is no fatter than it was several years back—he is "earning" more, but he may actually be getting less.

The trade-union leaders, trapped between their commitment to increasing welfare expenditures and their disillusioned membership, are forced to be more "militant" than they, in their heart of hearts, know to be justifiable. As a result, "collective bargaining" today is increasingly irrational, with an awful lot of "militant" play-acting going on in the foreground, while behind the scenes union leaders, company representatives, and mediators try desperately to figure out what package they can "sell" to the restless workers this time.

Labor Day 1969: Affluence and Quiet

Young Unionists Often Eschew Liberal Goals

By WILLIAM BORDERS
Special to The New York Times

FLINT, Mich., Aug. 31—The Labor Day weekend is passing quietly in Flint this year, with no speeches and no parades.

There used to be plenty of both, as workers from the General Motors plants that dominate this industrial city gloried in the successes that made Flint in the 1930's a nationwide symbol of the strength of organized labor.

"Those were the days right after we, the workers, conquered G.M., and we stood proud," recalled 76-year-old Lloyd E. Metiva, who helped stack up engine parts to block the doors of the Buick plant here during the crucial sitdown strike of 1937.

This quiet little city 60 miles northwest of Detroit is still very much a union town, with one out of every four residents a member of the United Automobile Workers of America.

But in Flint, as in many other American cities where unions have flourished, organized labor these days has gone into a second generation, and old attitudes have changed.

The American Federation of Labor and Congress of Industrial Organizations has found that 46 per cent of the nation's union members earn between $7,500 and $15,000 a year. Of the union members under 40, about 75 per cent now live in the suburbs.

Nearly half of the union members are 39 or younger— too young to remember the days before the sitdown strikes and, as Mr. Metiva puts it, "the youngsters don't care what we cared about."

As union leaders all over America are discovering, there is less loyalty to the old causes. George Meany, president of the labor federation, acknowledged the other day that labor "to some extent has become middle class."

Explaining why such tactics as the sitdown strike had become passé, he said:

"When you have no property, you don't have anything, you have nothing to lose by these radical actions. But when you become a person who has a home and has property, to some extent, you become conservative."

Instead of marching in parades or singing about solidarity, the workers of Flint preferred to spend this sunny weekend playing golf or vacationing at lake resorts in the cool pine forests, to the north.

The union has won prosperity for them, and many have moved from downtown Flint to pleasant tracts far from town.

Often they have taken their loyalties with them, leaving the union "stung by its own success," as one official here put it. The membership, which is now financially comfortable, tends to eschew many of the union's liberal goals and to consider the bloody sitdown strikes of 1937 as simply a moment in history.

Those strikes, in which National Guardsmen patrolled Flint with machine guns and 14 union men were shot, were a turning point in trade union history because they won for labor the organization of the automobile industry.

Describing company attempts to starve the workers out of one Fisher Body plant that they had seized here, a union newspaper wrote at the time:

"When outside strikers came with food for the evening meal, they found the door blocked. They began passing it through the windows. Guards attempted to prevent that. A teargas bomb went through the window.

"Then came the first shot! A striker fell. Police were firing into the crowd. Union sympathizers were retaliating with the only means of defense they had — stones, lumps of coal, steel hinges, milk bottles."

But that was 1937, and W. W. Wilson, who now earns $3.68 an hour spraying paint on Buicks, had not even been born yet.

Barry Edmonds for The New York Times

Workers' cars streaming out of automobile plant on Chevrolet Avenue in Flint, Mich., at the end of work shift on Friday. Lake-bound motorist—boat atop car—leads the pack.

"I can't really care that much about the sitdowns and all," 29-year-old Mr. Wilson said as he began the three-day weekend with a beer in Ethel's Bar, a squat brick building across the street from the huge Fisher plant, where he has worked since 1962.

"That's when I came up from North Carolina. I was making $1.25 there, unskilled. Now I still have got no skills, but I can live the life of an average class person."

Benefits Already Won

"I'll admit the reason we don't care so much about the union is that we've already got all those benefits, and, sure, they're benefits that this guy fought for," said Mr. Wilson, gesturing down the bar toward an older man who had just told him, with some heat, "You're getting twice what I got when I was a kid."

Mr. Wilson, and others who think as he does, would rather toss a baseball with his son in the back yard than lounge around the union hall, and the result is that the halls that dot this city are seldom the scene of dances or bull sessions any more, and most of them are open only during regular business hours.

"The union used to be like a church, and you'd do everything, even social things, together," said a concerned U.A.W. official in Flint. "But now, everyone's got their cars, and it's easy, for example, to drive to the ball game in Detroit on your own, so they think, why go together in a bus?"

Last Friday — outside the plants where the first generation of union men here bloodied the heads of strikebreakers in a struggle for job security — cars were parked with boats already tied to the top, so their owners could get a quick start on fishing trips at the end of the shift.

Others in the plant were picked up in campers or station wagons by well-dressed wives who had already packed up the children for what was, to these families, the last weekend of summer rather than a holiday to celebrate the dignity of labor.

The new rank-and-file conservatism of organized labor in Flint takes many forms, and some of them are causing deep distress among union leaders

Barry Edmonds for The New York Times

UNION MEN: Lloyd E. Metiva, right, and his son, Lloyd D., outside the son's home in a suburb of Flint, Mich. With them are the younger Metiva's wife, Joan, and their children, Kim and Scott. The father can remember when he helped barricade the doors of the Buick plant in Flint during the 1937 sitdown strikes. The son, a Buick worker and U.A.W. member, believes that "the union's at a crossroads . . . It's going to have to change."

trained in automatic allegiance to certain progressive goals.

Although virtually no one here contends that they would ignore a strike call, the modern young members of the auto union often care more about suburban school taxes and the sanctity of their neighborhoods than they do about workmen's compensation or the union shop.

"I don't even know what the minimum wage is nowadays, but pulling down $3.54 an hour myself, I guess it's not too important to me," said Dennis Comstock, a curly-haired 29-year-old truck driver at Fisher.

He said that he had "never experienced a hard time, like the old guys did."

Says Unionists Forget

In a survey two years ago, the labor federation found that 75 per cent of the American union members under the age of 40 were living in the suburbs, often with a different point of view from the city dweller or from the trade union orthodoxy.

Civil rights, for example, is a goal that labor traditionalists talk a great deal about. But 12 per cent of Flint voted for George C. Wallace for President last year, and in some neighborhoods the percentage was 20 or 30.

The union leadership, in fact, had feared a much larger Wallace vote here, perhaps 25 per cent citywide, and it waged an intensive last-minute campaign against the former Alabama Governor.

The average union member here, said one man who knows many members well, is also "very anti all this student turmoil on the campuses." "He for-

gets that the sitdown was just exactly how he got where he is, that the union, too, was once revolutionary, not establishment, as it is now," he said.

Like the boy who accepts his father's color television set as a fact of life without worrying about the work that was done to get it, the young union members sometimes irritate their elders, like Mr. Metiva, who said:

"They should have been there when I was there, when we got raised from 25 cents to 40 cents."

"In those days, why, the foreman just looked at you crossways and you could be done for —laid off and not taken back. I just don't understand these younger ones."

But Mr. Metiva's son, Lloyd D. Metiva, also a Buick worker, is 39 years old, and he understands.

Young Workers Are Raising Voices to Demand Factory and Union Changes

By AGIS SALPUKAS
Special to The New York Times

WIXOM, Mich., May 29—The older workers at the Ford auto plant here like to tell about the young kid, fresh from high school, getting his first taste of work on the assembly line.

The foreman told him to watch a 15-year veteran weld the sections of the bodies together.

The youth watched the white sparks cascade around the welder. "Do those things hurt?" he asked. The oldtimer opened his shirt and showed him the scars on his chest and neck where he had been burned in the past.

"Forget it," the young man said. He turned in his overalls and he hasn't been back since.

The younger generation, which has already shaken the campuses, is showing signs of restlessness in the plants of industrial America.

Many young workers are calling for immediate changes in working conditions and are rejecting the disciplines of factory work that older workers have accepted as routine.

Not only are they talking back to their foremen, but they also are raising their voices in the union halls complaining that their union leaders are not moving fast enough.

Leaders and young workers from such giant unions as the 1.5 - million - member United Automobile Workers and the 1.2-million United Steelworkers of America said in recent interviews that they saw increasing dissatisfaction and militancy.

The new, younger workers, they say:

¶Are better educated and want treatment as equals from the bosses on a plant floor. They are not as afraid of losing their job as the older men and often challenge the foreman's orders.

¶Do not want work they think hurts their health or safety, even though oldtimers have done the same work for years.

¶Want fast changes and sometimes bypass their own union leaders and start wildcat strikes.

And at the heart of the new mood, the union men said, there is a challenge to management's authority to run its plants, an issue that has resulted in some of the hardest-fought battles between industry and labor in the past.

The worker wants the same rights he has on the street after he walks in the plant door, said Jim Babbs, a 24-year-old worker who is a U.A.W. officer at Wixom. "This is a general feeling of this generation whether it's a guy in a plant or a student on a campus, not wanting to be an I.B.M. number," he said.

Pat Stafford, the president of U.A.W. Local 36 here, which has 5,000 members, most of whom are under 30, pointed to a paragraph in a 1967 contract and said:

"If there isn't a change in this section soon there's going to be a revolt against the union here."

The Company's Rights

The section says that the company retains the sole right to maintain order and efficiency in its plants and operations; to hire, lay off, assign, tranfer and promote employes, and to determine the starting and quitting time and the hours worked.

"To the young guy this means the company has all the rights and he's just part of the machinery," Mr. Stafford said. "They want to equalize things a little."

The young fight back, he said, by challenging the orders of foremen in the sprawling assembly plant that turns out luxury Lincoln and Thunderbird cars.

"If a guy's car breaks down and the foreman tells him to take a cab and pay for it out of his pocket the older guy will take his hat in hand and accept it. The young guy will speak up and say it's unfair," he explained.

When they challenge a foreman, he added, they may be disciplined, and that raises another cry of injustice.

'Willing to Strike'

The foreman can immediately discipline a worker by barring him from the plant but a worker who feels he has been punished unjustly must follow a grievance procedure that sometimes lasts up to a year.

"They're willing to strike to win that one," Mr. Stafford said. "They want to change the idea that you're guilty until proven innocent. And just like the students they want it changed now."

Leaders of the steel workers, from all sections of the nation, described similar unrest at a conference just held in Pittsburgh. About 20 union leaders met for three days with 15 young workers to find out what their complaints were.

Manuel Fernandez, the staff representative of District 32 in East Chicago, said: "Most of the older workers in my area are immigrants. They're somewhat afraid of authority. When a foreman pushes them around they take it. The young generation coming in now won't take that. They want to be asked to do something, not to be told to do it."

He recalled that young workers had sparked several wildcat strikes over the way an employe had been treated by a foreman. Last month, he said, young workers led a three-day wildcat strike in a brick manufacturing plant after a foreman disciplined a worker for carelessness in operating a lift truck.

"The older generation would have filed a grievance," he said. "The young people have no faith in that. They want it settled right away. There's a big explosion coming in the industrial unions and the young people are going to come out on top."

Ronald Koontz, a 22-year-old steel worker at the Bethlehem steel plant in Johnstown, Pa., said that the younger workers often refused to do hazardous, dirty jobs in the plant, such as sealing the coke ovens.

"You wear two to three shirts a day it's so hot. There's lots of gas, smoke, dirt. Some guys just tell the foreman 'No' and then rely on the union to protect their jobs."

Many young workers, he added, quit after a few months and go back to school or find other jobs. One of the reasons the steel union called the conference was that a recent survey showed the 1.2-million-member union had a turnover of 187,000 workers each year.

I. W. Abel, the president of the steel workers union, said that one cause of the unrest was that "young workers don't appreciate what the union has built."

"They didn't go through the rough times," he said.

The young men, he added, do not read the contract or attend the union meetings but come into the plants and start calling for the elimination of the "no strike" clause, which outlaws strikes in between contracts. "We've got a big job of education ahead," he said.

George Meany, the president of the American Federation of Labor and Congress of Industrial Organizations, said that he was encouraged by the militant mood of the young workers.

"All the labor leaders of the past," he said, "were young men dissatisfied with working conditions when they started to build unions. And from what I've seen of today's young worker I think the future of labor is going to be in good hands."

UNIONS ARE URGED TO UPGRADE JOBS

Study Warns on Discontent Bred by Dead-End Work

A study of worker opportunities in 11 major industries has warned of "danger signs" requiring a call for more effort in upgrading jobs. It suggests skills advancement as a new goal for labor unions needing to eliminate worker discontent.

The study, made for the American Foundation on Automation and Employment, estimated that 34 per cent of the nonsupervisory jobs in these nationwide industries—2.39 million jobs of a total of 7.02 million—were "dead-end jobs."

These were defined as jobs "which allow a minimum opportunity for the exercise of independent judgment and which do not provide a reasonable expectation of advancement either through formal or informal job-related training." Other millions of advancement opportunities were held to be going unused.

The motor vehicle and apparel manufacturing industries were held to have "the least opportunities for the bulk of entry-level workers," with "tasks simplified to the point that al-most anyone, once trained, can perform the tasks of other employes throughout the facility."

In department stores, the study reported "a structure exists which does not provide genuine upgrading opportunity." In hotels, it found "a majority of employes" in units so set up that "no meaningful progression exists."

By contrast, the study described the steel, rubber-tire, banking and insurance industries as providing a number of steps to go up a skills ladder. The printing industry was set forth as an example of a craft system with apprentices progressing to skilled journeyman status.

In air transportation and telephone communications, 40 to 45 per cent of employes were termed "closely akin" to craft progressions, with other clerical or white-collar jobs possessing upgrading potential.

Used Ford Fund Grant

The 273-page study was made by E. F. Shelley and Company, consultants, with William J. Grinker, Donald D. Cooke and Arthur W. Kirsch as authors. The automation foundation said it had been made possible by a grant from the Ford Foundation.

The study said industry had thus far shown "coolness" to Federal efforts to subsidize upgrading through Labor Department manpower training contacts.

Nevertheless, it asserted "the worker who has a strong desire to advance in even the most 'dead-end' industries usually can satisfy such ambitions eventually." It said this sometimes meant his switching jobs or getting training on his own.

The study contended, "either most workers are not very interested in moving up or they have not clearly articulated the idea."

In some industries, this lack of interest was linked to the type of worker. In banking and insurance, low-level duties have been assumed by young women regarded as "not really very serious" about an office career.

Retail merchandising was said to depend on many women who only supplement family incomes. Apparel and hotel jobs with low wages, the study said, attract workers either unable to get other work or preferring sewing and domestic tasks.

As for "danger signs," the study said new technology was making some jobs simpler, while creating others with higher skills in maintenance and operating.

"This," the study said, "is opening a chasm between low-skill and higher-skill jobs which is becoming increasingly difficult for an individual worker to bridge through traditional, on-the-job training techniques.

"Also, newly imposed requirements for higher education in first-line management and technical positions cut off such jobs from those workers in the production work force with limited educational backgrounds.

"Furthermore, the introduction of hard-core workers and minority-group members into the lower levels of the mainstream of American economic life is creating pressures from the blacks who want to move up in the system and resentment among whites over special favoritism accorded to blacks.

"For these reasons, evidences of job dissatisfaction by those at the lower level seem destined to increase."

The study reported "high turnover and worker restlessness" as a reason for concern, including discontent by "the white, lower-middle-class industrial worker who flirted so longingly with the George Wallace-for-President drive in the last election."

Beyond this, the study cited contentions that business should provide "general enrichment programs for employes in order to somehow counteract the dissatisfaction with institutions now rampant among students and blacks, a dissatisfaction which is predicted to spread to the industrial situation."

When unions have become interested in upgrading, notably in steel and hotel industries, the study reported "real movement."

Because many union goals have been achieved in the last 30 years, the study suggested unons ned new and imaginative issues to prevent "erosion." Facing "increasingly rebellious factions in their ranks," unions "might find upgrading an appealing objective to pursue," it suggested.

February 8, 1970

U.S. URGED TO AID BLUE-COLLAR MAN

White House Panel Outlines Plan in Confidential Study

By JACK ROSENTHAL
Special to The New York Times

WASHINGTON, June 29—In a confidential report to the President, a special White House panel recommends urgent Administration assistance for millions of blue-collar workers, described as economically trapped, socially scorned and "overripe for a political response to the pressing needs they feel so keenly."

The report, a copy of which has been obtained by The New York Times, proposes an 11-point program for lower-middle-income families, ranging from new tax advantages to the issuance of postage stamps honoring craftsmen.

Work on the report began a year ago. It was submitted late last week, at the time of rising attention here to the alienation and apparent antiblack hostility of ethnic and working class groups.

The report, however, is explicitly addressed to both blacks and whites in the lower-middle-income category, defined as $5,000 to $10,000 a year.

Administration officials stress, nevertheless, that this response to a widespread problem should not be interpreted, in the words of one panel member, "as just a play for the hard hats."

The report was the last major one submitted to the White House by the panel chairman, George P. Shultz, in his capacity as Secretary of Labor. Mr. Shultz has now become the President's new management and budget director.

The report, entitled "The Problem of the Blue Collar Worker," was drafted by Jerome M. Rosow, Assistant Secretary of Labor.

Economically, the report said, blue-collar workers and their families—some 70 million people—are trapped, "chasing the quicksilver of money wage increases" and, in fact, are falling steadily behind as their family needs increase.

Socially, meanwhile, they are embattled by what the report calls "the social squeeze." Manual and skilled labor have become so badly denigrated in status that "fathers hesitate—and even apologize—for their occupations instead of holding [them] up as an aspiration for their sons."

The study panel acknowledged that almost anything the Government could do to ease these pressures would cost money. Accordingly it envisions a program starting in phases, "so the price tag should not be a major impediment," one panel member said, asking anonymity.

"But some of these steps are not all that expensive anyway," he said. "The urgent need is to show these people that they are not, in fact, forgotten."

The 11 proposals fall into three categories — improving earning capacity, improving social status and assistance from Federal social programs.

For many working-class families, the report said, needs rise far faster than income. Workers reach their earnings peak from promotion and seniority fairly quickly, but costs continue to rise as children reach their teens.

The panel submitted a table showing the economic pressure on a typical steelworker.

"If he does not anticipate later family needs by adequate early savings—and usually he does not," the report said, "he begins to be squeezed in his later thirties and finds himself in deeper straits as his children reach their teens.

Since 1965, money wages have increased 20 per cent, but "real earnings, measured in true purchasing power remained almost static. These men are on a treadmill," the report said. They are, Mr. Shultz said in his covering letter to the President, "cashing the quicksilver of money wage increases."

The improved earning proposals call for a broadening of training programs now limited to the poor, greatly enlarged adult education for improvement of job skills or for new jobs, and tax subsidies of day care for children of working mothers. Referring to day care aid, the report notes that the Administration's proposed welfare reform plan would provide direct subsidies to welfare mothers who took jobs. Lower-middle-income families, however, must pay the full cost of child care if wives work.

The proposed solution is to permit families earning up to $10,000 to deduct child care costs from Federal taxes. The present eligibility ceiling is $6,900. The proposed change would involve little loss to the Government, the report said—possibly $60-million.

The panel took social pressures on blue-collar workers as seriously as the economic. "To a considerable extent, they feel like 'forgotten people,'" the report said. They live close to high-crime areas—but cannot afford to flee. They see welfare programs at close hand, yet their wages "are only a notch above the liberal states' welfare payments," and they as taxpayers, get no visible share.

Less educated, they are more prone to transfer their frustrations "to radical and ethnic prejudices, and, of late, to overt hostilities," it was said.

Worst of all, their jobs have become not decent, respected careers, but jobs of last resort, ignored or scorned by schools and media.

To combat this loss of self-respect, the report proposed more effective guidance and placement in blue-collar jobs, national awards for outstanding craftsmen, a Federal job environment body and portrayal of various skilled trades on postage stamps.

Proposals for Federal assistance inclued possible increases of tax benefits for older children; close, visible recreational facilities like vest-pocket parks; improve dpublic transportation; "no-blame" auto insurance if it in fact reduces costs as much as contended; and increased low-income housing supply.

The panel arose last summer after the President circulated a magazine article about blue-collar problems with a hand-written note saying, "This is very disturbing. What can we do about it?"

The panel arose last summer—Attorney General John N. Mitchell, Donald Rumsfeld, director of the Office of Economic Opportunity, and John Ehrlichman, Daniel Patrick Moynihan, Harry Dent and other White House aides.

June 30, 1970

A Wallace Backer Stirred by Busing

By NAN ROBERTSON
Special to The New York Times

DETROIT, May 13—Dewey Burton is going to vote for George C. Wallace for President in the Michigan primary on Tuesday.

He is 26 years old, short and thick, with a gravelly voice and a gap-toothed grin. He lives with a warm-hearted, pretty wife, a rollicking 5-year-old son a scramble-footed Great Dane puppy in an immaculate bungalow he owns in Redford Township, a white working class suburb on Detroit's western edge.

He struggles out of bed at 4 A.M. five days a week. He drives 20 miles to the Ford Motor Company plant at Wixom. His job begins at 5:42 A.M. as the first car moves past him on the assembly line. It ends at 2:12 P.M. after he has wiped clean one side of 217 Thunderbirds, Mark IV's and Lincoln Continentals before their first coat of paint.

He then drives his beat-up 1960 Thunderbird back to the tiny house with the orchid colored front door and a plaster reproduction of Rodin's "The Kiss" near the living room sofa. After supper, he goes to his neighbor's garage to work long hours on the family heirloom—a shark-nosed 1963 Stingray he "customized" himself. The neighbor, thrown out of steady work 18 months ago, has posted a sign by his back entrance: "Our God Is Not Dead—Sorry About Yours."

A Man of Contrasts

Dewey Burton is a man of contrasts: independent, energetic and sensitive, yet seeming old and trapped.

He is in love with cars; he hates his job at the auto plant, which he finds boring, brutalizing and endlessly repetitive.

He is smart, driving, a compulsive worker, spilling over with ideas; he cannot be promoted.

He does not read newspapers; but he speaks his mind and his friends listen.

He resents welfare cheats; he was on welfare as a child after his parents deserted him.

He calls the black man who is president of his local union "the best president we've ever had." He has no qualms about his son David going to school with blacks. And if a black family moved on his block—and he would not object—he bets they would take better care of their home than the white folks on welfare down near the corner, whose conduct scandalizes him.

But he is violently opposed to busing, even one-way busing that would bring black children into his son's school three blocks away, saying:

"My child will never be bused into Detroit or anywhere for integral purposes. Busing—that's the only issue I'm interested in. It's the biggest issue in this campaign."

A Liberal Tradition

Like Dewey Burton, there are hundreds of thousands in the state of Michigan who will vote for George Wallace in Tuesday's primary — and they make the Alabama Governor the most important political phenomenon in this traditionally liberal state.

Dewey Burton will count for not one vote but four. He is the undeniable head of an affectionate, trusting, but disheartened family that would include his wife, Ilona, a platinum blond with a 5,000 watt smile; his mother-in-law, Violet Kish, a lickety-split talker who makes Edith Bunker of "All in the Family" seem positively taciturn by comparison; and his father-in-law Stephen Kish, who works at Detroit Edison by day and is a gas station attendant at night.

As Mr. Burton votes, so will the three others.

He buys a Sunday newspaper mainly to pore over the classified ads for hotrods.

But there are about 150 books in his house, ranging from Jean-Francois Steiner's "Treblinka," through volumes on algebra and trigonometry, Erich Segal's "Love Story," Gordon Seagrave's "Burma Surgeon," and "Inside the Ku Klux Klan."

Mr. Burton rarely watches television. Saturday nights, however, he and his wife invariably sit down to watch "All in the Family."

We Call Him 'Archie'

"We all call him 'Archie' now," Mr. Burton said. "He's

486

The New York Times/Frank Lodge

Dewey Burton with his wife and son at Detroit home. Opposed to busing, Mr. Burton says, "I'm voting for Wallace."

a fool. He's taken hate and bigotry and turned them into the most fun things I know. It's like Mark Twain's satire —it's hilarious."

It is one of his few diversions. He has not had a vacation since he and Ilona went to Niagara Falls on their honeymoon eight years ago— work has been his whole life.

He was born in Detroit of Southern parents who were on the verge of divorce. When he was 3 days old, his mother turned him over to his grandmother, who lived in Mount Vernon in southern Illinois.

It galls him to this day that, when he was 11, he and his grandmother spent Saturdays packing rice, beans and flour at the welfare outlet to get a pound of cheese in pay. "Then those guys setting on their cans all week at home came in to pick up their food. We didn't get no meat or cheese because I wasn't her legal child," he said.

Now there is the white welfare family on Mr. Burton's block in Redford—an unmarried mother with eight children and many male visitors. Mrs. Kish railed against them: "Filthy-mouthed, busted for

drugs, kicking in the storm doors, boys turning into girls. There she is, having a ball in bed every day and we got to go out and work our tails off for them. They're giving America away free."

The young Burton was sent back to Detroit when he was 12, supported by an aunt. That year, he was putting roofs on houses for $1 a day. Other jobs followed: short-order cook, gas station attendant, playing drums and guitar in bars in a band that he formed at the age of 16.

He became a "line rat" at Ford's Wixom plant when he was 18 years old, full of hope for the future. His son David was born. Five years ago, he and his wife bought their bungalow for $14,800.

"There are two things you buy a home for—how close you are to a school and how close you are to a shopping center," Mr. Burton said. "What burns me to the bottom of my bones is that I paid an excessive amount of money so that my son could walk three blocks to school. I'm not going to pay big high school taxes and pay more for a home so that somebody

can ship my son **30 miles** away to get an inferior education."

But he also insists, "If a black mom and daddy buy or rent a house here and send their kids to David's school and pay their taxes, that's fine."

Busing black kids to white neighborhoods, and white kids to black neighborhoods is never going to achieve integration. It's upsetting. It's baloney." He went on. "Who's going to pick up the tab for the buses? I'm going to wind up paying part of it anyway."

Only his family, and cars, give him solace now. Mr. Burton spends almost all of his time outside the factory fashioning cars into wondrous shapes and painting them with exotic designs and colors: candy apple, diamond dust, metal flake, pearl. He can build a car from scratch.

For three years, while his wife took one job after another, including hiring out as a maid, Mr. Burton struggled toward an industrial management degree in a community college, going "half

whipped" to his regular job. Often he would be able to snatch only two hours of sleep, parked in his car at the plant after the night shift before going to early morning classes. In late 1970, he quit six months short of "that piece of paper" and it almost broke his wife's heart. Last year he spent six months trying to run a small bumper and paint shop— "Dewey's Custom Illusions" —on the side. It went bankrupt.

He passed tests for foreman and skilled trades apprentice, but he's never moved up. He's still at what Ilona bitterly calls "a dummy type job."

'I Hate My Job'

"I hate my job. I hate the people I work for. I hate having to drive so far to work," he said. "I'm doing the same job as the fellow working across from me and he quit in the eighth grade. It's kinda stupid to work that hard and achieve so little.

"Once you're there, there's no other way to make as much money and get the benefits. Ford's our security blanket. I'm a scaredy-cat. If I leave, I lose eight years seniority."

During those years at Wixom, Mr. Burton has been given every kind of work on the line except what he wants to do most — the difficult status job of painting cars with a spray gun.

What his wife calls his "mouthing off" at the plant has led to a bad record of disciplinary actions for what seem to be minor infractions of the rules. His foremen find him "pushy" and much too outspoken about his complaints.

At the age of 26, Mr. Burton feels exhausted and deeply frustrated. He has arthritic gout. His wife has an ulcer.

The Burtons think his wages — his gross pay was $189.90 last week and his take-home pay $134.68 — are enough to carry them. But "I don't have no self-satisfaction in my job," the husband said.

Backed Humphrey in '68

In 1968, Mr. Burton voted for Hubert H. Humphrey, "as a union man coming from a long line of F.D.R. Democrats."

"People have been telling me since I was a child that when the Democrats were in office, everybody was put to work," he said.

He thinks President Nixon means unemployment but he would not vote for Humphrey now. The reason is that he is convinced that Mr. Humphrey "said right here in Detroit, in simple, plain English, 'I believe in forced integration through busing.' I will not send somebody to the White House who doesn't represent what I believe in."

"I used to think Muskie was one candidate for me. He seemed to be a guy who could stop and look sensibly at things. But all of a sudden I began to feel it was just his way of talking around issues and not taking a stand. He's not a decision maker. If you're President, whether you decide right or wrong, you've got to make decisions 24 hours a day."

"McGovern to me is like a dark shadow—like McCarthy —he strikes me as the kids' candidate."

Mr. Burton, never a soldier, does "not give a deadly dam about the war."

"It has never concerned me," he said. "People getting killed concerns me. When this war is over, there'll be another one. Maybe it's because it keeps big industry going, keeps people employed."

"The trouble with this war is that we're not fighting a Hitler or Mussolini or little slant-eyed Japs who bombed Pearl Harbor," he said. "We're fighting a civil war You see 30 Vietnamese running down a road in the newsreels and you don't know if they're friends or enemies."

Mr. Burton has never seen a Presidential candidate, or been to a political rally, or even put on a button or a bumper sticker.

But he'll vote Tuesday. He will vote against the dreariness of his dead-end job, the threat to take his child away, and the dollars he thinks he's forced to pay to support welfare drones.

Dewey Burton knows only one way to protest now:

"I'm voting for Wallace."

see also
pp 482-484
two article

May 14, 1972

Taft-Hartley at 25— How It's Worked

Did the Act Turn Out As Was Expected?

By A. H. RASKIN

With the end of World War II and of the non-strike pledge given by organized labor to assure full production in the "arsenal of democracy" came an unparalleled wave of strikes. Virtually every major industry was shut down for some period in 1946, bringing the volume of strike losses on an economy-wide basis to one day out of every 60 of scheduled work time, a record never approached before or since.

That record engendered widespread clamor for revising the Wagner Act of 1935, labor's Magna Carta, to establish more dependable safeguards for the public against crippling tie-ups and abuses of union strength. The result was passage of the Taft-Hartley Act, hailed by its Republican sponsors as a

measure to redress the balance of industrial power but condemned by unions as a "slave-labor law."

The new statute made unions as well as management subject to National Labor Relations Board cease-and-desist orders if found guilty of unfair labor practices.

The closed shop, under which workers had to belong to a union before they could be hired, was abolished. Unions and employers were left free to sign agreements requiring all workers to become union members within a fixed time after they got their jobs, provided a majority sanctioned such an arrangement in a secret election. But even this right was not absolute. All forms of compulsory union membership could be prohibited in states that adopted so-called "right-to-work" laws.

Also included in Taft-Hartley were provisions empowering the N.L.R.B. to get injunctions to stop featherbedding, jurisdictional strikes and secondary boycotts; separating the board's investigative, prosecuting and judicial functions and making Federal mediators independent of the Department of Labor.

But more controversial than any of these changes was the law's machinery for

dealing with national emergency disputes. It gave the President authority to get Federal court orders halting for 80 days any strike that might imperil the national health or safety.

Despite the feverish conflict that surrounded the birth of Taft-Hartley, most observers are convinced that the law has become a negligible factor in labor-management relations in steel, automobiles and most other basic industries.

Strong unions have become stronger in the face of the law's limitations; whether the continuing weakness of weak unions, especially those in the South, is primarily attributable to Taft-Hartley is decidedly conjectural.

The ban on the closed shop has been almost meaningless in the urban strongholds of the construction and printing crafts.

The requirement for secret votes to sanction the union shop was repealed after unions found it a useful device for whipping up militancy in wage negotiations.

Court rulings turned the supposed prohibition on featherbedding into a dead letter.

The provision for 80-day injunctions in emergency strikes is now viewed by labor as a shield against Ad-

ministration pressure for compulsory arbitration.

Indeed, many civil-service unionists now seek the same type of cooling-off provision in public agencies as a substitute for the present total prohibition on government strikes.

One thing Taft-Hartley did accomplish. It got unions into politics on a year-round basis. The old Congress of Industrial Organization, child of the New Deal, did not need the new law as a spur. But it was resolve to get Taft-Hartley repealed that moved the American Federation of Labor far beyond the old Samuel Gompers concept of cranking up to "reward your friends and punish your enemies" at election time.

Out of that resolve developed the sustained, large-scale activity that now makes the merged labor federation a principal source of political funds and manpower, usually in support of the Democrats.

Even though out-right repeal was scrapped long ago as a primary labor goal, the focus on political involvement and Congressional lobbying gets stronger every year. That was not exactly what the law's Republican authors had in mind, but it has been the most clear-cut effect of their efforts.

Harris & Ewing

Representative Fred A. Hartley, left, and Senator Robert A. Taft at the time the labor bill was pending in Congress.

June 18, 1972

Management:

By R. HEATH LARRY

In 1935 Congress gave legal status and regulation to collective bargaining. A reluctant and apprehensive management was escorted to the Congressional altar and required by the National Labor Relations Act to pledge its unilateral vows to a beaming labor bride.

Twelve years later, Congress concluded that the public interest would be better served if the bride also took some vows, and thus, under Taft-Hartley, she was recalled to the altar, kicking and screaming, to make some pledges of her own.

President Truman refused to preside at the ceremony, predicting in a veto message that marriage under Taft-Hartley would ruin the relationship:

"It [will] contribute neither to industrial peace nor to economic stability. It contains the seeds of discord which will plague the nation for years to come," he said.

Some within the high ranks of labor went so far as to call it a "slave-labor act."

Yet, now as the time nears to commemorate the act's 25th anniversary, those early forecasts of union doom have long since been totally shown to have been totally lacking in substance. Those who either feared—or hoped—that Taft-Hartley would destroy or reduce union power would have to conclude that it did not happen.

After all, what Taft-Hartley did in terms of secondary boycotts, jurisdictional disputes and threats of coercion of individual employes was in no way unfair to unions.

Insofar as the then-imposed reciprocal duty of unions to bargain in good faith, it seems hard to imagine that the law had not earlier required it. And as for the law's confirmation of the right to file suits for breach of labor agreement and to recover damages for certain illegal union activities, neither has proved to be the undoing of the union movement.

To be sure, the act's provisions concerning national-emergency disputes have often been called into question. But with every questioning, the challenge has always been to cast up something better. No one yet seems to have done so.

In some ways, the climate surrounding the collective-bargaining process can be said to have improved throughout the last 25 years. There has, I believe, been a lessening of those types of disruptive union activities that were inconsistent with the bargaining process and with the best interests of the economy.

Bargaining relationships have continued to take on more sophistication, as collective agreements have long since gone beyond some of the early basic provisions covering wages, seniority and grievances, into those dealing constructively with a long list of matters, including insurance, pensions, unemployment programs, remedial training, apprenticeship, safety, civil rights and so on.

It has to be said, however, that, after 25 years, the worry over union power is greater than ever. It still has the ability to produce great injury to the economic health of the country. In short, it has been well said that the power of labor unions is too great, even for the good of their own membership.

Certain unions are beginning to recognize that with such power must come greater responsibility.

During the last 25 years, the United States has moved from the postwar time during which it seemed to have unquestioned industrial and economic superiority in the non-Communist world to a today in which its competitiveness in world markets is most seriously challenged.

Thus, whereas at the beginning of the period, the level of settlements emerging from collective bargaining and the manner of their achievement could be viewed primarily as private matters for the parties to the bargain to slug out, now the economic results of collective bargaining, fully as much as the monetary and fiscal policies of our Government, can shape the potential for future

The New York Times
R. Heath Larry

economic progress for all the people of the United States.

Not only has the world economy become more interrelated and more competitive; but within our own domestic economy, the structure of unions and the industrial structure both point to a greater interdependence of all of the more important segments of the economy.

Unquestionably, what were previously purely private matters have increasingly taken on the coloration of public interest. This has focused new attention upon the strike weapon. Unquestionably, the nature of the risks and injuries both to the parties and to those affected by their actions have undergone considerable change. If it were not so, we would not be undergoing Phase Two right now.

It would be hard, even now, to find anyone, either in management or unions, who would argue for permanent removal from the parties to collective bargaining of the right to strike or lock out under all circumstances.

Nevertheless, spokesmen on both sides have lately begun critically to question whether a more qualified use of the strike weapon must now be found, because both sides recognize that such freedom can exist only as long as its exercise does not unduly impair the public interest.

It surely is increasingly hard to justify "trial by combat," as the modern-day means for resolving economic disputes. The evidence is clear that real wages in the long-term improve only in relation to productivity improvement, no matter how much dollar wages increase.

Efforts by unions to "over-achieve" by use of force in the end destroy job opportunities — because they impair their employers' ability to compete and harm profits. In fact, the portion of the G.N.P. represented by profits has declined sufficiently over the 25-year period that it constitutes a real concern for our future economic growth.

Our country is at a point where better economic results must be expected from the institution of collective bargaining—in terms of reducing the economic damage of strikes and strike threats, and in terms of achieving more constructive trends in unit-labor costs.

The chance to achieve such progress under Taft-Hartley still exists. Failure to do so could mean a new law much less congenial to the traditions of freedom that both management and labor have long supported.

Mr. Lary is vice-chairman of the board of the United States Steel Corporation and is the steel industry's chief labor negotiator.

Labor:

By GEORGE MEANY

The Taft-Hartley Act, passed over President Truman's veto 25 years ago, cannot be evaluated in isolation, for it was a revision of the Wagner Act (1935), designed to alter both the broad policies and the detailed rules established by that statute, and it must be judged in that context.

The Wagner Act, like the rest of the New Deal, was a child of the Depression. It rejected the laissez-faire economics of the nineteen-twenties in favor of affirmative encouragement of unionization, and it likewise rejected the trickle-down economics of the Coolidge and Hoover Administrations.

Its preamble recited, and this is still in the National Labor Relations Act, that "the inequality of bargaining power between employes . . . and employers . . . tends to aggravate recurrent business depressions, by depressing wage rates and the purchasing power of wage earners . . ." As a remedy, the act, and this is still in the law too, declares it to be the policy of the United States to encourage the practice of collective bargaining by protecting the rights of workers to organize.

The Taft-Hartley Act contains no such frank avowals of its purposes. Its main purpose was to check the spread of unionization, and it has done just that. It has likewise served to perpetuate low wage rates in certain indutries whose workers have been unable to achieve the full benefits of unionization and collective bargaining because of the barriers raised by Taft-Hartley.

During the 12 years of the Wagner Act, unionization spread rapidly. During the 25 years of Taft-Hartley, union membership has increased only moderately, and has, indeed, declined as a per cent of the total work force. According to the Bureau of Labor Statistics, union membership increased from about 3.5 million in 1935 to about 15 million in 1947. Union membership actually declined during the years immediately following Taft-Hartley, and has increased only slowly and intermittently since, reaching

18.9 million in 1968. Union membership as a per cent of the total work force was slightly lower in 1968 than in 1947, standing at 23 per cent in 1968 against 24 per cent the year Taft-Hartley was enacted.

It is, of course, impossible to demonstrate mathematically what part, or how much, of this diminution in unionization is attributable to the Taft-Hartley Act. The rate of increase would necessarily have slowed at some point, even had the Wagner Act continued unchanged.

It is the opinion of every union official and organizer, and it is certainly my opinion, that the changes Taft-Hartley made in the Wagner Act have been major obstacles to organizing.

●

Some major segments of the economy, such as the Southern textile industry, are today still substantially nonunion and low wage, and Taft-Hartley has surely played a major role in perpetuating those conditions.

Among the Taft-Hartley provisions that have had an antiunion impact are:

¶The so-called employer free speech provision, which was specifically intended to sanction employer harangues to captive audiences of employes required to attend on company time. This sort of compelled listening is demeaning to the employes and is inherently coercive in its parading of the employer's power and authority over his workers. Two-thirds of the employers use captive audience speeches during organizing campaigns.

¶Taft-Hartley required the N.L.R.B. to conduct a hearing before every election. This bogged down the board's election machinery and gave employers abundant time to pressure and brainwash employes.

¶Taft-Hartley broadly prohibited secondary boycotts, thereby preventing unions from helping each other, although employers are under no such disability.

¶The Taft-Hartley Act invites the states to legislate the compulsory open shop, while forbidding them to permit the closed shop. The 19 so-called "right-to-work" states are exactly one-half as organized as the rest of the

Associated Press

George Meany

country: union membership averages 16 per cent of the nonfarm work force, as against 32 per cent in the rest of the country.

The main impact of the Taft-Hartley Act has been its adverse effect upon new organizing, and it has had relatively little effect where unions were already strongly established by 1947. The act is largely concerned with regulating the conduct of employes and unions during organizing campaigns, and as Frank W. McCulloch, former chairman of the N.L.R.B., has noted, "the bulk of [the N.L.R.B.'s] unfair labor practice caseload arises out of organizing and election situations."

●

Once a union has been recognized and accepted by the employer, the Labor Act is of only peripheral significance.

In consequence, the wage gap has widened during the years since 1947 between industries that were solidly organized then and industries that were then unorganized, or where the percentage of organization was too small for unions to bargain effectively, and where Taft-Hartley has blocked subsequent unionization.

For example, none of the big three textile chains, Burlington, J. P. Stevens, or Deering-Milliken, has even signed a contract with a union covering a mill in the Southeastern states, where most of their plants are located. These companies, and particularly J. P. Stevens, have been held in innumerable cases to have violated the Labor Act; but no major consequences, such as recog-

nition of the union, have ensued.

In 1947 the average hourly wage in the textile industry was $1.04, while in primary metals it was $1.39. In 1971 the average textile wage was $2.57 while in primary metals it had risen to $4.23. During those 22 years of Taft-Hartley the wage gap had widened from 35 cents an hour to $1.66.

This perpetuation of nonunion plants and low wages has not been good for the workers in those plants, or for the nation as a whole. National prosperity depends, in my view, on high wages and an equitable distribution of the national income. Apart from and above these economic issues, the denial to workers in certain areas and industries of the basic right to form unions and bargain collectively has deprived them of the personal security and human dignity that are the right of every man.

Taft-Hartley is one part of an over-all approach to government and economics that has stopped the progress toward social justice that this country made during the years from 1933 to 1947. It is one bad tile in a faulty mosaic.

The question remains as to what sort of revision of the Taft-Hartley Act the A.F.L.-C.I.O. would support.

In general, we would like to see two things done. First, the act should be strengthened to make real once more its purported guarantees of the rights to organize and bargain collectively. Second, the act should be revised so as to make it fair as between unions and workers on

The A.F.L.-C.I.O. News
The passage of the Taft-Hartley Act triggered protests by labor like this one in Madison Square Garden in 1947.

the one hand and employers on the other.

●

These problems are interrelated. For example, the act mandates prompt and drastic remedies against various types of union activities that are forbidden by the act and that have major impact upon employers. Among these union practices are secondary boycotts, jurisdictional disputes, hot-cargo clauses and organizational and recognition picketing.

Once a charge is filed that a union has engaged in a practice of this sort, the general counsel of the Labor Board undertakes, as a matter of priority, a preliminary investigation, and, if the investigation discloses "reasonable cause to believe that such charge is true," he is required by the act to petition the District Court for injunctive relief pending board hearing and adjudication of the matter.

The very fast and effective enforcement mechanism safeguards employers against all of these forbidden union practices, which are apt to be most harmful to employers.

In marked contrast, there is no provision for mandatory injunctions against employers, no matter how crass their violations of the act and no matter how injurious they may be to unions and workers. The commonest violation of the act, after nearly 30 years, is still the discharge of workers for joining a union. Ordinarily no remedy whatever is forthcoming in these cases for three or four years, during which the discharged employes may be thrown on relief and the organizing efforts will certainly be permanently thwarted. Is this evenhanded justice?

Again, the Taft-Hartley Act provides for private damage suits by employers against unions for any violation of the secondary boycott and jurisdictional dispute provisions, but it affords no right of action to unions or workers against employers for any conduct, however unlawful or however harmful to employes or unions.

These illustrations could be added to almost endlessly.

As long as the Taft-Hartley Act fails to protect the basic rights of workers and unions, and is heavily and unfairly slanted in favor of employers, unions must and will refuse to accept it and will and must seek to change it. It is not a matter of doctrinal dogmatism but of simple justice.

Mr. Meany is president of the American Federation of Labor and Congress of Industrial Organizations.

Labor and Management
The Great Contemporaty
   Issues
Richard B. Morris, Ed.
   The New York Times
   Arno Press, N. Y., 1973

A Brief Chronology:
Labor and Management History

1866	National Labor Union founded; pushes for eight-hour day and political reform
1876	"Molly Maguire" revolt in Pennsylvania coal fields crushed
July 1877	Violent railroad strikes put down by state militia and federal troops
1878	Knights of Labor organized on a national, industrial basis
Nov. 1881	Federation of Organized Trades and Labor Unions founded—a forerunner of the A.F. of L.
May 1886	Haymarket bombing in Chicago is attributed to labor agitation
Dec. 1886	American Federation of Labor organized; Samuel Gompers elected president; tight organization along craft lines and specific economic goals stressed
1890	Sherman Anti-Trust Act—later used against labor
1892	Violent mining strike in Coeur d'Alene, Idaho
July 1892	Homestead, Pennsylvania, steel strike; Pinkerton detectives battle strikers
1894	Labor Day established by act of Congress
June 1894	Strike by American Railway Union led by Eugene V. Debs—stymied by a federal injunction
May 1895	*In Re Debs:* Supreme Court supports use of federal injunctions to halt labor disputes involving interstate commerce
1895	National Association of Manufacturers formed
June 1898	Erdman Act provides arbitration machinery for labor disputes on the railroads
1900	National Civic Federation formed; it promotes peaceful resolution of industrial conflicts
May 1902	Anthracite coal strike; settled following year as a result of Theodore Roosevelt's mediation
June 1903	Organization of the American Anti-Boycott Asociation
Nov. 1903	American Federation of Labor formally rejects socialism
June 1905	Founding of the Industrial Workers of the World
1905	*Lochner* v. *New York:* Supreme Court strikes down New York State law setting maximum hours for bakers
1908	*Adair* v. *U.S.:* Supreme Court holds that Erdman Act does not prevent railroads from forcing workers to pledge not to join a union (yellow dog contract)
1908	*Loewe* v. *Lawler* (Danbury Hatters Case): Supreme Court holds that a secondary boycott is a conspiracy under the Sherman Act
1908	*Muller* v. *Oregon:* Supreme Court sanctions a state law limiting the working hours for women
Sept. 1910	Settlement of cloak makers strike brings permanent arbitration machinery to garment industry
Mar. 1911	Triangle fire in New York City kills 146 workers and spurs factory legislation and organizing by the International Ladies Garment Workers Union
Jan. 1912	Violent textile strike in Lawrence, Massachusetts, spearheaded by the Industrial Workers of the World; wage gains later dissipated by management speedup
Mar. 1913	Department of Labor created
July 1913	Newlands Act improves arbitration machinery for the railroads
1914	Women and children massacred in suppressing of mining strike at Ludlow, Colorado
Jan. 1914	Henry Ford announces he will pay all workers five dollars a day
Oct. 1914	Clayton Anti-Trust Act exempts labor from its provisions and restricts the use of injunctions
Mar. 1915	LaFollette Seamen's Act
Sept. 1916	Owen-Keating Child Labor Act
Sept. 1916	Adamson Act provides for the eight-hour day on the railroads
Dec. 1917	Supreme Court rules in the Hitchman Coal case that the open shop is valid
Apr. 1918	National War Labor Board set up to mediate Labor disputes for the duration of World War I
June 1918	*Hammer* v. *Dagenhart:* Supreme Court strikes down the federal child labor law
1919	Rash of postwar strikes; steel workers lose
Oct. 1919	Industrial Conference called by President Wilson ends in labor-management acrimony
Feb. 1920	Esch-Cummins Act provides for a nine-member presidential board to mediate rail disputes
Sept. 1922	John L. Lewis leads anthracite coal miners to victory in a bloody strike
Apr. 1923	*Adkins* v. *Children's Hospital:* Supreme Court strikes down a federal law setting minimum wage for women
Dec. 1924	Gompers dies and William Green succeeds him as president of the A.F. of L.
June 1929	Violent textile strike in Gastonia, North Carolina, is one of many in this industry
Nov. 1929	Hawthorne industrial psychology experiments reported by General Electric
Mar. 1932	Norris-LaGuardia Act curbs use of injunctions to break strikes
June 1933	Section 7a of the National Industrial Recovery Act provides for collective bargaining; it is only partially successful
1934	Extensive organizing in the coal industry; violent strikes in Toledo and Minneapolis and a four-day general strike in San Francisco growing out of a labor dispute on the docks

June 1934	Railway Labor Act establishes National Railway Adjustment Board
July 1934	Franklin D. Roosevelt sets up the National Labor Relations Board
May 1935	The Supreme Court in the Shechter case strikes down the National Industrial Recovery Act
July 1935	Wagner Act protects union organizing and leads to vast increase in membership—upheld by Supreme Court in 1937
Aug. 1935	Social Security Act
Nov. 1935	Committee for Industrial Organization formed within the A.F. of L.; expelled in 1938 and becomes the Congress of Industrial Organizations (CIO) under leadership of John L. Lewis
1937	CIO organizes the steel and auto industries
Mar. 1937	*West Coast Hotel* v. *Parrish:* Supreme Court upholds minimum wage for women
May 1937	Massacre at Republic Steel
June 1938	Fair Labor Standards Act sets federal minimum wage
Nov. 1940	Philip Murray elected president of the CIO
June 1941	Roosevelt sets up the Fair Employment Practices Committee to keep discrimination out of the defense industries; strengthened in 1943 but abandoned after World War II
Jan. 1942	War Labor Board established; ties wage increases to "Little Steel" formula
Apr. 1943	Roosevelt freezes wages and prices
1943	Roosevelt seizes coal mines and railroads to prevent strikes
June 1943	Smith-Connally Act forces unions to give advance notice of strikes; President gets wide powers to seize plants
Aug. 1945	Truman eases wage curbs; rash of reconversion strikes with biggest in auto, steel and coal industries
Dec. 1945	Truman's labor-management conference unable to produce accord
May 1946	Truman forces end of railroad strike with threat to draft workers
Nov. 1946	End of wage and price controls
Nov. 1946	Coal strike leads to contempt of court judgment against John L. Lewis
June 1947	Taft-Hartley Act
1948	Strikes: United Auto Workers (UAW) get escalator clause from General Motors; miners get welfare benefts
Nov. 1949	CIO expels Communist unions
Aug. 1950	Truman seizes railroads to prevent a strike
Jan. 1951	Korean War wage and price freeze; labor successfully pressures Wage Stabilization Board for more liberal raises
Apr. 1952	Steel strike: Supreme Court forces Truman to return seized steel mills
Dec. 1952	George Meany and Walter Reuther become new leaders of A.F. of L. and CIO following deaths of William Green and Philip Murray
Dec. 1952	Waterfront crime in New York City exposed—leads to the expulsion of the International Longshoreman's Association from the A.F. of L.
Feb. 1953	Eisenhower ends wage and price controls
June 1953	A.F. of L. and CIO agree to a no-raiding pact
June 1955	UAW get Supplementary Unemployment Benefits from Ford
Dec. 1955	Merger of the A.F. of L. and the CIO
1957	White collar workers outnumber blue collar workers for the first time
Feb. 1957	McClellan Committee investigates corruption in labor and management
July 1959	Six-month steel strike: work rules become an important issue
Sept. 1959	Landrum-Griffen Act
Oct. 1960	West Coast longshoremen agree to use of containers for loading and shipping goods
Jan. 1962	Kennedy's economic advisers suggest wage-price guideline of about 3%
Jan. 1962	Kennedy's executive order grants federal employees the right to join unions
Feb. 1962	Kennedy administration announces it will assert the national interest in labor-management negotiations
Apr. 1962	Kennedy forces U.S. Steel to roll back prices
June 1963	Equal Pay Act requires equal wages for equal work in industries involved in commerce
Aug. 1963	After the Supreme Court, in March, upheld the railroads' right to change work rules, Congress imimposes arbitration of the featherbedding issue
June 1964	Title VII of the Civil Rights Act deals with fair employment opportunity
Sept. 1964	U.A.W. achieves early retirement as a contract right
Mar. 1965	Practice of importing Mexican laborers (Braceros) for western farms is ended by the federal government
Jan. 1966	Transit strike cripples New York City
Jan. 1967	Federal government abandons 3.2% wage guideline
Sept. 1967	New York City teachers strike (and again the following year)
May 1968	UAW leaves the A.F. of L.—CIO
July 1968	New York City hospital workers get $100/week minimum pay
Nov. 1968	Large number of blue collar workers vote for George C. Wallace
Sept. 1969	Nixon offers Philadelphia Plan to increase number of black construction workers
Jan. 1970	Joseph Yablonski of the United Mine Workers murdered
Apr. 1970	U.S. postal strike
May 1970	Leonard Woodcock succeeds the late Walter Reuther as president of the UAW
July 1970	Cesar Chavez successfully concludes Delano grape pickers strike
Aug. 1970	Nixon issues first inflation alert; reluctantly signs bill authorizing wage and price controls
Aug. 1971	Nixon declares wage-price freeze
Nov. 1971	Phase Two of economic controls in effect; Pay Board monitors wages, sets 5.5% standard
Apr. 1972	Pay Board cuts settlement in longest dock strike; George Meany and three other labor members of the Board quit over its decisions on wages

Suggested Reading

Adamic, Louis. *Dynamite: The Story of Class Violence in America*. New York: Viking Press, 1931.

Baritz, Loren. *The Servants of Power: A History of the Use of Social Science in American Industry*. New York: Wiley Science Editions, 1965.

Bernstein, Irving. *The Lean Years: A History of the American Worker*. Boston: Houghton Mifflin, 1960.

———. *The Turbulent Years: A History of the American Worker, 1933-1941*. Boston: Houghton Mifflin, 1970.

Brooks, Thomas R. *Toil and Trouble: A History Of American Labor*. New York: Delacorte Press, 1964.

Cochrane, Thomas C., and William Miller. *The Age of Enterprise: A Social History of Industrial America*. Revised Edition. New York: Harper Torchbooks, 1961.

Cohen, Sanford. *Labor in the United States*. Columbus: C. E. Merrill Books, 1966.

Commons, John R., *et. al. History of Labor in the United States*. 4 Volumes. New York: Macmillan, 1918-1935.

Derber, Milton. *The American Idea of Industrial Democracy, 1865-1965*. Urbana: University of Illinois Press, 1970.

Dubofsky, Max. *We Shall Be All: A History of the IWW*. Chicago: Quadrangle, 1969.

Dulles, Foster R. *Labor in America*. 2nd Revised Edition. New York: Crowell, 1960.

Fine, Sidney. *Sit-Down: The General Motors Strike of 1936-1937*. Ann Arbor: University of Michigan Press, 1969.

Ginger, Ray. *The Bending Cross: A Biography of Eugene Victor Debs*. New Brunswick: Rutgers University Press, 1949.

Jacobson, Julius, editor. *The Negro and the American Labor Movement*. Garden City: Doubleday, 1968.

Kampelman, Max. *The Communist Party vs. the CIO*. New York: Praeger, 1957.

McClure, Arthur F. *The Truman Administration and the Problems of Postwar Labor, 1945-1948*. Rutherford: Fairleigh Dickinson University Press, 1969.

Madison, Charles A. *American Labor Leaders: Personalities and Forces in the Labor Movement*. New York: Harper & Brothers, 1950.

Morris, Richard B. *Government and Labor in Early America*. New York: Octagon Books, 1965.

Millis, H.A., and E.C. Brown. *From the Wagner Act to Taft-Hartley: A Study of National Labor Policy and Labor Relations*. Chicago: University of Chicago Press, 1950.

Radosh, Ronald. *American Labor and United States Foreign Policy*. New York: Random House, 1969.

Seidman, Joel. *American Labor from Defense to Reconversion*. Chicago: University of Chicago Press, 1953.

Taft, Philip. *The A.F. of L. in the Time of Gompers*. New York. Harper, 1957.

———. *The A.F. of L. from the Death of Gompers to the Merger*. New York: Harper, 1959.

Ware, Norman. *The Industrial Worker, 1840-1860*. Boston: Houghton Mifflin, 1924.

Wortman, Max. *Critical Issues in Labor: Text and Readings*. New York: Macmillan, 1969.

Index

Abel, I. W., 448–49, 455, 460, 484
Actors' Equity Association, 276, 320
Adamson Eight-Hour Act (1916), 113
Aderholdt, O. F., 114–16
Adkins v. *Children's Hospital*, 131–33
AFL, *see* American Federation of Labor
Agency shop, 212, 460
Aishton, R. H., 50–51, 103
Akron Rubber Strike (1943), 160
Alliance for Labor Action, 469–73
Allied Industrial Workers, 298, 303
Altgeld, John P., 22, 53, 231
Amalgamated Association of Iron, Steel and Tin Workers, 97, 141
Amalgamated Clothing Workers of America, 113, 140, 147, 294, 356, 476
Amalgamated Meat Cutters, 252, 387
American Anti-Boycott Association, 31
American Arbitration Association, 276
American Communications Association, 174
American Farm Bureau Federation, 80, 370
American Federation of Government Employees, 321
American Federation of Labor, 33, 69, 125, 130, 159, 166, 192–93, 292: and boycotts, 31, 35; Buck Stove and Range Company, 34; labor legislation, 55, 79, 146–47, 173, 194, 330, 489; formation, 61–64; opposes Socialism, 68; World War I, 85; strikes, 92–93, 96–97, 169, 190–91; ousts radicals, 97; party politics, 100–01, 140; coal industry, 102, 209; company unions, 106–09, 127–28; membership decline (1920's), 110; William Green, 111–12; unionization of South, 114, 117–19; Depression (1930's), 122; opposes industrial unions, 140–41; and Committee for Industrial Organization, 148, 152–53, 246–54; Truman Administration, 167–68, 172–73; George Meany, 250–52; racketeering, 280–81; longshoremen, 290–94; blacks, 349–52; *see also* AFL-CIO; affiliated unions
AFL-CIO (American Federation of Labor-Congress of Industrial Organizations), 254–55, 297, 390–91, 471–74, 482: formation, 253–54; longshoremen, 294; teamsters, 299–310; anti-racketeering codes, 300–01; union suspensions, 303, 469; white collar workers, 318–35; postal strike (1970), 323–24; blacks, 355–59, 362–66; farm workers, 370–77; wage-price policy, 428, 436–39, 445–46; international trade, 438; Nixon's wage-price policy, 451–56, 460; organization in South, 467; and U.A.W., 469; United Transportation Union, 470; *see also* American Federation of Labor; Congress of Industrial Organizations; affiliated unions
American Federation of State, County and Municipal Employees, 318–22, 331–33, 338–39, 452
American Federation of Teachers, 320–22, 325–29, 333–34, 338
American Iron and Steel Institute, 177, 271
American Labor Movement and Foreign Policy, The (Radosh), 480
American Labor Party, 161
American Management Association, 214, 266–67, 318, 386–87
American Negro Labor Congress, 350–51
American Railway Union, 21–26
Ammons, Elias M., 44–47
Anarchism, 11–13, 17, 53, 64–66, 88
Anastasia, Anthony, 282, 287

Anderson, Harry W., 171, 177, 217
Anthony, Susan B., 59
Anti-trust laws, *see* specific legislation
Apprenticeship, 4, 8, 51, 104, 138, 357, 360–67
Association of American Railroads, 162, 181, 292, 401
Automation, 382–87: shipping industry, 399–400, 411–14; and American economy (1947–62, charts), 407–08; steel industry, 409; coal industry (table), 410; and strikes, 411, 467; automobile industry, 416–23
Automobile industry, 117, 416–23, 444, *see also* United Automobile Workers

Baer, George F., 53, 72, 75, 272
Baker's International Union, 66–67
Baldwin-Felts Detective Agency, 41
Ball, Joseph, 161, 174, 197
Ballard, S. Thurston, 50–52
Baltimore and Ohio Railroad, 6–8, 17–19, 22
Barr, William H., 86–87, 106
Baruch, Bernard M., 93
Beal, Fred Erwin, 114–116
Beck, Dave, 291–92, 299–309
Beirne, Joseph A., 299, 320
Bell, Sherman, 46
Belmont, August, 112
Berkman, Alexander, 17
Bernard, Fred, 98–99
Berry, George L., 140, 146
Bethlehem Steel Corporation, 106–07, 155, 208–09, 234–35, 270–71, 367
Biddle, Francis, 130, 274
"Bill of Grievances" (1906), 32–33
Birthright, W. C., 118–19
Black, Hugo L., 188–89, 232, 237, 411, 467
Blacklisting, 9, 29, 48, 60, 75, 293
Blacks, 78, 256, 436: strikes, 94–95, 338, 346, 378–79, 478; in South, 344–45; Illinois race riots, 348–49; and Communism, 350–51; discrimination, 352–55, 358–61; armed services, 354–55; building trades, 356–57, 362–67; Meany on, 471–72
Blue-collar workers, 485–86
Boldt, George H., 459–61
Bonnett, Clarence E., 105–06
Boulware, Lemuel R., 390
Bowen, Margaret, 118–19
Bowers, Mickey, 287, 289
Bowles, Chester, 175–76
Boyle, W. A. (Tony), 314–15, 410
Braden, Spruille, 280–81, 296
Bradley, William V., 291–94, 399
Brandeis, Elizabeth, 54
Brandeis, Louis D., 54, 76, 102, 131, 134, 215
Braun, Robert J., 325–27
Brennan, Owen, 304–07, 310
Bricklayers and Masons' International Union of America, 58, 61, 65

7 FLINT 482

> Teamsters - see INT'L BRO. OF T.

Wright, Carroll D., 72, 75
Wright, George, 163
Wurf, Jerry, 320–22, 331, 452

Yablonski, Joseph A., 314–15

"Yellow Dog" Bill, *see* Norris-LaGuardia Act
Young, Nelson, Sr., 66

Zaritsky, M., 140

Byline Index